Sefer HaChinukh

On 613 Mitzvahs

of the Torah

By

Anonymously Rabbi

There is no known book without mistakes. Therefore, I ask in every language of application if anyone has any questions, comments, clarifications, corrections, please send to: book@simchatchaim.com

All material used in this section may not be used for commercial purposes, but only for study and teaching.
To get this book or books and information Email me at:
book@simchatchaim.com

Copyright©All Rights Reserved to
www.simchatchaim.com

YB"S©All rights reserved

First Edition 2022

Sefer HaChinukh

TABLE OF CONTENTS

Author's Introduction
Opening Letter by the Author
Mitzvah 1 - The commandment of procreation:
Mitzvah 2 - The commandment to circumcise:
Mitzvah 3 - Not to eat the sciatic nerve:
Mitzvah 4 - The commandment of sanctifying the new month:
Mitzvah 5 - The commandment to slaughter the Pesach sacrifice:
Mitzvah 6 - The commandment of eating the meat of the Pesach sacrifice:
Mitzvah 7 - To not eat the Pesach sacrifice uncooked or boiled:
Mitzvah 8 - To not leave from the meat of the Pesach sacrifice:
Mitzvah 9 - The commandment of disposing of chamets:
Mitzvah 10 - The commandment of eating matsah:
Mitzvah 11 - That chamets not be found in our possession on Pesach:
Mitzvah 12 - To not eat from anything that has chamets in it:
Mitzvah 13 - That we not feed of the Pesach sacrifice to an apostate Jew:
Mitzvah 14 - That we not feed of the Pesach sacrifice to a stranger or a resident:
Mitzvah 15 - Not to take out from the meat of the Pesach offering outside:
Mitzvah 16 - To not break a bone from the Pesach sacrifice:
Mitzvah 17 - That an uncircumcised man not eat from the Pesach sacrifice:
Mitzvah 18 - The commandment of sanctifying the first-born in the Land of Israel:
Mitzvah 19 - To not eat chamets [leavened grain products] on Pesach:
Mitzvah 20 - That chamets not be found to us on Pesach:
Mitzvah 21 - The commandment to recount the exodus from Egypt:
Mitzvah 22 - The commandment of the redemption of a [first-born] donkey:
Mitzvah 23 - The commandment of beheading a [first-born] donkey:
Mitzvah 24 - That we should not go outside of the boundary [techum] on Shabbat:
Mitzvah 25 - The commandment of belief in God:
Mitzvah 26 - That we not believe in a god besides God alone:
Mitzvah 27 - To not make a statue:
Mitzvah 28 - To not bow down to idolatry:
Mitzvah 29 - To not worship idolatry in that which is its way to be worshiped:
Mitzvah 30 - To not swear in vain:
Mitzvah 31 - The commandment of the sanctification of Shabbat with words:
Mitzvah 32 - To not do work on Shabbat:
Mitzvah 33 - The commandment to honor father and mother:
Mitzvah 34 - To not kill the innocent:
Mitzvah 35 - To not reveal the nakedness of a man's wife:
Mitzvah 36 - To not steal a soul of Israel:
Mitzvah 37 - To not testify falsely:
Mitzvah 38 - To not covet:
Mitzvah 39 - Not to make the form of a man, even for decoration:
Mitzvah 40 - To not build [with] hewn stones:
Mitzvah 41 - To not take steps on the altar:
Mitzvah 42 - The commandment of the law of a Hebrew slave:
Mitzvah 43 - The commandment of designation of a Hebrew bondwoman:
Mitzvah 44 - The commandment of redemption of a Hebrew bondwoman:
Mitzvah 45 - That the one who acquires the Hebrew bondwoman from the father not sell her:
Mitzvah 46 - Not to reduce her flesh, covering and time period:
Mitzvah 47 - The commandment on the court [beit din] to kill with strangulation one who is liable:
Mitzvah 48 - Not to strike father and mother:
Mitzvah 49 - The commandment of the laws of penalties:

Sefer HaChinukh

Mitzvah 50 - The commandment on the court to kill with the sword one who is liable:
Mitzvah 51 - The commandment on the court to judge the damages of an animal:
Mitzvah 52 - Not to eat from the meat of a ox that was stoned:
Mitzvah 53 - The commandment on the court to judge the damages of a pit:
Mitzvah 54 - The commandment on the court to judge a thief with repayment or the death penalty:
Mitzvah 55 - The commandment on the court to judge concerning damages of destruction:
Mitzvah 56 - The commandment on the court to judge damages from fire:
Mitzvah 57 - The commandment on the court to judge the case of an unpaid guardian:
Mitzvah 58 - The commandment on the court to judge the case of a plaintiff and a defendant:
Mitzvah 59 - The commandment on the court to judge the case of one who takes a wage and of a renter:
Mitzvah 60 - The commandment to judge the case of the borrower:
Mitzvah 61 - The commandment on the court to judge the case of a seducer:
Mitzvah 62 - To not keep a witch alive:
Mitzvah 63 - To not oppress the convert with words:
Mitzvah 64 - To not oppress the convert regarding money:
Mitzvah 65 - To not abuse the orphan and the widow:
Mitzvah 66 - The commandment of lending to the poor person:
Mitzvah 67 - That we not demand the debt of a poor person that does not have with what to pay:
Mitzvah 68 - That we not give a hand between the borrower and the creditor with interest:
Mitzvah 69 - To not curse the judge:
Mitzvah 70 - The negative commandment of 'blessing' the Name:
Mitzvah 71 - To not curse a chieftain [nassi]:
Mitzvah 72 - To not skip in the laws of produce:
Mitzvah 73 - To not eat a torn animal:
Mitzvah 74 - To not hear the claim of a litigant when it is not in front of his fellow litigant:
Mitzvah 75 - Not to have a sinner testify:
Mitzvah 76 - Not to incline after the many in capital punishments because of one:
Mitzvah 77 - That the one who advocated innocence at the beginning of capital cases not advocate guilt:
Mitzvah 78 - The commandment of inclining towards the many:
Mitzvah 79 - To not have mercy upon a poor person in his case:
Mitzvah 80 - The commandment of removing a burden
Mitzvah 81 - To not tip the judgment of an evildoer:
Mitzvah 82 - To not conclude the judgment by estimation:
Mitzvah 83 - To not take a bribe:
Mitzvah 84 - The commandment of the releasing [shmitat] of lands:
Mitzvah 85 - The commandment to rest on Shabbat:
Mitzvah 86 - To not swear by idolatry:
Mitzvah 87 - To not entice the Children of Israel towards idolatry:
Mitzvah 88 - The commandment of celebration on the festivals:
Mitzvah 89 - That we not slaughter the lamb of the Pesach offering on the fourteenth of Nissan while chamets is still in our possession:
Mitzvah 90 - To not leave the entrails of the Pesach sacrifice to stay overnight:
Mitzvah 91 - The commandment of bringing the first-fruits:
Mitzvah 92 - To not cook meat in milk:
Mitzvah 93 - To not make a covenant with the seven nations and likewise with any worshiper of idolatry:
Mitzvah 94 - To not have worshipers of idols dwell in our land:
Mitzvah 95 - The commandment of building the Choice House:
Mitzvah 96 - To not remove the poles of the ark from it:
Mitzvah 97 - The commandment of arranging the bread of display and the frankincense:
Mitzvah 98 - The commandment of arranging lights in the Temple:
Mitzvah 99 - The commandment of wearing the priestly clothes:
Mitzvah 100 - That the breastplate not move from on top of the apron:
Mitzvah 101 - To not tear the coat of the priests:
Mitzvah 102 - The commandment of eating the meat of sin-offerings and guilt-offerings:
Mitzvah 103 - The commandment of burning the incense:
Mitzvah 104 - To not burn incense and not to bring sacrifices upon the gold altar:
Mitzvah 105 - The commandment of the giving of the half shekel during the year:

Sefer HaChinukh

Mitzvah 106 - The commandment of sanctifying the hands and the feet at the time of the service:
Mitzvah 107 - The commandment of anointing the high priest and the kings of the House of David with anointing oil:
Mitzvah 108 - To not rub a foreigner [layman] with anointing oil:
Mitzvah 109 - To not make [oil] according to the specification of the anointing oil:
Mitzvah 110 - To not make [incense] according to the specification of the incense:
Mitzvah 111 - To not eat and drink a gift to idol worship:
Mitzvah 112 - The commandment of the land resting on the seventh year:
Mitzvah 113 - To not eat meat with milk:
Mitzvah 114 - That the court not administer a death sentence on the Shabbat:
Mitzvah 115 - The commandment of the procedure of the burnt-offering:
Mitzvah 116 - The commandment of the meal-offering [mincha]:
Mitzvah 117 - To not offer leaven or honey:
Mitzvah 118 - To not offer a sacrifice without salt:
Mitzvah 119 - The commandment of salting the sacrifice:
Mitzvah 120 - The commandment of the sacrifice of the court if they erred in instruction:
Mitzvah 121 - The commandment of a sin-offering for an individual who sinned inadvertently in a commandment for which we are liable excision:
Mitzvah 122 - The commandment of testimony:
Mitzvah 123 - The commandment of the sacrifice that varies up and down:
Mitzvah 124 - Not to sever a fowl sin-offering:
Mitzvah 125 - To not place olive oil in the meal-offering of a sinner:
Mitzvah 126 - To not put frankincense in the meal-offering of a sinner:
Mitzvah 127 - The commandment of the addition of a fifth for one who eats from the consecrated or misappropriates it:
Mitzvah 128 - The commandment of the sacrifice of an undetermined guilt-offering:
Mitzvah 129 - The commandment of a definite guilt-offering:
Mitzvah 130 - The commandment of returning theft:
Mitzvah 131 - The commandment of the lifting of the ashes:
Mitzvah 132 - The commandment of lighting fire on the altar every day:
Mitzvah 133 - To not extinguish the fire upon the altar:
Mitzvah 134 - The commandment of eating the remainders of the meal-offering:
Mitzvah 135 - To not make the remainders of the meal-offering chamets [leavened]:
Mitzvah 136 - The commandment of the daily meal-offering of the high priest:
Mitzvah 137 - To not eat the meal-offering of the priest:
Mitzvah 138 - The commandment of the procedure of the sin-offering:
Mitzvah 139 - To not eat from the meat of the sin-offerings processed inside:
Mitzvah 140 - The commandment of the procedure of the guilt-offering:
Mitzvah 141 - The commandment of the procedure of the sacrifice of the peace-offerings:
Mitzvah 142 - To not leave over meat from the thanksgiving sacrifice:
Mitzvah 143 - The commandment of the burning of the remnant [notar] of the [sacrifices]:
Mitzvah 144 - To not eat piggul:
Mitzvah 145 - To not eat meat of [the sacrifices] that has become impure:
Mitzvah 146 - The commandment of burning meat of [sacrifices] that has become impure:
Mitzvah 147 - That we not eat forbidden fat [chelev]:
Mitzvah 148 - That we not eat the blood of a [domesticated] beast, a [wild] animal or a bird:
Mitzvah 149 - That the priests not enter the Temple with grown hair:
Mitzvah 150 - That the priests not enter the Temple with torn clothes:
Mitzvah 151 - That the priests not go out from the Temple at the time of the service:
Mitzvah 152 - To not enter the Temple intoxicated, and likewise to not give a ruling intoxicated:
Mitzvah 153 - The command of checking the signs of a beast or animal:
Mitzvah 154 - To not eat an impure beast or animal:
Mitzvah 155 - The commandment to check the signs of fish:
Mitzvah 155 - The commandment to check the signs of fish:
Mitzvah 156 - To not eat impure fish:
Mitzvah 157 - To not eat impure fowl:
Mitzvah 158 - The commandment of checking the signs of grasshoppers:

Sefer HaChinukh

Mitzvah 159 - The commandment of the impurity of the eight swarming creatures
Mitzvah 160 - The commandment of the matter of impurity of foods:
Mitzvah 161 - The commandment of the matter of the impurity of a carcass:
Mitzvah 162 - To not eat the swarming creature of the ground:
Mitzvah 163 - To not eat species of minute swarming creatures born in seeds and fruits:
Mitzvah 164 - To not eat of the swarming creatures of the waters:
Mitzvah 165 - To not eat of swarming creatures that exist from decay:
Mitzvah 166 - The commandment of the matter of the impurity of a woman who has given birth:
Mitzvah 167 - That one impure not eat consecrated foods:
Mitzvah 168 - The law of the sacrifice of the woman that has given birth:
Mitzvah 169 - The commandment of the matter of the impurity of a metsora:
Mitzvah 170 - To not shave the hair of the scab:
Mitzvah 171 - The practice of wildness and rending of a metsora and all who render a person impure:
Mitzvah 172 - The commandment of the matter of ailments of clothing:
Mitzvah 173 - The commandment of purification from tsaraat that it be with certain species:
Mitzvah 174 - The commandment of shaving the metsora on the seventh day:
Mitzvah 175 - The commandment of immersion for the impure:
Mitzvah 176 - The law of the commandment of a metsora when he is healed from his tsaraat:
Mitzvah 177 - The commandment of the matter of the impurity of a house that has an ailment:
Mitzvah 178 - The commandment of the matter of impurity of a zav [one with a discharge] to be impure and to render impure:
Mitzvah 179 - The commandment of the sacrifice of the zav when he is healed from his discharge:
Mitzvah 180 - The commandment of the matter of the impurity of semen, which is impure and renders impure:
Mitzvah 181 - The commandment of the matter of the impurity of the menstruant, that is impure and renders impure:
Mitzvah 182 - The commandment of the matter of the impurity of the zavah [woman with an irregular discharge], that is impure and renders impure:
Mitzvah 183 - The commandment of the sacrifice of the zavah when she is healed from her discharge:
Mitzvah 184 - That the priests not enter at any time into the Temple - and all the more so, non-priests:
Mitzvah 185 - The commandment of the service of Yom Kippur:
Mitzvah 186 - Not to slaughter consecrated animals outside of the [Temple] yard:
Mitzvah 187 - The commandment of covering the blood:
Mitzvah 188 - To not marry one of all the sexual prohibitions:
Mitzvah 189 - To not reveal the nakedness of the father:
Mitzvah 190 - To not reveal the nakedness of the mother:
Mitzvah 191 - To not reveal the nakedness of the wife of the father, even though she is not his mother:
Mitzvah 192 - To not reveal the nakedness of his sister, from any angle that she is his sister:
Mitzvah 193 - To not reveal the nakedness of the daughter of the son:
Mitzvah 194 - To not reveal the nakedness of the daughter of the daughter:
Mitzvah 195 - To not reveal the nakedness of the daughter:
Mitzvah 196 - To not uncover the nakedness of his sister from the father, and she is the daughter of the wife of the father:
Mitzvah 197 - To not reveal the nakedness of the sister of the father:
Mitzvah 198 - The nakedness of the sister of your mother you shall not reveal:
Mitzvah 199 - The nakedness of the brother of your father you shall not reveal:
Mitzvah 200 - The nakedness of the wife of the brother of your father, you shall not reveal:
Mitzvah 201 - The nakedness of your daughter-in-law you shall not reveal:
Mitzvah 202 - The nakedness of the wife of your brother you shall not reveal:
Mitzvah 203 - The nakedness of a woman and her daughter, you shall not reveal:
Mitzvah 204 - The nakedness of a woman and the daughter of her son:
Mitzvah 205 - To not reveal the nakedness of a woman and the daughter of her daughter:
Mitzvah 206 - The nakedness of a woman and her sister:
Mitzvah 207 - To not have intercourse with a menstruant woman:
Mitzvah 208 - That we should not give from our seed to Molekh:
Mitzvah 209 - [For a man] to not have intercourse with males:
Mitzvah 210 - To not lay with a beast:
Mitzvah 211 - Those women not lay with the beasts:

Sefer HaChinukh

Mitzvah 212 - The commandment of the reverence of father and mother:
Mitzvah 213 - To not turn after the worship of idols - not in thought, not in speech and not in vision:
Mitzvah 214 - To not make [idols] not for himself and not for those besides him:
Mitzvah 215 - To not eat notar:
Mitzvah 216 - To leave over the corner of the field:
Mitzvah 217 - To not finish the corner in the field:
Mitzvah 218 - To leave the gleanings in the field:
Mitzvah 219 - To not take the sheaves that fall at the time of the harvesting:
Mitzvah 220 - The commandment of leaving over the corner of the vineyard:
Mitzvah 221 - To not finish the corner of the vineyard:
Mitzvah 222 - The commandment of leaving the peret of the vineyard:
Mitzvah 223 - To not gather the peret of the vineyard:
Mitzvah 224 - To not steal any money:
Mitzvah 225 - That we do not disavow money that is in our hand from another:
Mitzvah 226 - To not swear about the denial of money:
Mitzvah 227 - To not swear falsely:
Mitzvah 228 - To not oppress:
Mitzvah 229 - To not rob:
Mitzvah 230 - To not delay the wage of a wage worker:
Mitzvah 231 - To not curse an Israelite, whether a man or a woman:
Mitzvah 232 - To not make an innocent one stumble on the way:
Mitzvah 233 - To not vitiate justice:
Mitzvah 234 - To not honor a great person in judgement:
Mitzvah 235 - The commandment to judge with righteousness:
Mitzvah 236 - To not spy:
Mitzvah 237 - To not stand over the blood of neighbors:
Mitzvah 238 - To not hate brothers:
Mitzvah 239 - The commandment of rebuke to an Israelite who does not behave properly:
Mitzvah 240 - To not whiten the face of an Israelite:
Mitzvah 241 - To not avenge:
Mitzvah 242 - To not begrudge:
Mitzvah 243 - The commandment of love of Israel:
Mitzvah 244 - To not mate a beast, a specie with not its specie:
Mitzvah 245 - To not sow seeds of forbidden mixtures and not graft in any place in the Land:
Mitzvah 246 - To not eat orlah:
Mitzvah 247 - The commandment of the fourth-year plant:
Mitzvah 248 - To not eat or to drink in the way of a glutton and a drunkard:
Mitzvah 249 - To not divine:
Mitzvah 250 - To not soothsay:
Mitzvah 251 - To not encircle the corner of the head:
Mitzvah 252 - To not destroy the corner of the beard:
Mitzvah 253 - That we not imprint an imprinted tatoo into our flesh:
Mitzvah 254 - The commandment of awe for the Temple:
Mitzvah 255 - To not do an act of ov:
Mitzvah 256 - To not do an act of yidaaoni:
Mitzvah 257 - The commandment to honor sages:
Mitzvah 258 - To not cheat in measures, and all measures are included:
Mitzvah 259 - The commandment of having just scales, weights and measures:
Mitzvah 260 - To not curse father and mother:
Mitzvah 261 - The commandment to burn one who is liable for burning:
Mitzvah 262 - To not follow the practices of the gentiles:
Mitzvah 263 - That a common priest not become defiled with a dead:
Mitzvah 264 - The commandment of the matter of the impurity of the priests for their relatives, and included in it is that each one in Israel should mourn for their six relatives [the identify of which is] well-known:
Mitzvah 265 - That a priest who immersed that day [tevul yom] not serve until his sun set:
Mitzvah 266 - That a priest not marry a licentious woman [zonah]:
Mitzvah 267 - That a priest not marry a profaned woman [challalah]:

Sefer HaChinukh

Mitzvah 268 - That a priest not marry a divorcee:
Mitzvah 269 - The commandment of sanctifying the seed of Aharon:
Mitzvah 270 - That a high priest not enter the tent of a dead body:
Mitzvah 271 - That the high priest not become impure with any impurity:
Mitzvah 272 - The commandment of a high priest to marry a virgin maiden:
Mitzvah 273 - That a high priest not marry a widow:
Mitzvah 274 - That a high priest not have intercourse with a widow:
Mitzvah 275 - That a priest with a blemish not serve in the Temple:
Mitzvah 276 - That a priest with a transient blemish not serve:
Mitzvah 277 - That one with a blemish not enter the entire sanctuary:
Mitzvah 278 - That an impure priest not serve:
Mitzvah 279 - That an impure priest not eat priestly tithe:
Mitzvah 280 - That no foreigner eats priestly tithe:
Mitzvah 281 - That the boarder of a priest and the hired worker not eat priestly tithe:
Mitzvah 282 - That an uncircumcised one not eat priestly tithe:
Mitzvah 283 - That a profaned woman not eat from the holy:
Mitzvah 284 - To not eat tevel:
Mitzvah 285 - That we not consecrate [animals] with blemishes for the altar:
Mitzvah 286 - The commandment of the sacrifice being unblemished:
Mitzvah 287 - That we not place a blemish upon consecrated animals:
Mitzvah 288 - That we not sprinkle blood of an [animal] with a blemish on the altar:
Mitzvah 289 - That we not slaughter an [animal with a blemish] for the sake of a sacrifice:
Mitzvah 290 - That we not incinerate the entrails of [animals] with blemishes:
Mitzvah 291 - Not to castrate one of all of the species:
Mitzvah 292 - Not to sacrifice a sacrifice that is one with a blemish from the hand of the stranger:
Mitzvah 293 - The commandment of a sacrifice that it be from eight days and above:
Mitzvah 294 - To not slaughter a beast and its child on one day:
Mitzvah 295 - That we not do anything through which the name of the Heavens is profaned among people:
Mitzvah 296 - The commandment of sanctification of the Name:
Mitzvah 297 - The commandment of resting on the first day of Pesach:
Mitzvah 298 - To not do work on the first day of Pesach:
Mitzvah 299 - The commandment of the additional sacrifices all of the seven days of Pesach:
Mitzvah 300 - The commandment of resting on the seventh [day] of Pesach:
Mitzvah 301 - To not do work on the seventh day of Pesach:
Mitzvah 302 - The commandment of the sacrifice of the omer of barley:
Mitzvah 303 - To not eat from the new grain before the end of the sixteenth of Nissan:
Mitzvah 304 - To not eat roasted grain from the new grain until that day:
Mitzvah 305 - To not eat fresh grain from the new grain until that day:
Mitzvah 306 - The commandment of counting the omer:
Mitzvah 307 - The commandment of the sacrifice of the new meal-offering from wheat on the day of [Shavuot]:
Mitzvah 308 - The commandment of resting from work on the day of [Shavuot]:
Mitzvah 309 - To not do work on the day of the holiday of Shavuot:
Mitzvah 310 - The commandment of resting on the day of Rosh Hashanah:
Mitzvah 311 - To not do work on the first day of Tishrei:
Mitzvah 312 - The commandment of the additional sacrifice on the day of Rosh Hashanah:
Mitzvah 313 - The commandment of the fast on the tenth day of Tishrei:
Mitzvah 314 - The commandment of the additional sacrifice of Yom Kippur:
Mitzvah 315 - To not do work on the tenth of Tishrei:
Mitzvah 316 - To not eat and drink on Yom Kippur:
Mitzvah 317 - The commandment of resting from work on Yom Kippur:
Mitzvah 318 - The commandment of resting on the first day of the holiday of Sukkot:
Mitzvah 319 - To not do work on the first day of the holiday of Sukkot:
Mitzvah 320 - The commandment of the additional sacrifice on each day of the seven days of Sukkot:
Mitzvah 321 - The commandment of resting from work on the eighth day of Sukkot:
Mitzvah 322 - The commandment of the additional sacrifice on the eighth day of Sukkot, which is called Shemini Atseret:
Mitzvah 323 - To not do work on day of the holiday of Shemini Atseret:

Sefer HaChinukh

Mitzvah 324 - The commandment of taking the lulav:
Mitzvah 325 - The commandment of sitting in a sukkah [booth]:
Mitzvah 326 - That we not work the land on the seventh year:
Mitzvah 327 - That we also not do work with the trees:
Mitzvah 328 - That we not harvest the aftergrowth on the seventh year:
Mitzvah 329 - That we not gather the fruit of the trees in the seventh [year] in the manner that we gather them in every year:
Mitzvah 330 - The commandment of counting the seven [cycles] of seven years:
Mitzvah 331 - The commandment of blowing the shofar on Yom Yippur of the Jubilee:
Mitzvah 332 - The commandment of the sanctification of the Jubilee year:
Mitzvah 333 - That we not work the land on the Jubilee year:
Mitzvah 334 - To not harvest the aftergrowth of the produce of the Jubilee year:
Mitzvah 335 - To not gather the fruits of the trees on the Jubilee year in the manner that we gather them in other years:
Mitzvah 336 - The commandment of adjudicating between the buyer and the seller:
Mitzvah 337 - To not mistreat in buying and selling:
Mitzvah 338 - To not mistreat any Israelite with words:
Mitzvah 339 - That we not sell a field in the Land of Israel in perpetuity:
Mitzvah 340 - The commandment of returning land to its owners on the Jubilee:
Mitzvah 341 - The law of redemption of houses of walled cities until the completion of a year:
Mitzvah 342 - To not change the open areas of the Levites:
Mitzvah 343 - To not lend with interest to an Israelite:
Mitzvah 344 - That we not make a Hebrew slave perform demeaning work, like the work of a Canaanite [gentile] slave:
Mitzvah 345 - That we not sell a Hebrew slave upon the auctioning stone:
Mitzvah 346 - To not make a Hebrew slave perform oppressive work:
Mitzvah 347 - The commandment of work with a Canaanite slave forever:
Mitzvah 348 - To not allow a gentile to work a Hebrew slave sold to him:
Mitzvah 349 - That we not prostrate ourselves on a figured stone, even to God:
Mitzvah 350 - The commandment that one who appraises a man give the value delineated in the Torah:
Mitzvah 351 - To not exchange consecrated things:
Mitzvah 352 - The commandment of the one who exchanges the beast of a sacrifice with another beast, such that both of them be consecrated:
Mitzvah 353 - The commandment of the appraisal of a beast, such that one give according to what the priest appraises:
Mitzvah 354 - The commandment of appraising houses, such that he give the appraisal that the priest appraises and the addition of a fifth:
Mitzvah 355 - The commandment of appraising a field, that he give the appraisal specified in the section of the Torah:
Mitzvah 356 - To not change the consecrated from a sacrifice to a sacrifice:
Mitzvah 357 - The commandment of the law of one who dedicates from his properties, that it is of the priests:
Mitzvah 358 - That owners that dedicated land not sell it, but that it rather be given to the priests:
Mitzvah 359 - That a dedicated field not be redeemed:
Mitzvah 360 - The commandment of the tithe of pure beasts every year:
Mitzvah 361 - To not sell the tithe of beasts, but rather that it be eaten in Jerusalem:
Mitzvah 362 - The commandment to send the impure out of the camp of the Divine Presence:
Mitzvah 363 - That an impure person not enter the entire Temple:
Mitzvah 364 - The commandment of confession of sin:
Mitzvah 365 - The commandment of the suspected adulteress [sotah] for the husband to bring her to the priest and that he do to her according to the statute that is written:
Mitzvah 366 - That we not put oil on the sotah sacrifice:
Mitzvah 367 - Not to place frankincense on the sotah sacrifice:
Mitzvah 368 - That the nazirite not drink wine or all types of spirits:
Mitzvah 369 - That the nazirite not eat damp grapes:
Mitzvah 370 - That the nazirite not eat raisins:
Mitzvah 371 - That the nazirite not eat the seeds of the grapes:
Mitzvah 372 - That the nazirite not eat the peel of the grapes:

Sefer HaChinukh

Mitzvah 373 - That the nazirite not shave his hair:
Mitzvah 374 - The commandment of growing the hair of the nazirite:
Mitzvah 375 - That the nazirite not enter the tent of a dead body:
Mitzvah 376 - That the nazirite not become impure through a dead body or through other impurities:
Mitzvah 377 - The commandment of shaving the nazirite and bringing his sacrifices:
Mitzvah 378 - The commandment of the priestly blessing every day:
Mitzvah 379 - The commandment of carrying the Ark on the shoulder:
Mitzvah 380 - The commandment of the second Pesach [Pesach Sheni] on the fourteenth of Iyar:
Mitzvah 381 - The commandment that the second Pesach [Pesach Sheni] offering be eaten with matsot and maror [bitter herbs]:
Mitzvah 382 - Not to leave any meat from the Pesach Sheni sacrifice to its morrow:
Mitzvah 383 - Not to break a bone from the bones of the Pesach Sheni sacrifice:
Mitzvah 384 - The commandment of blowing the trumpets in the Temple and in war:
Mitzvah 385 - The commandment of challah [dough-offering]:
Mitzvah 386 - The commandment of fringes [tsitsit]:
Mitzvah 387 - To not wander after the thoughts of the heart and the vision of the eyes:
Mitzvah 388 - The commandment to guard the Temple:
Mitzvah 389 - That the priests not be involved in the service of the Levites and the Levites in the service of the priests:
Mitzvah 390 - That a foreigner not serve in the Temple:
Mitzvah 391 - To not nullify the guarding of the Temple:
Mitzvah 392 - The commandment of redeeming the first-born of a man:
Mitzvah 393 - To not redeem the first-born of a pure animal: That we should
Mitzvah 394 - The commandment of the service of the Levites in the Temple:
Mitzvah 395 - The commandment of the first tithe:
Mitzvah 396 - The commandment of the Levites to give a tithe from the tithe:
Mitzvah 397 - The commandment of the red heifer:
Mitzvah 398 - The commandment of the impurity of a dead body:
Mitzvah 399 - The Commandment of the niddah waters which render the pure, impure and only purify someone impure from the impurity of a dead body:
Mitzvah 400 - The commandment of the laws of inheritance:
Mitzvah 401 - The commandment of the regular [sacrifices] daily:
Mitzvah 402 - The commandment of the additional sacrifice of Shabbat:
Mitzvah 403 - The commandment of the additional sacrifice on each and every month:
Mitzvah 404 - The commandment of the additional sacrifice on the day of the festival of Shavouot:
Mitzvah 405 - The commandment of shofar [horn] on Rosh Hashanah:
Mitzvah 406 - The commandment of the law of the abrogation of vows:
Mitzvah 407 - That we not profane our words from vows:
Mitzvah 408 - The commandment on Israel to give cities within which the Levites may dwell, and they shelter:
Mitzvah 409 - To not kill someone liable before he is brought to justice:
Mitzvah 410 - The commandment on the court to send one who smites a soul inadvertently from his city to the cities of refuge and upon the killer himself to go there:
Mitzvah 411 - That the witness not issue a ruling in the case that he is testifying about in capital punishments:
Mitzvah 412 - Not to take ransom to save the murderer from the death penalty:
Mitzvah 413 - Not to take ransom from one liable for exile to exempt him from exile:
Mitzvah 414 - Not to appoint a judge that that does not know the laws of the Torah:
Mitzvah 415 - That a judge not fear in judgement:
Mitzvah 416 - Not to desire the money of your friend:
Mitzvah 417 - The commandment of the unification of God:
Mitzvah 418 - The commandment of loving God:
Mitzvah 419 - The commandment of Torah study:
Mitzvah 420 - The law of the recitation of Shema morning and evening:
Mitzvah 421 - The commandment of the tefillin of the arm:
Mitzvah 422 - The commandment of the tefillin of the head:
Mitzvah 423 - To affix a mezuzah on entrances:
Mitzvah 424 - To not test a true prophet more than is necessary:
Mitzvah 425 - The commandment of killing the seven nations:

Sefer HaChinukh

Mitzvah 426 - To not grace and to have mercy on an idolater:
Mitzvah 427 - To not marry with idolaters:
Mitzvah 428 - To not derive benefit from the coverings of idolatry and from its auxiliaries:
Mitzvah 429 - To not benefit from an offering to idolatry:
Mitzvah 430 - To bless God after eating food:
Mitzvah 431 - The commandment of loving the strangers [converts]:
Mitzvah 432 - The commandment of fearing God:
Mitzvah 433 - The commandment of prayer:
Mitzvah 434 - To cling to Torah sages:
Mitzvah 435 - To swear in His name, may He be Blessed, truthfully:
Mitzvah 436 - To destroy idolatry and its auxiliaries:
Mitzvah 437 - Not to destroy things upon which His name, may He be Blessed, are called:
Mitzvah 438 - That one brings all of his vows on the first festival:
Mitzvah 439 - Not to sacrifice a sacrifice outside of the [Temple] yard:
Mitzvah 440 - The commandment to sacrifice all the sacrifices in the Choice House:
Mitzvah 441 - To redeem consecrated things upon which a blemish developed:
Mitzvah 442 - To not eat from the second tithe of grain outside of Jerusalem:
Mitzvah 443 - To not eat the second tithe of wine outside of Jerusalem:
Mitzvah 444 - To not eat the second tithe of oil outside of Jerusalem:
Mitzvah 445 - To not eat an unblemished first-born [animal] outside of Jerusalem:
Mitzvah 446 - To not eat higher-level consecrated foods [kodshai kodashim] outside of the [Temple] yard:
Mitzvah 447 - To not eat meat of a burnt-offering:
Mitzvah 448 - To not eat lower-level consecrated foods [kodashim kalim] before the sprinkling of the bloods:
Mitzvah 449 - That the priest not eat the first-fruits [bikkurim] before their placement in the [Temple] yard:
Mitzvah 450 - To not forsake the Levite, from giving him his gifts:
Mitzvah 451 - The commandment of slaughter:
Mitzvah 452 - To not eat a limb from the living:
Mitzvah 453 - To bring consecrated things to the Choice House [Temple]:
Mitzvah 454 - To not add to the commandments and their understanding:
Mitzvah 455 - To not subtract from the commandments of the Torah:
Mitzvah 456 - To not listen to one who prophecies in the name of idolatry:
Mitzvah 457 - To not love the seducer:
Mitzvah 458 - To not leave the hatred towards the seducer:
Mitzvah 459 - To not save the seducer:
Mitzvah 460 - Not to advocate innocence for a seducer:
Mitzvah 461 - Not to refrain from advocating guilt for the seducer:
Mitzvah 462 - To not seduce one of Israel to worship idolatry:
Mitzvah 463 - The commandment of investigating the witnesses well:
Mitzvah 464 - The burning of an enticed city and to kill its people:
Mitzvah 465 - To not rebuild an enticed city:
Mitzvah 466 - To not benefit from the property of an enticed city:
Mitzvah 467 - To not gash ourselves, like the worshipers of idolatry:
Mitzvah 468 - To not make a bald spot for the dead:
Mitzvah 469 - To not eat from consecrated [animals] that have been disqualified:
Mitzvah 470 - To check the signs of a bird:
Mitzvah 471 - To not eat from the flying swarming creatures:
Mitzvah 472 - To not eat from the meat of a [domesticated] beast, a [wild] animal or a bird that has died by itself:
Mitzvah 473 - The commandment of the second tithe:
Mitzvah 474 - To separate the poor tithe:
Mitzvah 475 - To not claim a debt that the seventh year passed:
Mitzvah 476 - The commandment to press the foreigner:
Mitzvah 477 - That he releases all of his loans in the seventh [year]:
Mitzvah 478 - To not steel his heart against the poor:
Mitzvah 479 - The commandment of charity [tsedekah]:
Mitzvah 480 - To not refrain from lending before the sabbatical year:
Mitzvah 481 - To not send a Hebrew slave empty:

Sefer HaChinukh

Mitzvah 482 - To endow him upon his leaving to freedom:
Mitzvah 483 - To not work with consecrated things:
Mitzvah 484 - To not shear the wool of consecrated [animals]:
Mitzvah 485 - To not eat chamets after midday:
Mitzvah 486 - To not leave over from the festive [chagigah] sacrifice to the third day:
Mitzvah 487 - To not sacrifice the Pesach sacrifice on the bamah [altar] of an individual:
Mitzvah 488 - The commandment to rejoice on the festivals:
Mitzvah 489 - To appear on the festivals in the Choice House:
Mitzvah 490 - To not go up for the festival without a sacrifice:
Mitzvah 491 - To appoint judges and officers:
Mitzvah 492 - To not plant any tree-idols:
Mitzvah 493 - To not erect a matsevah:
Mitzvah 494 - To not offer a sacrifice of [an animal] with a temporary blemish:
Mitzvah 495 - To listen to the voice of the court at all times:
Mitzvah 496 - To not stray from their words:
Mitzvah 497 - To appoint a king from Israel:
Mitzvah 498 - To not establish a foreign king over us:
Mitzvah 499 - That the king not amass many horses:
Mitzvah 500 - To not ever dwell in the Land of Egypt:
Mitzvah 501 - That the king not amass many wives:
Mitzvah 502 - That the king not amass much silver and gold for himself:
Mitzvah 503 - That the king write a second Torah scroll for himself:
Mitzvah 504 - That the tribe of Levi not inherit in the Land of Israel:
Mitzvah 505 - That the tribe of Levi not take a portion in the spoils:
Mitzvah 506 - To give the foreleg, the jaw and the maw to the priest:
Mitzvah 507 - To separate the great tithe for the priest:
Mitzvah 508 - To give the first shearing to the priest:
Mitzvah 509 - That the priests and the Levites work in the Temple in shifts:
Mitzvah 510 - To not engage in clairvoyance:
Mitzvah 511 - To not do magic:
Mitzvah 512 - To not invoke a charm:
Mitzvah 513 - To not ask a master of ov:
Mitzvah 514 - To not ask a yidaaoni:
Mitzvah 515 - To not inquire of the dead:
Mitzvah 516 - The commandment to heed a true prophet:
Mitzvah 517 - To not prophecy falsely:
Mitzvah 518 - To not prophesy in the name of idolatry:
Mitzvah 519 - That we not fear from the killing of a false prophet:
Mitzvah 520 - The commandment to prepare six cities of refuge:
Mitzvah 521 - To not show pity upon the killer or injurer:
Mitzvah 522 - To not remove a landmark:
Mitzvah 523 - To not establish a matter of testimony with one witness:
Mitzvah 524 - To do to the collusive witness like he colluded:
Mitzvah 525 - To not be terrified or to be afraid in war:
Mitzvah 526 - The commandment to anoint a priest for war:
Mitzvah 527 - To send peace to the cities that we besiege:
Mitzvah 528 - To not keep alive a soul of the seven nations:
Mitzvah 529 - To not destroy fruit trees:
Mitzvah 530 - To behead the calf in the riverbed:
Mitzvah 531 - To not work or sow in that land:
Mitzvah 532 - To execute the law of the one of beautiful form [yefat toar] as is written in the Torah:
Mitzvah 533 - To not sell one of beautiful of form:
Mitzvah 534 - Not to make her serve after he has intercourse with her:
Mitzvah 535 - To hang one who is liable for hanging:
Mitzvah 536 - To not leave one that is hung overnight:
Mitzvah 537 - To bury him on the same day, and so [too] all the dead:
Mitzvah 538 - To return a lost item to an Israelite:

Sefer HaChinukh

Mitzvah 539 - To not avoid his eyes from it:
Mitzvah 540 - To not leave the beast of his fellow falling under its load:
Mitzvah 541 - To load the load that has fallen [together] with his fellow:
Mitzvah 542 - That a woman should not wear the adornments of a man:
Mitzvah 543 - That a man should not wear the clothes of a woman:
Mitzvah 544 - To not take the mother upon the young:
Mitzvah 545 - To send away the mother [bird] if he takes it upon the young:
Mitzvah 546 - The commandment of a parapet:
Mitzvah 547 - To not leave a stumbling block:
Mitzvah 548 - To not plant forbidden mixtures in a vineyard:
Mitzvah 549 - To not eat forbidden mixtures of the vineyard:
Mitzvah 550 - To not do work with two species of animals:
Mitzvah 551 - To not wear shaatnez:
Mitzvah 552 - To marry a woman with a marriage contract and betrothal:
Mitzvah 553 - The commandment that the wife of one who 'puts out a bad name' [about her] dwell with him forever:
Mitzvah 554 - That he should not divorce her all of his days:
Mitzvah 555 - The commandment upon the court to stone the one liable:
Mitzvah 556 - Not to punish one coerced into a sin:
Mitzvah 557 - The commandment on the rapist to marry the one he has raped:
Mitzvah 558 - That he not divorces her all of his days:
Mitzvah 559 - That a eunuch not marry a daughter of Israel:
Mitzvah 560 - That a mamzer [a child born from a forbidden marriage] should not marry a daughter of Israel:
Mitzvah 561 - That an Ammonite or a Moabite not enter the Congregation of the Lord:
Mitzvah 562 - Not to seek their peace in a war:
Mitzvah 563 - Not to distance an Edomite of the third generation from coming into the congregation:
Mitzvah 564 - To not distance an Egyptian of the third generation:
Mitzvah 565 - That one impure should not enter the Temple mount:
Mitzvah 566 - The commandment to set up a place in which to defecate:
Mitzvah 567 - The commandment to set up a spike to dig with:
Mitzvah 568 - Not to turn over a slave that fled from his master:
Mitzvah 569 - To not oppress a slave who has fled to us, from outside the Land, to the Land [of Israel]:
Mitzvah 570 - Not to have sexual relations with a woman without a marriage contract and betrothal:
Mitzvah 571 - Not to bring the fee of a prostitute or the price of a dog:
Mitzvah 572 - That the borrower not give interest to an Israelite:
Mitzvah 573 - To lend to the gentile with interest:
Mitzvah 574 - Not to delay his vows for more than three festivals:
Mitzvah 575 - To fulfill what has come out of his lips, as he vowed:
Mitzvah 576 - The commandment to allow the wage-worker to eat from the attached [produce] upon which he is working:
Mitzvah 577 - That the worker not take into his hand more than his eating:
Mitzvah 578 - That the worker not eat during work time:
Mitzvah 579 - That one who wants to divorce his wife divorce her with a bill [get]:
Mitzvah 580 - That he not brings back his ex-wife from when she has married:
Mitzvah 581 - That a groom should not go out from his home the whole year, even for the needs of the community:
Mitzvah 582 - The commandment that a groom rejoices with his wife for one year:
Mitzvah 583 - That we not take as surety vessels in which life-sustaining food [ochel nefesh] is made:
Mitzvah 584 - To not detach signs of tzaraat [a Biblical skin disease]:
Mitzvah 585 - To not take surety from a debtor by force:
Mitzvah 586 - To not prevent surety from its needy owner:
Mitzvah 587 - To return the surety to the owners at the time that he needs it:
Mitzvah 588 - To give the wage of a wage-worker on its day:
Mitzvah 589 - That a relative not testify, one about the other:
Mitzvah 590 - To not sway the judgement of a stranger or an orphan:
Mitzvah 591 - To not take the garment of a widow as surety:
Mitzvah 592 - To leave what is forgotten to the poor:

Sefer HaChinukh

Mitzvah 593 - To not go back to take what is forgotten:
Mitzvah 594 - The commandment to lash the evildoer:
Mitzvah 595 - To not increase in flogging him:
Mitzvah 596 - To not muzzle an animal at the time of its work:
Mitzvah 597 - That a levirate wife not marry another until she is released:
Mitzvah 598 - The commandment of levirate marriage:
Mitzvah 599 - The commandment of release [chalitsah]:
Mitzvah 600 - The commandment to save the pursued with the life of the pursuer:
Mitzvah 601 - To not have concern about the pursuer:
Mitzvah 602 - To not hold over deficient weights and measures:
Mitzvah 603 - To remember what Amalek did to us:
Mitzvah 604 - To blot out his seed from the world:
Mitzvah 605 - To not forget what he did to us:
Mitzvah 606 - The commandment of recital over the first-fruits:
Mitzvah 607 - The commandment of declaration of tithes:
Mitzvah 608 - To not eat the second tithe in bereavement:
Mitzvah 609 - To not eat the second tithe in impurity:
Mitzvah 610 - To only expend monies of the second tithe for eating and drinking:
Mitzvah 611 - The commandment to walk in - and make oneself similar through - the ways of God, may He be Blessed:
Mitzvah 612 - To gather all of Israel on the festival of Sukkot:
Mitzvah 613 - For everyone to write a Torah scroll for himself:

Sefer HaChinukh

Sefer HaChinukh

Author's Introduction

Introduction of the Rabbi, the author of the Sefer Hachinukh

The clear truth in the human species is that which most people in the world have agreed about - and the opinion of all people has already agreed with it - to believe the testimony of people. And with the proliferation of those testifying about a thing about which they are testifying, the thing is more established in the eyes of its hearers. And in those testifying being few, a bit of doubt develops in the thing for those that are sharp. And this matter has become so strong among people to the point that they fixed it in the practices of each and every nation to kill a man according to the testimony of two or three witnesses. And since three is more honored [than two], the perfect Torah also [mentioned it]. And from this reason also did the opinion of all agree to accept from the mouths of the testimony of their fathers, their elders, about that which they tell them that happened in their days or in the days of their fathers or in the days of the fathers of their fathers. And there is no doubt that in the fathers testifying being many - and in the ones that the event happened in their days being many - the thing is strengthened in the hearts of the children that hear [it]. Therefore, when God wanted to give the Torah to His people, Israel, He gave it to them in the eyes of six hundred thousand adult men, besides the many infants and women, that they all be believable witnesses about the things. Also, in order that the testimony, be stronger and more believable, they all merited prophecy [at that time]. As doubt never develops about that which one knows by way of prophecy. And that is [the meaning of] that which God said to Moshe, "in order that the people hear My speaking to you, and they also believe in you forever" (Exodus 19:9) - meaning to say, they and their children will believe in you and your prophecy forever. As they will then know [with] a trustworthy knowledge that God speaks with a man and he can live, and that all of your prophecy is true. And had it not been that they merited prophecy, a claimant could have argued about all of the signs that Moshe did in the eyes of Pharaoh and in their eyes and said, "Who knows if he did it with machinations of the wisdom of demons or with the power of the names of the angels. And even though the wise men of Egypt and all of its magicians, who were more expert in the wisdom of demons and magic than all the rest of the world, conceded to Moshe against their will and said to Pharaoh that it it was through the power of God that he did [it] - as it is written (Exodus 8:15), "it is the finger of God" - nonetheless, one who wants to be stubborn will say it was from his greater wisdom that he did it and they conceded to him. But after the prophecy, no type of hesitation remained about the matter. And [so] they knew clearly that all of the events were done by the command of the Master of the world, and that everything come to them from His hand. And they - who saw with their eyes and knew the thing with a true knowing that people do not have any stronger truth than this - testified to their children that were born afterwards that all the words of the Torah, from the [first letter] bet of the [first word], Bereshit to the lamed [at the end of the final words] le'einei kol Yisrael, that they received from Moshe in the eyes of all of Israel were true and clear without any hesitation in the world. And their children also testified to their children and their children to their children until [it reached] us. It comes out that the Torah that is in our hands is a true Torah according to six hundred thousand believable witnesses - which is the tally that includes all the opinions of the men, besides the infants and the women. And now if a seducer, 'whose heart turns away from the Lord, our God,' would claim to us and say, "What is it with you, Jew-man, and your tradition? And what is with you to 'ask your father and your elder?' Investigate and search well with your intellect and establish your reasoning. 'Open your eyes and see' what is in your world - the movement of the sphere and the four basic elements of the land. From them you will you will see and understand the hidden things of wisdom. And investigate with your reason and you shall learn how the One unified"; we would [then] respond to him: From the angle of our investigation, we could never grasp anything of the word of God. As even in matters of the lowly world, all the wise men of science have not been able to come to fullness [of understanding]. As through the wisdom of investigation, who will reveal the mystery of the grasses and the fruit, the mystery of precious stones and vegetables and the cause of the movement of iron with magnetic rocks? As all of the wise men of science and all the men of understanding have stood wondering [about these things]. Even more [would they not be helpful] if we would say to understand from them the glorious wisdoms and the knowledge of God's existence. God forbid for us, God forbid, to come behind the King in our arrogance and to raise our hand and to think thoughts from that which is above our thoughts and for which we have no need. As behold our ancestors, may their memory be Blessed, set up a table in front of us - they probed deeply and they come to the fullness of true knowledge. They grasped knowing that God speaks to a man and he can live. And [hence] what is it to us after this to investigate and to examine if the truth is with them? Rather [it is] for us to drink their words with thirst, according to their words and according to their expressions. And the parable for this is one to whom it has been testified by thousands of thousands of people to not drink from the waters of a river, because they have seen these waters kill its drinkers. And the thing was experienced a thousand times at different time periods and with people [from] different lands. And a sage expert physician said to him, "Do not believe all of them, as I am informing you from the perspective of wisdom that these waters are not fitting to kill, since they are clear and light and the dirt that goes through them is goodly. Drink them until your soul is satiated." Would it be good for this one to leave the famous testimony of all and to do like the words of the sage? Truly the matter is not good and an intelligent person will not listen to him and will not do like his words. This is the matter that we have prefaced - that the truth of matters of the world is known by the multitude of people that testify about it more than by those that prove their words from the angle of their intellect and investigation. Since because man is lacking perfection, his intellect does not grasp the fullness of things. And therefore, the chosen path is for a man to fulfill all the words of the Torah, which was received by trustworthy witnesses, which the Master of wisdom gave to people. And in it is included all precious knowledge and all glorious wisdom.

And [maybe] one would ask, "What is the matter that God gave such a precious Torah to people? Does not God have everything, and there is no measure to His elevation and to His glory? And there is no addition to His glory from the knowing of men of the power of His deeds; as there can be no addition or subtraction to complete glory and majesty on account of something [else]. The answer to this is obvious: That the mind of people does not grasp the ways of his Creator to know what is the reason for His deeds; as higher are 'His ways than our ways and His thoughts than our thoughts.' And even though the reason for the thing is not revealed to us, we should believe that the Father of wisdoms, the Master of all, does everything that He does for a purpose and for a positive matter. And nonetheless it is possible for us to find a little reason and to say that people's knowledge of the ways of God is necessitated by His loftiness, may He be Blessed. As since it came up in His thought in front of Him to create the world, it is fitting that it be with complete perfection - since all of the acts of the Perfect One are perfect. And this is the truth, since Blessed be He was perfect in everything, as nothing is lacking from Him, such that a man could say, "Why did He not do this in His world?" As he knows His advantage over him in wisdom. As behold, He created separated intellects in His world - and they are the angels. And He also created intellects in permanent bodies - and they are the heavens and all of their hosts. And He created physical bodies without any intellect at all in the world - and they are the beasts and the birds and the other species that are similar to them. And he also created physical creatures with intellect - and that is the human species - to make known that that nothing is prevented from Him (He can do anything). As even though the physical and the intellect are complete opposites, He mixed them together in the greatness of His wisdom and made man with them. And if so, it was nonetheless necessary that this intellect mixed with the physical - and that is man - know his Creator and recognize Him, so as to fulfill the intention of his creation. And if it were not for the Torah that He gave him, the intellect would be completely drawn to the physical in all of its desires, and he would be 'compared in similarity to beasts.' And as such, the work would not be perfected, since the body of a man and the body of a beast would be one in the matter - even if they are not one in their form - and it would come out that there is a lack in the creation. And it comes out according to our words that the giving of the Torah to educate the hearts of men is necessitated for the perfection of the designs. And [perhaps] one might ask further, "Since it is the perfection of the designs, why was it given to one people from the peoples of the world, and not to all of them?" In this also would

Sefer HaChinukh

it be an obvious answer to respond that the intellect of the one designed will not grasp the intention of his Designer. But nonetheless with this too is it possible to find a little reason according to the way of the world: Is it not known that in all the things of the world, the chaff is greater than the core? And even in the core, there is a part of it that is more select in it than the whole. It is as if you would say most of the land in the world is not prime, but rather only its minority. But even in the prime, part of it is the prime of the prime. And so is the matter also with the fruits of the world and with types of beasts and fowl. And, if so, also with the human species shall the thing be like this, to make it similar to the lowly world. Since it shares some of itself with it - as it has a finite body like them - it is no wonder about the thing. And so, one part of the human species was chosen - and that is Israel, and it is the 'smallest from all the nations.' And Blessed is God who knows that they are the choicest of the human species and chose them to be called His people and gave them all the main parts of wisdom. However even with the rest of the human species, He gave them a way to distinguish themselves from beasts - and that is the seven commandments that all the people of the world were commanded as a whole, as we shall write about each one of them, with God's help. And also, with the people of Israel itself - part of them are more choice, and that is the tribe of Levi, which was chosen for His permanent service. And so [too,] is the thing with planet Earth, that there is a part of it that is choicest from all of it and God knew that the choicest in it is the Land of Israel. And [so] His will was to settle the choicest of the Human species in it. Also, in it, the best in it was Jerusalem. And so, it was chosen to be the dwelling of the Torah and place of his Service. And from it is the entire planet of the earth Blessed, as God commanded blessing to be there. And perhaps one would ask further - since I said that the essence of all, and the chosen portion, is the people of Israel - how is the thing that they always suffer exile and troubles? And the answer is that it is well-known and famous among the people of the world that the Master of all created two worlds - the world of bodies and the world of souls. And the world of bodies is considered like nothing and emptiness in contrast to the world of souls. As this one is like a passing shadow, whereas that one remains forever and ever. And the body serves as a vessel for the soul for a short time, and afterwards it decomposes and becomes vile. [Accordingly,] God bequeathed to His people the world of souls, which is the eternal world and the enjoyment of which has no measure. And perhaps one who asks would ask further, "And why did God not give to His people, that He chose, two portions of enjoyment - the world of bodies and the world of souls?" The answer is that it is well-known to every intelligent person that it is impossible for a physical being to be in the world without sinning. And among the fixed traits forever and ever of God, Blessed be He, is the trait of justice; and it obligates every intelligent person to go in the way of the intellect and to be liable when he veers [from it]. And once the trait of justice has made him liable, it is impossible for him to be exempted without any [punishment]; since he left the court of the trait of justice [with a] guilty [verdict]. And hence it is from the kindnesses of God to us that He placed our share to have sin purged from us in this finite world, [so that] our souls be clean and survive to the world of souls; as one hour there is better than all of the life in this world. However, we should believe that a time will come that we will merit the two portions, and that is the days of the messiah. And the reason is that in those days, we will not need the purging of the bodies at all, since the evil impulse will be nullified from us; as it is written (Ezekiel 36:26), "and I will remove the heart of stone, etc." And also, if a little dross of sin remains at that time, it will fall on the goat (sacrificed scapegoat), as at the beginning. And this is what is written in the Torah (Leviticus 26:4), "If you will go in My ways," I will bequeath the good of this world to you - meaning to say, if you will be whole and not require purging of the body, you will also merit the good of this world. And that is what is written about our father, Avraham - peace be upon him - that God Blessed him, even with the good of this world. As he did not need purging of the body at all at that time. And after this, there is no [cause] to wonder about the pain of Israel in the exiles more than all of the nations; as it is all for their good and for their glory. And you who asks - place your eyes and your heart to this as it is a big thing that all of the evildoers will not understand, but the intelligent will understand. As many of of the Jews are destitute from the many great troubles that follow [one another against] them in the exiles and they do not know nor understand the good of the world of souls - their 'feet almost strayed' from the many worries, and 'their hearts were not constant with them' from the many ruminations.

Sefer HaChinukh

May God, in His kindnesses, remove thoughts of wickedness and impart upon us proper intellect and correct opinions to fulfill His desire - amen, may He do so. And he may ask further, "Since you said that the essence of all is the world of the souls and the final reward of commandments is in it, why did the Torah not mention it and state, 'When you do My commandments, I will bequeath you the world to come.'" The answer is because the matter of the world to come is well-known and revealed to all intelligent people and clear as the sun. There is no people nor language that do not agree that there is permanence to souls after the termination of the bodies. And there is also no one that disagrees that it is according to the good of the soul, its wisdom and the propriety of its actions, that its enjoyment will be greater. As the source of the intellectual soul from which it is extracted is the Intellect, and anyone that comes closer to its nature - the place of its extraction - will have greater pleasure. These words do not require support with proofs and witnesses - they are their own witnesses and their proofs are basic knowledge. And so, the Torah never elaborates about that which is well-known from human logic. And this is [the meaning] of their, may their memory be Blessed, saying in every place, "It is logical" - meaning, there is no need for a verse about that which logic reveals. And hence the Torah promised us with the fulfillment of the commandments in this world to say that we not be preoccupied with sustenance and with wars [against] the enemies and that we be able to put efforts into the service of God and fathom His will. And there is no need to elaborate further and to say, "And when you accomplish His will, you will merit the pleasure of the world to come" - since the thing is self-evident that any creature that accomplishes the will of his Creator, may He be elevated, approaches Him and will enjoy from His radiance. And another reason [for this] is that if the Torah had promised about the reward of the world to come and not this one, the promise would not have been seen while [people are still] alive; and the heart of those of little faith may have disturbed [them] with words.

And from the fundamentals of this Torah that we said that God gave to His people through Moshe, His prophet, is to know that the Lord God in the Heavens that gave the Torah to Israel is the First Being - such that there is no beginning nor end to His being, may He be Blessed - and that He made exist and created from His will and His power all that was created, ex nihilo. And [likewise] that He keeps in existence everything that He created the whole time that He wishes, but no longer - [not] even an instant. And that He is not prevented from doing anything. And [also from the fundamentals is] to believe that He is one without any conjunction; to believe that in a man fulfilling that which is written in [the Torah], his soul will merit great enjoyment forever; and to believe that God oversees the actions of people and knows all the details of their deeds and repays everyone according to his action. And also, from the fundamentals of the Torah is to believe that the true explanation of the Torah is the traditional received explanation that is in our hands from the early Sages of Israel. And anyone who explains about it something that is the opposite of their intention is [expressing] a mistake and a completely void thing. As our Sages received the explanation of the Torah from our teacher, Moshe - peace be upon him - who received it from God, Blessed be He, when he stood on the mountain forty days. And even though it was possible to learn [it] in less time than this due to the power of the Teacher, God wanted to hint to the learners that they learn it with deliberation. And this true explanation that we wrote is the explanation that is written in the Babylonian and Jerusalem Talmuds (Gemara), which [was] composed [by] our early Sages, who received it one generation after another from our teacher Moshe, peace be upon him. And the Babylonian is lengthier and more elucidated, and [so] we rely upon it more. And it is made up of six orders, and there are sixty tractates in it, according to the division of the contents. Their mnemonic is 'there are sixty queens.' And there are five hundred and twenty-two chapters. And the true explanation of the Torah is likewise elucidated from other books that some of our early Sages composed. And [these books] are called Sifra, Sifrei, Tosefta and Mekhilta. All of these are books that all of Israel believe and [they] rely upon the words of theirs which are there without a disagreement. And about those that there is a disagreement, they have already also explained the ruling that we should take from them. Everything is nicely elucidated without any doubt or confusion to those that understand. And anyone whose heart troubles him about these matters is not included in the holy (Jewish) people - since we would never agree about the truth from the simple understanding of the verses of the Torah without their explanations and their true tradition. As there are several verses in the Torah that appear to contradict one another. But the one who knows their explanation understands and sees that the ways of God are straight: Behold it is written in the Torah (Exodus 12:40), "And the inhabitation of the Children of Israel [which they dwelt in Egypt was four hundred and thirty years]." And [yet] we found that Kehat the son of Levi was from those that went down to Egypt; and if you count the days of his life and the years of the life of Amram, his son, and the eighty years of Moshe - as he was eighty in his standing in front of Pharaoh to speak to him to take out the Children of Israel from Egypt - they all only add up to three hundred and fifty years. However, the explanation of this is that the tally of four hundred and thirty begins from the time that it was stated to Avraham, "that your seed will be a stranger" (Genesis 15:13). And the explanation of the verse is thus: "And the inhabitation of the Children of Israel which they dwelt in Egypt" and other lands - meaning that they began to be exiled - "was four hundred and thirty years." As from the time that it was stated to Avraham, "that your seed will be a stranger," did the distress begin for him - and [so] the beginning of the tally is from there. And do not let its stating, "the Children of Israel," be difficult for you - as behold they said in the Midrash (Bereshit Rabbah 63:3), "Avraham is called Israel, as it is stated, 'And the inhabitation of the Children of Israel.'" And that which it states, "the Children of Israel" is meaning to say the Children of Israel and Israel (referring to Avraham); but Scripture expressed it in this language since the distress began to the father with the proclamation of the exile of the children. And that which it is stated, "Egypt," is also not specific, but rather meaning to say in exile. And that which it expressed it all with the [word,] Egypt, is because the core of the exile was there; and everything goes according to the core, and it is always called by it. And so [too,] is it written in the Torah (Deuteronomy 10:22), "With seventy souls did your forefathers go down to Egypt." But when you count their enumeration, you find [only] sixty-nine souls. But rather the explanation (Bava Batra 123b) comes that Yocheved was born 'betwixt the walls' (of Egypt, though she was conceived before they arrived), and [so] was not counted in the enumeration. And likewise, one verse (Exodus 12:15) states, "Seven days shall you eat matsot" and one verse (Deuteronomy 16:8) states, "Six days." And many like this would not be elucidated without the traditional explanation that is in our hands, that was given to us from our teacher, Moshe.

And now, you should know that according to what we have received from our Sages, may their memory be Blessed and from their explanations, the tally of commandment that are practiced for [all of] the generations that are included in the Book of the Torah that God gave to us adds up to six hundred and thirteen commandments - between the commandments that it commanded us to do and those that it warned us not to do, as they are all called commandment[s]. And those that it commanded us to do add up to two hundred and forty-eight; and to not do, three hundred and sixty-five. And some of them are [those] that all of Israel are obligated - including males and females - at all times and in every place. And some of them are [those] that only Israelites are obligated in every place and at all times, but not priests and Levites. And some of them are [those] that only Levites alone are obligated; and some of them are [those] that only priests alone are obligated - in every place and at all times. And among the commandments, there are those that a person is obligated to do constantly, such as the commandment of loving God, and fearing Him, and that which is similar to it. And there are some that he is obligated to do at a specific time and not before then - such as the commandment of sukkah (dwelling in a hut), lulav, resting on the holidays, recitation of Shema and all that is similar to them - that have a set time to do them in the year or in the day. And there are some of them that a person is never obligated to do unless he is caused by a matter that comes to his hand that requires that commandment that is fitting for that matter. Such that you can say that giving the wage of a wage-worker in its time is a commandment, while a man is certainly not obligated to hire workers in order to fulfill this commandment. And so [too,] some that are like this - as we shall clarify it all, with God's help, about every commandment that we write. And one of the commandments is the root and principle that all lean upon - and that is Torah study - as through study will a person know the commandments and fulfill them. And hence our Sages, may their memory be Blessed, fixed for us to read a portion of the Book of the Torah each and every week in the place of the gathering of people - which is the synagogue - to arouse the heart of a man about the words of the Torah and the commandments, until they finish the whole Book. And according to that which we heard, most of

Sefer HaChinukh

Israel today practices reading it all in one year. And the Sages, may their memory be Blessed, further obligated us that every one of Israel read it in his home each and every week in the way that we read it in the place of gathering. And that is [the meaning of] their, may their memory be Blessed, saying (Berakhot 8a), "A person should always finish his sections with the community" - so that he understands things better with his reading them at home. And now since the six hundred and thirteen commandments are dispersed in the Book, scattered in it, here and there, in different stories that are written in the Book - for a great principle or for the need that is to be found in it - the reader will perhaps not place his heart in the [weekly reading] to see how many commandments he read that week; and he will not arouse his heart to urge himself about them. Hence I - 'the poorest of my thousand,' a student of the students in my time, a Jew from the House of Levi in Barcelona - saw it good to write the commandments by way of the [weekly] orders and in the order that they are written in the Torah, one after the other. [This is] to arouse the heart of the youth - my son and his friends - each and every week about the tally of the commandments after they study that [reading]. And [this is also in order] to accustom them to [the commandments] and to attach their thoughts to the thought of purity; and to the calculation of the essential, before they put in their hearts, calculations of joking and 'what is it to you,' and of 'what is the point.' And [so] 'even when they age, it will not depart from them.' And my [thought] is to write about each one a hint of the roots of (reason for) the commandment - when it is revealed in Scripture, I will write it as it is; and when it is hidden, I will say what I have heard about it from the mouth of sages and that which I understand about the things. And I do not think and insist to get to the truth regardless - as who 'is a worm and not a man,' like I, who did not see the lights of wisdom all of the days, to raise the hand about that which wizened sages have not grasped. I have not, however, lacked intelligence to know that ants cannot carry the load of camels; and [that] a 'child that does not know to Whom we recite blessings' should not expound about the 'Story of the Chariot,' and the secret of the chasmalim. Except that the greatness of my desire 'to dip the tip of the staff into the honeycomb' of the commandments has pushed me to enter the forest that has no limits, with my awareness that many great ones who entered there brought out [only] charcoals. However I said, "Who will give that my thought be preoccupied with this all of the days - and not be disqualified and not rendered defective by the intrigues 'of travail and sorrow,' like the guilty evildoers - and that I place them 'as a signet ring upon my right hand,' and that I put all of my wellsprings all of the day in their work. I shall make a faithful house in my heart, a strong dwelling. And the rest of all my deeds - eating, drinking and the occupation of men and women - their time is enough for them. Are [the commandments] not all refined and pure - 'every precious stone is their adornment.' And if there sometimes be sediment in that which is written in their explanation, the food should be separated from it for oil, and [sediment] returned to the house of the owners. And let the one who wants to eat with me, 'eat the meat and leave the bones and peels on the table.'" And at the beginning of my words, I mention as a merit for me that which my teachers said, "All chatter is bad, [but] Torah chatter is good." And they, may their memory be Blessed, further expounded to strengthen the heart of the learner, "His skipping is love to Me, his stuttering is love to Me" (Shir HaShirim Rabbah 2:4). And these [readings] of the year in which the commandments are [found] is according to the calculation of the great Rabbi, known for his great wisdom and stature among his people, Rambam - may the memory of the righteous be Blessed.

Opening Letter by the Author
A letter from the author of the Sefer HaChinukh:
Perhaps one who delves into this book will think that its author gathered all of its laws in his effort and his good research from the words of the Tannaim (early Talmudic sages) and the Amoraim (later Talmudic sages). And if this were so, it would require that the author be an expert in all of the corners of our Gemara - the Babylonian and the Jerusalem [Talmuds], the Sifra, the Sifri and the Tosefta. Hence, he who knows himself and what wisdom he has is fitting to publicize the truth to all who listen to his voice. And he should not make the unblemished craft of God into 'a bow of duplicity' and trickery, as one who is glorified 'by the children of foreigners,' as a weak one that arms himself with 'the shields of the mighty,' as a lowly one among men who crowns himself with the crowns of kings.

Sefer HaChinukh

Behold he calls - from his place he informs and testifies with trustworthy testimony to all readers that the majority of the words of the book are taken from the books of the pillars of the world that are famous in stature and wisdom from all of the nations: Rabbi Yitschak Alfasi (Rif) and Rabbi Moshe bar Maimon (Rambam), they should be remembered for the good. 'The statute of the first-born,' the glory and the greatness in this book is theirs. And [also] upon the 'three-fold string' in wisdom, understanding and knowledge is Rabbi Moshe bar Nachman, may his memory be Blessed. He composed a very esteemed book about the tally of the commandments besides several, several precious compositions. These are the 'mighty ones from yore' who spent most of their time clarifying the words of the Sages, Blessed is their memory. They 'plunged into the powerful waters' and brought up pearls in their hands from the words of the Gemara. And the day that we came to their sanctuary and to the room of their instruction, we found 'a well of living waters,' gardens and orchards, loaves and vessels of cloth' set up there. I said, "With what would it be pleasing to serve in front of the mighty ones, as they have already clarified all the things for us? Would it not be in ordering the six hundred and thirteen commandments according to the [weekly readings]? Perhaps the youths will be more stimulated in them from this; they will put their hearts into them on Shabbat and holidays; and return from going crazy in the plaza of the cities, 'to the light of the living light.' The delicate children will ask, 'one to his neighbor,' 'How many are the commandments of this Shabbat,' and the land will be full of 'knowledge and foresight.' And behold the explanation of each one is arranged in front of them, and without toil will they find pleasing words in their listings. The holy seed will be Blessed from God - 'they and their children and all that they have in all of the places of their dwellings.' And I will be included in the blessing with them." And I bring an oath with the ineffable name [of God] upon any transcriber [of this book], that he write this letter at its beginning - and [so] life and peace shall be with him - in order that all will give its splendor and its glory to its bearer and its parent. And may one who corrects any error after concentrated investigation receive his full compensation from the Omnipresent God. And let there be peace upon Israel, amen.

There are commandments that are practiced today and, all counted, they are three hundred and sixty-nine. And from these that are practiced, there are some that a person only be obligated in them by a cause. And sometimes the cause will never come to a person all of his days, such that it will come out that he never do [that commandment] - such as the commandment of giving the wage to a wage-worker on its day, and that which is similar to it; as there are people that will never employ a wage-worker [all] their days. And so [too,] from the negative commandments, there are some of them that a person not be obligated without his will, and through the cause of his deeds. And with his avoiding that deed, there will not be any sin to him and nothing will be lacking from him. For example, one who puts out a bad name [on his wife], that he may never divorce his wife - as he caused it to himself to be obligated in this negative commandment, as he is the one who put out a bad name. And so [too,] with the negative commandment of "do not delay" with vows, it is also he who causes it. And one who refrains from vowing will not have a sin. And so, all that is similar to this. And, all counted, they are ninety-nine, from which there are seventy-eight positive commandments and twenty-one negative commandments. But the commandments that every man of Israel is commanded without his creating a cause for it in the world are, all counted, two hundred and seventy. And the mnemonic is "I am sleeping, but my heart is awake (the numerical equivalent of its letters being two hundred and seventy). Forty-eight of them are positive commandments and two hundred and twenty-two are negative commandments. And you will find each one in its [weekly reading] in the book. And the obligation with them is not at all times, but rather at specific times of the year or of the day - except for six commandments, the obligation of which is constant. It does not cease from being upon a man even an instant in all of his days. And these are them: 1) to believe in God; 2) to not believe in anything besides Him; 3) to conceive of His oneness; 4) to love Him; 5) to fear Him; and 6) to not wander after the thought of the heart and the vision of the eyes. Their mnemonic is 'six cities of refuge shall there be for you.'

Sefer HaChinukh

Mitzvah 1
The commandment of procreation: [Parshat] Bereshit has one positive commandment and that is the commandment of procreation, as it is stated (Genesis 1:28), "And God Blessed them and told them to procreate."

It is from the roots of this commandment (i.e the reason behind this commandment) that the world should be settled (Gittin 41b) because God wants the world to be settled, as it says (Isaiah 45:18), "I did not create it for naught, but [rather] formed it for habitation." This is a great commandment, through which all the commandments are observed, as [the Torah] was given to people and not to the ministering angels (Berakhot 25b).

The laws of this commandment - when a man is obligated to be involved with it; how many sons he needs to have; what other commandments he is exempt from due to his involvement in procreation; and the rest of its details - are [all] explained in the sixth chapter of Yevamot and in Berachot. (see Shulchan Arukh Even HaEzer 1 and Orach Chaim 70:3)

And [it] is practiced in every place and at all times (Kiddushin 36b), and a person is obligated to be involved with it from when it is fitting for him, and this is the age which the sages (Avot 5:21) designated to marry a woman. And this commandment is not incumbent upon women. And one who negates it violates a positive commandment; and his punishment is very great (Kiddushin 29b), as he shows that he does not want to fulfill God's will to settle His world.

Mitzvah 2
The commandment to circumcise: Parshat Lekh Lekha [has] one positive commandment, and that is the commandment to circumcise; as it is stated (Genesis 17:10), "This is My covenant which you shall keep, between you and I, and with your descendants after you, circumcise all males." And [the commandment] is repeated in the Order of Eesha ki Tazria, as it is stated (Leviticus 12:3), "And on the eighth day circumcise the flesh of his foreskin." There are many commandments which are repeated in many places in the Torah; and all of them are necessary as the sages explained (Shabbat 132a and Shabbat 135a). And the content of this commandment is that we cut the foreskin that covers the head of the member and then tearing the sorting skin which is below it so that the glans of the member will be exposed. As is known to those that understand, the completion of the form of man comes with the removal of this foreskin which is extraneous.

It is from the roots of this commandment [that it is] because God wanted to establish in His nation, that He separated to be called by His name, a permanent sign on their body; to separate them from the other nations in the form of their bodies just like they are separated from them in the form of their souls, the going out and coming in of which are not similar. He established this difference in the 'golden fountain,' because this is the reason for the existence of people, besides being a completion of the physical body as we mentioned. God wanted to complete His plan with the chosen nation. He wanted men to complete the creation of his body, as He did not create him complete from the womb; [so as] to hint to him that just like the completion of the form of his body is through him, so [too] is it in his hand to complete the form of his soul, by refining his actions.

The laws of the commandment - upon whom is the circumcision of infants incumbent, as well as the circumcision of slaves, the homeborn (a Canaanite slave that a maidservant gave birth to in the house of a Jew) and those acquired with money (which means a Canaanite slave that was acquired from when he was born), and the difference between them; in which way is Shabbat and holidays pushed off for him; which infant has his circumcision delayed for more than eight days; and its other details - are [all] elucidated in Chapter Nineteen of Shabbat and in Chapter Four of Yevamot. And there in Shabbat, it is elucidated that the one who circumcises recites the blessing, "Blessed are You, Lord our God, King of the universe, who has sanctified us with Your commandments, and commanded us concerning the circumcision." And the father of the child - or the court when there is no father [present] - recites the blessing, "Blessed are You, Lord our God, King of the universe, who has sanctified us with Your commandments, and commanded us to bring him into the covenant of Avraham, our father." And the ones standing there respond, "Just as he had merit for the circumcision, may God let have him merit for the wedding canopy and for good deeds" (see Shulchan Arukh Yoreh

Deah 260-266).
And [it] is practiced in every place and at all times. And women are not obligated regarding the circumcision of their sons (Kiddushin 29a); just the father - or the court when there is no father [present]. And one who transgresses this commandment and does not circumcise himself when he reaches the category of [those who can receive] punishments - which is thirteen year and a day - [each day, that he transgresses it from when he is grown and does not circumcise himself, violates a positive commandment. And if he dies and was uncircumcised by volition,] he is liable for excision. But the father is not liable for excision for the [lack of] circumcision of his son (Shabbat 133a), but he does transgress a positive commandment. And there is no positive commandment in all of the Torah the negation of which makes one liable for excision besides this and the slaughtering of the Pesach sacrifice (Keritot 2a).

Mitzvah 3
Not to eat the sciatic nerve: Parshat Vayishlach has one negative commandment, and it is the prohibition of [eating] the sciatic nerve; as it is stated (Genesis 32:33), "Therefore the Children of Israel shall not eat the sciatic nerve." And this [phrase] "they shall not eat" is not to be taken as part of the story, to mean that because this event occurred to [our] forefather, [we, his] descendants refrain from eating that nerve. Rather, it is a warning (prohibition) of God that they shall not eat it.
It is from the roots of this commandment [that it is to serve as] a hint to Israel that though they will suffer many troubles in the exile by the hand of the nations and by the hand of the [descendants] of Esav [the Jews] should trust that they will not perish, but rather that their descendants and name will stand firm forever, and that their redeemer will come and redeem them from their oppressor. And in continually remembering this idea through the commandment that serves as a reminder, they will stand firm in their faith and righteousness forever. And this hint [stems from the fact that] that the angel who fought with Yaakov our forefather - who according to tradition (Bereshit Rabbah 78) was the guardian angel of Esav - wished to eliminate Yaakov from the world, he and his descendants; but he could not [get the better] of him, (Genesis 32:26) but anguished him in injuring his thigh. Likewise, Esav's seed anguishes the seed of Yaakov; but in the end, [the latter] will be saved from them. As we find (Genesis 32:32) with respect to [our] forefather that the sun shone to heal him and he was saved from pain, so will the sun of the messiah shine and he will heal us from our pain and redeem us speedily in our days, amen!
The laws of this commandment - which sinew is prohibited; the clearing out, that we are obligated to clear out [its area] after it; with regards to which beast, it applies; who is trustworthy regarding its removal; and the rest of its details - are explained in the seventh chapter of Chullin (see Tur, Yoreh Deah 65.)
And [it] is practiced in every place and at all times by males and by females. And one who transgresses it and eats a [whole sciatic nerve], even if it is less than an olive's-worth - or eats a kazayit (the size of a large olive) from a large sciatic nerve - is lashed (see Chullin 96a).
From here until the end of Genesis there are no commandments. The Book of Genesis is complete.

Mitzvah 4
The commandment of sanctifying the new month: To sanctify months and intercalate [months into] years in the court [whose members are the] great in wisdom and ordained in the Land of Israel, and to establish the year's holidays according to that sanctification; as it is stated (Exodus 12:2), "This month shall be to you the first of months." This means, when you see the renewal of the moon, establish for yourselves the new month - or even if you do not see it, since it is appropriate for [the moon] to appear according to the accepted calculation. Likewise, this commandment includes the commandment of intercalation, since the basis of the commandment to sanctify the month is for Israel to observe God's holidays at their appointed times. And the commandment of intercalation has the same basis. However, beyond this verse are more Torah passages concerning the commandment of intercalation, and that is what is written (Exodus 13:10), "You shall observe this commandment in its proper time"; and likewise, "Observe the month of Spring" (Deuteronomy 16:11).

Sefer HaChinukh

The content of the commandment is that two Jews fit to testify come before the court and testify before them that they saw the renewed moon. [The judges then] establish the new month on the basis of their [testimony] and say, "Today has been sanctified." The reason why this commandment applies only with ordained judges is because it came with the explanation [of the verse], "This month shall be for you" - great [in Torah] and ordained, like you (Rosh Hashanah 22a), since it was said to Moshe and Aharon. This matter was further expounded, as it is juxtaposed to "speak to the entire congregation of the children of Israel," meaning that they who sanctify the month must have the assent of all Israel, meaning the wisest men of Israel, such as the Great Court (the Sanhedrin). And so [too] any great sage in Israel who was ordained in the Land of Israel. And since ordination is no longer practiced, as is known, [the sage] has permission to perform this commandment even outside the Land of Israel, so long as there is no one of his stature in the Land of Israel. And so we find that Chananiah ben Achai, Rabbi Yehoshua, and Akiva ben Yosef did so in this regard (Berakhot 23a). But without these conditions, no one of Israel is permitted to establish the months or intercalate. And perhaps you will ask, "If so, how do we conduct ourselves today, when we lack ordained sages?" Know that so have we received it; since Rabbi Hillel the Prince, son of Rabbi Yehudah the Prince, who was the greatest of his generation and ordained in the Land of Israel - he was the sage who fixed for us the calculation of intercalation, sanctified future months, and intercalated future [months into] years until the coming of Eliyahu, and it is upon this that we rely today. That which we have said all follows the opinion of Rambam. However, Ramban (in the Sefer HaMitzvot LaRambam, Mitzvot Ase 153), considers the sanctification of the month as one commandment and intercalation a separate commandment. His proofs (for dividing these into two separate commandments are) in his Book of Commandments. And so [too] the Ba'al Halakhot (considers these separate commandments). And the verse that teaches about the commandment of intercalation, that is, that we calculate the seasons in order to make the holidays in their (proper,) established times, is "You shall observe this commandment in its proper time," (Exodus 13:10) and so, "Observe the month of Spring," (Deuteronomy 16:11) as we have written.

It is from the roots of this commandment [that it is] so that Israel shall make God's holidays in their (proper) times, as God commanded that we make Pesach in the time that the produce is in [bloom], as it is written (Deuteronomy 16:1), "Observe the month of Spring, and you shall offer the Pesach sacrifice." And the holiday of Sukkot is [to fall] at the time of the harvest, as is written, "And the holiday of the harvest at the turn of the year." (Exodus 34:22) And were it not for intercalation, the holidays would come not at these times, since Israel calculates their months and festivals according to the lunar year, which has three hundred and fifty-four days, eight hours, and eight hundred and seventy-six parts, which is less than the solar year by ten days, twenty-one hours and two hundred and four parts - its mnemonic is ten, twenty-one, two hundred and four. Due to the ripening of the produce and fruit from the power of the sun, it turns out that but for intercalation - by which we align the lunar and solar years - Pesach would not come in the Spring, nor Sukkot at the time of the harvest. And this matter is to be fixed by the greatest [sages] of the generation, since it is a matter requiring great wisdom. And since it is also said that from this [calculation, one comes to know] the agricultural happenings of the year, it is appropriate to give [this task] only to great and pious men.

The laws of the commandment - for example, interrogating [those who offer] testimony concerning the new month; instilling fear in the witnesses on occasion; the law concerning circumstances under which the Shabbat may be desecrated for this testimony; for what [considerations] we do or do not intercalate; which month they would intercalate, i.e. Adar, as they, may their memory be Blessed, expounded, "'You shall observe this commandment in its proper time' (Exodus 13:10), this teaches that we only intercalate at the time near the holiday"; and they, may their memory be Blessed, further expounded on this verse, "From where do we know that we only intercalate the month during daytime? [We learn this from the] verse, [which] states, 'from year to year' (yamim yemima, literally from day to day) (Sanhedrin 10b); and they, may their memory be Blessed, further expounded, "'For the months of the year' (Exodus 12:2) - it is months you calculate towards the year, not days" (Megillah 5a); furthermore did they say on this matter, "'A month of days' (Numbers 11:20), it is days you calculate towards the month, not hours" (Megillah 5a); and the rest of its details - are [all] elucidated in Tractate Rosh Hashanah, and in the first chapter of Sanhedrin, and similarly in Berakhot (see Mishneh Torah, Laws of Sanctification of the New Month 1).

And [it] is practiced in every place and at all times when we have ordained sages, according to the aforementioned conditions. One who transgresses it and does not [sanctify the new month or intercalate the month] - if he be a sage for whom it is appropriate - has violated a positive commandment; and his punishment is very great since he causes the ruining of the holidays. And now that – due to our iniquities - we do no intercalate by ordained [sages], our calculation relies on the accepted calculation from Rabbi Hillel, as we have said.

Mitzvah 5

The commandment to slaughter the Pesach sacrifice: To slaughter on the day of the fourteenth of Nissan in the late afternoon an unblemished one-year-old male lamb, or kid, in the Chosen House (Temple), and this is called the Pesach (Passover) sacrifice, as it is stated (Exodus 12:6), "The entire assembly of the congregation of Israel shall slaughter it in the afternoon." The content of this commandment is that all the people of Israel divide into assemblages, take from the market or from their houses an unblemished one-year-old male kid or lamb, and slaughter it in the courtyard of the Temple on the fourteenth day of Nissan in the afternoon. Afterwards in the evening, they eat it, [dividing it up] amongst themselves, after [eating their other] food; since its commandment is that it should be eaten while satiated (Pesachim 70a).

From the roots of this commandment are so that the Jews will remember forever the great miracles that God performed for them during the exodus from Egypt.

The laws of this commandment - for example, the time of slaughter (Pesachim 58a); that it is slaughtered in three groups in the Temple courtyard (Pesachim 64a); that it supersedes the Sabbath (Pesachim 65b); the laws of its designating [the members of the assemblage]; the recitation of Hallel over it; the blowing of the trumpets; and the rest of its details - are explained in Tractate Pesachim (see Mishneh Torah, Laws of Paschal Offering 1:12).

And [it] is practiced by males and by females at the time of the [Temple]. And one who transgresses it volitionally and does not offer the Pesach sacrifice is liable for excision. [One who transgresses] inadvertently does not bring a sacrifice, since this [commandment] is one of three sins whose volitional transgression is punishable by excision, but whose inadvertent transgression does not [mandate bringing] a sin-offering. And they are this one, one who blasphemes and one who negates circumcision.

Mitzvah 6

The commandment of eating the meat of the Pesach sacrifice: To eat the meat of the Pesach sacrifice on the fifteenth night of Nissan, according to the specifications of the verse, as it is stated (Exodus 12:8), "And they shall eat the meat on this night."

That which we wrote about its slaughtering (Sefer HaChinukh 5) is from the roots of this commandment - so as to remember the great miracles which God did for us when He took us out of slavery.

The laws of this commandment - what is the minimum amount required to be eaten by each person (Pesachim 69a); how he should act before he eats it; that he should not leave his assemblage (Pesachim 66b in the Mishnah); that he should not sleep (Pesachim 120a); and the rest of its details - are [all] explained in Pesachim (See Mishneh Torah, Laws of Paschal Offering 1).

And [it] is practiced by males and females. One who transgresses it has negated a positive commandment. An important principle in the entire Torah about anyone who says that he will negate a positive commandment is that he is coerced by the court (a beit din) - if they have the power in their hands - until he fulfills it (Ketuvot 86a, Chullin 132b).

Mitzvah 7

To not eat the Pesach sacrifice uncooked or boiled: To not eat from the meat of the Pesach sacrifice uncooked or boiled, but rather roasted with fire, as it is stated (Exodus 12:9), "Do not eat any of it raw (na), or surely boiled with water, but only roasted with fire." The content of this is not to eat it before it is completely cooked, even if roasted. And this is the explanation of na (Pesachim 41a) - as the meat that the process of heating has begun upon and is roasted a bit but is not [yet] fit for a person to eat is still called na. But when it is completely raw - whereby the heating process has not begun upon it at all - it is not included in the prohibition of na; such as to administer lashes, because of "Do not eat any of it na." But [it] is [still] prohibited by the Torah, as the Torah prohibited more generally anything that is not roasted with fire. And the explanation of "boiled" (literally, cooked) is that it is boiled in water or in any liquid or fruit juice; as it is stated, "surely boiled" - [to] include all [of these]. That which we have written about its slaughtering (Sefer HaChinukh 5) is from the roots of this commandment - to remember the miracle of the exodus from Egypt. And that which we have been commanded to specifically eat it roasted is because such is the way of the children of kings and ministers, to eat roasted meat - as it is a good and tasty food. And the rest of the people only eat the little meat that they [are able to acquire] boiled, in order to fill their stomachs. And it is certainly fitting for us - that eat the Pesach sacrifice [to remember] that we went out into freedom to be a nation of priests and a holy nation - to behave in a manner of freedom and lordship in its eating. [This is] besides (Guide for the Perplexed 3:46) that the eating of roast indicates the haste [with] which they left Egypt and could not delay, that it should cook in a pot.

The laws of the commandment - for example, what is its law if one made it as a pot roast, or [roasted it basted] with fruit juices or water or with tithed oil; and the rest of its details - are elucidated in Pesachim (See Mishneh Torah, Laws of Paschal Offering 8).

And [it] is practiced by males and females at the time of the [Temple]. And one who transgresses it and eats it uncooked or boiled is lashed. And so, if he ate both of them, he is lashed one [set of] lashes - since both of them are [the same] negative prohibition, according to the opinion of Rambam (Mishneh Torah, Laws of Paschal Offering 8:4 and Sefer HaMitzvot LaRambam, Shorashim 9). But Ramban, may his memory be Blessed, (on Sefer HaMitzvot LaRambam, Shorashim 9, s.v. hamin hashlishi) counted them as two [separate] negative commandments and wrote that one receives lashes for each one [of them]. As since it is written, "Do not eat [...] but only roasted with fire," why do I [need] "raw and boiled?" It is understood from it that we should give lashes for each one of the components. And he, may he Blessed, said that the count is like this with all of the commandments - that any that are specified individually, which are two separate things, are each counted in the tally of the commandments. [An] example is this of 'uncooked and boiled'; and so [too], 'the wage and the price'; and 'leaven and honey,' and others [besides them].

However, regarding the matter of lashes, there is a difference between [the examples]. As all those [simply] specified in one negative commandment only receive one [set of] lashes - for example, "the wage of a harlot and the price of a dog"(Deuteronomy 23:19); and "leaven and [...] honey" (Leviticus 2:11); "the case of a stranger [or] an orphan" (Deuteronomy 24:17), and all that is similar to them. But the negative commandments that [also] have a general category and are specified at the beginning or end [of the category] - for example, this negative commandment that specified "uncooked and boiled" and is [then] generalized, "Do not eat [...] but only roasted with fire"; and so [too], with a nazerite (Numbers 6:4), "from anything that is obtained from the grapevine [...] may he not eat," and afterwards it specifies, "seeds [...] or skin," ('and grapes wet and dry,' Numbers 6:3) - with these and those similar to them, we give lashes for each and every one. [This is] because the inclusion of the specification that was not needed, indicates lashes for each one [of them], as we have said. And the teacher was prolific in his proofs about this in the ninth shoresh in his Book of the Commandments - that the calculation of commandments is not the same as the calculation of [which commandments require] lashes [independently]. And that which I have said that Ramban, may his memory be Blessed, will count each of the ones specified by their names individually - each one by itself - only when they are separate in their content, as we have written; [it] is, for example, [in the case of] 'leaven and honey,' [and] 'the wage and the price.' But in a case where it is the same content - even if they are specified by different names - they are only counted as one commandment. For example, "All male first-borns that are born in your herd and in your flock" (Deuteronomy 15:19) is only one commandment to sanctify all of the first-borns; and the specification is [also] only one commandment.

And so [too], "All tithes of the herd or flock" (Leviticus 27:32) is only one commandment to separate to give the tithes of these animals. And so [too], "Judges and officers" (Deuteronomy 16:18) is only that we should establish justice through these people and it is one commandment. And so [too], "An honest balance, honest weights, an honest ephah, and an honest hin " (Leviticus 19:36) is all one commandment, that we should not lie about measures.

Mitzvah 8
To not leave from the meat of the Pesach sacrifice: To not leave any of the meat of the Pesach sacrifice to the next day (overnight), which is the fifteenth of Nissan, as it is stated (Exodus 12:10), "You shall not leave any of it over until morning."

That which is written about its slaughter (Sefer HaChinukh 5) is from the roots of this commandment - to remember the miracles of Egypt. And the essence of that which we were commanded to not leave over from it, is that it is in the way of kings and ministers who do not need to leave over from their meals from one day to the next. And therefore, it states that if there remains from it, one should burn it like something that he does not desire, in the way of the kings of the land. And all of this is to remember and establish in our hearts that at this time, God, may He be Blessed, redeemed us and we became free and merited majesty and greatness.

The law of this commandment is in Pesachim (See Mishneh Torah, Laws of Paschal Offering 9). And [it] is practiced by males and females at the time of the [Temple]. And one who transgresses it and leaves [it] over violates a negative commandment. And we do not give lashes for this negative commandment, since it is rectifiable by a positive commandment (Mishneh Torah, Laws of Paschal Offering 10:11) - as it is stated (Exodus 12:10), "and that which remains until the morning, you shall burn with fire." And it is a law that we do not give lashes for [the transgression of] a negative commandment that is rectifiable by a positive commandment.

Mitzvah 9
The commandment of disposing of chamets: To remove all leavened bread from our dwellings on the fourteenth day of Nissan, as it is stated (Exodus 12:15), "but on the first day, you shall dispose of leaven from your homes" - and the understanding of "first" is before Pesach.

It is from the roots of this commandment [that it is] in order that we should remember the miracles in Egypt, as it is written with the Pesach sacrifice (Sefer HaChinukh 5).

The laws of this commandment - for example what time of the day is its destruction; what is its disposal (Pesachim 21a); in which place one needs to search for it (Pesachim 5a) and in which place one does not need; from when the commandment is incumbent upon him if he goes on the road (Pesachim 6a); how is its law if the fourteenth of Nissan falls out on Shabbat (Pesachim 49a); the oral negation that he needs to do in addition to the destruction (Pesachim 6b); and the rest of its details - are [all] elucidated in [the] first [section of] Pesach[im] (see Tur, Orach Chaim 431-440).

And this commandment is practiced in every place and at all times by males and females. And one who transgresses it and does not dispose of [his chamets], has violated the commandment of 'you shall dispose of it.' And if there is chamets in his dwellings, he also transgresses a negative commandment - as it stated (Exodus 12:19), "leaven is not to be found in your homes." But we do not administer lashes for this negative commandment, if he has not done an act - as it is the law that we do not administer lashes for a negative commandment that does not have an act [involved] with it.

Mitzvah 10 - The commandment of eating matsah:
To eat matsah-bread that is made from a species of grain on the night of the fifteenth of Nissan (Pesachim 35a), as it is stated (Exodus 12:18), "in the evening, you shall eat matsot." And the understanding [of "evening"] is the night of the fifteenth of Nissan - whether it be at a time when the Pesach sacrifice is present or whether it be at a time that it is not present.

That which is written about the Pesach sacrifice (Sefer HaChinukh 5) is from the roots of this commandment.

The laws of the commandment - for example, the guarding needed for the matsah (Pesachim 40a); the matter of their kneading (Pesachim 42a); with which water they are kneaded; the minimal amount of time for their eating; and the rest of its details - are elucidated in [the] first [section of] Pesach[im] (see Tur, Orach Chaim 453-466).

And it is practiced in every place and at all times by males and females. And one who transgresses it violates a positive commandment. And we have already said that the court enforces [observance, in the case of the] negation of a positive commandment.

Mitzvah 11

That chamets not be found in our possession on Pesach: That chamets not be found in our possession on all the days of Pesach, as it is stated (Exodus 12:19), "Seven days shall leaven not be found in all of your homes." And our Sages, may their memory be Blessed, elucidated (Pesachim 5b) that it is not specifically one's home, but rather anything that is in his possession; and not specifically leaven which makes rise, but the same is true of [any grain product] that has risen - as leaven and leavened grain products are one [and the same] concerning the matter of its prohibition (Beitzah 7b).

It is from the roots of the commandment [that it is] so that we should always remember the miracles that were done for us in the exodus from Egypt, as is written with the lamb of the Pesach sacrifice (Sefer HaChinukh 5). And we should remember that which occurred to us with this matter - that as a result of the haste of the exodus, we baked the dough [into] matsah. As they could not wait until it rose, as it is written (Exodus 12:39), "And they baked the dough, etc."

The laws of this commandment - for example if he deposits his chamets in the hand of others or [that of] others [is deposited] into his hand, and also chamets that is sacred property that is in his hand or that of a gentile, with responsibility or without responsibility, and the law of a violent [gentile] that deposited chamets with him; the law of whether one transgresses for a mixture that includes chamets; what is the law of bread that has rotted (Pesachim 45b); and the rest of its details - are elucidated in [the] first [section of] Pesach[im] (See Tur, Orach Chaim 440-442).

And [it] is practiced by males and females in every place and at all times. And one who transgresses it and chamets is volitionally found in his possession violates two negative commandments, on account of 'that it not be seen and it not be found.' And he is lashed anytime he does an act with it - for example [if] he had dough rise and left it in his home, or he purchased chamets and stored it in his home. But if he did not do any act, but it [just] remained at home from before Pesach, he is not lashed (Mishneh Torah, Laws of Leavened and Unleavened Bread 1:3). As it is the law that we do not administer lashes for a negative commandment that does not have an act [involved] with it, as we have said.

Mitzvah 12

To not eat from anything that has chamets in it: To not eat from things that have chamets in them, even though the main part is not a chamets product - for example, Babylonian kutach (a type of bread pudding) and similar to it. As it is stated (Exodus 12:20), "All that is leavened shall you not eat" - and they, may their memory be Blessed, explained (Pesachim 43a) that the subject of the verse instructs about this; as so did they receive the understanding about it. And the opinion of Rambam (Sefer HaMitzvot LaRambam, Mitzvot Lo Taase 198), may his memory be Blessed, is that if there is in these foods a kazayit (the size of a large olive) of chamets [that is eaten] in the time it takes to eat a peras (a half-loaf of bread), it is forbidden by the Torah as a negative commandment - meaning to say for lashes, but not for excision, since it is mixed with a majority [of non-chamets products]. But if there is not in them a kazayit of chamets [that is eaten] in the time it takes to eat a peras, there are no [formal] lashes, but rather [just] lashes of rebellion - as it is only prohibited rabbinically. And so is it written in his great essay (Mishneh Torah, Laws of Leavened and Unleavened Bread 1:6). And if so - according to his opinion - this prohibition of "All that is leavened" comes when a kazayit of chamets [that is eaten] in the time it takes to eat a peras, is mixed in. [This is such] that there should be a negative commandment - meaning to say [for] lashes, not excision. And Ramban, may his memory be Blessed, wrote the opposite of this (on Sefer HaMitzvot LaRambam, Mitzvot Lo Taase 198) and said that this negative commandment is not considered [a separate commandment] among the negative commandments, but rather is one of the many negative commandments [included in the prohibition] of leaven and chamets. And this prohibition (of "All that is leavened") is coming to teach about that which the Sages, may their memory be Blessed, said in the Gemara (Pesachim 28b), "I only have if it became leavened on its own. From where [do I know] if it became leavened due to another substance? [Hence] we learn to teach, 'All that is leavened.'" But concerning chamets that is mixed, anytime there is a kazayit of chamets [that is eaten] in the time it takes to eat a peras, there is no need for a separate negative commandment about it - as behold, it is as if it is intact, and it [comes with] excision. And if there is not a kazayit of chamets [that is eaten] in the time it takes to eat a peras, one who eats it is exempt [from the prohibition], but [still doing something] forbidden. As the law is like the words of the sages (Pesachim 43a) that said [that] on complete leavened grain products, one is punished with excision. And anything that is a kazayit of chamets [that is eaten] in the time it takes to eat a peras is called a complete leavened grain product. And about its mixture - meaning less than a kazayit of chamets [that is eaten] in the time it takes to eat a peras - [there] is no [prohibition]. And [the law] is not like Rabbi Eliezer who disagrees with them in the Gemara and said that its mixture is a negative commandment.

From the roots of this commandment is that which we have written about leaven. However, the Torah distanced it from us so much in order to strengthen the matter in our hearts.

The laws of the commandment - for example, what are the things that are included in this prohibition; what are their names; and the rest of its details - are in Pesachim (See Tur, Orach Chaim 446).

And [it] is practiced by males and females in every place and at all times. And one who transgresses it is lashed - and on condition that there be in it a kazayit of chamets [that is eaten] in the time it takes to eat a peras, as we have said - but there is no excision for it. [This is] according to the opinion of Rambam. But according to the opinion of Ramban, may his memory be Blessed, there is excision. But if there is not in it a kazayit of chamets [that is eaten] in the time it takes to eat a peras, there is no liability for lashes. Rather is is like the law of a half size [of something prohibited], which is forbidden by the Torah, but we do not give lashes for it. And about this they, may their memories be Blessed, both [agreed].

Mitzvah 13

That we not feed of the Pesach sacrifice to an apostate Jew: That we not feed of (allow to eat from) the Pesach sacrifice to a Jew that is a habitual sinner of idolatry, as it is stated (Exodus 12:43), "no foreigner shall eat of it." And the understanding (Mekhilta DeRabbi Shimon Bar Yochai 12:43) comes upon it that [this 'foreigner'] is a Jew whose actions have become foreign to his Father in Heaven. And so, did Onkelos translate.

From the roots of this commandment is like that which is written about its slaughter (Sefer HaChinukh 5) - that it is to remember the miracles of Egypt. And therefore, it is fitting that a habitual sinner (apostate) not eat from it. Since we are doing it as a sign and as a memory device that we came at that time to take refuge under the wings of the Divine Presence and that we entered into the covenant of Torah and faith, it is not fitting that we feed him - someone who is the opposite of this and went out from the group and denied the faith - of it. And sometimes it is said in the Gemara about things similar to this, "It is logical" - meaning to say that there is no need for a [further] proof (Mishneh Torah, Laws of Paschal Offering 9).

And [it] is practiced by males and females at the time of the [Temple], where there is a Pesach sacrifice. And the one who transgresses it and feeds a 'foreigner' from it violates this negative commandment. And there are no lashes for it, since there is no act [involved] with it (Mishneh Torah, Laws of Paschal Offering 9:7).

Mitzvah 14

That we not feed of the Pesach sacrifice to a stranger or a resident: To not give (allow) to eat from the meat of the Pesach sacrifice to a stranger or resident, as it is stated (Exodus 12:45), "The resident or wage-worker shall not eat it." And a "resident" is a man from the [other] nations who takes

Sefer HaChinukh

upon himself not to worship idolatry, but eats carcasses. And a "hired laborer" is a convert who has circumcised himself but not immersed [in a mikveh] - as so did our Sages, may their memory be Blessed, explain (Yevamot 71a).

From the roots of this commandment is that which we have written in others [about Pesach above] - to remember the exodus from Egypt. And because this sacrifice is to remember our freedom and our coming into the steadfast covenant with God, may He be Blessed, it is fitting that only those that have completed the faith benefit from it - and those are complete Jews; not those that have not yet come together with us in the complete covenant. And the content of the distancing of the uncircumcised from its eating is also from this root (Yevamot 71a).

And [it] is practiced at the time of the [Temple] by males and females. And one who transgresses it and gives these to eat [it], transgresses a negative commandment. But we do not administer lashes for it, as it does not have an act.

Mitzvah 15
Not to take out from the meat of the Pesach offering outside: Not to take from the meat of the Pesach offering out of the place of the assemblage (Pesachim 85b), as it is stated (Exodus 12:46), "you shall not take any of the meat outside the house."

From the roots of this commandment is that which we have written - to remember the miracles of Egypt. And since we were made into free men and lords, this commandment came to us that we should eat [it] in the place of the assemblage and not take it outside - like the kings of the land. As everything that is prepared for them is eaten in their chambers with their large retinues. But when the poor of the land prepare a large meal, they send portions to their friends

outside, since it is a novelty for them (to have a lavish meal).

The laws of the commandment - for example, what is the law of [the] meat when he takes [it] out (Pesachim 85a); the border that they must make (Mishneh Torah, Laws of Paschal Offering 9:3); the law of a partition between two assemblages that is breached (Pesachim 60b); and the rest of its details - are [all] elucidated in Pesachim.

And [it] is practiced at the time of the [Temple] by males and females. And one who transgresses it and takes of the meat outside violates a negative commandment. And we administer lashes for it - and that is when he dislodges [it] from the house and places [it] outside, like the well-known law about [carrying on] Shabbat (Pesachim 60b).

Mitzvah 16
To not break a bone from the Pesach sacrifice: To not break any from all of the bones of the Pesach sacrifice, as it is stated (Exodus 12:46), "and a bone of it, you shall not break."

From the roots of the commandment is to remember the miracles of Egypt, as we have written in the other [related commandments]. And this is also a trunk from the root mentioned: For it is not honorable for the sons of kings and the advisers of the land to drag the bones and break them like dogs. Except for the impoverished among the people and the starving, it is not a proper thing to do this. And therefore, as we began to become the chosen of all nations, 'a kingdom of priests and a holy nation' - and in each and every year at that time - it is fitting for us to do acts that show the great stature which we achieved at that hour, about us. And in the act and reenactment that we do, this thing is placed in our souls for eternity. My son, do not think to pounce upon my words and say, "Why would God, may He be Blessed, command us to do all of these commandments to commemorate that miracle; would we not remember it with one commemoration, [such that] it not be forgotten from the mouth of our offspring?" You must know that it is not from wisdom that you would [question] me about this, and it is your youthful thoughts that lead you to this. And now, my son, 'If you have understanding,' 'incline your ear and hear,' and I will teach you to benefit from Torah and the commandments: You must know, that a man is acted upon according to his actions; and his heart and all his thoughts always follow after the actions that he does - whether good or bad. And even he who in his heart is a complete sinner and all the desires of his heart are only for evil; if his spirit shall be enlightened and he will put his efforts and actions to persist in Torah and commandments - even if not for the sake of Heaven - he shall immediately incline towards the good. And from that which is not for its own sake comes that which is for its own sake [as opposed to being for personal gain]; for the hearts are drawn after the actions. And even if a man is perfectly righteous and his heart is straight and innocent, desiring of Torah and the commandments; if he shall constantly deal with improper things, you could compare it to someone who was forced by the king to work a wicked craft - if he constantly works in that wicked craft - eventually, from his righteousness, he shall have become completely evil. For it is known and true that every man is acted upon according to his actions, as we have said. And the Sages, may their memory be Blessed, said about this (Makkot 23b), "God wanted to grant merits to Israel, therefore he gave them many laws and commandments," to occupy all of our thoughts and all our deeds, to benefit us at our end [i.e. in the world to come]. Because from the good actions we are acted upon to be good and merit eternal life. And the Sages hinted at this (Menachot 43b) with their statement that anyone who has a mezuzah on his door, tsitsit on his garment and tefillin on his head is promised that he shall not sin - for these are constant commandments, and [so] he is constantly acted upon by them.

Therefore, surely observe what [you choose] to be your craft and your dealings, since you will be pulled by them and you will not pull them. And do not let your [evil] impulse assure you by saying, "Since my heart is complete and pure in the faith of God, what loss is there if I enjoy the pleasures of men in the markets and the plazas - to joke with the jokers and to speak finely and similar to these things that do not bring guilt and sins - do I not have a heart like them, 'my small finger is thicker than their loins,' and how would they pull me in behind them?" Do not [say this], my son. Guard yourself from them, lest you be trapped in their snare. Many have drunk the cup of poison from this, but you should save your soul. And once you know this, the multitude of commandments about the matter of remembering the miracles of Egypt will no longer be a challenge to you - as they are a great pillar in our Torah. Since by greatly engaging in them, we will be acted upon about by the matter, as we have said.

The laws of the commandment - for example, the breaking of one of its bones even after the time of its eating; the law if there is a kazayit of meat upon it, what is its law; the law of cartilages and soft tendons that would ultimately harden; and the rest of its details - are elucidated in Pesachim.

And [it] is practiced by males and females at the time of the [Temple]. And one who transgresses it and breaks a bone of a pure Pesach sacrifice is lashed.

Mitzvah 17

That an uncircumcised man not eat from the Pesach sacrifice: That the uncircumcised man not eat from the Pesach sacrifice, as it is stated (Exodus 12:48), "and no uncircumcised man shall eat from it." And that is the uncircumcised man whose brothers have died because of circuicision, and it is not necessary to say [also] the sinner (the apostate) regarding being uncircumcised. And it is "from it" that he shall not eat, but he shall eat from the matsah and the marror. And so [too], the [gentile] resident and wage-worker.

From the roots of this commandment are that which we have written about a resident and a wage-worker.

The laws of this commandment - for example, if the [need to administer the] circumcision of his children and his slaves prevents him from slaughtering and eating the Pesach sacrifice; and the rest of its details - are elucidated in Pesachim.

And [it] is practiced at the time of the [Temple]. And one who transgresses it - for example, an uncircumcised man who eats a kazayit from it - is lashed.

Mitzvah 18

The commandment of sanctifying the first-born in the Land of Israel: To sanctify the first-born; meaning to say that all those that are born first, which is to say [that] come out first from the womb of the female - whether with people or with beasts - the males are holy to God; as it is stated (Exodus 13:2), "Sanctify for Me every first-born; the first issue of every womb among the Israelites - man and beast - is Mine." And specifically, the beast (behamah) - which is an ox and and a sheep and a goat -

but not a wild animal (chayah). And from the impure beasts, only the donkey is [included] in this commandment (Bekhorot 10a). And the content of the commandment with a pure beast is that it is a commandment upon the owners to sanctify it and say, "Behold this is holy." And they are obligated to give the first-born to the priests (Kohanim); and [the latter] offer its fat and its blood on the altar and eat the meat in Jerusalem. And he does not give it immediately when it is born, but rather takes care of it - with [sheep and goats] for thirty days; and with [cattle] for fifty days (Bekhorot 10a). And outside the Land, where we do not have a Temple - according to some commentators (Mordechai in the name of Rabbi Eliezer MiMetz on Avodah Zarah, Chapter 1) - he locks the door in front of it and it dies on its own. But there are [others] of them (Mishneh Torah, Laws of Firstlings 1:10) that said we should always kill it. And if a blemish developed upon it, he can feed it to any man and in any place that the priest wants to give it to him. And it is considered like unsanctified meat (as it is like unsanctified meat) - as it is stated (Deuteronomy 15:22), "the impure and the pure shall eat it, like the gazelle and the deer." And so wrote Ramban, may his memory be Blessed, in his Laws of Firstlings (at the end of Chapter 5). And we shall explain the topics of the first-born of a man and the [first-born] of a donkey with the commandment of the redemption of each of them, with the help of God. And they are in this Order and in the Order of Vayikach Korach.

It is from the roots of this commandment that God, may He be Blessed, wanted to make us merit to do a commandment with the beginning of His fruit, in order that all should know that everything is His; and that man has nothing in the world, except that which God, may He be Blessed, apportions to us, in His kindness. And he will understand this in his seeing that after a man exerted himself [with] many exertions and put himself through many troubles in His world and reached the time when it makes a fruit - and his first fruit is beloved to him like the [apple] of his eye - he immediately gives it to the Holy One, Blessed be He, and empties his possession of it and of his properties [to put it] into the possession of his Creator. And it is also to remember the great miracle that God, may He be Blessed, did for us with the first-born of Egypt - as He killed them and saved us from their hand.

The laws of this commandment - in which place it is sacrificed and eaten; until which time is it a commandment to eat it; the matter of blemishes that disqualify it; which one is a fixed blemish or a passing blemish and the difference between them; who is [considered] trustworthy about the blemishes and if they developed on it or were made on purpose; which sage is fitting to judge his [own] blemishes; the law of a first-born of Jewish partners or of a gentile partner; and in what case a beast is, or is not, exempted from the [status of the] first-born; what is the law of a questionable first-born; the matter of a cesarean section; [a firstborn the sex of which is in doubt]; and the rest of its details -are [all] elucidated in Tractate Bekhorot (See Tur, Yoreh Deah 306-320).

And the commandment of the sanctification of the first-born pure animal is practiced according to the Torah in the Land of Israel alone, at all times; and like the rabbis expounded (Temurah 21b, and see Mishneh Torah, Laws of Firstlings 1:5), "From that which is written (Deuteronomy 14:23), 'And you shall eat in front of the Lord, your God, the tithes of your new grain and wine and oil, and the first-born of your herds' - it compares, etc." And rabbinically even outside the Land and with males and females, whether [of] Israelites, [of] priests or [of] Levites (Bekhorot 13a). And even though a first-born that is born to a priest is his, nonetheless he is obligated to sacrifice its fat and its blood and to eat the meat according to the laws of first-borns. But the first-born of a man and the [first-born] of a donkey are not practiced with a priest or a Levite, as we will write with God's help. And this is from the commandments mandated as a result of something [that happened historically].

Mitzvah 19

To not eat chamets (leavened grain products) on Pesach: To not eat chamets on Pesach, as it is stated (Exodus 13:3), "no chamets shall be eaten."

That which we have written about the other commandments of Pesach is from the roots of this commandment.

The laws of the commandment - for example, which are the things that are forbidden because of chamets and they are five types of grain; the law of kneading with fruit juice; the law of soaking [grain kernels]; a cooked food within which chamets is found, while it is hot or while it is cold; and

the rest of its details - are [all] elucidated in Pesachim 35 (See Tur, Orach Chaim 446-468).
And [it] is practiced in every place and at all times by males and
females. And one who transgresses it and eats a kazayit of chamets on Pesach volitionally is liable for excision. [And if it is] inadvertent, he is obligated a fixed sin-offering.

Mitzvah 20
That chamets not be found to us on Pesach: That chamets should not be seen in all of our dwellings all seven days of Pesach, as it is stated (Exodus 13:7), "and no chamets shall be seen with you, and no leaven shall be seen with you in all your territory (seven days)." And these are not two negative commandments about two topics, but rather one negative commandment; as they, may their memory be Blessed, said (Beitzah 7b), "The verse opened with chametz and ended with leaven, to say to you that chamets is leaven" - meaning to say [that] there is no difference between chamets itself and something that causes it to become chamets.
That which we have written about the other commandments of Pesach is from the roots of this commandment. Its laws are elucidated in Pesachim (See Tur, Orach Chaim 434).
And [it] is practiced in every place and at all times by males and females. And one who transgresses it and buys chamets on Pesach and places it in his domain is lashed. But if he does not remove if from before Pesach from his house, he is not lashed, since there is no act [involved] in it. And [so] we do not administer lashes for it, as we have said.

Mitzvah 21
The commandment to recount the exodus from Egypt: To tell about the exodus from Egypt on the night of the fifteenth of Nissan (the first night of Pesach) - each person according to his own power of expression - to laud and to praise God, may He be Blessed, for all the miracles He performed for us there, as it is stated (Exodus 13:8), "And you shall tell your son." [Although the verse doesn't specify when this should be done,] the Sages have already explained (Mekhilta d'Rabbi Yishmael 13:8) that this commandment of retelling is on the night of the fifteenth of Nissan - which is the time of the eating of the matsah. And that which the verse states, "[and you shall tell] your son," [does not mean] exclusively one's son; but rather even with any creature (Pesachim 116a).
The content of the commandment is that one mentions the miracles
and the [related] matters that happened to our forefathers during the exodus from Egypt, and how the Almighty, may He be Blessed, exacted our revenge from [the Egyptians]. And even one who is by himself - if no other people are present - is obligated to verbally express these matters, so that his heart will be inspired in this matter; for the heart is inspired through verbal expression (see Sefer HaMitzvot LaRambam, Mitzvot Ase 157).
That which we have written about the Pesach sacrifice (Sefer HaChinukh 5) is from the roots of this commandment. And it is no wonder if there are many commandments that came about this - positive commandments and negative commandments - since it is a great foundation and a strong pillar in our Torah and in our faith. And therefore we always say, "in memory of the exodus from Egypt," in our blessing and in our prayers" - since it is a sign and a total proof for the creation of the world and that there is a primordial God that has will [and] ability: He controls all of what exists and it is in His hand to change them according to what He desires at any time - as He did in Egypt when He changed the natural processes of the world for our sake, and made for us novel, great and powerful signs. Does this not silence all that deny the creation of the world and support the faith with the knowledge of God, may He be Blessed; and that His providence and power is upon all of the general categories [as well as upon] the particulars!
The laws of the commandment - for example, the Order (Seder) that Israel is obligated to do on this night in the matter of their meal; the cups of wine, their measurements, their pouring and their order; and the rest of their details - are [all] elucidated at the end of Pesachim (See Tur, Orach Chaim 469-482). And behold, my son, I will write for you the Seder in short - exactly as I have heard it from the sages of the generation: In the beginning, we bring water and wash one hand for the sake of the cup of Kiddush which needs to be held. And this is how it is in Berakhot 43a in the Chapter [entitled]

Sefer HaChinukh

Keitsad Mevarkhin - that with the cup, washing one hand is sufficient. And we do not recite a blessing on this washing. And if he wants to wash two hands for the cup, he washes them without a blessing. And afterwards, he washes both hands and recites the blessing, "upon the washing of the hands," and dips with a vegetable (the vegetable, according to the Vilna edition) and recites the blessing, "who creates the fruit of the ground," before [eating it]. But he does not recite the blessing, "who creates souls, etc.," after it - since he waits until he eats the marror; and then he recites the blessing, "who creates souls," upon the marror and upon the vegetable. And everything that he did is not an interruption, as we will explain. And after they ate from the vegetable in charoset (a thick sweet dip), we pour a second cup and read the Haggadah with two chapters of Psalms and recite the blessing, "who has redeemed us, etc.," upon the second cup, and we drink it. And we do not recite the blessing, "who creates the fruit of the vine," upon it, nor "upon the vine," after it. And after they drink the second cup, we wash our hands and recite the blessing, "upon the washing of the hands." And [then] we take half of a matsah and we place it on the complete one and recite the blessing upon the half, "who brings forth" and "to eat matsah." And we take bitter herbs and we recite the blessing, "to eat marror," and eat from it dipped in charoset; but we do not recite the blessing, "who creates the fruit of the ground," upon it, since he is exempted by the blessing that he recited upon the vegetable at the beginning. As this is how it is concluded in the Gemara (Pesachim 103b) - that it is never [considered] an interruption unless there is [one of] two things: That he removes his thoughts from the matter - for example when they say, "Let us bless (say Grace after the Meal)," and similar to it. And also, that [he be engaged in something else, such] that it not be possible to do the two things together - for example that which they, may their memory be Blessed, said (Chullin 87a and Rashi there), "Drinking and blessing together is not possible." And after we eat from the marror with the dip, we wrap some of it on top of matsah and eat a little bit, in memory of the Pesach sacrifice that was eaten upon satiation. And we do not eat more the whole night, so as not to remove the taste of matsah from the mouth; as it is written (Psalms 113:103), "than honey to my mouth." But we can certainly drink water, since water does not spoil the taste. And we also drink the two cups of the commandment, as we do not push off the commandment [on account of] this reason. And afterwards, we wash our hands, but we do not recite the blessing, "upon the washing of the hands." And we pour the third cup and recite the Grace after the meals and "who has created the fruit of the vine" over it; but not "upon the vine," after it (see Baal HaMeor on the end of Arevei Pesachim). And afterwards, we pour the fourth cup and finish Hallel over it. And we do not recite the blessing, "who has created the fruit of the vine," upon it; but we do recite the blessing, "upon the vine," after it. And that is if he does not have in mind to still drink a fifth cup. It comes out according to this that we only recite the blessing, "who has created the fruit of the vine," twice - on the cup of Kiddush and on the cup of the Grace. And [we only recite the blessing,] "upon the vine," once, after all of the cups. And the four cups and the matsah of the commandment requires leaning.

And [it] is practiced by males and females (Pesachim 36a and Pesachim 115b) in every place and at all times. And one who transgresses it violates a positive commandment.

Mitzvah 22

The commandment of the redemption of a [first-born] donkey: To redeem the male offspring of a donkey that was born first, as it is stated (Exodus 13:13), "And the first-born of a donkey, you shall redeem with a sheep." And its content is that the Israelite takes one sheep and gives it to the priest as redemption for the first-born donkey, which is to God, for the reason that we wrote above. And He, Blessed be He, gave it to the priest. And hence the Israelite redeems it from him, since God, may He be Blessed, wanted that there should be a redemption for it with a sheep. And if he does not have a sheep, he redeems it with the money [value] of a sheep. And since the money of sheep is not the same [in all cases], the Rabbis, may their memory be Blessed, said (Bekhorot 11a), "A good eye (a generous price) is a sela, a bad eye (a miserly price) is half a sela, an intermediate [one] is three zuz." And the time of the redemption is until thirty days. And the sheep is non-sanctified in the hand of the priest and the donkey is [likewise] in the hand of the Israelite.

It is from the roots of this commandment [that it is] so that the Jews will always remember the miracle that God did for them during the exodus from Egypt - that He killed all of their first-born, as it is written.

The laws of the commandment - for example, the partnership of a gentile or if he receives a donkey from him to take care of; the law of a gentile who separated out a [firstborn] donkey as to what is its law; the law of a donkey that gave birth to a type of horse; the law of one who buys a donkey from a gentile; what is the law in the matter of a doubt if it already gave birth to a first-born; the law of one who gives the donkey itself to the priest; and the rest of its details - are [all] elucidated in Tractate Bekhorot (See Tur, Yoreh Deah 221).

And [it] is practiced in all places and at all times by Israelite males and females. but not by priests or Levites. And one who transgresses this violates a positive commandment.

Mitzvah 23

The commandment of beheading a [first-born] donkey: To behead a [first-born] donkey, if he does not want to redeem it, as it is stated (Exodus 13:13), "and if he does not redeem it, he shall behead it." Its content is that he kills the offspring of the donkey if he does not want to redeem it. And God decreed that he should not benefit from it, since he did not redeem it. And [this is such] that even the carcass is forbidden for him to benefit from.

That which is written with redemption (in the previous commandment) is from the roots of this commandment.

The laws of the commandment - that which they said (Bekhorot 13a) that the commandment of redemption takes precedence over beheading; that it is forbidden to benefit from it if it dies before the redemption and that it should [then] be buried; so [too,] that he should kill it with a kofits (a large knife), and not with something else; and the rest of its details - are elucidated in Bekhorot (See Tur, Yoreh Deah 221). And it is practiced like the redemption regarding everything.

Mitzvah 24

That we should not go outside of the boundary (techum) on Shabbat: That we have been prevented from going outside of the known boundaries on Shabbat, as it is stated (Exodus 16:29), "let no one leave his place on the seventh day." And the explanation comes about this that "his place" is called anywhere that is no further than three parsa from outside of the city (Mishneh Torah, Laws of Sabbath 27:1-2). And a parsa is four mil, and a mil is two thousand ells. And we measure it from the outermost house in the city, even if it is as large as Nineveh. This is according to the law of the Torah, but the Sages made a fence and forbade that one should walk more than two thousand ells outside of the city.

From the roots of this commandment are that we should remember and know that the world is created and not primordial, as it is written explicitly about the commandment of Shabbat (Exodus 20:11), "For in six days the Lord made the heavens and the earth, the sea and all that is in them, and He rested on the seventh day." Hence to remember this thing, it is fitting that we rest in one place; meaning to say that we not go to a faraway place, but rather only stroll and have delight [from our walks]. And the walking of [up to] twelve mil (the limit of what is allowed by the Torah) does not have much strain to it.

The laws of the commandment - for example, what is the law about one who spends Shabbat in the wilderness or in a cave (Eruvin 61b); and so [too,] one who goes outside of the boundary - volitionally or inadvertently, or by permission of the court (Eruvin 52b); what is the law if he surrounded himself with a partition on Shabbat (Eruvin 42a); what are the laws regarding the city of a house that goes out more than the other houses of the city seventy ells and a bit, a synagogue that has a domicile for the sextons, a house of idolatry that has domiciles for priests, or storehouses that have domiciles or three barriers that do not have a roof or pitch (Eruvin 55b); and how one measures a long or square or round city, or one that is made like the shape of a gamma or like an arch (Eruvin 55a); and with which string do we measure; and what is the size of the string (Eruvin 53b); and how does one measure from one valley to [another] valley, or to a mountain or to a wall; and upon whom do we rely for the measurement; and who is [considered] trustworthy to testify about the boundaries; and the rest of its details - are [all] found in the tractate that is built upon it, and that is Eruvin.

And [it] is practiced in every place and at all times by males and females. And one who transgresses and goes even one more ell than three parsa [outside of the city] is lashed. And so [too], if he goes even one more ell outside of the two thousand ells adjacent to the city, he is struck with rabbinic lashes for rebellion. And Ramban, may his memory be Blessed, wrote (on Sefer HaMitzvot LaRambam, Mitzvot Lo Taase 321) that that which Rambam, may his memory be Blessed, said in his Book of the Commandments (Sefer HaMitzvot) that the prohibition of boundaries is forbidden from the Torah past two thousand ells [from the city] - and so [too], what he said in his great composition (Mishneh Torah, Laws of Sabbath 27:1) that he recanted from this and wrote that the measurement of the Torah is three parsa - is all a mistake, since we do not have a prohibition of boundaries from the Torah at all. And so is it elucidated from many places in our Gemara, which is the Babylonian [Talmud] that we rely upon in all of our words. And the teacher (Ramban) gave numerous proofs for this on Commandment 313 (it should read, 321) of the negative commandments. And he understands, "let no one leave (yetseh)," to be like "let no one carry out (yotsee)" - [just] like there is an opinion in Tractate Eruvin 16b that understands it this way.

Mitzvah 25

The commandment of belief in God: To believe that the world has one God that caused all that exists, and that all that is, and was, and will be forever and ever, is from His power and His will; and that He took us out out of Egypt and gave us the Torah - as it is stated (Exodus 20:2), "I am the Lord, your God, who took you out of the land of Egypt, etc." And its understanding is as if it said, "Know and believe that there is one God" - since the word, "I," indicates existence. And that which it stated, "who took you out, etc.," is to say that your hearts not seduce you to take the matter of your leaving the slavery of Egypt and the plagues of Egypt as the way of happenstance; but rather you should know that I am the One who took you out with will and providence - as He promised our forefathers, Avraham, Yitschak and Yaakov.

The root of this commandment does not need elucidation. The matter is known and revealed to all that this belief is the foundation of the religion, and that one who does not believe in it denies a fundamental principle and has no share and merit with Israel. And the content of the belief is that he fix in his soul that such is the truth and that a change of (about a change of) this in any way be impossible. And if he be asked about it, he will respond to any enquirer that his heart believes this and he will not assent to a change in it, even if they say they will kill him [as a result]. As all of this - when he takes the thing from the potential to actuality, by which I mean to say when he puts into the words of his mouth what his heart decides - strengthens and fixes the belief of the heart. And if one merits to rise in the levels of wisdom, 'his heart will understand and his eyes will see' with a sealed proof that this belief that he believed is true and clear - it is impossible that there be something besides this - then he will fulfill this positive commandment [in the best way].

The laws of this commandment - for example, that which it obligates us to believe about Him that all power and all greatness and strength and glory and all majesty and all blessing and all existence are in Him, and that we do not have the power or the intellect to grasp and to speak out His greatness and goodness, since His great virtue and majesty is only grasped by Himself; to deny about Him with all of our strength any lacking and anything that is the opposite of all perfections and all virtues, and the matters that come out from this, for example, to know that He is a perfect Being, without a body and not a power of a body, since lackings effect bodies, whereas He, may He be Blessed, is not effected by any type of lacking, as we have said; and all the many things about this matter - are all elucidated in the books of those that know the wisdom of theology. Happy are those that merit it, as they can then fulfill this commandment with clarity (Mishneh Torah, Laws of Foundations of the Torah 1).

And [it] is practiced in every place and at all times by males and females. And one who transgresses it has no portion and merit with Israel, as we have said. And this is from the commandments that does not have a specific time, since a man must live with this thought all the days of his life.

Sefer HaChinukh

Mitzvah 26

That we not believe in a god besides God alone: That we not believe in a god besides God, may He be Blessed, alone, as it is stated (Exodus 20:3), "You shall have no other gods in front of Me." And its understanding is [that] you not believe in another god, except Me. And Ramban, may his memory be Blessed wrote (Ramban on Exodus 20:3) [that] you will only find that Scripture states, "other gods," about belief of the heart. But concerning their making, it will never state, "do not make other gods," since the expression, "making," does not sit with others (since they cannot be made). And he, may his memory be Blessed, was nicely precise [in this] - 'the words of the wise are grace!' And this commandment is the great fundamental principle of the Torah, as everything is dependent upon it - as they, may their memory be Blessed, said (Sifrei Bamidbar 111:1), "Anyone who concedes to idolatry is as if he denied the whole entire Torah." And it is the same whether he accepts anything as a god besides only God, or whether he worships it according to its worship - meaning to say, in the way that those that believe in it worship it - or even not according to its worship, if he worships it according to the four well-known [forms of] worship, and they are sacrificing, bringing incense, pouring and bowing; he has transgressed upon "you shall have no." And pouring and sprinkling are one thing, and those that sprinkle are liable, [just] like those that pour.

The root of this commandment is revealed and known. Its particulars - for example, that which they said that if one accepts any of the creations as a god, and even if he concedes that the Holy One, Blessed be He, rules over him and over his god, transgresses upon "you shall have no"; what is the thing which is called, "according to the way of its worship," and "not according to the way of its worship"; what is the law if he worships it by disgracing it and that is its [standard] worship; how far does the prohibition extend regarding the four worships forbidden with all of the gods, like the matter that they, may their memory be Blessed, said (Avodah Zarah 51a) that one who breaks a stick in front of it is included in sacrificing; so [too], what they, may their memory be Blessed, forbade (Shabbat 149a) to read from the books of idolatry written about matters of their worship or about other things (matters) of it, anything that causes belief in it in any way; the prohibition of meditation of the heart [to go] after it; what is the law about an Israelite that worshiped it even once; and that if he took it on as a god and recanted during the time of speech (immediately after the first speech), he is liable (Bava Batra 129b), since we do not say "during the time of speech is like the speech," about this and also regarding the matter of marriages; and worship from love, wherein one loves the shape due to its beautiful form, or from fear that it not harm him and it is not that he accepts it as a god; so [too], what is the law of prohibiting one who gives it honors such as hugging, kissing, anointing, clothing, shoeing (Sanhedrin 60b, Sanhedrin 61b); how are the laws of the negation of idolatry and the distinction between that of an Israelite and that of an idolater regarding its negation; how far does the law of benefit from idolatry go; the distinction between something disconnected [from the ground] that was worshiped and something that was originally connected; from when does it become an idol; the law of those objects that service the idolatry, and if he negated it, what happens with these objects (Avodah Zarah 52b); what is the law of that sacrificed to it (Avodah Zarah 29b); an idol that was abandoned by its worshipers; the distancing of its worshipers on the day of its worship and near to [that day]; the things that are always prohibited to sell to them, out of concern for disgrace; the distancing of a city that has idolatry in it; and the rest of its many details - are [all] elucidated in the tractate that is built upon it and that it is Avodah Zarah.

And [it] is practiced by males and females in every place and at all times. And one who transgresses it and worshiped idolatry according to the way of its worship or - with the four worships that we wrote - [even] not according to the way of its worship, with witnesses and a warning, is stoned. And if it is inadvertent, he is obligated to bring a fixed sin-offering. And this commandment is included in the seven commandments that all the people of the world were commanded (Sanhedrin 56a). However, there are differences between Israel and the other nations in the details, and it is all elucidated there in Avodah Zarah. And among the differences between Israel and the other nations in the matter of the commandments that are incumbent upon all is that an Israelite will never be liable [for the death penalty] without witnesses and a warning, but the other nations do not require a warning, since there is no difference for them between inadvertent and volitional. And also, they can become liable with the admission of their [own] mouths, which is not the case with Israel, who requires witnesses. And there is yet another difference - as when the nations transgress one of their commandments, they are always liable for the death penalty; but Israel is sometimes liable for a sacrifice, sometimes lashes, sometimes the death penalty and sometimes not liable for any of these, but is [simply] like someone who transgresses the commandment of the King and he carries [the weight of] his iniquity.

Mitzvah 27
To not make a statue: To not make statues that will be worshiped; even if the one that makes them does not worship them, the making is itself forbidden, [so as] to push off the stumbling block. And there is no difference between his making it with his hand or commanding someone else to make it, as it is stated (Exodus 20:4), "You shall not make for yourself a statue or any depiction." And the one who commands to make it is the one who causes its making - that is the opinion of Rambam, may his memory be Blessed (Sefer HaMitzvot LaRambam, Mitzvot Lo Taase 4). And the opinion of Ramban, may his memory be Blessed, (on that entry in Sefer HaMitzvot) it that there is no prohibition here except for not making idols with the intention of worshiping them. He also wrote that this negative commandment should not be counted from this scripture, as this verse only warns about the prohibition of idolatry which comes with the death penalty; but with the making of idols, the whole time that he does not worship them, the only thing he is liable for is lashes. And he, may his memory be Blessed, wrote that this whole verse of "You shall have no," is considered one negative commandment [that] warns not to concede the divinity of anything besides Him; whether he accepts it as a god - meaning to say that he says to it, "You are my god" - or bows down to it, or worships it in one the four forbidden worships or worships it with the worship that is particular to it. Rather, he wrote that the [prohibition] of making idols and their preservation is extrapolated from the verse (Leviticus 19:4) of "Do not turn to idols or make molten gods for yourselves." And I wonder about that which Rambam, may his memory be Blessed, wrote that there is no difference if he made it with his hand or if he commanded to make it - as behold, the one who commands is a dispatcher, and it is an established [principle] for us that a dispatcher is exempt.

The root of this commandment is known, that it is to distance the idols (idolatry).

The laws of the commandment - for example, [regarding] one who makes forms, which one is forbidden to make and which one is permissible; the distinction between a protruding [form] and a sunken [one]; the law of a ring that has a seal upon it; and the rest of its details - are [all] elucidated in Tractate Avodah Zarah 43b (See Tur, Yoreh Deah 139-141).

And [it] is practiced in every place and at all times by males and females. And one who transgresses it volitionally and makes idols that will be worshiped is lashed.

Mitzvah 28
To not bow down to idolatry: To not bow down to idolatry - and idolatry is anything that is worshiped besides God, Blessed be He - as it is stated (Exodus 20:5), "You shall not bow down to them or serve them." And the explanation of the verse is not "do not bow down to them with the intention of worship," [so] that we would learn that bowing down, by itself - without the intention of worship - would not be forbidden. As behold, in another place, it is stated in the Torah (Exodus 34:14), "For you must not bow down to another god," which forbade bowing down by itself, from any angle. Rather, [the reason] it made "or serve them" adjacent, [is] to say that bowing down is one of the ways of worship. And we learn from here, with the assistance of other verses, that there are four worships about which the Torah is insistent with any idolatry in the world - and even if it is not the way of its worship, we are liable for it. And one of [these four] is bowing down.

The root of this commandment is known. The laws of the commandment - for example, what is [considered] bowing down, if it is the spreading out of hands and feet or if it is from the time he puts his face to the ground (Horayot 4a); the distancing of the matter, as for example, what they said (Avodah Zarah 16a) that if a thorn is stuck in his foot or his coins scattered in front of idolatry that he is not permitted to bend over to get them because it appears like bowing down; and the rest of its details - are elucidated in Tractate Avodah Zarah.

And [it] is practiced in every place and at all times by males and females. And one who transgresses it and bows down to any idolatry in the world - or sacrifices, or gives incense, or pours or sprinkles [libations] - volitionally is liable for excision. And [if it is] in front of witnesses, he is stoned; and inadvertently, he is liable for a sin-offering. And the elucidation of the statutes of the punishments are in the seventh chapter of Sanhedrin.

Mitzvah 29
To not worship idolatry in that which is its way to be worshiped: That we not worship any idolatry in the world with the things that are the way of those that believe in it to worship it. And even though its worship is not with one of the four worships that we said above, since he worshiped it with that which is its way to be worshiped, he is liable. And even [if] its worship is in a way of disgrace - for example, one who defecates to Peor, or one who throws stones at Markulis or one who passes his seed to Kamosh - as it is stated (Exodus 20:5), "or worship them," meaning to say with what is their way to be worshiped, whatever worship it may be.

Its root is known. Its laws - for example, what the law is for one who worships it in the way of its worship with the intention of disgracing it (Sanhedrin 64a); and the rest of its details - are in Tractate Avodah Zarah.

And [it] is practiced in every place and at all times by males and females. And one who transgresses it volitionally and there are witnesses is stoned. And this law is also elucidated in Chapter Seven of Sanhedrin. These two commandments that Rambam, may his memory be Blessed, counted - which are bowing down to idolatry and also not to worship it according to how it is its way to be worshiped - Ramban, may his memory be Blessed, included in the commandment of "you shall have no," and as we wrote above (Sefer HaChinukh 27). It comes out that he removes two commandments here from the calculation of Rabbi Moshe Maimonides (Rambam), may his memory be Blessed.

Mitzvah 30
To not swear in vain: That we not swear pointlessly, as it is stated (Exodus 20:7), "You shall not take the name of the Lord, your God, in vain." And the notion of pointlessness has four angles: [The first is,] for example (Shevuot 29a), that he swears about something known [to be true] that it is not so, like swearing about a pillar of marble that it is a pillar of gold. And so [too], anything like this. The second angle is, for example [Talmud Yerushalmi Shevuot 3:8], that he swears about what is known to be so, like about a stone that it is a stone and about a tree that it is a tree, and all that is like this. The third angle is that he swears to negate this commandment or the commandments that God, Blessed be He, commanded us; as this is also completely pointless, since it is not in his hand to swear [to negate] that which God has already obligated him - and it is like the one who swears about something known that it is not so. The fourth angle is that he swears to do something that he does not have the power to do; for example (Shevuot 25a) that he will not sleep for three consecutive days, or that he will not eat for seven consecutive days. And so [too], anything like this.

It is from the roots of this commandment [that it is] for people to know and fix in their souls and strengthen the faith in their hearts about God, Blessed be He - who is in the Heavens above and exists forever - that there is nothing else like His existence. And it is fitting and obligatory upon us when we mention His great name upon our actions and upon our words, to mention it with fear, with awe, with trembling and perspiration; and not like those that joke and speak about something light, such as the things that exist and perish and do not continue to exist - like us people, and the other things of the lowly world. Hence (it is fitting) [in order] to fix this matter in our hearts and that His awe should be in front of us to give us life and merit, it obligated us in this commandment that we not mention His holy name pointlessly; and punished with lashes the one who is lenient and transgresses it.

And from this root itself is the matter of a false oath (shevuah), meaning to say when he swears to fulfill something and does not fulfill it. [This] is called an oath of speech, about which another separate commandment comes in the Order of Kedoshim Tehiyu, as it is stated (Leviticus 19:12), "And you shall not swear falsely by My name." As one who swears by the great name [of God] to say something was and [yet] he knows that there is falsehood in his mouth, behold, he is acting lightly with the awe of God; as if to say in his heart that He is not true - 'let his lips be silent.' And so the one who swears to do something and afterwards does not do it is, behold, also among the rebels against light, the deniers of truth. As the understanding of "swore," is, according to my opinion, that he concludes in his heart and says with his mouth to fulfill that thing that he swore about and that he will never change it, [just] as God, may He be Blessed, exists and does not change forever and ever. And that is [why] the expression, sworn nishbaa always comes in the passive; meaning to say that he is acted upon by his words to make it exist, [just] like he said about His existence, Blessed be He.

And regarding a vow (neder), a different approach pertains to it - as it is like placing something permissible into the category of the forbidden, and [it is] as if he would say thing x which is permissible will be forbidden to him, like a sacrifice that God, may He be Blessed, forbade. And they, may their memory be Blessed, said (Nedarim 14a) that only when he makes the vow with a thing that is vowed (that changes status) does his vow stand, and not in another way. As if he says, "Thing x is forbidden to me like a sacrifice," as we have said; in this [way], the vow will stand (Nedarim 13a). But if he says, "like the meat of a pig," this is not a vow; as the Torah stated (Numbers 30:3), "If he vows a vow," meaning to say, "if he vows with something that is vowed." And so, one who forbids something to his fellow or to himself like the matters of a sacrifice that God, may He be Blessed, forbade, is like this matter (like something vowed); since it is as if he said [that] thing x will be forbidden to him or to his friend, [just] like God, may He Blessed, forbade us the matters of a sacrifice. And this matter that we have the power to forbid the permissible is because the Torah taught us this, from that which is written (Numbers 30:3), "If [...] he creates a prohibition [...], he may not break his word."

And this matter is similar to consecration (hekdesh). As we have found in the Torah that a person has the power to consecrate what is his, with the words of his mouth; and they will immediately be forbidden to him and to the whole world, as it is written (Leviticus 27:14), "And if a man consecrates his home to be holy." And so [too], does he have power over himself to forbid things upon his body. This is their, may their memory be Blessed, always saying in the expressions of vows (Nedarim 15a), "Behold, it is upon me" - or (Nedarim 13b), "my mouth" for speech - meaning to say that he distances that thing from him. And he has the power to bind himself with a prohibition of that thing, [just] like he has the power to forbid his possessions. And that is itself the law and the reason why [only] an oath can rest upon something of substance [as well as] something that is not of substance (Nedarim 15b), since the oath lodges upon the body of the person, meaning to say that his body is obligated to do that thing - and behold, the body has substance. However, a vow only rests upon something that has substance, as it is like him placing something into the category of other things that are forbidden; meaning to say that thing x will be forbidden to him like the category of the sacrifice that is forbidden to him. And if there is no substance to that which he is [literally] placing in the category, he has not done anything and it is nothing.

And so, from this reason, an oath cannot rest upon an oath [about the same matter], but a vow can rest upon a vow [about the same matter]. As with an oath, behold once a man has himself entered into the partition of [something's] existence, as we have said, even if he repeats his word that he is entering there a thousand times, the entrance of his body into another place is done [only] one time. And this that he does after that is only repeating words pointlessly. But with a vow in which he is like one that accepts upon himself that something permissible is as if it is forbidden; with each time that he repeats his acceptance, he adds [a further] prohibition if he [breaks his vow]. And hence he is liable for each and every one. And it is the same matter itself that an oath cannot rest upon the matter of a commandment (Nedarim 16a), but a vow can rest even upon the matter of a commandment. As one who makes an oath speaks about his body, and his body is already obligated in that matter [of the commandment] from Mount Sinai. But with a vow, he is only speaking about the object that he wants to bring into the category of the forbidden, and about this specific object, he was never obligated. And hence [his new] prohibition rests upon it. And we do not feed a person something that is forbidden for him [because of an oath or a vow]. And this is what they, may their memory be Blessed, said (Ran on Nedarim 8a, s. v. Vehalo mushva) that the one who makes an oath forbids himself to the object and the one who makes a vow forbids the object to himself.

Sefer HaChinukh

And you may ask, "How is it that the one who makes a vow not to eat something that he is commanded about to eat, does not eat it - as behold, he is commanded about that thing with a positive commandment; and a positive commandment comes and pushes off the negative commandment of 'he shall not break.' As so did the Sages say in every place, 'a positive commandments comes and pushes off a negative commandment.'" The answer to you is that the vow is a positive commandment and there is [also] a negative commandment in it: the negative commandment is "he shall not break," and the positive commandment is "everything that comes out of his mouth he shall do." And from the reason that we gave [before] that his body is acted upon with an oath, they said (Shevuot 20a) [that] one that is added on with an oath [of someone else] is exempt [from it]; but with vows, he is obligated. How so? If he heard that his fellow made a vow and he said, "I am also like you," within the time of speech (immediately after it), behold this one is forbidden, since the intention of this one is to say, [just] like you are forbidden from this thing, so too will I be forbidden from it, and with this, it will be sufficient for him. But with an oath, wherein we picture the first one as if he acts upon his body with his words - as we have said - he has not removed something else away from his body; they, may their memory be Blessed, did not see that this later one is included in this movement by saying, "I am also like you." [Rather,] he must speak out the expression of this movement with his actual mouth - for example, if he says, "I too swear like you"; or if he hears from the mouth of someone who moves him [specifically] to that thing, and he fulfills it and indicates that he wants this movement, like when another man says to him, "I put an oath upon you," and he answers, "Amen."

The general principle of the thing is that the language of the oath must be said by his own mouth or that someone else specifically refers it to him and he accepts [it]. But he is not moved by the movement of another man, since his [own] body needs the movement; [but this] is not the case with a vow. [It is also] possible to say that it is from the strictness of a vow that they were stricter about it, that one should be added on more quickly than with an oath; since it is stricter than an oath, as behold, they compare it to the life of the King (Sifrei Bamidbar 123:3, see Ramban on Numbers 30:3). And from the reason that we wrote about an oath, that its content is that a man concludes to fulfill his words and to confirm [them by that which] he believes in the Divine existence, we would have learned that his oath cannot be nullified from any angle. But it was from the kindnesses of God to us - in His knowing the frailty of the structure of our body and the smallness of our opinions and the constancy of the change of our wills - to give us counsel to get out from the prison of the oath with the [change] of our will at any time: he allowed us to make the claim regarding the matter of the oath that it was under duress or inadvertent, as is explained in its place in Shevuot 26a and Nedarim 20b.

However, we were not permitted to go out from it [wantonly, but] rather [only] with the stratagem and counsel of the sage; that the one who swore come in front of the man who is wise and understanding of the ways of the Torah and confess to him that [the oath] was from his lack of knowledge - that he did not know at the time that he swore something that he knew afterwards - that he wants to annul what he swore about (Nedarim 71a); and that he recognizes that the smallness of his knowledge and his lacking caused the annulment, not something else or an external thought that would be in his heart, God forbid. And after the confession of his mouth about this, the sage recognizes and sees that there is substance in his words that something new happened to him that if he had had to agree to it at the time that he swore, he would not have sworn and that this is why he regrets [it]; he accepts his confession and he releases him from his oath. And this is what they, may their memory be Blessed, said (Berachot 32b), "He cannot forgive [it], but others can forgive it to him." Therefore, it is never possible to annul an oath, except with the reason of something new to the one who swore - for example, that he will say, "If I had known thing x, I would never have sworn." As this is like duress. But if he says, "Annul me my oath," without a claim, no man has the power to annul it. And based on this, they, may their memory be Blessed, said (Nedarim 64a) that we do not create an opening (to annul the vow) with something new that is not found (that has not happened). As [with this] he does not clearly say that he regrets that he swore - that we should consider it duress - but rather that his will today is like it was at the beginning, but he [just] wants it annulled now. How is this? He swears that he not benefits from **x** and [**x**] becomes the town scribe or butcher, and he says, "My will [still] stands that I did not want to benefit from him and I [also] did not want him to become the scribe or the butcher." We do not annul [it] for him until he says, "Since I see that this man has become the scribe, I regret that I swore [off] his benefit forever. And if only I had not sworn!" In this way, we annul [it] for him; as behold, he concedes that his will has changed and that he regrets his deeds completely, due to the lack of his knowledge - as had he known at the time of the oath what he knows today, he never would have sworn. And it is like duress. And we expound (Shevuot 26a), "'A man with an oath' (Leviticus 5:4) - to exclude duress."

And from this foundation - also when he makes his oath depend on the mind of others, it is difficult to annul it. As since he has removed his [own] mind from the thing and made it depend on the mind of others, afterwards the claim of duress or inadvertence is not found with him. And this is what they said (Gittin 36a) that one who swears upon the mind of others does not have annulment. And nonetheless for a matter of a commandment, the Sages agreed to annul [it. This is] because [regarding] everything that a man does, which is something that causes the negation of a commandment or that a commandment is performed by not doing that thing, the heart of any Jew would [want] to negate the private action and do the commandment. And [so] we see [it] as if all of the [others] upon whose minds he swore were with him in front of him [now] and say that if they knew [about] the negation of the commandment [coming from] his oath, their minds would not have agreed with him. And behold, we have a claim of duress and inadvertence. And therefore they, may their memory be Blessed, said (Nedarim 16b), "But there is annulment for the matter of a commandment."

And do not think to challenge me about the giving of this reason that I have said - that the main annulment [comes from] something new happening to a man; that had he known about it from the beginning, he would not have sworn – [such that] you would say, "Behold, we have found annulment regarding the oaths of God, may He be Blessed, as they, may their memory be Blessed, expounded (Berakhot 32b) about 'And Moshe beseeched' (Exodus 32:11), that, as if it were possible, he annulled His oath [for] Him; and the matter of Zerubavel the son of Shaltiel, [about whom] they, may their memory be Blessed, said (Sanhedrin 38a) that he was asked by God [to annul] His oath." And God forbid that there should be a change of will with Him. As one can answer you - and it is [perfectly] true - that everything that comes in Scripture similar to these matters is all stated from the angle of the receivers, which are people. As God forbid to Him and for our hearts to believe that the Master of all would need to swear about something, or that He would need to annul it and negate it afterwards. Rather this thing is said from the angle of receiving punishment which comes to the one punished - that if a man is liable, due to the greatness of his sin, that he be punished regardless, to the point where it is not fitting to give him [the possibility] of repentance, the notion of an oath of God will come upon such a man; meaning to say [that] his punishment and decree is strongly upon him as if there were an oath on the thing. And so [too], for the good: if a man merited, from his great significance, to receive good - he and his children - the verse will also state that God, may He be Blessed, swore to benefit him.

And about this and that which is similar to it, they, may their memory be Blessed, said (Mekhilta d'Rabbi Yishmael 19:18:2) [it is] in order to (assuage - Vilna edition) break the ear to that which it can hear (make it understandable). As the strength and persistence of a thing cannot be illustrated to people except with that which they strengthen and keep their [own] words. And in this way exactly did they, may their memory be Blessed, expound the annulment of the oath of God, may He be Blessed: They wanted to say that He is 'graceful and merciful, slow to anger and of great kindness,' and atones for sins; even though their sins are great and strong to the point that if a man sinned to another so much, [the one offended] would swear never to forgive [the other]. And upon this approach, they, may their memory be Blessed, said that Moshe annulled it; meaning to say that it was the merit of Moshe's good prayer that caused God, may He be Blessed - who is the Listener to prayer - to have forgiven their sin. And this is [why] you will not find that our Rabbis, may their memory be Blessed, expound about the matter of the annulment of an oath of His, may He be Blessed, except with a great sin - such that every listener will [understand] that it not given to atonement; meaning to say it is fitting to swear about it that it should not be atoned. But His mercies, Blessed be He, were greater than all of our thoughts, and He atones for all those who return to Him - and even if their sin is too heavy to bear - according to my opinion.

And the proof to these words of ours is that which they said (Rosh Hashanah 18a) concerning a [Divine] decree that has an oath with it, as Rava concludes there, that it is not atoned with a sacrifice or a grain offering, but rather it is atoned with words of Torah; and they have no mention there that God would need to annul [His oath]. As the matters are known and clear to all who see the sun that it is all said metaphorically for the receivers. And in order to direct you on this path in many places, I have been lengthy about this until now.

And [regarding] that which I said that our Sages, may their memory be Blessed, ascribe the term, annulment, to an oath of God, may He be Blessed; you will only find this in a place that they attributed to Him an oath to make a creature liable. But in a place where they attributed to Him an oath to give merit to a creature, they never mention annulment - as the One of great kindness, inclines towards kindness. I mean to say that once a person appears meritorious at one time in front of the Omnipresent, it is so fitting for him to receive the good [that] it is as if the Holy One, Blessed be He, swore the goodly reward to him. It is like the matter that is stated (Psalms 132:11), "The Lord swore to David," and similar to it - [it means] the merit will no longer go away from him, even if he sins greatly. And this is from His precious traits, Blessed be He.

The laws of the commandment - for example, appellations for oaths, [about] which they, may their memory be Blessed, said that they are like an oath [and the explanation of appellations for oaths are the many terms that exist among people, according to their places, like what they, may their memory be Blessed, said (Nedarim 10a), " Shevuta, shekuka, etc. "]; so [too], the law [if one says,] "a curse (allah)" or "cursed (aroor)" whether they are like oaths (Shevout 36a); one who says "no" with the mention of God, and so [too], "right or left (Nazir 3b); the law of his mouth and heart being [in agreement], and that which we learned from this law of his mouth and heart being [in agreement], that we are able to make [deceptive] oaths to killers and plunderers, like [if] he say that all the fruits in the world are forbidden to him if there be such and such, and in his heart is that they only be forbidden for today (Nedarim 27b), and even though it generally implies forever, but it is only permitted to us like this, when the words of his mouth do not completely contradict the thought of his heart, and not in any other way; and the rest of its many details - are [all] in Shevuot and Nedarim (See Tur, Yoreh Deah 236).

And [it] is practiced in every place and at all times by males and females. And one who transgresses it and swears that a pillar of marble is of gold; or of gold that it is of gold; or to negate this commandment; or to do something that is not in the power of a man to do it is lashed, when volitional. And even though there is no act, the Torah made him liable for lashes due to the severity of the matter (Shevuot 27b). And he is exempted from a sacrifice for this, when inadvertent. But with a false oath - and that is what is called an oath of expression - the Torah obligated a sacrifice for inadvertence, as we shall write (Sefer HaChinukh 123) with God's help.

Mitzvah 31
The commandment of the sanctification of Shabbat with words: To speak words on the Shabbat upon its entry and also its departure - that there be in them cognizance of the greatness of the day and its stature and its positive distinction from the other days before it and after it; as it is stated (Exodus 20:8), "Remember the Shabbat day, to sanctify it," meaning to say, remember it with a memory of [its] holiness and greatness. And in explanation, our Sages told us (Pesachim 110a) that we are commanded to say these things upon wine - as so does the explanation come: remember it over wine. And the content is that we place into a cup a reviit or more of pure or mixed wine - but not less than this (Pesachim 108b). And it is known that the [proportions of the] mixture is one part pure good wine to three parts water. And we recite the blessing of the Kiddush (sanctification) of Shabbat upon it, according to the wording that is known among the Jews. And so [too], at the departure of Shabbat, we recite the blessing over the wine in honor of the day - and that blessing of the conclusion of Shabbat is called Havdalah (Berakhot 52a).

It is from the roots of this commandment [that it is] in order that we be aroused through this act to remember the greatness of the day and that we fix upon our hearts faith in the creation of the world, "that in six days the Lord made, etc." (Exodus 20:11). And therefore, we are obligated to do an act with wine - since the nature of man is to be greatly aroused by it (Berakhot 35b), as it satiates and causes joy. And I have already said to you that according to the arousal of a man and his acts will he always be acted upon towards things. And from this root did they, may their memory be Blessed, say in the Gemara (Pesachim 106b), that if bread is more beloved to a person, he should sanctify [the day] over bread - since then his nature will be more aroused by that which he craves. And even though in the departure of the day, they did not say this, but rather obligated him to recite Havdalah with wine nonetheless, they were correct with this as well; since they, may their memory be Blessed, as well as the perfect Torah, will always choose to go according to the majority. And in truth, the majority of the world will desire drinking over eating at the conclusion of Shabbat; since they have already [eaten] a large meal during the day in honor of the Shabbat. And there is no need to give a reason for their obligating us that there be a reviit of wine in the cup; since less than this amount is not fitting and will not arouse the heart of a man upon it. And that which they obligated us in rinsing the cup (Berakhot 51a), and not to drink anything until he recites the Kiddush (Pesachim 105a) and that he recites the Kiddush at the location of his meal - all of [these] are branches of the root of arousal that I [discussed].

The laws of the commandment - for example, which is the wording of the Kiddush and the Havdalah; which wine is fitting upon to recite the Kiddush and which is not (Bava Batra 97a); if we sanctify or recite Havdalah over ale (Pesachim 107a); one who eats on the eve of Shabbat and the Shabbat [begins] (Pesachim 100a), or on Shabbat and Shabbat departs; so [too] the wording of the Kiddush and Havdalah of holidays; the laws of the blessings we are obligated to recite upon the candle on the conclusion of Shabbat and Yom Kippur; the laws of the blessing that we are obligated to recite over the spices and which spices are fitting to bless upon them or not fitting (Berakhot 51b); and the rest of its details - are [all] elucidated at the end of Pesachim and in places in Berakhot (See Tur, Orach Chaim 262, 271).

And [it] is practiced in every place and at all times by males and females - even though it is from the commandments that is caused by time (from which women are generally exempt). As so did our Rabbis, may their memory be Blessed, teach us (Berakhot 20b) that women are obligated in Kiddush and Havdalah. And one who transgresses it and does not perform the Kiddush with words has nullified this positive commandment. And if he performs the Kiddush with words without wine and without bread, he has fulfilled it ex post facto [according to] the Torah.

Mitzvah 32

To not do work on Shabbat: To not do work on the day of Shabbat ourselves; and not allow our children, slaves and animals to do so, as it is stated (Exodus 20:10), "you shall not do work, etc." There is no doubt that even though the verse issues a [single blanket] prohibition on us, our children, servants, and animals, they are not all equal; as we see that one who volitionaly does work with his own body will be liable for the death penalty in a court. But with the work of others - even though he is warned about them with a negative commandment - he is not liable for them; [not] even with lashes, as lashes are never for the act of others. And from the language of Rambam, may his memory be Blessed, (Mishneh Torah, Laws of Sabbath 20:1) it is implied that he holds that this prohibition of " you shall not do work, you [...] and your animal," comes upon letting an animal work (mechamer) while being behind it - for example, that he is using it to plow. As, according to his opinion, letting an animal work by itself is only a prohibition [embedded] in a positive commandment. And hence, according to his opinion, they said in the Gemara (Shabbat 154a) that this negative commandment of letting your animals do work is a negative commandment that is given over to the warning of a death penalty from the court - meaning to say, that a man is killed for it, and [so] there are no lashes for it. But Ramban, may his memory be Blessed, (on Sefer HaMitzvot LaRambam, Shorashim 14) wrangles with him greatly on this explanation, and says that this negative commandment of letting your animals do work is only about walking behind his animal laden with his load, while the man does not do any act with his hands. And therefore, neither lashes nor the death penalty would ever come to him; and it is as that which has been established for us, we do not administer lashes for any negative commandment that does not have an act. [And it is] like they, may their memory be Blessed, expounded (Shabbat 154b), "'You [...] and your animal' - let it write, you shall not do work and your animal'; why do I need 'you?' [To tell you] that when he does work, he is liable; but for the work of his animal, he is not lia work ble." Rather, he is [just] warned about it with a negative commandment, like with the work of his young child and his Canaanite slave. But for his own actual work - for that there was no reason to say that he is liable, as behold, his punishment is explicit (Exodus 34:2), "any one who does work on it shall die." And according to the opinion of Ramban, may his memory be Blessed, the explanation of that which they said in the Gemara about the negative commandment of letting your animal do work, that it is a negative commandment that is given over to the warning of a death penalty from the court, is that since it also includes the other [types of] work which [come] with a warning of a death penalty from the court - even though with letting your animal work there is certainly only a negative commandment, as there is also not [even] lashes with it - nonetheless, this negative commandment is [called] a negative commandment that is given over to the warning of a death penalty from the court because of those things that it includes that have death penalties of the court. And similar to this did they, may their memory be Blessed, say in the first chapter of Eruvin 17b about the negative commandment of "let no man leave his place": Since it also includes carrying out from one domain to another - like the teaching that they expounded, [read, do not go out (yetseh), as] do not carry out (yotsee) - that it is from now a negative commandment that is given over to the warning of a death penalty from the court in some of its matters. And since it is so, we can say that we do not administer lashes for it, in all of its matters. And in exactly the same way, we can explain the negative commandment of not letting your animal do work here.

It is from the roots of this commandment that we should be free from our preoccupations in honor of the day [of Shabbat], in order to instill within our soul's faithfulness to the [concept of the] universe's creation, which is [a concept that affects many fundamental principles in Judaism] (lit. a rope that drags along all the foundations of our religion). And we remember once a week, every week, that the universe was created in six distinct days, that nothing was created on the seventh day, and that different [types of creations] were brought into being each day. [All of this confirms the Torah's philosophical idea of God's] Simple (Single) Will, which differs from the philosophers' view, that disgusts us in their idea regarding this matter that [alongside] the Blessed One['s existence] was everything. And through our rest on the seventh day we are reminded of the universe's creation; because, when everyone simultaneously rests once a week, curious people will ask what is the point of this rest? And the answer will be "because [in] six days God created, etc." (Exodus 31:17). [And through that answer], everyone will be strengthened in the true faith. And in addition to remembering the universe's creation, there is in [Shabbat] also a remembering of the miracle of [the exodus from] Egypt - that we were slaves there and we were not able to rest whenever we desired to rest, and God saved us from their hands and commanded us to rest on the seventh day (Shabbat). Therefore, the second root is mentioned in Deuteronomy (lit. the repetition of the Torah), as it states in the [context of] the commandment of Shabbat, "And you should remember that you were a slave in the land of Egypt, etc. therefore the Lord, your God, commanded you to [observe] (lit. make) the day of Shabbat" (Deuteronomy 5:15).

The laws of the commandments - for example, what are the things that are called the main types of work (melakhot) to make one liable for those that do them, like the forty minus one types of work counted by the Sages and their derivatives, and the light types of work that they, may their memory be Blessed, forbade [so as] to make a fence, and the things that were also called Shabbat prohibitions (shevootin); and that which they, may their memory be Blessed, learned from the verse that everything is pushed off for saving lives (Yoma 85) and that one who shows alacrity to profane the Shabbat to save lives, behold it is praiseworthy, and the reason is that the cause of the doing of the commandments is man and preserving the cause is [therefore] preserving everything, and because of this, they, may their memory be Blessed, said (Yoma 83a), that any patient is believed to say I need that you profane the Shabbat for me, and any patient with fever laying on a sick bed is included [in the category of being in] danger that we profane the Shabbat for him (Avodah Zarah 28a); and the rest of its many details - are [all] elucidated in Tractate Shabbat and Yom Tov (See Tur, Orach Chaim 328).

And [it] is practiced in every place and at all times by males and females. And one who transgresses it volitionally is stoned, and that is when there are witnesses and a warning there. [Let] this rule be in your hand always - that the death penalty or lashes is only administered with witnesses and a warning - and the warning is always to distinguish between [the] inadvertent and [the] volitional. And know this fundamental and do not ask from me to review it. And if he did thoughtful work (melekhet machshevet) inadvertently, he brings a fixed sin offering (Beitzah 13b).

Mitzvah 33
The commandment to honor father and mother: To honor father and mother, as it is stated (Exodus 20:12), "You shall honor your father and your mother." And the explanation (Kiddushin 31b) comes to [define it], "What does it mean to 'honor'? To feed, give drink, dress, bring in, and take out."

From the roots of this commandment is that it is fitting for a person to acknowledge and return kindness to people who were good to him, and not to be an ungrateful scoundrel, because that is a bad and repulsive attribute before God and people. And he should take to heart that the father and the mother are the cause of his being in the world; and hence it is truly fitting to honor them in every way and give every benefit he can to them, because they brought him to the world, and worked hard for him when he was little. And once he fixes this idea in his soul, he will move up from it to recognize the good of God, Blessed be He, who is his cause and the cause of all his ancestors until the first man (Adam), and that he took him out into the world's air, and fulfilled his needs every day, and made his body strong and able to stand, and gave him a mind that knows and learns - for without the mind that God granted him, he would be 'like a horse or a mule who does not understand.' And he should think at length about how very fitting it is to be careful in his worship of the Blessed be He.

The laws of this commandment - for example, whose property should be spent on this honor, the child's or the parent's, and the ruling (Kiddushin 32a) is that it is out of the parent's if the parent has assets, but if not, the child must even beg door to door (see Talmud Yerushalmi Kiddushin 1:7) in order to feed their parent; which takes priority, honoring the father or the mother; if [the parent] waives that honor [if it is effective]; if the child sees the parent violating the Torah's words, with what words should they stop them; if his father commands him to violate the Torah's words, that he should not believe him about it; that the child is obligated to honor [the parent] in life and in death, and how is the honor in death; and the rest of its details - are [all] elucidated in Tractate Kiddushin and in a few other places in the Gemara (See Tur, Yoreh Deah 260).

And [it] is practiced in every place and at all times by males; and by females (Kiddushin 31a) any time it is possible for them - meaning to say when their husbands do not prevent them. And one who transgressed it violated a positive commandment, and his punishment is very great; for they are like one who ignores their Heavenly Father. And if the court has the power, they coerce him; as we wrote above (in Sefer HaChinukh 6) that the court coerces with regards to the negation of a positive commandment.

Mitzvah 34
To not kill the innocent: To not kill a soul, as it is stated (Exodus 20:13), "You shall not kill."

The root of this commandment is well-known and revealed to all that see the sun. As God, may He be Blessed, created the world and commanded us be fruitful and multiply, in order to settle it in front of Him. And [so] He prevented us, that we not destroy it with our hands, to kill and destroy the creatures which are the settlers of the world. However, the total evildoers - for example, the heretics and the talebearers - are not from the settlers of the world. And about them, the verse states (Proverbs 11:10), "with the destruction of the evildoers is there glee" - because they do not settle (civilize) the world, but rather destroy it with all their might. And this is what one sage from our Sages, may their memory be Blessed, said about the destruction of the evildoers (Bava Metzia 83b), "I am ridding the thorns from the vineyard" - meaning to say that with the destruction of these, the world will be more settled, [just] like with the removal of thorns (weeds), the fruits of the vineyard multiply and are better.

From the laws of this commandment - that which they, may their memory be Blessed, said (Sanhedrin

88a) [that] it is the same whether one kills a healthy person or a sick person close to death - and even if he is dying from a sickness by the hand of the Heavens - he is [still] killed for it; the law of the trial of a murderer; and the rest of its details - are elucidated in the ninth chapter of Sanhedrin and the second chapter of Makkot (See Tur, Choshen Mishpat 425).

And [it] is practiced in every place and at all times by males and females. And we kill with the sword one who transgresses it and kills volitionally, [if] there are witnesses who warned him (Sanhedrin 71b). About inadvertence, we will write its law below, with God's help in the Order of Eleh Masaaei (Sefer HaChinukh 409).

Mitzvah 35

To not reveal the nakedness of a man's wife: To not have intercourse with a man's wife, as it is stated (Exodus 20:13), "You shall not commit adultery." And the explanation comes that the undifferentiated expression, "adultery," indicates with a man's wife, as they, may their memory be Blessed, said (Rashi on Exodus 20:13), "Adultery is only with a man's wife." And this negative commandment is repeated in the Order of Achrei Mot, as there it is written explicitly (Leviticus 18:20), "And to your neighbor's wife, etc."

It is from the roots of this commandment [that it is] so that the world be settled as God desired. And God, Blessed be He, wanted that all of His world makes their fruit, each and every one according to their species, and not that one specie mix with another specie. And so [too], did He want that the seed of men be known to whom it is, and not that they be mixed, one with the other. And also, there are several losses found with adultery: That it would be the cause of negating several of the commandments of God to us, as He commanded us in the honor of fathers and they would not be recognized by their children due to adultery; and there would be a stumbling block in that which we were also commanded not to have intercourse with the sisters and with many women - and it is all uprooted by reason of adultery, as people will not recognize their relatives. And there is an angle of theft, which is something clear that everybody pushes off. It is also a cause for the destruction of life, as it is very known in the nature of people that they are jealous about the adultery of their spouse with others, and [so] they will fight [to the death] with the adulterer. And there are several other mishaps besides these.

The laws of the commandment - for example, distancing the matter [by] not isolating ourselves with them; and the sentence of the adulterer and also the adulteress, since the adulteress also [has] the prohibition and the penalty; and the rest of its details - are [all] elucidated in Tractate Sanhedrin and [other] places in the Gemara (Mishneh Torah, Laws of Forbidden Intercourse 6). And there in Sanhedrin 51a, it is elucidated that [in the case of] an adulterer with a totally married women, both of them [get] strangulation. And [in the case of] an adulterer with a betrothed maiden, both of them [get] stoning. And with the daughter of a priest, she is burnt and he is strangled. And the prohibition of a man's wife is from the commandments that are upon all people in the world more generally, whether Jew or whether gentile. But there is a small difference in the matter, as there is no marriage for a gentile except through intercourse; whereas a Israelite acquires her with sanctification (kiddushin) (Sanhedrin 57b).

Mitzvah 36

To not steal a soul of Israel: To not steal a soul of Israel, as it is stated (Exodus 20:13), "You shall not steal." And the explanation comes that the verse is speaking about stealing souls (kidnapping) (Sanhedrin 86a).

The root of the commandment is revealed.

The laws of the commandment - for example, that which they said (Mishneh Torah, Laws of Theft 9:6) [that] there is no difference between an adult and a child or between a man and a woman, as "a soul" implies all cases; the law of a father who steals his son or a master who steals his student; and the rest of its details - are [all] elucidated in Chapter Eleven of Sanhedrin. And its prohibition is practiced in every place and at all times. And one who transgresses it and steals a soul is liable for strangulation, and that is if he has already sold that soul. As so came the explanation (Sanhedrin 85b) that the liability does not rest upon him until he sells; since another verse reveals this, as it is written (Exodus 21:16), "And he steals a man and sells him [...], he will surely be killed."

Mitzvah 37
To not testify falsely: To not testify [with] false testimony, as it states (Exodus 20:13), "You shall not bear false witness against your neighbor." And it is repeated in another place in another negative commandment - the "vain witness."

The root of this commandment is revealed, as falsehood is 'disgraceful and vile' in the eye of any intelligent one; also, because the world stands upon true testimony, since all [types] of arguments can be [settled by] the testimony of people. And, if so, false testimony is a cause for the destruction of the world.

The laws of the commandment - for example, from whom do we accept testimony (Mishneh Torah, Laws of Testimony 9:1) and from whom do we not accept [it]; what is it that disqualifies people from testifying; how is [the process] of accepting testimony; that there are people that do not testify for anyone, due to their great stature; examination of the testimony and the interrogation; the differences between testimony in financial cases and capital cases; the difference between investigation and corroboration; the difference between [written] testimony and oral; and the rest of its many details are elucidated in Sanhedrin and in [other places] in the Gemara (See Tur, Choshen Mishpat 38).

And [it] is practiced in every place and at all time by males, but not by females. As women are not [included] in the category of testimony, since testimony requires focus and much concentration. And the verse put a limit on the punishment of the one who transgresses this negative prohibition and testifies falsely against his fellow, to do unto him as he thought to do his fellow (Deuteronomy 19:19). And there are also lashes for it (Makkot 2a). And it is also elucidated there in Sanhedrin.

Mitzvah 38
To not covet: To not bring up to our thoughts to do a machination to take for ourselves that which is someone else's of our brothers, as it is stated (Exodus 20:14), "You shall not covet the house of your neighbor, etc." And they, may their memory be Blessed, have already proven (Mekhilta d'Rabbi Yishmael 20:14:3) from a different verse [in which] it is written (Deuteronomy 7:25), "do not covet, etc. and you shall take for yourself," that the negative commandment of "you shall not covet" is not completed until he acts upon it. And even if he gives money to his fellow for the object [that he coveted], he [still] transgresses the negative commandment of "you shall not covet." As the negative commandment of "you shall not covet" is not rectified by the giving of money, so long as he took it from him coercively. Such is the true explanation of our Rabbis; may their memory be Blessed.

It is from the roots of this commandment that it is since it is a bad thought and causes a person many mishaps. As once he fixes it into his thought to take the thing that he covets from him, that bad desire will not pay attention to anything; and if his fellow will not want to sell it to him, he will take it from him by force. And if he stands up to him, it is possible that he will [even] kill him; as we found (I Kings 21) that Navot was killed for his vineyard that Ahav coveted from him (See Mishneh Torah, Laws of Robbery and Lost Property 1:11).

The laws of this commandment [and] how it is fitting to greatly distance oneself from this bad trait are elucidated in scattered places in the Gemara and in the Midrash (See Tur, Choshen Mishpat 359 at the end).

And [it] is practiced in every place and at all times by males and females. But one who transgresses it and covets - even if he does some act with it - is not liable for lashes, as it is something that is given to returning. As behold, even if he took it from him by force, it is [still] given to returning. And nonetheless, behold, he is like one that transgresses the commandment of the King, may He be elevated - and how many are the messengers of the King, may He be elevated, to take His vengeance from him!

Mitzvah 39
Not to make the form of a man, even for decoration: Not to make the form of a man from any

object - whether from metals, whether from wood, or stone, or anything else - and even for decoration, as it is stated (Exodus 20:20), "Do not make with me (eeti)." And they, may their memory be Blessed, expounded (Rosh Hashanah 24b), "Do not make Me (oti," which can be spelled with the same letters as eeti), meaning to say, do not make a replica of that form - being the body of man - about which I wrote in My Torah (Genesis 1:26), "Let us make man in Our image." And the intention of the verse is from the angle of the intellect that He gave in him. And that which it stated, "in Our image," about the intellectual side of man is because all intellect is in Him, Blessed be He. But there is no other comparison between Him, Blessed be he, and any creature (that preceded its matter) of His creatures, God forbid. And the negative commandment of "You shall not make a statue" is that we not make any form that will be worshiped, [whereas] this prohibition is specifically about the form of a man - that we should not make it at all, even for decoration. And this is to distance idolatry.

The laws of the commandment - for example, what is the law of one who makes the form of a man lacking one or more limbs; and the rest of its details - are elucidated in the third chapter of Avodah Zarah. And in Tractate Sanhedrin 7b, they said that this negative commandment [also] includes other topics. However, the main negative commandment is about that which we have mentioned. And so [too], did they say in the Mekhilta (see Shulchan Arukh, Yoreh Deah 141:7).

And [it] is practiced in every place and at all times by males and females. And one who transgresses it and makes the form of a man - even for decoration - violates the commandment of the King, but there is no liability for lashes.

Mitzvah 40

To not build [with] hewn stones: That we should not build an altar of stones that metal would touch, as it is stated (Exodus 20:22), "do not build of hewn (gazit) stones." The explanation of hewn (Ramban on Exodus 20:22) is when we chisel from the stone with an iron tool. And if [the altar] is built with hewn stones, it is disqualified.

It is from the roots of this commandment that we should fix into our souls from the day that we make [the altar], that forgiveness of iniquity, blessing and peace will come [through] it afterwards. And hence to remember this thing, we were commanded to not do anything upon it with tools that are fit for destruction - and that is [those made from] iron that cuts and is constantly ready to spill blood. And I have already prefaced for you at the beginning, that man is acted upon according to his actions, and [that] his thoughts always follow his deeds. Therefore, it is fitting for us to do symbolic actions, according to the intention of the things. And when the fool who is [too] rushed hears these things, he will not know nor understand [them].

The laws of the commandment - for example, from where they would bring these stones with which they would build the altar, that they, may their memory be Blessed, said (Mishnah Middot 3:4) that they would bring them from virgin ground or from the Great Sea; the law of if metal touched a stone after the altar was built, whether all of it is disqualified or only it alone is disqualified; that which they, may their memory be Blessed, said (Mishnah Middot 3:4), [that] when they whitewashed the altar twice a year, that they did not whitewash it with a tool that had iron in it, so that the iron not touch a stone; and the rest of its details - are [all] elucidated in Tractate Middot (See Mishneh Torah, Laws of The Chosen Temple 1).

And [it] is practiced at the time of the [Temple] by males and females. And one that transgresses it and builds the altar or [its] ramp with a stone that iron touched is lashed.

Mitzvah 41

To not take steps on the altar: To not ascend the altar with stairs, so that he not make large steps in his going up - as it is stated (Exodus 20:23), "And you shall not ascend My altar by stairs, that your nakedness not be exposed upon it." Rather, when he ascends there, he should walk slowly and with awe, [placing] his heel in front of his toe. And so is it said in the Mekhilta d'Rabbi Yishmael 20:23.

That which we have written in the commandment that is before it is from the roots of this commandment - to fix the awe of the place and its importance in our souls. And, therefore, we were warned not to act with light-headedness there in any way. And everyone knows that the stones would not be exacting about any disgrace [to them], since they do not see and do not hear. Rather, the whole matter is to give an illustration in our heart of the awe of the place and its importance and great glory - as through action, the heart is acted upon, as we have written.

The laws of the commandment - how we make the ramp so that they will not come to transgressing this negative commandment, its form and all of its content - are elucidated in the third chapter of Middot (See Mishneh Torah, Laws of The Chosen Temple 2:13).

And [it] is practiced at the time of the [Temple] by males and females. And one who transgresses it and takes a large step, to the point that he reveals his nakedness, on the altar is lashed. And 'the humble ones will dwell in the land.'

Mitzvah 42

The commandment of the law of a Hebrew slave: To adjudicate the law of a Hebrew slave according to what is written in the section, as it is stated (Exodus 21:2), "When you acquire a Hebrew slave, etc." [This] means to say that we do the things to him that we are commanded about: For example, to send him away in the seventh year (Kiddushin 14b), or within the six years if the Jubilee occurs [before the end of his term], or by subtracting [with] money, or with the death of a master who did not leave a male child. And [we] also [do] for the "pierced one," according to the laws that are written about him. Everything is like our Rabbis, may their memory be Blessed, taught us form the verse, as it is explained in the first chapter of Kiddushin 14b.

It is from the roots of this commandment that God wanted His people Israel that He chose, to be a holy nation, full of - and crowned with - good and lofty traits; as blessing rests upon them from this. And kindness and mercy are from the most praiseworthy traits in the world. And therefore, he warned us have mercy on the one under our hand and to do kindness towards him, as is written in the section, and as we know also from the tradition (Sifra, Behar).

The laws of the commandment - for example, the differences between one who sells himself and one who is sold by the court; the things for which he is sold and those for which he goes free; and the rest of its laws - are [all] elucidated there in Kiddushin (see Tur, Yoreh Deah 263).

And the commandment is practiced by males, but not by females - as a woman does not acquire a Hebrew slave (Bava Metzia 71a). And [this is] specifically when Israel is dwelling on its land - as so does the received explanation (Arakhin 29a) come [to tell us], that [the law of] a Hebrew slave is only practiced when the Jubilee is practiced. And it is explicit (Arakhin 32b) that the law of Jubilee is only in the Land. And one who transgresses it and does not do to the slave that which is written about him, negates a positive commandment, and also teaches his soul to be cruel. And it is almost as if he testifies about himself that he is not from the Children of Israel, since they are merciful ones [who are] the children of merciful ones (Shabbat 97a; Yevamot 79a).

Mitzvah 43

The commandment of designation of a Hebrew bondwoman: To designate a Hebrew bondwoman, meaning to say that the Israelite that acquired a Hebrew bondwoman marry her as a wife or give her to his son as a wife, as it is stated (Exodus 21:8), "If she is bad in the eyes of her master, who designated her for himself, he must let her be redeemed." And they, may their memory be Blessed, said (Rashi on Exodus 21:8) that here is a hint for you that there is a commandment of designation. And they, may their memory be Blessed, explicitly said (Bekhorot 19a) that the commandment of designation is before the commandment of redemption.

It is from the roots of this commandment that God had mercy on the poor one that is sold and upon her father who needed to sell her. And [so] He commanded the one who acquires her to marry her as a wife and to make her a patroness - as He is a graceful and merciful God. And if the acquirer does not want her for himself, [he is commanded] to marry her to his son, as she will also be happy and rejoice [to be married] to the son of her master; or - in any event - to reduce her redemption [price] and help her that she should go out from slavery. And, in any case, he should not cause her to stay under his hand until the time of her sale [is completed] - even if her work is very [good] in his eyes. And all of this is from the kindnesses of God upon his creatures and from His elevated traits.

Sefer HaChinukh

The laws of the commandment - for example, until when the daughter can be sold; that she cannot be sold by her master, meaning to say that even if he transgressed and sold her, his sale is nothing (ineffective); that the father can sell her several times; the things for which she is sold and those for which she goes free and how many more ways out she has than the [male] slave; the law of the girl who has just become an adult (bogeret); the time of [waiting before determining a woman to be] a sterile woman; and the rest of its details - are [all] elucidated in the first [chapter] of Kiddushin.

And [it] is only practiced at the time that the Jubilee is practiced (Gittin 65a). And one who transgresses it and does not designate her - not for him, and not for his son - and does not help with her redemption, has not performed this commandment. However, it appears that we do not coerce him about the fulfillment of this commandment; as behold, it is written there explicitly (Exodus 21:11), "And if he does not do these three to her." [From here,] it is implied that the Torah left the thing up to his will. But if he married her as a wife or married her to his son, as we have written, he has done what his fitting. And a blessing will come upon him and good and proper children are fitting to come from their union.

Mitzvah 44
The commandment of redemption of a Hebrew bondwoman: To redeem a Hebrew bondwoman, as it is stated (Exodus 21:8), "he must let her be redeemed." And that is a positive commandment, meaning to say that the master that acquired her, help her in her redemption and give her room to go back to the house of her father. [It is] like they, may their memory be Blessed, said (Kiddushin 14b), "He reduces the price and she leaves." [This] means to say that if he took her for [the price of] sixty dinars over six years and she worked three years and gathered thirty dinars, that he should take them and send her away. And he should not claim about her that she must finish the years of her bondage regardless, or say, "My money was sitting idly with you; if you want to leave, add the profit to me [that the money should have produced while it was idle]" - as this is only evil-heartedness. And for the Children of Israel who are the children of kings, merciful ones [who are] the children of merciful ones, it is fitting to do kindness with the creatures, even those who serve them, and even [if it is] for one day.

That which we have written about [the previous commandment of] designation (Sefer HaChinukh 43) is from the roots of this commandments. And its details are also there in Kiddushin.

Mitzvah 45
That the one who acquires the Hebrew bondwoman from the father not sell her: That anyone who acquires a Hebrew bondwoman not sell her to another man ever, as it is stated (Exodus 21:8), "he shall not have the right to sell her to a foreign people, etc." And the explanation [of the phrase] is like [Onkelos' Aramaic] translation, "to another man." And it was stated with this wording to distance this thing - meaning to say that if he sells her to a second man, it is for this poor little one similar to if he sold her to a foreign people.

From the roots of this commandment is that God wanted to give us merit and commanded us to act with the trait of compassion, which is beloved in front of Him.

The laws of the commandment are written above in the commandment of designation (Sefer HaChinukh 43) (See Mishneh Torah, Laws of Slaves 4).

Mitzvah 46
Not to reduce her flesh, covering and time period: That anyone who acquires a Hebrew bondwoman and designates her may not reduce her flesh, her covering and her time period. And the explanation (Ketuvot 47b) of "flesh" is food, of "covering" is like its simple understanding and of "time period" is the way of the world (conjugal rights). And included in this negative commandment are all daughters of Israel (as well), not to reduce from them any thing from these [categories]. [This inclusion] is a fortiori (kal ve'chomer): If he does not reduce for [bondwomen], all the more so for free [women]. And [about] that which is written (Exodus 21:9), "like the statute of the daughters he shall do for her" - they said in the Mekhilta d'Rabbi Yishmael 21:9:2 that it came to learn [from

the others], but it ends up to teach, as the [law of the other] daughters are learned form her.

From the laws of this commandment - that which our Rabbis, may their memory be Blessed, said (Ketuvot 56a) what is the law of one who stipulates [to marry] his wife "on condition that you do not have [the rights] from me of flesh, covering and time period"; that which they said (Ketuvot 61a), "A woman rises with [the economic standards of a new] husband, but does not descend," and hence we calculate her food and clothing [allowance] according to his elevation; the matter of the differentiation of time periods, which is according to the strain of the man's profession, to the point where they, may their memory be Blessed, said (Ketuvot 62b) that the time period of a sailor is twice a year, a camel rider once a month and a Torah scholar once a week and it is fitting for him that it be on Shabbat night; and the rest of its details - are [all] elucidated scattered in the Order of Nashim.

And this commandment is practiced regarding a free woman in every place and at all times by males. And one who transgresses it and reduced one of these three from his wife willingly, from the angle of intending to hurt her, has violated this negative commandment (Sefer HaMitzvot LaRambam, Mitzvot Lo Taase 262). And it is like he has transgressed the warning of the King. But we do not administer lashes for it, since there is no act [involved] with it.

Mitzvah 47

The commandment on the court (beit din) to kill with strangulation one who is liable: That we have been commanded to kill the transgressors of some of the commandments of the Torah with strangulation, as it is stated (Exodus 21:12), "He who strikes a man and [that man] dies shall surely be put to death." And this one of "One who strikes a man" is one of the ones whose death penalty is with strangulation. Since it is written about it, "[he] shall surely die" - and in the explanation, they, may their memory be Blessed, said (Sanhedrin 52b), "Any death penalty stated in the Torah undifferentiated is only strangulation." We have learned that those that are liable for the death penalty do not have repayment, as it is stated (Exodus 21:11-12), "there is no money. He who strikes a man and [that man] dies, etc." - Mekhilta.

The root of this commandment is revealed to all, as 'by justice a king sustains the land.' As were it not for the fear of judgment, people would kill one another. Therefore, God, Blessed be He, commanded us to kill the murderer. And in His wisdom, Blessed be He, He saw that it is fitting to punish him with the death penalty of strangulation. And the matter is beautiful, also according to our [understanding], since 'as he has done, so shall it be done to him' - since the intention of the killer was to kill the murdered quickly, as from [the killer's] fear of him, he will quicken his death with all of his might. And so too was the Torah lenient with his judgment to kill him with strangulation, which is a quick death penalty; and not with stoning and burning, which are with great pain. (In the other editions, it is written, "The truth is that the death penalty of the murderer is with the sword, [whereas] he who hits his father and mother has a death penalty of strangulation.") However with the statutes of licentiousness, in which the transgressors derived pleasure from the sin and the pleasure continued a bit, they sometimes get burning and sometimes stoning.

How are the laws of the commandments - for example that which they, may their memory be Blessed, said (Mishnah Sanhedrin 7:3) that we place the guilty one in manure up to his knees and tie a hard handkerchief onto his neck, one pulls towards himself and [the other] one pulls towards himself until his soul departs; and the rest of its details - are elucidated in the seventh chapter of Sanhedrin 52 (see Mishneh Torah, Laws of Murderer and the Preservation of Life 1).

And this commandment is only practiced in the Land [of Israel], since we only judge capital cases in the Land. And whoever has [it] in his hand to make a judgment and does not do so, has negated this positive commandment. And his punishment is great - 'as were it no for the fear of [judgment], man would swallow his fellow alive.' And Ramban, may his memory be Blessed (on Sefer HaMitzvot LaRambam, Shorashim 14) does not count this commandment in his calculation. And so [too] does he not count any of the four death penalties of the court - which are stoning, burning, killing (decapitation) and strangulation - that Rambam, may his memory be Blessed, counted as four commandments. And [Ramban] said that through the verse of "and you shall destroy the evil from within you" (Deuteronomy 17:7), the Torah commanded more generally that we destroy those that do evil from among us; and within it are included all of the laws. And when Scripture specifies the laws according to their punishments afterwards, it is not considered a [separate] commandment, as it is only an elucidation of the topic. And 'the sage will choose for himself that which is straight in his eyes.

Mitzvah 48

Not to strike father and mother: That a child should not strike the father and the mother, even if they strike him [very much], so long as their souls do not bring them to kill him, as it is stated (Exodus 21:15), "He who strikes his father or his mother shall surely be put to death." And even though the verse does not explicitly warn him about this, that it says to him, "Do not strike the fathers," but rather it only wrote the punishment of the one who strikes them - and it is the way of the Gemara to always ask about a matter like this and to say, "We have heard the punishment, from where is the warning" - here too, we have a warning: as behold, we are warned (Makkot 9a) for every person, not to strike him. As it is written about one who is liable for lashes (Deuteronomy 25:3), "Forty shall he strike him, he shall not add." And it is a fortiori (kal ve'chomer) about someone who is not liable [for lashes] - and the father is included in Israel. And [so] the warning [for the commandment] is from here. And [this must be the case] even though this negative commandment of "he shall not add," is considered a separate negative commandment on its own. Since we have a rule in our hands that anything that has for it excision or a death penalty must also have a negative commandment - except for the Pesach offering and circumcision - and behold with the striking of father and mother, [we know] that there is excision without witnesses and the death penalty with witnesses! And therefore, we have to say that we nonetheless learn the warning for it from the Scripture of "he shall not add," as we did not find it in [any] other place. And the main idea of the warning will be [about] all of Israel; but [also] included in it, we learn about the one who strikes mother and father. And they, may their memory be Blessed, said (Sanhedrin 85b) that the case of this liability for death of the one that strikes is specifically when he brings out blood from them. [But it is] not the same with any other person - as even if he extracts blood from them, he is [only] liable for money.

From the roots of this commandment are to punish scoundrels and informers that raised their hand against the ones that brought them to the world by the will of God and did for them many goodnesses. And 'by justice does the King sustain the land.'

The laws of the commandment - for example, one who strikes him after death is exempt; the one that strikes him on his ear and makes him go deaf is liable, as it is impossible that a drop of blood did not go out inside [his ear]; the one who makes a wound for healing is exempt and that he should not, at the outset, perform healing that requires a wound if it is possible [to be done] by another; the law of a foundling (Mishneh Torah, Laws of Rebels 5:14) that he is liable for his mother but not for his father; the law of a convert whose conception was not in holiness (before his mother's conversion) that he is not liable for either of them; and the law of the convert that he is [nonetheless] forbidden to strike his gentile father [from] rabbinic law; the law of one whose father and mother are completely [and] famously wicked that he is exempt for striking them until they repent, but it is nonetheless forbidden even before repentance; [that] in all [cases] except for an inciter to idolatry, the son is not made the agent of the court to [lash] his father; and the rest of its details - are [all] at the end of Sanhedrin (See Tur, Yoreh Deah 242).

And [it] is practiced in every place and at all times by males and females and [those the sex of which is in doubt]. And one who transgresses it and strikes them with a blow that has a wound from it with witnesses and a warning, [receives] his death penalty by strangulation. But without a wound, he is liable towards them like any other man: As one who strikes his fellow for which there is a repayment worth [even] a small coin (perutah), pays and does not get lashed. But if there is no repayment of the worth of a small coin, he is lashed and does not pay. As the law is that a man does not die and pay (Ketuvot 36b); and so [too], he is not lashed and [obligated to] pay.

Mitzvah 49

The commandment of the laws of penalties: That we were commanded about the law of one who injures his fellow to penalize that person, as it is written in the Torah in the section of "And if men fight" (Exodus 21:18). And this is called the laws of penalties. And in another verse, it includes all of the laws of penalties, and it is the verse, "as he did, so shall it be done to him" (Leviticus 24:19) – it means to say that what he pained [his fellow] should be taken away from his money, in accordance with that which he injured his fellow, as the tradition comes about it (Bava Kamma 83b). And even if he did not hit him, but only embarrassed him, the court must cause him pain through his money, that he should pay the one embarrassed, according to this amount. And these laws that are called the laws of penalties – for example, the laws of a man [who hurt another] man; an ox, an ox; an animal, a man; a man, an animal – must be judged in a court that has been ordained in the Land of Israel (Bava Kamma 84a).

The root of this commandment – and more generally – everything that the Torah commanded about the matter of law – does not require me to exert myself to [find] its reason for the matter. As it is a rational thing, since if there is no justice, people would never dwell and stand together. And [civilization] is impossible without justice.

The laws of this commandment – for example, that one who hurts his fellow is liable for five well-known items and how we calculate them; the law of embarrassment, wherein everything is according to the one who embarrasses and the one who is embarrassed; and the law of one who is sleeping and embarrasses or is embarrassed; what is the law of one who dies on account of his embarrassment; what are the laws of those that embarrass a mentally incapacitated person, a deaf-mute or a minor (Bava Kamma 86b); one who embarrasses a convert or slave (Bava Kamma 87a); one who embarrasses with words (Bava Kamma 91a); what are the laws [about] the difference between a Torah scholar and other people; (Mishneh Torah, Laws of One Who Injures a Person or Property 3:5); the law of one who kicks his fellow or hits him with his palm, or slaps him in the face, slits his ear, pulls out his hair, spits at him and the spit lands on him; and the rest of its details - are [all] elucidated in the chapter [entitled] Hachovel (of Bava Kamma). And there it is clarified that there is a difference in the laws of penalties for that which is common and there is a loss of money, as we serve as an agent with the matter for that, [whereas] when it is a matter that is not common - and the same is true when it is common but there is no loss of money - we do not serve as an agent in those matters. And our Rabbi Alfasi (Rif), may his memory be a blessing, wrote [that] it is the practice of [the] two academies (Sura and Pompedita) that even though we don't collect penalties, we excommunicate [the offender] until he appeases his claimant, and when enough time for it passes, we release him immediately, whether he has appeased the [opposing] litigant, or whether he has not (see Tur, Choshen Mishpat 420-424).

And this commandment that we are obligated to judge and to punish one who injures is practiced by males, as it was given to them to administer justice; not by women (Talmud Yerushalmi Sanhedrin 3:9), who do not judge. But they are nonetheless included in the law of payments, whether they embarrassed or whether they were embarrassed. And the way in which payments of damage to a married woman are divided is also clarified there (Ketuvot 65b).

Mitzvah 50

The commandment on the court to kill with the sword one who is liable: That we have been commanded to kill the transgressors of some of the commandments of the Torah with the sword. And this law is called killing by our Rabbis. And it is a [relatively] light death penalty, but strangulation is nonetheless lighter than it (Sanhedrin 49b). And one of the ones killed by this death penalty is the one who strikes his slave - even a Canaanite [one] - if he dies from his hand, as it is stated (Exodus 21:20), "he shall surely be avenged." And the explanation comes [to tell us] that his striker should be killed by the sword. I have already written above (Sefer HaChinukh 47) that Ramban, may his memory be Blessed, does not count the four death penalties of the court as four [distinct] commandments, as does Rambam, may his memory be Blessed.

It is from the roots of this commandment that God wanted to uproot evil-heartedness and severe cruelty from His holy people. And therefore, He commanded that anyone, whose great anger overpowers him to the point that he strikes his slave who is in his home and has no savior, should be killed. Even though the slave is an acquisition of his money and he has destroyed his [own asset] with [his slave's] death, he is still killed - since his anger overcame him so much. And this is a fitting and proper law - 'the judgments of the Lord are true, righteous altogether.'

The laws of the commandment - for example, the law of [one who does not die until after] a day or two days; and the rest of its details - are elucidated in Bava Kamma (see Mishneh Torah, Laws of The Sanhedrin and the Penalties within their Jurisdiction 14). And one who transgresses it and did not administer justice upon him, if he has the power in his hand, has violated a positive commandment. And his punishment is great, since he has caused mishaps to [happen to] people.

Mitzvah 51

The commandment on the court to judge the damages of an animal: To judge in the case of a damaging ox - whether it [injures] a person, as it is written in the section of (Exodus 21:28), "If it gores," or whether it damages [assets], as it is written in the section of (Exodus 21:35), "If it hurts (yigof)." And the main understanding of hurting [here] is to push (Rashi on Exodus 21:35). However, whether it damages with its body or its feet, or it bites with its teeth, or even if it damages with its horns, it is all implied by the expression of hurting. But goring only implies with the horn (Bava Kamma 2b). [Still,] the [other] injuries of a man by an ox have already been included; as it is written in the section of "If it gores," "and it kills" (Exodus 21:26) - since it implies killing in any case, whether it is with goring or whether it is with other things (Mekhilta d'Rabbi Yishmael 21:28:2). And it is not specifically an ox, but rather we are even obligated for any domesticated animal or wild animal or bird that has damaged. [However], it is only that the verse stated [that] which was common. And we have already said that all of the commandments that come about the matter of justice have one root to them and it is a rational thing. And [so] I do not have to review it with each and every one.

The laws of the commandment - for example, which is a muad (known as likely to cause damage) or a tam (tame) and the difference between them (Bava Kamma 23b) and the things that an animal is muad about from the beginning (Bava Kamma 16b) and the things for which it is not a muad until we saw that it is accustomed to them; how is this matter of getting accustomed to the point that we assume it to be a muad, and in what way does it give up this custom, such that it returns to being a tam ; the five types of wild animals that are muad from the beginning; the distinction [created] by the domain wherein it damages; that which is called the main categories (avot) of damages (Bava Kamma 2a) and that which is called the derivatives (toledot), and the distinction that exists between them in one [of the derivatives]; the laws of guarding (Bava Kamma 45b) in which a person is obligated to guard them that they not damage, and how does he become obligated or exempt from them; and the rest of their many details - are [all] elucidated in the first six chapters of Bava Kamma (see Tur, Choshen Mishpat 291). And we have already said [about] these laws that are called the laws of penalties, that only a court of ordained [judges] in the Land of Israel can judge them (Sefer HaChinukh 49:1). But the damager must nonetheless pay by the laws of the Heavens (Bava Metzia 91a); and if [the injured party] grabbed the [value of] the damage, we certainly do not remove it from him (Bava Kamma 15b).

Mitzvah 52

Not to eat from the meat of a ox that was stoned: Not to eat the meat of an ox that was stoned, even if it was properly slaughtered - once its case is finished, its meat is prohibited. So is it explained in the Mekhilta d'Rabbi Yishmael 21:28:2, as it is stated (Exodus 21:28), "and its meat shall not be eaten" And it is not specifically an ox, but rather any domesticated animal, wild animal or bird, however the Torah stated that which is common?

It is from the roots of the commandment [that it is] in order to establish in our mind that anyone that has a mishap happen through him is distanced and disgusting for God and for people; even if it is inadvertent - like with an animal that has no intelligence - and all the more so, if it is volitional. And when we put our minds to this thing, it will cause us to be very careful in all of our actions, so that a mishap never come from our hands.

From the laws of the commandment is that which they, may their memory be Blessed, explained

(Bava Kamma 41a) that whether it is a muad (known as likely to cause damage) or a tam (tame), it is stoned for any [person] that it kills, be it a man or a woman or a child or a slave; that we only finish its judgment in front of it owners, if it has owners (Sanhedrin 99b); and [that which] they also said (Sanhedrin 44a) that there are many angles through which the ox kills but is not stoned. And the rest of its details - are elucidated in [Bava] Kamma (see Mishneh Torah, Laws of Forbidden Foods 4).

And the commandment of the prohibition of its meat is practiced by males and females. And the judgment to stone an ox is only practiced in the Land of Israel by ordained judges in a court of twenty-three [judges]. And one who transgresses it and eats a kazayit of its meat is lashed.

Mitzvah 53
The commandment on the court to judge the damages of a pit: To judge about the laws of one who opens a pit in a place where it is an obstacle for people, as it is stated (Exodus 21:33), "If a man opens a pit" - as it is explained in the section. And it is not specifically a pit, but rather even a ditch or a cave (Bava Kamma 50b), but it only stated, "pit" to teach that there needs to be enough [depth] to it to kill - which is twenty fingerbreadths.

Its roots have already been written. Its laws are, for example, that which they said (Bava Kamma 53b), "'An ox' and not a man - 'a donkey' and not vessels; one who digs a pit in his [own] domain and abandons his domain but not his pit is liable, [but] if he abandons his pit as well, he is exempt, since he dug it in his [own] domain - which is not the case if he dug in the public domain, since he was not allowed to dig it to begin with, and therefore he is liable in every way; so [too] one who digs a pit in his domain, immediately adjacent to the public domain and did not abandon his pit but there is nothing intervening between the pit and the public domain - like those that dig for ooshin, the understanding of which is foundations - is exempt, even though it is impossible for the public to guard itself from it, since it is so adjacent to the path, as it is impossible to inhabit the world without everyone [building] foundations for their homes; the law of one who opens a pit even though he did not dig it, [about] which they, may their memory be Blessed, said (Bava Kamma 49b), that he is liable, since he is nonetheless the responsible party for the mishap; the difference among the laws that come with the matter of opening of a pit according to the strength or weakness of the pit's cover; the law of partners in the matter of the covering (Bava Kamma 51a); the law of a pit that was dug by two people, one after another, as to which of them has the liability (Bava Kamma 51a); and the laws of the obligation that a person has to distance the [danger], so that damage does not happen to people through his waters, his thorns and his glass (Bava Kamma 31a). And the rest of its details - are elucidated in the third and fifth chapters of Bava Kamma and in Bava Batra (see Tur, Choshen Mishpat 410).

And [it] is practiced by males, since it is upon them to administer justice; but not upon females, since they do not judge. But nonetheless, [women] are included in the law of payments, whether they caused damage or had damage caused to them.

Mitzvah 54
The commandment on the court to judge a thief with repayment or the death penalty: To judge the laws of a thief, as it is written in the section of "If a man steals, etc." (Exodus 21:37). And the matter of theft is one who takes a thing of [from the] money of his fellow, from his house or from his pocket at a time when the owner is not looking and does not know; and so [too] all that is similar to this (see Tur, Choshen Mishpat 348). The root of the commandment of justice is well-known. Its laws are for example, the payment of double, four or five; the law to kill the thief that comes surreptitiously or to sell him for his theft; the law of a stolen object that became more valuable in the house of the thief, on its own or due to expenditure [upon it], and the law of a stolen object that went up in price, wherein he pays the [repayment] according to what he stole and the payment of multiples according to the time that he is being judged; the law of a thief that stole from a thief, that he does not have to pay double to [such a one], even before there was a losing of hope of retrieval; the law of a thief who stole consecrated assets or the assets of a gentile, or one who steals slaves, deeds or lands; what is the law concerning repayment by one who who steals on Shabbat, and the liability for desecration of the Shabbat and [the liability for] the theft came together; from which assets does the court collect

payment from him; that if he is sold for his theft that his value needs to be like the value of the theft or less, but that if it is more, he is not sold; the laws of a guardian that stole or had property stolen from his house; the law prohibiting the purchase from the hand of the thief of that which was stolen, and what is the law with regards to the owners if he bought it. And the rest of its details are elucidated in the seventh chapter of Bava Kamma, in the eighth of Sanhedrin, in the third of Bava Metzia and in a few places in Ketuvot, in Kiddushin, and in Shevuot (see Mishneh Torah, Laws of Theft 1). And [it] is practiced by males, as it is upon them to administer law. And in any place where there is a court of judges ordained in the Land [of Israel], they obligate to pay four and five times [in the relevant cases]. And if there are no ordained judges, they do not have the power to obligate [this], but [they do have the power] to return the stolen object or its value. But the actual selling of a thief is only practiced when the Jubilee year is practiced - even by ordained judges.

Mitzvah 55
The commandment on the court to judge concerning damages of destruction: To judge concerning the damages of the tooth and the foot - meaning to say one who damaged his fellow with a damage that came as a result of [his animal's] foot or tooth - that we must obligate him in payment from his choice properties for all that he destroyed, as it is stated (Exodus 22:4), "If a man destroys the field, etc. For example, one who brings his animal into the field of his fellow and he ate there; or destroyed those things that sustain themselves from it, when it passed through there with its feet. And they, may their memory be Blessed, explained that it is [referring to] the tooth (Bava Kamma 2b). And they, may their memory be Blessed, explained that that which is written afterwards, "and he sent its destroyer, etc." [refers to] the foot. And it is stated about both of them, "and with the best of his field and the best of his vineyard shall he pay.
The root of the commandment of jurisprudence is well-known.
Its laws are, for example, what are the places in which one is liable for the tooth and the foot and what are the ones in which one is not liable for them (Bava Kamma 24b); the difference in the law if it eats what is fitting for it to eat or it eats something not fitting, and so [too,] that which is fitting under duress - for example a cow that ate barley, a donkey that ate vetch or fish, a pig that ate meat, a dog that licked oil or a cat that ate dates - that if it derived benefit, it pays according to what it benefited. And the rest of its details - are in Gittin and in [Bava] Kamma. And there in the chapter [entitled] Hachovel (Bava Kamma 84b), they said that that which Rava said that we collect, with an ox against an ox, for the tooth or the foot, is with those that are muad from the beginning (see Tur, Choshen Mishpat 399-406).
And [it] is practiced by males, since it is upon them to administer justice. But women are, nonetheless, included in the law of payments, whether they caused damage or had damage caused to them. And a court that transgresses it and does not judge this law as it is written has negated a positive commandment.

Mitzvah 56
The commandment on the court to judge damages from fire: To judge and obligate one, who has damaged his fellow with fire, to pay - for example, [if] he lit his stockpile or burned anything of his - as it is stated (Exodus 22:5), "If a fire goes out, etc." The understanding of "goes out" implies even if it went out on its own (Bava Batra 22b), and it comes to warn even if one lit [a fire] on his own [property] and it went out on its own and it damaged, that he is liable - since he did not watch his coals. As a man is obligated to watch his fire that it not [spread] and damage, since it is the way of fire to spread on its own, even though it is not a living being.
Its root is well-known, as we said.
Its laws - for example, the quantity of the distance that we must distance the [fire] from the [property's] border, which is according to the height of the fire (Bava Batra 61a); the law of one who sends it in the hand of a deaf-mute, someone mentally incapacitated, a child, or [he sends it with] someone capable; the law of a group in which one brings the fire, another brings the wood and another stokes [it]; if he stoked it and the wind stoked it; the law of vessels hidden in the stockpile or hidden in the

compound; what is the law (Bava Batra 62b) of a passing camel laden with flax that was lit by the the candle of a storekeeper or by a Channukah light; and the rest of its details - are [all] elucidated in the second and sixth chapters of [Bava] Kamma (see Mishneh Torah, Laws of Damages to Property 14). And [it] is practiced by males, as it is upon them to administer justice. And a court that transgresses it and does not judge the damager with payments - [according to what] is written - has violated a positive commandment.

Mitzvah 57

The commandment on the court to judge the case of an unpaid guardian: To judge the case of an unpaid guardian, as it is stated (Exodus 22:6), "If a man gives his neighbor silver or vessels to keep, etc." And the explanation that comes for it (Bava Metzia 94b) is that this section is stated about an unpaid guardian. And therefore, it exempted him from [liability for] theft. And the understanding of "unpaid" is that the [guardian] did not receive any wage for his guardianship from the [owner].

The root is well-known. Its laws - for example, what is the law of one who makes the claim of theft about the deposited item and swears [that it is so] and afterwards witnesses come [and testify] that it is on his property, and he goes back and [again] makes the claim of theft and swears and afterwards witnesses come that it is on his property (Bava Metzia 108a); the law of one who makes the claim of [it being] lost; what is the law of one who makes a claim of it being deposited; the law of one who makes a claim and goes back and makes a claim of theft and afterwards witnesses come that it is on his property; the law of one who makes the claim of theft about the deposited item of a minor; and the rest of its details - are elucidated in the ninth chapter of [Bava] Kamma and the third of [Bava] Metzia and the eighth of Shevuot (see Tur, Choshen Mishpat 291).

And [it] is practiced in every place and at all times. And a court that transgresses it has violated a positive commandment.

Mitzvah 58

The commandment on the court to judge the case of a plaintiff and a defendant: That we have been commanded to judge the case of a plaintiff and a defendant in a court, meaning to say that we adjudicate the case of anyone who makes a claim against his fellow about anything - or that he lent him or deposited with him or that [the other] stole from him or exploited him or extorted him - as it is stated (Exodus 22:8), "About any misdeed, etc. about which he will say that this is it." And the explanation comes about this expression of "that this is it," that we do not make an oath by writ of the Torah unless the defendant admits to part of the loan. But if he says, "There never were [such] things," or " I returned it all," with a loan and even with a deposit, he is exempted from an oath by writ of the Torah (Bava Kamma 106b). And this is what they, may their memory be Blessed, said in the Gemara (Bava Kamma 107a) that when it is written, "that this is it," it is written about a loan; meaning to say about the claim of a loan, which is that I paid it or that there were never [such] things. But about the claim of guardians - which is a claim of matters beyond his control or [of] theft - even if he does not admit to part [of the claim] but rather says that everything was beyond his control, he is obligated to take an oath. And included in this verse are all of the claims between people that bring with them admission or denial.

The root of the laws are well-known.

Its laws are, for example, one who admits partially must take an oath by Torah writ - the explanation [of which] is one who admits to [owing] a perutah (the smallest bronze coin) but denies [owing] two meah of silver (the smallest silver coin), as [for] less then that he never takes an oath from Torah writ, unless a witness testifies against him, [then] he must swear even when he denies less than two meah (Shevuot 39b), but for less than a perutah, he never swears unless [the] claim was for vessels, as with vessels - even if they claimed two needles, and he admitted about one and denied one, he must swear; when he swears from his partial admission when they claimed something measured, numbered or weighed; the law of one who denies everything; an admission from the [same] type as the claim; the admission of a litigant; the laws of guardians; one who is obligated an oath by Torah or rabbinic writ; the law of one who swears and becomes exempt, and one who swears and takes [the disputed money

Sefer HaChinukh

or item]; the law of one who is suspect for an oath; reversals of the oath; for which sin does he become suspect; what repentance extricates him from the suspicion; the one who was not known not to be suspect and won money [in the case], and afterwards witnesses came [to testify] that he was suspect, that he is obligated to return the money; what is the law of someone who is obligated an oath that he cannot swear (Bava Batra 34a); the laws of migo (a logic establishing credibility, Ketuvot 12a); the laws of a certain claim [as opposed to] a possible claim (Bava Batra 118a); the laws of adding an oath [onto another] (Shevuot 45a), whether it is a certain one onto a certain one or onto a possible one, or even a possible one onto a possible one, and [that] for every type of oath there is addition - whether [the oath] is from the Torah, or rabbinic, or even from the decree of the later authorities; the laws of claims wherein we treat the defendant like one who returns a lost object (Shevuot 31b); things about which we do not make an oath from Torah writ; if we judge produce that has reached shoulders (is ready to be harvested) like land regarding an oath; whether we coerce one who says to his fellow, "There is a deed in your hand and I have a right to it," to bring it out; the law of one who comes to pay, not in front of the creditor; the law of one who gives a loan upon collateral and the collateral is lost, when they disagree with each other about the number of the coins loaned; the law of the creditor who is in the settlement, but [the debtor] wants to pay in the wilderness; the law of the borrower who says, "I payed half," and the witnesses testify that he paid it all; the law of the borrower who admits that they wrote the deed and claims that he paid it, whether the creditor must keep [the deed]; the law of a deed upon which he made a loan and the deed was paid back (Ketuvot 85a); the law of one who sends an amount in the hand of an agent to someone to whom he owes it, and wants to retract [the agency]; the law of a claim that it was paid for a deed in the hand of a third party; the law of whether a deed that does not have the time or place [written] on it is valid (Ketuvot 110b); the law of responsibility for an error of the scribe in all deeds besides a deed of gifting; the law of one who puts a lien on his movable goods, and one who makes his field or slave into collateral, [implicitly] or explicitly (Gittin 41a); the law of tearing [away] the profit and the fruit, whether it is the victim of theft or the creditor [that is coming to do so] (Gittin 48b); the law of the one who lost his deed or it was erased; the law of who is the one who must give the wage for the writing of the deed; the law that the appropriation [to pay a debt] can always be reversed, unless he sold the place or gave it as a gift (Bav Metzia 35a); the law of the things about which there is no oath, but just a general excommunication; that we do not swear based on the claim of a deaf-mute, a mentally incapacitated person or a minor (Shevuot 38b); the laws [of cases] that come from them with adults; that we only take testimony in front of the litigant; that a minor is like naught, even when he is in front of him; that a blind man is like a healthy one, for everything except for testimony; the law of the storekeeper [recording] on his ledger (Shevuot 44b); [that] the gathering of the three [parties, engenders] acquisition and that it is a law without an explanation, and everything related to this matter;

the laws of one given power of attorney (Bava Kamma 70a) towards the one he was appointed against and towards the one who appointed him, and the wording of appointment - which is, "take it to court and own it and take it for yourself"; and [that] the law of one who says, "I did not take out a loan," is as if he said, "I did not repay [it]" (Shevuot 41b); the laws of one who is assumed to be [dishonest] (Bava Metzia 17a); the law of one to whom the court says, "Go out and pay him," and he says, "I payed," or [if they say,] "You are obligated to give [it] to him"; the one who says, "Do not repay me without witnesses," or "[Repay me] in front of x and y," and what the law would be if they went to the country of the sea (far away); the law of whether witnesses of repayment are effective for a [borrower] who trusts the creditor with a deed as if there were two witnesses (Shevuot 42b); the law of in which matter a person can [effectively] say, "I was fooling you," or if a person cannot say [it at all] (Sanhedrin 29a); the law of the one who [wants to] extract [something] from his fellow, and the things wherein [there is validity to continued] possession - such that the one who claims them is [considered] the one who [wants to] extract them; the laws of possession (Bava Batra 28a); the laws of collections, for what do we go down to (impound) his properties; the laws of guarantees (Bava Batra 176b); the laws of protests (Bava Batra 38b); the law of the people against whom we do not establish possession, and that do not establish possession towards another; and all the laws of [making the first offer to neighbors]. And the rest of its many details - are [all] elucidated in [Bava] Kamma, mostly in the third chapter, and in [Bava] Metzia, mostly in the first chapter, and in the eighth of [Bava] Batra, and in Shevuot in the fifth, sixth and seventh chapters, and a few laws are in many scattered places in the Gemara (see Tur, Choshen Mishpat 89-94, etc.)

And this commandment that we are obligated to judge is practiced by males, but not by females, as they do not judge. But nonetheless, women are included in the law of payments for everything, though there is a small difference in the claims of married women in well-known things, as we will explain in the places that we mentioned. And [it] is also practiced in every place and at all times. And a court that transgresses it and did not administer justice - if it had the power [to do so] - has violated a positive commandment. And its punishment is very great, as it causes destruction to the world - since the world is only civilized with justice. And it is like they, may their memory be Blessed, said (Avot 1:18), "On three things the world stands" - and one of them is justice. And this is one of the commandments that all of the people of the world are commanded more generally, since the civilization of the world is impossible without it.

Mitzvah 59

The commandment on the court to judge the case of one who takes a wage and of a renter: To judge the case of one who takes a wage and a renter. And the understanding of one who takes a wage is someone who guards a deposited item for a wage they give to him for guarding [it]; and [of] a renter is like its simple meaning, that he rented an animal from his fellow to ride or to do work, or he rented movable objects from him. And [if a] disagreement arose between the renter and the owner or between the owner of the deposited item and the one guarding it for a wage, it is a commandment upon us to adjudicate between them, as it is written in this section (Exodus 22:9), "If a man gives to another a donkey, an ox, a sheep or any animal to guard, etc." **The** root of the laws is well-known. **Its** laws are for example, that which they, may their memory be Blessed, said (Bava Metzia 93a) that we take an oath on the things of great duress (out of one's control), but pay for theft or loss - since there is some negligence and some duress in this and because of the wage that we take for this, we are obligated to pay, which is not the case with the free guardian, who is exempt from everything except for negligence; the laws of the rental of workers (Bava Metzia 75b), the rental of animals and houses; the law of a craftsman that ruins [an item] (Bava Kamma 98b); one who shows a coin to a storekeeper and it is found to be bad (Bava Kamma 99b); the law that one who rents [the item, as well as hiring the] owners is exempted (Bava Metzia 4a); the laws of beginning with negligence and ending with duress (Bava Metzia 42a); the laws of a guardian who gave [the item] over to [another] guardian and the latter added or reduced its [level] of guardianship (Bava Metzia 36b); the matter that anyone who deposits, deposits with the knowledge that it is [also deposited to the guardian's] wife and adult children (Bava Metzia 36b); that which they, may their memory be Blessed, said (Bava Metzia 29b) that the renter is not permitted to rent it out. And Ramban, may his memory be Blessed, wrote (it seems that the correct version reads Rambam, the source being Mishneh Torah, Laws of Hiring 2:5) that they only said this about movable objects - since it is not his will that his deposit be in the hand of another. But one who rents a house and wants to rent it out to another is permitted, so long as the later [inhabitants] be the same as the number of the first; and so [too] with a boat. But there are those that disagree with him (Raavad on MT, Hiring 2:5). And the rest of its details - are elucidated in the sixth and seventh chapters of [Bava] Kamma, the third and sixth of [Bava] Metzia and the eighth of Shevout (see Tur, Choshen Mishpat 303-313).

And [it] is practiced by males in every place and at all times. And if [one] transgressed it and did not judge - if he was fitting for it - he violated a positive commandment. And even though we were commanded to judge more generally with the law of the plaintiff and the defendant, the Torah added the command of guardians in particular, because they are common matters in human communities.

Mitzvah 60

The commandment to judge the case of the borrower: To judge the case of the borrower, meaning to say a man who borrows any object or animal from his fellow. And borrowing is without a wage at all, but rather, he is doing a kindness for him to do him this favor. And if a disagreement breaks out between them about the matter, we must judge the law that is stated about this [upon] them, as it is written in this section (Exodus 22:13), "And if a man borrows from his neighbor, etc." And regarding the law of the borrower, the Torah made [him] liable even for things of duress (out of his control) - as it is his responsibility: Since he borrowed it and did not put out any thing of his for it, behold he is like one who took out a monetary loan - who if something beyond his control occurred to him could not be exempt from [paying the] creditor, with the claim that it was duress. And about the matter that he is exempt if borrowing in the presence of the owners, we can say according to the simple understanding that the Torah did not make the borrower liable since the owner of the vessel or or the animal is with him - as since he is there, he will guard what is his. And even though the borrower is [still] exempt after the owners left [him], if they were there at the time of the borrowing - it is possible to answer about this that the Torah did not want to give different measures for its words and state that if the owners stay long, he will be exempt, but if [only] a little, he will be liable. [Instead,] the Torah commanded more generally that so long as the owners are there at the time of the borrowing, he will be exempt. And this is the reason that they, may their memory be Blessed, said (Bava Metzia 95b), that if he was there with him at the time of the borrowing – even if he was not with him at the time of it breaking or dying – he is exempt; but if he was with him at the time of the breaking or the dying but he was not there at the time of the borrowing, he is liable. As the procedure depends on the beginning of the matter. And this very same reason suffices for us regarding that which he is also exempt if he rents [something] in the presence of the owners.

The laws of the commandment are that which our Rabbis, may their memory be Blessed, said (Bava Metzia 96b) that if the animal dies because of its work - and so [too,] if a tool breaks because of its work - that he is exempt, but if he deviated from that which the owners commanded him, even if it died because of work, he is liable; [that] if he took it to a place where onlookers are found, he is obligated to bring a proof about his claim that it died because of its work (Bava Metzia 83a); [that] when we exact payment from the one liable to pay, we estimate the payments like with damages (Bava Metzia 97a); that the borrower is obligated for its food from when he pulls it until the end of the borrowing (Ketuvot 34b); the law [if] their father left them a borrowed cow and it died; (Ketuvot 34b); the law of one who says to his fellow, "Let me borrow thing x by your goodness," [such] that he can use it forever and return the fragments to him; how long is implied by one who borrows without specification and the many differences about this matter; which [items] can be borrowed by a teacher from his students (Bava Metzia 97a) and which can they borrow from him; the law of one who says to his agents, "Go lend out my cow"; one who borrows from a woman and she asks her husband; one who borrows from his wife; partners that borrowed from one another, or from someone else and it is borrowed by one of them; the laws of one who borrows a cow and sends it away; one who borrows it for a borrower - upon his command or not upon his command; and that which they said that the borrower is not allowed to lend it out. And the rest of its details - are elucidated in the eighth chapter [of Bava] Metzia and also the eighth chapter of Shevout (see Tur, Choshen Mishpat 340-346).

And [it] is practiced by males, as it is upon them to administer justice. And a court that transgresses it and does not adjudicate [these cases] has violated a positive commandment.

Mitzvah 61

The commandment on the court to judge the case of a seducer: To judge the case of a seducer - meaning to say one who seduces a virgin – that we should judge him according to his statute that is written about him in the section, as it is stated (Exodus 22:15), "And if a man seduces a virgin, etc." And the matter of seduction is that he tells her things that are false or [even] true until she gives in to him.

The root of the commandment is well-known. And do not wonder here – since 'all of the honor of the king's daughter is inside' (Psalms 45:14), [how is it that] she is sold to the [seducer] for fifty silver pieces, whether she is wealthy or whether she is poor? As the penalty is only the value of the enjoyment of laying [with her] alone. But from another angle, the one who lays with her is liable to give [the money] of embarrassment and damage according to her lineage and her importance. And all the commands of God, may He be Blessed, are faithful.

Sefer HaChinukh

The laws of the commandment: Rambam, may his memory be Blessed, wrote (Mishneh Torah, Laws of Virgin Maiden 1:2) [that] anything that is in the city is assumed to be seduction until witnesses testify that it was rape, and anything that is in the field is assumed to be rape. And they, may their memory be Blessed, said (Ketuvot 39a) that the marriage of a seducer is dependent upon the will of the father, the daughter and the seducer. And if he marries her, there is no penalty. The law of the High Priest who seduced or raped; the law of the penalty when intercourse was in its way; that the time of the penalty is only from three years until she becomes an adult; [that] that which is written, "to her father," [means] specifically to her father, but if she does not have a [living] father, there is no law of penalty towards her - as seduction is with her consent, which is not the case with rape, as we we will write in its place with God's help; and the women that do not have a penalty and they are ten; and the rest of its details - are [all] elucidated in the third and fourth chapter of Ketuvot (see Mishneh Torah, Laws of Virgin Maiden 1)

And [it] is practiced in every place that there is a court of ordained judges, as we only judge cases of penalties with ordained judges. And one who transgresses it and does not fulfill this law has violated a positive commandment.

Mitzvah 62

To not keep a witch alive: To not keep a witch alive. Rather, we kill her, as it is stated (Exodus 22:17), "You shall not keep a witch alive." And it is not specifically a witch, but rather anyone that does magic. It is just that it stated it according to what is common, as women are more involved with magic than men (Sanhedrin 67a).

From the roots of the commandment are that it is known that magic is a very bad thing and causes many mishaps to people. I do not have to write at length about it, as the things are well-known. And therefore, we were commanded to put away from the world someone who makes efforts with this, as he is coming against the will of God, as He desires [the world's] settlement and that everything should be administered in a natural way. As nature was at the beginning of creation and this one wants to change everything. And according to my opinion, the matter of magic is that at the beginning of creation, God, Blessed be He, placed for each and every thing in the world a nature [through which] to accomplish its action well and straight, for the good of the creatures of the world that He created; and He commanded each one to act according to its species, as it is written about all the creatures, in Parshat Bereshit (Genesis 1:12), "according to its species." And He also made a higher force govern each and every one from above, to compel it to perform its action; as they, may their memory be Blessed, said (Bereshit Rabbah 1), "There is no [blade of] grass below that does not have a constellation above that tells it, 'Grow!'"And besides the action that each and every one does according to its nature, there is another action that they have, by mixing one specie with another. And in the craft of this mixing there are some angles that were not permitted for people to utilize, because God knows that the end result that will come out for people from these angles will be bad for them. And on account of this, He prevented them from them. And this is what they, may their memory be Blessed, said more generally (Shabbat 67b), "Anything that has healing in it does not have the 'ways of the Amorite' in it"; meaning to say, it should not be forbidden from the perspective of magic – since there is a benefit to it that is found from true experience, it is not from the forbidden angles, as they are only forbidden because of the perspective of their damage. And there is another matter in these forbidden angles of mixture and machinations for which they were forbidden. [It is] because the power of this mixture is so strong that it negates the power of the constellations that are assigned upon the two species. And the illustration of this is that it is just like that which you see with the grafting of one specie with a different one, that a new third specie is created. It comes out that the grafting negates the power of both of them. And so, we have been prevented from bringing up to our minds to switch the perfect acts of God, even if something that appears to be pleasing comes out in our hand.

And it is possible that a hint will come up in our hands from the roots of the forbidden mixtures of seeds and animals and shatnez (the mixture of linen and wool). And we will write at length about them in their places, with God's help. And that which they, may their memory be Blessed, said

(Sanhedrin 67b, Chullin 7b), "Why is its name called kishufim (magic)? Because it contradicts the retinue (makhishin pamaliah) on high and on low," is meaning to say that their power temporarily overrides the power of those forces appointed over them. And see the precision of their words, may their memory Blessed, as they said, "the retinue on high," and they did not say, "the decree of High – since God, Blessed be He, decreed it and wanted from the beginning of creation that this action would come out from the two of them when they are mixed. And there is an open rebuke from it towards those appointed over them [about their lack of absolute power]. Rather, they said that the power of the retinue on high is [that which is] contradicted regardless. And one, whose intellect is close to the light of the face of the King and the power of his merit overrides the power of those appointed, will not fear from this phenomenon, as we found that the sage said to the witch in the Gemara (Shabbat 81, Sanhedrin 67b).

And the knowledge of the difference [between] these things – which is the mixing He permitted to us and there is no angle of magic and which is the one that has an angle of magic and is forbidden as the science of magic – is well-known. And do not think that the craft of magic and [of] demons (shedim) is the same thing. As behold, they, may their memory be Blessed, said (Sanhedrin 67b), "'With their tricks,' that is the work of demons; 'with their spells,' that is the work of magic." It is implied from this that the matter of magic is possible to do without demons. However, sometimes it is also done with demons. And those demons that are used for the craft of magic are called angels of destruction. So did Rashi, may his memory be Blessed, explain – since the matter of magic is always only done to destroy. And about the details of the laws of magic, we will write at more length in the negative commandment of the witch, with God's help, as its place is there. As here there is only the warning of the law, meaning to say that we will not forgive them, but [rather] kill them (see Mishneh Torah, Laws of The Sanhedrin and the Penalties within their Jurisdiction 15).

And this commandment to administer the laws of those that do magic is practiced by males - since it is fitting [for] and it was given to them to administer justice - and not females. And [this is] specifically in the Land of Israel with ordained judges and in a court of twenty-three [judges]. And a court that transgresses - it if it has the power to administer justice - has violated this negative commandment, besides that it violated the positive commandment, which is more generally to administer justice against those that are liable. And there are no lashes for this, as there is no act [involved] with it. And we do not give lashes for any negative commandment with which no act is involved - except for one who takes an oath, a rebel, and one who curses his fellow with the name [of God] (Makkot 16a).

Mitzvah 63
To not oppress the convert with words: That we have been prevented from oppressing converts, even [only] with words - and that is one from the [other] nations who converted and entered our religion - such that is forbidden for [one] to disgrace him even with words, as it is stated (Exodus 22:20), "and you shall not oppress a convert." And even though we are warned about this with [Jews] and since this one entered our religion, behold is like [any other Jew], Scripture added a warning to us and also redoubled the prohibition for him, as it is written (Leviticus 19:33), "do not oppress" another time; because the issue of oppression is more relevant to a convert than it is to [another Jew], as [another Jew] has redeemers who will redress his insult. And there is another reason, [and that is] because there is a concern that [the convert] might return to his deviance out of anger over the disgraces. And they said in the Sifra (Sifra, Kedoshim, Chapter 8:2) that one shouldn't say, "Yesterday you were an idolater and now you entered under the wings of the Divine Presence."

Aside from what we have [already] written, it is from the roots of the commandment [that it is] in order to permanently train our negative inclination not to do whatever evil is in our power to do. Therefore, we are warned regarding this person who is among us without [a full support system], and over whom each and every one of us - with his friends - can exert some power; that we not exclude him from the general [sensitivity that we show to everyone among us]. And through boundaries such as these we will acquire a soul of higher worth - raised-up and crowned with [positive] characteristics and worthy of receiving good. And we will fulfill in ourselves the desire of God, may He be Blessed, who desires to give benefit?

The laws of the commandment are, for example, the many [prohibitions] that they, may their memory be Blessed, warned us about; that they made known to us - in order to warn us more about the thing - that the Torah warned about it in twenty-one (and see the Lemberg edition, that reads, twenty-four) places (Bava Metzia 39b); that they also wrote to strengthen the commandment, that with the same expression that we were commanded about the love of the Omnipresent, we were [also] commanded about the love of the convert - as with the Omnipresent, it is written (Deuteronomy 6:5), "And you shall love your God"; and with the convert, it is written (Deuteronomy 10:19), "And you shall love the convert." And many things like this are in Midrash and in a few places in the
Gemara (see Tur, Choshen Mishpat, 307).

And [it] is practiced in all places and at all times by males and by females. And one who transgresses it and disgraces him, has violated a negative commandment. But we do not give lashes for it, since it does not have an act [involved] with it.

Mitzvah 64

To not oppress the convert regarding money: That we have been prevented to not oppress the convert regarding money - that if we have give and take (business matters) with him, to not oppress him - as it is stated (Exodus 22:20), "you shall not pressure him." And they said in the Mekhilta d'Rabbi Yishmael 22:2, "'You shall not pressure him' is regarding money." And this negative commandment is in addition to the negative commandment in which he is included with all of Israel, as they are [covered] by the [that] negative commandment of monetary oppression. And they are warned about him [both] regarding words and regarding money, due to the reason that we have written. All of its statutes are in the commandment that preceded this (Sefer HaChinukh 63). And in the negative commandment of monetary oppression of Israel (Sefer HaChinukh 337), we will write a few of the details of fraud, with God's help (see Tur, Choshen Mishpat 307).

Mitzvah 65

To not abuse the orphan and the widow: That we have been prevented from burdening - by action or even by speech - the orphans and the widows, as it is stated (Exodus 22:20), "Every widow and orphan you shall not abuse." Rather, all of a person's give and take (business matters) with them should be calm and with kindness and pity.

That which I have written adjacently regarding the matter of a convert is from the roots of the commandment - it is because these are of weak (weary) power; as they have no one to make their claim against any one - as would have done the husband of the widow and the father of the orphans had he been alive. And therefore, our perfect Torah warned us to acquire the trait of kindness and mercy for our souls, so that we be straight in all of our deeds as if there were a claimant making a strong claim against us. And we should be concerned and have pity upon them, and see their [side] in every thing; [even] more than we would have done if their father and husband had been alive.

From the laws of the commandment is that which they said (Mishneh Torah, Human Dispositions 6:10) that even the widow of the king and his orphans are [included] in this prohibition and how to behave towards them: That we should only speak softly with them; that a person should only behave honorably towards towards them, and not hurt them in their bodies with work, nor embarrass them with words; and be concerned about their money more than about his own money. And because of this, they, may their memory be Blessed, said (Shevuot 45a), that one who comes to collect [a debt] from their monies - even if he has a validated deed - may not collect without [taking] an oath, which is not the case with another. And they, may their memory be Blessed, said (Bava Batra 23a) that if they have a quarrel with anyone - that the court is obligated to make a claim for them, against the one who sues them, and they claim for their benefit anything they think that their father would have been able to claim; and if they have money, that the court must force anyone they find that is wealthy - beyond possessions that are liened - and that is a trustworthy man who loves peace and is upstanding, and deposit the money of the orphans with him, to do business with (invest) it in a way that is likely to profit the orphans and be far from loss (low-risk) (Bava Metzia 70b), which they did not permit

Sefer HaChinukh

with another person due to a rabbinic prohibition on interest. And they also force any person that is good for them to put his eye on their properties, if their father had not left any custodian for them. And they also said about them (Gittin 52a) that their hand be on the higher (they be given the advantage) in all give and take that they have with anyone, as [is this case] with consecrated property; and in one [case], even more than consecrated property. How is this? [If] the orphans sold their fruit and the purchaser dragged some of them towards him but did not yet give the money and [their value] appreciated in the interim, they can retract, since their properties are only acquired through money - like consecrated property, about which it is written, "and he gives him the money and it is established for him" (and not by dragging as is otherwise the standard). If the fruits depreciated, the buyers may not retract, as the power of a commoner should not be weightier than their power. And so [too], if they bought the fruit and they dragged them and did not give the value, and they appreciated, the seller cannot retract, so that the power of the commoner not be greater than their power. But if they depreciated, they could retract; however, for the sake of their welfare, [the rabbis] said they are not able to retract - so that they will be able to find someone to sell them fruit on credit. If they gave the value to the seller for fruit and they did not drag the fruit, and the fruit depreciated - they can recall [it]. And this is the one [case] that we said they have an advantage over consecrated property. As consecrated property cannot be recalled in this case - as since in the same case with a commoner there is a [curse called] the One who repayed [placed upon the one who retract, the sages did not want to apply a lowly trait for [such] a small gain for consecrated property. But with orphans, it is enough for them to be like the rest of the people; and since the rest of the people can retract [in this case], according to [the letter of] the law - except that they [are given a curse] - it is correct that (orphans, who do not receive a curse), [be allowed] to retract. [If] the orphans gave the value, but did not drag the fruit, and they appreciated - the sellers may reretract, [though] they retract and receive [a curse]. But this is for the welfare [of the orphans], as if their law would be that they acquire with the giving of money, the seller would tell them that they burned up or got lost from duress (it was beyond his control). And you might say, they should be in their possession for any benefit of theirs - that if they want, they take them regardless; and if they do not, they do not take them - so that the buyer not give this answer. [If so,] your answer is that it is impossible to do all this for them - as it is not correct to give them the property of [other] people. It is enough for them that for their benefit we sometimes [administer] Torah law upon them and sometimes [administer] rabbinic law upon them. But above all this, it is not correct to give them the money of the [rest of] the world, and similar to that which they said about them in the Gemara, (Bava Metzia 70a), "Orphans that consume what is not theirs will follow those that left them (and die)." [If] the orphans took the value for their fruit, but the buyer did not drag some of them, and they depreciated - the buyers can retract according to the law and receive [a curse]. As if you say, "Let us [administer] Torah law upon them, and since the buyers gave the money, they acquired the fruit and the buyers may not retract" - this would be bad for the orphans, as they would never find someone who will advance them money for their fruits. And it is possible that they will need money at that time; and it will come out for them that this advantage will sometimes be a great loss. And so [the Rabbis] investigated every side of their benefit that was possible and arranged it for them.

And the orphans never receive [a curse] for anything that the custodian does; nor also does the custodian - since he is recalling on their behalf (Bava Metzia 74b). And so [too] is the law more generally regarding an agent who gives and takes with the knowledge of his sender, that neither of them receive [a curse]. And nonetheless, they said about them that it is permitted to oppress them a little for their benefit - for example a teacher towards his student in Torah or in a craft. However even for their benefit, it is a commandment to be more lenient upon them than upon other people. And they also said that there is a covenant made with them that their cries will be answered, as it is stated (Exodus 22:22), "I will surely hear his cry"; and that they are called orphans regarding the matter of this commandment until they do not need an adult for their business affairs, but rather administer all of their own needs like all other adults. And the rest of its details are elucidated in scattered places in the Gemara and in Midrash (see Mishneh Torah, Laws of Human Dispositions 6).

And this commandment is practiced in every place and at all times by males and by females, that all people are obligated to treat them gently and honorably. And behold, one who transgresses it and angers them or taunts them or afflicts them or subjugates them or destroys their money - and all the more so, if he hits them - violates a negative commandment. And even though we do not administer lashes for this - as the affliction is not something [clearly] defined, such that we can give lashes for it, since the evil afflicter can make the lying claim that he afflicted them according to the law or for their benefit - God, may He be Blessed, who examines the hearts, will [redress] their pain. And behold his punishment is explicit in the Torah, as it is stated (Exodus 22:23), "and I shall kill you with the sword" - meaning to say, measure for measure, such that the wives of the afflicters become widows and their children, orphans, and not find someone who has mercy upon them. As in the way that a person measures, so will he be measured (Sotah 8b). And if the afflicter is a female, she will die and her husband will marry another woman who will afflict her children. And they, may their memory be Blessed, expounded, "if he will surely cry to Me" - a son complains to his father, a wife to her husband, a widow and orphan to Me, "and I will listen, as I am gracious" (Exodus 22:26). And Ramban, may his memory be Blessed, (on Sefer HaMitzvot LaRambam, Mitzvot Lo Taase 256) counts the prohibition towards the orphan and the widow as two negative commandments, because of the reason we wrote above (Sefer HaChinukh 7).

Mitzvah 66
The commandment of lending to the poor person: To lend to the poor person - according to what is in reach of one's hand - in accordance with what [the poor person] needs, in order to give him space and to lighten his distress from upon him. And this commandment of lending is stronger and more obligatory than the commandment of giving charity. As the duress and the darkness of one who whose duress is [already] known and revealed among people and has [already] asked from them is not the same as the one who has not yet come to this embarrassment and is [still] afraid to enter into it. And if he would have a little assistance of a loan with which to make a little profit, maybe he will never need to come to asking. And [then] if God has mercy upon him with profit, he will pay his creditors, and he will live on the remainder (Sefer HaMitzvot LaRambam, Mitzvot Ase 197). And therefore, our perfect Torah warned us about this to assist the impoverished man with a loan before he needs to come to ask, as it is stated (Exodus 22:24), "If you lend money to My people." And they, may their memory be Blessed, said in Mekhilta d'Rabbi Yishmael 22:24:1 [that] each and every, "if" in the Torah is optional except for three that are obligatory - and this is one of them. And they proved the matter from that which it is written in the way of a command in a different place, "you shall surely pledge" (Deuteronomy 15:8).

The root of the commandment is that God wanted His creations to be trained and habituated to the trait of kindness and of mercy, since it is a praiseworthy trait. And from the refinement of their bodies with good character traits, they will be fit to receive the good; as we have said that the good and blessing always descend upon the good, and not upon its opposite. And when God, may He be Blessed, does good to the good, He fulfills His will, since He desires to do good to the world. And if it were not from the angle of this root, does He, Blessed be He, not have enough for the lacking of the poor person without us? Rather, it was from His kindness, Blessed be He, that He made us His messengers to give us merit. And there is also another reason in the matter - that God, Blessed be He, wanted to support the poor person through [other] people because of the greatness of [that person's] sin, so that he be chastised by pain in two ways: by the contracting of embarrassment through those his age; and by the reduction of his food. And in the manner that we said [that it is] in order to give us merit did a sage from our Sages answer a certain heretic who asked him if God loves the poor - as He commanded [to help] them - why does He not provide for them, etc., as it appears in Tractate Bava Batra 10a.

The laws of the commandment are for example, which poor person is prioritized for this commandment; the many warnings that they, may their memory be Blessed, warned us about it - as they said (Bava Batra 10a), that a person who has [the wherewithal] but withdraws his hand from this commandment is pushed off and disgraceful and abominable and disgusting and detestable until his vileness is close to being like the vileness of idolatry; and how beautiful and beloved and favored and

Blessed from several blessings is the one who supports it. It is all elucidated in [various] places in Ketuvot and in [Bava] Batra and in many [other] places in the Gemara (see Tur, Choshen Mishpat 97.)

Mitzvah 67

That we not demand the debt of a poor person that does not have with what to pay: That we have been prevented from demanding the debt of the borrower at the time that we know that he can not pay his debt, since he does not have [the money] - as it is stated (Exodus 22:24), "do not be to him as a creditor." And know that this preventing also includes not to lend with interest to [another Jew].

It is from the roots of the commandment [that it is] to fix within us the trait of kindness and pity. And when they are fixed within us, we will then be fit to receive the good, and God will fulfill His will through us, as He desires [to do good] in this world and in the next world.

From the laws of the commandment is that which they, may their memory be Blessed, said (Bava Metzia 45b), "From where [do we know] about one who gave a hundred to his fellow and knows that he does not have it, that it is forbidden to pass in front of him (across from his home)? As it is stated, 'do not be to him as a creditor'"; and that which they also said in Mekhilta d'Rabbi Yishmael 22:24:4, "do not be to him as a creditor" - that he should not see him all the time. And other things are said about this matter in [Bava] Metzia and in [various] places in the Gemara (see Tur, Choshen Mishpat 97).

And [it] is practiced by males and females in every place and at all times. And one who transgresses it and demands his loan [back] from his fellow and knows that he does not have it, but demands it [regardless] in order to cause him pain, has violated this negative commandment and it is as if he has violated the commandment of the King.

Mitzvah 68

That we not give a hand between the borrower and the creditor with interest: To not be involved in an interest loan between the borrower and the creditor - meaning to say that we do not act as a guarantor for them and that we do not write a deed for them that has a mention of interest - as it is stated (Exodus 22:24), "you shall not place interest upon him." And the explanation comes in Bava Metzia 75b that this negative commandment is stated about those involved in the matter, such as the guarantor, the witnesses and the scribe. And there it is said also that the creditor is included with them in this negative commandment, besides the other negative commandments that are specific to him. And the general principle of the matter is that which Abbaye said there that the creditor transgresses six negative commandments, the borrower two and those involved, one. **It** is from the roots of this commandment [that it is] because the good God desired the settlement of His people which He chose. And therefore, He commanded to remove the obstacle from their path, that one should not swallow up the wealth of his friend without his [even] feeling it, until he finds his house empty of all good. As this is the way of interest, and the matter is well-known, and that is why it is called, "bite (neshekh)." And in the avoidance of this matter by the guarantor, the scribe and the witnesses, people will [also] avoid it. And the rest of its details are in [Bava] Metzia (see Tur, Yoreh Deah 160). **And** [it] is practiced in every place and at all times by males and females. And one who transgresses it and becomes a scribe or a guarantor or a witness for the loan violates this negative commandment. But we do not administer lashes for it, since even the creditor does not [receive] lashes - as behold, it is given to returning. And [so] it is not right that these that come because of him be liable for lashes.

Mitzvah 69

To not curse the judge: To not curse the judges, as it is stated (Exodus 22:27), "Lords (elohim) shall you not curse." And the understanding of elohim [here] is judges, as [in] (Exodus 22:8), "that the elohim deem guilty." And the verse [chose] this expression [which can also mean, God], so that another negative commandment would be included in this negative commandment, and that is the negative commandment of 'blessing' God. As they, may their memory be Blessed, said in the Mekhilta and the Sifri, "The warning for 'blessing God' is from that it is written, ' Elohim shall you not curse.'" And that which is written in another place, "And the one that blasphemes the name of the Lord will surely die" (Leviticus 24:16), is [the mention of] its punishment. But the warning (prohibition) is from here. As mention of the punishment of a commandment without its warning is not sufficient for us. And this is what our Rabbis, may their memory be Blessed, always said (Sanhedrin 54a), "We have heard the punishment, from where is the warning?" And the matter is because of this: That if the prevention of God did not come to us in the matter, but it would [only] state, "One who does thing x will be punished with this," it would be implied that there is permission to transgress the commandment in the hand of anyone who is willing to take the punishment and is not concerned with his pain, and that he will not go against the will of God and His commandment with this. And [so] the matter of the commandment will turn into a type of give and take, meaning to say that one who wants to do thing x, can give such and such and do it, or bare his shoulder to suffer such and do it. And the intention of the commandments is not like this, but rather that God prevented us from things for our [own] good, and informed us in some of them of the punishment that comes to us immediately, besides transgressing His will, which is weightier than anything. And this is [the meaning] of that which they, may their memory be Blessed, said in every place (Yoma 81a), "He did not punish, unless He warned," meaning to say, God did not inform of the punishment that comes for a sin, unless He first informed us that His will is that we do not do that thing for which the punishment is coming.

It is from the roots of the commandment to remove fear of the accused and his curse from the judges, so that they will pronounce the true judgment. And it also warned about this in another place in the Torah. And there is also another benefit found in the commandment, as many mishaps come with the cursing of judges; since the masses hate him, in their foolishness - and if they were not warned about his curse, maybe they would curse him and get aroused from this to stand against him. As the sage said to the king about the masses, "Be careful lest they say; as if they say, they will do, and there will be much evil with this, since he 'holds up the land with judgment.'"

From the laws of the commandment with judges - that which they said [that] the liability of the negative commandment is only with a name from the names of God, such as Lord, or Omnipotent, and God and similar to them, or with an appellation, such as Gracious or Zealous and similar to them, but without a name or appellation, such as [if he says,] "cursed is x," or "let him not be Blessed," he does not have liability for the negative commandment, but it is [still] forbidden; that which they, may their memory be Blessed, also explained about this matter that the liability is not only if he curses him in the Holy Tongue, but even in any language (Mishneh Torah, Laws of The Sanhedrin and the Penalties within their Jurisdiction 26:3), and that there is a need for witnesses and warning for this, as in all liabilities of negative commandments; and the rest of its details - are elucidated in Sanhedrin (see Mishneh Torah, Laws of The Sanhedrin and the Penalties within their Jurisdiction 6).

And [it] is practiced in every place and at all times by males and females. And one who transgresses it and curses the judge with a name or with an appellation [of God] is lashed two [sets] of lashes; [one,] since [the judge] is like any proper [member] of Israel, whom are included in this prohibition - and as we will write in the Order of Kedoshim Tehiyu (Sefer HaChinukh 231) - and [another] one because he is a judge.

Mitzvah 70

The negative commandment of 'blessing' the Name: And it is from the roots of the commandment of 'blessing' the Name that it empties out the man from any good, through this bad speech. And all the glory of his soul becomes something destructive, and he is considered like the animals. As it is with this exact thing through which God separated him for the good and with-it man was created - and that is speech - [and] through which he is separated from the animals, that he is separating himself to evil. And he extracts himself completely from any parameter of knowledge and becomes like a disgusting and repulsive creeping animal, and lower than it. And therefore, the Torah warns us about this - since the good God will desire our good. And each and every word that causes the denial of good to [a person] goes against God's desire, may He be Blessed.

Sefer HaChinukh

Some of the laws of the commandments – for example, that which they explained that there is no guilt unless he pronounces the specific name, which is (yod-hay-vav-hay), or of (alef-dalet-nun-yod) according to the opinion of some commentators (Mishneh Torah, Laws of Foreign Worship and Customs of the Nations 2:7); that which they said (Sanhedrin 56a), that they would each and every day ask the witnesses with a nickname, "Yose should strike Yose," when the case was finished they would move all the people outside and ask the senior witness and say to him, "Say with your mouth what you heard," and he would say [it], they would [then] stand on their feet and tear [their clothing] and not [ever] mend [them], and the second witness would say, "I also heard like him," and if there were many witnesses, they all say like this; that which they, may their memory be Blessed said (Nedarim 87a), that the blasphemer, even though he recants within the time of speaking (right away) is [still] stoned; that one who curses God in the name of idolatry is to be attacked by zealots, but if they did not attack him and he comes to court, he is not stoned unless he 'blesses' with a name from the specific names [of God], and the reason he is not stoned is because, even at the time of his anger, he himself knows that his words are complete foolishness, but zealots attack him nonetheless, since he was destructive and caused abomination and was brazen-faced to speak bad things like these; that which they said that anyone who hears the 'blessing' of God from the mouth of an Israelite is obligated to tear [his clothes], but that one who hears it from a gentile is not obligated to tear, and Eliyakim and Shevna only tore because Ravshakeh was an apostate (Sanhedrin 60a); [that] all of the witnesses and the judges lean their hands one by one upon the head of the blasphemer and say to him, "Your blood is upon your head, since you caused [it to] yourself," and there is none else in all of those killed by the court besides only the blasphemer that we lean upon, as it is stated (Leviticus 24:14), "and all those who heard lean, etc."; and the rest of its details - are [all] elucidated in Sanhedrin, Chapter 7.

And this prohibition is practiced in every place and at all times. And one who transgresses it and 'blesses' the Name, in the way we said, is stoned in the Land by the mouth of ordained judges. And today, outside the Land - where we do not have ordained judges - all of Israel distance themselves from him and place a ban upon him (see Tur, Choshen Mishpat 27).

Mitzvah 71
To not curse a chieftain (nassi): To not curse a chieftain, as it is stated (Exodus 22:27), "and a chieftain among your people shall you not malign." And the explanation upon it came that the nassi is the king (Mishneh Torah, Laws of The Sanhedrin and the Penalties within their Jurisdiction 26:1). But nonetheless, this negative commandment also includes the nassi of Israel and that is the head of the Great Sanhedrin, who is also called the nassi ; since the intention of the verse is about anyone who is the head authority over Israel, whether it is the government of the kingdom or whether it is the government of the Torah.

It is from the roots of the commandment that it is because it is impossible for the settlement of people without their making one of them head over the others, to do his command and fulfill his decrees. As the opinions of people are different and they will never all agree to one opinion - to do one thing from among the many things. And from this, the result will be idleness and a cessation of actions. And therefore, they need to accept the opinion of one of them - whether it is good or whether it is bad - so that they will be successful and be involved in the business of the world, sometimes finding great benefit from his will and counsel and sometimes [finding] the opposite. And all of this is better than disagreement which causes complete idleness. And since the one appointed as head is the cause for the benefit that we said - whether he is big in leading us in the ways of religion or whether he is big in the kingdom to guard a man from his neighbor that is more powerful than he - the matter is fitting and proper that we not [treat] his honor lightly, and also that we not curse him. [We should not do this] even not in front of him, and all the more so [not] in front of witnesses; as a bad habit that a person accustoms himself [to do] by himself will in the end become his action [in public]. And we have already [talked about] the great loss that comes because of disagreement (see Bemidbar Rabbah 18).

From the laws of the commandments - what they, may their memory be Blessed, said (Shevuot 35b), that the only one who is liable is one who curses with a name or with an appellation [of God]; that the one who curses him is lashed three [sets] of lashes, because of " Elohim shall you not curse," because of "and a chieftain among your people shall you not malign," and because of "You shall not curse a deaf person" (Leviticus 19:14), which is a negative commandment that includes all of Israel; and the rest of its details - are elucidated in Sanhedrin (see Tur, Choshen Mishpat 27).

And it is practiced by males and females in the Land and in every place that we are with our king or with the head of the Great Sanhedrin. And one who transgresses it and curses him with a name or an appellation is lashed three [sets] of lashes. And if the son of the nassi curses him, he is lashed four - three as we have said, and one for one who curses his father.

Mitzvah 72

To not skip in the laws of produce: To not skip in the laws of produce - some of them over [others] of them - but we should rather extract them in order. The elucidation of the matter is that after the wheat is threshed and cleaned, it is tevel, and the understanding of tevel is produce that has not been separated. And the obligation upon us with it, is to first remove the priestly tithe from it. And by Torah writ, even one [kernel of] wheat exempts the threshing floor (Kiddushin 29b), but the Sages said that [the mandatory amount] is one part in fifty. And afterwards, the obligation upon us from that which is left over is to remove the tithe from it, and that is called the first tithe. And afterwards, the obligation upon us from that which is left over is to remove another tithe, and that is the second tithe. And the priestly tithe is given to the priest, the first tithe to the Levite, and the second tithe [is kept,] that it be eaten by its owner in Jerusalem. And we are obligated to separate these portions from the produce in this order. And upon this came the preventing, that we not do first from this what is fitting to delay, and not delay what is fitting to do first (Mishnah Terumot 3:10) - as it is stated (Exodus 22:28), "Your fullness and your offering you shall not delay." And it is as if it stated, "From your fullness and your offering, you shall not delay what is fitting to do first."

It is from the roots of the commandment that in doing things in their order, they will not come to a mix-up and a mistake; but when we do not do them like this, a mistake will always be found in them. And since priestly tithes and [other] tithes are a big thing in the fulfillment of our religion - as we will explain with God's help in the Order of Reeh and of Shoftim - God, may He be Blessed, commanded us to be very careful with them, so as not to ever come to a mistake in their calculations. And when we hear [something] better than this from the mystics (mekubalim), we will accept (nekabel) [it].

From the laws of the commandment - that which they, may their memory be Blessed, said (Mishnah Terumot 3:10) that if he transgressed and first did in this matter something that it is not fitting to do first, what is done is done, and we are not obligated to go back and mix everything and separate them a second time; so [too], what they expounded in Tractate Terumot (Mishnah Terumot 3:7) and in the Mekhilta d'Rabbi Yishmael 22:28, "'Its fullness,' those are the first-fruits that are taken from what is full," meaning to say, before he takes anything from the thing, [as that is the expression of fullness, meaning to say it is completely full, "'and your offering,' that is the priestly tithe; 'do not delay,' that you not do first the priestly tithes before the first-fruits, etc"; and the rest of its details - are in Tractate Terumot (see Mishneh Torah, Laws of Heave Offerings 3).

And [it] is practiced by males and females in the Land of Israel and at the time that Israel is there - according to the opinion of Rambam (Mishneh Torah, Laws of Heave Offerings 1:26), who wrote that the commandment of the priestly tithe and [other] tithes is by Torah writ only at the time that the Land of Israel is settled [by the Jewish people]. And one who transgresses it and does these things first - this one over that one - his judgement is as for one who has violated the commandment of the King. But we do not administer lashes for it; as so is it elucidated there in Terumot (see Mishnah Terumot 3:6) - that there are no lashes for this negative commandment.

Mitzvah 73

To not eat a torn animal: To not eat from a torn animal, as it is stated (Exodus 22:30), "and meat in the field of a torn animal, you shall not eat." And the obvious understanding of this verse is to warn us about an animal that a wolf or a lion tore in the field, and that it is torn in a way that it is inclined to die from this tearing. As certainly, its understanding does not include that if [the wolf or lion] touched the tip of its ear or tore from its wool, that it be called a torn animal for this. Rather, its correct understanding - and the tradition supports this - is that it was torn enough that it will die in the hour, or soon, because of that tearing. And they, may their memory be Blessed, said (Chullin 57b) that this time is [up to] a year. And it should also be understood by all those that understand, that the Torah is not exacting that the tearing be by a wolf or a lion or a bear, but rather any animal that inflicts a wound which brings [another animal] to die is forbidden regardless. And those are the wounds that the sages enumerated that kill, and it is as it comes in the Mishnah (Chullin 42a), "This is the general rule: anything that nothing like it stays alive is a torn animal." And that which the verse stated, "in the field," is not specific, but rather it is the way of Scripture to always state what is common, and it is the way of animals to get torn in the field. And so is it [found] in the Mekhilta d'Rabbi Yishmael 23:30), "The Torah stated what is common." And it was also needed to write, "in the field," in order to teach many other things. As the words of the Torah are expounded in different ways - outside, they wear clothing of majesty, pure linen and silk and embroidery, and inside, there is gold and many pearls. And the clothing of this verse that is revealed and more obvious at the beginning of its study is to teach only about the torn animal, as we have written; and [also] about meat from a living animal, which is included in the [concept of] meat of a torn animal. And that which is inside is this - that it teaches about any meat that went out of its boundary, that it is forbidden and becomes like a torn animal - for example consecrated meats that went outside [the Temple] courtyard, and lightly consecrated meats that went outside of [Jerusalem's] wall, and the meat of a Pesach sacrifice that went outside of its assemblage and so [too,] a limb that went out from its mother's womb. And the understanding of the Scripture comes like this, as if it stated, "and meat in the 'field' is 'torn,'" meaning to say, meat that went out of its boundary - as that is [the meaning of] the expression, 'field,' that it has no boundaries - is a 'torn' animal. And the law of all of these that we mentioned is like a torn animal, and one who ate a kazayit from them is lashed.

It is from the roots of this commandment [that it is] because the body is an instrument of the soul - with it, it carries out its activity; without it, it can never complete its work. And hence it is in its shadow truly for its good, and not for its bad; as God does not do bad but does good to all. Thus, we find that the body at its command is like a pair of tongs in the hand of a blacksmith: with it he can produce a tool fit for its purpose. Now in truth, if the tongs are strong and properly shaped to grasp tools in them, the craftsman can make them well. But if the tongs are not good, the tools will never come out properly shaped and fit. In the same way, if there is any damage in the body, of any kind, some function of the intelligence will be nullified, corresponding to that damage. For this reason, our whole and perfect Torah removed us far from anything that causes [such] a defect. In this vein, according to the simple understanding, would we say [that] we were given a ban by the Torah against all forbidden foods. And if there are some among them whose harm is known [understood] neither by us nor by the wise men of medicine, do not wonder about them; as the faithful, trustworthy Physician who adjured us about them is wiser than both you and them. And how foolish and impulsive is the one who thinks that things don't have damage or benefit, except for that which he can grasp. And you should know that their reasons were not revealed, for our benefit; lest people who hold themselves to be great sages get up and feign wisdom to say, "X damage that the Torah stated in thing y is only in place a, whose nature is such," or "with person b, whose nature is such and such," and lest one of the dim-witted be seduced by their words. Therefore, their reason was not revealed, to aid us [avoid] this obstacle.

And it is known from the paths of medicine that the meat of all torn animals that are forbidden to us brings damage to the body of its eater, as the state of being 'torn' indicates sickness in the animal. And do not ask yourself to say, "What damage can there be in an animal that was torn and immediately slaughtered?" As it is not from wisdom that you would ask about this. Do you not know that there is a beginning to everything? And if you admit to me that in the course of time, the damage will be found in it due to its being in a status of being 'torn,' you will be obligated to admit that the damage begins from the first instant, except that it is small at first. Yet there is no doubt that even a little damage is bad. And also, all of the laws of the Torah and anything that has endurance must be like this, as if you place measurements on your words, nothing will ever be established in your hand.

Sefer HaChinukh

The laws of the commandment: For example, the [types of] 'torn' animals that were [instructed] to Moshe at Sinai, and they are the eight main categories (avot, Chullin 54a): the clawed; the pierced; the lacking; the removed; the split; the torn; the fallen and the broken. And the clawed is the most severe of all, since it is explicit in the Torah. And hence, they, may their memory be Blessed, said (Mishneh Torah, Laws of Ritual Slaughter 5:3) that any doubt that comes about it [renders it] forbidden. And with other 'torn' animals, there are some wherein a doubt is permissible. And each and every one of these main categories has many, many derivatives, as their listings come in the Gemara. And the tally of all the 'torn' animals that it is possible to find in a domesticated animal, a wild animal or a bird that comes in our hand from their listing - as it would appear from the words of the Gemara - is seventy-two, with one more in the birds than the animals. And they cannot be added to and they cannot be subtracted from; since it is possible that a domesticated animal or a wild animal or a bird could survive from any wound contracted by [other ailments], except for these that the Sages enumerated in the early generations and about which the Israelite courts agreed - and even [if] we know by way of medicine that its end is not to survive. And all of these wounds that they enumerated and said that they were [in the category of] 'torn' animals - even if it appears according to the ways of medicine in our hands that some of them do not kill and it is possible that it will survive it - you only have what the Sages enumerated, as it is stated (Deuteronomy 17:1), "According to the instruction." And each one of the seventy-two 'torn' animals that we mentioned is elucidated at length with all of its conditions in Tractate Chullin.

And a person need not search for all of these 'tearings' that the sages enumerated in animals and in birds and check them before he eats the meat of an animal or bird - since most animals are assumed to be fit (kosher), as we assume most living creatures to be healthy - except for one of them that the Sages required to check before we eat the meat, because this 'tearing' is much found. And that is the 'tearing' in the lung in which mucous membranes called sirkhot (adhesions) are found. And there is a concern with them that they not pull the tissue of the lung and puncture it. Hence, a person must always see on which side these mucous membranes are found in the lung before he eats from the animal. And if he finds them in [such] a way that it is possible that from their movement, the lung would be punctured, it is a 'torn' animal - as we say that we consider anything that stands to be punctured regardless as punctured [already]; and it is as if it is dead, since it is impossible for it to be saved from death. And it is known that this sickness that brings these mucous membranes in places that they will puncture in the future is the beginning of a sickness that brings death, as the mucous membranes have [already] formed in those places.

And these are the places that the mucous membranes 'tear' according to the principle that has come into our hands from the words of the Gemara with the good commentaries: Any place where there is an adhesion on the central bronchial tube is 'torn' and it is not permitted by way of examination, except in one way - if the adhesion is on the wall and there is a wound on the wall and the entire adhesion comes out of the place of the wound. As in this case, we say [to] check, and some permit it without checking. And there are those (Rashi on Chullin 46b) that remove from this principle [of what is automatically 'torn'] if the adhesion is on the side of the lobe from one [end of the] division to the [other end of the] division, and so is it our custom today to permit [this]. Any time that the small pink lobe which is on the right side has an adhesion, it is 'torn.' And the lobes of the lung are five, besides the small lobe, and there are three on the right side of the lobe when the animal is suspended by its legs, according to the way the butchers suspend it, and two on the left. [But] if they have adhesions or are [connected] one to the other and the adhesion comes out from one [end of the] division to the [other end of the] division, and so [too,] if the adhesions are on the ribs of the animal among which [the lungs] crouch and the adhesion goes out from the back of the lobe to the rib and clings to the ribs and the flesh between the ribs - and all the more so [if it clings] to the flesh itself - we determine all of this to be permissible. But if the adhesion come out between them from the division of the lobe to the back of [another lobe] or from one back to [the other] back, and so [too,] if it goes out from the lobe to the ribs and only clings to the bones themselves, and so [too,] in any other place in the animal at all that the lobe has an adhesion there or is [connected], we determine it to be forbidden.

And Rambam, may his memory be Blessed, removed from this principle anytime the adhesions are on the breast or the fat of the breast and determines it to be permissible (Mishneh Torah, Laws of Ritual Slaughter 11:7). But this is not our custom. An adhesion that is suspended in any place - whether from the lobe or whether from the central bronchial tube - is fit (kosher). And there are those that render it 'torn,' but our custom is to permit it. If the lobes are not to be found in this order or are lacking from this sum, it is 'torn.' And the small pink lobe replaces one lack [of a lobe]. But if [even] many more than this sum are found, it is nothing - so long as the addition is not on the side of their back. As if it is on the side of their back - even one that is as small as a myrtle leaf or smaller - it is forbidden. And there are those that permit it when it is smaller than a myrtle leaf (Mishneh Torah, Laws of Ritual Slaughter 8:4).

And the rest of the many details of this commandment are elucidated in the third chapter of Chullin. And the laws of the other prohibitions that we wrote above which are understood from the understanding of the language of the verse inside [of it] are in this same exact chapter and in the last chapter of Makkot and the first of Bekhorot. And this warning was repeated in the Prophets in the book of Ezekiel 44:31 for the priests alone, as it is written, "Any carcass or torn animal [...] the priests shall not eat." And the Sages informed us (Menachot 45a) that it was repeated [specifically] for them, as Scripture commanded them to eat the bird sin-offering with melikah (ritual decapitation), even though it is forbidden to [other Jews] like a carcass. And maybe you would think from this that non-consecrated meat would also be permissible for them with melikah or an inferior slaughtering, as the Torah is not exacting with them. As since they were excluded for one thing, they would would be excluded regarding all matters of slaughter. And therefore, the prophet warned them explicitly to inform us that melikah alone is only permissible with a sacrifice, but with non-consecrated meat, they are still forbidden like [other Jews].

And this commandment is practiced in every place and at all times by males and females. And one who transgresses it and eats a kazayit of a 'torn' animal and from all of those [things] that are implied from the understanding of the verse, "that went out of their boundaries," is lashed. And let it not be difficult to you [to ask,] "And how is he lashed - it is established for us that we do not administer lashes for a negative commandment that is part of a group, and behold, this [is a negative commandment] that included several things," as we have said." As two greats of the generations have already elucidated it in the Book of the Commandments in the ninth principle - and they are Rambam, may his memory be Blessed, and Ramban, may his memory be Blessed. And there they wrote their explanations and their proofs in detail, to clarify the thing well. And the matter would be long. Therefore, I have left it, as is my custom in [this] book. And nonetheless, you should know that it comes out of the words of both of them that this is not included as a negative commandment that is part of a group.

Mitzvah 74
To not hear the claim of a litigant when it is not in front of his fellow litigant: That the judge not hear the claim of one, not in front of his adversary, as it is stated (Exodus 23:1), "You shall not raise a false report." And the reason is because people will speak idle words when not in front of their adversary. And the judge is commanded about this so that he not bring the untruths of one of them into his soul. And so does Mekhilta d'Rabbi Yishmael 23:1 come [to tell us] that this warning of "You shall not raise, etc." is said about this. And they also said there that it is also a warning to the litigant, for him too, not to make his claims to the judge not in front of his adversary, and even if the judge wants to hear it. And about this, it is also said (Exodus 23:7), "From a false matter, distance yourself." And they, may their memory be Blessed, also said (Makkot 23a) that this negative commandment includes telling evil speech, and accepting it, and giving false testimony.

The root of this commandment is well-known, as falsehood is abominable and vile in the eyes of all. There is nothing more disgusting than it, and malediction and curse are in the house of its lovers. [This is] because God, may He be Blessed, is a truthful God, and everything that is with Him is true. And blessing is only found and resting upon those that make themselves similar to Him in their deeds: to be truthful, like He is truthful; to be merciful, like He is merciful; and to be purveyors of kindness, like He is of great kindness. But [regarding] anyone whose deeds are the opposite of His good traits and are masters of falsehood - which is exactly the opposite of His traits - the opposite of His traits will similarly always rest upon them. And the opposite of the trait of blessing which is with Him is malediction and curse; and the opposite of joy and peace and enjoyment which are with Him is worry, strife and pain. All of these are the 'evildoer's portion from God.' And therefore, the Torah warned us to distance ourselves much form falsehood, as it is written, "From a false matter, distance yourself," And behold, it used an expression of distancing, due to it being very disgusting; something it did not mention in all the other warnings. And from the side of distancing, it warned us not to bend our ears at all to anything that is considered falsehood - and even if we do not know with certainly that it is a false matter. And [this is] similar to what they, may their memory be Blessed, said (Chullin 44b), "Distance yourself from what is ugly, and from what is similar to it." And in my saying, "the traits of the Holy One, Blessed be He," I am pulled after the words of our Rabbis, may their memory be Blessed, who related to Him, may He be Blessed, the name of traits according to the side of those receiving them (people). But to Him, may He be Blessed, from His side - in His greatness and His uniqueness - one cannot ascribe traits. As He and His wisdom and His will and His power and His traits are [all] one, without any combination or division in the world.

From the laws of the commandment is that which they, may their memory be Blessed, said (Shevuot 30b) that any judge who knows about a case that it is rigged, that he is obligated to remove himself from it, and not say, "I will conclude it and the chain will be around the neck of the [lying] witnesses"; and the great praises with which the sages praised the seeking of truth and the distancing of falsehood in judgment. And the rest of its many details - are elucidated in Sanhedrin and also in the Midrash (see Mishneh Torah, Laws of The Sanhedrin and the Penalties within their Jurisdiction 25).

And [it] is practiced in every place and at all times by males, but not by females, since they do not judge. And hence they are not included in this warning, not to accept the claim of one litigant not in front of his adversary. Nonetheless, they are included in this negative commandment, that they should not make their claims to the judge not in front of the adversary. And so [too,] they are warned to distance themselves from all falsehood, like men. And behold, one who transgresses it is like he violates the commandment of the King. But we do not administer lashes for this negative commandment, as there is no act [involved] with it.

Mitzvah 75
Not to have a sinner testify: That we not accept the testimony of a man who sins, and we not do anything on account of his testimony, as it is stated (Exodus 23:1), "do not place your hand with an evildoer to be a violent witness." And the explanation comes about this (Sanhedrin 27a), "Do not place an evildoer as a witness, do not place a violent one as a witness," meaning a violent person - to exclude violent people and thieves who are disqualified from testimony, as it is stated (Deuteronomy 19:16), "If a violent witness comes upon a man."

The roots of the commandment are revealed - that anyone who is not concerned about himself and not concerned about his evil deeds will not be concerned about others. And therefore, it is not fit to believe him about a thing.

From the laws of the commandment is that which they, may their memory be Blessed, said (Mishneh Torah, Laws of Testimony 9:1) that there are ten [categories] that are disqualified from Torah writ. And they are women, slaves, minors, deaf-mutes, the mentally incapacitated, the blind, evildoers, especially disgraceful people, relatives, those that are invested in their testimony - behold, these are ten. And [those whose sex is unclear] are in the category of women (Mishneh Torah, Laws of Testimony 9:3), one who is half a slave is in the category of slaves and the epileptic is in the category of the mentally incapacitated at the time of his epilepsy. And even not during the time of his epilepsy, the judge must consider whether his mind is confused from the side of the sickness. And so [too,] the very dim-witted that do not understand [when] things contradict one another, and so [too,] people that are impulsive and rash in their thinking and very [unstable] - all of these are in the category of the mentally incapacitated. And so [too,] that which they, may their memory be Blessed, said (Sanhedrin 24b) [about] who is the one that is called an evildoer, such that he is disqualified by Torah writ, and who is the evildoer who is disqualified [rabbinically]. And among them is the dice player who does not have any other craft besides it, and the one who flies pigeons in the settlement, and those that raise [sheep and goats]. And the distinction between the [Torah's] disqualification and the [rabbinic] disqualification, that they, may their memory be Blessed, said - that the Torah's disqualification is that [if] he testified, his testimony is void even before they have proclaimed [his status], but [with] the rabbinic disqualification, his testimony stands until they proclaim [his status]. And what repentance brings him back to his being fit - and it is like Rav Idi said in the the chapter [entitled], Zeh Borer (Sanhedrin 25a); as Rav Idi bar Avin said, "One who is suspected of [selling] 'torn' animals [has no remedy to restore his fitness to bear witness] until he goes to a locale where they do not recognize him and returns a lost item of substantial value, or removes his own 'torn' animal of significant value from his possession'" and so [too] is it said similarly about another sin. And the rest of its details are elucidated there in Sanhedrin.

And this commandment is practiced in every place and at all time by males, but not by females; since they do not judge, that they should need to accept testimony. And one who transgresses it and accepted the testimony of an evil man and enacted something on account of his testimony has violated a negative commandment. But we do not administer lashes for this negative commandment, as there is no act [involved] with it. And regarding anything that [has to do with] money, even if he does an act, we [still] do not administer lashes, since it is given to return.

Mitzvah 76

Not to incline after the many in capital punishments because of one: That a judge should not go after the opinion of the majority in capital punishments when the difference will only be one man (see Sefer HaMitzvot LaRambam, Mitzvot Lo Taase 282). And the elucidation of this is that when there is a disagreement among the judges about the case of a man, and some say that he is liable for the death penalty and some say that he is not liable - and those who [would] make him liable are one more than those who [would] make him innocent - that the judge should not do with the [suspected] sinner according to the words of those who make him liable; as it is stated (Exodus 23:2), "Do not be after the many to do bad" - meaning to say, do not go after the majority that would result in concluding a verdict of death. And this is the expression stated in the Scripture, "to do bad" - meaning to say, to a liability for the death penalty. And that is when there is an exact majority, meaning to say that the decision is only because of one person. But if the decision is with two, we follow their words, even 'to do bad.' And in the Mekhilta d'Rabbi Yishmael 23:2, "Leaning to the good is according to one, but to the bad is according to two."

It is from the roots of this commandment [that it is] since we have been commanded to resemble the characteristics of God, Blessed be He, in our actions. And among His traits is that He is of great kindness, meaning that He goes beyond the letter of the law with people. And [so] we too are commanded about this, that innocence be greater than liability in capital cases, as it is something that has no repayment. And the judgments of the commandment are in the fourth chapter of Sanhedrin, as we have written above in the positive commandment of inclining towards the many (Sefer HaChinukh 78). And one who transgresses it and makes [someone] liable with a majority decided by one, has violated the commandment of the King. And his punishment is very great, as he caused the loss of a soul not in accordance with the law.

Mitzvah 77

That the one who advocated innocence at the beginning of capital cases not advocate guilt: That one of the judges not go after the opinion of another greater judge or even after the opinion of the majority, because he trusts him - to make liable or to make innocent - if the matter is not understood to him in his mind. And if it is a case that is dependent upon a decree of scripture (gezerat hakatuv), a gezerah shava or a hekesh (the latter two being exegetical inferences based on similar wording in two sections), he must know it himself and not rely and trust one of the [other] judges or the majority; as it is stated (Exodus 23:2), "and you shall not answer about a dispute to incline." [This is] meaning to say, do not say something about a dispute to incline - meaning only from the side of leaning towards

Sefer HaChinukh

the words of a great judge or towards the majority - and not from the side of your understanding. Or if you want to be silent from [saying] that which is in your heart about the case and [instead] to incline after their words, do not do so. And the language of the Mekhilta d'Rabbi Yishmael 23:2 is "'You shall not answer about a dispute to incline' - that you not say, 'It is enough for me that I be like Rabbi x,' but rather, say what is in your heart. Maybe, monetary cases are also like this? [Hence] we learn to say, 'to lean after the majority.'" And within this very negative commandment is included that the one who advocates innocence in capital cases not go back and advocate guilt; as it stated, "and you shall not answer about a dispute to incline" - meaning to say, "let not your words be inclined towards guilt" (Sanhedrin 34a). And so, too, included is that we do not open towards guilt in capital case. And the explanation then comes, "and you shall not answer about a dispute to incline," meaning to say, the opening of your words should not be for guilt. As per force, we must explain it about the beginning of the case, since it is impossible to say that it warns that you not answer guilt about about the whole case. As, if so, no man would ever be prosecuted.

And likewise, we have understood from this negative commandment (Sanhedrin 36a) that we do not begin in capital cases from the great one, but rather the one below him should first say his opinion. And this is [the understanding of] "and you shall not answer about a dispute (riv)" - [that it is] like "upon a rav (teacher); as [the word, riv,] is written without [the letter] yod [such that it could also be read as rav] - meaning to say, do not answer the great one; but rather he will answer you, since you will speak first. All these things we learned from "and you shall not answer about a dispute to incline." And this matter is from the power of the Torah's wisdom, that many things are to be learned from one thing from it. And this is [the meaning] of that which they, may their memory be Blessed, said, "There are seventy faces to the Torah" (The Letters of Rabbi Akiva). And since God knew that the people that received the Torah - in their acting in the way that they were commanded by it - would be prepared for wisdom and understanding and would understand what they need to about the functioning of the world in it, He kept the words [unelucidated] in [various] places and gave over the understanding through the great intermediary (Moshe) between them and Him. And [so] He did not give it with longer words; as all of its words are decreed, and obligated to be like they are in their count and form. As besides the understanding of its precious commandments that we understand in them, great and majestic wisdom is [also] included in it - to the point that our Rabbis, may their memory be Blessed, exalted the wisdom that God, Blessed be He, placed in it; such that they said about it (Bereshit Rabbah 1) that the Holy One, Blessed be He, looked into it and created the world. From the roots of this commandment is like that which we said at the beginning - that one of the judged not go after his colleagues, but rather he should understand the things on his own. The reason is because it is possible that from this the case will sometimes be totally [decided] by the opinion of [only] one of them. Understand the matter, as it is such. And God, may He be Blessed, did not want to give over a capital case to one opinion. But with the case of money - which is given to repayment - we are not concerned with all of this. And it is even given over to three from the outset, relying upon it being impossible that there not be any of them that did not study. And the rest of the things that we learned from it - such as the one who advocated innocence may not advocate guilt; that we do not open with guilt; and that we do not begin from the great one - all of it is out of the pity of God, may He be Blessed, upon His creatures. [It is] metaphorically like a man who has pity on his children, as it is written (Deuteronomy 14:10), "Children are you to the Lord, your God." And work upon yourself [to understand it] by way of a parable: If a man fathered a hundred and he built a city for them and placed them there, but saw that they would not survive in the community unless he decreed upon them that anyone who hits his neighbor would be punished with his money; and if he kills him, he shall be killed. And one of them got up and transgressed his decree [and killed another] - if he forgave him, behold, the community would be lost; as fear would not stay upon the [others. So] what is there for him to do and not see the death of his second son? He would nonetheless seek any way he can to exempt him according to the law. If he can, that is best, but if it is impossible in any way, he would command to kill him, so as to preserve the community [for] the others. And so is this matter - understand it.

Sefer HaChinukh

From the laws of the commandment is that which they, may their memory be Blessed, said (Sanhedrin 17a) that if they all [advocated] for guilt, that he is exempt; [that] if the ones that make him innocent and the ones that make him guilty are equal, that we add [more judges] upon them, and until how many do we add (Sanhedrin 41a); what will be if one said, "I do not know." And that which they said, that one who advocates innocence may not go back and advocate guilt, is only said about the time of give and take; but he may go back and be counted with those that make him guilty at the end of the trial. And [that] if one opened and said, "I have guilt to advocate," and became paralyzed or died, he is like one who does not know; but we see one who [would] make him innocent that dies, as if he is in his place at the end of the trial. And [that] we silence a student who comes to advocate guilt; but if he wanted to advocated innocence, we elevate him to the Sanhedrin - and if there is substance to his words, we listen to him and he never goes down from there ever; and [even] if there is no substance to his words, he does not go down from there the whole day, by way of edification. And [that] we [even] listen to the accused himself that says, "I have innocence to advocate about myself" - and that is when there is substance to his words. And the rest of its details - are [all] elucidated in the seventh chapter of Sanhedrin.

And this commandment is practiced by males but not by females, as they do not judge - as we have said above in many places. And do not let that which is written about Devorah the prophetess (Judges 4:4), "and she judged Israel," be difficult to you. As it is possible for us to answer that the judgement was not concluded according to her [word]. Rather, [since] she was a wise woman and a prophetess, they would give and take with her - even about matters of the prohibited and the permitted and also civil laws. And hence it is written about her, "and she judged Israel, etc." Or we can say that the heads of Israel accepted her upon them - and after them, everyone - to decide according to her [word]. As everyone is fit [to judge] with acceptance [of the parties involved], since any condition upon money is valid (Ketuvot 56a). And nonetheless, all this that we have said that they do not judge is according to the opinion of some commentators and the opinion of the Yerushalmi (Talmud Yerushalmi Sanhedrin 3:9) - as such is it found there explicitly. But according to the opinion of some commentators, they are fit to judge. And they said that it is an open verse [that proves this] - as it is stated, "and she judged." And [about] that which they said in Sanhedrin 34b that anyone who is not fit to testify is not fit to judge - and women are certainly not fit to testify, as is proven there - it is possible that they would say, according to their opinion, that this is [not an issue] since we do not learn from general principles (Eruvin 27a). But what appears [correct] from the [sources] and from logic is that they are not [included] in the category of judgment, as it is found in the Yerushalmi and as it is implied in our Gemara (Bavli) by way of simple understanding.

And this commandment is practiced only in the Land of Israel, as we only judge capital cases there. And one who transgresses it and does not want to advocate that which he sees in his mind in the case and relies upon his colleagues; or opens with guilt; or goes back and advocates guilt after [he advocated] innocence; or a great one that opens first - has violated a negative commandment. But we do not administer lashes for it, as there is no act [involved] with it.

Mitzvah 78

The commandment of inclining towards the many: To incline towards the many, and that is when there arise a disagreement among the sages in a law of all the Torah laws - and so too in a private case, meaning to say a case that would be between Reuven and Shimon, for example - when there would be a disagreement between the judges of their city, that some of them rule guilty and some rule innocent, to always go after the majority; as it is stated (Exodus 32:2), "to incline towards the many." And in the elucidation, they, may their memory be Blessed, said (Chullin 11a), "The majority is by writ of the Torah." And this choice of the majority appears to be when the two opposing groups are equally known for their Torah wisdom - as it cannot be said that a small group of sages would not be decisive against a great group of ignoramuses, and even like [the number] that went out from Egypt. But with approximately equal wisdom, the Torah informed us that the many opinions will always conform to the truth more than the minority. But whether - according to the opinion of the listener - they agree to the truth or they do not agree to the truth, logic dictates that we do not swerve from the path of the majority. And that which I say that the choice of the majority is always with two groups that disagree that are equal in the wisdom of truth is said so about every place except for the Sanhedrin. As with them, we are not exacting when they disagree as to which group knows more; but rather we always do like the words of their majority. And the reason is because they had an obligatory number [of people] by writ of the Torah; and it is as if the Torah explicitly commanded, "Do all of your matters according to the majority of these" - and also, as they were all great sages.

It is from the roots of the commandment that we were commanded through this to strengthen the fulfillment of our religion. As if we were commanded, "Keep the Torah, according to how you are able to understand its intended truth," each and every one in Israel would say, "It follows from my opinion that the truth of matter x is such." And [so,] even if the whole world would say its opposite, he would not be allowed to do the matter contrary to the truth, according to his opinion. And destruction would come from this, as the Torah would turn into many Torahs - since every one would judge according to the poverty of his [own] opinion. But now that we have been explicitly commanded to accept the opinion of the sages about it, there is one Torah for all of us, and its performance is great through this. And we may not budge from their opinion, whatever the case. And so, in our doing their commandments, we are executing the commandments of God. And even if the sages sometimes do not reach [come to] the truth - God forbid - the sin will be upon them and not upon us. And this is the matter that they, may their memory be Blessed, said in Horayot 2a that [if] a court erred in a ruling and an individual acted upon their [word], they have liability for a sacrifice, [while] the individual does not at all, except in the [cases] that are explained there.

The laws of the commandment are, for example, the differences that there is about this majority if it is in monetary cases or capital cases - as capital case require that the majority be more distinct; how many people we need for capital cases, whereby we are commanded to follow the words of the majority and [that] it is not fit to kill a man with two judges, which are a majority, against one. So [too,] that which they, may their memory be Blessed, said (Sanhedrin 37a) that those that make a majority in capital cases must also be ordained, and that ordination testifies about them that they are wise, understanding and fit, [such] that everything should be done through them. And [this is so] that we not kill people through people lacking wisdom, lest they err in judgment - as there is no repayment for the death penalty. And that those that advocate innocence in capital cases may not go back and advocate guilt and that it is not so in monetary cases; that we open with innocence in capital cases, and behold, the one who opened like this is removed from the group advocating guilt; and that anyone may advocate innocence, whether a teacher or a student. And the rest of its details are elucidated at the end of Sanhedrin.

And [it] is practiced in every place and at all times by males and females. And one that transgresses it and did not incline towards them has violated a positive commandment; and his punishment is very great, as [this] is the pillar upon which the Torah rests.

Mitzvah 79
To not have mercy upon a poor person in his case: To not have pity in judgment upon the weak and impoverished at the time of the judgment, but rather one must judge the case truthfully. [It should not be] from the angle of pity upon him, but rather [the judge] must treat [all] the same - whether he is rich or impoverished - to force him to pay what he is obligated; as it is stated (Exodus 23:3), "And you shall not favor an impoverished man in his dispute." And this matter is repeated in another place (Leviticus 19:15), "do not lift up the face of the impoverished." And the language of Sifra, Kedoshim, Chapter 4:2 is "Do not say, 'He is a poor man and since I and this rich man are obliged to sustain him, I shall vindicate him in judgment, so that he can support himself honorably.' [Hence,] we learn to say, 'do not lift up the face of the impoverished.'"

And the root of this commandment is well-known, as the intellect testifies to equitability in judgment - since it is a fit and proper thing.

And [it] is practiced in every place and at all times by males. And one who transgresses it and [tips] the judgment in pity of the impoverished has violated the commandment of [the] King. But there are no lashes for it, since there is no act [involved] with it.

Sefer HaChinukh

Mitzvah 80
The commandment of removing a burden: To remove a burden from upon the donkey that is weary from its burden upon the way, as it is stated (Exodus 23:5), "If you see the donkey of your enemy, etc." - and the understanding of this enemy, is [another Jew]. And even though it is written (Leviticus 19:17), "Do not hate your brother in your heart," which [refers to a Jew] - the Sages said (Pesachim 113b) that this matter is for example that he saw him commit a sin privately, and he warned [the one sinning] but he did not yield, such that he is [then] permitted to hate him. And that which it states, "donkey," is not specifically a donkey, but rather that the Scripture expressed that which is common - as donkeys are [used for carrying] a burden. And it is written, "you must certainly relieve with him" - meaning to say, help him, from the usage (Nehemiah 3:8), "and they relieved Jerusalem," which is an expression of strengthening.

It is from the roots of the commandment to train our souls in the trait of compassion, which is a praiseworthy trait. And there is no need to say that there is an obligation to have compassion on a person in pain in his body. But even [upon] one who is in pain due to the loss of his money is there a commandment upon us to have compassion upon him and save him.

The laws of this commandment are, for example, if the animal is of a gentile and his load is of [a Jew] or the opposite; and the law of one who runs into his friend and his enemy [both of whom are Jewish], such that the commandment is towards the enemy in order to constrain the [evil] impulse, and even when it is to unload the friend and to load the enemy (Bava Metzia 32b), and that the enemy [in this case] is not the enemy we mentioned - coming from a sin - but is one with whom his heart is not complete. And from when is the obligation understood by "If you see," and that the sages estimated it to be one in seven and a half parts of a mil and that is a ris (Mishneh Torah, Laws of Murderer and the Preservation of Life 13:6); but further than this measure, there is no obligation to go out of one's way for him - yet one who goes beyond the letter of the law is fit for a blessing. And the law of an elder and it is not according to his station, which is all determined according to what he would do for his own [property] (Bava Metzia 30b). And the law of unloading for free and loading for a wage; that he goes with him for a parsah, and that he receives a wage for the accompaniment, as is elucidated (Bava Metzia 33a). It is all in the second chapter of [Bava] Metzia (see Tur, Choshen Mishpat 84).

And [it] is practiced in every place and at all times by males and females. And one who transgresses it has violated a positive commandment and shown the trait of cruelty in himself, which is an ugly trait. And anyone who does not have mercy, is not shown mercy from the Heavens, as his body is not fit for mercy (Shabbat 151b).

Mitzvah 81
To not tip the judgment of an evildoer: To not tip the judgment of one of the litigants when one knows that he is an evildoer and a master of sin, as it is stated (Exodus 23:6), "You shall not sway the judgment of your destitute in his quarrel." And its explanation is that he is destitute in commandments, as its understanding is not that he is destitute in money; since it is not necessary to say that he not sway the judgment against him, to steal from him in his poverty. Rather, we have been commanded that even though he is an evildoer, the judge should not say, "Since he is an evildoer, I will sway the judgment against him" - as the judgment of evildoers is for God, and not for you. And so is it in Mekhilta, "[If] an evildoer and a proper man stand in front of you in judgment, you might say, etc."

The root of equitablity in judgment for all men is something rational.

And [it] is practiced in all places and at all times by males, but not by females, as they do not judge. And [one who] transgresses it and sways the judgment against an evildoer, has violated the commandment of [the] King.

Mitzvah 82
To not conclude the judgment by estimation: That a court only kill the accused with witnesses that testify about the same matter about which he is to be killed; that they actually saw him with their eyes, [not] that they testify against him based on strong indications. And about this is it stated (Exodus

23:7), "and an innocent one and a righteous one you shall not kill" - meaning to say, be very careful not to kill a person about whom it is possible that he did not do what they said that he did. And so is it explained in Mekhilta d'Rabbi Yishmael 23:7:2, as there they said, "If they saw him pursuing another to kill him, the knife in his hand, and they [warned him, 'If you kill him, you will be killed.' And the witnesses] averted their eyes [and did not see him striking him] and afterwards they found him (the victim) in the death throes, the knife dripping blood in the hand of the murderer — I might understand that he is liable [for execution. Hence,] we learn to say, 'and a clean one and righteous one you shall not kill.'" Behold, because they averted their eyes at the time of the striking, this one is exempted. And the matter is proper and fitting to be like this. As if the Torah had permitted to establish the parameters of punishment with strong possibilities, it would come out from the matter that sometimes we would kill people for something they did not do, as there is great breadth to the possible. And know this and understand it, as it is a clear thing. And therefore, He, may He be elevated, closed this gate and commanded us about it. And all of "the precepts of the Lord are just, rejoicing the heart" (Psalms 19:9). And also included in this negative commandment is one about whom two witnesses have testified that he committed a [different] sin; for example, that one testifies that he did work on Shabbat and one testifies that he worshiped idolatry, such that this one is not condemned by their testimony, as it is stated, "and an innocent one and a righteous one do not kill." And so did they, may their memory be Blessed, say (Mekhilta d'Rabbi Yishmael 23:7:2), "If one testified against another that he worshiped the sun, and another, [that he worshiped] the moon, I might understand that they combine (to constitute the necessary two witnesses). [Hence,] we learn to say, 'and an innocent one and righteous one you shall not kill.'"

The root of this commandment is revealed to all, as we have said.

Its laws - that which they, may their memory be Blessed, said (Makkot 6b), that their testimony is not combined even if they testify about the same sin unless they both saw it [together]; also that they saw each other at the time of the act, to exclude if this one saw it from this window and the other from another window and they could not see each other, but the one who gives the warning combines them if he saw both of them; and the rest of its details - are in Sanhedrin.

And [it] is practiced in the Land of Israel by males, since justice is with them, as we have said many times; but not by females, as they do not judge. And one who transgresses it and judges according to testimony that is not precise - as we have said - has violated a commandment of [the] King. And his punishment is very great, as he causes souls to be killed, not according to the law. And Ramban (on Sefer HaMitzvot LaRambam, Mitzvot Lo Taase 290), may his memory be Blessed, counted this verse as two negative commandments about a different matter. And that is that [the accused] is exempted in capital cases, in ways through which he would be liable in monetary cases. And he relied upon that which they said in the Gemara (Sanhedrin 33b), "The Sages taught, 'From where is it derived that one who is leaving the court liable, and someone said, "I can advocate his innocence," that we bring [the accused] back [to be judged again]? The verse states, "and an innocent one you shall not kill"'" - meaning to say [that] this one is innocent, as maybe this one will advocate that he is innocent. "And from where is it derived that one who is leaving the court innocent, and someone says, 'I can advocate his guilt,' that we do not bring [the accused] back [to be judged again]? The verse states, 'a righteous one you shall not kill'" - and this one is righteous, as he already left [the court] righteous (innocent). And all of these matters are from the root that I have written - that God wanted that we mull every merit for the accused, as he may repent and regret the evil that he did and become from those that civilize the world. And He, Blessed be He, desires its civilization.

Mitzvah 83

To not take a bribe: That the judge not take a bribe from the litigants - even to judge truthfully - as it is stated (Exodus 23:8), "And you shall not take a bribe." And this negative commandment is repeated in the Torah about this matter in another place (Deuteronomy 16:19). And so did they say in Sifrei Devarim 144:10, "'You shall not take a bribe' - even to make the innocent, innocent and the liable, liable."

It is from the roots of the commandment that it was forbidden to us to take a bribe even to judge a case truthfully, in order to remove this bad practice from among us, lest we will come from this to judge falsely with bribes. And it is a clear thing - it does not need a proof.

From the laws of the commandment is that which they, may their memory be Blessed, said (Mishneh Torah, Laws of The Sanhedrin and the Penalties within their Jurisdiction 23:1, 3) that the one who gives and the one who takes it [both] transgress a negative commandment - the one who gives it because of (Leviticus 19:14), "before the blind," and the one who takes it is included in the curse (Deuteronomy 27:25). And [that] he is obligated to return it; and that it is forbidden for a judge to raise his stature on purpose in order to provide more pay for his scribes. And that it is even forbidden to take an oral bribe - but rather if maybe the litigants honor him with words, he should show himself as if he does not pay attention at all to the words. The general principle of the thing is that it is forbidden for the judge to accept any benefit from the litigants at all for his judgments. But if the judge is a craftsman, the Sages allowed him to take a wage while he is involved in their case, for his idleness from his craft - and that is when the matter is recognizable that it is only a wage for idleness, but not more; and he takes equally from both of them. And the rest of its details - are in Sanhedrin (see Mishneh Torah, Laws of The Sanhedrin and the Penalties within their Jurisdiction 23).

And [it] is practiced in every place and at all times by males, as they judge. And one who transgresses it and receives a bribe, violates the commandment of [the] King. But he is not lashed, as it is given to returning.

Mitzvah 84

The commandment of the releasing (shmitat) of lands: To make ownerless everything that the earth put out in the seventh year, which is called the shmitta (release) year, because of this process in which we are obligated; and that all who want to [take] its fruits may do so - as it is stated (Exodus 23:11), "But the seventh you shall release it and abandon it, and the needy among your people will eat of it, and what they leave the beasts will eat; you shall do the same with your vineyards and your olive groves." And the language of Mekhilta DeRabbi Shimon bar Yochai 23:11: "And were the vineyared and the olive groves not included?" [This] means to say that the beginning of the verse that stated, "release it and abandon it" includes everything that grows in the earth, whether they are fruits of the tree or fruits of the ground. And [so] why did Scripture specify these two? "To compare the other types of trees to the vineyard, to teach that like there is a positive commandment and a negative commandment with the vineyard - as behold, it is written explicitly about it (Leviticus 25:5), "and the grapes that you set aside, do not reap" - so too, is there a positive commandment and a negative commandment in all of the other trees." And hence, it specified vineyard and olive grove, to teach about this matter. As the intention of the verse was not specifically about the vineyard and olive grove alone, but rather it is the same with all the other fruits of the tree. Rather, it mentioned one of them and it teaches about all of them, as this is one of the devices through which the Torah is expounded. And this commandment to make all of the fruits ownerless and the other commandment that God commanded us to rest in it - as it is stated (Exodus 34:21), "and rest from plowing and reaping" - are [both] connected.

It is from the roots of this commandment to affix in our hearts and make a strong impression in our minds [about] the matter of the world having been created. As (Exodus 20, 11) "in six days did God make the heavens and the earth, and on the seventh day" - in which He did not create anything - He imposed rest on Himself. And in order to remove and uproot and eradicate from our thoughts the idea of the eternity [of the world] - which the deniers of the Torah believe in, through which they destroy all its principles and break through its walls - did the requirement come upon us to expend all our time, day by day and year by year, for this matter, by counting six years and resting on the seventh so that this matter will never depart from between our eyes for all time. And this is similar to the manner in which we count the days of the week [by dividing them] into six days of work and the seventh is a day of rest. Therefore, He, Blessed be He, did command to render ownerless all that the land produces in this year - in addition to resting during it (i.e. during the year) - so that a person will remember that the land which produces fruits for him every year does not produce them by its [own] might and virtue. For there is a Master over it and over its master - and when He wishes, He commands him (i.e. the master of the land) to render them (i.e. the fruit) ownerless. And there is another benefit in this matter - to acquire the trait of letting go (i.e. of one's possessions), for there is no one more generous than he who gives without hope for recompense. And there is another benefit - the outcome of this is that a person will add to his trust in God, may He be Blessed, since anyone who finds it in his heart to give and abandon to the world all of the produce of his lands and his ancestral inheritance for an entire year - and educates himself and his family through this for all of his days - will never have the trait of stinginess overcome him too much, nor will he have a deficient amount of trust.

From the laws of the commandment is what are the [types] of work on the land about which there is an obligation of rest by Torah writ - such as planting, pruning, reaping and harvesting; and that are forbidden by rabbinic writ - such as fertilizing, digging and work on trees such as cutting off excrescences, removing dry leave or stalks from it, placing dust [on exposed roots], raising smoke below it to kill insects, oiling saplings, pruning and removing trees; and that which they permitted to do, such as reddening with dye, hoeing under grape vines. And the law of an irrigated field. And that they should not make a dungpile in his field until the time of fertilizing is over; and that afterwards it be big and not appear like fertilizing - and its size is from one hundred and fifty seah and above. That which they said (Moed Katan 3b) that the obligation to refrain from working the land is from thirty days before the seventh year and that this is a law given to Moshe at Sinai (halacha le'Moshe miSinai). And the law of how much time from the sixth year is forbidden to work in a field of trees, and what is called a field of trees. And the prohibition of implanting shoots in the ground and grafting; what is [to be done with] his saplings; what is the law of the fruits of the seventh [year] - as we do not make a medicinal chew or a bandage from anything that is uniquely for human food, such as wheat and barley and fruits, as with them it states, "to eat it." But we do make a medicinal chew or a bandage for humans - though not for animals - from anything that is uniquely for animal food, such as thorns and thistles. And behold, that which is not uniquely for humans or animals - such as rubia, hyssop and thyme - depends on the designation of the person: [If] he designated them for food, their law is like food; but [if] he designated them for wood, their law is like wood. And the rest of its many details are elucidated in the tractate that is built upon this, and that is Tractate Sheviit (see Mishneh Torah, Laws of Sabbatical Year and the Jubilee 4).

And [it] is practiced by males and females in the Land of Israel only, at the time that [the people of] Israel is there - as it is stated about it (Leviticus 25:2), "When you come to the land." And it is practiced rabbinically even at this time, only in the Land. And any place (Mishnah Sheviit 5:1) that those [Jews] that came up form Babylonia controlled until Keziv - but not including Keziv - is included in the prohibition of work, and all of the aftergrowth that grows there is forbidden to eat. As [these Jews] sanctified the places that they controlled forever. But in the places that those [Jews] that came up from Egypt controlled, but not those that came up from Babylonia - which is from Keziv to the river and to Amanah - even though, since they were stringent about [it], they are rabbinically forbidden today regarding work on the seventh [year], [nonetheless] the aftergrowth that grows there is permissible to eat; as it was not sanctified by those that that came up from Babylonia. And it is permissible even [for work] from the river and from Amanah and further. [With regards to] Syria, even though the seventh [year] is not practiced in it from Torah writ, they decreed that those places should be forbidden in work like the Land of Israel. And Syria is from the places that David conquered before all of the Land of Israel was conquered - and that is what our Rabbis, may their memory be Blessed, called the conquest of an individual (Mishneh Torah, Laws of Heave Offerings 1:3, 9). And that land corresponds to Aram Nehorayim and Aram Tsovah, all along the Euprates to Babylonia, [including] such [places] as Damascus and Allepo and Charan and other places close to these. But the seventh [year] is not practiced in Ammon, Moav, Egypt and Shinnar, even though they are obligated in tithing (Mishnah Yadayim 4:3). And all the more so is it not practiced in the other places outside of the Land. And one who transgresses it and seals his vineyard or his field on the seventh [year] - or gathered all of his fruits into his house at the time that Israel is on their land - has violated a positive commandment. And nonetheless it is permissible to gather from them to his house a little bit at a time to eat - so long as the hand of everyone is equal in them, as if there were no known owners to the land.

Mitzvah 85
The commandment to rest on Shabbat: To rest from work on the Shabbat day, as it is stated (Exodus 23:12), "on the seventh day you shall rest" (Sefer HaMitzvot LaRambam, Mitzvot Ase 154). All of its content is written above in the negative commandment that comes about it (Sefer HaChinukh 32). And the commandment of Shabbat is repeated up to twelve times.

Mitzvah 86
To not swear by idolatry: That we not swear by idolatry - and even to its worshipers - and that we not make a gentile swear by it, as it is stated (Exodus 23:13), "and you shall not mention the name of other gods." And we have understood that included in this mentioning is whether one swears or causes to swear. And there are some that explain that the main negative commandment [here] is only coming about one who does business with a gentile on his holiday and makes him profit, as he goes and thanks [his god], and [so] he transgresses "you shall not mention"; meaning that others should not mention it in the forbidden manner, which is with intention to serve them. As this is forbidden also to [gentiles] by Torah writ, since the Children of Noach are prohibited in idolatry. And they, may their memory be Blessed, added a distancing and said (Sanhedrin 63b) that a man should not say to his fellow, "Wait for me by the side of idolatry x."

It is from the roots of the commandment to distance any matter of idolatry - whether in deed or in speech - to the point that its memory not rise up in our hearts ever. And our Rabbis, may their memory be Blessed, noted and said that the Torah warned us about it forty-four times, due to its great vileness. Go and count [them].

From the laws of the commandment is that which they said that it is forbidden to mention the name of idolatry even not by way of an oath; and that the name of all idolatry written in the Holy Books (Bible) is permissible to mention - such as Peor (Numbers 23:28), and Bel and Nevo (Isaiah 46:1), and similar to them. And that it is forbidden to cause others to vow or to affirm with the name of idolatry, but the only one to get lashed is the one that makes the oath or the one that makes the affirmation in its name - meaning the one who swears, himself, and not the one who makes him swear, even though the one who makes someone swear is also included in this negative commandment, according to the opinion of Rambam, may his memory be Blessed. And the rest of its details are elucidated in the seventh chapter of Sanhedrin.

And [it] is practiced in every place and at all times by males and by females. And one who transgresses it and swears by something from all of the creatures in which foolish heretics believe on account of the greatness [of these creatures] is liable for lashes - so wrote the rabbi (Rambam), may his memory be Blessed. [This is so] even though there is no act [involved] with it, due to the great stringency of idolatry.

Mitzvah 87
To not entice the Children of Israel towards idolatry: To not call people to worship idolatry and to urge them about it. And even though the one who calls does not worship it and does not do any of the actions [of idolatry] - just the calling alone - this is called an enticer. And so did they say in Sanhedrin 63b), "'It should not be heard on your mouth' - that is a warning to the enticer." And so did they say in the Mekhilta.

The root of this commandment is well-known.

Its laws are in the tenth chapter of Sanhedrin. And one who only entices one person in this manner is not called an enticer (mediach) but rather a seducer (mesit). And in the Order of Reeh Anochi (Sefer HaChinukh 462), we will write [about] the prohibition of the seducer, with God's help. But when he entices two people or more, he is called an enticer. And [about] that which you find all of these distancings about idolatry and the greatness of the punishment for it and that it is repeated in forty-four places in the Torah and that Torah refers to God, Blessed be He, as jealous about its worshipers

- do not let it come into your heart that the jealousy of God and all of these distancings were written except from the side of the worshippers. As there is no angle of addition or subtraction that occurs in the glory of God, Blessed be He and Blessed be His name, if people worship Him or worship an angel or a sphere or a star or one of all of His creatures. As total glory and majesty cannot be added to or subtracted from, on account of anything - even as we are His creations, His doings, the people of bodies. Rather, know that truthfully all of these matters are said from the angle of the receivers - that it be said that at the time that a person completely removes himself and strips [his] faith in God, Blessed be He, and takes his body and entangles his thoughts to follow vanity, he will not be fit at all that any blessing and any good should rest upon him. Rather, he will be fit that everything that is the opposite of blessing - and that is curse and malediction and sicknesses and all bad things - rest upon him. As he has completely distanced all boundaries of the good from himself and, so, only evil will come to him from every angle. And by way of a metaphor, it is said about Him, as if God, may He be Blessed, who is the Master of good, becomes his enemy and blocks all good from him; and as if He is jealous about him, due to his leaving His service and serving others. However, God, Blessed be He, is not indebted to any man, nor jealous of any man. As it is in His hand to reverse them all - together with the rest of the world - to null and void, by resting His will on nullification; in the same way that He created them by resting his Will on creation. [Rather], God, Blessed be He, is referred to as jealous, by way of the deeds of men. As there is no greater hatred among them than one who is jealous of a man about any thing, or one who is jealous about his wife for her licentiousness with others. And hence, these comparisons were written in the Torah about Him, Blessed be He, in order that they should enter the ears of the hearer (see Mishneh Torah, Laws of Foreign Worship and Customs of the Nations 4).

And this prohibition is practiced in every place and at all times by males and females. But the law of one who transgresses it - whether a man or a woman - which is stoning, is only in the place that is fitting for judgement, and that is the Chosen Land.

Mitzvah 88

The commandment of celebration on the festivals: To celebrate on the festivals; and that is that we have been commanded to come up for the festival to the Temple three times a year - and they are [before] Pesach, Shavouot and Sukkot, in order to celebrate there, as it is stated (Exodus 23:14), "Three festivals shall you celebrate for Me in the year." And the matter of celebration is that we should go up there with a sacrifice and we slaughter it as peace-offerings (shelamim) in honor of the festival. And this commandment is repeated twice in the Torah. And they, may their memory be Blessed, said in Tractate Chagigah 10b [that] three commandments was Israel commanded on the holiday - celebration, being seen and joy.

It is from the roots of this commandment [that it is] because it is not appropriate to come in front of Him, Blessed be He, with empty hands. And even though the truth is that He does not need a thing from our hands, as it is written (Psalms 50:12), "Were I hungry, I would not tell you" - nonetheless in the imagination of our thoughts, we see [it] as if we were standing in front of Him. And the truth is that the souls are closer to the good in that place than in other places and [that] the light of the face of [the] King shines upon them there. And therefore, it is fit for us to do the act of sacrifice at that time. As through the action of the sacrifice, we become prepared for receiving the good and our souls rise ever higher - as we shall write, with God's help.

From the laws of the commandment is that which they, may their memory be Blessed, said (Mishnah Peah 1:1 at the beginning) that these sacrifices do not have a measure - that even one would suffice, whether it be an animal or whether it be a bird, a dove or a chick. And that he needs to go up to Jerusalem regardless with a sacrifice in his hand, or with money to buy the sacrifice in Jerusalem. But he is not exempted with [an object that has] the value of money. And [that] if he did not sacrifice his sacrifice on the first day, he is able to make it up for seven full days (Chagigah 9a) - so long as he be there on the first days. And the rest of its details - are [all] elucidated in Tractate Chagigah (see Mishneh Torah, Laws of Festival Offering 1).

Sefer HaChinukh

And [it] is practiced at the time of the Temple by males, but not by females. And it is not all males [that are obligated]. As anyone who is lame or blind - even in one of his eyes - or sick or old or very pampered, such that he could not go up by foot is exempt; and so [too, those the sex of which is in doubt] and slaves. But all other males are obligated, and even if they have an ugly trade, such as a manure collector, a smith and a tanner (Chagigah 4a). They clean their bodies and clothes and go up in front of God, may He be Blessed, and are accepted like the rest of Israel. As a dirty soul is that which is disgusting about people in front of the Omnipresent, and not a craft - so long as it is done honestly. And one who transgresses it and appears in the courtyard on the first day of the festival and does not bring a sacrifice has violated a positive commandment. And he has also violated a negative commandment, as it is stated about this (Exodus 23:15), "and they shall not see My face empty-handed."

Mitzvah 89
That we not slaughter the lamb of the Pesach offering on the fourteenth of Nissan while chamets is still in our possession: That we not slaughter the lamb of the Pesach offering on the fourteenth of Nissan while chamets still be in our possession - until half of the day, as they, may their memory be Blessed, expounded (Pesachim 5a),"[The word,] 'but,' divides" - as it is stated (Exodus 23:18), "Do not slaughter upon chamets the blood of my slaughtering." And the explanation of it comes [to tell us] not to slaughter the lamb of the Pesach sacrifice while chamets still exist in your possession. And this preventing is repeated in the Torah, with a different expression. And we have also understood that included in the explanation is that chamets not be with the one who slaughters it (Pesachim 13b) and not be with the one that sprinkles its blood and not be with the one that makes its fat smoke and not be with one of the assemblages that is counted upon it (Pesachim 63b).

It is from the roots of the commandment [that it is] because it is something known to every man that setting the time for all matters is the preservation of their doing. And so, with the matter of Pesach - which is a big thing for us in preserving the religion, as we have written above (Sefer HaChinukh 21) - God, Blessed be He, commanded that we do its content in order, and in set times for each and every part of its things; and that no commandment from the matter of the commandments of this time period come into the boundary of its fellow. And therefore, we were warned to first dispose of the chamets which is disgusting in our eyes at its time; and afterwards to begin with the Pesach sacrifice, which is the beginning of the good time period. But also, if we hear better than this, we will hold from it.

From the laws of the commandment - that which they said (Pesachim 61a), that the time of its slaughter is after midday and that if it is slaughtered before midday it is disqualified; that even though its time is after midday, it is ideally not slaughtered until after the daily afternoon sacrifice, after they burnt the incense of the afternoon, [and] also after [a priest] has prepared the lights [of the menorah]; and the rest of its details - are in Pesachim (see Mishneh Torah, Laws of Paschal Offering 1).

And [it] is practiced in the time of the Temple by males and by females. And one who transgresses it and consciously leaves a kazayit of chamets in his possession at the time of its sacrifice - whether he sacrifices it or sprinkles [its blood] or burns the portions to be burnt or even [if he is] one from all of those counted in the assemblage for its eating - is lashed. But the Pesach sacrifice is fit nonetheless.

Mitzvah 90
To not leave the entrails of the Pesach sacrifice to stay overnight: Not to leave the entrails of the Pesach sacrifice until the morning, [such] that they not be sacrificed, and [so] become disqualified with this leaving over and become called notar (what is left over); as it is stated (Exodus 23:18), "and the fat of My festival offering shall not be left lying until morning." And the same is true of other portions to be burned in other sacrifices. And the language of Mekhilta d'Rabbi Yishmael 23:18 is "'The fat shall not be left lying' - the verse comes to teach that the fats are disqualified by lying over." And this preventing was already repeated in another place, as it is stated (Exodus 34:25), "and the sacrifice of the festival of Pesach shall not be left lying until morning."

Sefer HaChinukh

It is from the roots of the commandment [that it is] because it is the honor of a sacrifice to sacrifice it at its time that is set for it. And one who passes the set time appears like one who abandons [it] and throws the matter over his back; and he does not arouse himself and properly place his intentions upon the service. And because of this, [the portions to be burned] become disqualified with it.

From the laws of the commandment - that which they said (Pesachim 64b) that it is a commandment to burn the entrails of each and every sacrifice on its own; that which they said (Menachot 72a), that the commandment of their burning is after their slaughter, close upon [it], and if he did not burn them like this, he can burn them the whole night until the dawn (amud hashachar), and [this is] specifically when the fourteenth of Nissan comes out to be on Shabbat, since the fats of Shabbat [sacrifices] can be sacrificed on a holiday, but if the fourteenth of Nissan fell out to be [a weekday], we do not burn them at night, as we do not burn the fats of [weekday sacrifices] on a holiday, since [the sanctity of a] holiday is a positive and a negative commandment and [so] push off the negative commandment of "it shall not be left lying;" and the rest of its details - are found in Pesachim (see Mishneh Torah, Laws of Paschal Offering 1).

And [it] is practiced at the time of the Temple by male priests. And one who transgresses it and does not sacrifice them is not lashed, as there is no act [involved] with it.

Mitzvah 91
The commandment of bringing the first-fruits: To bring the first-fruits to the Temple - and that is that we are obligated to bring there the first fruit that ripens on a tree and to give it to a priest. And not all trees are in this commandment from Torah writ, but rather only the seven species through which the Land of Israel is praised - and they are wheat, barley, the [fruit of the] vine, figs, pomegranates, olives and dates - as it is stated (Exodus 23:19), "The first fruits of your land you shall bring, etc." and the explanation comes that it is only stated about these seven fruits. And according to what it appears, it is in this way that they, may their memory be Blessed, learned to say like this: Since no other fruits at all are mentioned in any place in the Torah besides these, and He, Blessed be He, commanded us to bring undifferentiated first-fruits from our land, it follows that it is about the fruits that He informed us about in the Torah that are in the Land of Israel and through which it is praised, that He commanded us. And it is possible that our Rabbis, may their memory be Blessed, have another [indication] from the verse, or maybe they are words of transmission. And so was it their way to bring them, that those close to Jerusalem would bring them soft (fresh) and those far would dry them [first].

It is from the roots of the commandment [that it is] in order to put the word of God, may He be Blessed, 'at the top of our joy,' and that we remember and we know that it is from Him, Blessed be He, that all of the blessings of the world come to us. Therefore, we were commanded to bring the first fruit that ripens in the trees to those that serve His house. And through the remembering and the acceptance of His kingdom and our thanking in front of Him that the fruits and the rest of all of the good comes from Him, we will be fit for blessing and our fruits will be Blessed.

From the laws of the commandment - that which they, may their memory be Blessed, said (Makkot 19b) that they are forbidden once they enter Jerusalem to a [non-priest] like the priestly tithe; from which fruits do we bring first-fruits from rabbinic writ; that we give first-fruits to the men of the [priestly] watch [on duty]; that they require a vessel and it [goes] to the priest, if they are of wood; that a person should not bring them mixed up, but rather in a beautiful way, for example that he place palm leaves or [other] leaves between each and every specie and surround the basket of figs with clusters of grapes around its rim; [that] they bring in their hands turtle-doves and pigeons in honor of the first-fruits and give them to the priests; how they would bring them up, and the joy about them which the ones who brought them up and the ones going out to greet them would show; the psalms that they would read close to the city; and the rest of its details - are elucidated in Tractate Bikkurim (see Mishneh Torah, Laws of First Fruits and other Gifts to Priests Outside the Sanctuary 4).

And [it] is practiced at the time of the Temple by males with fruits of the Land of Israel and of Syria and of Transjordan, but not with fruits from outside of the Land. And one who transgresses it has violated a positive commandment.

Sefer HaChinukh

Mitzvah 92
To not cook meat in milk: That we not cook animal meat in animal milk, as it is stated (Exodus 23:19), "you shall not cook a kid in its mother's milk." And the explanation came (Chullin 113a) that it is not specifically a kid, but rather all meat of an animal is implied - as the expression, "kid" is an expression that only [applies to] animal meat. And the verse [chose] the expression, "kid," since meat is a soft thing, like a kid. And how is it that you learn like this? From that which you find in several places in the Torah where it is written, "kid," and it was necessary [for the Torah] to explain, "a goat kid." Behold, you have learned [from this] that in a place where is stated only, "kid," it is not specifically, a goat kid, but rather all animal meat like it is implied.

It is from the roots of this commandment, according to what appears, that it is similar to the matter that we wrote about the commandment of the witch (Sefer HaChinukh 62), that there are things in the world the mixture of which are forbidden to us, for the reason of the matter that we said there. And it is possible that the reason for the prohibition of the mixture of meat and milk through the process of cooking is from this foundation. And there is somewhat of a proof to this, since the prohibition comes to us with the action of mixing, even though we do not eat it; such that we see from this that its prohibition is not because of the damage [caused by] its eating at all. Rather [it is] that we do not do the action of that mixing, for the sake of the distancing of that matter that we said. And we have also been warned in another place, that if we maybe make the mixture, we should not eat it and not derive benefit from it, to distance the matter [further]. And he is lashed even if he ate it without deriving benefit (enjoyment) from it at all (Pesachim 25a), which is not the case with all the other forbidden foods. And all of this teaches that the foundation of its reason is because of the mixture, and like the matter that we said about magic. This is said out of duress, and we still need the knowledge of the mystic. And Rambam, may his memory be Blessed, said (Guide for the Perplexed 3:48) that there are some idolaters that worship through the act of mixing meat and milk. And that is why the Torah distanced that mixture. 'But none of this is worthwhile for me.

We will write the laws of the commandment in brief, with God's help - as is our custom - in the commandment of the prohibition of eating and benefit, in the Order of Ki Tissa (Sefer HaChinukh 113).

And [it] is practiced in every place and at all times by males and females. And one who transgresses it and cooks' meat with milk is lashed - and even though he does not eat it.

Mitzvah 93
To not make a covenant with the seven nations and likewise with any worshiper of idolatry: That we not make a covenant, meaning to say that we promise our friendship to the bad nation of heretics - which are the seven nations in the Torah which were holding our land before our arriving there, and they are the Hittite, the Emorite, etc. - as it is stated (Exodus 23:32), "You shall not make a covenant with them and their gods." [This] means to say that we should not make peace with them and leave them to worship idolatry.

It is from the roots of this commandment to destroy idolatry and all of those who serve it from the world. And these seven nations were the center of idolatry and its first foundation; and because of this, they were uprooted from their land. And we were commanded to uproot them and to destroy their memory forever. And it is as it is written about them in the Torah (Deuteronomy 7:2), "and you shall surely annihilate them" - and that is a positive commandment in the Order of Ve'etchanan. And there I will write at length about this commandment, with God's help, and tell the reason for why these bad nations are in the world and that this commandment is included in the commandments that are practiced. And from the warning about them, we understand a warning not to make a covenant with any worshipers of idolatry. But there is a distinction between the seven nations and the other peoples that are worshipers of idolatry (Gittin 45a); as there is no commandment to kill the other peoples if they do not fight with us, but these seven nations, we are commanded to kill in any place that we are able to - unless they abandon their idolatry. And the matter is because they were the center of idolatry and its first foundation, as I have written. And anyone who has one of them come to his hand and he can kill him without danger, but does not [do so], has transgressed a negative commandment. And that which we said that we do not kill worshipers of idolatry when they are not fighting with us, is specifically [regarding] worshipers of idolatry from the [other] peoples. However, it is a commandment upon us to kill an Israelite that worships idolatry - such as the sectarians, the apostates and the heretics - because they oppose Israel. And it is better that a thousand like these be destroyed than one proper Israelite.

From the laws of the commandment - that which they said that we accept them if they want to return and repent; and the rest of its details - are elucidated in Sanhedrin (see Tur, Yoreh Deah 191).

Mitzvah 94

To not have worshipers of idols dwell in our land: To not have worshipers of idolatry dwell in our land, as it is stated (Exodus 23:33), "They shall not dwell in your land, lest they cause you to sin against Me."

From the roots of the commandment is what is revealed in the verse - so that we not learn from their heresy.

The laws of the commandment: For example, that which they, may their memory be Blessed, said (Avodah Zarah 64b) that if they wanted to leave idolatry, even though they worshiped it at their beginning, they are permitted to live in our land, and that is what is called a resident stranger (convert) - meaning to say, he is a convert regarding that he is permitted to reside in our land. [It is] as they, may their memory be Blessed, said (Avodah Zarah 64b), "Who is a resident convert? The one who accepted not to worship idolatry." But, if he did not leave idolatry, it is not necessary to say that we do not sell him land to dwell in our land; but rather even to rent him a house is forbidden (Avodah Zarah 21a), so long as he rents it as a residence - since he will bring idolatry [into it]. But it is permitted for his business, so long as he not rent it to three people [or more] - since three is a matter of permanence, and it is not fit to make them permanent. And the difference in laws that our Rabbis, may their memory be Blessed, said there is between houses, and fields and vineyards, and between Syria and the Land of Israel. And the rest of its details are elucidated in Sanhedrin and Avodah Zarah (see Tur, Yoreh Deah 191).

And [it] is practiced by males and females in the Land. And one who transgresses it and sells them land or rents it to them in a place that is not permitted has transgressed the commandment of [the] King. But he is not lashed - as it is possible to sell them land or rent [it] without an act.

Mitzvah 95

The commandment of building the Choice House: To build a house for the sake of God, meaning to say that we would bring Him sacrifices there and that pilgrimage and yearly gathering of all of Israel be there, as it is stated (Exodus 25:8), "And let them make Me a sanctuary." And with it, this commandment includes the vessels needed for the service of the House of God - such as the menorah, the table, the altar, and all of the other vessels.

From the roots of the commandment are what you will see at the end of my words. However, I am afraid of drawing close to the Dwelling of God, as I know that 'anyone who comes close, who comes close' that has not sufficiently sanctified himself 'will not see the House and live.' Even the priests that come forward for the service sanctify themselves in their coming to the sanctum inside; and before the Levites [came] to raise their voices in the sanctuary of God, they purified themselves and Aharon waved them as a wave-offering. [Hence] I said, I too will say my counsel and arrange my apology in front of my elders, and 'I will wash my palms in innocence' before I go up to the House of God.

It is well-known and famous among us - the people that accepted the commandments - that there are seventy faces to the Torah. And in each one of them, there are many great and numerous roots, and to each and every root, [is there] branches - each one supports a great cluster of fruits that are pleasant for hearts to ponder. Each day they put out a flower for those that are constant over them - flowers of wisdom and good reasoning. The depth of its wisdom enlightens the eyes, [it] is broad and surrounding, to the point that a man does not have the power to grasp its end; as the wise king testified

Sefer HaChinukh

(Ecclesiastes 7:23), "I said that I would fathom it, but it is far from me." And with all of this, the hands of the one who is involved with it should not tire, for whether he eats little or much, it is all sweet. And if there are many whose hand will not reach the fruit to take it, let them take the leaves for themselves as medication. And I - with the knowledge of its great value and enormous depth and that 'it is a wonder and sublime for me' - have opened my mouth to speak about it. And I will rely upon what my teachers have taught me (Avodah Zarah 19a), "Let a person recite (ligris), and even though he does not know what he said, as it is stated (Psalms 119:20), 'My soul is crushed (garsah) for desire.'"

Know, my son, that all of God's desire that human beings perform His commandments is only to do good to us. And by virtue of a person being prepared and ready - by doing those commandments to receive the good - then God will do good to him. Therefore, God informed them of the good path to be good, and that path is the path of the Torah; for through it will a man be good. It comes out that all who uphold (accept) God's commandments, fulfill His desire [to do good to us] - in his then being fit to receive His goodness. But [regarding] anyone who does not ready himself for this, his evil is great - as he knows God's desire in this, and he [still] makes his actions contrary to God's will. And one section of the Torah was written specifically to inform us of this fundamental principle - and that is what is written in the Order of Vehaya Ekev (Devarim 10:12-13), "And now, Israel, what does the Lord, your God, request from you, etc. for your benefit." [That is] to say, He is not asking anything from you, in your performing His commandments, besides His wanting, in His great goodness, to do good to you. And, as it says afterwards, "Behold, to the Lord your God belongs the heavens and the heavens of the heavens, and all that is in it." [That is] to say, He doesn't require your commandments, except out of His love for you, and for your merit.

And among those that do the commandments, there are some that only place the direction of their focus upon the future reward to them for doing them, as they know that because of them, blessing and good will rest upon them. And they will always be involved with [the commandments] with this intention, and '[this is] their portion in life,' and they merit Eden, the Garden of God. However, there are those that merit that God, may He be Blessed, gave them a heart to know and to recognize His elevated characteristics. And from their recognition, they connect the 'thoughts of their hearts' to His love with a strong and powerful connection - to the point that they make all of the intention of the preparation of their bodies to fulfill the desire of God, may He be Blessed, due to their great longing for Him. And they do not place their [thoughts] upon the future benefit from this involvement. And this is the great level to which the three holy forefathers - and many of their children after them, may all of their memory be Blessed - climbed. And this is the highest level to which a person can climb.

And from here, in that this is the grounding of our opinion about the matter of His commandments, Blessed be He, we are obligated to say that the building of the House for God, may He be Blessed, for us to do our prayers and sacrifices to Him in it - it is all to prepare our hearts to His service, may He be elevated. [It is] not from His need to sit in the house of people and to come under the shade of their beams - whether they build it from cedars of Lebanon or from cypresses, 'as the heavens and the heavens of the heavens cannot contain Him,' and they [only] stand by His spirit; 'surely the house that people built' would [not] be needed for His glory, God forbid. Are the things not known and clear that it is all for the refinement of our bodies? As bodies are refined by actions; and by the multiplication of good actions and their great constancy, the thoughts of the heart become purified, cleansed [and] sanitized - and God desires the good of the creatures, as we have said. And therefore, He commanded us to fix a place that would be pure and completely clean to purify the thoughts of people there and to refine their [our] hearts towards Him in it. And maybe He, Blessed be He, chose that place and prepared it for the good of people from its being exactly at the center of the world, and the center is choicer than the ends; or for [another] reason that He, Blessed be He, would be [its] Knower. And through the refinement of action and the purification of thought that we will have there, our minds will rise to clinging with the Highest mind.

And we will explain the dwelling of the Divine Presence in this place in this way according to the simple understanding: Even though, in truth, our Rabbis, may their memory be Blessed, said (Megillah 28a) [that] their sanctity is upon them, even when they are desolate - which implies that there is no reason at all for the dwelling of the Divine Presence from the side of the worshipers - [still,] it is possible to say that God chose this place to bless from it people that He crated, as we have said. And [just] like it was His desire to send a prophet to people to teach them the path in which they should walk and [so] merit to preserve their souls, so too did He desire, in His great kindnesses, to fix a place on earth for them that would be prepared for the good of people and their merit - and all of this is from His kindnesses to His creatures. And regardless, blessing and holiness will increase there according to the good actions that people do there. And then with the good actions, the channels of good will open up corresponding to it; since in truth the holiness of a place in its destruction is not similar to its holiness in its inhabitation (use).

And the laying down of this reason in the matter of the Temple obligates us also to make the matter of the sacrifices and the tribe of its workers and the precious well-known vessels rely on the very same reason, according to the simple understanding. Did we not say that the main [inclinations] of the heart follow after the actions? And, if so, the heart of a person will not be properly purified only with the word of the lips, that he say between himself and the wall, "I have sinned, I will not [do it] again." But when he does a great act for his sin, to take 'he-goats from his pens' and to exert himself to bring them to the prepared house to the priest, and [do] all of the procedure that it written about the sacrifices of the sinners - from all of this great action - he will fix the badness of sin in his soul, and it will be avoided by him the [next] time.

And I found with Ramban, may his memory be Blessed, [an explanation] on the [level] of the simple meaning, similar to this reason. As he wrote (Ramban on Leviticus 1:9) in the name of others, and this is his language: Since the deeds of people are determined by thought, speech and action, God, may He be Blessed, commanded that when he sins, he brings a sacrifice and place his hands upon him corresponding to the deed, and confess with his mouth corresponding to the speech, and burn the innards and the kidneys, as they are the instruments of thought and desire. And the limbs [of the sacrifice] correspond to the hands and feet of a person that does all of his work. And he sprinkles the blood on the altar corresponding to the blood of his soul, so that a person think in doing all of this that he sinned to God with his body and his soul, and it is fit for him that his blood be spilled and his body burnt; were it not for the kindness of the Creator, who took an exchange and ransom from him [in] the sacrifice - that its blood be instead of his blood and its soul be instead of his soul. And the central limbs correspond to his central limbs. And the portions with which to sustain the teachers of Torah [are so] that they will pray for him. And the daily sacrifice is because there is no saving the community from always sinning. And these words are tenable [and] grab the heart, like the words of classic homiletic teachings (Shabbat 87a). To here [are his words]. And he wrote at more length about the matter and wrote, "And in the way of truth (mysticism), the sacrifices contain a hidden secret, etc.," as he wrote in his commentary on Parshat Vaykra.

And we will add other things on the [level] of the simple meaning, and say that it is from this root that God commanded us to always sacrifice from things about which the heart of man covets, like meat and wine and bread, so that the heart be more aroused with this matter. And it [likewise] obligated the poor person to bring from his little [supply] of flour that his eyes and heart are upon all of the day. And there is another arousal of the heart with animal sacrifices from the angle of similarity, as human and animal bodies are similar in all of their matters - they are only differentiated that in this one, intellect was given into it, and not into that one. And when the human body goes out of the realm of the intellect at the time of the sin, he must know that he has entered the realm of animals at that time, as this is the only thing that differentiates them. And therefore he is commanded to take a body of flesh like him and to bring it to the place chosen for the raising of the intellect and to burn it there, and to forget its memory - it shall be completely [incinerated], 'it shall not be remembered and it shall not be thought of,' corresponding to his body - in order to form a strong image in his heart that any matter of a body without intellect is lost and completely null. And he should [thus] rejoice in his portion of an intelligent soul with which God has graced him, [and] which exists forever. And the body that cooperates with it will also exist in the revival [of the dead] on its account, in its following its counsel, meaning to say in its guarding itself from sin. And in his fixing this image in his soul, he will be very careful about sin. And the Torah promises that through this great act and through the obedience of its doer that he regrets his sin from his heart and from his soul, [that] his accidental sin will be atoned. But this similarity will not suffice to atone for volitional sins, as one who sins volitionally will not be chastised by similarities and words, but only by "the rod for the back of fools" (Proverbs 26:3).

And let it not be difficult to you in putting down this reason, how it is that we would ever bring a voluntary offering, as our reason also [explains] voluntary offerings: Since we have said that a sacrifice is an illustration of the lowering of bodies and the elevation of soul, the sacrificer will find benefit to [learn this] lesson, even without a known sin.

And about the sacrifice of Azazel that would be sent alive to a place of destruction and of extinction, we will say about the simple understanding of the matter [as follows]: The complete sinner should not imagine that after his soul receive the punishment for [the] sins, it will return to stand in the place of the good or [that] there will be some survival and good - even if he is like Yerovam the son of Nevat and his colleagues - just like he sees the whole entire year that the body of the animal that is an illustration for the body of the sinner has some remnants in the House of God, may He be Blessed, in the ashes that stay there at the time of the burning. [As] they do not take them out from the Temple until after much time. Therefore in [this] living goat that carries all of the sins, they will see a hint that a sinner whose sins are great - like the heretics and those that deny Torah or the revival of the dead, and all of those that oppose Israel are included [as well] - will never see any good, and 'their worm will never die and their fire will never be extinguished.' [It is] like the procedure of this goat - [that] in his carrying the multitude of sins of all of Israel, is sent completely to a desolate land. He is not found in the House of God, not for slaughter and not for sprinkling - 'its memory will be lost from the earth.' And this is [the meaning of] what they, may their memory be Blessed, said (Talmud Yerushalmi Yoma 6:3) that at the time that Israel was accepted, [the goat] would not reach halfway [down] the mountain before it would become [detached,] limb [from] limb - to show them the illustration of a compete sinner. As so will he be quickly destroyed, and he will be entirely, completely destroyed. [This is] in order that they would learn and [understand] the lesson and improve their ways. And this sign is good for them, as only he who loves one teaches him lessons, as it is written (Proverbs 13:24), "but he who loves him disciplines him early."

And regarding the division of the sacrifices in their slaughtering and the giving of the blood and the portion of the priests and the rest of its many details, were we to say that the thought of the servant [making the sacrifice] be directed to the [parts of the] multitudinous service - as the distinctions would require the direction of thought to the matter - the only thing that would come up in our hands would be the words of youths. And the principle of the thing is that even in the simple understandings, we cannot find our hand or feet without the support of the mystics (kabbalists). And we bow our heads to them and they should open our eyes about all of this.

However, we should not be called from the group of fools, in our spending all of our breath on [empty] words; as in much waste, a little food can sometimes be found. Also because we have seen our Rabbis, may their memory be Blessed, saying [words] similar to our words: As they said about the sacrifice of a sotah (a suspect of adultery) (Sotah 14a), "She did an animal act, therefore she should bring barley (animal food)"; and with the sacrifice of a metsora (Vayikra Rabbah 16, Arakhin 16b), "He did an act of chatter, he should bring birds." And similar to this, they, may their memory be Blessed, said regarding the matter of a menstruant woman, "Why did the Torah say that she sit seven clean days? That she be most dear to him." And in truth, none of all this is in their opinion the ultimate intent of the things. Rather, it is to inform that the matter of the commandment includes many hints, besides the great and strong fundamentals.

From the laws of the commandment is that which they, may their memory be Blessed, said (Zevachim 112b) that before the Temple was built in Jerusalem, they would sacrifice in other places; but from when the Temple was built, all of the places were forbidden to build a house for the sake of God and to sacrifice there - as it is stated (Psalms 132:14), "This is the place of My resting forever and ever. And these are the things that are the main part of the building of the Temple: We make a Holy and a Holy of Holies there; and in front of the Holy is another place and it is called the chamber, and the three of them are called the sanctuary (Mishnah Middot 4:6); and we make a partition around the sanctuary distant from it, like the curtains of the courtyard that were in the wilderness; and everything that is encircled by this partition, which is like the courtyard of the tent of meeting is called the yard - and the whole thing is called the Temple (mikdash) - and we make the vessels in the Temple that are written in the Torah that we need there. And that which they said (Zevachim 88a) that we immediately melt down all holy vessels that become pierced or cracked and make new ones; and [that] we do not fix a knife, the blade of which is detached or dented, but rather bury it immediately, as there is no poverty in a place of wealth. And [that] we make boundaries in the yard - up until here for Israel, up until here for the priests. And [that] close to it, we build enclosures to use for all the needs of the Temple, and each one is called a compartment. And the rest of its details, such as how was the building of the Temple, its form, all of its measurements, the building of the altar and its ordinances – are [all] elucidated in Tractate Middot. And so [too,] the form of the menorah, the table, and the golden altar and their place in the chamber are in the Gemara, [in] Meanchot and Yoma.

And this commandment is practiced at the time that most of Israel is upon their land. And this is from the commandments that are not impingent upon the individual, but rather upon all of the community. When the Temple is built, speedily in our days, a positive commandment will be fulfilled.

Mitzvah 96

To not remove the poles of the ark from it: To not remove the poles of the ark from the rings, as it is stated (Exodus 25:15), "The poles shall be in the rings of the ark; they shall not be removed from it." And it is elucidated that this commandment is among the commandments practiced throughout the generations. As the understanding of 'practiced throughout the generations' is not that the doing of that commandment never cease from Israel ever at any time. Rather the matter is like this: Any commandment that was only commanded to do at a specific time and not more - such as that which is written (Exodus 19:15), "Be in preparation for three days"; and so [too,] the warning of Sinai (Exodus 34:3), "neither shall the flocks and the herds graze across from that mountain"; and all that is similar to it, wherein the command was only temporary - those are called commandments that are not practiced throughout the generations. But any commandment that we were not commanded about [only] for a specific time - even though there is a pause at any given time because of our exile or by reason of something else, such as now when, on account of our sins, we do not have the ark - is called a commandment practiced throughout the generations. As any time that we have the ark, we are obligated not to remove its poles from it, so that the Levites [may] take [the ark] out with them, if we need to bring it from one place to another place as a result of war or from whatever reason that [may] arise.

It is from the roots of the commandment [that it is] because the ark is the residence of the Torah, and [the latter] is our essence and our glory. And [so], we have been commanded all glory and all majesty towards it, to all of our ability. Therefore, we were commanded not to remove the poles of the ark from it, lest we need to go out with the ark to any place quickly, and maybe due to the preoccupation and the rush, we will not check well that its poles are strong enough; and lest, God forbid, it will fall from their hands, and this is not [fit for] its glory. But with their always being ready and not being removed from it, we will make them very strong, and [so] there will not be a mishap with them. And another reason [is] that the forms of all of the vessels of the Temple are required to hint to great and lofty matters, so that a person is impressed by them for the good, in the course of his thinking about them. And for our good, God wanted that that form not be lost even temporarily.

The three commandments of this Order are not practiced today.

Mitzvah 97

The commandment of arranging the bread of display and the frankincense: To always place bread in the Temple in front of God, as it is stated (Exodus 25:30), "And on the table you shall set the bread of display, to be before Me always" (See Sefer HaMitzvot LaRambam, Mitzvot Ase 27).

It is from the roots of this commandment that God, Blessed be He, commanded us the constant commandment of the bread, on account that through it a man lives; and as a result, [the commandment] is needed by him for blessing to always be found in [his bread]. And from our

Sefer HaChinukh

involvement in it to fulfill the commandment of God, may He be Blessed, the [Divine] will and blessing will descend upon us, and that which is similar to it will be Blessed. And according to each and every matter upon which he places the conglomeration of his focus, his thoughts and his activities by way of a commandment - according to them, a similar blessing will emerge upon him. And so I have found [in] Ramban (Ramban on Exodus 25:24). And [it] is like the matter that they, may their memory be Blessed, said (Rosh HaShanah 16:1), "Bring the omer (barley offering) in front of Me at Pesach, in order that the grain in the fields will be Blessed for you; pour the water in front of Me on the Festival (Sukkot), in order that the rains of blessing will be Blessed for you in the coming year; blow the ram's horn (shofar) in front of Me, in order to remember the binding of Yitschak." And they said about this very same bread (Megillah 26b) that because it is an accessory of the commandment, and through it the will of God is done, blessing would cling to it more. And [so] each one of the priests who had from it coming to him would be twice as satiated.

We were commanded in all of these things, such as the table, the menorah, the bread of display and the sacrifices, from the angle of the receivers (people), and like the matter that I wrote. There is no doubt or qualm to anyone who understands, or student that is not lacking in comprehension in the world who would think that with the arrangement of bread in the Temple upon the table, which we place complete and we take [away] complete, that there is any benefit (enjoyment) accrued by the Above, God forbid - not in its appearance, not in its smell and not from any angle. Rather, He commanded us like this in His desire, Blessed be He, that we be Blessed from Him, in His great trait of kindness. And [this is] also [true about] the frankincense that comes with the bread, about which it is written, "a burnt offering to the Lord." And [when] some of the commentators (Rashi on Leviticus 24:7) said that there is nothing from the bread that is for the Above except for the frankincense, their intention was not, God forbid, that there be any distinction between the frankincense and the bread for the Above. And the fulfillment of the commandment of God is the same with the bread and the frankincense: As just like God, Blessed be He, commanded to arrange the bread in front of Him, so too is His will done, with the frankincense that He commanded to burn, and they burned it - one standard for all. Rather, all of these matters were written from the angle of those involved [in them]. As it cannot be written about the bread - that we feed the priests - that it is all for God; as others have a portion in it. But with anything that man does not have any benefit in it at all, and it is completely consumed in the commandment - with that we can say about it that it is completely for God. [That] means to say that all of it is included in the commandment - no man ate from it, nor enjoyed any physical benefit from it at all. And since smell is not from the pleasures of the body, but rather from the pleasures of the spirit - as the body only receives tangible pleasure - the matter of smell is always attributed to God, Blessed be He. [This is] even though He, Blessed be He and Blessed be His name, is not - due to His supernal level and His greatness - connected to these matters at all; as He is not a body, and not the attribute of a body. This is known to all that understand. And they, may their memory be Blessed, already explained (Rashi on Zevachim 46b, s.v. hanachat ruach) [that] every place that it is stated, "a pleasing smell to the Lord" (for example, Leviticus 1:9), [it means] "I said something, and My will was done." And so [too,] "And the Lord smelled the pleasant smell" (Genesis 8:21), [should be understood] in this way. This is what appears [correct] to us regarding the matter of the arranging of the bread in the House of God. And Rambam, may his memory be Blessed, wrote (Guide for the Perplexed 3:45), and this is his language: But I do not know a reason for the table and the bread always being put upon it; and to this day, I do not know to what thing to ascribe it.

From the laws of the commandment is that which they, may their memory be Blessed, said (Sifra, Emor Chapter 18 5) that in each array, they would put a vessel that would have a fistful of frankincense in it, as it is stated (Leviticus 24:7), "And you shall set on the array," meaning to say on each one of them, "pure frankincense" - and this vessel is called a bazakh (bowl), And [that which] they, may their memory be Blessed, said (Menachot 26a) that [the absence of one of] the two sets [of loaves] impinges on the other, and [that] the two bowls impinge upon one another; that they would remove the bread and arrange other bread immediately, from one Shabbat day to another Shabbat day (Menachot 99b); [that] that which they take out is what is split by the two shifts, the incoming [one] and the departing [one], along with the high priest, and they [would all] eat it (Yoma 17b); and how it was arranged, that four would come in with the bread and the bowls, and four would precede them to take the [old] bread from upon the table. And they, may their memory be Blessed, said (Menachot 99b) that they would orchestrate [it], that in their setting them down, the [edge] of [the new one] would be alongside the [edge] of the [old one] - to fulfill that which it states, "before Me always," And the form of the bread; how was the matter of its placement, such that it [be exposed] to the air; and the rest of its details - are [all] elucidated in the eleventh chapter of Menachot (see Mishneh Torah, Laws of Daily Offerings and Additional Offerings 5).

And [it] is practiced at the time of the Temple by male priests, as the service is theirs, and not women's.

Mitzvah 98

The commandment of arranging lights in the Temple: To prepare perpetual lights in front of God, may He be Blessed, as it stated (Exodus 27:21), "Aharon and his sons will arrange it," meaning to say, he will set it up in front of God, may He be Blessed. And this is the law of preparing the lights that is mentioned in the Gemara (Yoma 14b).

It is from the roots of the commandment that God, may He be Blessed, commanded us that there be a lit light in the Temple for the aggrandizement of the Temple, for [its] glory and splendor in the eyes of the seers. As it is the way of people to be glorified in their homes with lit lights. And the whole matter of its aggrandizement is in order that fear and humility enter a man's heart when he sees it. And we have already said (Sefer HaMitzvot 16) that the soul is refined by good action. And all of this revolves around the principle established for us that everything is defined according to the side of the receivers (people); in that I truly believe that there is great wisdom and amazing secrets for the receivers in these matters. And notwithstanding, we will also write that which appears from the simple understanding of the words, everything for the sake of Heaven.

The laws of the commandment - for example, that which they said (Sifra, Emor, Section 13:11) [that] the lighting of the lights pushes off Shabbat like the sacrifices, since they have a set time, as it is stated about it, "always"; that (Menachot 89a) half a log of oil was placed in each and every light, as it states, "from evening until morning," and the sages estimated that this is the amount that would suffice for the nights of Tevet (in the winter), and so [too], was it given on all of the nights, and if there would be a surplus, there is nothing [wrong] in that; about the matter of arrangement, [that] it is the cleaning; [that] cleaning the menorah and setting it up is a positive commandment in the morning and in the afternoon; [that] the cleaning is, that [with] each light that became extinguished, he removes the wick and all of the oil that was extinguished, cleans [the bowl] and places another wick and other oil in it, but he [only] fixes a light that has not become extinguished; [that] if the middle (eastern) light becomes extinguished, he lights it from fire that is in the outer altar, but the others he lights one from another by pulling the wick and inclining it until it catches on fire, since it is not [fit] the honor of the commandment to light it from another light; and the rest of its details - are [all] elucidated in the eighth chapter of Menachot and in places in Tamid.

This is the opinion of Rambam, may his memory be Blessed, (Mishneh Torah, Laws of Daily Offerings and Additional Offerings 3) - that in this commandment, the arrangement of the lights is the lighting, as we have explained. However, the opinion of other commentators (Rashi on Exodus 30:7) is that the arranging is the removal of the ashes, the cleaning, and the fixing of the wicks; and that it is a commandment in of itself (besides the lighting). And so does it appear in the chapter [entitled] Hatekhelet in Tractate Menachot 49b-50a (see Mishneh Torah, Laws of Daily Offerings and Additional Offerings 3).

And [it] is practiced at the time of the Temple by priests. And a priest that transgresses it and does not arrange the candles, as is commanded, violates a positive commandment.

Mitzvah 99

The commandment of wearing the priestly clothes: That the priests were commanded to wear special clothes for aggrandizement and glory - and then they may serve in the Temple - as it is stated (Exodus 28:4), "and they shall make priestly clothes for Aharon your brother and his sons."

Sefer HaChinukh

From the roots of the commandment is the principle established for us, that a person is impacted according to his actions and pursuant to his thoughts and intentions. And the agent that atones must attach all of his thoughts and intentions to the [Divine] service. Therefore, it is fit that he wears special clothes for it; as when he stares at any place of his body, he will immediately remember and be aroused in his heart as to in front of Whom he is serving. And this is like the tefillin that all have been commanded to place on a part of the body, that it be to remember proper thought. And even though the priest also wears tefillin, due to the greatness of his matter, he needs this too.

And from this reason we can [explain that] which is said (Pesachim 65b) that the length of the robe is obligated to be upon all of his body, from above to the heel below; the length of its sleeve be to the palm of his hand (Yoma 72b); the length of the turban be sixteen ells (Mishneh Torah, Laws of Vessels of the Sanctuary and Those who Serve Therein 9:19) and wrap the whole head, so that he see it any time he raises his eyes; and the length of the sash that he wraps on his loins be thirty-two ells and he wraps and rewraps it on his body, one layer over another, and it comes out that he feels it with his forearms all the time, as due to its thickness from all the wrappings, his forearms touch it regardless. And all of this is a proof to that which we have said, for the one who concedes the truth. Besides [this reason], there is glory to the Temple and to the [Divine] service in the matter that the servant wears special clothes for the service. And we have already written (Sefer HaChinukh 95) that with the aggrandizement of the Temple and its fear, the hearts of sinners will be softened and they will repent to God.

And the laws of the commandment are, for example, the elucidation of the clothes, which are three types, one type of regular priestly clothes and two types of high priestly clothes - the gold clothes and the white clothes. And [the garments] of a regular priest are four, and their names are like this: robe (ketonet), trousers (mikhnasayim), turban (migbaat) and sash (avnet . The robe is like a wide Yishmaelite cloak. And the form of the trousers is well-known in every place, but theirs were big, from the loins to the thighs - meaning to say until the [part of the] thighs which [in the vernacular] is called the genoi (knee). However, the turban is a garment that is placed upon the head, made like a hat. The sash is a type of belt with which he girds himself, except that they wrap it around themselves many [times], which we do not do with a belt. And these four linen garments were white and their string was six-stranded (Yoma 71b). And only the sash was embroidered with wool (Yoma 12b). And the regular priest would always serve in them, and it is permissible for him to wear them during the day, whether during the time of the service or not during the time of the service - as it is permitted to derive benefit from them. [This is] except for the sash, since it is shatnez (an otherwise forbidden mixture of fibers). And therefore, it is forbidden not during the time of the service.

And [the garments] of the high priest are eight, and their names are like this: robe (ketonet), trousers (mikhnasayim) and sash (avnet) - like the names of the three of the regular priest - and mitsnefet (miter) was for the high priest instead of the turban of the regular priest. As this and that were [both] placed on the head, except that the the miter is made like a long type of cloth that women coil around their heads - and the high priest would coil himself with it - but the turban is made like a type of hat (that does not require coiling). Behold, [these] four of the high priest, which were only of linen, were white, six-stranded and embroidered, but their embroidery was not similar to the embroidery of the regular priest's sash. And he also had four others of gold and their names were breastplate (choshen), apron (ephod), coat (me'il) [and] headband (tsits). And he would do the external service with all of the eight, but inside - which is past the partition - he would never serve with anything but the [linen] clothes. And after he served with them for one Yom Kippur, he does not repeat to ever serve with them (Yoma 24a), as it is stated (Leviticus 16:3), "and he leaves them there." And anytime a priest - whether a regular or a high [priest] - serves with less than the clothes that are designated for that service, or more than them, his service is disqualified. And he is also liable for the death penalty by the hand of the Heavens, as our rabbis, may their memory be Blessed, learned (Sanhedrin 83b, Zevachim 17b-18a) from "And you shall gird them with a sash [...] and they would have priesthood" (Exodus 29:9) - at the time when their clothes are upon them, their priesthood is upon them; when their clothes are not upon them, their priesthood is not upon them. And they are [hence] considered like a stranger (a non-priest) who transgresses, which is [punishable] by death. [These] and the rest of its details are elucidated in the second chapter of Zevachim and in places in Yoma and Sukkah (see Mishneh Torah, Laws of Vessels of the Sanctuary and Those who Serve Therein 10).

And this commandment is practiced at the time of the Temple by males of the priesthood. And one who transgresses it and served lacking [priestly] clothes or [with too many] is liable for the death penalty by the hand of the Heavens, as we have written.

Mitzvah 100

That the breastplate not move from on top of the apron: That we not move the breastplate from on top of the apron. And above we have already mentioned the matter of the breastplate and the apron, which are two of the eight clothes of the high priest. And the breastplate was set in line [and] in front of the heart of the priest. And the apron is behind him across from the breastplate that is in front of him. And there was within the apron, from the cloth of the apron itself, like a type of two handles that come out from it, that the priest girds himself with; and it is called the band (cheshev) of the apron. And after he girds himself with the band of the apron, and placed the breastplate on his heart, it would sit under the breastplate. And Scripture commanded to tie rings that were fixed onto the breastplate and rings that were fixed onto the apron with a string of blue (tekhelet), so that the breastplate would be set upon the band in a fixed and dignified way. As if he did not tie them with those rings, the breastplate would wander and be separated from the band of the apron and bang upon the chamber of the priest's heart. And about this is it stated (Exodus 28:28), "and the breastplate shall not budge from the apron" - meaning to say from upon the band of the apron. And its [official Aramaic] translation (Onkelos) is to break apart (yitparak). And one who severs its connection at the time of the service is lashed for this negative commandment.

It is from the roots of the commandment that God, may He be Blessed, wanted for our good to bring us merit by the aggrandizement of that holy house, [such that] everything in it be proper and set in its place. Whether in the matter of its vessels, that they should be completely perfect, or whether in the matter of the vessels of its servants - such as these clothes that they wear at the time of the service - everything should be proper and completely perfect. No beauty should be lacking from any of [these] things. And in truth, it is from the beauty of the matter that the breastplate should not be loose and wandering upon the chamber of his heart, but it should rather sit fixed like a type of [thing set in] plaster. And we will hold to this [explanation], until we hear better than it.

The laws of the commandment - for example, the design of the breastplate and the apron; the order of their being adorned; and the rest of its details - are elucidated in Middot.

And this commandment that we not remove the breastplate from the apron is practiced at the time of the [Temple] by males and females. [This] means to say that it is the same; [both] a man or a woman that severs their connection is lashed.

Mitzvah 101

To not tear the coat of the priests: To not tear the opening of the coat of the high priest, as it is stated (Exodus 28:32), "it shall not be torn."

It is from the roots of the commandment [that] because tearing is a thing of disgrace for us and a matter of destruction, we have been distanced from the thing and warned about it with a negative commandment. [This is] so that its wearer will put it on with trepidation, fear and care. And it is the way of honor that he should fear from tearing it and from destroying anything in it.

And [it] is practiced at the time of the [Temple] by males and females. [This is] meaning to say whoever volitionally tears it - whether a man or a woman - or even cuts it with scissors is lashed.

Mitzvah 102

The commandment of eating the meat of sin-offerings and guilt-offerings: That the priests were commanded to eat the meat of some of the sacrifices - such as the guilt offering and the sin offering, as it is stated about them (Exodus 29:33), "They shall eat that with which atonement was done." And they, may their memory be Blessed, said (Pesachim 59b), "The priests eat, and the owners are atoned." And with God's help, we will write about the matter of the procedure of the sin-offering and the guilt-offering, how they would do it, and the time of its eating in their Order (Sefer HaChinukh 138, 140). And the principle of the matter is that all the meat of the sacrifices of the sin-offering and the guilt-offering was eaten by the males of the priesthood in the [Temple] yard, except for their entrails; and the owners do not have any [part] in it. And there it will also be explained what are the parts that are to be burned. And also included in this positive commandment is that they eat the portion that is coming to them from the group of sacrifices called lightly consecrated. And the eating of the priestly tithe is also included in the commandment. However, the eating of the lightly consecrated, and so [too,] the priestly tithe, is not like the eating of the meat of a sin-offering and a guilt offering. As with the eating of a sin-offering and a guilt-offering, the atonement of the penitent is accomplished - as they, may their memory be Blessed, said, "The priests eat, and the owners are atoned." But the eating of the lightly consecrated and the priestly tithe does not add or subtract from the commandment of the one who brings [the sacrifice] or gives the [tithe].

It is from the roots of the commandment [that] the fundamental principle for us is that all of the acts of the sacrifices are to prepare our thoughts and our intentions for the good, to submerge the spirit of desire within us and to enlarge and strengthen the intellectual spirit towards the commandments. And hence we were commanded to behave in all matters of the [Temple] and the sacrifices in the manner of loftiness and greatness and honor, so that awe and humility and lowliness of spirit descend upon our hearts when we are there, and also when we remember it in our places. And in truth it is from acting with honor towards the sacrifice upon which atonement is dependent that it be eaten by the servants, themselves, and that they not give it to their slaves and dogs or sell it to all buyers. And so [too,] it is from [its] honor that he eats [it] in a holy place; and also, that he not leave its eating [for a long time] so that it not smell bad and the soul [then] be disgusted by it. Does all of this not show the matter of greatness and importance?

The laws of the commandment: We will write at a bit of length about them in their place, as is our custom.

And this commandment is practiced at the time of the [Temple] by the males of the priesthood. And one who transgresses it and does not eat his portion that is coming to him from them in the limited time for it, has violated a positive commandment. And he is also punished from the side of the atonement of the owners that is dependent upon it, as we have said. And Ramban (on Sefer HaMitzvot LaRambam, Shoresh 12), may his memory be Blessed, does not count this commandment [separately]. As he said that who eats them and for whom they should be is a part of the [various] parts of the commandment of sacrifices, that God, may He be Blessed, commanded about them; and the truth is that atonement is dependent upon this.

Mitzvah 103

The commandment of burning the incense: That the priests were commanded to burn the incense of spices twice every day upon the golden altar, as it is stated (Exodus 30:7), "And Aharon will burn incense of spices each morning in his arranging, etc." And in each and every year, it is a commandment upon them to make some of it so as to burn it, as we have said. And its making and the commandment [of burning] that is done with it every day is considered one commandment, since the end of the commandment of making it is only to burn it. And even though we find two passages of commandment between the making and the burning - as it is stated about its making in Parshat Ki Tissa (Exodus 30:34), "Take for yourself spices, etc." and here it is written, "And Aharon will burn incense, etc." - nonetheless, I have seen that the enumerators of the commandments count it all as one commandment, and there is no disagreement about this among them at all. But they do disagree about another matter in it - as Rambam, may his memory be Blessed, counts the burning in the morning and in the evening as one commandment, but Ramban (at the end of Sefer HaMitzvot LaRambam), may his memory be Blessed, counts them as two. And his proofs are in his book.

And it is also from the roots of this commandment to aggrandize the glory of the [Temple] and to have its loftiness and awe upon the face of every person. And it is only possible to aggrandize something in the heart of people and their thoughts with things that one [associates with] greatness, and in which he will find delight and joy. And it is known that a good smell is a thing that the spirit of a person enjoys and desires and [that] it draws the heart much. And the smell of the incense was the best that can possibly be made by a man - to the point that they, may their memory be Blessed, said in the chapter [entitled] Amar Lahem HaMemuneh (Mishnah Tamid 3:8) that they would smell its smell at the time of its burning from Jericho to Jerusalem.

From the laws of the commandment is that which they said in a bereita in Keritot 6a that the composition of the incense was eleven spices, four of which are explicit in the Torah and seven of which are a tradition. And that which they said (Yoma 26a; Mishnah Tamid 7:3) that the incense is made either by the high priest or by a regular priest. And [that] which they said (Menachot 49a) that if he did not burn it in the morning, he burns the whole amount of the day - which is the weight of a hundred dinar - in the afternoon. And the weight of a dinar is well known. And [that] every day he would burn half of it in the morning and half of it in the evening, after the afternoon sacrifice before the arrangement of all of the lights, after the [lighting] of five of their wicks - as they were not lit consecutively (Yoma 14b). And [that] they would do this matter [as follows], the priest that merited to burn the incense takes a vessel - the name of which is a teni - heaped full of incense (Mishnah Tamid 6:3), and all of the people leave from between the sanctuary and between the chamber and the altar, as it states (Leviticus 16:17), "And no man will be in the tent of meeting, etc." And he [then] burns [it] in the way that is explained there in the Gemara (Mishnah Tamid 6:3) - that he gently throws the incense upon the coals in the gold pan, and he bows down and exits. And the rest of its details, how it is done, and that which they said during the grinding of the spices, "Crush well, well" - because our Rabbis, may their memory be Blessed, said (Keritot 6a) that the voice is good for spices while they grind them - is all in Keritot and in Tamid (see Mishneh Torah, Laws of Daily Offerings and Additional Offerings 3).

And [it] is practiced at the time of the [Temple] by the males of the priesthood. And one who burns [it] according to its law, has fulfilled this positive commandment.

Mitzvah 104

To not burn incense and not to bring sacrifices upon the gold altar: To not bring sacrifices upon the gold altar in the chamber except for the daily incense, besides the sprinkling of bloods from [one] Yom Kippur to [another] Yom Kippur, as it is stated (Exodus 30:9), "You shall not offer foreign incense on it, or a burnt offering or a meal offering; nor shall you pour a libation on it."

We have already written an answer above (Sefer HaChinukh 95) to the one that asks according to the simple [level] about the matter of the building of the Temple for God, Blessed be He, and the matter of there being precious vessels there for His service and a table and a menorah. And after this, we should not tire our thoughts about that which is not necessary and to search for a reason why God commanded that we not burn a foreign incense on the gold altar. As, if so, we would be obligated to search why He commanded us that the lights of the menorah be seven and not eight. And there is no [possibility of] analysis about the details for us, and [our] thinking will never grasp it. And if you pressure me to answer about the details nonetheless, I will say according to the simple [level] - unless the mystical tradition (kabbalah) shows that according to the words of our holy rabbis, the kabbalists, may their memory be Blessed, there be in the details another reason - that since we have been obligated to build a [Temple] and to make vessels, we were commanded about them as one of several possibilities; and one of the calculations came to us, as it is impossible to act without one of them. However, once we have been commanded about one of them, the commandment came about them to do the commandment in [this] fixed way forever, and not to add and to subtract - as addition or reduction in that which is perfectly set is corruption. And all of God's commandments are perfection and purity. However, I have heard that the mystics have amazing reasons and deep secrets for each one of the details.

And this commandment to only bring incense on the gold altar is practiced at the time of the [Temple] by priests. And one who transgresses it and sacrifices or sprinkles upon it anything not fit to bring upon it, as we have said, is liable for lashes.

Sefer HaChinukh

Mitzvah 105
The commandment of the giving of the half shekel during the year: That each one of Israel from twenty years and up - whether poor or rich - give the half shekel, which is the weight of ten gerah of silver, each year to the hand of the priests, as it is stated (Exodus 30:13), "This is what everyone who passes the count shall give." And they would place all of it in a compartment in the Temple. And from there they would take them out (Mishnah Shekalim 4) to buy daily offerings, additional offerings and any sacrifice brought for the community and their libations, the salt with which they would salt the sacrifices, the wood for the arrangement, the bread of display and the wage of the one making the bread of display, the omer, the two-breads, the red heifer, the goat sent away and the golden strip [it would carry].

It is from the roots of the commandment that the Holy One, Blessed be He, wanted for the good of all of Israel and for their merit, that the hand of all be equal in the matter of the sacrifices that are brought in front of Him regularly the whole year, and in these matters that were mentioned. [It is] also that all be equal - both poor and rich - in one commandment in front of Him, to bring up their thought for the good in front of Him, through the commandment that they are all included in. And raising up the thought is all said from the side of the receiver (people), as we have written above (Sefer HaChinukh 97).

From the laws of the commandment is for example, that which they, may their memory be Blessed, said (Mishnah Shekalim 1:1) that on the 1st of Adar, we announce about the shekel-coins; that even the poorest of the poor is liable for it, and if he does not have it, he borrows from others or sells the cloak that is upon him and gives it, as it is stated (Exodus 30:16), "and the poor may not lessen." And [that] he does not give [it] over several times, but rather all at one time; that its weight is [equal to] eighty grains of barley, as the weight of the whole shekel that was in the days of Moshe was one hundred and sixty barleys [grains]. And that all are obligated to give it, priests, Levites, Israelites, converts and freed slaves; but not women, slaves and minors. But if they give it, we accept [it] from them, but not from gentiles - they do not have a share and inheritance among us. And [that] they, may their memory be Blessed, also said (Mishnah Shekalim 1:6) that anyone who does not give an exact half-shekel which was a coin at that time; but gives silver of its weight for it or [its equivalent] in small bronze coins (perutot) [instead], must add a little to the weight of his shekel - and that little was called a kalbon (small coin). And that this little is the wage of the moneychanger who gets his wage for changing the perutot into the half shekel that was fixed. And therefore, two that brought a whole shekel between the two of them [also] require a kalbon - since if they wanted to exchange it, they would need to give the moneychanger a kalbon. And so too must they give it to the [Temple] treasurer, since Scripture obligated them in a half shekel (and not a whole one) - and so they are obligated about it or its value precisely. And so [too,] that which they, may their memory be Blessed, said (Mishnah Shekalim 2:1) is the law about one who loses his shekel on the way. And the rest of its many details are [all] elucidated in the Tractate built upon this, and that is Tractate Shekalim (see Mishneh Torah, Laws of Sheqel Dues 1).

And [it] is practiced at the time of the [Temple], such that all of Israel is obligated to give it - whether those that are standing in the Land or those outside of the Land. And not during the time of the [Temple], no man is obligated about it - even those standing in the Land. And one who transgresses it and does not give it, has violated a positive commandment and his punishment is very great; as he has separated himself from the community and is not included in their atonement. And now, in our sins, that we do not have a Temple, all of Israel is accustomed to remember the thing by reading this section of Ki Tissa until "And you shall take the money of the atonements" in the synagogue every year, always on the Shabbat that is before Rosh Chodesh (the first day of) Adar (Megillah 29a).

Mitzvah 106
The commandment of sanctifying the hands and the feet at the time of the service: To wash (Sefer HaMitzvot LaRambam, Mitzvot Ase 24) the hands and the feet at all times when one enters into the sanctuary and when one comes to do the service (see Tosefot on Yoma 5b, s.v. lehavi) - and

that is the commandment of the sanctification of the hands and the feet - as it is stated (Exodus 30:19-20), "And let Aharon and his sons wash their hands and feet [...] When they enter the Tent of Meeting, etc. or when they approach the altar to serve, etc."

From the roots of the commandment is the fixed foundation that we have said [that it is] to aggrandize the glory of the [Temple] and all of the [activities] that are done there. And therefore it is fitting to clean the hands, which are the [things] that are involved in the work at all times when the priests are touching the contents of the [Temple]. And from this root, they, may their memory be Blessed, said (Zevachim 19b) that the priest does not need to sanctify his hands between one service and [another] service, but rather once during the morning, and he may [then] serve the whole day and the whole night - and that is when he does not sleep and does not urinate and does not remove his mind. It appears from all of this that the intention of the washing at the beginning is only for the aggrandizement of the glory of the [Temple], since even if he was pure and clean from the beginning of his arrival there, he [still] needs to wash. And once he has started the service, he does not need to wash again between one service and [another] service, except for on Yom Kippur, due to the stringency of the day. [This is all] since we hold and see in our hearts all of the business of the service of the [Temple] as pure, clean and holy.

From the laws of the commandment is that which they, may their memory be Blessed, said (Zevachim 20b) that one who goes out of the wall of the yard requires sanctification of the hands. And that if he sanctified his hands today, he needs to go back and sanctify [them] tomorrow - even if he did not sleep the whole night - as the hands are disqualified by [passing the night]. And that the commandment is ideally to wash the face, the hands and the feet in the morning; that it is a commandment to sanctify with the water of the basin (Zevachim 22b), and that if he sanctified [his hands] from one of the serving vessels, it is fit, ex post facto - but not from a non-sacred vessel, even ex post facto. And that they do not put their hands into [the water], but we pour it over their hands - and this is also the way of honor. But we do not require this regarding the [washing] of the hands for non-sacred foods - to [wash] from a vessel and not into it. As even though we require a vessel for the [washing] for the non-sacred, and the foundation of the matter is because we found [the requirement] for a vessel by [washing] for the sanctified - nonetheless it is with the sanctified that the [Torah] excluded it, but with the non-sacred, there is no exclusion. And even though the [washing] for the non-sacred is by extension of the priestly tithe - and as they, may their memory be Blessed, said (Chullin 106a), "By extension of the priestly tithe" - still we do not make them the same in all of their laws. And [so] it is enough for us to obligate [washing] and a vessel for the non-sacred - by extension of the priestly tithe - and to leave the exclusion [derived from] "from it," that is said about it in its place. And even about the priestly tithe itself, its [washing] of the hands is rabbinic; as by Torah writ, one only finds purity for the entire body at once, and that which they, may their memory be Blessed, said (Chullin 106a) that the [washing] is [derived] from that which is written (Leviticus 15:11), "and he did not wash his hands, etc." - that is just a memory device (asmakhta). And so is it written in the Sefer HaMitzvot of Ramban, may his memory be Blessed (see Sefer HaMitzvot LaRambam, Shoresh 1, s.v. beteshuvah hashenit).

And so [too,] that which they, may their memory be Blessed, said (Zevachim 21b), [about] how much water needs to be in the basin - [that it is] no less than water that is fit for the [washing] of four people - as it is is stated, "And let Aharon and his sons wash their hands and their feet." And they were Aharon and Elazar and Itamar, and Pinchas was with them. And that all water is fit for sanctification - whether the water from a spring or the water of a pool (mikveh) - and they are disqualified by [passing the night]. And how is the commandment of the sanctification (Zevachim 19b) - that he places his right hand on his right foot and his left hand on his left foot and washes standing up and not sitting. As the sanctification of the hands and feet is included in the service, and all of the services of the Temple are [done while] standing up - as it is stated (Deuteronomy 18:5), "to stand and to serve." And all of this is for the loftiness of the [Temple]. And the rest of its details are elucidated in the second chapter of Zevachim.

And it is practiced at the time of the Temple by the males of the priesthood alone. And one who transgresses it and does not sanctify his hands and his feet in the morning, or if he goes out from the

Temple and removes his thoughts and comes back and serves without sanctification, is liable for death at the hands of Heaven - and his service is disqualified - whether he is a high priest or a regular priest.

Mitzvah 107
The commandment of anointing the high priest and the kings of the House of David with anointing oil: To make the anointing oil according to the way that the Torah commanded to make it, as it is stated (Exodus 30:25), "And you shall make it, a holy anointing oil, etc." [This is] so that it be ready to anoint every high priest that is appointed, as it is written (Leviticus 21:10), "The priest who is exalted above his fellows, on whose head the anointing oil has been poured." And so [too], we anoint some of the kings. And so [too,] they also anointed the vessels of the Temple with it, but they will not need to anoint [them] in the future, as they will be sanctified by their service. And this is [the meaning] of what is written (Exodus 30:31), "and it will be for Me for the generations." And so, did they, may their memory be Blessed, say in Sifrei Bemidbar 44.

It is from the roots of the commandments that God, Blessed be He, wanted us to to do an act, ourselves, on the day that we go up to be inaugurated to the honor of His holy service that indicates greatness and praise in us. And that is the anointing of the oil, since only kings and great ministers do the matter of anointing with good oil. And it is also from the foundation of the commandment that it be ready in the [Temple] for the time [it will be] needed, due to the loftiness of the place. As it is known, by way of a metaphor, that it is from the loftiness of an honored patron to have his house ready for every need in it and that no work be delayed until the time it is needed.

The laws of the commandment - for example, the process of how the oil was made, five hundred shekel [weight] of myrrh, cinnamon and cassia, each, except that the cinnamon is weighed in two [batches] to increase the two [toppings off] with it, and two hundred and fifty shekel of fragrant cane, and they are all found in the Indian islands, and the measure of olive oil is a hin which is twelve log ; that after it is all properly cooked, it all comes back to the measure of the oil, which is twelve log, and its mnemonic is zeh (made up of the Hebrew letters, zayin, hey), [which] is twelve in its numerical count (gematria); and the rest of its details - are in the first chapter of Keritot.

And [it] is practiced at the time of the [Temple], and it is from the commandments that is impingement upon the community - like the building of the [Temple] and its vessels.

Mitzvah 108
To not rub a foreigner (layman) with anointing oil: To not anoint [anyone] with the anointing oil that Moshe made, except for priests alone - as it is stated (Exodus 30:32), "It must not be rubbed on any person's flesh." And it is elucidated in the Scripture that one who anoints (is anointed) with it volitionally is liable for excision, as it is stated (Exodus 30:33), "and one who puts any of it on a foreigner, shall be cut off." And if he is anointed by accident, he is liable for a fixed sin-offering - meaning to say that there is no difference between the poor and the wealthy, but rather it is a set thing for all.

It is from the roots of this commandment also [that it is] for the aggrandizement of the [Temple] and everything that is in it. And therefore, it is not fit for commoners to use this precious oil in the [Temple], only the chosen ones of the people alone - and they are the priests and the kings. And likewise, in the prevention of the masses from it, it will be become very dear in their eyes and they will desire it. As the great value of things in the heart of most people is according to the scarcity of its being found among them.

From the laws of the commandment - for example, that which they, may their memory be Blessed, said (Keritot 6b) that the liability for excision and the sacrifice is not until he rubs the amount of a kazayit of it; that the Scripture did not make us liable except for that which Moshe made, and not for another that is made by any [other] man (Keritot 5b), and it is a tradition in our hands that a miracle happened with it, that it will suffice forever (Keritot 5b); that which they, may their memory be Blessed, said (Keritot 5b) that we do not anoint all of the priests for [all] the generations with it, but rather the high priest and the one anointed for war and the kings of the House of David, but all of the other kings are not anointed with this oil but with afarsimon oil; the distinction that there is between the process of anointing a king and the process for anointing a priest; that which they, may their memory be Blessed, said (Keritot 5b) that we do not anoint a king who is the son of a king except if there is a disagreement about him, and hence Shlomo was annointed; and the rest of its details - are [all] elucidated in the third [first] chapter of Keritot (see Mishneh Torah, Laws of Vessels of the Sanctuary and Those who Serve Therein 1-2).

And this commandment of the prohibition of anointing the oil is practiced in every place that it is found and at all times by males and females. And one who transgresses it and rubs a kazayit of it volitionally is liable for excision; [and, if] accidental, a fixed sacrifice.

Mitzvah 109

To not make [oil] according to the specification of the anointing oil: To not make the anointing oil, as it is stated (Exodus 30:32), "and you shall not make according to its specification."

From the roots of the commandment is what we have written in the prohibition of its anointing (Sefer HaMitzvot 108). The content of the commandment - [that which] they, may their memory be Blessed, said (Keritot 5b), that none of it was ever made besides the one that Moshe made in the wilderness; and they said that a miracle was performed with it, that it is all preserved for the future to come, and [its] blessing replaced that which they expended from it to anoint the tabernacle and its vessels; that one is not liable for its making unless he makes it according to the amount of its spices, and that is the [meaning of the] expression, "specification,' which expresses a calculation, [as] in the calculation of its spices; and the rest of its details - are elucidated in the first chapter of Keritot.

And this commandment of the prohibition of making the oil is practiced in every place and at all times by males and females. And one who transgresses it and made of it volitionally is liable for excision; [and, if] accidental, a fixed sacrifice.

Mitzvah 110

To not make [incense] according to the specification of the incense: To not make incense identical to the [Temple] incense, meaning to say that its composition be the same weight measurements and he have the intention to provide incense for himself, as it is stated (Exodus 30:37), "and you shall not make for yourselves according to its specification." And it is stated (Exodus 30:38), "A man that makes any like it, to smell of it" - meaning to say that when he is making it, he intends to provide incense for himself.

From the roots of the commandment are what is written in the prohibition of anointing the oil (Sefer HaChinukh 108).

The laws of the commandment - that which they, may their memory be Blessed, said (Keritot 5a) that one who makes it to practice or to sell it to the public is exempted; [that] one who makes even a little of it, anytime he does that little according to the proportions of the incense, is liable; that which they said (Keritot 6a) that the incense was made at the time of the Temple each and every year; that if he reduced one spice from it, he would be liable for the death penalty; and the rest of its details - are elucidated in the first chapter of Keritot (see Mishneh Torah, Laws of Vessels of the Sanctuary and Those who Serve Therein 2).

And this commandment of the prohibition of making it is practiced in every place and at all times by males and females. And one who transgresses it volitionally and made of it according to its proportions, [in order] to smell from it, is liable for excision; [and, if] accidental, a fixed sacrifice. But one who only smells from it and did not make it, is not liable for excision; but rather his ruling is like the ruling for anyone who has benefit (enjoys) from the consecrated.

Mitzvah 111

To not eat and drink a gift to idol worship: To not eat and drink a gift to idolatry, as it is stated (Exodus 34:12-15), "Guard yourself lest you make a covenant with the inhabitants of the land, etc. and he will call to you and you will eat from his offering."

Sefer HaChinukh

It is from the roots of the commandment to distance and remove all matter of idolatry and any matter that is related to it from [in front] of our eyes and from our thoughts. And we have written above (Sefer HaChinukh 26 and 86) what we have known about the foundation of distancing idolatry.

From the laws of the commandment is that which they, may their memory be Blessed, said (Avodah Zarah 51b) that every thing from which they made a gift to idol worship is forbidden, even water and salt - meaning to say that even though water and salt are lesser things and it is possible to say about them that they are not for a gift and that they did not place them in front of idols for the sake of [its] glory at all - nonetheless, it is forbidden. And for great distancing, they, may their memory be Blessed, also forbade (Avodah Zarah 29b) all wine of a gentile, even though we do not know that he used it as an idolatrous libation. And this is called their undifferentiated wine (stam yeinam). However, they, may their memory be Blessed, distinguished (Avodah Zarah 74a) between known libations and their undifferentiated wine - as the prohibition of the known is [prohibited] by Torah writ for the smallest amount. And we administer lashes for it, as it is written (Deuteronomy 13:18), "Nothing is to cling to your hand from the anathema." But with the prohibition of their undifferentiated wines, which is only rabbinic, the [punishment] for its drinking is only lashes of rebellion for one who drinks a revi'it of it. But it does not [carry] lashes of rebellion for less than a revi'it. And nonetheless even the smallest amount is rabbinically forbidden to benefit from. And regarding other things in the world besides wine, they, may their memory be Blessed, were not stringent to forbid everything found in their hand undifferentiated - out of the concern for sacrifices to idol worship or the concern [that it is] itself idolatry, besides with things that are [specifically] made for it; for example, that which they, may their memory be Blessed, said (Avodah Zarah 41a) regarding idols, that undifferentiated idols are made for idol worship. And therefore, they forbade them. And even one who finds them discarded is not allowed to take them without well-known conditions, as they, may their memory be Blessed, explained (Avodah Zarah 41a). And so [too,] is it certainly with anything that an Israelite think was made as a sacrifice - that it is forbidden to take of them.

And they also made many distancings about the matter of wine, as it was the main [source] for the joy of the offering; and also since the Torah mentioned its prohibition explicitly, as it is written in Parshat Haazinu (Deuteronomy 32:38), "drank the wine of their libations." And hence they, may their memory be Blessed, were stringent and said (Avodah Zarah 58a) - in order to distance the matter - that even the wine of a Jew when it is touched by a gentile is immediately prohibited, even to benefit from it. And do not let it be difficult to you, how is it that a gentile can forbid the wine of an Israelite, since we have it established that a person can not bring a prohibition to something that is not his (Chullin 40b). As this is not said except in a case such as if he bows down to his friend's animal, where he did not do an act to the body of the thing. But anytime he does an act to the body of the thing - and even a minor act, like this of touching - he has the power to forbid a thing that is not his, rabbinically. However, it is not [forbidden] by Torah writ until he does a major act, such as slaughtering his animal, which is a major act; and so [too,] if he poured wine in front of the actual idol, that is also a major act. But regarding touching the wine not in front of the idol, it is a minor act. And since it is minor and the prohibition is only rabbinic, they, may their memory be Blessed, permitted (Avodah Zarah 59b) one to take repayment from the one who made it forbidden for that which he made forbidden. And even though they were stringent about the body of the thing to forbid its benefit, they were not stringent about its payment; as payment [here] is only a type of repayment for damage. And [so] he does not benefit from the forbidden thing, but rather takes payment for his damage from the one who made it forbidden.

And so [too,] were they, may their memory be Blessed, very strict in the distancing of wine that has been libated in front of an actual idol or about any thing of idolatry more than with any other prohibitions in the Torah. As you don't have anything [else] in all of the Torah the benefit of which is forbidden, that when it is mixed with something permissible and it is not recognizable, does not have a remedy, [so] as to benefit [from what was permissible] - even something wet in something wet - with that which Rabban Shimon ben Gamliel said in the Gemara (Avodah Zarah 74a): that he should sell it all to gentiles except for the value of the prohibited matter in it. And that is when it is from the things that are not purchased [by Jews] from a gentile, so that no Israelite man will stumble through them and purchase it from the gentile. But with true wine libations and with all idolatrous things, they do not have the remedy of selling it all to the gentile, etc. And all the more so, do they not have the remedy of taking [its] benefit to the Dead Sea. However, [it is] only when true wine libations were mixed - and even one drop of it - that there is no remedy for its benefit ever. But if a barrel of it got mixed with other barrels of kosher wine - since the actual body of the prohibition did not mix, but rather each [barrel] stands on its own - it has a remedy with the remedy of Rabban Shimon ben Gamliel, that he sell all of it to the gentiles, etc. And so [too,] with their undifferentiated wine, do they have a remedy with the remedy of Rabban Shimon ben Gamliel - even when they actually got mixed - like the law of other prohibitions; as it is not fully wine libations.

And you must also know that [in] all of the prohibitions of the Torah, the mixture of which is forbidden to benefit from, it is only forbidden if there is enough of the forbidden food mixed into the permissible food to give off taste into the permissible food - unless that forbidden food is an important thing. As any important thing, such as a portion [with which it] is fit to honor [others] and similar to it, is forbidden in the smallest amount. But anything that is not an important thing does not forbid a mixture unless there is enough in it to give off taste. [This is] except for, wine libations and all matters of idolatry which forbid in the smallest amount, to benefit from everything that is mixed with them (Avodah Zarah 73a), as we said. And there is nothing else in the world at all that is an exception to this principle except for forbidden mixtures of the vineyard (and orlah, the fruit of trees for the first three years), and chamets on Pesach, according to the opinion of some commentators who forbid their mixture of one in two hundred - whether in its own type [of food] or whether not in its type - and (tithes) (orlah) [a burnt offering] with [a mixture] of one in a hundred. And regarding the matter of the remedy that they have, we have already said that there is the remedy of Rabban Shimon ben Gamliel for all of the prohibitions, except for all of the prohibitions of idolatry wherein the prohibited object was itself actually added. As there is no remedy for it ever, and this is from the stringency of idolatry. 'And turn and turn in' the Gemara, as you will find all of this elucidated with the good commentaries. And hold on to [these] things, as you will need them in many places in the Talmud. Hence, I wrote at length about them, which is not like my custom in these annals.

And they, may their memory be Blessed, further distanced us from the prohibition of wine libations, saying that even the payment for wine libations is prohibited to benefit from (Avodah Zarah 62a). They also stressed its distancing by saying that [perhaps] the payment of one who is paid to break barrels of wine libations should be prohibited, because he desires its existence for a short time; meaning to say that he wants that the wine should be preserved in the barrels until he breaks them, so that he will gain his payment for breaking them. As they, may their memory be Blessed, wanted to uproot [it] from our thoughts that we should not want its preservation for even one moment, due to our great disgust with all types of idolatry. And the answer [to their query] was, let him break it and a blessing will come to him, as he diminished the idiocy.

And the rest of its many details - for example, who is it that makes [wine into] wine libations to render it prohibited even to benefit from, and who is it that renders it prohibited only for drinking; from when does it become a wine libation; the law of the gentile's intentional and unintentional touch; his propulsion and the propulsion of that propulsion, and if the Jew is aiding him; which guarding will suffice for us with our wine in the house of the gentile or in our house if there is a gentile there or a carriage and he left a gentile there, such as coming in and out, such that the wine will be permissible; the prohibition that we have with the vessels of their wine, and the law of how to make it fit (kosher); the many details that come to us also about the vessels of their cooking and that is the matter called, "expurgations [of the vessels] of the gentiles"; the laws of our distancing that we not defile our souls also in the matters that are extensions of these disgusting things, such as that which they, may their memory be Blessed, said (Makkot 16b) not to eat and drink in disgusting vessels such as urinals, vessels for feces and a blood-letting horn, since the soul is disgusted in the matter; and the rest of its details - are elucidated in the last chapters of Avodah Zarah, and some of them are in Chullin.

And this warning (prohibition) is practiced in every place and at all times by males and females. And one who transgresses it and eats the smallest amount - or drinks even a drop of true wine libation - is lashed. As the law of these things is not like the law of other laws of prohibited foods, which are with a kazayit, and the law of drinking [which] is with a reviit ; since the Torah warned about idolatry and stated (Deuteronomy 13:18), "Nothing is to cling to your hand from the anathema" - meaning to say even the smallest amount.

In this prevention of wine libations, both Rambam (in Sefer HaMitzvot LaRambam, Mitzvot Lo Taase 194), may his memory be Blessed, and Ramban (in his gloss to the Sefer HaMitzvot), may his memory be Blessed, conceded that there is a negative commandment in this and that it is counted in the tally of the negative commandments. However they did disagree about it in the [following] matter: that Rambam extracts the prohibition of wine libations from the verse that is written in Parshat Haazinu (Deuteronomy 32:38), "drank the wine of their libations"; and the prohibition of other gifts to idolatry from, "Nothing is to cling to your hand from the anathema"(Deuteronomy 13:18) and from "You shall not bring an abomination" (Deuteronomy 7:26); [whereas] Ramban, may his memory be Blessed, wrote that we learn the prohibition of all of the gifts of idolatry from this verse of "Guard yourself," and wine libations are included. And I have written this verse, like his opinion - not like my custom in all of the book, as I have written all [of the other verses] according to the opinion of Rambam, may his memory be Blessed. But in this [case] I saw that this verse is very fit to expound the matter from it; and also, that there is a warning in it. And [it is] as they, may their memory be Blessed, said (Eruvin 96a), [that] every place where it states, "guard yourself," or "lest" or "do not," it is nothing but a negative commandment. However, in the verse, "drank the wine of their libations," there is no warning. And I also saw great ones from the enumerators of the commandment that wrote like this.

Mitzvah 112

The commandment of the land resting on the seventh year: To cease work on the land on the seventh year, as it is stated (Exodus 34:21), "from plowing and from reaping you shall rest." And the explanation comes that it is speaking about the seventh year, that we were commanded not to be occupied with work on the land at all. And this commandment is repeated in its stating in another place (Leviticus 25:5), "it shall be a year of complete rest for the land." And so [too,] "the land shall observe a Shabbat for the Lord" (Leviticus 25:2). And above I have already written all of its content completely (Sefer HaChinukh 84) in the Order of Eem Kesef Talveh et Ami in the commandment of "But in the seventh you shall let it rest and lie fallow" (Exodus 23:11) - even though its place is here.

Mitzvah 113

To not eat meat with milk: To not eat meat with milk that has been cooked together, as it is stated (Exodus 34:26), "you shall not cook a kid in its mother's milk." And this verse comes to forbid eating and deriving benefit (pleasure) from the meat with milk. And let it not be difficult to you - [that] if so, why is its prohibition not stated explicitly, as "you shall not eat," and [instead] expressed with an expression of cooking. As the answer to this [is] because there is a novelty in the prohibition of its eating above the eating of the other prohibitions. As with other prohibitions, the liability is only if he enjoys his eating. But here even if he does not enjoy his eating, once he swallows it - and even if he swallows it hot and he burns his throat with it, and similar to it - he is lashed nonetheless. [It is] as they, may their memory be Blessed, said in Pesachim 25a, "For this reason did [the Torah] not write, 'eating' in [the verse] itself: To say that one is lashed [even when consumed] not in the way of its enjoyment." And nonetheless, we do not administer lashes for it unless it is by way of cooking (Chullin 108a), according to the language that the verse expressed its prohibition.

And even though they, may their memory be Blessed, said (Chullin 115b) that that which the prohibition of cooking is written three times in the Torah is to teach the prohibition of eating, the prohibition of cooking and the prohibition of benefiting - it is only fit for us to count two [of them] in the tally of negative commandments; as the prohibition of eating and benefiting is one thing. [It is] like they, may their memory be Blessed, said (Chullin 115b), "Every place that it is stated, 'You (singular) shall not eat,' 'You (plural) shall not eat,' both the prohibition of eating and the prohibition of benefiting are implied." As the Torah expresses all of the enjoyments more generally with an expression of eating, since it is a constant enjoyment for a person, and he needs it; and like the matter that is written (Exodus 24:11), "they beheld God, and they ate and drank" - that it calls enjoyment 'eating.'

And if you will grab me [and say], "If so, why are three prohibitions written?" As two suffice, according to what I have said. [Then] one can answer you that certainly if in [one] place it was written, "You shall not cook," to teach about the prohibition of cooking and in another place, "You shall not eat," which would include the prohibition of benefiting and the prohibition of eating, as we have said - it would have been correct not to write the third. As there would not be any need for it, since we would have already learned eating and benefiting from "You shall not eat" - from the principle in our hand, that included in eating is the implication about benefiting. But now that eating is not mentioned in any place, we would not have learned [about] benefiting without the third negative [statement]. And you should not ask further, "And why did the [Torah] not write, 'You shall not eat' in one of them and it would suffice with two?" As I have informed you that it was for a purpose that Scripture did not mention it with the expression of eating, as the liability for it is even if it is not in the way of its enjoyment. We have learned from here that the intention of that which they, may their memory be Blessed, said (Chullin 115b) "One is for the prohibition of eating, one is for the prohibition of benefiting and one is for the prohibition of cooking," is not that the third verse be a [separate] negative commandment, but rather that we need to learn from it about benefiting. And Blessed be [the One] Who chose their words.

We have written (Sefer HaChinukh 92) what we could from the roots of the commandment from the angle of the simple meaning, in the prohibition of cooking in Parshat Eleh HaMishpatim.

From the laws of the commandment: That which they, may their memory be Blessed, said (Chullin 113a), that the prohibition of meat with milk from Torah writ is only with meat of a beast (domesticated animal) that is pure (kosher); but not from an impure beast, not from a [wild] animal - even a pure [one] - and not from a bird, whether pure or impure. And they relied for this upon that which it is written, "kid" three times in the Torah, which is an expression of exclusion, as it should have [otherwise] written, "meat." And the explanation about this came (Chullin 113a), "'A kid' and not an impure beast, 'a kid' and not a [wild] animal, 'a kid' and not a bird." And therefore, they, may their memory be Blessed, said that it is permitted to cook these three with milk, and they are permitted in benefit. But they, may their memory be Blessed, prohibited them in eating to make a fence for the meat of a beast, which is forbidden by Torah writ, so that people do not switch [one] meat for [another] meat. And hence since the thing is [plausible] that [one] meat will be switched with [another] meat, they were also stringent with this fence, exactly like they were with the meat of beast in some matters, such that they forbade that they be brought up [together] on a table at all. And according to the opinion of some commentators, they obligated about them that there be a pause between their eating and the eating of cheese, like with the main prohibition, which is the meat of a beast. But with the meat of fish and locusts, they did not make a fence with them all, as their meat is not at all similar to the meat of a beast, and people will not come to err in this.

And they were also stringent in this matter according to some of the commentators to [deduce] a novel prohibition in this, more than in other prohibitions of food (Chullin 108a). [It is] in that with the matter of meat with milk, if milk is mixed with meat, and there is not sixty parts in the piece of meat corresponding to the milk, we see both of them as one piece of prohibited food. And if this piece fell into a stew of meat or a stew of milk, we measure against all of [the piece]. And this is what, they, may their memory be Blessed, said (Chullin 108a) "The piece itself becomes a carcass." And the reason is because their mixture is what makes them prohibited. And hence, after they have mixed, behold, they are like a piece of carcass. And with other prohibitions, it is not such; as [with] prohibited food that is mixed with a piece of permissible food and there is not sixty parts in the permissible food to negate the prohibited food, and afterwards they fall into a stew, we only measure according to the measurement of the prohibited food that fell into it, and [the permissible portion of the piece] itself helps to [count against] the prohibited food. [This is] because that piece does not become a carcass, and [so] the permissible food in it is found to be like the rest of the permissible food in the stew - and [so] it assists [in counting against] the prohibited food. However if it is recognizable, the piece itself is forbidden forever, according to the opinion of some of the commentators.

And they, may their memory be Blessed, said (Temurah 33a) that the ashes of meat [that was cooked together] with milk is prohibited; like the ashes of all things that are prohibited to benefit from, which require burial. And they also said (Chullin 111b) that the Torah only prohibited meat with milk, regarding the milk of a living beast. But with the milk of a dead [one], it is not prohibited. And therefore, the udder is permitted [to be eaten] with its milk, according to Torah writ. However, the sages forbade it as a fence, until one removes its milk from it, as is elucidated in its place (Chullin 109b). And there are two dispensations for milk that is found in the stomach [of an animal]: one, that it is included in [the category of] the milk of a dead [one]; and also, since it is only like refuse more generally - as it has already been digested there. And therefore, it is permissible from the outset. And it is not necessary to say that that which is found coagulated there is permissible - as it is certainly like refuse - but even that which is liquid was permitted by the Geonim. One who cooks an embryo in milk is liable, and so [too,] one who eats it. But one who cooks a placenta or skin or tendons or bones or the roots of the horns or hoof nails is exempted. [These] and the rest of the commandment's details are elucidated in the eighth chapter of Chullin.

And [it] is practiced in every place and at all times by males and females. And one who transgresses it and volitionally eats a kazayit from the meat with milk that has been cooked together is lashed. But if he benefited from it - for example, [if] he gave it or sold it - he is not lashed, since it is possible to [derive] benefit without an act. And we do not administer lashes for anything that does not have an act [involved] with it. And it is possible that he is not lashed even if he rubs with it - since it is not in the way of its enjoyment, as it is not made for rubbing. But there is also an argument about it [to say] that he is lashed.

Mitzvah 114

That the court not administer a death sentence on the Shabbat: That the judges not administer sentences on Shabbat, meaning to say that they not kill on the Shabbat one who has been made liable for the death penalty by the court, as it is stated (Exodus 35:3), "You shall not kindle fire throughout your settlements on the Shabbat day." And the explanation comes about this (Yevamot 6b) that the court should not burn someone who has become liable for burning. And the same is true for the other death penalties. And it is [correct] for us to expound this thing from [this verse]; as behold, it is not necessary for itself, as behold, it is already written in another place, "you shall not do work" (Exodus 20:10) - and kindling is for the sake of work. Rather, it is written to teach [another] matter. And they explained about it that it came to teach us this [matter] that we said. And this is the language of Mekhilta d'Rabbi Yishmael 35:3:2 (at the beginning of Parshat Vayakhel): "'You shall not kindle fire' - burning was in the general category [of forbidden work], yet it was [specified, in order] to teach that just like burning is particular in that it is one of the death penalties of the court and [we see here] that it does not push off the Shabbat, so too all of the other death penalties do not push off the Shabbat." And even with all that we have learned in this verse, it should also be expounded [for] that which they also expounded on it (Yevamot 6b), "Kindling was [specified] to separate" - meaning to say that one who does many principle categories of work at one time in one forgetful spell would be liable a sin-offering for each and every [type of] work by itself. And in the Gemara of the Westerners they said (Talmud Yerushalmi Sanhedrin 4:6), "'In all of your settlements' - Rabbi Ila said in the name of Rabbi Yannai, 'From here [we learn] about courts, that they should not judge on Shabbat.'"

It is from the roots of the commandment that God, may He be Blessed, wanted to honor this day, that everyone find rest on it - even sinners and guilty ones. [There is a relevant] parable about a great king who called the people of his state to a feast, such that he does not prevent [its] entryway to any man. And after the day of the feast, he will administer justice. So [too] is this thing, as God, may He be Blessed commanded us to sanctify and honor the Shabbat day for our good and for our merit, as I have written above (Sefer HaChinukh 31, 32) - and this is also from the honor of this day.

And this commandment is practiced at the time of the [Temple] by males, as they are the ones in charge of justice. And they are obligated to be careful that they not administer a sentence on the Shabbat. And if they transgressed and commanded to burn a creature on the Shabbat, they have violated this negative commandment. But we do not administer lashes for it, as there is no act [involved] with it. And if they did do an act with it, such as burning him with their hands - if there are witnesses and a warning - they are stoned; [and if] accidental, they bring a sin-offering for atonement. Parshat Eleh Pikudei does not have a commandment in it.

Mitzvah 115
The commandment of the procedure of the burnt-offering: To execute the burn-offering according to its statue, as it is stated (Leviticus 1:3), "If his sacrifice is a burnt-offering, etc." - as it is written in the section.
What I have written in the commandment of the Temple about the matter of sacrifices in the Order on Vayikchu Li (Sefer HaChinukh 95) is from the roots of the commandment.
From the laws of the commandment is that which they, may their memory be Blessed, said about the procedure of the burnt-offering that it was executed thus: We slaughter the beast in the [Temple] yard - and the slaughter is fit even with non-priests, but from the reception of the blood and onward, it is a commandment of the priesthood. And the priest would sprinkle the blood and flay it and dissect the limbs whole - as it is written (Leviticus 1:6), "into sections," and they, may their memory be Blessed, explained (Chullin 11:1), "And not sections into sections." And when he dissects [it], he removes the sciatic nerve from the thigh, and incinerates all of the sections on top of the altar. And the wool on the heads of the sheep, the hair of the beards of the male goats, the bones, the tendons, the horns and the hooves - when they are attached - we incinerate it all, as it is stated (Leviticus 1:9), "and the priest incinerates it all." [But if] they were separated, they do not go up, as it is stated (Deuteronomy 12:26), "And you shall execute your burnt-offerings, the meat and the blood."
And how was the order of the dissection (see Mishnah Tamid 4); how was the rinsing of the intestines; with how many people they would move the limbs to the altar - that they, may their memory be Blessed, said (Yoma 26b) that the sheep is with six, the ox with twenty-four for communal burnt-offerings and less [for] burnt-offerings of individuals. And the content of the burnt-offering of fowl - how it was done - and the rest of its details are elucidated in Zevachim.
And [it] is practiced at the time of the [Temple] by the males of the priesthood. And a priest that transgressed and did not execute it according to this order has violated a positive commandment.

Mitzvah 116
The commandment of the meal-offering (mincha): To execute the procedure of the meal offering in the matter that is mentioned in the Torah in its sections, as it is stated (Leviticus 2:1), "And if a soul offers a meal-offering," and it is written (Leviticus 2:5), "If it is a meal-offering on a griddle," and it is written further (Leviticus 2:6), "If it is a meal-offering in a pan."
And the content of the meal-offerings is an offering that comes from types of flour and not from animals. And I have already written above (Sefer HaChinukh 95) that the sacrifice of animals is truthfully a strong resemblance to people, [in order] to humble and lower the desiring and sinful soul when he sees that a living thing like him - except that it does not have intellect - is burnt and finished. And so too is the sinning soul, from the angle of the weakness of its intellect, ending and lost also, if it becomes habituated to animal actions which are the sins - as sin only comes from an animal root. But [this] offering in that it is not a living thing - even though it also comes to humble the impulse, such that it sees that because of his sin, a man needs to burn [from] his money and finish it - the resemblance is not strong like with living things. And it appears according to the simple understanding that therefore is it called a gift (mincha) - as its content is less than a living sacrifice; just like gifts of people are usually with little. And also, because many of them come as voluntary offerings - and that which is not obligated among people is called a gift.
And these are all the types of meal-offerings that they would offer at the time of the [Temple] that come on their own - meaning to say that they do not come as meal-offerings of libations, meaning in the context of another sacrifice: There are three meal-offerings that come for the sake of the entire community and they are (Menachot 68b) the omer of Pesach, the two breads of [Shavouot] and the bread of display of each Shabbat - and the three of them are called, ' mincha.' And there are nine of the individual and these are them:

Sefer HaChinukh

1. The meal-offering of a sinner - and that is the meal-offering that a poor person offers when he is liable for a sin-offering, but his hand does not reach [a more expensive sacrifice];

2. the meal-offering of the sotah, which is the meal-offering of jealousy that is written in Parshat Nasso (Numbers 5:15);

3. the meal-offering that every priest offers when he enters the service that he offers in his hand, and this is called the meal-offering of inauguration;

4. the meal-offering that the high priest offers every day, and it is called the griddled meal-offering;

5. the meal-offering of fine flour, and it comes as an oath or a vow;

6. the meal-offering of the griddle, and it comes as an oath or a vow;

7. the meal-offering of the pan, and it comes as an oath or a vow;

8. the oven-baked meal-offering that is loaves, and it comes as an oath or a vow;

9. the oven-baked meal-offering that comes soaked in oil, and it comes as an oath or a vow;

From these meal-offerings, some of them are fine wheat flour and some are barley; some of them are eaten by the priests except for the handful and some are all burnt. And one of them is chamets and that is the two breads of the day of Shavouot, as they are also called ' mincha,' but they are not offered on top of the altar. And it was not stated in the Torah about the two breads, when it more generally forbade, "Any meal-offering that you offer to the Lord, you shall not make chamets" (Leviticus 2:11). [Rather,] it specified these and excluded them from the rule. And about them is it stated there (Leviticus 2:12), "A first sacrifice shall you bring them to the Lord" - meaning to say, with these I did not prohibit chamets to you. And nonetheless, they would not go up on the altar, since there was chamets in them, and as it is stated about them, "upon the altar they shall not be brought up as a pleasing smell." And all of the rest was matsa. And the order of their bringing was thus (Sotah 14b): A man brings fine flour from his house in a vessel of silver or gold or of [another] metal and carries it to the priest; and the priest carries it to the altar, [he] skims a handful from it with the tips of his fingers and incinerates the handful; and the rest is eaten by the priests. This is the order of those eaten. And the order of those burned; the processes done with meal-offerings by non-priests and those done [only] by priests; and the rest of its details are elucidated in the tractate that is built upon this, and that its Tractate Menachot.

And the execution of meal-offerings was practiced at the time of the [Temple] by the males of the priesthood. And a priest that transgressed and changed the procedure of the meal-offering that is explicit about it has violated a positive commandment.

Mitzvah 117

To not offer leaven or honey: To not offer leaven or honey on top of the altar, as it is stated (Leviticus 2:11), "for any leaven and any honey you shall not burn from it as a fire to the Lord." And the prevention is repeated at the beginning of the verse, as it is stated, "Any meal-offering that you offer to the Lord, you shall not make chamets." And honey is a general name for the well-known honey, as well as for the honey of dates - which is the undifferentiated honey of the Torah - and also for the sap that exudes from [other] sweet fruits. And included in "you shall not burn," is also not to put from it into the filling of the incense. And [it is] as the incense-makers say, "Honey is good for incense, but the Torah forbade it."

The roots of this commandment are very hidden to find even a small hint from them. However, since I already made known at the opening of my words that my intention with these reasons that I write is to accustom the youth and give them explanations at the beginning of their coming to hear the words of the Book, since the words of Torah have explanations and benefits - and they shall accept them according to their custom and according to the weakness of their intellect - and let not the commandments be like 'words of a sealed book' at first, lest they rebel against them from this in their youth, leave them forever and go (to emptiness) in emptiness. Hence, I will write everything that first comes into my thoughts. And once he knows my intention, let not the [critic criticize] me in any thing. And I will say that the matter of all of the sacrifices is to arouse the thoughts of the one that offers [them]; and according to that act, he shall take its similarities into his soul - all as we have already written (Sefer HaChinukh 95, 116). Hence in distancing chamets, which is made with great delay, he will take the similarity from his sacrifice to acquire the trait of alacrity, of lightness and of speed in [doing] the act of God, Blessed be He. And as they, may their memory be Blessed, said (Mishnah Avot 5:20), "Be[...] light like the eagle, swift like the deer, and mighty like the lion to do, etc." And we are obligated in the matter with the meal-offering of individuals more than with the communal meal-offering; since discouragement and laziness are found more with the individual - as the many will flag one another. And therefore, the Torah did not concern itself about this with a communal meal-offering that comes from time to time, such as two breads of [Shavouot]. But with the bread of display - even though it is also called a communal meal-offering - since it is a constant meal-offering on each and every Shabbat, the Torah concerned itself about it and also commanded us about it that it should be matsa.

And regarding the distancing of honey, we shall say to the tender children in order to discipline them that the cause is to make a similarity that a person should minimize running after food that are sweet to the palate, like the custom of the gluttons and drunkards that are always drawn after everything sweet. And he should place into his heart [to seek] only foods that are beneficial for the body, necessary for his sustenance and [that] protect the health of his limbs. And for this [reason], it is fit for any intelligent person to not plan his food and his drink towards the intention of the pleasure of the sensation of his throat. And if only people were wise, they would understand this. As the whole matter of sensation is a disgrace for them, all the more so is it not fitting for them to intend it and to enjoy it - only that which is required by nature perforce. And there are from the wise men that wrote, "The sense of touch, which is a disgrace for us."

And I have further heard a reason about the prohibition of leaven and honey, because leaven raises itself and honey likewise brings up much foam. And therefore, they were distanced [from us] to hint that 'an abomination to the Lord is every haughty person.' And I saw further in the commentary of Ramban, may his memory be Blessed, who wrote (Ramban on Leviticus 2:11) and this is his language: "And since the sacrifices are for the will of the glorious God, they should not come from things that have a strong hand to change the nature [of things]; and so [too], they should not come from things that are completely sweet like honey, but rather from [things that are] mixtures - as they, may their memory be Blessed, said (Bereishit Rabbah 12:15) about the creation of the world, 'He combined the trait of mercy with the trait of kindness and created it.'" To here [are his words].

The laws of the commandment: That which they, may their memory be Blessed, said (Menachot 52b) that all meal-offerings that are offered on top of the altar come [as] matsa, as we said. And so [too, that] the remainders of the meal-offerings that the priests eat are not eaten chamets - even though [the priests] are permitted to eat them with any food or with honey - as it is stated (Leviticus 6:10), "You shall not bake their portion chamets," and [included] in its understanding is [that] even their portion shall they not render chamets. And if he renders its remainders chamets, he is lashed. And we administer lashes for each and every doing within it. How is this? [If] he kneaded it chamets or set it up chamets or cut it up chamets or broke it up chamets or baked it chamets, he is lashed - as it is stated, "you shall not make chamets," "you shall not bake chamets," to make liable for a single action in making it chamets; [he is] liable for lashes. And we do not dampen wheat kernels of meal-offerings lest they become chamets (Rashi on Pesachim 36a). And nonetheless they, may their memory be Blessed, said (Menachot 55a) that baked meal-offerings were kneaded in lukewarm water, and they would guard them that they not become chamets, as priests are alacritous. And leaven and honey are forbidden (forbid) with the smallest amount, as it is stated, "you shall not burn from it" - meaning to say, even the smallest amount. And he is not liable unless he burns them with the offering or for the sake of the offering (Mishneh Torah, Laws of Things Forbidden on the Altar 5:1). And it is one whether he burns them by themselves or their mixture - he is lashed (Menachot 58a). But if he burned them on their own for the sake of [fire]wood, he is exempted; as it is stated (Leviticus 2:12), "upon the altar they shall not be brought up as a pleasing smell" - for a pleasing smell you shall not bring up, but you may bring up for the sake of wood (Zevachim 76b). And the rest of its details are elucidated in Tractate Menachot.

Rambam, may his memory be Blessed, (in Sefer HaMitzvot LaRambam, Mitzvot Lo Taase 98 and in Mishneh Torah, Laws of Things Forbidden on the Altar 5:1) calculated the prohibition of leaven and

Sefer HaChinukh

honey as one negative commandment - meaning to say, if he offered both of them, leaven and honey, together, he is only lashed once. [But] if he offered each one on its own, he is lashed one [set of] lashes for each one. And he gave a reason for his words: That this is a general negative commandment; and with a general negative commandment like this, we administer one [set of] lashes for two things. And the teacher, our Rabbi Moshe bar Nachman (Ramban), may this memory be Blessed, (in his glosses on the Sefer HaMitzvot above) disagreed with him, to calculate leaven and honey as two negative commandments. And he said that he does not see a general negative commandment here; as behold with chamets, it specifies its negative commandment explicitly, as it is written, "you shall not bake chamets." And if so, [with regards to] the negative commandment of honey - even though there is leaven with it (after it), we should say that the honey is learned by itself. And [so] a negative commandment is found for each one. And the rest of their proofs are in their book.

And [it] is practiced at the time of the [Temple] by male priests, as the service is theirs.

Mitzvah 118

To not offer a sacrifice without salt: To not suppress salt from upon the sacrifice or upon the meal-offering; meaning to say that the priests not offer any sacrifice or any meal-offering unless they place salt in them, as it is stated (Leviticus 2:13), "you shall not suppress the salt of your covenant with God from your meal-offering." And it is also written (there), "upon all your offerings you shall offer salt."

I have written from the roots of the commandment above at the beginning of the Order.

From the laws of the commandment is [that which] they, may their memory be Blessed, said (Menachot 21a) that it is a commandment to salt the meat properly - similar to the salting of meat for roasting - such that he salts it from both sides. But it is fit, ex post facto, even if he salted it a tiny bit (Mishneh Torah, Laws of Things Forbidden on the Altar 5:11). And the salt with which we salt the sacrifices is the communities, like the [fire]wood. And an individual does not bring salt or wood for the sacrifices. And all of this is from the aggrandizement of the [Temple]; as 'in a place of wealth, there is no poverty' (Shabbat 102b). And they would put the salt in three places: in the chamber of salt; on top of the ramp; and at the top of the altar. They would salt the limbs in the chamber of salt, and they would salt the handful, the frankincense, the burnt meal-offerings and the burnt offering of the fowl at the top of the altar. And the rest of its details are in the seventh chapter of Zevachim.

And [it] is practiced at the time of the [Temple] by the males of the priesthood, as it for them to complete the requirements of the sacrifice. And a priest that transgresses and offers a sacrifice or meal-offering without salt at all, has violated a positive commandment and also violated this negative commandment. And he is lashed - as behold, there is an act here when he offers the bland meat, about which he has been warned not to offer it without salt.

Mitzvah 119

The commandment of salting the sacrifice: To offer salt on all of the sacrifices; meaning to say, that he places salt in the meat of the sacrifice and so [too,] in the flour of the meal-offerings, as it is stated (Leviticus 2:13), "upon all your offerings you shall offer salt."

We have already said in the commandment of the building of the [Temple] (Sefer HaChinukh 95) that it is from the roots of the commandment of the sacrifice to render fit and straighten the soul of the one who offers it. And therefore, in order to arouse the soul of the one who offers, he is commanded offering things that are good, pleasant and beloved to him - and as we wrote above. And the salt in it is also from this root, so that his action be complete, [that] it not lacks anything according to the practice of people; since then, will his heart be more aroused. As anything without salt is not pleasant to a person - not its flavor and not even its smell. And besides this, there is another matter hinted to with salt, as salt preserves everything and saves from spoiling and rotting. And so [too,] with the procedure of the sacrifice, a man is saved from loss, preserves his soul and will remain in existence forever.

From the laws of the commandment is that which they, may their memory be Blessed said (Menachot 20a) that all the sacrifices are salted before they go up to the altar. And you do not have anything that approached the altar without salt, except for the libations, blood and wood. And this thing is a tradition and it does not have a [source in] Scripture. And if he transgressed and sacrificed without salt, the sacrifice is fit and acceptable - except for the meal-offering, [for which] the salt impedes it. As about it is it stated explicitly (Leviticus 2:13), "you shall not suppress the salt of your covenant with God from your meal-offering." And the rest of its details are elucidated in Sifra and in [various] places in Menachot (see Mishneh Torah, Laws of Things Forbidden on the Altar 5:11).

And [it] is practiced at the time of the [Temple] by the males of the priesthood. And one who transgresses this and offers a meal-offering or sacrifice without salt has violated this positive commandment; and he further violates a negative commandment, as it is written, "you shall not suppress the salt, etc."

Mitzvah 120
The commandment of the sacrifice of the court if they erred in instruction: That the Great Sanhedrins offer a sacrifice if they erred and instructed not like the law about weighty sins for which we are liable excision and the community or their leader acted according to their word; as it is stated (Leviticus 4:13), "If the whole community of Israel erred and the thing was hidden, etc."

I have already written above (Sefer HaChinukh 95) that the sacrifice is intended to humble the desiring soul and to enlarge the intellectual soul. And therefore, when a mistake comes to the great ones in something, it is well-known that it happened to them from the weakness of the intellect. And it is fitting to strengthen it in any case. And hence they come to the House upon which the Intellect impacts, do the act of the sacrifice and, by force of the action, put back into their hearts the inferiority of the erring animal soul and the importance of the straight and clear intellect. And from this pure thought, they will pay attention and comprehend with [the execution of] all of their rulings forever.

From the laws of the commandment is (for example,) that which they, may their memory be Blessed, said (Horayot 4b) that there is a mistake in the instructions [for which] the court is liable to bring a sacrifice, and not (upon) the one who does according to their word, and there is [one] where the doer is liable and not them. And these are from the necessary conditions for which the court would be liable and not the ones doing according to their word: That the instructors be seventy-one; that the head of the yeshiva be with them at the time they instructed; that they all be fit for instruction, as it is stated (Numbers 25:24), "if from the eyes if the community" - [not] until they be eyes for them, meaning to say, until they are fit for instruction; and the majority of them err in this matter that they instructed about; that they instructed explicitly, such that they said to the people, "You are permitted to do [it]"; that all of the congregation - or most of them - do according to their word; that the ones doing it are inadvertent according to their word and imagine that the court instructed properly, and not that those doing knew that they erred and did [it] nonetheless. And also, that they instructed to nullify part [of the law] and preserve part of it (Horayot 3b), but not to uproot all of one commandment, as it is stated, "and the thing was hidden," - and not the whole body [of the commandment]. And this is a (teaching) decree of Scripture (gezerat hakatuv). And it is possible that the reason of the matter it that there is no concern that a mistake of uprooting the whole body of the commandment will not be revealed quickly. And when the sin become known to them, that they knew the actual thing that they instructed in error, and not that they were in doubt about which thing the error occurred to them - and even if they knew that they certainly erred in one [part]. And even if the sinners informed them and told them, "You erred in this" - since they do not remember that thing exactly, they are exempt; as it is stated (Leviticus 4:14), "And the sin is known" - meaning to say, to them, and not those others inform them. All of these conditions need to be in the thing, such that the court is liable for a sacrifice and not the ones that act according to their word.

And their saying that the court is liable a sacrifice means to say that the the tribes of Israel bring a sacrifice for them, as it is elucidated in Horayot 5b. And if they erred in an instruction about idolatry, the twelve tribes bring twelve bulls for a burnt-offering and twelve goats for a sin-offering; and if in the instruction of other sins of excision for which one is liable a sin-offering when inadvertent, they bring [only] twelve bulls.

And if one [of the conditions] is lacking, one who does according to their word is liable for a fixed sin-offering and [the judges] are exempt. As the Torah only made the court liable for this sacrifice when they are complete - since there is in this instruction for sin of all the people, that their heads err and they be in their completeness.

And the rest of the many angles by which an individual is liable and they are exempt or they are liable and he is exempt; the difference in sacrifices between them, such as that which they, may their memory be Blessed, said (Horayot 9a), "All of the commandments in the Torah for the volitional transgression of which one is liable excision and for the inadvertent transgression of which one is liable a sin-offering, the individual brings a ewe or female goat, the chieftain brings a male goat and an anointed priest and a court bring a bull" - and that is the high priest that was anointed with anointing oil (Horayot 11b); and the rest of its details are elucidated in Tractate Horayot and in [various] places in Zevachim (see Mishneh Torah, Laws of Offerings for Unintentional Transgressions 14)

And [it] is practiced at the time of the [Temple] when we have Great Sanhedrins.

Mitzvah 121

The commandment of a sin-offering for an individual who sinned inadvertently in a commandment for which we are liable excision: That anyone that sins inadvertently from the big well-known sins offer a sin offering, as it is stated (Leviticus 4:27), "And if a soul sin inadvertently from the people of the land, etc." And this is what is called a fixed sin-offering; meaning to say that it is always a sacrifice of a beast and it does not vary up or down according to the wealth or poverty of the one who brings it. And the sins for which they would be liable a sin-offering are always the ones for which we are liable excision for their volitional transgression (Yevamot 9b) - and on condition that it be a negative commandment and that there be an act [involved] with it (Makkot 13b). We have already said that it is from the roots of the commandment of the sacrifice to abase the sinning soul - 'like the sin-offering, like the guilt-offering, there is one law for them.' I do not need to repeat it for each and every one.

From the laws of the commandment is, for example, that which they, may their memory be Blessed, said (Horayot 9a) that the liability of the one that sins inadvertently to bring a sin-offering is only for a sin for which we are liable excision for its volitional transgression. But there are three sins in the Torah that, even though there is excision for their volitional transgression, there is no sin-offering for their inadvertent transgression. And these are them: one who curses; one who undoes circumcision; and one who refrains from enacting the Pesach sacrifice. And they give a reason for each one and it is explained in its place. And all other sins for which their volitional transgression has excision, their inadvertent transgression has a fixed sin-offering - except for an impure person that eats consecrated [foods] and an impure person that enters the Temple; as even though their volitional transgression has excision, we do not bring a fixed sin-offering, but rather a sacrifice that varies up and down - which is fowl or flour, as is explained in the verse (Leviticus 5:6,13). You come out learning that all of the sins in the Torah for which an individual brings a fixed sin-offering for their inadvertent transgression are forty-three (Mishneh Torah, Laws of Offerings for Unintentional Transgressions 1:4) - go and count, because you will find it so. And most of them are for forbidden sexual relationships. And so [too,] from this matter is that which they, may their memory be Blessed, said (Shabbat 112a) that there is only liability for a sacrifice when he is inadvertent from beginning to end. And the different awarenesses that it is possible for an inadvertent sinner to have in his inadvertence are many. And the rest of its many details are elucidated in Horayot and Keritiot, and in [various] places in Shabbat and Zevachim.

And [it] is practiced at the time of the [Temple] by males and females. And one who transgresses it and does not offer a fixed sin-offering for his inadvertent sin has violated a positive commandment.

Mitzvah 122

The commandment of testimony: To say the testimony in front of the judges, in all that we know of it - whether with the testimony, [the accused] will become liable for death or money that is earmarked for him, or whether it will be his salvation for his money or for his life - as it is stated (Leviticus 5:1), "and he is a witness or saw or knew, if he does not say, he will carry his iniquity." In every matter, it is an obligation (Mishneh Torah, Laws of Testimony 1:1) upon us to say the testimony in front of the court (Bava Kamma 55b).

However, there is a difference between monetary laws, and capital and other laws in the Torah. As with monetary laws, a man is not obligated to testify about them on his own, unless a party in the case or the court solicits him. But with capital laws and other prohibitions in the Torah - for example, he saw someone that transgressed a prohibition; and so [too,] with capital testimony, that he saw someone kill his fellow; or in the testimony of blows, that one hit his fellow - with all of this, a man is obligated to come on his own and say the testimony in front of a court, so as to destroy the evil and to separate a man from a prohibition.

It is from the roots of the commandment [that it is] because there is great benefit to people with this commandment. It is not necessary to write at length about it, as the things are known to all who see the sun.

The laws of the commandment: For example, the differences that the Sages, may their memory be Blessed, revealed to us that there are in this commandment between one man and another, such that not every man is obligated to come in front of the court to testify to them: As if the witness was a great sage and the court less than he, he may - if he wants - withhold from testifying in front of them; as the positive commandment of honor of the Torah pushes off the positive commandment of testimony (as is elucidated in Shevuot 36b). And a high priest is also not obligated to testify except only for testimony [that pertains] to a king (Mishneh Torah, Laws of Testimony 1:3). And kings of Israel do not testify about others, and others [do not testify] about them, because of a case that happened, as it appears in Sanhedrin 19a in the chapter [entitled] Kohen Gadol. But kings of the House of David testify and [others] testify about them and judge them. And we do not withhold from accepting the testimony on account of love or hate, as 'the remnant of Israel will not do injustice' in their testimony (Sanhedrin 27b). But regarding judgement, it is not so; as a friend and an enemy may not judge, because the enemy cannot see a merit and the friend cannot see a liability.

And Rambam, may his memory be Blessed, wrote (Mishneh Torah, Laws of Testimony 3:4) that the main testimony of the Torah is from the mouth of witnesses and not from the mouth of their writing, as it is stated (Deuteronomy 17:6), "By the mouth, etc."; except that because of the betterment of the world, such that people would find [those from whom] to borrow, the Sages ordained that we establish law with regard to money according to witnesses in a deed, the same as from their mouth. But Ramban, may his memory be Blessed, (in the Sefer HaMitzvot at the end of the second root) challenged him greatly about this in the Sefer HaMitzvot. And if I would come to write the whole matter, it would be lengthy. But the essence of the thing is that Ramban, may his memory be Blessed, holds that the testimony of a deed is from Torah writ, as it is written (Jeremiah 32:44), "write in the book, and seal."

And from the laws of the commandment is also that which they, may their memory be Blessed, said (Ketuvot 18b) that any man who said (testified) his testimony in front of a court and they investigated him according to their will, may not go back and contradict anything from all that he said in front of them, and say that he erred or was inadvertent or that he remembered afterwards that the matter was not like he testified. And even if he gave a reason for his words, we do not listen to him. And also testimony in a deed is like testimony that the court investigated according to their will, and [so] the witnesses may not recant on anything in the deed. And we judge [the case] according to the signatories about everything written in the deed - and that is when we are sure that those signatories are are the ones that signed the deed, not that a forger forged them. And this investigation we should do by way of men that recognized those signatures - that they are the writing of those people that are signed. And we need two witnesses that recognize the two signatures - each one of them that recognizes both of the witnesses. And so [too,] if two of the judges, themselves, recognize them, it is enough for us with that (Ketuvot 21b); or if the signatories, themselves, are in front of us and each one testifies about his signature, it is enough with that. But one cannot testify about his writing and the writing of his fellow (Ketuvot 20b). And so [too,] if the writing of their hand is [validated] from another place that is in front of us, we certify them from it. And it is explained in the Gemara (Ketuvot 20a) that we only certify a deed from two [other] deeds of two fields [through which] their owners ate [from] them openly without fear or trepidation about a claim from the [previous] owners; or from two marriage deeds (ketuvot) - and that is when they come from under the hand of another, not from under the hand of this one that wants validation [of the document], as we are concerned lest it is all a forgery. And so [too, we validate] from another deed that was challenged and [then] ratified by the court.

And that which they, may their memory be Blessed, also said (Ketuvot 28a) that with testimony about a signature, a relative is trusted to testify about the writing of his relative, that he recognizes it - and he combines with another to validate the deed. And with this testimony a man is trusted when he is an adult to testify and say, "When I was small, I saw the writing of my father - or my brother - and I recognize it now, that it is the one that I saw." And that which they said that ten creatures are disqualified for testimony from Torah writ, and like I wrote above in the commandment of "do not place your hand with an evildoer to be a witness" (Sefer HaChinukh 75). And so [too,] one who is not [involved] in Scripture, nor in Mishnah, nor in the way of the world (productive work) is disqualified by the words of [the Rabbis], as there is an assumption about him that he is an evildoer - and behold, it is written (Exodus 23:1), "do not place [...] an evildoer to be a witness." But if he has [involvement] in the way of the world and is involved in some commandments, we accept his testimony, even though he is an ignoramus. You will be found to say that any Torah scholar is assumed to be fit until he is disqualified and [any] ignoramus is assumed to be disqualified until his status is established with us for the good. And so [too,] the most debased men are disqualified [rabbinically], such as those that eat in the marketplace in front of everyone. And included in the debased (Sanhedrin 26b) are those that consume the charity of gentiles publicly. And the rest of its details are elucidated in Sanhedrin and in Shevuot (see Mishneh Torah, Laws of Testimony 1).

And [it] is practiced in every place and at all times by males, but not by women - as women are not in the category of testimony due to the weakness of their minds. And one who transgresses it and does not testify - in monetary laws when he is solicited by a party in the case or [by] the court; and with capital laws, or blows or Torah prohibitions, on his own - has violated a positive commandment. And his punishment is very great, as civilizations are preserved with the power of testimony. Therefore, it it written about it (Leviticus 5:1), "if he does not say, he will carry his iniquity." And if the testimony that he suppressed was monetary testimony and the witness denied it and swore about it - meaning to say, he swore that he does not know testimony for him - he is obligated to bring a sacrifice that varies up and down; and under the conditions that are known about the matter, as it is explained in its place in Shevuot 30a. And it is one of three sacrifices that come whether [it is] inadvertent or whether [it is] volitional.

Mitzvah 123
The commandment of the sacrifice that varies up and down: To sacrifice the sacrifice that varies up and down for specific sins - and they are: Impurity of the Temple, meaning to say a man who is impure with a primary source of impurity and enters the Temple inadvertently; likewise, the impurity of its consecrated [foods], that he is impure and ate consecrated meat inadvertently; an oath of expression, meaning to say that he swore falsely about a thing to do it or not to do it, and the other known angles of an oath of expression, and he transgresses it inadvertently; likewise an oath of testimony, meaning to say that he swore to his fellow that he does not have testimony for him [when he actually does], whether inadvertently or volitionally. For these sins, a person is obligated to bring a sacrifice that varies up and down - meaning to say, according to the wealth or poverty of a person; as it is explicit in the verse (Leviticus 5:1), "And if a soul shall sin and he heard the voice of an oath" - meaning to say the voice of the oath that they swore him to, whether he knows testimony, "if he does not say, he will carry his iniquity." And the end of the matter is (Leviticus 5:6), "And he shall bring his guilt-offering." And it is not stated there, "and it was hidden from him," to teach that he is liable for the sacrifice, whether [he is] inadvertent or volitional.

And it is written about impurity of the Temple and its consecrated foods (Leviticus 5:2), "Or a soul that touches anything impure, etc. and it was hidden from him"; and it is stated about it all at the end of the matter (Leviticus 5:6), "And he shall bring his guilt-offering." And the verse does not come explicitly that the liability of the impure one there would be with his entering the Temple or with his eating consecrated meat. Rather, we have understood from the tradition that it speaks about this (Shevuot 6b). And even though the thing is from the tradition, we have found the liability for excision for one who ate consecrated [food] or entered the Temple explicit in another place, as it is stated (Leviticus 7:20), "And the soul that eats meat from the sacrifice of the peace-offering that is to the Lord and his impurity is upon him, he shall be excised"; and another verse (Numbers 19:20) states about the impure one that enters the Temple, "for the Temple of the Lord he has made impure, and he shall be excised." And once excision has been written about its volitional transgression, there is a sacrifice for its inadvertent transgression - with our rule, that everything that is with excision for its volitional transgression, is with a sin-offering for its inadvertent transgression. And it is written about an oath of expression (Leviticus 5:4-6), "Or if a soul swears to express with his lips, etc. and it was hidden from him, etc. And he shall bring his guilt-offering." And from where [do we know] that the liability there [for them] is with a sacrifice that varies up and down? As it is written in the section (Leviticus 5:11), "And if his hand does not reach, etc."

From the roots of the commandment, we have already said (Sefer HaChinukh 95) that the matter of the sacrifice is to remind - and to have the thinker place in his heart - by force of action that he made his deeds bad; and that he requests forgiveness about the past and be careful about the future. And it is from His wisdom, Blessed be He, and His awareness of the lightness of people's intellect, the limitation of their understanding and the weakness of their power, that He was lenient upon them [regarding] the atonement of these sins that are mentioned - that they be according to the wealth of people or their poverty - as stumbling in them is [common] for people. As there is no doubt that (every) sin of the the tongue is more [common] and frequent than the sin of action. And this will suffice for you about oaths.

And also, regarding the impurity of the Temple and its consecrated [foods], it is known that stumbling is common with it. As the matter of purity is very difficult for any man to guard it, to the point that the pure man must be careful from approaching [other] people out of the concern for impurity. And the matter would be lengthy if I had come to write of the several angles of stumbling that are found with it - however, it is known to all that understand (See Guide for the Perplexed 3:41).

And from this root that we have said - that stumbling in these matters is [common] - He was further lenient upon them with testimony of an oath that they bring atonement whether [he was] inadvertent or volitional. As since the matter of testimony is very frequent, 'and the impulse of the heart of man is bad,' they [can] attribute the falsehood to forgetting and not be precise in their testimony. There are also some among the creatures that do not [pay so much attention] to the great evil they are doing in swaying the direction of the testimony - since they did not steal and did not extort with their hands. Even though a man is oppressed and broken because of them, they do not [pay attention] to this. And so, from the frequency of the matter and its lightness in the eyes of the masses of people, it was from His kindnesses, may He be Blessed, that the atonement be whether for the inadvertent or for the volitional.

And yet one who is understanding among people knows that everything from which God distances us - even if He gives atonement for the thing - is fitting for us to distance with the utmost distancing. And the matter is as if God, Blessed be He, informs people, "It is not My will that you do thing x in any fashion. However, one of you who stumbles and transgresses it should repent with all of his might, protect himself with many fences and bring a sacrifice to fix the thing in his heart, that he not stumbles in it again." And nonetheless, that person is not saved from having transgressed the commandment of his Creator.

From the laws of the commandment is that each one of these four sins obligates its doer to bring a ewe or a female goat, like the well-known law of the fixed sin-offering; and he is only exempted with fowl or flour if he is poor. But if he is poor and he brings a ewe or a female goat, he has not fulfilled his obligation. And the reason is that since God, Blessed be He, had mercy upon him and exempted him with [something less expensive] it is not appropriate that he push himself to bring more than what his hand can reach. And from this, every understanding person will acquire good counsel: to not make expenditures [that are] more than what is fitting according to his money - as this is a cause to steal from the creatures when he seeks that to which he is accustomed and does not find [it]. And they also said (Keritot 27b) that one who was wealthy and separated money to buy a ewe or a female goat with it and became poor and needs the money, should take two doves or two young pigeons; and he should say, "Behold this money is rendered profane upon these birds." And afterwards, he may benefit from all of the money. And so [too, if] he separated money for fowl and became poor and needed them, he renders them profane on a tenth of an eifah of flour, and benefits from [the money]. And so [too,] a poor person who separated money for a tenth of an eifah [of flour] and became wealthy, adds upon it and brings a ewe or a female goat. And for this matter, a wealthy person is called one so long as he has [the wealth]. And the liability for these sacrifices is only when inadvertent - and with an oath of testimony even when volitional - but if under duress, there is no liability for a sacrifice with any of them (Shevuot 31b). As the Torah exempts any [one under] duress from any liability (Pesachim 71b). The sides that are in oaths through which a person is called under duress and exempt or inadvertent and liable, and the sides that he is only liable for one sacrifice even for many oaths (Shevuot 31b) or a sacrifice for each and every oath. And so [too,] the sides to make liable or exempt regarding the sacrifice for the impurity of the Temple and impurity of its consecrated [foods] - the side to obligate is when the sinner has awareness of the impurity and the consecrated [food] or the Temple, at first and likewise at the end, but it was hidden [from him] in the middle. How is this? He became impure and he knew that he became impure, and consecrated meat came to his hand and he knows that it is consecrated meat, or he comes to enter the Temple and he knows that it is the Temple - such that he has awareness of the impurity and of the consecrated at the beginning. And afterwards [it is] hidden, as he forgot his impurity and thought that he was pure, and likewise that the consecrated [foods] or the Temple became hidden from him and he thought them to be non-sacred, and he ate from the consecrated [foods] or he entered the Temple, such that this is hiddenness in the middle. And afterwards, it becomes known to him that he was impure or that the meat was consecrated or that they were in the Temple, such that this is awareness at the end. In such a manner [must] he brings a sacrifice; and about this did our Rabbis, may their memory be Blessed, say, (Shevuot 2a), "Awareness at the beginning and at the end and hiddenness in the middle."

And the side of exemption is (for example,) that he became impure and he did not know that he became impure and he entered the Temple or ate consecrated meat, and afterwards it became known to him that he had become impure. In this manner, he is exempt from a sacrifice. And this law is not like other liabilities for excision [when volitional and a sacrifice when inadvertent] in the Torah. As with other excisions - once he knows at the end, even if did not know at the beginning, he is liable for a sacrifice. And the verse determines to judge like this here, as it is written about the impurity of the Temple and its consecrated [foods] (Leviticus 5:2), "and it was hidden from him" - [which] implies that there was a time of awareness at the beginning; and afterwards it is stated, "and he knew." Behold, you have learned that that it needs awareness at the beginning and awareness at the end and hiddenness in the middle. But with other [instances of those] that are liable for excisions, it is written (Leviticus 4:27-28), "in his doing one of the commandments of the Lord which shall not be done, etc. Or his sin is made known to him" - meaning to say, once he knew at the end, even if he did not know at the beginning. As behold, it is not written there, "and it was hidden," from which we would learn awareness at the beginning.

And also, from the matter of the commandment is that which they said (Shevuot 2a) that one who has awareness at the beginning but not at the end may not bring atonement, as they said that the goat of Yom Kippur, that is executed inside, and Yom Kippur itself, puts it into the balance until it is made known to him and he brings the sacrifice for his atonement. But one who has no awareness at the beginning, but has awareness at the end - about which we said, he does not bring a sacrifice - the goat executed outside, and Yom Kippur, atone for him. And for the one that has no awareness, not at the beginning and not at the end, the goats of the holidays, and the goats of Rosh Chodesh, atone. And for volitional impurity of the Temple and its consecrated [foods], the bull of the high priest atones - if the volitional [party] is a priest. But if he was from Israel, the blood that is executed inside and Yom Kippur atone, as it stated (Leviticus 16:16), "And atone for the Holy from the impurities of the Children of Israel." And that which they, may their memory be Blessed, said (Horayot 9a), "As with these four sins, all are equal in the sacrifice - the king, the anointed priest and the commoner" - as there is no distinction among them in their sacrifice except for the commandments for which they are obligated a fixed sin offering for their inadvertent transgression, but all are equal with these that their liability is [for a sacrifice] that varies up and down. And the rest of its details are elucidated in Keritot and Shevuot.

And [it] is practiced at the time of the Temple by males and females; except for the sacrifice of the oaths of testimony, which is not practiced by females - since they are not in the category of testimony, as we have written above (Sefer HaChinukh 122). And one who transgresses it and does not offer his sacrifice for one of these has violated a positive commandment.

Mitzvah 124
Not to sever a fowl sin-offering: That the priest not sever the head from the fowl that comes as a sacrifice - and that is what is called the fowl sin-offering - when he cuts (yimalek) it, as it is stated (Leviticus 5:8), "and he shall malak its head across from its nape, and he shall not sever." And the understanding of melikah (Rashi on Zevachim 65a) is that the priest plants his fingernail across from the nape - which is the bone that is called the neck-bone - and cuts the bone with his fingernail until he reaches the benchmarks, and [then] cuts the benchmarks (the esophagus and the trachea) with his fingernail, or the majority of one of them. And this is the slaughter of the fowl sin-offering. And the priest needs to not cut it all completely until the head be severed from the body. And about this is it stated, "and he shall not sever." We have already said in the commandment of building the [Temple] (Sefer haChinukh 95) that we do not have the ability - nor does one whose 'small finger is thicker than our loins' - to find an argument about the details of the sacrifices even from the angle of its simple understanding. And it is enough for this work of ours to make known a little explanation about the content of the sacrifices more generally from the angle of the simple meaning. And I have already written above (Sefer HaChinukh 95) that which I have known and heard.

And the matter of melikah and the warning not to sever is also from the details of the sacrifice. However, the one who is not concerned about expending all of his spirit can answer that maybe with the matter of melikah that is done by the hand of the priest on the fowl sin-offering, which is the sacrifice of the poor person, there is a hint that every person should by extremely quick with the needs of the poor person. And therefore, his sacrifice does not need slaughter, so that the priest not need to look for the knife and to check it, and the poor person be [delayed] there in the meantime from his work. Also, to expedite the speed, it stated that he begins across from its nape, since that is what is prepared [for] his hand, and that he not need to turn the neck to the side of the benchmarks. And there is also a further hint in the matter of melikah that is across from the nape of doves and young pigeons, that are compared to Israel, that we not be stiff-necked.

And the matter of the prohibition of severing the head from the body is something that is fit to embellish the sacrifice - as truly when the head of the fowl clings to it, it is more embellished. And it is fitting for us to embellish the sacrifice of the poor person with all of our might; it is enough for him [to suffer] with his poverty - we should not add to his paucity by reducing the stature of his sacrifice. And all of this is from the foundation that we have built at the beginning - that it is from the roots of the sacrifices to acquire good and lofty traits for our souls, and to refine our deeds through the power of comparisons with that in which we are involved. As since man is physical, he cannot fashion and fix the things with a strong fashioning in his soul, except with actions. And until we hear another reason, we will hold on to this.

From the laws of the commandment is, for example, that which they, may their memory be Blessed, said (Zevachim 64b), "How does the priest grab the fowl sin-offering at the time of melikah? He grabs the fowl's two legs between two of his fingers and its two wings between two of his fingers, and he stretches its neck upon the width of two of his fingers and does melikah. And this is from the hardest services in the Temple." But if he alters and grabs any place it is [still] fit. And any place on the altar is fit for melikah (Zevachim 63a). We can say that the explanation of this is also to quicken the matter of the poor person - and hence, it has no specific place. And the rest of its details are elucidated in Zevachim (see Mishneh Torah, Laws of Sacrificial Procedure 6).

And it is practiced at the time of the [Temple] by priests and by every person, as anyone who severs a foul sin-offering is lashed.

Mitzvah 125
To not place olive oil in the meal-offering of a sinner: That a priest not place oil in the meal-offering of a poor sinner, as it is stated (Leviticus 5:11), "he shall not place oil on it" - and even though they would put oil on other meal-offerings. And I said, "the meal-offering of a poor sinner," because of [the following] - since a rich sinner never brings a meal-offering of flour, but rather a sacrifice of a beast, as is explicit in the Torah.

It is from the roots of the commandment [that it is] because oil is a hint for stature and greatness - since if you mix it with any liquid, it floats above them all; and it is a very significant thing. And the significance of good oil is well-known - and therefore they would anoint those inaugurated to the stature of monarchy or priesthood with it. Hence it is not fit to place [some] of it in the meal-offering of the sinner who needs to show concern and lowliness about himself, that the matter of a sin came to his hand. And we can further say [it is] from compassion for the poor person, that he need not burden himself more than necessary to bring oil - as God, Blessed be He, does not burden a creature. And because of this, it also obligated him only a little flour - as it is impossible for any person, even the most destitute of the destitute, [not to have] a little four. And this will suffice for us also about the frankincense.

From the laws of the commandment is that which they, may their memory be Blessed, explained (Menachot 76b) that the meal-offering of a sinner was one issaron - not less and not more. And all of the meal-offerings (Menachot 59a) offered on top of the altar require oil and frankincense. And [it is] one log of oil for one issaron of flour, and one handful of frankincense for any meal-offering - whether it was one issaron or sixty issaron, but we do not bring one meal-offering from more than sixty issaron - except for the meal-offering of jealousy and the meal-offering of the sinner, in which there is no oil or frankincense; as it is stated, "he shall not place oil on it, nor shall he put frankincense on it." And the rest of its details are elucidated in Menachot.

And [it] is practiced at the time of the [Temple] by the males of the priesthood, as the service is theirs. And a priest that transgresses it and puts oil on this meal-offering of the poor sinner is lashed.

Mitzvah 126
To not put frankincense in the meal-offering of a sinner: To not put frankincense in this meal-offering of the poor sinner that we said, as it is stated (Leviticus 5:11), "nor shall he put frankincense on it." And the language of the Mishnah (Menachot 59b) is "And he is liable for the oil on its own and the frankincense on its own" - as they are two negative commandments, without a doubt. All the content of frankincense is like the content of oil that we wrote (Sefer HaChinukh 125) - there is no point in writing at length about it.

Mitzvah 127
The commandment of the addition of a fifth for one who eats from the consecrated or misappropriates it: That one who benefits from the consecrated (see Sefer HaMitzvot LaRambam, Mitzvot Ase 118) pay - it is one whether it is the consecrated [foods] of the altar or the consecrated things of the [Temple], and even lower level consecrated [foods] or if he eats the consecrated inadvertently, meaning the priestly tithe - all that he eats or benefits from it, with the addition of a fifth. And he [also] brings a sacrifice for his inadvertent transgression - a ram of two sela or more - and this is what is called the guilt-offering of misappropriations - and it is one of five definite guilt-offerings. [The source of adding the fifth is] as it is stated (Leviticus 5:15), "A soul that misappropriates a misappropriation, etc. he shall bring his guilt-offering, etc." And it is stated (Leviticus 5:16), "And that which he has sinned from the consecrated he shall pay, and its fifth shall he add to it."

It is from the roots of the commandment [that it is to put trepidation and awe upon every person about approaching holy things. And we have already written above (Sefer HaChinukh 95, 101) [about] the benefit for people of awe and aggrandizement of the holy.

From the laws of the commandment is that which our Rabbis, may their memory be Blessed, said (Kiddushin 54b) [regarding] one who misappropriates after someone misappropriates: if the first was inadvertent, the latter is exempt - since the consecrated already became desanctified once the first became liable for payment and a sacrifice. But if the first was volitional - which is not in the category of a sacrifice - the latter is in the category of misappropriation. And there is only misappropriation after misappropriation of the consecrated with a beast or ministering vessels alone (Meilah 19b). And one who takes a coin [of minimal value] from the consecrated in order that it be his does not misappropriate until he spends it on his wants. If he gives it to his fellow, he has misappropriated, and his fellow has not misappropriated - as there is only misappropriation after misappropriation with a beast or vessels alone, as we said.

And the laws of misappropriation are whether with the consecrated for the altar or the consecrated of the [Temple] upkeep. And the measure of misappropriation is [the value of] a small coin (Meilah 18a). There is no misappropriation for those things that have become permissible to eat among the sacrifices - such as meat of the sin-offering and guilt-offering after the sprinkling of their blood; or the two breads after the sprinkling of the blood of the two lambs. Even if a commoner ate from one of these and similar to them - since they are permissible for some people to benefit from, anyone who benefits from them has not misappropriated. And even if they became disqualified and forbidden to eat - since there was a time that they were permitted, one is not [any longer] liable for misappropriation for them. If he is in doubt if he misappropriated or did not misappropriate, he is exempted from the payments and from the sacrifice. The payment of the principal and the bringing of the guilt-offering impede the atonement, but not the fifth; as it is stated about the ram of the guilt offering (Leviticus 5:16), "and he shall be forgiven" - the ram and the guilt-offering impede, but the fifth does not impede [it]. And once the one who adds has added the fifth, if he benefited from the fifth, he adds a fifth to [the] fifth; since it is considered like the beginning of the consecrated things. And the fifth is one of four [parts] of the principal, [such that] it and its fifth are five. And the rest of its details are elucidated in Meilah and Temurah.

And [it] is practiced at the time of the [Temple] by males and females. And one who transgresses it and ate or benefited [the value of] a small coin from the consecrated by the execution of an act volitionally is lashed and only pays what he lessened from the consecrated, since volitional transgression does not have the addition of a fifth. And the warning of misappropriation to administer lashes upon him is from that which is written (Deuteronomy 12:17), "You may not eat in your gates," and as we will write with God's help in the Order of Reeh. [But if] he misappropriated inadvertently he pays that which he benefited from, adds a fifth and brings a sacrifice, as we have written.

Mitzvah 128
The commandment of the sacrifice of an undetermined guilt-offering: That one who is in doubt if he sinned one of the big sins for which a man is liable excision when he does it volitionally and a fixed sin-offering when inadvertent, bring a sacrifice (Keritot 25a). And the doubt emerges for him in this way: As you might say, by way of an archetype, that there were two pieces in front of him - one of forbidden fat and one of permissible fat - and he ate one of them and the other got lost. And [so] he worries to himself as he does not know if he ate the one of forbidden fat or the one of permissible fat. This sacrifice that is brought upon this doubt is called an undetermined guilt-offering. And the word undetermined (talui) is said about anything about which it is fitting that a matter come afterwards that reveals about it that which was not known previously. For example, if [one] knows that the sinner ate forbidden fat - behold, it is revealed that the first [sacrifice] was not sufficient for him and he needs to still bring another sacrifice that is called a fixed sin-offering to complete his atonement; but if one knows about him that he ate what was permissible - behold it is revealed that the first was sufficient and he does not need to bring another sacrifice after it. This is the explanation of its being undetermined. And the command for this sacrifice is from that which it is written

(Leviticus 5:17-18), "And if a soul sins and does one of all of the commandments of the Lord which you shall not do and he does not know, but he is guilty and he shall bear his iniquity. And he shall bring an unblemished ram from the flock, according to your assessment for a guilt-offering to the priest, and the priest shall atone for his inadvertent transgression which he transgressed and did not know" - meaning to say, about his not knowing if he transgressed inadvertently or [not]. And the Sages called this matter, "not known."

It is from the roots of the commandment that a man should be careful, fear sin and analyze his deeds with a proper analysis that he not stumbles in the matter of a sin. And hence the Torah required him to bring a sacrifice when he was not careful [enough] in his deeds to the point that this doubt would not have come up. And the proof that this only comes to atone for his laziness is that behold it does not uproot [it for] him, to atone for the sin at all. [Rather,] when the sin is made known to him, he immediately needs a complete sacrifice; [just] as he would have been liable if he had not offered the first one.

From the laws of the commandment is that which they, may their memory be Blessed, said (Keritot 18a) that there is never a liability for this sacrifice until there is an established prohibition there. For example, that there be two pieces in front of him and one of them is certainly forbidden fat - as behold there is an established prohibition here, and he ate one of them. And so [too,] if he ate a certain forbidden fat, but he is in doubt if there was a whole kazayit or not (Keritot 17a) - this too is an established prohibition. But if there was one [piece] in front of him and it is a doubt if it was forbidden fat or permitted fat, and he ate it - he is exempted from the sacrifice, as there is no established prohibition here; as lest there is no prohibition here at all. And from this reason they said that one who has sexual relations with a woman the divorce of which is in doubt is liable for a sacrifice; as behold there is an established prohibition here, such that we evaluate her according to [that which is] established about her. But one who has sexual relations with a woman the marriage of which is in doubt is exempted from a sacrifice, as there is no established prohibition here; and behold it is like one piece with a doubt if it is forbidden fat or permitted fat, such that he is exempted from a sacrifice (Ketuvot 22b), as we have said. And the rest of its details are elucidated in Keritot (see Mishneh Torah, Laws of Offerings for Unintentional Transgressions 8).

And [it] is practiced at the time of the [Temple] by males and females. And one who transgresses it and does not offer this sacrifice if a doubt happens to him that makes him liable for it has violated a positive commandment.

Mitzvah 129

The commandment of a definite guilt-offering: To offer a sacrifice for well-known sins - that we will explain. And this sacrifice is called a definite guilt-offering. And it is a sacrifice of a ram that needs to be worth two sela (Keritot 22b). And there are some of these sins for which this sacrifice comes, that are whether he sinned inadvertently or whether volitionally; and there are some for which it only comes specifically for the inadvertent, but not for the volitional.

And one of these sins is one that illegally has money of a Jew in his hand, from the worth of a small coin and up - for example, he robs him or steals from him, or [money] that remained in his hand from a deposit that was deposited with him or because of a loan or a partnership. The principle of the matter is that [in a case] if he were to admit to him, he would be liable to pay by law, and the robbed or oppressed - or his inheritor or one that comes by his authority - sues him for it, but he denies it and swears falsely about it; when he repents and regrets his sin and returns the 'loot that is in his hand,' he is liable to bring this sacrifice that we said for his sin, besides the fifth that he is obligated to add on the principle and to give to the robbed, as it is stated (Leviticus 5:21), "A soul that sinned and misappropriated a misappropriation from God and denies his kinsman, etc." And Rabbi Akiva says, "What do we learn to say [from] 'a misappropriation from God?' Because any lender and borrower act only with witnesses, [therefore] when he denies, he only denies the witnesses; but one who borrows without witnesses and denies it, he denies the Third Party among them" - the Divine Presence - "That is why it states, 'and misappropriated a misappropriation from God and denies his kinsman, etc.'" (Sifra, Vayikra Dibbura d'Chovah, Chapter 22:4). And it is written after it (Leviticus 5 23-25),

Sefer HaChinukh

"And it shall be when he sins and is guilty" - meaning to say that he will repent, such that he takes responsibility for his own guilt - "and return the theft, etc. and he shall pay it from its principle, and a fifth shall he add upon it, etc. And he shall bring his guilt-offering to the Lord, a ram, etc." And this is what is called the guilt-offering of thefts; and this is from those that come whether for the inadvertent or for the volitional.

And in this section, there are no guilt-offerings mentioned besides this one that we said. But in the section above, there is a definite guilt-offering mentioned, similar to this, that is also called a definite guilt-offering; and it is (called) the guilt-offering of misappropriations - meaning to say, [for] one who misappropriates and derives benefit from the consecrated things. And therefore, the expression, meilah is applied to it, which is something very bad. And one who extends his hand to derive benefit from the money of the Heavens is similar to giving over (the property of others). And this guilt-offering comes only for the inadvertent, and as we wrote above in its place (Sefer HaChinukh 127).

And the Torah further also obligated this sacrifice of the definite guilt-offering - and it is a ram of two sela - for a nazirite that became impure - and as we will write, with God's help, in the Order of Nasso (Sefer HaChinukh 277). And this is also whether he became impure volitionally or indavertently. And the Torah further also obligated this sacrifice for a metsora when he is purified from his tsaraat - and as we will write with God's help in the Order of Zot Tehiyeh Torat Hametsora (Sefer HaChinukh 177). And there is no need to explain inadvertent and volitional about this, as the notion of inadvertent and volitional is not relevant here.

And the Torah further also obligated this sacrifice for one who has sexual relations with a designated maidservant; and as it is written in the Order of Kedoshim Tehiyu, as it is stated (Leviticus 19:20-21), "If a man lays with a woman, etc. and she is a maidservant designated (charufah) for a man, but has not been redeemed with redemption, etc. there shall be an investigation, etc. And he shall bring his guilt-offering [etc.] a ram of guilt." And this is from those that come whether for inadvertent transgression or volitional (Keritot 9a). It comes out that with all of them, there are five definite guilt-offerings. And so did the Sages, may their memory be Blessed, count in the Mishnah, such that they said (Mishnah Zevachim 5:5), "These are the guilt-offerings: 1) The guilt-offering of thefts; 2) the guilt-offering of misappropriations; 3) the guilt-offering of the designated maidservant; 4) the guilt-offering of the nazirite; 5) the guilt offering of the metsora." And [regarding] the undetermined guilt-offering which is counted there, its name is upon it [to show] that it is not from the group of definite guilt-offerings. And from these five, three of them come whether they are inadvertent or volitional - and they are the guilt-offering of thefts, the guilt-offering of the designated maidservant and the guilt-offering of the nazirite; and one of them only comes for inadvertent transgression and not for volitional transgression - and that is the guilt-offering of misappropriations; and [for] the fifth - which is the guilt offering of the metsora - the expression, inadvertent and volitional, is not relevant, as we said.

And since the designated maidservant 'has come to our hand, let us say a thing about her.' And even though it is not from this Order - since it is not from the tally of the commandments, I have no [other] place to speak about it besides here. The understanding of charufah is, designated, meaning to say, betrothed. And they said in the Gemara at the beginning of the first chapter of Kiddushin 6a, that so [was it] in Yehudah, that they would call a betrothed woman, a charufah. And the verse is speaking about a Canaanite (gentile) maidservant that is half a maidservant and half a free woman. And this is that which is written about her, "but has not been redeemed with redemption" - meaning to say she is redeemed but not redeemed: for example, she paid her master half of her money. And she is betrothed (to an Israelite slave or) to another Israelite (see Mishneh Torah, Laws of Forbidden Intercourse 3:13). About this is it stated that if another man has sexual relations with her - whether inadvertently or volitionally - he is liable to bring this sacrifice that is called a guilt-offering, and it is a ram that is worth two sela or more. And because of this, the atonement of a sacrifice is enough for the one that has sexual relations with her - since her betrothal is not full betrothal as if she had been a free woman. As with a betrothed free woman, the one who has sexual relations with her is liable for the death penalty. But with this one, her betrothal is not full because of the half of her that is still in the category of being a maidservant; and therefore, it is enough with the atonement of a sacrifice for the one that stumbles with her. The Torah was also lenient with her sexual relations to exempt one with a sacrifice even when volitional - which is not the way of other volitional transgressions, to exempt them with a sacrifice - since a woman maidservant, even though she is half redeemed, is light in the eyes of every man; and [so] stumbling is very easy with her, since the masses do not not think of her sexual relations to be a great sin. And hence their iniquity is removed and their sin is atoned with the sacrifice. And similar to that which they, may their memory be Blessed, said about other matters (Sanhedrin 106b), we can say here, "The Merciful One wants the heart."

And nonetheless the maidservant is liable for lashes, as we cannot say about her that she is light in her [own] eyes - and that because of that, she did not guard herself from licentiousness. But still, she also is not liable for lashes unless she has intercourse in the regular fashion, is an adult and volitional. And about her is it said, "there shall be an investigation (bikoret tehiyeh)" - as our Rabbis, may their memory be Blessed, expounded (Keritot 22a), "bikrai tehe (she shall be with verses)," meaning to say with lashes. And they, may their memory be Blessed, said (Keritot 22a), "She is lashed, and not he." And because of this did the Scripture express the lashes with this language of 'reading' - since they would read verses of rebuke over the one lashed while they were still lashing him, so that he understands and take instruction. And [these verses] are "And the Lord will make wondrous, etc." (Deuteronomy 28:59).

It is from the the roots of the commandment [that] a person not think that even though the matter of the prohibition of robbery is rectified by a positive commandment, as it is stated (Leviticus 5:23), "and return the theft" - that each one should go and rob what he wants from his fellow and imagine in his heart to say that when he has it and he return the theft, his iniquity will be atoned and he will be purified from it; and behold, it will be as if he never did it. And this would be an opening for sinners. Hence the Torah made known that even with the repayment with the addition of a fifth, he [still] needs a sacrifice for atonement, for his having sinned. And I have already written above (Sefer HaChinukh 123) about this matter, that nonetheless, it does not save him from having transgressed the will of his Creator. And it is a pity on his head that He transgressed the will of the Master of the Heavens, [even if] he sacrificed several [fat] sheep (peace-offerings) for burnt-offerings. And there I also wrote that the sacrifice and the principle impede the atonement, but the fifth does not impede [it].

The laws of the commandment - for example, in which manner he would be obligated for this oath such that he be liable for this guilt-offering, and in which manner he would be exempt from it; in which way he would be liable for many guilt-offerings according to the number of the obligation of oaths, and in which way he would only be liable one guilt-offering; and the rest of its details - are elucidated in Keritot and in Shevuot (see Mishneh Torah, Laws of Offerings for Unintentional Transgressions 9).

And the commandment of the liability for this sacrifice is practiced at the time of the [Temple] by males and females. And [regarding] one who transgresses it and does not offer [it] - even though he has returned his theft - his sin will not be atoned. However, we can suppose that his punishment will not be so strong as it would have been, had he not returned the money. And the parable for this is about one who struck his fellow and became liable for a penalty to the king; and [then] he appeased the one struck, [such that] the only thing that remained upon him was the claim of the king.

Mitzvah 130

The commandment of returning theft: That we were commanded to return the theft intact (Bava Kamma 66a) - meaning to say that if the thing itself that he robbed is with him and it has not changed in his possession, he is obligated to return it to the one robbed; and not take it for himself, and give its value to the one robbed - as it is stated (Leviticus 5:23), "and return the theft that he robbed." And we say in Bava Kamma 102a in the chapter [known as] HaGozel Batra, "The Rabbis learned, 'And return the theft that he robbed' - what do we learn to say [from] 'that he robbed?' That he return the intact item that he robbed." But if the theft changed in the possession of the robber, he is [only] obligated to repay its value, and he is exempted with that - even though the owners did not forsake it (Bava Kamma 66b). And what is a change that exempts from returning the theft? Like the change that he cannot reverse afterwards to its original state - for example, one who robs wood and burns it or cuts some of it up or digs holes in it; and so [too,] one who robs wool and dyes it or robs spun fabric and makes a garment out of it, and all that is similar to it. But one who robs boards of wood, even if he builds a box out of them - this is not a change that cannot revert to its original state. As behold, it is possible to dismantle them and they will go back [to being] boards as they had been. And therefore, he is obligated to return them intact. And so, with all that is similar to this.

The root of the commandment is well-known.

It laws: For example, that which our Rabbis, may their memory be Blessed, said (Sanhedrin 57a) how much would the theft be that obligates the robber in repayment? Any theft that is worth a small coin (perutah). But less than that is not in the category of repayment, even though he has transgressed a Torah prohibition. And as we shall write at length in the negative commandment of "You shall not rob" (Sefer HaChinukh, 20, 29), [it is] because Israelites are the children of Avraham, Yitschak and Yaakov - generous men, the children of generous men. And it is a well-known thing that that even a poor Israelite will pardon less than the worth of a perutah that was stolen from him, and he will not want to seek it at all. And therefore, they, may their memory be Blessed, said (Bava Kamma 105a) that one who robs three bundles, worth three perutah at the time of the theft, and they depreciate in the hand of the robber and became worth two perutah - even though he returned two - he is obligated to return the third; since we judge according to the time of the robbery, and [the] third was already worth a perutah at that time. [If] he stole two that are worth one perutah [together] and he returned one, there is robbery here [but] there is not repayment here.

And the laws of forsaking (yiush) and the transfer of domain are many. But the principle of the matter is thus according to that which appears from the Gemara: That any time that the [actual] theft is in the robber's hands - or even his son's - and it has not changed, they are obligated according to Torah writ to return it like it is to the one robbed. [And this is] even though we knew with certainty that the one robbed has forsaken it; and that is like they said in the Gemara (Bava Metzia 23a), "For example, that people heard him saying, 'Woe to him for his loss'" - meaning to say, that he concedes in his mind about that thing, that it is already lost from him, and his mind does not rely upon seeing it again. Even if [its value] appreciated in the hand of the robber, the appreciation is to the one who was robbed. And this is [the understanding] of that which is written in the Torah, "and return the theft that he robbed." And the explanation comes - if it is the same as what he robbed, meaning that it has not changed, he must return it as it is, and even if it appreciated much.

But the Sages ordained (Bava Kamma 94b), as a result of the Ordinance of the Penitents, that anything that appreciates in the hand of the robber after the forsaking be his. And [so] when he comes to return it, he calculates with the robbed one how much it was worth at the time of the robbery; and the robbed one pays him the money of that which it appreciated, and takes it. And the Sages have the power to do this thing, since they may do according to their will in a monetary matter - and even against the commands of the Torah. As it is well-known that what the court makes ownerless is ownerless (Yevamot 89b, Gittin 36b). And therefore if a gentile (to which the Ordinance does not apply) robbed and [the item] appreciated, whether before the forsaking or whether after the forsaking; or if an Israelite robbed it and he sold [it] to a gentile, and the gentile makes [it] appreciate - [the appreciation is for the one robbed. If he sold it (Minchat Yitschak)] before the forsaking, the law of the [purchaser] is like the law of the [robber] - as transfer of domain does not create acquisition without forsaking. But after the forsaking - whether that forsaking was after the theft came to the hand of the purchaser, or when it was still in the hand of the robber - since there was forsaking and a transfer of domain with this theft, the purchaser has acquired the body of the theft. And if that robber that sold it to him is a robber that is not famous, it is completely his; and he is not obligated to return anything to the one robbed. Rather the robbed one should go and sue the robber. But if he is a famous robber, the purchaser is obligated to return the value of the theft to the robbed one, and he sues the robber.

And the laws of the theft as to how far he is to burden himself to return it to its owners is like that which our Rabbis, may their memory be Blessed, said (Bava Kamma 103a) that one who robs the worth of a perutah from his fellow is obligated to bring it after him, even to Medea - meaning to say to a far place. But in order to lighten his burden if the expense [to do this] is great, our Rabbis, may their memory be Blessed, said that he leave it with the court and they know that this money is for x, and they give it to him when he happens by.

And the law of what will be with a beam that he built into a mansion (Gittin 55a); and the law of one who robbed in a settlement and he wants to return it in the wilderness (Bava Kamma 118b); and the law of one who robs and consecrates [it]. And what is the law of one who robs a lamb and it becomes a ram; and the law of the appreciation that comes from inflation - which is not under the Ordinance, but rather goes to the robbed one, as they only ordained that the appreciation be for the robber after the forsaking, in such a case as with shearings or offspring, but not appreciation from inflation; the law of one who overpowers the slave of his fellow and does work with him, or overpowers his ship; the law of one who lives in the courtyard of his fellow without [the latter]'s knowledge; and the rest of its details are elucidated in the final chapters of [Bava] Kamma.

And [it] is practiced in all places and at all times by males and females. And one who transgresses it and robs but does not return has violated this positive commandment, besides the negative commandment that he violated at the time of the robbery. And woe to the one who has it in his hand to 'fix the twisted,' and does not fix it before his death (Yoma 85b)!

Mitzvah 131

The commandment of the lifting of the ashes: That the priest remove the ashes each and every day from on the altar - and this is what is called the lifting of the ashes (trumat hadeshen), which was done every day - as it is stated (Leviticus 6:3), "And the priest shall dress in linen, etc. and he shall lift the ashes."

That which we wrote above (Sefer HaChinukh 95) to aggrandize the honor of the [Temple] and to glorify it with all of our ability - because of the reason that we said there - is from the roots of the commandment. And it is adorning the altar to remove the ashes in the place in which it is fitting to light the fire. And also, that the fire burns nicely when there are no ashes underneath it.

From the laws of the commandment is that which they, may their memory be Blessed, said (Yoma 23b) that the lifting of the ashes is one of the services of the priesthood. But the priestly garments in which they would lift the ashes were lowlier than the vestments that he would use for the other services; as it is stated (Leviticus 6:4), "And he shall take off his clothes and wear other clothes." And even thought this verse was stated about the removal of the ashes to outside of the camp, nonetheless also with the lifting of the ashes – which is when he removes it from on the altar and puts it down on the floor next to the altar – we should learn that it also not fitting to do that service with those clothes in which he serves (otherwise). And it is said about this metaphorically (Shabbat 114a), "He should not mix the cup for his master with the clothes that he cooked the food for his master."

And when would they lift the ashes every day? From the rising of the dawn. And on the festivals, from the (last) [middle] third of the night (see Yoma 20); and on Yom Kippur, from midnight. And how would they lift it? Whoever would win the lottery to remove it would immerse and wear the garments of lifting and sanctify (wash) his hands and feet. And his brothers, the priests, would say to him, "Be careful, lest you touch a (sanctified) vessel before you sanctify your hands and your feet." And afterwards he would take the censer – and it was of silver, placed in the corners between the ramp and the altar, to the East of the ramp – pick up the censer, go up to the top of the altar, remove the coals hither and thither, collect the coals that have been consumed at the heart of the fire, go down to the ground, turn his head to the North, walk on the ground to the East of the ramp about ten ells towards the North and gather the coals that he collected on the floor three handbreadths away from the altar in the place of the crop of the birds and the ashes of the inner altar and the menorah. And this sweeping that he sweeps with the censer and brings down to the ground is the daily commandment. And after the one that lifted comes down, his brothers, the priests, run and quickly sanctify their hands and feet, take rakes and pitchforks, go up to the top of the altar, rake the ashes from all the sides of the altar and make from it a pile on top of the mound (tapuach) – and that is a place on the altar that is called like this. And when this mound was big, they would bring some [of the ashes] down from it into a large vessel holding a letech, called a psachther. And it would stay there until they would take it all out of the camp. And the rest of its details are in Tractate Tamid and Yoma.

Sefer HaChinukh

And it is practiced at the time of the [Temple] by the males of the priesthood. And one who transgresses it and did not remove it according to its commandment, has violated a positive commandment.

Mitzvah 132
The commandment of lighting fire on the altar every day: To burn (some have the textual variant, to have) fire on the altar every day perpetually, as it is stated (Leviticus 6:6), "A perpetual fire shall burn on the altar." And the explanation of perpetual came [that] it means to say to place wood in the morning and in the afternoon. And in the elucidation, they, may their memory be Blessed, said (Yoma 21b), "Even though the fire descends from the Heavens, it is a commandment to bring [it also] from the commoners. And do not let it be difficult for you, to say, "What is this commandment – is it not that they, in any case, had to burn a fire for the sake of the sacrifice that they were obligated to bring, as it is impossible [to do so] without fire." As this is a commandment on its own; since besides the fire for the sacrifice, they would place fire on the altar for this commandment – and as they, may their memory be Blessed, expounded (Yoma 45a), there were three arrangements of fire [derived] from the verses, as we will write in the laws of this commandment.

From the roots of the commandment, [we need to] preface [that] the thing is known amongst us and among every sage that the great miracles that God does for people in His great goodness, He always does hiddenly. And these matters appear a little as if they were truly done by way of nature, or close to nature. As even with the miracle of the splitting of the sea – which was an open miracle – it is written there (Exodus 14:21), "and the Lord moved the sea with a powerful Eastern wind all of the night, and He made the sea into a dry place and He split the waters." And the enlightened ones will understand that this matter of concealment is because of the loftiness of the Master and the lowliness of the receiver. And due to this matter did He command us to burn fire on the altar, even though fire descended there from the Heavens – in order to hide the miracle. It [also] appears that the fire that came down from the Heavens was not visible when it came down because of the reason that we said – except for the eighth day of the inauguration and that of Gidon (Judges 6:21), Manoach (Judges 13:20) (and of Eliyahu), which was visible.

But we still need to say what is the idea of the commandment to light a fire on the altar, besides the fire that is needed there for the sacrifice. [And we shall say] (And it appears) on the level of the simple understanding that it is like the matter that we wrote about the commandment of the bread of display (Sefer HaChinukh 97); that man is Blessed, according to his deeds in which he is involved, in accordance with the will of his Creator. And through this approach, we said that blessing is found in all ordinary bread as a result of our involvement in the commandment of holy bread. [It is] as if you would say metaphorically that the blessing spreads in its type [of object]. And so too is the involvement in the commandment of the daily fire; that a person will be Blessed in the matter of fire that he has.

And what is the fire that he has? It is a person's nature – since of the four elements in a person, fire is the head of those four; as with it does a man strengthen himself and move to act. And therefore, he needs more blessing in it; and the matter of blessing is completeness – meaning to say a thing in which there is no lack, nor excess. And the fire in a person requires this blessing, such that a man will have what he needs: Not less, since his strength will weaken; and not more, since he will be burnt through it, in the way of people that die from too much of a supplement of it – and that is a burning fever. And the sons of Aharon increased fire without being commanded, and [so] fire was also increased in them, and they were burnt – as according to the actions of people does their punishment come, or does the blessing of God rest [in him] (upon them).

From the laws of the commandment is that which they, may their memory be Blessed, said that even though the fire descended from the Heavens in the days of Moshe, it is a commandment to bring [it] from the commoners, as it is stated (Leviticus 1:7), "And the sons of Aharon shall place fire, etc." And (Mishnah Tamid 2) they would set up wood in the morning and make a large arrangement of wood at the top of the altar, as it is stated (Leviticus 6:5), "and the priest would burn wood each morning." And besides the wood that was set up in the arrangement, it was a commandment upon the priest to bring up two blocks of wood, as it is stated, "and the priest would burn wood (etsim, which is plural)" - and the minimum of etsim is two. And so [too,] would they add two blocks of wood with the daily afternoon sacrifice; and two priests would bring them up, as it is stated, "and they shall set up" - but [for that] of the morning, [it was only] one priest.

And they would make three arrangements of fire on the altar every day. The first one was large, [and] upon it were the daily sacrifice and the other sacrifices offered; the second one on its side was smaller than it, [and] the fire was taken from it in the censer to burn the incense every day; and the third arrangement did not have anything upon it, so as to fulfill the commandment of the fire, as it is stated, "A perpetual fire shall burn, etc." (Yoma 43b). And there are three passages about the topic, which instruct about these three arrangements, as we learned from the tradition. As they, may their memory be Blessed, said (Yoma 45b), "'Upon its burning' (Leviticus 6:2), that is the large arrangement; 'and the fire of the altar shall burn upon it' (Leviticus 6:2), that is the second arrangement of the incense; 'And the fire of the altar shall burn upon it' (Leviticus 6:5), that is the third arrangement for the fulfillment of the fire." And the rest of its details are elucidated in the fourth chapter of Yoma and the second of Tamid.

And it is practiced at the time of the Temple by the males of the priesthood. And if the priests did not burn the third arrangement on the altar, they violated this positive commandment.

Mitzvah 133

To not extinguish the fire upon the altar: To not extinguish the fire upon the altar, as it is stated (Leviticus 6:6), "A perpetual fire shall burn on the altar, it shall not be extinguished."

I have written from the roots of the commandment, above in the positive commandment of 'A fire shall burn.' And the root of the commandment of the fire to burn it and not to extinguish it are one, and there is no need to repeat it.

From the laws of the commandment is that which they, may their memory be Blessed, said (Yoma 46b) that even if the brought down the fire from upon the altar and [then] extinguished it, he is lashed. But the fire of the censer and the fire of the menorah that were prepared on the altar to light from it - even if he extinguishes it at the top of the altar, he is exempt. As it was severed from the altar, and I do not call it, 'fire of the altar.' And we were only warned about extinguishing the fire of the altar; as it is stated, "A perpetual fire shall burn on the altar, it shall not be extinguished." And we say in Sifra, Tzav 2:7, "'It shall not be extinguished' teaches that the one who extinguishes transgresses a negative commandment." And the rest of its details are in the tenth chapter of Zevachim.

And it is practiced at the time of the [Temple] by males and females - even Israelites. And one who transgresses it and extinguishes even one coal from the fire of the altar is lashed.

Mitzvah 134

The commandment of eating the remainders of the meal-offering: That the priests were commanded to eat the remainders of the meal-offerings - meaning to say after they separated from it that which they would offer on the altar, they would eat all the rest, as it is stated (Leviticus 6:9), "What is left of it shall be eaten by Aharon and his sons; as matsahs shall it be eaten, etc." And the language of Sifra, Tzav 2:9 is "'As matsahs shall it be eaten' is a commadmeent; 'her levirate husband shall have sexual relations with her' (Deuteronomy 25:5) is a commandment" - meaning to say that both of them are positive commandments, not optional.

I have written from the roots of the commandment above (Sefer HaChinukh 102) in the commandment of "They shall eat that with which atonement was done" in Ve'atah Tetsaveh - that it is an honor for the sacrifice that the actual servants of God, may He be Blessed, eat it, and not that it be given to lesser ones to eat it, etc. as it is written there.

From the laws of the commandment is that which they, may their memory be Blessed, said (Menachot 72b) that all of the meal-offerings that were offered on the altar were skimmed - and the skimming was completely incinerated on the altar, and the rest was eaten by the priests - except for the meal offering of the males of the priesthood, which ia not skimmed, as it is stated (Leviticus 6:16), "And every meal-offering of a priest shall be whole; it shall not be eaten." It comes out that the inauguratory meal-offerings and the griddled ones, and a priest that brought a sinner's meal-offering or a voluntary meal-offering - [all these offerings] were burnt on the altar and not skimmed. The meal-offering of a priestess (Sotah 23a) is skimmed and its remnants are eaten; as we say, it is specifically a priest [that is stated by the Torah], and not a priestess. And the rest of its details are elucidated in Menachot (see Mishneh Torah, Laws of Sacrificial Procedure 10).

And it is practiced at the time of the [Temple] by the males of the priesthood, as it is stated (Leviticus 6:11), "Every male of the Children of Aharon shall eat it." [If] he transgressed and did not eat it, he has violated this positive commandment.

Mitzvah 135
To not make the remainders of the meal-offering chamets (leavened): To not cook the remainders of the meal-offerings [to make them] chamets - and that is the portion of the meal-offerings that is of the priests - as it is stated (Leviticus 6:10), "It shall not be baked chamets, their portion have I given it of my fire-offerings." And it is as if it said, "Their portion - which is the remainders of the meal-offering - you shall not bake chamets." And in the explanation, they, may their memory be Blessed, said in the Mishnah (Menachot 55a), "And they are liable for its baking [to make it] chamets."

From the laws of the commandment is, for example, that which they, may their memory be Blessed, said (Menachot 56a) that one who renders it chamets after [another has already] rendered it chamets is liable; and one who renders a disqualified meal-offering chamets is exempt, as it is stated (Leviticus 2:11), "that you shall offer to the Lord, you shall not make chamets" - one that is proper for God and not one that is disqualified. [If] he rendered it chamets on top of the altar, he is not lashed, as it is stated, "that you shall offer to the Lord, you shall not make chamets" - and this one was already offered. And the rest of its details are elucidated in Chapter Five of Menachot.

And this commandment is practiced at the time of the [Temple] by males and females. Even an Israelite that transgressed and baked it chamets is liable for lashes, and there is no need to say [that it is so] about a priest.

Mitzvah 136
The commandment of the daily meal-offering of the high priest: That we were commanded that the high priest offer a daily meal-offering twice - in the morning and in the afternoon - as it is stated (Leviticus 6:13), "This is the sacrifice of Aharon and his sons that they shall bring to the Lord, etc." And it is what is called the grilled ones of the high priest, and it is also called the meal-offering of the anointed priest (so is it [written] in the Sefer HaMitzvot LaRambam, Mitzvot Ase 40).

It is from the roots of the commandment [that it is] because the high priest is the agent between Israel and their Father in Heaven - meaning to say, that he is the one that carries prayer to Him for their sake; and through his prayers and the act of his sacrifices, they are atoned. And hence it is fitting that there be a private daily sacrifice for a man like this, like the daily sacrifices of the community. And [just like those] were two a day, he too is obligated to bring his meal-offering twice a day. And all of this is based on the reason that we said about the sacrifice: In order that all of his thoughts be aroused and he place his mind and intention towards God, Blessed be He. And on account of this, he will be effective for himself and for them. And there is no doubt that the arousal of a man when he brings his own private sacrifice is not the same as when he brings a sacrifice that he shares. And this is something well-known and tested with every man - that he is more aroused by what is private only to him. There is no need to speak at length [about this].

From the laws of the commandment is that which they, may their memory be Blessed, said (Menachot 50b), "How is the making of the grilled ones of the high priest? He brings a whole issaron of flour, and divides it" with the half issaron measure in the Temple. As even though the meal-offering of the issaron was offered in halves - meaning to say, half of it in the morning and half of it in the evening - it is not sanctified in halves; meaning he brings it all together. And he brings with it three log of oil and mixes the fine flour with the oil and scalds it in boiling water. And he kneads six loaves from each half issaron - it comes out that there were twelve loaves - and they were made one by one. And how does he make [it]? He divides the three log with the reviit measure in the Temple - one reviit for each loaf - he bakes it a little and afterwards roasts it on the griddle with its oil, but he does not cook it much. And afterwards he divides each loaf into two, so that he offer half [of it] in in the morning and half in the evening. And he takes the halves, doubles each one up into two and crumbles it, until you find each crumbling doubled up into two. And he offers the halves with half a handful of frankincense in the morning, and the remaining half [of the offering] with the [other] half handful of frankincense in the evening. And it is completely for the fire.

And it is practiced at the time of the [Temple] by the high priest. And the meal-offering of the morning and of the evening is one positive commandment - there is no one that disagrees about this. As even Ramban, may his memory be Blessed, (at the end of Sefer HaMitzvot LaRambam, s.v. veatah eem tavin) - who counted the two daily [communal] offerings as two commandments - concedes this.

Mitzvah 137

To not eat the meal-offering of the priest: To not eat of the meal-offering of the priest, as it is stated (Leviticus 6:16), "And every meal-offering of a priest shall be whole; it shall not be eaten."

The foundation that we said at the beginning that the intention of the sacrifice is to arouse the heart of the one that offers it is from the roots of the commandment. [For] if the priest eats his meal-offering, his heart will not properly be aroused about it; as it is similar in his eyes to his baking bread for his need and eating it. And even though his fellows will eat from his and he from theirs, it will all add up to one. Hence it commanded that it be completely burnt; it cannot be eaten by any man.

From the laws of the commandment is that which they, may their memory be Blessed, said (Menachot 72b) [that] all of the meal-offerings that were offered on the altar were skimmed - and the skimming was completely incinerated on the altar, and the rest was eaten by the priests - except for the meal offering of the males of the priesthood, which is not skimmed, but we rather incinerate it completely, as it is stated (Leviticus 6:16), "And every meal-offering of a priest shall be whole; it shall not be eaten." We have learned from here that the inauguratory meal-offerings and the griddled ones, and a priest that brought a sinner's meal-offering or a voluntary meal-offering - all these [offerings] were burnt on the altar and not skimmed, as we said above in this order (Sefer HaChinukh 134). And the content of skimming is that the priest take from the flour with his handful - meaning to say with the tips of his fingers - in the way that any man skims: That he extends the palm of his hand and skims with the tips of his fingers (Menachot 11a) - meaning to say that his fingers cling to the palm and he does not hold much flour. But if he adds upon the handful, such as [if] he widened his fingers and [then] skimmed, he disqualified [it]. And the rest of the details of the commandment are in Menachot. And the prohibition of the eating of the meal-offering of the priest is practiced by males and females at the time of the [Temple]. And one who transgresses it and ate a kazayit is lashed. And the language of Sifra, Tzav 5:4 is "'Shall be whole; it shall not be eaten' - anything that is in 'shall be whole,' to place a negative commandment upon [it, about] its eating."

Mitzvah 138

The commandment of the procedure of the sin-offering: That we were commanded that the priests process the sin-offering in the manner that is mentioned in Scripture - whatever sin-offering it should be of a beast or fowl - as it is stated (Leviticus 6:18), "This is the law of the sin-offering."

We have already said above (Sefer HaChinukh 95) that about the details of the sacrifices - meaning to say the order of their sacrifice, in which place, the manner of their bringing and their sprinkling, the place and time of their eating or with some of them, their burning - we can not strain our thoughts towards the roots of these matters that have no comparison, and we do not have any acquisition of the intellect that is acquired about this. There will be one in a city - a wise mystic - who will merit to know some of the main things of the matter. And it is enough for us once we have [already] written that which came up into our thoughts of the reason - by way of the simple understanding - of the sacrifices more generally. And with this I exempt myself from writing the root - as is my custom with the rest - about the sin-offering and all that is similar to it, since they are included in the specifics of the sacrifice. As the general principle is the offering of the sacrifice and the specifics are the laws of how to sacrifice it.

Sefer HaChinukh

And behold, Ramban, may his memory be Blessed, (on Sefer HaMitzvot, Root 12) does not calculate the law of the sin-offering, the guilt-offering, the burnt-offering and the peace-offerings in the tally of the commandments, based on the fundamental principle that I have said. As the main commandment comes about the obligation of the bringing of the sacrifice. But it is not right to calculate the order of its processing afterwards as a commandment on its own. As perforce Scripture had to teach us the process of each one of them, once we became obligated about them. And this is his language: "Every process of the sacrifices is one commandment and all of the seed of Aharon were commanded in its service, as it is stated (Numbers 18:7), 'and you shall serve, the service of the gift that I gave your priesthood.' And its explanation is that they shall serve all of the service of the priesthood, since it is a service and a gift of Mine and a gift to you, that you get reward for it when you take from the table of the Higher realm, may He be Blessed." To here [are his words]. And with all of this, we shall not veer from the path of the tally of Rambam, may his memory be Blessed, which (we have taken hold of) [permeates] the commandments. And the thing that is difficult, the difficulty should be attributed to us and not to him - as he is truthfully our source in this endeavor, and from his hand did we merit it. The righteous man should rest in his resting place.

From the laws of the commandment is that which they, may their memory be Blessed, said (Mishneh Torah, Laws of Sacrificial Procedure 1:9) that the sin-offerings come from five species: sheep; goats; cattle, whether large or small - and we will explain the matter of their big ones and small ones in the peace-offerings, with God's help (Sefer HaChinukh 141) - and whether male or female; doves; and young pigeons. And we have already written some of the laws above, with the sin-offerings of the fowl (Sefer HaChinukh 124). And there were some of the sin-offerings that came for the entire community and some that came for the individual. And from them, there were some for the congregation and some for the individual that were all burned on the outer altar, and some of them that were all eaten - except for their entrails, which were burnt on the outer altar. As the whole year, all we burn on the inner [altar] is incense, as we have said above (Sefer HaChinukh 104).

And these are the entrails of an ox or a goat: the fat that is on the innards - and included in it is the fat that is on the maw; the two kidneys with the fat that is on them and the fat that is on the flanks; the protuberances of the livers that are called polegar in the vernacular, and a little of the liver is taken with the protuberances. And the entrails of the species of sheep are these same ones. And in addition to them, with the sheep, we also take the whole fatty tail with the vertebrae of the backbone until the place of the kidneys, as it is stated (Leviticus 3:9), "opposite the kidneys (aatzah) shall you remove" - meaning to say above the place of the kidneys (Sifra, Tzav 14:8). And it referred to that place [with this word that is spelled like the word for counsel] because they, may their memory be Blessed, said (Berakhot 61a) that the kidneys give counsel. And also that which they, may their memory be Blessed, explained about the process of the sin-offering that is eaten, about its slaughter and its sprinkling, and all the rest of its content; and also regarding the process of the sin-offering that is burnt; and what is their law if any act of destruction is done upon them; and the rest of its details are [all] in Zevachim. And it is practiced at the time of the [Temple] by the males of the priesthood. And a priest that transgresses and does not do the sin-offering according to its statute, has violated this positive commandment.

Mitzvah 139
To not eat from the meat of the sin-offerings processed inside: To not have the priests eat from the meat of the sin-offerings inside - meaning to say from those sin-offerings that were sprinkled on the inner altar that was in the Sanctuary, as it stated (Leviticus 6:23), "And any sin-offering the blood of which is brought to the tent of meeting to atone in the Holy shall not be eaten; it shall be burned with fire." And the language of Sifra, Tzav 5:4 [is] "'It shall be burned with fire' - anything that requires burning, to [make] transgress a negative commandment for its eating." The matter is well-known [and famous] and explicit in the verses [that] all the sin offerings the blood of which required sprinkling inside - meaning to say, on the altar that was in the Sanctuary - were burned. And all the sin-offerings the blood of which was only sprinkled on the altar outside, were eaten. And about this is this verse stated, such that they not eat from any sin-offering, the law of which is with burning.

And the details of the sin-offerings - which of them are burned and which of them are eaten is explicit in Scripture. And that which is not elucidated well in the verses is explained to us by our Sages, may their memory be Blessed, in Zevachim. We have already said (Sefer HaChinukh 138), that we do not have any involvement in the details of the sacrifices. And this too - if it is eaten or if it is not eaten - is from their details.

From the laws of the commandment is that which they, may their memory be Blessed, said (Zevachim 81b), that once blood of a sin-offering that was eaten enters the Tent of Meeting, it is disqualified. And they learned to say this from this verse, as it stated, "And any sin-offering the blood of which is brought, etc. shall not be eaten; it shall be burned with fire." And [this is] specifically when it enters through the gate of the Sanctuary, as it is written, "which is brought" - meaning to say, by the [standard] way of its entering. But if he brought it through the small gates or through the window or the roof, it is not disqualified - as that is not the way of its entering. And the law is the same for sin-offerings that were burnt, the blood of which is sprinkled on the inner altar; that if its blood was brought inwards of the curtain (parokhet) - which is the Holy of Holies - it was disqualified. As also with them do I read, "And any sin-offering the blood of which is brought" inwards - as this place is inwards from its place. And the rest of its details are in Zevachim.

And this prohibition of eating the inner sin-offering is practiced by the priests. And the law is the same for Israelites; as it is more generally stated, "it shall not be eaten." And one who transgresses and eats a kazayit of it is lashed.

Mitzvah 140
The commandment of the procedure of the guilt-offering: That we were commanded that the priests execute the process of the guilt-offering according to the manner described in Scripture, as it is stated (Leviticus 7:1), "This is the law of the guilt-offering, etc.," as it is written in the passage. Did I not tell you (Sefer HaChinukh 138) that we should not write the root in these processes, since they are similar to the details of the sacrifices - and one should not seek after their reasons, as they are things that are blocked and sealed.

I have mentioned a few of the laws of the guilt-offering in Parshat Vayikra (Sefer HaChinukh 129). But we shall still inform that a sin-offering always only comes from male sheep - there are some guilt-offerings that come from the large animals of the species and there are some from the small ones. Its procedure in slaughtering, sprinkling, salting the entrails and the waving is the same in [all of] the guilt-offerings - except for the guilt-offering of the metsora, which has a little difference regarding the reception of its blood. And the rest of the details of the commandment are in Zevachim.

And it is practiced at the time of the [Temple] by the males of the priesthood. And a priest that transgresses it and does not offer the guilt-offering according to its statute has violated this positive commandment.

Mitzvah 141
The commandment of the procedure of the sacrifice of the peace-offerings: That the priests were commanded that they should execute the peace-offerings (sacrifice) according to the statute that is written in the passage, as it is stated (Leviticus 3:1), "If his sacrifice is a sacrifice of peace-offerings, etc." And it states further in the completion of the process (Leviticus 7:11-12), "And this is the law of the sacrifice of the peace offerings[...] If he offers it as a thanksgiving-offering." And under four names are all matters of sacrifices included. And they are the burnt-offering; the sin-offering; the guilt-offering; and the peace-offerings. As any sacrifice offered by the community or the individual is always from one of them. I have already written twice that we should not write the roots for these processes (Sefer HaChinukh 138).

The laws of the commandment are that which they, may their memory be Blessed, said (Menachot 107b) that the peace-offerings come from sheep, goats and cattle, whether male or female and whether large or small. And fowl does not come as peace-offerings. And from eight days old to a full year - from day to day (according to the calendar date) - is called small. If the year is intercalated, it is intercalated for it - meaning to say, it will be small until the completion of the [extra month]. And

Sefer HaChinukh

from one year until three years is called large with cattle; and from a year until two full years with sheep. More than this is old and we do not sacrifice it. And there are four types of peace offerings: one is a communal peace-offering and three are individual peace-offerings. Communal peace-offerings are called higher-level consecrated foods (kodshei kodashim); but regarding peace-offerings, the community only has one [type] of sacrifice - and that is the two sheep that come with the two breads on [Shavouot]. These two sheep are called the sacrifices of the communal peace-offerings and are eaten by priests - except for the entrails - like the sin-offering and the guilt-offering. Their processes - such as their slaughter, sprinkling, flaying, dissection, salting and the incineration of their entrails - are explained in Menachot 20a. And individual peace-offerings are called lower-level consecrated foods (kodshim kalim). And the place of their slaughter and the procedure of the sprinkling, flaying, dissection, waving and the separation of the entrails is explained in Menachot 61a. And these three types of individual peace-offerings are the same in these processes. But you should know the matter of the difference between them in some of their matters more generally.

You should know that of the three types of individual peace-offerings: The first is the sacrifice of peace-offerings which comes without bread, and those are the peace-offerings of the festival and of joy - and these are called [just] peace-offerings; and the second are peace-offerings that come with the well-known bread, and those are the ones that come for a vow or an oath - and these peace-offerings are called thanksgiving, and the bread that comes with it is called the bread of thanksgiving; and the third type of peace-offerings are the ones that a nazirite brings on the day of the fulfillment of the days of his naziriteship, and they also come with bread - and these peace-offerings are called the ram of the nazirite. And they, may their memory be Blessed, elucidated there in the Gemara (Chullin 134b) what is the measure of their breast and leg that were eaten by the priests, and also the measure of the cooked forearm from the ram of the nazirite that was eaten besides the breast and the leg, and in which place of the [Temple] they cooked it.

And the laws of the bread (Menachot 76b) that comes with the two types of peace-offerings - and they are the thanksgiving and the ram of the nazirite: from how many issaron it is (made); which one of them comes [also] as chamets and which one comes only as matsa; how the one that comes as chamets and matsa is divided; how they are leavened; the tally of the loaves that come as matsa - how many of them are baked in the oven and how many are soaked with oil or roasted in oil - it is all in Zevachim (it should say Menachot).

And the content of those that came as matsa with the thanksgiving offering was like this: They would make thirty loaves from the ten issaron of flour. Ten of them were made by baking in the oven, meaning to say that nothing was done to them, except for putting an eighth of a log of oil into its dough, as such is a law of Moshe from Sinai. And ten of them are called rekikin (soaked in oil); but there is no difference between the ten that were soaked and the ten that were oven-baked, except that with the ten that were oven-baked, they would mix the eighth of a log of oil at the time of kneading, but with the soaked ones, they would smear the eighth of a log of oil after their being baked in the oven. And ten of them are called murbakhot (roasted in oil) - and the understanding of roasting is that they would scald the loaf in boiling water and bake it a little, and afterwards roast it in oil, in the way that people roast (fry) donuts in a pan. And it is roasted in the oil of the ten roasted ones, as the oil in which [each one] was roasted was a fourth of a log, [which when totaled] is the measure of all the oil of the [other] twenty loaves - and the measure of oil of the roasted ones is also a law of Moshe from Sinai. And that which we said is the understanding of murbakhot in every place in the Torah. And it is explained there (Menachot 77b), how much the share of the priest is in the loaves - and the rest is eaten by the owners. And the rest of all of its details are in Tractate Zevachim.

And the commandment of peace-offerings is practiced by the males of the priesthood, as the obligation of the service is upon them. And one who transgresses it and changes their arrangement in ways that are known in the Gemara has violated a positive commandment - aside from [the fact] that there are ways through which the sacrifice is disqualified.

Mitzvah 142

Sefer HaChinukh

To not leave over meat from the thanksgiving sacrifice: To not leave over anything from the thanksgiving sacrifice until the morning - meaning to say on the morrow of the day of its sacrifice - as it is stated (Leviticus 7:15) about the thanksgiving sacrifice, "you shall not leave it until the morning." And we learned from it to the other [sacrifices] as well, that anything that remains of it after the time of its eating is notar. And one is obligated to burn it, as burning is the positive commandment that rectifies it, as we have written above in this order (Sefer HaChinukh 143). And there, we wrote a hint from its roots and a little of its laws, as is our custom.

Mitzvah 143

The commandment of the burning of the remnant (notar) of the [sacrifices]: That we were commanded to burn the notar - and that is meat of the [sacrifices] that remains after the time limited for their eating has passed - as it is stated (Leviticus 7:17), "And the notar of the meat of the sacrifice on the third day, it shall be brunt with fire." And this burning is a positive commandment - as so they say in Mekhilta concerning Pesach (Exodus 12:10), "'You shall not leave any of it, etc., and the notar you shall burn with fire, etc.' - the verse comes to give a positive commandment upon the negative commandment." It is implied that the commandment of burning notar is a positive commandment. And the law of piggul and notar are the same in this, that there is also a positive commandment in its burning, such that we have found Scripture expressing piggul, with the word, notar.

It is from the roots of the commandment [that it is] since the nature of all meat is (to spoil) [to become disqualified] by sitting out and coming to (putrification) [loss]. And therefore, for the aggrandizement of the matter of the sacrifice - as we have said above (Sefer HaChinukh 102) - we were commanded to burn it immediately and to destroy it from the world, that a man not be disgusted by it and its smell. And the most extreme destruction is by way of fire, more than by separating and scattering in the wind, or any other thing. And besides this, there is also a hint in the matter to have trust in God, may He be Blessed, Blessed be He - that a person not [starve] himself regarding his food more than is necessary, to save it for tomorrow - in his seeing that God commanded to completely destroy the holy meat from when its time passed. And He did not want any other creature to benefit from it - whether a man or whether a beast.

From the laws of the commandment is that which they, may their memory be Blessed, said (Pesachim 82b) that included in notar and piggul are all disqualified [sacrifices], such that all of them are also burned. And a sacrifice that is definitely disqualified or made piggul is burned immediately. But if there is a doubt, its form is left to be altered, and it is burnt afterwards (Mishneh Torah, Laws of Sacrifices Rendered Unfit 19:2). And any meat that is found in the [Temple] yard as limbs is burnt-offerings - the understanding of which is that we treat them like burnt-offerings; and if it is found as pieces, they are sin-offerings; and that which is found in Jerusalem is a peace-offering (Mishnah Shekalim 7:2). And the difference that comes out of this is if one transgressed and ate from them, he brings his atonement according to this assumption. But they, may their memory be Blessed, said about all [of them], "Let their form be altered and [then] go out to the House of Burning, lest [they were] notar." And we only burn notar during the day, as it is stated, "on the third day, it shall be brunt with fire" (Pesachim 3a). And even though the peace-offerings are forbidden to eat from the beginning of the second night, we only burn them during the day. And the rest of its details are elucidated in Pesachim and at the end of Terumah (see Mishneh Torah, Laws of Sacrifices Rendered Unfit 19).

And [it] is practiced at the time of the [Temple] by the males of the priesthood, as the service is for them. And a priest that transgresses and does not burn the notar has violated this positive commandment and has [also] violated the negative commandment of "you shall not leave over." But we do not administer lashes for this negative commandment, as there is no act [involved] with it.

Mitzvah 144

To not eat piggul: To not eat piggul - And piggul is a sacrifice that the priest who is sacrificing it had a disqualifying thought at the time of the slaughter or offering. And a disqualifying thought is, for example, that he made up his mind at the time of the slaughter or offering that he would eat from that sacrifice after the limit for its eating or burn from it that which requires burning after the time

Sefer HaChinukh

limit for burning – as the 'eating' of the altar and the eating of a person is all expressed by eating. And the verse elucidated, that one who eats from it carries his iniquity, as it is stated (Leviticus 7:18), "And if it is surely eaten, etc. and the soul who eats from it shall carry its iniquity." And the carrying of iniquity here is excision, as we shall learn in the Gemara (Zevachim 28b) through an inferential comparison (gezara shava).

And yet its warning – meaning to say, the explicit negative commandment, besides the punishment that is mentioned here – is from that which is written in the inauguration [of the tabernacle], "it shall not be eaten, as it is holy" (Exodus 29:34). And they, may their memory be Blessed, said (Pesachim 24a) that this verse includes in its warning all that which has been spoiled of the [sacrifices] and is not fitting to eat, like notar and piggul. And likewise, did they, may their memory be Blessed, say (Avodah Zarah 66a) that they are included in the warnings, "You shall not eat any abomination" (Deuteronomy 14:3) - which they expounded (Chullin 114b), "Anything that is abominable for me, is forbidden to eat." And since this is so, we shall say that [that warning (negative commandment) is to make one liable for] additional negative commandments; and the verse here is speaking about the punishment of the one who eats it, as so did the explanation come about it. And that which it stated (Leviticus 7:18), "If it shall surely be eaten on the third day," is meaning to say that he thought about it to eat it on the third day. As so did they, may their memory be Blessed, expound (Zevachim 29a), "'And if it shall surely be eaten, etc.' – that is piggul." Bend your ear to hear that the verse is speaking about one who thinks to eat his sacrifice on the third day, that it is spoiled with this thought. And one who eats it is liable for excision, as it is stated about it, "and the soul that eats from it will carry his iniquity." And it is stated about notar (Leviticus 19:8), "And the one who eats it will carry his iniquity, as he has profaned the holy of the Lord, and he shall be excised." And we learned [about] it in Keritot 5a, "Let not an inferential comparison (gezara shava) be light in your eyes; as behold piggul is one of the [important] bodies of Torah, and Scripture only taught it through a gezara shava." As we learn it] from notar, from [the use of] 'iniquity' [in both cases] – "just like there it is excision, here too it is excision."

From the roots of this commandment is the foundation that we have built at first – as we have said that the matter of the sacrifice is to refine the thoughts of people; and through the acts in their hands to fashion in their souls the evil of sin and the good of straight paths. Therefore, in that the main cause of something is thoughts, it is fit to disqualify on account of a thought that leans away from that which is straight in any of his deeds. And this thing is clear, close to the intellect and ancillary of truth.

From the laws of the commandment is that which they, may their memory be Blessed, said (Zevachim 43a) that the liability of excision is only for one that eats that part of the sacrifice which is for the person or the altar. But one is not liable for excision on account of piggul from the part of it that permits the sacrifice. How is this? One is not liable for excision on account of piggul when one eats a kazayit of the blood from a sacrifice that is made piggul - as behold, the blood is the part of the sacrifice that permits; since after the sprinkling of the blood, it is permitted to offer the entrails, but not before then. And nonetheless, we administer lashes for it – even if there is no excision with it. But one who eats a kazayit of meat from the sacrifice – or even from the entrails – is liable for excision on account of piggul. As it is the blood that permits the entrails [to be put] on the altar. And after the first thing that permits, we follow this law, to make liable one who eats from any of the rest – and therefore, one who eats even from the entrails is liable. And even though they also permit the meat for a person, it makes no difference; as we follow the blood, which is the first thing that permits, as we have said.

And so [too,] one who eats a kazayit from the remainder of a flour-offering that became piggul is liable on account of piggul. But one who eats a kazayit of its handful or from the frankincense – which are the things that permit it – is not liable excision for it. And nonetheless, he is lashed for them, as we have said. And these are the things for which one is never liable for piggul: the handful; frankincense; blood, as we have said; wine; and flour offerings that are completely burned, as behold they do not have a handful that permits them. And one is not liable on account of piggul for anything that does not have something that permits it, beside it. And one is also not liable for it with a log of oil of the metsora. And if you say, "But does not the blood of the guilt-offering permit it" – the answer is that it is not dependent upon it. As behold, a man brings his guilt-offering today and the log after several days.

And so [too,] from the matter of the commandment is that which they also said that one who sacrifices who has a disqualifying thought transgresses a negative commandment; as it is stated (Leviticus 7:18), "it shall not be counted (yichashev) for him (which can also be read as, 'he shall not think about it')." And we learned from the tradition (Zevachim 29b) that included in this warning (negative commandment) is about one who sacrifices, that he not have a disqualifying thought. But nonetheless, it is not considered to be from the tally of the three hundred and sixty-five negative commandments, since it is similar to one of the extensions of another negative commandment, which is calculated in the tally – and that is that which is written in the Order of Emor el HaKohanim, "There shall be no blemish in it" (Leviticus 22:21) – and they, may their memory be Blessed, expounded (Berakhot 33b), on account of the negative commandment of one who places a blemish in [sacrifices]; as we shall write with God's help (Sefer Ha Chinukh 287). And also, the content of one who has a disqualifying thought is considered similar to one who places a blemish. And hence they did not consider it in the tally. And in any event, he is not lashed for it, since there is no act [involved] with it, but rather only thought. And the rest of the laws of thoughts: which thought disqualifies, for example the thought of changing a name, the thought of a place and the thought of a time; and in which sacrifice; and which process, for example slaughter, sprinkling, reception, taking; and all of the details of the laws of piggul - and also of notar, which is similar to it - are elucidated in many places in the Order of Kedoshim.

And the prohibition of eating piggul is practiced at the time of the [Temple] by males and females - even Israelites, as the Torah prohibited it in general, whether to priests or whether to Israelites. And one who transgresses it and eats a kazayit from it volitionally is liable for excision; inadvertently, he brings a fixed sin-offering. And I have already explained twice (Sefer HaChinukh 108, 121) that a sacrifice that does not vary up and down according to poverty and wealth is called fixed.

Mitzvah 145

To not eat meat of [the sacrifices] that has become impure: That we do not eat meat of [the sacrifices] that has become impure, as it is stated (Leviticus 7:19), "And meat that touches anything impure shall not be eaten." And the same is the law for an impure man, that it is forbidden for him to eat meat [that is] pure – and as we will write (Sefer HaChinukh 167) in a separate negative commandment, with God's help. And in the second chapter of Pesachim 24b, they said [that] impurity of the body is with excision; impurity of the meat is with a negative commandment.

That which we have written above that we were commanded to aggrandize matters of the sacrifice in every way is from the roots of this commandment. And it is certainly from its loftiness to only eat it in purity and with a clean body. And we have already written the reason of what is the benefit for us in its aggrandizement (Sefer HaChinukh 103).

From the laws of the commandment is, for example, that which they, may their memory be Blessed, said (Makkot 14b) that it is forbidden to render [sacrifices] impure or to bring about their impurity. But one who makes them impure is not lashed. Rather it is the pure one who eats them that are impure that is lashed – from that which is written (Leviticus 7:19), "it shall not be eaten." And even though this verse was about the inauguration, the law is the same for all of the other sacrifices. And even one who eats a kazayit of frankincense from the meal-offering which became impure after it was sanctified in a vessel is lashed; as it too is a part of the sacrifice. And the liability only comes with becoming impure [from] a primary source of impurity or its derivative by Torah writ. But on account of rabbinic impurity, he is not lashed [by Torah writ], but we do administer rabbinic lashes of rebellion upon him. And the rest of its details are in the thirteenth chapter of Zevachim.

And it is practiced at the time of the [Temple] by males and females. And one who transgresses it and eats a kazayit of sacrificial meat that has become impure volitionally is lashed.

Mitzvah 146

Sefer HaChinukh

The commandment of burning meat of [sacrifices] that has become impure: That we were commanded to burn meat of [sacrifices] that has become impure, as it is stated (Leviticus 7:19), "And meat that touches anything impure shall not be eaten; it shall be burnt with fire."

What we have written about notar (Sefer HaChinukh 143) is from the roots of the commandment.

From the laws of the commandment is that which they, may their memory be Blessed, said (Mishnah Shekalim 8:6) that if it became impure on the interior, we burn it on the interior; if it became impure on the exterior, we burn it on the exterior. And we burn it, whether it became impure from a main category of impurity or its immediate derivative. The owners burn notar of lower level [sacrifices] in their homes. And no bones of [sacrifices] that do not have marrow require burning, except for the bones of the Pesach sacrifice. And this matter strengthens a little our argument that we said about the spoiling of meat. And therefore, the bones that do not come to spoiling do not require burning - except for the bones of the Pesach sacrifice: Since they are in the [negative commandment] of "and you shall not break a bone in it" (Exodus 12:46), there is usually a little meat upon them, because of the fear of breaking. And therefore, they said in general about all of [their bones] that they require burning. And these are [the items] that are burned: Meat of [sacrifices] that have become impure or notar, or of a sacrifice that has become disqualified; also a meal-offering that has become impure, notar or disqualified; an undetermined guilt-offering about which it has become known (after) [before] its blood was sprinkled that the owner did not sin; a fowl sin-offering that came about a doubt; the hair of a pure nazirite; orlah (fruit of the first three years); and forbidden mixtures of the vineyard (so is it found in most hand-written manuscripts) - behold, these are burnt. And [while we are on this], we will write [the items] that are buried, and these are them: consecrated [animals] that died - whether consecrated for the altar or consecrated for the upkeep of the [Temple]; the fetus of consecrated [animals] that miscarried is to be buried, [and] if it passed a placenta, it is [also] buried; an ox that is stoned; a beheaded calf; the birds of a metsora ; the hair of an impure nazirite; a firstborn donkey; meat with milk; and non-sacred animals slaughtered in the [Temple] yard. And the rest of the details of the commandment are elucidated in Pesachim and at the end of Temurah.

And the burning of [sacrifices] that became impure is practiced at the time of the [Temple] by priests and by Israelites. How is this? The burning of [sacrifices] that require burning in the Temple is incumbent upon the priests. And the [Israelite] owners burn those that are burned in the whole city, such as lower order [sacrifices] if they became impure or notar in their homes. And one who transgresses this and did not burn impure meat or notar that is in his hand has violated this positive commandment.

Mitzvah 147

That we not eat forbidden fat (chelev): That we not eat the forbidden fat of a pure animal, as it is stated (Leviticus 7:23), "Any chelev of an ox or sheep or goat you shall not eat."

I have already written in the prohibition of 'torn' animals (treifa) in the Order of Mishpatim (Sefer HaChinukh 73) that in that the body is the vessel for the soul and with it does it act properly - and according to his merit and the quality of his constitution does he understand the wisdom placed in it and believes its counsel and follows it - because of this a man must regardless make efforts for the welfare of his body, to preserve its order, health and strength. And the thing is well-known and famous among people that the body functions for health or illness, according to foods [that it consumes]. As the flesh of the body spoils on each and every day, and it is formed in return by good nourishment. And it was from God's great kindnesses towards us - His people that He chose - that He distanced from us all food that injures the body and that produces bad fluids in it. And this is the principle that I have according to the simple understanding about all prohibitions of foods, as we said above. And it is well-known that forbidden fat clings and produces bad fluids.

From the laws of the commandment is, for example, that which they, may their memory be Blessed, explained (Keritot 4b) that the prohibition of forbidden fat is only with the three beasts in Scripture - the ox, the sheep and the goat. And one is liable for the chelev of these three, whether they are fit (kosher), torn or carcasses. But the chelev of other types of animals - whether impure or pure - is like its meat. And so [too,] there is no prohibition of chelev in the fetus that is called the embryo that is in the innards of the three beasts mentioned. And therefore, they said (Chullin 74b) [about] one who slaughters an animal and found an embryo in it, [that] all of its chelev is permitted - and even if he found it alive. But if it finished its months and he found it alive - even though it did not hover over the ground and it does not require slaughter - its chelev is forbidden, and we are liable excision for it. And behold, its law is like [adult] beasts regarding its chelev. And hence we must remove all the fibers and all of the forbidden membranes from it. This is the opinion of Rambam, may his memory be Blessed, (Mishneh Torah, Laws of Forbidden Foods 7:3) regarding an embryo that has finished its months - that there is a liability for excision with its chelev. But the majority of the commentators disagree with this and say that its chelev is permissible. And the words of the Gemara (Chullin 92b) decide like them. As behold we found Rabbi Meir and Rabbi Yehudah disagreeing about its chelev; and Rabbi Yehudah - whom we follow - is the one that permits it.

And they, may their memory be Blessed, also taught us (Chullin 75a) about the law of the embryo, that [the Torah] permits it with four benchmarks (its two and the two of its mother) - such that if its mother becomes 'torn,' one can slaughter the embryo and it is permissible; as it is not the 'thigh of its mother.' And that which they said (Chullin 75b) that if it hovered over the ground it requires slaughter; it is only because of appearances that we need to slaughter it. And therefore, we do not disqualify it with pausing, pressing and the other types of [causing it to be] 'torn.' And there are three forbidden fats in a beast that have a liability of excision: that on the innards; that on the kidneys; and that on the flanks. And the understanding of the three of them is [found] with great elucidation in its place in the Gemara (Chullin 93a). And more generally, they, may their memory be Blessed, said in Chullin 93a, "Chelev that meat surrounds is permissible; as [the Torah] stated, 'upon the flanks,' and not 'within the flanks.'"

And besides these three, there are also fibers and membranes that are forbidden on account of chelev. And they, may their memory be Blessed, said (Chullin 89b) that slaughterers that are expert in removing the chelev are trusted about the matter, so long they do not leave their status of their being expert and fit. And the chelev of the heart and the chelev of the intestines - and that is the small [tissues] wrapped around [them] - are permitted, and behold they are like shuman (permitted fats); except for the head of the intestines which is adjacent the maw, which is at the beginning of the intestines, as a man needs to scrape the chelev from upon it. And about it, they, may their memory be Blessed, said in the Gemara (Chullin 93a), "The head of the intestines requires an ell of scraping" (Rashi: Where the small [tissues] exit from the maw, there is a need to scrape the chelev from on top of them the length of an ell). And there are some of the Geonim that said (Mishneh Torah, Laws of Forbidden Foods 7:15) that this intestine is the intestine from which the rectum comes out, which is the end of the intestines. And the rest of the details of the commandment and all of its content are elucidated in the seventh chapter of Chullin (see Tur, Yoreh Deah 64).

And it is practiced in every place and at all times by males and females. And one who transgress it and eats a kazayit of chelev volitionally is lashed; inadvertently, he must bring a fixed sin-offering.

Mitzvah 148

That we not eat the blood of a [domesticated] beast, a [wild] animal or a bird: That we not eat the blood of a [domesticated] beast, a [wild] animal or a bird (Keritot 20b), as it is stated (Leviticus 3:17), "And any blood you shall not eat.' And it is stated in another place (Leviticus 7:26) - "from a bird or a beast" - and a [wild] animal is included in "beast" (Chullin 71a). And the prevention of blood is repeated in many places in the Torah.

I have already written what I think on the level of the simple understanding about forbidden foods, in the prohibitions of the 'torn' [animals] (Sefer HaChinukh 73) and of forbidden fat (Sefer HaChinukh 147). But it is also possible to say about blood that besides the bad constitution [that it brings] - as it is of bad constitution - there would be in its eating a little acquisition of the trait of cruelty. As a man swallows from living beings, like him in the body, that thing in them that life is actually dependent upon and to which their spirit is connected. As it is well-known that beasts have spirits, which the wise men call a living spirit, meaning to say it is not an intelligent spirit. We can also see that their spirits have that aspect to guard from falling into one of the traps, and in a few other things. And

Sefer HaChinukh

Ramban, may his memory be Blessed, wrote (Ramban on Leviticus 17:11) about the reason of blood, that it is well-known that that which is eaten returns to (dwells within) the body of the eater. And [so] if a man eats blood, there will be density and coarseness in the spirit of the man, just like the beast is dense and coarse. And he further wrote similar to that which I said, myself - that is not fitting for a spirit to eat a spirit.

From the laws of the commandment is that which they, may their memory be Blessed, said (Keritot 21a) that one is not liable for excision on account of blood, with the blood of fish, locusts, disgusting animals and creeping animals, nor the blood of people. And therefore, they said that the blood of fish and locusts is permissible, that it is permissible to eat their blood - and even if he put it into a vessel. And that is when it is recognizable to all that it is the blood of fish. And, like they said in the Gemara (Keritot 21b), that there be a few of the scales of the fish in the vessel. But the blood of forbidden fish is forbidden, since it is like the milk of an impure beast, which is forbidden from the principle that is in our hands - food that comes out of the impure is impure. As we see that the Torah forbade the egg of an ostrich, since it came out from the impure (ostrich).

But the Sages forbade the blood of people because of appearances. And therefore, they said (Keritot 22a), "Blood that is between the teeth, he should suck and swallow; and that is on the bread, he should scrape it off of it and eat the bread." And so [too] is the blood of eggs permitted - as I do not call it the blood of the fowl, and it is not from the meat, even if it has started to form. And such is the opinion of our teachers, the Masters of the Tosafot on Chullin 64b, s.v. vehu, and as is implied from the simple meaning of the bereita in Keritot 21a. This is the law of the Torah. But the Sages forbade an egg that has [been] formed, and supported the thing with the verse of "the swarming creature that swarms" (Leviticus 11:42). And hence they forbade the blood of eggs on account of the doubt - that [perhaps] it formed. But anything that does not have a doubt of formation, they only forbade on account of appearances. And so, [regarding] blood of eggs found in the white, one should throw out the blood and eat the rest. But there are those that are stringent when it is found on the union and outside of the union [of the egg], to forbid the whole egg.

And [of] the blood that is forbidden by Torah writ, there is some the prohibition of which is with excision and some with a negative commandment. Lifeblood is with excision - as in the place that excision for blood comes in the Torah, there it is stated life (literally, spirit), as it is stated (Leviticus 17:11), "For the life of the flesh is in the blood." But the prohibition of that which is not lifeblood, but rather the blood of the limbs is only with a negative commandment - since about it is it stated (Leviticus 7:26), "And any blood you shall not eat." And therefore they, may their memory be Blessed, elucidated and said (Keritot 22a) that we are liable for excision with the blood that comes out at the time of slaughter, stabbing or decapitation, so long as it has redness in it; with blood stored in the heart; and blood that is let, so long as it flows and comes out - as it too is lifeblood, and therefore we are liable for it. And specifically flowing - to exclude the dripping at the beginning of the letting and at its end, which is not lifeblood, such that we are not liable excision [for it]. And so [too,] the concentrated blood - meaning to say the blood that oozes a little at a time at the time of slaughter, after the pouring blood came out; and so [too,] the blood of the limbs, such as the blood of the spleen, the blood of the kidneys, the blood in the testicles and the blood that lodges in the heart at the time of slaughter - we are not liable excision for it, but rather lashes. And that is when he eats a kazayit of it. The blood that is absorbed in the rest of the meat, which is also called blood of the limbs; so long as it has not separated, it is permitted to eat the meat with [this] blood absorbed inside it. As this blood is considered like meat for us, so long as it has not separated from the meat. And therefore, they, may their memory be Blessed, allowed [us] to eat raw meat without salting it; so long as it was properly rinsed, that there should not be actual blood on its surface. But at the time when the blood absorbed in the meat separates and goes out, we are liable for it with a negative commandment - as with the blood of the limbs that we enumerated above, which are with a negative commandment.

And therefore, the Sages obligated one who wants to eat meat cooked in a pot to extract the blood from it [that it not] (that it) separate from it and go out into the broth in the cooking. And the only scheme they found to take it out was salt, as it draws the blood and dries it naturally. And its power is great and goes into the meat - and even with a very thick piece, it has the power to extract the blood

Sefer HaChinukh

from [its] thickness. And so is this thing well-known and tried - that if a man salts a piece of meat properly according to the measure that the Sages gave for salting, he will find the taste of the salt in all of the meat, even in a big piece of a fattened ox. And since the thing is clearly so and recognizable to the eye, it is permissible to put all meat that has been salted according to its measure in a pot - whether the water is boiling, lukewarm or cold. [This is so] since we see the meat after salting according to its measure, as if - for all purposes - all forbidden blood was drained from it. And even if after the salting, we see a little blood that comes out from it; it does not have the status of blood, but rather it is considered as red brine. And about that which is similar to it, it is said in the Gemara (Chullin 112b), "Rabbi x called this, 'the wine of meat' and permitted it."

And there are a few limbs in the beast [with] much blood, which all of Israel is accustomed to extract the blood in them with the power of fire before they cook them in the pot, and they did not want to rely on salting alone for them - and these are the brain and the liver. They roast them a little on the fire and afterwards cook them - whether they wanted to cook them on their own or with other meat. And the custom of Israel is Torah. If he transgressed and cooked them with other meat after salting alone, it is all permissible - and [that is] so long as he did not plan to do so at the outset, so that the matter returns to [be permitted] for him ex post facto after the cooking. As with regards to anyone who does this with prohibitions, we forbid it all for him, as if it were at the outset. And I read upon him, 'one who breaches a fence will be bitten by a snake.'

And the order of salting is like this: He rinses the meat properly from the blood on it, and afterwards places medium salt upon it - not very thick, so that a little will cling, and not very fine (so that it not cling more than necessary - Venice edition). And he leaves it in its salt enough to walk a mil; and it is enough with that even for a thick ox. And after it sits in its salt this measure [of time] on a diagonal place upon which the blood can properly flow or on a vessel with holes, he takes the meat in his hands and raises it and shakes off the salt from upon it, and then rinses it properly with water in the vessel three or more times, until the salt is removed and the water that he rinses the meat with is clear. And if the meat stays in its salting more than the fitting measure for salting, we do not concern ourselves lest the meat went back and absorbed from the blood on the surface of the salt; as we say that after the meat expunged its forbidden blood, it expunges its brine - meaning to say the meat's liquid, and that is the moisture in the meat. And so long as the meat expunges this brine, it is not its nature to be be able to absorb blood, since blood is very smooth by nature and is only absorbed slowly - meaning to say, [only] all of the time that the meat is not expunging anything, not blood and not brine.

And how long is this staying [with salt] that we can assume that the meat is still exuding brine? The rabbis said that it is up to twelve hours. If it stays more than this in its salt, it is forbidden to eat it until he peels the entire surface of the meat. And nonetheless it is sufficient with peeling, since we hold that salting is like the heating of a roast; and with a prohibited [food] that touches a roast, we hold [it is enough with] peeling, when there is not a prohibition that gushes - and blood does not gush. And if he did not want to peel the meat, it is permitted to eat it with roasting. As even though we say that salt does not have the power to extract the blood that comes to the meat from another place, the power of fire to extract it is stronger than salt. And therefore, it is permitted to eat meat that sat in salt longer than is necessary, roasted without peeling; and with peeling, even in a pot, as we said.

And the rest of the many laws of salting - such as fish and poultry that were salted one with the other; pure fish salted with impure fish; what is the law about ceramic vessels or wooden vessels that were salted in; what is the law of the salt itself that was [used] to salt; and the rest of the many details of salting are elucidated in Chullin in the chapter [entitled] Kol Habasar (see Tur, Yoreh Deah 69). And the laws of blood and the differences between lifeblood and blood of the limbs is also elucidated in the fifth chapter of Keritot.

And [it] is practiced in every place and at all times by males and females. And one who transgresses it and ate a kazayit of lifeblood volitionally is liable for excision; inadvertently, he brings a fixed sin-offering. And if he ate kazayit of blood of the limbs volitionally, he is lashed; inadvertently, he is exempted.

Mitzvah 149

Sefer HaChinukh

That the priests not enter the Temple with grown hair: That the priests not enter the Temple with grown hair, like mourners do - meaning to say that they not grow their hair long, as it is stated (Leviticus 10:6), "you shall not let your head be wild." And the Targum (Aramaic translation of Onkelos) said, "Do not increase locks." And Yechezkel the prophet elucidated and said (Ezekiel 44:20), "and they shall not send forth locks." And so too with the metsora (Leviticus 13:45), "and his head shall be wild" - and they said in Sifra [that it means], "He grows locks."

And the prevention was already repeated with the high priest, and it stated (Leviticus 10:6), "and he shall not let his head be wild." However it is repeated in order that we not think that that which is stated to Elazar and Itamar, "you shall not let your head be wild," would only be from the angle of the dead alone; and that when they do this not from the angle of mourning, it would be permissible. Therefore, it is elucidated with the high priest that it is because of the service, that God, may He be Blessed, commanded them to cut their hair (see Sefer HaMitzvot LaRambam, Mitzvot Lo Taase 163). The aggrandizement of the [Temple] is from the roots of the commandment. And [it is] as we said above (Sefer HaChinukh 95) that we were commanded to aggrandize it with all of our might for the reason that we said. And therefore, it is fitting that we not arrive there with grown hair, in the way of mourners. And [this is] similar to what is stated in the Scroll of Esther 4:2, "for one could not enter the palace gate wearing sackcloth" - meaning, it is fitting to only come to the house of the monarchy in the manner of gladness, joy and enjoyment; and not in the manner of mourning and distress. And all of this strengthens the foundation built at the beginning that all matters of the [Temple] and its procedures are to strengthen and to illustrate [the good] in the hearts of those that do proper action; and to distance all ugliness and all sin from their hearts and from their thoughts. And therefore, since the intention of the [Temple] is for this, it is fitting for us to come there in the manner of glory, awe, greatness and joy. And from fixing the importance of the place and its greatness, its splendor and its majesty in our thoughts, our hearts will soften and we will be fitting to receive the good.

From the laws of the commandment is, for example, that which they, may their memory be Blessed, said (Sanhedrin 22b) that the prohibition of growing locks with the common priests is only at the time of entering the Temple. But anytime that the common priest does not enter the Temple, he is not [transgressing] the prohibition of growing locks at all. But because the high priest is constantly in the Temple, he is always forbidden to grow locks - as if you were to say, that if by way of duress he stays outside of the Temple a few days, he is nonetheless obligated to not grow locks. And how [long] is the growing of locks? Thirty days, like the nazirite - as undifferentiated naziriteship is no less thirty days. And the rest of its details are elucidated.

And [it] is practiced at the time of the [Temple] by the males of the priesthood. And one who transgresses it and enters the Temple with wild [hair] - meaning after he grows his hair for thirty days - and serves there is liable for death by the hand of the Heavens; as it is stated, (Leviticus 10:6), "you shall not let your head be wild [...] and you shall not die." And the words of the Torah are [in short] - meaning to say, behold if they let their heads be wild, they will die. Nonetheless their service is not disqualified. And one who entered there but did not serve, is with a warning - meaning to say, he violated a negative commandment and is lashed. But he is only in [the category of] the death penalty if he served - since so did the explanation come. And Ramban, may his memory be Blessed, wrote (in Sefer HaMitzvot, Mitzvot Lo Taase 163) that one with wild [hair] not enter the Temple is an embellishment from [the Rabbis] and is not from Torah writ; and his proofs are in his book. And he said that the verse is only coming to forbid drawing close for service, and it is included in the negative commandment of one with a blemish who served. And he wrote further that even the Sages only forbade the place that is called, "between the chamber and the altar"; but they did not forbid in front of the altar itself - which is thirty-two ells, as we learned (Mishnah Middot 3:1, 6), "The altar was thirty-two ells [...]; between the chamber and the altar was twenty-two."

Mitzvah 150

That the priests not enter the Temple with torn clothes: That the priests not enter the Temple with torn clothes, as it is stated (Leviticus 10:6), "and you shall not rend your clothes" - the understanding is, do not tear your clothes. And the prevention is repeated with the high priest, as it is stated about him (Leviticus 21:10), "and he shall not rend his clothes." And repeating the prevention about it is because of the addition of a thing with him: That he is not permitted to tear for a dead when he dies - and even not during the time of the service. And they said in Sifra, Emor, Section 2:3, "'And he shall not let his hair be wild and he shall not rend his clothes' - for his dead, as [other] people do for their dead. Behold, how is it? The high-priest rends from the bottom (of his garment), and common [priests], from the top."

And I have written in the previous [commandment of] wildness of the [hair] (Sefer HaChinukh 149) from the roots of this commandment. And the law of wild [hair] and [that of] torn clothes are the same in all of their [particulars].

From the laws of the commandment is that which they, may their memory be Blessed, said (Sifra, Emor, Section 2:3), that the [measure required for] liability for this tearing be like the tearing that we tear for the dead. And it appears that this is a handbreadth - as so did they say in Moed Katan 22b that there is no tear that is less than a handbreadth. And the rest of its details are elucidated.

And [it] is practiced at the time of the [Temple] by the males of the priesthood. And one who transgresses it and enters the Temple - from the altar and inward - with torn clothes and served, is liable for death by the hand of the Heavens. But if he did not serve, behold it is with a warning (negative commandment) and he is lashed. This is according to the opinion of Rambam, may his memory be Blessed (Mishneh Torah, Laws of Admission into the Sanctuary 1:15). But according to the opinion of Ramban, may his memory be Blessed (in Sefer HaMitzvot, Mitzvot Lo Taase 163), there are no lashes for one who enters the Temple with torn clothes; as the prohibition to enter without [doing] service is only an embellishment from [the Rabbis]. But if he served and he was with torn clothes, he is lashed - according to what he wrote in the name of Baal Halakhot.

Mitzvah 151
That the priests not go out from the Temple at the time of the service: That the priests not go out from the Temple at the time of the service, as it stated (Leviticus 10:7), "And from the entrance of the Tent of Meeting you shall not go out, lest you die." And this prevention was repeated likewise with the high priest, and it stated (Leviticus 21:12), "And from the sanctuary he shall not go out." And the language of Sifra, Shemini, Mechilta d'Miluim 42-43 is "'And from the entrance of the Tent of Meeting' - it could be [that they shall not go out] at the time of the service and [also] not at the time of the service. [Hence] we learn to say, 'And from the sanctuary he shall not go out and he will not profane' - [...] it would be said, when he is officiating. [...] 'For the anointing oil of the Lord is upon you' - I only have Aharon and his sons who were anointed with the oil of anointment, if they went out while serving, they would be liable for death; from where [do I know] for all of the priests of the generations? As it is stated, 'for the anointing oil of the Lord is upon you.'"

The transcriber wrote in the name of Rambam, may his memory be Blessed, (Sefer HaMitzvot LaRambam, Mitzvot Lo Taase 165), "Know that there is an addition with the high priest, that he not go out after the coffin. And this is revealed in the language of Scripture in its stating, 'And from the sanctuary he shall not go out.' And so is it elucidated in the second chapter of Sanhedrin 18a - that it is if a [relative] dies on him, he does not go out after the coffin. And they brought a proof about this from its stating, 'And from the sanctuary he shall not go out.' And we learn from this that it is permitted for him to serve on the day that a [relative] dies on him. And so, did they, may their memory be Blessed, say in Tractate Sanhedrin 84a, '"And from the sanctuary he shall not go out and he shall not profane" - behold, another who serves [that he does not go out], profanes.' [This is] meaning to say for a common priest, the service is not permitted for him when he is bereaved. And so too is this principle elucidated at the end of Horayot 12b, that a common priest that is bereaved may not serve, but a high priest serves when he is bereaved. Behold, it is elucidated for you that its stating, 'and he shall not profane,' is to make it a negation - and not a prevention (negative commandment) - to say that his service is not profane, even though he is bereaved."

And from that which appears from the words of Ramban, may his memory be Blessed, he reasons that "and he shall not profane" is a prevention for the high priest, who is commanded that he not go out of the Temple because of his dead relative and not profance the service of God, may He be

Blessed. As it would be a profanation of the service that the great servant leave it for anything else in the world. And he explains this whole matter in a different way, as he wrote in his commentary on the Torah (Ramban on Leviticus 21:12).

The foundation built for it about the aggrandizement of the [Temple] and the services done there is from the roots of the commandment. And therefore, it is fitting in any case to not go out and leave the precious service for anything in the world. As truly if they leave it, it would be a demeaning of it. And they would be showing about themselves that there is something greater in the world than the service of God, since it is pushed off even temporarily for something else. And therefore, they were warned about this with death.

The laws of the commandment: For example, that which our Rabbis, may their memory be Blessed, said [regarding] a common priest, that even though he is not permitted to go out from the Temple at the time of service - as it is stated, "And from the entrance of the Tent of Meeting you shall not go out, lest you die" - nonetheless, if a [relative] that is fit (closely enough related) for him to mourn dies on him, he does not serve, as he is bereaved; and one bereaved is forbidden in the service. And even though he does not serve, he is warned not to go out of there until he finishes the service in which he is occupied, so that it not appear like he is occupied with something transient. And the high priest is more than he, as he is obligated not to go out of the Temple and also not to leave his service at all on account of bereavement, as it is stated, "And from the sanctuary he shall not go out and he shall not profane, etc." And the explanation comes about this verse [that it is] meaning to say, that he not go out, but rather do the service in which he is involved, and that his service is not profaned on account of bereavement (see Mishneh Torah, Laws of Admission into the Sanctuary 2).

And [it] is practiced at the time of the [Temple] by the males of the priesthood. And if he transgressed and went out at the time of service, he is lashed.

Mitzvah 152

To not enter the Temple intoxicated, and likewise to not give a ruling intoxicated: To not enter the Temple intoxicated, and likewise to not give a ruling - meaning to say to judge something of the laws of the Torah - while a man is still drunk, as it is stated (Leviticus 10:9), "Wine and strong drink you shall not drink, etc. in your coming to the Tent of Meeting." And the language of the Talmud (Eruvin 64a) is "If he drank a reviit, he may not give a ruling." And the language of Sifra, Shmini, Section 1:2 is "'Wine [...] you shall not drink' - I only have wine. From where [do I know] all the other intoxicants? [Hence] we learn to say, 'strong drink.' If so, why is it stated, 'wine?' For wine, [one is liable] for death. For all other intoxicants, [one is liable] for a negative commandment." And there it is stated, "From where [do I know] that he is only liable at the time of the service? [Hence] we learn to say, 'you and your sons, and you shall not die' - you and your sons are with death, but Israelites are not liable for death for giving a ruling."

The root of the commandment is well known - that it is only fitting to be involved in extremely precious things, like matters of the Temple and words of Torah, at the time that a man is settled in his thoughts and focused in all of his actions. There is no need to write at length about obvious things.

From the laws of the commandment is that which they, may their memory be Blessed, said (Sanhedrin 22b) [regarding] any priest that is fit to do the service - if he drinks wine, he is forbidden to enter from the altar and inwards. And if he entered and served, his service is disqualified and he is liable for death by the hand of the Heavens, as it is stated, "and you shall not die." And so [too,] is it forbidden for any man - whether priest or Israelite - to enter the entire Temple, from the beginning of the yard of the Israelites and inwards, when he is drunk from wine or strong drink; with wild [hair] in the way of slovenliness - meaning to say, the hair of his head is very long; or with torn clothes. And even though it is not with a negative commandment, there is a prohibition in the thing; and the prohibition is only due to the honor of the [Temple]. And therefore, an Israelite is permitted to enter there with the hair of his head grown more than thirty days - since that is not slovenliness for people. And even though the priests were warned about this due to their great holiness and closeness to the holy house - such that it is not fitting that there be anything superfluous at all with them, but rather that they all be 'beautiful and that no blemish be upon them' - the rest of the people are not in their category; just that they not enter there with very long hair, as we said.

And the measure of wine (Keritot 13b) that a man drink and be forbidden to enter the Temple or to give a ruling is a quarter (reviit) of a log - which is [the volume of] one and a half [large] eggs - and he must drink it unmixed and at one time, and on condition that forty days have transpired since the wine was made. If one of these [things] is missing, he is exempt, but forbidden [from doing so], and his service is not disqualified by it. If he drank more than a reviit of wine - even though he interrupted it and drank [it] bit by bit - he is liable for death and disqualifies his service. If he was drunk from other intoxicating beverages, he is forbidden from entering the Temple. And if he entered and served and was drunk from other intoxicating beverages - even from milk or from figs - behold, he is lashed and his service is fit (kosher); as we are only liable for death for wine at the time of the service, and it is only disqualified by one drunk from wine.

And just like it is forbidden for a priest to come to the Temple on account of drunkenness, so is it forbidden for any man - whether priest or Israelite - to give a ruling when he is drunk. Even if he drunk the honey of dates or milk and his mind is mixed up, he should not issue a ruling; as in the section of "Wine and strong drink you shall not drink," it is stated (Leviticus 10:11), "And to instruct the Children of Israel." But if he gave a ruling about a thing that is explicit in the Torah to the point that the Sadducees (conceded) [know] it, it is permitted - for example, if he gave a ruling that a sherets (certain swarming animals) is impure or that blood is forbidden, or similar to them. And it is permitted for a drunk to read the Torah, and even laws and homilies (midrash) - and that is when he does not give a ruling. And if he was a sage that regularly gave rulings, he should not teach - as his teaching is [legal] instruction. If he drank only enough for a reviit and there was the smallest amount of water in it or he slept a little or he walked [the distance] of a mil, the wine has already passed and he is permitted to serve. But if he drinks more than a reviit - even if it is mixed - if he a slept a little or walked on the way, it adds to his drunkenness. Rather he should wait according to his drunkenness until there is nothing at all left from his drunkenness. The [priests] of the shift were permitted to drink wine during the nights, but not during the days, of their week (Taanit 15b) - and even the other clans of the shift whose service was not on that day, lest the service be heavy for the clan of that day and they require other men from their shift to help them. But the men of the shift from that day are forbidden to drink both night and day, lest he drink at night and get up early for his service while his wine has still not gone away from upon him.

A priest, that knows from which clan he is and knows that his clan was fixed for the service of today, is forbidden to drink all of that day. If he knew from which shift, he is, but he does not know which is his clan, he is forbidden to drink the whole week that his shift is serving. If he was not aware of his shift or his clan, the law should be that he is always forbidden to drink wine. But his solution is his mishap: behold, he is permitted to always drink, since he may not serve until, he becomes fixed in his clan and his shift.

And the prohibition of coming to the Temple in drunkenness is practiced at the time of the [Temple] by males and females. And the prevention of giving a ruling is [practiced] in every place and at all times by males, and so [too,] by a sage woman that is fitting to give a ruling. And anyone who is a great sage that people rely upon for his rulings is forbidden to teach to his students when he is intoxicated - since his study is like a ruling, as we have said.

And one who transgresses it and enters, between the chamber and the altar, and inwards intoxicated from wine is liable for lashes; and if did a service, he is liable for death by the hand of the Heavens. But if he drank form other intoxicants and served, he is only liable for lashes, not death. And likewise, anyone how gave a ruling and was intoxicated - whether a priest or an Israelite; whether he was intoxicated from wine or intoxicated from other intoxicants - has violated a negative commandment. And Ramban, may his memory be Blessed, wrote (in Sefer HaMitzvot, Mitzvot Lo Taase 73) that it is a [rabbinic] embellishment not to enter the Temple intoxicated with wine; and only not to serve intoxicated is from Torah writ.

Mitzvah 153

Sefer HaChinukh

The command of checking the signs of a beast or animal: That we were commanded to check the signs of a [domesticated] beast or [wild] animal when we want to eat of them - and they are that it brings up (chews) its cud and completely splits [its hoof], as it is stated (Leviticus 11:2-3), "This is the animal that you shall eat, from every beast upon the earth: All that separate the hoof, etc." And the language of Sifri, Shemini, Chapter 3:1 is "'It shall you eat' - it is for eating, but an impure animal is not for eating"; meaning to say, and we learn from it a negative commandment for an impure animal. And a negative commandment like this is called a negative commandment that comes from the implication of a positive commandment. And it is stated in another place, "And you shall differentiate between a pure beast and an impure, etc." (Leviticus 20:25). And it is also written (Leviticus 11:47), "To differentiate between the impure, etc."

We have written in the warning of the 'torn' animal (Sefer HaChinukh 73) and forbidden fat (Sefer HaChinukh 143) that which we have known from the roots of the commandments of forbidden foods. And that root suffices according to the simple understanding for them all. And the matter of the command to check the signs goes after the reason for their prohibition; as it is fitting and obligatory upon us to properly check anything about which a prohibition comes to us. And I have not spared my pen here from writing the words of Rambam, may this memory be Blessed (Sefer HaMitzvot LaRambam, Mitzvot Ase 149) - who calculates this verse as a positive commandment - because I have set out at the beginning of my words to write the commandments according to the order that he counted. [This is] even though my heart is grabbed in this matter by the logic of Ramban, may his memory be Blessed, (in his glosses of the Sefer HaMitzvot, Root 6) that it is not fitting that we count the checking of the signs of beasts as a commandment - since in truth once the Torah had forbidden us some of the beasts, it becomes necessary to inform us of the signs of the pure ones in order to separate us from [the one] that is forbidden. And this is not fitting at all to count as a commandment in the tally. And the law is the same - and the reason is the same - also with the checking of fowl, fish and locusts, which Rambam, may his memory be Blessed, counts as three; however, Ramban, may his memory be Blessed, does not count them [in the tally].

From the laws of the commandment is that every beast and animal that brings up the cud does not have teeth in its upper (rear) jaw. And every beast in the world that brings up the cud separates its hoof except for the camel. And all that separate its hoof brings up the cud except for the pig. And there are ten species of beasts and animals that are permitted: Three [domesticated] beasts that are well-known and they are the ox, the sheep and the goat; and seven species of [wild] animals that are explicit in Scripture - "The deer, the gazelle, etc." (Deuteronomy 14:5). And [just] like we need to know the signs of the fit (kosher) ones to differentiate them from the impure ones, likewise must we know which is a species of beast and which is a species of animal regarding the chelev (forbidden fat) - as the chelev of a beast is forbidden, but the chelev of an animal is permissible, as we we wrote above in the warning of chelev; and also, as the blood of an animal requires covering, but not the blood of a beast. And the signs of the [wild] animal, as to how it is distinguished from a [domesticated] beast is not stated in the Torah. Rather, we learned from the heard tradition (Chullin 59b) that it is recognizable by its horns, as the horns of an animal are scaled, notched and circular: scaled like the horns of an ox; notched like the horns of a goat - such that the notch be absorbed in them (tight); and round like the horns of a gazelle. Therefore [with] any [being] that does not have these signs in its horns, a man must practice the prohibition of its chelev. And one who finds a [wild] animal without horns - such that he is not able to check its horns - if he recognizes it clearly by its shape, such as that which he is used to, it is permitted for him to trust his recognition. And it is not said that he has to check with the horns no matter what. And the rest of its details are in Chullin.

And [it] is practiced in every place and at all times by males and females. And if he transgressed it and did not check, but he saw one sign and relied upon it and ate it - even though afterwards he found that he ate something permissible - he violated this positive commandment of checking the signs.

Mitzvah 154

To not eat an impure beast or animal: To not eat an impure beast or animal, as it is stated (Leviticus 11:4), "this shall you not eat from those that bring up the cud and separate their hoof, the camel," "and the pig" (Leviticus 11:7), "and the hare" (Leviticus 11:6), "and the daman" (Leviticus 11:5). And a clear negative commandment about the other species of impure beasts does not appear. But since the Torah stated (Leviticus 11:3), "All that separate the hoof and [...] bring up the cud in an animal, it shall you eat," we know that we are prevented from eating anything that does not have these two signs together. And this is a negative commandment that comes from the implication of a positive commandment. And the principle that we have is [that] a negative commandment that comes from the implication of a positive commandment, is a positive commandment, and [so] we do not administer lashes for it.

However [the] other beasts and animals were forbidden to us by an a fortiori argument (kal vechomer): As we say that [since] we administer lashes for the pig and the camel which have one sign of purity; all the more so do we administer lashes for other beasts and animals that do not have any sign of purity at all. And the language of Sifri, Shemini, Chapter 3:1-2 is "'It shall you eat' - it is for eating, but an impure animal is not for eating. I only have a positive commandment. From where [do I know it is also a] negative commandment? [Hence] we learn to say, 'this shall you not eat from those that bring up the cud, etc.' I only have these alone. From where [do I know] other impure beasts? It is inferred: And just like these that have one sign of purity, behold, their eating is with a negative commandment; is it not [then] inferred that the eating of other impure beasts that do not have any sign of purity would be with a negative commandment? It comes out that the camel, the hare, the daman and the pig are from Scripture, and the other impure beasts are from an a fortiori argument." However it is only just revealing a matter - meaning to say, that the a fortiori argument about this matter is elucidated in Scripture; as if it warned about those that have one sign of purity, all the more so [is it the case] about those that do not have any sign of purity at all. And it is not relevant here to say, 'we do not punish from an inference.' And hence anyone that ate a kazayit from an impure animal - from whatever species it be - is lashed from Torah writ. And the understanding of "separates the hoof," is that its hooves are split. And the understanding of "completely splits," is meaning to say totally divided from above and below; but if it was split below and attached above, or the opposite, it is impure. And the understanding of "bring up the cud," is that it regurgitates the food from its intestines to its mouth to grate it and grind it fine.

What we wrote in the warning of the 'torn' animal in the Order of Mishpatim (Sefer HaChinukh 73) is from the roots of the commandment - as God knows that all of the foods that he distanced from His people that He chose, have [properties] in them [that] injure bodies, [and] that stop the souls from activating them and elevating them with good deeds. Therefore, He distanced us from them, in order that the souls will make their impact; and that a bad constitution and a blockage of the heart not seal the door in front of them, as I wrote there.

From the laws of the commandment is that which they, may their memory be Blessed, said (Zevachim 70a) that Scripture did not distinguish with an impure beast or animal between its meat and its chelev - as it is all forbidden. And [regarding] flesh of a person, his flesh is not included in the prohibition of an impure beast, to transgress a negative commandment for it, even though man is called a living (or animal) soul and he does not bring up the cud or completely divide [his foot]. And therefore, we do not administer lashes for one who eats from his flesh or drinks from his chelev - whether alive or dead. But it is nonetheless forbidden with a positive commandment, as behold Scripture numbered seven species of animals and stated about them (Leviticus 14:4), "this is the animal that you may eat." And a negative commandment that comes from the implication of a positive commandment, is a positive commandment. This is the opinion of Rambam, may his memory be Blessed (Mishneh Torah, Laws of Forbidden Foods 2:3). But Ramban, may his memory be Blessed, wrote (Ramban on Leviticus 11:3) that there is not even a positive commandment about the flesh of a man. And he brought a proof from that which they, may their memory be Blessed, said (Keritot 21a), "There is not even a commandment of separation from the blood and chelev of those that walk on two [legs]." And he, may his memory be Blessed, wrote that the law is the same for flesh, that it is permitted like the blood. As if not, how could blood be permissible - and as they, may their memory be Blessed, said (Keritot 22a), "Blood that is between the teeth, he should suck and swallow" - and it is established for us (Bekhorot 5a) "All that comes out of the impure is impure." And nonetheless, the flesh of the dead (Israelite) is forbidden to benefit from. And the rest of his proofs are in his book. And the rest of the details of the commandment are elucidated in the third chapter of Chullin and in other places (see Mishneh Torah, Laws of Forbidden Foods 2).

And [it] is practiced in every place and at all times by males and females. And one who transgresses it and eats a kazayit of an impure animal or a reviit of chelev volitionally is lashed; and inadvertently, is exempted.

Mitzvah 155
The commandment to check the signs of fish: To check the signs of fish, meaning to say that one who wants to eat fish first check properly for the signs that the Torah gave about them - and they are fins and scales, as it is stated (Leviticus 11:9), "And this shall you eat from all that is in the water, etc." We have already written in the commandment preceding this (Sefer HaChinukh 153, in the commandment of checking the signs of beasts and animals) that Ramban, may his memory be Blessed, does not calculate the checking of signs in the species that the Torah permitted; and that the truth is with him, according to what appears to us. And even though we have found explicitly in the Gemara (Chullin 66b) with some of them, "This is a positive commandment," the intention of the matter is to make liable for impure species with a positive commandment [as well as] a negative commandment - from the principle that is well known to us, [that] a negative commandment that comes from the implication of a positive commandment, is a positive commandment. And [that is] like we shall write with God's help in the commandment of lending to a gentile (Sefer HaChinukh 173), such that Rambam, may his memory be Blessed, counted it as a commandment (Sefer HaMitzvot LaRambam, Mitzvot Ase 198), [whereas] according to what it appears, the verse only comes to make liable for a positive commandment [as well] as a negative commandment for the lending to a Jew with interest.

I have also written the root of the commandment above in the signs of the beast. And it is the general principle for the four species.

From the laws of the commandment is, for example, that which they, may their memory be Blessed, said (Chullin 59a) that fins are what in the fish is like a type of wings with which to fly; and scales are that covering that clings to all of its body. And even if scales are only found on part of its body - and even it is only one - it is enough for it and it is fit (kosher). And they said in Tosefta Chullin 3:9, "And that is when it is under its jaw or under its tail or under its fins; but on the rest of its body, it is not enough for us with less than two." And everything in which scales are found - even one in the places mentioned - need not be checked [to ascertain] if it has fins; as it certainly has [them]. But if fins are found on it, it needs to be checked [to ascertain] if it has scales - as there are many impure fish that have fins. And any fish the nature of which is to have scales, even though they are not produced on it when it is still small until it grows up - such as the sultanit and the afian - behold it is permissible. And anything that has scales when it is still in the sea, even though it drops them at the time that it goes out from the sea - such as the akonas, the afonas, the bisifityas, the afnasetiyas and the tunny that is called biret in the vernacular - behold, it is fit (Chullin 66). As the Torah is only concerned with the species that it have scales and fins - since that is what is seemly for the nature of people, and from the reason that we wrote in the prohibition of foods according to the simple understanding.

And [it] is practiced in every place and at all times by males and females. And if one transgressed it and did not check properly, such that he saw only one sign and relied [upon it] for the other, without checking - even though afterwards it was found to be fit - he violated this positive commandment.

Mitzvah 156
To not eat impure fish: To not eat impure fish, as it is stated (Leviticus 11:11), "you shall not eat of their meat and you shall abominate their carcasses." And we have written the signs of the fit (kosher) fish in the positive commandment (Sefer HaChinukh 155) - which is to check the signs of the fish - which we have counted in the tally [of the commandments] in deference to Rambam, may his memory be Blessed.

That which we wrote above regarding the matter of the prohibition of foods (Sefer HaChinukh 93) is from the roots of the commandment - that God, Blessed be He, distanced all in which injury is found from His people, whether beast, fowl or fish, from the reason that we said there.

We have also written the laws of the commandment above, and they are in Chullin, Chapter 3 (see Tur, Yoreh Deah 83).

And [it] is practiced in every place and at all times by males and females. And one who transgresses it and eats a kazayit of an impure fish is lashed; and inadvertently, is exempted.

Mitzvah 157

To not eat impure fowl: To not eat impure fowl, as it is stated (Leviticus 11:13), "And these you shall abominate from the fowl; they shall not be eaten, etc."

That which we have written about the forbidden foods (Sefer HaChinukh 73, 147) is from the roots of the commandment.

From the laws of the commandment is that which they, may their memory be Blessed, said (Chullin 59a), "The signs of the the beast and animal are stated from the Torah" - meaning to say they are explicit in the Torah, and that is a hoof completely divided, like the ox and the sheep, and [that] it brings up the cud - "but the signs of the fowl were not stated," since the Torah delineated for us by name all of the impure ones in the world. And since it is so, there is no need to write their signs - as any bird that is found in the world besides them is fit (kosher). And nonetheless since not every man is an expert in all of the species of which the Torah informed us, the Sages informed us of signs through which any man may recognize them and he be able to eat of fowl, even though he not recognize even one of the many impure species that are delineated in Scripture.

It comes out according to our words that anyone who knows well all those delineated in the Torah - which are twenty-four species - can eat from any other bird that he finds; as they said that any bird not mentioned in the tally of the impure ones in the Torah is fit. And [it is] like they, may their memory be Blessed, said (Chullin 63b), "It is revealed and known in front of the One that spoke and the world came into being, that the pure birds are more than the impure ones - therefore he specified the impure ones," meaning that he specified all of the impure ones in the world. That is the explanation according to most of the rabbis, that all of the impure ones in the world are mentioned in the Torah. And [for] the ones that do not recognize them, the Sages, may their memory be Blessed, said (Chullin 59a) that these are their signs: It is known that any bird that tramples (is a predator) is from the impure ones in the Torah. And the understanding of a predator is meaning to say that he sinks his claws into another bird and injects poison into him, as is the custom of the hawk and other birds that people hunt with. And there are some that are not predators, but are also from the impure species.

And the Sages, may their memory be Blessed, said to us as a general rule that anything that has in its body these three signs: That it has an extra digit - and that is the large digit that protrudes more than the other digits; a crop - that is a broad place at the end of the esophagus wherein the bird gathers the food at the beginning of the eating; and a gizzard that peels [away] - and that is a place in which the bird grinds the food, which is called ventrai in the vernacular, and it has a thin membrane inside the flesh, and that membrane peels off in some birds - once a bird has these three signs, it is known that it is not from an impure species, and it is permitted. These two general rules that we have generalized - one to forbid and one to permit all birds that have them - no man need ask an expert in birds about them. Rather he may forbid the forbidden and allow the permitted immediately, as there is no hesitation about this.

And it comes out according to this general principle that there are four signs of purity in fowl. And these are them: it is not a predator; an extra digit; a crop; and a gizzard that peels. And we have already generalized that any bird that is found to be lacking one of them, and that is the unique one among them - which is that it is not a predator, meaning that it is a predator - is always impure and one need not check any other sign. And it is not necessary to say if it is lacking all of them - that it does not have even one of these signs of purity - that it is forbidden. As behold, even the one - the unique one - forbids by itself, as we said; all the more so if all of them are lacking. And the eagle is also one that does not have any of the signs of purity. If a bird is found that is lacking two - meaning to say that it only has two signs of purity and is lacking the two others, and one of the two [signs] of purity found in it is that it is not a predator - any bird that is like this is pure to eat for anyone who recognizes the raven and any species of raven. As there is none among the impure like this except for the raven, since it does not trample but it has one sign in its body of the signs of purity. And that sign of purity is not fixed in each species of raven. Rather there is a type that has an extra digit and is not a predator; one that has a crop and is not a predator; and one that has a gizzard that peels and is not a predator. The general rule of the matter is that these two signs of purity are found in its species and not another species - so did some of the commentators explain. And there are some that said that the raven has two signs of purity in its body besides that it is not a predator.

If a bird is found that is lacking the three signs of purity and there is none remaining to it besides the unique one - and that is that it is not a predator - it is always pure. As there is none among the impure birds that do not have one of all the signs of purity in their bodies but is not a predator except for the ossifrage and the osprey, which are like this. And they are not found in settlements - and since they are not found in settlements, we are not in doubt about them. And there are some of the commentators that said that they were not found with our Rabbis, may their memory be Blessed, but they are found now. And I [say] about them, 'do not be greatly righteous.' As [the Rabbis] said that they are not found in settlements - meaning to say, that they are always distant from inhabited places - and since their nature is like this, 'the world stands forever,' and the law is the same at all times. If three signs of purity are found in its body - and they are an extra digit, a crop and a gizzard that peels - it is known that it is fit, and [that also] the fourth is [in it] (like this); meaning to say that it is not a predator. As there is no bird in the world with these three signs that is a predator. And [so] he does not need to check about it at all, but rather he may eat it immediately. But if three signs of purity are found in it and one of the three is that it is not a predator, one must certainly be in doubt about it; as most of the impure ones are like this, that they have three signs like these. And every man must ask about such a bird if he does not recognize all of (the impure) the enumerated ones in the Torah. It comes out, according to our words, that any bird that is in doubt for us whether it is impure or pure will be in one of two ways: that it have three signs of purity, and one of them is that it is not a predator, as we said, that it should be in doubt [of being] among the many species of the impure; or that it have two signs of impurity and one of them is that it is not a predator, that it should be in doubt of being a raven and its species. But all of the other ways do not bring a doubt, but rather we judge it as pure or impure immediately. Place your mind to the thing, as it is so, according to this general rule of ours. And we have written this general rule according to some of the commentators, as there are many explanations given in these matters of birds. And our Rabbis, may their memory be Blessed, said (Chullin 64b) that all birds that are in doubt are eaten according to tradition - meaning to say that if the people of a place received [a tradition] and were accustomed to eat it [with no question] under the assumption that it is pure - that we should have no hesitation about it at all, and there is no need to check it. And the rest of its details are in the third chapter of Chullin (see Tur, Yoreh Deah 82).

And [it] is practiced in every place and at all times by males and females. And one who transgresses it and eats a kazayit of impure fowl volitionally is lashed; and inadvertently, is exempted.

Mitzvah 158

The commandment of checking the signs of grasshoppers: To check the signs of grasshoppers - and these are the signs that are written in the Torah, "that has jointed legs above its feet, etc." (Leviticus 11:21) - as it is stated, "this you may eat from all the winged swarming things." And the content of its root is like with the other species.

Its laws: They, may their memory be Blessed, explained (Chullin 65a) that eight types of grasshoppers are pure. And these are them: The first is called grasshopper; the second is called duvanit, and it is a type of grasshopper; the third is called cricket; the fourth is the utsravia, and it is a type of cricket; the fifth is the locust; the sixth is the 'bird of the vineyards,' and it is a type of locust; the seventh is the bald locust; [and] the eighth is the Jerusalem yochana and it is a type of bald locust. One who is an expert can check them based on his expertise and their names, and eat [them]. And an Israelite trapper is trusted about them and about fowl. And one who is not an expert about them checks with the signs that the Torah gave about them. And there are three signs - and these are them: Four wings that cover most of the length and most of the width of its body; four legs; and two jointed legs with which to hop on the ground. And some say that he needs to know the name of the grasshopper. And the rest of its details are elucidated in the third chapter of Chullin (see Tur, Yoreh Deah 85).

And [it] is practiced in all places and at all times by males and females. And one who transgresses it and eats without checking properly has violated a positive commandment.

Mitzvah 159
The commandment of the impurity of the eight swarming creatures: That the eight swarming creatures are impure and render impure, as it is stated (Leviticus 11:29), "And this shall be impure for you from the swarming creatures that swarm on the ground: the mole, the mouse and the lizard, etc."

From the roots of the commandment, [we need to] preface [that] anyone who has intelligence will not have a doubt that there was never a man that grasped to know all wisdom to its end, that nothing of it be hidden from him. As behold even about our teacher Moshe, peace be upon him, they, may their memory be Blessed, said (Rosh Hashanah 21b), "There are fifty gates of understanding, and they were all given over to Moshe, except for one." And likewise, the wise King Shlomo said about himself (Ecclesiastes 7:23), "I said, 'I will be wise,' but it is distant from me." And also any one with a brain in his skull will not have a doubt that God, may He be Blessed, is the Father of wisdom and it is from Him - it comes out that it is all included in Him. And there is also not any doubt that the Father of all good would only command something to His creatures for their good and for their benefit, and to distance any injury from them. And therefore, when we grasp some of the commandments with our wisdom, to know the benefit that accrues to us from them, we shall rejoice about it. But when we do not grasp the benefit to us from them, with our wisdom, we must nonetheless think that with the extra wisdom that God, may He be Blessed, has over every creature, He knows the benefit to us in that commandment. And therefore, He commanded us about it.

And they, may their memory be Blessed, already informed us (Sanhedrin 21b) why we do not know the reason for all of the commandments; and they said that the thing is that it not become a stumbling block for us. And they brought a proof, as behold, the reason for three of them was revealed, and a great man of the world stumbled upon them. And let not a quibbler think to come against me with the metaphor that they, may their memory be Blessed, said (Pesachim 28a), "The spoon carved by the carpenter will burn his mouth with mustard," about that which I said now: That God, may He be Blessed, hid the reasons from the commandments from us, and [yet] I have raised my hand to speak about them to my youth. As my teachers have already preceded me to speak several things about them in the Midrashim and in other places, by way of their simple understanding. And the depth of their wisdom, the strength of their understanding and their great holiness is stored in them - and even all the winds of the world cannot move them. And [regarding] anyone who is [able to] deepen counsel in their simple understanding, because he longs to 'peer through the lattice,' to delight in the splendor of their vision and to gather from their leaves to gird himself with them - it is not fit to place blame upon him, but to bless him and to mention him for praise, 'in that he is there.'

And now after this preface of ours - that the wisdom of God is greater than all wisdom and that He only commands a thing for our good and for our great benefit - we have no difficulty or question in all of the prohibition of foods and distancing of impurity, in everything that the benefit to us is not known and graspable by investigation; as we truthfully know, it is all for the good. And do not wonder, my son, about the matters of impurity, if it is very hidden from every creature - as it is possible that impurity injures the soul and makes it a little sick. And so [too,] have I heard the thing from the mouth of sages. And [it is] similar to that which they, may their memory be Blessed, said (Yoma 39a), "'And become impure (nitmeitem) through them' (Leviticus 11:43) - it is written 'and you shall become foolish (nitamtem)'; meaning to say that the springs of the intellect, which is the living soul, is spoiled a little with the matter of impurity.

And do not wonder about the intellect being spoiled with physical things, even though that is not its type. As due to the partnership of the the soul with the body, such occurs to it regardless. And if so,

Sefer HaChinukh

we - the sons of man - in the poverty of our intelligence, do not know the soul and its nature. And [so] how are we to tire ourselves to know its healing or sickness by way of investigation? Is it not that there [can be] no strategy for physicians in healing until they know the essence of the sickness? And therefore, regarding all of the distancings of impurity that are in the Torah, we should not dig for their roots until we come to complete knowledge of the matters of the soul - to know its nature, where it comes from and where it is going. And understand this and know it, as in it there is a bit of an answer to all the roots of the commandments of impurity and purity. [This is the case] to the point that there is like a veil over our faces regarding the novelty of the red heifer that renders the pure impure, but purifies the impure. And there too will we write at length about the matter, with God's help, [so as] to receive reward for the effort to find desirable words.

The laws of the commandment: For example, that which they, may their memory be Blessed, said (Mishnah Kelim 1:1) that eight swarming creatures are called a primary source (av) of impurity, meaning to say that they render a man and vessels impure by touch; and if the vessels are of clay, they render them impure once they enter its space (hollow). And this is the distinction that there is in the matter between that which is called a primary source and that which is called a derivative (velad) - as that which is called a primary source renders a man and vessels impure, but that which is called a derivative does not render a man and vessels impure. And the swarming creatures only render impure after they die, as it is stated (Leviticus 11:31), "in their being dead, he shall become impure." And it is specifically these swarming creatures that render impure, but all other swarming creatures - the snake, the scorpion and all that are similar to them - do not render impure at all. And the law of the swarming creatures is that they do not render impure by carrying without touching [directly]; and that one that touches them does not render his clothes impure when they are upon him at the time that he touches them. And the measure of the impurity of the swarming creature is like [the size of] a lentil. As behold, we found that the Torah renders them pure undifferentiatedly, and there are some of these swarming creatures that are only like a lentil. And all of the swarming creatures combine to [the measure of] like a lentil - meaning to say, even a little of this one and a little of that one combine to [form the size of] a lentil, to render impure; such that you not say that the liability is only like a lentil from one [creature] by itself (Meilah 15b).

And the law of living flesh that is separated from a swarming creature, a complete limb, the kidney, the liver, and the tongue (Chullin 128b); the law of their blood, their tendons, their claws, their skins and their eggs (Meilah 17a); the law that anyone that is rendered impure by them is forbidden from eating the priestly tithe and consecrated food and entering the Temple until he immerses [in a ritual bath] - and the matter of immersion is like we will explain in its commandment (Sefer HaChinukh 175), with God's help - and that even after his immersion, he is forbidden to eat even the priestly tithe until the sun sets, and afterwards he is pure and eats; and the rest of its details are elucidated in the Order of Tahorot, and mostly in Tractate Kelim and Tahorot (see Mishneh Torah, Laws of Other Sources of Defilement 4).

And [it] is practiced in every place and at all times by males and females, regarding that anyone who is rendered impure by swarming creatures is called impure and does not emerge from his impurity until he immerses in water, like his law. And nonetheless now that - on account of our iniquities - we do not have a Temple nor pure objects; we should not count it in the tally of commandments practiced. And anyone who is rendered impure - and even on purpose - at any time, does not have a sin with this; but rather he is not permitted to touch consecrated things until he becomes pure. And nonetheless anyone who understands, should distance impurity, as the soul is elevated with purity.

And Ramban, may his memory be Blessed, wrote that we should not count all the laws of impurities in the tally of the commandments; and in his Book of Commandments (on Sefer HaMitzvot LaRambam, Mitzvot Ase 96), he wrote a correct reason for his words, and the intellect inclines towards him. And from my desire for brevity in this composition, I did not want to write all of his arguments, but behold in Commandment 96 in his book, you will find the matter at length. And at the end of the matter, he said that God prevented us from doing [certain] things in impurity, and [so] it remained to make known to us what thing is impure; and he said that they are the touching of the dead and the swarming creatures and the others - all that are mentioned in the Torah - and that we should not truthfully count them as commandments of their own. And this is [like] that which we said that the [Temple service] of someone with a blemish is prevented, and [so] it remained for us to know which thing is a blemish. And in fact, we do not count each and every blemish as a commandment.

Mitzvah 160
The commandment of the matter of impurity of foods: That we were commanded about the guarding of the impurity of foods and drinks and to act in this matter according to the Torah, which informed us how to determine every matter of impurity of food and drinks, and the vessels through which they become impure, as it is stated (Leviticus 11:34), "From any food that is eaten, which water comes upon."

In the previous commandment, you will see much to ponder from the roots of impurity and purity - there is no need to repeat it.

From the laws of the commandment is that which they, may their memory be Blessed, said (Sifra, Shemini, Chapter 9:1) that the understanding of that which is stated in the Torah, "From any food that is eaten," is that it is eaten by man. And therefore they, may their memory be Blessed, said (Mishnah Tahorot 8:6) that any food that is not designated for man does not contract impurity at all. And they also explained that it is not called food regarding the contracting of impurity until it is detached from the ground. But the whole time that it is connected - even by a small root from which it can be sustained - it is not called food regarding the contraction of impurity. And even if all the impurities touched it, it is [still] pure.

And so, there is no food in the world [that is] called food, to contract impurity, until water comes upon it after it has been detached from the ground - and as it is written, "which water comes upon, etc." And even though they said this is a decree of Scripture (gezerat hakatuv), it can be based a little upon a reason according to what first comes to mind. And [accordingly we would] say that the matter is because the Torah does not consider anything to be ready for its laws until the time when its processing is finished - as is known regarding priestly tithes and tithes; and also, challah, the time of which is not until the flour has been rolled [into a dough]. And this is [the reason why in the case of] one who separates his challah [as] flour, it is not [considered] challah, but [rather] it is robbery in the hand of the priest.

And therefore, also regarding impurity, we can say that we do not judge the impurity of fruits and their purity until the end of their processing. And since it is the way of people with some fruits and vegetables to rinse them from their dirt before they eat them, it was relevant to say about all of them more generally that they not be called food until they are prepared with water. And from this reason itself, they said that their preparation is when they were rinsed with the intention of the owners - meaning to say that the owners considered as liquid, the water with which they were rinsed - in the way that people rinse their vegetables with liquid. And this is the understanding of consent and duress that is mentioned in the Gemara about this matter, according to the good commentaries. But if they do not consider it as water - even though they, themselves, put it on the fruits - it is not intention. And hence they, may their memory be Blessed, said (Mishnah Tahorot 1:6) that his fruits are not prepared [to become impure] when one buries them in water on account of thieves, as the water is not considered a liquid for the owners. As they only placed them in it to bury them, in the same [way] that they would have also buried them in shearings of wool or something else. And from this matter is that which they, may their memory be Blessed, said (Mishnah Makhshirin 4:3) that one who covers his wall with a bowl on a rainy day - if he does it that his bowl should be rinsed, [the water] is fit to prepare [the fruits]; since now we can judge this water as liquid with the consent of the owners, as it is the way of the world to rinse things with something that is liquid. But if he leaves it there so that the wall not be damaged, they do not prepare [the fruits].

And the laws of the appendages of food are many. And the rest of its details are elucidated in Tractate Tahorot and Oktzin and Makhshirin (see Mishneh Torah, Laws of Defilement of Foods 1).

And [it] is practiced in every place and at all times by males and females - that we determine the impurity of foods and drinks in this manner. And nonetheless now that, outside of the Land - on account of our iniquities - we do not have a Temple nor pure objects, the laws of impurities are annulled for us. But nonetheless, if one wants to practice them on his own - the practice of the holy ones - as if he was in the Land, and be careful about foods to eat them in purity; for this one, it is fit to determine them. And I have already written in the previous commandment the opinion of Ramban, may his memory be Blessed, about the laws of the impurities - and it sits well in the heart of its listener. But I do not not need to review it with each and every [commandment].

Mitzvah 161
The commandment of the matter of the impurity of a carcass: That a carcass be impure and render impure, as it is stated (Leviticus 11:39), "And if a beast dies that is for you to eat, etc." Rambam, may his memory be Blessed, wrote about this commandment (Sefer HaMitzvot LaRambam, Mitzvot Ase 96), and this is his language: "And I will mention to you here now a nice preface, that you should remember about all that we mention of the types of impurities. And it is that that which we count each and every type of the impurities as a positive commandment, its substance is not that we would be obligated to become impure with this impurity, and likewise not that we are prevented from becoming impure from it and that is should be a negative commandment. However since the Torah states that one who approaches this species is impure or that this thing becomes impure in this way by the one who approaches it, that is a positive commandment - meaning to say that this law that we are commanded about is a commandment. And that [commandment] is that which we said, that the one who approaches such in this way becomes impure, and the one in that way does not become impure. And as to one becoming impure, himself, the option is in the hand of each man: As if he wants, he becomes impure; and if he wants, he does not become impure. And the language of Sifra, Shemini, Chapter 4:10 is '"And their carcass you shall not touch" - it is possible that if one touched a carcass he receives forty stripes; [hence] we learn to say "and to these you shall become impure" (Leviticus 11:24). It is possible that if one saw a carcass, he should go and become impure from it; [hence] we learn to say "their carcass you shall not touch." How is this? I would say [it is an] option.' And the commandment is that which is said to us about these laws - that the one who approaches this becomes impure and will be impure; and he will be obligated that which the impure are obligated - to go out of the encampment of the Divine Presence and not to eat from the holy, and not come close to it and other than this. And that is the commandment, meaning to say his being impure with this species, when he approaches it or be with it in this manner. And remember this matter with each and every type of impurity." To here is his language. And with all of this, it does not sit well with the heart for us to think of this matter as a commandment. And nonetheless we shall not veer from the path of our rabbi in our tally to the right or the left, as we set out at the beginning.
The root is written above (Sefer HaChinukh 159).
From the laws of the commandment is that which they, may their memory be Blessed, said (Mishnah Kelim 1:2) that a carcass is a primary source (av) from the primary sources of impurity; and that a kazayit of its flesh makes a man and vessels impure by touching, and a clay pot from its hollow; and makes a man impure from carrying to make [his] clothes impure. And it is one whether it is a permitted beast or animal or a forbidden one that died - the flesh of all of them transfer impurity with a kazayit. And the slaughter of a pure beast or animal purifies them and they do not transfer impurity afterwards. And even the slaughter of non-sacred [animals] in the courtyard or consecrated ones outside purifies them from being a carcass. And anything that dies on its own or a disqualification occurred in its slaughter, behold it is a carcass - and like they, may their memory be Blessed, said in Chullin 32a, "This is the general principle: All that became disqualified in its slaughter is a carcass; and all that something else caused it to become disqualified, is 'torn' (tereifah)." But slaughter does not purify an impure beast or animal from being a carcass. And hence they are carcasses in any way that they die. And nonetheless, they do not transfer impurity - not them and not the pure ones - until they die completely, and not while they are still twitching. And the rest of its many details are elucidated scattered in the Order of Tahorot, but mostly in Tractate Kelim and Tractate Tahorot (see Mishneh Torah, Laws of Defilement of Foods 1)

Mitzvah 162

Sefer HaChinukh

To not eat the swarming creature of the ground: To not eat the swarming creature of the ground, as it is stated (Leviticus 11:41), "And any swarming creature that swarms on the ground is an abomination; it shall not be eaten."

I have already written above (Sefer HaChinukh 159) that which I know about the roots of this commandment, with all that comes about the prohibition of foods. There is no need to review it with each [commandment].

From the laws of the commandment is, for example, the distinction that they, may their memory be Blessed, made between the eight swarming creatures that are mentioned in the Torah and the other swarming things such as snakes, scorpions, the beetle, the centipede and those similar to them - such that they said that the measure for the liability for eating the eight swarming creatures stated in the Torah is like the measure of their impurity, which is like a lentil; and the measure for the others is a kazayit. And all of the measurements are a law of Moshe from Sinai (Eruvin 4a). And the rest of its details are elucidated in Tractate Chullin (see Tur, Yoreh Deah 84).

And [it] is practiced in every place and at all times by males and females. And one who transgresses it and eats a kazayit of insects that are on the ground volitionally is lashed - and if he ate from the eight swarming creatures, even like [the size of] a lentil, he is lashed - and inadvertently, he is exempted.

Mitzvah 163

To not eat species of minute swarming creatures born in seeds and fruits: To not eat species of minute swarming creatures born in seeds and fruits, from the time they go out and swarm on the ground (Chullin 67a) - and the law is the same the whole time that they are produced in the fruit when it is still connected to the ground, even though they did not go out and swarm on the ground; as it is called "swarms on the ground," since it it is produced in the fruit while [in its being] connected - as it is stated (Leviticus 11:42), "for any of the swarming creature that swarms on the ground; you shall not eat them." But if they went out on the ground - even though they returned afterwards into the fruit - it is also called, "swarms on the ground," since it went out. And so is it in Sifra, Shmini, Chapter 12:2, "'(And you shall not render impure) [You shall not abominate) your souls from any of the swarming creatures that swarms' - to [include] those that separated to the ground and returned." [This is] meaning to say, even though they are now in their holes, since they went out to the ground, they became forbidden, and are called, "swarms on the ground."

In this explanation that I wrote here that the liability for minute swarming creatures is from the time that they go out on the ground and not before this, I am ignoring that which Rambam, may his memory be Blessed, wrote about it - and even though I set out to hold on to his path. As he wrote in his book of commandments (Sefer HaMitzvot LaRambam, Mitzvot Lo Taase 179) that this negative commandment is from when they went out into the air or walked on the surface of the fruit. And we should wonder much about him with this, as we found explicitly in Chullin 67b, that this matter remains [unresolved] there - as it appears there, "Rav Yosef asks, 'If it separated to the air of the world, what is [the law]; on top of a date, what is [the law]?'" And even the rabbi himself wrote in his great essay (Mishneh Torah, Laws of Forbidden Foods 2:14, 16) that this matter is a doubt and [so] we do not administer lashes for it. And therefore, I put aside his explanation here, and I wrote [the commandment] by way of the truth. And here too did I find afterwards that Ramban, may his memory be Blessed, (on the Sefer HaMitzvot LaRambam, Root 9) wondered greatly about him on this mistake. I have written above (Sefer HaChinukh 159) about the roots of the commandment.

Its laws are [for example,] that which they, may their memory be Blessed, said (Chullin 67b), "'That swarms on the ground' - to exclude mites that are in lentils, worms (that are in aklusinim) [that are in klisin]" - which is a type of legume - "and worms in dates and cakes of figs." And the law is the same for all insects that are produced in the fruits internally after they are detached, and [the insects] did not separate from within them - that they are not [prohibited] by this negative commandment of that which swarms on the ground. And they are permissible from [the letter] of the law, except that there is a little disgust to the soul of the one that is eating them. And if there is a doubt if the insects were produced in the fruit before they were detached or afterwards, he should check for them properly. And if they are very minute to the point that he cannot check, he should wait twelve months.

Sefer HaChinukh

And afterwards, they are permissible to eat, from the outset, without checking. [This is] due to the principle known to our Rabbis, may their memory be Blessed (Chullin 58a) that all insects of fruits do not exist twelve months. The explanation of, "do not exist," is to say that once twelve months have passed over it, it is like total dirt. And because of this, they, may their memory be Blessed, said (Chullin 58b), "Those dates in the jug are permitted after the time of twelve months." And if the insects of the fruits separated into the air but they did not touch the ground, as when they went out from the fruit and fell into the mouth of the eater; and so [too,] if they separated and crawled on top of the fruit, whether we consider on the fruit to be on the ground; and so [too,] if the insect separated form the fruit and fell to the ground after it died - all of this is forbidden from the doubt if we determine and say that it like one that swarms on the ground or not.

And so [too,] that which they, may their memory be Blessed, said (Chullin 67b) [that] worms that are found in the intestines of fish are forbidden on account of [being] a swarming creature, since they come from the outside; but those found in them between the skin and the flesh or in the flesh are permitted. Those that are found in the intestines of the beast are forbidden, since they came from the outside. But even those found in the brain of the beast or in its flesh are forbidden, since there is not anything in the beast that is permitted without slaughter, and they are not susceptible to slaughter. And also since the Torah added them [by implication] to the forbidden. And [it is] like they, may their memory be Blessed, said (Chullin 67b), "You shall abominate their carcasses' (Leviticus 11:11) - is to include deranin (the understanding of which is insects found between the skin and the flesh) that are in the beast." And if you will [ask], how is it that the embryo is permitted without slaughter; [it is] because the Torah permitted it - as we expound in the Gemara (Chullin 69a) from "among (which can also be read as, 'in') the beast[...] you may eat" (Leviticus 11:3). And so [too,] did they, may their memory be Blessed, permit (Chullin 66b) water in vessels that became worm-ridden, or even [if they were] in ditches and caves - meaning to say, any gathered waters. And they said (Chullin 66b) that a man [may] swim and drink from them, so long as the insects have not separated to a different place. And even if they have separated to the sides of the vessel or the pit - once they returned to it, he may drink and not prevent himself [from drinking], as this is their habitat. And it appears that there is not even [an issue] of 'you shall not be disgusting' with them. And that is [the meaning] of their saying, "and he may drink and not prevent himself." And it appears that the reason is because they found explicit permissibility from Scripture for them - as they, may their memory be Blessed, expounded (Chullin 66b), "'In the seas and in the streams' - [is it] that what has [signs], you may eat; what does not have signs, you may not eat. But in vessels, and similar to vessels, whether they have or whether they do not have, it is permitted."

And also, from the laws of the commandment is that which they said (Chullin 67a) that a man should not pour ale through tsavta at night, because of the concern for insects that stay in the tsavta, and afterwards fall into the cup - and the understanding of tsavta is straw that is on top of the vessel (which serves as a filter). And once the swarming creature is on the tsavta, its status is like a swarming creature on the ground.

And the law of a creature which they, may their memory be Blessed, said (Chullin 96b) that it is not ever neutralized. [This is] meaning to say that even if it fell into a thousand pieces like it of permissible matter, it is not neutralized by them, and [the whole mixture] is forbidden. As just like it is significant regarding lashes, such that we administer lashes for it for the smallest amount - as it is [found] in Tractate Makkot 13a - so too, is it significant concerning prohibitions, such that it is never neutralized. And even though in Talmud Yerushalmi, Terumot in the chapter [entitled] Batsal, they said, "Rabbi Yose bar Bon taught about a mouse, 'One in a thousand'" - our Gemara (the Babylonian Talmud), which says that it is not neutralized even in a thousand, is preferable to us.

And the understanding of a creature is meaning to say any living animal; and even the smallest worm, since it has life. This is the main understanding of creature. [However,] they, may their memory be Blessed, also said that concerning it not being ever neutralized and [not] even in a thousand, anything that is forbidden from the beginning of its creation and is all whole like as its creation, is called a creature - to exclude if it is lacking even the smallest amount, which does not have the status of a creature, and we only administer lashes for it with a kazayit. And it must be from an animal, like the sciatic nerve which has all of this - to exclude any fruit, which is not a living animal, and anything similar to it.

And [related] to the creature that we are saying that it is significant and not neutralized - we will say that which they, may their memory be Blessed, said (Mishnah Orlah 3:7) that any significant thing is not neutralized, such as nuts with brittle shells, Badan pomegranates, sealed barrels [of wine], beet shoots, cabbage heads, Greek gourds and loaves [of bread] of homeowners. And Rambam, may his memory be Blessed, wrote (Mishneh Torah, Laws of Forbidden Foods 16:9) that it is not specifically these seven things, but rather any significant thing; except that these were the significant things at the time of the Sages of the Mishnah, may their memory be Blessed.

And that which we said that a creature is not neutralized and the intention was to say whether alive or dead - [that is] specifically a creature that is forbidden from the beginning of its creation, such as an impure beast or an impure swarming creature; and so [too,] a sciatic nerve, as it too is forbidden from the beginning of its creation. But a beast that is fit (kosher) from its beginning is only not neutralized when it is still alive - on account of living animals being significant and [so,] not neutralized (Zevachim 73a). But after it dies, it certainly [can have] neutralization; and we say that it [can be] neutralized, even with a large dead ox. And this is according to Rabbi Yochanan - as the law follows him - who said in the Gemara (Beitzah 3b) regarding significant things that are not neutralized, "We learned things that it is their way to be counted." [This is] meaning to say that we learned that the things that are not neutralized are those that it is the way of people to always count due to their importance, such as the seven designated above. But it is not the way of people to always consider an ox significant in their hearts; since it is not fit at the time, and [so] its benefit is not close to the hearts of people like those seven things.

And do not wonder to say, [how is it that] a piece from it with which it is fitting to honor guests will be considered significant and will not be neutralized, whereas all of it together will be neutralized; as in truth, it is so. As the benefit of one piece from it is close and the hearts of people are close to it and render it significant - and hence they said that it is not neutralized, even though all of it can be neutralized. And know this and understand it.

And there are some commentators that said (Shulchan Arukh, Yoreh Deah 101:3) that the law of a piece with which it is fitting to honor is not neutralized, was only said with one that is cooked - as then is it fitting to honor with [it]. And there are some of them that said that it is said even when it is raw. And there are some commentators that also said that we only say that a piece with which it is fitting to honor is not neutralized, when it is forbidden on account of itself. But if a prohibited substance fell into it and gave it taste, it [can be] neutralized - since the prohibited substance it not fitting to honor. And even though we find that even with a piece of meat into which milk fell, they said in Avodah Zarah 74b that it is not neutralized - meat with milk is different, as their mixture makes them like a piece of forbidden substance on account of itself. And the rest of these many detailed matters are in Chullin and in Avodah Zarah (see Tur, Yoreh Deah 105).

And [it] is practiced in every place and at all times by males and females. And one who transgresses it and eats a completely whole impure creature volitionally - whether it is alive or dead, and even if it is less than a mustard seed, and even if it was putrid; and whether it [came about] by way of male and female or from all the decay that is in the world - and it came out on the ground, one who eats it all is lashed for it. But if it is lacking even one leg, he is not lashed until he eats a kazayit of it.

Mitzvah 164

To not eat of the swarming creatures of the waters: To not eat of the swarming creatures of the waters, as it is stated (Leviticus 11:43), "You shall not abominate your souls with any swarming creature that swarms, and you shall not defile yourselves with them and become impure through them." And the substance of a swarming creature of the waters is well-known; that it is from the minute creatures that swim in the water - and they are called the swarming creatures of the waters. And this negative commandment is specific to them, [and] besides the negative commandment that is specific to the impure fish; as these are not included as fish at all, since they are a completely different species of its own. That is the opinion of Rambam, may his memory be Blessed, (Sefer

Sefer HaChinukh

HaMitzvot LaRambam, Mitzvot Lo Taase 179), about this verse, that it comes to teach about this. But Ramban, may this memory be Blessed, (on Sefer HaMitzvot, Root 9, s.v. veraiti lerav z"l) disagrees with him on this and wrote, that this negative commandment is not a specific negative commandment about any swarming creature; but rather that it is from the general negative commandments for which we do not administer lashes, like "You shall not eat any abomination" in Deuteronomy 14:3 at the beginning of the sections of the prohibited animals. And so [too,] here at the end of all of them, it stated, "You shall not abominate your souls" with all of the walkers of the ground that I have prohibited. And grouped in this was the prohibition of the impure beast, the prohibition of the impure fowl, the flying swarming creature and the swarming creature of the ground. As all the forbidden and the distanced is included in abomination, as [with] "For He did not disparage nor abominate the plea of the lowly" (Psalms 22:25). And both of them, may their memories be Blessed, wrote at length about this negative commandment and involved in it that which [the Sages], may their memory be Blessed, said in the Gemara [in] Makkot 16b, "If he ate a putita, he is lashed four [sets], an ant five, a wasp six." And each one explains what appears [correct to him] about the matter.

And if I had come to write all of their arguments about the thing such as they are, the matter would be lengthy, to the point that a large parchment would not hold it and I would go out of this task of mine. However, according to my opinion, their main disagreement in the matter is dependent upon whether we administer two [sets of] lashes for one prohibition or not. As Rambam, may his memory be Blessed, wrote (Sefer HaMitzvot LaRambam, Root 9) in the roots of the commandments [such] that he made and fixed with screws that we can never be lashed two [sets of] lashes for one sin - and even if several negative commandments come about it in Scripture. [It is] as if you would say by way of illustration that "You shall not eat pig" would come in the Torah in five verses - or even one hundred; if he ate it, he would always only be lashed for one eating. And even though those negative commandments do not come to have anything expounded from them besides the additional prohibitions - nonetheless, a man is always lashed only one [set of] lashes for a single prohibition.

And from the angle of this root that it is fixed for him, he had to greatly strain the explanation of that teaching of the Gemara of Makkot and to explain it not like the explanation of all of the commentators that preceded him. And he, himself, wrote that he did not see the commentary of any man before him who explains it like him. And the general rule of his commentary about the thing is that which he always reviews; that that which they said that a man is lashed for the eating of one creature [for] many negative commandments is such that that creature has the addition of an aspect, such that that [additional] negative commandment is designated for that addition; and not that he ever be lashed two [sets of] lashes for one prohibition alone - and even if there are a thousand negative commandments stated in the Torah about it, as we said. And therefore, he said that the creature for which the Sages, may their memory be Blessed, made liable several [sets] of lashes is such a one as brings together in its body several species. For example, [it is] such that you would say that its character is such that it is possible to call it a swarming creature of the ground and a flying swarming creature - for example that it has wings - and a swarming creature of the waters, that it also swims in the water even as it flies in the air. [This is] as we sometimes see in a few species of swarming creatures. And in this way with some strain that he strains in his explanation, he explains this teaching in the Gemara of Makkot: "If he ate a putita, he is lashed four [sets], an ant five, etc." And he exerts himself to find six separate matters in the body of one creature.

And Ramban, may his memory be Blessed does not require all of this. As he reasons that we should administer several [sets of] lashes for one prohibition if there are multiple negative commandments in the Torah about it and they are not required by us for other teachings. And he [presented] many proofs about this - proofs that appear 'strong as a mirror of cast metal.' And he explained the teaching of the Gemara Makkot nicely like the understanding of the early scholars. And Ramban, may his memory be Blessed, expounds the negative commandment of the swarming creatures of the water from that which is written in the section of the prohibition of fish, "And anything that does not have fins and scales, etc. from any swarming creature of the waters, etc. it shall be an abomination for you" (Leviticus 11:10). And this is truly a thing that is learned from its context, as it is speaking in the section about the prohibition of fish, and there it is also speaking about the swarming creature of the waters. Understand this, my son; and if you merit, choose for yourself according to your opinion - these and those are the words of the living God.

We have written above (Sefer HaChinukh 73, 155) from the roots of the prohibition of food.

Its laws are short, and the general principle of the matter is that all those small creatures - like worms, leeches and similar to them - that grow in the waters, are called swarming creatures of the waters.

And [it] is practiced in every place and at all times by males and females. And one who transgresses it and eats a whole creature of them - and even if it is the smallest - is lashed. But if it is not whole, he is not lashed until he eats a kazayit of them. And nonetheless, it is forbidden to eat even less than a kazayit from Torah writ; as half of a measure [that would result in punishment] is forbidden by the Torah. But there is only liability for lashes for eating the transmitted measure.

Mitzvah 165

To not eat of swarming creatures that exist from decay: To not eat of swarming creatures that exist from decaying matter - even though they are not from a known species and do not exist from male and female - as it is stated (Leviticus 11:44), "and you shall not defile your souls with any swarming creature that crawls upon the ground." And the language of Sifra, Shemini, Chapter 12:4 is "'Swarming creature that crawls upon the ground' - even though it does not give fruit and multiply." And Rambam, may his memory be Blessed, wrote that "swarming" is stated about a swarming thing that is born from a male and female and "crawling" is stated about one that is made from decay. But Ramban, may his memory be Blessed (on Sefer HaMitzvot, Root 9, s.v. vehaperush) challenged him from verses that are written; and he wrote that in all of them, [both] swarming and crawling are stated. Its root is well-known.

Its laws are short, such that all of its details can be gathered in one general principle: That all swarming creatures of decayed matter in the world that crawl on the earth have been prohibited to us; except for swarming creatures from the decay of fruit that were produced there after they were detached [and] swarming creatures from decaying matter in the waters that are in vessels - it is all like we said above (Sefer HaChinukh 163).

And it is practiced in every place and at all times by males and females. And one who transgresses it and eats a creature from any of the decaying matter in garbage dumps or in any place, even the smallest of the small - once he has eaten it and it was whole - is lashed for it. And if it was not whole, its measure is with a kazayit, as we said.

Mitzvah 166

The commandment of the matter of the impurity of a woman who has given birth: To render a woman who has given birth impure; meaning to say that when a woman gives birth, she be impure for her husband - and all the more so for pure items - seven days for a male and two weeks for a female, as it is stated (Leviticus 12:2, 5), "If a woman conceives and gives birth to a male, she will be impure for seven days, etc. And if she gives birth to a female, she will be impure for two weeks, etc."

From the roots of the commandment, [there is a need] for a preface: There is no doubt that all of the sicknesses of people come either because of an excess in the body or from the angle of a deficit that happens from whatever reason it might be. As in truth, so long as [a person's] constitution is in total equilibrium and it not have a deficit, the body will not become ill. And the sin of people brings them to have an excess or a deficit from what people need for their constitution, and they become sick.

And we have already said in the warning of the 'torn' animal (Sefer HaChinukh 73) and in the prohibitions of foods (Sefer HaChinukh 147, 148) that God, Blessed be He, distanced His people that He chose from all the things that hurt the body, in that it is a vessel for the soul that knows its Creator. And so too from this root did He distance us from the woman who has given birth, from the menstruant and from the zavah (a woman with an irregular discharge) for a few days, until they become cleansed from that excess that they have, which is a bad and infectious thing. Therefore they, may their memory be Blessed, said (Rashi on Leviticus 12:2) that a woman never [experiences] blood unless her head and limbs are heavy upon her. And there is no doubt that this excess makes them, and anyone who comes close to them at all, sick. And all the more so with sexual relations, which is the epitome of physical closeness. And also the offspring that is born [from a union] while that excess overpowers her is destined for bad illnesses. And from this root that we said from the angle of excess, the Torah commanded that she be impure from the male seven [days] and two weeks from the female. As there is no doubt that the excesses of the woman that gives birth to a female are greater than one who gives birth to a male - since conception of a male indicates heat in the female. And [it is] like they, may their memory be Blessed, said (Berakhot 60a), "'If a woman conceives (literally, gives seed) and gives birth to a male - [if] a woman gives seed first, she gives birth to a male." And it is well-known that the excesses of heat are few and its action is always quick - it is a logical thing. And therefore, seven days of cleansing suffices with the pregnancy of a male.

And the conception of a female indicates coldness in the constitution of the female. And in coldness, excesses abound; and hence she needs two weeks for the cleansing of her body. And so did I find the matter after I wrote this [in] Ramban, may his memory be Blessed, and these are his words (Ramban on Leviticus 12:4): "Because the constitution of the female is cold and wet, and the dampness in the womb of the mother is very great and cold. And therefore, she gave birth to a female. And hence she requires a big cleansing because of the multitude of dampness and the blood decaying in her and because of her coldness. And it is well-known that the cold sicknesses require a longer time to be cleansed than the hot ones." To here [are his words].

And similar to this is also the matter of the menstruant and the zavah. As the menstruant is purified after seven days - and even if she gushes all of the seven, so long as she stops on the seventh while it is still day - by the law of the Torah. But the the zavah requires seven clean [days after her bleeding], because the flow indicates the extent of the excesses of the woman - and that is the continuation of the emptying of blood many days after the days that are customary in most women. And it is possible for us to say that the sickness of discharging blood in women from month to month was so that their weak minds not become haughty. Or [it is] so as to distance their closeness from man a little, so that he not run after them all of the days. As the thing of this messiness that he knows about them will be a little disgusting in his eyes and he will not always err in his love of them.

And our Rabbis, may their memory be Blessed, said in Niddah 31b from the angle of the simple understanding - I mean to say that they intended to reveal one of the great benefits that there is in the commandment besides its great and strong principles - and they wrote that there is a benefit in the distancing of the wife a little time so as to make her more beloved to her husband at the fit time, and that they should not get sick one of the other from the great constancy of their closeness and they give their eyes to other bodies - like most of the other nations, who are not restrained by our strict fences, do. And likewise, this reason of theirs suffices from the angle of the simple understanding with the woman who has given birth; such that he not disgrace himself with her immediately, and lest she be disgusting in his eyes and he be sick of her, like we said in Niddah 31b.

From the laws of the commandment is, for example, that which they, may their memory be Blessed, said (Niddah 66a) that all women who give birth are impure - and even if they did not see blood, as it is impossible to have an opening of the womb without blood. And it is one whether the woman gives birth to a live [baby] or to a dead one, and even if she miscarried - and that is when its form is completed - she is impure with the impurity of birth. And even if she miscarried a placenta or an amnion full of water or blood, behold this one [must be] concerned about a birth; as it established for us that there is no placenta without a fetus. And even though they do not find the fetus in the placenta now, we are concerned lest it dissolved inside it. And from the doubt, she sits [out] the days of impurity for a female which is two weeks, and the days of purification for a male which are thirty-three days and not more - as from a doubt, we are stringent [to this side] and [that side]. And this that we say that she must be concerned about a birth is specifically when forty days have passed over her since she conceived. But if forty days have not passed over her, she does not concern herself about a birth - and even on the actual fortieth day, as the fortieth day is considered like before the [end of] forty days. And nonetheless even though she does not concern herself about a birth - meaning to say, and she will not have the days of purification like a woman who has given birth - she concerns herself, nonetheless, about the impurity of a menstruant. And even if the 'birth' was a dry birth - meaning to say that she did not see blood at all - we say that since she gave birth, it is impossible to have an opening of the womb without blood, and lest it was little and it got lost. And any woman that has days of birth for impurity has days of purification from Torah writ. And the days of purification are thirty-three for a male and sixty-six for a female. And the matter is like this [regarding] the law of the Torah: That after she gave birth, the woman counts seven days from the day she gave birth. And whether she gave birth at the beginning of the night or at midday or even near sunset, she counts that day of birth as one day and completes six [more] days upon it. And whether she [experiences blood] a few of the days of the seven or all of the seven, she immerses on the evening of the seventh, which is the eighth night, and she is pure for her husband. And even if she is gushing blood on that eighth night, she immerses and is pure for her husband; as the Torah permitted all blood that a woman has given birth will see after the seven days within the thirty-three days for a male, and after fourteen within sixty-six days for a female.

And about this they, may their memory be Blessed, said (Niddah 35b) that there is one 'wellspring' and the Torah made it impure, and the Torah [also] made it pure. [This is] meaning to say that the blood of birth that the Torah made impure and the blood of purification that the Torah made pure are from one place; and that is [that] both of them come out from the source (the uterus), which is a place of impurity. However, the Torah made the matter depend on time and made impure the blood that comes from her at one time and made [it] pure at a second time. And Blessed is the One that knows all wisdom, as He did every thing for a correct and necessary reason. And He, Blessed be He, knows that up to a certain time, the blood is damaging; and [that] from then on, it is not damaging.

But now all of Israel has girded itself and has become accustomed to treat the blood of purification like the blood of impurity. And the general principle of the matter is that a woman today does not ever emerge from her impurity until she undergoes seven full days clean from all blood. And she begins counting them from the evening. And this is a great principle and it is practiced until this day in all the places of the proper Israelites. And through this, we are saved from several doubts. And the laws of the doubts that sometimes arise upon the woman giving birth - for example, if she is obligated to sit [out] for the impurity of a male or the impurity of a female, as sometimes she must sit [out] for a male and a female and for [being] a menstruant from the doubt; the law of what is the law of one who has a miscarriage of a type of beast or bird; what is the law if their faces are like the faces of people or if their faces are not like the faces of people; what is the law of one who has a miscarriage of types of gnats [or] types of hairs; one who has a miscarriage of the image of a man that has wings of flesh; likewise one who has a miscarriage of the image of a man with one eye and one thigh; one who has a miscarriage of a male together with a sandal, and that is a creature that it not recognizable whether it is male or female; the law of a woman that goes out full and comes back empty and errs in her calculation - and the rest of its many details regarding her impurity are all in Tractate Niddah (see Tur, Yoreh Deah 191). And the matter of the laws of sacrifices are scattered in many tractates, and many of them are in Zevachim, Arakhin, Keritot and Negaim.

And this commandment is practiced in every place and at all times regarding that woman giving birth are impure. And one who transgresses it and has sexual relations with her volitionally during the time specified for prohibition - or even after the specified time, so long as she has not immersed - has violated this positive commandment, besides that he has violated a negative commandment, as with a menstruant. And [it is] like the matter that is written (Leviticus 12:2), "like the days of her menstrual illness, shall she be impure." And [so] he is liable for excision. If inadvertent, he is liable to bring a fixed sin-offering at the time of the [Temple].

Mitzvah 167
That one impure not eat consecrated foods: That one impure not eat consecrated foods until he immerses and his sun sets and - if he is an impure one that requires atonement - until he brings his atonement, as it is stated (Leviticus 12:4), "every consecrated thing shall he not touch." And the language of Sifra, Shemini Parashat Yoledet, Chapter 1:8, "'Every consecrated thing shall he not touch and to the sanctuary shall he not come' - just like the one who enters the sanctuary in impurity

is punished excision, so too one who eats consecrated foods in impurity is punished excision." And we say in Makkot 14b, "'Every consecrated thing shall he not touch' is a warning for the eater. You say it is for the eater or is it only for the one who touches, etc.," as it is [found] there.

What we wrote above (Sefer HaChinukh 95), [that it is] to fix awe of the Temple and its holy things, is from the roots of the commandment. And hence, it is fitting that only pure ones should eat them, as purity is an embellishment and glory for a man, as is well-known to all that understand.

From the laws of the commandment is that which they, may their memory be Blessed, said (Zevachim 33b) that the impurity for which we are liable is when one is made impure by a Torah-level impurity, for which we are liable excision - the understanding is for approaching the Temple and its consecrated things, as we wrote above (Sefer HaChinukh 123). And that which they, may their memory be Blessed, said (Zevachim 34a) that we are not liable for eating of the holy that has things that permit it, until those things that permit it have been brought - meaning to say its entrails. And likewise, did they, may their memory be Blessed, instruct us (Meilah 10a) that we are not liable on account of pigul or notar or on account of [being] impure, until those things that permit it have been properly brought. And [regarding] anything that does not have things that permit it, once it has been consecrated in a vessel, we are [potentially] liable for it. And the rest of its details are in the thirteenth chapter of Zevachim (see Mishneh Torah, Laws of Sacrifices Rendered Unfit 18).

And [it] is practiced at the time of the [Temple] by males and females. And one who transgresses it and eats a kazayit of pure holy meat or impure holy meat while he is still impure with a Torah-level impurity volitionally is liable for excision; inadvertently, he brings a sacrifice that varies up and down, as is written above. And if he ate after he immersed [but] before his sun set or before he brought his atonement - like a woman who gave birth who needs to bring a sacrifice; and so [too,] all who need an atonement - he is lashed. But he is not liable for excision, as it is stated regarding the matter of this excision (Leviticus 7:20), "and his impurity is upon him"; and they, may their memory be Blessed, explained, "until all of his impurity be upon him." And if he was impure from a [rabbinic] impurity, he is not lashed - and there is no need to say that he is not liable excision - but rather he is struck with lashes of rebellion.

Mitzvah 168
The law of the sacrifice of the woman that has given birth: That a woman who has given birth bring a sacrifice when the days of her purification for a son or a daughter are completed. And it is a one-year-old lamb for a burnt-offering and a young pigeon or a dove for a sin-offering. And if she is poor, she brings two doves or two young pigeons - one for a burnt-offering and one for a sin offering, as it is stated (Leviticus 12:6), "On the completion of the days of purification for a son or daughter, she shall bring, etc." And she is lacking atonement until she brings her sacrifice.

It is from the roots of the commandment [that it is] in order that she be aroused by action to give thanks to God, Blessed be He, who saved her from the pangs of her birth, which is a miraculous thing. And also, they, may their memory be Blessed, said (Niddah 31b) that a woman rushes to swear at the time of her throes that she will no longer [have sexual relations with] a man. And therefore, she requires atonement, and hence her sacrifice is called a sin-offering, and it is stated about her, "and the priest shall atone for her" (Leviticus 12:8).

From its laws is, for example, that which they, may their memory be Blessed, said that a woman that has given birth does not bring her sacrifice on the fortieth day for a male and on the eightieth day for a female, but rather on the morrow, which is the forty-first day, and likewise the eighty-first day, as it is stated, "On the completion of the days of purification" - meaning to say that they are totally completed. And if she brought it during the days of completion, she has not fulfilled her obligation (Zevachim 112b). If the time has passed and she did not bring her atonement, she brings it after the time. And the whole time that she has not brought it, she is forbidden to eat consecrated foods - and as they, may their memory be Blessed, said (Mishnah Negaim 4:3), "[When] she brought her atonement, she eats from consecrated foods." And all those lacking atonements have the same status in this regard. And [regarding] all those that are obligated to bring a sacrifice, we may not bring their sacrifice without their consent; except for [the sacrifice of] those lacking atonement, which does not require consent of the owners (Nedarim 35b). And the rest of its details are in Tractate Niddah (see Mishneh Torah, Laws of Offerings for Those with Incomplete Atonement 1).

And [it] is practiced at the time of the [Temple] by females. And one who transgresses it and does not bring her sacrifice has violated this positive commandment, and she is lacking atonement and forbidden to eat from consecrated foods. And woe is to her if she dies before she brings it and [so] carries her iniquity upon her soul.

Mitzvah 169
The commandment of the matter of the impurity of a metsora: To make a man that is metsora (has a type of skin disease) impure - meaning to say that it is a commandment upon us that anyone who is a metsora come to the priest to ask about his tsaraat, and the priest will render him impure or render him pure; and he will act according to the written Torah, as the priest will command him; and he should not take the thing as an illness that comes by chance, but rather put his [mind] to it and know that the greatness of his iniquity caused it, as it is stated (Leviticus 13:2), "When a man has on the skin of his flesh, etc. it shall be brought to Aharon the priest or to one of his sons, the priests." And this commandment includes all the statutes of tsaraat of a person: that from which one is impure, and that from which one is pure; that from which one requires quarantine and that from which one does not require quarantine; that which requires shaving with the quarantine or does not require shaving - meaning to say shaving of the scab - and many laws besides this.

And the matter of tsaraat is that one or more places on the skin of the flesh of a man become white - and these places be very white until their white resembles the white of the membrane of an egg and more than it in its whiteness. But the whole time that it is less dark in its appearance than the membrane of an egg, it is not tsaraat but rather a shiny spot (bohak) - meaning to say, a different illness that is not a type of tsaraat at all, but rather like types of rash and other types of [skin] ailments that occur with a person. There are four appearances to the tsaraat on the skin of a man's flesh: Two are primary sources (avot) - and they are the se'et and the baheret - and two are their derivatives. And that is [the meaning] of their, may their memory be Blessed, saying (Mishnah Negaim 1:1), "The appearances of ailments are two which are four: Baheret [...] and its adjunct; se'et [...] and its adjunct." And the understanding of its adjunct is meaning to say, its derivative; as the expression, adjunct (sapachat) is only an expression of [being] secondary. And the Sages likened these four appearances: one to clean white wool, and that is the se'et; one to snow, and that is the baheret; one to the lime of the sanctuary, and that is the derivative of the baheret; and one to the membrane of an egg, and that is the derivative of the se'et (Mishnah Negaim 1:1). These are the impure ones and they combine, one with the other, to render impure (Mishnah Negaim 1:3). And anyone who does not recognize them through their differences and their names should only determine them by the mouth of someone who recognizes [them] (Shevuot 6a) - and as it is stated below in the laws of the commandment.

It is from the roots of the commandment to fix in our hearts that the providence of God, Blessed be He, is individualized upon everyone among people, and that His eyes are observing all of their ways, as it is written (Job 34:21), 'For His eyes are upon a man's ways; all of his steps He sees." And therefore, he warned us to put our [minds] to this bad illness, and to think that it is sin that caused it - and as they, may their memory be Blessed, said (Arakhin 16b) that it generally comes from evil speech, and we should not take it [as being] by way of happenstance. And we need to come to the priest, who is the one that is ready [to effect] the atonement of sinners. And in the company of the one who atones, maybe he will contemplate repentance. And he is put in quarantine for a few days, in order that he put his matters into his heart with deliberation, and examine his deeds (Berakhot 5a). And sometimes he is put into two [consecutive] quarantines, lest he contemplated repentance, but not complete full repentance. It is as if you would say by way of illustration, that he thought to return half of his robbery; and then God, Blessed be He, renewed some of the signs that he should be quarantined a second time - perhaps he will complete his repentance and purify himself completely.

And the whole matter of these quarantines indicates His providence, Blessed be He, on all the ways of man - one by one. And because the opinions are many about the providence of God upon all of his creatures, many verses in Scripture and many commandments come about it, to instruct about the

Sefer HaChinukh

matter - given that it is a cornerstone in our Torah. As there are groups of people that think that the providence of God, may He be Blessed, is [individualized upon all of the species - whether people or all other animals. And there are groups that think that the providence of God, Blessed be He, is] upon all the matters of the world - whether animals or all other things - meaning to say that no small thing in the world moves without His will, Blessed be He, and His decree; to the point that they think regarding the falling of one leaf from a tree, [that] He decreed about it that it should fall, and [so] it is impossible that the time of its falling be even a second later or earlier. And this opinion is very removed from the intellect. And there are evil groups that think that His providence, Blessed be He, is not put upon any matters of this lowly world at all - whether upon people or other animals. And this is the opinion of the heretics - it is evil and bitter. And we who have the correct opinion, according to what I have heard, place His generalized providence, Blessed be He, upon all the species of animals, such that each and every species that was created in the world, survive in the world - [that] it not completely finish and be lost - as with His providence does everything find existence in the world. But with the human species, we believe that His providence, Blessed be He, is upon each and every one individually, and He is 'the One who understands about all of their deeds.' And so [too,] have we received from all of our great ones; and there are also many verses that instruct that the matter is so. And therefore, the Torah warned us that when this bad illness - and that is tsaraat - reach a man, he should not take it [as being] by way of happenstance. Rather, he should immediately think that his iniquities caused [it]. And he should distance himself from the company of people, like a man who is distanced due to the evil of his deeds. And he should associate with the one who can atone - the one who can heal the fracture of the sin - and show his ailment to him. And through his counsel and through his words, and through the examination of his deeds, the ailment will be removed from him - since God, Blessed be He, who constantly watches him, will see the act of his repentance and heal him. And this matter is the matter of the quarantines, as we said.

From the laws of the commandment is that which they, may their memory be Blessed, said (Shevuot 6b) that these appearances of ailments that we said do not render impure until they appear deeper than the skin. And it is not that they actually be deeper to the touch, but rather that they appear so with the vision of the eye - similar to the appearance of sunny areas that appear deeper than the shade to viewers. And that which they said (Mishnah Negaim 6:1) that the measure of tsaraat is like [the size of] a Cilician bean - meaning to say that if those appearances like this size appear in the skin of a man, it is called tsaraat. And that measure is a rectangular surface on the skin that holds six hairs across and is six [hairs] long, which in arithmetic is thirty-six hairs. If it [only held] five hairs in its width - even [if] its length was an ell - that is not tsaraat ; as we need six hairs.

Every place that " baheret " is stated in the Torah, the law is the same for the four appearances. And there are three signs of impurity: a white hair; raw flesh; and spreading. How is this? If someone had a se'et or an adjunct or a baheret develop on him - when the priest sees him, he says to him immediately that he is definitively impure. If he did not have a white hair, nor raw skin, he should quarantine him seven days. And if [during that time] the ailment spread, he likewise renders him definitive - since spreading is also a sign of impurity, as we said. [If] none of these signs of impurity develop on him during the week of the first quarantine, he quarantines him during the second week. If one of these three signs of impurity develop on him [then], he renders him definitively impure; and if not, he renders him pure. As there is no quarantining for tsaraat of the skin of flesh [for] more than two weeks. And if afterwards from when he purified him, one of the three signs of impurity develop on him, he also renders him impure immediately; as these three signs of impurity always render impure - whether at the beginning, or after the quarantines. [Regarding] an ailment of tsaraat that was very white like white wool or snow, and afterwards dimmed and returned to be like the appearance of the membrane of an egg or like the lime of the sanctuary, this is not a sign of purity at all. But rather, behold, it is actually in its state of impurity as at the beginning until it dims beyond the white of the membrane of an egg. And then it is called a shiny spot and it is pure.

And if you will ask - if so, what is that which is stated in the Torah (Leviticus 13:6), "and behold, the ailment dimmed [...] the priest shall render him pure"; your answer is that this is stated about the ailment dimming beyond the membrane of an egg. But with the membrane of an egg and above it, this is not [considered] dimming, as it is still included in the appearances of impurity. And that which is stated (Leviticus 13:6), "and the ailment did not spread in the skin, the priest shall render him pure," instructs that any time it did not spread at all and none of the other signs of impurity that we said developed - even though it did not dim, but rather stayed in its hue - since it did not spread, he is pure. And the places in a person that do not become impure on account of tsaraat; the laws of the measures of how much raw skin, spreading and also white hair [are required to] render impure; the laws of the ailments of the head and the beard - and its substance is that it is the shedding of their hair from its roots and the place become empty, and this is a scab (netek), which is no less than the size of a split bean (kegris); the laws of how we shave them and the signs of its impurity and its purity; the law of that which they said that all become impure with ailments, and even a one-day old child and slaves, but not gentiles nor a resident stranger; the law of that which they said that all are fit to see the ailments but the purity and impurity is in the hand of the priest, how is this - an Israelite sage sees it [for] a priest who does not know how to see it, and he says to the priest [to] say, impure, and he says, "Impure," or he says [to] say pure, and he says, "Pure"; and the rest of its details are elucidated in Tractate Negaim (see Mishneh Torah, Laws of Defilement by Leprosy 10).

And the laws of tsaraat are practiced by males and females at all times when there are expert priests seeing them. So does it appear from the words of Rambam, may his memory be Blessed, (Mishneh Torah, Laws of Defilement by Leprosy 11:6). And even though it is impossible to bring a sacrifice now, he will bring a sacrifice when the Temple is built and it will be possible to bring a sacrifice with the purification from his tsaraat. Any anyone who developed tsaraat and did not act act according to the Torah that is written about the metsora, but rather took the thing [as being] by way of happenstance, and did not concern himself with coming to the priest and showing it to him, has violated this positive commandment. And truthfully his punishment should be that his tsaraat should cling to him forever. But God, may He be Blessed, will do good to the good, and he will be healed. And I have already written above [in] the Order of Bayom HaShemini in commandment 159 about the impurity of the eight swarming creatures (Sefer HaChinukh 159) that Ramban, may his memory be Blessed, does not count all of the laws of the impurities - such as the impurity of carcasses, swarming creatures, food and drink, the menstruant, the woman who has given birth, the zavah, the zav, semen, the tsaraat of a man, a house or a garment, the impurity of a corpse and the impurity of the sprinkling water and its purification - in the tally of the commandments. And he wrote clear proofs about this matter, that draw all hearts that listen to them, in his Book of the Commandments (on Sefer HaMitzvot LaRambam, Mitzvot Ase 96). But with all of this, we will not swerve in the tally from the path of Rambam, may his memory be Blessed; as we set out at the beginning of the structure (in most printed versions, "the matter").

Mitzvah 170
To not shave the hair of the scab: To not shave the hair of the scab (netek), as it is stated (Leviticus 13:33), "but the scab, he shall not shave" - meaning to say that hair that is on the place of the scab, he shall not shave. And the language of Sifra, Tazria, Parashat Nega'im, Chapter 9:7 is "From where [do I know] that one who detaches the signs of impurity from within his scab, that he violates a negative commandment? As it is stated, 'but the scab, he shall not shave.'" And the matter is that the priest recognize the signs of impurity in the hairs.

It is from the roots of the commandment to hint that every person should tolerate whatever pain and whatever punishment God, Blessed be He, punishes him and not rebel against them. And he should not think that there will be ability in his hand to negate them and to hide them from the creatures. Rather, he should request grace from God, Blessed be he - that He should heal the crushing of his afflictions. And this root will also suffice for the negative commandment that he should not cut off his baheret that is in the Order of Ki Tetseh (Sefer HaChinukh 584).

From the laws of the commandment is that which they, may their memory be Blessed, said (Mishnah Negaim 10:5), "How does one shave the scab? He shaves outside of it and leaves two hairs adjacent to it, so that he will recognize the expansion. And that which they also said (Sifra, Tazria, Parashat Nega'im, Chapter 9:4) that the shaving is proper by any man, as it is stated, "and he shall be shaved"

- and undifferentiated [as it is], it implies by any man. And that which they said that one is not liable until he shaves the entire scab with a razor. And the rest of its details are elucidated in Tractate Negaim (see Mishneh Torah, Laws of Defilement by Leprosy 10).

And it is practiced by males and females in every place and at all times that there is a priest that has the wisdom to [recognize these] ailments. And one who transgresses it and shaves the scab is lashed.

Mitzvah 171
The practice of wildness and rending of a metsora and all who render a person impure: That a metsora act like the statute written in the section of the Torah, as it is stated (Leviticus 13:45), "his clothes shall be rent, his head shall be wild." And likewise, all other impure ones must let themselves be known. And the language of Sifra, Tazria, Parashat Nega'im, Chapter 12:9 is "One who is impure from a dead body, one who has intercourse with a menstruant and all who render a person impure - from where [do I know they are included? Hence] we learn to say, '"impure, impure," he shall call out' (Leviticus 13:45)." And the calling is that he should do a matter in his body that people will recognize about him that he is impure and veer away from him.

It is from the root of the commandment that he take his distancing from people as an example for his soul. As a person is distanced from all good as a result of sin, in order that he will repent from his evil way. And this is [the meaning] of their, may their memory be Blessed saying (Arakhin 16b), "With evil speech, he separated a man from his wife and a man from his fellow. And therefore, his tent is outside of the camp." And therefore, it is fitting that he should call to every man that they veer away from him. And the general principle in all things is "With the measure that a man measures, [so] will he be measured" (Sotah 8b). And many do not know the understanding of this thing. As they think to explain this thing with God, may He be Blessed, modeled on the recompense of men - that each one will recompense his fellow according to the good that he did by him, or according to the bad [that he did]. But the matter is not like this with God, Blessed be He, - God forbid. As there is always only kindness and mercy with God, Blessed be He; and His goodness is ready at every instant and every hour for all who are fitting to receive it. And 'the Guardian of Israel does not slumber and does not sleep.' [Rather] the intention of that which they, may their memory be Blessed said about Him, Blessed be He, "With the measure that a man measures, [so] will he be measured," is to say that according to the action of a man - whether for the good or the opposite - will he be set to receive recompense. As always in the same manner that a person sets his thoughts and does his actions - in that exact mold - will blessing or its opposite be drawn to him.

And so does the verse state, "For He does not oppress from His heart, nor bring grief to man" (Lamentations 3:33). And it is also written, "For You are not a God who desires wickedness, etc." (Psalms 5:5) - meaning to say that God, may He be Blessed, does not obligate liability to any creature from His desire for the liability, as the good God always desires good. Rather, it is a man who makes himself liable in his moving from righteousness; and [so] removes from himself the preparations that allow him to receive the good. And the parable for this is the one who walks on a straight path that is free of stones and from anything that makes one stumble, but there is a hedge of thorns from this [side] and from that [side]. And one went and rubbed the hedge and was hurt - truthfully, one cannot say about this man that God desired his hurt. [Rather,] he was the cause, since he was not careful to walk straight. And so too, with one who sins, it is the attribute of justice that makes him liable for his sin regardless. And one cannot say that the good God desired his liability. [Rather,] in his preventing himself from the good, from the angle of his sin, did evil become [drawn] found to him. And similar to this thing did they, may their memory be Blessed, say - "No evil thing descends from Above" (Bereshit Rabbah 51:3).

And the general principle of our words is that every bad event that happens to a man is an action that happens to a man by God, may He be Blessed, hiding His face from the man - meaning to say, that God, may He be Blessed, removes His guarding from upon him, from the angle of his sin, until he receives the fitting punishment according to his sin. And then He commands His angels to guard him, as at first. And [it is] as it is written (Deuteronomy 31:17), "And I will hide My face from them and they will be for food, and many evils and troubles will find them; and they will say on that day, 'It is because our God is not among us, they found us, etc.'" And one sage wrote, "We know that God is one and the change [only] comes from the recievers. And God will not change His deeds, as they are all with wisdom" (Sefer Kuzari 4:3).

From the laws of the commandment is that which they, may their memory be Blessed, said (Megillah 8b), "There is no difference between a quarantined metsorah and a definitive metsorah except renting and wildness, [...] shaving and [offering] birds" - meaning to say that the quarantined one does not become wild and rent. And the explanation of becoming wild is the growing of hair; and of rending is that he tears his clothes. And the one who is pure [after] the quarantine is exempt from shaving and birds, but the one who is pure [after being] definitive is obligated about shaving and birds. But the impurity of both of them is the same in everything. And the matters of their impurity and how it is; whether they are prohibited in inquiring about [others'] welfare; whether they are permitted to study [Torah] while they are still in their impurity; whether they are forbidden to get a haircut and to wash clothing; whether they are permitted in bathing, anointing, the wearing of shoes and sexual relations; the law of a metsoraat (a woman that contacts tsaraat), how is her law and her practice; and the rest of its details are elucidated in Negaim (see Mishneh Torah, Laws of Defilement by Leprosy 10).

And [it] is practiced at all times that we have priests and sages that know the ailments, that are fitting to render pure and to render impure. And one who transgresses it and does not do like this statute for himself has violated this positive commandment.

Mitzvah 172

The commandment of the matter of ailments of clothing: To act with ailments of clothing like the statute written in the section of the Torah, as it is stated (Leviticus 13:47), "And the garment that has an ailment in it, etc." And this commandment includes all of the laws of the tsaraat of clothing: how they become impure and how they do not become impure; which ones of them require quarantine, or tearing or burning, or washing and purification.

It is from the roots of the commandment that God wanted in His great goodness to chasten us, 'like a man chasten his child.' As this matter is not natural, but [rather] a sign with the holy people, in order that they learn and take rebuke in the changing of the items that are particularly for their use - and they are clothes of wool and flax, as most usage of people is with them - and they repent through this from their evil way, before the tsaraat breaks out also in their bodies.

From the laws of the commandment is that which they, may their memory be Blessed, said (Sifra, Tazria, Parashat Nega'im, Chapter 13:1) that only clothes of wool and flax alone become impure with aliments; and the measure of their impurity is a split bean, like the measure in a person. And there are three signs of impurity with them (Mishnah Negaim 3:7): deep green; deep red; and spreading - the understanding of deep green is green among the greens, like the wing of a peacock; and of deep red is red among the reds, like crimson fabric. And the laws of spreading (Mishnah Negaim 11:7); the law of green that spread red or red that spread green; the law that all [cloths] are fitting to become impure - as they, may their memory be Blessed, said (Mishnah Negaim 11:11) that it becomes impure with ailments, even though it does not become impure as the base (midras) of a zav - like sails of a ship, a partition, the decorative piece of a hairnet, scribes' hankerchiefs, a belt, the laces of a shoe or of a sandal that has the width of a split bean, and similar to them, and there is no need to say other [cloths] like bedspreads and pillows; and the rest of its details are elucidated in [the Order] of Tahorot, and most of them are in Tracate Negaim (see Mishneh Torah, Laws of Defilement by Leprosy 12).

And [it] is practiced with the clothes of males and females. And one who transgresses it and does not act in this matter like the law that is written in [this] section of the Torah has violated a positive commandment.

Mitzvah 173

The commandment of purification from tsaraat that it be with certain species: That purification from tsaraat - whether tsaraat of a person, a garment or a house - be with cedar wood, hyssop, wool dyed red, two birds and living water, and that he do with them everything that is written about the matter, as it is stated (Leviticus 14:2), "This is the law of the metsora, etc." to the end of the section.

Sefer HaChinukh

And three types of purifications are mentioned in the Torah, and these are them: Water, and this type, by water, includes the purification of every impurity - meaning to say it is impossible for any impure thing to emerge from impurity without water; and the second type is sprinkling water, and that is the type that is specific for the impurity of a dead body; and the third type, the cedar wood, hyssop, wool dyed red, two birds and living water, and it is the type that is specific for tsaraat. The Sages informed us of a bit of a hint in the matters of the purification of the metsora with these things. As they, may their memory be Blessed, said (Pesikta D'Rav Kahanna 14) that the matter is to fix in the soul of the metsora that if, before the illness came to him, he was haughty-hearted like the cedar - by way of metaphor, since it is a tall tree - he should lower himself like the hyssop. It is said about the reason of the birds (Arakhin 16b) [that] he did an act of chattering - meaning to say, he spoke many words of evil speech - therefore, he must sacrifice birds that constantly chirp. And with the wool dyed red (shani tolaat), I do not know or remember anything that they, may their memory be Blessed, said about it. And it is possible that it is also a hint that he should lower himself; and it would be a hint from its name [as it is called,] worm (tolaat).

And about the reason that water purifies everything impure, I would think on the side of the simple understanding that it is in order that a man see himself with the immersion as if he is created at that time, [just] like the whole world was water before man was upon it - as it is written (Genesis 1:2), "and the spirit of God floated upon the face of the waters." And through this comparison, he place upon his heart that [just] like he is renewed in his body, he also renew his actions for the good, fix his actions and be exacting in the way of God, Blessed be He. And therefore, the Sages said that the purification is not fit with water that is in a vessel, but rather only with living water - or collected [water], which is on the ground and, in any case, not in a vessel - in order to place in his heart, the thought as if the world was entirely water, and [that] he is renewed with his emerging from them, as we said. But if the water was in a vessel - or even if it passed through a vessel - this matter that we said would not be set in the thought of the one immersing. As there is a limit to all that is in a vessel, which is the creation of the hands of man. And therefore, when he immerses in a vessel, he will not think as if the whole world is water like at the beginning [of Creation], and that he is renewed at that time. 'And the one who accepts, will accept; and the one who refrains will refrain.'

From the laws of the commandment is that which they, may their memory be Blessed, said (Mishnah Negaim 14:1), "How does one purify the metsora? He would bring a new earthenware pitcher and place within it a reviit of living water," with which it would be fitting to consecrate the sprinkling water - and that measure is [rabbinic] (Sotah 16b) - "and he would bring two wild birds" that are pure, for the sake of the purification of the metsora; as it is stated (Leviticus 14:4), "and it shall be taken for the one being purified." He slaughters the clarified (meaning, choice) of the two of them upon the water in the earthenware vessel and squeezes until the blood is recognizable in the water. And he digs and buries the slaughtered bird before him - and this is a tradition from what was heard. He takes cedar wood - and its commandment is that it be an ell long and its width be like a quarter of a foot of the feet of a bed; and not less than a handbreadth of hyssop that does not have an adjunct name; wool dyed red, the weight of which is a shekel, and if he mixed [its color], he disqualified it, like the dying of the aquamarine, which is disqualified by mixing. And all the measures are a law [from Moshe at Sinai] (Eruvin 4a). And he takes the living bird with the three of them; and the four species impede one another (Menachot 27a); and cedar wood or hyssop that have been peeled are disqualified. He ties the hyssop to the cedar wood with a strip of crimson fabric and surrounds them with the tips of the wings and the tip of the tail of the living bird. And he dips the four of them in water that is in the vessel and in the blood that is [in] it; "and sprinkles seven times on the back of the hand of the metsora." And he sends away the bird. And how does he send it away? If he is standing in the city, he throws it out of the wall (Kiddushin 57b). "He does not face the sea nor the city, but the desert, as it is stated (Leviticus 14:53), 'to outside the city toward the field'"(Mishnah Negaim 14:2). [If] he sent it and it comes back, he again sends it away - even a hundred times.

And afterwards, the priest shaves the metsora. And how does he shave him? He passes the razor over his visible flesh - and even [on] the underarm and the pubic area and all the rest of the body - until he becomes [smooth] like a gourd, as it is stated (Leviticus 14:9), "all of his hair." If so, why does it state, "his head, his beard, and his eyebrows?" To include everything that is like them and to exclude hair that is in the nose, since it is not seen. And afterwards he washes his clothes and immerses, and is purified with this from passing on impurity from his resting and sitting [upon something]; and he can come inside the [city] wall. And he counts seven days; and during those seven days, he is prohibited in sexual relations, as it is stated, "outside of his tent" - teaching he is forbidden in sexual relations. But a metsora'at is permitted in sexual relations. All of these seven days, he is still a source of impurity and renders a person and vessels impure with touch, but he does render impure with carrying - as behold it states (Leviticus 14:9), "And it shall be on the seventh day, etc. and he shall wash his clothes" - teaching that he was rendering clothes impure. And [just] like he was rendering clothes impure, so [too] was he rendering a man impure with touch - since all that renders a person impure, renders clothes impure; and all that does not render a person impure, does not render clothes impure (Mishnah Kelim 1:1). And on the seventh day, the priest shaves him a second [time] like the first shaving. And [the metsora] washes his clothes and immerses and is purified from rendering others impure. And behold he is like all who have immersed during the day, and can eat from the tithe; when his sun sets, he can eat from the priestly tithe; [and] when he brings his atonement, he can eat from consecrated foods. The slaughter of the bird, the shaving and the sprinkling are during the day, but all the other procedures are whether during the day or during the night. These [three things] are with men, but all the rest are even with women. These are with priests, but all the rest are even through an Israelite. And it is a commandment for the same priest who rendered him impure [to render him pure, as it is stated (Leviticus 13:59)], "to render him pure or to render him impure." And the rest of its details are in Tractate Negaim.

And this purification is practiced in every place and at all times that there is a priest that is wise about ailments. So did Rambam, may his memory be Blessed, explain (and so did I see in Sifra). And one who transgresses it and did not do it like its statute, has violated a positive commandment.

Mitzvah 174

The commandment of shaving the metsora on the seventh day: That the metsora shave all of his hair - and that is the second purification, as they, may their memory be Blessed, said in Negaim (Mishnah Negaim 14:3) - as it is stated (Leviticus 14:9), "And it shall be on the seventh day and he shall shave all of his hair, etc." And they, may their memory be Blessed, said (Mishnah Negaim 14:4), "Three shave, and their shaving is a commandment: the nazirite; the metsora; and the Levites." And the Levites require [the same] shaving as the metsora, and it was in the wilderness (after the Exodus). A little of the reason that we said above about the water (Sefer HaChinuch 173) is from the roots of the commandment: So that a man appears as if he was created today, and today his hair starts growing and he start his actions for the good. As when a man is cleansed from all [the] hair, he is properly cleansed from all dirt. And therefore in order to emerge from the impurity of his tsaraat it is fitting for him to, himself, do an act of cleansing with all of his might; so that he also cleanse his actions with all of his might and change them from evil to good and to make them fit.

From its laws is that which they, may their memory be Blessed, said (Sotah 16a), "How is the shaving? He passes the razor over his visible flesh - and even [on] the underarm and the pubic area and all the rest of the body - until he becomes [smooth] like a gourd, as it is stated (Leviticus 14:9), 'all of his hair.'" And when he shaves the two shavings, he only shaves with a razor. But if he shaved not with a razor - or he left two hairs - [it is as if] he has not done anything. And the rest of its details are in Tractate Negaim (see Mishneh Torah, Laws of Defilement by Leprosy 10).

And Rambam, may his memory be Blessed, said regarding this commandment (Sefer HaMitzvot LaRambam, Mitzvot Ase 111) and this is the language of the transcriber: And I will now elucidate what is the reason for us [that] the shaving of the metsora is a commandment on its own and the bringing of his sacrifices is a commandment on its own, and we did not do this with the nazirite (Sefer HaChinukh 377), but rather placed his shaving and the bringing of his sacrifices as one commandment. And that is that there is no connection between the shaving and the bringing of sacrifices of the metsora; and the purpose that comes from his shaving is not the purpose that comes from his sacrifices. And that is [because] the purification of the metsora is dependent upon his shaving: And in the sixth chapter of Nazir 44b, they said, "What is [the difference] between a nazarite and a metsora? Rather the purification of this one is dependent upon his day - meaning the nazirite - and the the purification of the metsora is dependent upon his shaving. And [so] when the metsora shaves and completes his second shaving, he is pure from giving off the impurity like a swarming creature, as is elucidated at the end of Mishnah Negaim 14:3. And [then] he remains lacking his atonement until he brings his sacrifices, like the rest of those that lack atonement, as is elucidated there.

And that is that the purpose of his shaving is his purification from giving off impurity like a swarming creature - whether he brought his sacrifices or he did not bring [them]. But the purpose of his bringing his sacrifices is the completion of his atonement, like the rest of those lacking in atonement - meaning to say, the zav, the zavah and the woman who has given birth. And the language of their statement has already preceded us, "There are four who are lacking atonement" (Keritot 8b). And there it is elucidated that the nazirite is not lacking atonement, but [rather] the procedure in its entirety - the shaving and the bringing of the sacrifice - [is what] permit him in drinking wine. And the one will not suffice without the other; and [so] the shaving is connected with the sacrifice and the sacrifice is connected with the shaving. And with their combination, the purpose comes at once - and that is that the things from which he was prevented during the days of his naziriteship will be permitted to him. And in the sixth chapter of Nazir 46b, they said "If he shaved over the sacrifice, and the sacrifice was found disqualified, his shaving is disqualified, and his sacrifices did not count for him." Behold, it is elucidated that the shaving is from the conditions of the sacrifice, and [that] the sacrifice is from its conditions.

And in Tosefta Nazir 2, it is likewise elucidated that the nazirite who completed his days is forbidden to shave, drink wine and to become impure to the dead, until he does the complete procedure. And that is the shaving of purification, as is elucidated in the sixth chapter of Nazir 45; and that is that he shaves at the opening of the Tent of Meeting, throw his hair under the cauldron and offer the sacrifices that come in the verse. And you will find (at the end of the commandments) [in most places], that they call the bringing of [these] sacrifices, "shaving." And in the elucidation they said, in explaining the Mishnah (Nazir 11b) [that states that one who says,] "Behold, I am a nazirite, and it is upon me to shave as a nazarite," [that] he means to say with this that he will bring the sacrifices of [another] nazirite and he will sacrifice them for him. Behold, it has been elucidated to you that the shaving [also means] the bringing of sacrifices. And the reason for this is their being a part of them, as we explained. And in their combination, the law of naziriteship is removed and the nazirite may drink wine. Moreover, the shaving of impurity (if a nazirite becomes impure) is from the detail[s] - the understanding of which is, from the substance - of the commandment, and not a commandment on its own, as we explained in what preceded (Sefer Ha Mitzvot LaRambam, Mitzvot Ase 93). To here [are his words].

And [it] is practiced by males and females in every place and at all times when there are great wise priests that are fitting to give rulings about tsaraat. And one who transgresses it and does not shave has violated a positive commandment, and is [still] impure.

Mitzvah 175

The commandment of immersion for the impure: That we should immerse in the waters of a mikveh (ritual bath) and then become pure from any type of the types of impurity with which we have become impure, as it is stated (Leviticus 14:9), "and he shall wash his flesh." And the tradition came about it, [that it is] water in which all of his flesh can go. And the Sages estimated this as forty seah (Eruvin 4b), and that is the measure of a mikveh. And from the Torah - whether the water is drawn, or it is pulled from the springs or from rain water - it is all fit. But the Sages disqualified any mikveh, the water of which is drawn. And not only that, but rather even if the water passed through a whole vessel at the time that it was flowing into the pit, they disqualified it. And this measure of forty seah regarding the waters of a mikveh is even to immerse a needle, according to some commentators. But with gushing water - meaning to say, water that comes out of springs - it does not have a measure at all. Rather, any time that all of his body together is covered by it, or that the impure vessels are covered together by it, it is fit to immerse in it.

And Rambam, may his memory be Blessed, wrote (Sefer Hamitzvot LaRambam, Mitzvot Ase 109), "And our intention in writing that immersion is a positive commandment is not that it is a commandment upon everyone impure to become purified regardless, like anyone who is covered by a cloak must make fringes (tsisit), and so [too,] all who have a roof are obligated to make a parapet for it. [Rather,] the matter is that the Torah informed us that one who wants to become pure from his impurity will not have a possibility to do this without immersion in water. And [so] it commanded us to accept the matter and to do it like this when we want to become pure. But if one wants to stay in in his impurity and not to enter the encampment of the Divine Presence for a long time, the option is in his hand." An addition: But nonetheless it is not from the trait of piety and men of [good] action to be defiled in their impurity - as impurity is disgusting, and purity is beloved. And the soul of a person is elevated and purified with purity. To here [is the addition]. "And the language of Sifra, Achrei Mot, Section 5:3 is '"And wash his flesh" - perhaps it is a decree of the King? [Hence] we learn to say, "and after, he may come to the encampment."' [This is] meaning to say that a person is not commanded to purify himself. [Rather,] if he wants to purify himself, it is a commandment upon him to do this procedure for his purification."

What I wrote above at the beginning of this Order (Sefer HaChinukh 173) is from the roots of this commandment of the purification of the water; to answer the children - according to the simple understanding of things, in the way of those that seek the simple understanding - until they grow up and understand that which they will understand. And we shall also say about the matter that there is a hint in immersion to the one immersing that he clean his soul from all sin, just like the nature of water is to clean every thing that is washed in it.

From the laws of the commandment is that which they, may their memory be Blessed, (Mishnah Mikvaot 1:8) said that the waters of the mikveh are fitting to purify in them from any impurity, such as [that of] the menstruant, the zavah and the other types of impurity of men and vessels - except for only a zav, since Scripture made explicit only for it [that] living waters are his purification - the understanding of which is gushing water. And also that which they, may their memory be Blessed, said (Yevamot 74b) that even though the immersion of some of them is during the day, their purification is not completed until the sunset, as it is written (Leviticus 11:32), "it shall come in water and be impure, until the night and it shall become pure." And he needs to immerse his body revealed - meaning to say, that all of it is [in contact] with the water, meaning that there not be anything separating between all of the body and the water. But if he immersed in his clothes, the immersion counted for him, ex post facto - since the water goes into them. And the menstruant is also [included] in this law, ex post facto, and is permitted to her husband - and that is so long as the clothes are not extremely tight. And the immersion of all of those obligated to immerse is during the day, except for the menstruant and the woman that has given birth, such that their immersion is during the night. And one impure from a seminal emission may immerse from the beginning of the night and on, until the sunset [of the next day].

The laws of separations [from the water] that they, may their memory be Blessed, said (Eruvin 4b) is that it is the word of the Torah if there was something separating, covering most of the person or the vessel, the immersion would not count for them - and that is when the person is concerned about the thing. But if he is not concerned, the immersion counts. But if the thing that separated was only on its lesser part, the immersion counts for him from Torah writ, even if he is concerned about it. But [rabbinically, with] anything - even the smallest amount - that separates that he is concerned about, his immersion does not count; [as a] decree of its lesser part, on account of its majority, which is forbidden from the Torah when he is concerned. And if the thing that separated covered most of him - even if he is not concerned - his immersion does not count; [as a] decree of the majority about which he is not concerned, on account of the majority about which he is concerned, which is forbidden from Torah writ. It comes out that if there was something on his lesser part and he is not concerned, the immersion counted for him - even rabbinically - as now there are two advantages to the thing.

And the laws of mikvaot are many. And [there is] the law of drawn water - how much disqualifies the mikveh and how it is [that it is disqualified]; and with which vessel is the water called drawn water - as if one drew it with a vessel that has a hole the size of a pomegranate, it is not called drawn. As from then, it no longer has the status of a vessel. And even if he filled the hole with a filling that is not proper, which still leaves holes or cracks when the liquid enters [it] - such as if he placed a stone of a fruit in it temporarily - I have heard from my teacher that this is not called drawn, and [so, it is] fitting to immerse in it.

And the law of carving out a vessel before he fixed it [in the ground], or if he fixed it and afterwards carved it out; and how much carving out is [needed] to disqualify - and the difference between an earthenware vessel and other vessels, as an earthenware vessel is not disqualified until it be carved out enough to hold a reviit, whereas a wooden vessel [is disqualified] with the smallest amount. And that which they said (Shabbat 14a) that a mikveh is not disqualified with a change of smell or a change of taste, but rather only with a change of appearance. And any [liquid] from which we do not make a mikveh from the outset - such as wine, milk, blood and also the juice of any fruit - disqualifies the mikveh with a change in appearance. But if some of it fell into [the mikveh] and it did not change its appearance, it is not disqualified. As it is only with drawn water that they decreed and said that three log disqualifies. But fruit juice does not [disqualify] until the appearance of the water changes from their mixing [in] (see Mishnah Mikvaot 7:5).

And the law of separations are many. But the end of the things is the general principle that we require, [which] is this: From Torah writ (Bava Kamma 82a), any woman should have [only] needed to inspect all of our body proximate to her immersion - so that there not be anything separating on her body, and that would suffice for her. But Ezra and his court ordained that she scrub in hot water any place she has hair, and comb or loosen her hair with her hands - or a comb, if she has one - very well; such that if her hair was knotted, she would undo them. And the daughters of Israel were stringent upon themselves to cleanse all of their bodies with hot water. And anyone who differs from their custom should be stretched on the pole [to be whipped] (see Makkot 22b).

And this scrubbing needs to be proximate to her immersion - meaning to say that she not be involved in anything in between. And nonetheless if the immersion of a woman happened to be on Shabbat or a holiday, they permitted even from the outset that she scrub during the day and immerse at night. And likewise, the Sages, may their memory be Blessed, said (Niddah 67a) that on account of the concern that water should enter onto all parts of here body, a woman needs to stand at the time of the immersion in such a way that she appear like a weaver or one nursing her child standing under her breast. And she also needs to be careful about rings on her hand and bracelets - and if they are tight, she must take them off her hands at the time of immersion; and so [too,] to untie the bands on her hair, and to rinse her mouth and teeth. As even though water does not need to come into any of the hidden places, they need be fit for the water to come in. And there was a case (Niddah 66b) of a woman who immersed and a bone was found between her teeth, and the Sages required her another immersion. If she immersed and then something else separating was found upon her, such as dough or tar or dry blood and what is similar to them from all of the things that the Sages enumerated as separating - even it if is as small as a mustard seed, so long as she is concerned about it and her way is to remove it - her immersion did not count for her. And even if the thing was under the fingernail, and even if it was [impressed on] the flesh - since she is concerned - it is [considered to be] separating. And therefore, the daughters of Israel have been accustomed to cut their nails at the time of immersion. And the rest of its many details of the laws of separations and the laws of mikvaot and one who has immersed on that day are elucidated in Tractate Mikvaot and and in Tractate Tevul Yom.

And this commandment of immersion is practiced in every place and at all time by males and females. As it is a commandment upon them when they want to become pure from their impurity that they immerse in water, like the matter that we said about fitting waters, and that there not be something separating upon them and the rest of the matters that we wrote. But nonetheless the commandment is not that they purify themselves regardless if they want to stay in their impurity, unless they came to enter the Temple or to eat consecrated foods. And [the latter] is at the time of the Temple. As then - at that time - if one did like that, he [would have] violated this positive commandment, besides the liability that is upon him in his eating the holy in impurity and his entering the Temple, as we wrote above (Sefer HaChinukh 167).

Mitzvah 176
The law of the commandment of a metsora when he is healed from his tsaraat: That every metsora bring up a sacrifice when he is healed from his illness. And that is three beasts - one for a burnt-offering, one for a sin-offering and one for a guilt-offering - and also a log of oil; and if he is poor, a lamb for the guilt-offering, a tenth of a log of oil and two doves or two young pigeons - one for the sin-offering and one for the burnt-offering. As it is stated (Leviticus 14:10), "And on the eighth day he shall take two unblemished male lambs and one female lamb." And it is written in the section that is after this (Leviticus 14:21), "And if he is poor, etc." And this metsora is called, 'one lacking atonement,' until he sacrifices this sacrifice. And there are four lacking atonement (Keritot 8b): this one that we said; the zav ; the zavah ; and the woman who has given birth. And the substance of [their being] called lacking atonement is to say that each one of them - even though he is pure from his impurity, immersed and his sun set for him on the seventh day - is still lacking this atonement and he cannot eat the consecrated foods until he sacrifices them on the eighth day. And let it not be difficult upon you why we count the sacrifice of each one of these four as a [distinct] commandment, and do not group them all as one commandment - that we say that the four who are lacking atonement offer a sacrifice, and afterwards they will be atoned; as we say about the purification of the waters of the mikveh, that any impure one immerse, and afterwards he will be pure - and we do not distinguish among the types of impurity to count each one as a commandment. As the matter is because the sacrifices of these four are not the same, and it comes out that the thing that completes the purification of one of them does not complete the purification of the other. And therefore, they counted each one a [distinct] commandment. [But this] is not the case with the waters of the mikveh, as the purification is the same with all of them. So answered Rambam, may his memory be Blessed (in Sefer HaMitzvot LaRambam, Mitzvot Ase 77).
I have written above (Sefer HaChinukh 95), from the angle of the simple meaning from the roots of the matter of the sacrifice, that there is a resemblance [to the animal], to lower the impulse of the body of the sinner and to enlarge the level of the soul. And hence the metsora is liable for it, as tsaraat is only in a man from the angle of his being pulled after the desires of his body - in word or deed - and [so,] he is fitting to be afflicted.
From the laws of the commandment is what they, may their memory be Blessed, said (Nedarim 35b) that all others may not offer a sacrifice for one who is liable a sacrifice without his consent - except for those lacking atonement, which do not require the consent of the owners. And because of this, they said (Nedarim 35b) that a man may bring a sacrifice for his young sons or daughters if they were lacking atonement, and [then] feed them from sacrifices. And the rest of its details are elucidated in many places in the Gemara, but mainly in Zevachim in the second chapter and Arakhin [in] the sixth chapter and at the end of Negaim and Kinin (see Mishneh Torah, Laws of Offerings for Those with Incomplete Atonement 4).
And [it] is practiced at the time of the [Temple] by males and females. And one who transgresses it and does not sacrifice his sacrifice at its time has violated this positive commandment.

Mitzvah 177
The commandment of the matter of the impurity of a house that has an ailment: To render an ailing house impure; meaning to say that we do with a house that has tsaraat according to the statute that is written in the section of the Torah, as it is stated (Leviticus 14:35), "And the one who the house is his shall come, etc.," as it is written there; and that we assume one who entered the house [to be] impure, as it is written (Leviticus 14:46), "And the one who entered the house [...] shall be impure, etc." And this commandment includes all of the matters of the impurity of houses - which one requires quarantine or destruction of some of the walls or all of them. And I have heard (see Ramban on Leviticus 14:35) that this matter of tsaraat existing in stones is not a natural matter, but rather a miraculous matter, [and] it sometimes comes to the houses of Israel to rebuke them. As it is from

God's loving them that He afflicts them with something outside of their bodies, so that they will repent before they are liable for [Him] to punish them with their bodies. And so was the matter, that if one did not repent, the aliment would also spread to his clothes; if he still did not sense it, it would also spread to his body. And they, may their memory be Blessed, said (Vayikra Rabbah 17:6) that at the beginning when they conquered the land, God, may He be Blessed, brought the ailment of tsaraat to some of their houses for their good, in order to destroy the house and reveal the buried treasure that the Amorites buried there. And even though it was possible to inform them [of] this through a prophet without an ailment, it is known that God will do miracles for people in a hidden way, as we wrote above.

From the laws of the commandment is that which they, may their memory be Blessed, said (Mishnah Negaim 14:3), that the measure of the ailments of houses is like two gris (split beans), one next to the other. And there are three signs of impurity in the house: deep green; deep red; and spreading, and all of them are explicit in Scripture. And two appearances combine, one with the other, for the measure of two gris. And all measures are a law of Moshe from Sinai. And when one sees an appearance in a house - even if he is a sage who knows that it is an ailment - he does not decree and say, "An ailment has appeared to me," but rather, "[Something] like an ailment has appeared to me." As it is for a priest to render ailments impure and pure, and not for another man. And a dark house cannot become impure from an ailment, as we do not open up [new] windows with which to see the ailment, as it is stated (Leviticus 14:35), "appeared to me" - and our Rabbis, may their memory be Blessed, explained (Sifra, Metzora, Section 5:11), "to me," and not "to my light." And lest you say, he should see the ailment with a candle, sight with a candle is not complete. And therefore, a dark house is never rendered impure by an ailment.

And likewise, a house cannot be rendered impure until there are four square ells or more in it; as less than this is not called a house - and the Torah stated, "house." And so [too,] it must be in a way that it has four walls and is built on the ground, with stones, wood and dirt, as it is stated (Leviticus 14:45), "its stones, its wood, and all of its dirt." And bricks and marble are not considered [to be] like stones. And Jerusalem, and outside the Land [of Israel] as well, do not have the law of impurity of houses, as it is stated (Leviticus 14:34), "upon a house in the land of your holding." And outside the Land is not a holding; and Jerusalem was also never divided for the tribes - and therefore it is not included in "your holding." And the rest of its details are in Negaim (see Mishneh Torah, Laws of Defilement by Leprosy 14).

And it is practiced in the house of a male or female in the Land [of Israel], at any time that there are priests fitting for the thing. And one who transgresses it has violated a positive commandment.

Mitzvah 178
The commandment of the matter of impurity of a zav (one with a discharge) to be impure and to render impure: That a zav be impure and render others impure, as it is stated (Leviticus 15:2-3), "when there be any man with a discharge from his flesh, etc." And the explanation comes, "from his flesh," is meaning a flow from the orifice of the member. And [it is] as they, may their memory be Blessed, expounded, "'When there be a discharge' - it is possible, a discharge from any place would be impure. [Hence,] we learn to say, 'from his flesh' and not all of his flesh. Once Scripture has distinguished between flesh and flesh, I have merited to learn out the law of impurity with a zav and with a zavah. Just like a zavah is from the place that she become impure, etc."

And the content of discharge is that which issues as a type of fluid from a man from the orifice of the member and he has no desire or pleasure from its emission. And they, may their memory be Blessed, said (Niddah 35b) that it is similar to barley dough and, likewise, similar to the white of an addled egg; but semen is not like this, since it is similar to the white of an egg that is not addled. And that is the difference between them to distinguish between this and that.

And Scripture commanded that anyone to whom this matter happens, that issues a discharge, be impure and render impure, until he is purified. And the explanation comes that he is not impure on account of one appearance alone, but rather for two appearances - meaning to say that this matter flow from him twice - whether they are proximate or distant, so long as they are on one day and that they not flow exactly at one time. And it has no measure, but rather even the smallest amount [is impure] (Niddah 40a). And this is their, may their memory be Blessed, saying (Megillah 8a), "The verse enumerated two and it called [it] impure, three and called [it] impure. How is this? Two for impurity and three for a sacrifice" - meaning to say that even though he is impure with two, he is not obligated to bring a sacrifice with his purification until [there were] three. And nonetheless if he [experienced] an appearance as long as three appearances, which is found to be from its beginning to its end like two immersions and two wiping downs, behold it is considered like three appearances, and he brings a sacrifice.

It is from the roots of the commandment [that it is] since God, Blessed be He, distanced us greatly from the excesses and commanded us to be holy and righteous regarding food and drink and in all other matters of man. And there is no doubt that the matter of a discharge happens to a person from his constantly leaving the straight path in his foods and drinks. And that putrid, disgusting and impure excess develops in his body, from this. And it is like they, may their memory be Blessed, said (Kiddushin 2b), "It is the way of excessive drinking to lead to discharge." And the Torah informed us that a man who has this in him is called impure; and impurity is a general name for anything disgusting and vile. And in our distancing, ourselves from this, we acquire the trait of righteousness and balance in all of our dispositions and in all of our abilities. And it is from this matter that he is not impure from one appearance. As that fluid has not [yet] become so strong in his body. And [so,] this small amount is not an indication of his being very habituated to leave the straight path. And since that is so, it is not fitting to render him impure with a small amount - as a person is built in a way that it is impossible for him to prevent himself from not leaving the straight line at all. But in his leaving it much, he will then be called guilty; and it is fitting that he should be impure. And even though they, may their memory be Blessed said (Mishnah Zavim 2:2), "There are seven ways a zav is examined: with regard to food; drink; a load; a jump; illness; a sight; or [improper] thoughts" - meaning to say if it happened to him because of this, he is not impure - our argument is not contradicted by this. As the matter is that we need to examine if his discharge was by way of a one-time event and he should not be made impure for that; or whether it has become strong in his body from a bad habit to which he has become accustomed many times, and [so,] it is fitting to render him impure. And so did Ramban, may his memory be Blessed, write (in Ramban on Leviticus 15:11) and this is his language: "And the reason for the impurity of the discharge is because of its being a heavy illness, from the contagious illnesses." To here [are his words]. And if it were from the angle of an event - meaning to say from one of the [seven] well-known ways - it would not be a contagious disease, and it would not be fitting to render him impure. And we only do this inspection with the second appearance, as there is no impurity of discharge without two appearances, as we said. As so did the true explanation come to us.

The laws of the commandment [includes] that which they, may their memory be Blessed, said that the zav imparts impurity to the [place of] sitting, laying and riding in five ways, and these are them: standing, sitting, laying, hanging from and leaning. And the understanding of riding is that it is that board which is a vessel that is made for riding (to hold on to it) that is called artson (Rashi on Leviticus 15:9). As we cannot say that we sit upon it - as if so, it would be [the same as] sitting - and this is an obvious thing. And the rest of its many details are elucidated in the tractate that is built upon it, and that is Tractate Zavim (see Mishneh Torah, Laws of Those Who Defile Bed or Seat 7).

And this matter that one with a discharge is called impure is practiced in every place and at at all times. But now - due to our iniquities - that we do not have a Temple or pure objects, we should not count the impurity of a zav as a commandment that is practiced; since we do not have anything to do regarding the matter of a discharge. But at the time of the [Temple], he practices the bringing of a sacrifice for it. And one who transgresses it and goes into the Temple or eats holy [foods] before he has become purified has violated this commandment - besides that he has a punishment for it, as we wrote above (Sefer HaChinukh 167).

Mitzvah 179

Sefer HaChinukh

The commandment of the sacrifice of the zav when he is healed from his discharge: That the zav offer his sacrifice after he is healed from his discharge, as it is stated (Leviticus 16:13-14), "When the zav is purified from his discharge, etc. And on the eighth day, he shall take two doves, etc." And this sacrifice is two doves or two young pigeons - one for a sin-offering and one for a burnt-offering. And he is called, 'lacking atonement,' until he offers it.

That which I have written above (Sefer HaChinukh 95), that the matter of the sacrifice is to hint to the lowering of the impulse of the desiring body and raise up the intellectual soul, is from the roots of the commandment. And hence when the zav is healed, it is fitting for him to recognize the evil of his desire and to straighten out his body with all of his strength. And with the matter of the sacrifice, he will begin to take instruction.

From the laws of the commandment is that which they, may their memory be Blessed, said (Nedarim 35b) that a sacrifice of one lacking atonement does not need the consent of the owners, as we wrote above (Sefer HaChinukh 176). And the rest of its details are elucidated in the places we wrote above with the sacrifice of the metsora.

And [it] is practiced at the time of the [Temple]. And one who transgresses it and does not offer a sacrifice has violated a positive commandment and is lacking atonement. And [it is] a pity on his head if he dies and he carries his iniquity on his body.

Mitzvah 180

The commandment of the matter of the impurity of semen, which is impure and renders impure: That semen be impure and render impure, as it is stated (Leviticus 15:16), "And if semen come out from a man."

It is from the roots of the commandment [that] since this matter only happens from the angle of thoughts of physical desires, the perfect Torah informed us that the body is called impure with them. As the essence of his being in the world is only to understand ideas and to serve his Creator. Hence when that thing that shows about him [that he is] leaning to physical desire, happens to him; it is fitting to stop in his impurity for a day, in order that he cleans his thoughts properly, and then become pure.

From the laws of the commandment is that which they, may their memory be Blessed, said (Niddah 43b) that the measure for one who touches [it] is like [the size of] a lentil, and for one who [experiences] the emission is with the smallest amount. And it is one, whether he [experiences] the emission accidentally or volitionally, he is impure. And the seed of a young child does not render impure. And red seed does not render impure, but rather [only] white. And any seed that a man does not feel - not at the beginning and not at the end - is not impure. And one who has [improper] thoughts at night, and saw in a dream that he had sexual relations and got up and found his flesh [to be] warm, is impure - even though he did not [knowingly experience] semen. And the rest of its details are elucidated in Tractate Zavim (see Mishneh Torah, Laws of Offerings for Those with Incomplete Atonement 1).

And the impurity of semen is practiced in every place and at all times. But today that - due to our sins - we have neither a Temple nor consecrated things, we do not need to be careful about the matter of impurity. And nonetheless, Ezra and his court ordained immersion for those with an emission, so that they be cleaner and purer in their thoughts, and that men not be found with their wives [constantly] like chicken. And in his time, no man would pray or study Torah until after immersion. But at this time, they ruled in the Gemara (Berakhot 22a) that the Sages rescinded [the law of this] immersion. And from [then], no man prevents himself from praying or studying - also placing tefillin - because of an emission. And they also rescinded taking [of waters] - which is rinsing the body with nine kav of water. And [so] now, they do not immerse, nor rinse [off] at all. And nonetheless, a soulful person who purifies himself from his emission also today [is exhibiting] a good and praiseworthy trait, and a blessing will come to him. And one who knows the way of purity and much good should hold on to it.

Mitzvah 181

Sefer HaChinukh

The commandment of the matter of the impurity of the menstruant, that is impure and renders impure: That the menstruant be impure and render others impure, as it is stated (Leviticus 15:19), "and anyone who touches her shall be impure until the evening."

We will write the root of the commandment and a little of its details - as per our custom - in the negative commandment of the menstruant in the Order of Achrei Mot (Sefer HaChinukh 207), with God's help.

And [it] is practiced in every place and at all times. And one who transgresses it and does not act with her [according to her] impurity - and likewise if she, herself, acts [according to] the practice of purity (and not impurity) - has violated this positive commandment, besides the punishment that there is with it, as we shall write below with God's help.

Mitzvah 182

The commandment of the matter of the impurity of the zavah (woman with an irregular discharge), that is impure and renders impure: That the zavah be impure and render impure, as it is stated (Leviticus 15:25), "And a woman who discharges a discharge of her blood many days, etc."

I have written a hint of the root of the commandment with the woman that has given birth (Sefer HaChinukh 166) - that the matter of distancing from them and their impurity is because of the illness that they have, which hurts many people; and all the more so, one who lays with her. As the hurt is greater, according to the greatness of the closeness.

From the laws of the commandment is that which they, may their memory be Blessed, said (Niddah 72b) that there are eleven days between [one] menstruation (niddah) and [another] menstruation - meaning to say, that she becomes a zavah upon them. This is a law of Moshe from Sinai. And the explanation of the matter is like this: That every woman at the time that she [experiences] blood, at the beginning of her [experiencing] it, is called a 'menstruant.' And the law of the matter of the menstruant is like this: That if she [experiences] blood one day, or even seven consecutive days - so long as the blood stops on the seventh day while it is still day - immerses at night; which is the night, the morrow of which is the eighth from the beginning of her experiencing [it]. And after her immersion, she is pure for her husband. But after the seven days of menstruation, if she [experiences] blood within the eleven days after the seven, that blood is called, 'blood of discharge,' and its law is [as follows]: That if she [experience] it for one day - whether she [experiences] it at the beginning of the night or the end of the day - she watches one day corresponding to it and immerses, and she is pure for her husband in the evening. And her immersion is even during the day, from when the sun rises. And this is called a 'small zavah.' And so [too,] if she [experiences] blood two days and stops on the third, her law is likewise to watch one day. And this is sufficient for her - even for two days - and she is purified. And this is also called a 'small zavah.' But if she [experiences] blood during these eleven days [over] three consecutive days, she is called a 'big zavah,' and needs to sit [out] seven clean days. And afterwards, she immerses and is pure for her husband. And after these eleven days, if she [experiences blood], she goes back to the beginning of menstruation; and she has seven days [to be] like the law of the menstruant, as we said above. And so is the matter always - that after [the days of] menstruation, she has eleven days in which she [can] become a zavah. And after those eleven days pass, she never becomes a zavah until the seven days of menstruation have passed.

And because others have already erred in this - and thought that the equation is that she count seven days of menstruation and afterwards eleven day of discharge, and seven of menstruation and eleven of discharge and so on, forever - I have spoken at length about this matter, to say that it is not like that. Rather, there are never days of discharge besides [the] eleven days after the seven of [actual] menstruation; and never afterwards until she returns to the beginning of [actual] menstruation. I mean to say that if she stops and does not [experience blood] after the eleven days - even [for] a year - she does not have the status of a zavah, until seven days of menstruation pass over her.

And the rest of its details are in Tractate Zavim, and a few of the laws of discharge are also in Tractate Niddah (see Tur, Yoreh Deah 183). And in the negative commandment of the menstruant in the Order of Achrei Mot (Sefer HaChinukh 207), we will write, with God's help, that which is practiced today. And one who transgresses this commandment and is lenient in these matters and in the matter of impurity has violated this positive commandment; besides the punishment of the one who lays with her, which is with excision, as we will write in the negative commandment of the menstruant, with God's help.

Mitzvah 183
The commandment of the sacrifice of the zavah when she is healed from her discharge: That the zavah offer her sacrifice after she is healed from her discharge - and it is two doves or two young pigeons, as it is stated (Leviticus 16:28-29), "And if she is purified from her discharge, etc. And on the eighth day, she shall take two doves, etc."

And the root of this commandment and some of its details are similar to what we have written above (Sefer HaChinukh 179) about this sacrifice. And Rambam, may his memory be Blessed, wrote (Sefer HaMitzvot LaRambam, Mitzvot Ase 75) that because of [the following] did we consider these two sacrifices of the zav and the zavah as two commandments, even though they are totally [the same] sacrifice - which we have not done with many other sacrifices, as we are not concerned to count each and every sacrifice as a commandment of its own, because of the distinction of who brings them, so long as it is one sacrifice: Because the impurity of these is not the same at all - as the man becomes impure with white and the woman becomes impure with red. And with the opposite, [neither] becomes impure, neither this [one] nor that [one]. And since they are so different, it is fitting to count them as two commandments. And this matter is not at all similar to the metsora and the metsoraat, which is considered one commandment - as tsaraat is the same thing for all of them. And he brought a bit of a proof for his words, from that which they said in Keritot 8b, "There are four who are lacking atonement and these are them: the zav ; the zavah ; the woman who gave birth; and the metsora." Behold they counted zav and zavah as two, because they are different in their illnesses; but metsora and metsoraat as one, because the illness is the same in both of them.

And it is practiced at the time of the [Temple]. And one who transgresses and does not bring her sacrifice when she is healed from her discharge has violated this positive commandment, besides that she is lacking atonement.

Mitzvah 184
That the priests not enter at any time into the Temple - and all the more so, non-priests: That the priests not enter at any time into the Temple, bur rather only at the time of the service, as it is stated (Leviticus 16:2), "and let him not come at any time." And with this, the high priest is warned not to come into the house of the holy of holies - and even on Yom Kippur - except at the time of the service. [And likewise brought into (this) warning is a common priest from entering the sanctuary all of the year except at the time of the service (according to the Venice edition)]. And the elucidation of the matter of the prevention is to say that any priest not enter into any place that is fitting, except at the time that is fitting to enter it - which is the time of service. And the language of Sifra, Achrei Mot, Section 1:8, 10 is "'And let him not come at any time' - that is Yom Kippur; 'to the holy' - to include the other days of the year. 'Within the partition' - maybe for all of the sanctuary, [the punishment is] death. [Hence] we learn to say, 'before the ark cover which is on the ark, that he not die.' Behold, how is this? 'Before the ark cover' [is punishable] by death; (if he enters) the other parts of the sanctuary, (he is only in transgression of) a warning. And in the Gemara Menachot 27b, they, may their memory be Blessed, said, about the chamber that it is with forty [lashes].

It is from the roots of the commandment that the servants fix the greatness of the place and its loftiness in their souls, and that its awe always be upon their faces.

From the laws of the commandment is that which they, may their memory be Blessed, said (Mishnah Kelim 1:9) that the high priest only enter the Holy of Holies on Yom Kippur, when he enters four times and not more. As if he enters a fifth, he is liable for death by the hands of the Heavens. And a common priest may enter the chamber for the service every day. But anyone who enters the chamber not for the sake of the service - whether a high priest or a common priest, such as one who enters even to bow down - is lashed, but he is not liable for death. As it is stated 'Before the ark cover [...], that he not die' - for the Holy of Holies, he is liable for death; for the other parts of the sanctuary, (he is only in transgression of) a negative commandment. This is the opinion of Rambam, may his memory be Blessed, about this negative commandment (Mishneh Torah, Laws of Admission into the Sanctuary 2:4). And I have already written the opinion of Ramban, may his memory be Blessed, above (Sefer HaChinukh 149, 150), who said that entrance to the sanctuary, not for service, with wild [hair] and torn clothes is a rabbinic embellishment. And if so, according to his opinion, it is possible that anyone who entered to bow down is not [punished] with lashes at all; and this prohibition of "he shall not come" would only be in a completely empty coming - as such would be a disparagement to the honor of the [Temple], to enter into it for nothing. And the rest of its details are elucidated in Menachot and Sifra (see Mishneh Torah, Admission into the Sanctuary 2).

And [it] is practiced at the time of the [Temple] by the priests. And even today - not at the time of the [Temple] - they, may their memory be Blessed, said (Megillah 28a) that we are warned not to enter the Temple [grounds]. And they expounded the matter, from that which is written (Leviticus 26:31) "and I will make your sanctuaries desolate," and it did not state, "your sanctuaries will I make a desolation." As it is implied that their holiness is [still] upon them, even when they are desolate. And since that is so, I should count this prohibition among the prohibitions that are observed today.

Mitzvah 185

The commandment of the service of Yom Kippur: That the high priest do all the procedure of Yom Kippur, with the order of the sacrifices, the confessions, the sending away of the goat and the rest of the service, as it is written in the section of the Torah - as it is stated (Leviticus 16:3), "With this shall Aharon enter the Holy, etc." until the end of the section.

It is from the roots of the commandment that it was from the kindnesses of God towards His creatures to fix one day in the year for the atonement of sins, with the repentance that they repent. As if the iniquities of the creatures would accumulate year by year, their measure would be full at the end of two or three years or more, and the world would be liable for destruction. And therefore He, Blessed be He, saw in His wisdom - for the survival of the world - to fix one day a year for the atonement of sins for penitents. And from the beginning of the creation of the world (Bereshit Rabbah 2:3), He designated it and sanctified it for this. And since God, Blessed be He, designated that day for atonement, the day was sanctified and received the power of merit from Him, may He be elevated, to the point that it aids atonement. And this is [the meaning] of their, may their memory be Blessed, saying in many places (Yoma 85b), "Yom Kippur atones" - meaning to say that there is power in Yom Kippur, itself, to atone for light sins.

From the laws of the commandment is that which they, may their memory be Blessed, said (Yoma 70a) that on that day they would offer the daily morning sacrifice and the daily afternoon sacrifice according to the order of each and every day. And they would offer the additional (musaf) sacrifice of the day - a bull and a ram and seven sheep, all burnt-offerings, and a goat for a sin-offering, and it was processed outside, and eaten in the evening. And they would further offer beyond this, a young bull for a sin-offering, and it was burnt; a ram for a burnt-offering - and they were both of the high priest's; and the ram that came from that of the community that is stated in this section, and it is the ram stated in the Book of Numbers as part of the additional service, and it is called the 'ram of the people.' And they would also bring two male goats from that of the community - one they would offer as a sin-offering and it was burnt, and the second was the goat sent away (the scapegoat). All of the beasts that would be offered on the day of the fast - besides the goat sent away, which was not offered - come out to fifteen: two daily ones; a bull; two rams; seven sheep - all of them burnt-offerings; two goats for sin-offerings, one was processed outside and eaten in the evening, and the second was processed inside and burned; and also, a young bull for a sin-offering. All fifteen of the beasts that were offered on this day were only [offered] by the high priest anointed by the anointing oil or who [simply] had more [officiating] garments. And if it was Shabbat, only the priest would offer the additional [offering]. And likewise, the other procedures of the day, such as the incense of every day and the arrangement of the lights - all was [done] by a married high priest, as it is stated (Leviticus 16:11), "and he shall atone for himself and for his home" - [the meaning of] his home is his wife.

And the rest of all of the procedures: the change of garments from the white garments to the gold garments, and from the gold garments to the white garments; the five immersions that he would immerse on this day; the ten times he would sanctify his hands and feet; the matter of separating. that they would separate him seven days before the fast day; the honor that they would [show] him; the confessions that he would say; and all the rest of the laws of this day - it is all in the tractate that is built upon it, and that is Tractate Yoma (see Mishneh Torah, Laws of Service on the Day of Atonement 1).

And all of this commandment is practiced at the time of the [Temple]. And now that - due to our iniquities - we have neither a Temple nor a high priest, neither serving garments nor sacrifices, all of Israel has been accustomed to serve on this day though our prayers and supplications. And [it is] as it is written (Hoshea 14:3), "and we shall pay the bulls of our lips."

Mitzvah 186
Not to slaughter consecrated animals outside of the [Temple] yard: Not to sacrifice consecrated animals outside of the [Temple] yard - and that is called 'those slaughtered outside' - as it is stated (Leviticus 17:3-4), "that slaughters an ox or sheep or goat, etc. And does not bring it to the opening of the Tent of Meeting, etc., he has shed blood and shall be cut off." And the warning (negative commandment) does not come to us from this verse, as this verse only expresses the punishment. And it is established for us, [that] He does not punish unless he warned (Sanhedrin 56b). And our Rabbis, may their memory be Blessed, said that we learn the warning for this with an inferential comparison, as it is [found] in the Gemara, Zevachim 106a. As there, they, may their memory be Blessed, said, "One who slaughters and brings up outside is liable for the slaughter and liable for the bringing up" - the understanding of bringing up is burning with fire. And they challenged there, "Bringing up is fine, the punishment is written, and the warning is written - the punishment, 'And does not bring it to the opening of the Tent of Meeting [...] and shall be cut off'; the warning, 'guard yourself lest you bring up your burnt-offering' (Deuteronomy 12:13), like Rabbi Avin, as Rabbi Avin said, 'Every place that it is stated, "guard," "lest" or "not," it is nothing but a negative commandment'; but slaughter, it is fine that the punishment is written, 'And to the opening of the Tent of Meeting, etc.,' but from where is the warning?" And after great effort, they said there that since Scripture states (Deuteronomy 12:14), "there you shall do, and there you shall bring up," it compares bringing up and doing: Just like bringing up, it punished and warned; so too doing, it punished and warned - and the understanding of doing includes everything, whether slaughter or burning.

It is from the roots of the commandment [that it is] since God, Blessed be He, fixed a place for Israel to bring their sacrifices there and to prepare their hearts to Him there. And from the fixing of the place and its aggrandizement and its awe in the hearts of people, their souls are moved there for the good; and the hearts are softened and humbled to fully accept the kingdom of the Heavens there. Therefore, God, may He be Blessed, prevented us from doing the procedure of the sacrifices except in that place, so that the atonement for us be complete. And the principle of the matter is that all that He commanded us is for our good, as we have written - as God wants the good of His creatures in His great goodness. And [so] He said that it is considered blood upon whoever sacrifices outside of that chosen place. And the matter is that God only permitted the meat of animals to people for atonement or the needs of people, such as food or healing or anything that has some need for people. But to kill them without any benefit at all is destruction and called, 'spilling blood.' And even though it is not like spilling the blood of man, due to the loftiness of man and the lowness of beasts, nonetheless, it is [still] called, 'spilling blood,' as Scripture did not permit it, to spill it without benefit. And therefore, it stated undifferentiatedly that it is like the spilling of blood, since he is spilling its blood in a place that he was not commanded to slaughter, and there is no benefit to this slaughter at all. [Rather] there is damage in the thing, as he transgressed the commandment of his Creator. And so the verse punishes him with excision.

The laws of the commandment: For example, that which they, may their memory be Blessed, said (Zevachim 106a) that if he slaughtered outside - even though he brought up inside - he is liable, since with both the slaughter and bringing up, each one is a negative commandment by itself; and the negative commandment of bringing up is in the Order of Reeh Anokhi (Sefer HaChinukh 439); and a person is only liable for the slaughter of consecrated animals that are fitting to bring on the altar, but one who slaughters outside, one of those prohibited on the altar, behold, he is exempted, as it is stated (Leviticus 17:4), "in front of the tabernacle of the Lord" - anything that is not fitting to go to the tabernacle, we are not liable for it; and the rest of its details are elucidated in the thirteenth chapter of Zevachim (see Mishneh Torah, Laws of Sacrificial Procedure 19).

The prohibition of sacrificing outside is practiced in every place and at all times, as even one who slaughters a beast for the sake of consecrated animals today is liable. And so do we say in the Gemara, Tractate Zevachim 107b, about one who brings up [a sacrifice] at this time, "Rabbi Yochanan says, 'He is liable'" - and that is the law. And one who transgresses it and slaughters consecrated animals outside volitionally is liable excision. And even though he did not bring them up - from the time that he slaughtered them, he is liable. And so did they, may their memory be Blessed, say (Zevachim 106b), "He is liable for the slaughter and liable for the bringing up." And if he transgressed and slaughters inadvertently, he is liable to bring a fixed sin-offering at the time of the [Temple].

Mitzvah 187

The commandment of covering the blood: To cover the blood after slaughtering a [wild] animal or fowl, as it is stated (Leviticus 17:13), "who hunts game, an animal or a bird that is to be eaten, and spills its blood, he must cover it with dirt."

It is from the roots of the commandment [that it is] because the soul is dependent upon the blood, as we said about the prohibition of blood (Sefer HaChinuch 148). And therefore, it is fitting for us to cover the soul and to hide it from the eye of its seers, before we eat the meat. As we acquire a bit of cruelty in our souls when we eat the meat, and the soul is spilled in front of us. And with [domesticated] beasts, we were not commanded so, since the blood of beasts is given for a sacrifice of atonement for our souls, and it is impossible to cover [that]. And since it is so, the Torah did not want to differentiate for us between consecrated ones and non-sacred ones. And even while in the species of fowl, there are some of them that are offered on top of the altar, [they are] few. And the Torah never concerns itself with a lesser thing. And because of that, the Torah obligated us about covering the blood of all fowl.

From the laws of the commandment is, for example, that which they, may their memory be Blessed, said (Chullin 83b) that covering of the blood is practiced with every bird and with every animal - whether it was at hand or it was not at hand. "Who hunts" is only stated for what is common, etc. And it is practiced with non-sacred animals, but not with consecrated ones. And it is practiced with the koy, because it is a doubt whether it is a type of animal or beast; but we do not recite a blessing on its covering, due to the doubt. And blood that splattered and that is on the knife is obligated in covering when there is no blood besides it. But if there is any blood besides it, he does not need [to do so], as it is written, "he must cover it with dirt" - its understanding is even some of its blood (Chullin 83b). And the one who covers it must put dirt below and above [it]. And any dirt in the world that is fine enough that a potter does not need to pound it, is fitting to cover [it] (Chullin 28a). And likewise, we [may] cover with all that is called dirt - even though it is not actually dirt, such as shaved gold, which is called dirt (dust), as it is stated (Job 28:6), "and it has gold dirt." And one who saw his fellow slaughter but not cover is obligated to cover; as it is stated about this commandment (Leviticus 17:14), "and I say to the Children of Israel" - and they, may their memory be Blessed, elucidated, "this commandment is to all of the Children of Israel (Chullin 86-87a). And the rest of its details are in Chullin in the chapter [entitled] Kisui Hadam (see Tur, Yoreh Deah 28).

And [it] is practiced in every place and at all times by males and females. And one who transgresses it and does not cover the blood of an animal or a bird has violated a positive commandment.

Mitzvah 188

To not marry one of all the sexual prohibitions: To not indulge [we not indulge] in one of all of the [women forbidden by] sexual prohibitions - and they are the [close] relatives, a married woman and a menstruant - and even without intercourse, such as hugging and kissing and all that is similar to these evil acts that licentious ones, 'that go after vanity and become vanity,' develop expertise about. As it is stated (Leviticus 18:6), "Any man shall not approach any of his own flesh, to reveal nakedness" - and its understanding is as if it stated, "Do not do any approaching, which is what causes and brings a person to reveal nakedness." And so did they, may their memory be Blessed expound (Sifra, Achrei Mot, Chapter 13:15, 21), "'Shall not approach to reveal' - I only have not to reveal. From where [do I know] not to approach? [Hence] we learn to say, 'And to a woman in the impurity of her menstruation you shall not approach' (Deuteronomy 18:19). I only have a menstruant with 'do not [approach' and 'do not] reveal.' From where [do I know] for all sexual prohibitions? [Hence] we learn to say, 'do not approach to reveal.'" And there it is said, "'And the souls that do, will be cut off' (Deuteronomy 18:29) - lest you say they will be liable for excision with approaching alone. [Hence] we learn to say, 'that do,' and not 'that approach.'"

And the negative commandment of this prohibition was repeated in its stating, "and you shall not do from any of [these] abominations" (Leviticus 18:26), which includes all of these matters which are an abomination to God, may He be Blessed. [This] means to say, that one who does them distances himself from the good and removes from himself the providence of God, Blessed be He. And this is the understanding of the abominable to the Lord, may He be Blessed, in every place, according to that which I have heard. And also, that which is written at the end of the matter, "for all of these abominations did the people of the land that were before you do" (Leviticus 18:27), "and I was disgusted with them" (Leviticus 20:23). And the matter is to say that the trait is very disgusting. And every thing that is bad and very vile, Scripture describes as if God, may He be Blessed, hates. And it is all according to the matter that we said; and similar to what they, may their memory be Blessed, said in every place (Mekhilta d'Rabbi Yishmael 19:18:2), [it is] in order to break [to assuage] the ear to that which it can hear. And the language of Sifra, Achrei Mot, Section 8:8 is "'Like the deed of the land of Egypt and like the deed of the land of Canaan, etc.' (Leviticus 18:27) - perhaps they should not build or plant as they do? [Hence] we learn to say, 'and in their statutes you shall not walk.' I have only said those statutes which were instituted for them, and not their buildings. What did they do? A man would wed a man, and a woman, a woman; and a woman would wed two men."

I have written in the Parsha of Vayishma Yitro in the negative commandment of "You shall not commit adultery" (Sefer HaChinukh 35) that which I have known about the root of distancing from licentiousness. And this commandment is also from that root - that we were prevented from approaching the sexual prohibition with any approach. As it is known that approaching is the cause of the revealing of nakedness (sexual transgression) - [which, in turn] draws (finds) several mishaps and several losses, as I wrote there. However, that reason will [only] suffice for a married woman. But for relatives, we still need another reason. And in the warning (prohibition) of the nakedness of the mother (Sefer HaChinukh 190), we shall write that which we shall know about it.

From the laws of the commandment is that which they, may their memory be Blessed, said (Avot 3:13; Avot D'Rabbi Natan 2) about this for a fence, and that is that a man not motion with his hand nor hint with eyes to one of the sexual prohibitions, nor to joke with them at all. And it is even forbidden to smell perfume that is on them; and not to gaze at women at all, and even at a bride - with the intention to derive pleasure. And they forbade to stare even at their small finger. [This is] besides the wife of a man, as it is permitted for him to gaze at her beauty, and even while she is still menstruant, as she will be permitted to him later. And there is an assumption about an Israelite that his impulse is given over to his hand (under control) in an example like this, that is dependent upon time. And it is specifically at the revealed places upon her that they permitted to stare while she is still a menstruant, but not at the covered [places] so that his evil impulse not cover (overcome) him. And our Rabbis, may their memory be Blessed, also said (Berakhot 24a) that it is forbidden to stare even at the hair of a woman that is forbidden to him. And even to hear her voice with the intention to derive pleasure from it is forbidden. And even to stare at the colored clothes of a woman - meaning to say, beautiful clothes, the way of which is to make them from colored fabric - is forbidden, so long as he knows the woman that wears them, since by seeing the garment, he will come to have improper thoughts about her. And they also distanced [us] that we should not ask about the welfare of a married woman at all, and even through her husband (Kiddushin 70b and Tosefot s.v. ein shoelin).

Sefer HaChinukh

And there are many details of the distancings that they warned about this matter, but the general principle of the matter is that a man should not do anything in the world that brings him to improper thoughts about women - not in action, not in speech and not with any hint to bring close the weak mind of a woman to his mind - except for only his wife. And like this matter did the prophet rebuke the men of his generation, in his saying to them (Jeremiah 5:8), "each one is neighing at his neighbor's wife" - meaning to say, according to their way that they appear as if they do not intend this, they hint to the wives of their neighbors' hints of adultery, and raise their voices in such a way that these women should listen to them and their impulse be aroused towards love of the adulterer. And it is not from the possible to say [all of] the details of the matters that a man will know to do to bring the mind of a woman, which is weak, close to him. And therefore they, may their memory be Blessed, [only] mentioned a few of them. But with the rest, each and every one should be careful to guard himself according to what he finds with his person, 'as the Lord sees to the heart.'

And in any case, according to what appears from all that they, may their memory be Blessed, have warned us, a man is not permitted to budge from their good teaching. And even if he finds himself a little devoid of desire, he should not say, "Since I find myself so, what do I care if I stare at women, since I know about myself that my impulse will not be aroused by this" - as many have said like this and stumbled. And about this, they, may their memory be Blessed, hinted when they said (Sukkah 52a) that the impulse is very weak at first and continues to [grow until it] greatly overpower a man. And you, my son, be very careful about this and do not let your impulse promise you [that it will not overpower you], even if it gives you a thousand pledges. And that which you find a few stories in the Gemara that appear to contradict these words of mine - meaning to say that a few of them were not concerned about even that which our Rabbis, may their memory be Blessed, forbade with women - this is not a contradiction to my words at all. As they were only a little lenient in the place of a commandment, as we found with Rabbi Yochanan who would sit at the gates of the [place of] immersion in order that the women would stare at him and give birth to sons as beautiful as he (Berakhot 20a), but he did not stare at them, God forbid; and Rebbi, and Rav Acha, who would take a bride on his shoulders for a commandment, as he did this in order to have her rejoice (Ketuvot 17a); and a few matters similar to this.

And also, as they, may their memory be Blessed, were like angels, as they had no other occupation - even for a short time - beside Torah and the commandments; and their intention was famous to the whole world like the sun; and they would not feel any evil feeling about anything, due to their great clinging to the Torah and the commandments. But we now should not even breach a small fence in these matters at all, but rather guard all of the ditancinings that they, may their memory be Blessed, informed us [about] in particular. And regarding that which they did not mention, each and every one should do according to that which he finds his person ready, as we said. As if he finds about himself that he needs a fence even about the permissible, he should fence himself - as we found (Kiddushin 81b) one of the Sages who said, "Be careful with me because of my daughter," even though it is permitted for a man to isolate himself with his daughter, as we will write with God's will - since this matter is very difficult, and the evil impulse about it is strong.

Therefore, every man should increase his guarding. And if upon running into a beautiful woman, a man will think that Gehinnom is open between her eyelids and that any who approaches her will burn in a perpetual fire, and review his thoughts about these things, 'it will not be a cause of stumbling for him.' And they, may their memory be Blessed, said (Berakhot 5a) that if [he] does not have the power in his hand to kill the impulse and to distance its thought from him, he should recite the reading of Shema or involve himself with Torah [study]. And they informed us that it will die with this in any event - as they, may their memory be Blessed, said (Kiddushin 31a), "If it is a stone it will dissolve, and if it is iron, it will explode, as it is stated (Jeremiah 23:29), 'Is My word not thus, like fire, etc.'"

And our Rabbis, may their memory be Blessed, also said (Kiddushin 80b) about this commandment that it is forbidden to isolate oneself with all of the Torah-level sexual prohibitions - whether old or young - as isolation brings to revealing nakedness. [This is the case] except for a mother with her son, a father with his daughter and a husband with his wife who is a menstruant - who are permitted, except for a groom whose wife has become menstruant before he has intercourse. And it is permissible to isolate oneself with a male and with a beast, as Israelites are not suspected about this. And when the story of Amnon and Tamar occurred, David and his court decreed [to forbid] isolation with a single woman (Avodah Zarah 36b). Shammai and Hillel decreed [to forbid] isolation with [gentiles]. And they, may their memory be Blessed, permitted (Kiddushin 41a) to stare at a single woman by one who stares to know if he he will marry her as a wife if she is beautiful in his eyes. And they also said that it is fitting to do so, that a man not marry until he see her; so that he not come to divorce her afterwards, if she become unsightly in hie eyes. And the rest of the details of the commandment are elucidated in many scattered places in the Talmud (see Tur, Even HaEzer 21).

And [it] is practiced in every place and at all times by males and females; as it is forbidden for them as well to have improper thoughts about men besides their husbands. As it is fitting for them to draw all of the their yearning and desire towards [their husbands]; and so do the proper daughters of Israel do. And one who transgresses it and approaches a sexual prohibition with approaching of the flesh, in order that he derive pleasure from it, is lashed when warned and volitional. And if he transgressed on the remaining things that they, may their memory be Blessed, forbade as a distancing - such as laughing and light-headedness - and they warned him but he did not prevent himself [from it], they would strike him with lashes of rebellion. And Ramban, may this memory be Blessed, wrote (on Sefer HaMitzvot LaRambam, Mitzvot Lo Taase 353) that we should not count this negative commandment of approaching in the tally of the negative commandments, as all distancing of approaching is rabbinic. And the proof is that which they, may their memory be Blessed, said (Talmud Yerushalmi Sanhedrin 7:7), "Rabbi Yose beRebbi Bon said, 'It is "do not approach," it is "do not reveal"'" - meaning to say, that there is no negative commandment of approaching besides the negative commandment of revealing. And the rest of his many proofs are in his Book of Commandments 347 (it should say 353).

Mitzvah 189

To not reveal the nakedness of the father: That a man not reveal the nakedness of his father - meaning to say that he not lay with him, the layings of a woman, as it is stated (Leviticus 18:7), "The nakedness of your father [...] you shall not reveal." And this warning (negative commandment) about one who lays with his father is in addition to the general warning of laying with males about all men (Sefer HaChinukh 209), as it is stated (Leviticus 18:22), "And with a male you shall not lay, the layings of a woman." And so did they, may their memory be Blessed, say in Sanhedrin 54a, "'The nakedness of your father [...] you shall not reveal' - your actual father." And they asked there, "That is extracted from, 'And with a male you shall not lay, the laying.'" And the one who answered, answered, "So as to make him liable for two [prohibitions], and it is like Rav Yehudah, as Rav Yehudah said, 'A gentile who has intercourse with his father is liable for two.'" And there they elucidated and said, "It is likely that the word of Rav Yehudah is with an Israelite, and inadvertent and with a sacrifice; and that which he said, 'a gentile,' is [because] he took a euphemistic expression." [This is] meaning to say that he did not want to mention this disgraceful matter with an Israelite, since it was possible to establish it with a gentile; as they are also commanded about sexual prohibitions, but the law is the same with an Israelite - that he is liable for two with his father, meaning that if he lay with him inadvertently, he is liable to bring two sin-offerings. The substance of this matter is revealed to all. There is no reason to be lengthy about its root, as it is fitting to distance this great ugliness from people, and to punish one who transgresses it [with] a great punishment. And therefore it made him liable for stoning.

From the laws of the commandment is that which they, may their memory be Blessed, said (Yevamot 53b) that the liability is with the insertion of the corona immediately, but not before then. And the law is the same for all of the sexual prohibitions, that the liability with them is with the insertion of the corona immediately - except for one who has relations with a maidservant, [for] which the liability is with the completion of his intercourse. And we will inform the place of the rest of its details together with the rest of all the sexual prohibitions at the end of the Order, with God's help (see Tur, Even HaEzer 21).

And this prohibition is practiced in every place and at all times. And one who transgresses this and lays with his father volitionally with witnesses and a warning is stoned from when he inserts the head of the corona; inadvertently, he brings two sin-offerings at the time of the [Temple] - one on account of the negative commandment of 'his father, and one on account of the negative commandment of 'a male.'

Mitzvah 190
To not reveal the nakedness of the mother: That a son not reveal the nakedness of the mother, as it is stated (Leviticus 18:7), "it is your mother, do not reveal her nakedness." About the reason for relatives, Rambam, may his memory be Blessed, wrote (Guide for the Perplexed 3:49) that the matter is because the Torah distanced sexuality from people besides that which is needed for being fruitful and multiplying, or for the commandment. Therefore, the Torah forbade [close] relatives to us - as stumbling is found with them more, since they are always found (proximate). And Ramban, may his memory be Blessed, said (Ramban on Leviticus 18:6) that this reason is very weak - that the Torah should make one liable for excision for one of these because of their being always found near him; and from another side, permit a man to marry one hundred women - or a thousand - if he wants. [Rather,] he, may his memory be Blessed, said - and this is his language: "But according to logic, there is a matter of a secret from the foundations of creation this is implanted in the soul, and it is included in the 'secret of intercalation' (a play on words that can also mean conception), that we have already hinted to." To here [are his words]. And I have seen that Rambam, may his memory be Blessed, wrote another reason about the matter (Guide for the Perplexed 3:49): From the angle of the simple understanding - according to my opinion - did he say [it is] because the Torah distanced [it], that he should not be brazen-faced to have intercourse with the woman that he is to treat with honor. And he pushes [it] to explain most of [the sexual prohibitions] from this angle, meaning to say on account of the trait of shame - all as it appears in his book; the matter would be [too] lengthy if we came to write it all.

From the laws of the commandment is that which they, may their memory be Blessed, said (Sanhedrin 54a) that the prohibition of the mother is even if she was raped by his father, as behold she is his mother in any event. And so [too,] that which they said (Sanhedrin 53a) that one who has intercourse with his mother that is the wife of his father - meaning that she was not raped by him - is liable for two, on account of his mother and on account of the wife of his father. And there is no distinction in this whether he had intercourse in his father's lifetime or after his death, as she is always called the wife of his father, and [so] he is liable for two, as we said. And so [too,] that which our Rabbis, may their memory be Blessed, forbade (Yevamot 21a) as a fence of this prohibition of the mother, the mother of his mother - meaning to say, his grandmother - and likewise the mother of his grandmother, going way back even to a thousand generations if it was possible to see them all; they are all forbidden by the words of the [Rabbis]. And so [too] they forbade the mother of his father - meaning to say, his grandmother from the father's side - as a fence for the mother, and likewise the mother of his grandmother, going way back. And so [too,] they forbade just the mother of the father of his father, and just the mother of the father of his mother only, as a fence of this [prohibition] of the mother. And there are some (Rashi on Yevamot 21a s.v. dalet nashim) that explained that these are also forbidden way back. And if you ask why the prohibition extends way back with the first ones - according to the first opinion - more than with these last two; the reason is because the first ones approach the prohibition of the mother which is the main prohibition, as behold they have a forbidden grandmother, which is the mother of the mother or the mother of the father. And therefore, is it fitting to decree about them even going way back? But with these last two, they do not have a forbidden grandmother. And since the matter does not approach the mothers which is the main prohibition, they, may their memory be Blessed saw (said) that it is enough that we decree with these two alone. And 'the words of the Sages are grace.' And these that are forbidden rabbinically are called secondary ones - meaning to say, they are secondary to those sexual prohibitions that were prohibited by the Torah.

And this prohibition is practiced in every place and at all times. And one who transgresses this and lays with his mother volitionally is liable for excision, and is stoned if there are witnesses;

inadvertently, he is liable to bring a fixed sin-offering at the time of the [Temple]. And if he laid with one of the secondary ones, he is struck with lashes of rebellion. And this is from the sexual prohibitions that all people of the world were prohibited more generally. But there is a distinction between Israel and the rest of the nations regarding the secondary ones; as Israel made a fence regarding the secondary ones, but [with] the rest of the nations, only the mother alone is forbidden to them.

Mitzvah 191
To not reveal the nakedness of the wife of the father, even though she is not his mother: To not reveal the nakedness of the wife of the father, even though she is not his mother, as it is stated (Leviticus 18:8), "The nakedness of the wife of your father you shall not reveal."
What we wrote (above, Sefer HaChinukh 190) regarding the [close] relatives is from the roots of the commandment. But we should also say that the reason for this is because there would be a disgrace to the father in the matter. And we have already written in the commandment of honoring the father (Sefer HaChinukh 33), the benefit that is found for us with honoring the parents.
From the laws of the commandment is that which they, may their memory be Blessed, said (Sanhedrin 53a) that the wife of his father is forbidden by Torah writ, whether [she is his wife by virtue of] betrothal - the understanding of which is kiddushin (designation) - or from marriage; whether in the lifetime of his father and even if he divorced her, or after his death. And so [too,] that which they forbade (Yevamot 21a) the wife of his father's father - meaning to say the wife of his grandfather - even though she is not his grandmother, to make a fence for this prohibition. And so [too,] did they also forbid the wife of the father of his grandfather and so [too,] the wife of the father of the mother of his grandfather, and likewise going way back, even to Yaakov. And they also forbade just the wife of the father of his mother, as a fence for this prohibition. And the reason is because the essence of this prohibition is from the side of the father - meaning the wife of the father. Therefore they, may their memory be Blessed, were more stringent with the side of the fathers and said that it be forbidden going way back forever; but from the side of the mother, they only decreed just with the wife of the father of the mother. And this is similar to the distinction that we wrote above with the prohibition of the mother. And the rest of its details are in the places that we will write below (Sefer HaChinukh 211) at the end of the Order (see Tur, Even HaEzer 21). And this is from the sexual prohibitions that all people of the world were prohibited more generally. But there is a distinction between Israel and the rest of the nations - as with the rest of the nations, [one] is only called the wife of the father by way of intercourse, but with Israel, even by way of designation; and likewise, regarding the secondary ones, as there is no prohibition of the secondary ones among the nations, as we said.
And this prohibition is practiced in every place and at all times. And one who transgresses it and lays with the wife of his father volitionally is liable for excision, and is stoned if there are witnesses and a warning; inadvertently, he is obligated to bring a fixed sin-offering at the time of the [Temple]. And if he laid with one of the secondary ones, he is struck with lashes of rebellion.

Mitzvah 192
To not reveal the nakedness of his sister, from any angle that she is his sister: To not reveal the nakedness of his sister - whether she is a sister only from the father or whether she is a sister only from the mother; whether she is a sister from a woman raped by his father, or whether she is a sister from a mother from infidelity. From all of these angles, she is called his sister, and [he] is liable for her, as it is stated (Leviticus 18:9), "The nakedness of your sister - the daughter of your father or the daughter of your mother, whether born into the household or born outside." And if you shall say, "If so, what is this that is stated in the Torah (Leviticus 18:11), 'The nakedness of the daughter of the wife of your father, who has born into your father's household'; and what was the need for this verse, is he not liable for her on account of [her being] his sister" - this verse was truthfully only stated to make the daughter of the wife of the father when she is his sister, a sexual prohibition on its own, and as we will write below in its place (below, Sefer HaChinukh 196). And it comes out that one who has intercourse with his sister, who is the daughter from the marriage of his father, is liable for two: on

account of the nakedness of his sister and the nakedness of the daughter of the wife of his father. (Yevamot 22b). And if he has intercourse with her inadvertently, he is liable for two sin-offerings.

We have written in the sexual prohibition of the mother (Sefer HaChinukh 190) that which we have known about the roots of the prohibition of relatives (see Tur, Even HaEzer 21).

From the laws of the commandment is, for example, that which they, may their memory be Blessed, said (Sotah 43b) that only the daughter of his father who is his sister - meaning to say, who was conceived by his father - is forbidden to him. But the daughter of his father's wife who is not his sister - such as when the wife of his father had a daughter from another man - is not forbidden to him at all. Rather, it is permitted for a man to marry her at the outset, and we do not decree because of his sister - as there is no place for a decree here at all.

And [it] is practiced in every place and at all times. And one who transgresses it and lays with his sister volitionally is only liable for excision, meaning to say [that there is no death penalty of the court. But with witnesses and a warning, the court lashes him, like the law of all those who are liable for excision, that they are lashed] (that even with witnesses and a warning, there is nothing in the matter besides excision alone). And inadvertently, he brings a fixed sin-offering. And this is from the sexual prohibitions that all people of the world were prohibited more generally. But there is a distinction between Israel and the rest of the nations; as with the rest of the nations, there is no prohibition except with their sister from the mother alone, but with Israel it is whether from the mother or the father.

And [let] this principle be in your hand about all that the [other] nations were commanded: that so long as they are under our hands, it is upon us to judge them when they transgress their commandments. And I have already written above in the Order of Vayishma Yitro in the negative commandment of 'there shall not be' (Sefer HaChinukh 26) that their judgement is always with the death penalty - whether they are volitional or inadvertent - and that they do not need a warning. But they do need two witnesses or the admission of their [own] mouths. And it appears that even though they are not fit to testify about an Israelite, they are fitting to testify one about the other - and so did the elder instruct (Mishneh Torah, Laws of Kings and Wars 9:14).

Mitzvah 193

To not reveal the nakedness of the daughter of the son: To not reveal the nakedness of the daughter of the son, as it is stated (Leviticus 18:10), "The nakedness of the daughter of your son, etc. do not reveal." And according to what appears, the prohibition is whether the son is fit or even if he is a mamzer - he is his son regardless - and whether the daughter of the son is fit or even if she is a mamzeret.

I have written in the sexual prohibition of the mother (Sefer HaChinukh 190) about the root of the prohibition of relatives.

From the laws of the commandment is that which they, may their memory be Blessed, forbade (Yevamot 22a) as a fence for this prohibition - and that is just the daughter of the daughter of his son and, likewise, just the daughter of the son of his son. And some say that there is no end to these prohibitions ever, since they forbade a man all that 'come out from his thigh' for all generations. And you will see where the rest of its details are at the end of the Order (Sefer HaChinukh 211) (see Even HaEzer 21).

And this prohibition is practiced in every place and at all times. And one who transgresses it and laid with the daughter of his son volitionally - and there are witnesses - is liable for burning, as they, may their memory be Blessed, said in Sanhedrin 75a; and if there are no witnesses, he is liable for excision; inadvertently, he brings a fixed sin-offering at the time of the [Temple]. And if he laid with the daughter of the daughter of the son and all the other secondary ones, he is struck with lashes of rebellion.

Mitzvah 194

To not reveal the nakedness of the daughter of the daughter: To not reveal the nakedness of the daughter of the daughter, as it is stated (Leviticus 18:10) "or the daughter of your daughter, you shall not reveal, as it is your nakedness." All of its laws are like the law of the daughter of the son; and the ones secondary to her are also the daughter of the daughter of daughter and, likewise the daughter of the son of the daughter. And some say that there is no end to [the generations of] these prohibitions ever.

Mitzvah 195

To not reveal the nakedness of the daughter: To not reveal the nakedness of the daughter, and this is not elucidated in the language of the Torah, that the verse would state, "The nakedness of your daughter you shall not reveal." And because of [the following] did a verse not come about it explicitly, since there is no need for it: As since the Torah forbade the daughter of the son and the daughter of the daughter which are more distant than she, there is no reason to say that she is forbidden - as it is an a fortiori argument (kal vachomer). And they, may their memory be Blessed, also learned it from a inferential comparison (gezearah shavah). As if we had only extracted it with an fortiori argument, no one would have ever been judged for it - as it is established for us (Sanhedrin 76a) [that] 'we do not punish from an inference.'

We have written above (Sefer HaChinukh 190) from the roots of the commandment, that which we were able about all of the sexual prohibitions more generally.

The laws of this commandment - meaning to say how did they, may their memory be Blessed, learn it and from which verse - are in the Gemara Yevamot. As there (Yevamot 3a) they said, "The main prohibition of his daughter from a woman he raped, comes by interpretation (drasha), as Rava said [that] Rav Yitzḥak bar Avdimi said to [me], 'This prohibition comes [by means of an inferential comparison between] "their" (hena) and "their"; it comes [by an inferential comparison of] "licentiousness" and licentiousness - meaning to say, that the verse states with the son's daughter and the daughter's daughter, "it is their nakedness"; like it is written at the end of the section (Leviticus 18:17), "their flesh." Just like over there, it is explicit that her daughter is forbidden; so too here, wherein the verse prohibits the daughter of his son, the law is the same for his daughter even though the verse did not explain it - as we learn it from this inferential comparison. And they, may their memory be Blessed, also learned with which death one who has intercourse with his daughter or with the daughter of his son or the daughter of his daughter is judged, from the strength of this inferential comparison. They, may their memory be Blessed, learned it from it, after it was learned about it from another place. And from what other place was it learned about it? From that which is written (Leviticus 20:14), "And a man that takes a woman and her mother, it is licentiousness; with fire shall they be burnt, him and them." And they, may their memory be Blessed, said (Sanhedrin 75b) [that] just like there, with a woman and her mother, about them which is written, "licentiousness," it is with burning; so too here, with a woman and her daughter or the daughter of her son or the daughter of her daughter, about them which is written, "their flesh, it is licentiousness," he is judged with burning. And from now, since we found that the judgement of one who has intercourse with a woman and her daughter or the daughter of her son or the daughter of her daughter is with burning - since we have already learned the prohibition of his daughter from it by the inferential comparison of "their, their"; we can further learn from all of the other laws in it, and say that the judgement of one who has intercourse with his daughter is also with burning. And about that which is similar to this, they say in the Gemara (Yevamot 78b), "Infer from it and from it" - meaning to say, when we learn one verse from its fellow, we do not learn it for only one thing about it, but rather we learn it for all its laws from it. And [this is the case] even when those laws that are with it are not like the understanding of that verse itself, but rather learned from other verses. Nonetheless, we learn from everything that is in it - whether from the verse itself or whether it is learned from another place. And they, may their memory be Blessed, said in the Gemara Keritot 5a, "Let not an inferential comparison (gezara shava) be light in your eyes; as behold, his daughter from a woman he raped is one of the [important] bodies of Torah, and Scripture only taught it through a gezara shava - it comes by 'their, their'; 'licentiousness, licentiousness.'" [This is] meaning to say that we learned its prohibition and its judgement from these two inferential comparisons, as we explained. But his daughter from a woman he married is explicit in Scripture, as it is stated (Leviticus 18:17), "The nakedness of a woman and her daughter" - and there is no distinction whether she is his daughter and her daughter, or from another man. And this is speaking about a married woman, since it is written, "woman" (eeshah, which is also the word for wife), which implies the language of marriage (eeshut). And it is also written "you shall not take" - and taking also implies through marriage. But regarding his daughter from a woman, he raped or the daughter of her son or daughter of her daughter, only, "you shall not reveal," is written. And Rambam, may his memory be Blessed, wrote (in Sefer HaMitzvot LaRambam, Mitzvot Lo Taase 336), "Observe their, may their memory be Blessed, saying 'The verse did not teach it,' and they did not say, 'We did not learn it' - since all of these matters are a transmission from the messenger (Moshe), peace be upon him, who transmitted the understanding [of the Torah] to the elders. And that is [the meaning] of their saying, 'body of Torah,' about this." And [this] brought the rabbi, may his memory be Blessed, to write this as a fixed major principle for himself - that only what is explicit in the verse or that which they, may their memory be Blessed, said explicitly that it is from the Torah, is in the tally of the six hundred and thirteen commandments, but not that which we learn from the thirteen hermeneutic principles. And Ramban, may his memory be Blessed, already contradicted this with clear proofs (in Sefer HaMitzvot LaRambam, Root 2).

We will write the place of the laws of the commandment at the end of the Order, with all of the sexual prohibitions more generally (see Tur, Even HaEzer 21).

And this prohibition is practiced in every place and at all times. And one who transgresses it and volitionally lays with his daughter from a woman he raped, and there are witnesses, is judged with burning; without witnesses, he is liable for excision; inadvertently, he is liable for a fixed sin-offering. And if he laid with his daughter from a woman he married, he is liable for two sin-offerings - one on account of 'his daughter' and one on account of "the nakedness of a woman and her daughter." As the liability for "the nakedness of a woman and her daughter" is only with marriage of the first one, as behold it is explicitly written, "you shall not take" - whether in the place of the warning about them or whether in the place of the punishment - and the language of taking implies the language of marriage for us. And on account of this, they, may their memory be Blessed, said (Yevamot 97a) that it is from the law of the Torah that if a man raped a woman, it would have been permitted to marry her daughter [from another man], except that the Sages, may their memory be Blessed, made a fence and forbade the thing. And they said (Yevamot 97a) that one who has adultery with a woman is forbidden to marry one of her seven [delineated] relatives so long as the unfaithful woman is alive, because the unfaithful woman comes to visit them and [so] he will isolate himself with her; and [since] his heart is coarse with her, he will come to a sin, as he will have intercourse with the sexual prohibition. And not only that, but even one who is claimed (the explanation of which is suspected) about a woman, behold this one shall not marry one of her relatives until the one who he is claimed about dies. However, if he [married] this one who is a relative of the one with which he was licentious, we do not require him to remove (divorce) her. And they, may their memory be Blessed, also said about this matter (Kiddushin 12b) that anyone, who is claimed about a sexual prohibition or that a bad name went out about him with her, shall not live in the same passage with her and not be seen in the same neighborhood. [If it was] his father or his son or his brother that raped a woman or seduced her, behold he is permitted to marry her - as only by way of marriage are they forbidden. And they, may their memory be Blessed, were also not stringent to make a fence for another because of the licentiousness of his relative.

Mitzvah 196
To not uncover the nakedness of his sister from the father, and she is the daughter of the wife of the father: To not uncover the nakedness of the daughter of the wife of the father when she is his sister - meaning to say, that she is the daughter of his father. As if she was the daughter of the wife of his father that is not his sister, we have already said above (Sefer HaChinukh 192) that he is permitted to marry her from the outset. Rather, the understanding [of the prohibition] is that it is the daughter of the wife of his father and she is his sister, as it is stated (Leviticus 18:11), "The nakedness of the daughter of your father [...] you shall not reveal." And I have already written above regarding the nakedness of the sister that this negative commandment comes in order to make his sister from the

Sefer HaChinukh

wife of his father a sexual prohibition by itself - and similar to what I wrote about his mother (Sefer HaChinukh 190): that if she is the wife of the father, he is liable with her for two - on account of the mother and on account of the wife of the father. And the proof is from that which they, may their memory be Blessed, said in Yevamot 22b, "The Sages learned, 'He who has intercourse with his sister who is the daughter of his father's wife, is liable on account of his sister and on account of the daughter of his father's wife.' Rabbi Yose beRebbi Yehudah says, 'He is liable only on account of his sister alone.' What is the reason for the opinion of the rabbis? They said, 'How is it? Since it is written in the Torah, "The nakedness of your sister, the daughter of your father, etc." (Leviticus 18:9), for what do I need, "The nakedness of the daughter of the wife of your father, who has born into your father's household," (Leviticus 18:11)? We understand from this, [that] it is to make him liable on account of his sister and on account of the daughter of his father's wife.'" It comes out that there is only one negative commandment with one who lays with his sister who is from a woman that his father raped; but one who lays with his sister from a woman that his father married is liable for [the transgression of] two negative commandments - and [so] if inadvertent, he is obligated to bring two sin-offerings. And 'the judgments of God are righteous': Since the Torah distanced the sister, it is fitting to be stringent with the one that is his full sister - meaning to say from marriage, as she is called the [true] sister (of her mother). And like this matter did Ramban, may his memory be Blessed, write (Ramban on Leviticus 18:9).

And at the end of the Order (Sefer HaChinukh 211), we will see where the laws of the commandments are (see Tur, Even HaEzer 21).

And this prohibition is practiced in every place and at all times. And one who transgresses it and laid volitionally with his sister from a woman that his father married is liable for excision; inadvertently, he is liable two sin offerings, as we said.

Mitzvah 197

To not reveal the nakedness of the sister of the father: To not have intercourse with the sister of the father, as it is stated (Leviticus 18:12), "The nakedness of the sister of your father you shall not reveal, etc."

We have written what we know of the roots of sexual prohibitions (Sefer HaChinukh 190).

From the laws of the commandment is, for example, that which they, may their memory be Blessed, said (Yevamot 54b) that the prohibition of the sister of the father is whether she is the sister of his father from the father only or from the mother only; whether she is the sister from marriage or whether from licentiousness - as each one of these is called his sister regardless. And there is no room for secondary [prohibitions] here.

You will see the place of the laws of the commandment at the end of the Order (see Tur, Even HaEzer 21). And this prohibition is practiced in all places and at all times. And one who transgresses it and lays with the sister of his father volitionally is liable excision; inadvertently, he brings a fixed sin-offering.

Mitzvah 198

The nakedness of the sister of your mother you shall not reveal: To not have intercourse with the sister of the mother, as it is stated (Leviticus 18:13), "The nakedness of the sister of your mother you shall not reveal, etc." All of its content is like the sister of the father (Sefer HaChinukh 197).

Mitzvah 199

The nakedness of the brother of your father you shall not reveal: To not have intercourse with the brother of the father. And it is from what appears that there is no difference whether he is the brother of his father from the father or from the mother, whether he is from marriage or whether from licentiousness; as it stated (Leviticus 18:14), "The nakedness of the brother of your father you shall not reveal" - and he is called the brother of his father regardless. And even though [a man] who has intercourse with any male is liable on account of "and with a male you shall not lay, etc.," this negative commandment is in addition [to that] for the one that has intercourse with the brother of his father.

And if he was inadvertent, he is liable for two sin-offerings - on account of the negative commandment of the one who has intercourse with the male, and [on account of] the negative commandment of one who has intercourse with the brother of his father - and as we said also with his father (Sefer HaChinukh 189). And in the Gemara Sanhedrin 54a, they, may their memory be Blessed, said, [that] one who has intercourse with the brother of his father is liable for two, according to the words of all.

And this prohibition is practiced in all places and at all times. And [in the case of] one who transgresses it and laid with the brother of his father, both of them are stoned - the layer and the one who is lain with - if they are both volitional and [it occurred] with witnesses and a warning; if there are no witnesses, they are both [liable] for excision. And when inadvertent, one is liable for two sin-offerings - as we said, that one who has intercourse with the brother of his father is liable for two sin-offerings - and one is liable one sin-offering.

Mitzvah 200
The nakedness of the wife of the brother of your father, you shall not reveal: Not to have intercourse with the wife of the brother of your father. And this one is called his aunt (dodah) in Scripture, since she is the wife of his uncle (dod), as it is stated (Leviticus 18:14), "to his wife you shall not approach, she is your aunt (dodah)." And this warning is from when she was betrothed to his uncle - meaning to say, she was designated for him - and there is no need to say, after she married him. And [this is the case] whether [it is] in the lifetime of his uncle and even after he divorced her, or whether after his death (Yevamot 97a).

We have written above about the roots of the commandment (Sefer HaChinukh 190).

The laws of the commandment: For example, that which they, may their memory be Blessed, said (Yevamot 54b) that he is called the brother of his father regarding this prohibition of his wife when he is the brother of his father from the father's side. But the brother of the father from the mother's side is not [included] in this prohibition of "to his wife you shall not approach" by Torah writ. However, the Sages made a fence and forbade even the wife of the brother of his father from the mother's side, in order to distance us greatly so as not to touch a prohibition of the Torah. And likewise, they also forbade the wife of the brother of his mother - whether she is a sister from the father's side alone or from the mother's side alone. And even though the wife of the brother of his mother is not forbidden at all from Torah writ; since the Torah forbade the wife of the brother of his father from the side of the father - who is called, 'his uncle' - they added upon the prohibition to make a fence with all of these that are similar to it.

And this prohibition is practiced in every place and at all times. And [in the case of] one who transgresses it and laid with the wife of the brother of his father from the father's side during the lifetime of his uncle volitionally - and there were witnesses - the death of both of them is with strangulation, as this is the law of the one who has intercourse with a married woman, with strangulation. And if he laid with her volitionally after the death of his uncle, he is liable for excision; and if there are witnesses, he is lashed; inadvertently, he brings a fixed sin-offering - as it is well-known to us that with anything for which there is excision if volitional, its inadvertent transgression is with a sin-offering. And if he laid with the wife of the brother of his father from the mother's side or the wife of the brother of the mother - whether from the father's side of from the mother's side - we strike him with lashes of rebellion when volitional, and he is exempt when inadvertent.

Mitzvah 201
The nakedness of your daughter-in-law you shall not reveal: To not have intercourse with the wife of the son, which is his wife from the betrothal - and all the more so from the marriage - whether during his lifetime and even after he divorced her, or whether after his death. In any manner [above], she is called the wife of his son and she is forbidden to him, as it is stated (Leviticus 18:15), "The nakedness of your daughter-in-law you shall not reveal." And from that which appears, the liability is even with a son that is a mamzer - he is his son regardless. But the son from a maidservant or from a gentile is not called "his son" for anything.

We have written the root of the prohibition (Sefer HaChinukh 190).

From the laws of the commandment is, for example, that which they, may their memory be Blessed, forbade (Yevamot 21b) - to make a fence for this - the daughter-in-law of his son and likewise the daughter-in-law of the son of his son, to the end of the world. And they also forbade only the daughter-in-law of his daughter. And the reason is similar to that which we said above - since the prohibition came in the verse about his daughter-in-law, they decreed about all daughters-in-law that come on account of the son; and they decreed with [the daughter-in-law of] the daughter only, and that is enough for us with that. And these are called secondary [prohibitions].

And this prohibition is practiced in every place and at all times. And one who transgresses it and laid with his daughter-in-law volitionally - and there are witnesses and a warning - is [punished] with stoning; and if there are no witnesses, with excision; inadvertently, he brings a fixed sin-offering. And if he laid with the daughter-in-law of his son or the son of his son, to the end of the world - or the daughter-in-law of his daughter, we strike him with lashes of rebellion.

Mitzvah 202

The nakedness of the wife of your brother you shall not reveal: To not have intercourse with the wife of your brother, as it is stated (Leviticus 18:16), "The nakedness of the wife of your brother you shall not reveal." And it is one whether it is his brother from only his father or only his mother; and whether it is from marriage or whether from licentiousness - his wife is a sexual prohibition for him, since he is called, "his brother," regardless. And from when he betrothed her, she is called, "the wife of his brother," and is forbidden - and all the more so after he marries her. And it is whether it is in the lifetime of his brother or whether after he died, that she is forbidden to him on account of "the wife of the brother." [This is] except for the wife of the brother that did not leave a child, as the Torah commanded explicitly about that, that the brother should marry her. And that is the commandment of levirate marriage, as we will explain with God's help (Sefer HaChinukh 598).

And this prohibition is practiced in every place and at all times. And one who transgresses it and laid with the wife of his brother is liable excision if he was volitional; and if he was inadvertent, he is obligated to bring a fixed sin-offering. And this is after the death of his brother and he left children, or after he divorced her. As if it was in his life when she is still [with] him, it is well-known that the law of the one who lays with the wife of his brother (it should say, with a married woman) [is that] his death is with strangulation. And there is no room to prohibit secondary [prohibitions] with the prohibition of the wife of the brother.

Mitzvah 203

The nakedness of a woman and her daughter, you shall not reveal: To not reveal the nakedness of a woman and her mother, as it is stated (Leviticus 18:17), "The nakedness of a woman and her daughter, you shall not reveal." And the explanation came that the liability is only in such a case that he married one first; and then when he had intercourse with the second, he becomes liable. But if he did not marry one of them, he does not become liable for them. [This is] since an expression of marriage is written about them - "taking," which implies through marriage. As so is it understood to us, that the expression of taking is an expression of marriage in every place. But the Sages decreed a fence and said that if a man has adultery with a woman, it is forbidden to marry her daughter - [even] all of her seven [delineated] relatives - so long as the unfaithful woman is alive. [This is] because the unfaithful woman comes to visit them and [so] he will isolate himself with her; and [since] his heart is coarse with her, he will perhaps come to a sin.

And this prohibition is practiced in every place and at all times. And [in a case of a man] who transgresses it and laid with a woman and with her daughter, both of them are burnt - he and the one he laid with last. As the first one has no sin, since [it was] permitted [for] him [to] marry her. And if he had intercourse with the second after the death of his first wife, behold they are [punished] with excision and they do not [receive] a death penalty of the court. As it is stated in another place in the Order of Kedoshim Tehiyu (Leviticus 20:14), "they shall be burned with fire, he and them (ethen)." And Rabbi Eliezer explained in Sanhedrin 66b, "'They shall be burned with fire, he and' one of them (echat mehen)" - which is the later one, as we said. But that is only when both of them are alive - as so came the explanation. But when both of them are not alive, there is no burning there. Rather, they are [punished] with a liability for excision when volitional; and he brings a fixed sin-offering when inadvertent. However, Rabbi Akiva explains there, "He and both of them" - for example that he [was] forbidden to marry both of them, and this is found when he married a daughter, her mother and the mother of her mother. And what they disagree about is explained there.

Mitzvah 204
The nakedness of a woman and the daughter of her son: To not reveal the nakedness of a woman and the daughter of her son. And we have already said that this prohibition is always with marriage to the first one (as a condition), as it is stated (Leviticus 18:17), "the daughter of her son [...] you shall not take."

From the laws of the commandment is that which they, may their memory be Blessed, forbade (Yevamot 21a) the daughter of the son of her son as a fence for this - and it is included in the secondary [prohibitions]. As everything the prohibition of which is from the words of the [Rabbis] is called a secondary prohibition. And so [too,] did they forbid only the mother of the mother of the father of his wife.

And this prohibition is practiced in every place and at all times. And [in the case of] one who transgresses it and volitionally laid [with] a woman and the daughter of her son, with the marriage of the first one - in the lifetime of the first - both of them are burned; but if the first one died, both of them are [punished] with excision. If it was inadvertent, they bring a fixed sin-offering. And if he laid with the secondary [prohibition], he is struck with rabbinic lashes of rebellion.

Mitzvah 205
To not reveal the nakedness of a woman and the daughter of her daughter: To not reveal the nakedness of a woman and the daughter of her daughter. And we have already said that this prohibition is always with marriage to the first one (as a condition), as it is stated (Leviticus 18:17), "the daughter of her daughter you shall not take." And the expression of taking is understood by us to be an expression of marriage.

From the laws of the commandment is that which they, may their memory be Blessed, forbade - as a fence to this - only the daughter of her daughter of her daughter, and only the mother of the mother of the mother of his wife, and only the mother of the father of the mother of his wife. The general rule of the matter of the prohibition of a woman and her daughter or the daughter of her son or the daughter of her daughter is that the Torah forbids a man from marrying six relatives of his wife besides the sister: three above, which are her mother and her two grandmothers; and three below, which are her daughter, the daughter of her daughter and the daughter of her son. And the Sages also added six others upon them as a fence - four above and two below. As the matter is proper to be like this perforce - as the two grandmothers drag along four others as a fence for them, whereas it is impossible for the daughter of her son and the daughter of her daughter to have [anyone] besides the two corresponding to them as a fence. And there is nothing to add upon the mother and the daughter, as behold there are women below them and above them [already] forbidden from the Torah.

And this prohibition is practiced in every place and at all times. And [in the case of] one who transgresses it and volitionally laid [with] a woman and the daughter of her daughter - in the lifetime of the first - both of them are burned; but if the first one died, both of them are [punished] with excision. And if it was inadvertent, they bring a fixed sin-offering. And if he laid with the secondary [prohibitions], they would strike him with rabbinic lashes of rebellion.

Mitzvah 206
The nakedness of a woman and her sister: To not have intercourse with two sisters, meaning to say that a man not marry two sisters together - and not even this one after that one - during the lifetime of the first one; and even if he divorced the first one, as it is stated (Leviticus 18:18), "And a woman upon her sister shall you not take to be a rival, to reveal her nakedness upon her during her life." The

explanation is a woman and her sister together, "shall you not take to be a rival," [which] is an expression of rivalry - meaning to say that he should not make one the rival of her friend; "during her life" comes to teach that even [if] he divorced the first, he shall not marry her sister - and that is [the meaning of] the expression, "during her life," meaning to say all the time that she is alive. But after the death of one, there is no doubt that it is permitted to marry the other. And that is what the verse stated, "during her life." And likewise, if he lays in the way of licentiousness with the sister after he married the first one or designated her, is also included in the prohibition; as the Torah was concerned about the the marriage of [only] the first one.

The matter of the sexual prohibitions is from the roots of the commandment, [about which] we wrote that which we knew above (Sefer HaChinukh 190). And also, my heart tells me about this matter that Scripture forbade to marry two sisters, that the Master of peace wants peace [for] all of his creatures and, all the more so, those creatures that nature and intellect obligate to have peace between them - and not constant quarrel and competition the whole day.

From the laws of the commandment is that which they, may their memory be Blessed, said (Yevamot 54b) that she is called the sister of his wife, whether she is the sister from her mother or the sister from her father; whether from marriage or whether from licentiousness. And they also explained that the prohibition comes into force from when he designates her, and as the expression of taking of a woman is always understood by us, as we said. And also, that which they, may their memory be Blessed, forbade the sister of his bound one, as a fence for this prohibition. And the understanding of his bound one is such a case as one who has a brother and he dies and does not leave children, such that he is obligated by the Torah to marry his wife or to release her, as it appears explicitly in the written commandment (Sefer HaChinukh 597, 599). And that is the woman that is bound to the brother, meaning to say that she is in the domain of the brother to marry her if he wants. Since she is acquired by him from the Heavens, she is called, "his bound one." And they, may their memory be Blessed, forbade (Yevamot 41a) him from marrying her sister from when she is bound to him, even though he did not designate her and did not do any action.

And likewise, they also forbade him (Yevamot 40a) as a fence for this, the sister of his released one (chalitsato); meaning to say, they forbade him form marrying her sister, even after he released her. Just like Scripture forbade the sister of his divorcee, as we explained; so too did [the Sages] also forbid the sister of his released one - since release is similar to a bill of divorce. And nonetheless, it is established for us on the legal level that the prohibition of the sister of his released one - and even the sister of his bound one - is rabbinic. As the Torah only forbade the sister of a woman that he married or betrothed. But the sister of a woman bound to him - even if [the latter] was acquired by him from the Heavens - is not included in the Torah prohibition. Rather, [it is] they, may their memory be Blessed, that prohibited her, so as not to touch the Torah prohibition. And since this prohibition is [only] rabbinic, as we said, they were sometimes a little lenient in that matter - to the point that they, may their memory be Blessed, said (Yevamot 41a) that we say to one of the brothers required for levirate marriage who designated the sister of [this] levirate wife, "Wait. Do not divorce her and do not marry her until your brother performs levirate marriage or releases this levirate wife that is bound to all of you." [If] his brother released her or performed levirate marriage, or [if] the levirate wife dies, he can [marry] his betrothed. But if all of the [other] brothers die, he divorces his betrothed with a bill of divorce, and his levirate wife with release (chalitsah). And if his betrothed dies - whether she died before the death of the brothers or whether she died after their death - the levirate wife comes back to be permitted [to him]. If he wants, he releases [her]; if he wants, he performs levirate marriage. And in the commandment of levirate marriage, we will write a little further about these matters (Sefer HaChinukh 498) - as is our custom - with God's help; as here is not its place.

And this warning (negative commandment) is practiced in every place and at all times. And one who transgresses it and volitionally laid with the sister - whether by way of marriage, or by way of licentiousness - during the lifetime of the first, is liable for excision; and he is lashed, if there are witnesses and a warning; inadvertently, he brings a sin-offering. And if he laid with the sister of his bound one or the sister of his released one, he is struck by rabbinic lashes of rebellion. And nonetheless, his wife - that is the sister that he married first - is not forbidden to him, because of the marriage to the second or (her licentiousness) because he was licentious with her. Rather, his wife is permitted to him, and this second one should go away (Yevamot 94a). And even if he married [the second] with 'a canopy and designation,' she does not require a bill of divorce from him - as designation is not effective with sexual prohibitions, to have her require a bill of divorce. But nonetheless one who does an act of designation (kiddushin) with them makes himself liable, as the Torah stated, "you shall not take" - which implies a language of designation. And even though if he transgressed and took, meaning designated, [her], it does not help him - meaning, she is not 'taken' by him for any matter, and [so] she does not require a bill of divorce from him - nonetheless, he becomes liable with this, as we said.

And this law is not only with sisters, but rather also with all the other sexual prohibitions: that if he marries them with the assumption [that they are] permitted and they turn out to be sexual prohibitions, they do not require a bill of divorce from the reason that we said - that the designation is not effective with sexual prohibitions. And likewise, if he married or transgressed and was adulterous with one of the six women that we said above (Sefer HaChinuch 205) are sexual prohibitions for him - on account of his wife - from Torah writ, they do not prohibit his wife to him; but rather they should go away without a bill of divorce. And his wife remains permitted to him, as we said. [This is the case] except with the sister of his betrothed, wherewith the Sages were stringent and forbade even the first one, because of the second one. As they, may their memory be Blessed, said (Yevamot 94b) that if a man betroths a woman - meaning to say, he designates her - and afterwards marries her sister, both of them are forbidden to him and [both] require a bill of divorce from him (Mishneh Torah, Laws of Divorce 10:9, 10). And because of what did they say this, and they did not say that he [stays] married to the first one and the second one goes away without a bill of divorce, as we wrote above? Because the Sages were concerned, lest the creatures say since there was only designation alone with the first one, that there was some condition in that designation - and as a result, he married the second; and he married her legally. And therefore, they required a bill of divorce for her. And since they required a bill of divorce for the later one - because of the concern that we said - they needed to also forbid his first betrothed; so that the creatures not say, he married the sister of the woman he divorced.

Mitzvah 207

To not have intercourse with a menstruant woman: To not have intercourse with a woman when she is menstruant, as it is stated (Leviticus 18:19), "And to a woman in menstrual impurity, you shall not approach." And the time of her menstruation continues for seven days, as it is written (Leviticus 15:19), "seven days shall she be in her menstruation." And whether she [experiences blood] once during them or gushes all seven, she is a menstruant (Niddah 73a). And the entire time that she does not immerse (in a mikveh) - even after the seven - she is [considered] a menstruant; since the verse made it dependent upon days and immersion, as it is stated with impure people (Leviticus 15:18), "and they shall wash in water." And they, may their memory be Blessed, said [that it is] a constructive paradigm (binyan av) to any impure one, that he is with his impurity until he immerses (see Rabbenu Bachya on Leviticus 15:19 in the name of the Geonim). And likewise, they, may their memory be Blessed, also expounded (Shabbat 64b), "'Shall she be in her menstruation' - she shall be in her menstruation until she goes into water."

And the content of menstruation is that there is a matter with women, such that blood flows from them through their nakedness (vagina) two or three days or more - up to seven - each and every month. And Scripture commanded that the law is the same with them whether the blood flows from her for one day only or even all of the seven. As if it flows all seven and stopped on the seventh while [it was] still day, she immerses in the evening, which is the night the morrow of which is the eight day, and is pure. And likewise, if it only flowed one day of all of the seven - and even blood that is a drop the size of a mustard seed - she observes [herself] seven days and immerses in the evening, which is the night of the eighth, and is pure for her husband.

I have written that which I know from the roots of the menstruant in Parashat Zot Tehieh (Sefer HaChinukh 166, 182). And the general principle of the matter is that God, may He be Blessed, distanced all impurity, all dirt and all damage from His people that He chose. And there I also said what appears to be the substance of God's, may He be Blessed, making women sick with this illness. From the laws of the commandment is that which they, may their memory be Blessed, said (Niddah 32a) that a woman becomes impure as a menstruant even on the day of her birth; whereas the law is not like this with a zavah - as a woman does not become impure with a discharge until ten days [of age]. And this thing is by way of the heard tradition. And all women are included in this prohibition, and even Canaanite (gentile) maidservants - since they are included in the commandments, they are like Israelitesses for this matter (Sifra, Metzora Parashat Zavim, Section 5:1). But the women of the [other] nations of the world are not included in the prohibition of menstruation and discharge from Torah writ, but rather [only] rabbinically. As they decreed about them - whether males or whether females - that they be like a zav for all their matters (Niddah 34a). And that which they said in the Gemara (Avodah Zarah 36b) that one who has intercourse with a gentile woman is liable because of her on account of nashgaz (the acrostic of the four prohibitions about to be named) - the explanation of which is a menstruant, a maidservant, a gentile woman and an unfaithful woman (zonah). And this liability is only rabbinic for an Israelite. But for a man who is a priest, he is liable because of her from Torah writ on account of an unfaithful woman (Temurah 29b); and he is lashed because of her.

And that which they, may their memory be Blessed, said (Niddah 19a) that there are five appearances of blood that the Torah made impure and the rest of the appearances of blood are pure - its content is [that it is] because the Sages knew in their wisdom that every blood that is not of those five appearances is not from an impure place. As there is a specific place in a woman, that only blood which comes from it is impure - it is called the source. And in the language of the Sages, it is called, "the room." And in their days, [since] they were experts in every wisdom, all the women were accustomed to practicing the law of the Torah for menstruation and discharge; such that a zavah would sit [out] for seven clean days, and a menstruant would immerse on the night of the eighth - and even if she was gushing all of the seven - since the blood stopped on the seventh while [it was] still day. And from when the troubles multiplied, the hearts (understanding) of sages and those that know the Torah shrunk and they did not want to rely on their opinions to judge appearances of blood at all. And therefore, now at this time, anyone who has [a spot that has] an appearance that is at all red or an appearance of black - whether it is deep or light, meaning, that it is not deep - is impure. But green and white - even if it is thick - behold, it is pure. And a woman is believed to say, "I saw an appearance like this and I lost it." And if she said [it was] green or white, we render her pure (Niddah 20b).

And when Rebbe arrived and saw that wisdom shrunk in the world, and that the Sages were [no longer] expert in appearances of blood, and that the women were acting in accordance with the law of the Torah, and were counting the days of menstruation for menstruation and the days of discharge for discharge, he was concerned about the thing. [As] sometimes a woman will [experience] blood which is pure [according to] the Torah, but because she will not find a sage who would recognize it, she would be concerned about it [based on] the doubt and sit [out] for it. And if you have her practice the Torah law, behold she will count seven days from that day that she starts [experiencing] the blood, and on the night of the eighth - even if she was gushing all of the seven - if the blood stopped on the seventh, she will immerse in the evening, as we said above. And it will come out that sometimes we would come to a prohibition of excision because of her - as we should be concerned that all of the blood that she [experienced] on the [first] six days was pure blood, and [only that] of the seventh was impure blood. And [so] she began to count the seven days of menstruation from the first day that she [experienced] it, whereas she should have started to count from the seventh, as that is the beginning of her menstruation, since [only] it was impure blood. And from this mistake, she will come to err many times from menstruation to discharge and from discharge to menstruation - that she will figure that she is in the days of menstruation whereas she is [actually] in the days of discharge. Therefore, Rebbe rose and ordained (Niddah 66a) that every woman that [experiences blood] one day, sit [out] six clean days, and likewise if she [experienced] two days, she also sits six clean ones. When she sits six clean days for them, there is no longer any room for doubt: As if both of those days were in the days of menstruation, she will be pure at the end of seven days. And if they are in the days of discharge, there was only a need to wait one day. And even if the first was in the days of discharge

Sefer HaChinukh

and the second was in the days of menstruation, there is no [problem] with this - as behold, she sits after this six clean days, and one of those six clean days counts for that day of discharge. And even though all of them were in the days of menstruation, the law is that days of menstruation in which she does not [experience blood] count for the days of discharge. And if she [experienced blood] three days, he ordained that she sit seven clean days, as we should be concerned that all of the three days are in the days of discharge, and behold she [would be] a big zavah, which requires sitting seven clean [days] from Torah law.

That was the ordinance of Rebbe, and with that ordinance, no doubt in the matter remained. And after that ordinance, the daughters of Israel added [to it] further and were stringent upon themselves (Niddah 66a), such that even if they [experienced] a drop of blood like a mustard seed - meaning to say even with one appearance - they would sit [out] seven clean days, as they did not want to differentiate between [experiencing] blood one or two days, and [experiencing it] three days. And the matter of the stringency about which they were stringent is not on account of the blood being little as a mustard seed, as from the law of the Torah, there is no distinction between a little blood and much blood - as she always needs to sit seven consecutive days [regardless], as we said. [Rather,] the stringency is that they made themselves to be like a zavah even with one appearance. And this stringency that they took upon themselves is mentioned in many place in the Talmud; and it appears from this that the Sages saw their stringency as good and needed, and they conceded to the words of [the Daughters of Israel].

And it comes out that all women today are like a big zavah and need to count seven clean days, even with one appearance; and likewise, any woman that found a [blood] stain in a place that it is fitting to be concerned about it. Even though stains are rabbinic (Niddah 58b) - as from Torah writ, a woman does not become impure until she feels impure blood herself, as it is stated (Leviticus 15:19), "blood flowing in her flesh," meaning that that she feels the impure blood in herself - nonetheless, the Sages were already stringent about stains and required the counting of seven [clean days] and a break of purity (hefsek tahara) for them. And therefore, if she found a stain of the size that forbids in a place that it is fitting to be concerned about it, she also needs to sit seven clean days for it. And from when does a woman count her seven clean days? From the morrow of the day that the blood stopped completely. How is this? If she [experienced blood] for two or three days, she checks herself constantly. If the blood stopped on the second day or on the third day - even in the morning - she does not count her seven from that day in which the blood stopped, but rather she checks herself another time on the morrow and begins to count seven from that day. And what are these words speaking about? When she [experienced blood] two days or three or more. But if she only [experienced it] one day - even though she checked herself on that day and she had a break of purity, she does not count from the next day. As there is an assumption that the first day will be completely impure and the source is assumed to be open that whole day, and [so,] we are concerned lest her blood came back to her after her checking, and she was gushing the whole night. And [so] this second day from her [experiencing blood] is not from the number [of clean days]. And even if she checked herself from the evening, we are concerned lest with the removal of her hands [to check], she [experienced blood. This is] except if her hands were between her 'eyes' all of the twilight (bein hashmashot) - meaning to say that she checked herself and left the [checking cloth] inside while it was still day and it stayed there all of the twilight until the night - and she did not find blood on it at all. In such a way, it is possible that we should say that she starts counting from the next day (see Mishneh Torah, Laws of Forbidden Intercourse 6:20).

And we are not so stringent with one who finds a stain to require her a day of a break of purity besides the day upon which she found the stain, as we said about one who [experienced blood] only one day. Rather, certainly since she checked herself after she found the stain and found it pure, she counts seven clean ones besides that day that she found the stain. [This is] meaning to say that she counts her tally from the morrow of the day upon which she found the stain, like the law of a woman who [experienced] blood two or three days, as we said above. From the outset, a woman needs an examination on each and every day of all seven days (Niddah 68b). But ex post facto, if she only checked on the first day - which is the morrow of the day she stopped [bleeding] - and she did not check again, even if several days after the seven passed, she checks herself at the time of immersion; and that is enough for her, as she already had a pause of purity before then. [If] she did not check herself on the first day, but rather only on the day of her stopping alone (the day before the first day), she checks herself on the seventh day; and that is enough for her, and [so] she immerses on the night of the eighth. [If] she did not check herself, neither on the first day nor on the seventh day - even if she checked herself on the night of the eighth - even though she made a pause of purity before then (before the first day), those seven days that passed do not count for her at all. As she did not check during them, not at the beginning and not at the end, and she needs to count seven clean days from the time that she checked. And it is possible that the essence of this matter is because the Torah commanded (Leviticus 15:28), "and she shall count for herself [...] and she shall become pure." And since she did not check - not at the beginning and not at the end - there is no counting here.

And a woman needs to do this examination with cotton, which is called coton in the vernacular, or with clean and soft wool or with an old flax garment that is soft because of its oldness. And they all should be white, so that any appearance of redness be properly recognized upon it (Niddah 17a). And these cloths that she checks with are called, "witnesses," in the Talmud. And when she checks, she needs to insert the witness into all of the holes and cracks that are in that place. And if she found any appearance of red on it afterwards, she is impure. Any examination that is not done like this is not an examination. Even if she inserts the witness into that place, but she did not check in the holes and cracks, it is not a proper examination, as that is only called a wiping - and all the more so does a change of her cloak not count for her as an examination. These seven clean days need to be consecutive, such that impurity not intervene between them. Even if she sat all of the days and she did not [experience blood], but on the seventh day [towards] the evening, she [experienced blood] - behold, this breaks up her whole count, and she needs to count seven consecutive clean days afterwards.

And the laws of the measure of the stain (Niddah 58b), and in which case it is attributed to a stain [from something else] and in which case it is not attributed [to it]. And one who has a wound in that place, if she attributes it to it until the wound heals. And the matter of what is the law of a girl minor who has had intercourse and has blood flow from her (Niddah 64b). And the blood of virginity (breaking the hymen), that the Sages determined to be like menstrual blood (Niddah 65b). And the many laws of the regular times, and the law of separation before her regular time, which is the [menstrual] period - meaning to say that day or that night that she is accustomed to [experiencing blood] upon it - is forbidden for sexual relations. [This is] from that which it is written (Leviticus 15:31), "And you shall separate the Children of Israel from their impurity," and the epalanation came that they should separate from their wives before their regular times. But after the period of the regular time has passed [without blood], they are permitted in sexual relations. And the matter of the distancing from the wife that they, may their memory be Blessed, commanded (Shabbat 11a) regarding the matter of menstruation, in order that a man not stumble in sin - and it is that a man should not eat with his menstruant wife from the same tray, nor pass a thing from his hand to her hand (Shabbat 13a), nor speak to her about things that often cause sin nor similar to these things.

And the matter of their immersion that the Sages required them to immerse at night. And even though the immersion of a zavah is even during the day by Torah writ and they are all today like a zavah; nonetheless the Sages said that the immersion of all of them is at night, because of the dragging of her daughter (who will misconstrue the law), and as the topic is explained in the Gemara (Niddah 67b). And in a place of duress - for example that the gates of the city are closed at night, and similar to this - they permitted to immerse even during the day. But nonetheless, she is forbidden to have sexual relations until the night, lest she [experience blood before then] and break up her whole count; and it [would] come out that he had intercourse with an impure woman - as Scripture made her purity dependent on days and immersion.

And this prohibition is practiced in every place and at all times. And one who transgresses it and volitionally laid with a menstruant is liable excision from when he inserts himself in her; inadvertently he brings a fixed sin-offering. And the son of a menstruant (who was conceived while she was impure), is not called a mamzer, but rather a defective offspring. And we shall elucidate this in the negative commandment of "a mamzer shall not enter" in the Order of Ki Tetseh (Sefer HaChinukh 465), with God's help.

Mitzvah 208

That we should not give from our seed to Molekh: That we should not give some of our sons, to pass them in front of an idol that people would make during the time of the giving of the Torah, the name of which was Molekh; as it is stated (Leviticus 18:21), "And from your seed, you shall not give to pass to Molekh" - meaning some of your seed. And the warning is repeated in a different place, as it is written (Deuteronomy 18:10), "There shall not be found in you, one who passes his son or his daughter in the fire." And so would they do - the father would hand him over to the priests for the sake of the abominations (idols), similar to that which is written about fit offerings (Leviticus 15:14), "and he shall give them to the priest." And it is possible that the priests would do a waving or a presentation in front of the Molekh, and they would give him back to the father afterwards. And they would burn a big fire in front of the Molekh and the father would take his son and pass him through the flame of the fire. And so, did they say in Talmud Yerushalmi Sanhedrin 7:10, "He is not liable until he gives [him] over to the priests and he takes him and passes him through. But the opinion of the rabbi, Rashi, may his memory be Blessed (Rashi on Sanhedrin 64b, s.v. shragah) and Rambam (Mishneh Torah, Laws of Foreign Worship and Customs of the Nations 6:3), may his memory be Blessed, is that he would not burn him, but rather the worship was to pass him through alone. And once he passed him as it was their way of passing, he is liable. And the opinion of Ramban, may his memory be Blessed, (Ramban on Leviticus 18:21) is that he would pass him through the flame until his soul departs - and his proofs are in the commentary to the Pentateuch that he made.

I wrote what I have known above about a hint from the roots of the distancing of idolatry more generally in the Order of Vayishma Yitro (Sefer HaChinukh 26). And the matter of this idolatry of Molekh [is that] since it was an extremely bad worship and [its followers] were very fervent at that time, a warning (negative commandment) was specified about it, besides all of the many warnings about idolatry in the Torah. And this is said according to the opinion of Rambam, may his memory be Blessed. But according to what appears is the opinion of Ramban, may his memory be Blessed, (Ramban on Leviticus 20:5) we do not require this; since he reasons that there is a novel matter in this worship of Molekh [compared to] all of the other idolatries. As with any [other] idolatry, he is only liable if it is not its way [of worship] except for the four well-known [ways] of worship. But in this style of Molekh, one is liable who does this act of Molekh with any idolatry. And therefore, a warning was specified for it. And because the matter was extremely ugly, the Torah was so strict with it, to make one liable for it with any idolatry, even it is not its way with this. This is what appears from the sum of his words. And [regarding] this matter (see Sefer Mitzvot Gadol, Negative Commandments 40) that the liability only comes with some of the seed and not with all of it, it is possible that it was because the lying priests would promise the father of the child that through the sacrifice of this child, the rest of his seed would succeed in everything to which they would turn, and blessing and good be found in his home. And from their great trickery, they did not want to fix the law at first except for one who would have seed remain besides the one that he gives to them, lest they refuse to listen to them - whether to completely burn him or whether to pass him through the flame, according to the opinion of some of the commentators; and in order that they could also promise blessing and good to those remaining; and from this, the fools could be deceived. And therefore, the Torah only made liable in the matter, just when it was similar to their worship, and not in any other way.

From the laws of the commandment is that which they, may their memory be Blessed, said (Sanhedrin 64a), "[If] he gave over but did not pass, passed but did not give over, he is exempt"; that he is not liable until he passes part of his seed and leaves some of it, as we said; that he is liable whether with his fit seed, or whether with his disqualified seed; and that he is liable for all of those that 'come out of his thigh' - sons or daughters, whether children or grandchildren, forever. But if he passes his brothers or sisters or fathers or passed himself, he is exempt. And the rest of its details are in the seventh chapter of Sanhedrin (see Tur, Even HaEzer 86).

And it is practiced in every place and at all times by males and females (Sifra, Kedoshim, Section 4:1). And one who transgresses this negative commandment volitionally and there are witnesses and a warning is stoned at the time that we judge capital cases. And if there are no witnesses and warning, he is liable for excision. And when inadvertent, he is obligated to bring a fixed sin-offering. And I have already written above in the Order of Vayishma Yitro (Sefer HaChinukh 26) that the prohibition of idolatry is upon all people of the world, more generally.

Mitzvah 209
[For a man] to not have intercourse with males: To not have intercourse with males, as it is stated (Leviticus 18:22), "And with a male you shall not lay, the layings of a woman." And Rambam, may his memory be Blessed, wrote (Sefer HaMitzvot, Mitzvot Lo Taase 350), "And this negative commandment about this very matter is repeated in another place, as it is written (Deuteronomy 23:18), 'and there shall not be a kadesh from the Children of Israel.'" It appears that the rabbi, may his memory be Blessed, does not agree with that which Onkelos translated (Onkelos on Deuteronomy 21:18), "and a man of the Children of Israel shall not marry a woman maidservant" - the understanding of which is a Canaanite (gentile) maidservant. Rather, his opinion is that "there shall not be a kadesh" only comes as additional negative commandments for male homosexuality, [just] as there are several [other] warnings (negative commandments) that are repeated with different words. And I have seen about Ramban, may his memory be Blessed, (Ramban on Deuteronomy 21:18) that he also does not agree with the translation, but would say that the negative commandment of "there shall not be a kadesh " comes to warn that we not allow there to be among us - the holy nation - a kadesh ; and that is a man who is designated to lay with men, as is known about them in the lands of the Yishmaelites to this day. And because of this, it is stated "from the Children of Israel" - since we are not warned from this with the [other] nations. As if there was a kadesh from the nations - and even amongst us - we are not warned about him; as we are not warned (commanded) about others besides us, except for idolatry alone.

And let it not be difficult to you [that], if so that we do not say like the words of the translator (Onkelos) - from which verse do we learn the negative commandment of marrying a maidservant? And lest you say, from that which is written (Deuteronomy 7:3), "Do not get married with them" - that is not [correct], as behold, it is explained in the Gemara that this is coming [specifically] for the seven [Canaanite] nations, and about them is it written. And [it is speaking about] specifically in their conversion; as in their gentileness, the expression, "marriage," is not applicable - and as we will write with God's help in its place, in the Order of Ve'etchanan (Sefer HaChinukh 427). But it is possible to say that we learn the prohibition of a maidservant as included in the prohibition of all the nations that are not Israelites, that it is prohibited to cling to them. And [it is] like the Sages expounded (Kiddushin 68b) from that which is written (Deuteronomy 7:4), "For they will remove your son from after Me" - to include all who remove. And likewise, a Canaanite maidservant is included in those who remove, since she is not a full Israelite; as behold, there are some commandments about which she is not obligated. And those are the ones in the section of the Torah in which it is explicitly written, "Speak to the Children of Israel" (e. g. Leviticus 18:2), to exclude anyone who is not from the Children of Israel, as it is explained in the Gemara in a few places. And with this, they are included in those that remove.

It comes out according to our words that the explanation of the translator of Aramaic (it should say, is true) that there is a negative commandment with a maidservant, except that we learn it from another place. And [regarding that which] Ramban, may his memory be Blessed considers the negative commandment of "there shall not be a kadesh," that we not allow there to be among us a man who is designated for licentiousness in the manner of the Yishmaelites, as we said - there is no negative commandment about this for Rambam, may his memory be Blessed. And hence he wrote that this verse only came to strengthen the warning not to have intercourse with males, as we wrote. And this is his language that he wrote about this matter: "And this is the true opinion, that this negative commandment is repeated for strengthening; not so there be a warning (separate negative commandment) for the one laid with - as we learn the warning for the one laying and the one laid with, from its stating, 'you shall not lay.' And it is elucidated in the Gemara Sanhedrin 54b that Rabbi Yishmael is the one that puts 'there shall not be a kadesh,' as a warning for the one laid with. And according to his opinion, [a man] who has intercourse with a male and brings a male upon him in one [period of lack of] knowledge, he is liable two [sin-offerings]. But Rabbi Akiva says, 'He does not need two. Behold it states, "And with a male you shall not lay (tishkhav), the layings of a woman" - read it as be laid (tishakhev).' And hence for him, one who has intercourse with a male and brings a male upon him in one [period of lack of] knowledge is only liable one. And he said in this reasoning, '"You shall not lay" is [all] one.'" To here [are his words].

It is from the roots of the commandment [that it is] because God, Blessed be He, desired the settling of His world that He created. And therefore, He commanded that [men] not destroy their seed with male homosexuality. As it is truly destruction, since there is neither [reproductive] benefit, nor a commandment of [a wife's] appointed time - besides that the matter of this craziness is disgusting and ugly to anyone with intelligence. And it is not fitting for a man who is born for the service of his Creator to become distorted (some have the textual variant, to become repulsive) with these ugly acts. And from this root, they, may their memory be Blessed, said (Sanhedrin 76b) that it is forbidden to marry a woman to a minor, as it is similar to licentiousness; and so [too,] that a man not marry an elderly woman nor a sterile woman that is not [able] to give birth (see Yevamot 68b).

From the laws of the commandment is that which they, may their memory be Blessed, said (Sanhedrin 54a) that [in a case of a man] who has intercourse with a male or brings a male upon him, both of them are stoned, if they are both adults. But if one is an adult and one is a minor less that nine years old and a day, they are both exempt from Torah writ - but we strike the adult with rabbinic lashes of rebellion. And if the one was a minor who did not reach the category of thirteen yeas and a day, but he is nonetheless nine years and a day and up, the adult is stoned - whether he had intercourse with him or brought him upon himself - and the minor is exempt from Torah writ, but we strike him [with rabbinic lashes] (see Mishneh Torah, Laws of Theft 1:10). And it is one if he had intercourse with a male or with a hermaphrodite [anally], he is liable; but [vaginally], he is exempt (Yevamot 83b) from Torah writ, but we strike him [with rabbinic lashes]. About a tumtum (one whose sexual organ is covered by flesh), there is a doubt, and he is therefore forbidden rabbinically (see Mishneh Torah, Laws of Forbidden Foods 5:8). But it is permitted for a hermaphrodite to marry a woman. And because of the concern for homosexuality, they, may their memory be Blessed, forbade (Avodah Zarah 15b) to give over an Israelite child to a gentile to teach him a book or a craft - as they are all suspect about homosexuality. And the place of the rest of its details is written at the end of the Order. And this prohibition is practiced in every place and at all times. And one who transgresses it is liable for stoning once he inserts himself - meaning to say [even if] he only inserts the tip of the corona, as we have said. And if there are no witnesses and warning, he is liable for excision when volitional; when inadvertent, he is obligated to bring a sin-offering. And this is from the sexual prohibitions that all the people of the world - whether Israelites or all the other nations - are commanded more generally. And Rambam, may his memory be Blessed, wrote (Mishneh Torah, Laws of Forbidden Intercourse 14:18) that he saw himself that even Canaanite (gentile) slaves are included in this prohibition of the male and are killed for it. Even though they are not included in the prohibition of the sexual prohibitions of relatives - as they are even permitted with their mothers and their sisters - since they have left the category of [gentiles] and not entered the category of Israelites; nonetheless, they are forbidden. And likewise, the prohibition of [bestiality] is forbidden to all men.

Mitzvah 210

To not lay with a beast: To not lay with a beast - whether the man had intercourse with the beast or brought the beast upon himself, it is all included (Sanhedrin 54b); and also included in beast is a [wild] animal - as it is stated (Leviticus 18:23), "And to any beast you shall not give your laying."

It is from the roots of the commandment that God, Blessed be He, desired that all the species that He created in His world make offspring according to their species and like it appears in Scripture at the beginning of the Creation, such that it is written with each and every species, "according to its species." And since it is His will like this, blessing and greatness will not be found in that which is the opposite - as is known to us with mules that come from a mixture of two species, that they do not become fruitful and multiply. And so [too,] any tree that is grafted from two species will not be successful to make fruit like it. And all the more so with man - who is select from all of the species - is it not fitting to mix with a species of low and inferior beasts.

From the laws of the commandment is that which they, may their memory be Blessed, explained (Sanhedrin 54b) that there is no distinction between a large beast and a small [one], as it is stated, "And to any beast" - meaning to say, even on the day of its birth. And there is no difference whether he has intercourse with it in its way, or not in its way. In any fashion, once he has inserted himself in it - meaning to say, when he inserted the tip of the corona - or the beast inserted itself into him, they are both stoned, he and it. [This is] if he is an adult - meaning to say he has reached the category of punishments - and he was volitional. But if inadvertent, the animal is not stoned. And if he is from nine years old and a day and up, the animal is stoned, but he is exempt until he reaches the category of punishments, but it is nonetheless fitting to chastise him. However, if he is less than nine years and a day, even the animal is not stoned because of him. And we will write the place of all the rest of its details at the end of the Order, with God's help.

And this prohibition is forbidden in every place and at all times. And one who transgresses it volitionally and there are witnesses and a warning is stoned, as we have said; but if there are no witnesses, it is [punishable] with excision. And if inadvertent, he is obligated to bring a fixed sin offering at the time of the [Temple].

Mitzvah 211

That women not lay with the beasts: That women not lay with the beasts, as it is stated (Leviticus 18:23), "and a woman shall not stand in front of a beast to mate with it." And Rambam, may his memory be Blessed, wrote (Sefer HaMitzvot, Mitzvot Lo Taase 349) that this a commandment on its own in the tally of the commandments and it is not subsumed in the commandment before it. As the prohibition of the male to have intercourse with the beast and the prohibition of the woman to not bring the beast upon herself are two distinct prohibitions. And were it not for the negative commandment that came explicitly about [the women], we would not have learned this one from that one. And he brought a proof from that which they, may their memory be Blessed, said in the first chapter of Keritot 2a, "There are thirty-six excisions in the Torah," and they enumerated them. And they counted among them [a man] who has intercourse with a beast as one, and the woman who brings a beast upon herself as another, even as they were [only] counting the main categories of things there. The root of this commandment is included with the one before it.

From the laws of the commandment is that which they, may their memory be Blessed, said (Sanhedrin 55a) that an adult woman - meaning to say that she has reached the category of punishments, which is twelve years and a day - that brought a beast upon herself, whether large or small; once it has inserted itself in her - whether in her [conventional] way or not in her way - they are both stoned, the beast and her. And if the woman is a minor - meaning, less than twelve years and a day - the animal is stoned and she is exempt, but it is fitting to chastise her. However, if she is less than three years and a day, even the animal is not stoned because of her. And the rest of its details [together] with the details of all of the sexual prohibitions that are written in this Order - whether the matter of their prohibitions and their distinctions, or whether the distinctions of the judgments of their transgressors - it is all in Tractate Sanhedrin and Tractate Keritot and in [some] places in Yevamot, Ketuvot and Kiddushin.

And Rambam, may his memory be Blessed, wrote (Sefer HaMitzvot, Mitzvot Lo Taase 352) that excision came from the Torah with a clear language about these sexual prohibitions that we wrote are with excision (karet, literally, cutting off). And it is like the verse stated after their enumeration (Leviticus 18:29), "For all who do from all of these abominations shall be cut off from their people." And likewise, that which we have written about them that one who transgresses them is liable for the death penalty of the court, is likewise the language of the Torah. However, the variation of the death penalty and our saying about some of them, stoning, about some of them, strangulation, and about some of them, burning - some of them are from Scripture and some are through tradition. And [with]

Sefer HaChinukh

all of the sexual prohibitions, in all of them in which one was an adult and the other a minor, the adult is liable and the child is exempt, as we said above. And likewise, if they were both adults, but one was sleeping, the one sleeping is exempt - even though it is possible that he had a little pleasure when he was still sleeping. And with all of the sexual prohibitions - and so [too,] with all of the sins that a liability of the court comes upon them - there needs to be two or more fit witnesses there, warning the transgressor and seeing him violate the transgression with their [own] eyes (see Sanhedrin 37a). And nonetheless regarding the matter of the sexual prohibitions, our Sages have instructed us (Makkot 7a) that there is no need for the witnesses to see the matter of adultery completely - meaning to say that they see the evil act like a brush in a tube. Rather, from when they see them [acting] like adulterers - meaning to say like the way of all those having intercourse - behold, they are killed with this sight. And we do not say, maybe he did not insert [himself] - as the assumption of this position is that he inserted. And they, may their memory be Blessed, also said (Kiddushin 80a) about this matter that anyone who is assumed to be from the same flesh is killed according to [that] assumption - even though there is no clear proof about the relation besides the assumption alone. [This means] that people say x is the son of y or the brother of z or her father. And we lash, burn, stone and strangulate [based] on this assumption.

And this prohibition is in every place and at all times. And one who transgresses it and brings a beast upon herself is liable for stoning for it, as we said. And if there were no witnesses and a warning, she is [punished] with excision; and when inadvertent, she is obligated to bring a fixed sin-offering. And we have already said that in all [cases] of inadvertence, the beast is not stoned. And even though they, may their memory be Blessed, said (Sanhedrin 55a) as the reason for stoning the beast, [that it is] so that people not say, "This is [the beast] that x stumbled with"; that is only said when volitional, as that is the big stumbling. But there is a bit of accidentality in inadvertence.

It comes out according to our words that the only prohibition for the [gentiles] on account of sexual prohibition is the mother, the wife of the father, the sister from the mother, a married woman - as we wrote in the Order of Vayishma Yitro (Sefer HaChinukh 35) - a male and a beast. And slaves are not included in the sexual prohibitions of relationship, and are permitted even with their mothers and their sisters - and as we wrote above (Sefer HaChinukh 209) - since they have already left the category of [gentiles] but have not come into the category of Israelites.

And they, may their memory be Blessed, said further as a reason for this (Yevamot 62b) that a Canaanite slave does not have relationship - meaning to say that behold, he is like a beast in this matter. And Scripture indicates this, from that which it is written (Genesis 22:5), "Sit here with (eem) the donkey" - and they, may their memory be Blessed, expounded, "A people (am, which is spelled the same way as eem) similar to a donkey"; and they were the slaves of Avraham, our father. And nonetheless, they are [included] in the prohibition of males and beasts, according to the opinion of Rambam, may his memory be Blessed. And the reason is correct; as about this, it is not applicable to say [that] he has no relationship. And they are also forbidden from having intercourse with the married woman of an Israelite; as also about them is it not applicable to say [that] he has no relationship. And they are likewise forbidden with a menstruant, and even [in the case of] a maidservant - as [the latter] are liable for all of the punishments in the Torah. And explicitly did they, may their memory be Blessed, expound (Sifra, Metzora Parashat Zavim, Section 5:1), "'And when a woman discharges' (Leviticus 15:19) - whether an Israelitess or whether a maidservant; whether a convert or a freed [maidservant]."

And they, may their memory be Blessed, said (Yevamot 22a) that if someone from the [other] nations convert - and likewise, if a slave is freed - behold, they are like a newborn child. And all of the relationship of flesh that he had from the beginning in their being gentiles are no [longer] their flesh relatives at all and they are permitted to marry them - even their mother or their sister. That is from Torah writ. But the Sages forbade the thing, so that [people] not say that they came from a stringent holiness to a light holiness. And they ordained the thing like this: That if he was married to his mother or to his sister when he was a [gentile] or a slave, they would separate them - since these were forbidden even in [being a gentile]. But if he was married to the other sexual prohibitions and they converted, they would not separate them; as there is no concern here that they will say, etc. - as behold the rest of the sexual prohibitions were permitted to them in their being [gentiles]. And from this reason, they, may their memory be Blessed, only decreed with the relatives of the mother, but not with the relatives of the father. And therefore, they, may their memory be Blessed, said (Yevamot 97b) that it is permitted for a convert to marry his daughter who converted; and likewise the wife of his brother from his father but not from his mother; and he is likewise permitted with the wife of his son. And it is permitted for him to marry two sisters from the father, but not from the mother. And so [too,] with all the secondary [prohibitions], they did not decree them for converts. And behold, slaves that were freed are like converts, and everything that is permitted to [the latter] is permitted to [the former]. And the same is the law with prohibition.

Mitzvah 212

The commandment of the reverence of father and mother: To be in reverence from parents - meaning to say that a person act with his mother and his father as he would with someone for whom he has reverence, as it is stated (Leviticus 19:3), "His mother and father shall a man revere." And the language of Sifra, Kedoshim, Section 1:10 (also Kiddushin 31b) is "Which is reverence? He shall not sit in his place, and he shall not speak in his place, and he shall not contradict his words."

I have written from the roots of the commandment on the commandment of honoring parents in Parshat Vayishma Yitro (Sefer HaChinukh 33).

From the laws of the commandment is that which they, may their memory be Blessed, said (Kiddushin 31a). "To what point is the reverence of father and mother? That even if they strike him and they spit in his face, he does not embarrass them." And even so, the sages commanded (Moed Katan 17a) a person not to strike his adult son, since there is in the thing [a possible violation of], "do not put a stumbling block in front of the blind" (Sefer HaChinukh 232) - (lest he kick his father, and it will be he that made him stumble - Rashi there). And we excommunicate someone for that. And they, may their memory be Blessed, said (Kiddushin 31b) about the stringency of this commandment that even if the father or mother lose their mind, the son must make efforts to behave in a way of honor towards them, according to their perception. But if they become extremely insane, he is able to leave them and command others over them to treat them as is fit, if he has [this possibility]. And a mamzer is obligated in the honor of parents and their reverence (Yevamot 22b), even though they are exempted from the statute of hitting them or cursing them. And they, may their memory be Blessed, taught us about this matter (Bava Metzia 32a) that if the parents command to transgress words of Torah - and even a rabbinic commandment - we do not listen to them. [These] and the rest of its details are in [sactered] places in the Gemara, but the most are in Kiddushin, according to my opinion (see Tur, Yoreh Deah 240).

And it is practiced in every place and at all times by males and females. And [if] he transgresses it and treats their reverence lightly, he has violated this positive commandment; unless he does it with the agreement of his father and his relinquishment - as the honor of a father who relinquishes it, is relinquished (it is effective).

Mitzvah 213

To not turn after the worship of idols - not in thought, not in speech and not in vision to not turn after idolatry with thought or speech and not even only with sight; so that he not come from this to serve it, as it is stated (Leviticus 19:4), "You shall not turn to the idols." And they, may their memory be Blessed, said in Sifra, Kedoshim, Section 1:11, "If you turn after them, you make them gods"; meaning to say, if you involve yourself with their matters - meaning to ponder after the follies that those that believe in them say about it, that constellation x or star y does this action, and so [too,] incense x or service y; or you constantly observe the forms that their worshipers make in order to know the manner of its worship. All of this [can cause] you to be seduced after it and that you would worship it.

And explicitly is it stated there in Sifra, Kedoshim, Section 1:10 that even observing alone is prohibited - as they said there, "Rabbi Yehudah says, 'Do not turn, to see them.'" And the matter is from the reason that we said, which is that it causes [one] to see it and to stray after it. And also, so that he not wastes a portion of [his] time and be involved in these vanities, whereas man is only created to be involved in the service of his Creator. And this is what they, may their memory be Blessed, said in Shabbat 149a in the chapter [entitled] Shoel Adam Mechavero, "And [regarding] an image itself, even on a weekday it is prohibited to stare at it, because it is stated, 'You shall not turn to the idols.' What is the inference? Rabbi Yochanan said, '"Do not remove God (Al tefannu El " a play on the words of the verse) out of your minds.'"

And this negative commandment - meaning, the prohibition of thought about idolatry - is repeated in another place, as it is stated (Deuteronomy 11:16), "Guard yourselves, lest your hearts be seduced and you serve, etc." [This is] meaning to say that if your heart spends much time in thinking about it, it will be a cause to divert you from the straight path and to be involved in its service. And it is also stated about this matter (Deuteronomy 4:19), "And lest you lift your eyes to the heavens and see, etc." As the content [of this verse] is not that a man not lift up his eyes to the sky and observe the heavens, but [rather] the intention of the thing is that he not observe them with his heart's eye - to know their power and their makeup in order to serve them. And [it is] like it is stated in another place (Deuteronomy 12:30), "and lest you inquire of their gods, saying, 'How do these nations serve their gods, and I will do so, me too, etc.'" The verse prevents us from asking about the manner of their worship, since all of this is a cause to err about it.

The root of distancing ourselves from idolatry is well-known to every man.

The laws of the commandment and its details are elucidated in many scattered places in the Gemara, such that they, may their memory be Blessed, warned us about it, not to ponder thoughts of idolatry (i.e. Berakhot 12b); and they, may their memory be Blessed, said that it is not only the thought of idolatry that is forbidden, but rather any thought that causes a person to uproot something from the Torah. And Scripture prohibited this explicitly, as it is written (Numbers 15:39), "and you shall not stray after your hearts." And they may their memories be Blessed, said (Kiddushin 40a) that for Israel, the Holy One, Blessed be He, does not consider a thought of sin to be like the act - except for the thought of idolatry, which is considered for a man to be like the act (see Mishneh Torah, Laws of Foreign Worship and Customs of the Nations 2).

And this prohibition is practiced in every place and at all times by males and females. And one who transgresses it and turns after idolatry in a way that there be an act [involved] with it, is lashed (see Mishneh Torah, Laws of The Sanhedrin and the Penalties within their Jurisdiction 19:4).

Mitzvah 214
To not make [idols] not for himself and not for those besides him: To not make [idols] for one that will worship it, not for himself and not for those besides him, and even if the one who orders that it be made is an idolater - as it is stated (Leviticus 19:4), "and molten gods do not make for yourselves." And they, may their memory be Blessed, said in Sifra, Kedoshim, Section 1:12, even for others. And there is it said, "One who makes [an idol] for himself, transgresses on account of two warnings" - meaning to say, on account of "do not make," and on account of "for yourselves, etc."

The root of distancing ourselves from idolatry is well-known.

Its laws are, for example, that which they, may their memory be Blessed, said (Mishneh Torah, Laws of Foreign Worship and Customs of the Nations 7:4; Avodah Zarah 51b), "What is [the difference] between [an idol] of an Israelite and [the idol] of a gentile? The [idol] of a gentile is immediately forbidden to benefit from, as it is stated (Deuteronomy 7:25), 'The statues of their gods shall you burn with fire, etc.' - from when they became statues, it becomes a god for him. But for the Israelite, it does not become forbidden to benefit from until it is worshiped, as it is stated (Deuteronomy 27:15), 'and places [it] secretly' - until he does things to it secretly, which are its worship. But the auxiliaries of idolatry - whether of a gentile or whether of an Israelite are not forbidden until they use them for idolatry. And the wage of the one who makes [the idol] is permissible, even though he is lashed - and even if he makes it for a gentile, such that it is forbidden when it is finished even before it is worshiped. Nonetheless, it is not forbidden until it is finished, and the last hammer-blow is not worth the value of a small coin (such that all the tangible value was invested before it was forbidden)." [These] and the rest of its many details are in Tractate Avodah Zarah (see Tur, Yoreh Deah 141).

And this prohibition is practiced in every place and at all times by males and females. And one who transgresses it and makes an [idol] for someone else - whether he made it for a gentile or an Israelite - is lashed one [set of lashes]. And if he made it for himself, he is lashed two [sets], as we have said. And both of them are because of the manufacture with the intention of worship, alone - even though he did not worship it.

Mitzvah 215
To not eat notar: To not eat notar - and that is what remains from the meat of consecrated animals, from a sacrifice that was brought according to its commanded [specifications] after the time that it is fit to eat from it, as it is stated about the inauguratory sacrifices (Exodus 29:33), "it shall not be eaten, they are holy." And the explanation came about this (Meilah 17b), "[It refers to] anything that is consecrated [that is] disqualified, to give a negative commandment on its eating." And this is hinted to by the verse, in its stating, "they are holy": This third person, which is "they," includes all that which is disqualified of the consecrated animals. But we should not learn from this that notar and pigul (sacrifices disqualified by the wrong thought) are considered one negative commandment, as they are two topics - as I have written above on the prohibition of pigul in the Order of Tsav (Sefer HaChinukh 144). And we found about them that two [different] verses came concerning the punishments, as it is written (Leviticus 7:18), "And if it is surely eaten, etc."; and it is written, after it, "and the soul that eats it will carry its iniquity" - and this carrying of iniquity is excision, as we learn from a comparison with notar. As here, it is written concerning notar (Leviticus 19:6-8), "and that which remains to the third day[...] is piggul, it is not acceptable. And one who eats them will carry his iniquity, since he profaned the holy of God, and excised, etc." And hence, even if the warning for both of them is from one verse, it is not made impossible because of this to consider them two [separate] negative commandments. And so did they say in Meilah 17b, " Pigul and notar do not combine because they are two topics, etc." - as it is explained there that there are things that do not combine and there are things that combine.
I have written what I have known about the roots of the matter in the prohibition of pigul.
From the laws of notar is that which they, may their memory be Blessed, said (Zevachim 35a) [that if one] ate from the skin, from the gravy, from the spice, from the remnants of meat stuck to the skin, from the crop, from the sinews, from the horns, from the hooves, from the nails, from the beak, from the eggs of the bird and from its feather, he is not liable for excision. And so [too,] with blood (Zevachim 45b), one is not liable on account of notar; and so [too,] with the frankincense, the incense and the wood, as we wrote about pigul. But [if he ate] from the embryo or from the placenta, he is liable for excision. And so [too,] what they said (Zevachim 45a) that consecrated animals of the gentiles - meaning to say vows and pledges that we accept from them - do not have [liability] on account of notar and pigul. [These] and the rest of the details of the prohibition of notar - and also of pigul - are elucidated in many places in the Order of Kodashim (see Mishneh Torah, Laws of Sacrifices Rendered Unfit 1).
And this prohibition is practiced at the time of the [Temple] by males and females. And one who transgresses it and eats a kazayit of notar volitionally is liable for excision; and he is obligated to bring a fixed sin-offering, if inadvertent. And so [too,] is the law if he ate a kazayit of notar and pigul in combination - since with regards to eating, they combine (see Meilah 17b).

Mitzvah 216
To leave over the corner of the field: To leave over a corner from the produce, as it is stated (Leviticus 19:10), "to the poor and to the stranger shall you leave them," after it mentioned, "you shall not finish the corner of your field" (Leviticus 19:9). And the understanding of stranger [here] is a righteous convert (see Sifra Kedoshim 3:4). And so [too], any "stranger" stated in [the context of] gifts to the poor - as behold, it is written about the second tithe (Deuteronomy 26:12), "to the stranger, to the orphan and to the widow." And that is certainly the righteous convert - when undifferentiated - as its witnesses (the orphan and the widow) are by its side. And the same is the case for all of the gifts to the poor. And nonetheless they, may their memory be Blessed, said (Gittin 59b) that we do

not prevent them from the poor of the idolaters, due to the ways of peace. And the content of the corner, is that a person leaves a little of his produce at the end of his field at the time that he reaps. And there is no measure to this remnant by Torah writ, but the Sages gave a measurement to the thing
(Mishnah Peah 1:2), and it is one in sixty parts.

It is from the roots of the commandment that God, Blessed be He, wanted that His people that He chose be crowned with every good and dear trait and that they would have a Blessed soul and a generous spirit. And I have already written (Sefer HaChinukh 16) that through the actions is the soul acted upon and it become good and the blessing of God descend upon it. And there is no doubt that when a man leaves a portion of his fruits in his field and he abandons them so that those in need should benefit from it, he shows about himself a satisfied will and a correct and Blessed spirit, and that God, may He be Blessed, has satiated him with His good, 'and his soul will also recline in the good.' But the one who gathers it all into his home and does not leave over blessing that the destitute - who saw the field in its fullness and had a desire to fill themselves with it, because they were hungry - not benefit from it, shows, without a doubt, about himself an evil heart and a bad spirit and evil will come to him. And it is like they, may their memory be Blessed, said (Sotah 8b), "In the measure that a person measures, so will he be measured." And this matter will suffice for us on the level of its simple understanding also for gleanings, forgotten sheaves, fallen grapes of the vineyard and bunchless grapes.

From the laws of the commandment is, for example, that which they, may their memory be Blessed, said (Chullin 137a) that it is one, whether he is a harvester (cutter) or a plucker, he is liable for the corner - and even though the verse stated, "In your harvesting," [it is] not specifically [about] a harvester. And if he transgressed and harvested everything (Bava Kamma 94a), he gives a little of the harvested [produce] to the poor. And that which they, may their memory be Blessed, said (Chullin 131a) that there is no [right] for the owners to benefit [by choosing who receives] the favor, but rather [the poor can] take it against their will. And the law of from when is any person permitted to them. And that which they, may their memory be Blessed, said (Chullin 134b) that if there are no poor to take the corner, that the owner of the field is permitted to take it; as it is stated, "to the poor and to the stranger," and they, may their memory be Blessed, expounded, "and not to the ravens and to the bats." And they, may their memory be Blessed, gave this general principle about the obligation of the corner, whether from the produce or whether from the trees: Any food that grows from the ground, is guarded, cut all at once and brought in to be preserved - for example produce, legumes, carobs, walnuts, almonds, grapes, olives and that which is similar to them that have these five [characteristics] that we said - is obligated in the corner. But woad and rubia and what is similar to them are exempted because they are not food; and so [too,] truffles and mushrooms are exempted because they are not guarded; and so [too,] figs are not obligated since their cutting is not at once; and so [too] vegetables are exempt, because they are not brought in to be preserved (see Shabbat 68a).

And so [too,] that which they, may their memory be Blessed, said (Talmud Yerushalmi Peah 4:4) that the obligation of the corner is only after the fruits have reached a third [of their ripeness], and that we leave the corner only at the end of the field, so that the poor will know its place (Shabbat 22a). And what is the law of brothers that split a field (Mishnah Peah 3:5), and so [too,] the law of partners that split [it]; the law of one who sells parts of his field to [different] people; the law of [a group of poor people, in which] one poor person says to divide the corner among them and his fellows say to plunder, that we listen to the one - and even against many - since he is saying like the law (Mishnah Peah 4:1); the law of at which times of day we distribute the corner (Mishnah Peah 4:5); the law of a poor man who took a little of the corner and threw [it] on the rest, or he spread his cloak over it [to acquire it] (Mishnah Peah 4:3); the law of poor people standing over the corner, that if [another] poor person came and took it, he acquires it, since a poor person does not acquire gleanings, forgotten sheaves and the corner - nor any person a found coin - until it reaches his hand (see Bava Metzia 118a); so [too] that which they, may their memory be Blessed, said that a man is obligated to add to the corner according to the size of the field, according to the number of the poor and according to the blessing of the seed (crop); and the rest of its details are in the tractate that is built on this, and that is

Sefer HaChinukh

Tractate Peah. And it is practiced by Torah writ by males and females - whether by Israelites, by Levites or by priests - specifically in the Land of Israel and at the time that Israel is there, as with the priestly tithe and the tithes. [This is] according to the opinion of Rambam, may his memory be Blessed (Mishneh Torah, Laws of Heave Offerings 1:26), who said that the priestly tithe and the tithes are only practiced in the Land and specifically at the time that Israel is there, and as we will write with God's help in the Order of Shoftim on the commandment of separating the great priestly tithe (Sefer HaChinukh 507). And rabbinically, it is practiced even outside the Land. And he, may his memory be Blessed, wrote (Mishneh Torah, Laws of Gifts to the Poor 1:14) that it appears to him that the law is the same for the other gifts to the poor, that they are all practiced outside the Land rabbinically. And one who transgresses it and does not leave the corner in the Land at the time that it is in its inhabitation has nullified this positive commandment and is obligated to give the measure of the corner from the [produce] to the poor. And if all of the [produce] is lost or burnt before he gives anything from it to the poor, he is lashed on account of the negative commandment of "you shall not finish the corner of your field, etc." (Sefer HaChinukh 217), since he no longer has anything in his hand with which to fix [his violation of] the negative commandment. But so long as he has from the [produce] in his hand, he gives from them and [becomes] exempt with this; since this negative commandment is a negative commandment that is rectified by a positive commandment - and so [too,] the negative commandment of gleanings (Sefer HaChinukh 219), as it is elucidated in Peah and Makkot (see Tur, Yoreh Deah, 332).

Mitzvah 217

To not finish the corner in the field: Not to harvest all of what is planted, but rather to leave a remnant from it to the poor in the edge of the field, as it is stated (Leviticus 19:9), "you shall not finish the corner of your field in your harvesting." And this negative commandment is rectified by a positive commandment, as it is stated (Leviticus 19:10), "to the poor and to the stranger shall you leave them, etc." - meaning to say, that if he transgressed and harvested all of the field, that he gives the measure of the corner to the poor from that which is harvested. And that is rabbinically one in sixty parts, as they obligated us so; but from the Torah, it has no measure, as we learned in Mishnah Peah 1:1, "These are the things that do not have a measure: the corner, etc."

I have written above what I have known about the roots of the commandment, its laws and all of its content on the positive commandment in this Order (Sefer HaChinukh 216).

Mitzvah 218

To leave the gleanings in the field: To leave the gleanings to the poor - and that is what falls from the sickle at the time of the harvesting, or from the hand at the time of the plucking, as it is stated with the gleanings (Leviticus 19:10), "to the poor and to the stranger shall you leave them."

I have written what I have known from the roots of the commandment on the commandment of the corner (Sefer HaChinukh 216).

From the laws of the commandment is that which they, may their memory be Blessed, said (Mishnah Peah 6:5), "One or two sheaves are gleanings, three are not gleanings" - meaning to say, if three sheaves or more fall together from the hand of the harvester, the three of them [go] to the owner of the field; as the law of gleanings is only with a little, and specifically when the gleanings fell from the harvester without duress (Mishnah Peah 4:10). But if a thorn struck his hand and they fell, this is not gleanings. And [if there] is a doubt [whether they are] gleanings, they are [considered] gleanings; as it is stated (Psalms 82:3), "the poor and destitute shall you justify" - justify from what is yours and give [it] to him. And the law of produce that is found in ant holes (Mishnah Peah 4:10); the law of a sheaf of gleanings that is mixed up in a pile (Mishnah Peah 4:2); and the rest of its details are elucidated in Tractate Peah. And with regards to in which place it is practiced and who is obligated about it and the punishment of one who transgresses it, it is all like the corner.

Mitzvah 219

To not take the sheaves that fall at the time of the harvesting: To not take the sheaves that fall at the time of the harvesting, but [rather] we leave them them for the poor, as it is stated (Leviticus 19:9), "and the gleanings of your harvest you shall not glean." And that is also rectified by a positive commandment, as we have elucidated about the corner (Sefer HaChinukh 217). And all of the content of this commandment you will also find above in the positive commandment of gleanings (Sefer HaChinukh 218).

Mitzvah 220
The commandment of leaving over the corner of the vineyard: To leave over the corner of the vineyard. And this corner of the vineyard, the verse [chose to convey] with the expression of bunchless grapes (ollalot) - meaning to say that we were commanded that we leave over all of the bunchless grapes of the vineyard as the corner. And this is [the meaning of] that which it is written (Leviticus 19:10), "to the poor and to the stranger shall you leave them," after it mentioned, "And [in] your vineyard, you shall not take the bunchless grapes." This is the opinion of Rambam, may his memory be Blessed, about the bunchless grapes of the vineyard, that they are in place of the corner that is with the other trees. And Ramban, may his memory be Blessed, did not explain like this. And I will write the essence of their disagreement at length in the negative commandment of "And [in] your vineyard, you shall not take the bunchless grapes" (Sefer HaChinukh 221). And there I will further explain from where [is] the obligation of the corner with all trees, and all of the matters of the commandment, as is my custom, with God's help.

Mitzvah 221
To not finish the corner of the vineyard: To not finish all of the fruit of the vineyard at the time of the grape harvest, but [rather, one] leaves a corner from them to the poor, as it is stated (Leviticus 19:10), "And [in] your vineyard, you shall not take the bunchless grapes" - this is the corner of the vineyard. So wrote Rambam, may his memory be Blessed. And he said further that, that which is written (Deuteronomy 24:20), "you shall not take from the branchlets after you" with olives, also instructs about the corner of the olive tree. As the corner of the olive trees is called branchlets (porot), and the corner of the vineyard is called bunchless grapes (ollalot). And from the both of them we learn [this] for all the trees. And Ramban, may his memory be Blessed, argued against him about this and said (in his introduction to the details of the commandments) that it is all a mistake. And he said that the negative commandment of "And [in] your vineyard," is unique specifically to the vineyard - and it is that we leave over all of the small grapes in it that do no have a katef or a natef. And the understanding of katef is sprigs one over the other (clusters); [of] natef is that they all hang and descend. And it comes out according to this that the ollalot are the small grapes sometimes found in the vineyard that are called gatimas in the vernacular. And this is certainly a small thing, according to that which we see in our vineyards. And so, did they, may their memory be Blessed say (Mishnah Peah 7:4), "Which are ollalot? All that do not have a katef nor a natef."

And (for Ramban,) besides this obligation of bunchless grapes, there is an obligation upon us to leave over the corner. And with the corner of the vineyard, the verse did not come clearly about it, but rather we learn [by a comparison of the words], "after you," from olives. And [it is] as we say in the Gemara Chullin 131a explicitly, "There are four gifts in the vineyard: the fallen grapes; the bunchless grapes; the forgotten [grapes]; and the corner. [There are] two in the trees: forgotten [fruit]; and the corner." And there, it learns the corner in the vineyard, from that which it is written (Deuteronomy 24:21), "you shall not take the bunchless grapes after you": And Rabbi Levi said, "'After you' is the forgotten [grapes]" - meaning what remains after you, which is the forgotten [grapes]. And the corner we learn [from a comparison of] "after you" [and] "after you" from olives, as it is written about the olive tree (Deuteronomy 24:20), "When you beat your olive tree, you shall not take from the branchlets (tefaer) after you" - and the House of Rabbi Yishmael learned, "That you should not takes its splendor (tiferet) from it" - which is the corner. And Ramban, may his memory be Blessed, learns the corner of all trees from the olive tree - for which the verse explicitly obligated the corner - and from the vineyard, about which we learned it from the expression, "after you." And he, may his memory be Blessed, said that

Rambam, may his memory be Blessed, wrote the matter corrected in his great essay (Mishneh Torah, Laws of Gifts to the Poor 4:17). But there is no addition or subtraction in the tally of the negative commandments implied in this disagreement of theirs. As the disagreement is only that Rambam, may his memory be Blessed, explains "you shall not take the bunchless grapes," [to be] for the corner, whereas Ramban, may his memory be Blessed, explains it literally as bunchless grapes, and learns the corner of the vineyard from the expression, "after you"; as we have written that we learn [by a comparison of the words], "after you," from olives. And this negative commandment is also rectified by a positive commandment - as if he transgressed and finished all [of the grape harvest], he is obligated to give the bunchless grapes to the poor (see Mishneh Torah, Laws of Gifts to the Poor 4). I have written above in this Order on the commandment of the corner (Sefer HaChinukh) a little of the roots of the commandment and its laws. And there, it is written in which place it and all of the other gifts to the poor are practiced, and that the details of the commandment of the corner are elucidated in Tractate Peah. And we still must write here that which they, may their memory be Blessed, said about bunchless grapes (Mishnah Peah 7:7): That if the whole vineyard was bunchless grapes, all of it is for the poor, as it is stated, "And [in] your vineyard, you shall not take the bunchless grapes" - and they, may their memory be Blessed, expounded (Mishnah Peah 7:7), "even all of it [being] bunchless grapes." And [also that] the poor do not have the right to take the bunchless grapes until the owner of the vineyard begins to harvest his vineyard, as it is stated (Deuteronomy 24:21), "When you harvest your vineyard, you shall not take the bunchless grapes."

Mitzvah 222

The commandment of leaving the peret of the vineyard: To leave the peret of the vineyard to the poor. And that is that which separates and falls from the grapes at the time of the grape harvest, as it is stated (Leviticus 19:10), "to the poor and to the stranger shall you leave them," after it mentioned, "and the fallen grapes of your vineyard, you shall not gather."
And I will write all of the matters of the commandment in the negative commandment after this of "do not gather" (Sefer HaChinukh 223), with God's help.

Mitzvah 223

To not gather the peret of the vineyard: To not gather the peret of the vineyard, but [rather] to leave them over to the poor, as it is stated (Leviticus 19:10), "and the peret of your vineyard, you shall not gather." And that is the berries that shed at the time of the reaping of the grapes. And the law is the same for other trees that are similar to a vineyard - that we are obligated not to gather the berries that shed.
A hint of the roots of the commandment is like the matter that I wrote above about the corner (Sefer HaChinukh 216).
From the laws of the commandment is that which they, may their memory be Blessed, said (Mishnah Peah 6:5), "Which is fallen grapes? That is one or two [grapes]" that separate from the cluster at the time of the grape harvest." But three [grapes]" that fell at one time "are not fallen grapes." If he was harvesting and he threw them to the ground, when he removes the clusters, even half of a cluster that is found [all separated] there is fallen grapes; and so [too,] a whole cluster that separated there, behold it is fallen grapes. And [regarding] the one who places his basket under the vine at the time of the grape harvest - behold, this one robs the poor (Mishnah Peah 7:5). [These] and the rest of its details are in Tractate Peah (see Tur, Yoreh Deah 332).
And the content of the commandment, in which place it is practiced and by who - is [all] written above in the commandment of the corner (Sefer HaChinukh 216, 220).

Mitzvah 224

To not steal any money: To not steal any money, as it is stated (Leviticus 19:11), "You shall not steal." And they, may their memory be Blessed, said (Sanhedrin 86a) that this is the warning [about] stealing money. And the content of theft is like I explained in the Order of Mishpatim (Sefer HaChinukh 54).

Sefer HaChinukh

The root of this commandment is well-known, since it is from the commandments obligated by the intellect.

From the laws of the commandment is that which they, may their memory be Blessed, said (Bava Metzia 61b) that it is forbidden from the Torah to steal even in order to return [what was stolen] or in order to vex - meaning to say, to anger the owner of the stolen item, to confound him temporarily, and to give the thing back to him afterwards. And so, did they say in Sifra Kedoshim, Section 2:1-2, "Because it is written [with respect to] theft (Exodus 22:3), 'he shall pay double,' we know the punishment. From where is the warning? [Hence,] we learn to say, 'You shall not steal.' 'You shall not steal,' even in order to vex'; 'You shall not steal,' even in order to pay four or five [times the price]."

And [also] the laws of one who steals a sela from the purse of his friend or from his house and returned the stolen thing to its place with the owner's knowledge or without the owner's knowledge, and in what way [the owner's] count (inventory) exempts him; and the difference there is in this matter between something that has life such as beasts, and something that does not have life, and as it appears in Bava Kamma 118a in the tenth chapter. And [also] that which they said that it is forbidden to purchase from the hand of a thief, since it strengthens the hand of sinners; and so [too,] is it forbidden to buy anything that is assumed to be stolen. And therefore they, may their memory be Blessed, said that we do not buy wool, milk and goats from shepherds; and so [too], we do not buy from the guardians of wood or fruit, except in places that are known (public); and so [too,] we only buy objects that are known [to usually be sold by them] from women, slaves and minors. And more generally, they said that it is forbidden to buy from any of them that say, "Cover them."

And [also] that which they said (Bava Kamma 115a) that they did not make the Ordinance of the Marketplace for a famous thief, and [so,] one who buys from him returns the vessel [to the original owner] and [takes] the thief [to court]; but if he is not famous, there is the Ordinance of the Marketplace for him, and [so,] the owner of the stolen item returns the money to the purchaser and he takes his vessels, and afterwards [the owner takes] the thief [to court]. And Rambam, may his memory be Blessed, wrote (Mishneh Torah, Laws of Theft 1:1) and this is his language: "Anyone who steals from the value of a small coin and upwards transgresses a negative commandment, as it is written, 'You shall not steal.' And we do not administer lashes for this negative commandment, since it is given to repayment. And it is one if he steals the money of an Israelite or steals the money of a gentile, if he steals the money of an adult or steals the money of a child." To here [are his words]. And the rest of its details are in the tenth chapter of [Bava] Kamma and in other places (see Tur, Choshen Mishpat, 348).

And this prohibition is practiced in every place and at all times by males and females. And one who transgresses this negative commandment is obligated to pay, as is explicit in Scripture (Exodus 21:37, 22:3). If he stole a gold coin or clothing or a donkey or a camel, he pays twice their value, and it comes out that he loses that which he sought to remove from his fellow. And payments of double are practiced for everything except for an ox and a sheep, as there are situations in which he pays four and five for them - such as if he slaughtered or sold [them], as appears clearly in Scripture. And when he pays double - or four or five for an ox and a sheep - it is specifically when witnesses testified about him, and he paid according to their [testimony] in a court. But one who admits on his own (Bava Kamma 75a) is exempted with the payment of the principal alone, as it is stated (Exodus 22:8), "the one that the powers deem guilty shall pay two" - and they, may their memory be Blessed, expounded (Bava Kamma 64b), "To exclude one who deems himself guilty." And this is the law for all penalties, that one who admits [his guilt] is exempt. And I have already written above (Sefer HaChinukh 49) that we only judge cases of penalties in the Land.

Mitzvah 225

That we do not disavow money that is in our hand from another: That we not disavow that which is deposited into our hand, and about anything that is to us of someone else's, as it is stated (Leviticus 19:11), "you shall not disavow." And the explanation came (Shevuot 37b) that the verse is referring to money. And the language of Sifra, Kedoshim, Section 2:3 is: "Since it is stated (Leviticus 5:22),

Sefer HaChinukh

'and he disavows it and swears falsely,' we have learned the punishment. From where is the warning? [Hence,] we learn to say, 'and you shall not disavow.'" This is also from the commandments about which the intellect testifies.

From the laws of the commandment is that which they, may their memory be Blessed, said (Bava Metzia 5b) that one who denies a deposit is disqualified from testimony - and even though he did not make an oath. And they said in the Gemara, [this is] specifically when the witnesses say that the deposit is in his house at that time. Its details are elucidated in [scattered] places in Tracatate Shevuot (see Tur, Choshen Mishpat 94).

And this prohibition is practiced in every place and at all times by males and females. And one who transgresses it and disavows to his compatriot [having] something of monetary value violates this negative commandment, and it is like he violates a commandment of the King. But there are no lashes for it.

Mitzvah 226

To not swear about the denial of money: To not swear about the disavowal, as it stated (Leviticus 19:11), "and you shall not lie" - meaning to say that if a man denied a deposit, he transgressed, "you shall not disavow"; and if he swore about the denial afterwards, he transgressed, "and you shall not lie." As so has the understanding of this verse come to us, that it is to warn about one who swears about the denial of money. And [it is] like it appears in Sifra, Kedoshim, Section 2:3, "'And you shall not lie' - what do we learn to say? Since it is stated (Leviticus 5:22), 'and he swears falsely,' we have learned the punishment. From where is the warning? [Hence,] we learn to say, 'and you shall not lie.'"

And it is elucidated in Tractate Shevuot 49b that anyone who swears an oath about the denial of money, transgresses two negative commandments - on account of "And you shall not swear in My name falsely" (Leviticus 19:12), and on account of "and you shall not lie towards your compatriot."

I have written in Parshat Vayishma Yitro in the commandment of "You shall not take" (Sefer HaChinukh 32) about the roots of the prohibition of a false oath.

And the laws of this commandment are in the fifth chapter of Shevuot.

And it is practiced in every place and at all times. And one who transgresses it and lies and volitionally takes an oath on his denial is lashed. And even though there is no act [involved] with it, the Torah made him liable for lashes, due to the weightiness of oaths.

Mitzvah 227

To not swear falsely: To not swear falsely, as it is stated (Leviticus 19:12), "And you shall not swear in My name falsely." And they, may their memory be Blessed, explained (Shevout 21a) that this verse warns about an oath of speech. And an oath of speech is what is stated in the Torah (Leviticus 5:4), "Or a soul that swears to express with the lips to do bad or to do good." And it is divided into four parts - two of the future and two of the past, such as swearing on something that was done or not done, and on something that in the future he will do or will not do. And an oath of speech is only practiced with things that it is possible for a person to do, whether in the past or in the future. How is of the past? "I ate," or "I did not eat"; and so [too,] "I threw," or "I did not throw a stone into the sea." And how is of the future? "I will eat," or "I will not eat"; or "I will throw," or "I will not throw." But with things that have a prevention from the Torah, an oath of speech is not practiced. As an oath only rests upon an optional matter - that if he wants, he does it and if he wants, he does not do it - as it is stated, "to do bad or to do good." But with any matter of a commandment, there is an obligation upon him to do it. Therefore, an oath of speech does not rest upon him, whether in the past or in the future - in the case that he swears to perform a commandment, and he did not perform it; and so [too,] if he swears that he performed a commandment, and he did not perform it. As [just] like a liability [for punishment for a false oath] does not rest upon the matter of a commandment in the future, so too does it not rest upon it in the past. And so is the matter elucidated in its place in Shevuot 27a.

And from this reason that we said - that the liability of an oath only rests upon something that he is permitted to do - they, may their memory be Blessed, exempted from an oath of speech anyone who swears to do bad to others, since he is commanded to not do bad to his fellow. And Rambam, may his memory be Blessed, wrote (Mishneh Torah, Laws of Oaths 5:16) that it appears to him that he is lashed nonetheless, on account of [making] a vain oath. And one who swears to do bad to himself - even though he is not allowed - is liable on account of an oath of speech, if he does not do [the] bad. [If] he swears to do good to others in something that is in his hand to do, and he did not do [it], he is liable on account of an oath of speech. [These] and the rest of the many details of oaths and the matter of their annulment are all elucidated nicely in the tractate that is built on this, and that is Tractate Shevuot. And I have already written more than this regarding this commandment - and I wrote at length - on the commandment of "You shall not take" in the Order of Vayishma Yitro (Sefer HaChinukh 32).

And this prohibition is practiced in every place and at all times by males and females. And one who transgresses it - if he was volitional - is lashed, and specifically with witnesses and a warning, as is well-known in all of the commandments. And if he was inadvertent, he is obligated to bring a sliding-scale sacrifice. And so did they say in Shevuout 27b, "This is an oath of speech, which we are liable for lashes for its volitional transgression, and a sliding-scale sacrifice for its inadvertent transgression." And that which they said, "This is" has no novelty other than from the side of the sacrifice, which is a sliding-scale offering

Mitzvah 228
To not oppress: To not hold on to that which is in our hand of someone else's by way of force or delay or deception - like delinquents who delay people, saying, "Go and return," so as to cause that what is in their hand of someone else's to remain with them. And this is an extremely bad trait, and [so] our perfect Torah distanced us from it and warned us about it in this place, as it is written (Leviticus 19:13), "You shall not oppress your neighbor" - as one who holds the money of someone else in this manner that we said is called an oppressor. And also included in oppression is anyone who is liable specific money to his fellow and he oppresses him, such as one who suppresses the wage of a wage worker and similar to it. As we do not require that the money actually come from the hand of the oppressed to the hand of the oppressor; but rather anyone that has a claim of specific money against him and he delays it as a result of his violence or any angle of deception is called an oppressor. And even though oppression, robbery and theft are one matter even if the act of one is different from the another, as the intention of the three of them is that a man not take that which is someone else's in any way; since people pilfer each other in these three ways, Scripture specified all of them and warned about each one on its own. And similar to this is what they, may their memory be Blessed, said in Metzia (Bava Metzia 111a), "Rava said, 'This is oppression, this is [also] robbery. And [so] why did Scripture divide them [and specify each one]? To [have one who commits it] transgress two negative commandments.'"

And the explanation of this matter and the main reason according to my opinion is from two angles. The one is that [in] everything that God, Blessed be He, wanted to distance from us a great distancing for our good, He multiplied for us many warnings (negative commandments) about it. And there is also a [direct] benefit found for us in the multiplication of the warnings. And it is like they, may their memory be Blessed, said (Makkot 23b) that the Omnipresent wanted to give merit to Israel; therefore he multiplied the commandments for them. And the intention in their saying commandments is also about the warnings (and not just the positive commandments). As He multiplied many warnings about that which was possible to inform with one warning; like here that it was possible to warn them more generally, "You shall not take the money of others not according to the law." But [instead] the warnings to us about the thing were multiplied, so that we can receive much reward for separating from sin. And so too, in every place where they, may their memory be Blessed, said, "[So as] to [make one] transgress it with many negative commandments," we will explain the matter like this. As it should not be explained, God forbid, that God, may He be Blessed, wanted to come to His creatures with ploys, so that He would multiply the vengeance upon them. As God, Blessed be He and Blessed be His name, desires to give merit to His creatures, not to make [them] liable. But He prompts them with one prompting after another, in order that they learn to take rebuke and merit greatly in their distancing from sin. And this reason for those that know knowledge is honey and milk.

The root of the commandment is well-known, since it is from from the commandments that the intellect obligates.

The laws of the commandment are in Bava Kamma, and primarily in the ninth chapter and the tenth chapter (see Tur, Choshen Mishpat 359).

And this prohibition is practiced in every place and at all times. And one who transgresses it and oppresses his fellow violates this negative commandment. But it is a negative commandment that is rectified by a positive commandment - meaning to say that he restores the loot that is in his hands and appease his fellow about having irritated him and angered him. And they, may their memory be Blessed, already informed us (Berakhot 32a), that the power of those that repent is great. And the French rabbi (Rabbi Moshe of Coucy, in SeMaG, Mitzvot Lo Taase 156), wrote in the tally of the commandments that since we find that Rava said that oppression and robbery are one, we will not count oppression in the number of the negative commandments. And he counts in place of this, "and not be like Korach and his congregation" - meaning to say, that we not [take part] in a controversy. And in our opinion - ours - the intention of Rava was not that they should not be counted as two negative commandments, but rather to have one transgress robbery with two negative commandments, and so too [in the case of] oppression. And since their content is different, we will count them as two negative commandments - like robbery and theft. As even thought the matter of both of them is that that we not take the money of others, there is no doubt that they are considered two negative commandments of the six hundred and thirteen commandments.

Mitzvah 229

To not rob: To not rob - meaning to say, to not take with strength and force and publicity that to which we do not have a right, as it is stated (Leviticus 19:13), "and you shall not rob." And the explanation came about it (Bava Kamma 79b), that the expression, "robbery (gezelah)" relates to one that grabs something from the hand of his fellow or takes it out of his domain against his will by way of force and in the open, like the matter that is stated (II Samuel 23:21), "and he robbed the spear from the hand of the Egyptian."

The root of the commandment is well-known, as it is something that the intellect distances greatly. And it is fitting to distance it, since the one who robs one weaker than he, knows that when one more powerful than he comes upon him, he will also be robbed, etc. And it is a reason for the destruction of civilization.

From the laws of the commandment is that which they, may their memory be Blessed, said (Sanhedrin 57a) that it is forbidden from Torah writ to rob even the smallest amount. But the negative commandment of "you shall not rob" only applies to the value of a small coin (perutah), since the Torah only makes liable [here] for something that is money; and less than the value of a small coin is not called money. But nonetheless, it is forbidden from Torah writ - like half a measure, for which we do not administer lashes, but it is [still] a Torah prohibition. And Rambam, may his memory be Blessed, wrote (Mishneh Torah, Robbery and Lost Property 1:2), "It is forbidden to rob or oppress even a gentile and an idolater. And if he robbed him or oppressed him, he must return [it]." And in the Gemara (Bava Kamma 119a), they, may their memory be Blessed, said that it is even forbidden to destroy the money of, and to rob and steal from, people that it is permitted to destroy their persons, such as the heretics. And they said as the reason for this, lest proper seed will come from them and their money would go to them. And it is also possible to say that their, may their memory be Blessed, intention in the distancing of this was so that a man not accustom his nature to this, as habituation to lowly and bad traits would be lack in the soul. And it is a strong 'rope to drag iniquity.'

And also from the laws of the commandment is that which they, may their memory be Blessed, said (Bava Kamma 98b), that the robber is obligated to return the stolen object itself, as it is stated (Leviticus 5:23), "the stolen object that he robbed" - and they, may their memory be Blessed, explained, "he returns like what he robbed." And because of this they said (Gittin 55a; Rashi s.v. mipnei), it is according to the law that even if he robbed a mareish - the explanation of which is a beam - and he built it into a mansion, he takes apart all of the mansion and returns the beam to its owner. But as a result of the Ordinance of the Penitents, they ordained that he gives its money and he become exempt. And I have already written above (Sefer HaChinukh 130) how the court has the power to do this. And [also] what is the law of the one who robs his fellow in a settlement and wants to return it in the wilderness. And the law of one who robs his fellow and absorbs it into the account [of what is owed], that he fulfills his obligation with this. And if he returned it to his purse, he has fulfilled [it], and that is when there is money in it - since we establish [the law] like Rabbi Yitschak, that says (Bava Kamma 118b), "a man is in the habit of feeling in his purse and he will count his money"; and counting without intention exempts [the one who returns it from further action] with regards to [items] that are not living things. And the law of one who robbed and died [that is] - whether he 'fed' the stolen object to his sons before the loss of hope [by the owners] or after the loss of hope - if he left them land, the sons are obligated to pay the money of the stolen object, but the orphans are not obligated to pay from the movable objects [that the father leaves them]. But because of the Ordinance of the Gaonim that they ordained thus for the betterment of the world, the movable properties of orphans are liened even for an orally agreed loan. And the law of one who buys from the robber is like the law of one who buys from the thief - that there is a distinction between [a thief] who is famous and one who is not famous. And that which they said (Bava Kamma 119a) that it is forbidden to benefit from a man about whom it is assumed that all that he has is from stolen property; but if a little of what is in his hand is not from stolen property - even though it is sparse - it is permitted to benefit from him, until one knows clearly that that actual thing from which he benefits is stolen. And the rest of the laws of robbery, the laws of giving up hope and of changing domains and the rest of its details are elucidated in the ninth and tenth chapters of [Bava] Kamma. And I have written a few of them in the Order of Vayikra (Sefer HaChinukh 130).

And this prohibiton is practiced in every place and at all times by males and females. And one who transgresses it and robs from the worth of a small coin and up has violated a negative commandment. But we do not administer lashes for this negative commandment, since it is rectified by the positive commandment of returning [it], as it is stated (Leviticus 5:23), "that he shall return the stolen object that he robbed, etc." And even if he negated the positive commandment about it - meaning to say, that he burned the stolen object or hurled it to the Great Sea - he is not lashed, since it is a negative commandment that is given to repayment, such that he repay what it was worth. And if he denied it and swore falsely, he adds a fifth and brings a guilt-offering, as it is elucidated in [Bava] Kamma and at the end of Makkot 16a.

Mitzvah 230

To not delay the wage of a wage worker: That we not delay the wage of a wage worker, as it is stated (Leviticus 19:13), "you shall not lay over the salary of a wage worker with you until the morning." And they, may their memory be Blessed, said that this verse is referring to a day wage worker (Bava Metzia 110b). And the Torah extended the time of his payment the entire night, as it is stated, "until morning." And we learned about a night wage worker from another place, that the time of his payment is the whole day, as it is stated (Deuteronomy 24:15), "On its day you shall give his wage, and the sun should not set upon it." And they, may their memory be Blessed, explained (Bava Metzia 110b) that this verse is referring to a night wage worker. And the language of the Mishnah is "A day wage worker collects the whole night, and a night wage worker collects the whole day. And even though two verses came about this commandment, they are only one commandment; and the one is stated to complete the law of the commandment. And we should not count that which the Torah has come to complete the law of a commandment [to be a commandment] on its own. And the content of this commandment - that we not delay payment to the wage worker, but rather we pay him at a set time - that is the principle of the commandment. And with the two negative statements mentioned about it, we knew when is the time of the payment of wage workers - whether a day wage worker or a night wage worker. And remember this principle [mentioned above] for all of the commandments; as it is a great principle in the calculation of the commandments. And it is a principle that two of the pillars of the world agreed about - Rambam, may his memory be Blessed (Sefer HaMitzvot LaRambam, Mitzvot Lo Taase 238), and Ramban, may his memory be Blessed.

It is from the roots of the commandment [that it is] because God, Blessed be He, desires the preservation of Man which He created. And it is well-known that with the delay of nourishment, the body will be destroyed. And therefore, we were commanded to give the wage of the wage earner - as 'he urgently depends upon it,' to sustain himself from it. And it appears that therefore did he place the limit of its time to be one day and not more - as it is the way of people to sometimes fast for a day. And explicitly did the verse give a reason for the thing, in its stating (Deuteronomy 24:15), "he urgently depends upon it." And even though they, may their memory be Blessed, expounded it for a different matter, its simple understanding implies that which we wrote.

From the laws of the commandment are that which they, may their memory be Blessed, said (Bava Metzia 110a) [that] it is one whether it is the wage for a person or the wage for an animal or for vessels - [for them all, he transgress] on account of "You must pay him his wages on the same day" and on account of, 'do not lay over.' And so [too,] that which they, may their memory be Blessed, said (Bava Metzia 110a) that a day hourly wage-worker collects the whole day and a night hourly wage-worker collects the whole night. A monthly wage worker, a weekly wage worker, a yearly wage worker, a seven-year wage worker - [if] he leaves during the day, he collects [that] whole day, [and if] he leaves during the night, he collects [that] whole night. And [also] the law of one who gives his cloak to a craftsman - when he has finished it and informed him - the whole time that it is in the hand of the craftsman, he does not transgress; if he gave it to him and [the owner] did not pay him on the day that [the craftsman] gave it to him, he has transgressed. As contractual work is like wage work - so did they, may their memory be Blessed, explain.

And [also] the law of an agent who hired wage workers, who [is it that] transgresses on account of 'do not lay over' - he or the owner - that everything goes according to the expression that he [used] with the workers. And that which they said (Bava Metzia 110a) that the employer only transgresses at the time that the wage worker claims [the wage from] him and he does not give it to him, but if he does not claim [it from] him, he does not transgress. [(Scribal) emendation: Or if he claimed (it from) him and he did not have with what to pay, and he does not find someone who will lend to him, he does not transgress. To here (is the emendation).] And so [too,] if he assigned to the worker that someone else pay him and the worker accepted, the employer is exempt, even though the other one did not pay him later. And that which they, may their memory be Blessed, said (Bava Metzia 110b), that one who delays the wage of a wage worker until after its time - even though he has already transgressed a positive commandment and a negative commandment - he is obligated to give [it] to him as soon as he demands it. And all the time that he delays his payment - even after the time - he transgresses a negative commandment from the rabbis, may their memory be Blessed; and they based it on this verse, that is written (Proverbs 3:28), "Do not say to your fellow, 'Go, and come back, etc.'" And [also] the law of the wage worker, that he makes an oath (that the money is still owed) and takes [it], so long as he claims his wages within its time - and even if the wage worker was a minor, he too makes an oath and takes - and they, may their memory be Blessed, gave a reason for this (Bava Metzia 112b): since the [employer] is preoccupied with his workers. [These] and the rest of its details are elucidated in the ninth chapter of [Bava] Metzia (see Tur, Choshen Mishpat 339).

And it is practiced in every place and at all times. And one who transgresses it and delays the wage of a wage worker until after the set time has violated a positive commandment and violates a negative commandment. But we do not administer lashes for this negative commandment, since it is given to repayment - as behold, he is obligated to pay his wage at all times. And they, may their memory be Blessed, said (Bava Metzia 111a) about one who suppresses the wage of a wage worker that he transgresses on account of, 'do not oppress,' 'do not rob,' and 'do not lay over,' and on account of "the sun should not set upon it." And they said (Bava Metzia 111a) about a resident alien that, "On its day you shall give his wage" [applies to] him, but we do not transgress, 'do not lay over,' with him. And this law of the resident alien is explicit in the Mishnah of the chapter [entitled] HaMekabel. And Rambam, may his memory be Blessed, wrote (Sefer HaMitzvot LaRambam, Mitzvot Ase 200) that the law is the same with [any] Noachide.

Mitzvah 231

Sefer HaChinukh

To not curse an Israelite, whether a man or a woman: To not curse an Israelite, whether a man or a woman; and even though he does not hear the curse, as it is stated (Leviticus 19:14), "You shall not curse the deaf" - and the explanation comes about this [that it is] one who does not hear your curse. And so did Onkelos translate [it]. And the language of Sifra, Kedoshim, Section 2:13 [is] "I only have a deaf person, from where do I include every man? [Hence] we learn to say (Exodus 22:27), 'among your people, you shall not maledict.' If so, why does it state, 'deaf?' Just like a deaf person is unique that he is alive - to exclude the dead that is not alive." Even thought we do not have the power to know in which way a curse impacts upon the one cursed, and with what power within speech there is to bring [that impact] upon him, we know more generally that people are concerned about curses - whether Israel or other nations - and say that curses of people, and even curses of commoners, have an impact on the one cursed and attaches malediction and distress to him. And since we know this thing from the mouth of the creatures, we will say that it is from the roots of the commandment that God prevented us from injuring others with our mouths, [just] like he prevented us from injuring them with action. And similar to this did they, may their memory be Blessed, say (Moed Katan 18a), "A covenant is made with the lips" - meaning to say that there is power in the words of a person's mouth. And it is possible for us to stay - according to the paucity of our intelligence - that since the speaking soul in man is the elevated part, and as it is written (Genesis 2:7), "He blew into his nostrils the breath of life," and it is translated (by Onkelos) as "a speaking spirit"; He gave it great power to impact even on that which is external to it. And hence we have known and it is always seen that to the extent of the importance of a man's soul and its clinging to the elevated things - like [is the case with] the souls of the righteous and the pious - will their words be quick to impact upon all that they speak about. And this is something well-known and famous among those that know knowledge and understand science. And it possible to say also that the matter is to stifle a quarrel between people and that there be peace between them; since the birds of the sky make the voice travel, and maybe the words of the one that cursed will come to the ears of the one that he cursed. And Rambam, may his memory be Blessed, said (Sefer HaMitzvot LaRambam, Mitzvot Lo Taase 317) as the reason of the commandment [that is is] in order that the soul of the one that curses not be moved to vengeance and that he not become used to anger. And he wrote at further length about this in his book. And it appears to me from his words that, in his opinion, he does not see any injury to the one cursed from the curse, but rather that the Torah is distancing the matter from the perspective of the one that curses - that he not accustom himself to vengeance and anger and to lowly traits. And we shall accept all the words of our rabbis, though our hearts hold more of what we have written.

From the laws of the commandment is that which they, may their memory be Blessed, said (Shevuot 35a) that it is forbidden to curse in any way. But nonetheless, he is not lashed unless he cursed with a name of one of the names [of God], such as Y-ah, Sha-dai, E-loah and similar to them, or with any appellation of one of the appellations [of God], such as Compassionate, Jealous and similar to them. And he is liable in any language that he curses with a name or appellation, as the names that the gentiles call the Holy One, Blessed be He, are among the appellations (even though they are in their languages). And [also] that which they said (Shevuot 36a) that even one who curses himself is lashed, as it is stated (Deuteronomy 4:9), "But you shall guard yourself and guard your soul much." And also, that [which they said] in Mekhilta (see Sanhedrin 66a), "'You shall not curse the deaf' - [it is speaking] about the wretched among men." And they also said there (Mekhilta d'Rabbi Yismael 22:27) that when the verse (Exodus 22:27) states, "a chieftain (nassi) among your people, you shall not maledict, etc.," it implies both a chieftain and a judge. What [then] do we learn by saying, "[Judges] shall you not curse"? To impose liability for this one in itself and for that one in itself. From here they said, "One may speak one thing and be liable for four things. (How so?) If the son of a chieftain curses his father, he is liable on account of chieftain, on account of father, on account of judge, and on account of 'among your people you shall not maledict'" (see Tur, Choshen Mishpat 26).

And it is practiced in every place and at all times by males and females. And one who transgresses this and volitionally curses an Israelite with a name or an appellation [of God] - and there are witnesses and a warning - is lashed. As this is one of three negative commandments (Temurah 3a) for which we administer lashes, even though there is no act [involved] with them and lashes are not stated explicitly about them in the Torah. And the other two are one who makes an oath and one who exchanges, as is explained in the Gemara Sanhedrin.

Mitzvah 232
To not make an innocent one stumble on the way: To not make the Children of Israel stumble, to give them bad advice; but rather we right them when they ask advice, with that which we believe to be right and good advice, as it is stated (Leviticus 19:14), "and you shall not put a stumbling block in front of the blind." And the language of Sifra, Kedoshim, Section 2:14 [is] "In front of one who is blind about a thing and he takes advice from you, do not give him advice that is not appropriate for him." And they, may their memory be Blessed, said [there also], "A man should not say to his fellow, 'Sell your field, and buy a donkey,' and he stalks him and takes it from him." And this negative commandment also includes one who helps one who commits a sin, since he brings him to being seduced to also transgress other times besides this. And from this angle, they, may their memory be Blessed, said that the both the lender and the borrower with interest transgress with regards to "in front of the blind, etc."

The root of the commandment is well-known, since the guidance of people and to give them good advice for all of their actions [is needed for] the ordering of the world and its civilization.

From the laws of the commandment is that which they, may their memory be Blessed, said (Avodah Zarah 14a), that we are concerned about "in front of," but we are not concerned about "in front of" of "in front of." And because of this they explained there that when we had the question in the Gemara (Avodah Zarah 6a) [regarding] the reason for our Mishnah (Avodah Zarah 2a), if it is on account of that he will go and thank [his idol] or if it is on account of "in front of the blind" - that we were only in doubt about the reason of the Mishnah regarding buying and selling with them, that an Israelite give the gentile something fit for a sacrifice. And in such a way, it is possible that there would be [a violation] of it. But in all the rest of our Mishnah - for example to give loans, to redeem them and to have them borrow - it is forbidden on account of that he will go and thank. As it cannot be said that it is on account of "in front of the blind"; as he must return the actual item he borrowed, and also in giving them loans and redeeming them - he gave him coins, and coins are not fit for a sacrifice. What [might] you have said? Maybe he will buy a sacrifice with them. [But] that would be "in front of" of "in front of." And we are not concerned about such a way, as they said - and so [too,] all that is similar to it. And so [too,] that which they, may their memory be Blessed, said (Avodah Zarah 15b) that it is forbidden to sell any weapons and anything that can injure the public, unless he sells them so that they will defend us. And so [too,] is it forbidden to sell them to an Israelite who sells them to idolaters, and so [too, if he sells them] to Israelite brigands. And it is all forbidden on account of "and in front of the blind." And the rest of its details are in scattered places of the Talmud (see Mishneh Torah, Laws of Murderer and the Preservation of Life 11).

And it is practiced in every place and at all times by males and females. And one who transgresses it and consciously raises advice to his fellow that is not appropriate for him; or helped him in the matter of a sin - such as handing a cup of wine to a nazirite and all that is similar to this - has violated this negative commandment, and it is like violating the commandment of the King. But we do not administer lashes for it, since there is no act [involved] with it.

Mitzvah 233
To not vitiate justice: That the judge not cause vitiation in a decision. And vitiation is with anything where he deviates from that which the Torah commanded us regarding the law, unless he did so with the consent of the litigants. And about this is it stated (Leviticus 19:15), "You shall not vitiate judgement."

The root of this commandment is well-known, since the civilization of men is preserved with righteous judgement.

From the laws of the commandment is that which they, may their memory be Blessed, said (Ketuvot 105a) that one who [unnecessarily] prolongs the judgment is included in one vitiating judgement. And that which they said (Mishnah Avot 1:1), "Be deliberate in judgement," so that they not come to vitiation of the judgement. And they, may their memory be Blessed, said (Yevamot 109b) that it is fitting for someone judging to consult with someone greater than he, if he is near him. And they said in warning about this matter (Mishnah Avot 4:7), "Anyone who prevents himself from judging - prevents from himself enmity, theft, and the false oath." And all of this is to teach us that the thing requires deliberation and much composure, so that they not err in the decision. As there are many things [involved] in legal decisions, and one must be a great sage in a decision - and it is like they, may their memory be Blessed, said (Bava Batra 175b), "One who wants to become wise should engage in monetary laws, as there is no greater discipline in the Torah than them, as they are like a flowing spring." And they also warned us that the judgement of a small coin should be beloved to us like the judgement of a thousand expensive coins, to judge it according to its truth. And because of the weightiness of judgement, they greatly praised the one who can bring a compromise between the litigants. And about him is it said (Zechariah 8:16), "truth and peaceful justice shall you rule" - as this is the judgement of peace. And so too about David does it state (II Samuel 8:15), "and David executed judgement and righteousness (tzedekah, which is also the word for charity) for all of his people" - which is the judgment that also has charity? One can say, a settlement. And the rest of the many warnings that they, may their memory be Blessed, warned us about equitability in judgement and the rest of the details of the commandment are scattered in the Order of Nezikin, and are primarily in Tractate Sanhedrin (see Tur, Choshen Mishpat 17).

And it is practiced in every place and at all times by males, since judgement is for them. And one who transgresses it and vitiates a judgement - meaning to say, he consciously judges not like the law of the Torah - has violated this negative commandment. But we do not administer lashes for it, as we do not administer lashes for a negative commandment that does not have an act [involved] with it, but rather only speech - except for those that we mentioned above (Sefer HaChinukh 239). And also behold, anyone who judges not according to the law of the Torah, his decision is overturned; and hence we do not administer lashes for it. And [it is] as we say in Sanhedrin 33a in the chapter [entitled] Echad Dinei Mammonot, that anyone who errs in the matter of Mishnah is always overturned. And the matter is to say that there is no doubt that the judgement of anyone who errs to make a judgement which is the opposite of the Torah's intent is completely negated - and behold, it is as if it was never said. And there, it is elucidated that there are situations in which if he judged a case opposite to the truth, his decision [stands]; but he is obligated to pay from his estate to the one to whom he vitiated the judgement. And [even] with all this, he does not become liable for lashes - and even if he did an act with it, such as giving and taking [property in question] with [his own] hand - due to the rule that is in our hands, that we do not administer lashes for anything that is given to repayment.

And if it were not that the matter would be [so] long and we would leave the bounds of our work, we would explain at length all of the situations wherein the decision is overturned and the situations when it is not overturned but the court is liable to pay from its estate, and the situations wherein it is not overturned and the court is exempted from paying. And it appears from the general rule of the matter that anytime that they judged without acceptance [beforehand by the litigants] and there is a greater [authority] in the city than them and they erred - even in [their] course of thought - their judgement is overturned. And that is when they did not give and take by hand; for if they did give and take by hand, their decision is not overturned, but they are obligated to pay. [If it is] in a different way, their decision is not overturned. And when they judged by permission, whereby it cannot be said that they were negligent when they came to judge, they are exempted from paying. But when it was without permission - or also in any situation that one can say that they were negligent at all when they come to judge - they are obligated to pay. And in all that they said that the decision is overturned, they are exempted from paying even if the thing that they decided upon was lost or consumed, unless they actually gave and took by hand - since they are [then] nonetheless liable to pay from the law of damagers. Behold, if it is not like this, they are exempt. And my teacher - God should protect him - explained to us, that that which we said above above that anyone who errs in the matter of Mishnah is always overturned, is not literally only the Mishnah, but rather anything explicit in the Talmud in the words of the Amoraim (Rabbis of the Talmudic era) as the law; if he erred in judgment about it, it is also called erring in the matter of a Mishnah. And they further expanded their ways by also saying that even one who errs in a decision that was decided by one of the Geonim or from the sages famous among us for their wisdom - we treat it like one who erred in the matter of a Mishnah. [That is the case] unless that court says that it is not deciding like him and will not defer from judging its decisions like its opinion on account of him and that it knows and remembers the opinion of that Goan or sage - and that is when it is fit for it [to do so].

Mitzvah 234

To not honor a great person in judgement: That the judge not honor one of the litigants at the time of the dispute - and even if he was great, honored and esteemed - as it is stated (Leviticus 19: 15), "and do not dignify the face of a great man." And they said in Sifra Kedoshim, Chapter 4:3, "That you not say, 'This one is a wealthy man, he is the son of great ones. How can I shame him?'" - meaning to say that I should not honor him more than his opponent who is not great like him. "Hence it is stated, 'and do not dignify the face of a great man.'"

And the root of the commandment is well-known, and I have written it at the beginning of the Order (Sefer HaChinukh 235).

And from the laws of the commandment is that which they, may their memory be Blessed, said (Shevuot 30a) that it not be that one stand and one sit, but rather both of them stand. As in that they are in front of the court, it is fitting for them to stand as if they were in front of the Divine Presence; since the spirit of God dwells among the congregation of the judges of Israel, as it is stated (Psalms 82a), "God stands in the congregation of God." And nonetheless, they, may their memory be Blessed, said (Shevuot 30b) that if they wanted to seat the litigants, the option is in their hand. And about what are these words speaking? At the time of give and take. But at the time of the final judgement, there is an obligation to stand, as it is stated (Exodus 18:13), "and the people stood over Moshe." Except that all of the courts of Israel after the Talmud have become accustomed to seat them [in order to avoid] controversy. And even [regarding] the witnesses about whom it is written (Deuteronomy 19:17), "and the two men stand," they have also become accustomed today to seat them (Mishneh Torah, Laws of The Sanhedrin and the Penalties within their Jurisdiction 21:5). [This] and the rest of its details are elucidated in [various] places in Sanhedrin and Shevuot (see Tur, Choshen Mishpat 17). And it is practiced in every place and at all times by males, since judgement is for them. And one who transgresses it and honors one litigant more than his fellow volitionally has violated this negative commandment and violated a positive commandment, as it is written (Leviticus 19:15), "you shall judge your people with righteousness." And [regarding] that which, they may their memory be Blessed, permitted an advantage for the sage over the ignoramus in a few of the commandments, we will write later on the next commandment adjacently (Sefer HaChinukh 235).

Mitzvah 235

The commandment to judge with righteousness: To judge with righteousness, as it is stated (Leviticus 19:15), "you shall judge your people with righteousness." And the explanation of it comes that the judges were commanded to treat the parties to the dispute equally - meaning to say that the judge not honor one of the litigants more than the other. And so, they said in Sifra, Kedoshim, Chapter 4:4 that one not speak all that he needs, and [the judge] say to the other, "Speak briefly." And so [too,] in the chapter [entitled] Shevuot HaEdut (Shevuot 30a), "Our Rabbis learned, '"You shall judge your people with righteousness" - that it not be that one stand and one sit; one not speak all that he needs, and [the judge] say to the other, "Speak briefly."'" And so [too,] included in this commandment is that every man that is wise in the laws of the Torah and righteous in his ways is commanded to judge the law of the Torah between parties of a dispute, if he has the power in his hand [to do so]. And even an individual can judge from Torah writ - and like they, may their memory be Blessed, said (Sanhedrin 3a), "One can judge his fellow from Torah writ, as it is stated, 'You shall judge your people with righteousness.'" But the sages warned (Mishnah Avot 4:8), that a man not judge alone. And also included in this commandment is that it is fit for every person to judge his fellow favorably, and only to understand his deeds and his words favorably.

The root of the commandment is revealed to all - as with equitability in judgement, the world is civilized. But if a judge honors one of the litigants over the other, the [latter] disputant will fear to say all of his claims in front of him. And from this, the judgement will come out twisted. And about that which we said that it is a commandment upon one wise in words of Torah - and he be a righteous man - to judge those who disagree, that this is included in the commandment as well; there is benefit in this as well, as he will judge a true judgement. But if this one that knows does not want to judge, other people who are not wise will judge them, and they will slant the judgement towards one of the litigants without knowing. Also, about that which we said that every person is obligated to judge his fellow favorably - that it is included in the commandment - is a cause for there to be peace and amity among people. And [so] it comes out that the essence of the whole intent of the commandment is to help in the civilization of people with righteousness of judgement, and to bring peace among them with the removal of suspicion of one man towards another.

From the laws of the commandment is that which they, may their memory be Blessed, said (Shevuot 31a) [regarding] two litigants, whereby one was dressed in expensive clothes and the other in worn clothes, we say to the honored one, "Dress him like you, or dress like him; and afterwards, we will judge between you" - so that they be equal. And now in our time, we have not seen a court that did this. And they, may their memory be Blessed, also said (Mishneh Torah, Laws of The Sanhedrin and the Penalties within their Jurisdiction 21:3) that it is a commandment to sit them equally, and not that one be above his fellow or that one be sitting and the other be standing - except for a Torah scholar and an ignoramus, about which they said that we seat the Torah scholar and say to the ignoramus, "Sit"; but if he does not sit, we are not concerned about this (Mishneh Torah, Laws of The Sanhedrin and the Penalties within their Jurisdiction 21:4). And they, may their memory be Blessed, said (Mishneh Torah, Laws of The Sanhedrin and the Penalties within their Jurisdiction 21:6) that if many cases came in front of you, and among them was a case of an orphan or a widow, that it is a commandment to have them precede [the others]; as it is stated (Isaiah 1:17), "judge the orphan, dispute for the widow" - meaning to say that we were commanded to quicken their cases more than with the case of others. And so [too,] did they, may their memory be Blessed, say (Ketuvot 105b) that the case of a Torah scholar precedes the case of an ignoramus, and the case of a woman precedes the case of a man - since the embarrassment of a woman is great. And all this that we said is included in "you shall judge with righteousness." And these matters, together with the rest of the details of the commandment are in scattered places in the Talmud, and many among them are in Sanhedrin and Shevuot (see Tur, Choshen Mishpat 17).

And this commandment is practiced in every place and at all times by males - as they are obligated to judge, and not females. However, also females are obligated about that which we said is included in this commandment, and that is to judge one's fellow favorably.

Mitzvah 236

To not spy: That we have been prevented from talebearing, as it is stated (Leviticus 19:16), "You shall not go talebearing (rachil)." And the matter is that if a person hears something bad about his fellow, that he should not go to him and tell him "x" is saying so and so, unless his intention is to remove damages or to stop a quarrel. And our sages, may their memory be Blessed, said (Ketuvot 46a) about the meaning of rachil, rach la'zeh ve kashe la'zeh (soft to this one and hard to that one). A different explanation: Do not be like a rochel (peddler), who picks up things and goes [with them to others].

It is from the roots of the commandment that God in His goodness desires the good of the creatures that He created, and commanded them in this so that there will be peace among us, since talebearing leads to quarrel and strife.

The details of the commandment and the great amount of warnings that they, may their memory be Blessed, warned us about talebearing and about its partner - evil speech - are explained in scattered locations in the Talmud and in the Midrash (see Mishneh Torah, Laws of Human Dispositions 7). And they explicitly said about evil speech (Arakhin 15b), that it kills its speaker and its receiver (listener), (and) that it is said about it, "and the receiver more than all of them [does it kill]." And they warned much about it to the point that they said (Bava Metzia 59b), "One who has someone who was hung in his [family] record, let him not say, 'Hang me a fish [on the grill].'" And they said, (Arakhin 16a), "Within the category of 'the dust of (adjunct)' evil speech is one who praises his friend in front of [his friend's] hater, as it is stated (Proverbs 27:14), 'He who blesses his friend, etc.'"

And [this commandment] is practiced in every place and at all times by males and females. And one who transgresses it and has talebearing on his tongue, violates a negative commandment and it is like one who violates a commandment of the King. And there are no lashes, because it is a negative commandment that does not have an act [involved] with it - but [nonetheless] there are several agents to the Omnipresent to give lashes besides a whip of a calf [skin] or a cow's [skin]. And even though this negative commandment does not have lashes because it does not have an act [involved] with it, there are times that it even has a death penalty, as is known in the law of the informer. And this law the sages permitted to do outside of the land [of Israel] for the improvement of the world: it is better that one man die and not damage and destroy the bodies - or even the property - of the many.

And I will write for you, my son, a little of that which is in the Gemara about this matter; and if you will merit knowledge, you will see everything in its place. We follow the textual variant in the chapter [entitled] HaGozel Batra (Bava Kamma 116b), "A certain man who showed piles of wheat of the Exilarch's household [...] Rav Naḥman obligated him to pay." And the reason is because of the law of causation (garmi, Bava Kamma 117b). And [that is] specifically when he showed him on his own. But as a result of duress, he is exempt - and as "We learned, 'An Israelite who was under the duress of gentiles and he showed them the money of his friend is exempt'" (Bava Kamma 117a). And our teachers, may their memory be Blessed, explained it, that it is not the last word [that] they put his body under duress; but even if they put him under duress with money - that they would take money from him, if he does not show the money of his fellow - he is exempt. As anyone who shows [it] out of duress is exempt, and he is only obligated if he shows it on his own. And so wrote Rabbi Avraham bar Rabbi David, may his memory be Blessed. But if he gave and took with [his] hand, he is liable - and even because of duress [to his life]. And if you will say [that] there is nothing that stands in front of saving a soul, it can be said, "Do we tell him to die? We say to him that he should give and pay, and not save himself with the money of others." And even with someone pursued who is fleeing the pursuer and breaks vessels, [he is] liable [to pay for this damage] - and even though he did not break them intentionally, but rather unintentionally, and at the time that he was fleeing from the pursuer to save himself - and all the more so is he liable for repayment, when he gave and took with [his] hand. But if he gave and took with [his] hand after he showed them from duress, we see the thing as if it is burned from the time that he showed them, and he is no longer liable on account of his giving and taking. And he is also not liable on account of showing, since he showed [it] because of duress, as we have written. And so do we say there (Bava Kamma 117a), "A certain man who showed the wine of Rav Mari and Rav Pinhas, the sons of Rav Pappa" - the explanation [of which] is because of duress - "They said to him, 'Carry [it] and bring [it],' [and] he carried and brought [it]." And it was concluded that once "he brought them to it [at the outset, it is as if] he burned it" - and he is no longer liable for it. But when he shows it on his own without a claim of duress, he is liable for death and repayment. As we follow the textual variant there, "A certain man who desired to show his fellow's straw shed came before Rav. Rav said to him, 'Do not do this.'" - meaning to say, he warned him. "He did not obey him. Rav Kahana was sitting before Rav; Rav Kahana rose and dislodged his neck" - meaning to say, he killed him. And this is proven [by] that which "Rav said to Rav Kahana, 'Now is the [time] of the monarchy of the Persians, and they are particular about bloodshed.'" And we also say in the Gemara (Bava Kamma 119a) concerning the question we had whether it is permitted to destroy the money of an informer, that we respond to it, "His money should not be more severe than his body" - hence it is permitted to destroy his body. However, that is only at the time of the act and with a warning, and like the story of Rav Kahana - but he does not have to accept the warning, as with other death penalties. And it appears that one who is established as an informer is as if he is warned and standing, and [so] it is permitted to kill him at any time.

And the opinion of Rambam, may his memory be Blessed, that he wrote (Mishneh Torah, Laws of One Who Injures a Person or Property 8:10-11) about the law of an informer is thus: "Once he said,

'Behold, I am informing about the body or money of **x**' - and even if it is negligent money - behold, this one has permitted himself for death. And we warn him and say to him, 'Do not inform.' If he was brazen-faced and said, 'No, rather I will inform' - it is a commandment to kill him, and whoever is first to kill him, merits. [If] the informer did that which he plotted and informed, it appears to me that it is forbidden to kill him; unless he is established as an informer, lest he inform [on] others." To here is the language of the rabbi. He required a warning for one who is not established as an informer and that he accept the warning. And for the one who is established as an informer, it appears from his words, that he does not need a warning. And an informer may not say, "Because x was afflicting me, I am informing [on] him to the gentiles" - as this does not exempt him from his punishment. But it is permitted for the community to inform to the gentiles about one who is afflicting the community. And so did Rambam, may his memory be Blessed, write (Mishneh Torah, Laws of One Who Injures a Person or Property 8:11). And it is forbidden to destroy the money of an informer, on account of [An evildoer] "Prepares but the righteous one wears" (Job 27:17). And so is it concluded in the chapter [entitled] HaGozel (Bava Kamma 119a).

Mitzvah 237

To not stand over the blood of neighbors: That we not refrain from saving the soul of an Israelite when we see him in danger of death and destruction and we have the ability to save him from any side, as it is stated (Leviticus 19:16), "you shall not stand over the blood of your neighbor." And we say in Sanhedrin 73a, "We learn, 'From where [do we know] about one who sees his fellow drowning in a river, or being dragged away by a wild animal, or [that there are] bandits coming against him, that he is obligated to save him with his life? As it is stated, "you shall not stand over the blood of your neighbor."' It is not needed that he is obligated with his life, but he is also obligated to tarry and hire [others to do so]." And our Rabbis, may their memory be Blessed also included in this warning (negative commandment) not to suppress testimony so that his fellow not lose money. And so is it in Sifra, Kedoshim, Chapter 4:8, "From where [do we know] that if testimony is known to him that he is not permitted to remain silent about it? As it is stated, 'you shall not stand over the blood of your neighbor.' And from where [do we know] if you see someone drowning in the river, etc. And from where [do we know about] one pursuing his fellow to kill him, that you are obligated to rescue him with [the soul of the pursuer]? As it is stated, 'you shall not stand, etc.'"

The root of this commandment is well-known - as [just] like one will save his fellow, so [too,] will his fellow save him. And the world will be inhabited like this, and God desires its habitation, as 'He created it to be inhabited.' And the laws of this commandment have already been elucidated in Tractate Sanhedrin.

And it is practiced in every place and at all times by males and females. And one who transgresses it and refrains from saving [a Jew in danger] and has the ability [to do so] has violated this negative commandment. But we do not administer lashes for it, since it is a negative commandment that does not have an act [involved] with it - and it is established for us that we do not administer lashes [in such a case].

Mitzvah 238

To not hate brothers: To not hate with hatred of the heart any Israelite, as it is stated (Leviticus 19:17), "You shall not hate your brother in your heart." And the language of Sifra Kedoshim, Chapter 4:8 is "I have only said hatred that is in the heart." And likewise, in Arakhin 16b, "The verse is speaking about hatred in the heart." But when he shows him hatred, and [the other] knows that he is his enemy, he does not violate this negative commandment. However, he does violate "You shall not take vengeance and not bear a grudge." And he likewise violates a positive commandment, as it is stated (Leviticus 19:18), "and you shall love your neighbor as yourself." And nonetheless hatred of the heart is worse than all revealed hatred, and [so] the Torah especially warns about it.

The root of the commandment is well-known - as hatred of the heart causes great evils among people, being a constant 'sword between a man and his brother' and a man and his neighbor. And it is a cause for all of the informing that is done among people, and it is a lowly and completely disgusting trait among all people of intellect.

The details of the commandment and the many warnings that our Rabbis, may their memory be Blessed, warned us about it - not to accustom ourselves to this evil - are elucidated in the Talmud in scattered [places] and in the Midrash.

And it is practiced in every place and at all times by males and females. And one who transgresses it and fixes hatred in his heart towards any proper Israelite has violated this negative commandment. But we do not administer lashes for it, as there is no act [involved] with it. But there is no prohibition in the hatred of the evildoers, but rather [it is] a commandment to hate them, after we rebuke them about their sin many times and they do not want to return, as it is stated (Psalms 139:21), "Do I not, Lord, hate Your enemies, and argue with those that come against You."

Mitzvah 239

The commandment of rebuke to an Israelite who does not behave properly: To rebuke an Israelite who does not behave properly - whether about things that are between a man and his fellow or between a man and the Omnipresent - as it is stated (Leviticus 19:17), "you shall surely rebuke your compatriot, and you shall not bear a sin for him." And they said in Sifra, Kedoshim 4:8, "From where [do we know] that if you rebuked him four or five times and he did not return, that you are obligated to go back and rebuke [him again]? [Hence] we learn to say, 'you shall surely rebuke.'" And they, may their memory be Blessed, also said in the Gemara (Bava Metzia 31a), "'You shall surely rebuke' - even a hundred times." And they said in the Sifra, "Perhaps, he should rebuke and his face change [color]? [Hence] we learn to say, 'and you shall not bear a sin for him.'" And this teaches that at the beginning of the rebuke it is fitting for a person to rebuke privately, with soft expressions and calm words, so that he not be embarrassed. But there is no doubt that if he does not return with this, that we shame the sinner in public and publicize his sin and insult him, until he returns to the better.

It is from the roots of the commandment [that it is] because there is peace and goodness between people with this. As when a man sins to a man, and he rebukes him privately, he will apologize in front of him, and [the other] will accept his apology and he will be whole (some have the variant, at peace) with him. But if he does not rebuke him, he will loathe him in his heart and injure him at the time or at some [other] point in time, as it is stated about evildoers (Samuel II 13:22), "And Avshalom did not speak with Amnon." And 'all the ways of the Torah are pleasant and its paths are peace.'

From the laws of the commandment is that which they, may their memory be Blessed, said (Arakhin 16b) that the obligation of this commandment is until hitting - meaning to say that the one rebuking is obligated to multiply his rebukes upon the sinner until it is enough that the sinner is close to hitting the one rebuking. And nonetheless they, may their memory be Blessed, also said (Arakhin 16b) that if the one rebuking sees that there is no benefit at all found from the words of his rebukes - from the greatness of the sinner's evil, or that he is deaf [to it] and extremely evil and [the rebuker] is afraid of him that he not stand against him and kill him - that he is not obligated in this commandment with this man. And this is what they, may their memory be Blessed, said (Yevamot 65b), "In the same way as it is a commandment to say something that will be heard, so [too,] is it a commandment to be quiet in a place where the thing will not be heard" - since there would be disgrace in the matter for the one who is rebuking and no benefit to the one who is rebuked. And nonetheless, it is for every careful person to consider and to pay great attention to these matters and to think and see if there will be a benefit to the sinner with his words, such that he should rebuke him and trust in God, may He be Blessed - as He will help him in his fight with His enemies. And let his heart not be soft and let him not fear, since 'the Lord protects all those that love Him and He obliterates all of the evildoers.' And if the sinner returns, he will have great reward for this. But the one who has in his hand [the possibility of] bringing him back and rebuking him, and does not rebuke him, is caught in his sin. And this is something clear from the words of our Rabbis (Shabbat 55a) and also from Scripture (Isaiah 3:14). And they, may their memory be Blessed, also said (Yevamot 65b) that even a minor is obligated to rebuke an adult if he sees the adult going in a path that is not good. [These] and the rest of the details of the commandment are elucidated in scattered [places] in the Talmud (see Mishneh Torah, Laws of Human Dispositions 6).

And this commandment is practiced in every place and at all times by males and females. And one who transgresses it and does not rebuke in the manner that we said has violated this positive commandment; and he is also from the group of evildoers who do this.

Mitzvah 240

To not whiten the face of an Israelite: To not embarrass an Israelite; and our Rabbis, may their memory be Blessed, called this sin (Avot 3:15), "whitening the face of his fellow in public. And the negative commandment that comes about this [in the Torah] is that which is written (Leviticus 19:17), "you shall surely rebuke your compatriot, and you shall not bear a sin for him." And they said in Sifra, Kedoshim 4:8, "From where [do we know] that if you rebuked him four or five times [...] go back and rebuke [him again]? [Hence] we learn to say, 'you shall surely rebuke.' Perhaps, he should rebuke and his face change [color]? [Hence] we learn to say, 'and you shall not bear a sin for him.'"

The root of the commandment is well-known - since embarrassment is very painful for the creatures - there is nothing greater than it. Therefore, God prevented us from causing so much pain to His creatures, since it is possible to rebuke them in private and not to embarrass the sinner so much.

From the laws of the commandment is that which they, may their memory be Blessed, said (Yoma 86b) that we were not warned like this about all things, but rather [only] about things between a man and his fellow. But with Heavenly matters - if he does not return after the private rebuke - it is a commandment to shame him publicly, to publicize his sin and to disgrace and curse him until he returns to the good, as the prophets did to Israel. And [also] that which they, may their memory be Blessed, said (Berakhot 43b) by way of a warning about this matter, " From where do we [know that] it is better for a man to descend into a fiery furnace, and not to whiten the face of his fellow in public? From Tamar," who did not want to whiten the face of her father-in-law, to say in public that she was pregnant from him. And had she not found the pledge and let the matter be known through a hint, she would have been condemned to burning; but she did not whiten his face. And the rest of the details of the commandment are in scattered places in the Gemara and in the Midrash.

And [it] is practiced in every place and at all times. And [if one] transgresses it and volitionally whitened the face of his fellow publicly - not for a sin in the way that we have said - he has violated a commandment of the King. But he is not lashed, since there is no act [involved] with it. And the Omnipresent has many agents to pay back those that transgress His will.

Mitzvah 241

To not avenge: To not avenge, meaning to say that we have been prevented form taking revenge from an Israelite. And the content is, for example, that an Israelite did evil or caused pain to his fellow in one of the things that it is customary among most people to not veer from searching for the one who did evil do them until they pay him back like his evil deed, or they hurt him like he hurt them. And God, may He be Blessed, has prevented us from this matter, by His stating (Leviticus 19:18), "You shall not avenge." And the language of Sifra, Kedoshim, Chapter 4:10 [is] "How far is the power of revenge? If [one] said to [another], 'Lend me your sickle,' and he did not lend him. The next day [the other] said to him, 'Lend me your spade.' [So] he said [back], 'I will not lend you [it], just as you did not lend me your sickle.' Hence, it is written, 'You shall not avenge.'" And compare like this to all things.

It is from the roots of the commandment that a person know and put into his heart that everything that happens to him - good and bad - the cause of it coming to him is from God, Blessed be He. And from the hand of man - from the hand of a man to his brother - there would not be anything without the will of God, Blessed be He. Hence, when a person caused him pain or hurt him, he should know for himself that his [own] sins caused [it], and that God, may He be Blessed, ordained this for him. And he should not place his thoughts to taking vengeance from [the one who pained him], since he is not the cause of his evil, but rather the sin is the cause; like David, peace be upon him, stated (II Samuel 16:11), "leave him to curse, since the Lord told him [so]" - he made the matter depend upon his [own] sin, and not upon Shimei ben Gera. And there is also a great benefit found in this commandment, in quieting a dispute and removing enmity from the heart of people. And when there is peace among people, God, may He be Blessed, will make peace for them.

And the laws of the commandment are short. We have already mentioned what appears to be most of them.

And [it is] practiced in every place and at all times by males and females. And one who transgresses it, and fixes into his heart to hate his fellow about his doing him evil until he pays him back like [the other's] evil, has violated this negative commandment. And its evil is very great, as it is a cause for great mishap. But we do not administer lashes for it, since there is no action [involved] with it. And take this rule into your hand for every place where it is said, "We do not administer lashes for a negative commandment that does not have an act [involved] with it": That even though he did some act, he is [still] not lashed as a result - since it is possible to transgress the negative commandment without an act. And remember this thing in all of them, since it it is a clear thing - there is no need to repeat it in another place.

Mitzvah 242

To not begrudge: To not begrudge, meaning to say that we have been prevented from bearing a grudge in our hearts [about] an Israelite having done evil to us. And even though we have consented in our souls not to pay him back for his deeds, we have even been prevented from just remembering his sin in the heart. And about this is it stated, (Leviticus 19:18), "you shall not begrudge." And the language of Sifra, Kedoshim, Chapter 4:11 is "How far is the power of begrudging? If [one] said to [another], 'Lend me your sickle,' and he did not lend him. The next day, the [other] said to him, 'Lend me your spade.' [So] he said [back] to him, 'Here it is; I am not like you, who did not lend me your sickle.' Hence, it is written, 'you shall not begrudge.'"

All of the content of this commandment is like the commandment of vengeance that preceded [it].

Mitzvah 243

The commandment of love of Israel: To love [with] love of the soul each one of Israel - meaning to say that we have compassion for an Israelite and for his money, [just] like a person has compassion for himself and for his [own] money; as it stated (Leviticus 19:18), "you shall love your neighbor as yourself." And they, may their memory be Blessed, said (Shabbat 31a), "What is hateful to you, do not do to your fellow." And they said in Sifra, Kedoshim, Chapter 4:12, "Rabbi Akiva said, 'This is a great principle in the Torah'" - meaning to say that many commandments are dependent upon it. As one that loves his fellow like himself will not steal his money, have adultery with his wife, cheat his money from him nor hurt him from any angle. And so [too,] are there several other commandments dependent on this - the thing is well-known [revealed] to all who have intellect.

The root of the commandment is well-known - as in the way that he acts to his fellow, so will his fellow act to him. And there will be peace among the creatures with this.

And the laws of this commandment are included in the commandment, as the general principle of everything is that a man behave with his fellow in the way that a man behaves [with] himself - to guard his money and to distance all injury from him. And if he recounts things about him, he recounts them for praise, and he relate to his honor; and he does not become honored through his disgrace - and as they, may their memory be Blessed, said (Talmud Yerushalmi Chagigah 2:1), "One who is honored by the disgrace of his fellow has no share in the world to come, but one who treats his fellow with love, peace and neighborliness, seeks their benefit and is happy about their good, the verse states about him, 'Israel, about you will I be glorified' (Isaiah 49:3)."

And this commandment is practiced in every place and at all times. And one who transgresses it and is not careful about the money of his fellow, to guard it - and all the more so, if he injures him with money or caused him pain in any matter, volitionally - has violated this positive commandment; besides the liability that there is in it according to the matter in which he injured him, as is explained in its place.

Sefer HaChinukh

Mitzvah 244

To not mate a beast, a specie with not its specie: To not mate a beast [in a] forbidden mixture - meaning to say that we not graft a male with any specie of [domesticated] beast or [wild] animal which is not its specie - as it is stated (Leviticus 19:19), "your beast shall you not mate [in a] forbidden mixture." And in its explanation, they, may their memory be Blessed, said (Bava Metzia 91a) that the obligation is from when he inserts like 'the brush into the tube' - and then is he lashed.

It is from the roots of the commandment that God, Blessed be He, created His world with wisdom, with understanding and with knowledge, and [so] He made and formed all of the forms according to that which it was fitting for its matter to be, to be designed [according to] the design of the world - and Blessed is He that knows [this]. And this is what is stated about the story of creation (Genesis 1:31), "And God saw everything that He had done, and behold, it was very good." And his seeing, Blessed be He, is His knowledge and contemplation about things; as He, Blessed be He, does not need seeing things with the eye after the act, due to His great level; since everything is revealed and known and apparent in front of Him before the act, [just] like after the act. But the Torah speaks to people with words directed to them, and it calls things by the name of things that are aimed at them, as it only possible to speak with a creature with what is known to him - as who can understand what he does not have the power to understand? And about what is similar to this, they, may their memory be Blessed, said (Mekhilta d'Rabbi Yishmael 19:18:2), [it is] in order to break [to assuage] the ear to that which it can hear. And in that God knew that everything He made was designed perfectly for its matter that it needed in His world, He commanded to each and every specie to make its 'fruit' for its specie - as it is written in the Order of Bereshit - and that the species not mix, lest it will take away from their perfection and He [therefore] not command His blessing upon them. And according to what it seems in our thoughts, it is from this root that we were prevented from mating beasts [in a] forbidden mixture. And likewise, from this reason where we warned about this, combined with another reason that we already wrote about species of seeds and trees (Sefer HaChinukh 62).

From the laws of the commandment is that which they, may their memory be Blessed, said (Bava Kamma 54b) that it is not specifically [domesticated] beasts that are [under] this prohibition, but even a [wild] animal or a bird - so long as he mates them with what is not their specie, he is lashed for them. And even if he mates a [domesticated] beast or a [wild] animal with an animal in the sea, he is lashed. And it is one, whether it is a [domesticated] beast, a [wild] animal or a bird of his, or [one] of his fellow - he is lashed for them. And that which they said (Bava Metzia 91b) that it is permissible to bring in two species into one pen; and if they mate, he is not required to separate them. And that which they said (Bava Metzia 90a) that it is forbidden for an Israelite to mate his beast [in a] forbidden mixture, by way of a gentile. And so [too,] that which they said that one who transgressed and grafted [it] with what is not its specie, what is born from them is permitted in benefit and in eating - so long as they are both pure animals. And anything that is two species is included in this prohibition, even if they are similar to one another. And anything that is one specie, even though one lives in the wild and the other [with man], is permissible. But the domesticated goose and the wild goose are not [included] in this dispensation, since they are two species, as the testicles of the domesticated are internal and the testicles of the wild are external. And a koi is a forbidden mixture with a [domesticated] beast and with a [wild] animal; but we do not administer lashes for it, since [its status] is a doubt.

And regarding this prohibition, everything follows the mother, such that we are not concerned about the seed of the father at all, according to that which is apparent from the decision of Rabbi Alfasi, may his memory be Blessed. But there are other commentators (Tosafot s.v. aeyil on Chullin 79a) that decided that since they were in doubt about this matter in the Gemara - whether we are concerned about the seed of the father or not concerned - we always go towards the stringent about it. And regarding "it and its child," we are concerned about the seed of the father, and [so] we do not slaughter the father with the child if we know [who] he [is]. But concerning mating, plowing and leading one with the other, we are not concerned about the seed of the father - to consider him [as] one specie with the son, so long as the mother is of a different specie. This is what comes out of the discussion with the good commentary in the chapter [entitled] Oto ve'et Beno (Chullin 79a). And there in the

Gemara, they mentioned for us the signs [with which] to recognize the species of mules: that are like the mother with the ears, the tail and the voice. And there is no doubt that in that the specie of the mother of mules is [all] the same, the specie of their fathers is also the same - this is known to all men. And the rest of the details of the commandment are in Tractate Kilayim (see Tur, Yoreh Deah 297).

And it is practiced in every place and at all times by males and females. And one who transgresses it and mates forbidden mixtures - and that is when he inserts like 'the brush into the tube' - is lashed from Torah writ. But if he [only] puts this one on that one or helps them with the voice, we strike him with lashes of rebellion.

Mitzvah 245

To not sow seeds of forbidden mixtures and not graft in any place in the Land: To not sow two species of seed, such as wheat and barley or fava beans and peas, together - only in the Land of Israel - as it is stated (Leviticus 19:19), "your field shall you not sow [with] a forbidden mixture." And the explanation comes about it (Kiddushin 39a) that the verse is speaking about a field that we have in the Land.

I have written what I have known from the roots of the commandment on the preceding commandment, and likewise on the commandment of a witch in the Order of Mishpatim (Sefer HaChinukh 62).

From the laws of the commandment is that which they, may their memory be Blessed, said (Moed Katan 2b) that it is one whether one sows or weeds or covers with dirt - they are all included in sowing, to be lashed for them. And whether he covered [the seeds] with his hand, with his foot or even with a tool - he is lashed for all of them. And one who sows them in a holed pot, is like he sows in the actual ground (Mishnah Kilayim 7:8). And that which they said (Talmud Yerushalmi Kilayim 1:1) that there is only a prohibition on account of forbidden mixtures of seeds with seeds that are fitting for human food. But the bitter seeds - even those that are capable of healing people - do not have [the prohibition] of forbidden mixtures of seeds. And behold, forbidden mixtures of trees are included in this negative commandment of "your field shall you not sow [with] a forbidden mixture." However, the prohibition of forbidden mixtures of trees is only by way of grafting - for example, that he grafted a sprig of an apple tree to a citron (etrog) tree, and all that is similar to it, that are two species. But by way of sowing - for example, to sow the seed of a tree with [other] seeds - this thing is permissible even from the outset; except for the vineyard, as we will explain in the Order of Ki Tetseh (Sefer HaChinukh 549), with God's help.

And they, may their memory be Blessed, said (Mishnah Kilayim 8:1) that even though there is lashes for both one who sows seeds of a forbidden mixture and one who grafts trees of a forbidden mixture - behold, they are permitted to be eaten; as it is only their planting that was forbidden. And so [too,] they permitted planting a sprig of a tree that was grafted with a forbidden mixture, and to plant a seed that was sowed in a forbidden mixture. And seeds are divided into three groups and three names and these are them: grains, legumes and garden seeds - and there are some of the garden seeds that are called types of vegetables. And even though it was forbidden to us to mix two types of seeds even if they are of one name - for example, wheat with barley, in that both of them are called grain; and so [too,] fava beans and peas, even though both of them are called legumes - nonetheless, there is a small distinction between them in the difference of the name. How is this? That if one part of wheat bigger than the twenty-three [individual] parts of barley was mixed unintentionally, there is no need to separate it out; less than this, he must separate it. But if it was from the garden seeds that was mixed, its measure is one in twenty-four of that which we plant from that type of garden seed in [a field, the measure of which is] a beit seah. And grain and legumes are like one specie concerning this, and their measurement is one part in twenty-four of grain [regardless of how much of that type is planted in a field]. And they, may their memory be Blessed, said (Mishnah Shekalim 1:1) that we announce about the shekalim and forbidden mixtures on the first of Adar; and everyone goes out to his garden and to his field, and cleans it from [these mixtures]. And everything that is two species, even though they are similar in their shape, are forbidden on account of forbidden mixtures. And everything that is one specie, even though their shapes are different because of the variation of location or the variation in the work on the land - behold, it is like one specie.

And the laws of the measure of distancing needed between two species are many (Mishnah Kilayim 2:10). And they, may their memory be Blessed, said (Rashi s.v. vaechat be'emtsa on Shabbat 84b) that the measure of distancing of two species of vegetables such that they not feed one from the other is a handbreadth and a half for each one, such that it comes out that the gap [between] the two of them is three handbreadths. And that which they said in Mishnah Kilayim 3:1 - and it was also brought in Shabbat in the chapter [entitled] Amar Rabbi Akiva (Mishnah Shabbat 9:2) - that we plant five [types] of seeds in a garden bed that is six handbreadths by six handbreadths. And that, which according to our words, they should have said nine - eight on the four sides and one in the middle - is not difficult; as they already resolved it in the Talmud Yerushalmi Shabbat 9:2), that [the Mishnah] was learned about a garden bed [surrounded by other] garden beds.

And the principle that comes out in our hands from their words, may their memory be Blessed, regarding forbidden mixtures of seeds is that anytime that there is a proper distance between the two types - and that is one and a half handbreadths, as we said - even if the leaves are mixed up, we do not concern ourselves about them; and likewise, anytime they appear separated one from the other, such that the leaves of one garden bed lean to one side and the leaves of the garden bed adjacent to it [lean] to another side - even though they are feeding one from the other - we do not concern ourselves with their feeding. As the Torah [only] paid heed to both of them together - that they feed one from the other and that their feeding be seen clearly by the eyes of the onlookers. And about what are these words speaking, that it needs distancing, or something that separates? When he sowed in his [own] field. But if his field is planted with wheat, it is permitted for his fellow to sow barley adjacent to it; as it is stated, "your field shall you not sow [with] a forbidden mixture" - meaning to say, specifically, your field - as it was not written, "the land shall you not sow [with] a forbidden mixture." And they, may their memory be Blessed, also learned (Kiddushin 39a) [from] "your field," to say that it is only in the Land that the prohibition of forbidden mixtures of seeds is practiced, but not outside of the Land. [This is the case,] even though they did not say thus regarding the grafting of trees, which is also derived from "your field," but which is rather practiced in every place - and as Shmuel said [there] in the first chapter of Kiddushin, since he compares the grafting of trees to the mating of beasts which is practiced in every place. They, may their memory be Blessed have already resolved [this difficulty] there in Kiddushin. And if you desire, my son, to know [their resolution], see it there. And the rest of its details are in Tractate Kilayim.

And the prohibition of forbidden mixtures of seeds is practiced by males and females only in the Land of Israel, as we said. But outside of the Land, it is permitted to mix seeds from the outset and to sow them. And even in the Land, the prohibition is only on an Israelite, but it is permitted to say to a gentile to sow a forbidden mixture for him. Nonetheless, it is forbidden for [the Israelite] to maintain them in his field once they grow. And all that we have said is specifically with forbidden mixtures of seeds. But forbidden mixtures of trees - meaning to say, the grafting which is forbidden with them - is practiced even outside the Land, as we said; and it is forbidden for an Israelite to allow a gentile to graft his tree, even outside of the Land. And one who transgresses this - whether a man or a woman - and sows forbidden mixtures of seeds in the Land of Israel is liable for lashes. And one who grafts a tree to a tree that is not its specie, or a vegetable with a tree or a tree with a vegetable - even outside of the Land, and all the more so in in the Land - is also liable for lashes.

Mitzvah 246

To not eat orlah: That we not eat from the fruits of a tree during the time of its orlah, which is the first three years from its being planted. And it is the same if one planted a sapling or a sprig from a tree, as it is stated (Leviticus 19:23) "three years shall it be orlah for you, it shall not be eaten."

I have written from the roots of this commandment on the commandment of the fourth-year plant (Sefer HaChinukh 247) in this Order, in the name of Rambam, may his memory be Blessed.

From the laws of the commandment is that which they, may their memory be Blessed, said (Mishnah Orlah 1:1) that one who plants for a hedge or for beams is exempted from orlah, as it is written, "food tree" - meaning to say that he did not plant it with the intention to eat its fruits, but rather that the tree will be a hedge around his garden, or with the intention that he will make beams for his house with it. [If] he planted it for a hedge or for a beam and went back and thought about it that it should be for food, he is obligated in orlah - once he mixed a thought of obligation into it, he is obligated. And what protects the fruit is [also] obligated in orlah; and like they expounded (Berakhot 36b), "'Its fruit (et piryo," the word et not being essential to the meaning), [to include] that which is secondary to the fruit" - meaning to say that which protects it. And it is with certain conditions known to our Rabbis, may their memory be Blessed, that that which protects the fruit is forbidden, until the time that the fruit reaches the category of the prohibition of orlah. And also, that the fruit needs it so much that if you took that which protects it, the fruit would die. And therefore, they, may their memory be Blessed, said that only the berries of the caper tree are obligated in orlah, but the capers (themselves, which covers the berries) are permitted, from this reason that we said; as it is well-known that if you take the capers before the fruits reach the prohibition of orlah, the fruit does not die. And the law of what is planted for the many (Mishnah Orlah 1:2), one who plants for a commandment and one who plants in a holed pot that he is obligated in orlah ; and the law of a young plant that is enmeshed in an old plant (Nedarim 57b). And the rest of its laws are elucidated in Tractate Orlah.

And [it] is practiced in every place and at all times by males and females. And Rambam, may his memory be Blessed, wrote (Sefer HaMitzvot LaRambam, Mitzvot Lo Taaseh 192) and this is his language: "As the prohibition of orlah outside of the Land is a law of Moshe from Sinai. However, the language of the Torah is that it is only in the Land." To here [are his words]. Since in the Torah it is stated explicitly, "And when you come to the land and plant" - which implies specifically in the Land. And explicitly did they, may their memory be Blessed, say (Kiddushin 39a) that so was it said about it [that] the law of Moshe from Sinai [is that] its definite is forbidden, but its doubt is permitted - meaning to say that its prohibition is not like the other prohibitions in the Torah, such that any time we encounter a doubt in a thing that is of Torah writ, we should forbid it from the doubt; since it is established for us that [in a case of] doubt about a Torah law, it is forbidden. And likewise, have we elucidated with the good commentaries that [a case of] doubt about a law of Moshe from Sinai [should be decided] towards stringency? But about the prohibition of orlah, we have received [from the tradition] that it was specifically said to Moshe that its doubt is permitted. And since this is so, that the prohibition of orlah does not rest at all [upon it] in a doubt, an Israelite that has a tree that is orlah in his garden is not at all required to inform his fellow that comes to eat from it, that it is orlah. And regarding this, we have found in the Gemara that they said (Kiddushin 39a), "It is a doubt to me and I will eat" - meaning to say that any time that a person does not know with certainty that it is orlah, it is permitted for him to eat from it. And one who transgresses it and eats a kazayit from fruits of a tree in its years of orlah - or even from that which protects the fruit, [in the case] that it was known as that which was forbidden with it - is liable for lashes.

Mitzvah 247

The commandment of the fourth year plant: That the fourth year plant be completely holy - the explanation [of which] is that all fruits that come out of the tree in the fourth year from its planting are holy; meaning to say, that they are eaten by the owners in Jerusalem, like the second tithe, and that is their holiness - as it is stated (Leviticus 19:23-24), "and you shall plant any food tree[...] And in the fourth year all of its fruit shall be holy, for praising to the Lord." And the explanation comes about it that it is for the owners - and the explanation of praising is that the owners should eat it in Jerusalem, and that is rejoicing. And the Sages called it the fourth-year plant, in every place. And in Sifrei Bamidbar 6:1, it expounds that the fourth-year plant is for the owners, from that which is written (Numbers 5:10), "And a man's consecrated things shall be his." As they said there, "'A man's consecrated things, etc.' - it pulled back all of the consecrated things and gave them to the priests; and there is nothing remaining for them except for the thanksgiving-offering, the peace offering, the Pesach offering, the animal tithe, the second tithe and the fourth-year plant, which are for the owners. It is from the roots of the commandment that God wanted man to be inspired to praise God, Blessed be He, with the beginning of the best fruits of his trees; so that the pleasantness of God, may He be

Sefer HaChinukh

Blessed, and His blessing rest upon him, and [that] his fruits be Blessed. Because the Good God wants the good of His creatures; therefore, He commanded us to bring them up and to eat them in the place He chose long ago for His service, Blessed be He - for there has He commanded blessing. And the best of the fruits of the tree come out in the fourth year. And there is another benefit to man that he is commanded to eat some of his fruits - such as this and the second tithe and also the animal tithe - in that place; because through this, his dwelling or the dwelling of some of his sons will be fixed in that place, to study Torah there. Since the teachers of Torah and the center of wisdom is there, and as we will write on the commandment of the second tithe (Sefer HaChinukh 473), with God's help.

And Ramban, may his memory be Blessed, wrote about the reason for the commandment in his commentaries (Ramban on Leviticus 19:23) [that it is] to honor God, may He be Blessed, from the beginning of all our produce, and not to eat from them until we bring all of the fruits of one year [as] 'praising to the Lord.' And behold, within the first three years, the fruit is not fit to offer, since it is meager; and also, because [the tree] does not give taste or a good fragrance into its fruit [then]; also, because most trees do not put out fruit at all until the fourth year from their planting - and so we wait for them all. And this commandment is similar to the first-fruits. And he also wrote that the truth of the thing is also that the fruit at the beginning of its planting until the fourth year is full of moisture that is very clingy, [which] injures the body and [so] is not good to eat; like the fish that have no scales, and the [other] foods prohibited by the Torah, which are bad also for the body.

From the laws of the commandment is that which they, may their memory be Blessed, said (Berakhot 35a) that one who wants to redeem the fourth-year plant, redeems it like the second tithe, which [can be] redeemed - meaning to say, that he redeems it with money and brings [that] up to Jerusalem. And if he redeems it himself, he adds a fifth. As so is the law with the second tithe, from that which it is written about it (Leviticus 27:31), "And if a man surely redeems his tithes." But one who redeems the second tithe for others, does not add a fifth. And he does not redeem [the fourth-year plant] until it reaches the season of the tithe; as it is stated about it (Leviticus 19:25), "to increase its produce for yourselves" - and they, may their memory be Blessed, expounded (Sifra, Kedoshim, Section 3:10), "Until it becomes produce" - meaning to say that it reaches the season of the tithe, and that is a third of its ripeness. And according to Rambam (Mishneh Torah, Laws of Second Tithes and Fourth Year's Fruit 9:2), may his memory be Blessed, we do not redeem it when it is attached [to the tree], like the tithe. But others explain (Rash on Orlah 5:5) that we redeem it even attached. And it is called money of the Higher Realm, like the tithe. And therefore, it cannot be acquired as a gift - unless he gave it when it is still unripe fruit, as the obligation has not yet rested upon it, as we said. And its law in the other things - such as eating, drinking and anointment - is like the tithe. And on the commandment of the second tithe in Parshat Reeh Anochi (Sefer HaChinukh 473), we will write more about it at length with God's help.

And one who redeems a fourth-year vineyard - [if] he wants he redeems it [as] grapes, [and if] he wants, he redeems it [as] wine; and so [too,] olives. But with other fruits, he redeems them before they change from their natural state. And the redemption is that he say, "These fruits are desanctified upon this money" - and behold, they are desanctified with this. And he [then] brings up the money and consumes [that which is purchased with it] in Jerusalem. And Shmuel said in the Gemara (Kiddushin 11b) that consecrated things worth a maneh (a hundred large coins) that is desanctified upon the value of a perutah (the smallest coin) is desanctified (is effective) - but not less than the value of a small coin, as it does not have the legal status of money, for any [purpose]. And the same is the law for the fruits of the fourth year. And a fourth-year vineyard does not have [the law of] forgotten [grapes] and the corner (Mishnah Maasrot 5:3), nor fallen grapes and bunchless grapes. And we do not separate the priestly tithe and the [other] tithes from it, but rather it all goes up to Jerusalem, or he redeems it and brings up the money and consumes it in Jerusalem. And the law of that which they, may their memory be Blessed, said from when do we count the new year for fourth year plant, and so [too,] (Talmud Yerushalmi Orlah 1:1) that everything that is obligated in orlah is obligated in the fourth year. And in the commandment of orlah (Sefer HaChinukh 246), we will write about this at length, with God's help - and we will write which tree is obligated in it, and what [part] of the tree.

And from it, we will learn to the fourth year. And the rest of all of its details are elucidated in the last chapter of Maaser Sheni (see Mishneh Torah, Laws of Second Tithes and Fourth Year's Fruit 9).

And this commandment is practiced at the time of the [Temple] in the Land by males and females, but not outside the Land. And so wrote Rambam, may his memory be Blessed (Mishneh Torah, Laws of Second Tithes and Fourth Year's Fruit 9:1): "In the same way as there is no second tithe in Syria, so is there no fourth-year plant in Syria." To here [are his words]. And all the more so outside of the Land. But there are some of our rabbis who instructed (see Tosafot s.v. ouleman on Berakhot 35a) us today that the obligation of this commandment is even now in the Land; and [that] even outside the Land, fourth year vineyard is practiced rabbinically. And according to this, every man should now redeem the fruits of his fourth-year vineyard upon the worth of a small coin or more. They also said that we recite a blessing over the redemption and, afterwards, we throw the redemption into the Dead Sea - meaning to say a desolate place - so that no creature benefit from it, as it is [still] holy today, rabbinically. And afterwards he eats the fruit of his vineyard. But fourth year plants are not practiced at all outside the Land, even rabbinically. And one who transgresses this commandment and does not bring up the fruits or their redemption to Jerusalem at the time of the [Temple] - or does not redeem it in the Land, according to the opinion of some commentators, even today - has violated this positive commandment, and has not desired blessing. And one who fulfills it will be Blessed.

Mitzvah 248
To not eat or to drink in the way of a glutton and a drunkard: To not indulge in much eating and drinking in the days of youth, according to the conditions described with a rebellious son (ben sorrer oumoreh) in Scripture, with what the Sages, may their memory be Blessed, explained about it in Tractate Sanhedrin. And the warning to us about this is from that it is written (Leviticus 19:26), "You shall not eat upon the blood." As so did they say explicitly in Sanhedrin 63a, "From where is the warning for a rebellious son? [Hence] we learn to say, 'You shall not eat upon the blood'" - meaning to say, do not eat an eating that leads to shedding blood, and that is the eating of the rebellious son, such that he is liable the death penalty for such a bad eating. And Rambam, may his memory be Blessed, wrote (Sefer HaMitzvot LaRambam, Mitzvot Lo Taase 195), "And even though this is a general negative commandment as we have explained in the ninth principle, it is not distant [to say] that when the punishment is explicit - meaning to say the punishment of the rebellious son, the statute of which is stoning, being explicit in Scripture - we are not concerned about whether the warning is from the general negative commandments." And he gave a reason for his words, as it is written in his book, Negative Commandment 195, and in the ninth principle. And Ramban, may his memory be Blessed, wrangled with him greatly about this. However, they both concede that the negative commandment of "You shall not eat upon the blood," and anything similar to it that includes many things - as we will write here - and their content and the reason for their prohibition is not the same, except that Scripture forbids them all in one negative commandment and in one category (literally, with one name), is called a general negative commandment. And it a law that we do not administer lashes for a general negative commandment. But Rambam, may his memory be Blessed, would say that because of this is the rebellious son punished with the death penalty for this eating - since Scripture explicitly revealed that his punishment is stoning in another place. And he elucidated at the the introduction to his book (Sefer HaMitzvot LaRambam, Root 14 at the end) that anything about which Scripture makes liable for excision or the death penalty of the court is a negative commandment, except for the Pesach sacrifice and circumcision - as they have excision but they are positive commandments. And from this principle was it derived by the Rabbi that the law of the warning of the rebellious son - even though it is learned from a general negative commandment - is like the law of other warnings, since Scripture made the punishment of the death penalty about it explicit.

And Ramban, may his memory be Blessed, does not hold of this approach and he does not lean towards it; but [rather] he holds that there always be an explicit warning about the one to be lashed or about the one being killed - and not from a general negative commandment. And even if Scripture makes his death penalty explicit a hundred times, the Rabbi will still say that it does not punish unless

Sefer HaChinukh

it warns (and not from a general negative commandment). And he does not consider a general negative commandment as a warning in the place of lashes, because of that which is a famous law in our hands, "We do not administer lashes for a general negative commandment." And therefore he, may his memory be Blessed, said that they already clarified in the Gemara from which verse we learned to administer lashes to the rebellious son: And they said in Sanhedrin 71b, "It is like Rabbi Abahu, as Rabbi Abahu said, 'We learned lashes for one who puts out a bad name, as it is written about him (Deuteronomy 22:18), "and they shall chasten him," from "and they chastised him" (Deuteronomy 21:18) that is written about the rebellious son; and "son" from "son" [in] "And if the evildoer be a son of (liable for) lashing" (Deuteronomy 25:2).'" And there is also a difficulty for Rambam, may his memory be Blessed, in this, [since] he writes in the second root, that we do not give lashes by the power of a comparison (which is what seems to be indicated here). And he also challenged the Rabbi about his statement that the rebellious son is liable for the death penalty for his indulging in much eating and he did not distinguish between the first eating and the second. But they said explicitly in the Gemara in Sanhedrin 71 that we do not punish the first eating of the rebellious son with the death penalty, but rather lashes, as they said, "We warn him in front of two [witnesses] and we lash him in front of three. [If] he goes back and goes bad, he is judged by twenty-three [judges for the death penalty]." He, may his memory be Blessed, also wrote and this is his language, "And what is fit to take out from this is that the first eating is prevented (forbidden) and its punishment is lashes, and the punishment of the second is death, and they are two preventions (negative commandments) in the tally of commandments, and they are [both] included in 'You shall not eat upon the blood.'" To here [are his words].

And behold I will mention to you from the things that they, may their memory be Blessed, explained (Sanhedrin 63a) are included in this negative commandment: They, may their memory be Blessed, said that there is a warning to [not] eat an animal before its soul departs; and also, to [not] eat consecrated meat before the sprinkling of the blood, and like they said (Sanhedrin 63a), "Do not eat the meat and the blood is still in the bowl." And so [too,] did they learn from it that we do not provide a consolation meal over those killed by the court; and so [too,] that a Sanhedrin that killed a soul not taste anything all of that day; and that a person not taste anything before he prays (Berakhot 10b); and so [too] the warning to the rebellious son, as we said.

It is from the roots of the commandment [that it is] because most sins of people are done as a result of much eating and drinking, as it is written (Deuteronomy 32:15), "And Yeshurun grew fat and kicked." And so [too,] "you became fat, you became thick, you became covered; and he abandoned the God that made him, etc." And so [too,] did they, may their memory be Blessed, say [about a man's cow] (Berakhot 32a), "Who caused you to kick (rebel against) me? The vetch which I fed you." And more generally they said, "Filling his stomach is a type of sin" - meaning to say after filling the stomach, a person come to do bad sins. And the matter is that foodstuffs are the dough for the physical, whereas contemplation of the intellect and of the fear of God and His precious commandments is the dough of the soul. And the soul and the physical are complete opposites, as I have written at the beginning of the book. And so with the strengthening of the dough of the physical, the dough of the soul is weakened a little. And from this root there were some of the Sages, may their memory be Blessed, that would only benefit from foodstuffs just what they required, only to keep their souls alive; and as it is written (Proverbs 13:28), "A righteous person eats to the satiation of his soul." And therefore, for our good, did our perfect Torah prevent us form indulging in eating and drinking more than is necessary - lest the physical overcome the soul greatly, until it makes it ill and destroys it completely. And so in order to distance this matter fully, it warned us about this with a strong punishment - and that is the death penalty. And this is what appears [correct] to me about the topic. And a man is warned about this at the start of the power of the passion of his youth and at the beginning of his obligation to guard his soul (to observe the commandments) - and these are the first three months from when he begins to grow two [pubic] hairs until [the hair] surrounds the whole member. And from that time, he is to take ethical teaching for all of his days. As in those foods are a constant matter with man - it is impossible for him without it - the Torah did not command about it at every instance, but rather it 'teaches him early' at one time, to benefit him for all of the times.

Sefer HaChinukh

From the laws of the commandment is that which they, may their memory be Blessed, said (Sanhedrin 70a) that a rebellious son is not liable until he steals from his father and buys meat and wine on the cheap; he eats them outside of his father's domain in an assemblage where they are all empty and lowly people; he eats meat raw but not [fully] raw, like the thieves are wont to eat, and drinks the wine diluted but not [fully] diluted, like the guzzlers are wont to drink; and he eats the weight of fifty dinar of this meat in one mouthful and drinks half a log of this wine at once. And that which they said (Sanhedrin 70a) that if he eats this ugly eating from forbidden meat or on a day that it is forbidden to eat - and even on a rabbinic fast - he is not liable, as it is stated (Deuteronomy 21:20), "he does not listen to our voice" - one who only transgresses their voice with this eating, to exclude this one that also transgresses words of Torah. And that which they said, if he ate from any other food but did not eat the meat of a [domesticated] beast [or] drank from any drink but did not drink wine, he is exempt. And the reason is from the root that we wrote, as the nature [of a person] is not drawn to anything so much as to these. And the law of how we judge him, how they warn him (Sanhedrin 71a) and how we proclaim about him. And that which they said (Sanhedrin 71a) that the law of the rebellious son is not enacted unless both the father and the mother want it, as it is stated (Deuteronomy 21:19), "And his father and mother shall grab him." And if one of them was stump-armed or mute or blind, he is not made a rebellious son, as it is stated, "shall grab him" - and not stump-armed people; "and bring him out" - and not lame people; "And they shall say" - and not mutes; "This son of ours" - and not blind people; "he will not obey our voices," - and not deaf people. And because of all these matters, there were some of the Sages that said in the Gemara that the law of the rebellious son was never executed. But there is one that testified that he saw him and even sat on his grave. And that which they said (Sanhedrin 71a) that at the beginning we lash him, as it is stated, "and they disciplined him" - and they, may their memory be Blessed, explained "they disciplined him" is lashes. And the rest of its details are in the eighth chapter of Sanhedrin.

And it is practiced in the Land of Israel alone - as we only judge capital cases there, and with a court of at least twenty-three. And this law is only practiced by males and not be females, as it is not their way to be drawn to eating and drinking like men. And that is what is stated, "a gluttonous and drunkard son" - and not daughter, and not [a child the sex of which is in doubt]. And even [one] who was cut open and found to be a male, does not become a rebellious son, as it is stated, "When there is to a man a gluttonous son" - until he is a son from the time that he existed. And one who transgresses this and becomes a rebellious son, according to all of the things that we wrote, is stoned. And behold, he is like all those killed by the court, such that their money [goes] to their inheritors - as even if his father caused him stoning, behold, he inherits all of his properties.

Mitzvah 249
To not divine: That we not follow divinations, as it is stated (Leviticus 19:26), "you shall not divine." And it is repeated in another place, as it is stated (Deuteronomy 18:10), "There shall not be found in you, etc. or a diviner." And they said in Sifrei Devarim (Shoftim), "'A diviner' - such as one who says, 'My bread fell from my mouth, the stick fell from my hand, a snake passed on my right and a fox on my left,' and he refrains from some act because of it." And in Sifra, Kedoshim, Chapter 6:2 they said, "'You shall not divine' - such as those that divine with weasels, birds, stars and what is similar to them." To here [are the words of the Sifra]. And such as that which the silly masses among the nations say: Since he came back from his path that he was walking, a deer passed in front of him, or a yelling crow passed over his head or if he saw thing x at the beginning of the day - he will not have profit today or any [other] bad event will come to him. And all of these acts and similar to them are included in this negative commandment.

It is from the roots of the commandment [that it is] because these matters are crazy things and total foolishness; and it is not fitting for the holy true people that God chose that they pay attention to false words. And also, because they are a cause to push man away from faith in God, may He be Blessed, and from His holy Torah and to come through them to complete denial [of God and/or Torah]; as he will think that all of his good and all of his evil and all that happens to him is coincidental, and not from the supervision of his Creator. And it will happen that through this he will go out from all of the principles of the religion. Therefore, since God, may He be Blessed, wanted our good, He commanded us to remove this thought from our hearts. As all the bad and the good comes out of the mouth of the Highest, according to the actions of man - if they are good, or if they are evil. And the divinations do not [help or hurt], and as it is written (Numbers 23:23), "As there is no divination in Yaakov and no clairvoyance in Israel." The details of the commandment are in the seventh chapter of Shabbat [in Chapter 6 of Sanhedrin] and in the Tosefta Shabbat, Chapter 8.

And [it] is practiced in every place and at all times by males and females. And one who transgresses it and does any act according to divination with witnesses and a warning is lashed - and specifically with a court of twenty-three. In every place that we wrote "lashed," in that which preceded and that which we will write, the intention is in the Holy Land - since it is the place of the judgement of twenty-three. As we do not judge capital cases outside of the Land, except only with a talebearer; since his death is the salvation and resuscitation of others better than he.

Mitzvah 250

To not soothsay: To not soothsay, as it is stated (Leviticus 19:26), "and you shall not soothsay (teonenu)." And the understanding of the matter is like they said in Sifra, Kedoshim, Chapter 6:2, that it is an expression of a time period (onah). [This] means to say that we do not fix time periods to say time x is good to do action y; and anyone who does it at that time will be successful, but one who does it at time z will not be successful - like the empty clairvoyants say. And the negative commandment about this matter is repeated in the Order of Shoftim, as it is written there (Deuteronomy 18:10), "There shall not be found in you, etc. a soothsayer." And they, may their memory be Blessed, said (Sanhedrin 65b) that included in this negative commandment of the soothsayer is the fooling the eyes that people do. And this matter is a great type of machination that is connected with lightness of hand and its powerful quickness to the point that it appears to people that the trickster is doing fantastic things, meaning to say that they are supernatural. As what those that make efforts in this always do, such that they take a rope and put it into the corner of their clothes in front of people's eyes, and afterwards they take out a snake; and so [too,] they throw a ring into the air, and afterwards they take it out from the mouth of one of the bystanders in front of them; and many things similar to these. And each one of these evil acts is forbidden, and one who does it is called a fooler of the eyes. And it is included in the prohibition of the soothsayer and we administer lashes for it. And even though [the prohibition of the] soothsayer is stated next to the sorcerer in one verse, it is not precisely a type of magic. As if the prohibition about it was on account of the negative commandment of the sorcerer, we would not administer lashes for it, since the negative commandment of the sorcerer is given over to the warning of a death penalty from the court, as it is stated (Exodus 22:17), "You shall not keep a witch alive." And it is established for us (Eruvin 17b) that we do not administer lashes for any negative commandment that is given over to the warning of a death penalty from the court.

What we wrote about the negative commandment of the diviner adjacently is from the roots of the commandment. And there is another very great damage that is found with this, since it will [cause that] the masses and the women and the youths will accept that which is completely impossible as possible. And it will be sweet for their minds to accept the impossible and that it be possible without the matter of a miracle from the Creator. And perhaps a bad outcome will result from this for them; to deny a fundamental principle, and their souls will be excised - and understand this. The details of the commandment are there in Sifra and in [various] places in the Gemara and in the Midrash.

And this prohibition is practiced in every place and at all times by males and females. And one who transgresses it and says time periods to people that they should perform their actions in order that they be successful - and also the one who does his actions according to [these] time periods - is liable for lashes. And a man who asks of one who knows [these time periods] does not have a liability for lashes with the question alone, until he designs his action to be with the known time, and does his work during it. And then is he lashed on its account, since he did an act.

Mitzvah 251

Sefer HaChinukh

To not encircle the corner of the head: To not encircle the corner of the head, as it is stated (Leviticus 19:27), "You shall not encircle the corner of your head." And they, may their memory be Blessed, explained that the matter is that it is forbidden for an Israelite to shave and even out the hair of his head behind his ears and to his forehead, like the idolaters and their priests do also today. And this is what they, may their memory be Blessed, said in Tractate Makkot 20b, "Which is [the prohibition of] the corner of the head? That is the one that evens his temples to the back of his ears and to his forehead."

It is from the roots of the commandment [that it is] in order to distance from ourselves any matter of idolatry and anything that is done for its sake, and to make it forgotten from between our eyes and from all of our actions. And the warning comes explicitly about a thing that people do on their bodies, since it is 'a perpetual reminder of iniquity,' as it is something that is fixed in the body. And since this is from the central reasons for the commandment, they, may their memory be Blessed, needed to elucidate that encircling the entire head is also included in the commandment. That you not say that the point of that which was forbidden to us was that we not resemble them and they do not shave the entire head, they taught us that this too is included in this prohibition - as it appears in Yevamot 5a; that they said there, "Encircling the entire head is [called] encircling." And it is possible that the Torah forbade it all because of that which is similar to that which is similar (see Sefer HaMitzvot LaRambam, Mitzvot Lo Taase 43).

From the laws of the commandment is that which they, may their memory be Blessed, said in Makkot 20b, that it is one for the shaver and the one who is shaved so long as he assists - they are both liable. But if he did not assist, only the shaver is liable. And one who shaves a minor is [also] liable. And regarding the measurement of the corner of the head, the sages did not give a measurement. But Rambam, may his memory be Blessed, wrote (Mishneh Torah, Laws of Foreign Worship and Customs of the Nations 12:6), "We have heard from our elders that we do not leave less than forty hairs" - this is his language - "but it is permitted to shave the corner with scissors, as the Torah only forbade destruction of the blade;" or one who evens his temples to the back of his ears. And I have heard that regarding the corner of the head, even scissors that are like a blade are forbidden (all of this [after the quote] is in in the first Venice edition). And the rest of its details are at the end of Makkot (see Tur, Yoreh Deah 180-181).

And [it] is practiced in every place and at all times by males. But females - whether they shaved or whether they were shaved - are exempt. And [it is] like they, may their memory be Blessed, expounded (Kiddushin 35b), "'You shall not encircle the corner of your head and you shall not destroy the corner of your beard' - whoever has, do not destroy, etc." And nonetheless it is forbidden for them to shave the male, and even a minor. And slaves - even though they are in the category of women regarding many commandments - are liable for this, since they have a beard. And [those the sex of which is in doubt], behold [the law is in] doubt, and we give them the stringencies of the male and the female in this. And they are [accordingly] obligated in everything in every place. But if they transgressed - [because of the] doubt they are not lashed. And related to this matter, I will write the principle that they, may their memory be Blessed, taught us about the commandments for women - even though my way is to write it specifically about each and every commandment; since from between the principle and the specific case, the reader will remember it. And this is it: It is one, that [both] men and women are obligated in all of the negative commandments in the Torah, except for do not encircle, do not destroy and do not become impure by the dead. And women are exempt from all positive commandments determined by time, except for kiddush, matsa, eating the Pesach sacrifice, gathering and joy [on the holiday]. But they also said that we do not learn from principles - even in a place in which it is said about them, "except" [to conclude that these are the only exceptions]. As in order to shorten his principles, the one who generalizes will not concern himself with small things that differ from the principle, to put them into the book. And one who transgresses this and shaves one corner of the head is liable for one [set of] lashes. But if he shaved two temples - and even at one time with one warning - he is liable for two [sets of] lashes (see Makkot 20a). And the transcriber wrote in the name of Rambam, may his memory be Blessed (Sefer HaMitzvot LaRambam, Mitzvot Lo Taase 43), "And it is fitting that we not count them as two commandments, even though he is lashed [twice], since both of them are written within one negative commandment. As had it stated, 'You shall not encircle the right corner of your head and the left corner of your head,' and we had found that they are liable two [sets of lashes] for them; then it would have been permitted to say that we count them as two commandments. However, in that it is one word and one subject, it is truly [only] one commandment. And even though it comes in the explanation that it includes various parts of the body and that he is obligated for each one of them by itself; nonetheless, it does not require that they be several commandments." To here is his language.

Mitzvah 252
To not destroy the corner of the beard: To not destroy the corner of the beard, as it is stated (Leviticus 19:27), "and you shall not destroy the corner of your beard." And there are five corners to the beard, and there is a [separate] liability for lashes for each one, even if he removed them all at once and with one warning. And these are them: the upper and lower jaw on the right; the upper and lower on the left - behold, that is four - and the chin of the beard, and that is the place of connection of the jaws below, which is called menton in the vernacular - behold, that is five. And the language of the Mishnah (Mishnah Makkot 3:5) is "For the beard, five: two from here and two from there and one at their bottom." And the transcriber wrote in the name of Rambam, may his memory be Blessed, (on Sefer HaMitzvot LaRambam, Mitzvot Lo Taase 44), "And the prevention came about this with these words, 'and you shall not destroy the corner of your beard,' and it did not say, 'and you shall not destroy your beard' - even though it is all called the beard. It wanted to say with this that you should not shave even one corner from the whole of the beard. And we administer one [set of] lashes for each one. And even if he shaved all of them at one time, he is liable five [sets of] lashes for it."
That which we have written on the previous commandment to distance all matter of idolatry is from the roots of the commandment. And this was also a custom of the priests of idolatry, to destroy the corner of their beard. And he also wrote about this - and this is the language of the transcriber: "And that which determines that the five corners of the beard are not counted as five commandments is because the prevention comes with [one] distinct word, and it is [one] distinct subject; as we explained in the commandment before it." To here [are his words].
From the laws of the commandment is that which they, may their memory be Blessed, said (Makkot 21a) that the liability is only with shaving of a blade, as it is stated, "and you shall not destroy" - specifically a shaving that has destruction, and that is a blade. And so, did they, may their memory be Blessed, explain it. And Rambam, may his memory be Blessed, wrote (Mishneh Torah, Laws of Foreign Worship and Customs of the Nations 12:7), "And if he shaved with scissors, he is exempt." [It appears from his words that he is specifically exempt, but it is (still rabbinically) prohibited to do so. And it is possible that the matter is regarding shaving with scissors that are similar to a blade,] and as the matters appears to be in Tractate Nazir 59b. As they said there, "Rav said, 'A person may lighten all of his body with a blade'" - and we establish it to be [referring to] scissors similar to a blade; except for the underarm and the pubic area, which is forbidden even thus (this follows the first edition). [And it is permissible to shave the mustache with a blade, as there is no concern of a corner there at all.] And there are some great ones that are stringent not to pass a blade over any of their skin. And the rest of its details are elucidated at the end of Makkot.
And [it] is practiced in every place and at all times by males. But females are permitted regarding destruction of the beard - if they have hair there - [and a woman is exempt also for destroying the beard of man. But slaves are liable for the destruction of the beard], as we have written above (Sefer HaChinukh 251). And so [too], those [the sex of which is in doubt] are forbidden [based on the] doubt.

Mitzvah 253
That we not imprint an imprinted tatoo into our flesh: To not imprint an imprinted tatoo into our flesh, as it is stated (Leviticus 19:28), "and an imprinted tattoo you shall not put into your flesh." And the content is like that which the Yishmaelites do today, as they imprint an imprint that is inscribed and stuck into their flesh, such that it is never erased. And the liability is only with an imprint that is inscribed and impressed with ink or blue dye or with other colors that make an impression. And so

did they say in Makkot 21a, "[If] he tattooed, but did not imprint" - meaning to say, he did not make an impression with color - "[if] he imprinted, but did not tattoo" - meaning to say that he did make an impression [on] his flesh with a color, but he did not make a marking in his flesh - " he is not liable, until he imprints, and tattoos with ink, or with blue dye or with anything that makes an impression." That which we wrote on encircling the head and destroying the beard, which is to distance all matters of idolatry from our bodies and from between our eyes, is from the roots of the commandment. And this too is from this very root, as it was the custom of the [other] nations to make an impression upon themselves for their idolatry - meaning to say that he is a slave sold to it and marked for its service. From the laws of the commandment is that which they, may their memory be Blessed, said (Mishneh Torah, Laws of Foreign Worship and Customs of the Nations 12:11) that every place on the body - whether it is revealed, or whether it is covered by clothes - is included in this prohibition. And the rest of its details are at the end of Tractate Makkot.

And [it] is practiced in every place and at all times by males and females. And one who transgresses it and writes even one letter on any place of his body in the manner that we have said - that it be inscribed and generate an impression with one of the colors that make an impression - is lashed. But if others made an impression upon him, he is not lashed unless he assisted - due to the well-known principle [that] we do not administer lashes for a negative commandment that does not have an act [involved] with it.

Mitzvah 254

The commandment of awe for the Temple: To be inawed from the Temple, meaning to say that we set it up in our souls as a place of fear and awe, so that our hearts soften in our coming there to pray or to offer sacrifices, as it is stated (Leviticus 19:30), "and be inawed by My Temple." And they, may their memory be Blessed, explained in Sifra, Kedoshim, Chapter 7:9 and likewise in Berakhot 54a, "Which is awe? One may not enter the Temple Mount with his staff, with his shoes, with his money belt, with the dust on his feet or with money bundled into his cloak; and he may not make it a shortcut" - meaning to say he enter from one opening and exit from an opening across from it, only in order to shorten his path - "and through an a fortiori inference, spit" - and there is no need to say that the place is forbidden for spitting. And they also elucidated in Sanhedrin 101a that it is only fit for kings of the House of David to sit in the [Temple] yard, due to the honor of the monarchy - as it is stated (II Samuel 7:18), "And King David came and sat before the Lord." And they said in Sifra, Kedoshim, Chapter 7:7, "Not from the Temple should you be inawed, but from the One who commanded about the Temple."

I have written above on the commandment of "And let them make Me a sanctuary" (Sefer HaChinukh 95) [in the] Order of Vayikchu Li Trumah and in other places about the roots of this commandment. From the laws of the commandment is that which they, may their memory be Blessed, said (Megillah 28b) that a person may only enter any of the Temple Mount for the matter of a commandment. And anyone who has finished his service in the [Temple] and retires, walks backwards a little at a time; and so [too,] the men of the shift, the men of the watch and the Levites from their platforms, would leave like this from the Temple. And [also] that which they, may their memory be Blessed, said (Berachot 61b) [that] it is always forbidden to defecate or sleep between east and west, because the Sanctuary is in the West. And so [too,] (Rosh Hashanah 24a) is it forbidden for a person to build a house in the form of the Sanctuary, nor a portico in the form of the chamber nor a courtyard in the form of the [Temple] yard. And all of this is from the awe of the place. And the rest of the details of the honor of the [Temple] and its awe are in Middot and Tamid (see Mishneh Torah, Laws of The Chosen Temple 7).

And this commandment is practiced [even today] by males and females. As even though the Temple is destroyed today on account of our iniquities, every person is [still] obligated in its awe. And [so] he should only enter a place that it is permitted to enter when it is built, and he should not even sit in the courtyard; and he should not be light-headed opposite the Eastern Gate - as it is stated (Leviticus 19:30), "You shall keep my Shabbats and be inawed by My Temple"; and they said in Sifra, Kedoshim, Chapter 7:8, "Just like keeping the Shabbat is forever, so too is awe of the Temple forever." And one who transgresses it and acts light-headedly in these matters that we have said has violated this positive commandment.

Mitzvah 255
To not do an act of ov: To not do an act of ov - and that we not turn to it; meaning to say, that we not ask of it, as it is stated (Leviticus 19:31), "Do not turn to the ovs." And the content is that they offer well-known incense and perform well-known acts; and through these things, it appears to a person that he hears speech from under the armpit that answers what he will ask. And this is one of its types. And the language of Sifra, Kedoshim, Chapter 7:10 [is] " Ov is pitom which speaks from his armpit."

That which we have written on the prohibition of the diviner and the soothsayer (Sefer HaChinukh 249) is from the roots of this commandment. And [it is] since all of these nullities cause a person to leave the true fundamental religion and faith in God, may He be Blessed; and to turn to emptiness and think that everything that happens to him, happens by way of circumstance; and that it is in his hand to better himself and remove all injury from him with those questions and nullities that he will do. And all of this is not worth it for him, since everything is decreed by the Master of the World. And according to the proper deed or the sin that a person does, do things occur to him - whether good or whether bad - and as it is written (Job 34:11), "For the action of a man does He pay to him." And upon this it is fitting for a person to order all of his thoughts and to prepare all of his ways. And this is the thought of every person of the good Children of Israel. And also, as there is a tinge of idolatry in this matter of ov and yidaaoni. The details of the commandment are in the seventh chapter of Sanhedrin (see Mishneh Torah, Laws of Foreign Worship and Customs of the Nations 6).

And [it] is practiced in every place and at all times by males and females. And one who transgresses it and does [an act of] the ov volitionally and [in view of] witnesses is stoned. And if there are no witnesses [or] warning, it is with excision; [and if done] inadvertently, he brings a fixed sin-offering. And one who inquires of them [only violates] a negative commandment; but if he plans his actions and does according to their words, he is lashed.

Mitzvah 256
To not do an act of yidaaoni: To not do an act of yidaaoni, as it is stated (Leviticus 19:31), "Do not turn to the ovs and to the yidaaonis." And Rambam, may his memory be Blessed, explained (Sefer Ha Mitzvot, Mitzvot Lo Taaseh 9) and this is his language: "That the matter is that he takes a bone of a bird the name of which is yidoaa, places it into his mouth, burns types of incense to it, makes incantations and performs actions, until he is connected with the matter of the disease of epilepsy - like the disease that is called sovat - and speaks out predictions. And so did they, may their memory be Blessed, say (Sanhedrin 65a), ' Yidaaoni [is that] he places a well-known bone into his mouth and it speaks on its own.' And do not think that this is a general negative commandment, as it already separated them: When it mentioned the punishment, it stated, ' ov or a yidaaoni ' and made one liable for stoning and excision for each of the two of them, when volitional. And that is its stating (Leviticus 10:1), 'And a man or a woman that has an ov or a yidaaoni with them shall surely be killed, etc.' And the language of Sifra, Kedoshim, Chapter 9:1 [is] 'Since it states, "And a man or a woman, etc." We have heard the punishment; from where [do I know] the warning? [Hence] we learn to say, "Do not turn to the ovs and to the yidaaonis."'" Its neighbor, ov (Sefer HaChinukh 255), will speak about all of the content of yidaaoni. And there in Sanhedrin [in] the sixth chapter are its laws also elucidated.

Mitzvah 257
The commandment to honor sages: To honor sages and to rise in front of them, as it is stated (Leviticus 19:32), "Before an elder rise" - and Onkelos translated [it as], "Before one who understands the Torah rise" - "and dignify the face of the aged (zaken)." They, may their memory be Blessed, explained (Kiddushin 32b), "A zaken is only one who has acquired (shekanah) wisdom. And the reason that the verse expressed, the sage, with the language of "aged," is because the young sage has seen with his wisdom that which the aged has seen from his many years.

It is from the roots of the commandment [that it is] since the main [purpose] of man being in the world is wisdom, so that he can recognize his Creator. Therefore, it is fitting to honor someone who has attained it; and through this, others will be aroused to it. And from this root, Eesi ben Yehudah explained in the Gemara in Kiddushin that even a simple aged one - meaning to say that is not wise - is included in this commandment, such that it is fitting to honor him. Because from his many years, he saw and understood some of the works of God and his wonders. And as a result of this, he is fit for honor. And that is what Rabbi Yochanan said there in Kiddushin, "The law is like Eesi ben Yehudhah"; and that which they said (Sanhedrin 85a) [that it is] on condition that he is not a man of sins; as if so, he has prevented himself from honor.

From the laws of the commandment is that which they, may their memory be Blessed, said that there is no need to say that someone who is not a sage is obligated in the honor of a sage, but rather even a sage is obligated in the honor of [another] sage; as they, may their memory be Blessed, said (Bava Metzia 33a), "The Torah scholars in Babylonia get up for one another." And that which they also elucidated that with the honor of a teacher upon his student, there is a great addition upon the honor that he is obligated to any other sage. And they emphasized this to the point that they said (Avot 4:12) "The reverence of your teacher [should be] like the reverence of Heaven." And in the explanation, they said [between] his father and his teacher, his teacher has precedence in honor, in a lost object, in a load and in captivity. But if his father was a sage - even though he was not equivalent to his teacher - his father has precedence. And in the chapter [entitled] Chelek (Sanhedrin 110a), they said, "Anyone who disagrees with his teacher is as if he disagrees with the Divine Presence, as it is stated (Numbers 26:9), 'in their quarreling with the Lord.'" And they spoke at much length about this matter there.

And that which they, may their memory be Blessed, said (Kiddushin 31b) about the awe of his teacher, that he should not sit in his place, and not sustain his words, not contradict his words and never make a ruling in front of him - and even if he is within twelve mil of him, it is forbidden to make a ruling. And how should he stop him if he saw him transgressing words of the Torah; the distinction between his primary teacher - meaning to say, that most of his wisdom is from him - and a teacher that the majority of his wisdom is not from him; from when is he obligated to stand in front of his teacher, and in front of another sage; in which place and in which way is he exempt from rising; and the rest of the many details of these matters are in Kiddushin in the first chapter and in other places (see Tur, Yoreh Deah 244).

And likewise, from the laws of the commandment are matters from which the sages are exempted from the angle of their honor and awe - such as building and digging for the country and similar to them; and likewise, taxes that the kings impose on the people of the land, whether it is a tax that is fixed on all of the people of the city together (as a lump sum) or whether it is fixed on each and every man or whether it is not fixed at all. They are exempt from all of this, as it is stated (Hoshea 8:10), "Though they have hired among the nations, now I will gather them, and they will begin to be diminished by reason of the burden of kings and princes" (which is understood regarding this in Bava Batra 8a, "If all learn [Torah], I will gather them already now; and if only a few, they will be excused from the burden imposed by kings and princes").

And [it] is practiced in every place and at all times by males and females. And one who transgresses it has violated a positive commandment and his punishment is great, since this is a strong pillar in the religion.

Mitzvah 258

To not cheat in measures, and all measures are included: To not cheat in liquid and dry measures, and not with scales; and included in measures is also the measuring of lands; and anything that is measured by people, such as clothes and that which is similar to them - as it is stated (Leviticus 19:35), "You shall not pervert justice with measures of length, weight, or capacity (mesurah)." And they, may their memory be Blessed, explained (Bava Metzia 61b) that mesurah is a liquid and a dry measure; and it is the smallest measure, as it is one thirty-third of a log. And we learn from this that the Torah is concerned about the smallest amount with measures; meaning to say that even though the Torah was only concerned about [the value of] a small coin with other thefts, regarding measures, it was concerned about the smallest amount.

And the explanation of the verse is thus: "You shall not pervert justice" - and what is justice that is learned here? It is the 'measures of length, weight, or capacity.' And they, may their memory be Blessed, learned (Sifra, Kedoshim, Chapter 8:5) from this that the verse mentioned justice here since the measurer is called a judge. And if he lies about the measure, it is like he corrupts the judgement and it is called perversion, disgusting, anathema and abomination. And he causes five things that are said about a judge: he defiles the land; profanes God; removes the Divine Presence; brings Israel down with the sword; and exiles them from their land. And they emphasized the stringency of this commandment further and said (Bava Batra 88b), that its punishment is greater than the punishment for forbidden sexual relations; as [the latter] is between man and the Omnipresent and [the other] is between man and his fellow.

The root of this commandment is well-known, as I have written above in the positive commandment in this Order (Sefer HaChinukh 259).

From the laws of the commandment is that which they said (Bava Metzia 61b) that one who measures or weighs perversely - even though he is stealing without a doubt - does not pay double payment, but rather pays that which he caused him to lack from the measure or the weight. And so [too,] that which they, may their memory be Blessed, said (Bav Metzia 52a) to guard this commandment, that one should not make a sela that has been damaged into a weight, lest it get damaged further and the weight will be lacking; and he should not leave them in a place that others can [find and] make into a weight. And that which they spoke at length about this, to say that if it lacked and stood at exactly half, he can keep [it]. And that which they said [that] a person can make his measurements a seah and a half seah, etc.; but he should not make them two kav, so that it not be mixed up with a quarter seah, which is one and a half kav. And so [too,] with liquid measures, one can make a hin and a half hin, etc. - as it is found in a bereita in Bava Batra 89b.

And that which they said that one who measures land with a rope not measure it for one in the summer and for the other in the winter, because the rope contracts in the summer. And that which they said (Bava Batra 117b) that every person must be very exacting in the measurement of land, since there are many differences in the measurement of land between a mountain and a valley; and one must also also investigate the [differences] between the circles, the rectangles and the angles in it. And also many other matters which are elucidated in the books of the wisdom of mathematics and geometry that distinguish between a right angle, a broad angle and a narrow angle - and these are the three shapes ([pictured are] a right angle, a broad angle and a narrow angle); between a triangle of three equal sides (equilateral), a triangle in which only two sides are equal, and it is called a triangle of equal legs (isocles), and a triangle in which none of the sides are equal, which is called of varying sides (scalene); between a rectangle that is an even square, a rectangle that is elongated, a rhombus and a rhomboid. And there are several aspects to these - a large parchment could not contain [them] due to the many shapes that the masters of the wisdom of arithmetic and sizes that are called engineers have made about these matters. And we must be very careful about all aspects in the measurement of land.

And remember with this that the principles that the Sages, may their memory be Blessed, set down regarding matters of mathematics - such as that which they said (Eruvin 57a), "Any ell in a square is an ell and two fifths in diagonal"; and so [too,] "Everything that has three handbreadths in its circumference has a width of one handbreadth"; and so [too,] "How much more is a square than a circle? One fourth"; and similar to these principles - they, may their memory be Blessed, did not say with complete exactitude, but rather in approximation. And therefore, do not rely on it in the division of things among people. And do not wonder, how did they write things that were not exact, since they are men of truth, that God stands in their assembly. As they only needed the calculations for the perimeters of Shabbat or the planting of forbidden mixtures or their planting of trees, and similar to these things; and in this, that which they were not exact about it brings us to a stringency and does not damage any person's money. And nonetheless, they testified in most of these places that the calculation is not precise there. As they said in each and every place according to what is fit about it,

"That is that it is not precise, and it is not precise for stringency," and similar to this that they informed us in every place; such that we not attribute lack of concern or knowledge to them in any thing of this. And the rest of the details of the commandment are in [Bava] Batra and in other places (see Tur, Choshen Mishpat 230).

And [it] is practiced in every place and at all times by males and females. And one who transgresses it and lies about measures of length, weight, or capacity has transgressed a negative commandment. But we do not administer lashes for it, because it is given to repayment. And (Ramban) [Rambam], may his memory be Blessed, wrote (Mishneh Torah, Laws of Theft 7:8) that if one lied in measures even to a gentile that worships idolatry, he has transgressed a negative commandment and he is obligated to return [it]. And likewise is it forbidden to fool gentiles in calculations, as it is stated (Leviticus 25:50), "And calculate with his owner" - even if he is subjugated under your hand; all the more so towards a gentile that is not subjugated under your hand? And behold, it states (Deuteronomy 25:16), "For it is an abomination of God [...] anyone who does perversion" - in any case.

Mitzvah 259

The commandment of having just scales, weights and measures: To have just scales, weights and measures and to be very careful about them, as it is stated (Leviticus 19:36), "You shall have just scales, just weights, a just eiphah, and a just hin." And the language of Sifra, Kedoshim, Chapter 8:7 [is] "'Just weights' - justify the scales precisely" - meaning to say, that the scales be righteous. And the matter is well-known regarding scales that there are important adjustments to make, as it is possible to do many types of falsehood with them. "'Just weights' - justify the weights precisely" - also with weights, it is also possible to do many types of falsehood, and similar to that which they, may their memory be Blessed, said (Bava Metzia 61b), "I will repay in the future anyone who submersed his weights in salt." "'A just eiphah' - justify the eiphahs precisely; 'and a just hin' - justify the hin precisely." And an eiphah is a dry measure and a hin is a liquid measure. And the Torah warned us about each and every one of these things specifically, due to the severity of the matter - and even though it is all included in the principle of "And a man shall not cheat his compatriot." And the language of Sifra, Kedoshim, Chapter 8:10 [is] "On condition of this, I took you out from the Land of Egypt - that you accept upon yourselves the commandment of measures." And they, may their memory be Blessed, also said (Bava Metzia 61b), "I am He Who distinguished in Egypt between the drop of a firstborn and the drop that is not of a firstborn, and I am [He Who is] destined to exact punishment from one who submerses his weights in salt" in order to cheat the creatures, since they do not notice it.

The root of the commandment of righteousness and the distancing from robbery and deceit among people is well-known to all intelligent people.

From the laws of the commandment is, for example, that which they, may their memory be Blessed, said (Bava Batra 89a), that we do not make weights out of tin and lead and from any of the other types of metal, since they bring up rust and become lacking, but we [rather] make them out of stone and glass and what is similar to them; and the things that they said regarding the measurement of land; and that which they taught us about the shape of the leveler, that they call rasero in the vernacular. And they also said (Bava Batra 89b) that he should not cause foam in a liquid measure at the time that he measures, and even if it was the smallest measure. As behold, we have found that the Torah is concerned with measures about the smallest amount. As it is stated (Leviticus 19:35), "You shall not pervert justice with measures of length, weight, or capacity (mesurah)"; and mesurah is the smallest measure, as it is one thirty-third of a log. And the sizes that they, may their memory be Blessed, gave to the length of the bar of the scales and the length of the strings; and the distinction that they said between scales that are made to weigh one type and the scales for another type; and that which they said that the court is obligated to set up supervisors in each and every place to make rounds to regulate the scales and weights, and they have the authority to fine the money, and [even] the body of anyone with whom lacking scales are found; and the rest of its details [are] in the fifth chapter of [Bava] Batra (see Tur, Choshen Mishpat 231).

And [it] is practiced in every place and at all times by males and females. And one who transgresses it violates a positive commandment, besides having violated the negative commandment of cheating, of robbing and of stealing - if there is the value of a small coin in it. And that which is most difficult regarding the matter is that one who lies with measures will not pay attention to all of the customers; and [so] he does not know from whom he robbed, such that he return his theft to him. And this is what they, may their memory be Blessed, said (Bava Batra 88b), "Very difficult is the punishment for measures."

Mitzvah 260
To not curse father and mother: To not curse father and mother, as it is stated (Leviticus 20:9), "Any man that curses his father and his mother, etc." And the truth is that the main warning of cursing father and mother is not from Scripture, since here it only mentions the punishment of the one that curses; and so [too,] that which is written in the Order of Mishpatim (Exodus 21:17), "And he who curses his father and his mother shall surely be killed" - there too, it only spoke about the punishment. And that is what they said in Mekhilta d'Rabbi Yishmael 21:17:3, "'And he who curses his father and his mother, etc.' - we have heard the punishment, but from where is the warning? [Hence] we learn to say (Exodus 22:27) 'Lords you shall not curse, [etc.]' If his father is a chieftain (nassi), behold he is included in 'and a chieftain in your people you shall not malign.' If he is a boor, behold he is included in 'You shall not curse the deaf.' Hence it is to be derived by a constructive paradigm (binyan av) through the three of them, etc." until, "Their common denominator is that they are 'in your people,' and you are exhorted against cursing them. Your father, too, is 'in your people,' and you are exhorted against cursing him." And so did they say in Sifra, Kedoshim, Chapter 10:7, "'And he who curses his father and his mother - we have heard the punishment, etc." exactly like the language of the Mekhilta. And since there is no specific [textual] negative commandment to this warning - but rather it is comes out from the principle [understand by an analysis] of three negative commandments - I have written it on this verse that is speaking about the punishment [for it]. And likewise, Rambam, may his memory be Blessed, wrote about "he who curses his father and his mother shall surely be killed," that it is speaking about the punishment (Sefer Ha Mitzot LaRambam, Mitzvot Lo Taase 318).

I have written about the roots of the commandment in Mishpatim on the negative commandment to not curse judges (Sefer HaChinukh 48).

From the laws of the commandment is, for example, that which they said (Sanhedrin 85a), that the liability for the cursing of father and mother is whether they are alive, or even after their death; which is not the case with hitting - as the liability in it is only in their lifetimes; but after death, he is exempt for hitting them. And that which they said (Shevuot 35a) that there is no liability for death on the son until he curses them with one of the explicit names [of God]; but one who curses them with an appellation is exempt from stoning, and is [only] lashed - as is the way that one is lashed for the curse of a proper man. And that which they said (Makkot 12a) that the law of one who curses the father of his father or the father of his mother is like one who curses [any]one from the rest of the congregation. And [in the case of] a father that is obligated an oath, the son should not administer the oath, with an oath that has a curse; but rather he administers an oath that does not have a curse. And they also said that it is forbidden to disgrace him at all, as it is not about the curse that the Torah was concerned, but rather about the disgrace. And one who disgraces him is cursed, as it is stated (Deuteronomy 27:16), "Cursed is the one who belittles his father and mother." And the court should strike one who does this and punish him according to that which is fitting. And the rest of its details are in the seventh chapter of Sanhedrin (see Tur, Yoreh Deah 241).

And [it] is practiced in all places and at all times by males and females, and so [too,] by [those the sex of which is in doubt]. And a child of unknown paternity is obligated towards his mother, but he is not obligated towards his father, even if his mother was questioned and she said that he is the son of x. And it appears that a mamzer is liable for cursing his father and his mother - as behold, he is fit to inherit them from Torah writ. And he also has the status of a fit son regarding mourning and for everything. But the son of a female slave or of a gentile woman is not liable for their curse. And so [too,] a convert whose conception was not in holiness - for example, if his mother converted when she was pregnant - is not liable for cursing his mother. And just like he is not liable for cursing his father, so too is he not liable for cursing his mother, even though she was Jewish when she bore him; and like they, may their memory be Blessed, expounded (Sifra, Kedoshim, Chapter 9:9), "'And he who curses his father and his mother' - one who is obligated for his father, is obligated for his mother, etc." And it should not be asked about this teaching based on the son of unknown paternity who is only obligated for his mother - as [there] the father is not known and recognizable. And a convert is rabbinically forbidden to curse his gentile father, so that [people] not say he came from a stringent [level] of holiness to a light one (see Yevamot 22a). But a slave has no lineage, and behold his father is like someone who in all respects is not his father - and even after he is freed. And one who transgresses this and curses them with one of the names [of God] is stoned; and that is when there are witnesses and a warning there - as is well known in every place. But if he [only] curses them with one of the appellations [of God], he is lashed.

Mitzvah 261
The commandment to burn one who is liable for burning: That the court burn with fire - meaning to say that the court is commanded to enact the statute of burning for some sins. And one of them is for the one that has sexual relations with a woman and her mother, as it is stated (Leviticus 20:14), "And a man that takes a woman and her mother - that is depravity - they shall be burned with fire, he and them, etc." And I have already written above in the Order of Achrei Mot on the commandment not to have sexual relations with a woman and her daughter (Sefer HaChinukh 203), in which manner one who takes a woman and her daughter is liable, and that only one of them is included in the liability - and that is the last one. And [regarding] that which is written, "and them (hen)," its understanding is "one of them." As so does the explanation come in Tractate Sanhedrin 76b. And they said so there, that in [a certain] place they call one, " hen," etc., as I have written there.
I have written above in Achrei Mot (Sefer HaChinukh 190) that which I have known and heard about the matter of the roots of the prohibition of forbidden sexual relations.
From the laws of the commandment is that which they, may their memory be Blessed, said (Sanhedrin 52b) "The commandment of those that were burned is that they would submerge him in dung up to his knees, and they place a rough scarf within a soft one, and wrap [them] around his neck." And his two witnesses, "this one pulls toward himself, and that one pulls toward himself, until he opens his mouth." And they melt the tin or the lead or what is similar to it, "and [someone] throws it into his mouth, and it goes down and burns his intestines." And the rest of its details are in the seventh chapter of Sanhedrin.
And this commandment is practiced by males, as judgement is for them; and only in the land of Israel, as it is the place of judgement. And a court that transgresses it and did not judge someone liable according to his law has violated a positive commandment. And their punishment is great as the world is civilized by judgement. And I have already written on this positive commandment above in the Order of Mishpatim (Sefer HaChinukh 47) that Ramban, may his memory be Blessed, does not count the four death penalties of the court in his tally of the commandments. And there I brought a little of the reason that he wrote about the matter.

Mitzvah 262
To not follow the practices of the gentiles: To not follow the practices of the Amorites and so [too,] the practices of the gentiles, as it is stated (Leviticus 20:23), "And you shall not follow the practice of the nation that I am driving out before you." And the law is the same for all the nations, since the matter is that they turn away from [following] God, and worship idolatry. And the content of the commandment is that we not behave like them in our clothing and our matters. And it is like they said in Sifra, Achrei Mot, Chapter 13:8, "'And do not follow their practices - that you not follow their mores with things that are fixed for them, such as theaters, circuses and amphitheaters" - and all of these are types of frivolity that they would do in their gatherings, when they gathered to do craziness, licentiousness and idolatry. And they said there, "'The practice of the nation' - Rabbi Meir says, 'These are the ways of the Amorites that the sages numbered (see Shabbat 67a).' Rabbi Yehudah ben Betira

says, 'That you should not grow a tassel of the head and not cut its growth'" - meaning to say that he not shave from the sides and leave hair in the middle, which is called a forelock. And this negative commandment is repeated in another place with other words, as it is stated (Deuteronomy 12:30), "Guard yourself lest you be ensnared to follow them." And the language of Sifrei is "'Guard' is with a negative commandment; 'lest' is with a negative commandment; 'you be ensnared to follow them' is lest you imitate them and do like their deeds; 'and it shall be a snare for you' is that you not say, 'Since they go out with velvet, I will go out with velvet, since they go with helmets, I will go with a helmet'" - and that is a type of knight's armor. And the language of the books of prophecy (Zephaniah 1:8) is "and upon all of the dressed, there is a foreign dress."

It is from the roots of the commandment [that it is] in order to distance ourselves from them and disparage all of their customs, and even in dress.

We have written a little from the laws of the commandment. And they, may their memory be Blessed, brought some of these, along with the rest of its details, in the seventh chapter of Shabbat and in (Chapter 8 of the) Tosefta of Shabbat (see Tur, Yoreh Deah 177).

And [it] is practiced in every place and at all times by males and females. And one who transgresses it and does a thing of those that we mentioned, to imitate them, is liable for lashes. And one who distances himself from all of their customs and from all of their mores, and places all of his heart and his thoughts to God, may He be Blessed, and to His precious commandments, 'his soul will rest in the good, and his seed will inherit the land.'

Mitzvah 263

That a common priest not become defiled with a dead body except for the relatives elucidated in Scripture: That a common priest not become defiled with a dead body except for the relatives elucidated in Scripture, as it is stated (Leviticus 21:1), "shall not become impure for his people" - meaning to say, each one of the priests should not become impure for a dead soul. And even though a good soul does not die, the verse referred to the body with the name, soul, since it is the essence [of a person].

It is from the roots of the commandment [that] since the priests were chosen for the service of God, Blessed be He - as the verse stated, "they shall be holy to their God" (Leviticus 21:6) - therefore, He distanced them from the dead. And I have already written above (Sefer HaChinukh 159) that the substance of impurity is something that is disgusting and vile. And the Sages explained about the body of a dead person that it is the primary source of the primary sources (avi avot) of impurity - meaning to say that it has very strong impurity, above all [other] impurity. And the matter is that in the separation from him of the living, good form of the intellect, [the body] remains by itself, as 'he is also only flesh' - base and inferior, and seeking evil things; and also in its great evil, it led the precious soul to sin when it was still dwelling with it. Hence it is fitting that it make impure all that is around it, in the stripping of its glory from it - and that is the soul - and [when] only the evil substance remains in it. And it is truly fitting that the servants of God, may He be Blessed, distance themselves from it - except for the relatives that are permitted to them, as they are their brothers, their flesh. As all the ways of the Torah 'are pleasant and its paths are peace,' and it did not want to grieve them so much. As their hearts would be heated about the dead relative, that they could not approach into the tent that he is in and pour out their spirits and satiate their souls with crying about him. And I saw a hint about the reason which I wrote about the impurity of the dead; as they, may their memory be Blessed, said (Talmud Yerushalmi Berakhot 3:1) that the completely righteous do not render impure. And from what appears, the intention is [that it is] because their bodies are pure and clean and they did not bring their soul to sin, but [rather] aided it to receive merit. And therefore, their soul rose in a 'kiss,' and upon their cadaver sown light will shine forever.

From the laws of the commandment is that which they, may their memory be Blessed, said (Mishneh Torah, Laws of Defilement by a Corpse 1:1) that a dead body renders impure through touch, through carrying and through a tent (being under its roof). And the impurity of carrying they, may their memory be Blessed, learned from an a fortiori argument (kal vechomer) from the impurity of an (animal) carcass. And the matter of impurity of touch that is said in every place - whether with a dead body or whether with the others that render impure - is that a person should touch the impure object itself, either with his hand, or his foot or with the rest of his body; and even with his tongue is [considered] touching. And Rambam, may his memory be Blessed, wrote (Mishneh Torah, Laws of Defilement by a Corpse 1:1) that even touching with the fingernail or with the teeth is touching, and [that] they are considered like the body. And the impurity of carrying that is said in every place is that a man carry the impure object, even though he does not touch it. And even if there were several vessels between him and the impure object - since he carried it, he has become impure. And it is one whether he carries it with his hand or with any other [part] of his body, behold he is in the category of carrying and is impure.

And moving is also included in carrying. And how is moving? For example, when there is something impure at the end of the beam: once a man moves the beam in any way, since he moved it from his power - even though the impure object is on the other end of the beam - behold, that is moving and it is impure. And this [manner of transmitting] impurity and all that is similar to it is the impurity of moving that is said in every place. And even though an impure object [in] an enclosed place [in the body] does not render impure for touching - as an enclosed place is not [considered] touching - it renders impure from the law of carrying; such that one who carries in an enclosed place is called, carrying, and he is impure. And only a person is rendered impure from carrying without touching, but not vessels. And the impurity of the tent is only exclusively with the impurity of a dead body and not with other impure objects. And even though tsaraat renders impure with entering [into a covered space], he does not render impure through a tent [if he was there to begin with]. But a dead body renders impure with a tent - whether a man or vessels or foods and drinks. And it is one whether all of the man enters the tent of the dead body or only part of him, such as if he inserted his hand there or the tips of his fingers or his nose - behold, all of him is impure (see Nazir 43a). And even though their limbs have not become joined, dead fetuses render impure (Nazir 50a); a kazayit of flesh from a dead body; and a complete single limb, even though it does not have a kazayit of flesh - all of these renders impure through touch, through carrying and through a tent. And each one of the two hundred and forty-eight limbs in a person is called a limb, as each and every one of them has flesh, sinews and bones. But teeth are not from the tally. If the form of a man was recognizable in the bones of the dead body, they render impure in a tent, even if there is no flesh upon them. And these are the bones that they, may their memory be Blessed, said render impure even in a tent: the spine; the skeleton; and the majority of its structure or the majority of its number - meaning to say the majority of the number of the bones. And the spine and the skull that they said is specifically when they are whole. But if the spine was missing even one ring or the skull even like a sela coin, they do not render impure in a tent. And the majority of its number is one hundred and twenty-five bones from the two hundred and forty-eight limbs that are in a person. And [regarding] the rest of the bones that do not have the majority of the structure or the majority of the number, if they have a quarter of a kav of bones, they render impure even in a tent. But if not, they do not render impure in a tent. And the impurity of a dead body is seven days. And the rest of its details are elucidated in the Order of Tahorot, and mainly in Tractate Oholot (see Tur, Yoreh Deah 372).

And this commandment is practiced by the male priests in every place and at all times. But [it is not practiced] by females, as so came the explanation [of], "Speak to the priests, the sons of Aharon, 'For a soul he shall not become impure for his people'" - specifically the sons of Aharon and not the daughters of Aharon. And a priest that transgresses this and volitionally became impure for any dead body besides the six commanded [relatives] is lashed.

Mitzvah 264
The commandment of the matter of the impurity of the priests for their relatives, and included in it is that each one in Israel should mourn for their six relatives [the identify of which is] well-known: That the priests should become impure for the dead bodies (the relatives) that are mentioned in the Torah, as it is stated (Leviticus 21:3), "for her, he shall become impure." And this is a positive commandment, as so did the explanation come. And so is it explained in Sifra, Emor, Section 1:12, "'For her, he shall become impure' - is a commandment. If he does not want to become impure, we

Sefer HaChinukh

make him impure by force." And were it not that we received this explanation from our Sages, I would have reasoned to say that it be optional - if he wants, he becomes impure; if he does not want, he does not become impure - since Scripture prevented him from becoming impure for the rest of his relatives. And I would have said that regarding these mentioned in the section of the Torah, they were permitted to become impure if they wanted. Hence the explanation about it came to us - that it is not optional, but rather a commandment. And the Sages, may their memory be Blessed, mentioned a story that Yosef the priest came when his wife died on the eve of Pesach and he did not want to become impure, and the Sages pushed him and made him impure by force. And Rambam, may his memory be Blessed, wrote (Sefer HaMitzvot LaRambam, Mitzvot Ase 37), "And this itself is the commandment of mourning - meaning to say that each person in Israel is obligated to mourn for his relatives, meaning the six relatives mentioned in Scripture." And the verse that the Rabbi brought [as a source] (Mishneh Torah, Laws of Mourning 1:1) for the commandment of mourning is that which is stated by Aharon, "if I had eaten the sin-offering today, would it have been good in the eyes of the Lord?" (Leviticus 10:19). And he said, "And for the strengthening of this commandment did they elucidate about the priest that he is warned about impurity, that he should become impure regardless like other Israelites, in order that the laws of mourning not become weakened. And it was already elucidated that mourning of the first day is by Torah writ - and that is the day of death and burial. And they said in the elucidation in Moed Katan 14b [that] it is not practiced on the holiday - the positive commandment of the many comes and pushes off the positive commandment of the individual. And behold, it is elucidated [from this] that the obligation of mourning is from Torah writ and that it is a positive commandment - but only on the first day. And the remaining six [days] are rabbinic. And even a priest observes mourning on the first day, as he becomes impure for his relatives. And understand this." To here [are his words].

What I have written many times about previous commandments is from the roots of this commandment - that man is acted upon according to his actions that he does. As since he is a physical being, he is not impacted by something in potential, until he takes matters from the potential to the actual. Hence when a punishment of an incident of death of one of his relatives - about which it is natural for him to love them - comes to him, the Torah obligates him to do acts with himself that arouse him to focus his thoughts on the anguish that has come to him. And then he will know and contemplate to himself that his iniquities caused it to him, that this anguish came upon him. As God, may He be Blessed, 'does not afflict man from His heart, nor causes woe to the sons of man,' except from the angle of sins. And this is our - we, the practitioners of the precious Jewish faith - perfect belief. And when a man puts this matter into his heart with the act of mourning, he will move his mind to repent and improve his deeds, according to his ability. And behold, we have found with this a great benefit for people in the commandment of mourning. But the heretics that want to be wise that make empty the matters of the world and the acts of God, may He be Blessed, place perversity and evil on their hearts: They make the death of the sons of man dependent on the happenstance of time, and think - in their evil thoughts - that 'the incident of man and beast, it is the same incident for them; and like the death of one is the death of the other.' And hence they wrote in their books - they should only be burnt - "Unfortunate is the one who worries [about this] at all." And in order to uproot and to pull out this evil belief of theirs from our hearts, the Torah obligated us in this commandment. [This is] besides the benefit of what we mentioned.

From the laws of the commandment is that which they, may their memory be Blessed, said (Rif, Ramban and Rashba on Moed Katan 14b) that the first day is by Torah writ and the [next] six are rabbinic. And even though it is stated (Genesis 50:10), "and he made a mourning for his father seven days," [when] the Torah was given, the law was recreated (a new law came into being). And nonetheless they, may their memory be Blessed, said (Mishneh Torah, Laws of Mourning 1:1) that Moshe, our teacher, ordained seven days of mourning and seven days of festivity. And they, may their memory be Blessed, said (Moed Katan 27a) that the obligation of mourning does not begin until the coffin cover is closed - meaning to say that the whole time that he is not buried, the mourner is not forbidden in anything from all of the things of mourning. And because of this reason, King David bathed and anointed [himself] when [his] child died, before [the child] was buried. And that which they said (Shabbat 136a) that we do not mourn for any [infant] that has not [been alive] for thirty days, is because of a doubt. But they, may their memory be Blessed, said in the Gemara that if we clearly know that he has finished his months [of gestation], his law is like the law of other dead people regarding mourning; and likewise for all the other things is his law like a complete person.

And so [too,] did they, may their memory be Blessed, say (Mishneh Torah, Laws of Mourning 1:10) [regarding] those that separate themselves from all the ways of the community, and likewise heretics, apostates and informants - that we do not mourn at all for all of them, since their death is gladness for the world. And this is not a punishment for their relatives, but rather a merit for them. And this is all from the root that I wrote. And about them is stated (Psalms 139:21), "Do I not hate those You hate?" And likewise, we do not mourn for one who kills himself on purpose. And in its place, it is clarified how we know that he struck himself on purpose. And also from the laws of the commandment are the things that they, may their memory be Blessed, said (Moed Katan 21a) that the mourner is forbidden with on the first day from Torah writ and the rest of the days rabbinically; the law of seven and thirty [days]; the law of twelve months of mourning for father and mother; the law of tearing - who are the relatives who tear and what is the time [for it], how is it for [other] relatives and how is it for father and mother, for which of his relatives, and his teacher and his greats, for which places in the Land of Israel in their destruction; the law of the tear that we darn immediately or after a time and the law that a woman darns immediately so as not be disgraced; the law of the holidays that interrupt [the count] and do not count [in the tally], and that which they said (Moed Katan 19a) that the decree of seven is negated for anyone who buries his dead even an hour before the holiday, and the decree of thirty is negated if seven days passed before the holiday and he began even one hour of the thirty [days], and that the status of Rosh Hashanah and Yom Kippur is the same as the holidays of Pesach, Shevouot and Sukkot; that which they said (Moed Katan 24b) that even though there is no mourning on the intermediate days of the festival, a man tears for a dead [relative] for which he is obligated to mourn; the law that we only observe one day and do not tear for a distant report [of death] after thirty days, - since the law is like Rabbi Mani, who said like this in the Gemara [Moed Katan 21b] - but he tears even for a distant report for his father and for his mother according to the opinion of Ramban, may this memory be Blessed, (Torat HaAdam 61b), but not according to the opinion of the rabbi, Rabbi Avraham beRebbi David (Ravad), may his memory be Blessed.

And regarding the eulogy, for whom do we eulogize and how, and what is [the relation] of Shabbat, holidays, intermediate festival days, Channukah and Purim to it; for the death of whom do we cancel Torah study; the matter of justification of the decree, the blessings and consolations that are made in the house of the mourner; the matter of gathering the bones of relatives and likewise the gathering of the bones of his father and his mother; that which they said (Moed Katan 20b) that we mourn with mourners, who are relatives for which we would mourn, in front of them [for their honor] from the words of the [Rabbis]; that which they said that a man mourns for his wife - and she for her husband - and for brothers from the mother from the words of the [Rabbis]; that he does not mourn for his son or his brother from a maidservant or an idolatress (gentile) - even if they convert - not from Torah writ and not from the words of the [Rabbis]; that a priest becomes impure for his wife - even though the mourning of a man for his wife is only from the words of the [Rabbis], they made her like a dead body that one is commanded to be involved with (met mitzvah) - but once the coffin cover is closed, he may no longer become impure; that which they said that the obligation of mourning is rabbinic for three relatives and these are them - a brother or sister from the mother, a married or betrothed sister from either the father or the mother and [even if the mother] was raped or seduced - and therefore a priest does not become impure for these relatives. And these matters with the rest of its details are elucidated in Tractate [Moed Katan] and in other places in Berakhot, Ketuvot and Yevamot and in Sifra, Parashat Emor el HaKohanim (see Tur, Yoreh Deah 372-374).

And this commandment of the obligations of impurity for the dead body of a relative is practiced by a priest in every place and at all times. And so is it with males of the priesthood, but the women are not [commanded] in this obligation. As so did the explanation come - that the one who is prevented from becoming impure for others than the relatives, he is the one who is commanded to become impure for the relatives. But since women priests were not prevented from becoming impure for a dead body - as is explained in its place (Sefer HaChinukh 263) - so too, were they not commanded to become impure to the relatives regardless; but they must nonetheless mourn. And thy have a choice whether to become impure if they want. And know this and remember it. And the commandment of the obligation of mourning - that is dragged along with his commandment, as we said - is practiced in every place and at all times by every person, whether priest, Israelite, male or female. And a priest who transgresses this and does not want to become impure for the six relatives mentioned in Scripture - and likewise, a priest or an Israelite who did not want to mourn for his relatives with the things that the Sages enumerated in the obligation of the main mourning of the first day - has violated this positive commandment. And I have already written above (Sefer HaChinukh 6) that the court coerces [one who refrains from] a positive commandment. And there are some of the commentators that wrote that the commandment of mourning is not considered a commandment from the Torah. Maybe their opinion is to say that even though one bereaved (onen) is forbidden in consecrated foods from Torah writ, the whole matter of mourning is nonetheless rabbinic.

Mitzvah 265
That a priest who immersed that day (tevul yom) not serve until his sun set: That a priest who immersed that day not serve until his sun sets. And even though he immersed and became pure, he needs the setting of the sun - since he is like a secondary impurity until his sun sets. As so did they, may their memory be Blessed, explain, "it shall be brought into water and be impure until evening and become pure" (Leviticus 11:32): The verse called one who immersed that day impure, even though he immersed, until his sun set (Mishneh Torah, Laws of Other Sources of Defilement 10:1). But nonetheless he is not impure like he was before the immersion. As at the beginning, he was a primary impurity and after the immersion he is called a secondary impurity. And about this is it stated (Leviticus 21:6), "and they shall not desecrate the name of their God." As so did the received explanation come about it, and so is it in the ninth chapter of Sanhedrin 83b. As there they said, "'Holy shall they be to their God, and they shall not desecrate the name of their God'; if it is not regarding one impure - as it was already elucidated (Sefer Hachinukh 178) - teach it for the matter of the one who has immersed on that day." And it is learned over there from [the inferential comparison] of "desecration" [and] "desecration."

It is from the roots of the commandment [that it is] since the priest is the messenger between Israel and their Father in the heavens (based on Yoma 18b). And through his actions and his sacrifices will a man become reconciled in front of his Creator, and his iniquity atoned. Therefore, it is an obligation upon him to be completely clean in body at the time of the service. And perhaps the spirit of impurity has not fully passed from him until the sunset. And Blessed is the Master of wisdom, as He is the one who knows - and not us - at what time it becomes fit for someone who became impure to be involved in His service, Blessed be He. And He told us that it is the time of the sunset for some impurities.

From the laws of the commandment is that which they, may their memory be Blessed, said that one who immersed on that day is the same whether it was from a stringent impurity such as the impurity of a dead body, discharge or tsaraat; or from light impurity such as the impurity of a swarming animal or similar to it - it requires the sun setting. And this matter is whether it is with a man or vessels, whether it is with an impurity from Torah writ or even with a rabbinic impurity - it requires the sun setting. And the understanding of one who immersed on that day (tevul yom) is to say one who immersed, but his sun did not set. And this is its understanding in every place. And if he touched foods and drinks of the priestly tithe, he disqualifies them and makes them a tertiary impurity - as he is like a secondary impurity, as we have said. If they afterwards touched other foods, they do not disqualify them, as a tertiary does not create a quaternary with priestly tithe. And if the one who immersed that day touches consecrated foods or drinks, he makes them a quaternary - meaning to say, he disqualifies them; but they do not go back and render others impure. As even though a tertiary creates a quaternary with consecrated foods, the impurity of one who immersed that day is not so stringent as to render impure to [the point that it reach] the quaternary. But if one who immersed that day touched non-sacred foods, behold they are pure - as a secondary does not create a tertiary with non-sacred foods. So have we received the things from our Sages, may their memory be Blessed

(Sotah 29a). And behold it is elucidated from this that neither a tertiary impurity in the priestly tithe, nor a quaternary impurity in consecrated foods, renders another drink or another food impure. And it is not necessary to say that they do not render vessels impure - since a man and vessels only acquire impurity from a primary source of impurity. And all that render impure - whether stringent or whether light - the law of liquids that come out of them, such as their spit or their urine, is like that of liquids that they touched. And the rest of its details are in Tractate Tevul Yom (see Mishneh Torah, Laws of Admission into the Sanctuary).

And this commandment is practiced by male priests at the time of the [Temple] - since they are warned about the service and to be careful from impurity, and not priestesses. And one who transgresses this and serves [while a] tevul yom is liable for death by the hands of the Heavens. And a clear verse in the Torah does not come about this. Rather, the Sages, may their memory be Blessed, learned the matter there in Sanhedrin 83b with an inferential comparison of "desecration" [and] "desecration."

Mitzvah 266
That a priest not marry a licentious woman (zonah): That a priest - whether a common priest or a high priest - not marry a licentious woman as a wife, as it is stated (Leviticus 21:7), "A woman who is licentious or profaned they shall not take." And the expression, "take," implies by way of marriage. Therefore, he is not lashed for her unless he marries her and has intercourse with her. As so did the explanation come, that there is no liability until he has intercourse with her, as we shall write with God's help.

It is from the roots of the commandment [that it is] since the priests were chosen to always perform the service of God, may He be Blessed. And hence it is fitting and obligatory that they be holier and cleaner than all the rest of the people in all of their matters - even in the matter of marital union, which is an essential thing with a man; and some of the thoughts of a man are always about his spouse. Therefore, he became obligated not to marry a licentious woman, whose constitution is evil and bitter, lest she divert and move him from his good way and acceptable intention, 'with her frequent oratory.' She is also an embarrassment and a defect for all who draw close to her, as all of the people jest about her, from 'the impurity that is in the bottom of her skirts.'

From the laws of the commandment is that which they, may their memory be Blessed, said (Yevamot 61a) that the licentious woman spoken about in the Torah is anyone who is not a daughter of Israel - as they are all in the category of licentious women; and also, since marriage to them is not effective, it is licentiousness (by definition). And also called a licentious woman is any daughter of Israel that has had intercourse with a man that it is forbidden for her to marry - the prohibition of which is the same under all circumstances. [The latter is] to exclude a widow that has had intercourse with a high priest or a divorcee with a common priest, as this prohibition is not the same with every man; and [so] she is not [defined as] a licentious woman with it. And likewise, also called a licentious woman is all who have had intercourse with a profaned priest (challal) - and even though she is permitted to marry him. As her being [defined as] a licentious woman is not dependent on prohibited intercourse, but rather on her becoming defective. And we learned from the heard tradition that she is only defective from a man that is forbidden for him to marry her or from a profaned priest.

And from [this], we learned that one who has mated with a beast does not become a licentious woman, even though she is [punishable] with stoning - as it is specifically the intercourse of a man that makes her a licentious woman (Yevamot 59b). And so [too,] if she had intercourse when she was still a menstruant with someone to whom it is fitting for her to be married; she does not become a licentious woman with that, even though it is [punishable] with excision. And likewise [in a case of] one who has intercourse with a single woman - even if she was a prostitute, meaning she made herself available to all - she does not become a licentiousness woman so long as she has not had intercourse with someone she is forbidden to marry, meaning that she is a sexual prohibition for him. And even prohibitions of [only] a negative commandment or even [those forbidden by] the obligations of a positive commandment are included in this prohibition. And therefore, they said that if one of [the following] - a [gentile], a slave, a natin, a mamzer, an Ammonite or Moavite convert, an Egyptian or Edomite [convert] of the first or second [generation], one whose testes are crushed or whose member is cut off - had intercourse with a Jewish woman, he makes her into a licentious woman and she is disqualified to the priesthood. And if she is a priestess, she is disqualified from the priesthood. And so [a woman] who has had intercourse with someone who makes her a licentious woman is disqualified on account of [being] a licentious woman, from when he inserts himself in her - whether through rape, through consent, through inadvertence, and whether in her [conventional] way or not in her way - and [that is] only when she was three years and a day [old] and above, and the [man] was nine years and a day and above. And also from the matter of the commandment is that which they said (Nedarim 90b) about the wife of a priest who says to her husband, "I was raped," - and even if a witness testifies to him that it was so, like her words, that she was [made] licentious - that she does not become forbidden to him with this. As we say, maybe she put her eyes on someone else [and is seeking a pretext for divorce]. And nonetheless, she is forbidden to any [other] priest after the death of her husband; as she made herself into a 'piece of forbidden matter.' And if she was trusted by him or the witness was trusted, behold this one should [divorce] her in any case to remove the doubt. And our teachers, God should keep them, instructed us (see Teshuvot HaRashba 1268) [that the latter is] specifically when she came to say this - whether she or the witness - from amidst peace between him and her. But if she said this - whether she or the witness - from amidst a spat between him and her, we should determine the matter, [such] that he is not obliged to [divorce] her regardless. As there is [then] an assumption that she was lying, and [hence] it is not fitting to believe her in her words with one witness, but rather [only] with two fit witnesses. But nonetheless, if his opinion is very reliant upon her words or the words of the witness, it is fitting to be concerned [and not] have intercourse with her. And the rest of the many details of the commandment are in Yevamot and in Kiddushin (see Mishneh Torah, Laws of Forbidden Intercourse 18).

And [it] is practiced by priests in every place and at all times. And a priest who transgresses it and marries a licentious woman - from those that we elucidated - by way of marriage, and has intercourse with her is lashed.

Mitzvah 267

That a priest not marry a profaned woman (challalah): That a priest - whether a high [priest] or a common [one] - not marry a profaned woman, as it is stated (Leviticus 21:7), "A woman who is licentious or profaned they shall not take." And profaned is called one who was born from those disqualified from the priesthood - such as the daughter of a widow from the high priest or the daughter of a divorcee from a common priest - or was profaned by the intercourse of one of those disqualified to the priesthood.

That which I wrote about the prohibition of the licentious woman previous to this is from the roots of the commandment.

From the laws of the commandment is that which they, may their memory be Blessed, said (Kiddushin 78a) that there is no liability for lashes until he has intercourse. But [if] he married her and did not have intercourse, he is not lashed - as there is no liability for lashes without intercourse. And [both] he and her are lashed; and that which they, may their memory be Blessed, said (Yevamot 84b), "Fitting women are not [prohibited] from marrying disqualified men," is not from this matter at all - and we will explain the thing below on this page. As this one who has had intercourse with someone to whom she is forbidden, is also included in the obligation - and like the matter that they, may their memory be Blessed, said that there is no difference between a woman and a man regarding all of the punishments of the Torah, except for the designated maidservant, [about] which I have written above in the Order of Vayikra in the commandment of a definite guilt-offering (Sefer HaChinukh 129).

And likewise, from the laws of the commandment is that which they, may their memory be Blessed, said (Sotah 23a) that the body of the priest himself who transgresses the sin - who has intercourse with the profaned woman - is not profaned with this, even though his seed is profaned. And from when he inserts himself in her - whether she had intercourse through rape or through inadvertence, and whether in her [conventional] way or not in her way - she becomes profaned; and that is when the priest was nine years and a day and above, and she was three years and a day [old] and above -

she is [then] profaned. And that which they, may their memory be Blessed, said (Yevamot 56b) that she is not made a profaned woman except with intercourse, but with designation alone she is not rendered profane. However, with [actual] marriage, she is made a profaned woman even if she did not have intercourse; because every married woman is assumed to have had intercourse, even if she is found to be a virgin. And that which they said (Yevamot 60a) that a priest who has intercourse with a menstruant - even if it [punishable] with excision - does not make her profane; as the matter of profanation is only with a prohibition that is specific to the priests, such as a widow, a divorcee, a profaned woman, a licentious woman or one who has had intercourse with one of those disqualified to the priesthood, such as the profaned priests. And that which they, may their memory be Blessed, said (Yevamot 85a) that there are profaned priests from the words of the [Rabbis]. How is this? A priest that had intercourse with a released woman (chalutsah), who is forbidden to a priest rabbinically, and [so] she is a profaned woman rabbinically and her seed are profaned priests rabbinically. But [regarding] a priest that has intercourse with one of the secondary [prohibitions], his seed from her are not profaned priests - not even rabbinically - as it is a prohibition that is the same for everyone and is not specific to the priests, and as we wrote above.

A priest that has intercourse with a possibly licentious woman, such as a possible convert or freed [maidservant], or with a possible divorcee; and so [too,] a high priest who has intercourse with a possible widow - behold this is a doubtfully profaned woman and the offspring is a doubtfully profaned priest. It comes out that there are three [types of] profaned priests: a profaned priest from Torah writ; a profaned priest from the words of [the Rabbis]; and a doubtfully profaned priest. And we give upon any doubtfully profaned priest or profaned priest from the words of [the Rabbis], the stringencies of the priests and the stringencies of the Israelites. He does not eat from the priestly tithe and does not become impure for the dead and he must marry a woman that is fitting for a priest. And if he ate priestly tithe or became impure or married a divorcee, a profaned woman [or a] licentious woman, we strike him with rabbinic lashes of rebellion. But behold, a certainly profaned priest from Torah writ is like a non-priest and marries a divorcee and becomes impure for the dead; as it is stated (Leviticus 21:1), "Speak to the priests, the sons of Aharon" - even though they are sons of Aharon, [not] until they are in the [their] priesthood. And they, may their memory be Blessed, also received (Sifra, Emor, Section 1:2) as the explanation of that verse, "'The sons of Aharon,' and not the daughters of Aharon - from here that fit women are not warned (prohibited) from marrying disqualified ones." And so, a priestess is permitted to marry a profaned priest, a convert and a freed [slave]. And therefore they, may their memory be Blessed, said (Kiddushin 73a) that a convert is permitted to marry a priestess and a mamzeret: a priestess for the reason we said, that they were not warned from marrying ones disqualified; and a mamzeret on account that the congregation of converts is not called a congregation - and with the prohibition of the mamzer, it is written (Deuteronomy 23:3), "A mamzer shall not come into the congregation of the Lord." And that which they said (Kiddushin 77a) that all the seed of a profaned priest that married a fit woman are profaned priests and disqualified to the priesthood; since the offspring goes after the father in this matter, as it is stated (Numbers 1:18), "and they shall be pedigreed by their families [according to the houses of their fathers]." And any widow from a family into which a possible profaned priest was mixed is forbidden to a priest at the outset. But if she married [him], she should not leave (be divorced) - since there is a double doubt. And we are not concerned about a double doubt, even in a [law] of Torah writ. But if a certainly profaned priest is mixed into a family, every woman from it is forbidden to marry a priest, until he examines [her lineage]. And the rest of its details are in Kiddushin and Yevamot.

And [it] is practiced in every place and at all times. And one who transgresses it and married a certainly profaned woman and has intercourse with her is liable for lashes. [If] he married a possibly profaned woman or a woman profaned rabbinically, we strike him with lashes of rebellion. And that is at the time when the Israelites would judge capital cases. But at this time, we do not administer lashes - and as we will write below with God's help in the Order of Ki Tetseh (Sefer HaChinukh 594) in the positive commandment of lashes.

Mitzvah 268

Sefer HaChinukh

That a priest not marry a divorcee: That a priest - whether a high [priest] or a common [one] - not marry a divorcee, as it is stated (Leviticus 21:7), "and a woman divorced from her husband they shall not take."

That which I wrote about the prohibition of the licentious woman previous to this (Sefer HaMitzvot 266) is from the roots of the commandment.

From the laws of the commandment, it that which they, may their memory be Blessed, said (Yevamot 59a) that she is called a divorcee even from betrothal, and there is no need to say from marriage. But one who refused (child marriage) - even if he divorced her with a bill of divorce and brought her back and she refused him - behold she is permitted to a priest (Yevamot 108a). And a released woman (chalutsah) - meaning to say a woman that went out from [the domain of] her levirate husband with release - is forbidden to a priest rabbinically, since they gave her the legal status of a divorcee (Yevamot 24a). A priest that brought in (married) a possible divorcee or licentious woman or profaned woman turns her out with a bill of divorce. But if he brought in a possibly released woman, he does not turn her out with a bill of divorce; as the Sages only decreed about a certainly released woman. And any [woman] that is not fitting to be released is not disqualified to the priesthood if she was released. If a rumor went out about her that she was released, we do not concern ourselves with that rumor. As the Sages are the ones that decreed about a released woman that she be like a divorcee, and they are [also] the ones that were lenient in these matters that we said. And the rest of its details are in Kiddushin and Yevamot.

And [it] is practiced by priests in every place and at all times. And one who transgresses it and marries a divorcee and has intercourse is liable for lashes. But so long as he does not have intercourse, he does not become liable for lashes. And even a high priest, who is liable for two negative commandments - on account of "he shall not take, and on account of "He shall not profane," as we will write below with God's help (Sefer HaChinukh 274) - and is lashed for both of them, is never lashed for [even] one of them, except after he has intercourse. But if he did not have intercourse, he is [also] not lashed for "he shall not take" - as "he shall not take" is bound with the negative commandment of "He shall not profane" (Mishneh Torah, Laws of Forbidden Intercourse 17:4). And there are times when the high priest will become liable for four [sets] of lashes with one intercourse - for example if she was a widow and became a divorcee and [then] became a profaned woman and [then] became a licentious woman. And about what is similar to this, the Sages, may their memory be Blessed, would say (Kiddushin 77b) it is a supplementary prohibition. As behold, at first the widow was permitted to a common priest. But when she got divorced, a prohibition was added to her - that she became forbidden to a common [priest]. Yet she was still permitted to eat priestly tithe. But when she became profaned, a prohibition was added to her - that she became forbidden from eating priestly tithe. Yet she was still permitted to an Israelite. But when she became a licentious woman, a prohibition was added to her concerning an Israelite - as behold, we have found a prohibition for an Israelite with a licentious woman: As a woman who is volitionally licentious while in her husband's [domain] is forbidden to the husband and to the one who had intercourse [with her]. But if this order is changed - for example that she first became a licentious woman, etc. - we are only liable for one [set of] lashes for her intercourse; as this is not a supplementary prohibition. And there is a great principle about all of the prohibitions of the Torah: A prohibition does not rest upon [another] prohibition unless the prohibitions came together or one adds other things - as we said - or [it was] an inclusive prohibition (issur kollel).

Mitzvah 269

The commandment of sanctifying the seed of Aharon: To sanctify the seed of Aharon - meaning to say, to sanctify them and to bring them in to the sacrifice - and that is the essence of the positive commandment - and likewise to have them precede in every thing of holiness. And if they refuse this, we do not listen to them. And this is all for the honor of God, may He be elevated, since He took them and chose them for His service. As it is stated (Leviticus 21:8), "And you shall make him holy" - for every thing in holiness: to open first; to bless first; and to take a nice piece first. And the language of Sifra, Emor, Chapter 1:13 is "'And you shall make him holy,' against his will" - meaning to say that we are commanded in this commandment and it is not the choice of the priest. And they also said (Sifra, Emor, Chapter 1:13), "'Holy shall they be to their God' (Leviticus 21:6) - against their will; 'and they will be holy' - to include those with blemishes, that we not say, 'Since those are not fitting "to offer the bread of their Lord," why should we have this one precede and we honor him?' Hence, its stating, 'and they will be holy'" - meaning that all of the seed is holy, [both] those unblemished and those with blemishes.

It is from the roots of the commandment [that it is] since it is known that honoring his servants is from the honor of the master. And every time we honor the priests, we remember and fix His honor, Blessed be He, and His greatness in our thoughts. And in the merit of this pure thought and loftiness and good will, His blessing and his great goodness will descend upon us. And He desires blessing, as we have informed several times.

From the laws of the commandment is that which they said (Gittin 39a) that the order of the communal reading of the Torah is like this - that the priest (Kohen) always reads first; and a Levite after him; and an Israelite after him. But if there is no priest there, the package is undone. And if there is no Levite, a priest reads twice. But a priest does not read after a priest, because of [the appearance of] the defect of the first. And a Levite does not read after a Levite, because of [the appearance of] the defect of both of them. And this honor is done for them if they are fitting it. But if they are sinners, we prevent them from honor. And they, may their memory be Blessed, already said (Horayot 13a) that a mamzer Torah scholar precedes an ignoramus high priest. But today at this time, we have not seen [anyone] who had himself precede any priest, because of his wisdom - and 'following modesty is the fear of the Lord.' And the rest of its details are elucidated in scattered places of the Gemara: Makkot; Chullin; Bekhorot; Shabbat; and the rest of them (see Mishneh Torah, Laws of Vessels of the Sanctuary and Those who Serve Therein 8).

And [it] is practiced in every place and at all times by males and females, as it is a commandment upon all of them to honor the seed of Aharon. And one who transgresses it and does not honor them in a place that is fitting and [with] a priest that is fitting to honor has violated this positive commandment.

Mitzvah 270

That a high priest not enter the tent of a dead body: That a high priest not enter the tent of a dead body - and even for one of the six commanded dead [relatives], as it is stated (Leviticus 21;11), "And for all dead souls, he shall not come" - meaning to say, he should not enter into the house with them. As the expression, "he shall not come" implies entering [entering a house].

What I wrote above in Mitzvah 266 in this Order (Sefer HaChinukh 263) is from the roots of the commandment - that it is fitting to distance the priests, who are the holy ones who do the service of God, from the matter of impurity. And [regarding] the high priest who is distinguished to be Holy of Holies; though he has a body, his soul always dwells among the elevated servants. Therefore, the Torah is not concerned to ever permit him impurity - even for the relatives which the Torah is concerned about for the ordinary priests, which I wrote about above (Sefer HaChinukh 263), who will pour out their souls in the house of [mourning] because their hearts are heated for their relatives. The high priest, by contrast, is thoroughly bound to loftier pursuits and entirely separate from human nature. He will lose any memory of this fleeting world; he will not weep for the loss of one of his society because he was already apart from them in life. As far as the laws of impurity from the dead and the tent of the dead, I have already spoken some according to my custom in this Order; it is not fitting to repeat it, lest it become burdensome for the reader (see Mishneh Torah, Laws of Mourning 3).

And this prohibition is practiced at the time of the [Temple] and there was a High Priest there. And in any place that he may be - even if on some occasion he exited the Land - he is [still forbidden] from entering into the tent of a dead body. And if he transgressed and entered there volotionally - even [if it was] his father or mother [that] were dead in the house - he is lashed.

Mitzvah 271

Sefer HaChinukh

That the high priest not become impure with any impurity: That the high priest not become impure - even with a dead body from among his relatives, and all the more so with all the other dead bodies in the world - with a type from the types of impurity, whether through touching or whether through carrying, as it is stated (Leviticus 21:11), "for his mother or for his father, he shall not become impure." [This is] meaning to say, even for these which are his relatives. And even though it forbade him from becoming impure for all souls at the beginning of the verse, that is impurity of coming into the tent of a dead body, as we explained there (Sefer HaChinukh 270). As behold, there it is written, "he shall not come," which implies coming into a tent. Whereas here all of the other types of impurity are forbidden more generally. And do not think that that which it stated, "for his father and for his mother, etc.," is an explanation of the beginning of the verse that stated, "And for all dead souls, etc." - as the matter is not like this. But [rather,] they are two [distinct] negative commandments, "he shall not come," and "he shall not become impure." And the language of Sifra, Emor, Section 2:4 is "He is liable for 'he shall not come,' and he is liable for 'he shall not become impure.'" And they, may their memory be Blessed likewise said, that a common priest is liable for "he shall not come," and "he shall not become impure" - even though it is not written about him - stemming from the law of an inferential comparison; as both of them were forbidden from becoming impure with a soul, and as it appears in the Gemara. However, we should not count "he shall not come" and "he shall not become impure" for a common priest as two negative commandments, such as we counted them for a high priest. [This is] as they are written explicitly with a high priest; while with a common priest, one is learned from an inferential comparison. And the elder has already instructed - that is Rambam, may his memory be Blessed - that we should only count those that are explicit in Scriputre in the tally of the six hundred and thirteen commandments, but not those that are learned through the hermeneutic principles through which the Torah is expounded.

That which we wrote about the commandment preceding this is from the roots of the commandment. And it is the same law and it the same reason; as the intention of both of them - of "he shall not come" and of "he shall not become impure" - is one matter.

And we have already written a few of the laws of the impurity of a dead body above in this Order in Commandment 263 (Sefer HaChinukh 263).

And this prohibition is practiced at the time of the [Temple], as then was there a high priest there. And this prohibition is also practiced in any place that the [high] priest is there. And if he transgressed and became impure with a type of the types of impurity - and even for his relatives - he is liable for lashes.

Mitzvah 272

The commandment of a high priest to marry a virgin maiden: That a high priest marries a virgin maiden, as it is stated (Leviticus 21:13), "And he shall take a woman in her virginity." The proof that this is considered to be from the positive commandments is that which they, may their memory be Blessed, said (Ketuvot 30a), "Rabbi Akiva would make a mamzer (one illegitimate) even from those liable from a positive commandment." And they elucidated that this is when a high priest has intercourse with a woman who is not a virgin, who is prohibited to him by a positive commandment. As it is a principle with us that a negative commandment inferred from a positive commandment is a positive commandment. And they, may their memory be Blessed, also said (Horayot 11b), "He is cautioned about the widow and commanded about the virgin."

It is from the roots of the commandment [that it is] since the essence of good in a person is that he have thoughts of purity and cleanliness - for after the thoughts are the deeds of bodies drawn. Therefore, it is fitting for the highest servant to cling to a woman who has never fixed her thought towards another man besides him who is Holy of Holies. And through that, the seed that God, may He be Blessed, gives him from her will be pure and clean; fitting to serve in holiness. And lest you say, "And who knows if the virgin has also fixed her thought towards a man besides him and set her eyes on another," the answer to this is that for as long as the thought has not gone from the potential to the actual, she is not disqualified. But anytime she had intercourse with him, she is disqualified. And even though they, may their memory be Blessed, said (Yevamot 59a) that when she becomes an adult, she is prohibited to him, the matter is that once she has matured so much, the thought of her impulse is only evil; and perhaps she fixed her thought towards another. And from when she is an adult, her evil thought counts as an act. And so [too,] from this reason did they say (Yevamot 59a) that if she was widowed from betrothal - even as a minor - she is forbidden to the [high] priest. As from when the act of designation (kiddushin) was done with her, she already fixed her thought towards another man via the act of betrothal and was [so] disqualified - as an act disqualifies even with minors, and thought [does] with adults. And likewise, they said (Yevamot 59a) that if she had intercourse not in her (customary) way, she is also disqualified - as she already did a big act, even though her virginity (hymen) is intact. And so [too,] they said (Yevamot 59a) that even [if she is one] struck by wood (on her hymen), she is disqualified. And the reason with her is apparently that she will not fix her thought greatly on the high priest. As once she lost her virginity, she does not cut (form) a strong covenant with a man ever. And [this is] similar to that which they, may their memory be Blessed, said (Sanhedrin 22b) that a woman only cuts a covenant with one who 'makes her a vessel' - and behold, this one did not 'make her a vessel.' However, they, may their memory be Blessed, were not very stringent with these [laws], and they said (Yevamot 60a) that if he married an adult or one struck by wood, he keeps [the marriage], ex post facto.

From the laws of the commandment is that which they, may their memory be Blessed, said (Horayot 12b) that it is one [if it is] a high priest that was anointed by the anointing oil or with many clothes, and it is one [if it is] a high priest that is serving or a high priest who they appointed and he left [the service], and likewise a priest anointed for war - they are all commanded about the virgin and forbidden with the widow. And that which they said (Yevamot 58b) that even if he betrothed a minor and she became an adult while [in his domain] before the marriage, behold this one should not [marry her]. But if he did [marry her], he does not [divorce her]. And that which they said (Yevamot 59a) that he never marry two women together, as it is stated, "And he shall take a woman in her virginity" - specifically one woman, and not two. And that which they said (Yevamot 61a) that if he [married] a widow while he was still a common [priest] and became appointed as high priest, he does not [divorce] her. And even if he [only] betrothed her before he was appointed high priest, he [marries] her after he is appointed. And the rest of its details are in the sixth chapter of Yevamot and in [various] places of Ketuvot and Kiddushin (see Rambam, Laws of Forbidden Intercourse 17).

And [it] is practiced in the Land at the time of the [Temple] and the service; as the high priest is appointed there, not in another place. And a high priest that transgresses this and marries one - who is neither a widow nor a divorcee - who has had intercourse with a man, has violated this commandment and [must] put her out with a bill of divorce.

Mitzvah 273

That a high priest not marry a widow: That only a high priest not marry a widow, as it is stated (Leviticus 21:14), "A widow and a divorcee and a profaned woman, a licentious woman - these he shall not take." And the verse did not need to repeat the prohibition of "a divorcee and a profaned woman, a licentious woman" with a high priest - as they were forbidden more generally to any priest, and he is the head of the priests. And therefore, they, may their memory be Blessed, explained (Kiddushin 77a), that the repetition of this warning of "a divorcee and a profaned woman, a licentious woman" with a high priest comes to teach us this matter: And they said in the Gemara in Kiddushin that it comes to teach that at a time that it happens that all of these prohibitions happen with one woman in this order - that at first, she is widowed; and afterwards she divorces; and afterwards she is profaned; and afterwards she becomes a licentious woman - and the high priest has intercourse with her, he is liable four [sets] of lashes for one intercourse. And this is when he was warned about [the] four negative commandments. And if a common priest had intercourse with her, he will be lashed three [sets]. And the reason that they are liable for several [sets of] lashes when [her status changed] in this order is because there is a supplementary prohibition in this matter. And [it is] as we wrote above close by in the commandment of the prohibition of a divorcee to a priest (Sefer HaChinukh 268) - that a prohibition does not rest upon [another] prohibition except when it is a supplementary prohibition or [it was] an inclusive prohibition (issur kollel) or [several prohibitions come] at one time, as it is explained in Tractate Keritot 14b. And it is not necessary to say that if he had intercourse with four women and one of them was a widow, one was a divorcee, one was a profaned woman and one was a licentious woman and he was warned about all of them, he is liable for four [sets] of lashes - whether he has intercourse in the order or not in the order - since they are different bodies.

And if you will ask and say, how can he be lashed several [sets of] lashes - whether for one woman or several - take heed, it is established for us that we do not administer lashes for a general negative commandment; [and] behold, this is a general negative commandment, as behold the prevention of all of them comes from one negative commandment - and as we wrote above (Sefer HaChinukh 7) according to the opinion of Rambam, may his memory be Blessed! The answer is - know that they, may their memory be Blessed, elucidated this matter; and that is their saying in the Gemara Kiddushin 77b about that which is written about a common priest (Leviticus 21:7), "and a woman divorced from a man they shall not take," that it is for this reason that the divorcee was separated with [its own] negative commandment - to teach that we administer lashes for the divorcee on her own. And [just] like we administer lashes for the divorcee on her own, so do we administer lashes for the profaned woman and for the licentious woman on her own. And they said there, "In the same way that a divorcee and a profaned woman and a licentious woman [are] divided [into separate negative commandments] with a common priest, so too [are they] divided with a high priest." And to teach these things was the prevention repeated with a high priest, as we said.

It is from the roots of the commandment [that it is] because there are foreign (external) thoughts in marriage to a widow. [It is] similar to that which they, may their memory be Blessed, said (Pesachim 112a), "[When] a young man marries a widow, there are three dispositions in the bed, etc."

From the laws of the commandment are that which they, may their memory be Blessed, said (Yevamot 59a) that she is called a widow even from the betrothal; and that [in the case] of a high priest whose brother dies [and leaves a widow] even from betrothal, behold this one should not do levirate marriage, but rather release [her]. If she was designated by a questionable designation and her betrothed died, behold she is a questionable widow and forbidden - as any doubt in a Torah law is forbidden from Torah writ. And therefore they, may their memory be Blessed, said in every place that [in the case of] a doubt in Torah law, [we go] towards stringency. And the rest of its details are in Yevamot and Kiddushin. And a high priest who transgresses it and designates a widow and has intercourse with her, is lashed twice - one on account of 'a widow he shall not take,' and one on account of "he shall not profane his seed" - which is a negative commandment on its own, and as we will write nearby (Sefer HaChinukh 274). But if he designated her and did not have intercourse afterwards, he is not lashed at all - and even on account of 'he shall not take.' And [it is] like they said there in Kiddushin 78a, "If he had intercourse, he is lashed; if he did not have intercourse, he is not lashed [...]. For what reason is he commanded 'he shall not take'? On account of 'he shall not profane.'" But if he had intercourse with the widow - even though he did not designate her, it is implied that he is lashed one [set], on account of "he shall not profane." As so did they, may their memory be Blessed, explain (Kiddushin 78a), "He shall not profane": not her and not his seed. And likewise, did they say there in Kiddushin, "And Rava concedes in [the case of] a high priest with a widow, that if he had intercourse and did not designate [her], he is lashed. What is the reason? As [the Torah] states, 'And he shall not profane his seed,' and behold, he profaned" - meaning to say, it is included in "And he shall not profane." [Hence] it is implied that 'he shall not profane' proper ones [such as the widow], nor [shall he profane] 'his seed.'

Mitzvah 274

That a high priest not have intercourse with a widow: That a high priest not have intercourse with a widow - and even without designation (kiddushin), as it is stated (Leviticus 21:15), "And he shall not profane his seed among his people." And they said in Kiddushin 78a, "A high priest with a widow is lashed two [sets], on account of 'he shall not take,' and on account of 'he shall not profane'" - meaning that if he married her and had intercourse with her, he is lashed two [sets of] lashes. But if he had intercourse with her without having designated her, he is lashed on account of "he shall not profane"; and like Rava says there: "Rava concedes in [the case of] a high priest with a widow, that if he had intercourse and did not designate [her], he is lashed. What is the reason? As [the Torah] states, 'And he shall not profane his seed,' and behold, he profaned." If he designated her and did not have intercourse with her, he is not lashed on account of 'he shall not take' - as behold, we say there, "For what reason is he commanded 'he shall not take?' On account of 'he shall not profane.'" It is implied that the whole time that he does not profane, he is not lashed.

And this reason we learned even with a common priest regarding the women forbidden to him. And even though this verse of "he shall profane," is regarding the high priest and with a widow, we learned from it that the common [priest] is also not liable for lashes with the women forbidden to him until he has intercourse. As [the Torah] was certainly not more stringent with the common [priest] than with the high. And [it is] as they elucidated it there in Kiddushin, "If he had intercourse, he is lashed; if he did not have intercourse, he is not lashed." And they said that this law is also with a common priest - that he is not liable for the women forbidden him until he first designates [her] and afterwards has intercourse. But if he had intercourse with a licentious woman or a divorcee or a profaned woman without dedication - even though it is forbidden to him and he becomes disqualified for the priesthood - he is not lashed; since the prevention is not elucidated about this explicitly - as "he shall not profane," is written in the section of the high priest and specifically about a widow. But with with a licentious woman or a divorcee or a profaned woman, the high priest is only lashed one [set] for them when he marries them and afterwards has intercourse with them; however, if he has intercourse with them without dedication - even though it is forbidden and he becomes disqualified for the priesthood - he does not have a liability for lashes for this. Rather, his law is exactly like the law of the common priest. As specifically regarding the widow is it that a negative commandment was designated for the high priest, to make him liable for "he shall not profane" - meaning for intercourse without designation, as we said - but not with the three others. As the three others were only repeated with a high priest for that matter that we said above (Sefer HaChinukh 273), to divide - meaning to say to make liable for each and every one [on its own]. And there is still another reason in the matter: That with a widow, there is a profaning in the intercourse. As she was fitting for common [priests], and she became disqualified with the intercourse. And hence he should be made liable for her, and on account of "he shall not profane." But with the other three, we should not make him liable for lashes because of intercourse without designation - as behold, we cannot say, "profane," about them; as behold, they are [already] profaned for a common priest before the intercourse.

In the [commandment] previous to it [can be found] from the roots of the commandment and also a few of its laws.

And this commandment is practiced at the time of the [Temple] when we had a high priest. If he transgressed and had intercourse with a widow - even without designation - he is lashed on account of "he shall not profane." As behold, he profaned the widow; as she was fitting to a common priest and now, she is forbidden to him. And we have already said that he is obligated not to profane - neither her nor his seed. And the profaning of his seed is relevant to say when he has intercourse with a divorcee, a profaned woman [and] a licentious woman, who are profaned. And when he has intercourse with them, he does not profane them; as behold, they are [already] profaned. [Rather] it is his seed that he profanes, as his seed is in a place of profanation. And it is relevant to say profaning of the woman when he has intercourse with a widow, as she is still fitting to a common priest. And with this intercourse of the high priest, she is made a licentious woman; and behold, he profaned her from her being fit. And there is no doubt that the seed is also profaned, as the seed is also profaned in her automatically. But the distinction that there is between the profaning with her and the profaning of the seed is that she is profaned with insertion, but the seed [is only profaned] from the completion of intercourse - as it is [found] in the Gemara (Kiddushin 78a).

Mitzvah 275
That a priest with a blemish not serve in the Temple: That a priest with a blemish not serve in the Temple service, as it is stated (Leviticus 21:17), "A man from your seed in their generations who has a blemish shall not approach to offer the bread of his God." [This is] meaning that he may not approach for the service, because all types of food are called bread in many places (see Rashi on

Sefer HaChinukh

Genesis 31:54). And this blemish [referred to in this context] is permanent. As so did they explain in Sifra, Emor, Section 3:5, "'Who has a blemish shall not approach' - I only have a permanent blemish. From where [do we know] a transient blemish? [Hence] we learn to say in the same section (Leviticus 21:18), 'any man who has a blemish shall not come close'" (meaning it is from another verse and not this one). And a permanent blemish is like a boil-scar or a protrusion, and that is a growth.

It is from the roots of the commandment [that it is] since most activities of people are pleasing to the hearts of their observers based on the importance of the ones doing them. As when a person appears important and of good deeds, 'he will find favor and appreciation' in all that he does in the eyes of those who see him. And if he is the opposite of this - of lowly form and having unusual limbs and if his actions are not straight - his actions will not be so pleasing to the heart of those who see him. It is therefore truly fitting that the messenger upon whom atonement depends be a man of favor, of nice form and nice appearance [and] pleasing in all his ways, so that the thoughts of people will attach themselves to him. Aside from this, it is possible that there is in the perfection of his form, a hint to concepts through which the thoughts of a person about them will purify his soul and he be elevated. And therefore it is not fitting in any way for there to be [anything unusual] in any of his forms, lest the soul of the thinker be scattered due to the anomaly and he be moved from the purpose.

The laws of the commandment: That which they, may their memory be Blessed, said (Bekhorot 43a) that there are three kinds of blemishes. There are some blemishes that disqualify a priest from serving, and if they are in a beast, they disqualify it from being offered. And there are some other blemishes that only disqualify a person from the service, but do not disqualify a beast from being offered. And there are some blemishes that disqualify neither man nor beast, and [our concern] is because of [their] appearance. Any priest that has any of these three types of blemishes may not serve. Only revealed blemishes that are revealed (external) disqualify a person, but blemishes that are inside of his body, such as a removed kidney or spleen, or a punctured intestine - even though they render him a treifah (terminally ill) - his service is still fit. As it is stated (Leviticus 21:9), "a broken leg or a broken hand" - just as those are revealed, so too must all disqualifying blemishes be revealed. The Sages enumerated (Mishneh Torah, Laws of Admission into the Sanctuary 7-8) that the blemishes that disqualify both people and beast are fifty, besides the blemishes that are unique to beasts and they are twenty-three; and [so] it comes out that there are seventy-three in beasts. And there are also blemishes that are unique to people and they are ninety; and [so] it comes out that the blemishes in people are one hundred and forty. This is the grouping of the ninety that are unique to people: there are eight in the head; two in the neck; four in the ears; five in the eyebrows; four in the eyelids; eleven in the eyes; six in the nose; three in the lips; three in the belly; three in a man's back; six in the hands; four in the genital organs; fifteen in the thighs and legs; four over the entire body; eight in the skin of the flesh. And there are also four more big blemishes in people and they are not external, and these are them: a deaf[-mute]; one mentally incapacitated; an epileptic, even if [only on certain] days; and one who is bewildered by an evil spirit, even [only] at set times. In addition to these there are two more that disqualify because of their appearance, and these are them: one whose eyelashes have fallen off, even though the hair remains at the root; and one whose teeth have been removed.

And this is the grouping of the fifty disqualifying blemishes that apply to people and to beasts: five in the ear; three in the eyelid, and these three are included in [the term,] charuts that is stated in the Torah; eight in the eye; three in the nose; six in the mouth; twelve in the genital organs; six in the arms and legs; four that are fitting to be [anywhere on] the body, and these are them: the boil-scar (garav), and it is the one stated in the Torah; a protrusion that has a bone in it, and this is the yabelet that is stated in the Torah; one who has an Egyptian growth of [even] the smallest size on him, and that is the yalefet stated in the Torah; and any bone that is revealed in which a crevice formed, and it is included in charuts that is stated in the Torah. But ribs are not included in bones that are revealed. And there are three others: an old one who has reached [the point that he] shakes and trembles when he stands; a sick one who trembles because of his sickness and the failing of his strength - but a treifah is fit with men, but a disqualification with a beast, and likewise one who had a Caesarian birth is fit with men, but a disqualification with a beast; and one who has a bad smell. Behold fifty. And the rest of its details are in the seventh chapter of Tractate Bekhorot.

And it is practiced at the time of the [Temple] by priests. And so [in the case of] one who transgressed this and served and was one with a blemish: If it was from the blemishes that disqualify a man and a beast - whether inadvertently or whether volitionally - his service is disqualified. And if he was volitional, he is liable for lashes. And so, did they say in Sifra, Emor, Chapter 3:11, "One with a blemish is not with the death penalty; but [only] with a warning (a negative commandment)." And if it was from the ninety that are unique to people - even though he is lashed - he did not profane his service. But if it was one of the blemishes the disqualification of which was only because of appearance, he is not lashed and his service is fit.

Mitzvah 276
That a priest with a transient blemish not serve: That a priest with a transient blemish not serve, as it is stated (Leviticus 21:21), "Any man that has a blemish from the seed of Aharon the priest shall not come forth" - [the] word, "any," is an inclusion; and it includes a transient blemish. As at the beginning, it warns about a permanent blemish, such that I would reason that it is permitted to serve with a transient blemish which is less weighty than it. Therefore, it warned about the transient, and that is the garav and the yalefet.

Similar to what we wrote about the commandment previous to it is from the roots of the commandment.

From the laws of the commandment is that which they, may their memory be Blessed, said (Kiddushin 66b) that both one with a permanent blemish or [one with] a transient blemish disqualifies the service and is lashed - if he served (transgressed) volitionally. And that which they, may their memory be Blessed, said (Mishnah Middot 5:4) that the Great Court would sit in the chamber of hewn stone and their main constant activity was to check the priests in their pedigree and their blemishes. And any priest that was found to be disqualified in his pedigree wears black, wraps himself in black and goes out of the [Temple] yard. But one found complete and fit wears white, enters and serves with his brother priests. And one who was found fit in his pedigree but a blemish was found on him sits in the chamber of wood and removes the wormy wood for the arrangement [of wood]. And he divides the holy foods with his clan and eats, as it is stated (Leviticus 21:22), "The bread of His God from the holy of the holies and from the holy he may eat." And the rest of the laws of all of the blemishes are in Bekhorot, the seventh chapter.

And [it] is practiced at the time of the [Temple] by the priests. If he transgressed and served with a transient blemish volitionally, he is lashed. And Ramban, may his memory be Blessed, (on Sefer HaMitzvot LaRambam, Mitzvot Lo Taase 71) does not count the negative commandment of a transient blemish as a negative commandment on its own. And he wrote that it is included in the negative commandment of a permanent blemish, and that it is like a section of the [various] sections of the commandment. And he and Rambam, may his memory be Blessed, (Sefer HaMitzvot LaRambam, Shorashim 11) have already agreed - and it is a clear thing - that we should not consider a section of a commandment, a commandment on its own.

Mitzvah 277
That one with a blemish not enter the entire sanctuary: That one with a blemish not enter the sanctuary in its entirety - meaning to say the altar, between the chamber and the altar and all the rest of the places in the sanctuary, as it is stated (Leviticus 21:23), "But to the curtain he shall not come and to the altar he shall not come." And it is elucidated in Sifra, Emor, Chapter 3:10 that these two negative commandments of the curtain and the altar do not suffice, one without the [other]. And each of them comes to complete the law as one matter - and it is to distance the place that is forbidden for them to enter in [from them].

It is from the roots of the commandment to aggrandize the glory of the [Temple] and its beauty. Therefore, it is not fitting for someone with a blemish to go there - since it is the place of perfection, it is not appropriate for someone with any lack to stand there. And I have already written above many times (e. g. Sefer HaChinukh 95) the benefit that is found for us in our aggrandizing the loftiness of the holy [Temple] and its glory.

I mentioned the laws of the commandment – meaning what are the blemishes for which a priest refrains from entering - with hints (in outline form), above close by in the law of the one with a permanent blessing (Sefer HaChinukh 175). And there I made known their place in the Gemara and all of the content, as is my custom. And Ramban, may his memory be Blessed, wrote (on Sefer HaMitzvot, Mitzvot Lo Taase 69) that we should not count this negative commandment as one of the tally of the negative commandments; that the prohibition for one with a blemish to enter into the Sanctuary - and also one with wild [hair], torn clothes or drunk with wine - is an embellishment from the words of [the Rabbis]. And this verse is only coming to forbid drawing close for service and it is included in the negative commandment that one with a blemish not serve. And he wrote further that even they only forbade the place that is called, "between the chamber and the altar," which is twenty-two ells; but in front of the altar itself, which is thirty-two ells, they did not forbid. And [it is] as I wrote above in the Order of Vayehi Bayom Hashmini (Sefer HaChinukh 149) in the warning of the one with wild [hair] in the name of the teacher, may his memory be Blessed (see Mishneh Torah, Laws of Admission into the Sanctuary 6).

Mitzvah 278

That an impure priest not serve: That a priest not serve when he is still impure, as it is stated (Leviticus 22:2), "and they shall separate from the holy things of the Children of Israel and they shall not profane My holy name." And they, may their memory be Blessed, said in the ninth chapter of Sanhedrin 83b, "From where [do we know] about an impure one who served that he is [punished] with death" - meaning to say, with death by the hands of the Heavens? "As it is written, 'Speak to Aharon and to his sons, and they shall separate from the holy things of the Children of Israel and they shall not profane'"; and it is written in another place (Leviticus 22:9), "and die for it, since they profaned it."

That which we have written in many places is from the roots of the commandment - [that] because of the glory of the [Temple] and the loftiness of the service, we distance from it anything that is not in its loftiness and its importance - and the loftiness of a man in purity is known to all who understand. The laws of the commandment are for example, what are the impurities that render impure rabbinically; in what ways one impure purifies himself from his impurity: which impurity requires sprinkling and a sacrifice for its purification and which only needs immersion and the setting of the sun - and included in the matter is that it is impossible to emerge from any impurity [without] immersion; which impurity requires seven days for its purification and which suffices with one day. And the rest of its many matters which 'became very numerous,' are all elucidated in the Order of Tahorot (see Mishneh Torah, Laws of Admission into the Sanctuary 4).

And [it] is practiced by priests at the time of the [Temple]. And a priest that transgresses it and serves in impurity is liable for death by the hands of the Heavens (see Mishneh Torah, Laws of Admission into the Sanctuary 4:1).

Mitzvah 279

That an impure priest not eat priestly tithe: That an impure priest not eat priestly tithe, as it is stated (Leviticus 22:4), "Every man from the seed of Aharon, etc. from the holy things he shall not eat, until he becomes pure." And we say in Tractate Makkot 14b, "From where [do I know about] a warning for priestly tithe" - meaning to say, that he not eat it [while he is] impure? "As it is stated, 'Every man, etc.'; what is the thing that is equal to the seed of Aharon" - meaning to say, that all of the seed eat it, males and females? "I would say, 'that is the priestly tithe.'" And the warning about this matter is repeated, as it is written (Leviticus 22:9), "And they shall keep My charge." And [it is] like they said in Sanhedrin 83a [in] the ninth chapter concerning those liable for death by the hands of the Heavens, that they learn [about] the one who is impure that eats priestly tithe, from "And they shall keep My charge and they shall not bear a sin for it."

It is from the roots of the commandment [that it is] to aggrandize and make dear all that is [part of] the holy in the heart of every man. And I have already mentioned many times the benefit that comes out to us in the thing. And it is well-known [that] to eat it in purity is from the embellishments of the holy.

From the laws of the commandment is that which they, may their memory be Blessed, said (Mishneh Torah, Laws of Heave Offerings 7:1) that an impure priest that ate pure priestly tithe is [punishable] with the death penalty and is lashed for it. But if he ate impure priestly tithe - even though it is [forbidden] with a negative commandment - he is not lashed, as it is not holy. And that which they said (Berakhot 2a) that impure ones eat priestly tithe with the sun setting and they see three medium stars in the firmament - and that time period is like a third of an hour after the setting of the sun. And that which they, may their memory be Blessed, said about one who was eating priestly tithe and felt that his limbs shuddered to ejaculate semen, and that which they said about camel drivers. And that which they said (Bekhorot 27a) about the priestly tithe of outside the Land, that it is permitted to a priest that the impurity does not come out to him from his body - such as a boy minor who did not experience an emission or a girl minor who has not [yet] become menstruant. And that which they said (Chullin 130b) that all ignoramuses are assumed to be impure, and so we only give the priestly tithe to priests who know to keep it in purity. And I have also mentioned above (Sefer HaChinukh 159) some of the laws of the impurities in general and in particular.

And [it] is practiced by male and female priests in the Land and at the time that it is in its settlement - as then the obligation of the priestly tithe is from Torah writ there, according to the opinion of Rambam, may his memory be Blessed (Mishneh Torah, Laws of Heave Offerings 1:26). And one who transgresses it and eats priestly tithe volitionally and is impure, is liable for death by the hands of the Heavens. And [it is] as it is mentioned in Sanhedrin 83a [in] the ninth chapter, such that they enumerated those liable for death there, and enumerated an impure priest that ate priestly tithe among them. And at this time, there is a rabbinical prohibition with the fruits of the Land of Israel (see Tur, Yoreh Deah 231).

Mitzvah 280

That no foreigner eats priestly tithe: That no foreigner (non-priest) eat priestly tithe, as it is stated (Leviticus 22:10), "And any foreigner shall not eat the holy." And the received (traditional) understanding (Pesachim 23a) came that this "holy" is only the priestly tithe and anything that is called priestly tithe (terumah), but it does not come here to warn about other types of holy things. And that which is also called priestly tithe is the first fruits, as they, may their memory be Blessed, expound from the tradition (Pesachim 36b), "'And the terumah of your hand' (Deuteronomy 12:17) - these are the first fruits."

From the roots of the commandment [is] like [that which is written about] the preceding commandment. And it is from the embellishments of the holy that only the servants of God and their wives, their children, and their slaves that they acquired eat it; and that they give it to their beasts and to all of their animals, but not to others.

From the laws of the commandment is that which they, may their memory be Blessed, said (Gittin 12b) that a runaway slave of a priest eats priestly tithe, since he is his acquired property in any case. And so [too,] a rebellious wife, behold she eats; and any wife of a priest [may] eat, even if she is only three years and one day old. Also, the betrothed of a priest would have been fitting to eat, except the Sages decreed that she not eat until they are married, as it appears in the beginning of the fifth chapter of Ketubot 57b. A Hebrew slave does not eat, as behold the Torah forbade both the perennial worker and the annual worker, as it is written (Leviticus 22:10), "the boarder of a priest and the hired worker may not eat the holy." But a Canaanite (gentile) slave eats, because he is his acquired property. Also, if the slave acquires other slaves, they [may] also eat through him, since it is written (Leviticus 22:11), "when he acquires an acquired soul" - which has an implication that the acquired soul makes an acquisition. If, however, the second-tier slave acquires a third-tier slave, [the latter] may not eat. Since the [Torah] stated, "when an acquired soul makes an acquisition," and not "an acquisition of an acquisition." Any priestess who had intercourse with someone who disqualifies from the priesthood is permanently forbidden from eating priestly tithe (Yevamot 65a). The same is true for a hermaphrodite [priest], whether he had intercourse through his male organ or through his female organ. And even a stretched - and that is a person who stretched his foreskin so that he would appear as if he was uncircumcised - is rabbinically forbidden from eating until he is circumcised a second time (Yevamot 72a). And the rest of its many details are elucidated in Tractate Terumot.

And the prohibition of the eating of priestly tithes for non-priests is practiced by all of Israel, males and females, in any place that there is priestly tithe from Torah writ - that is at the time that the Land of Israel is in its settlement, for then the obligation of priestly tithe is from Torah writ, as we will write in the Order of Shoftim (Sefer HaChinukh, 507) in the commandment of separating the great priestly tithe, with God's help. And at this time, this prohibition is practiced rabbinically with the fruits of the Land of Israel, and as we will write there. One who transgressed this and ate priestly tithe and is a "foreigner," such as an Israelite - who is a foreigner - or even a priest or priestess who was profaned from [their status in the] priesthood through one of the well-known [mechanisms of] profanation that our Sages, may their memory be Blessed, have instructed us, is liable for death by the hands of the Heavens, as it appears in the ninth chapter of Sanhedrin 83b, from that which is written (Leviticus 22:9), "and die for it, since they profaned it," and afterwards, "And any foreigner shall not eat the holy."

Mitzvah 281

That the boarder of a priest and the hired worker not eat priestly tithe: That the boarder of a priest and the hired worker not eat priestly tithe, as it is written (Leviticus 22:10), "the boarder of a priest and the hired worker may not eat the holy."

The root of the commandment and all of its content is included in the previous commandment, since the reason for their prohibition is that they are considered like "foreigners," since he is not his acquired property - as "the boarder" is the perennial worker, and "the hired worker" is the annual worker (see Yevamot 70a).

Mitzvah 282

That an uncircumcised one not eat priestly tithe: That an uncircumcised one not eat priestly tithe; meaning to say, a priest that is not circumcised - whether he is volitional or inadvertent or from duress, such as when his brothers died because of circumcision, so that the fear of death prevented him from being circumcised; in any manner that it be - since he is uncircumcised, he is forbidden to eat priestly tithe. And the same is the law - that he is forbidden - with other consecrated foods. And this prevention is not elucidated in Scripture, but we rather learn it from an inferential comparison. And the transcriber wrote in the name of Rambam, may his memory be Blessed, (Sefer HaMitzvot, Mitzvot Lo Taase 135), "The ones that received the tradition elucidated with this, that this prohibition is from Torah writ and not rabbinic. And the language of Yevamot 70a is, 'From where [do we know] that an uncircumcised does not eat priestly tithe? It is stated, "a boarder and a hired worker" (Exodus 12:45) with regard to the Pesach [sacrifice], and it is stated, "a boarder and a hired worker" (Leviticus 22:10) with regard to priestly tithe. Just as "a boarder and a hired worker" with regard to the Pesach, an uncircumcised is prohibited [from eating] it, so too, "a boarder and a hired worker" stated with regard to priestly tithe, an uncircumcised is prohibited [from eating] it.' And the same is the law for other holy foods. And this is likewise the language of Sifra, Emor, Chapter 4:18. And there it is stated, 'Rabbi Akiva says, "Every man (literally, A man, a man)" (Leviticus 22:4), [is] to include the uncircumcised.' And there - meaning in the Gemara Yevamot 72a - it is elucidated that a stretched [may] eat from priestly tithe from the word of the Torah, but [the Rabbis] decreed [that he may not] because he appears like one uncircumcised. And a stretched is one who stretched his foreskin in a way that he would appear as if he was uncircumcised, after he was circumcised. Behold, it is already elucidated that an uncircumcised is forbidden from the Torah and a stretched is forbidden rabbinically. And understand this. And there it is said that a stretched must be circumcised [again] rabbinically." To here [are his words].

And according to that which appears, the entire lengthiness of his words here is because in the second root of the Sefer HaMitzvot, it is written that not everything that we learn from the thirteen hermenutic principles through which the Torah is expounded or by an inclusion is fitting to count in the tally of the commandments. And behold the inferential comparison (gezara shava) is one of the thirteen principles, and [yet] he himself counted the prohibition of an uncircumcised one with priestly tithe as one - and even though it is learned like this. And therefore, he is apologizing, with his saying that the ones that received the tradition elucidated that this prohibition is from Torah writ and not rabbinic. And it appears that his intention is to say that any time they, may their memory be Blessed, elucidated that the matter is from Torah writ [and] not rabbinic, we count it as a commandment. [And this is] even though we learn it from one of the principles, since the Sages testified about the matter that it is from Torah writ. And were it not that it is fitting to be very careful with the coal of the Rabbi and that I am afraid, I would say that he entered this topic with great duress. And Ramban, may his memory be Blessed already wrangled with him in his Sefer HaMitzvot on the second root, and he [produced] many proofs from the words of the Gemara and the Midrash - how the words were prolific, to the point that seven large folios would not contain them. And [as the] final word, the Rabbi said that the contents of Sefer Hamitzvot of Rambam, may his memory be Blessed, are sweet things and it is all delights, except for this root (ikar) that 'uproots (oker) mountains.'

It is from the roots of the commandments [that it is] because the uncircumcised is considered like a foreigner, since he did not enter the covenant of the circumcision - which is a great matter - with [the rest of] Israel. And there is one root to the distancing of a foreigner from priestly tithe and impure ones from the holy, and it is written above close by (Sefer HaChinukh 279).

And [it] is practiced in every place that there is priestly tithe from Torah writ there, as we said in the previous commandment (Sefer HaChinukh 281). And one who transgresses this and eats priestly tithe - whether pure or impure - and is uncircumcised is liable for lashes.

Mitzvah 283
That a profaned woman not eat from the holy: That a profaned woman not eat from the holy - meaning to say from the priestly tithe, the breast and the thigh that fit daughters of the Children of Aharon are fitting to eat - as it is stated (Leviticus 22:12), "And the daughter of a priest when she shall be to a foreign man, she shall not eat that which is raised of the consecrated things." And we say in the Gemara Yevamot 68a, "'When she shall be to a foreign man' - such that she had intercourse with one disqualified to her, that he disqualified her." And from that which is written, "that which is raised of the consecrated things," they, may their memory be Blessed, said (Yevamot 68b), "With that which is raised from the consecrated things, they shall not eat" - meaning from the breast and the thigh. And there it is said, "Let the verse write, 'she shall not eat the consecrated things.' What is [the meaning of] 'that which is raised of the consecrated things?' We hear two [things] from it: One is that when she had intercourse with one disqualified, she is disqualified from eating priestly tithe, the breast and the thigh; and the other is that when she was married to a 'foreigner' and her husband dies, she returns to eating the tithe but does not return to [eating] the breast and the thigh." And it comes out that included in this negative commandment is the warning of the priestess that married a foreigner not to eat the breast and thigh even though her husband died or divorced her, which is not what we determine with priestly tithe - as a priestess that marries a foreigner and her husband dies, returns to eat priestly tithe. And the understanding of the verse is such: "when she shall be to a man foreign with that which is raised of the consecrated things" - meaning to say when she has intercourse with a foreigner, meaning one disqualified to her, and this is his foreignness, [then] she shall not eat that which is raised of the consecrated things, which is the priestly tithe, the breast and the thigh, as I have explained. And further there is also in the understanding of the verse, "when she shall be to a foreign man" - one who is not a priest; and so, did Rashi, may his memory be Blessed, write (Rashi on Leviticus 22:12), "To a Levite or Israelite," meaning to say that he is foreign from the priesthood - she does not eat "that which is raised of the consecrated things" at the time that she is his. But after his death or that he divorces her, when she eats of that which is raised of the holy things - as behold, she has left from being [in the domain] of the foreigner - she [still] does not eat from the breast and the thigh. As once she has married a foreigner, she is disqualified from the breast and the thigh forever. However, you should know that we did not learn the prohibition of a priestess eating from priestly tithe when she is still [in the domain of] her Israelite husband from this verse at all - as the [traditional]

commentary does not come to expound this from that, but rather only that which we wrote. But this prohibition, the Sages - the masters of the received tradition - may their memory be Blessed, learned (Yevamot 68b) from another place - from that which is written (Leviticus 12:10), "And any foreigner shall not eat the holy." As the commentary comes about it, that all the time that the woman is [in the domain of] her husband - meaning her Israelite husband - who is a foreigner from the priesthood, she 'shall not eat the holy.' [This is] since the wife of a foreigner is considered like a foreigner - and behold, she is like one of his ribs. And know this it and receive it, as it is the received truth.

And this commandment is practiced in every place [and at all times] where there is priestly tithe from Torah writ, as we said in the previous commandments. A priestess that transgressed and ate priestly tithe or the breast or the thigh, and she is profaned, meaning to say she has had intercourse with someone who disqualifies her from the priesthood; and so [too,] if she transgressed and ate the breast or the thigh after her Israelite husband died or she became divorced from him; and likewise if she transgressed and ate priestly tithe or the breast or the thigh while she is still [in the domain of] her Israelite husband - in all of these ways, she is liable for lashes.

Mitzvah 284
To not eat tevel: To not eat tevel - whether an Israelite or a priest - and that is a thing that tithes and priestly tithes have not been taken away from it, as it is stated (Leviticus 22:15), "And they shall not profane the consecrated things of the Children of Israel that they shall raise to the Lord." And the received (traditional) explanation comes about this (Sanhedrin 83a) that the verse is speaking about tevel. And the content of the verse is to say that they should not profane the consecrated things in their still being mixed with the non-sacred. And that is [why] the expression is [in] future tense - meaning to say that it has not yet been raised. And so [too], is it in the Gemara Sanhedrin 83a, "From where [do we know] about the one who eats tevel that he is [punishable by] death? As it is stated, 'And they shall not profane the consecrated things of the Children of Israel that they shall raise to the Lord' - the verse is speaking about those that will be raised in the future; such that we learn [a comparison of] 'profane' [and] 'profane' from priestly tithe," about which it is written (Numbers 18:32), "and the consecrated things of the Children of Israel you shall not profane and not die." And [the latter] is with the death penalty - as we wrote above (Sefer HaChinukh 280), from that which is written (Leviticus 22:9), "and die for it, since they profaned it," and adjacent to it, "And any foreigner shall not eat the holy." And they, may their memory be Blessed, also said about this matter in the Gemara Makkot 16b, "Perhaps one is only liable for eating tevel from which no [gifts] were taken at all; but if the great priestly tithe was taken from [the produce], but not the tithe of the tithe, or the first tithe or the second tithe, or even if only the poor tithe [was not separated]; from where [is it derived] that there is a liability in the thing? [Hence] we learn to say, 'You may not eat in your gates' (Deuteronomy 12:17), and later it states, 'and they shall eat within your gates and be satisfied' (Deuteronomy 26:12). Just as there, it is poor tithe, here too, it is poor tithe - and the [Torah] states, 'You may not.'

However, this liability is for lashes, but the iniquity [punishable by]
death is only for tevel that has not had the great priestly tithe taken from it; and likewise, for one who eats tithe before the priestly tithe of the tithe has been taken from it. And this is what is stated in the commandment to the Levites when it commanded to take out the tithe from the tithe (Numbers 18:32), "and the consecrated things of the Children of Israel you shall not profane and you shall not die." That is a prevention that they should not eat the first tithe in its mixture [with gifts that still need to be separated]. So, did they, may their memory be Blessed, explain (Yevamot 86a). And therefore, they are liable for death for it, as it is elucidated in Tractate Dammai. It comes out from the sum of our words that one who eats tevel before he takes the great priestly tithe from it - and likewise before he took the priestly tithe from the tithe - is with death. But if he ate from it after the great priestly tithe was taken from it, and also the priestly tithe of the tithe was taken - for example that he preceded to take the priestly tithe of the tithe before the tithe, even though it is still mixed with the two tithes, which are the first tithe and the second tithe, or poor tithe; he is not liable for death, but rather he has a liability for lashes. And so [too,] the whole time when it is mixed [with] one of the tithes, it is with

lashes. And its warning is from, "You may not eat in your gates, etc.," as we will write in the Order of Re'eh Anochi (Sefer HaChinukh 473-4). And hold on to this matter, as you will find the truth to be like this if you merit to study the words of our Sages - the masters of the tradition - may their memory be Blessed.

That which I have written above close by in the negative commandment of an impure priest with priestly tithe (Sefer HaChinukh 279) is from the roots of the commandment.

From the laws of the commandment is that which they, may their memory be Blessed, said (Avodah Zarah 73a) about the prohibition of tevel that it forbids its mixture with the smallest amount - which is not the case with other prohibitions in the Torah besides idolatrous wine and chamets on Pesach, as I have written in its place (Sefer HaChinukh 111). And they gave a reason with tevel - [it is] because its prohibition is like its permissibility with the smallest amount: As they, may their memory be Blessed, said that priestly tithe does not have a measure from Torah writ, but rather even one [grain] of wheat exempts a large threshing floor of wheat. [And so], even its prohibition is like this, with the smallest amount. And it comes out that if a little tevel got mixed in several of the non-holy [produce], they are all forbidden. And in the Order of Seeds in Tractate Terumot and Maaser Sheni and Maaserot, it is elucidated which thing is liable for priestly tithe and [other] tithes - and they make [other] fruits tevel - and which thing is exempt; which is liable from Torah writ and which is from the words of [the Rabbis]. And the rest of the statutes of tevel are there and in Tractate Dammai (see Tur, Yoreh Deah 331).

And this prohibition of tevel is practiced by all of Israel, by males and females - and even priests and Levites (Mishneh Torah, Laws of Tithes 1:3), even though that they are the ones who eat the priestly tithes, and even with their [own] grain. And so [too,] is this prohibition practiced in every place - meaning to say that it is forbidden to eat tevel of the fruits of the Land of Israel in every place. But [regarding] the obligation of priestly tithes and [other] tithes from the fruits, it is well-known, that the Torah only obligated us about them in the Land of Israel, and at the time that Israel is there, as it is stated with the priestly tithe (Numbers 15:2), "in your coming." And they, may their memory be Blessed, expounded (Ketuvot 25a), "'The coming' of all of you, and not the coming of some of you." And so, did Rambam, may his memory be Blessed, determine (Mishneh Torah, Laws of Heave Offerings 1:26). And therefore, there is only a prohibition of tevel from Torah writ on the fruits of the Land of Israel - and specifically with the grain, the wine and the oil, as we will write in the commandment of tithing in the Order of Vayikach Korach (Sefer HaChinuch 395).

And I have already written some of the differences of the places surrounding the Land of Israel concerning the seventh [year] in the Order of Eem Kesef Talveh. And I will still write at length [about] the whole matter of priestly tithes and [other] tithes and the distinctions of the places and that which is from Torah writ and what is rabbinic in the Order of Shoftim in the commandment of the separation of the great priestly tithe (Sefer HaChinukh 507) - take it from there. And I will also inform you there of a disagreement among the commentators regarding whether the priestly tithe is from Torah writ or rabbinic today even in the Land. And [regarding] one who is in a place about which he is in doubt if it is from the Land of Israel or not, at the time when the land is in its inhabitation - it is fitting for him to be stringent nonetheless, since it is prohibition from Torah writ; and it is established for us that [in the case of] a doubt in Torah law, [we go] towards stringency (Beitzah 3b). And from that which it appears, the Sages, may their memory be Blessed, were stringent (Chullin 6b) in the places about which they were in doubt if they were from the Land of Israel, even about the fruits the tithing obligation of which was only rabbinic - even after the destruction of the Temple, even though this prohibition is only practiced [altogether] from Torah writ [when the Temple is standing]. And one who transgresses this and ate a kazayit of tevel before they separated the great priestly tithe from it - and likewise before they separated the priestly tithe of the tithe - is liable for death by the hands of the Heavens, and as we said above. But if he ate a kazayit of tevel from which the great priestly tithe and the priestly tithe of the tithe were taken, but they still did not separate the tithes from it - and even if only the poor tithe remained in it - he is liable for lashes. And if it was tevel from their words - meaning something that the obligation of priestly tithes and [other] tithes from which is only rabbinic, such as all the fruits besides grain, wine and [olive] oil of the Land of Israel and at the time of the

Temple - we strike him with lashes of rebellion. And the liquids that come out of the fruits that are tevel are forbidden like them. And nonetheless even though they are are forbidden from Torah writ, the liability for lashes is not on the liquids but only only on the body of the fruits - except for wine and [olive] oil, such that we administer lashes for them in the same way that we administer lashes for the olives and grapes [themselves]. And the reason, according to that which appears, is because the essence of those fruits for the creatures is for [their] liquids.

Mitzvah 285
That we not consecrate [animals] with blemishes for the altar: That we not consecrate [animals] with blemishes, to sacrifice, them for the altar. And even though he did not sacrifice them, there is a negative commandment for the consecration alone. And about the consecration alone is it stated (Leviticus 22:20), "All that has a blemish in it, you shall not offer" - on account of you shall not consecrate (Temurah 6a).

That which we wrote above (Sefer HaChinukh 277) in the negative commandment that [a priest] with a blemish not enter all of the sanctuary is from the roots of the commandment. And look in the commandment of the sacrifice (Sefer HaChinukh 286) to be complete (unblemished), and you will find it there if you seek it.

And I have written a little about the laws of the commandment - meaning to say which are the blemishes that disqualify and which do not disqualify - above in the commandment that a priest who is one with a blemish not serve in the service of the Temple (Sefer HaChinukh 275). And it is all in [detail] in Tractate Bekhorot (see Mishneh Torah, Laws of Things Forbidden on the Altar 1).

And [it] is practiced in every place and at all times by males and females. Anyone who transgresses it and consecrates an [animal] with a blemish - and even at this time - violates this negative commandment. And from what appears, there would not be lashes with this, since there is no act [involved] with it; but I saw that Rambam, may his memory be Blessed, wrote (Mishneh Torah, Laws of Things Forbidden on the Altar 1:2) [that] one who consecrates an [animal] with a blemish is lashed. And maybe he makes it like one who exchanges [a sacrifice] about which there is lashes even though there is no act [involved] with it - as [in that case, we see the impact of his words - since] this and that are consecrated. And to him shall we listen 'and we will seek Torah from his mouth, as he is an angel of the Lord of hosts.'

Mitzvah 286
The commandment of the sacrifice being unblemished: That every sacrifice that we sacrifice be perfect from blemishes that come in Scripture and from those that the tradition comes about that they are blemishes for its specie. And that is [the understanding of] what is stated about this (Leviticus 22:21), "unblemished shall it be acceptable." And they said in Sifra, Emor, Section 7:9, "'Unblemished shall it be' - is a positive commandment." And they brought a proof (Menachot 87a) that the libations and flours and oils [also] be completely perfect from degeneration from that which is written (Numbers 28:31), "they shall be unblemished, and their libations."

The root of the commandment is revealed with that which we [wrote] previously above regarding sacrifices from the angle of the simple understanding, [which is] that they are to arouse and direct the thoughts of people towards God, Blessed be He. As a man is affected by the strength of his actions - hence it is fitting no matter what that the sacrifice be without a blemish, given that the intentions of man do not rest nor become focused upon a lesser type as they will a more important [one]. As hearts will be more aroused by the important and perfect in its species and this is something well-known to all who understand.

From the laws of the commandment are the blemishes that disqualify a sacrifice that the Sages, may their memory be Blessed, enumerated (Mishneh Torah, Laws of Things Forbidden on the Altar 1:2) that are seventy-three. Fifty of them are whether with a man or with a beast, and twenty-three are unique to beasts and are not fitting to be with a man. And likewise, there are blemishes that are unique to man that are not fitting to be with a beast and they are ninety, as we shall write in this Order (Sefer HaChinukh 275) concerning blemishes that disqualify a priest. And so [too,] that which they, may their memory be Blessed, distinguished between a permanent blemish and a transient blemish; and that which they said (Zevachim 116a) that the blemishes do not disqualify a sacrifice of fowl, as it does not state about them, "an unblemished male." And about what are these words speaking? About small blemishes. But a fowl the wing of which has dried up, or its eye was blinded or its leg cut off is forbidden on top of the altar. And the rest of its details are elucidated in the eighth chapter of Menachot (see Mishneh Torah, Laws of Things Forbidden on the Altar 1).

And this commandment is practiced at the time of the [Temple]. And one who transgresses it and slaughters or sprinkles the blood or incinerates the entrails upon the altar, from a beast that is one with a blemish, has violated this positive commandment - besides that he has violated a negative commandment; and as we shall write with God's help (Sefer HaChinukh 288-290). And Rambam, may his memory be Blessed, wrote (Mishneh Torah, Laws of Things Forbidden on the Altar 1:4), "It comes out that you learned that if he consecrated an [animal] with a blemish and slaughtered it, and sprinkled its blood and incinerated its entrails upon the altar, he is lashed four [sets] of lashes." And about that which he said that if he consecrated, he is lashed, it requires [further] study.

Mitzvah 287
That we not place a blemish upon consecrated animals: - That we not place a blemish upon consecrated animals; meaning to say that we not make any wound or any fracture upon a beast that is consecrated for the altar that disqualifies it as an offering - as it is stated (Leviticus 22:21), "and no blemish shall be upon it." And they, may their memory be Blessed, said (Menachot 56b), "Read it as 'shall not be made in it.'" And the language of Sifra, Emor, Section 7:9 is, "'No blemish shall be upon it' - do not place a blemish upon it."

It is from the roots of the commandment [that it is] since there would be a disgrace to the consecrated animals with this. And I have already written many times (Sefer HaChinukh 95) [about] the benefit to the heart of man that comes out [from] the endearment of the glory of the Temple, its servants and its offerings.

From the laws of the commandment is that which they said that one who puts a blemish in consecrated animals themselves or their exchanges transgresses a negative commandment and is lashed, except for the first-born or the tithe. As one who puts a blemish on their exchange is not lashed, because they are not fitting as sacrifices - as is elucidated in Temurah 21b. And the rest of its details are elucidated in scattered places in Zevachim and Temurah.

And this prohibition is practiced in every place and at all times by males and females. But there is only a liability for lashes at the time that the Temple is in existence; such that the beast would be fitting as a sacrifice, as is elucidated in the Gemara, Avodah Zarah 13b.

Mitzvah 288
That we not sprinkle blood of an [animal] with a blemish on the altar: That we not sprinkle blood of [animals] with a blemish on top of the altar, as it is stated (Leviticus 22:22), "A blind or broken or creviced (charuts) or protrusion (yabelet) or boil-scar (garav) or yalefet ; you shall not sacrifice these to the Lord." And the tradition comes about this negative commandment that it is a prevention of sprinkling the blood of [animals] with blemishes. And that is the opinion of the first teacher (tanna kamma) in the Gemara, Temurah 6b, and that is the law. As it says there, "And [for] the first teacher, why do I need this 'you shall not sacrifice to the Lord.' He requires it for sprinkling of the blood." All of the content of this warning (negative commandment) is like the warning of the placing of a blemish upon holy [animals] (Sefer HaChinukh 287) and the sacrifice of an [animal] with a blemish (Sefer HaChinukh 289) and the incineration of the entrails (Sefer HaChinukh 290). However, we should not count it with the prohibitions that are practiced today; as due to our iniquities, we do not have an altar.

Mitzvah 289
That we not slaughter an [animal with a blemish] for the sake of a sacrifice: That we not slaughter [animals] with blemishes for the sake of a sacrifice, as it is stated (Leviticus 22:22), "you shall not sacrifice these to the Lord." And the language of Sifra, Emor, Chapter 7:1 is "'You shall not sacrifice'

- on account of you shall not slaughter." All of the content of this commandment is explained in the commandment preceding it. However, we should not count this prohibition with those that are practiced today; as due to our iniquities, we do not have an altar to slaughter the sacrifices there.

Mitzvah 290
That we not incinerate the entrails of [animals] with blemishes: Not to incinerate the entrails of [animals] with blemishes. I have written the understanding of entrails in the Order of Tsav in the commandment of the procedure of the sin-offering. And about this is it stated (Leviticus 22:22), "a fire-offering you shall not give of them upon the altar." The content of this commandment as well, and the elucidation of the place of its laws is written in the commandment prior to its colleague (Sefer HaChinukh 287). However, we should not count this prohibition with those that are practiced today; as due to our iniquities, we do not have an altar upon which to incinerate.

Mitzvah 291
Not to castrate one of all of the species: To not castrate one of all of the species - not a man and not a beast and not a bird, as it is stated (Leviticus 22:24), "and in your land you shall not do [it]." After the verse mentioned, "And a crushed, and a pounded and a disconnected and a cut," which is stated about the [sexual organs], it stated, "and in your land you shall not do [it]." And the explanation came about it (Chagigah 14b), "[To] all in your land you shall not do [it]" - meaning to say this shall not be done among Israel; or its explanation is from every species in your land you shall not do [it]. And "[to] all in your land you shall not do [it]" includes man and beast and all animals. And the content of the verse is not to say that there only be a prohibition of castration in the Land. And explicitly did they, may their memory be Blessed, say in Shabbat 110b in the chapter [entitled] Shmoneh Sheratsim, "We learned, 'From where [do we know] about castration of a man, that it is forbidden? [Hence] we learn to say, "and in your land you shall not do [it]" - you shall not do it in (to) you.'"

It is from the roots of the commandment [that it is] since God, Blessed be He, created His world with absolute perfection - He did not miss nor add a thing in it from all that is fitting to be for its perfection. And it was from His will to bless animals that they should be fruitful and multiply. And He also commanded the males from the human species about this in order that they survive. As otherwise, the species would cease, since death finishes them. And hence, one who destroys the [sexual organs] shows himself to be as if he is disgusted by the act of the Creator and wants the destruction of His good world.

From the laws of the commandment is that which they, may their memory be Blessed, said (Bava Metzia 90b) that even to tell a gentile to castrate the beast of an Israelite is forbidden. But if the gentile took it on his own and castrated it, it is permissible to take [the beast] from his hand and eat it. However, if the Israelite was being sly, such as if he said things in front of the gentile that show his desire for this - and similar to these matters, such as the lowly sly ones do - we penalize him, such that he take it out from under his hand and sell it to another Israelite. And they, may their memory be Blessed, permitted him to sell it even to his adult son; as they only decreed that it should go out from under his hand and that he sell it to another Israelite. But he [may] not sell nor give it to his minor son.

And that which they also said (Shabbat 111a) that one who castrates after [another] who castrates is liable, and like Rabbi Chiya bar Avin said that Rabbi Yochanan said, "Everyone concedes that one who leavens after [another] leavened is liable, as it is stated (Leviticus 6:10), 'It shall not be baked leavened,' and (Leviticus 2:11) 'it shall not be made leavened'; that one who castrates after [another] castrates is liable, as it is stated (Leviticus 22:24), 'And a crushed, and a pounded and a disconnected and a cut' - if one is liable for one cut, is one not all the more so [liable] for one disconnected? Rather, [this comes] to include that one who disconnects after one who cuts is liable." How is this? Behold, one came and cut the member, and another came and cut the testicles or disconnected them, the last one is also liable; and so [too,] if one came and crushed the member, and another came and disconnected it, they are all lashed - even though the last one does not castrate, as it is already castrated. And that which they, may their memory be Blessed, said (Shabbat 111a) that if one neuters a female - whether a person or of the other species - he is exempt. And that which they said (Shabbat 110a) that [it] is forbidden to give a cup of roots to a man or to other creatures in order to sterilize them, but we do not administer lashes for this. And so [too,] one who places his fellow in water or in snow, until the power of his reproductive organs is neutralized, is not lashed until he castrates [him] manually. But it is fitting to strike [such a one with] lashes of rebellion. And a woman is permitted to drink a cup of roots that sterilize her, such that she not gives birth; as women are not commanded about being fruitful and multiplying - as I wrote in the first commandment of the book. And the rest of its details are elucidated in [various] places in Tractate Shabbat and Yevamot (see Tur, Even HaEzer 5).

And this commandment is practiced in every place and at all times by males and females. As it also forbidden for them to castrate the males - though not themselves with a cup of roots, as we have said. And one who transgresses this and castrates one of all the species of animals - whether a man, whether a beast or a fowl; whether pure [animals] or impure [ones] - is lashed.

Mitzvah 292

Not to sacrifice a sacrifice that is one with a blemish from the hand of the stranger: Not to sacrifice [animals] with blemishes from the hands of gentiles, as it is stated (Leviticus 22:25), "And from the hand of the stranger you shall not offer the bread of your God from all of these" - such that we not say, "Since he is a gentile, we can sacrifice one with a blemish for his sake." And it required a warning about this for them, since the Torah already permitted us to accept unblemished sacrifices from them; as it is stated (Leviticus 22:18), "Every man from the House of Israel and from the sojourner in Israel that offers his sacrifice for all of their vows and for all of their pledges." And the explanation comes about this (Menachot 73b; Chullin 13b), "'Man' to include the gentiles that promise vows and pledges." And we accept it from them.

The glory of the [Temple] is from the roots of the commandment; and as I wrote in the negative commandment that a blemish not be placed on consecrated animals, in this Order (Sefer HaChinukh 287).

From the laws of the commandment is that which they, may their memory be Blessed, said (Temurah 7a) that every blemish of the blemishes that disqualify for our sacrifices, such as the seventy-three well-known blemishes, also disqualify with that which we accept from them. And we do not say that only that which they consider a blemish, like a missing limb, will be a blemish in their sacrifices. And the little of the rest of its details is scattered in [various] places of the Talmud.

And [it] is practiced by the priests at the time that Israel is dwelling on its land, because then is the time of offering. And a priest who transgresses this and sacrifices an [animal] with a blemish, even though it is from a stranger, is lashed.

Mitzvah 293

The commandment of a sacrifice that it be from eight days and above: That every sacrifice that we sacrifice of the beast be from eight days [old] and above, not less than that; and this is the commandment of the lacking in time of its body. And the verse that warns us about this is that which is written (Leviticus 22:27), "An ox or a sheep or a goat when it is born shall be with its mother seven days; and from the eighth day and onward, it shall be accepted." And the words of the Torah are [in short]; and the verse teaches that before then, the sacrifice is not accepted. And this - and that which is like this - they, may their memory be Blessed, called 'a negative commandment inferred from a positive commandment is a positive commandment.' And therefore, we do not administer lashes for it. And [it is] like they, may their memory be Blessed, elucidated in Chullin 80b in the chapter [entitled] Oto ve'etvBeno - as there they said regarding the matter of lashes, "Leave lacking time alone, as Scripture has [connected] it to a positive commandment."

That which we [wrote] previously regarding sacrifices from the angle of the simple understanding is from the roots of the commandment - that a man is aroused by the strength of his action to improve his deed[s]. And therefore, he was commanded that the action though which he is to improve his deed[s] be [as] perfect as he is able. And it is from the perfection of the sacrifice that it be from eight days [old] and onward. As before then, it is not fitting for anything - and no man would desire it for eating or for commerce or for a gift.

From the laws of the commandment is that which they, may their memory be Blessed, said (Chullin 22a), that doves that have not reached their time are forbidden for a sacrifice like a beast that has not reached its time. And so [too,] young pigeons that are very big are forbidden. And the reason with them is that largeness is considered like a blemish with them. And they, may their memory be Blessed, said (Chullin 22a) in the Mishnah more generally about doves and young pigeons that the beginning of yellowness in this and in that disqualifies" - as it is [a sign of] largeness in pigeons and smallness in doves. And they, may their memory be Blessed, expounded (Chullin 38b) about this verse, "'When it is born,' to exclude a cesarean section; 'with its mother,' to exclude an orphan" - meaning to say that it was born after its mother was slaughtered. And it is from that which appears that in all of [these], it is possible to say that perfection with them is not like with those born in the [normal] way of the world. And I have already written (Sefer HaChinukh 286) that the obligation is for the sacrifice to be in absolute perfection from every angle. And the rest of its details are elucidated in Sifra and the end of Tractate Zevachim (see Mishneh Torah, Laws of Things Forbidden on the Altar 3).

And [it] is practiced at the time of the [Temple] by the males of the priesthood - as the commandment of the sacrifice is upon them, and they will be sacrificed though them, and [so] it appears that they are warned (commanded) about the matter. But regardless, I saw with Rambam, may his memory be Blessed, that he wrote (Mishneh Torah, Laws of Things Forbidden on the Altar 3:10) - and this is his language - "And so [too,] one who consecrates [an animal] lacking in time, behold he is like one who consecrates one with a transient blemish, but he is not lashed, as we heave elucidated." To here [are his words]. It appears from his words that he reasons that the liability of this commandment is also upon an Israelite who consecrates it. And since this is so, we should say according to his opinion that the liability of this commandment is whether with priests or whether with Israelites, and with males and females. And one who transgresses this and sacrifices [an animal] lacking in time - or consecrates it according to the opinion of Rambam, may his memory be Blessed - has violated a positive commandment. But he is not lashed, since it is a negative commandment inferred from a positive commandment, as we wrote.

Mitzvah 294

To not slaughter a beast and its child on one day: That we not slaughter a beast and its child on one day - whether consecrated or mundane - as it is written (Leviticus 22:28), "it and its child you shall not slaughter on one day."

It is from the roots of the commandment that a person should place upon his heart that the providence of God, Blessed be He, is upon all species of animals more generally. And with His providence over them, they shall endure eternally; as His providence over things is [itself] their sustenance. And therefore no species will ever become completely extinct. And even though His providence over the human species is individual - and as I explained earlier in the Order of Eesha ki Tazria (Sefer HaChinukh, 169) - this is not the case for other species of animals. Rather His providence, Blessed be He, is for the species as a whole. And we are therefore prevented from finishing 'the tree and its branches' together to hint [about] this. And we can also say about the matter from the angle of the simple understanding as well, that this is to fix in our souls the trait of compassion and to distance us from the trait of cruelty - which is a bad trait. And therefore, even though God permitted us [to eat] species of animals for our sustenance, He [also] commanded us that we not kill it and its child on one day to fix the trait of compassion in our souls.

The laws of the commandment: That which they, may their memory be Blessed, said (Chullin 82a) that there is no distinction between it and its child and its child and it (the order is not important). And that which they said (Chullin 83a) that at four periods during the year, one who sells a beast to his fellow must inform him, "I sold the mother for slaughter" - because at these four times, all purchasers presumably buy to slaughter [immediately]. And these are them: the eve of the last holiday of [Sukkot]; the eve of the first holiday of Pesach; the eve of [Shavuot]; and the eve of Rosh HaShanah. And according to the words of Rabbi Yose HaGalili, also on the eve of Yom Kippur in

Sefer HaChinukh

the Galilee. And behold, that which we learned that he needs to inform him - it is specifically the seller that has to inform [of] the thing. But the buyer need not ask, as it is a double doubt for him: Lest it does not have a mother; and [even] if it does, perhaps [the seller] did not sell it for slaughter. And that which they said (Chullin 82a) [regarding] two people that bought a cow and its child - that the one who purchased first, slaughters first; but if the second preceded him and slaughtered against the law, the first is forbidden to slaughter. And the law of slaughtering a cow and two of her children, or her two children and her afterwards; and so [too,] it and her daughter and the daughter of her daughter. And it is permitted to slaughter the mother and the daughter of her daughter, as the Torah only forbade "it and its child."

And that which they said that if one slaughters the mother and the daughter of her daughter, and then the daughter, he is only lashed forty [lashes]. And [that is] even though he transgresses two negative commandments on account of "it and its child" and on account of 'its child and it' - nonetheless it is [still] one deed.

And that which they, may their memory be Blessed, said (Chullin 78b) that the prohibition of "it and its child" is only practiced with females (mothers) - as they said in explanation of "its child," the one who the child is attached to, which is the [mother]. And nevertheless, we conclude in Chullin 79a - with the good commentaries - that if the thing becomes clear to us that this is certainly its father, we [may] not slaughter it and its child on the same day; because we determine there that the law [follows] Rabbi Yehudah. And according to what is implied from his words, Rabbi Yehudah is in doubt if we concern ourselves with the seed of the father or not - [as] he says regarding the forbidden mixtures with mules [that] we do not mate a horse nor a donkey with it, but only its [own] specie. And if he reasoned that we certainly do not concern ourselves with the seed of the father, he would not have said that. Rather, he would have had to say thus: "We only mate it [with] it specie from the side of the mother." But rather Rabbi Yehudah is certainly in doubt. And when he said [that] we do not concern ourselves with the seed of the father, his intention was to say that we do not concern ourselves with the seed of the father to be lenient about a thing; but to be stringent, we definitely concern ourselves with the seed of the father. And [likewise,] in any place that a stringency will result from saying that we are not concerned, then we say that we are not concerned for [the father]. As since it was a doubt for him, we go towards stringency in every case. And according to this, when we definitively know the [identity of the father] we should be concerned for him regarding "it and its child." And the rest of its details are in the eighth chapter of Chullin (see Tur, Yoreh Deah 16).

The commandment is practiced in every place and at all times by males and females. And one who transgresses this and slaughtered "it and its child on one day" - or its child and it - is lashed.

Mitzvah 295
That we not do anything through which the name of the Heavens is profaned among people:
That we were prevented from profanation of God, may He be Blessed, and that is the opposite of that sanctification of God about which we are commanded - as we will write in the commandment after this - as it is stated (Leviticus 22:32), "And you shall not profane My holy Name." The transcriber wrote in the name of Rambam (Sefer HaMitzvot LaRambam, Mitzvot Lo Taase 63) "This iniquity is divided into three parts - two are upon the collective, and one on the individual. The first collective part [is] in any case that one is asked to transgress one of the commandments during a time of persecution, and the enforcer intends for [him] to transgress - whether from the light commandments or from the weighty - or if one is asked to transgress idolatry, sexual immorality, or murder even not during a a time of persecution; he is obligated to give his life and be killed rather than transgressing. And if he transgressed and was not killed, he has already profaned God in public and has violated its stating, 'And you shall not profane My holy Name,' and his sin is very giant. However, he is not lashed, as he was coerced - since the court only has the ability [to give out] lashes or death for volitional [acts], with desire, with witnesses and with a warning. The language of Sifra Kedoshim, Section 4:13 about one who gives from his seed to Molech, [that] I will place 'My face against that person' (Leviticus 20:5), is that they, may their memory be Blessed, said '"That" one, and not coercion, nor inadvertent, nor mistaken.' It has already been elucidated to you that a person who worships

idolatry under coercion is not liable for excision, and all the more so, death of the court. However, he has violated profanation of the Name.

The second collective part is when a person commits a sin without desire for it or pleasure; but [rather] with his action, he intends to anger [God]. This is also profaning the Name of the Heavens and he is lashed. And therefore, it stated (Leviticus 19:12), 'And you shall not swear falsely in My name and profane the Name of your God.' As this one displays the causation of anger with this thing, since there is no physical pleasure in it. And the part which is upon the individual is when a person who is famous for acts of kindness and good deeds commits an act which appears to the public as a sin, such that this act is unfitting for a pious person like this to do - even if it is a permissible act, he has profaned the Name. And this is [the understanding of] their, may their memory be Blessed, saying (Yoma 86a), 'How is profaning the Name? [...] "Such as if I purchase meat from the butcher and do not give him money immediately." [...] Rabbi x said, "Such as if I walk four ells without tefillin and without words of Torah."' And this negative commandment is already repeated elsewhere and it is stated (Leviticus 18:21), 'and you shall not profane the Name of your God, I am the Lord.'" To here [are his words.]

I will write the root of this commandment and some of its laws and all of its content - as is my custom - in the commandment of sanctification of the Name, which is adjacent.

Mitzvah 296

The commandment of sanctification of the Name: That we were commanded to sanctify the Name, as it is stated (Leviticus 22:32), "and I will be sanctified in the midst of the Children of Israel," - meaning to say that we surrender our souls for the observance of the commandments of the religion. And they, may their memory be Blessed, have already elucidated from the tradition and from the verses in which manner and for which commandment, we are commanded about this. And even though it is written in the Torah, "and live by them" (Leviticus 18:5), which implies, and not that you should die by them - they already received that this verse is not stated in every matter and for every sin. And [it is] through the tradition that we live in all [the] words of the Torah. And in explanation, they, may their memory be Blessed, said (Sanhedrin 74a) that there are three commandments which one is always obligated to be killed and not transgress them. And these are: idolatry and any of its trappings - meaning, all of its matters that are prohibited on the strength of its specific negative commandments, as we will explain below with God's help; and also, sexual immorality and all of its trappings; and murder. Such that if they say to a person, "Worship idolatry or we will kill you," he should be killed and not worship. Even though his heart is pure in his faith with the fear of God, nonetheless he is commanded that he be killed and not commit this evil act, and not give room to the assailant to think that he has denied God. And the language of Sifra, Emor, Chapter 9:6, "For this reason I took you out of the Land of Egypt, so that you will publicly sanctify My name." And likewise, for the other two that we mentioned - he must be killed and not transgress, as we said.

The root of this commandment is well-known. As Man was only created to serve his Creator. And one who does not sacrifice his body in the service of his master is not a good servant. And behold [since] people do give their souls for their masters, all the more so [should we] for the commandment of the King of kings, the Holy One, Blessed be He.

From the laws of the commandment is that which they, may their memory be Blessed, said (Sanhedrin 74a) that for these three sins that we mentioned, a person is obligated to give his life under any circumstance - whether at a time of persecution or not at a time of persecution, whether in public or even in private, whether the gentile intends to have him transgress or even for his own benefit. For other sins, however, they said if it is not at a time of persecution and it is in private, he should transgress and not be killed - and even if the gentile intends to have him transgress. But if it is in public - meaning, in the presence of ten Jews - if the coercer intends [it] for his [own] benefit, he should transgress and not be killed. However, if it is to have him transgress, he should be killed and not transgress. At a time of persecution, even in private and even for his benefit and even for a trivial commandment, he should be killed and not transgress. And a light commandment is similar to what they, may their memory be Blessed, said (Sanhedrin 74b), "Even a shoe strap," such that an Israelite should not make the shape of his shoe like the gentiles that worship idolatry, that he should not appear to be an idolater like them.

That which we said, the trappings of idolatry, the matter is to say, anything that is prohibited for us from any prohibition specific to idolatry. And [it is] similar to that which they, may their memory be Blessed, said in [Pesachim 25a], "One who is in peril may be healed by anything except for asheirah (a tree-god) wood." And they said about this in Yerushalmi Shabbat 14:4 [that] it is not only if the physician said, "Bring me leaves of asheirah x," that he would [then] seem like he concedes to it. Rather even if he just said to him, "Bring me leaves of tree x," and he went and he only found [them] on the asheirah, he should be killed and not transgress. And even though when he is healed with the wood of the asheirah, it is not truly idolatry - for he did not worship it - nonetheless he benefited from it, and there is in it the matter of the negative commandment of "Nothing is to cling to your hand from the anathema" (Deuteronomy 13:18), which is a negative commandment specific to idolatry. But the many prohibitions of idolatry that exist, which we learn from the negative commandment of "in front of the blind you shall not place a stumbling block" (Leviticus 19:14), are not included in trappings of idolatry to be killed for them - since the negative commandment of "in front of the blind," is not specific to idolatry itself, as it is also with all of the [other] commandments.

After I wrote this I found in some of the novellae of my master - may God protect him - that he wrote that it is implied in the Yerushalmi Avodah Zarah 2:2 [about] anything that the physician says generally (without mentioning the idol), [that] he should transgress and not be killed.

The matter of murder, they, may their memory be Blessed, learned by way of reasoning (Sanhedrin 74a); and they said by way of a metaphor, "What do you see that your blood is redder? Perhaps the blood of that man is redder." [That is] meaning, the murdered might be fitting to perform more commandments than the one that killed him. And therefore, it is not right that anyone kill his fellow, even if he will be killed for [not doing so]. And they may their memory be Blessed, said further (Yerushalmi Terumot 8:4) that even if there were several thousand Israelites and the coercers said to them, "Give us one of you; and if not, we will kill all of you" - they should all be killed and not give over one soul of Israel. And [that is] only when they say "one," unspecifically. But if they specified him explicitly, such that they said, "Give us x; and if not, we will kill all of you," they are permitted to give him over - like the well-known matter of Sheva ben Bichri. This is also the law with women - if the gentiles say to them, "Give us one of you [to rape], etc.," as it is [found] in Tractate Terumot, the eighth chapter (Mishnah Terumot 8:12).

And the Sages, may their memory be Blessed, learned the matter that we are killed [rather than transgress] sexual immorality (Sanhedrin 74a), because the betrothed maiden is compared [by the Torah] to a murderer: Just as a murderer should be killed and not transgress, as we said; so too must a man be killed and not have intercourse with her. As the Torah does not tell metaphors for nothing, but only to teach a matter. They also had support from the tradition, which is an iron wall for all of their words. And the early authorities (rishonim) wrote that we only say a person must be killed and not transgress [about] transgressing a sin. But to not perform a commandment, he should transgress and not be killed, and not perform the commandment. And [it is] similar to what they, may their memory be Blessed, said about Esther (Sanhedrin 74b), "She was ground of the earth" - meaning, it was similar to [a situation of] 'sit and do not act,' as behold a woman has intercourse against her will. And even if the woman assisted in the intercourse after her impulse covered her, she is not liable with this - as there is no greater coercion than this. And that which we find stories about the early pious ones that were killed even [so that they not participate in] the negation of a [positive] commandment - and similar to what they, may their memory be Blessed, said (Mekhilta d'Rabbi Yishmael 20:6), "What is to you to go out to stoning? Because I circumcised my son. What is to you to go out to hanging? Because I took the lulav" - that was an [extra] measure of piety that they did and they saw that [their] generation needed this. And they were great sages fitting for this, to decide about this. As otherwise they would not have been permitted to give over their souls to die - as not everyone has permission to be killed for [other matters] than those that they, may their memory be Blessed, obligated us about. Moreover, [such a person] would be liable for his life (Mishneh Torah, Foundations of the Torah 5:4).

Sefer HaChinukh

I have also seen about the matter of this commandment in the books of my teacher, may God protect him, that any woman for which betrothal (kiddushin) is effective - such as a widow to a high priest, a divorcee or released woman to a common priest, a mamzeret or a netinah to an Israelite and an Israelitess to a mamzer - are not included in the sexual prohibitions, for which one must die. Still, we nonetheless do not instruct any man to have intercourse with any woman - even if she is single, we do not instruct [it]. He should instead die from the illness that has come from his lust and not have her have intercourse with him or [even] speak with her, etc. - [as we see] in Sanhedrin 75a and the Book of Knowledge (Mishneh Torah, Foundations of the Torah 5:9). And the rest of its details are elucidated in Chapter 8 of Sanhedrin and in Pesachim and Yoma and in other places (see Tur, Yoreh Deah 157).

This commandment is practiced in every place and at all times by males and females. And one who transgresses it and did not sanctify the Name in a circumstance where he was obligated to do so, has violated this positive commandment; besides that, he has also violated the negative commandment of "And you shall not profane My holy Name," and as we wrote above adjacently (Sefer HaChinukh 295). The iniquity of profaning the Name is great and very severe to the point that they, may their memory be Blessed, said that repentance, Yom Kippur, and afflicitons do not have the power to atone for it, but only death - as it is [found] in the last chapter of Yoma 86a.

Mitzvah 297

The commandment of resting on the first day of Pesach: To rest on the first day of Pesach, as it states about it (Leviticus 22:7), "On the first day, a holy occasion." And about all about which it is stated in the Torah, "a holy occasion," they, may their memory be Blessed, explained (Sifra, Emor, Chapter 12:4), "Make it holy." And the content of its holiness is that no work be done on it, except for that which is specific to eating; as the verse elucidated (Exodus 12:16), "but that which is eaten by every soul, that alone shall be done for you." And the proof that the rest of the holiday is considered a positive commandment is their, may their memory be Blessed, saying (Shabbat 25a), "This 'shabbaton' is a positive commandment." And we learn from now that in every place that shabbaton is stated in the Torah with regards to a holiday, it is a positive commandment. And [what] also appears much in the Talmud is, "The holiday is a positive commandment and a negative commandment."

It is from the roots of the commandment [that it is] in order that we think about the content of the holiday in the miracle that was done for us on it, and that we praise and laud in our thoughts the One, Blessed be He, who commanded us about it and did miracles for us at this time. And if a man is preoccupied in his work, he will not be free to think about anything. And we will further write at length about its root and its laws in the negative commandment of work on the holiday in this Order (Sefer HaChinukh 288) with God's help.

And [it] is practiced in every place and at all times by males and females. And one who transgresses it and does work not for the needs of food for the soul has violated this positive commandment, besides that he violated a negative commandment - as we will write in its place.

The laws of the commandment are elucidated in [Beitzah] (see Mishneh Torah, Laws of Rest on a Holiday 1).

Mitzvah 298

To not do work on the first day of Pesach: That we not do work on the first day of the holiday of Pesach - which is the fifteenth of Nissan - as it is stated (Leviticus 23:7), "On the first day, a holy occasion shall it be for you; all work of labor shall you not do." And Scripture already warned about this in the Order of Bo el Pharoah in the command of the holiday of Pesach; as it is stated there (Exodus 12:16), "all work shall not be done upon them." And Rambam, may his memory be Blessed, brought that verse (in Sefer HaMitzvot LaRambam, Mitzvot Lo Taase 223) in his tally. But I have written this other one, so that the holidays be organized in one order. But it all comes to the same thing.

And the verse stated here, "work of labor," and it did not state, "all work" - since the needs of food for the soul were permitted to be done on the holiday; as Scripture comes in another place (Exodus

Sefer HaChinukh

12:16), "but that which is eaten by every soul, that alone shall be done for you." And this is the understanding of work of labor - meaning to say, work that is not for the needs of food for the soul, like the matter that is stated (Exodus 1:14), "labor in the field"; and so [too,] "Kain was a laborer of the field" (Genesis 4:2); "a king over a field that is labored" (Ecclesiastes 5:8); "labors his land" (Proverbs 12:11). But work that is for food for the soul like cooking and similar to it is work of enjoyment, not work of labor. So did Ramban, may his memory be Blessed, explain. And he wrote further (Ramban on Leviticus 23:7) that this understanding is elucidated in the Torah [itself], since with the Festival of Matsot, [about which] it first stated, "all work shall not be done upon them" in the Order of Bo el Pharoah, it was required to explain, "but that which is eaten by every soul, that alone shall be done for you." But with all of the other holidays, it was brief and it stated, "all work of labor you shall not do," to forbid all work that is not [for] food for the soul, and to inform that food for the soul is permitted on them. And Scripture did not ever state in one of the other holidays, "all work," nor explain the permissibility of food for the soul - since "all work of labor" teaches about this. But in the section, Kol HaBekhor on the Festival of Matsot, it states (Deuteronomy 16:8), "and on the seventh day, it is a convocation to the Lord, your God; you shall not do work." And the reason is because it already explicitly permitted food for the soul on this holiday in the Order of Bo el Pharoah. And afterwards in this Order, it mentions "work of labor," which also implies the permissibility of food for the soul. And therefore, when it repeated and mentioned it another time in the section of Kol HaBekhor, it was not needed for it to state a further explanation about it; and [so] it mentioned just, "work," and relied on that which is known [from the earlier entries]. And nonetheless, it did not state, "all work," as [it does] with Shabbat and Yom Kippur, but [rather just] stated, "work" - meaning to say, the work which I have warned you about.

It is from the roots of the commandment that it is so that the great miracles that God, may He be Blessed, did for them and for their forefathers be remembered, and that they speak about them and inform their children and the children of their children about them. As with the rest from the business of the world, they will be free to be involved with this. As if they were permitted work - and even light work - each and every one would turn to his business. And the honor of the festival would be forgotten from 'the mouths of babes'; also from the mouths of adults. And there are also many [other] benefits to its rest: As all the people gather in the synagogues and study halls to listen to the words of the book, and the heads of the people guide them and teach them knowledge. And [it is] similar to that which they, may their memory be Blessed, said (Megillah 32a), "Moshe ordained for Israel that they should expound the laws of Pesach on Pesach and the Laws of [Shavuot] on [Shavuot and the laws of the Holiday (Sukkot) on the Holiday].

From the laws of the commandment is that which they, may their memory be Blessed, said (Beitzah 28b) that even though Scripture permitted work for the sake of food for the soul, it is specifically things that are impossible to do from the eve of the holiday, such as kneading, slaughtering, baking [and] cooking - as all of these types of work become a little defective from delay [after them]. And likewise, for this reason, they permitted to pound spices on the holiday, on account that their taste becomes fainter with delay after they are pounded. But it is forbidden to do types of work on the holiday that are possible to do from the eve of the holiday and do not deteriorate at all - such as harvesting, threshing, separating, grinding, sifting and what is similar to them; and they are not included in the needs of food for the soul at all. And we administer lashes for them like [for] plowing in the field - which is actually a work of labor. And the later commentators elucidated this matter further and said that truly that which is called the need of food for the soul is only that which is made for its day - meaning to say, for a short time, like cooking and baking and what is similar to it, as we have said - and also [only] that which a person's mind relies upon to make for that time. [This is] to exclude hunting, as the mind of a man is not upon it, since perhaps game will not appear to him today. And they said further that that which we permit food for the soul with that which is made for that time - as we said - is only if he uses the body of the work. But if he uses the removal of the work, it is forbidden. And this is [the understanding of] that which they, may their memory be Blessed, forbade (Beitzah 22a) to extinguish the log, even though his mind in extinguishing it is so that [the stew in] the pot not get smoky. And regarding the roasting of meat over coals - which is the bisra agumrei mentioned in the Gemara (Beitzah 23a) - even though the fire is extinguished from the [liquids] of the meat, this is not called using the removal of the work, since it is for the needs of the roasting to do this. And [so] he is using the body of the work and it is permissible.

And so [too,] that which they, may their memory be Blessed, said (Beitzah 12a) that included in the dispensation of the needs of food for the soul is not specifically food and drink only. Rather, even every thing that a person needs on the day: [Something] which is a matter of a commandment, such as to circumcise an infant, and a lulav to fulfill [the commandment] with it, and a Torah scroll to read from it - as each and every day is the time for Torah; or whether it is not a matter of a commandment but a need of the body on that day, such as the washing of the feet with hot water that was heated on the holiday or to make a fire to warm oneself with it. All of these things are permitted and included in the dispensation of food for the soul. So did our Sages, may their memory be Blessed, explain (Mishneh Torah, Laws of Rest on a Holiday 1:16).

And nonetheless it is specifically [regarding] things that are the same for all people's bodies that we permit and we say that it is included in this dispensation of food for the soul - such as washing the feet, as everyone washes like this sometimes. But that which is not the same for every person, such as mugmar (a type of incense) - since not all people burn mugmar, as we say in Ketuvot 7a - is certainly forbidden [along with] all that is similar to it. And it is only in these things that we need that it be the same for every person. However, regarding eating, every person is permitted to make even a food that is not its way to be made except by kings and great ministers - since the basic concept of eating is something that is the same for every soul. And so [too,] that which they said (Beitzah 2b) about the prohibition of preparation, that a holiday cannot prepare for Shabbat, nor a Shabbat prepare for a holiday. And you will only find a prohibition of preparation from Torah writ in my opinion - if you have studied the words of the Gemara well - with an egg alone. And its main prohibition is when it was born on a holiday after Shabbat or on a Shabbat after a holiday. In this way is the preparation of Rabbah established with an egg, and with this is there a Torah prohibition - and in no other way. As behold, that which we prohibit when it is born on Shabbat on the holiday that is after it, and so [too,] when it is born on the holiday on the Shabbat that is after it, and so [too,] when it it is born on the holiday [on the holiday] itself is [only] a rabbinic prohibition - and it is all on account of a decree [to make a fence for] the one that is born on a holiday after Shabbat, as we said. And the matter would be [too] lengthy if I came to write it with a broad elucidation. And in its place at the beginning of Beitzah, I have written at length about it, as my teachers - may God protect them - have taught me.

And the law that it is forbidden to make tools that prepare food for the soul, on account of its being written (Exodus 12:16), "that alone" - and not what prepares it. And the law of inviting gentiles on a holiday (Beitzah 21b), which is forbidden, as it is written, "for you" - and not for gentiles. And so [too,] that we do not bake anything for dogs, as it is written, "for you" - and not for dogs. And that which they, may their memory be Blessed, said (Beitzah 4b) about the two days of the exiles - that an egg born on this one is permitted on that one; and that which is detached from the ground on this one is permitted on that one, as the [two days] are two [separate units of] holiness. And it is not like this on the two days of Rosh Hashanah. And the rest of its many details are all elucidated in the tractate that is built on this, and that is Tractate [Beitzah] (see Tur, Orach Chaim 495).

And it is practiced in every place and at all times by males and females. And one who transgresses it and does work from the forbidden types of work on a holiday volitionally is liable for lashes.

Mitzvah 299
The commandment of the additional sacrifices all of the seven days of Pesach: To sacrifice the additional sacrifice on all of the seven days of Pesach, as it is stated (Leviticus 23:8), "And you shall offer a fire-offering to the Lord seven days." And it is like the sacrifice of Rosh Chodesh (the new moon): two bulls; one ram; seven sheep - all of them burnt-offerings, and as it is written explicitly about all of them in the Order of Pinchas (Numbers 28:19), "a fire-offering, a burnt-offering," and I have already explained the statute of a burnt-offering above (Sefer HaChinukh 115) - [and one goat as a sin-offering, and it is eaten].

From the roots of the commandment is like the matter that we wrote above regarding the sacrifice (Sefer HaChinukh 95) - that a man is acted upon according to his deeds. As since he is a physical being, his thought only clings through actions. And from this root, Blessed be He, commanded us to do a specific action for the sake of the day, in order that we be impacted by this to put our hearts to the greatness of the day and its holiness, and [to] the miracles and the goodnesses that God, Blessed be He, has bestowed upon us at that time.

The laws of the commandment: That which they, may their memory be Blessed, said in the fourth chapter of Menachot 49a that the daily offerings do not impede the additional offerings and the [different] additional offerings do not impede one another. And so [too,] that which they, may their memory be Blessed, said (Menachot 44b), "'The bulls, the rams and the sheep do not impede one another; and the bull, the ram and the sheep do not impede the bread'" - meaning the offering of fine flour, as that is the bread - "'and the bread does not impede the sheep.' These are the words of Rabbi Akiva. Rabbi Shimon ben Nannas said, 'No, rather these sheep impede the bread, but the bread does not impede the sheep - as so did we find when Israel was in the wilderness forty years that they offered sheep without bread; so too here, they offer sheep without bread.' Rabbi Shimon said, 'The law is like the words of Ben Nannas, but the reason is not like his words, as everything that is stated in Chumash Pekudim '" - meaning in the Book of Numbers - "'they offered in the wilderness; and that which is stated in Torat Kohanim '" - meaning in the Book of Leviticus - "'they did not offer in the wilderness. When they came to the Land they offered these and those. And because of what do I say that they offer sheep without bread? As the sheep permit themselves, but bread without sheep does not have [what] to permit it.'" And so [too,] that which they said there, the ninth chapter (Menachot 89a), "We mix the libations of the bulls with the libations of the rams, but we do not mix the libations of the sheep with the libations of the bulls and the rams." And they also said there further (Menachot 87b), "Seven liquid measurements were in the Temple: a hin ; a half hin, etc. Rabbi Eleizer beRebbi Tsadok says, 'There were markers in the hin [measurement]: up to here for the bull; up to here for the ram; and up to here for the sheep.'" And the rest of its details are explained there and in [other] places in Kedoshim (see Mishneh Torah, Laws of Daily Offerings and Additional Offerings 4).

And [it] is practiced at the time of the [Temple] by the males of the priesthood. And if the priests transgressed this and did not sacrifice the additional sacrifice at its appointed time, they violated this positive commandment and they will carry their sin. But the Israelites are clean [of sin] - as the obligation of the sacrifices is more upon [the priests]. And if perhaps the Israelites sensed the thing, the transgression will also be upon them. As the entire matter of the Holy House - and, all the more so, the daily offerings and the additional offerings - is upon the community, and it is impingent upon them all.

Mitzvah 300

The commandment of resting on the seventh [day] of Pesach: To rest on the seventh day of Pesach, as it is stated (Leviticus 22:8), "and on the seventh day, a holy occasion." And I have already written above close by to this commandment (Sefer HaChinukh 297) that in every place in which it is stated in the Torah, "a holy occasion," its content is to say, make it holy, to not do work on it, and [that] it is a positive commandment. And a hint from the roots of the commandment from the angle of its simple understanding is also written there. And as is our custom, we will write a few of its laws with God's help in the negative commandment of the prohibition of work in this Order (Sefer HaChinukh 298). And the entire content of resting on the seventh [day] is like the rest of the first day. And they are both considered one festival with regards to that which we do not say [the blessing over] time (shehechiyanu) on the seventh; and so with every matter - which is not the case on Shemini Atseret, which is a holiday on its own (Yoma 2b), and as we will write in its place (Sefer HaChinukh 323), with God's help.

Mitzvah 301

Sefer HaChinukh

To not do work on the seventh day of Pesach: That we not do work on the seventh day of Pesach - which is the twenty-first day of Nissan - as it is stated (Leviticus 23:8), "and on the seventh day, a holy occasion, all work of labor shall you not do."

And the root of this commandment and all of its content is written in the previous commandment - which is the first day of Pesach (Sefer HaChinukh 298). However, it is fitting, my son, that I elucidate for you the matter of two days for each and every appointed time, whereas our Torah only obligated us one holiday - as it is written explicitly about Peasch (Leviticus 23:7-8), "On the first day, a holy occasion," and "on the seventh day"; and so with [Shavuot] and Rosh Hashanah and Sukkot.

And the truth is that the matter today is only a custom - [and] not [from] any other obligation. As we do not make that day because of a doubt, since all of Israel are now experts in the setting of the months and know the exact day of the appointed time according to the traditional calculation that is in their hand, as I wrote above in the Order of Bo el Pharaoh in Commandment 4 (Sefer HaChinukh 4). And the custom was set because at the beginning when there were ordained men in the Land, they would set the month according to sighting, which is the commandment of the Torah - as we have written there. And therefore all the places of Israel (Jewish settlement) far from the chosen place in which it was fixed there, that messengers could not reach to inform them of the day of the fixing, were in doubt about which day was fixed as the [first of the] month - whether the thirtieth [of the previous month] or the thirty-first. And [so] they would make the appointed time two days from this doubt. However, they were never in doubt about more than one day, as they would always fix the new moon on the thirtieth or the thirty-first - whether with witnesses or without witnesses. As the thing is well-known and clear that the new moon never delays more [than this]. And therefore, whether witnesses came or did not come, they would set the new month [no later than] the thirty-first. And because of this doubt that there is for those far from Jerusalem, they fixed for them at first to make two days of the holiday (Beitzah 4b). And the Sages, may their memory be Blessed, ordained (Pesachim 52a) also now for those far from the Land to make two days like the law that they would do at that time - even though all of Israel have become experts in the fixing of the month, as we said. But it is not fitting for those close and - all the more so - those living in the Land itself that they should do anything but one day, like the custom of the people of the place always. And so have they practiced, according to that which we have heard.

And from the reason that we said - that the thing is an ordinance of the sages, not a doubt - some of the commentators said that we do not say now on the two days of the exiles, what was born on this one (the first day) is permitted on that one (the second day). As it comes in the Gemara (Beitzah 4b) that at the time that the thing was a doubt, they would say this. But now since it is from an ordinance of the Sages and not at all from the status of a doubt, we should not say this. Rather their law is like one [unit of] holiness. And there were some that said the Sages, may their memory be Blessed, ordained it due to the first doubt, and we should not be more stringent about them than at first. And also, since when, "what is born on this one is permitted on that one," was said in the Gemara, the fixing according to sighting [had] already ceased, according to what appears. And so have they practiced today. And all that they said is specifically about the two days of holiday of the appointed times of the year except for Rosh Hashanah - as with Rosh Hashanah, it is like one [unit of] holiness. And what is born on this one is forbidden on that one, because also in the house of council they would sometimes make it two days of holiday not from the status of a doubt - for example, if the witnesses came from the [time of] mincha (afternoon) and onward - such that they would treat today as holy and the next day as holy. And nonetheless even on Rosh Hashanah it is [only on account of] the ordinance of the Sages today to do two days in every place, since we are experts in the fixing of the new month (Mishneh Torah, Sanctification of the New Month 5:12).

Mitzvah 302

The commandment of the sacrifice of the omer of barley: That we offer on the second day of Pesach, beyond the additional offering of the rest of the days of Pesach, a one-year-old sheep for a burnt-offering and one omer of barley, that is called the omer of waving - as it is stated (Leviticus 23:10-11), "When you come to the land, etc., you shall bring the omer, the beginning of your harvest, etc. And he shall wave the omer in front of the Lord from the morrow of the Shabbat." And Onkelos translates, "after the holiday" - meaning to say, on the second day of Pesach. As behold, it is referring to Pesach in the section before this. And it is stated there (Leviticus 23:12), "And you shall make on the day of your waving the omer an unblemished one-year old sheep, etc." And this sacrifice of the omer is called the offering of the first fruits. And it is a hint to this when He may He be Blessed, says (Leviticus 2:14), "And if you shall bring an offering of the first-fruits to the Lord, new roasted with fire, etc." And the language of Mekhilta d'Rabbi Yishmael 22:24 is "Each and every 'if' in the Torah is optional, etc. except for three that are obligatory and this is one of them." And they said there, "You say it is an obligation or is it only optional? [Hence] we learn to say, 'you shall offer the offering of your first fruits' - [it is] an obligation and not optional. And the matter of the offering is thus (Menachot 63b): That they would bring three seah of barley, and they would take out one issaron from all of it, which they would sift with thirteen sieves. And the rest would be redeemed and eaten by any person. And it is liable for the hallah -tithe but exempted from the [other] tithes. And we take this issaron of fine barley flour and we mix it with a log of oil and place a handful of frankincense upon it - like the other meal-offerings. And the priest waves it in the East - he extends [it] and brings [it back], raises [it] and lowers [it] - and presents it across from the point of the southwest corner, like the other meal offerings. And he takes a handful and incinerates [it], and the rest is eaten by the priests, like the remainders of all of the meal-offerings (Menachot 67b).

It is from the roots of the commandment [that it is] in order that we contemplate, through [this] deed, the great kindness that God, Blessed be He, does for His creatures, to renew the grain each year for [our] nourishment. Therefore, it is fitting for us that we should sacrifice to Him, Blessed be He, from it - so that we remember His kindness and His great goodness before we benefit from it. And from that which we become fitting for blessing by the refinement of our deeds in front of Him, our grain will be Blessed, and God's will for us will be fulfilled - as He desires blessing for His creatures, from His great goodness. And we were commanded about this on the second [day] of Pesach and not on the first, so that we not mix [one] joy with [another] joy - as the first is prepared to remember the great miracle that He, Blessed be He, took us out from slavery to freedom and from anguish to joy.

From the laws of the commandment is that which they, may their memory be Blessed, said (Menachot 68b) that the commandment of the omer is to bring it from barely - and not from wheat, nor spelt, oats or rye - and from what is close to Jerusalem that came out first. If the close ones did not come out, they would bring it from another place in the Land of Israel. And its commandment is to harvest it on the night of the sixteenth of Nissan - whether on [a weekday] or whether on Shabbat. And its commandment is from the [barley that is] damp (fresh) - its explanation [is that it] is in order that its being a first-fruit is more visible and recognizable to the eye. And all of the cities that are close to there gather, in order that it is harvested with a big deal. And all of this is from the root that we wrote - so that they can give their hearts to the word of God, may He be Blessed, through the deed and the joy.

And three men with three baskets and three sickles would harvest these three seah (Menachot 63b, 65a). And when it got dark, the harvester says to those standing there, "Did the sun set?" They say to him, "Yes," three times. "This sickle?" They say, "Yes," also three times. "This basket?" They say, "Yes" also three times. "Should I harvest?" They say to him, "Harvest," three times. And why so much? Because of those in error, who left from [being in the people of] Israel at the [time of] the Second [Temple], and would say that that which it is stated in the Torah, "from the morrow of the Shabbat," is the Shabbat of creation (the seventh day of the week). And the rest of its details are fully elucidated in Menachot (see Mishneh Torah, Laws of Daily Offerings and Additional Offerings 7).

And this commandment is practiced at the time of the [Temple] with males. And even Israelites are obligated to make efforts with this commandment, as behold the messengers of the court go out and make bundles in the field from the eve of the holiday, and as is explained in Menachot 65a. But nonetheless, the main obligation is the offering, the waving, the presenting, the taking of a handful and the incineration - and all of this is with the priests. And nonetheless since there is a portion in it for all of Israel and the foundation of the commandment is because of the renewal of the grain - which is something that is a necessary thing for all - we should write it in the tally of the commandments that are incumbent upon all the Children of Israel.

Mitzvah 303
To not eat from the new grain before the end of the sixteenth of Nissan: To not eat from the new grain before the end of the sixteenth of Nissan, as it is stated (Leviticus 23:14), "And bread and roasted grain and fresh grain you shall not eat until this very day."

It is from the roots of the commandment [that it is] since the main nourishment of the creatures is from grains. And therefore, it is fitting to offer from them a sacrifice to God who gave them, before the creatures benefit from them. And [it is] similar to that which they, may their memory be Blessed, said about [something] resembling this (Berakhot 35a), "Anyone who benefits from this world without a blessing has misappropriated." And all of this is to prepare ourselves that we should be fitting to receive from His goodness - and as I wrote in this book many times. And at the time of the [Temple], on the sixteenth of Nissan, we would offer the sacrifice of the omer from the new grain barley grain, since it is the grain that comes out first [before] the wheat. And it permits [us to benefit from] all of the grains.

From the laws of the commandment is that which they, may their memory be Blessed, said (Menachot 70a) that there are only five grains that are included in the prohibition of the new [grain]. And they are wheat, barley, spelt, oats and rye. And at the time of the [Temple] from the time that the omer was offered on the sixteenth of Nissan, the new [grain] was permitted in Jerusalem. And in places distant [from it], they would permit [it] after midnight, since the court would not be lazy with it until after midnight. And therefore, it was permitted for them in every place to rely upon this assumption. And today that - on account of our iniquities - there is no Temple, it is forbidden the whole day from Torah writ. And in places that they make two days of holiday, it is forbidden on the seventeenth until the evening rabbinically. And the rest of its details are in Menachot, the tenth chapter (see Sefer HaMitzvot LaRambam, Mitzvot Lo Taase 191) and in [some] places in [Shevuot], in Sheviit, Maasrot and Challah.

And this prohibition is practiced in every place and at all times - whether in the presence of the [Temple] (when it exists) or not in the presence of the [Temple] - by males and females. And one who transgressed it and ate a kazayit of new bread before the day of the offering of the omer is liable for lashes.

Mitzvah 304
To not eat roasted grain from the new grain until that day: To not eat roasted grain from the new grain until the time mentioned - meaning that even though he did not make bread from the grain and did not grind it and did not sift it, but rather roasted from the wheat or from the barley with fire, and ate from them, he is liable also for them. And about this is it stated (Leviticus 23:14), "and roasted grain, etc." And all of its content is in the previous commandment. And one who eats it is also liable for lashes for a kazayit of roasted grain.

Mitzvah 305
To not eat fresh grain from the new grain until that day: To not eat fresh grain from the new grain until the time mentioned, as it is stated (Leviticus 23:14), "and fresh grain shall you not eat." And grain roasted in its sheaves is called, "fresh grain" - granis in the vernacular. And we are also liable for fresh grain with a kazayit. And they, may their memory be Blessed, said (Keritot 5a), "[If] he ate bread, roasted grain, and fresh grain, he is liable for each and every one." And they also said it was not necessary to mention roasted grain, but Scripture mentioned it to distinguish, such as to make liable for roasted grain on its own, and upon the fresh grain and bread [each on its own]. And they said in the Gemara (Keritot 5a) from the angle of something pushed off, "Maybe he should become liable for roasted grain by itself, and so [too,] for fresh grain - since it is extra - but he would be liable one [set of] lashes for bread and fresh grain?" And the answer was, "For what law did the [Torah] write roasted grain in the middle? To say bread is like roasted grain, and fresh grain is like roasted

grain - and he shall [hence] be liable for each and every one [on its own]." All of its content is in the two previous commandments - its 'colleagues.'

Mitzvah 306
The commandment of counting the omer: To count forty-nine days from the bringing of the omer which is on the sixteenth day of Nissan, as it is stated (Leviticus 23:15), "And you shall count for yourselves from the morrow of the Shabbat from the day of your bringing the omer of waving." And this tallying is an obligation, and it is upon us to count the days on each day and, likewise, the weeks. As Scripture said to count fifty days and also said (Deuteronomy 16:9), "Seven weeks shall you count for yourself." And in explanation, Abbaye said in the Gemara in Menachot 66a, "It is a commandment to tally the days and it is a commandment to tally the weeks" (see Sefer HaMitzvot LaRambam, Mitzvot Ase 161). And there are some of the commentators (see the end of Ran on Pesachim) the opinion of which is that the intention of the verse is to tally the weeks specifically when they are full, but there is no need to mention [them] every day and say that they are such and such days and such and such weeks. And there are some that say (Rosh in his Responsa 24:13) that the [proper] way is to mention the tally of weeks with the days always on every day. And one who fears the Heavens will choose their way to remove [himself] from any doubt, and not be concerned about the elegance of the words. And so have they practiced today in all places of which we have heard.

And Rambam, may his memory be Blessed, wrote (Sefer HaMitzvot LaRambam, Mitzvot Ase 161), "And do not be misled by their, may their memory be Blessed, saying [that] it is a commandment to tally days and it is a commandment to tally weeks, and think that they are two commandments. As the intention of this is not to say that it be a commandment on its own, but [rather] it is a part of the [different] parts of the commandment. However, it would have been two commandments had they said, 'The tally of the days is a commandment and the tally of the weeks is a commandment.' And this is what will not be hidden from one who is exact in the thing and elucidates it - that when you say, 'It is obligated that he do such and such,' it is not obligatory from this statement that this matter be a commandment on its own. And the proof that elucidates this is our tallying the weeks as well on each night, in our saying that they are such and such weeks and such and such days. And if the weeks were a commandment on their own, their tally would have only been arranged on the nights of the [ends of] the weeks alone. And they would have had two blessings: 'and commanded us about the counting of the days of the omer '; and 'about the counting of the weeks of the omer ' - but the matter is not like this. [Rather] the commandment of the counting of the omer is its days and its weeks, as we have written." To here [are his words].

It is from the roots of the commandment from the angle of the simple understanding [that it is] since the entire essence of Israel is only the Torah, and because of the Torah were the heavens and earth created, and as it is stated (Jeremiah 33:25), "Were it not for my covenant day and night, etc." And it is the essence and the reason that they were redeemed and left from Egypt - in order that they receive the Torah at Sinai, and fulfill it. And [it is] like God said to Moshe (Exodus 3:12), "And this will be the sign for you that I have sent you; when you take out the people from Egypt, you shall worship God on this mountain." And the understanding of the verse is [that] your taking them out from Egypt is a sign for you that you shall worship God on this mountain - meaning that you shall receive the Torah, which is the great principle for which they were redeemed and it is their ultimate good. And it is a great matter for them, more than freedom from slavery. And hence God made a sign of their leaving Egypt for the receiving of the Torah; as we always make what is secondary into a sign for what is the essence.

And because of this - that it is [the] essence of Israel, and because of it were they redeemed and went up to all of the greatness to which they rose - we were commanded to tally from the morrow of the holiday of Pesach until the day of the giving of the Torah; to show about ourselves the great desire [we have] for the the honored day, which our hearts yearn [for] like 'a slave seeks shade' and always tallies when will come the yearned time that he goes out to freedom. As the tally shows about a man that all of his deliverance and all of his desire is to reach that time. And that which we count to the omer, meaning, "Such and such days have passed from the tally," and we do not tally "Such and such days do we have to the time," is because all of this shows us the great desire to reach the time [of Shavuot]. Therefore, we do not want to mention at the beginning of our counting the large number of days that we have to reach the offering of the two breads of [Shavuot]. And let it not be difficult for you, to say, "If so, after most of the days of these seven weeks have passed, why do we not mention the minority of the remaining days?" [It is] as one should not change the nature of the counting in the middle. And if you shall ask, "If so, why do we begin counting from the day after [Pesach] and not from the first day?" The answer [is that] it is because the first day is entirely dedicated to remembering the great miracle, which is the exodus from Egypt, that is a sign and a proof of the world having been created and of God's - may He be Blessed - providence over people. And we may not mix [something else into] its joy and mention anything else with it. And as such, the counting begins immediately from the second day. And we should not say, "Today is such and such days from the second day of Pesach" - as the count would not be fitting to say, "From the second day." And therefore, it was ordained to count the tally from that which is done on it - and this is the omer offering, which is a significant sacrifice. As through it is the remembrance that we believe that God, Blessed be He, wants - through His providence over people - to sustain them and [so] renews for them the seed of the grains in each and every year, to live through them.

From the laws of the commandment is that which they, may their memory be Blessed, said (Menachot 66a) that it is a commandment to tally them from the evening so that they be complete. As the verse stated, "complete shall they be" - and they, may their memory be Blessed, said, "From when are they complete? From when he begins from the evening." And nonetheless, the commentators (Tosafot in the name of Behag on Menachot, s.v. zecher) explained that if he forgot and did not tally from the evening, he [may] tally on the morrow the whole day. And some say there that one who forgot and did not tally one day may not tally again that year, since they are all one commandment; and since he forgot one day from them, the entire count is negated for him. And our teacher in our generation did not concede to this reasoning. Rather, one who forgot a day should say, "Yesterday was such," without a blessing; and tally the other [days] with all of Israel. And it is a choice [fulfillment] of the commandment to tally [while] standing (Mishneh Torah, Laws of Daily Offerings and Additional Offerings 7:23). And he recites the blessing, "who has sanctified us, etc." And one who has tallied without a blessing has fulfilled [the commandment], and [hence] he is not permitted to return and tally with a blessing (Mishneh Torah, Laws of Daily Offerings and Additional Offerings 7:25). And the rest of its details are in Tractate Menachot (see Tur, Orach Chaim 479).

And this commandment of counting the omer is practiced from Torah writ in every place by males at the time of the [Temple], such that the omer is there; and rabbinically in all places, even when the omer is not offered. And one who transgresses it and does not count these days has violated a positive commandment.

Mitzvah 307

The commandment of the sacrifice of the new meal-offering from wheat on the day of [Shavuot]: To sacrifice leavened bread from the new wheat on the day of the festival of Shavuot. And that is what is called in Scripture, "a new offering" (Leviticus 23:15). And they are two loaves, as it is written (Leviticus 23:16), "From your inhabitations you shall bring bread of waving, two of two issaron." And the matter was such that they would bring three seah of new wheat and rub them and pound them in the way of all of the meal-offerings. And they would grind them and sift two issaron in twelve sieves. And they would take them and make two loaves from them and bring leavening (Menachot 52b) and put it into the issaron. And the length of each loaf was three handbreadths and its width was four, and its height was [the span of] four fingers (Menachot 96a). And they were square; and they were baked on the eve of the holiday. And on the morrow after their waving, they were eaten by the priests that whole day and half the night (Menachot 100b). And that meal-offering is the first of all of the meal-offerings [of that crop] of wheat. And with the bread, they would sacrifice seven unblemished sheep, one young bull and two rams for a burnt-offering, a goat for a sin-offering and two lambs for a peace-offering - and these are the sacrifices spoken about in [the Book of Numbers]. All of this was brought with the bread besides the additional offering of the day which was two bulls, one ram and seven lambs for a burnt offering, and one goat for a sin-offering - and these are the sacrifices spoken about in the Book of Leviticus. And it was elucidated explicitly so in the fourth chapter of Menachot 45b that this sacrifice would come with the bread, separate from the additional sacrifice of the day. And after the waving of the bread, it was eaten by the priests with the lambs of the peace-offerings.

I have written from that which also suffices for the roots of the commandment of the two breads in the commandment of the omer, from the angle of the simple understanding. And my heart also tells me about the matter that because of [the following] was the commandment of wheat to be an offering of loaves of bread, and in the offering of barley with flour. Since wheat is for the food of man - and so it is fitting to prepare it in a way that man would enjoy and be nourished from it. And all of this is from the root that we planted at the beginning of the matter of the sacrifice from the angle of the simple understanding - that through the deed is the thought of a man aroused to things (Sefer HaChinukh 95). And therefore, according to the importance of the sacrifice and its goodly preparation is the heart of a man more aroused to it.

From the laws of the commandment is that which they said (Menachot 73b) that if they did not find new [wheat], they can bring it from the [storehouse]; and that one should not bring wheat that descended from the clouds at the outset, because there is a doubt if I call this, "from your inhabitations," or not. But if he brought it, it is fit. The kneading of the two breads and their forming is outside [the courtyard] and its baking is inside, like all of the meal-offerings. And their baking does not push off [the prohibition of work on] the holiday, as it is stated (Exodus 12:16), "shall be done for you" - and not for the higher realm. The waving of the bread with the lambs of the peace-offerings was done while they were still alive. And the high priest takes one of the loaves, and the second is divided for all of the shifts. And the rest of its details are elucidated in Menachot, Chapters 4, 5, 8 and 11 (see Mishneh Torah, Laws of Daily Offerings and Additional Offerings 8).

And this commandment is practiced by the males, etc. like we have written in the commandment of the omer.

Mitzvah 308

The commandment of resting from work on the day of [Shavuot]: To rest from all work on the sixth day of Sivan - and this is called the festival of Shavuot (Weeks) - except for that which is specific to the needs of the eating of the soul as it is stated (Leviticus 23:21), "And you shall call on that very day, a holy occasion." And I have already written in the commandment of resting on the first day of Pesach in this Order (Sefer HaChinukh 297) that in any place about which it is stated in the Torah, "a holy occasion," its content is to say, make it holy, to not do work on it.

And also, a hint from the roots of the commandment is written there from the angle of the simple understanding that suffices for all of the holidays. And we shall write some of its laws in the negative commandment after this, of the prohibition of work on the holiday (Sefer HaChinukh 298), with God's help (see Tur, Orach Chaim 497).

Mitzvah 309

To not do work on the day of the holiday of Shavuot: To not do work on the day of [Shavuot] - which is the sixth day of Sivan, as it is stated (Leviticus 23:15-16), "And you shall count for yourselves from the morrow of the Shabbat, etc. you shall count fifty days, etc." And the understanding of "from the morrow of the Shabbat," is meaning to say, the morrow of the first holiday of Pesach, about which it was speaking first. As if it was the Shabbat of creation (the seventh day of the week) - if so, it will not have informed us which. And it comes out that the fifty days end on the sixth of Sivan. How is this? Fifteen days from Nissan, which is always full (consisting of thirty days); and twenty-nine days of Iyar, which is always lacking (consisting of twenty-nine days); and six days of Sivan - behold, [that is] fifty. And this fiftieth day - which was the day that the Torah was given - is the holiday of the Assembly (atseret), and it is also called the holiday of Shavuot (Weeks). And it is also written at the end of the section about this glorious day (Leviticus 23:21), "all work of labor shall you not do" - we have already written that any labor that is not for the needs of food for the soul is called, work of labor.

The root of the commandment of this appointed time is hinted in the commandment of the counting of the omer (Sefer HaChinukh 306) - and take it from there.

And I have written some of its laws - as is my custom - in the commandment of the resting from work on the first day of Pesach in this Order (Sefer HaChinukh 298). And there is no need to write at length about the rest of the appointed times of the year. As the six well-known days of the appointed times of the year - and they are the first and seventh [days] of Pesach, the first and eighth days of [Sukkot, Shavuot] and Rosh Hashanah - all have one law for all of their dispensations and all of their prohibitions. And the elucidation of all of its laws at length is in the Tractate that is built on this, and that is Tractate Beitzah (see Tur, Orach Chaim 496).

Mitzvah 310

The commandment of resting on the day of Rosh Hashanah: To rest from all work on the first day of the month of Tishrei, except for that which is specific for the needs of food for the soul, as it is stated (Leviticus 23:24), "On the seventh month, on the first day it shall be a shabbaton for you." And the seventh month is the month of Tishrei, since Nissan is the new year for months and it is called the first in Scripture. And I wrote in the commandment of resting on the first day of Pesach (Sefer HaChinukh 297) that which they, may their memory be Blessed, said, (Rosh Hashanah 2a), "This ' shabbaton ' is a positive commandment." And all the rest of the content of the commandment is as it is written there.

Mitzvah 311

To not do work on the first day of Tishrei: To not do work on the first day of the month of Tishrei, as it is stated (Leviticus 23:24-25), "In the seventh month on the first of the month, etc. All work of labor shall you not do." And the seventh month is called 'Tishrei,' as it is the seventh from Nissan, which is the new year for [the count of] months. They, may their memory be Blessed, said (Rosh Hashanah 2a) that this day, the first of Tishrei, is called the new year to count from it the sabbatical years and the jubilees, and we also count plantings and vegetables from it. In the Gemara in Tractate Rosh Hashanah 8, 12a, the Sages elucidated what are the laws [that pertain] to their saying that is considered the new year for these things. They also said there (Rosh Hashanah 16a) that on this day all the inhabitants of the world are judged for their deeds. They explained His providence of the deeds of each and every [individual] and on the species more generally, such that metaphorically all people pass before Him like bnei maron (in an orderly procession) - meaning, one at a time and not mixed together.

It is from the roots of the commandment of this appointed time [that it] was from the kindnesses of God upon His creations that He remembers them and views their deeds one day each and every year; so that the iniquities should not mount so greatly, and there be room for atonement. He is abundantly kind and leans toward kindness; and since they are [resultantly] few, He forgives them. And if there are a few iniquities that require expiation, they will be retributed in small pieces. And [it] is like what they, may their memory Blessed, said (Avodah Zarah 4a), "For a friend, one is repaid in small pieces." If He did not remember them for a longer period, [the sins] would become so abundant that the whole world would be deserving of destruction, God forbid.

And it comes out that this glorious day is [responsible for] the sustaining of the world; and it is therefore fitting, to make it a holiday, and that it should be in the count of the dear appointed times of the year. And on the side that it is the day of judgement for all living things, it is proper to stand in fear and trepidation on this day more than on the other appointed times of the year. And this is the concept of the shofar blow (teruah) of remembrance that is mentioned in [connection with this day]; as the teruah is a broken sound, and it hints to the need for each person to break the power of his evil inclination and regret his evil deeds, as I will explain at length in the commandment of shofar (Sefer HaChinukh 405) in the Order of Pinchas, with God's help. It is for this reason that they, may their memory be Blessed, did not establish the recitation of Hallel on this appointed time. And as they said, that it is not proper for a person to sing songs of praise while he stands in judgement. And like Rabbi Abahu said in the final chapter of Rosh Hashanah 32b, "The ministering angels said in front of the Holy One, Blessed be He, 'Why does Israel not recite Hallel on Rosh Hashanah and Yom Kippur?' etc.," as it is [found] there.

I have written some of the laws of rest on the holiday - as is my custom - in the commandment of the appointed time of Pesach. And it is also fitting to write here some of the matters that are mentioned in Tractate Rosh Hashanah: That they said there that there are four 'new years'; the first of Nissan is the new year for kings and festivals - the understanding of festivals is meaning, the festival that is the first of the festivals, so is its definition in the Gemara (Rosh Hashanah 4a); the first of Elul is the New Year for tithing animals; the first of Tishrei is the new year for what we have written above; the first of Shevat is the new year for trees according to Beit Shammai, though Beit Hillel says that it is on the fifteenth in it. And there in the Gemara, it is elucidated for what matters these new years are [pertinent].

And there they said (Rosh Hashanah 16b) that four things tear up a person's [bad] decree: charity; crying out; changing the name; and changing the deeds. And the matter of changing a name seems to be so that a man should think of himself as if he is another person (see Mishnah Torah, Laws of Repentance 2:4) and improve all of his ways. [Thus] anytime he is called, he will remember this and pay attention to the matter. And that which they said [that] three books are opened on Rosh Hashanah, one for the completely righteous, one for the completely wicked and one for the ones in between. The substance of opening books seems to be metaphorical for the matter of His, Blessed be He, providence over them. Our rabbis always spoke about the familiar, in order that the things would penetrate the ears of the listeners. The completely righteous are immediately written and sealed for life. My teacher explained that 'completely righteous' here [means] that he is totally innocent, and likewise 'completely wicked' here [means] that he is totally guilty. And therefore, he is sealed immediately for death, since he has no merit to protect him. [The judgement of] those in between is left suspended until Yom Kippur, at which time a final verdict is sealed. And that which they said adjacent to this, "Beit Shammai said, 'There are three groups for the Day of Judgement'" - meaning after the death of each and every person, which is called the Day of Judgement - "one group of the completely righteous, a group of the completely wicked, and a group of those in between.'" Here the explanation of 'completely righteous' and 'completely wicked' is [that it is referring] to their judgement. And with this explanation, a great difficulty about the issue is removed. If you merit, my son, you will be sensitive to this and this toil of mine will put you at ease.

And that which they said there that the one who is completely righteous in judgement is sealed immediately for life in the **World To Come**. Do not think that the **World To Come** is something that is identical for all righteous people; for in that life there are countless gradations, and each righteous person rises to the fitting level according to his reward (See Shabbat 152a). And the rest of the details about these matters are there in the first chapter of Rosh Hashanah (see Tur, Orach Chaim 602-603). The prohibition of work on this day is practiced in every place and at all times by males and females. And one who transgresses it and did work that was not for the needs of food for the soul is liable for lashes, as we have written for the other appointed times.

Mitzvah 312
The commandment of the additional sacrifice on the day of Rosh Hashanah: To sacrifice the additional sacrifice on the day of Rosh Hashanah, as it is stated (Leviticus 23:24-25), "On the seventh month on the first of the month, etc. and you shall bring a fire-offering to the Lord, etc." And in the Order of Pinchas (Numbers 29:2-5), it mentions the sacrifice at length. And all of its content is like I wrote about the additional sacrifice of Pesach in the commandment of the additional offering of all of the seven days of Pesach in this Order (Sefer HaChinukh 299).

Mitzvah 313
The commandment of the fast on the tenth day of Tishrei: To fast on the tenth day of Tishrei, and this is called The Day of Atonements (Yom HaKippurim), as it is stated (Leviticus 23:27), "But on

Sefer HaChinukh

the tenth of the month, etc. you shall afflict your souls." The explanation appears is Sifra, Achrei Mot, Chapter 7:3): "[This refers to] affliction that causes a diminishing of the soul. What is this? This is eating and drinking." And so [too,] did they, may their memory be Blessed, explain in the Gemara (Yoma 74b). And the tradition also came about it, that it is forbidden for washing, anointing, wearing shoes, and sexual relations. And the language of Sifra, Parshat Achrei Mot, Chapter 8:3 is "From where [do we know] that Yom Kippur is forbidden for washing, anointing, [wearing shoes] and sexual relations? [Hence] we learn to say (Leviticus 23:32), 'A Shabbat of shabbaton'" - meaning that the doubling of Shabbat (rest) indicates resting from these things [as well as] resting from nourishment of the body.

It is from the roots of the commandment that it was from the kindnesses of God towards His creatures to establish one day to atone for their sins with repentance - and as I wrote at length in the Order of Achrei Mot (Sefer HaChinukh 185) in the commandment of the service for Yom Kippur. And we were therefore commanded to fast on this day; as food and drink and the rest of the sensual pleasures propel the physical matter toward desire and sin, and they cause people to negate the form of the wise soul from seeking truth - which is the service of God and His ethics [which are] good and sweet for anyone with knowledge. And it is not fitting to do [this] on the day of his coming to judgement in front of his Master; to come with a soul darkened and confused from the food and drink, with thoughts of the material which is in it. As we only judge a person according to his deeds of that time. Therefore, it is good for him to strengthen his wise soul and to subdue the physical in front of it on this glorious day, so that [the soul] will be fitting and prepared to receive its atonement, and [that] the veil of desires not prevent it.

From the laws of the commandment is that which they, may their memory be Blessed, said (Yoma 80a) that the measure of eating of fitting foods on Yom Kippur to be liable for it from Torah writ is a large kakotevet. And the reason that the measure of eating of Yom Kippur is differentiated from the measure of eating other prohibitions in the Torah - which are with a kazayit - is because the Torah forbade eating on that day with an expression of affliction. And it does not state, "you shall not eat," about it, like it states with other prohibitions. And the Sages explained that they received [the tradition] from those that were before them: that with a kazayit, it is called eating; but affliction in a man is so long as he has not eaten a kakotevet - since the mind of a man is not set at ease with less.

And the measure of a kotevet (large date) is more than a grogeret (fig cake) and less than a kabeitzah (the size of a large egg) and also less than three (textual variant - two) [large] olives (zayit) - as three (textual variant - two) olives are a kabeitzah. The principal of the matter is that one who is an expert was already exacting and measured on a scale that there is not in the measure of twelve argents and more, the measure of a kakotevet; and [so] its law is like [that of] half a measure. And so [too,] that which they said (Yoma 73a, 80b) that the measure of drinking is the fill of a man's cheek, which is a kabeitzah - as they have already measured that an egg fills the cheek of a man. And with less than this, there is no prohibition [the liability for which is with] excision. Rather its law is like [that of] half a measure. And therefore [in the case of] someone who is sick - even though there is no full danger with him - if he is very weak; it is fitting to feed him and give him drink little by little, less than the measure that we said. And we give a gap of [time] enough for the eating of a peras (half loaf of bread) - which is three eggs, according to the opinion of most commentators - between the eating and drinking of one time and [that of] another time, so that the eatings not combine and be considered one eating and [hence] one measure. But there is no need to pause between eating and drinking; as eating and drinking do not combine for this matter. And the measure between one drinking and [another] is [time] enough for the drinking of a reviit. And it is permitted to weigh and measure things on Yom Kippur at a time of need. And it is better that we be concerned and distance ourselves to not eat a measure and not be concerned to forbid measuring, which is [only] rabbinic. And also from the matter of the commandment is that which they, may their memory be Blessed, said (Yoma 77b) [regarding] these afflictions that are only rabbinic - such as washing and anointing - they only decreed that they should not be done for no need. But they did not decree [about] anyone who does them for a need - for example, one who has scabs on his head [may] anoint them in his [customary] way and not be concerned. And they, may their memory be Blessed (Yoma 77b), said that it is permitted to cross water until the neck even to guard fruits - and all the more so, for the matter of a commandment - whether going or returning.

And concerning the shoe (sandal), our teachers - God should protect them - explained that a shoe is always of leather. And that is what is forbidden on Yom Kippur, but not of a different type. And the principle of the matter according to some commentators is that anything that is fitting for the matter of release (chalitsah) - meaning to say, that it is of leather - is forbidden on Yom Kippur, and permitted to go out into a public domain with them (wearing them) on Shabbat. But anything that is not fitting for release - such as cork and reeds and palms (see Yoma 78b, that it is a shoe of grasses) and other types of grasses (plants) - are permitted on Yom Kippur, so long as they do not go out with them [to a public domain] in a place without an eruv, as we consider them like a burden (and not a piece of clothing, which is permitted). But from the commentators, there are [also] many honored ones that permit one to go out into the public domain with all of them.

And the law of the sick person who is in danger, that we feed him according to an expert physician, or according to himself - and even if the physician says that he does not need [to eat] (Yoma 83a); the law of a pregnant woman that smelled [food] (Yoma 82a, 83a); the law of one who was seized by bulimia; and the law of minors - whether a boy or a girl - from what time do we we afflict them all of the day rabbinically, and likewise from when do we teach them [to fast] with [some] hours. And the principle of the the matter according to a few of the commentators is that two years before the adulthood of a healthy child, they complete [the fast] rabbinically; and two years before that, we teach them [to fast] with [some] hours. And some explained that it is one year before adulthood that they complete [the fast] rabbinically - whether a boy or a girl. And some explained that only a girl alone completes [the fast] rabbinically one year before adulthood, but a boy does not complete [the fast] at all rabbinically. And adulthood for a boy is thirteen years and a day, and for a girl is twelve years and a day. And what is the law about washing for the king and the bride on this day (Yoma 73b).

And I will further mention to you here that which they, may their memory be Blessed, said about the matter of the 9th of Av, which is well-known to be rabbinic. And even though these two days are very distant in their reasons and their content; since the word, "fast," includes [both of] them, we will speak a little about it. And I will inform you that the Sages were stringent about it in all of its content like on Yom Kippur - to stop [eating] while it is still [the previous] day, and [about] anointing, wearing shoes and sexual relations. And pregnant and nursing women fast like the rest of the people - which they do not do on all other fasts, except for the middle three fasts of the stopping of rain. [This is] as it is mentioned in Tractate Taanit 14a at the end of the first chapter, where Rav Ashi concludes, "Take the middle [one] in your hand." And the rest of the details of the commandment [of fasting on Yom Kippur] are elucidated in Tractate Yoma (see Tur, Orach Chaim 612).

And [it] is practiced in every place and at all times by males and females. And one who transgresses it and ate like the measure of a ketovet on Yom Kippur has violated a positive commandment, and has [also] transgressed a negative commandment that has [a liability of] excision for it; as is is stated (Leviticus 23:29), "For any soul which is not afflicted on that very day shall be excised." [If] he ate or drink like this measure inadvertently, he is liable for a fixed sin-offering.

Mitzvah 314

The commandment of the additional sacrifice of Yom Kippur: To sacrifice the additional sacrifice on Yom Kippur, as it is stated (Leviticus 23:27), "But on the tenth of the month, etc. and you shall sacrifice a fire-offering to the Lord." And in the Order of Pinchas, the sacrifice is explained, as it is written there (Numbers 29:8), "And you shall sacrifice a burnt-offering to the Lord, a pleasing smell; one young bull, one ram, seven one-year old sheep, etc." And Rambam, may his memory be Blessed, brought this verse that is in Pinchas in his tally (Sefer HaMitzvot LaRambam, Mitzvot Ase 48), whereas I have written the one that is first in the Torah. But it all comes to the same thing.

I have already written what I have known from the roots of the commandment of the additional sacrifice and some of its laws in the additional sacrifice of Pesach in this Order (Sefer HaChinukh 299). And there is one connection to all of them that are similar.

Sefer HaChinukh

Mitzvah 315
To not do work on the tenth of Tishrei: To not do any work on Yom Kippur - and it is the tenth day of Tishrei - as it is stated (Leviticus 23:27), "on the tenth of the seventh month, etc."; and it is written after it (Leviticus 23:28), "And you shall not do any work on that very day, since it is the day of atonements, to atone for you." And the word, "since" (ki), [indicates] the giving of a reason for the cessation from work. And [it is] like the matter that I shall write later in this Order in the commandment of resting on Yom Kippur (Sefer HaChinukh 317). And you also find all of the content of this commandment there - and I will not write an addition for you about something that is not needed.

Mitzvah 316
To not eat and drink on Yom Kippur: To not eat and drink on Yom Kippur, as is is stated (Leviticus 23:29), "For any soul which is not afflicted on that very day shall be excised." And I have written all of the content of this commandment above in this Order in Commandment 313 (Sefer HaChinukh 313). See there, 'for it is close.'

Mitzvah 317
The commandment of resting from work on Yom Kippur: To rest from all work on Yom Kippur, as it is stated, (Leviticus 23:32), "A Shabbat of shabbaton is it to you." And I have written what they, may their memory be Blessed, said (Shabbat 25a), "This 'shabbaton' is a positive commandment" - meaning to say that its understanding is as if it says, "Rest on this day."
It is from the roots of the commandment from the angle of the simple understanding [that it is] so that we not be preoccupied with anything, and [so] place all of our thoughts and all of our intent to request pardon and forgiveness from the Master of all on that day, which is prepared for the forgiveness of iniquities from the day that the world was created - and as I have written in Achrei Mot in the commandment of the service of Yom Kippur (Sefer HaChinukh 185).
From the laws of the commandment is that which they, may their memory be Blessed, said (Megillah 7b) that anything which is forbidden to do on Shabbat - even though it is not totally work - is forbidden on Yom Kippur. The principle of the matter is, "There is no difference between Shabbat and Yom Kippur except that volitional work on Shabbat is [punishable] with stoning, and on Yom Kippur with excision." And nonetheless, they, may their memory be Blessed, permitted to trim vegetables on Yom Kippur from [the time of] the afternoon service and onward, so that it will be found ready immediately on the evening [after it] - which is not permitted on Shabbat. But the people have become accustomed to be strict about the thing and to practice prohibition in the matter, as [on] Shabbat for everything. And the rest of its details are elucidated in Tractate Yoma.
And it is practiced in every place and at all times by males and females. And one who transgresses it and does work has violated this positive commandment, besides that he has violated a negative commandment; and as we shall write with God's help (Sefer HaChinukh 215).

Mitzvah 318
The commandment of resting on the first day of the holiday of Sukkot: To rest from any work which is not for the needs of food for the soul on the first day of the holiday of Sukkot, as it is stated (Leviticus 23:35), "On the first day, a holy occasion."
I have already written what I have known from the roots of the commandment of rest on Shabbat and the holidays - and it is one reason for all of them. And I have written a few of its laws in the prohibition of work (Sefer HaChinukh 298) in this Order, with God's help.
And this commandment is practiced in every place and at all times by males and females. And one who transgresses it has nullified a positive commandment, besides that he has transgressed a negative commandment.

Mitzvah 319

To not do work on the first day of the holiday of Sukkot: To not do work that is not for the needs of food for the soul on the first day of the holiday of Sukkot - which is the fifteenth of Tishrei - as it is stated (Leviticus 23:34-35), "Speak to the Children of Israel, saying, 'On the fifteenth day of the seventh month, etc. On the first day is a holy occasion; all work of labor shall you not do.'" I have written the content of the prohibition of work on the holiday, above about Pesach in this Order (Sefer HaChinukh 298); and its content is the same in everything.

Mitzvah 320
The commandment of the additional sacrifice on each day of the seven days of Sukkot: To sacrifice a sacrifice on the holiday of Sukkot, as it is stated (Leviticus 23:36), "Seven days shall you sacrifice a fire-offering" - and this is the additional [sacrifice] of the holiday. And in the Order of Pinchas (Numbers 29:13-35), it writes at greater length and explains about the additional sacrifice of each and every day - how many beasts they would sacrifice - as each day was different than its fellow, since the bulls would diminish on each day. And they, may their memory be Blessed, said (see Rashi on Numbers 29:18) that in the merit of this commandment will the enemies of Israel diminish, just as the bulls diminish each day. And I have already written - from the angle of the simple understanding - about the additional sacrifice of Pesach, a root sufficient for all of the additional [sacrifices], according to my opinion. And Rambam, may his memory be Blessed, brought the verse that is in the Order of Pinchas in his tally (Sefer HaMitzvot LaRambam, Mitzvot Ase 50), whereas I have brought the one that is first in the Torah. But it all comes to the same [thing].

Mitzvah 321
The commandment of resting from work on the eighth day of Sukkot: To rest from any work which is not for the needs of food for the soul on the eighth day of the holiday of Sukkot, as it is stated (Leviticus 23:36), "on the eighth day, a holy occasion" - and that is the twenty-second day in Tishrei. I have written above (Sefer HaChinukh 297) about the roots of the commandment of rest on the festival. And we will write more about the matter with God's help in the prohibition of work on this day in this Order (Sefer HaChinukh 323). And there we will elucidate that this holiday is a holiday on its own.

And [it] is practiced in every place and at all times by males and females. And even though rest on the festival is from the positive commandments determined by time - since there is also the prohibition of a negative commandment in the doing of work, women are liable for it from the principle that is in our hands (Kiddushin 35a): "'A man or a woman, if they do from any of the sins of a person' (Numbers 5:6) - the verse equated a man and a woman for all of the punishments in the Torah." And one who transgresses it and did work on this day has violated a positive commandment, besides that he violated a negative commandment, as we shall write in this Order (Sefer HaChinukh 323) with God's help.

Mitzvah 322
The commandment of the additional sacrifice on the eighth day of Sukkot, which is called Shemini Atseret: To sacrifice the additional sacrifice on the eighth day of the holiday of Sukkot - and that is the additional [sacrifice] of Shemini Atseret - as it is stated (Leviticus 23:27), "and you shall sacrifice a fire-offering to the Lord; it is an atseret (convocation), etc." And in the Order of Pinchas (Numbers 29:36-38), it is explained at length. And in the explanation, they, may their memory be Blessed, said (Yoma 2b) that it is a festival on its own. And therefore, we should count this additional sacrifice as a commandment on its own.

I have already written what my hand has reached from the roots of this commandment and its content many times above.

Mitzvah 323
To not do work on day of the holiday of Shemini Atseret: To not do work on the eighth day of the holiday - and that is the twenty-second day of Tishrei - as it is stated (Leviticus 23:36), "on the eighth

day, a holy occasion; all work of labor shall you not do"; and this is what is called the holiday of convocation (atseret). And they, may their memory be Blessed, said (Rashi on Leviticus 23:36) that it is called like this because it is the end of the appointed times. And metaphorically, it is as if the Holy One, Blessed be He said to Israel, "Remain with me one day, as your departure is difficult for me."

We have already said many times that the prohibition of work on all of the appointed times is the same. However, I need to expand on the discussion here and inform you, my son, about the matter of this holiday which the Sages, may their memory be Blessed, informed us (Yoma 2b), which is that it is a holiday on its own - meaning, that it is not part of the holiday of Sukkot. And even though you see all of Israel sitting in their sukkot on one of the two days of the holiday of this holiday of Shemini Atseret - it is not because it is a part of the holiday [of Sukkot]. As behold, we explicitly say in its blessings, "the eighth day of the holiday of convocation," and there is no mention of the holiday of Sukkot in it at all. But because of the ordinance of the two days of the exiles, we must sit in the sukkah eight days; and seven - like the law of the Torah - will not suffice. And therefore, we sit in the sukkah on the eighth day of the holiday of Sukkot. And they, may their memory be Blessed, said (Sukkah 47a), "We do sit" in the sukkah, in order to fulfill the obligation: Since they, may their memory be Blessed, obligated us to add a day for each and every appointed time, we have also added to Sukkot and made the days of [the] sukkah eight days. But nonetheless, "we do not bless" over the sukkah on this day; as it is truthfully a different appointed time - since we are now experts in the fixing of the [new] moon. And it is more fitting for us to bless for the holiday of the convocation which is true than for the other which is because of the ordinance. And perhaps you will say, "Why did they not ordain to recite a blessing for both of them - and we would say, 'on this holiday of Sukkot and holiday of the convocation' - as on Shabbat and an appointed time, we mention both of them?" Behold, this is not [correct]. As Shabbat and an appointed time [can] both of them be as one day, but it is impossible for two appointed times to be together. And hence it is not fitting for us to recite the blessing like this. But it is fitting for us to sit in the sukkah - as sitting in the sukkah does not detract at all from the holiday of convocation; and there is in the thing, [a fulfillment of] the commandment of the ordinance of the two days of holiday of the exiles which they, may their memory be Blessed, ordained on every appointed time, as we have explained above (Sefer HaChinukh 301).

And I will also inform you, my son, a little of what they, may their memory be Blessed, said about the matter of the intermediate days of the festival - and they are the middle days that are in Pesach and Sukkot - which they, may their memory be Blessed - [found to be] forbidden in the doing of work by the Torah. However which work is forbidden on them and which is permitted did not appear explicitly in the Torah. Nonetheless, the Torah still forbade work on them, such that the Sages learned the thing from Scripture in the second chapter of Chagigah 18a. Some of them learned the thing from the verse of "The holiday of matsot you shall guard" (Exodus 23:15) - and that is Rabbi Yeshayah. As it was implied for him, "You shall guard all of the days of the holiday of matsot from the doing of work" - but not that they all be the same in the work [that is prohibited]. And Rabbi Yochanan [reasons that] it comes from an a fortiori (kal vechomer) argument there from the first and seventh [days], that do not have holiness [both] before them and after them, etc.

And there is one there that learns it from, "all work of labor shall you not do" (Leviticus 23:7) - and that is Rabbi Yose HaGalili. And this is how the verse is explained according to him - meaning, on the first day is it that all work of labor is forbidden besides what is needed for the food of the soul, but on the intermediate days of the festival, not all work is forbidden on it. Rather some are forbidden and some are permitted; and Scripture gave them over to the Sages [to decide]. And Rabbi Akiva learns it from, "These are the appointed times of the Lord, holy occasions" (Leviticus 23:4) - as he establishes it as [referring to] the intermediate days of the festival. And from that which is written in it, "holy occasions," it teaches that it is forbidden in the doing of work. And it is possible that according to him, permitted work is learned by him from (Leviticus 23:36) "it is an atseret (which can also mean, a cessation)" - meaning that the eighth day is stopped from all work, but not the other days. Or also, he learned it form [the letter] hay (which means, the) of "the seventh," written about Pesach in the Order of Reeh Anochi (Deuteronomy 16:8), "Six days shall you eat matsot," such that

Sefer HaChinukh

they, may their memory be Blessed, said "'And on the seventh day it is an atseret ' - the seventh is stopped from all work, but not the sixth. And which work is forbidden or permitted? Scripture gave them over to the Sages [to decide]." And since the matter is given over to their hand, such that the Torah only forbade what they said, they divided work according to their will and opinion. And it comes out that all work they, may their memory be Blessed, forbade, is forbidden to us from Torah writ; and that which they permitted is also permitted by Torah writ. As according to the understanding expounded from Scripture, this prohibition is given over to their hand.

And they said more generally that any work that if it is not done on the festival, will [result] in much deterioration is permitted to do. And this is [the meaning of] their saying (Moed Katan 2a), "We water an irrigated field (beit hashelachin) on the [intermediate days of the] festival" - meaning to say, a vegetable garden or what is similar to it which we water constantly, and it would deteriorate if we do not water it. The expression, shelachin is like shelahin, which is [known from the] usage, meshalhei, which is parched for water. And they, may their memory be Blessed, said that when he waters it, he should not water it from a pool or from rain water; as there is much toil in the thing. [Rather], he waters it from the spring - meaning, that he channels it and waters [his field] with it. Behold that they were a little stringent about this, that he should not toil with a great toil; since this is only done to keep his garden fresh, lest all of it or part of it will dry up. But with any work [that prevents a true] loss, or it will close to certainly deteriorate if he does not do it on the [intermediate days of the] festival - such as someone who has olives and he fears that they will deteriorate if he does not extract their oil immediately, or grapes if he does not stomp them immediately or anything that is similar to them - they were not stringent about it. And they were not concerned with great toil [in this case]. Rather, he should do all of his needs for them - without any alteration - the way that he does it on a regular workday. And they, may their memory be Blessed, likewise permitted (Moed Katan 12b) to harvest a vineyard that has reached the time to be harvested during the [intermediate days of the] festival. And they also said more generally (Moed Katan 8b) about this matter that a commoner (amateur) can sew in his [usual] way, but a craftsman must [alter his stitch]. And they certainly did not say this only about sewing, but rather the law is the same for all types of work, according to what appears. And I asked my teacher if we say so about writing - that a commoner can write in his [usual way] but he did not permit it to me. Maybe because we have found explicitly that they, may their memory be Blessed, forbade (Moed Katan 18b) to correct even one letter in a Torah scroll, we should be stringent about writing.

And they forbade every man (Moed Katan 12b) to not plan his work for the festival - meaning that he not purposely leave his work before the festival in a way that he will do it on the festival because he will be avialable. As the intermediate days of the festival were not established to be involved in work, but rather to rejoice in front of God; meaning to say, to gather in the study halls and to hear pleasantness of the words of the book - 'the laws of Pesach on Pesach, the laws of [Shavuot] on [Shavuot] and the laws of [Sukkot] on [Sukkot].' And the court destroys the work of anyone who plans his work for the festival and makes it ownerless for everyone [to take]. But if the one who planned his work for the festival died, they do not penalize the son after him; and they also do not prevent him from doing that work on the festival so that it not get wasted. And I [say] about this son, [An evildoer] 'Prepares but the righteous one wears.' And they, may their memory be Blessed, permitted (Moed Katan 13a) anyone who has a need - meaning who does not have what to eat - to do any work. And likewise they allowed the head of a household to do any work for the sake of someone (to hire him) who does not have what to eat. And according to what appears, the understanding of 'he does not have what to eat,' is one who does not have money with which to buy his requirements - and even if he has a house and furnishings, as we do not obligate a person to sell his vessels. And the rest of the details of the distinctions of work on the festival are very many, and they are elucidated nicely in Tractate Moed Katan.

And let this principle be in your hand: That the law of the [intermediate days of the] festival - as the laws of rabbinic enactments on Shabbat - are such that you cannot compare and extract one thing from [another] thing. As sometimes you will find that our Rabbis, may their memory be Blessed allowed a heavy [type of] work in one matter, and sometimes they were stringent about a light one in another matter. And do not wonder about the thing, given the introduction that I wrote - that the Torah only forbade and allowed on the intermediate days of the festival that about which [the Rabbis] agreed. And likewise with the matter of rabbinic enactments on Shabbat and holidays, we find places in the Gemara where they, may their memory be Blessed, upheld their words even in the place of [a] Torah law [that would be pushed aside]; and [yet] sometimes they were lenient with them in a place where they saw that it was good to be lenient - and there is nothing empty in all of their words. And remember, my son, this principle that the laws of the festival - as the laws of rabbinic enactments on Shabbat - are such that we do not determine a thing from [another] thing. And do not be mistaken about it, as it was said by the greats of the world. And the opinion of Rambam, may his memory be Blessed, (Mishneh Torah, Laws of Rest on a Holiday 7:2) is that every prohibition of work on the intermediate days of the festival is only from the words of the [Rabbis]. And the Rabbi would want to say that all of those verses that we said above, which are in the beginning of Tractate [Moed Katan], are only a memory device (asmakhta). But Ramban, may this memory be Blessed, (Ramban on Moed Katan and Ramban on Leviticus 23:7) - and many with him - said the essence of the prohibition of work on it is from the Torah, as we have written; but the specific [types of] work and their distinctions were given over to the Sages, may their memory be Blessed.

Mitzvah 324
The commandment of taking the lulav: The commandment of lulav, that we should take in our hands on the first day of the holiday of Sukkot the fruit of a hadar tree, palm fronds, the branches of a braided tree and willows of a brook, as it is stated (Leviticus 23:40), "And you shall take for yourselves on the first day the fruit of a hadar tree and palm fronds, the branches of a braided tree and willows of a brook." And the explanation came about it (Sukkah 35a) that the fruit of the hadar tree is the citron (etrog); the fronds (kappot) of date palms is the lulav - and it is written kappat, lacking [a letter] vav (which could make it singular), to hint that the obligations is that we take one lulav, and not two or three or more; the branch of a braided tree is the myrtle; and the willows of a brook is the willow that is well-known among Israelites.

From the roots of the commandment, [there is a need to] preface [that] I have already written to you several times in what preceded, my son - that a man is impacted according to his actions that he constantly does; and his thoughts and pursuits are all caught according to the deeds of his hands, whether good or bad. And therefore, since the Omnipresent wanted to give merit to His people Israel which he chose, He multiplied the commandments; such that their spirits constantly be effected by them for the good, all of the day. And among the commandments that He commanded us to grab our thoughts with His service in purity, is the commandment of tefillin - that they should lay across from the limbs of a man that are well-known as the dwelling place of the intellect. And [these limbs] are the heart and the brain. And from this constant action of his, he will dedicate all of his thoughts to the good, and always remember and be careful to calibrate all of his deeds in righteousness and justice.

And so too from this root is the commandment of the lulav with its three [other plants]. As the days of the holiday are days of great joy for Israel, since it is the time of the gathering of the grain and the fruit of the tree into the home; and all men rejoice a great rejoicing. And for this reason is it is called the holiday of the gathering (haasif). And God commanded His people to make a holiday in front of Him at that time to give them merit, such that the main joy will be for His sake, may He be Blessed. And since joy greatly elicits the physical and makes one forget the fear of God, God commanded us at that time to take in our hands things that remind us that all the joy of our heart is for His sake and His honor. And it was from His will that the reminder be from that which brings joy, just as the time is a time of joy - as all of the words of His mouth are just. And it is well-known that it is the nature of all of these four species to gladden the heart of those that see them.

And there is also another matter with these four things - that they are similar to precious limbs in a man (see Vayikra Rabbah 30:14; Midrash Tanchuma, Emor 19): As the citron is similar to the heart, which is the dwelling place of the intellect, to hint that he should serve His creator with his intellect; the lulav is similar to the backbone, which is the essence of a person, to hint that he should straighten himself completely for His service, Blessed be He; the myrtle [leaves are] similar to the eyes, to hint that he should not stray after his eyes 'on the day of the rejoicing of his heart'; and the willow [leaves are] similar to the lips, with which a man completes all of his acts of speech, to hint that he should put a muzzle to his mouth, calibrate his words and fear God, may He be Blessed, even at a time of joy. And the reason that it is only practiced one day in the country (outside of the Temple) is well-known - since the main joy is on the first day. And if you should ask, "Why would one not take it on Shemini Atseret, which has great joy on it for Israel" - the answer is that the day of Shemini Atseret is completely for God, may He be Blessed. And [it is] as they, may their memory be Blessed, said (Bemidbar Rabbah 21:22; Midrash HaGadol, Shemot 29:36), "A parable of a king who made a feast, etc.," as it is [found] in the Midrash. And at the end, He said to them, "Remain with me one day, as your departure is difficult for me." And therefore, it is called atseret (a stopping). And if so, there is no need for any other reminder. And the holiday of Pesach does not require another reminder with the lulav, as behold the matsa and marror and the body of the Pesach sacrifice are between his hands; and further since it is not a time of joy as [much as is] the holiday of the gathering. And the holiday of Shavuot also does not require another reminder, since the essence of [that] festival is only from the angle of the giving of our Torah - and that is the great reminder to straighten our ways. And this is what appears to me in these matters from the side of the simple understanding. And I have come to believe that the kabbalists (mystics) have wonderful secrets about the commandment of the lulav and the three [other plants].

From the laws of the commandment is that which they, may their memory be Blessed, said (Menachot 27a) that these four species are one commandment and impede one another when he does not have [one of them]. But if he has [all of them] and he takes them one after another, he has fulfilled [the commandment]; as it is established for us that the lulav does not need a binding (Tosafot on Menachot 27a, s.v. lo shanu, in the name of Bahag). And we take one lulav, two sprigs of willow, and three sprigs of fit myrtle - meaning that its leaves are formed in threes on the nodes, as is explained in the Gemara (Sukkah 32b), and the verse hints to this when it calls it "braided." And the minimum measure of the length of a lulav is four handbreadths; and [of] a myrtle and a willow is three handbreadths, which is [the span of] ten fingers of the thumb. And the measure of the citron is that it cannot be less than a kabeitsah (like a large egg). And the law of the things that disqualify (Sukkah 29, 34) the lulav, the citron, the willow and the myrtle; the law (Bava Batra 137b) of partners that have purchased a citron in partnership - or brothers that acquired it from the contents of a house - such that if they acquired it with the intention to fulfill [the commandment] with it, each one of them fulfills [it] and they do not need the acquisition of the one from the other. So did our teachers - may God protect them - instruct us. And the laws of shaking (Sukkah 38a), such that the obligation is to extend [it] and to bring [it back], to raise [it] and to lower [it]. And the matter is to arouse the soul, that it remembers at the time of joy that all belongs to God, may He be Blessed - from above to below and the four directions, as all is included in this. And the rest of its details are elucidated in Tractate Sukkah.

And this commandment is practiced in every place and at all times by males, but not by females. And one who transgresses it and does not take these four species on the first day of the holiday of Sukkot that does not fall on Shabbat in any place - and so [too,] on all seven [days of Sukkot] in the Temple - has violated this positive commandment. And in the Temple it was taken on the first day, even on Shabbat.

Mitzvah 325

The commandment of sitting in a sukkah (booth): The commandment of a sukkah, since we were commanded to sit in a sukkah for seven days - as it is stated (Leviticus 23:42), "In huts shall you sit for seven days." The first day [of these seven] is the fifteenth day of Tishrei.

What is explained in the verse is from the roots of the commandment - so that we recall the great miracles that God, Blessed be He, performed for our forefathers in the wilderness as they left Egypt. As He covered them with the clouds of glory, so that the sun would not harm them during the day nor the frost at night. And there are some that explained (Sukkah 11b) that the Children of Israel made actual huts in the wilderness. And through recalling His wonders that He did with us and our forefathers, we will be careful with His commandments, Blessed be He, and we will be fitting for the receiving of good from Him. And that is His desire, Blessed be He, as He desires to do good.

From the laws of the commandment is that which they said (Sukkah 2a) that a sukkah that is higher than 20 ells is disqualified, and so [too,] if it is lower than 10 handbreadths. Its area must be at least 7x7 handbreadths; less than that is disqualified. It needs three walls and the shape of an opening (tsurat hepetach) that it formed by two vertical posts and one on top of them. And the law that if it has more shade than sun, it is fit - but if not, it is disqualified; one who makes a thick house-style roof, it is fit. The law of one that makes his sukkah between trees, and the trees are its walls; the law of one who builds a sukkah on the top of a wagon or on the top of a boat. And the law of one who covered over a porch that has posts, whether they are inside or outside, that it is fit. The law of the covering (skhakh), that the obligation is to make it from something that does not contract impurity, such as the refuse of the threshing floor and the vineyard; but not from something that does contract impurity. And the law of disqualified covering in the middle or on the side; and the law of three [handbreadths] of airspace that disqualifies the covering, whether it is in the middle or on the side in a small sukkah. And the law of one that covers a sheet over [the sukkah] because of the sun or below [the cover] because of the shedding, that it is disqualified. [But] if they covered them to beautify them, it is fit - as anything that is to beautify [the sukkah] is fit.

And the law of a sukkah above [another] sukkah, the law of one who sleeps in a canopy in the sukkah, such that if it has a roof that is even one handbreadth wide, it is forbidden; but if not, it is permissible. And one who sleeps under a bed in the sukkah, such that if the bed is higher than ten handbreadths, it is forbidden; but if not, it is permissible. And even though [sleeping under a canopy held up by four posts] is forbidden even though it less than ten handbreadths - the bed is different because it is made for (to sleep on) its top. If one placed a sheet on [two] poles, it is permissible to sleep underneath it, as it has no roof; and behold, it is like making a space [by supporting it] with his two forearms, which is certainly permitted. And the law of a stolen sukkah, that it is fit - as land cannot be stolen; and even if one stole wood and made a sukkah out of them, it is fit due to an ordinance of the Sages - as they ordained [that he is only responsible] to pay for the value of the wood. And the law [that] one who is suffering is exempted from the sukkah - for the Torah stated, "you shall sit" [which is understood to mean,] as you [normally] reside - and all the more so an ill person, who is also exempted for this reason; and even those that serve the ill person are exempted. And all emissaries of a commandment; and so [too,] the bridegroom and all of his entourage - as they are performing a commandment. And the law of sojourners and watchmen for gardens and orchards, and city watchmen; the law of rain falling; the law of sukkot of ganba'kh (gentiles, women, animals and Cuthites) and rakba"sh (a shepherd, a summer field watchman, an outpost guardian, and a guardian of fruit), that they are fit; the law that the wood [used to build] the sukkah is forbidden from Torah writ [for any other use for] all seven days - and on the eighth and ninth day in the Diaspora, they are forbidden because they are [considered] set aside (muktseh) - and the decorations of the sukkah are forbidden because it is a degradation of the commandment; [so is it said] in the name of Ramban, may his memory be Blessed, (Milchamot Hashem on Beitzah 45a, Chapter 4); and the rest of its many details are [all] elucidated in the tractate built on this, which is Tractate Sukkah (see Tur, Orach Chaim 625).

And [it] is practiced in every place and at all times by males, but not by females. And one who transgressed it and did not eat [a meal] of bread in the sukkah or did not sleep in it, even if it was a nap - and it was not that he was sick or suffering or exempt due to the reasons we have said - has violated this positive commandment. And I have already written above (Sefer HaChinukh 6) that the court coerces [for the fulfillment of] a positive commandment. On the first night every man is obligated from Torah writ to eat at least a kazayit of bread; on the remaining days, it is optional - such that if a man wished to eat outside of the sukkah, he [may do so], so long as he eats his fixed meals of bread only in the sukkah. And the pious ones of old would not eat anything except in the sukkah (Sukkah 26b).

Mitzvah 326

Sefer HaChinukh

That we not work the land on the seventh year: That we not work the land on the seventh year, which is called the sabbatical (shmitah) year, as it is stated (Leviticus 25:4), "But on the seventh year, etc. your field you shall not sow."

The root of this commandment, its details and all of its content is written in Eem Kessef Talveh (Sefer HaChinukh 84) - take it from there. And one who transgresses it and works the land at the time of the [Temple] with one of the types of work that are forbidden from Torah writ - as we [explained] over there - is lashed.

Mitzvah 327

That we also not do work with the trees: That we also not do work with the trees on the seventh year, as it is stated (Leviticus 25:4), "and your vineyard you shall not prune." And the language of Sifra, Behar, Section 1:6 is "Sowing and pruning" - the understanding [of which is] "you shall not sow and [...] you shall not prune" - "were in the general category," meaning they were in the category of resting. "And why were they singled out? To compare to them: Just as sowing and pruning are distinct in being work on the land and on the trees, etc." - as it is [found] there. The content of this commandment is like the previous commandment. And I wrote a few of its laws also in the Parsha of Eem Kessef Talveh (Sefer HaChinukh 84) - you can see it from there.

Mitzvah 328

That we not harvest the aftergrowth on the seventh year: That we not harvest that which grows on its own from the land on the seventh year, nor the growth that occurs on this year from what was sown in the sixth year - and this is called aftergrowth - as it is stated (Leviticus 25:5), "The aftergrowth of your reaping you shall not harvest." This means to say that we not harvest it in the manner that we harvest our crops in other years (See Sefer HaMitzvot LaRambam, Mitzvot Lo Taase 222). Nevertheless, eating was permitted to us, provided that it is eaten in a way [that shows that it is] ownerless - meaning without preparation, as we will explain in the commandment after this (Sefer HaChinukh 329). As the Torah's only concern in these matters was that a person's actions during this year should indicate that he has no specific property, but that everything is the property of the Master of All - and as we said above.

What is written about this matter (in Sefer HaChinukh 84) is from the roots of the commandment.

From the laws of the commandment is that which they, may their memory be Blessed, said (Mishnah Sheviit 4:2) that even if a person transgressed and planted his field in the seventh [year] and [its produce] grew, the produce is permissible on a Torah level; so long as it is not harvested in the way of the harvesters on all other years - such that they harvest the whole field and bundle it into a threshing floor and thresh it with oxen. Rather from Torah writ, the law is to harvest a little at a time, to pound [it] and to eat. But the Sages decreed that [even] the aftergrowth be forbidden for eating, on account of the transgressors that would sow their garden in the Fall and say, "It is [only] aftergrowth." And this decree is only with vegetables, grains and legumes, as it is the way of people to plant them. But fruits of the trees and grasses - which is not the way of people to sow - are permitted (see Mishneh Torah, Laws of Sabbatical Year and the Jubilee 4).

And this commandment is practiced from Torah writ by males and females in the Land of Israel at the time that Israel is there. And regarding the other places, it is all as I have written (Sefer HaChinukh 84). And one who transgresses this at the time of the [Temple] and harvested the produce that he sowed in the way of the harvesters - such that he harvested the whole field and bundled it into a threshing floor and threshed it with oxen in the way that people do on other years - is lashed. And one who gathers from the aftergrowth of produce that is sown - even though he does not harvest it all together - is struck with lashes of rebellion; since the Sages decreed about it, as we said.

Mitzvah 329

That we not gather the fruit of the trees in the seventh [year] in the manner that we gather them in every year: That we not gather that which the trees produce on the seventh year in the manner that people gather the fruit of their trees in other years. Instead, we must do so differently to show that it is all as if ownerless in this year. And this is the explanation of, "and the grapes of your vines you shall not reap" (Leviticus 25:5) - meaning, you should not reap in the way of the reapers. As so did the traditional explanation come about it. And [it is as] the Sages explained, (Mishnah Sheviit 8:6) "From here they said that that fig [grown during] the seventh [year] may not be cut off with a fig-cutter, but may be cut with a knife. Grapes [grown during the sabbatical year] may not be stomped in a wine press, but may be stomped in a kneading trough. And olives may not be processed in an olive press or a small olive press, but he may crush and put them in a very small olive press."

And the understanding of "your vine," (nezirekha, literally that which is separated of yours) is that you have separated and removed them from other people and you have not made them ownerless, [such that] you may not reap them until you make them ownerless. This is the view of Rashi (Rashi on Leviticus 25:5), may his memory be Blessed; as he holds that the produce of one who guards his fields and his produce during the seventh [year] does not become forbidden. And so [too,] did he write in his commentary on Sukkah (Rashi on Sukkah 39b s.v. aval) and on Yevamot (Rashi on Yevamot 122a s.v. shel). And so is the thing learned - from Torah writ - with correct proofs.

And [regarding] that which the Sages said (Sifra, Behar, Chapter 1:3), "'The grapes of your vine you shall not reap' - from that which is watched on the land you shall not reap, [but you may reap from the ownerless": To our opinion, we will explain this, "from that which is watched on the land you shall not reap," [that it is] when it is still guarded that it is forbidden to reap from them, but not that the produce becomes forbidden through this. But Ramban (Ramban on Leviticus 25:5) explained " nezirekha " - meaning a vine that they did not work and did not prune. As he said that any vine that he does not prune and does not work is called like this. And the verse is stating that even an unworked vineyard cannot be reaped in the manner that we reap it in other years; and all the more so, a worked vineyard.

The root of this commandment is one with the the commandment of the seventh [year] preceding it - behold, I wrote for you where is its place (Sefer HaChinukh 84). And there you will find in which place and at what time it is practiced. And all of the laws of these commandments are elucidated at length in the tractate that is built upon these matters, and it is Tractate Sheviit - may you merit to study and teach [it].

Mitzvah 330

The commandment of counting the seven [cycles] of seven years: To count the years - seven years - seven times to the Jubilee year, when we are in the Land of Israel after we have settled it, as it is stated (Leviticus 25:8), "And you shall count for yourself, seven cycles of seven years; seven years seven times." And this commandment - meaning this counting of the the sabbatical years until the Jubilee year - is given over to the great court, meaning to say, the Sanhedrin. And the commandment is such that they would count each year and each cycle of seven years until the Jubilee year, like we count the days of the omer. Afterwards, they would sanctify the fiftieth year with resting the land and proclaiming freedom for all of the slaves and maid-servants. And all the lands return to their [ancestral] owners.

It is from the roots of the commandment from the angle of the simple understanding that God, may He be Blessed, wanted to inform His nation that everything is His; and in the end everything will return to those to whom He wanted to give it at first - for the earth is His, as it is written (Exodus 19:5), "for all the earth is Mine." And with this commandment of the counting of forty-nine years, they will distance themselves from stealing land of their fellows and they will not covet it in their hearts; in that they know that everything returns to the one that God wishes it to be his.

And this matter of Jubilee is a little similar to that which is practiced by the earthly monarchy - that from time to time, the [kings] take lands from the fortified cities that are [owned] by their ministers, to remind them of the fear of the master. And so [too,] is this thing - that God wanted that all the land return to the one who has a holding in the land from Him, Blessed be He. And so [too,] every slave of a man goes out from under his hand and will be in the domain of his Creator. However, the kings of the earth do this from their fear lest their minister's rebel against them; whereas God, Blessed be

Sefer HaChinukh

He, commanded this to His people to give them merit and to do good to them - as God, may He be Blessed, desires to do good to them in His great goodness.

And I have also heard from the mouth of sages that there is a great secret in the matter of the Jubilee and that all the days and years of the world are hinted to in it (see Ramban on Leviticus 25:2 and Ibn Ezra on Leviticus 25:2). Also, in the matter of the sevens - that we were commanded to count the years seven at a time, and not eight at a time or nine at a time, or less than [seven] - did they say that there is a great and goodly matter of wisdom about it as well. They have known it, but did not want to give it over to every person. And even though their secret was not revealed to us, we have paid heed to this thing - that the span of sevens is arranged in many of our commandments: Behold, we continue our work six days, and we rest on the seventh; we work the land six years, and we rest on the seventh; after seven cycles of seven years, we also rest a year - and that is the Jubilee that we have come [to write] about [here]; behold the holiday of Pesach is seven days, and likewise the holiday of Sukkot is seven, and after the seven, we celebrate [Shemini] Atseret; likewise, we count seven seven-year cycles from Pesach to [Shavuot], and after the tally of the seven, we celebrate [Shavuot]; likewise the cutting of a covenant (treaty), which is something done for preservation of a matter, is on the basis of seven, as it is written (Genesis 21:30), "Rather take these seven sheep from my hand"; likewise Bilaam, who was a wise man, made seven altars; so too, some of the sages said that the word, oath (shevuah) - which is translated [into Aramaic] as preservation - is derived from the expression, seven (shevah); and so [too,] many that I have not raised now on the tip of my pen. And you, my precious son, should merit and research and see and add to your knowledge and understand the matters. But I have already finished my work here to arouse your spirit about the question.

And if you shall ask, why did they, may their memory be Blessed, obligate to count the seven [cycles of] seven from that which is written, "And you shall count for yourself"; and [yet] we have never seen that the zav counts the days of his counting, nor the zavah the days of her counting, and even though it is written about them, "and he shall count for himself" (Leviticus 15:13), "and she shall count for herself" (Leviticus 15:28) - besides that they are obligated to pay attention to the days, but not that they be obligated to count them orally and recite a blessing on their count - the answer to this thing is what I prefaced at the beginning of my book: that every matter of the Torah is dependent upon the traditionally received explanation. And for the one that does not know this, how many verses will appear to be the opposite of one another, and how many difficulties and contradictions will arise? But for the one that knows it clearly, he will see that all of 'its ways are the ways of pleasantness and all of its paths are peace' and truth. And so, the tradition came to us that the command of, "And you shall count for yourself," of Jubilee requires an oral counting; whereas the command of counting, written about the zav and the zavah, is only paying heed to the days - and such is the practice of all of Israel in every place. "And even though they are not prophets, they are the children of prophets." And similar to this matter is that which we found in the Torah about the expression, remembering. As remembering is written about Amalek, and remembering [is written] about the [incident] of Miriam, and remembering is also written about the matter of leaving Egypt: And the tradition came to us about the remembering of Egypt to do it orally - and as they, may their memory be Blessed, said (Berakhot 21a), about the blessing of "True and firm" (which mentions the leaving of Egypt), "It is from Torah writ." But with the other rememberings, it is enough for us with just remembering of the heart and paying heed to the things.

From the laws of the commandment is that which they, may their memory be Blessed, said (Sifra, Behar, Section 1:2) that the obligation of the commandment of this count is only after the conquest and division of the land, as it is stated (Leviticus 25:3), "Six years shall you sow your field and six years shall you prune your vineyard" - until each and every one recognizes his land. And from when the tribe of Reuven and Gad and half [of the] tribe of Menashe were exiled, this commandment became negated, because the Jubilees were negated from that time and onward; as it is sated (Leviticus 25:10), "and you shall proclaim freedom in the land for all of its inhabitants" - only when all of its inhabitants are upon it; and also, that they not be mixed up (see Arakhin 32b), but rather sitting in their proper order. And at the time when the Jubilee is practiced in the Land [of Israel], it is [also] practiced outside of the Land; as it is stated (Leviticus 25:11), "It is a Jubilee" - meaning in every place (Kiddushin 38b). And at the time when the Jubilee is practiced, the law of the Hebrew slave is practiced, as well as the law of the houses of a walled city, the law of a consecrated (cherem) field and the field of a holding; and we accept a resident stranger (ger toshav).

The [laws of the sabbatical year] are practiced in the Land - and the release of monies in every place - from Torah writ. But at the time when the Jubilee is not practiced, none of these are practiced [either] - except for the release of land on the seventh [year] which is practiced in the Land [rabbincally]; and also the release of monies on the seventh [year] in every place [rabbincally]. And which is the sabbatical year? It was concluded like this in Tractate Avodah Zarah in the statement of Rav Huna, the son of Rav Yehoshua in the the first chapter (Avodah Zarah 9b) - that it is the seventeenth year (5017), specifically according to the opinion of Rashi, may his memory be Blessed; and the eighteenth year (5018) according to the opinion of Rabbenu Chananel, may his memory be Blessed. And all of the matter of the release of monies is elucidated nicely in the last chapter of Tractate Sheviit (see Mishneh Torah, Laws of Sabbatical Year and the Jubilee 10). And the rest of the details of all of the laws of the [seventh] year are there in the same tractate that is built on this. And they, may their memory be Blessed, mentioned the matter of this commandment - which is to count the years - in Sifra and in other places. And I have already written above that this commandment is given over to the Great Court - which is the Sanhedrin [and] which is called the eyes of the congregation - and that it is only practiced when the Jubilee is practiced.

Mitzvah 331

The commandment of blowing the shofar on Yom Yippur of the Jubilee: To blow the shofar on the tenth of Tishrei - which is Yom Kippur - as it is stated (Leviticus 25:9-10), "And you shall proclaim a shofar blow, etc. on Yom Kippur, you shall proclaim the shofar in all of your land, etc. and you shall proclaim freedom, etc." And it is known that the commandment of the blowing of the shofar on this day is to publicize the freedom of every Israelite slave to go out as a free man without money (see Rosh Hashanah 8b). And its substance is not like the substance of the blowing of the shofar on Rosh Hashanah, as that blowing, we do to fix our thoughts on the matter of the binding of Yitschak and to depict in our souls to also do like him from the love of God, may He be Blessed. And from that, our memory will go up well in front of God - meaning, that we be meriting (cleared in judgement) in front of Him. Whereas this blowing of the Jubilee is to publicize the freedom, as we have said (see Sefer HaMitzvot, Mitzvot Ase 137).

It is from the roots of the commandment [that it is] since the sound of the shofar is to arouse the hearts of all people - whether for peace or for war. And the matter of sending away the slave that served his master a long time is very difficult in the eyes of the master. Therefore, we were commanded about it to arouse the hearts of the creatures about the matter - to strengthen their souls and to warn them about the commandment when they hear the sound of the shofar, through their perceiving that the thing is the same in the whole land and that everyone [releases their slaves]. As there is nothing that strengthens the hearts of people like the action of the many; and like the statement of the sage, "The pain of the many is a consolation" (see Devarim Rabbah 2:22). Also, the slave himself is aroused to leave from under the hand of his master whom he loves, like all of the slaves, when he hears the sound of the shofar. And from that, the commandment is observed, such that everyone returns to the domain of the Master of all.

The laws of the commandment: For example, with which shofar do we blow on this day and which blessing do we recite for it - and they, may their memory be Blessed, have already said more generally in Tractate Rosh Hashanah 26b, "Jubilee and Rosh Hashanah are the same for blowing and for the blessings." And we will speak a little about it in the commandment of shofar of Rosh Hashanah (Sefer HaChinukh 405), with God's help - as is our custom. And nonetheless, even though they, may their memory be Blessed, said that they are the same, there is a little difference between them; as on Rosh Hashanah that falls out on Shabbat, they would only blow the shofar in the court; whereas on the Jubilee, each and every individual blows - whether in front of the court or whether not in front of the court - so long as the court meets (Rosh Hashanah 30a).

Sefer HaChinukh

And likewise, from the laws of the commandment is that which they, may their memory be Blessed, said (Rosh Hashanah 8b), "From Rosh Hashanah until Yom Kippur, the slaves would eat, drink, and rejoice in their masters' homes - they were not released to their homes and they were [also] not enslaved to their masters. Once Yom Kippur arrived, [and] the court would sound the shofar, they would be released to their homes; and likewise, fields would be returned to their owners." And many of the details of the laws of the Jubilee are in Arakhin and the laws of shofar are in Tractate Rosh Hashanah.

And this commandment is practiced in the Land of Israel at the time that Jubilee is practiced. And behold, I have written you adjacently (Sefer HaChinukh 330), which time the Jubilee is practiced and that the commandment of Jubilee is given over to the court. And if the court transgresses this and does not blow the shofar - even if the slaves are sent away and the fields go back to their owners without blowing - they have violated this positive commandment.

Mitzvah 332
The commandment of the sanctification of the Jubilee year: To sanctify the fiftieth year, like the sabbatical year - meaning to say with the stoppage of work on the land and the rendering ownerless of that which grows on it - as it is stated (Leviticus 25:10), "And you shall sanctify the fiftieth year." And the verse explained that the matter of the sanctity is that its fruit and its produce be ownerless, and that the slaves go out from under the hand of their master. As Scripture states after that, "and you shall proclaim freedom in the land for all of its inhabitants" - meaning freedom for slaves - "Since it is the Jubilee, it shall be holy to you; from the field shall you eat its produce" (Leviticus 25:12) - meaning that the produce will be ownerless, and not that each and every one gathers it into his domain. What I wrote about the commandment of the counting of the years (Sefer HaChinukh 330) is from the roots of the commandment - that God wanted to have His nation merit in the acceptance of His Kingdom, etc., as I wrote it there, but here was its [true] place.

From the laws of the commandment is that which they, may their memory be Blessed, said (Mishneh Torah, Laws of Sabbatical Year and the Jubilee 10:16-17) that everything that is forbidden from work on the land in the seventh year is [also] forbidden on the Jubilee; and everything that is permitted on [the one] is permitted on [the other]. And the liability for one who does [forbidden work] is the same in both of them. The seventh [year] is more than the Jubilee in that it releases [loans], and specifically at its end. And the Jubilee is more than the seventh [year] in that it releases land and removes slaves at [its] beginning. And the Jubilee year does not count in the tally of the years of the seven-year cycle. Rather we count forty-nine years, which are seven times seven years; and after the sabbatical year, which is in the last seven-year cycle, we make the Jubilee in the fiftieth year; and we begin to tally for [the next] Jubilee in the fifty-first year. And it is [also] the beginning of the six years of the seven-year cycle (see Nedarim 61a).

And this commandment is practiced in the Land of Israel at the time that all of its inhabitants (the Jews) are upon it, as I wrote above. And it is from what it appears that the Sanhedrin would gather for the sanctification of the year and recite the blessing, "to sanctify the years," upon it and blow the shofar afterwards. And so [too,] each and every individual would blow in his domain; and the sound would be heard in all of the land. And the slaves would leave to their homes and the lands would go back to their [original] owners. And the rest of its details are in Tractate Arakhin. And one who transgresses it and worked his land [with] a forbidden work on the Jubilee - and likewise one who did not want to send away his slave [to be] free - has violated this positive commandment, besides that he violated a negative commandment, and as we will write in this Order, with God's help (Sefer HaChinukh 333). And his punishment is very great, as he is like one who denies the creation of the world.

Mitzvah 333
That we not work the land on the Jubilee year: That we not work the land on the Jubilee year, in the same way that we were prevented from its work on the sabbatical year. As it is stated about the Jubilee (Leviticus 25:11), "you shall not sow," [just] like it is stated about the sabbatical (Leviticus

25:4), "your field shall you not sow." And [just] like the sabbatical year is forbidden whether regarding the working of the land or whether regarding the working of the trees, so is [it with] the Jubilee. And therefore, "you shall not sow," is a category that includes land and tree.

I have written in the previous commandment what I could of the roots of the commandment of the Jubilee.

Its laws regarding working the land and the trees is like in the seventh [year]. And in Eem Kesef Talveh (Sefer HaChinukh 84), I have written a little of its matters to arouse the heart of the reader about the matters of the commandment, as is my custom. Look there if you desire it.

Mitzvah 334

To not harvest the aftergrowth of the produce of the Jubilee year: That we not harvest and collect the aftergrowth of the produce of the Jubilee year in the way that a person reaps [it] in other years - rather we should perform an alteration in the things - as it is stated (Leviticus 25:11), "and you shall not harvest, etc." And the whole content is like we explained nearby with the aftergrowth of the seventh [year] (Sefer HaChinukh 328).

Mitzvah 335

To not gather the fruits of the trees on the Jubilee year in the manner that we gather them in other years: That we not gather the fruits of the trees on the Jubilee year in the manner that we gather them in other years, as it is stated (Leviticus 25:11), "and you shall not reap its vines" - and that is a general warning for all fruits of the tree. And Scripture gave for the Jubilee a warning about the fruits of the tree on its own and a warning about the produce on its own - as with the seventh [year], and as we wrote above (Sefer HaChinukh 333). And the law about about both of them - meaning about the sabbatical year and the Jubilee and about these negative commandments - is one. And according to what appears, it all arises from one root - and [so] there is no need to write at length about all of them. And I have already written (Sefer HaChinukh 330) that all of this is only practiced in the Land, and with the condition that all of its inhabitants be upon it, and that each and every tribe reside in its place.

Mitzvah 336

The commandment of adjudicating between the buyer and the seller: That we must adjudicate cases of a buyer and seller according to what the Torah commanded - meaning that there are circumstances that the sale between the seller and buyer stands, and there are circumstances when it does not stand; and it is an obligation upon us to adjudicate between them according to the commandment of the Torah. And even though there are other commandments that came about this - as we have written in Parshat Mishpatim (Sefer HaChinukh 58) that we were commanded to adjudicate between the claimant and the defendant and between the injurer and the injured and similar to them; and all buying and selling is included in a claimant and a defendant - nonetheless, this commandment came specifically about the matter of buying and selling, since it is a constant thing with the creatures. As it is impossible to go even one day without it. And the section of "And when you sell, etc." is stated about this. You find that this is the way of the Torah in many places - according to the necessity or severity of the matter will a commandment be specified for it. Likewise, will warnings be repeated many times [in such cases]. As you see with the prohibition of idolatry that it was repeated in forty-four places, but a warning about Molekh was [still] singled out because this evil worship was very common. And also, twelve warnings come about Shabbat in the Torah, but some types of work are [still] singled out with a warning - such as kindling and carrying. And even though there is a midrash about them [to ascertain] if they were [mentioned] to individualize [all the prohibitions of Shabbat] or to [reduce them] to a [simple] negative commandment, the midrash is not a contradiction for us, there are many [possibilities in explaining] the Torah.

The root of civil laws is well-known - as it is something to which human reason testifies and that it demands; for through law is civilization preserved among people.

From the laws of the commandment is that which they, may their memory be Blessed, said (Kiddushin 26a-28b) that the laws of buying and selling are different according to what is being bought and sold:

Sefer HaChinukh

Land and slaves are acquired with money, a contract or possession; and there are many details with each of these - how is it with money, how is it with the contract and so [too,] with possession - as it appears in the first chapter of Kiddushin. Movable items are acquired in other ways - some are acquired by lifting (see Bava Batra 76b) and that is the greatest [form] of acquisition, and it is sufficient for all movable items. And some are acquired through an acquisition [that is of a] lower level than this, and that is dragging; and some are acquired though a [still] lower level, and this is handing over. And they, may their memory be Blessed, brought a proof (Bava Metzia 47b) that movable items require these [ways of] acquisition and that they cannot be acquired like lands, from that which it is written (Leviticus 25:14), "or purchased from the hand of your fellow." And they, may their memory be Blessed, explained from the angle of the tradition in explanation of "or purchased from the hand" [as] meaning to say, something that is acquired from one hand to [another]. And likewise, did they bring proof from other verses about the acquisition of lands with money, with a contract and with possession, as it appears in Kiddushin.

And there is no doubt that all of these acquisitions are from rabbinic enactment, and they [only] brought the verses to support their words. And the truth is that their dear wisdom that would eventually be revealed by them was hinted and stored in the verses. And even though the essence of the verses are not about these supports, they are learned from them. And they, may their memory be Blessed, said (Bava Metzia 47b) [that] on a Torah level, money [is effective] even for movable properties, but the reason they required dragging it was a decree lest the seller say to the buyer "Your wheat burnt in the loft." And because the ordinance of dragging was made for this, they, may their memory be Blessed, said (Bava Metzia 49b) that if the movable items were in the buyer]s domain - even if he rented that place to the seller - since the domain is the buyer's and his eyes are always upon it and if any incident should happen to those movable items, he could also sense the matter like the buyer and attempt to rescue [them], as the seller could, in this case the sale is enacted only through money as the Torah prescribed, and not through dragging. And also, if the buyer rents that place that the movable items are located - in that case as well, they did not ordain dragging, giving over or lifting. And they also said (Bava Kamma 79b) that land is rented with the ways that it is bought - and that is money, a contract or possession - since renting is acquisition for its days. And they also said (Bava Batra 85b) that just as a person's place acquires for him, so too his vessels can acquire for him in any place that he is allowed to leave them. And once the movable items are placed inside the vessel, neither of them can retract about it; rather it is as if it was lifted, or placed inside his house. But in a place where the buyer is not allowed to place his vessel, his vessels will not (it does not) acquire for him there - such as the public domain or the seller's property. Nevertheless, the Sages said regarding the seller's domain that if the seller says to him, "Acquire with this vessel" - or even if he doesn't say it, but the buyer acquired another vessel from him in the domain of the seller by lifting it, and afterwards acquired fruits from him and placed them into the vessel - he has immediately acquired them. As due to the pleasure that the seller receives from the sale of the vessel, he is not concerned with the place of the vessel and it is considered as if the vessel is in the buyer's domain.

And handing over is not like this, as it only acquires in a public domain or a courtyard that belongs to neither of them (Bava Batra 76b). And acquisition by giving over is for that which is not the way of people to lift them, nor to even drag them, because of their great size - such as large ships and that which is similar to them that are impossible for people to move without much strain and many people (Mishneh Torah, Laws of Sales 3:3).

But dragging is not like this, as dragging only acquires in an alley - which is a place adjacent to the side of the public domain - where it is the way of people to leave their vessels there. [Any] vessels left in such a place may not be moved by [another person]. And dragging also acquires in a yard that [belongs] (does not belong) to both of them. But lifting acquires in all places; since he is lifting it with his body, and so (and with it), he acquires - because his body is his domain in all places that it is [present].

And there is yet another [method of] acquisition of lands and movable items on a Torah level, and that is exchange. And this acquisition was formerly common in Israel. And this matter of exchange is that a man trades his beast for his fellow's beast, or one vessel for another vessel, or vessels for

Sefer HaChinukh

land. And the Sages said about all of these (Mishneh Torah, Laws of Sales 5:5) that once the first dragged the object from his fellow; his fellow possessed the other object that he wanted to acquire from him, wherever it may be. And if anything happens that destroys the object, the loss is [absorbed by the purchaser]. And the law of acquisition by exchange is only with vessels, but not with produce; as produce cannot be used for exchange (Bava Batra 47a). As behold, we found explicitly in that verse from which we learned [about] exchange, that it is with a vessel (Ruth 4:7) - "And this was formerly common in Israel, a man would remove his shoe," meaning his glove, and this is a vessel. And nevertheless, even though produce cannot be the medium of barter, with which to acquire, produce can be acquired through barter like a vessel; i.e., a person can use a vessel to acquire produce through barter - such that he give a vessel to his fellow, and possess the produce of his fellow wherever it may be. The same is not true of coins, which can neither be bartered with nor be acquired with barter - because the mind of people is always on the imprint, and the imprint may be cancelled by the will of the king or the great ones of the states. And people do not rely upon that which is not a firm thing, to acquire with. And so it cannot be acquired in barter, nor used for barter. But a coin the value of which is not because of its imprint is acquired in barter and can be used for barter, like all other movable items. And which one is that? That is a coin that was cancelled by the monrachy - and as Reish Lakish said in the chapter [entitled] HaZahav (Bava Metzia 46b), "Even a purse filled with coins" and "Rabbi Abba translated it as anka dinars and anigera - dinars. One is that the kingdom invalidated and one is that the province invalidated."

When we said that it is not used as barter nor bartered for, the intention was not that the one who bought produce from his fellow for such and such money, is not obligated to pay him the money; for he is certainly obligated to pay him his money once he dragged the produce. Rather the matter is that it is not made into barter. As one who has a bag of coins that are not invalidated, as we said, and his fellow dragged vessels or a beast or produce and said to this fellow, "Behold, I am pulling this produce in exchange for that bag of coins that I have at home which has a hundred dinar" - his fellow does not possess those dinars at all. And if they get lost in any way - and even if it is beyond his control - they are not lost from [his fellow] at all. Rather [the original owner of the coins] is [still] obligated to give him one hundred dinar from any place. And this is [the meaning of] that which they, may their memory be Blessed, said (Bava Metzia 44a), "He pulled the produce, but he did not [yet] give him the money, he cannot renege on [the transaction]" - meaning he is obligated to pay him the value from any place. As it was not said with a status of barter, but with a status of value. And so was it elucidated at the beginning of the chapter [entitled] HaZahav. As there, they said (Bava Metzia 45b), "'The gold [coins] acquires the silver coins.' What, is it not with barter? No, with value." And it raises a difficulty there, "If so, [why the expression], 'acquires' - it should have been, 'obligates?'" [This] is meaning to say that the expression of acquisition only falls upon something known, but this one brings whatever [objects of] value he wants. And it answers, "[Emend the text and] teach, "obligates" - meaning, he is obligated to give him the value once he pulled the produce from him, and he may not renege on it. But [in the case of] one who gives his money to his fellow to acquire produce with it, the owner of the produce is not obligated to give it to him. As this is an ordinance of the Sages, may their memory be Blessed - not to acquire with money but with dragging. Nonetheless, the Sages, may their memory be Blessed, made him liable [if he does not give him the produce] to receive [the curse of] 'The One who dispenses' (Bava Metzia 44a); as he went back on his word after he did an act with his fellow and took money from him. And this acquisition of exchange - which is [just] called, 'acquisition' by the Sages, may their memory be Blessed - is a strong acquisition for every matter, whether for a sale, for a gift or for all of the conditions between a man and his fellow; as it is stated about it (Ruth 4:7), "to establish any matter [...] and this is a validation in Israel." And the law of who is fitting to sell and his sale stands and who is not fitting - such as a competent person and an incompetent person; the law of one who sells things undifferentiatedly and does not explain all the things that he must explain; and the law of one who leaves anything over in his sale, whether in an item or in produce; the law of the borders that a man must mention in the selling of land and what is its status if he mentioned some of them but not all of them. And the law of one who sells property that is not his; and what is the law of the one who is forced to sell his land - and the distinction between he was hung and he sold, and he was hung and he gave. And the law of one who makes a condition with his fellow that if he will want to sell his land, he will sell it to him. And the one who sells his land with the intention to do any [particular] thing and it did not come up in his hand to do it; such as one who sells it with the intention of going to the Land of Israel, and in the end, he does not go there, and all that is similar to this. And that which I say, with the intention to do any [particular] thing - it is not that the seller explicitly says the thing at the time of the sale, but rather that creatures know from his deeds and his words that this is his desire (see Kiddushin 49b and Tosefot there).

And the law of how is the selling of consecrated properties or synagogues, and for which matter is their selling permitted (Arakhin 21b). And the law of buying deeds - that they require the handing over of the deed and also writing that makes explicit that he is selling him the deed and any lien that it has (Bava Batra 76a). And the law of what would be if one gives money to his fellow to buy him something and he buys it for himself with that money; and the law of three that gave money to one, and he went and he bought with part of the money, how do they divide it. And the laws of that which they said, at four periods in the year does money [itself actually] acquire beasts - and therefore they, may their memory be Blessed, said in the chapter [entitled] Oto ve'et Beno (Chullin 83a) that we make a butcher slaughter [an animal once he received the buyers' money] against his will; and like the contextualization of Rabbi Eelai that Rabbi Yochanan said - which explained that [the Sages] stood their words upon the words of the Torah at these four times, and like Rabbi Yitschak said that Rabbi Yochanan said, "Money acquires from Torah writ." And what is the law (Ketuvot 76b) of one who sells a beast and it is found to be 'torn' (terminally ill and, so, unfit to eat). And the laws of a seller who says [the sale] is for a hundred and a buyer who says [it is] for fifty, and each one goes away, but he buys it afterwards undifferentiatedly. And the law of that which they said that a man may not sell what has not [yet] come to the world (Yevamot 93b). And the law of the owner of the sale; the law of a person's agent, and his partner in his buying and his selling regarding his loss and his profit. And the rest of the many details of the commandment are elucidated in the first chapter of Kiddushin and in the fourth, eighth and ninth chapter of [Bava] Metzia, and in the third, fourth, fifth, sixth and seventh chapter of [Bava] Batra. And a few of them are in scattered other places in the Gemara (see Tur, Choshen Mishpat). And [it] is practiced in every place and at all times by males, as it is upon them to administer justice. And a court that transgresses this and adjudicates between a buyer and a seller not according to the law that our perfect Torah commanded us about this has violated this commandment - unless if it did this with the consent of both of them, since it is allowed [to do so] with the acceptance of the two of them. As any condition with money is upheld.

Mitzvah 337

To not mistreat in buying and selling: To not mistreat one of Israel - whether male or female - in buying and selling, as it is stated (Leviticus 25:14), "And if you sell a sale to your countryman or buy from the hand of your countryman, a man should not mistreat his brother." And they, may their memory be Blessed, said in Sifra, Behar, Section 3:4, "'A man should not mistreat his brother' - that is mistreatment [with] money." And in the Gemara (Bava Metzia 56b), they, may their memory be Blessed, said "'From the hand of your countryman' - something that is acquired from a hand to a hand" - that is to say, movable items. And the intention of the midrash is not that the verse does not warn likewise about lands. Rather the matter is to say that the laws of mistreatment - such as the distinctions that they, may their memory be Blessed, said (Bava Metzia 50b) that it is returned if there is [overcharging that is] more than a sixth [above the market price], and its laws for less than a sixth and for a sixth - are not practiced with lands, but only with movable items. And they expounded further about this verse (Sifra, Behar, Section 3:1), "If you have come to purchase, purchase from an Israelite, as it is stated, 'or buy from the hand of your countryman.'" And perhaps that which they were exacting here that the laws of mistreatment are only with movable items is because the verse changed [its] expression - as it stated, "And if you sell a sale," which implies any sale, whether land or movable items; and afterwards it designated the warning for movable items, as it stated, "or buy from the hand," which implies specifically movable items that are acquired from a hand to a hand.

Sefer HaChinukh

They learned from this to say that there is a novel law with movable items which is not with land - and that is the return of money with it in certain cases.

But the essence of the warning – whether with land or whether with movable items - is truthfully that we have been warned not to mistreat the creatures on purpose. However, the difference between [movable items and land] is if there is mistreatment (overcharging) with movable items that is more than a sixth, the sale is nullified – as the mind of the creatures does not tolerate more [overcharging] than this with movable items. However, it is the way of the creatures to forgive all mistreatment regarding land after one has bought it, since land is something that exists forever. And it is similar to that which they, may their memory be Blessed, said by way of exaggeration (Bava Kamma 14b) that land is something worth all money. And the proof to these words of ours - meaning to say, that the prohibition of [overcharging] is also with land - is that behold, the main warning is written about lands, as is explained in this section of the Torah. And that is the opinion of Ramban regarding this - and as he wrote in his commentary of the Pentateuch (Ramban on Leviticus 25:14).

The root of the commandment is well-known, as it is something to which the intellect testifies. And if it were not written, it is appropriate that it would be written - as it is not fitting to take the money of people through falsehood and deceit. Rather, everyone should earn that which God has granted him through his toil, in truth and righteousness. And there is a benefit to each and every one with this thing; such that [just] like he will not mistreat others, others will also not mistreat him. And even if there be one who knows how to trick more than other people [do], maybe his children will not be so and people will deceive them. And [so] it comes out that the things are the same for all, and that it is of great benefit for the inhabitation of the world. And God, Blessed be He, created it to be inhabited.

From the laws of the commandment is that which they, may their memory be Blessed, said (Bava Metzia 51a) that both the buyer and the purchaser are warned by this warning (commandment), as it is stated, "And if you sell a sale to your countryman or buy." And the buyer should not say, "It is the way of the seller to know the worth of his sale. And given that he sold it to me for a little money, I do not have an iniquity [for buying it below its fair price]." As it is not like this, but they are rather both [included] in the warning. And likewise, both of them are [included] in the laws of mistreatments, in the manner that they, may their memory be Blessed, differentiated [the laws]. And so is it in the Mishnah (Bava Metzia 51a), "It is the same for the seller and the buyer that they have [the law of] mistreatment. And anyone that is [overcharged] is able to renege on [the sale]." And they, may their memory be Blessed, said (Bava Metzia 49b) that the measure of [overpricing] that we return [the extra amount] but the sale will stand is a sixth of the sold item or a sixth of the money; and the measure of [overcharging] that we do not even return it - and it is not necessary to say that we do not nullify the sale for it - is less than a sixth of the sold item or of the money, but if there was a sixth of one of them in the thing, [the extra amount] is returned; and the measure of [overcharging] for which the entire purchase is nullified is so long as it is more than a sixth of the purchase or the money. As the law is like Shmuel, who says in the Gemara (Bava Metzia 49b) that if the [overcharging] is not greater than either of them, the sale is not nullified, but he rather returns the [extra amount].

And that which we said that with [overcharging] that is more than a sixth, the sale is nullified - and even though this one went [back] to his house with his money, and this one went to his house with his produce - [that is] only if the one that was mistreated comes to renege on it. But if the one who mistreated comes to renege on it, because the produce had appreciated in between or [because of] another claim, we do not listen to him. [This is] because the one mistreated [could] say to him, "If you had not [overcharged] me, you would not have been able to go back on it; and now you have found that you want to go back on it?" And so is the language of the Gemara (Bava Batra 84a), and Rav Chisda is the one who said the teaching in the chapter [entitled] Hasefinah; and Rabbi Alfas, may his memory be Blessed, ruled [like] it regarding the nullification of a sale and of produce. [This is] meaning to say, that the one mistreated is saying to the one who mistreated, "At the time of the sale, the [extra] profit was already with you, and our sale or purchase was already standing because of you. What is it that comes to nullify it? The mistreatment that you did to me. Behold, I forgive it." As our Rabbis only nullified the acquisition because of the one mistreated. From when he wants the preservation of the [sale], behold, it is preserved. And that is [the meaning of that] which we learned

Sefer HaChinukh

(Bava Batra 83b), "Fine, and they were found to be inferior, the buyer can renege on it" - meaning to say, but not the seller; "Inferior and they were found to be fine, the buyer can renege on it" - meaning to say, but not the buyer.

And they, may their memory be Blessed, said (Bava Metzia 52a) about the matter of [overcharging] that it is not fitting that the law of reneging or nullification be forever; but they rather gave a set time about the things, so that the matters of buying and selling among people be preserved. And the time that they gave is not the same for all things and is also not the same for the buyer and the seller: As with any trade that [involves] the exchange of coins, they gave the measure [of time sufficient] for the buyer to show it to the money-changer if he is in the city. But if he is in a village, the measure is until the market day, that he can bring it to the city or to the place where the money-changer is [found]. And with all other goods there is no difference between a village and a city - and the measure for them is [time sufficient] for a person to show what he bought to a trader or to his relative. And this measure is according to what the eyes of the judge see; as it is impossible to set a calculation of hours about this matter. And Rava gave a reason in the Gemara (Bava Metzia 52b) about the distinction of a coin from other goods, and said it more generally, "Everyone is certain about a cloak, it is [only] a money-changer who is certain about a sela. If this time passed and the buyer did not renege on it, he may not legally renege on it - even if there is much more than a sixth of [overpayment]. However, the Sages said (Bava Metzia 52b) that it is fitting from the trait of piety to always [allow him] to renege on it. And these measures are for the buyer, but the seller can always renege on it; since the goods are not in his hand so that he can confer about them.

And these laws that we wrote are only said about one who purchased from a trader. But [regarding] one who buys from a homeowner, there is no [overcharging] in it and no nullification of the sale within the set time that we said nor afterwards. As these things were only said with traders for the improvement of the world and the settlements of the states. But homeowners only sell expensively - and in their knowing the matter that it is like this, people always forgive the matter with a homeowner. And these are the things (Bava Metzia 56a) that do not have the laws of [overcharging] for anyone, and even if they were sold for twice their worth - and even though there is a prohibition of [overcharging] about them, according to the opinion of Ramban, may his memory be Blessed: lands; slaves - since they were compared to lands, as is learned in the Gemara (Bava Metzia 56b), from that which it is written (Leviticus 25:46), "And you shall inherit them"; deeds; and consecrated properties. And [it is] as they, may their memory be Blessed, said, "'And if you sell, etc. or buy from the hand' - something that is acquired from a hand to a hand; [so] lands are excluded, as they are not movable items. Slaves are excluded, as they are compared to lands. Deeds are excluded, as Scripture stated, 'a sale' - that which it, itself, is sold; [so] deeds are excluded, as they are not sold themselves and they are not acquired themselves, but only for the proof in them. From here they said, one who sells his deeds to a perfumer has [the possibility of overcharging]." And the reason is because they do not sell it to him for the proof in them, but rather to use the paper. And it wonders about this in the Gemara, "What do we understand from it?" - meaning, isn't this obvious; is paper worse than any other thing? And it answers, "To exclude from that of Rav Kahana, as he says, 'There is no [overcharging] for perutot (the smallest coins) [and things of similar value].'" Consecrated property is excluded from the law of overcharging, from that which it is written, "your countryman."

And know that all of the matters of [overcharging] are said regarding the worth of an object, such as if he sold what is worth six for five or what is worth five for six. But one who [defrauds] about the measure of an object - in its length, width or thickness - or about its weight, [causes the sale to] go back; and even for a small thing. And that is [the meaning of] that which Rava said (Kiddushin 42b), "Anything with a measure, a weight or a number - even less than for [overcharging] - goes back." And one who wants to be saved from any concern of these matters that we wrote can say to the buyer, "I know that there is [overcharging] up to such and such [value] in this object that I am selling to you. If you want to buy it on condition that you do not [claim overcharging] against me, buy it; but if not, leave it." [Like this, the buyer] has no claim of [overcharging] against him afterwards, nor even words of grievance (as is elucidated in Bava Metzia 51b). And the rest of its details are in the fourth chapter of [Bava] Metzia (see Tur, Choshen Mishpat 227).

And [it] is practiced in every place and at all times by males and females. And one who transgresses it and [overcharges] his fellow on purpose by a sixth or more has violated this negative commandment. But they, may their memory be Blessed, permitted a trader to profit from less than a sixth for the betterment of civilization, so that people find their needs ready [for them] in every place. And we do not administer lashes for this negative commandment, as it is given to repayment.

Mitzvah 338
To not mistreat any Israelite with words: To not mistreat any Israelite with words, meaning to say that one not say to an Israelite words that hurt him or cause him pain and he doesn't have the strength to be helped by them. And in explanation, they, may their memory be Blessed, said (Baba Metzia 58b), "How is it? If he was a penitent, he should not say to him, 'Remember your previous deeds.' If ailments are coming upon him, he should not say to him in the way that Job's friends spoke (Job 4:6), 'Is not your reverence, your confidence, etc.' If one saw donkey drivers seeking [feed], he should not say, 'Go to x,' when he knows that he does not have any. And do not to say to a trader, 'How much is this item?' when he does not wish to buy it." And about this it is stated (Leviticus 25:17), "A person should not mistreat his countryman."

The root of this commandment is well-known - for it is to give peace among the creatures. And great is peace, as through it is blessing found in the world; and difficult is disagreement - how many curses and how many tragedies are dependent upon it.

From the laws of the commandment are many warnings and many prods with which they, may their memory be Blessed, warned us about this matter that we not hurt the creatures in anything nor embarrass them. And they expanded on the thing until they said (Baba Metzia 58b) that one should not place his eyes on a [possible] purchase at a time when he has no money. And it is fitting to be careful that no insult of people be heard even from a hint of his words. As the Torah was very concerned about mistreatment in words, since it is something very difficult for the heart of the creatures. And many people are more concerned about it than about money - and as they, may their memory be Blessed said (Baba Metzia 58b), "Mistreatment of words is greater than mistreatment of money; as with mistreatment of words, it states (Leviticus 25:17), 'and you shall fear your God, etc.'" And it would not be possible to write all of the things that [bring] pain to people individually. But everyone needs to be careful according to what he sees - as God, Blessed be He, knows all of his steps and all of his hints; 'since man looks to the eyes, but He looks to the heart.' And how many stories did they, may their memory be Blessed, write in midrashim to teach us ethics about this! And the essence of the matter is in the fourth chapter of [Bava] Metzia.

And this commandment is practiced in all places and at all times by males and females. And even to minors, it is proper to be careful not to pain them with words more than what is necessary - unless in regard to when they need a lot, so that they will take rebuke - and even to one's sons and daughters who live in a man's house. And one who is lenient with them, not to cause them pain in these matters, will find life, blessing, and honor. And one who transgresses this and pained his fellow with words, with the ones our Sages, may their memory be Blessed, specified - with a penitent or a sick man or those like them - has violated this negative commandment. But we do not administer lashes for it, since there is no act [involved] with it. But how many lashes - even without the whip of the calf (leather) - are there in the hands of the Master who commands about this, may He be exalted and Blessed.

However according to what it seems, it is not understood that if an Israelite came and began to be wicked to pain his fellow with his bad words, that the listener should not answer him. For it is not possible for a man to be 'like a stone that cannot be overturned' - moreover, that he will be in his silence like one who concedes to the insults. And in truth, the Torah did not command for a man to be like a stone, silent to those who insult him and to those who bless him alike. Rather it commands us to distance ourselves from this trait and that we should not begin to quarrel and insult people. And like this, every man will be saved from all this - since one who doesn't quarrel will not be insulted by people, except for [by] complete fools; and we should not pay attention to fools. And if perhaps some insulting person will force him to answer his words, it is fitting for a wise person to reply to him in a roundabout and pleasant way, and not become very angry; as 'anger rests on the bosom of fools.' And he will [so] save himself before those who listen to his insults, and he will cast the burden upon the one who insults [him]; and this is the way of the best among men. And we should learn this thing - that it is permitted to us to reply to a fool - according to what it seems from how the Torah permitted one who comes to rob secretly to be preceded and killed (Exodus 22:1). As there is no doubt that a man is not obligated to bear harm from his fellow; as he has permission to save himself from his hand - and similarly from the words of his mouth that are full of deceit and cunning - with anything that he is able to save himself from him. However, there is a group of people the righteousness of which rises so much that they do not want to include themselves in this teaching - to reply something to those that insult them, lest anger will overpower them and they become involved in the matter more than is necessary. And about them they, may their memory be Blessed, said (Shabbat 88b), "Those who are humiliated but do not humiliate [back], who hear their insult and do not reply - about them the verse states (Judges 5:31), 'but those who love Him are like the sun coming out in its strength.'"

Mitzvah 339
That we not sell a field in the Land of Israel in perpetuity: That we not sell a field in the Land of Israel in perpetuity, as it is stated (Leviticus 25:23), "But the land shall not be sold in perpetuity." That is, the buyer and seller should not stipulate between them that their sale be in perpetuity - and even though the Jubilee will void [it] against their will; as it is impossible for them to stipulate about this, since it is against the commandments of the Torah - nonetheless, if they did it, they have violated this negative commandment. That is the opinion of Rambam, may his memory be Blessed (Mishneh Torah, Laws of Sabbatical Year and the Jubilee 11:1). But Ramban, may his memory be Blessed, wrote (Ramban on Leviticus 25:23, and on Sefer HaMitzvot LaRambam, Mitzvot Lo Taase 227) that the words of the Master about this are like the matter that is mentioned in the first [chapter] of Temurah 4b, where Rava, differing with Abbaye said, "As anything that the [Torah] said not to do - if he did it, it is ineffective and he is lashed, as he has violated an edict of the King." But he, may his memory be Blessed, explained it in a different manner; that it warns (prohibits) us to not put the Land in the hand of the gentiles in perpetuity - meaning that we not sell it to them in perpetuity. He explained the verse like this: You shall not sell [it] to one who will hold it forever, and that is a gentile. But an Israelite will return it. And if he stipulated with the gentile to return it, it is permitted to sell it to him.

That which I have written in the commandment of the counting of the years of the Jubilee in this Order (Sefer HaChinukh 330) is from the roots of the commandment of the Jubilee.

From the laws of the commandment is that which they, may their memory be Blessed, said (Bava Metzia 79a) that [in a case of] one who sells his field for sixty years or more - meaning that he mentions a sum of years - it does not return in the Jubilee. As the only thing that returns in the Jubilee is something that was sold undifferentiatedly or in perpetuity. As we said above, when the sale is made in perpetuity, both [parties] have transgressed this law and their actions are ineffective - as one may not make conditions to violate the Torah, and the Torah stated, "But the land shall not be sold in perpetuity." But if, they mention a number of years between them, this is not perpetuity. And maybe (However) they, may their memory be Blessed, learned this thing from that which the verse stated, "shall not be sold in perpetuity," and it did not state "shall only be sold until the Jubilee" - which implies that anything other than a final (irreversible) sale does not return in the Jubilee.

And Ramban, may his memory be Blessed, explicitly wrote in his novellae (Ramban on Makkot, 3b) that [in the case of] one who stipulates, "On condition that the field will not return in the Jubilee," his condition is not a condition and it returns in the Jubilee - even though the same is not true for the sabbatical year. As if one [loans] on condition that it will not be released by the seventh [year], it is not released by the seventh [year] - since any condition about money stands. And he gave a reason about the thing: That regarding the sabbatical year, only the lender is warned about the cancellation of debts - and as it is written (Deuteronomy 15:2), "every creditor should release his hand from that which he lent his neighbor" - but not the borrower. As if he wants to repay, the option is in his hand. But regarding the Jubilee both of them, the buyer and the seller, are warned, and as we have written.

Sefer HaChinukh

As "shall not be sold in perpetuity," is stated to both of them, 'since the land is the Lord's,' and it is not in the hand of a person to sell it finally. And since the obligation is upon both of them, neither has the [authority] to forgive about the thing. Rather the land is forcibly returned to the one with the holding of the Land - and even if they make a thousand conditions that it should not return in the Jubilee. And it is a good reason.

And also, from the laws of the commandment is that which they, may their memory be Blessed, said (Arakhin 30a) that one who sells a field of holding and he had other lands - that is, land that he purchased or [others] gave to him as a gift - and [then] he sells those fields to redeem his field of holding that he sold, he is not heeded. As it is written in the section of the field of holding (Leviticus 25:26), "but he finds enough to redeem" - and the explanation comes about it, that it is until he finds something that was not available to him at the time of the sale. And so [too,] if he borrowed and wished to redeem with that loan, he is not heeded - as it is stated, "and his hand reached," and not that he borrowed.

Fields of holding are those that came as an inheritance to each Israelite in the division of the Land, as well as anyone who merited and had his holding added to, due to shifts in the possession by a daughter that inherits possession. As it is a well-known thing that "and the possession should not move" (Numbers 36:7), was only stated about that generation alone. These are the ones called the fields of holding, and their laws are a novelty from the Torah - differing from other lands for the purposes of redemption: As a field of holding can be redeemed by the seller or its redeemer after two years, against the will of the buyer; whereas other fields - which are called a purchased field - can only be redeemed with the buyer's consent, [or else] they stay with the buyer until the Jubilee.

And regarding the difference of houses from fields, we have already written their law later in its place (Sefer Hachinukh 340) - that the law of the houses of open (unwalled) towns is like the field of holding - meaning, that they [can also be redeemed] against the buyer's will; as it is written (Leviticus 25:31), "it may be redeemed." And their power is greater than the fields, in that they can be redeemed even within the [first] year, like the law of houses of walled cities. And the law of houses of walled cities is also explained in Scripture, and I have already written it later as well.

And from the content of the commandment is that which they, may their memory be Blessed, also said (Bava Metzia 108a) that if one purchased a field of holding and planted trees on it and thereby enhanced [the field]; when it returns, we evaluate the enhancement that is in it for the buyer. As it is stated (Leviticus 25:33), "the sale of the house shall go out," - and the traditional received explanation comes about it [that] the house goes back, but the enhancement does not go back. And that which they, may their memory be Blessed, also said (Arakhin 29b) that if one sells his field - whether it is a field of holding or another field - he is not permitted to redeem it in less than two years, even with the permission of the buyer. As Scripture commands that the sale stay intact for two years regardless, from that which it is written (Leviticus 25:15), "for the number of years of harvests shall he sell it to you" - that is the warning to the seller; the warning to the buyer is from that which it is written, "In the number of years shall you buy"; and the minimum of [what can be referred to as] "years" is two. It seems that the matter is so that no one will sell his land without difficulty, and he should not think that he will return and buy it from the hand of the buyer tomorrow. Rather he should know that he will not be able to eat from its produce in any way for two full years from the time of the sale. And they, may their memory be Blessed, also said (Arakhin 29b) that the buyer must consume two harvests during those two years, as it is stated, "years of harvests." Therefore, if one of these two years is a year of blight or plant-disease, or a [sabbatical year], it does not count in the tally. [But they, may their memory be Blessed, said that a fallow year is counted.] If he sold it in the Jubilee year itself, the sale is not a sale, and the money is returned to its owner. If he sold just the trees, they may [also] not be redeemed in less than two years. But if they are not redeemed during the Jubilee [cycle], they do not return in the Jubilee - as it is stated (Leviticus 27:25), "and return to his holding," but not to the trees. If he sold it to the first one and the first one [sold it] to the second one and the second one to the third one - and even if there were one hundred or more [buyers] - the field returns to the [original] owner at the Jubilee, as it is stated (Leviticus 27:24), "to he who has a holding of the land." And the rest of its details are at the end of Arakhin (see Mishneh Torah, Laws of Sabbatical Year and the Jubilee 10).

And [it] is practiced by males and females in the Land of Israel when its inhabitants are upon it; as all the matters of the Jubilee are only [applied] at the time when its inhabitants are upon it, as we wrote above. One who transgressed it and sold his field in perpetuity - and likewise one who purchased it from him in this way - is lashed, even though their words are not effective. And that is if they performed some act in the thing, as we do not administer lashes for a negative commandment that does not [involve] an act. This is the opinion of Rambam, may his memory be Blessed. But according to the opinion of Ramban, may his memory be Blessed, there are no lashes in this at all, as I wrote at the top of the commandment.

Mitzvah 340
The commandment of returning land to its owners on the Jubilee: To return all the lands - whether a house, or a field, or a vineyard or orchards - to their owners without money and without a price on the Jubilee year, as it is stated (Leviticus 25:24), "And in all the land of your holding, you shall give redemption to the land." [This is] to say in all the Land of Israel, which is your holding, you shall give redemption to the land. And Scripture elucidated the matter of redemption - which is return of the land to its owner; and as it is written (Leviticus 25:13), "In this jubilee year, each man shall return to his holding."

What we wrote at the beginning of this Order (Sefer HaChinukh 330) is from the roots of the commandment.

From the laws of the commandment: A few of them are elucidated in Scripture - how the law should be of the seller with the buyer when he wants to redeem his sold possession before the Jubilee year. And the distinction that Scripture elucidates is between one who sells a house in a walled city and one who sells one in open cities, that are called cities of chatserim in the language of Scripture. As the law of houses of open cities is like the law of fields. And they, may their memory be Blessed, also said (Arakhin 31a) about this commandment, that if [one] sold his house among the houses of walled cities to another and the first buyer sold it to a second within the [first] year, we count [the year according to] the first. And once the year comes to an end for the first, the house is finalized to the second (it is permanently his). As the matter of selling a house among the houses of the walled cities which is permanent [after] a year is a type of penalty, with which the Torah penalized the seller, on account of love of the Land. And since it stood for a year in the hand of someone besides him, it is fitting that it be finalized in the hand of the second. And further, since the first sold it to the second, all of the right [to it] is his. And had it stood for a full year in the hand of the first, it would already have been finalized in his hand.

And that which our Rabbis, may their memory be Blessed, also said (Arakhin 31b) that if the [last] day of the twelfth month arrives and [the original owner] does not find the buyer [to redeem it from him, behold he places his money in the court, breaks the door of the house and enters; and when the buyer comes,] he comes and takes his money. And that which they said (Arakhin 31b) that one who sells a house in the walled cities and the Jubilee arrives in the midst of the year of the sale, it does not go back immediately with the [start of the] Jubilee, but its law is like in other years in the years of the Jubilee [cycle] - that it is finalized with the [end of the] year if the seller does not want to redeem it. And that which they said (Arakhin 33a) [regarding] the seller of a house in the open cities - that if he wants, he can redeem [it] immediately like the law of a house from the houses of walled cities; and if does not want to redeem [it] immediately, he can redeem it even after a year like the law of fields. As they have the better power of [both] the fields, and the houses of the walled cities. And that which they said (Arakhin 32a) that the law of everything that is inside the wall, such as gardens, bathhouses, and birdhouses, is like the law of houses - as from that it is written (Leviticus 25:30), "that is in the city," it includes it all. But if there were fields inside the city, their law is like fields outside of the city, as it is stated, "the house will be established" - meaning to say, the house and all that is similar to a house, such as bathhouses, and birdhouses and even orchards, but not fields. And a house that does not have four ells by four ells is not called a house; and therefore, it is not finalized. And a house is not finalized in Jerusalem. And a city that its roofs are its walls does not have the status of of one surrounded by a wall, but rather we require that it has a wall besides its roofs. And we also require that it was first surrounded and settled afterwards, but if it was settled [first] and surrounded afterwards, that is not a walled city. And we only rely upon a wall that surrounded [a city] from the time that Yehoshua conquered the Land. And once they were exiled in the first destruction [of the Temple], the holiness of a walled city was nullified. But when Ezra came in the second coming [to the Land of Israel], all of the cities surrounded by walls at that time were sanctified; since their coming in the the time of Ezra which was the second coming, was like their coming in the time of Yehoshua: Just like their coming in the time of Yehoshua [provided that] they counted the sabbatical years and Jubilees, the walled cities were sanctified and they become obligated in the tithe; so too at the time of Ezra was it so. And so too, when the messiah will come with the third coming, we will begin to count the sabbatical years and Jubilees, the houses of walled cities that will be surrounded at that time will be sanctified and every place that will be conquered will be obligated in tithes. As it is stated (Deuteronomy 30:5), "And the Lord, your God, will bring you, etc." - and they said (Arakhin 32b), "It compares your inheriting to the inheriting of your ancestors, etc." And the rest of its details are elucidated in Tractate Arakhin (see Mishneh Torah, Laws of Sabbatical Year and the Jubilee 12).

And [it] is practiced by males and females in the Land of Israel and at the time that the Jubilee is practiced. And I have already written at which time the Jubilee is practiced, above - and it is at the time that all of Israel is on their land in their inhabitation. And one who transgresses this and holds the land that is in his hand and does not return it to its owner has violated this positive commandment; and his punishment is very great, as it is as if he denied the story of creation.

Mitzvah 341

The law of redemption of houses of walled cities until the completion of a year: That there be redemption of properties that are within a city surrounded by a wall until the completion of one year. And after the year, it will be in the possession of the one that buys them. And they do not go back in the Jubilee, as it is stated (Leviticus 25:29, "And if a man sells a dwelling house in a walled city, etc." I have already written above (Sefer HaChinukh 340) that the matter of the [sale of the] house of a walled city being finalized after a year is from the angle of love of the Land, in order that one who sells it makes efforts to redeem it quickly.

From the laws of the commandment is that which they, may their memory be Blessed, said (Arakhin 31a) that the seller may redeem it at any time that he wants within the year. And when he redeems it, he gives him all of the money that he received in its sale; and he does not deduct anything to him because of the time that he lived there [as rent]. And even though this is generally forbidden - as it is a method of interest - the Torah permitted it here, as is [found] in Arakhin 31a. And the other relatives may not redeem it, but rather only the seller himself. This is the opinion of Rambam, may his memory be Blessed, but it does not appear so in Kiddushin 21a. And he may not borrow and redeem [with that money]; but rather he may sell other properties if he has [any] and redeem it, or if he profited monies or [others] gave them to him, he may redeem it with them. But he may not redeem it in halves - meaning that he repays part of the money at [one] time and [part of it at] another [time], as they, may their memory be Blessed, said in Kiddushin 20b in the first chapter. And if the buyer died within the year, he may redeem from the hand of his son. And if the seller died, the son of the seller may also redeem it from the hand of the buyer. And the rest of its details are in Tractate Arakhin.

And [it] is practiced in the Land of Israel by males and females at the time that the Jubilee is practiced.

Mitzvah 342

To not change the open areas of the Levites: Not to change the open areas of the cities of the Levites and their fields - meaning to say, that a city may not be made into an open area, nor an open area into a city, a field into an open area, nor an open area into a field. And the law is the same about an open area (another textual variant: field) into a city and a city into an open area (another textual variant: field) - that one may not change anything about their content. And this matter is well-known, as the Torah commanded (Numbers 35:2-7) that the other tribes cede certain cities to the tribe of Levi; and these are forty-eight cities, with the six cities of refuge that were among them. And it also commanded that there be in these cities a thousand ells of open area - meaning a place open for space and beauty for the city; and two thousand ells beyond that for the sake of fields and vineyards, and this is also of the beauty of the city and from that which it needs, as it is explained in Sotah 27b. And this prevention comes about this, that these matters never be changed. And concerning this it states (Leviticus 25:34), "And the fields of open areas of their cities shall not be sold" - meaning, shall not be changed. As it is not speaking about actual selling, since it is explicitly written in Scripture (Leviticus 25:32), "a perpetual redemption shall there be for the Levites" - which implies that they are permitted to sell them.

It is from the roots of the commandment [that it is] because the cities of the Levites were prepared for the needs of all the other tribes; as it was the tribe that was selected for the service of God - and all of their efforts were about wisdom, as they were not preoccupied with the working of the land like the rest of the the tribes of Israel. And about them is it stated (Deuteronomy 33:10), "They shall teach Your statutes to Yaakov and Your law to Israel." And because of this - that wisdom was within them - the dealings of all of Israel were constantly with them; beside that there were among their cities, the cities of refuge for [those charged with manslaughter]. And from this also, the eyes of all of Israel were upon their cities, as a man cannot tell what [tomorrow will bring]. Hence it was appropriate that these cities - that the hand of all is equal with them and the heart of all are upon them - be of the utmost beauty and loveliness. And there is glory for all of Israel with this. And because of this, the command came about them, not to change any of their contents; for the Master of Wisdom established them, set them up and decided on their boundaries. And He saw that this was good, and [so] any reversal after His word is only detrimental and a disparagement.

From the laws of the commandment is that which, they, may their memory be Blessed, said (Makkot 12a) [that] beyond these three thousand ells that we said above that is of open space, fields and vineyards, we give to each city a cemetery, as it is stated (Numbers 35:3), "and their open spaces shall be for their beasts and their property and all their animals (chayatam)" - and the explanation came about this, that it was was given for the living (chayim), and not for burial. And that which they also said (Arakhin 33b) [about] priests or Levites that sold one of their fields or a house even in a walled city, [it can] always be redeemed, even from the hand of what is consecrated, as it is stated (Leviticus 25:33), "a perpetual redemption shall there be for the Levites." And [in the case of] an Israelite who inherits [property] from his mother's father who was a Levite, behold he may redeem like the Levites. And the rest of its details are elucidated at the end of Arakhin.

And this commandment is practiced in the Land of Israel at the time when Israel is there - whether by Levites or by Israelites - by males and females, as all are obligated never to change the three places spoken about: the city; the open space; and the fields and vineyards. And it would seem that anyone who did change them with witnesses and a warning would be liable for lashes. But I did not know the measure of this change - how much it would be for him to be liable for it. Be wise, my son, and know it. And Rambam, may his memory be Blessed, wrote concerning this commandment (Mishneh Torah, Laws of Sabbatical Year and the Jubilee 13:12), "Why did the Levites not merit [a portion] in the possession of the Land of Israel and in the spoils of war, with his brethren? Because they were set aside to serve God, may He be Blessed, and minister unto Him and to instruct His just paths. And therefore they were set apart from the ways of the world: They do not wage war like the remainder of the Israelites, nor do they [receive an inheritance], nor do they acquire [things] for themselves through the power of their bodies. Instead, they are God's legion - as it is stated (Deuteronomy 13:11), 'May the Lord bless His legion' - and He provides for them, as it is stated (Numbers 18:20), 'I am your portion and your possession.' And it is not only the tribe of Levi that is included in this, but each and every man that comes to the world whose spirit has moved him to be separated and to stand in front of God and to serve Him, to know His straight and righteous paths and to teach them to others - the yoke of the many calculations that people seek out is lifted from upon his neck. And behold, he is sanctified to become holy of holies, and God will be his possession for ever and ever. And he will acquire the thing that he needs in this world, just as the tribe of Levi acquired [it]. And so, David states (Psalms 16:5), 'The Lord is my appointed portion and my cup, you sustain my fate.'"

Sefer HaChinukh

Mitzvah 343
To not lend with interest to an Israelite: To not lend with interest to an Israelite, as it is written (Leviticus 25:37), "You shall not give your money with interest, nor should you give your sustenance with increase." And these are not two prohibitions - as increase is interest, and interest is increase; and as they, may their memory be Blessed, said in [Bava] Metzia, "You will not find interest without increase or increase without interest. So why did the verse divide them?" [That is] meaning to say, why did it divide them and not write, "Give neither your money nor your food with interest." "To cause the transgression of two prohibitions" - meaning to say, to give multiple warnings about it (Bava Metzia 61a). And this matter is what I have said above (Sefer HaChinukh 336), that the Torah will occasionally repeat warnings about that which it wanted to distance us from greatly. And it is possible for us to say about this, similar to what they, may their memory be Blessed, said about other matters, "The Torah speaks like the language of man" (Berakhot 31b). And likewise, the Torah is constantly warning about that which requires our vigilance in the way that people will repeat their conditions and speak much when they warn one another about a weighty matter - so that the [listener] be aware and vigilant about it in all circumstances. And even though it is fitting that a person should be most careful about the word of God - even if he heard the word through the slightest hint - this is all from His great kindnesses upon His creatures, that in a few places He repeated warnings for them many times - like a parent discipline his child. And we should therefore thank Him for all the goodness that He, Blessed be He, bestowed upon us.

What I have written about it in the warning (negative commandment) for the guarantor, witnesses and scribe that they should not be involved is loans with interest (Sefer HaChinukh 68) is from the root of the commandment:

The laws of the commandment: For example, the distinctions that they, may their memory be Blessed, taught us about this warning - that they said that there is interest that is prohibited from the Torah, which they call (Bava Metzia 61b) 'fixed interest'; and there is interest which is below this and it is rabbinically prohibited, which they, may their memory be Blessed, called 'the dust of interest'; and there is another interest, which is lower than these first two and it (should have been) is strictly speaking permitted, as it is far removed from Torah-level interest, to the point that it is not suited to decree about at all, but the Sages were strict in this matter, in their seeing, that the Torah was very strict about it, and the many warnings about the matter of interest, and they forbade it so that people would not cheat, [and] not for some other reason. And these are the three types of interest: Torah level interest is when anyone says to his fellow, "Lend me a maneh and I will give you a perutah every day for it," or thirty perutah a month, or more or less, until I pay it [back]; or if he says, "Lend me a hundred dinar, for a hundred and twenty [after] a year"; or if he lends money and takes a house or courtyard as collateral that he will hold and reap the produce until he returns his money, without subtracting something from the loan - that is fixed interest that is prohibited from the Torah. And they, may their memory be Blessed, said (Bava Metzia 63b) more generally, "And payment for 'Wait for me' is forbidden by the Torah," and that is so long as it came from the hand of the lender to the borrower - that is forbidden by Torah writ. And they, may their memory be Blessed, said about it, "Fixed interest can be extracted by judges" (Bava Metzia 61b). That is, the court may seize assets from the borrower and deduct from them, as is the law for theft and torts. But other commentators explain "extracted by judges" regarding coercion, meaning to say that the court coerces the borrower with whips to return it - as they do with anyone who says that he will not fulfill a positive commandment.

Every other form of interest aside from those mentioned is called rabbinic interest and is [also] called 'the dust of usury', and it cannot be extracted by judges. And the Sages prohibited these as a decree so that a person not come to [lending with] interest from Torah writ. And among them are like that which they, may their memory be Blessed, said (Bava Metzia 70b) that one cannot accept 'iron sheep' from an Israelite - the understanding of 'iron sheep' is one who takes money on condition that the principle will stay intact for the money's owner from the one who receives it, and [that] he [also] takes his share of the profit. And so [too,] may one not set [the price] for produce until the market rate is disseminated; though if the market rate is disseminated, we can set [a price] - for [even if] the [seller] may not have it, [someone else] has it. And to what do these words apply, that we never set [the price] until the market price has been disseminated? When he does not have it - meaning, from that type that he set [the price]; but if he does have some of it - and even if he only had a seah - he may set [the price] for several seah, [as with a loan]. For the law follows Shmuel who said like this in the Gemara (Bava Metzia 75a). And that which we said that he must have the same type, there are some of the commentators that said he must have exactly the same type (Beit Yosef, Yoreh De'ah 175), such that he may not set the price in new wheat if he only has old wheat - he must have exactly like the type for which he is setting [the price]. But there are others of them that said that there is no distinction between old and new, as so long as he has from the same type, it is permitted. And regardless, if he has from the same type, he may set [the price] with it even if it is lacking one or two [preparatory types of] work. But if it is lacking three [preparatory types] of work, behold, he is like one that does not have from that type. And in the Gemara, the chapter [entitled] Eizehu Nesekh (Bava Metzia 74a), the elucidation appears at length on the distinction of these [types of] work [involved] with wheat, as well as with the tools of a potter and with other things.

And so [too,] from the matter of the commandment is that which they prohibited to lend money with land [as collateral] and to make a condition with the borrower, "If you do not return the money from now until day x, the land will be mine" (Bava Metzia 66a); because the acquisition is not effective, as it is a dependence (asmakhta). [This is] meaning to say that the person's mind was depending on this at the time of the [loan] - that is that he would return the money - but his hand did not reach to fulfill the matter. And this is a type of duress. And [with] all that is of this type, we must be concerned about the eating of the produce on account of interest. And many types of dependence about the matter of interest and about other matters are spoken of in the Gemara. And my teacher, may God protect him, taught us more generally about the matter of dependences, that any time a person makes a condition with his fellow that is by way of a penalty - that is, if it not be so, he will be punished with such and such money - is called a dependence. And concerning this, they, may their memory be Blessed, said always (Bava Metzia 66b), "Dependences do not acquire." And with a different expression did they, may their memory be Blessed, also say, "Any 'that if' does not acquire." But any condition that a person makes with his fellow and says, "If you do such, I will do such and such" - as [is] the manner of people to make conditions in this way of speaking - is not included in dependencies at all, God forbid. For if so, how would we ever 'find our hands and feet' with any conditions people make with one another - as they are all with the expression, 'if'; since it is impossible without this. Moreover, what could we say about the many conditions that pertain to bills of divorce and marriages - as they are all with the expression, 'if?' Rather, that which we have written is certainly a correct explanation: That we only say, 'dependences do not acquire,' about that which people make conditions one with another by way of a penalty - such as "If I don't pay you by day x, the field will be yours," or whatever the collateral is, and all that is similar to it; but not for the great many other conditions that people make with each other - such as, "If you go to place x, I will give you such and such," or "If you do thing x for me, I will give you two hundred zuz," and anything like that. Understand this, my son, and give your heart to it, as through this you will remove a great cloud from between your eyes about the words of the Gemara in many places.

They also said (Bava Metzia 75b) that early or late interest is the 'dust of interest' and prohibited rabbinically. How is this? If one placed his eyes that he wanted to borrow money from someone and sent him gifts in order that he will lend to him - that is early interest. If he borrowed from him and returned the money to him, and then sent gifts [in recognition of the fact] that [the lender's] money was idle with him - that is late interest. And likewise, some of the commentators said (Mishneh Torah, Laws of Creditor and Debtor 6:7) that if one lends money to his fellow for [collateral of] a place that constantly produces value - such as a courtyard, bathhouse or store - [if it is] without a deduction [for that value], behold it is fixed interest; and with a deduction, behold it is 'dust of interest.' But one who lends money for a place that does not constantly produce value - such as a field or a vineyard, as its value is not always found, since sometimes the expense involved exceeds the revenues - without a deduction, it is 'dust of interest'; and with a deduction, it is permitted. But there are some of them that say that the Sages, may their memory be Blessed, prohibited even a field and a vineyard with a deduction; and the only permissible form of collateral that they found is the 'collateral of Sura,' [in which] they would write, "At the end of these years, this land will revert without money." And the truth according to what seemed from the Gemara to our teachers, may God protect them, with the good commentaries is that any collateral that is made with a deduction - whether it is a house or bathhouse that produces profits, and all the more so with a field or vineyard - it is all permitted with a deduction. And so, have they practiced in our land based on their words? But one who is concerned for the view of the great savants who were strict in this matter will be Blessed from the Heavens.

And what was the other interest that we said above that they, may their memory be Blessed, prohibited to prevent cheating on interest? Such as if a person says to his fellow, "Lend me a maneh (one hundred zuz)," and [the other responds], "I have no maneh, [but] I have a maneh's worth of wheat": [If] he gives him the wheat for a maneh and buys them back for ninety, this would certainly be logically permitted, except that the Sages forbade it because of cheating with interest. As behold, this thing appears like interest - as this one gave ninety dinar, but he is taking a hundred. Yet if he transgressed and did this, [the lender can] extract the full hundred, as there is not even the 'dust of interest' here. It is only as a fence that the Sages were strict about the matter. Also, if one had a field as collateral, he may not rent it to its owner, because of cheating with interest; and similar to these matters, as is found in the Gemara (Bava Metzia 68a). And even though they forbade these things only because of cheating with interest, there are some things they permitted, even though they are similar to true interest. And the Sages permitted them because they did not see a concern about them [in order] to make a decree at all: And that is that they permitted a person to sell a debt at a discount; and the Sages also permitted a person to give his fellow a dinar so that he will say to another Israelite that he lend [the first] a maneh. And they, may their memory be Blessed, said (Bava Metzia 69b) more generally that the Torah only forbade interest that goes from the hand of the borrower to the lender - as this is the way of the world. As the Torah always chooses the [more common case] and leaves out the details (unusual cases). And since the way of the world is like this, it [only] warned the borrower and the lender. And even though they said so and it is true, it is fitting for any scrupulous person to distance himself with all of his might from every matter that has cheating with interest in it. And anyone who pursues ways to take interest payments from an Israelite will eventually become poor - and as they, may their memory be Blessed, said (Bava Metzia 71a), that the property of anyone who deals in interest will shrink. [They] also said (Bava Metzia 75b) that a perutah of interest causes a loss of storehouses of money. And the rest of the many details of the commandment are in Bava Metzia, the chapter [entitled] Eizehu Nesekh (see Tur, Yoreh Deah 167).

And [it] is practiced in every place and at all times by males and females. And one who transgresses this and gave a loan with interest from Torah writ has violated a negative commandment, and [so] we extract money from him with judges; as the court may seize his assets in the way that the court seizes his assets for his theft or for his damages, according to the view of some of the commentators - or we extract if from him by way of coercion in the way that we coerce an Israelite who does not want to fulfill a positive commandment, according to the view of some of our rabbis, may God protect them. And if he lent with interest that is forbidden [rabbinically] that is called 'the dust of interest,' he has violated a rabbinic proscription, but the money cannot be extracted by judges. However if the borrower seized enough for the [value] of that interest from the lender, we do not extract it from his hand. And if he transgressed and lent with interest, which they, may their memory be Blessed, forbade only because of cheating with interest; there is no need to say that we do not extract it from the lender if he took it, as we even extract if from the borrower and give it to the lender - as they [already] transgressed and stipulated this between them. As since they, may their memory be Blessed, were only stringent about the thing because of cheating with interest, they did not concern themselves with the thing ex post facto. And this is called ex post facto, since the words between the lender and the borrower have [already] been fulfilled.

Mitzvah 344

Sefer HaChinukh

That we not make a Hebrew slave perform demeaning work, like the work of a Canaanite (gentile) slave: That we not make a Hebrew slave perform work that is very demeaning and humiliating, which is the way to make a Canaanite slave work - as it is written (Leviticus 25:29), "do not have him work with the work of a slave." And they, may their memory be Blessed, said in Sifra, Behar, Chapter 7:2 in explanation of this matter, "He should not carry your cushion" (see Sefer HaMitzvot LaRambam, Mitzvot Lo Taase 257) - which is a small cloth that people make to sit upon in every place if they tire - and it is the way of a demeaned slave to take this [item] and carry it behind his master. And they said likewise (Sifra, Behar, Chapter 7:2), "Nor should he carry his vessels in front of him into the bathhouse." And they, may their memory be Blessed, elucidated these types of work, and the law is the same for anything that is similar to them. It comes out that a person should be mindful of which type of work he orders his Hebrew slave to perform. And this is part of the principle which they, may their memory be Blessed, said (Kiddushin 22a), "Anyone who acquires a Hebrew slave is like he has acquired a master for himself." Nonetheless, from that which the verse states (Leviticus 25:40), "Like a laborer, like a boarder shall he be with you," it should be learned that a man may command him to do anything that it is the way of people to command a laborer or a boarder. And truthfully, a laborer - who is a free man - is usually not employed for degrading work; and likewise a boarder - who is a man who comes to live in a different land. And the way of boarders is is to do the work of the homeowner with whom they are living, from their [own] will - therefore [a householder] will not do very demeaning work with him. And hence Scripture sated, "Like a laborer, like a boarder shall he be with you," because these two men - even though they do work - their work is not usually demeaning work. Still, the slave must behave according to the way of a slave and honor his master with all of his might, and not become haughty with all that we have said.

It is from the roots of the commandment [that it is] so that a person place upon his heart that our nation is the most honored of all of them. And through that, he will love his people and his Torah. And he will also place upon his heart, that just as this slave was sold because of his desperation, so is it possible that the same could happen to the one who acquires him, or to one of his sons - if [their] sin causes it to them. And through honoring his slave, he will certainly think this thought; and through this thought he will be careful from sinning to God. And there is another purpose in the thing - that a man learn the traits of kindness and mercy, and distance himself from the evil trait of cruelty. And by preparing his soul for goodness, it will receive good - [as] God wishes to bestow from His blessings on His creations, as I have written many times before in previous commandments.

The laws of the commandment: That which they, may their memory be Blessed, were exacting about in the first chapter of Kiddushin 22b from that which the verse stated (Deuteronomy 15:16), "for it is good for him with you" - "'With you' regarding food, 'with you' regarding drink; that you should not eat refined bread and he eat coarse bread, nor should you drink aged wine and he drink unaged wine, nor should you sleep on pillows and he sleep on straw." They, may their memory be Blessed, likewise said (Sifra, Behar, Chapter 7:3) that the master should not live in the town and the slave in the village, as it is stated (Leviticus 25:41), "And he shall leave from with you." And the rest of its details are in the Sifra and in Kiddushin (See Tur, Yoreh Deah 267).

And [it] is practiced by males and females at the time that the Jubilee is practiced; and I have already written when the Jubilee is practiced at the beginning of the Order (Sefer HaChinukh 330). And even though it is not fitting for a woman to acquire a slave on account of suspicion, she is still included in the commandment nonetheless. And if one transgressed this commandment and had his Hebrew slave do degrading work, he has violated this negative commandment. Though from what it appears, there is no liability for lashes - as there is no act [involved] with it; since a slave is disciplined with words to get him him to do work - [whether] demeaning or honorable. And I already wrote above (Sefer HaChinuch, 241) that any negative commandment that can be transgressed without an act - even if he does any act with it, he should still not be made liable for lashes; as it is still termed a negative commandment without an act. This is my approach - it is clear in my eyes.

Mitzvah 345

Sefer HaChinukh

That we not sell a Hebrew slave upon the auctioning stone: - That we not sell a Hebrew slave in the way that we sell Canaanite (gentile) slaves, by announcement upon the auctioning stone, but rather discreetly and in an honorable fashion. And so did they say (Sifra, Behar, Section 6:1), "'They shall not be sold with the sale of a slave' (Leviticus 25:42) - that they not be sold in a market-stand and be placed up on the auctioning stone."

The root of this commandment is well-known - that it is not fitting for a person to treat the honor of his fellow lightly; even if his sins have brought him to be sold. As he does not know if maybe tomorrow, he will also come to this. The elucidation of this commandment is in Kiddushin and its laws are included in its essence - there is no need to be lengthy about them.

And [it] is practiced by males and females at the time that the Jubilee is practiced, as [the law of] Hebrew slaves is only practiced at the time of the Jubilee, as I wrote above (Sefer HaChinukh 330). And one who transgresses this and sells a Hebrew slave in the way that Canaanite slaves are sold has violated a negative commandment. But from what appears, there is no liability for lashes, since it is possible to transgress it without an act.

Mitzvah 346

To not make a Hebrew slave perform oppressive work: To not make a Hebrew slave do oppressive work, as it is stated (Leviticus 25:43), "do not subjugate him with oppressive work." And what is oppressive work? They, may their memory be Blessed, explained (Sifra, Behar, Section 6:2) that it is work that does not have a limit, and so [too,] work that a person does not need but he does it so that the slave not be idle - and like they, may their memory be Blessed said, "A man should not say to him, 'Hoe underneath the vines until I come,' as behold he has not given him a limit; but rather he should say to him, 'Hoe until x hour,' or 'until place y.' And they also said in Sifra that he should not say to him, "Heat this cup for me," when he does not need it; and all that is similar to it. But they, may their memory be Blessed, brought an example of the lightest type of work and the quickest to do - and all the more so [is it the case with] other ones. And the principle is that we only make him do work that we have a need for that work that we commanded him. The details of the commandment are short, and behold I have written a few of them.

And this commandment is practiced by males and females at the time the Jubilee is practiced. And we should not make him liable for lashes for it - since it is possible to transgress it with speech alone, without an act. And even though it is not practiced in our time, since the acquisition of Hebrew slaves is not practiced - nonetheless it is fitting for a person to be careful about the content of this commandment also today [if] the poor are members of his household. And he should be very careful about it and place upon his heart that wealth and poverty is a wheel that spins in the world, and it is from God. And He gives to the one that is straight in His eyes so long as He wants - but not a minute longer. As even if he gathers money like the dirt and buries it in the ground and acquires so many lands that they be countless, it will all be lost from him [if he sins] to God. But if he is righteous, the good will be preserved for him, as each type clings to its type.

Mitzvah 347

The commandment of work with a Canaanite slave forever: That we have a Canaanite slave work forever, meaning that we should never manumit him; and he should only go free for [suffering the loss of] a tooth or limb, as it appears in Scripture (Exodus 21:26-27) - or from the main limbs that are similar to them, meaning limbs that do not grow back, as the accepted traditional explanation comes about this (Kiddushin 24a) - as it is stated (Leviticus 25:46) "you shall work them forever." And they, may their memory be Blessed, said (Gittin 38a), "Rav Yehudah said, 'Anyone who manumits his slave is in violation of a positive commandment, as it says, "you shall work them forever."'" And [any] one from all of the [other] nations who was acquired by a Jew as a slave is called a Canaanite slave. But all slaves are attached with the name, Canaan, because Canaan was cursed to be a slave - he and his progeny - forever. And even though this section in which we were commanded to subjugate them is speaking about Canaanites - as it is written (Leviticus 25:44), "from the peoples that surround you may you purchase a slave or maid-servant," and it is written earlier (Leviticus 25:38), "to give to you the Land of Canaan" - it was known to the Sages, may their memory be Blessed, that it was not only Canaan and those in their land that were called Canaanite slaves. As the law is the same for all the rest of the nations - that they have the status of a Canaanite slave in every matter.

Also, if an Israelite has intercourse with a Canaanite slave woman - that is, a woman from the [other] nations who was purchased by an Israelite - behold the offspring from her is a Canaanite slave for all purposes (Yevamot 22a), and even if she is the slave of that Israelite that had intercourse with her. Similarly, [in the case of a free man] from the nations that had intercourse with a Canaanite slave woman of ours, the child is a Canaanite slave - as it it stated (Leviticus 25:45), "that they begot in your land." However [in the case of] one of our slaves that has intercourse with a [free woman] from the nations, the child is not a slave - as a slave has no [paternity]. And so [too,] a resident alien - that is, one that has accepted not to worship idolatry and he is living in our land - who sold himself to an Israelite, behold his status is that of a Canaanite slave. And they, may their memory be Blessed, said regarding a Canaanite slave (Yevamot 48b) that his master takes care of him up to twelve months; if he wants to deny and abandon idolatry, get circumcised and immerse for the sake of slavery and accept the commandments that Jewish women are obligated, it is good. But if not, it is forbidden for us to hold him in our homes longer than twelve months. Rather we sell him immediately. And [it is] about those slaves that were circumcised and immersed for the sake of slavery that we were commanded to work them forever.

It is from the roots of the commandment [that] since the people of Israel are the choicest of the human species and they were created to recognize their Creator and to serve in front of Him, it is fitting that they should have slaves to serve them. And if they do not have slaves from the nations, they would nonetheless need to subjugate their brethren, and [those subjugated] would be unable to strive in His service, Blessed be He. We were therefore commanded to retain these for our use - after they have been readied and have had idolatry removed from their mouths, lest they be a snare in our homes. And this [is the meaning of] the verse afterwards (Leviticus 25:46), "and as for your brothers, the Children of Israel, a man shall not subjugate his brother." That is to say that with this, you will not need to subjugate your brethren and you will all be prepared for the service of God. And even though the understanding of the verse is to warn not to subjugate a Hebrew slave with oppressive labor, there are seventy faces to the verses.

And given that the foundation of this commandment is in order to proliferate people's service of their Creator, the Sages, may their memory be Blessed, permitted [to transgress] this commandment whenever its nullification would cause [the fulfillment of] another commandment - and even for the sake of a rabbinic commandment, such as if there were not ten (a quorum) in the Synagogue and they needed to free the slave to complete the quorum (see Berakhot 47b). And let it not be difficult to you, how we can forsake this positive biblical commandment for the sake of a rabbinic one. As it is because the foundation of the commandment is only the proliferation of His service, Blessed be He: Since by manumitting him now, a commandment will be fulfilled. Moreover, he, himself will be increased in commandments that he was not obligated before the freeing. And this is [the understanding of] their, may their memory be Blessed, saying (Berakhot 47b) that is is permissible to free him - as they received the matter like this.

From the laws of the commandment is that which they, may their memory be Blessed, said (Kiddushin 22b) that he may acquire [his freedom] though money, a contract, or [an injury to] the main limbs that will not grow back - and they are twenty-four. And even though the law pertaining to him is to go out for the main limbs that do not grow back, he [still] requires a contract of manumission from the [master]; and we force the master to write [it] for him, since he caused him to lack one of the twenty-four well-known limbs. And they, may their memory be Blessed, said (Gittin 43b) that [in a case of] one who sells his slave to gentiles or Kuthites, or even to a resident alien, [the] slave goes out to freedom. And so [too, in the case of] an Israelite who lives in the Land [of Israel] who sold him to an Israelite who lives outside of the Land, in order that he take him outside of the Land - [the] slave goes out to freedom. And similarly, they, may their memory be Blessed, said (Gittin 40a) that if his master marries him to a free woman, or if lays tefillin on him, or [if] his master tells him to read three verses in a Torah scroll before the congregation or anything that is similar to these things about which only free men are obligated, [the slave] goes out to freedom with these and we force his master afterwards to write him a contract of manumission. And therefore, the master must be careful not to do any of these things at all, so that he will not violate this positive commandment, unless he did this for the honor of [another] commandment, as we explained. And the laws of the writing of the contract, its instruction and the rest of its details are in Kiddushin and Gittin (see Tur, Yoreh Deah 267 and Tur, Choshen Mishpat 197).

And [it] is practiced in every place and at all times by males and females. Even though women are forbidden to purchase slaves for themselves because of suspicion; if they did purchase them, it is forbidden for them to free them, but they must sell them instead. One who transgressed this and freed his slave not for the sake of a commandment - as we said - has violated this positive commandment.

Mitzvah 348

To not allow a gentile to work a Hebrew slave sold to him: That we not allow a gentile that dwells in our lands work a Hebrew slave, who sold himself to him, with oppressive work - as it is stated (Leviticus 25:53), "he shall not subjugate him oppressively in your eyes." And we should not say, "Since this Hebrew sinned against himself and sold himself to the gentile, let us leave him to suffer all the work. And they said in Sifra, Behar, Chapter 8:8), "'He shall not subjugate him oppressively in your eyes' - you are only commanded 'in your eyes.'" [This is] meaning to say that we are not obligated to look for it and to enter the house of the gentile to see if he has him work oppressively or not; but rather any time we see the thing, we have to prevent it from him.

The root of this commandment is revealed to all who see the sun. Its laws are included in its essence. And [it] is practiced by males and females at the time that our hand is powerful over the nations, that we have the power with us over them to command them to do a thing or not to do it. And one who transgresses it and saw the gentile make the Israelite work with oppressive work - and he has the power in his hand to prevent him - but he does not prevent him, violates this negative commandment. But we do not administer lashes for it, since there is no act [involved] with it.

Mitzvah 349

That we not prostrate ourselves on a figured stone, even to God: That we not prostrate ourselves on a figured stone, even to God, Blessed be He; as it is stated (Leviticus. 26:1), "and a figured stone you shall not place in your land, to prostate upon it." A figured stone refers to a stone that is adorned (see Sefer HaMitzvot LaRambam, Mitzvot Lo Taase 12). And so [too,] hewn stones that have been planed down with a scraper are also included in this prohibition of a figured stone.

From the roots of the commandment is what Rambam, may his memory be Blessed, wrote (Sefer HaMitzvotLaRambam, Mitzvot Lo Taase 12) that it is since they would do this for idolatry: They would place nicely figured stones before the idol and they would prostrate themselves upon [the stones] in front of it. It is [also] possible to say that the reason is because it seems like he is prostrating himself to the stone itself - since they prepared and beautified it, there is room for suspicion. But there is no room for suspicion for bowing on pretty clothing, as clothing is something that is quickly destroyed and [therefore] no one will make it into his god; whereas a stone, which is something lasting and has a [corresponding] minister in the Heavens - and like they, may their memory be Blessed, said (Chullin 40a), "Whether he speaks to the mountain, or to the gada of the mountain (to the angel that is appointed over the mountains)" - [he arouses] suspicion. And the Torah distances man greatly from doing anything about which [others might] suspect him; and also that they not stumble [by following his deeds].

From the laws of the commandment is that which they, may their memory be Blessed, said (Megillah 22b) that there is no liability for lashes unless he spreads his arms and legs, which would find him resting completely on the stone - as so did the accepted understanding come, that this is the prostration stated in the Torah. But without the spreading of the hands and legs, there is no lashes for it; but they would strike one who did this with lashes of rebellion. However, regarding [actual] idolatry there is no distinction between spreading of the hands and legs [and not] - as soon as one buries his face in the ground in front of it, he is stoned (Horayot 4a). And that which they, may their memory be Blessed, said (Mishneh Torah, Laws of Foreign Worship and Customs of the Nations 6:7) that if he placed mats on the stone floor and covered them, it is permissible to prostrate himself upon them. And that which they, may their memory be Blessed, said (Mishneh Torah, Laws of Foreign Worship and Customs of the Nations 6:7) that the prohibition [applies] everywhere except for the Temple, [where] it is permissible to prostate oneself to God on the stones; as it is stated, "you shall not place in your land" - in your lands you shall not prostrate yourselves, but you shall prostrate yourselves on the cut stones in the Temple. And from what it appears, this [distinction] is from the reason that I have said, that people will suspect the prostrater, that he not deify the stones. And since the Temple is chosen for the service of God, Blessed be He, and it is as [clear] to all as the sun in the middle of the day that there is no worship there except only to God, there is no room for suspicion. But according to the reason of Rambam, may his memory be Blessed - that it is to distance us from idolatry, since they were doing this for it - all the more so should it be fitting to distance all that is similar to it in the sanctified place, to avoid disqualifying the thoughts of the one who comes to prostrate himself to God in his thinking about them. However I know that our Rabbi had a correct reason for 'everything to which he turned' - but sometimes it is hidden from the inadequacy of the understanding of the listener. And the rest of the details of the commandment are in the Gemara, Megillah (See Mishneh Torah, Laws of Foreign Worship and Customs of the Nations 6).

And [it] is practiced in every place and at all times by males and females. And one who transgresses it and prostrated himself with spread arms and legs upon stones is flogged. 'But happy is he who guards the commandment.'

Mitzvah 350
The commandment that one who appraises a man give the value delineated in the Torah: To rule on appraisals of people; that is, one who says, "My appraisal is upon me" or "The appraisal of x is upon me," must give to the priest according to the amount that he said, and not less - as appears explicitly in Scripture about a male and female and according to the tally of [their] years - as it is stated (Leviticus 27:2), "If a man proclaims an oath of the appraisal of souls to the Lord." And the matter of appraisals is included in vows of consecration and we are therefore obligated to keep them on account of "he shall not profane his words" (Numbers 30:3), "you shall not delay" (Deuteronomy 23:22) and "he shall do like everything that comes out of his mouth" (Numbers 30:3).

It is from the roots of the commandment [that it is] since a person only belongs to the higher [realm] through speech, and this is the entire esteemed part in him. And it is what called the "living soul" (Genesis 2:7) of a man - as Onkelos' translates [this phrase as] "and there was a speaking spirit in man" - since the rest of the parts of the body die. And if a man loses this good part, the body remains dead and like an undesirable vessel. Therefore, he is obligated to [at least] fulfill his speech in whatever he uses it for matters of the Heavens, such as consecrations and with all matters of charity. And regarding all other matters of the world - even though there is no particular positive or negative commandment specified for them - the Sages commanded and warned with several warnings that a person should never change his words. And they also ordained to curse one who changes his words so long as an act is done with the matter. And that is the matter of [the curse of] "He who repaid" that is mentioned about them in many places, about which they said (Bava Metzia 44a), "Words and money [do not] acquire, but they said, etc." as it appears in the chapter [entitled] HaZahav. And I have already written at much length about the roots of oaths and vows in the Order of Vayishma Yitro in the commandment of "You shall not bear" (Sefer HaChinukh 30).

From the laws of the commandment is that which they, may their memory be Blessed, said (Arakhin 18b) that we received from the tradition that these years that are stated for appraisals are measured day to day - meaning from the day of birth - and also that all the shekel-coins stated there are the holy shekels. And we have known from the received tradition that the weight of a holy shekel is three hundred and twenty barley grains of pure silver. And the Sages have already added upon it and made its weight like the weight of the coin called the sela at the time of the Second [Temple], which is three hundred and eighty-four medium barley grains (so is it in Mishneh Torah, Laws of Sheqel Dues 1:2-3). And they, may their memory be Blessed, said that this sela is (four) dinar, and the dinar is six maah - and the maah is what was called gerah in the days of Moshe, as Onkelos translates gerah as maah - and its weight is sixteen barley grains.

And that which they, may their memory be Blessed, said (Arakhin 2a) that there is no distinction in appraisals whether he is handsome or ugly or sick or blind or stump-legged. Rather all are appraised according to [their] years, as the Torah commanded about them. And that which they said (Arakhin 2a) that the value is not like appraisal, such that one who says, "The value of x is upon me," gives according to what he is worth and we do not pay attention to the years at all - as the Torah only commanded to give the valuation according to years specifically for appraisal, as we explained. And [payment of] undifferentiated appraisals and values are for the upkeep of the [Temple] and we always give all of it into the cell that was prepared in the Temple for the consecrated items of the upkeep of the [Temple] (so is it found in Mishneh Torah, Laws of Appraisals and Devoted Property 1:10). And [also] the law of one [the sex of which is in doubt], a gentile or a slave who appraised or were appraised; the law of one who is dying that he has no appraisal or value; the law of one who is going out to be killed; the law of one who appraises one limb; the law of one who says, "My weight is upon me"; the law of one who says, "My height is upon me," or "My full height is upon me"; [the law of] one who says, "Gold and silver are upon me," but he did not specify from which [type of] coin (Menachot 104b); and the law of how it is that we arrange things for one who made an appraisal and his hand could not reach to pay what he appraised - and this is what the Sages said about this matter (Arakhin 23b): We take collateral from those obligated in appraisals and values, and we do not return the collateral during the day or the night; and we sell everything that is found to them of land and movable items - even clothing and household utensils, and there is no need to say, slaves and beasts. But we do not sell for them the clothing of their wives or their children - and not even clothes that he [just] dyed for their sake nor new shoes from when he bought them for their sake before he made the appraisal. And so [too,] one who consecrates all of his possessions, does not consecrate these.

And the matter of the arrangement is that we provide for the one that has appraisals or values [that he owes], thirty days of food and twelve months of clothing - clothes that are suitable for him - and his shoes and his tefillin, but not other books. And [we provide him with] a suitable bed and bedding. But we do not provide food and clothing for his wife and children, even though he is obligated in their food and clothing. And when we give him alone clothing for twelve months, it is only that which is suitable for him, but if he wore silk items and golden clothing, we take it off of him, and we provide him with suitable clothing for a man like him for weekdays, but not for Shabbat and holidays (Bava Metzia 113b). And if he was a craftsman, we provide him with tools of his trade - two craft tools from each and every type. How is this? If he was a carpenter, we provide him with two planes and two saws. And if he had many tools of one type and few of another type, we do not sell the many in order to buy him of the few. Rather we provide him with two of the many and all that he has of the few. But if he was a donkey driver or a shipowner, we do not provide him with the beast or the ship, even though their [sustenance] is only from them. And so [too,] if he is a Torah scholar and he has nothing with which to earn his livelihood besides his study, the commentators said that we do not leave him his books, as this is also not included in tools of a trade - and from here I have a proof that it is upon the student to bring the book to the teacher. But there are some of the commentators who said that we leave him the tractate that he is studying at that time - and they said Well, on account of the honor of the Torah.

And that which they, may their memory be Blessed, said (Arakhin 23a) that we ask about appraisals and values [in order to annul them] in the [same] way that we ask about other vows and consecrations. And they also said (Arakhin 24a) that if there were animals or slaves or jewels among the possessions of the appraiser and the traders say, "If he buys clothing of thirty dinar for this slave, he will increase his value by more than sixty"; or "If you wait on this animal for a month, its value will increase by double"; or "If they bring this jewel to place x, it will be worth much money" - we do not listen to them at all. Rather we sell everything in their place and in their time, as it is stated (Leviticus 27:23), "and he shall give the appraisal on that day, holy to the Lord." And the understanding came about this that this verse teaches about all consecrated things that we do not sustain them, we do not wait with them for the market day and we do not take them from one place to [another]. And this is the principle

- that they only have their place and time alone. And what are these words speaking about? About movable items. But we proclaim [the intention to sell] lands sixty consecutive days - morning and evening - and afterwards, we sell them.

And since the matter of arranging [this debt] has come to our hand, we shall write here that which they, may their memory be Blessed, said about a [general] debtor in the chapter [entitled] HaMekabel Sadeh Mechavero in Bava Metzia 113b: That there we say, "A teacher taught in front of Rav Nachman bar Yitzchak, 'In the [same] way that we arrange things with appraisals, so do we arrange things with a debtor.'" And they brought many challenges and solutions and the end of the matter is that which the Gemara brings, "A story of Eliyahu, who Rabbah bar Avoua found standing in a graveyard of gentiles. He said to him, 'What is [the law] about their arranging things for a debtor?'" And Rashi, may his memory be Blessed, and others had a textual variant [instead], "From where [do we know] about their arranging things for a debtor?" [This is] meaning to say, it was obvious to Rabbah bar Avoua that we arrange [things for a debtor], but he was asking Eliyahu, from which verse we learn it. "And Eliyahu answered him, 'That this is how we learn it, "destitution, destitution," from appraisals.'" [This is] meaning to say that it is written about a loan (Leviticus 25:35), "And if your brother becomes destitute and his hand falters with you, you shall strengthen him" - which is a loan, as it is written at its end (Leviticus 25:35), "Do not take from him interest or increase, etc."; and it is written about appraisals (Leviticus 27:8), "And if he is destitute from [paying] the appraisal" - and the received tradition (Arakhin 24a) comes [that its understanding is], revive him from his appraisal. And [so] we learn, "destitution, destitution," to arrange things with a debtor in the way that we arrange things with appraisals, and we should not hesitate about the words of Eliyahu. And so did all the Geonim and Rabbenu Alfasi rule. And even though Rabbi Yaakov in the name of Rabbi Pedat, and Rabbi Yirmiya in the name of Ilfa, said that we do not arrange things for a debtor, in the way of it being obvious in the Gemara - [nonetheless] we do not hesitate about the words of Eliyahu. And even though we found that Rabbenu Tam wrote like the opinion that we do not arrange things, and his proofs are in his book, 'after the many do we incline.' And Rambam, may his memory be Blessed, also ruled like the other Geonim that we arrange things (Mishneh Torah, Laws of Creditor and Debtor 1:7). And nonetheless, he wrote that the agent of the court only leaves the debtor items that are essential to him, such as a bed and bedding and that which he wears. And it appears that what forced the Teacher to say this is when he saw in this chapter [entitled] Mekabel regarding an agent of the court: That they said in the Mishnah (Bava Metzia 113a), "If he had two items, he takes one and returns one - the pillow at night, and the plow during the day." And they did not list tools of the trades. But from what it appears, this is certainly not a great compulsion [to rule as he did]. As since it is established to us that we arrange things with him in the way that we arrange things with appraisals, they are the same in every matter. And even though the Mishnah did not enumerate them, this is no matter; as it is not like a peddler that enumerates [all of his wears] and repeats [them] in every place. [Rather] it mentioned pillow and plow, and the law is the same for everything that is fitting to leave him. And the principle of the matter, according to that which seems - and that which is agreed by all the savants of the world whose fame about Torah has been disseminated - is that we arrange things with a debtor exactly in the way that we arrange things with appraisals. And they have what to rely upon from the words of the Gemara and from that of Eliyahu - may he be remembered for the good - as we have written.

And if you ask, "And how do we arrange his clothing; and behold, we say in the Gemara (Bava Kamma 11b), 'His clothing, and even the cloak that is on his shoulder'" - it is possible to say that it is an expression of exaggeration. And also [one could say it is referring to] a very precious cloak - such as [one] of silk and gold - from those that we said are not included in the arrangement [of what he keeps]. And the rest of the many laws of appraisals are elucidated in the tractate that is built upon this, and that is Tractate Arakhin (see Mishneh Torah, Laws of Appraisals and Devoted Property 4). And the commandment of appraisals is practiced in every place and at all times by males and females - meaning that it is practiced such that if they appraised, their appraisal is effective and [the amount] is consecrated. And nonetheless, the Sages said that at this time we should not appraise from the outset. And [it is] as we say in Tractate Avodah Zarah 13a [in the] first chapter, "We do not consecrate, and we do not appraise and we do not dedicate at this time. But if one did consecrate, or appraise or dedicate, a beast should be destroyed; produce, garments, or vessels should rot; money or metal vessels, he should take to the Dead Sea. And what is destroying? He locks the door before it, and it dies on its own." And the understanding of this consecration is consecration for the [Temple] upkeep - as with regards to appraisals, it was taught with it, that their undifferentiated [pledge] is also for the [Temple] upkeep. And even though Shmuel said in Arakhin 29a, "Consecrated items worth a maneh (a hundred large coins) that they desanctified upon that which is worth a perutah (the smallest coin), is desanctified (it is effective)" - and this is also about consecrated items of the [Temple] upkeep, as with consecration for the poor, it is certainly not something that can be desanctified, but rather we pay it in full; and that which Shmuel said, "desanctified," in the past is not [meant] to be precise, as he holds that we can desanctify it on the worth of the smallest coin at the outset, as is clearly proven in the Gemara - it is not a difficulty at all: That which we say about it here, "A beast should be destroyed, etc." - such is the law; but Shmuel said the solution [to the problem created by the law]. And it appears that this is how Rabbenu Alfasi, may his memory be Blessed, solves [it] in his Laws in the first chapter of Avodah Zarah, as he brings both of [these statements] together there.

And one who transgresses this and appraises at the time of the [Temple] and does not fulfill [it] to give the amount specified in the Torah; or that at this time he did not do in the thing that which they, may their memory be Blessed, said to destroy everything according to the law - or that which Shmuel said as its solution - has violated this positive commandment. And his punishment is very great, as he has 'misappropriated a misappropriation of the Lord.' And if three festivals have passed him by after he appraised, there is another punishment in the things, since he is [also] transgressing, 'do not delay.' And there are those that explained that he transgresses immediately also on account of 'do not delay': That in everything that he obligated himself and it is fit to pay, like charity and that which is similar to it, 'do not delay' [applies] immediately. [This is] to exclude a sacrifice, as he did not obligate himself, such that he does not transgress until three festivals - and like the words of Rabbi Shimon (Rosh Hashanah 4b), "Until three festivals, and the holiday of [Pesach] is first." And there are those that said that even regarding charity - and all the more so, other vows - we do not transgress on account of 'do not delay,' until three festivals. And [it is] like we find in the Gemara (Rosh Hashanah 5b) concerning gleanings, forgotten sheaves and the corner, "And we do not differentiate between if he obligated himself or he did not obligate himself." And that which they said in the Gemara, in Rosh Hashanah 6a, "And for charity, he is liable for it" - meaning, immediately - [means] he is liable for it with a positive commandment (see Mishneh Torah, Laws of Appraisals and Devoted Property 4).

Mitzvah 351

To not exchange consecrated things: To not exchange consecrated things - meaning to say one should not exchange a beast that has been consecrated for another beast afterwards, but it should rather be offered itself. And about this is it stated (Leviticus 27:10), "He shall not substitute nor exchange for it." And from when they exchanged it - meaning, that they said, "This instead of that"; "This in exchange for that"; or what is similar to these expressions, which is the essence of exchange (Temurah 26b) - there is liability for lashes in the thing, even though there is no act [involved] with it. [This is the case] even if there was somewhat of an error in the case. How is this? One who intends to say, "Behold this is in exchange for the burnt-offering that I have," but he says, "in exchange for the peace-offering that I have" - behold, this is an exchange and he is lashed; as nonetheless regarding the exchange it was volitional. But if his thought was that it was permissible to exchange, he is certainly not lashed. For one, it was inadvertent. And also, we only administer lashes with witnesses and a warning - and behold there is no warning [in such a case].

And if you will ask, "And why do we administer lashes for exchange - behold, it is a negative commandment that is rectifiable by a positive commandment, and that [commandment] is, 'and it and its exchange will be consecrated'"; the Sages, may their memory be Blessed, have already given a reason for that matter. And they said (Temurah 4b) it is because there are two negative commandments about it, as I have written in this Order (Sefer HaChinukh 352); and a positive commandment does not come and uproot two negative commandments. And they also said another reason - since the negative commandment of exchange is not the same as the positive commandment about it: As if the community, or partners make an exchange, they do not create an exchange (it is not effective), even if they are warned not to exchange (it is forbidden). And since the negative commandment is not the same as the positive commandment, we do not say about it that its law is like a negative commandment that is rectifiable by a positive commandment. And if you will ask further, "And why do we administer lashes for this negative commandment, as it is possible to transgress it without an act, with speech alone - and the principle is established for us that we do not administer lashes for any negative commandment that does not have an act [involved] with it"; we have already written the answer in many places: That they, may their memory be Blessed, explicitly excluded (Shevuot 21a) swearing, exchanging and cursing his fellow with [God's] name from this principle. As the Torah was very stringent about them to make them liable for lashes, even though there is no act [involved] with them.

And do not ruminate that it is on account of the bending of the lips, as it is an act. As behold, it is concluded in the Gemara in Sanhedrin 65a that it is not an act. Rather without an act at all is there a liability for lashes with some sins. And they are the three mentioned, one who puts out a bad name and a colluding witness. Some of them the lashes are explicit in the Torah about them - such as one who puts out a bad name and a colluding witness. And some of them we learned out from Scripture, such as swearing - as we learn in Shevuot 21a in the chapter [entitled] Shevuot Shtayim. And some commentators said about some of them that it is because an act will come out from it in the end - such as this of exchange, since the beast became consecrated with his speech and one who benefits from it will misappropriate it.

The root of this commandment and some of its laws are all written in this Order in the next commandment.

And this prohibition is practiced in every place and at all times by males and females. As even at this time, if a man transgressed and consecrated a beast for the altar and afterwards exchanged it [in front of] witnesses and [with] a warning, he is liable for lashes.

Mitzvah 352

The commandment of the one who exchanges the beast of a sacrifice with another beast, such that both of them be consecrated: That the exchange be consecrated - meaning to say, that both will be consecrated if one exchanges the beast of a sacrifice with another beast, such that he said, "This one will be for a sacrifice in exchange for that one," as it is stated (Leviticus 27:10), "and it and its exchange will be consecrated." And this passage is a positive commandment - meaning that the Torah commanded us that the exchange be holy and that we practice holiness with both of them. And the proof that this is a positive commandment is their, may their memory be Blessed, saying in Tractate Temurah 4b regarding the one who exchanges, "A positive commandment does not come and uproot two negative commandments." [This is] meaning to say that the prevention of exchange is repeated twice - as it is stated, "He shall not exchange nor substitute for it" - and the positive commandment of "and it and its exchange shall be" does not come and uproot these two negative commandments. Behold, what we wanted is elucidated, that it is a positive commandment.

It is from the roots of the commandment that God, Blessed be He, wanted to instill His fear in the hearts of people in all matters of sanctity, and as I wrote in the building of the the holy House and its vessels in the Order of Vayikchu Li Terumah (Sefer HaChinukh 95). In that commandment you will see our intent, from the angle of the simple understanding, about the great stringency that is fitting for us to practice with the holy. And therefore, in order to establish the awe of the matter of the holy in our hearts, the verse commanded us that we not change our words. Rather, from when the beast is sanctified, it is in its sanctity forever; and we should not think to remove it from its sanctity and to exchange it with another beast. But if he did [speak] this thing from his mouth, his thought and all of his action is reversed and both of them are holy. As he came with his actions to remove holiness and it shall be the opposite - that it expands more and be attached to all [of them]. And Rambam, may his memory be Blessed, wrote (Mishneh Torah, Laws of Substitution 4:13) about the reason for this commandment, and about that which we have been commanded to add a fifth for the redemption of consecrated things, that the Torah went down to the bottom of man's thinking and his evil impulse. As his nature is to multiply his [own] possessions and to be concerned with his money. And even though he vowed and sanctified, it is possible that he will go back on it and regret and want to redeem it for less than its worth. Therefore, he adds a fifth. And likewise, he will exchange the beast that he sanctified with one that is less than it. And if permission was given to him to exchange a bad one with a good one, he will exchange a good one with a bad one. And therefore, Scripture sealed the door in front of him. And he was further lengthy about this matter and wrote, "And even though all the statutes of the Torah are decrees, you are fitting to examine them (about) and give a reason for [everything] that you can." And the Teacher should be remembered for the good, as he aided me in this [project] of mine.

From the laws of the commandment is that which they, may their memory be Blessed, said (Temurah 17a) [that in the case of one] who exchanges with a forbidden mixture, a 'torn' (terminally ill) animal, or [one of unknown sex], sanctity does not descend upon it - since there is no sacrifice with its type. And therefore, he is not lashed. But a beast that has a blemish creates an exchange, since there is a sacrifice with its type. And like that which they said (Temurah 9a) that a man can not exchange his beast for a sacrifice that is not his. But if the owner of the sacrifice said, "Anyone who wants to exchange may exchange," any man can exchange for it. And one who exchanges cattle for sheep or sheep for cattle, sheep for goats or goats for sheep, males for females or females for males, or exchanged one beast for a hundred or a hundred for one - whether at one time or whether one after the other - behold, this is an exchange and he is lashed according to the calculation of the animals that he has exchanged. And the exchange cannot create a [further] exchange, nor can the offspring of a sanctified beast create an exchange, as it is stated, "and it and its exchange will be consecrated." And they, may their memory be Blessed, were precise, alongside the received traditional understanding (Temurah 13a): "'It,' and not its offspring; 'and its exchange,' and not the exchange of its exchange." But [in the case of] one who exchanges for a beast and goes back and exchanges for it even a thousand times, they are all an exchange and he is lashed for every one. And fowl and meal-offerings do not create an exchange, as only "beast" is stated in the verse. And the exchange for the sanctified things of gentiles [is not effective] from Torah writ. But rabbinically, [in the case of] a gentile who exchanges, it is exchanged (Mishneh Torah, Laws of Substitution 1:6). And everyone exchanges - both men and women. It is not that a man is permitted to exchange, but rather if he exchanges [an appropriate beast], it is exchanged and he absorbs the forty [lashes]. And that which they said how the law is of sacrificing the exchange; the law of its offspring and the offspring of its offspring; and the rest of its details, are elucidated in Tractate Temurah (see Mishneh Torah, Laws of Substitution 1).

And it is practiced in every place and at all times by males and females. And one who transgresses it and exchanges, but does not practice holiness towards both of the beasts - meaning, with the first and its exchange - has violated a positive commandment; besides the punishment that there is in the thing that he misappropriates what is holy.

Mitzvah 353

The commandment of the appraisal of a beast, such that one give according to what the priest appraises: To rule in the case of appraisals of beasts according to that which the Torah commanded us about it - as it is stated (Leviticus 27:11-12), "and he shall place the beast in front of the priest. And the priest shall appraise it" - and to give according to the appraisal that the priest appraises, and not less. As a man should not decrease and lie about that which he opens his mouth for the Heavens; and it is even forbidden to lie with common things, as I explained above (Sefer HaChinukh 350).

And what I wrote in the law of the appraisals of a man at the beginning of the Order (Sefer HaChinukh 350) is from the roots of the commandment.

From the laws of the commandment is that which they, may their memory be Blessed, said (Temurah 32b) that one who consecrates an unblemished beast for the altar and a blemish develops on it and it becomes disqualified, behold it is appraised and redeemed and he brings another beast instead of it. And about this is it stated (Leviticus 27:11), "And if it is any impure animal from which shall not be sacrificed to the Lord, he shall appraise the beast, etc." - as so did it come in the received traditional understanding, that Scripture expressed [this] with the expression of "impure." And whether a man consecrated a pure animal for the altar and a blemish developed upon it, as we said - or an impure [one] for the [Temple] upkeep - it requires being placed in front of the priest, as it is stated, "and he shall place the beast in front of the priest," and he appraises it. And if it died before it is appraised and redeemed, we do not appraise it and we do not redeem it after it died. But if he slaughtered two (the esophagus and the trachea) or the majority of two - even though it is like dead regarding slaughter, as it is established for us (Chullin 28a), as so was Moshe commanded about the majority of one with fowl and the majority of two with a beast - behold, it is living regrading appraisals. And [so] he brings it in front of the priest, and he appraises it. And the rest of its details are in [various] places in Temurah and Meilah (see Mishneh Torah, Laws of Substitution 4).

And this commandment is practiced by males and females at the time of the [Temple]. But at this time, the Sages, may their memory be Blessed, said (Avodah Zarah 13a) that "We do not consecrate, and we do not appraise and we do not dedicate [...]. But if one did consecrate, or appraise or dedicate," the law is that "a beast should be destroyed and produce, garments, or vessels should rot." But if he wants its solution, he can do to them like that of Shmuel, who said, "Consecrated items worth a maneh (a hundred large coins) that they desanctified upon that which is worth a perutah (the smallest coin), is desanctified (it is effective)" - as I wrote. And since this is so, we should write that the law of placing [it] in front of the priest is now not practiced at all. But nonetheless the law of appraisals of a beast is practiced with regards to that which if one did transgress and appraise his beast at this time, he needs to do what the Sages commanded with the thing. And since ex post facto we need a solution for the thing even at this time, I should count it and anything that is similar to it, among the commandments that are are practiced at this time.

Mitzvah 354

The commandment of appraising houses, such that he give the appraisal that the priest appraises and the addition of a fifth: To rule about the appraisals of homes; meaning [that] the priest appraise the house of one who consecrated it and wants to redeem it from that which is consecrated - he or his wife or his inheritors - and that [the redeemer] gives him according to the appraisal that he says to him, and also a fifth [of that sum]; as it is stated (Leviticus 27:14), "And if a man consecrates his house, holy, etc."

What I wrote about exchange in this Order (Sefer HaChinukh 352) is from the roots of the commandment - that God wanted for our good to place the fear of the holy in the hearts of people. And even though it was from His many kindnesses to give them room to redeem them, He wanted that they add a fifth to their redemption in order to distance [us], that we not reduce anything from the value of that which is consecrated. And even though there is no fifth with a purchased field, it is since it is not common that a man will consecrate his purchased field - as it is very beloved to him, since he acquired it with his money. Scripture is never concerned with what is not common.

From the laws of the commandment is that which they, may their memory be Blessed, said (Mishneh Torah, Laws of Appraisals and Devoted Property 5:3) that [in the case of] one who consecrates his house - and so [too,] his impure beast or movable items - that all of these are evaluated according to their worth, whether it is good or bad. And when the priests come to appraise them, we force the owners to open first and to say, "I would take it for me for such and such," and [that] value goes to the upkeep of the [Temple]. But they, may their memory be Blessed, said (Avodah Zarah 13a) that we do not consecrate at this time. And it appears certain that if [one] transgressed and consecrated his house at this time to the [Temple] upkeep - that we appraise its worth and he does like the solution of Shmuel or throws all of its value to the Dead Sea. And whether it was a house in the walled cities or whether it was in the unwalled cities, the owners or inheritors are always allowed to redeem them from the consecrated. But if another man redeemed it - if it was from the houses of the walled cities and it stood in the hand of the redeemer twelve months, it is finalized [to be his]; and if it was from the houses of the unwalled cities and the Jubilee came and it was in the hand of the redeemer, it goes back to its [original] owner at the Jubilee. And from that which the verse stated, "if a man consecrates his house," and it did not state, "a house," they, may their memory be Blessed were precise (Bava

Kamma 69b): "Just as one's house is in his possession, so too anything" that one wants to consecrate must be "in his possession." But if it is not in his possession, he many not consecrate it, even if it is his. And so [too,] did they, may their memory be Blessed, say (Bava Kamma 68b), "If he stole [something] but the owners did not despair, neither of them can consecrate it - this one because it is not his, and that one because it is not in his possession." And that is specifically with movable items; but land stays in the possession of its owners. And even with movable items that were deposited - he may consecrate anything that he can extract with judges. And the rest of its details are in Tractate Arakhin.

And [it] is practiced at the time that the Jubilee is practiced, as the law of appraisals of houses is only practiced - meaning to consecrate a house from the outset - at the time that the Jubilee is practiced. And one who transgresses it and consecrates his home and does not give its appraisal like the law written in the section of the Torah, at the time of the [Temple] - or did not solve the thing as we said, at this time - has nullified the positive commandment. And he also has a punishment since he misappropriated that which is consecrated.

Mitzvah 355
The commandment of appraising a field, that he gives the appraisal specified in the section of the Torah: To rule in the laws of appraisal of fields - meaning to say that one who consecrates his field and wants to redeem it, that he should give the appraisal fixed in the section of the Torah - "the seed of a chomer of barley for fifty shekel-coins of silver" (Leviticus 27:16), for all of the years of the Jubilee [cycle], which are forty-nine years. And according to the exact calculation, the appraisal of the field that is fitting to plant a chomer of barley is a sela and a pundyon a year. As the shekel-coin stated in the Torah is called an undifferentiated sela in the language of the Sages; and the gerah that is stated in the Torah is the maah in the words of the Sages - and the Sages added a sixth upon the shekel-coin, that is called a sela, as we have said. And that sela is equal to four dinars, and a dinar is four maah, and a maah is two pundyon. It comes out [to] a sela and a pundyon for each year. As even though the sela is forty-eight pundyon according to this calculation of ours - nonetheless, one who wants to take a sela from a money changer, needs to give forty-nine pundyon so that the money changer will earn one pundyon. And since he has to give forty-nine pundyon [in this case], we calculate it according to the calculation of what the consecrator would pay the money changer - as the hand of (terms for) the consecrated is always upon the higher. And we appraise it the same if he consecrates a field so good that there is none like it in the land or a field so bad that there is none as bad as it. As Scripture did not want to distinguish in this matter and made [the same] appraisal for all lands (Arakhin 14a).

And since we explained the shekel-coins, it is fitting that we explain how much is a chomer: You should know that the chomer is a measure that is [also] called a kor. And a kor is two letech, and a letech is fifteen seah. It comes out that a chomer is thirty seah, which is ten eipah - as an eipah is three seah. It is a well-known thing and we also already knew it from our Rabbis, may their memory be Blessed, (Eruvin 23b) that a place that has fifty ells by fifty ells is a beit seah - meaning that it is [what contains what grows from] a seah of barley - and that is two thousand five hundred [square ells] by arithmetic (multiplication). It comes out that a place that is fitting for the seed of a chomer of barley - which is thirty seah - is seventy-five thousand ells by arithmetic.

And what is the way of the calculation with the appraisal of fields? A field of holding is distinguished in its content from a purchased field. And when we measure [a field of holding], we only measure the places in it that are fitting for planting; and its appraisal is that stipulated by the Torah - "the seed of a chomer of barley for fifty shekel-coins of silver" - as we elucidated, whether it is good or bad; and he adds a fifth to this stipulated appraisal. And let this rule be in your hand: with every fifth stated in the Torah, it is a fourth of the principle, so that the principle and the fifth that is added to it are five [portions together]. And if the entire field that he consecrated is not fitting for seeding at all, we redeem it according to its worth. And which is that which is called a field of holding? That is a field that a man inherited from his bequeathers. And a purchased field is a field that a man purchased [on] his own, or that he received the rights to it in any way that is not because of inheritance.

And the law of one who consecrates his purchased field - that we estimate it worth - is [that] we see how much it is worth until the Jubilee year. And if the consecrator redeems it, he does not add a fifth onto it. And its redemption is for the upkeep of the [Temple], like other appraisals and values (Arakhin 24a). And when the Jubilee arrives, the field goes back to its [original] owners who sold it. Whether it was redeemed from the treasurer by any man and it goes out [now] from under his hand, or whether it was not redeemed and it goes out from the hand of the consecrated - it always returns to the one for which it is a holding in the Land. And it does not go out to the priests because a man cannot consecrate something that is not his, and this land was the purchaser's only until the Jubilee year. And this is not the case for a field of holding: As if the Jubilee arrived and the owners did not redeem it from the hand of the consecrated or from the hand of another who acquired it from the consecrated, the priests give its value - since the consecrated only goes out with redemption - and it is a holding for them forever. And those monies go to the consecrated for the upkeep of the [Temple]. And any field that we estimate for the consecrated, to sell it for its value, we announce sixty days - morning and evening, which is the time that the workers come in from their work and go out - so that all will hear about the thing. And we demarcate its borders and say, "Its quality is such and [price] x is its estimation." And whoever wants to buy comes and buys (Arakhin 21b). And the rest of its details are elucidated in the tractate that is built on this, and that is Tractate Arakhin.

And [it] is practiced by males and females at the time that the Jubilee is practiced. But at this time, the Sages, may their memory be Blessed, already said (Avodah Zarah 13a) that we do not consecrate and we do not appraise, as we wrote above (Sefer HaChinukh 360). But nonetheless, if one transgressed and did consecrate land now to the [Temple] upkeep, it is possible for him to solve it - like that of Shmuel - such that he desanctifies it upon that which is worth a perutah (the smallest coin) or more and he throws it to the Dead Sea. But if he does not want this solution, it appears certain that he must appraise it according to the statute that we have written and throw its money to the Dead Sea - so that it not be a stumbling block for him or for his children. It is better that [the money] be lost and that people not stumble with it, than that he leaves it in a corner for the [Temple] upkeep - as there will not be a lack of money in the future to support the House of our God.

Mitzvah 356
To not change the consecrated from a sacrifice to a sacrifice: To not change the consecrated from a sacrifice to a sacrifice, such that we turn a peace-offering back into a guilt-offering, or a guilt-offering we turn back into a sin-offering - there is a negative commandment in this and that which is similar to it. And about this thing is it stated (Leviticus 27:26), "a man may not consecrate it" - meaning that he not make the first-born a burnt-offering nor a peace-offering nor any other sacrifice. And the received tradition comes that it is not specifically with a first-born that the verse is concerned - that the law is the same for all that is consecrated [for] the altar. As so did they say in Sifra, Bechukotai, Section 8:3, "I only have the first born. From where [do we know] about all the consecrated that we do not change it from [one] holiness to [another] holiness? [Hence] we learn to say, 'with a beast, a man may not consecrate it.'" It hints that with every consecrated animal - whether the consecration of the consecrated for the altar or even for the upkeep of the [Temple] - we do not change it from its holiness, but it is [to be] left like it is; and "a man may not consecrate it" is stated about everything.

That which we wrote above in the commandment of exchange (Sefer HaChinukh 352) is from the roots of the commandment - that all this is from the awe of the holy.

From the law of the commandment is, for example, that which they, may their memory be Blessed, said (Mishneh Torah, Laws of Substitution 4:11) that if he consecrated [a beast] to the upkeep of the sanctuary, he should not change it to the upkeep of the altar. And they also said (Temurah 25a) that we are not to be tricky with a consecrated animal, to consecrate its embryo [with] a different holiness, but it is rather in the [same] holiness as its mother - as offspring of consecrated animals are consecrated from the innards of their mother. This is not the case with the first-born, as the first-born is consecrated upon its exit, as Scripture makes it depend on opening the womb. And therefore, it is possible to be tricky with a first-born before it is born, to consecrate it with a different holiness. And about this is it stated, "which becomes a first-born of [...], a man may not consecrate it" - from when it becomes a first-born, you may not consecrate it, but you can consecrate it in the belly. And therefore, one who said, "If the one that is first is a male, behold it is a burnt-offering," must sacrifice it as a burnt-offering. But he may not make it into a sacrifice of a peace-offering, since he cannot remove it from its holiness. As the holiness of peace-offerings is below that of the first-born; such that the first-born is only eaten by priests, whereas the peace-offerings [are eaten] by every person. And the rest of its details are in the fifth chapter of Temurah.

And this prohibition is practiced in every place and at all times by males and females. As even at this time that we do not consecrate, one who transgressed and did consecrate a beast for one consecration may not change it to another consecration. And one who transgresses this and changed it from [one] holiness to [another] holiness - for example if he consecrated it for a peace-offering and afterwards said that its holiness should be for a burnt-offering, or another sacrifice - has violated this negative commandment. But we do not administer lashes for it, since there is no act [involved] with it.

Mitzvah 357
The commandment of the law of one who dedicates from his properties, that it is of the priests:
To rule in matters of dedications (cherem, something that is put off limits) - that is, if anyone dedicated something of his possessions undifferentiatedly - for example, [if] he said, "Thing x of mine will become dedicated" - that thing must be given to the priest; as it is stated (Leviticus 27:28), "But any dedication that a man dedicates, etc." [That is,] unless he explicitly said that the dedication be to the Lord, or to the upkeep of the [Temple]. As so did the they, may their memory be Blessed, say (Arakhin 28b), "Undifferentiated dedications are for the priest." And their proof is from that which is written explicitly in the section, "like the dedicated field, his holding shall be of the priest."

It is from the roots of the commandment [that it is] because Israel is the nation that God chose from all the other nations for His service and to recognize His Name, and they are not under the rule of the constellations that God apportioned to all the other nations. They are instead [directly] under the hand of the Holy One, Blessed be He, without any intermediary of an angel or constellation; and as it is written (Deuteronomy 32:9), "For the portion of the Lord is His people, Yaakov is the measure of His inheritance." And as you find when He took them out from Egypt - which was a miracle that included all the people - that He took them out by Himself in His glory. And [this is] as they, may their memory be Blessed, expounded, "'I will pass through Egypt' (Exodus 12:12) - I and not an angel; 'and I will strike the first-born' - I and not a seraph," as it appears in the Haggadah. And therefore, anytime Israel maintains the Torah and crowns themselves with His service, only goodness will rest upon them, and the flow of blessing and a pure benevolent spirit will support them; and the opposite - the curse and the 'dedication' - will [rest] upon their enemies and haters. As such, if one of their tempers become short and he pronounces an expression of curse and 'dedication' on his money or his lands - which are under the blessing - the verse informs that it is impossible to remove it from the domain of the Blessed to another domain. [This is] since everything that belongs to Israel - who is the portion of God - is His; [as] whatever a slave acquired; his master acquired (Pesachim 88b). Still, since we truly know that the intention of the one who dedicates is to remove that thing from his domain, it is fitting to fulfill his will; and [so] it returns to the domain of his Master and it becomes holy.

And that is [the sense of that] which Scripture (Leviticus 27:29) states nearby, "Any dedication that is dedicated of a man you shall not redeem, he shall surely die"; as its content in the way of the simple meaning is that [in the case of] one who dedicates of a man that is not his - for example, those fighting against their enemies who make a vow, "If this nation is surely given into my hands, I will dedicate their cities" (Numbers 21:2) - [the objects of the vow] should die. As other nations are not included in the wellspring of blessings, as we have said; and [so] the expression of 'dedication' clings to them. And so, did Ramban (Rambam) explain this verse in the way of its simple understanding (Ramban on Leviticus 27:29). And even though there are many midrashic explanations about this verse, there are seventy faces to the Torah and 'they are all straight for the one who understands.' And from this root they, may their memory be Blessed, said (Arakhin 28a) that all that belongs to the Levites and the priests - whether land or whether movable items - cannot be dedicated. That is, even if the priest or the Levite said about his field that it be dedicated, it does not hold. As he is like one who dwells in his Master's house - the place of blessing and kindness and good - and all that he has is God's. And amidst blessing there is no place for 'dedication.'

From the laws of the commandment is that which they, may their memory be Blessed, said (Arakhin 28b), "What [is the difference] between dedications of the priests and dedications of the Heavens? That dedications of the Heavens are consecrated and are redeemed with their worth, their value goes to the [Temple] upkeep and the properties go out to the non-sacred. But the dedications of the priests" - meaning to say, an undifferentiated dedication, that [goes] to the priests - "never have redemption, but are rather given to the priests like priestly tithe." And it is concerning the dedications of the priests that it is stated, "it shall not be sold and it shall not be redeemed" (Leviticus 27:28) - "it shall not be sold" to another, "and it shall not be redeemed" for its [original] owners. It is one whether he dedicates land or movable items - they are given to the priests of that shift, [serving] at the time that he dedicates. And during the whole time that the dedications of the priests are in the house of the owners, they are consecrated for all of their purposes - as it is stated (Leviticus 27:28), "every dedication is holy of holies to the Lord." [Once] they are given to the priest, behold they are like the non-sacred for all of their purposes - as it is stated (Numbers 18:14), "Every dedication in Israel shall be for you." And a field that is dedicated to a priest never returns to the original owners. And the rest of its details are in the eight chapter of Arakhin and the first of Nedarim (see Mishneh Torah, Laws of Appraisals and Devoted Property 6).

And [it] is practiced at the time of the [Temple] by males and females. But at this time, we have already said in the first commandment of this Order (Sefer HaChinukh 350) that we do not dedicate. If, however, one transgressed and did dedicate [something] at this time, Rambam, may his memory be Blessed, wrote (Mishneh Torah, Laws of Appraisals and Devoted Property 8:11) that if one dedicated outside of the Land [of Israel] movable property undifferentiatedly or land explicitly to the priests - that they are given to the priests found in that place; as the status of land outside of the Land is like movable items for this matter. But if he dedicated land in the Land, it is not dedicated - as the field of dedications is only practiced when the Jubilee is practiced. And one who transgressed this and dedicated from his properties but did not give them to a priest or to the upkeep of the [Temple] - in the cases that we explained that they are given to the upkeep of the [Temple] - has violated this positive commandment. And his punishment is very great, as he has misappropriated from the holy.

Mitzvah 358

That owners that dedicated land not sell it, but that it rather be given to the priests: That one should not sell a dedicated field, and so [too,] all other lands. And the law is the same for movable items that have been dedicated by their owners. Rather, they should be given to the priests of that watch, as we wrote in this Order, positive commandment 6 (Sefer HaChinukh 357). And it is even forbidden for the owners to sell it to the treasurer of the consecrated, but rather [the latter] should attain the rights to it with nothing. As God gave the rights of dedications to the priests. And this is with undifferentiated dedications, as we said above. Since it established for us [that the law is] like the [opinion] that says, undifferentiated dedications - meaning to say that one who dedicated but did not specify to whom - are for the priests. As if he dedicates explicitly for the upkeep of the [Temple], the priests do not get rights to [it]. And about the dedications of the priests is it stated here (Leviticus 27:28), "any dedication [...] shall not be sold." But the priests can certainly sell them according to their will. As [with] the dedications of the priests - after they have gone out from the hand of their owners who dedicated them and have reached the hand of the priests - behold they are like the non-sacred for all of their purposes, as it is stated (Numbers 18:14), "Every dedication in Israel shall be for you." But so long as they are still under the hand of the owners, it is stated about them (Leviticus 27:28), "every dedication is holy of holies to the Lord."

And the root of the commandment and all of its content is written above (Sefer HaChinukh 357). See there, 'as it is close' (see Mishneh Torah, Laws of Appraisals and Devoted Property 6).

Mitzvah 359

Sefer HaChinukh

That a dedicated field not be redeemed: That a dedicated field not be redeemed; and the law is the same for all other lands and movable items that are dedicated - they do not have redemption but are rather given to the priests; and [the priests] do with them according to their will. And about this is it stated (Leviticus 27:28), "any dedication [...] shall not be redeemed." And they said in Sifra, Bechukotai, Chapter 12:4, "'It shall not be sold' to another, 'and it shall not be redeemed' for its [original] owners."

The roots of the commandment are written above (Sefer HaChinukh 357).

From the laws of the commandment is that which our Rabbis, may their memory be Blessed, said (Mishneh Torah, Laws of Appraisals and Devoted Property 6:4) that one who dedicates to the Heavens consecrates [the property], but he [may] redeem it for its worth, such that the value goes to upkeep of the [Temple] and the property goes out to the non-sacred. But dedications of the priests never have a redemption. Rather behold they belong to the priests and their children forever. And [in the case of] a priest who got the rights for a field of dedication and sold it, it goes back to him or his seed in the Jubilee; as is is stated (Leviticus 27:21), "for the priest shall it be a holding" - this teaches that his field of dedication is like a field of holding for an Israelite. And the rest of its details and of its content - all of it is like I wrote above (Sefer HaChinukh 357) and it is all elucidated in Tractate Arakhin. And there is no doubt that these two negative commandments - which are "it shall not be sold" and "it shall not be redeemed" - are practiced today according to the opinion of Rambam, may his memory be Blessed, as I wrote above: [In the case of] one who dedicates land or movable objects outside the Land at this time, it is given to the priests. [This is so] even though the field of dedication is not practiced in the Land [of Israel] today, but only at the time that the Jubilee is practiced. So did Rambam, may his memory be Blessed, write in the Book of Separation (Mishneh Torah, Laws of Appraisals and Devoted Property 8:11-12).

Mitzvah 360

The commandment of the tithe of pure beasts every year: To tithe all the pure beasts - which are cattle, sheep and goats (Bekhorot 53a) - that are born in our flocks each and every year, and to take that tithe and eat it in Jerusalem after the fat and blood have been offered on the altar (Zevchim 56b), as it is written (Leviticus 27:32), "And all the tithe of your cattle and sheep, all that passes beneath the rod, the tenth shall be holy to the Lord." And they, may their memory be Blessed, said in Bekhorot 58b, "How do we tithe? He brings them to a pen and makes for them a small opening, so that two cannot go out at the same time. He places their mothers outside, and they would moan, so that the lambs would hear their voices and exit the pen to meet them on their own and not from the effort of another. And he counts them with a rod, 'One, two, three, four' and so on, until ten. And the one that comes out tenth he marks with red chalk and he says, 'Behold, this is tithe.'"

It is from the roots of the commandment [that it is because] God chose the nation of Israel and wished for the sake of His righteousness that all of them be engaged with His Torah and be knowers of His Name. And in His Wisdom, he lured them with this commandment so that they would study [and] draw moral teachings. As God knows that most people are lured by lower physicality, 'as [they] are also flesh,' and they will not put their souls to the toil of the Torah and its constant involvement. Therefore, in His understanding, He caused [it] and gave them a place wherein everyone will know the words of His Torah regardless - for there is no doubt that every man will be drawn to establish his residence in the place that his money is there. And as such, when each person brings up the tithe of all his cattle and his sheep each year to the place where involvement with wisdom and Torah is found - that is Jerusalem, where is the Sanhedrin of those who master knowledge and understand information - and we similarly bring up the tithe of our grain in four years of the sabbatical [cycle], as we know that the second tithe is eaten there, and so [too,] the fourth year planting is eaten there; the owner of [these things] will perforce either go there and study Torah himself, or send one of his sons to study there and to be sustained by that produce.

And through this, each and every house in all of Israel will have someone who is wise and knowledgeable in the Torah who can [then] teach all of the household of his father with his wisdom. And with this, 'the land will be filled with knowledge of the Lord.' As if there was only one sage in

Sefer HaChinukh

each city - or even ten - there would be many men who would only come in front of them once a year, and all the more so the women and the children. And even if they heard their words once a week, they would [then] go to their home and throw all the words of the sage behind their back. But when the teacher is in each and every house, dwelling there evening, morning and afternoon and constantly reminding them; then they will all - men, women and children - be careful and aware and no matter of sin or iniquity will be found among them. And through this they will merit that which is written (Leviticus 26:11-12) "And I will place My dwelling amongst you [...] and you will be for Me a nation, and I will be for you God" (while the second part of this citation is likely meant to be a very similar quote from Leviticus 26:12, the actual quote is from Jeremiah 11:4).

From the laws of the commandment is that which they, may their memory be Blessed, said (Bekhorot 53a) that we do not tithe from cows onto sheep, or from sheep onto cows, but we do tithe from sheep onto goats and goats onto sheep, as Scripture used the expression, "sheep" for both of them, and they are considered like one species. We do not tithe from that which is born this year for [that born] another year, [just] as we do not tithe with the seed of the ground from the new onto the old, nor from the old onto the new, as it is written about it, "which comes out from your field each year" (Deuteronomy 14:22). Still, if one transgressed and nonetheless tithed from the old beasts onto the new or the new onto the old, Rambam, may his memory be Blessed, wrote (Mishneh Torah, Laws of Firstlings 7:5) that it appears to him that it is tithe, because of the severity of the tithes - as behold, "each year," is only written about the seed of the earth. And it is enough for us that we learn from it that the tithe of beasts be like it regarding [the law] from the outset, but not ex post facto.

And also, from the content of the commandment is that which they, may their memory be Blessed, said (Bekhorot 57b) that the newborn lambs are not like untithed produce, from which it is forbidden to eat until they are tithed. Rather, it is permissible to slaughter and eat all that he wants from the lambs; and when the times that the Sages have set for tithing arrive - and they are called the threshing floor of the beast - he tithes those [still] found with him. And once those times arrive, it is forbidden for him to eat or sell until he tithes them. But if one transgressed and slaughtered them, behold it is permissible [to eat them].

And there are three times set by them, may their memory be Blessed, and these are them: The last day of the month of Adar, the thirty-fifth day of the counting of the omer, and the last day of the month of Elul. And why did they set these times that are close to the holidays? So that animals should be available for pilgrims. For even though it is permissible to sell the animals before tithing, as we said - nonetheless people would refrain from selling until they tithed them, so as to fulfill the commandment with them. And the law that if one counted and erred in the number and called the eighth, the tenth; or the twelfth, the tenth - they are not consecrated. But if he erred in the ninth or the eleventh and called them the tenth - they are consecrated, since they are adjacent to the tenth. And we known this thing from the tradition (Bekhorot 23a). And that which they said (Bava Metzia 6b) that any beast about which there is a doubt as to whether it is obligated in tithing or it is not obligated in tithing, behold it is exempt from the tithe. And all - whether unblemished or blemished - are brought into the pen for the counting; except for forbidden mixtures, 'torn' (terminally ill) animals and one lacking time (very young ones), and so [too,] an orphan whose mother died or was slaughtered at its birth. And we have known these things from the heard tradition (Bekhorot 57a, Mishneh Torah, Laws of Firstlings 6:14). And the rest of its details are in the last chapter of Bekhorot.

And Rambam, may his memory be Blessed, wrote (Sefer HaMitzvot LaRambam, Mitzvot Ase 68), "This commandment is practiced by males and females - whether Israelites or whether priests and Levites; in the Land [of Israel] and outside of the Land - whether in the presence of the [Temple] or not in the presence of the [Temple]. And this is the Torah law; however as a rabbinic decree so that one not eat [tithe] without a blemish - since we do not have a Temple and he would come to a great prohibition which is slaughtering consecrated animals outside [the Temple] - they, may their memory be Blessed, said that it is only practiced in the presence of the [Temple]. But when there will be a Temple built there, it [will be] practiced in the Land and outside of the Land." To here is his language. And he further wrote in a different place (Mishneh Torah, Laws of Firstlings 6:2, 4) that if one transgressed and did it at this time, behold it is tithe and he eats it with its blemish (if and when it develops a blemish) in any place - as it is like the totally non-sacred. And the law of the unblemished that is eaten in Jerusalem at the time of the [Temple] is that all of it be eaten by the owners, like the Pesach sacrifice - except for the entrails and the blood which is offered, as we said above.

Mitzvah 361
To not sell the tithe of beasts, but rather that it be eaten in Jerusalem: To not sell the tithe of beasts in any way, but rather its owners - or whoever they want - eat it in Jerusalem. And regarding this is it stated here about the tithe of beasts (Leviticus 27:33), "it shall not be redeemed." And they said in Sifra, Bechukotai, Chapter 13:4, "With the tithe, it states, 'it shall not be redeemed' - it is not sold, neither alive nor slaughtered; neither unblemished nor blemished." And the expression of redemption is used here as an expression of sale, because redemption is similar to sale, since [redemption is when] a man gives value (money) and he purchases land.

That which I wrote in this Order in the commandment of the tithe of cattle and sheep (Sefer HaChinukh 360) is from the roots of the commandment. And from that reason that you will see there, we have been commanded not to sell the tithe in any way, but rather it must be eaten in Jerusalem regardless.

From the laws of the commandment is that which they, may their memory be Blessed, said (Zevachim 56b) the tithe of beasts was eaten completely by the owners in Jerusalem, and the priests have nothing in it. However, it was slaughtered in the courtyard and they would offer its entrails and sprinkle its blood with one sprinkling across from the base [of the altar]. And if it developed a blemish, it is eaten in any place. But the Sages forbade to sell it nonetheless, and even if it is a blemished one. And even if it is slaughtered is it forbidden to sell it [as a] decree lest one will sell it alive (Bekhorot 31b). And therefore, they said that we do not weigh one piece from it against [another] piece - as it appears like selling. And [this is the law] even though this thing is permitted to do even with an unblemished first-born; as they, may their memory be Blessed, said (Bekhorot 31a) [that] the priests that are designated for a first-born are permitted to weigh one piece against [another] piece. And that which they, may their memory be Blessed, said [regarding] the tithe of beasts that is slaughtered, [that] it is permissible to sell its fat, its tendons, its skin and its bones - as the they only forbade to sell its meat alone. And if the bones were expensive and he included the value of the meat in [that of] the bones, it is permitted. And Rambam, may his memory be Blessed, wrote (Mishneh Torah, Laws of Firstlings 6:5) that it appears to him that [in the case of] one who sells the tithe, the purchaser does not acquire [it]. And therefore, the seller is not lashed for it - since his actions were not effective. And [it is] like one who sells the dedications of the priests, such that the buyer did not acquire [it], and like one who sells a woman (captive) of beautiful form, such that the buyer did not acquire [it] - as is elucidated in its place. To here [are his words]. And the rest of the details of the commandment are elucidated in Tractate Bekhorot and in Tractate Maaser Sheni at the beginning.

And this prohibition is practiced by males and females - Israelites, priests and Levites - in every place and at all times. And even though the Sages forbade to tithe beasts at this time [as a] decree lest he eat them unblemished and there would be a prohibition of excision in the thing - which is the slaughter of consecrated animals outside [of the Temple], as we wrote above - nonetheless, [in the case of] one who transgressed and tithed at this time, it has the sanctity of the tithe. And if he sold it in any way, he has violated this negative commandment - which is "it shall not be redeemed." But we do not administer lashes for it, like we said adjacently in the name of Rambam, may his memory be Blessed. And praise to great and awesome God, we have completed the Book of Leviticus.

Mitzvah 362
The commandment to send the impure out of the camp of the Divine Presence: To send away the impure from the camp of the Divine Presence, as it is stated (Numbers 5:2), "Command the Children of Israel, and they shall send from the camp anyone with an eruption or a discharge and anyone impure of a soul." And until where was the boundary of the camp of the Divine Presence was known to them in the wilderness. And so [too,] in the [future] generations, the Temple and the whole yard which is in front of it is called the camp of the Divine Presence (Zevachim 116b), and it is

included in this commandment. And they said in Sifrei Bamidbar 1 that "and they shall send from the camp" is a warning (negative commandment) to the impure not to enter the Temple. And they said in Pesachim 68a, [that] "He shall exit to outside the camp" (Deuteronomy 23:11) is a positive commandment. And this commandment is [indeed] repeated in another place, "If there be among you a man who will not be pure of a nocturnal emission, he shall exit to outside the camp." And its explanation (Pesachim 68a) is [that it means] outside the camp of the Divine Presence. And, likewise, this itself is repeated, as it went back and stated (Numbers 5:3), "and send them out of the camp." And I have already written (Sefer HaChinukh 228) that the repetition of prohibitions within a [single] commandment indicates a little bit of the stringency of the commandment; as God wanted for the benefit of His creatures to warn them and go back and warn them about it. [It is like] the way of people that they warn each other many times about all things that have a great need. And if we have nonetheless found [important] bodies of the Torah stated by clues, everything is for a correct reason. It is from the roots of the commandment [that it is] because it is known to the Sages that the matter of impurity weakens the power of the intellect and mixes it up and separates between it and the pure and perfect Elevated Understanding. And it will be separated until it is purified. And [it is] as it is written regarding the matter of impurity (Leviticus 11:43), "and do not become impure with them and be impurified (venitmetem) in them" - and they, may their memory be Blessed, expounded (Yoma 39a), "and be stupefied (venitamtem) in them"; meaning to say that the the sources of intellect are stupefied by impurity. Hence it is not fitting for a person who is sullied by impurity to be in the holy and pure place, wherein the spirit of God is [found]. And this matter can be compared metaphorically to the palace of a king from which we distance any man that is leprous or disgusting in his body, or even in his clothing. And it is similar to that which is written (Esther 4:2), "for one can not enter the king's gate wearing sackcloth."

From the laws of the commandment is that which they, may their memory be Blessed, said (Sifrei Bamidbar 1:3-5 and Pesachim 67a), that the metsora who is more stringent in his impurity is also more stringent in his being sent out. And [so] he is sent out of three camps, which means out of Jerusalem; whereas those who have a genital flow whose impurity is not so stringent are [only] sent out of two camps, which are the camps of the priests and the camp of the Levites, and that is outside of the Temple mount; and one impure from a dead body whose impurity is [in some regards even less] stringent is only sent out from one camp - hence it is permissible for him to enter the Temple Mount. And what is the stringency of those with abnormal genital flows over one impure from a dead body? That the [former] renders impure that which is resting or sitting upon him, even when [separated by] a stone, whereas the one impure from a dead body does not impart impurity this way. And one impure from a dead body, and those that have intercourse with a menstruant and all gentiles more generally are sent out from the perimeter (chail), whereas someone who has immersed in purifying waters but only becomes pure at the end of the day (tevul yom) enters there. A tevul yom is sent out of they courtyard of the Israelites and the women's yard, whereas one lacking [only] the atonement sacrifice is not. But from the yard of the Israelites inwards, even one lacking the atonement sacrifice does not enter. [This] and the rest of its details are elucidated in the chapter [entitled] Avot HaTumaot, which is the first chapter of the Order of Taharot (see Mishneh Torah, Laws of Admission into the Sanctuary 3).

And this commandment is practiced by males and females at all times. As even at this time (according to the words of Rambam in Mishneh Torah, Laws of The Chosen Temple 6:15) when the Temple is desolate on account of our iniquities, it is forbidden for an impure person to enter there. And one who transgresses it and enters a place that he is not permitted while he is still impure, along the guidelines that we have explained, has violated a positive commandment; besides having violated a negative commandment, as we will explain in this Order (Sefer HaChinukh 363), with God's help.

Mitzvah 363

That an impure person not enter the entire Temple: That any impure person is prevented from entering the entire Temple - the likeness of which in the [future] generations is all of the yard from Nikanor Gate and inwards, which is the beginning of the yard of the Israelites - as it is stated (Numbers

5:3), "and they will not render your camps impure" - meaning to say the camp of the Divine Presence. And the proof of this being among the negative commandments is that which they, may their memory be Blessed, said in the Gemara (Makkot 14b), "One who enters the Temple while impure [is liable for excision], as both the punishment and the warning are written [in the Torah.] The punishment is written (Numbers 19:13) 'the Tabernacle of God he has defiled and he shall be cut off.' The warning is written (Numbers 5:3) 'and they will not render your camps impure.'" And they also said in the Mekhilta (Sifrei Zuta on Bamidbar 5:3), "'Command the Children of Israel, and they shall send from the camp' - [that is] a positive commandment. From where do we derive [the] negative commandment? Since it is written, 'and they will not render your camps impure.'" And they said in Sifra (Sifra, Tazria Parashat Yoledet, Section 1 1), "Since it is stated (Leviticus 15:31), 'And you shall separate the children of Israel from their uncleanliness[...],' I might understand, whether from its midst or from its back," meaning to say that one who approaches the Temple from its back while he is impure would be liable for excision; "it is, therefore, written in respect to a yoledet (a woman after childbirth) (Leviticus 12:4), 'and into the sanctuary she shall not come,'" meaning to say the expression of coming is only about one who enters from the front. And there it is elucidated that the law of a yoledet and the other [cases of] impurity are the same regarding this.

I have written above in this Order on the first commandment (Sefer HaChinukh 362) what I have known from the roots of the commandment regarding the distancing of impurity. And I have also written some of the laws of the commandment.

But I will still inform you of a general principle regarding this matter: Everything that requires going into water by Torah writ and it is from the impurity that the Torah's nazirite must shave [for its acquisition], is liable for excision for coming into the Temple if he goes in before immersion and the [end of the day]. But one who is impure from the impurity of a dead body, for which a nazirite does not shave - even though he is impure [with] an impurity [requiring] seven [days before being able to be pure] - is exempt [from excision] for coming into the Temple. And so [too,] one who touched vestments that touched a person who touched a dead body, or if he touched a person who touched vestments that touched a dead body - even though he is impure [on the] first [level] regarding impurity and to impart impurity to sanctified meat - behold, such a one is exempt for coming into the Temple. And these things are a law of Moshe from Sinai (halakha le'Moshe me'Sinai). And even though he is exempt, they would give him lashes of rebellion. And all of the impurities for which a nazirite must shave about or not shave about are elucidated in Tractate Nazir. And one who throws impure vestments into the Temple - even if they were impure vestment that touched a dead body - is exempt from excision, but liable for lashes. As it is stated (Leviticus 17:16), "And if he does not wash and his flesh he does not bathe" - and we learned form the tradition (Sifra, Acharei Mot, Chapter 12 13) that for [failure to] bathe his body, he is punished by excision, but for [failure to] wash his clothes, he is lashed forty [times]. [This] and the rest of its details are elucidated in the first chapter of Shevuot and in Horayot and in Keritot and in [scattered] places in Zevachim (see Mishneh Torah, Laws of Admission into the Sanctuary 3:13, 17).

And this commandment is practiced by males and females. And even at this time, one who enters there and is impure according to the guidelines that we wrote, will be liable for excision - since the holiness of God is upon it, even today when it is desolate. And [it is] like they, may their memory be Blessed, expounded (Megillah 28a) from that which it is written (Leviticus 21:31), "and I will make your sanctuaries desolate," as I wrote above in Acharei Mot (Sefer HaChinukh 184).

Mitzvah 364

The commandment of confession of sin: We are commanded to confess before God our sins that we have sinned, at such time that we feel remorse for them. And this is the content of confession: to say at the time of repentance, "Please, God, I have sinned, I have transgressed, I have rebelled [in] such and such," meaning to say that he mentions the sin that he did explicitly with his mouth. He should [then] seek atonement for it and extend his words in this matter according to his fluency. And they, may their memory be Blessed, said that even sins that require the bringing of a sin-offering still demand confession with the offering, and about this it states (Numbers 5:6), "Speak to the children of Israel [saying], a man or woman who commits from any of the sins of man and rebels against the Lord, that soul is guilty and they shall confess the sins that they did." [The Sages] said in the Mekhilta (Sifrei Zuta on Numbers 5:6), "Since it says 'confess the sin' (Leviticus 5:5) it means that the sin must be extant, that is that the sin-offering is alive and not slaughtered." This mean that the animal to be offered must still be alive. They also said there, "We see that one must confess if he renders impure the Temple and its holy things. From where do you know to include all other commandments?" That is that this verse in Parshat Vayikra only [discusses] one who renders impure the Temple and its holy things; from where do you know to include all other commandments? "As it is written, 'Speak to the children of Israel, etc. and they should confess.'" That is, that we expound the verse as if it is not written about a specific thing. "And from where do we know that its understanding [includes sins that are punishable by] death and excision? Since it is stated about the confession of Aharon in Acharei Mot (Leviticus 16:16 'for all their sins'." [The Sages], may their memory be Blessed, expounded [on this verse] to include negative commandments; and 'that they did' which is written here to include positive commandments, meaning to say that if he does not do a positive commandment that he could have done, he is obligated to confess about it. And they further expounded there in the Mekhilta, "'From any of the sins of man' - from that which is between him and his fellow, theft, robbery and evil speech." And this confession truthfully requires that he return the '[theft] that is in his hands,' as if he does not do so it would be better not to confess about it. "'To rebel' includes all those sentenced to death who must [also] confess. I might have thought to include even those convicted by false witnesses"; that is, even though he knows that he did not sin, except that false testimony was testified against him, that he be obligated to confess about this. "Hence the verse teaches, 'soul [that] is guilty' - I only said when there is guilt there, but not when he knows that he did not sin, except false testimony was testified against him. Hence we understand that [for] all iniquities, large and small - even positive commandments - a man is obligated to confess about them.

And since this commandment of confession comes with the obligation to bring an offering - as is written in Parshat Vayikra there (Leviticus 5:6), "And he shall bring his guilt-offering, etc." - one might think that the confession is not an independent commandment on its own, but rather only one of the things that are an extension of the sacrifice. Therefore, they had to elucidate in the Mekhilta that such is not the case, but rather it is indeed an independent commandment. And so they said there, "I might have thought that I only confess when they brought [offerings]. From where do I know even at the time that they do not bring [them]? Since it is stated, 'the children of Israel[...] and they shall confess'" - meaning to say that the tradition comes to expound [it] in this way. "Still, I might have thought that there is confession only in the Land"; that is, even though one may confess without the sacrifice, nonetheless, that the obligation for confession is only in the Land, as that is the locus of atonement, and the sacrifices are there and the locus of everything is there. "From where do I know to include the Diaspora? From that which is written (Leviticus 26:40), 'And they shall confess their iniquity and the iniquity of their fathers.'" That is, the iniquity of their fathers who sinned and were exiled from the Land. "And so [too,] did Daniel say outside of the Land (Daniel 9:7) 'For You, Lord, is the righteousness and for us is the shame on this day.'" Hence it is elucidated that confession is an independent commandment and that it is practiced in all places. And they also said in the Sifra (Sifra, Acharei Mot, Section 4 6), "'And they shall confess' - that is verbal confession."

It is from the roots of this commandment [that it is] because through the verbal admission of iniquity, the sinner reveals his thoughts and opinion: that he truly believes that all his deeds are revealed and known before God, Blessed be He, and that he will not act as if 'the Eye that sees' does not see. Furthermore, through mentioning the sin specifically, and through his remorse about it, he will be more careful about it on another occasion not to stumble in the same way again. Since he declares verbally, "I did such-and-such, and I stumbled in my deeds," he will have created a fence so he will not repeat what he did. And through this he will be wanted by his Creator. Blessed be He. And the Good God, who wants the good for His creations makes them walk in this way, [that] they merit with it.

From the laws of the commandment is that which they, may their memory be Blessed, said (Taanit 15a) that repentance is that the sinner leave the sin and remove it from his heart and from his thought, and he decide in his heart not to do like this again, as it is written (Isaiah 55:7), "Let the wicked give up his way, the sinful man his thoughts"; and afterwards, he must confess about it, meaning to say that he say the words of repentance orally, as it is stated (Exodus 32:31), "and they made for themselves a god of gold." And he must also mention explicitly that he will not return to do the sin again, as it is stated (Hosea 14:4), "and we will not again say 'our god' about the work of our hands, etc." And they, may their memory be Blessed, said (see Rambam, Mishneh Torah, Laws of Repentance 1:2) that the scapegoat would atone for all sins when one repented, light and weighty - whether he transgressed them volitionally or accidentally whether it was known to him or unknown to him. But if he did not repent, the scapegoat only atones for the light ones. And what are the light ones and what are the weighty ones? [Weighty ones] are sins for which one is liable for the death penalties of the court or excision; and also, vain and false oaths are from the weighty ones, even though they do not come with excision. And the other positive and negative commandments that do not come with excision are called light, in comparison to the weighty ones. And now that we do not have the Temple and the altar of atonement, on account of our iniquities, we only have repentance. And repentance atones for all sins. And even if one was a complete evildoer all of his days and he repented completely at the end, we do no mention any of his evil, as it is stated (Ezekiel 33:12), "and the wickedness of the wicked will not cause him to stumble when he turns back from his wickedness, etc." To what do these words apply that repentance alone suffices? To sins between man and the Omnipresent, such as one who eats something prohibited or has a prohibited sexual intercourse and so [too,] one who negates one of the positive commandments and similar to it. But [regarding[sins between a man and his fellow, such as one who injures his fellow, or robs his money or with any other thing through which he illegally injures him - whether in action or in speech - it is never forgiven him with repentance alone, until he gives his fellow what he owes him and until he is appeased. And they, may their memory be Blessed, have already said (Yoma 87a) what is his remedy if his fellow does not want to be appeased by him. And also, from the content of the commandment is that which they said in the Tosefta that there are twenty-four things that impede repentance, and they enumerate them there. [This] and the rest of the details of the commandment are elucidated in the last chapter of Yoma (see Mishneh Torah, Laws of Repentance 1).

And this commandment is practiced in every place and at all time by males and females. And one who transgresses it and does not confess about his sins on Yom Kippur, which is the day that is set from always for forgiveness and atonement, has violated this positive commandment. And woe to a man, if he dies without confession and carries his iniquity.

And the essence of confession that we received from our Rabbis and that is the custom of all of Israel to say during the Days of Repentance is, "However, we have sinned, we have been guilty, etc." And they, may their memory be Blessed, said in Shabbat 32a in the chapter [entitled] Bemeh Madlikin, "One who became ill and tended toward death, they say to him, 'Confess,' as it is the way of all those executed to confess." And so [too,] in Tractate Semachot, it is taught, "One who tended toward death, they say to him, 'Confess before you do not die. Many confessed and did not die, and many who did not confess died and many that are walking in the marketplace [have] confessed, as you live from the merit of your confessing.'" If he can confess orally, he [should do so], and if not, he [should] confess in his heart. And Rabbi Moshe ben Nachman (Ramban), may his memory be Blessed, wrote (in Torat HaAdam, Chapter of the End, regarding confession) that he received [a tradition] from pious men and men of good deeds, that such is the confession of someone on his deathbed: "I admit in front of You, Lord, my God and God of my fathers, that my healing is in Your hands and my death is in Your hands. May it be the will in front of You that You heal me [with] a complete healing. But if I die, let my death be atonement for all of my sins and my iniquities and my rebellion that I have sinned and been iniquitous and rebelled in front of You; and let my portion be in the Garden of Eden, and make me merit the World to Come that is safeguarded for the righteous." And remember this order, to say sins first, and afterwards iniquities and afterwards rebellion - the way we have mentioned, "I have sinned, I have been iniquitous, I have rebelled (chatati, aaviti, pashaati)." As Rabbi Meir and the Sages already disagreed about this in the Gemara (Yoma 36a): Rabbi Meir reasons that it is the opposite, that we say like Moshe said, "Who carries iniquity, rebellion and sin" (Exodus 34:7). But the law is like the Sages who reason that one mentions sins first. And the reason for the matter is explained in the Gemara.

Mitzvah 365
The commandment of the suspected adulteress (sotah) for the husband to bring her to the priest and that he do to her according to the statute that is written: To bring the sotah woman to the priest, so that he do to her according to the statute that is written about her in the [relevant] section of the Torah. And the matter of the sotah is explained in Scripture - that she is a woman whose husband has become jealous about her. And they, may their memory be Blessed, have already explained (Midrash Tanchuma, Nasso 5) what is [the meaning of] the expression, sotah, [that it is] meaning to say, she wandered from her husband - as most jealousy comes from the reason of the woman's licentiousness. And hence she is called a " sotah from her husband," since he is jealous about her. And the Scripture that teaches about this commandment is "If any man's wife stray, etc. And he shall bring his wife to the priest" (Numbers 5:12-15).

The root of this commandment is revealed to all that see the sun: that it is a great benefit within the nation that we have a mechanism to remove suspicion about our wives from our hearts and to truly know if she was unfaithful from her husband, which is impossible for any nation or country to have [something] like this among them. And about them, it is stated (Proverbs 30:20), "she eats, wipes her mouth, and says, 'I have done no wrong.'" As who will reveal 'about their daughters if they have been unfaithful, and about their daughters-in-law if they have been adulterous.' But our nation is sanctified with every matter of sanctification, and [so] God gave us a sign to know this matter which is hidden from the rest of the nations. And through this, love and peace between a man and his wife will be augmented and our seed will be holy. And [for] what [reason] should I write at more length about the details of these matters, as all of it is revealed to the heart of anyone with understanding. And therefore, in that the reason of the matter is a miracle with our people and a great honor for them, it stopped from the time they became corrupted by sins; as they, may their memory be Blessed, said (Sotah 47a), "From when adulterers proliferated, the sotah waters stopped; as it is stated (Hosea 12:4), 'I will not punish your daughters when they are unfaithful, etc.'" And the understanding of the verse is to say that He will [no longer] do this great miracle for them, that the waters should test whether the woman was unfaithful.

From the laws of the commandment is that which they, may their memory be Blessed, said (Sotah 2a) that the matter of jealousy is such that he said to his wife in front of two witnesses, "Do not seclude yourself with x" - and even if it were her father, or her brother or a gentile or slave or one impotent, and that is a man who cannot have children - and she secludes herself with one of them in front of witnesses [and] she remains with him enough [time] for impurity, which is enough to roast an egg and swallow it. Behold, [in this case] she is prohibited to her husband until she drinks the bitter waters, and the matter is tested. And at the time when there is no sotah waters, she is prohibited to her husband forever and she leaves [the marriage] without [collecting the value of her] marriage contract. But if he said to her, "Do not speak with Mr. x," this is not [considered] jealousy. And she is not prohibited to him with this jealousy, even though she secluded herself with him. If he was jealous in front of two witnesses, and he saw her seclude herself with the one with which he was jealous about her without witnesses, behold she is prohibited to him and he [must divorce her] and he gives her [the value of her] marriage contract - as he is not able to have her drink based on his own [testimony]. And so [too,] if he heard the people chattering about her that she was unfaithful with the man with whom he was jealous about her - to the point that the women who spin by the light of the moon are talking about her - he [must divorce her] and he gives her [the value of her] marriage contract.

And that which they, may their memory be Blessed, also said (Sotah 24a) that there are women that the court becomes jealous against; and they are the one whose husband has become deaf, or insane or that he has [gone] to another country or that he was imprisoned in a jail. And [it is not] to have her drink [that they do this], but rather to disqualify her from [collecting the value of] the marriage contract. And this matter is that if the court heard that the people are chattering about her [regarding] another man, they call her and say to her, "Do not seclude yourself with him." And if she secludes herself with him afterwards, the court prohibits her to her husband forever and they tear up her marriage contract. And when the husband arrives, he gives her a bill of divorce. And that which they said (Sotah 18b) that if she drank the bitter waters once about another man and she was rendered innocent by them, and he went back and was jealous about her from him [again], and she secluded herself with him [again] - she never drinks another time on his account. Rather, she is prohibited to her husband and leaves [the marriage] without [collecting the value of her] marriage contract. But if he became jealous about her [regarding] different men, she must drink, even a hundred times. And we never force her to drink - whether she said, "I have become impure," or she says, "I am not impure, but I will not drink." Rather, [if she refuses to drink,] she leaves [the marriage] without [collecting the value of her] marriage contract and she becomes prohibited to her husband forever. And if it is her husband that says, "I do not want to have her drink," she leaves [the marriage], but takes [the value of her] marriage contract.

And there are women that do not drink even though they and their husbands want [it]. And they are fifteen women and these are them: a raped woman (see note), and one waiting to preform levirate marriage, as it is written (Numbers 5:29), "underneath (tachat) her husband" - and these are not yet underneath a husband; a minor [who is] the wife of an adult, as it is written, "whereby a woman strays" - and this one is not yet a woman; an adult [who is] the wife of a minor, as it is written, "underneath her husband (literally, man)" - and this one is not yet a man; the wife of a man of unclear sex (androginos), as it is written, "her man" - and this one is not completely a man; the wife of a blind man, as it is written (Numbers 5:13), "and it is hidden from the eyes of her husband" - and this one has no eyes; a lame woman, as it is written (Numbers 5:18), "And the priest will make the woman stand" - and this one is not able to stand; one who does not have a palm of the hand, as it is written, "and he gives into her palms" - and this one does not have a palm; so [too] if her hand is crooked or paralyzed, such that she can only only take it with one hand alone, she does not drink, as it is written, "into her palms"; a mute, as it is written (Numbers 5:22), "and the woman says"; one who does not hear, as it is written (Numbers 5:19) "and he says to the woman"; so [too,] [if] he be lame or stump-armed or mute or deaf, and so [if] she is blind, as it is written (Numbers 5:29), "a woman tachat her husband" (here, the word, tachat, is understood as, corresponding to) - until she be complete like he, and he like her. [These] and the rest of all its details, the order of the drinking of the sotah and which angles does the water test and which angles does it not test is all well elucidated in the Tractate that is built on it, and that is Tractate Sotah (see Tur, Even HaEzer 148).

And this commandment is practiced at the time of the Temple by males, as it is incumbent upon them to do this process to women to test them, if they see that they require it. And [this is] only when there is a court of seventy-one [judges]. As so have we received in tradition (Sotah 7b), that we only make a sotah drink with the court of seventy-one in the Temple. And one who transgresses it and became jealous of his wife and she [then] isolated herself, and he did not bring her to the priest to do to her the process that is written in this section of the Torah, has violated this positive commandment.

Mitzvah 366

That we not put oil on the sotah sacrifice: That we not put oil on the sotah sacrifice, as it is stated (Numbers 5:15), "And he shall bring her sacrifice, etc. and he shall not pour oil upon it."

From the roots of the commandment is that which they, may their memory be Blessed said (Bamidbar Rabbah 9:13) [that it is] so that her sacrifice not be beautiful. As oil is called light and she did it in the dark; and she did the act of an animal which fornicates with all, therefore her offering is inferior, it being barley (Sotah 15a). And Rabbi Moshe ben Nachman, may his memory be Blessed, also wrote (Ramban on Numbers 5:15) regarding the matter of the sacrifice of the sotah, on the level of its simple meaning, that the husband brings this sacrifice from his [possessions] for the jealousy that he has towards her, so that God, may He be Blessed, will take vengeance from her. And the reason for the barley (seorim) is that there be 'an angry storm (saara) of the Lord going out, and the storm land on the head of the evildoer, that it land on the head' of the unfaithful woman; and like the matter of griddle bread of barley that is stated with Gidon (Judges 7:13), which they interpreted as a great, tumultuous storm. And so, [it being] in the clay vessel is a sign that she should be broken like the pot of a craftsman; and so, the dirt is a sign that she die and return to the dirt. But regarding the matter of the oil, he did not say anything. And I will answer my portion about it: [It is] because the oil is the highest of all the liquids, as it floats over all of them. And now that the sotah has corrupted her deeds and he has removed her from being the mistress and put her down to be lowly and contemptuous, it is not fitting to bring on her sacrifice, the glorious oil which is prepared for light and greatness, to anoint the kings and the high priests with it. And the principle of the matters that we have been commanded [is that they are] to refine the thought of those that do the process, and to place into their hearts that one who corrupts his actions [will have] all of his ways come to disgrace and shame, and [be] 'full of humiliation' and mockery; and that God will benefit the good, and 'joy and gladness and preciousness will reach them.' This commandment with its laws is elucidated in the Scripture and there is no need to write at length about it (see Mishneh Torah, Laws of Woman Suspected of Infidelity 3).

And it is practiced at the time of the Temple. And as we wrote above in this Order in the commandment of the sotah (Sefer HaChinukh 365), we only have a sotah drink with the court of seventy-one in the Temple. And a priest that transgresses this and pours oil on the offering of the sotah has violated a negative commandment and is lashed.

Mitzvah 367

Not to place frankincense on the sotah sacrifice: Not to place frankincense on the sotah sacrifice, as it is stated (Numbers 5:15), "and he shall not put frankincense on it."

From the roots of the commandment is that which we have written about oil, as frankincense is a beautification of the sacrifice and a pleasant smell. And hence it is not fitting for a sinful woman to beautify her sacrifice. And they, may their memory be Blessed, also said about this (Bamidbar Rabbah 9:13) that the proper and modest matriarchs were called frankincense, as it is stated (Song of Songs 4:6), "to the hill of frankincense" - and this one separated from their ways. And this commandment is also elucidated in the Scripture, and its matter is written in its 'colleague' - there is no need to write at length about it.

Mitzvah 368

That the nazirite not drink wine or all types of spirits: That the nazirite not drink wine or all types of spirits, the essential [ingredient] of which be wine, which is the juice of grapes. As with the juice of other fruits, even though they are called spirits, they are not prohibited to the nazirite, except when they are in a mixture of that which comes out of the grape. And about this is it stated (Numbers 6:3), "From wine and spirit shall he abstain, etc. and any marination of grapes shall he not drink" - meaning to say that any mixture that has grapes is included in the prohibition. And it broadened this prevention and stated that even if the wine or the spirit that wine mixed into became vinegar, it is prohibited to drink it. And about this, the Scripture stated, "wine vinegar and spirit vinegar shall he not drink." And these are not two [separate] negative commandments, meaning to say one about wine and one about vinegar; as behold, it did not state, "wine vinegar shall he not drink and spirit vinegar shall he not drink." And we have learned from here that one who drinks wine and vinegar is only lashed for one [commandment].

I will write that which I have known about the roots of the matter of naziriteness in the commandment of growing the hair of the nazirite in this Order (Sefer HaChinukh 374). And the distancing of the nazirite from all mixtures of wine is all from the reason that is written there.

From the laws of the commandment is that which they, may their memory be Blessed, said (Nazir 34b) that anything that comes out of the grape, whether it is the fruit or the refuse - meaning to say the zag which is the peel, and the chartsan, which is the seed that is inside it - is forbidden to the nazirite, and as it is explained in the Scripture. But behold, the leaves, the shoots, the vines and the immature berries (smadar), they are permissible; since they are not fruit and not refuse, but are considered like the tree. [This] and the rest of the many details of the commandment are elucidated in the tractate that is built on this, and that is Tractate Nazir.

Sefer HaChinukh

And this prohibition is practiced by males and females in every place and at all times, as anyone who vows [to become a] nazirite is obligated to abstain form wine, spirits, wine vinegar, spirit vinegar and from any grape marinade. And one who transgresses this and drinks a reviit of a log of wine, or ate a kazayit of grapes that are wet or dry, or from their refuse which is the seeds and the peels, is liable for lashes. And even if he ate a kazayit from among them all - meaning to say that he took a little from each one of those [items] that we mentioned, until among all of them, there was the measurement of a kazayit - and he ate it, he is lashed. As all prohibitions of the nazirite combine one with the other to a kazayit, to require lashes because of them. But other prohibitions in the Torah do not combine one with the other, except for the meat of a carcass with the meat of a 'torn' animal (tereifah), and a sacrifice disqualified by the wrong thought (pigul) with a sacrifice disqualified by its lateness (notar), which combine. And the six items in the thanksgiving sacrifice, which are fat, meat, fine flour, oil, wine, and bread also combine. And it is not necessary to say that everything that is of one name combines, such as the carcass of an ox, the carcass of a lamb and the carcass of a gazelle, and similar to this (Mishneh Torah, Laws of Forbidden Foods 4:17).

And they, may their memory be Blessed, taught us that it is a prohibited substance with a prohibited substance that combines to [form a] kazayit, like those that we mentioned. But a permitted substance does not combine with a prohibited substance, regarding all of the prohibitions in the Torah. [This] means to say that one who eats half a [kazayit] of a prohibited substance and half a [kazayit] of a permitted substance mixed together will not be liable for lashes - whether in the prohibitions of the nazirite, or whether in all of the other prohibitions. And also even with consecrated foods, meat and milk, and expurgations [of the vessels] of the gentiles - which [all] include novelties - when he did not eat a kazayit of the prohibited matter, there is never a liability for lashes in the thing, as is explained in Pesachim 44b and Nazir 37b. As the law is not like Rabbi Akiva, who holds like that in Tractate Nazir 37a [in] the chapter [entitled] Shloshah Minin, and learns it from the passage of "and any marination." Rather, the law is like the Rabbis who disagree with him and establish that verse there, and so [too] in Tractate Pesachim 44b, to learn from it that the taste of the prohibited matter is prohibited just like its essence (its solid mass) - whether for the nazirite or whether for all of the prohibited substances in the Torah. And so, is it said there, "And [does] this 'and any marination' come [to teach] that? That one is required to [teach] like that which was taught, '"And any marination" is to give [that] the taste be like its essence. As where one soaked grape in water and the water has the taste of wine, [it is forbidden]. From here you derive [the law] with regard to all prohibited substances in the Torah.' Just as with regard to a nazirite, etc. [continuing to] whose [opinion] is this? The Rabbis. However, some [and I] say [it is] like Rabbi Akiva."

And many interpretations have been said about the understanding of 'the taste is like the essence.' And one of them - and it appears to be the best - is that any prohibited substance that is not with its type, but rather is mixed into a permissible substance and gave taste to it; about this they, may their memory be Blessed, said that the taste of the prohibited matter is forbidden, like the essence of the prohibited matter. This excludes if it mixed into its [own] type [of substance], as there is no giving off [a different] taste here. And for [the previous matter], this passage of "and any marination" was required. As if it were not that we learned this thing from this passage, I would have determined that any prohibited substance that mixed into a permissible substance - in its type, or even not in its type - is nullified by the majority [constituted by the permissible substance], based on the well-known principle of the Torah, that one [part] is nullified in two [parts]. [This] means to say, in a majority, as the expression, 'two' is not [meant to be] exact. And once we have known this, we should determine the taste to be like the substance. And what is the law that is well-known to us regarding the substance without a mixture? That one who eats a kazayit of a prohibited substance without the elapsing of the measurement [of time] of eating a peras is lashed for it. But if more than this elapsed, he is exempted. And this same law is said with its taste: That if a kazayit of the taste of the prohibited substance mixed into the permissible substance [such that it could be eaten] within the [time] required to eat a peras, and he ate from it the measurement of eating a peras without the mentioned elapsing [of time], he is lashed for it. [But] if he ate less than this, or if less than this measurement of the prohibited substance mixed into it, he is not lashed for it. And, likewise, some of the commentators said that included in lashing for the prohibition of its taste without its essence is that any time the prohibited substance gave so much taste into the permitted substance as if a kazayit of the prohibited substance was mixed into it, [such that it could be eaten] within the [time] required to eat a peras - even though we do not know the measurement of how much of the prohibited substance [itself] entered into it. And this is not the opinion of Rabbi Moshe ben Maimon (Rambam), may his memory be Blessed, according to what appears from his words in Separation (Mishneh Torah, Laws of Naziriteship 5:4) and in Holiness (Mishneh Torah, Laws of Forbidden Foods 15:3). Rather, according to his opinion, we never administer lashes until we know that he ate a kazayit of the substance of the prohibited substance - either on its own or in a mixture [wherein it constitutes] a kazayit [such that it could be eaten] within the [time] required to eat a peras. And according to this reasoning, that which they said there, "'Marination' is to give [that] the taste be like its essence; such as where one soaked grapes in water," is said regarding the matter of the prohibition, and not about lashes.

Mitzvah 369
That the nazirite not eat damp grapes: That the nazirite not eat damp (fresh) grapes, as it is stated (Numbers 6:3), "and damp, etc. grapes shall he not eat." And they, may their memory be Blessed, said in Tractate Nazir 35b, "'And damp [etc.] grapes, shall he not eat' [is to include] unripe fruit (boser)." The entire content of this commandment is [found] in the commandment before it (Sefer HaChinukh 368).
I will write from the roots of the matter of naziriteness below in the commandment of growing the hair of the nazirite (Sefer HaChinukh 374).

Mitzvah 370
That the nazirite not eat raisins: That the nazirite not eat raisins, as it is stated (Numbers 6:3), "and damp and dry grapes shall he not eat." [It is] such that you should not say, since they have changed their name - as they are called raisins and not grapes - they have become permissible. Hence the verse elucidated the prohibition with them also. And all of its content is in the previous commandments. And one who ate a kazayit of them is lashed.

Mitzvah 371
That the nazirite not eat the seeds of the grapes: That the nazirite not eat the seed of the grapes, as it is stated (Numbers 6:4), "from the seeds to the skin shall he not eat." All of its content is in the previous commandments. And if he ate a kazayit of them, he is lashed.

Mitzvah 372
That the nazirite not eat the peel of the grapes: That the nazirite not eat the peel of the grapes, as it is stated (Numbers 6:4), "to the zag shall he not eat" - and the understanding of zag is the peel. All of its content is in the previous commandments. And if he ate a kazayit of them, he is lashed. And the warnings in the distancing of wine are multiplied, since there is a great power in everything that comes out of the vine to magnify the [evil] impulse. And this is well-known to the wise men of science.
And Rabbi Moshe ben Maimon (Rambam) wrote (Sefer HaMitzvot LaRambam, Mitzot Lo Taase 206), "The proof about each and every one of these five being an independent commandment - meaning wine, grapes, raisins, seeds and pits - is that, behold a person is liable for one [set of] lashes for each and every one. And [it is] like they, may their memory be Blessed, said in the Mishnah (Nazir 34b), 'He is liable for the wine by itself, and for the grapes by themselves.' And they said [as follows] in Tractate Nazir 38b, '[If] he ate grapes that were damp and dry [along with] seeds and skins, and squeezed a cluster of grapes and drank [the juice], he is lashed five times.' And when they wanted to establish that the teacher that taught [these five sets of] lashes taught [certain prohibitions] and omitted [others] and that the nazirite is liable for more than five [sets of] lashes, they said, \'What did he omit? Behold, he omitted the negative commandment of "He shall not profane his word" (Numbers 30:3),' and they did not say he omitted, the prohibition of vinegar. And the reason is because he would

not be liable for two [sets of lashes] for wine and for vinegar - as vinegar is prohibited for its essence which is wine, as we have said. And the content of the passage is as if it had stated that the essence of the prohibition of wine does not depart from it when [the wine] spoils, and as we mentioned above in its place (Sefer HaChinukh 368). And from that which is fitting for you to know is that these prohibitions of the nazirite all combine to [form] a kazayit and that we administer lashes for a kazayit." To here [are the words of Rambam].

Mitzvah 373

That the nazirite not shave his hair: That the nazirite not shave his hair, all of the days of his naziriteness, as it is stated (Numbers 6:5) "a razor shall not pass over his head."

I have written from the roots of the commandment below in the commandment of growing the hair of the nazirite (Sefer HaChinukh 374).

From the laws of the commandment - that which they, may their memory be Blessed, said (Nazir 39a) that it is the same whether he shaves with a blade or with scissors like a blade or he plucked his hair with his hand, anytime that he cut it from the root, he is lashed, but anytime he left enough of it to bend its head to its root, he is not lashed, as this is not like a blade; [that] if he passed a salve over his head that removes hair and it removed his hair, he is not lashed, [but he did violate a positive commandment; (that) a nazirite who shaves all of his head is only lashed] for one shaving, but if they warned him about it for each and every hair, and he shaves [regardless], he is lashed for each and every one; so [too,] from the matter of the commandment, that which they said in Tractate Shabbat (50a), "A nazirite washes and separates, but he does not comb," meaning to say he [may] wash his hair with his hand and separate it with his fingernails and if hairs fall from his washing and his separating, he [need] not be concerned, since it is not his intention to remove them, and it is also possible that they will not shed because of this, but he [may] not comb with a comb, since a comb will remove and shed hair without a doubt, and so [too,] he should not wash with dirt, as it will certainly remove hair, but if he does so, he is not lashed, and the rest of its details - are in Tractate Nazir.

And regarding who practices it, and at which time and the punishment of one who transgresses it, it is all like the law of the other commandments of the nazirite that we have written. And nonetheless, it should be clarified here that if he shaves even one hair, he would be liable for lashes for it, and like they said in Nazir 40a, "Rav Chisda said, 'To get lashes, [it is] with one hair; to invalidate, [it is] with two'" - meaning to say that he did not perform the commandment of shaving [at the end of his term] so long as two hairs remain on his head; "'and to interrupt, he only interrupts with the majority of his head'" - meaning to say he only interrupts the tally of the days of his naziriteness if he shaves the majority of his head. But if he shaves its minority, he does not interrupt the tally of the days of his naziriteness with this, even though he has transgressed the negative commandment of "a razor shall not pass over his head."

And this prohibition is practiced in all places and at all times by males and females, since anyone who accepts naziriteness upon himself - and even in our time - is prohibited from shaving even one hair. And one who transgresses this and shaved even one hair, is liable for lashes.

Mitzvah 374

The commandment of growing the hair of the nazirite: That the nazirite - who is the person who separated himself from wine - is commanded to let his head hair grow for all the days of his naziriteness for God, as it states (Numbers 6:5), "he shall grow the locks of his head." And the language of Mekhilta (Sifra Zuta on Numbers 6:5) is "'He shall grow the hair' is a positive commandment. From where [do I know there is also a] negative commandment? Hence, it teaches to say 'a blade shall not pass over his head.'"

From the root of the commandment, I have already written an introduction at the beginning of the book that there being something in the world of the Holy One, Blessed be He, that combines physicality and intellect - and that is Man - was something fitting and necessary for His praise, Blessed be He, to come up properly from His creatures; that with this creature, there would not be lacking any

Sefer HaChinukh

possibilities, which we have in our minds to grasp, from His world, etc., as I wrote there. And there is no doubt that without this reason that obligates our intellect to dwell within the physical, [which is involved with] desire and sin, it would have been fitting for our intellect to stand and serve in front of our Creator and to recognize His honor like one of the 'sons of God' that are stationed with Him. However, because of this obligation, it is subjugated to live in physical houses. And since it is subjugated to this, it must occasionally veer from the service of its Creator to tend to the needs of its home where it lives. For a home's structure and its lumber and its stones cannot stand without a person minding it. If so, as the intention of man's creation was according to what we have said, whenever the intellect can minimize physical work and focus on the service of its Master, that is good for it; so long as it does not completely ignore the work of the house and destroy it. As this would also be considered a sin for him, as the King wished to have a creature like this. It is like the saying of Rabbi Yose, (Taanit 22b) that a person may not afflict himself on a fast day, which Rav Yehudah explained in the name of Rav as stemming from the verse "and man was a living thing" (Genesis 2:7), [which implies that the soul should be allowed to live]. On the [same basis] the wise king stated (Ecclesiastes 7:15), "Do not be overly righteous; do not be overly wise. Why should you be desolate?" And this is the holiness of the nazirite and his loftiness, as he departs from the physical. [About this] Shimon the Righteous said (Nazir 4b), "In all my days [as a priest], I never ate the guilt-offering of an impure nazirite, apart from one man who came to me from the South, who had beautiful eyes and a fine countenance, and his locks were arranged in curls. I said to him, 'My son, what did you see to destroy this [beautiful] hair?' He said to me, 'I was a shepherd for my father in my town, and I went to draw water from the spring, and I looked at my reflection. And my evil inclination quickly rose against me and sought to drive me from the world. I said to my evil inclination, "Wicked one! For what reason are you proud in a world that is not yours, about one who in the future will be maggots and worms. [I swear by] the Temple service that I will shave you for the [sake of] Heaven.' Immediately, I arose and kissed him on his head, and said to him, 'My son, may there be more nazirites like you in Israel. With regard to you the verse states (Numbers 6:2), "When either a man or a woman shall clearly utter a vow, the vow of a nazirite, to consecrate himself to the Lord."'" Therefore, in order to suppress the [evil] inclination, he is commanded to shave his head at the end of the days of his [term]. And he is not permitted to fix it up and to take a little of them, so that his [evil] impulse does not come back against him as [it did] at first. Rather, he has become obligated to shave it all, for there is no doubt that both very long hair and completely shaven heads destroy the appearance of a person.

And do not wrangle [with] me from what they, may their memory be Blessed, said (Nazir 19a), "He must bring an atonement offering for himself, for he pained himself by avoiding wine." For this also works with our explanation. Since I have already said that a person does not have the right to destroy his house and to wreck anything of the building that was built by the First Builder, it is fitting for him to bring atonement for his soul. For perhaps he has overstepped the boundary that obligates him with regard to his body and his soul. As perhaps being a nazirite is overly afflicting to his soul according to his nature and constitution. And all 'the ways of God, may He be Blessed, are righteous and the just follow them.' And Ramban, may his memory be Blessed, wrote in his commentary (Ramban on Numbers 6:11) according to the simple understanding that the reason of the sin-offering that the nazirite bring for atonement [is] that he requires atonement for returning to become impure with the desires of the world. As once this person had had a 'spirit of God' upon him and began to become a nazirite to God, it would have been fit to stay that way for his whole life. And there are seventy faces to the Torah.

From the laws of the commandment is that which they, may their memory be Blessed, said (Nazir 39a) that if the nazirite shaves - whether volitionally or accidentally, or even under duress - behold, this interrupts his count, and he begins to count [another] thirty days; as we hold that a standard nazirite period is thirty days (Nazir, 5a), so that he will have a lock. To what do these words apply? If the majority of his head was shaved with a blade or something like a blade, and there is not enough to fold their tops over to their roots from that which remains of [what was shaved]. But if he only shaved the minority of the hair on his head, he does not interrupt his count for this. And so too, he does not interrupt his count by drinking wine, even if he drank [it] for several days. But he does interrupt his number by impurity, as the verse explains.

[Also among the laws is] that which they, may their memory be Blessed, said that all substitutes for the term of nazirite are effective - meaning to say, if a person had a speech impediment, or lived in a place where everyone has a speech impediment, and their way is instead of saying nazir, they say nazik, nazich or pazich and he said one of these expressions about himself, such that he said, "I will be a nazik, nazich or pazich," behold, he is a nazirite. As we do not say that the words of his mouth must be identical to [what is in] his heart, as we do for oaths. Rather, once he has [decided] in his heart to become a nazirite and he says [something by which] it can be understood that [he wants] to be a nazirite - even though these are words that themselves do not [positively identify] him as a nazirite - behold, he is a nazirite. And so [too,] that which they said that [adjunct expressions are effective]; for example where he says, "I shall be," as a nazirite passes before him. Or if he says, "I will be beautiful" and holds his hair, behold, he is a nazirite. And so, one who says, "I will be a nazirite from grape seeds only," or "shaving, or impurity only," behold, he is a complete nazirite. And one who says, "I will be a nazirite on the condition that I will drink wine", or "become impure," or "shave," behold, he is a nazirite, and all [the prohibitions of a nazirite] are prohibited to him; because [in the case of] one who makes a condition which violates the laws of the Torah, the condition is cancelled. One may request [annulment] on a nazirite vow in the same way that one requests on other vows. A father may make a nazirite oath for his son up until age thirteen, but the mother may not, and this thing is a tradition. Gentiles are not subject to [becoming a] nazirite, though women and slaves are. A husband or father may annul the nazirite vow of his wife or daughter like other vows, as may a master force his slave to drink wine or become impure (see Mishneh Torah, Laws of Nazariteship 1). This commandment, that anyone who vows to be a nazirite is obligated to grow his hair, is practiced in all places and at all times by males and females. As even though they, may their memory be Blessed, taught us (Nazir 19b) that being a nazirite is only practiced in the Land of Israel - meaning to say that every person must observe his days of his naziriteness that he vowed in the Land of Israel, and that only the days that he is a nazirite there count in his tally - [still], all of the stringencies of being a nazirite are upon him outside of [Israel] as well. Therefore, if one made a nazirite vow at this time, behold, he is a nazirite forever. As now, on account of our afflictions, we have no [Temple in order] to offer the sacrifices at the end of the period of being a nazirite. They, may their memory be Blessed, also said that if we have the ability, we coerce the nazirite to go to [Israel] and to fulfill his nazirite vow there until he dies or until the Temple is rebuilt and he can repay his sacrifices.

Mitzvah 375
That the nazirite not enter the tent of a dead body: That the nazirite not enter the tent of a dead body, as it is stated (Numbers 6:6), "to the soul of a dead person he shall not enter."
I have written what I have known from the roots of distancing impurity from a holy place in this Order in the first commandment (Sefer HaChinukh 362). And it is the same thing and the same reason for the distancing of a holy man from it. And I have also written what I grasped about the reason of the impurity of a dead body in the Order of Emor el HaKohanim (Sefer HaChinukh 563).
From the laws of the commandment - that which they, may their memory be Blessed, said (Nazir 43a) that the nazirite is not liable for coming into the tent of a dead body until he goes in completely, and even though he becomes impure regardless from the time when his nose or his toe goes in, it is not called entering until he goes in completely, therefore a nazirite that goes into a house where there is a dead body inside a chest, a box or a cabinet and his fellow opens the roof of [the relevant item] with his knowledge, is given two [sets] of lashes, one for "he shall not enter" and one for "he shall not become impure," as behold the impurity and the entering come at one time; [that] a nazirite that entered a tent of a dead body or a graveyard accidentally and, after it was known to him, remained there enough time to prostrate oneself in the Temple, is liable for lashes; and the rest of its details - are elucidated in Tractate Nazir.
And this prohibition is practiced in every place and at all times by males and females. And one who transgresses it and becomes impure according to the guidelines that we have said is liable for lashes.

Sefer HaChinukh

Mitzvah 376

That the nazirite not become impure through a dead body or through other impurities: That the nazirite not become impure through a dead body, as it is stated (Numbers 6:7), "For his father or for his mother, etc. he shall not become impure, etc." Even though I have already written the reason for the distancing of impurity from that which is holy in the first commandment of this Order (Sefer HaChinukh 362), I will still say that which comes to my spirit about the reason of the great stringency with the nazirite; as he is commanded not to become impure even for his father and his mother and - there is no need to say - other relatives, and [yet] a regular priest who is also holy, may become impure for [his close relatives]. And the matter is apparently because the holiness of the priest rests upon him automatically. He did not agree to it and it was not from his consent, but rather he was sanctified from birth and from the womb, by force of his tribe which is totally holy. And [so] his behavior towards his relatives is like all other people, since there is no difference between the priestly man and the rest of the people, except that sometimes he will do the service for his God. However, sometimes he will also dwell in his domicile and regale with his friends - he calls to his companions for joy and parties. Hence his heart will be warm towards them and theirs towards him. And because of this, the Torah permitted [him] to become impure for them - 'all the ways of the Torah are pleasant and all of its paths are peace.'

However, the man that is a nazirite to God is holy to God all the days of his nazirite vows and - as the verse attests to him (Numbers 6:7) - "as the crown of his God is upon him," he will not become impurified with worldly desires, and he will not be found at parties and the banquets of his companions. As his separation from wine shows about him that he has given his heart to prepare himself and to afflict himself before God, to improve the ways of his soul and to leave the pleasures of the benighted body. And since he has placed all of his heart and all of his thoughts towards his dear soul and he has abandoned all of his own needs and those of his flesh, what would be his desire for the drawing close of his companions and his friends - besides for the commandment, without a doubt. As with the raising of the soul, the pleasures of the body and all of its matters become very light in its eyes. All the more so will it not seek the company of other bodies, whether they be relatives or [others], and it will not find delight in any of their things, besides the holy service to which it is connected and to which its eyes are always directed. And hence from his great holiness and separation from his brothers, the Torah prevents him from becoming impure for them. And [it is] like the matter of the high priest - as since his matters are very elevated and he is separated from the company of his friends, and his pursuits and thoughts are only about the service of his God, may He be Blessed, the Torah prevents him from becoming impure for anyone of his relatives. And the stated explanation for his distancing from impurity is also stated about the nazirite; except that with the priest, it mentions oil, since he is anointed with it, but with the nazirite, it does not mention oil. As with the priest, it states (Leviticus 21:22), "as the crown of the anointing oil of his God is upon him." But with the nazirite, it [only] states, "as the crown of his God is upon him." And maybe you will think to respond to me, that when a temporary nazirite finishes his time, he will return to his obliviousness and chase after his desires; and, if so, why should he be more stringent than a regular priest? The answer is that after a person takes on being a nazirite one time, there is hope for him to sanctify himself and to add to his goodness each day. And he will be agreed to from the Heavens and like the matter that they, may their memory be Blessed, said (Shabbat 104a), "One who comes to purify himself, is assisted." And since he has taken on being a nazirite even one day, he is assisted and will finish all of his days in purity.

From the laws of the commandment is that which they, may their memory Blessed, said (Nazir 49b) that there is a [type of] impurity of a dead body that if the nazirite is made impure by it, he shaves and it interrupts his earlier [tally of] days, and begins to count the days of his naziriteness afterwards [from the beginning]; and there is [another type of] impurity of a dead body for which he does not shave and it does not interrupt his earlier days. [And the latter is such,] even though it is an impurity [that makes impure for] seven [days] (characteristic of impurity generated by a dead body); because it is not said about it, "and if he becomes impure for a soul," but rather (Numbers 6:9), "And if a dead

Sefer HaChinukh

body dies upon him" - which implies [only] when he becomes impure with impurities which are from the essence of the dead body. And these are the impurities for which the nazirite must shave: for a stillborn embryo, even if its limbs have not become attached to its tendons; for a kazayit from a dead body; for a kazayit of the discarded (netsel); for the bones that make up the numerical majority of the bones, even if they do not constiture one quarter of a kav ; for half a kav of bones, even if they do not constitute the majority of its structure or their numerical majority, so long as all of the bones are from one dead body and not from two dead bodies; for a backbone coming from a dead body; for the skull of one dead body; for the [detached] limb of a living person that has [enough] flesh to grow back on a living person; for half a log of blood from one dead body; and for a fist-full of rotted remains of a dead body. And what is netsel? It is flesh of a dead body that is dissolved and has become rotten liquid. And the rotten remains (rakav) of a dead person only render impure if he is buried naked in a marble coffin and he is all complete. If one limb was lacking from him or if he was buried with his cloak or in a coffin of boneware or metal, [his remains] are not [considered] rakav. And they only spoke about rakav regarding a dead body alone, which excludes someone killed, as behold, he is missing his blood. If they buried two dead bodies together or they cut his hair or his fingernails and buried them with him, or if a pregnant woman died and she was buried [with] the embryo in her innards and so [too,] if [someone] ground the dead body until it became rakav, their rakav does not render impure until [the body itself] rots on its own. And so [too,] if he became impure from a quarter [of a kav] of bones that come from the backbone or from the skull in their tent, behold it is a doubt whether he is impure.

[Regarding] all of these twelve [types of] impurity that we have enumerated - if the nazirite touched one of them or if he carried it, or if the nazirite hovered over it or the impurity hovered over the nazirite or the nazirite and one of the impurities were [together] in a tent (under anything over them) - behold he must shave the shaving of (caused by) impurity, and he brings a sacrifice for impurity and it interrupts all [of the days of his tally]. [This is true of all of the impurities] except for rakav, which does not render impure with touch, as it is impossible for him to touch it all, as behold, it is not one body. But if he carries it or becomes impure in its tent, he must shave. And so [too,] a nazirite who touches a bone of a dead body - even a bone that is [the size] of a barley grain - or he carries it, behold, this one must shave for it and bring a sacrifice for impurity and interrupts the previous [days]. But one [single] bone does not render impure in a tent.

But if he became impure from a clod of the land of the [other] peoples or of a field in which a grave was plowed - which render impure through touch and carrying; or if one of the twelve impurities mentioned was hovered over by shoots coming out of trees or protrusions coming out of a fence or a bed or a camel and that which is similar to it and he become impure in their hovering; or from a quarter [of a kav] of bones that do not constitute the majority of its structure or their numerical majority; or he became impure from a quarter [of a log] of blood - even though it renders impure through touch and carrying and in a tent; or he became impure from a grave-covering or [its] frame - which renders impure through touch and carrying; or he became impure from a limb from a living person or from a limb from a dead person, which does not have flesh that is fit, according to the matter that we described - behold this does not interrupt, even though he is impure from an impurity [that makes impure for] seven [days] and he sprinkles on the third and on the seventh, [nonetheless] he does not shave the shaving of impurity and he does not bring sacrifices and he does not interrupt the first ones. However, all of the days of impurity do not count for him in the tally of the days of being a nazirite.

And so [too,] from the matter of the commandment is that which they said (Nazir 44a), that one who causes a nazirite to become impure - if the nazirite was volitional - [the nazirite] is given lashes, and the one who rendered him impure transgresses on account of "in front of a blind man, etc." (Leviticus 19:14). But if the nazirite is indavertent, [even] if the one who makes him impure is volitional, neither one of them is lashed. And why is the one who makes him impure not lashed? Because it is stated (Numbers 6:9), "and he makes impure the head of his naziriteness" - meaning to say that the liability for lashes is only when he becomes impure with his consent. [These] and the rest of its details are in Tractate Nazir.

And this prohibition is practiced in every place and at all times by males and females. And one who transgresses it and makes himself impure volitionally according to the guidelines we have elucidated is lashed. And Ramban, may his memory be Blessed, wrote (the seemingly correct textual variant reads, Rambam, as the source is Mishneh Torah, Laws of Naziriteship 5:20-21) that a nazirite who makes himself impure volitionally is liable for four [different sets of] lashes: on account of "he shall not become impure"; on account of "he shall not profane his word"; on account of "he shall not delay to repay it"; and on account of "he shall not enter" - and that is when the entering and the impurity come together.

Mitzvah 377
The commandment of shaving the nazirite and bringing his sacrifices: That the nazirite shave his hair and bring sacrifices when he completes his naziriteness, and so [too,] if he becomes impure; as it is stated (Numbers 6:13), "and on the day that his term as nazirite is completed, etc." and also (Numbers 6:9), "If a dead body dies upon him, etc." And they said in Sifra, Metzora, Chapter 2:6, "Three shave, and their shaving is a commandment - the nazirite, the leper (metsora), and the Levites." However the three are not equal in all of their [characteristics], as the shaving of the Levites was for its time in the wilderness and not practiced [by future] generations; but the shaving of the leper and the nazirite is a commandment that is practiced [by future] generations. And Rambam, may his memory be Blessed, wrote (Sefer Ha Mitzvot LaRambam, Mitzvot Ase 93) that the two shavings of the nazirite - which are the shaving of impurity and the shaving of purification - are only fitting to be counted as one commandment; as the matter of the shaving of impurity is not a separate commandment at all, but rather one law of the laws of naziriteness. [That is] that the Scripture elucidated that if the nazirite becomes impure in the days of his being a nazirite, he must shave and bring a sacrifice and then he goes back to growing his locks in holiness for the days of naziriteness that he forbade to himself, like at the start. [It is] like the leper who also has two shavings and they are one commandment. And since it is not the essence of the commandment, but rather one law of its laws, it is not fitting to count it as a separate commandment - and as the Teacher, may his memory be Blessed, elucidated in his Book of the Commandments in the Seventh Root. And in the Order of Zot Tehiyeh (Metsora), I have also written in the name of the Teacher, may his memory be Blessed, the reason for our counting the shaving of the nazirite and his sacrifices as one commandment, and the shaving of the leper and his sacrifices as two commandments. And you will see it elucidated there, if you want to study [it].

I have written what I have known from the roots of this commandment, of shaving all of the hair with the completion of the days of being a nazirite and the bringing of sacrifices, within the root of the previous commandment (Sefer HaChinukh 374).

From the laws of the commandment - that which they, may their memory be Blessed, said (Mishnah Middot 2:5), "Where does he shave his hair? In the women's courtyard," and the chamber of nazirites was there in the southeast corner, and they would cook their peace-offerings there and throw the hair into the fire, and if he shaved in the [rest of the] country, he would have discharged [his obligation] (Mishneh Torah, Laws of Naziriteship 8:3); [that] in any place that he shaves, he throws it under the cauldron; [that] he does not shave until the opening of the courtyard be open, as it is stated (Numbers 6:18), "at the opening of the Tent of Meeting," and the understanding of the verse is not that he should shave in front of the opening, as there would be a disgrace to the Temple in this; so [too,] that which they, may their memory be Blessed, said about this commandment (Nazir 46a), [that] a nazirite who pulled out [his hair] does not need to pass a blade over [his head] even though he does not have hair, and so [too,] if he does not have palms [of the hand], behold, this one brings his sacrifices, and afterwards he can drink and become impure, and even if he has hair, once he has brought his sacrifices, even though he did not shave, the shaving does not impede [it], and he can drink and become impure in the evening, even though he did not give it on his palms and wave it, as all of these things are for [the fulfillment of] the commandment and not for an impediment; [that] even though the shaving does not impede, it is a commandment to shave even after much time; [that] a nazirite who shaved without a blade or shaved with a blade but left [at least] two hairs, did not do anything and did not fulfill the commandment of shaving, whether [in the case of] a pure nazirite, or whether [in the case of] an impure nazirite; that if he shaved upon his peace-offerings and they were found to be disqualified, his shaving is disqualified, [but] if he shaved upon [all] three animals that he is sacrificing, and it comes out that [at least] one of them is fit, his shaving is fit, and he shall bring the rest of his offerings [afterwards] and they are to be sacrificed, as per their law, [and] these three animals are a male lamb for a burnt-offering, a female lamb for a sin-offering and a ram for a peace-offering, and he brings six and two-thirds issaron of fine flour with the ram, and he bakes twenty loaves from it; and the rest of its details - are in Tractate Nazir.

And it is practiced at the time of the [Temple] by males and females. And one who transgresses it and does not shave it or shaves it without a blade or shaves but leaves [at least] two hairs has violated a positive commandment. But if he left one hair alone, the commandment is not violated for one hair. And even if he shaved and left two hairs, and afterwards, one of them sheds on its own; if he [now] shaves the other - even though there is no hair here, as behold, one strand is not considered hair, as we have said, [nonetheless] there is the commandment of shaving here, as he already shaved all of his head except for the two, and the shedding of one was nothing, as one strand is not considered anything - when he shaved the other, behold, he finished the shaving completely and fulfilled the commandment of shaving. And even though the shaving does not impede from drinking wine and becoming impure [at the end of his term], as we have said, the bringing of sacrifices impedes everything. And if he did not bring [them], he has violated this positive commandment, and he is prohibited from drinking wine and to become impure, until he brings them. And even though he has shaved, the commandment is not completed until he brings the sacrifices.

Mitzvah 378
The commandment of the priestly blessing every day: That the priests were commanded that they should bless Israel every day, as it is stated (Numbers 6:23), "Thus shall you bless the Children of Israel; say to them."

It is from the roots of the commandment that God wanted in His great goodness to bless His people through the servants that are always encamped in the House of God and all of their thoughts cling to His service and their souls are connected to His fear the whole day. And in their merit the blessing rests upon [the Jewish people] and all of their deeds are Blessed, and the pleasantness of God will be upon them. And do not wonder to say, "Were God to desire their blessing, He would command the blessing to them, and there is no need for the priestly blessing." As I have already anticipated [this] many times [by saying] that blessing rests upon us according to the preparation of our deeds. As His hand, Blessed be He, is open to all that ask if they are fit and prepared to receive the good. And therefore, when He chose us from all of the nations and wanted that we merit His goodness, He warned us and commanded us to prepare our deeds and refine our bodies with His commandments, so that we will be fit [to receive] the good. He also commanded us in His great goodness to request blessing from Him, and that we should ask for it through the pure servants. As all of this will be a merit for our souls, and through it, we will merit His goodness.

From the laws of the commandment is that which they, may their memory be Blessed, said (Megillah 23b) that the priests only raise their hands (to make the blessing) when there are ten (a prayer quorum), and the priests [are included in] the tally. And how is the raising of the hands? (Sotah 38b, Mishneh Torah, Laws of Prayer and the Priestly Blessing 14:3-4) At the time the prayer leader reaches the [blessing of] service, meaning to say when he wants to begin to say the blessing of Retseh, all the priests in the synagogue go up to the platform [with] their faces towards the ark, their backs towards the people, and their fingers bent upon their palms, until the prayer leader finishes the blessing of thanksgiving. And afterwards, they turn their faces towards the people, extend their fingers and raise their hands across from their shoulders and begin, "May He bless you." And the prayer leader dictates to them word by word, as it is stated, "say to them"; and they repeat after him with a pleasant tone. And when they finish the first verse [of the blessing], all of the people answer, "Amen." And so [too,] with the second verse, and the third. And when they finish [all] three verses, the prayer leader begins " Sim shalom, etc." (the next blessing) and the priests turn their faces towards the holy [ark] and bend their fingers and stand there on the platform until he finishes the blessing of Sim shalom, and [then] return to their places. And our custom today is that the priests do not go up to the platform, but rather stand in front of the ark and follow the [rest of the] order that we have written.

And before they turn their faces to bless the people, they recite the blessing, Blessed are You, Lord, our God, King of the universe, who has sanctified us with the holiness of Aharon and commanded us to bless His people, Israel, with love. And all of the turns that they turn - such as turning their faces to the congregation or to the chamber - should always be to the right. And six things prevent the priests from the 'raising of the hands' (Mishneh Torah, Laws of Prayer and the Priestly Blessing 15:1): the tongue; blemishes; sin; impurity of the hands; years; and wine. And the elucidation of these things together with the rest of the details of the commandment are all elucidated in the last chapter of Megillah and Taanit, and the seventh [one] of Sotah (see Tur, Orach Chaim 128).

And this commandment is practiced every day and at all times by the priests, as this commandment to bless Israel is upon them. And they are obligated to bless them in the morning service, in the additional service, and at the sealing of the gates (Neilah service on Yom Kippur). But in the afternoon service, there is no 'raising of the hands,' because all men have already had their [lunch] meal by the afternoon service, and [so] there is a concern of wine, as a drunk is forbidden in the 'raising of the hands.' They, may their memory be Blessed, decreed [not to say it] even in the afternoon service of a fast day, based on the afternoon service of every day, and as Rav Nachman decided in the last chapter of Taanit 26b. But over there, they said, "But nowadays, what is the reason [that] priests spread their hands in the afternoon prayer of a fast? Since they prayed it near sunset, it is considered like the Neilah service."

Mitzvah 379

The commandment of carrying the Ark on the shoulder: That the priests (Kohanim) are commanded to carry the Ark on their shoulders when the People of Israel move it from one place to another, as it is stated (Numbers 7:9), "for the holy service is upon them, they shall carry on their shoulders." Rabbi Moshe ben Maimon (Maimonides), may his memory be Blessed, wrote (Sefer HaMitzvot LaRambam, Mitzvot Ase 34) [that] even though this commandment came to the Levites, that was [only] at that time - meaning to say in the wilderness, due to the small number of Kohanim at that time. In [future] generations, however, the Kohanim were obligated in this commandment - and they shall carry it - as is elucidated from the Book of Joshua and the Book of Samuel.

And Rabbi Moshe ben Nachman (Nachmanides), may his memory be Blessed, wrote (in his glosses to the Sefer HaMitzvot LaRambam on the third Shoresh, s.v. veraiti) that that which the teacher said that the commandment was moved to the Kohanim is not true. God forbid that we should say that any commandment in the Torah changed, that the Levites were disqualified from carrying the Ark forever, and that he explained it well. [As we see that] the Levites carried it in the days of David, as it is stated (I Chronicles 15:26), "And it was in God's assisting the Levites who were carriers of the Ark of the Covenant of the Lord," and it is written (I Chronicles 15:27), "And all the Levites who were carrying the Ark, etc." But in truth, both the Kohanim and Levites are acceptable for carrying the Ark from Torah writ. As they are all called Levites, as it is written (Ezekiel 44:15), "the Levite Kohanim." And so [too,] is it written (I Chronicles 15:14-15), "And the Kohanim and Levites sanctified themselves to bring up the Ark of the Lord, the God of Israel, as Moshe had commanded by the word of the Lord, with the poles on their shoulders." And they said in the Sifrei, "Where did He command [this]? [From the verse] 'And to the sons of Kehat was not given any other, etc.'" - as they are all called the sons of Kehat. And he also wrote [regarding] what Maimonides, may his memory be Blessed, wrote that it is elucidated from the Book of Joshua and Samuel, that he did not find this elucidation. Rather, he found the opposite, as it is stated there (Joshua 3:3), "And he commanded the people saying, 'When you see the Ark of the Covenant of the Lord, your God, that is carried by the Kohanim, Levites." Rather, the truth is as we have said, that the whole tribe is eligible to carry the Ark. Moreover, the thing is explicit in Tractate Sotah 33b, where they, may their memory be Blessed, said, "How did the Israelites cross the Jordan? Every day the Levites carried the Ark, and on this day, it was carried by the Kohanim." That is, on the day that they crossed the Jordan, only the Kohanim carried it, as so is it written (Joshua

3:6), "And Yehoshua said to the Kohanim, 'Carry the Ark of the Covenant'" - so that the miracle would be done by the Kohanim, as they are the holiest members of the tribe.

It also seems that that which Maimonides, may his memory be Blessed, said that it is elucidated in Joshua is from this verse, but it is not a clear elucidation at all, as we have said. And that which is stated in I Kings 8:1, "And the Kohanim brought the Ark of the Covenant of the Lord to its place, to the sanctuary, to the Holy of Holies" should also not be difficult in your eyes. It is because the Levites were not permitted to enter the Holy of Holies that only the Kohanim brought it in. And [so] the main approach seems to be like the words of Nachmanides, may his memory be Blessed, that the entire tribe is fit to carry the Ark; and as it is written (II Chronicles 35:3), "And he said to the Levites, etc. 'place the Holy Ark in the Temple that was built by Solomon's son of David, the king of Israel, there is no longer a burden on your shoulders.'" Its matter is also that Israel would have no more need to carry the Ark form one place to another; but it does not indicate that if it were to move it, that it would not be done by the Levites, and this is clear and obvious to all. And [regarding] that which the Sages said (Chullin 24a) [that] blemishes disqualify the Kohanim but years do not, it is only the priestly duties that are not affected by age, but age does disqualify the Kohanim for the labor of carrying, as it does for the Levites (see Mishneh Torah, Laws of Vessels of the Sanctuary and Those who Serve Therein 2).

It is from the roots of the commandment that it is because the main glory of Israel is the Torah, through which they were made distinct from the other peoples and made into the portion of God. And it is therefore fitting and proper that it should be carried by the most dignified and holy people among us. And there is no need to elaborate on matters that any school child can understand. The entire content of the commandment is elucidated in the verse, and that is that the Kohanim and Levites would carry the Ark on their shoulders whenever they needed to move it from place to place, such as during war or for some other thing; and they would not carry it in a wagon or the back of an animal. And the Sages already castigated David for being mistaken about a thing that even toddlers read about, in his placing the Ark on a wagon (Sotah 34a).

And this commandment is practiced at the time when Israel is on their land; for there was a need then to carry the Ark of the Covenant of God because of war or when the king commanded. But today, on account of our iniquitis, we have no king and no Ark to carry in any place. And this commandment is incumbent upon the tribe of Levi; and upon the rest of the people to support them. And that to which they are accustomed today in the Diaspora to bring out the Torah to greet the [non-Jewish] kings is not governed by this commandment at all, as any of the Children of Israel may carry it. But if they choose a [Levite] even today as a way of showing honor to the Torah, [it is praiseworthy].

Mitzvah 380

The commandment of the second Pesach (Pesach Sheni) on the fourteenth of Iyar: That anyone who was unable to offer the first Pesach offering on the fourteenth day of Nissan - for example, due to impurity or because he was at a distance - [offer] the second Pesach offering on the fourteenth day of Iyar; as it is stated (Numbers 9:11), "On the second month on the fourteenth day in the afternoon, you shall offer it." The Sages taught us further (Pesachim 73a) that it is not specifically ritual impurity or distance, but any case of inadvertence or duress; or even if was volitional and he did not offer the first one, he may offer the second one.

It is from the roots of the commandment that it is because the commandment of the Pesach offering is a powerful and clear sign to all of the creation of the world. For at the time [of the exodus], God, Blessed be He, performed great miracles and wonders for us and changed the nature of the world in the eyes of many nations. And [so] all the peoples of the earth saw that His providence and power is over the lower (earthly) beings. And then at that time, everyone believed and all who came after them believed that He, Blessed be He, created the word ex nihilo at the time that He chose - and that was the well-known time. [As] even though creation ex nihilo is impossible according to the [laws of] nature, so too is splitting the depths of the sea to allow the passage of a great assemblage of people on dry land and returning them to their place, as is sustaining a large and numerous people for forty years on bread that would descend from the sky every day, and all the other signs and wonders that

Sefer HaChinukh

He performed for us at that time, as they all were novel and went against the laws of nature. This is the firm pillar of our faith and our Torah, for people who believe in the eternity of the universe have no Torah and no share in the World to Come. This thing is well-known and there is no need to elaborate on well-known matters. Therefore, it was His will, Blessed be He, to allow every man of Israel to merit in this important commandment, and that an accident or long-distance not impede him from fulfilling it. Rather, 'if trouble will occur to him' and he is prevented in the first month and he did not do it with the earlier ones, he may do it in the second month. And since this is a great fundamental principle in our religion, the obligation even extends to a convert who converted between the first Pesach and the second, and so [too, to] a child who reached maturity between the two Pesachs - that they are obligated to [offer] the Pesach Sheni sacrifice (see Mishneh Torah, Laws of Paschal Offering 6:7).

From the laws of the commandment is that which they, may their memory be Blessed, taught in Pesachim 95a in the chapter [entitled] Mi Shehaya Tamei, "What [are the differences] between first and second? On the first all leaven is forbidden to be seen or kept in one's possession; on the second both leaven and matsa are with him in the house. The second is only observed one day, and there is no holiday or prohibition of labor. The first requires Hallel while eating it; the second does not require Hallel while eating it - though this and that require Hallel during the offering. Both are eaten roasted with matsa and marror," as it is explicitly stated like that in the verse. "Both supersede the Shabbat, and neither may be left over or have bones broken in them," as the verse explicitly warns about this too, with "do not leave over" and "they shall not break a bone in it."

And if you ask, my son, why they are not completely equal, as behold, the verse explicitly states with respect to the Pesach Sheni sacrifice, "according to all the laws of the Pesach sacrifice shall you make it"; you should know that the Sages, may their memory be Blessed, already alerted us to this. And they clarified in the chapter [entitled] Mi Shehaya Tamei (Pesachim 95a) that the verse refers only to details that pertain to the body of the Pesach sacrifice, such as eating it with matsa and marror, not leaving any over, and not breaking bones, as we have explained. They taught us this from [the fact] that the verse singled out a few laws here with Pesach Sheni, while if the laws were truly identical it would have been sufficient to simply state, "according to all the laws of the Pesach sacrifice, etc." And so they said, "Just as the bone is remarkable in that is part of the body, so too anything, etc."

Also relevant to this commandment is that which they also said (Pesachim 93a) that the impure person that is delayed to Pesach Sheni is one who is impure in a severe way that impedes him from eating the Pesach sacrifice, such as someone who experienced a flow, or a menstruant, or a new mother, or one who had intercourse with a menstruant or someone who became impure through contact with the dead under circumstances that would require a nazirite to shave, as we explained in the Order of Nasso (Sefer HaChinukh 376). But if he became impure from the other impurities of the dead body for which the nazirite does not shave, and so [too,] if he touched a carcass or a crawling animal (sherets), or something like it - even on the fourteenth - behold, he will immerse [in the mikveh] and they slaughter [the Pesach sacrifice] after he immerses; and in the evening when the sun has set for him, he eats his Pesach sacrifice. Also relevant to this commandment is that which they, may their memory be Blessed, said there in the chapter [entitled] Mi Shehaya Tamei (Pesachim 93b) that a 'far distance' with regard to the established law [means anything] that is fifteen mil outside of the walls of Jerusalem, but less than that is not called a far distance. And the rest of its details are in Tractate Pesachim (see Mishneh Torah, Laws of Paschal Offering 5).

This commandment is practiced at the time of the [Temple] - by males in the category of obligation, and by females in the category of the optional. As so did they, may their memory be Blessed, instruct us (Pesachim 91b) [regarding] women who were delayed to Pesach Sheni because of impurity or because of one of the things that we mentioned, that the offering of the Pesach Sheni sacrifice is optional for them: If they wish [to], they slaughter, if they wish [not to], they do not slaughter. And for this reason we may not slaughter only on their behalf on the Shabbat. And a man who transgresses this and volitionally violated this positive commandment and did not bring the Pesach Sheni sacrifice, after he was under duress and was unable to offer the first Pesach sacrifice, is liable for excision. This is the opinion of Rabbi [Yehudah HaNasi] in the Mishnah (Pesachim 93a). But Rabbi Natan, Rabbi

Chaninah and Rabbi Akiva exempt him from excision, as he was not volitional in the first case. And we need not say that if he deliberately [did not partake of a sacrifice] the first time, and he also violated the second, whether willfully or not, that he incurs excision according to all, as he deliberately failed to offer the sacrifice of God in its proper time. And this is one of two positive commandments for which the punishment is excision, as we explained in the Order of Bo el Pharoah (Sefer HaChinukh 5).

Mitzvah 381
The commandment that the second Pesach (Pesach Sheni) offering be eaten with matsot and maror (bitter herbs): That anyone who is obligated in Pesach Sheni eat from the meat of the Pesach offering with matsot and bitter herbs, as it is stated (Numbers 9:11), "They shall eat it with unleavened bread and bitter herbs."

[Concerning] the roots of the commandment, I have written about all of the matter of Pesach in the Order of Bo el Pharaoh (Sefer HaChinukh 5). And there is no doubt that the entire matter of Pesach Sheni is all from the foundation of the first - the thing is well-known.

From the laws of the commandment - that which they, may their memory be Blessed, said (Pesachim 40a) that matsot require great watching, that they not come to rising, to the point that they, may their memory be Blessed, obligated us to be careful that no water come upon [the wheat], even from the time of reaping, lest it come to rising (Mishneh Torah, Laws of Leavened and Unleavened Bread 5:9); and the rest of its details - are [all] elucidated in [the] first [section of] Pesach[im]. And the general rule is that there be a great guarding upon them that they not come to rising. And so [too,] what they explained about marror, that any bitter (mar) herb is included in the marror mentioned by the verse, and that a person fulfills his obligation on Pesach with any of them. As the commandment to us about marror is in memory of "they made life bitter for them" (Exodus 1:14), and the matter is remembered with any bitter herb. But nonetheless, the Sages, may their memory be Blessed, chose for us (Pesachim 39a) to eat romaine lettuce. As with it, there is memory of the bitterness through the stalk, the taste of which is a little bitter, and there is also more beauty to the commandment than with other bitter herbs. And also its name is beautiful, as it is called chassa, [such that] a blessing is hinted in it - that the Merciful One pitied (chass) us and redeemed us from the hand of the harsh Egyptians. And from all of these [angles] there is arousal and remembrance in the heart of people of the matter of the miracles that were done for us in Egypt. And therefore, the law was fixed that it it fitting for us to look for romaine lettuce. Its details are also found in Pesachim.

And [it] is practiced at the time of the [Temple] by males, but not by females. As just like the slaughtering of the Pesach Sheni sacrifice is not obligatory [for them], but optional - as we said in the previous commandment - so too is the eating of matsa and marror with it not obligatory for them. And this is also elucidated there in Tractate Pesachim 95a. And one who transgresses this and eats the Pesach Sheni sacrifice without matsa and marror has violated this positive commandment.

Mitzvah 382
Not to leave any meat from the Pesach Sheni sacrifice to its morrow: Not to leave any meat from the Pesach Sheni sacrifice to its morrow, which is the fifteenth day of Iyar, as it is stated (Numbers 9:12), "They shall not leave any of it over until morning." All of its content is in the negative commandment that comes about this on the first Pesach which is written in the Order of Bo el Pharoah, and it is the second negative commandment there (Sefer HaChinukh 8).

Mitzvah 383
Not to break a bone from the bones of the Pesach Sheni sacrifice: Not to break a bone from all of the bones of the Pesach sacrifice, as it is stated (Numbers 9:12), "and a bone they shall not break in it." All of the content of this negative commandment is reflected in the negative commandment that comes about this also on the first Pesach, which is written in the Order of Bo el Pharoah (Sefer HaChinukh 8). And it is there - see it there if you want to know.

Sefer HaChinukh

Mitzvah 384

The commandment of blowing the trumpets in the Temple and in war: To blow trumpets in the Temple each day as every sacrifice is offered, and also at a time of troubles, as it is stated (Number 10:9), "When you come to war, etc." and it is written after it also (Number 10:10), "And on your joyous occasions, and your fixed festivals and new moon days, you shall blow the trumpets over your burnt-offerings and over the sacrifices of your peace-offerings, etc." And even though the verse warns about a joyous occasion, a fixed festival and a new moon day, this is not precise. As they would blow with the trumpets over the sacrifice every day in the Temple. And so is it explained in Rosh HaShannah 29a: "Everyone is obligated in the blowing of the shofar - priests, Levites, and Israelites." And the Talmud wonders about this in the Gemara, "Is this not obvious? [For] if they are not obligated, who would be obligated?" And it responds to it, "It was necessary [to say] priests, for it may enter your mind to say, 'Since it is written (Numbers 29:1), "It is a day of blowing, etc.," [you might have said that with regard to one who is obligated to sound only one day, he is obligated to sound the shofar on Rosh HaShanah.] But these priests, since they are [obligated] all year long, as it is written (Numbers 10:10), "you shall blow the trumpets over your burnt-offerings and over the sacrifices of your peace-offerings, etc." [you might say that they are not obligated].'" The Talmud then asks, "Are they similar? There it is a trumpet and here it is a shofar!" Nevertheless, we learned [from this] that throughout the whole year - meaning to say on each and every day - there were trumpets in the Temple. And they said in Tractate Arakhin 13a that we do not reduce to less than twenty-one blasts in the Temple and we do not increase to over forty-eight.

It is from the roots of the commandment that [it is] since at the time of the sacrifice they would need to properly focus their attention - as it is well-known that it is disqualified by certain thoughts - and also [that] the sacrifice requires complete awareness in front of the Master of all who commanded about them; and also at the time of trouble, a person needs great focus in his supplication before his Creator, that He should have mercy upon him and save him from his trouble; we are therefore commanded to blow the trumpets at these times. As since man is physical, he requires great arousal to these things. For the way of nature is to stand asleep, and there is nothing as arousing as the sounds of music, [as is] well known - and all the more so, the sounds of trumpets, which is the greatest sound of all musical instruments. And there is also another purpose, aside from arousal to focusing attention, that is realized through the sound of the trumpet; and that is that the sound of the trumpets removes all other worldly concerns from the heart of the listener, such that at that time he will only [direct] his heart to the matter of the sacrifice. But why should I go on so long? This is well-known to anyone who has ever bent his ear to hear the trumpets or the sound of a shofar with focus.

From the laws of the commandment - that which they, may their memory be Blessed, said (Menachot 28a) that the trumpets came from a block of silver, as [indicated] in Scripture, and [if it is] from other types of metals, it is disqualified; that which they, may their memory be Blessed, said (Arakhin 13a) that we do not ever reduce to less than two trumpets in the Temple and we do not increase above one hundred and twenty; and the rest of its details - are elucidated in Sifrei Bamidbar 77 (in Parshat Behaalotcha) and in Tractate Rosh HaShanah. And also, in Tractate Taanit (Taanit 19a), the Sages elucidated that we are commanded to blow the trumpets at a time of trouble (see Mishneh Torah, Laws of Fasts 1).

The commandment is practiced by priests at the time of the Temple, as the commandment to blow the trumpets is incumbent upon them, and like the matter that is written about them in the movements of the encampments (Numbers 10:8), "And the sons of Aharon, the priests, will blow with the trumpets." And lest you say that they did not blow over the sacrifices, but rather the Levites, this is not so. As behold, they explicitly said (Mishnah Tamid 7:3), "They gave him the wine to pour [for the libation]. The assistant stood on the horn [of the altar] with two handkerchiefs in his hand. Two priests stood in the table of (used for) fats and two trumpets were in their hands. They blew a teki'ah (long steady sound), then a teruah (a series of very short sounds) and then again a teki'ah." Behold, it is elucidated that this commandment was performed by the priests, and that it was a constant commandment to them, meaning to say that they would blow every day, and not only on a holiday or the day of the new month. However, I have seen that Rambam wrote (Mishnah Torah, Vessels of the

Sanctuary and Those who Serve Therein 3:5), "On all the festivals and on the the new moon days, the priests would sound the trumpets and the Levites would sing." It seems from his words that his opinion is that on other days, even the Levites blow the trumpets. And if the priests transgressed this and did not blow at the time of a sacrifice, and so [too,] if they did not blow at a time of trouble, they will have nullified this positive commandment.

Mitzvah 385
The commandment of challah (dough-offering): To separate some of our kneading and to give it to the priest, as it is written (Numbers 15:20), "The first of your kneading, set aside challah as a gift." And they, may their memory be Blessed, expounded (Eruvin, 93a) [that] "The first of your kneading (arissa)" [means] enough for your measure (issa), and the [dough] measure of the wilderness was an omer, which was one-tenth of an eifah, which is three saah, which is six kav, which is four log, which is six eggs' worth. It turns out that an eifah is four hundred and thirty-two eggs, one-tenth of which is forty-three and 1/5 eggs, and that is the measurement of dough that obligates [the separation] of challah.

It is from the roots of the commandment [that it is that] since the sustenance of a person is through food and most of the world will be sustained with bread, the Omnipresent desired to give us merit with a constant commandment in our bread, so that blessing should rest upon it through the commandment; and through it, we will receive merit for our souls. And [hence] it turns out that the dough is food for our body and food for our soul. Additionally, [it is] in order that the servants of God, those that are constantly involved in His service - and these are the priests - should be sustained without any toil at all. Whereas with the tithe of the threshing floor there is labor for them, to pass the grain through the sieve and to grind it; here, their ration will come to them without any pain whatsoever.

From the laws of the commandment is that which they, may their memory be Blessed, said (Mishnah Challah 3:1) that the obligation begins not from the time that the dough is placed into the trough, but from the time of rolling; that is to say that the obligation begins from the time that the water and flour are mixed. And the five types of grain that are obligated in challah are wheat, barley, spelt, oats, and rye; as it is stated (Numbers 15:19), "And it shall be when you eat from the bread of the land" - and only loaves made from these are called bread. And they all combine to [constitute] the measurement [of what requires the separation] of challah. And if one did not separate challah from the dough, he may separate it from the bread; as it says, "when you eat from the bread," which teaches that bread is also obligated. Even if one first kneaded a quantity that was insufficient [to be obligated] in challah, if he then kneaded another batch and mixed the whole loaf into one vessel that has an interior, such that the two combine to the requisite measurement, the vessel combines them [to be obligated in] challah. I heard from my teacher, may God protect him, that this is only if the bread was taken from the oven and put into a vessel that has an interior, but if it was placed on a board or on the floor, or anything else that has no interior, even though they were subsequently placed into a basket, they are already exempt from challah. This is what they meant when they said, "one who removes it into a basket;" it is only if it went from the oven to the basket at the time of [their] removal. And there is no need to say that the oven does not serve to combine [to obligate in] challah (Mishneh Torah, Laws of First Fruits and other Gifts to Priests Outside the Sanctuary 6:16). The bran that is in the dough is counted toward the requisite measurement before it is sifted; but if it is mixed back in after it is sifted, it does not count towards the requisite measurement (see Mishnah Challah 4:6).

The measurement [to be given] for challah is not [specified in] the Torah - and even if one separated only a barley grain from the kneading, he would exempt the whole kneading in the trough from the law of challah; as the Torah only says, "The first of your kneading, set aside challah." [Thus] anything that he sets aside [suffices] to exempt him. The Sages however obligated us (Mishnah Challah 2:7) to separate 1/24th, which they based upon what the verse stated about this commandment, "give to the Lord," meaning that the gift should be dignified, and this was [the amount] that they estimated. A baker who prepares his [dough] for sale in the market - and [the dough] is large, and he also needs to make a profit - was only obligated to give 1/48th. And whether it should happen that the professional prepares a small [amount] or the homeowner prepares a large [amount], their [laws] are [still] as we said above.

Dough that was kneaded from two ends of the trough and neither suffices to the measurement [of what is required for] challah is not obligated in challah, unless they touch each other and are from the same person.

Dough, whether it was kneaded with water or another liquid; whether it was baked in an oven or on the ground, in a [standard] pan, or in a deep-frying pan; and whether he first stuck the loaf [to the oven walls] and then heated - meaning that he lit the fire underneath it - or if he heated it and stuck it afterwards, in all instances there is an obligation of challah. As in all these cases it is called bread, since the law is not like the view (Pesachim 37a) that bread is only what is baked in an oven alone. But if one prepares dough that will be dried in the sun or boiled in a pot, it is not obligated in challah. Dough of the arnona (tax) - meaning to say that is shared by a Israelite and a gentile - is obligated in challah, if the Israelite's portion constitutes the measurement of [what is required for] challah. Dough that is made for animals is exempted from challah, but if it is for both animals and humans, it is obligated in challah (Mishnah Challah 1:8). If prepared dough - meaning to say, that from which challah had been separated - was mixed with other dough from which challah was not separated, what does he do? A new dough is brought and placed on [the mixture], and he takes challah for all of it. But if he has no other dough, he should take challah from [the mixture]; apparently without a blessing, for all of it has been rendered 'unseparated' (tevel). And even a small amount can render several prepared doughs, 'unseparated'; for 'unseparated' material creates a prohibition with the smallest amount, as I have written in the Order of Emor el HaKohanim (Sefer HaChinukh 284). And the rest of its details are elucidated in Tractate Challah and so [too,] in Tractate Orlah (see Mishneh Torah, Laws of First Fruits and other Gifts to Priests Outside the Sanctuary 5).

The commandment is practiced by males and females in the Land of Israel by Torah writ, as it is stated, "when you eat from the bread of the land," but specifically at the time that all of [the people of] Israel are there, meaning to say their majority. [This is], as it is stated, "when you come" - and the explanation came upon this (Ketubot 20a) [to mean] all of you, and not when some of you come. On a rabbinic level [we are obligated] to separate challah [even] outside of Israel, so that the concept of challah not be forgotten by Israel (Mishneh Torah, Laws of First Fruits and other Gifts to Priests Outside the Sanctuary 5:7). And because the obligation is so that it not be forgotten by Israel, we are accustomed to be lenient with it, such that we only separate a kazayit from a large dough, and throw it into the fire. And it is not given to any priest - child or adult. And I have heard that in some places they are accustomed to separate large challah according to the measurement that the Sages gave us for it, and they give it to a minor priest boy, that impurity does not come to him out of his body or to a minor priest girl who has not yet menstruated. And they even give it to an adult priest who has immersed [to purify himself from genital flows]. And even though he is impure due to contact with the dead, they give him to eat it in these places. It also seems that another leniency outside of Israel is that one may deliberately cancel it out by a majority [of permissible matter], as it [is found] in Tractate Yevamot (it should read, Bekhorot 27a) and in other places in the Gemara. And as far as I know, the same does not apply to any other prohibition in the Torah, with the exception of [branches] that fell into the oven on a festival which can have other [prepared] wood added to it to cancel those, as they said (Beitzah 4b), "a person may add wood to them and permit them." And they said that the reason of the thing is because the prohibited matter burns constantly, meaning to say it is something consumed by the fire, and we can therefore be lenient.

And Rambam, may his memory be Blessed, wrote in the Book of Seeds in the Laws of Tithes and First-fruits in the fifth chapter (Mishneh Torah, Laws of First Fruits and other Gifts to Priests Outside the Sanctuary 5:9-11), "At this time, when there is no pure dough because of impurity from contact with the dead, challah - [which is] 1/48th - is separated once in all Israel, and it is burned because it is impure. And this has a foundation from the Torah. But from Keziv to Amanah, a second challah is separated and given to the priest, but this has no required amount - as was the matter in the past.

Since its main obligation is only rabbinic, challah outside of [Israel] - even though it is impure - is not prohibited to be consumed by a priest unless he has impurity that emits from his body, such as those who have had seminal emissions or irregular genital flows, mestruant women, those who have recently birthed and lepers. Therefore, if there was a minor priest boy outside of Israel - whether in Syria or other lands - if they want to, they may separate one challah as 1/48th and it may be given to eat to a minor priest boy who has not yet seen a seminal emission or to a minor priest girl who has not yet menstruated, and there is no need to do a second separation to burn it. Also, if there is a an adult priest there who has immersed [to purify himself from genital flows] - even if the sun has not yet set for him [on the day of his immersion], and even though he is impure from contact with the dead - he may eat this first challah, and there is no need to do a second separation outside of Israel." To here [are the words of Rambam].

Mitzvah 386
The commandment of fringes (tsitsit): To put fringes on the clothes that we wear, as it is stated (Numbers 15:18), "and they shall make fringes for themselves." And this obligation applies to garments with four or more corners, as it is written (Deuteronomy 22:12), "on the four corners of your garment." And 'four' includes five or more (Mishneh Torah, Laws of Fringes 3:1), provided that the garment is large enough that the head and most of the body of a child who is old enough to walk unescorted in the marketplace can be wrapped in it. And it seems that this age is around six or seven years old. The garment must be made of wool or linen to be obligated in fringes when it is worn. If it is missing one of these [conditions], i.e. if it has fewer than four corners or is not as large as described, or it is made from some other material, it is exempted from fringes on a Torah level. Garments of silk, and even camel hair, rabbit hair, and goat hair are all exempted from fringes on a Torah level; as 'garment' in the Torah [refers] only to those made from sheep's or lamb's wool or linen, and so [too] in relation to tsara'at of clothing, as I have written in its place (Sefer HaChinukh 172).

The root of the commandment is revealed in the verse: It is in order that we always remember all of the commandments of God. And there is no better reminder in the world than carrying the seal of the Master on the clothes that one wears at all times, as a person is [always attentive] to his clothes. And this is what is stated in the verse (Numbers 15:39), "and you will recall all the commandments of the Lord." And they, may their memory be Blessed, said (Midrash Tanchuma, Korach 12) that the word 'tsitsit' alludes to the six hundred and thirteen commandments (in the numerical equivalent of the letters) when combined with the eight strings of the fringes and their five knots. And my heart also tells me that there is a reminder and allusion here that the soul and body of man all belong to God, Blessed be He. As the white portion corresponds to the body which is from the land, which was made from the snow, which is white, as we find in Pirkei D'Rabbi Eliezer 3, "From where is the land from? From the snow that is under the Holy Throne." And the threads [also] allude to the body, as the matter that they said, that the initial formation of a body is like threads. [It is] as they, may their memory be Blessed, said (Niddah 25b), "Rabbi Amram said, 'The two thighs are like two strands of crimson, the two forearms are like two strands of crimson.'" The blue (tekhelet), the appearance of which, is like the appearance of the sky hints to the soul which is from the upper beings. And they hinted to this in their saying (Menachot 47b), "What [makes] tekhelet different than all other colors? Because tekhelet is like the sea, and the sea is like the sky, and the sky is like the Throne of Glory, as it is stated (Exodus 24:10), 'And they saw the God of Israel, etc.' and it states (Ezekiel 1:26), 'The Throne appeared as sapphire stone'" - and the souls of the righteous are stored underneath the Throne. And because of this, they said (Menachot 39a) that we wrap the string of tekhelet around the white, as the soul is above and the body below. They said that we make seven or thirteen windings [around the white strings] to allude to the heavens and the divisions between them. And it is as they said (Menachot 39a), "It is taught, 'One who wishes to do fewer should not do fewer than seven, nor should he add more than thirteen, corresponding to the seven heavens and the six air-spaces between them.'"

From the laws of the commandment is that which they, may their memory be Blessed, said (Menachot 43b) that on a garment that has five or more corners we only put fringes in the four most distant corners. And [also] that which they said (Menachot 28a) that the four fringes impede one another, since all four of them are one commandment. And what they said (Menachot 38a) that the tekhelet does not impede the white [strings] and the white does not impede the tekhelet, which does not mean

Sefer HaChinukh

that they are actually two commandments, as it is all one commandment, but it means that that they do not impede one another. [This is the case] today where we cannot find tekhelet, such that we should still not hesitate to put white fringes without tekhelet onto our garments, and recite the blessing upon them as if it were complete with the tekhelet. Also - when the tekhelet is available - if one has no white strings, he may place the tekhelet on his garment, wrap himself in its garment and recite the blessing upon it.

The tekhelet dye that we are commanded to use, is similar to the appearance of a pure blue sky, and it is made from the blood of a fish called the chilazon, whose appearance is like the appearance of the ocean (Menachot 44a). And it is found in the Dead Sea, and we dye a string of wool in it. And it has been many days for Israel that we have not heard of anyone who merited [having] tekhelet in his talit. It must be dyed for the sake of its commandment, and the white strings also must be spun for the sake of the commandment. We may not use wool that was caught in thorns when the herd was crouching, nor from hairs that were torn from the animal, nor from the remnant left over from the loom, nor from stolen wool nor wool from a condemned city (of Jewish idolaters), nor from consecrated wool. If [any of these was used,] it is disqualified. Fringes that were spun (some have the textual variant, 'hung') by a non-Jew are disqualified, as it is stated, "Speak to the Children of Israel [...] and they shall make." But if a Jew made them without [proper] intention, it is fit, [nonetheless] ex post facto. And I have heard from great scholars that the making of fringes by women is not fit (see Rabbenu Tam, which is brought in the Ramah on Shulchan Arukh, Orach Chayim 12:1).

How are the fringes made? (Mishneh Torah, Laws of Fringes 1:6) Four strings are passed through the corner of the garment, such that there are now eight ends hanging from the corner. This is not done precisely at the corner, but [a half-] thumb's distance from the edge, as Rabbi Yaakov said that Rabbi Yochanan said in the Gemara (Menachot 42a), "It must be one large joint away." One of the strings should be longer so that it can be used for winding [around] the others. Five double knots are tied (Tosafot on Menachot 39a, s.v. lo); and between each knot, he makes three rings (windings), and between the final knot, four rings, so that there are a total of thirteen rings. The strings are made long so that it be enough for two [thirds] of the length to be branching; meaning to say without the knots and rings, besides the knots and rings. This is the main [approach to the] ideal fulfillment of the commandment. But ex post facto, even one ring suffices, and so [too,] ex post fact, even if the strings of the fringes shorten, even if there is only enough to make a basic bow, it is fit (Menachot 38b). But if even one string is completely torn, it is disqualified.

And one who owns a four cornered garment is not required to put fringes on it so long as he does not wear it. And the law is like [the view] of Rav who said, (Menachot 42a) [that] fringes is an obligation on the man, meaning that the obligation is for a person to put fringes on a garment when he wears it. But he is not obligated to put fringes on a garment that is sitting in a drawer, as the law is not like the other view, that it is an obligation on the garment itself. [This] would mean that if a person had many four cornered garments in his home, he would be obligated to put fringes on all of them, even if he never wears them. [But] this is not [the case], as the law is like Rav, as we have said.

And if one has a linen garment, he should place linen fringes in it, for the law is not like [the view of] Beit Shammai who taught (Menachot 40a) that a [linen] cloak is exempted from fringes. [This] means to say that since a linen garment could never have tekhelet placed on it, because [it would form] a forbidden mixture [of wool and linen] - as tekhelet must always be wool, since the tekhelet dye would never be absorbed properly by linen but rather only by wool, and the Torah obligates us in proper tekhelet - and since it would be impossible to ever put a string of wool into the linen because of the forbidden mixture, even white strings, meaning strings of linen, are not put on. This is what [they meant when] they said that Beit Shammai exempts a [linen] cloak from fringes. But the law is not like them, since their reason is because they did not expound adjacent verses; rather the law is like Beit Hillel who did expound adjacent verses. And they [therefore] held that there is no prohibition of forbidden mixtures in fringes, as the Torah stated (Deuteronomy 22:11-12), "Do not wear shaatnez (wool and linen together). Make fringes for yourself" - meaning to say, but fringes you may make for yourself from shaatnez. And therefore, Beit Hillel held that a [linen] cloak is obligated in fringes, and the law is like them. Still, we do not put tekhelet on [a linen garment] due to a concern about indigo;

that is, lest they would dye it with a non- tekhelet dye and then it would be shaatnez without the [performance of a] commandment. They asked in the Gemara in Menachot 40a, "Why? Is it not just white [strings]?" That is, for Beit Hillel who did expound adjacent verses, why should we make such a decree? As even if it is indigo, what is with that? Behold, we said that the forbidden mixture is permitted in fringes, meaning even with white [strings] - that is to say, even to put fringes of white wool in a garment of linen - and it is not [even] necessary to say that [it would be allowed] with fringes of wool that are dyed with tekhelet as is its commandment. And it was answered that these words that Beit Hillel said forbidden mixtures were permitted in fringes on the [strength of the] expounding of adjacent verses is only in cases where there is not from it; meaning to say when it is impossible from its own type - e.g. in a linen garment, if you want to place tekhelet in it, you will need wool regardless, as tekhelet is impossible without wool. [Only] in such cases did Beit Hillel rely on the expounding of adjacent verses and obligate the use of tekhelet in a linen garment. If however, there is 'from it,' meaning to say where you want to use white strings without tekhelet in a linen garment, it is not acceptable to use wool on the strength of the expounding of adjacent verses, as those white strings can be made of linen. This [follows] the principle of Reish Lakish; as Reish Lakish said that in any case where it is possible to maintain both the positive and negative commandments it is better [to do so], and only otherwise do we say that the positive commandment supersedes the negative. And here it is possible to maintain both commandments, for if you do not wish to place tekhelet with the white, linen suffices. And since this is so, if you use wool [you have violated the law of] forbidden mixtures and there is nothing [to help you]. Because there are many interpretations of these matters, I have spent some time on it for you. And from what I found in my trap I have set the table for you. But if you merit, my son, you will distinguish the truth. And if you perhaps find valid reason to challenge my words in this matter - or even in another - you should not mind the honor of your father and teacher, and I will then read (consider) your destruction as building.

And know that even though this commandment is only obligated by the Torah when he has a four cornered garment (Mishneh Torah 3:18) - like there is no obligation for the commandment [to build a] parapet unless one has a roof - the Sages still warned much about this commandment and said (Menachot 41a) that it is fitting to pursue it. They also said (Shabbat 32b) that a person who is careful [in the fulfillment of this commandment] will merit to be waited upon by many servants, as the Torah equated it to and depended upon it the fulfillment of all the other commandments, as it is stated, "And you will see it and remember all the commandments of the Lord." And Rabbi Elazar said that one who is careful in this and tefillin and mezuzah is assured that he will never sin, as it is stated (Ecclesiastes 4:12), "The three-fold thread will not easily break."

And you will find the laws of this commandment in Tractate Menachot in the fourth chapter (see Tur, Yoreh Deah 8-22.

This commandment is practiced by men in every place and at all times, but not by women. But if women want to [wear fringes, they may do so] without [reciting] a blessing, according to some commentators (Mishneh Torah, Laws of Fringes 3:9). But others say even with a blessing (Rabbenu Tam in Tosafot on Rosh Hashanah 33a, s.v. Rabbi Yehudah). And one who transgressed it and wore a wool or linen garment - that meets the size requirements above and it is his - without fringes has violated this positive commandment. And if it is [made] from other materials he has nullified a rabbinic commandment. But if it is not his own garment but rather it is borrowed, it is exempt for all thirty days. [This] means to say from the day that he borrowed it until the completion of the thirty days, he is exempt (Mishneh Torah, Laws of Fringes 3:4). From then on, he is obligated to put fringes on it.

Mitzvah 387

To not wander after the thoughts of the heart and the vision of the eyes: That we not wander after the thoughts of the heart and the vision of the eyes, as it is stated (Numbers 15:39), "Do not wander after your hearts and your eyes." The content of this negative commandment is that we were prevented from dedicating our thoughts to think about opinions that are antithetical to the ones on which the Torah is built, as that may lead one to apostasy. Rather, if the spirit to pursue these bad opinions should arise, one should minimize his thinking about them, and redouble his efforts to contemplate the true and good ways of the Torah. Similarly, one should not pursue the things he sees; and included in this is that we not pursue after the desires of this world, for in the end they are evil and 'there is much shame and wrath.' This is [the meaning of] what they, may their memory be Blessed, said (Berakhot 12b), "'Do not stray after your hearts' refers to apostasy. 'After your eyes' refers to licentiousness, as it is stated (Judges 14:3), 'And Samson said to his father, "Take her for me, as she is right in my eyes."'"

The root of this commandment is revealed, as through it a person is protected from sinning against God all his days. This commandment is really a fundamental principle in the religion, as evil thoughts are the progenitors of impurities, and the actions are their descendants. And if a person dies before having children, there is no record of the progeny; so it emerges that this prevention is the root that all good comes from. Understand my son, and let it be a jewel in your mouth, that which they, may their memory be Blessed, said (Avot 4:2), "One sin leads to another, and one commandment leads to another." As if you allow yourself to fulfill your evil desire one time, you will be drawn after it many times. But if you merit to be 'mighty in the land' and to conquer your evil inclination and close your eyes from seeing evil one time, it will be easier for you to do so many times. As lust pulls the body like wine draws the drinker. Drunkards can never be sated by wine, but they will rather have a great desire for it. And according to [the large quantity that] they have gotten themselves accustomed, the stronger their desire will become. And if only they would drink a cup of water, it would temper the burning fire of [their] desire for wine, and make it pleasant for them. The same is true here: The more a person allows himself to be governed by his desires and to allow them to become habit, the stronger his evil inclination becomes every day. But in his preventing himself from them, he will always be happy with his portion every day; and he will see that 'God made people straight, but they seek out many schemes' for no reason of any point.

The laws of this commandment are brief; behold, we have already elucidated the bulk of their essence here (see Mishneh Torah, Laws of Foreign Worship and Customs of the Nations 3).

And this commandment is practiced in all places and at all times by men and women. And one who transgresses it and dedicated his thought to these topics that we mentioned that cause a person to abandon the views of our perfect, pure Torah and to [partake of] the view of the empty heretics that are bitter and evil, or if he wandered after his eyes; that is, he chased the desires of the world - for example, if he constantly attempts to maximize great delights for himself without any attention paid to some positive gain that could be realized from it, meaning that he does not do it in order to be healthy and be able to strive in the service of his Creator, but just to maximize delights for himself - anyone who follows this path has violated this negative commandment constantly whenever he is involved in what we have said. But we do not administer lashes for this negative commandment, because there is no specific thing for which the transgressor can be warned, as man is made in such a way that it is impossible for his eyes not to sometimes see more than what is fitting, and it is similarly impossible for his thought not to sometimes go beyond what is fitting, so it is impossible to limit a man with clear boundaries about this. Also, this negative commandment can be transgressed without any deed at all; and I already wrote earlier (Sefer HaChinukh 346) that for any negative commandment that can be transgressed without a deed - even if a person does a deed - it seems that no lashes are administered to him.

Mitzvah 388

The commandment to guard the Temple: That the priests and the Levites were commanded to guard the Temple and walk around it constantly the whole night, on each and every night (see R. Chaim Heller - Sefer HaMitzvot LaRambam, Mitzvot Ase 22) - and this guarding is to honor it, to exalt it and to glorify it, and not from there being any fear from the enemy, God forbid - as it is stated (Numbers 18:4), "and they shall guard the guarding of the Tent of Meeting." And the language of Sifrei Bamidbar 116 is "'And you and your sons with you will be in front of the Tent of Testimony' (Numbers 18:2) - the priests inside and the Levites only outside"; meaning to say to guard it and to walk around it. And in the Mekhilta (Sifrei Zuta on Numbers 18:4), they said, "'And they shall guard the guarding of the Tent of Meeting' - I only know of a positive commandment, etc." Behold, it is elucidated that its guarding is a positive commandment. And there it says another greatness of the Temple is that it has guards - "A palace that has guards is not similar to a palace that does not have guards." And it is known that the palace is a name for the sanctuary.

What I have already written several times is from the roots of the commandment - that the glory of the [Temple] brings awe to the heart of people. And in our coming there to request supplication and pardon from the Master of All, [our] hearts will soften to quick repentance; and like the matter that we said at length in the Order of VeAtah Tetsaveh (Sefer HaChinukh 98). And it is from the glory of the [Temple] to appoint guards for it, like the way of great kings in the world that do such; and as it comes in the Mekhilta, "It is not similar, etc.," as is written adjacently (above).

From the laws of the commandment is that which they, may their memory be Blessed, said (Mishnah Middot 1:1-2) that twenty-four men guard it every night in twenty-four stations: the priests guard in three stations inside and the Levites outside. And they would appoint one who would circulate to the stations all of the night and there would be torches lit in front of him, and he was called the man of the Temple Mount. And it would be recognizable that any sentry that would not get up when the man of the Temple Mount would say to him, "Peace unto you," was asleep. And [the man of the Temple Mount] would hit him with his stick, and he had the right to burn his clothing, to the point that they would say in Jerusalem, "What is the voice in the Courtyard? It is the voice of a Levite being struck and his clothes burning, because he was sleeping at his sentry.

And the rest of its details, such as where did the Levites and the priests guard; if one of them had a nocturnal emission, how would he proceed; how was their order and their activities close to the dawn are all nicely elucidated in the first chapter of Tractate Tamid and Tractate Middot (see Mishneh Torah, Laws of The Chosen Temple 8).

And it is practiced by priests and Levites [that are] males at the time of the [Temple]. As they were designated in the command of guarding the Temple, and not the Israelites. And if they transgressed this and nullified this guarding, they have violated a positive commandment, besides violating a negative commandment, as we will write in this Order (Sefer HaChinukh 297), with God's help.

Mitzvah 389

That the priests not be involved in the service of the the Levites and the Levites in the service of the priests: That the priests not be involved in the service of the Levites and the priests in the business of the Levites, but rather each one does the work designated for him, from that which is written (Numbers 4:19), "each man to his service and his load." And the language of the prevention that comes about this is that which is stated about the Levites (Numbers 18:3), "but to the vessels of the Holy and to the Altar they shall not approach"; and afterwards the verse returns to speak about the priests, "and they shall not die, also they and also you" - meaning to say with this that you too, you are included in this negative commandment. Since just like the Levites are prevented from their work [when it is not assigned to them], so too are you prevented from your work [when it is not assigned to you]. And the language of the Sifrei on Numbers 18:3: "'To the vessels of the Holy and to the Altar' [is the] warning; 'and they shall not die' is the punishment. I only [know] that the Levites are punished and warned about the service of the priests; from where do I know [the same] about the priests [doing] the service of the Levites? [Hence] we learn to say, 'also you.'" And we have found (Sifrei on Numbers 18:3) that Rabbi Yehoshua ben Chananiah wanted to help Rabbi Yochanan ben Gudgodah in the closing of the doors, [and] he said to him, "Go back, as you are already liable with your soul (life), as I am from the gatesmen and you are from the singers." Behold, it is elucidated that any Levite that does work in the Temple that is not his designated work is liable for death by the hand of the Heavens. And so [too,] the priests are warned not to approach the work of the Levites. However, if they did transgress this, they are not killed, but rather [get] lashes. And they said in the Mekhilta (Sifra Zuta), "'To the vessels of the Holy and to the Altar they shall not approach' It is possible that they would be liable if they touched [them]. [Hence] we learn to say, 'but' - for the work they are liable, and not for touching. I only [know] about the Levites for the [work of the] priests, from where do I know about the priests for the [work of the] Levites? [Hence] we learn to say, 'also you.'" And there it is said that the Leivtes on that of the priests is [punished] with death, but the priests on that of the Levites is only with [the consequences of violating] a negative commandment.

It is from the roots of the commandment [that] because the service of these two groups is a very precious and holy service, therefore the work needs to be very guarded from abandon, from slothfulness and from forgetfulness. And there is no doubt that there is more negligence with any work incumbent upon two people or more, than work incumbent upon one alone. As many times each one of the two of them will rely upon his fellow, and the work will be neglected by both of them. This is something clear to all men. And by way of a parable, they, may their memory be Blessed, said about something similar to this (Bava Batra 24b), "A stew of partners is not hot and not cold."

From the laws of the commandment [is] that which they, may their memory be Blessed, said (Mishnah Shekalim 5:1), "There were fifteen appointees in the Temple: one was over the times," meaning to say to determine the time of the sacrifice. And he immediately envigorates them and says, "Priests, stand at your services; Levites, to the platform; and Israel, to serve!" And once they hear his voice, each one comes to his work. And specific priests and Levites would serve there. And it is like they, may their memory be Blessed, said that Moshe and Shmuel the Seer and King David divided them into twenty-four shifts, as it is found in Taanit 27a. And each shift would serve for a week and take turns in a cycle. And the head of the shift would divide all the men of the shift into clans. And each day of the week specific men would work, and the heads of the clans would divide specific men, each one to his service, and they would not be allowed to assist one another [in their tasks]. And so [too,] the Levites, the singer would not be allowed to help the gatekeeper; nor the gatekeeper, the singer. And of these fifteen appointees that we mentioned, we have already said that the first was appointed over the times; the second was appointed over the closing of the gates; third over the guards; fourth over the singers, etc., as it comes in the Mishnah. [This] and the rest of its details are in [various] places in the Order of Kedoshim and in Sifrei and in Mekhilta, as we have said above (see Mishneh Torah, Laws of Vessels of the Sanctuary and Those who Serve Therein 3).

And it is practiced at the time of the [Temple] by priests and Levites. And a Levite that transgresses it and does the work of the priest in the Temple, or even the work of his fellow Levite, is liable for death by the hand of the Heavens. And so [too,] a priest that transgressed and did the work of the Levite has violated a negative commandment, but he is not liable for death, as we said above. And apparently, a priest that assists in the work of a fellow priest is also [liable for] death.

Mitzvah 390
That a foreigner not serve in the Temple: That a foreigner not serve in the Temple - meaning to say anyone who is not from the seed of Aharon - as it is stated (Numbers 18:4), "and a foreigner will not approach you." And the prevention of this is repeated with a different expression in Scripture, and that is as it is stated (Numbers 18:22), "And the Children of Israel shall not again approach the Tent of Meeting, to carry guilt, to die."

I have written from the roots of the commandment above in this Order in the commandment of the service of the Temple (Sefer HaChinukh 394).

From the laws of the commandment is that which they, may their memory be Blessed, said that this warning of approaching is only [about] one who approaches to [do] a service from one of the services that are specific to a priest. And it is like they, may their memory be Blessed, said (Zevachim 32a), "From the receiving of the blood and onward, it is a commandment of the priesthood." For example, pourings, mixings, wavings, bringings and many other services like these that are explained in the Gemara that are commanded to be with a priest; behold, they are all with a warning to the foreigner, and the [effected] sacrifice is disqualified. But there are [also] services that are not included in this warning, such as slaughtering, which is fit, even a priori, with a foreigner, and even of sacrifices of the highest sanctity. And so [too,] lighting the lights; such that if a priest took them outside after he arranged them, it is permitted for a foreigner to light them. And there are only four specific services among them that are weighty, such that there is liability for the death penalty for them. And they are throwing, burning incense, placement [of the sacrifice] and pouring libations. And it is about them that it is stated, "and the foreigner that approaches shall die," as it is elucidated in the first chapter of

Yoma [entitled] Kol Mi Shehu Rotseh Litrom (Yoma 24a). [This] and the rest of its details are elucidated there in Yoma and in the last chapter of Tractate Zevachim (see Mishneh Torah, Laws of Admission into the Sanctuary 3).

And this prohibition is practiced by males and females at the time of the [Temple]; and even at this time, even though it is desolate, on account of our iniquities. And one who transgresses it and does one of the services that are specific to the priests in the Temple even today, violates a negative commandment, as we have written (Sefer HaChinukh 184, 263). And if he does one of the four services that we mentioned, he is liable for death by the hand of the Heavens.

Mitzvah 391
To not nullify the guarding of the Temple: To not nullify the guarding of the Temple, [but rather] to always walk around it every night, as it is stated (Numbers 18:5), "And you shall guard the guarding of the Holy." And it is well-known that the expression of guarding takes the place of a negative commandment. And [it is] as they, may their memory be Blessed, said (Eruvin 96a), "Every place in which it is stated, 'guard yourself,' 'lest,' and 'not,' is nothing but a negative commandment." And they said in Mekhilta, "'And they shall guard the guarding of the Tent of Meeting' (Numbers 18:4), - I only [know of] a positive commandment. From where [do I know] a negative commandment? [Hence], we learn to say, 'And you shall guard the guarding of the Holy.'" To here [are the words of Mekhilta]. And maybe they expounded a positive commandment and a negative commandment when they found two verses teaching one thing. And from the one that comes by way of a command in second person, they learned a negative commandment; and they expounded the command in third person - which is lighter than it - about a positive commandment. And anyone who weighs the things in just scales will concede about this - that the third person is lighter than a command in second person.

From the roots of the commandment - with some of its laws - are written, according to the rule of the book, in the first commandment [on this topic] (Sefer haChinukh 388).

Mitzvah 392
The commandment of redeeming the first-born of a man: To redeem the first-born of man; as it is a commandment upon every man in Israel to redeem, from the priest, his son who is the firstborn to his Israelite mother - as it is stated (Numbers 18:15), "but you shall redeem the first-born of man." Elsewhere we find that the Torah makes being firstborn dependent on exiting the womb, as it it is stated in the Order of Bo el Pharaoh (Exodus 13:2), "all the first-born, all that exit the womb of the Children of Israel - whether man or beast - is Mine." And the meaning of exit the womb is opening the womb, meaning who was the first to open the womb of the mother. And because of this, they, may their memory be Blessed, said (Bekhorot 46a) that one who is born after a stillborn - any stillborn for which the mother would be impure [as a result of it] - the one that comes after it is not a first-born to [be redeemed from] the priest, as the stillborn preceded him; but if the fetus [is not developed enough that] the mother [contracts] the impurity of birthing, the one that comes after it is a first-born. In Tractate Niddah (Niddah 21a) this distinction is elucidated, and likewise in Tractate Bekhorot (Bekhorot 46a) is elucidated which first-born children are considered first for the priest and not for inheritance, and which are first for inheritance but not for the priest. It also said there that there is a firstborn for everything and one that is not a firstborn for [even] one of them.

I have written what I have known from the roots of the commandment in the Order of Bo el Pharaoh. See there (Sefer HaChinukh 18).

From the laws of the commandment is that which they, may their memory be Blessed, said (Bekhorot 49a) that the commandment of redemption [begins when] the child is thirty days old, for [at that point he is no longer considered a potential] stillborn, as it is stated (Numbers 18:16), "And his redemption that you redeem, from one aged a month." And this commandment is the responsibility of the father (Kiddushin 29a). If the father transgressed and did not want to redeem him, the commandment devolves upon the son, to redeem himself when he becomes an adult. The amount of the redemption is five sela, whether it be money equivalent to five sela or commodities that are the equivalent of money, such that their makeup is money, to exclude slaves, land and deeds - as if one redeemed him with them, he is not redeemed. The five sela may be given to one priest or to several priests, and the obligation is to give it to a male priest, and not to a female priestess; as it is written regarding the money of redeeming the firstborn, "Aharon and his sons." If the priest wishes to return the redemption money after it is given to him, [the father] has [still] fulfilled his obligation, so long as the money is not given with this condition [in mind]. If he did give the money with this condition, the son is not redeemed, until he concludes in his heart to give it to him as a full gift. But if he did specify and gave the money with the condition that it be returned, and the priest was appeased to this, the child is redeemed.

Our Rabbis also taught us that in our time, we do the redemption of the first-born in an order like this: They bring a cup of wine and a myrtle branch to the home of the father of the son or to [some] other place, and the priest to whom the father chooses to give the redemption of his son blesses first over the wine and over the myrtle and then recites this blessing - "Blessed are You, our Lord, King of the Universe, Who sanctified the fetus in his mother's innards, and at forty days individuated his limbs into two hundred and forty-eight limbs, and then breathed in the spirit of life, as it is written (Genesis 2:7), 'and He breathed in his nostrils...'; He clothed him with skin and flesh, and covered him with bones and ligaments, as it is written (Job 10:11), 'He clothed me with flesh and skin and covered me with bones and ligaments.' He appointed food and drink for him, honey and milk to bring him joy, and appointed two ministering angels to guard him in his mother's womb, as it is written (Job 10:12), 'with life and kindness, etc.'" His mother says, "This is my firstborn son, with which God opened the doors of my belly." His father says, "This is my first-born and I am warned about redeeming him, as it is stated (Exodus 13:13), 'and all the first-born of man, your sons shall you redeem.' May it be the will in front of You, Lord, my God, that as You have allowed his father to merit to redeem him, so too should you allow him to merit Torah, marriage and good deeds. Blessed are You, Lord, who sanctified the first born of Israel to be redeemed." The father of the son then recites two blessings: 'on the redemption of the first born'; and 'Who has allowed us to live.' He gives the well-known redemption to the priest, which is five sela, as specified in the Torah. This is equal to sixty argents of refined silver in our land. And after the redemption, the priest recites these three blessings that we wrote.

Ramban, may his memory be Blessed, also wrote that when the father gives the money to the priest he should first give the child into the priest's hand, and the priest should say, "Which is more beloved to you, your son or these five sela?" And the father responds, "My son is more beloved to me." The priest immediately takes the silver coins and passes them over the head of the son and says, "This is in the place of this, traded for this, this is rendered no longer sacred through this. This goes out to the priest and this child should come to life and Torah and fear of heaven. May it be His will that as this one came to redemption, may he also come to Torah, marriage and good deeds, and let us say amen." The priest places his hands on the son's head and blesses him, according to how he knows to bless him, such as "May the Lord guard you, etc." (Psalms 121:5), or "As length of days and years of life, etc." (Proverbs 3:2) or "The Lord shall protect you from all evil and guard your soul, etc." (Psalms 121:7). And [the father] takes him out for all of his will. [This] and the rest of its details are elucidated in Tractate Bekhorot (see Tur, Yoreh Deah 308).

This commandment is practiced in every place and at all times by male Israelites, but not by females. As we have in our tradition that only a man who is obligated to [potentially] redeem himself is obligated to redeem his son; but not a woman, who is not [in the category of] redemption. The commandment is also not practiced by priests and Levites (Bekhorot 4a) from an a fortiori argument (kal vechomer): If they could exempt Israelites from redemption of the firstborn in the wilderness, it follows that they would exempt themselves. They, may their memory be Blessed, also said that even a son of an Israelite who has relations with a priestess or a Levite woman and his son is from her is exempt from redemption (Bekhorot 47a); since the matter is dependent upon the mother, as Scripture made it dependent on exiting the womb. And one who transgressed this and did not redeem his son from when he is fit, that is after thirty days have passed [from his birth]; if he dies before he has redeemed him, he has violated this positive commandment, and woe unto him for he carries his sin upon his soul. And even though there is no specified time for this commandment, as any time after thirty days have elapsed is appropriate, still the wise of heart will grab commandments and perform them at the first available moment, and 'the desire of God will prosper in his hand.' And it seems that the father is always obligated to redeem his son. And even after the son matures, the commandment is incumbent on the father, as the verse states (Exodus 13:17), "And all the first-born of man, your sons you shall redeem" - behold, that the commandment is made incumbent on the father. And so, does it seem in Kiddushin.

Mitzvah 393
To not redeem the first-born of a pure animal: That we should not redeem the first-born of a pure (kosher) animal. Since the Torah had commanded that the first-born donkey be redeemed, it may have come to our minds to also redeem the first-born of a pure animal with another animal. Therefore this prevention came to us, that we should never redeem it. And even if one transgressed and redeemed it, it is not redeemed. About this is it stated (Numbers 18:17), "But the first-born of an ox, the first-born of a sheep, or the first-born of a goat should not be redeemed; they are sacred." The verse elucidated the three types of pure (domesticated) beasts that are subject to the commandment of the first-born, as the seven varieties of wild animals are not included in the law of firstborns, and as I explained in the Order of Bo (Sefer HaChinukh 17).

I wrote about the roots of the commandment of the first-born to give it to the priest there. The matter of the warning not to redeem it is connected to it - so take it from there.

From the laws of the commandment: Rambam, may his memory be Blessed, wrote (Mishneh Torah, Laws of Firstlings 1:17), "Just as the first-born cannot be redeemed, so too can the priest not sell it while it is still unblemished. As since it stands to be offered as a sacrifice, the priest does not have the right to sell it. But at this time (when there is no Temple), since it is destined to be eaten, behold, it is permitted to sell it, even though it is unblemished - whether to a priest or an Israelite." To here [are his words]. Certainly, about that which our teacher, may his memory be Blessed, said that it is destined to be eaten, his intention was to say, when it gets a blemish. And a blemished first-born can be sold by the priest at any time, whether the Temple [is standing] or whether the Temple [is not standing], whether it is alive or whether it is slaughtered, to any person, even a non-Jew, as it is completely non-sacred, as it is written (Deuteronomy 12:15), "The pure and the impure together, like the gazelle and the deer." Still, the Sages warned not to sell it in the marketplace in public, but rather at home. The rest of its details are elucidated in Tractate Bekhorot [Chapter 5] (see Tur, Yoreh Deah 306).

And this commandment is practiced in the Land of Israel, like the commandment of sanctifying the first-born pure animals, which is only practiced in the Land of Israel, according to some commentators (see Beit Yosef, Yoreh Deah 306) - both when the Temple [is standing] and when the Temple [is not standing] - as it is stated (Deuteronomy 14:23), "And you shall eat before the Lord, Your God, the tithes of your grain, etc. and the first-born of your cattle and your sheep." And they, may their memory be Blessed, expounded [it to mean] (Temurah 21b), from the place that you bring your tithes - which is the Land of Israel - you shall bring your sheep and cattle. And if one brought a first-born animal from outside the Land, they would not accept it from him and it may not be sacrificed, as it is completely non-sacred. Everyone is obligated in this commandment, priests, Levites, and Israelites, as it stated (Deuteronomy 15:19), "Any first-born that is born, etc." (Mishneh Torah, Laws of Firstlings 1:7). And even though the priests and the Levites are exempt from redeeming the first-born of man and the one that exits the donkey, as we have written about each one of them in this Order (Sefer HaChinukh 392) and in the Order of Bo el Pharaoh (Sefer HaChinukh 22), they are obligated in this. And one who transgressed this and redeemed his first-born pure animal - even though his actions were not effective and it is not redeemed, but rather it is is sacred as it was [before] - he has violated a negative commandment. As regarding the transgression of the negative commandment, [the efficacy of] the violation of a negative commandment does not concern us, as is found in the first chapter of Temurah (Temurah 4b), in the disagreement of Abbaye and Rava. But he is not lashed, as he could transgress it without an act.

Sefer HaChinukh

Mitzvah 394

The commandment of the service of the Levites in the Temple: That the Levites serve in the Temple to be gatekeepers and to sing everyday over the sacrifice, as it is stated (Numbers 18:23), "And the Levite shall serve, he, etc." And the language of the Sifrei is "I can understand if he wants, he serves, and if he does not want, he does not serve. [Hence], we learn to say, 'And the Levite shall serve, he' - [even] against his will," meaning to say that this thing is an obligation, and that this matter is incumbent upon him perforce. And it is also elucidated in the second chapter of Arakhin 11a, that no one should ever say the song of the mouth (in the Temple) besides the Levite. And this commandment is repeated in the Torah with a different expression, as it is stated (Deuteronomy 18:7), "And he shall serve in the name of the Lord, his God." And they said there in Arakhin, "What is the service that is [done] in the name of the Lord? It should be said, it is song."

It is from the roots of the roots of the commandment [that it is] because it is the glory of the King and the place that there be specific people from a specific tribe, that are affixed to His service, and that foreigners not come to serve. [It is] similar to earthly monarchy, [wherein] they appoint specific respected people, such that all of the work of the king be done through them. As it is not fitting for a king that his servants in front of him should change every day, and that all would make use of the crown of the king's service. That is something clear.

From the laws of the commandment is that which they, may their memory be Blessed, said (Bekhorot 30b), that we do not accept a [Levite] who accepts all of the commandments of the Levites except for one thing, [but rather only if] he accepts all of them. And their service was that they would be guardsmen for the Temple, as we have written in this Order (Sefer HaChinukh 388). And some of them were gatekeepers, to open and close the gates of the Temple.

But the core of their service is to sing over the sacrifice. And they would only say song with communal burnt-offerings that are obligatory and upon the peace-offerings of [Shavouot] at the time of the wine libation; but not over voluntary offerings that the community would make for the 'end of the altar.' And so [too], they would not say song upon libations that came on their own. A Levite who is bereaved (onen) is permitted to serve and sing. We do not ever decrease below twelve Levites that stand on the platform to say song over the sacrifice, but we [may] increase [as much as is wanted]. And the song that the Levites would say was with the mouth, as the crux of song is with the mouth. And others would stand there that would play musical instruments - some of them Levites and some of them pedigreed Israelites that [their family be permitted to] be married to [priests] - as only the pedigreed are ever able to go up to the platform. And we never reduce below nine lyres, but we [may] increase [as much as is wanted]. And there was only one cymbals. And it appears that the reason is that the sound of cymbals is loud and a bit frightening; and [so] if there were many, the rest of the musical instruments that were there would not be heard - all the more so, the song of the mouth. And the hollow of the flutes that they would play with were of reed, since their sound is pleasant. And the flute would strike [play] in front of the altar twelve days a year. And it pushes off the Shabbat, since it is [a part of] the service of the sacrifice, and the sacrifice pushes off the Shabbat. And a [Levite] does not come to the service until they teach him for five years. and as they, may their memory be Blessed, learned from the verse. And from here, they, may their memory be Blessed, said (Chullin 24a) that a student that does not see a good sign of (some success) for five years, will never see [it]. And he does not ever come to serve until he is an adult, as it is stated (Numbers 4:49), "each man to his service." But a Levite is not disqualified by age and not by blemishes, but rather by deterioration of the voice, such as the old men whose voices deteriorate at the time of old age. And that which is stated in the Torah (Numbers 8:25), "But at the age of fifty they shall retire from the legion of service" is only at the time they were carrying the tabernacle from place to place. And even at the time of old age when his voice deteriorates, he is not disqualified from guarding the Temple and from closing the doors. And all of this and the rest of its details are nicely elucidated in [various] places in Tamid and Middot; also, some of this matter is elucidated in the second chapter of Arakhin. And I have written a little at length about this for you, my son, as the Temple will soon be built, and you will need it. Amen, so should God do (see Mishneh Torah, Laws of Vessels of the Sanctuary and Those who Serve Therein 9).

Sefer HaChinukh

And [it] is practiced at the time of the [Temple] by the Levites. And a Levite that transgresses it and did not sing over the sacrifice on his set day - as they had set days, according to the division of the shifts - but rather was silent, has violated this positive commandment. And his punishment is very great, as he appears as if the does not desire the glory of the service of God; and therefore God will prevent him from [any other] glory. But the one of the Levites who desires the service of his Creator; with him will be life, peace and blessing.

Mitzvah 395

The commandment of the first tithe: That the Children of Israel were obligated to give one tenth part of the seed of the land to the Levites, as is is stated (Numbers 18:24), "For it is the tithes of the Children of Israel that they will give to the Lord that I give to the Levites as a gift." And it is stated in the Order of Eem Bechukotai (Leviticus 27:30), "And all of the tithe of the land, etc. it is for the Lord." And that is what is called the first tithe (maaser rishon).

It is from the roots of the commandment [that] since God, may He be Blessed, chose the tribe of Levi from among his brothers for his service in the Temple always, therefore it was from His kindness to them to give them their sustenance in an honorable way. As so is it proper for the servants of the King that their meals should be readied for them by others - that they should prepare it for them and that [the Levites] should not have to toil in anything besides the precious service of the King. And even though they were twelve tribes - and according to their equal portion, it would have been fitting that they take one twelfth part - this advantage to them is also for their glory. As since they are from the house of the King, it is fitting that their portion be more than all [the rest] of them. And it is a big advantage that the tenth part come to them free from all of the expenses of the land. And the blessing of God, may He be Blessed, rests upon everything that belongs to the one who sustains the servants of God with his money. And this is what they, may their memory be Blessed, said (Mishnah Avot 3:13), "Tithes are a safeguarding fence around wealth." They, may their memory be Blessed, also said (Taanit 9a) that it is forbidden for a person to think in his heart and say, "I will test if God does good to me [for] my involvement in His commandments"; and about that which is similar to this is it stated (Deuteronomy 6:16), "Do not test the Lord, your God" - except for in this commandment. As it is permitted to test if God will bless him [for] his doing it and [for] his being alacritous about it. And it is made explicit by the prophets, as it is stated (Malachi 3:10), "Bring the entire tithe into the storehouse, etc. and put Me to the test with it, said the Lord."

From the laws of the commandment is that which they, may their memory be Blessed, said (Yevamot 85b), that this tithe that is of the Levites is completely non-sacred (chullin) and [so] permissible for any man to eat - whether a Levite or whether an Israelite - and even in impurity, as it is stated (Numbers 18:27), "This shall be accounted to you as your gift." [That is] to say that the tithe which is given as the tithe of Israel is for you "as the grain from the threshing floor or the flow from the vat." And they, may their memory be Blessed, expounded [that] just like the threshing floor and the vat are non-sacred for all purposes, so too is the first tithe that had its tithe taken non-sacred for all purposes. [And] the explanation of 'that had its tithe taken' is meaning to say after the Levites skimmed a tithe from their tithe and gave it to the priests. That is what is called 'its tithe.' And every place that it is stated about the tithe, "holy" or "redemption" is only about the second tithe. And they said in Sifrei that all that is food for people and guarded and its growth is from the earth is liable for the tithe and the priestly tithe (terumah). And they [derive] it from that it is written about the priestly tithe (Deuteronomy 18:4), "The beginning of your grain, etc." As they, may their memory be Blessed, expounded [that] just like grain, grapes and oil are food of people and its growth is from the earth and has owners, as it is stated, "your grain"; so too all that is similar to them are liable for the tithe and the priestly tithe. But even though vegetables are food of people, they are not liable for the tithe except rabbinically; as about the tithe it states (Deuteronomy 14:22), "all the produce of your seed," and vegetables are not called 'produce.' But from the words of the Gemara that we rely upon more, it appears that also in all [other] fruits besides grain, grapes and oil, is there no liability for the tithe, except rabbinically. And [according to this,] the verse that was brought [as a prooftext] in the Sifrei was only a memory device (asmakhta). This is the conclusion in the beginning of the chapter [entitled]

Sefer HaChinukh

Hasokher et HaPoalim (Bava Metzia 88a) concerning that which Rav Pappa answered that the fig tree stood in the garden, but its branches leaned into the courtyard. However, Rambam, may his memory be Blessed, wrote the opposite of this, and like he found [it] in the Sifrei. And so [too] from the topic of the commandment is that which they said that we do not separate the tithe of the new crop for the old crop, and not from the old for the new, not from that which is liable for that which is exempt and not from that which is exempt for that which is liable. And if one separated the tithe [like this], it is not [considered] a tithe. But we do take the tithe from that which is not encircled (close to the produce for which one is liable), even though it is not like this with the priestly tithe, as we only separate the priestly tithe from what is encircled. And nonetheless, with other things the tithe and the priestly tithe are the same; such that anything about which we say regarding the priestly tithe, "we do not take the priestly tithe, but if one [took it], his priestly tithe is a [valid] priestly tithe - so [too,] with the tithe, if he separated it, his tithe is a [valid] tithe. And everything that is exempt from the priestly tithe is exempt for the tithe. And in the Order of Shoftim, we will write at greater length, with God's help, and you can see it there. And so [too] from the topic of the commandment is that which they, may their memory be Blessed, said that a person is only obligated to separate the tithe from Torah writ if he finished [the work] on his fruit to eat them for himself, but one who finished them to sell them in the marketplace is exempted, as it is stated (Deuteronomy 14:22), "You shall surely tithe, etc. and you shall eat." And so [too,] one who buys [the produce] after its work has been completed - meaning to say it was put in the threshing floor by the seller - is exempt from Torah writ, but obligated from the words [of the Rabbis], as it is stated, "the produce of your seed," meaning to say that the work was finished in your domain. And the obligation of the tithe does not rest on the fruits until they reach the time of the tithe, as it is stated (Leviticus 27:30), "from the seed of the land, from the fruit of the tree"; meaning to say until it becomes a fruit. And from here, they, may their memory be Blessed, learned that the time of the tithe is from when the fruits reach [when they could] be seeded and grow. Everything is according to what [the specific] fruit is. How is this? Figs, from when they become soft such that they are ready to eat; apples and citrons from when they turn round. And so [too,] with each and every fruit, they established its time for the tithe. That is to say until this time that is established for them, we can eat as much as we need, as they are not in the category of the tithe at all. But after this time, it can only be eaten casually, until their threshing floor designates them for the tithe. And after their threshing floor has designated them for the tithe, it is forbidden to eat from them, even casually. And what is their threshing floor with regard to the tithe? Produce from when it is flattened, meaning to say that he flattens its top with a shovel, in the way that people do when they make it into a heap. And in the Talmud Yerushalmi Ma'asrot 1:4, we have found further that if his intention is not to flatten [it], it is a threshing floor for [the designation of] the tithe from when he sets up a pile from his produce. As the verse made it dependent on the threshing floor, and even without flattening, when his intention is not to flatten [it]. And even if he makes a threshing floor of it inside his house; even there, the threshing floor creates the designation for the tithe. And that which Rav Oshaya said, "A man may be crafty about his produce and bring it in with its chaff," so as to exempt it from the tithe - and it is a set law, as we say in Tractate Berakhot 31a - that is speaking when he did not set up a pile inside his house, and so [too,] that he did not flatten it, but rather that he pounded it and winnowed it, little by little without flattening, and put it into the storehouse, little by little. This is what appears in this matter; and in this way, all of the discussions go up in one 'stalk, healthy and well' (are all in agreement). And they, may their memory be Blessed, said that the season of squash and watermelon and pumpkin is from when they are rubbed, meaning from when the thin hair that is upon them is removed; and the season of a basket of fruit is from when he covers the fruit inside of it with leaves and fronds. And so [too,] with each and every fruit, they established the time of its threshing floor, according to what it is - everything like it comes in Tractate Maasrot (Mishna Maasrot 1:5). And I have also seen about the topic of designating the tithe by Torah writ that the opinion of some of the commentators is that there is never designation for the tithe from any angle until there is seeing the face of the house (that the produce enters the home), and also that the house be fit for it, as it is stated (Deuteronomy 26:13), "I have cleared out the consecrated from the house." And that is when he brought it in through the gate, as it is stated (Deuteronomy 26:12), "and they shall eat in your gates and they shall be satiated." But if he brought them in through the roofs or the enclosures, they are exempt from the tithe and the priestly tithe. And so did Rambam, may his memory be Blessed, write (Mishneh Torah, Laws of Tithes 4:2), "It appears to me that we do not administer lashes from Torah writ for the eating of unseparated produce until they are designated by his bringing them into his house. But if it is designated with the other things that designate for the tithe, we do not administer lashes, besides [rabbinic] lashes of rebellion." [This] and the rest of its details are elucidated in Tractate Maasrot (see Tur, Yoreh Deah 338).

And it is practiced by males and females, by Israelites and by priests and by Levites. As even though the priests and the Levites take the tithe from [the Israelites], they are [still] obligated to tithe their [own] fruits on their lands. And it stands in the prohibition of unseparated fruit until they tithe them, as it is stated (Numbers 18:28), "So shall you give, also you." And the explanation upon it comes, "You" [is] the Levites; "also you" [is] to include the priests. But after they tithe them; if they want, they can eat the tithe themselves, or [they can] give it to a different priest. And this commandment of the tithe and also the commandment of the priestly tithe is only practiced in the Land of Israel by Torah writ - so did Rambam, may his memory be Blessed, determine. And in the Order of Shoftim in the commandment of separating the great priestly tithe, we will elucidate more, with God's help, the differences that there are in the tithe and in the priestly tithe between the Land of Israel and Syria or (other places) outside the Land. If it is your desire to know, my son, learn it from there.

Mitzvah 396

The commandment of the Levites to give a tithe from the tithe: That the Levites were commanded to separate a tithe from the tithe they take from Israel and that they give it to the priests, as it is stated (Numbers 18:26), "And to the Levites you shall speak, etc. and they shall give from it a gift to the Lord, a tithe from the tithe." And this is what is called ' terumat ma'aser ' (literally, the gift of the tithe) in every place in the Gemara. They called it this expression in the way of the verse, which states, "a gift to the Lord." But the verse elucidates that he gives it to the priest, and as it states (Numbers 18:28), "and you shall give from it, the gift of the Lord, to Aharon the priest." And Scripture warns that he separates from the good and the choicest from the tithe, as it states (Numbers 18:29), "from all the fat that you sanctify from it." Moreover, it is stated about this (Numbers 18:32), "You shall bear no sin upon it in separating its fat from it" - teaching that if he takes it out from the inferior [portion], there will be a sin upon them. And this matter is like the matter of a negative commandment that comes by way of deduction from a positive commandment, and therefore it is not to be counted among the negative commandments.

From the roots of the commandment, [there is a need to] preface that there is no doubt that God separated the entire tribe of Levi from the congregation of Israel to always serve Him. And still, within that tribe itself, one [group] was selected to be the head, the officer and the minister over all of them - he and his seed forever, and it is the most sacred of all the tribe - to serve and to minister before God permanently. And He placed the rest of the whole tribe below it, to assist in the service - and as it states (Numbers 18:1), "And the Lord spoke to Aharon saying, 'You, your sons, and your patriarchal lineage shall bear the iniquity of the Temple - meaning to say, that the entire tribe will receive the guarding of the Temple. "But you and your sons with you will bear the iniquity of your priesthood" - meaning to say that the primary service - that is the priesthood - is upon you. And it is written after it (Numbers 18:2), "Also your brothers, the tribe of Levi, the tribe of your father, bring close with you, and they shall accompany you and serve you" - meaning to say that you are primary, and not them. And so [too,] is it written elsewhere (Numbers 3:9), "And you shall give the Levites to Aharon and to his sons; they are truly given to him." And so, since the priests are 'the foundation of the home' in the service of our God, they merited twenty-four gifts that are given to them, which are explicit in Scripture, and as the Sages, may their memory be Blessed, enumerated (Chullin 133b) - ten in the Temple, four in Jerusalem and ten [outside]. And the rest of the tribe that was chosen with it to assist it also merited to live [from gifts], without toil, with the tithe of the fruits that they take from all Israel. And in order that they know and contemplate that the cause of their portion being free and of the portion of their brothers is the service to God, they were commanded to give a tenth of all they take from the Children of Israel to the 'greater ministers.' And in this way, they will [remind themselves] that there are [others] above them, and that above all of them is the One Who guards all, may He be elevated. With this is also merit, honor and prestige for the Levites, without removing their names from the commandment of the tithe in their portion of the produce. And [the sons of the Israelites] will not [be able to] say to [the sons of the Levites], "You merited the grain, and we the commandment." And now the response will be, "There is 'Torah and there is flour.'"

From the laws of the commandment - that which they, may their memory be Blessed, said (Beitzah 13a) that a [Levite] who took sheaves as tithes, does not give sheaves to the priest from it, but he is fined to pound and winnow [it] and to give him a tithe of the tithe that is a tithe of grain, and he is not obligated to give a tithe of the straw [byproduct], after he pounded everything and winnowed [it], but if he first tithed the sheaths, and [then] pounded and winnowed [it], he must give [the priest] his portion in everything; that which they said (Mishnah Terumot 11:8) that only priestly tithes from the tithe with [at least] 1/64 of a log must he take to the priest, and so long as the priestly tithe is certain (not in doubt) and pure, [but] if it is less than this, he need not busy himself with taking it to the priest, but he rather throws it into the fire and burns it; that which they said (Mishnah Bikkurim 2:5) that the priestly tithe from the tithe can be separated from that which is not [close], as it is stated (Numbers 18:28-29), "From all the tithes [...] you shall gift," meaning to say even if you have a tithe in one country and [another] in another country, you may take one gift for all [of them], but nonetheless they, may their memory be Blessed, said (Gittin 30a) that Torah scholars should only take it from [what is close]; and the rest of its details - are elucidated in Tractate Terumot, Ma'asrot, and in parts of Demai (see Mishneh Torah, Laws of Heave Offerings 1).

This commandment is practiced in the place that the priestly tithe and the tithe are practiced. And in the Order of Shoftim in the commandment of the separation of the great priestly tithe (Sefer HaChinukh 507), we will explain everything.

Mitzvah 397

The commandment of the red heifer: That Israel was commanded to burn the red heifer so that its ashes will be ready for anyone who needs it to be purified from the impurity of the dead, as it is stated (Numbers 19:2), "Speak to the Children of Israel and they shall take to you a red heifer," and it is written below this (Numbers 19:9), "It will be a safeguard for the Children of Israel." Even though my heart has given me the gumption to write hints of the simple reasons for the previous commandments, with the excuse that [this] work is to instruct my son and his young friends, may God protect them; on this commandment my hands are weak and I am afraid to open my mouth about it at all, since I have seen that our Rabbis, may their memory be Blessed, spoke at length regarding the depth of its secret and greatness of its content; to the point that they said (Bemidbar Rabbah 19, Midrash Tanchuma 4:6:6) that King Solomon was able through his great wisdom to understand all the reasons of the Torah, except for this - as he stated about it (Ecclesiastes 7:23), "I have said that I will understand, but it is far from me." They also said in the Midrash Tanchuma 4:6:8, "Rabbi Yose BeRebbi Chanina says, 'The Holy One, Blessed be He, said to Moshe, "To you I will reveal the reason for the red heifer, but not to others."'" And there are many other similar statements. And now, the listener should not think that the matter of its secret and the matter of its being an arational commandment (chok) is that the ashes affect purification, as one will find a similar [process] with other sacrifices for the person with a discharge or a new mother, whose purification is completed by the offering of their sacrifices.

The real wonder, so far as I have heard, is in its purifying the impure, yet rendering impure those involved in its burning. And even though the same is true for all burnt-offerings from cows and goats - that the one who burns them makes his clothes impure at the time that he burns them until they become ashes - nonetheless, their ashes do not purify. Also [part of] its great wonder is that the [process] is done outside of the camp, unlike the way of other offerings. And about this point the [other] nations [have a claim against] Israel, as they will think that it is offered to the demons in the open field, as is their practice today. And yet many medicinal herbs of the field and [medicinal] trees - from the cedars that are in Lebanon to the hyssop on the wall - are full of mysteries [that operate] in

Sefer HaChinukh

opposite [ways]. They heat the cold and cool the hot. And if we understood the nature of the spirit, its root, its illness and its health, we would also understand [perhaps] (about the sickness), since the mystery of the heifer is also to sicken the soul and render impure those who are involved in the burning, while its ashes heal from the sickness of impurity. Yet it is not clear that this would yield any result, but the love of the sacred and the desire to understand the hidden moves the quill to write. From the laws of the commandment are that which they, may their memory be Blessed, said (Mishnah Parah 1:1) the commandment of the heifer is that it be three or four years old, but if it was [older], it is [also] acceptable. And [that] we do not take a calf and raise her to maturity; but rather a cow (heifer), as it stated (Numbers 19:2), "and they shall take to you a heifer." And [that] that which it states about it "pure" (temimah), is to speak about perfect redness, such that two black or white hairs disqualify it. Even if it was shrunken (other textual variants read, dwarfed, meaning a dwarf), it is acceptable, so long as it is all red - as it does not need to be more perfect than other offerings. And if it had hairs whose roots were red and the tips were another color, it all goes according to the roots. And [so,] he trims the tips with a scissors down to the red.

And work [with it] disqualifies it, as it is written (Numbers 19:12), "that has borne no yoke upon it." And any labor is [considered equivalent] to a yoke; therefore, they, may their memory be Blessed, said that even if he placed a cloak on it, it is disqualified. If, however, it needed to be guarded and it was tied by a rope, it is acceptable (Mishnah Parah 2:3, Mishneh Torah, Laws of Red Heifer 1:7), but if it did not need guarding, it is disqualified, as any protection that is unnecessary is a burden. And it was purchased with money from the collection of the cell (Mishnah Shekalim 4:2). And a heifer that became blemished can be redeemed and it goes out to being non-sacred. And [also] that which they, may their memory be Blessed, said (Yoma 88b) about the matter that it is the one who burns the heifer that is impure, that this is the one who assists in the burning - such as the one who turns over the meat, or throws in firewood, or [moves] the fire or stokes the coals to have the fire burn [better], and similar to these - but the one who lights the fire in the furnace, or arranges the wood, is pure, as is anyone who deals with it after it has become ashes.

And the Sages enacted great stringencies in the purity of the heifer in its burning (Mishneh Torah, Laws of Red Heifer 2:1). And from them is that they would separate the priest who would burn it from his home and from his wife for seven days before the burning; similar to how they would separate the high priest for the service of Yom Kippur. And this thing is from tradition. And on each and every day of the days of separation, they would sprinkle him with the ashes of a heifer from one of the heifers that had already been burnt. And this would only be done by someone who had never been rendered impure by a dead body, as the sprinkler must be pure. And if you say, "If so that the need is only that someone who is pure sprinkles him, [would it not] have been possible for someone who had been impure and was sprinkled upon, to sprinkle him" - it is not like this, as we are concerned that the one who sprinkled [the one sprinkling now] may have not been pure from the impurity of a dead body. And also, any vessels that were filled to be poured on the priest who would burn the heifer were all vessels of stone, since they [are not susceptible to] acquiring impurity.

And if you ask, "How we could ever find a man who had never been rendered impure by a dead body ever" - the Sages said (Mishnah Parah 3:2) that there were courtyards in Jerusalem built on rock [and] below them was hollow because of the [concern over the] graves of the deep. And they would bring pregnant women and they would give birth there and raise their children there. And when they wanted to sprinkle on the priest that would burn [the heifer], they would bring oxen - as their bellies were inflated - and they would place slats (literally, doors) on their backs and the children would be made to sit on top of the slats, so that there would be a 'tent,' separating between them and the ground, because of the [concern over the] graves of the deep; and there would be stone cups in the hands of the children. And they would be brought to the waters of Shiloach, and they would descend there and fill [the cups], as there was no concern there over the graves of the deep, since it is not the way of people to bury in rivers. And they would return and mount atop the slats on top of the oxen and go to the Temple Mount. And they would descend there and walk upon their feet, since all of the Temple Mount and the yards' underneaths were hollow, due to the concern over the graves of deep. And they would walk to the opening of the [Temple] yard and take from the ashes and place them in cups; and they would sprinkle the priest that burns [the heifer]. And the children would immerse due to the concern that they had become impure with another impurity. And all of these things are from the extra stringencies of the heifer. And it was burnt on the Mountain of Anointing (Mishnah Parah 3:6).

[These laws] and the the laws of how we burn it, and in which places we store its ashes, of how the water would be sanctified with the ashes of the heifer, of how we would purify those impure from the impurity of a dead body with the purifying waters, and the rest of its many details, are all elucidated in the tractate that is connected to this, and that is Tractate Parah (see Mishneh Torah, Laws of Red Heifer 1).

And [it] is practiced in the Land of Israel at the time of the [Temple]. And it is one of the commandments that we spoke about at the beginning of the book that are incumbent upon the whole community. And our Rabbis, may their memory be Blessed, said that there were nine heifers that were [processed] from the time we were commanded about this commandment until the destruction of the Second [Temple]. The first was [prepared] by Moshe, the second by Ezra, [and] there were seven from Ezra until the destruction of the [Temple]. And the tenth will be [prepared] by the King Messiah, may he redeem us speedily in our days, amen. And since this is a major matter with our people, as it would purify from the most severe impurity - and without it, it is impossible for one who is impure from the impurity of a dead body to [bring the] Pesach [sacrifice], which is a very great commandment - all of Israel has become accustomed to read this section [of the Torah] each and every year on the week before Parshat HaChodesh, and we never interrupt between Parshat Parah and Parshat HaChodesh. And Parshat HaChodesh is always read on the Shabbat before Nissan (see Shulchan Arukh, Orach Chaim 585:7).

Mitzvah 398

The commandment of the impurity of a dead body: That we were commanded regarding the matter of impurity from a dead body to behave as the Torah commanded us about it, as it is stated (Numbers 19:14), "This is the law; a man who dies in a tent - anyone who comes into the tent and everything that is in the tent will become impure seven days."

And I have written what I could from the roots of the matter of the impurity of the dead body in the Order of Emor el HaKohanim (Sefer HaChinukh 263); and so too, some of the laws - as is my custom - take it from there. And all the laws of the one rendered impure by a dead body are elucidated in Tractate Ohalot (see Mishneh Torah, Laws of Defilement by a Corpse 1). And in the Order of Vayehi Bayom HaShmini in the commandment of the impurity of the eight crawling animals (Sefer HaChinukh 159), you will also see it written that Ramban, may his memory be Blessed, disagrees with Rambam, may his memory be Blessed, not to count all the laws of the impurities in the tally of the commandments - and his reasoning is with him.

Mitzvah 399

The Commandment of the niddah waters which render the pure, impure and only purify someone impure from the impurity of a dead body: That we have been commanded about the laws of the niddah waters, meaning to say in the laws of the waters of sprinkling, which are 'living' waters mixed with the ashes of the heifer, which we sprinkle on the impure. And the expression, 'niddah,' is meaning to say, sprinkling, which is an expression of throwing, as in "and they threw (yadu) a stone at me" (Lamentations 3:53). And we were commanded with laws known from the Scripture: That we purify the impure, as it is stated (Numbers 19:19), "And the pure will sprinkle the impure, etc."; and render the pure impure [with] a severe impurity, as it is written (Numbers 19:21), "and the one who sprinkles the niddah waters, etc." And that which is stated about this commandment [to call it] the 'statute' (chukat) of the heifer, is [because] it is a lofty wonder - I cannot master it.

From the laws of the commandment - that which they said (Mishnah Parah 6:5) that we only fill the waters that we put on the ashes, with a vessel, from the bubbling springs and from the flowing rivers; [that] the placing of the waters on the ashes is called by our Rabbis, may their memory be Blessed, the "sanctification of the sin-offering waters"; [that] the waters that he places upon the ashes are called the " niddah waters" by the verse; [that] all are fit to fill the waters and to sanctify, except for a deaf-mute, a mentally incapacitated person or a minor (Mishnah Parah 10:4); [that] one who is involved in another work at the time of filling the waters or in bringing them, disqualifies them (Mishnah Parah 4:4), but that after he puts the ashes in them, [other] work does not disqualify them; [that] a wage also disqualifies in the sanctification and the sprinkling (Bekhorot 29a), [such that] the waters and ashes of one who takes a wage to sanctify or sprinkle are like the [regular] waters of a cave and like the [regular] ashes of an oven, but one who takes a wage for the filling [of the waters] does not disqualify [them]; and the rest of its many details - are [all] elucidated in Tractate Parah (see Mishneh Torah, Laws of Red Heifer 1).

And [it] is practiced at the time of the [Temple] by males and females; as they all need sprinkling before they enter the Temple or eat the sanctified foods if they became impure with a dead body. And one who transgressed this and did not receive sprinkling if he needs it, has violated this positive commandment. And I have already written in the previous commandment that Ramban, may his memory be Blessed, would not count all of the laws of impurity in the tally of the commandments. And his strong proofs are in his Book of the Commandments in Commandment 96.

There are no commandments in Parshat Balak.

Mitzvah 400

The commandment of the laws of inheritance: That we were commanded with the laws of inheritances; that is, that it is a commandment upon us to act and rule in the matter of inheritance, as the Torah ruled about it, as it is stated (Numbers 27:8-9), "If a man dies and has no son, you shall pass his inheritance to his daughter. And if he has no daughter, etc." And the end of the section [is], "and this shall be for the Children of Israel as an eternal statute, as the Lord commanded Moshe." But do not think that its stating in this that in the matter of inheritance we act as the Torah ruled about it, means to say that a man is commanded by God to give what he has to his heirs in all cases; as God, Blessed be He, did not wish to extract the properties of a person from his control, for the sake of his heir, that he should not do all of his desire [with them], so long as his soul is in him, as [is the view] of the wise men of the nations. Rather, it informs us that the right of the heirs is entwined with the property of their [progenitor]. And [so] when the [ownership] of the bequeather elapses with his death, the right of the heirs immediately rests upon them; like the matter of procreation that the Creator, Blessed be He, wanted without interruption. Our Rabbis, may their memory be Blessed, designated this right of assertion of the heir in the properties of his bequeather, with the expression, "touching," as in the expression in their statement in many places (e. g. Bava Batra 115b), "Inheritance touches and continues." [This] means that the right of the heir upon the bequeather is like two bodies clinging to each other, such that what comes out from one, rests upon the other.

And because of this, they, may their memory be Blessed, said (Bava Batra 126b) that if the bequeather commanded and said, "My son shall not inherit me," or "My son x shall not inherit with his brothers" or "My daughter x shall inherit me," when he has a son, or similar to these words; his words have no force, as he does not have the power to uproot the word of God, who said that the heir inherits the bequeather. And even though we said that his properties are in his hands for all of his desires, the matter is to say that he may give them to whom he wants and to do whatever is his desire - and even to destroy his property - with any expression, except for that of inheritance; as this statement is against the statement of the Omnipresent and His decree. As He stated that the heir inherits, and hence a person has no power to say [that] he shall not inherit. And this is [the meaning] of our teaching in our Mishanh in [the chapter entitled] Yesh Nochalin (Bava Batra 130a), "One who says, 'X shall not inherit with his brothers,' has said nothing, for he has stipulated against what is written in the Torah. And so [too,] one who says, 'Y (stranger) shall inherit me,' when he has a daughter, or 'My daughter shall inherit me,' when he has a son, has said nothing, for he has stipulated against what is written in the Torah. Rabbi Yochanan ben Beroka says, 'If he said [it] about one who is qualified to inherit from him, his words are valid, but about one who is not qualified to inherit from him, his words are not valid.'" The explanation is if he said about one son among his sons, or one daughter among his daughters that only [that] one among them inherit him, his words are valid. And it is expounded in the Gemara from that which is written (Deuteronomy 21:16), "And it shall be on the day that he gives

Sefer HaChinukh

his inheritance to his sons" - that the Torah gave the father permission to bequeath to whom he wants from those qualified to inherit. And the law about this is decided like Rabbi Yochanan regarding common [children], but not regarding the first-born; about which the father does not have the power to uproot the inheritance from the first-born in this matter.

They also said there (Bava Batra 126b), "The one who divides his properties, gives a large portion to one and a small portion to another, or gives a standard portion to the first-born, his words are valid. But if he said it as 'inheritance' he has said nothing. If he wrote it - whether at the beginning of his words, or in the middle of his words or at the end - as a gift, his words are valid." And it seems that even though there is no validity to the words of the one who [employs] an expression of inheritance and his actions [in this regard] are nothing - as is explicit in the Mishnah - through his commanding this, he has violated this positive commandment of inheritance, for he has transgressed against the decree of the King. And so [too,] if maybe after he dies, the court affirms these words of his, they also have the iniquity of violating this positive commandment, besides the punishment for the negative commandment of "Do not pervert justice." And according to what appears from the words of Rambam, may his memory be Blessed, the entire thrust of this warning is only upon the court that judged about the matter of inheritance like this. And this is his language that he wrote "It is a commandment to judge the laws of inheritance." And it is as he elucidated the matter about the commandment of annulling vows, before it.

It is from the root of the commandment [that it is] so that a person should reflect that the world is in the hand of the Master that oversees all of His creatures, and it is in His desire and His goodly will, that each and every person acquires the portion of possessions that he attains in this world. And His gift is Blessed, that it stay forever with the one He gave it to, were it not that the world was penalized with death because of the original sin. Yet it is not correct that the removal of his body should end the Blessed gift of God. Rather it should extend on its own [to] the body that descends from this one, i.e. his son or his daughter. And if he dies in his iniquity and he has no children, it is proper for the blessing of God to revert to the closest relative to him; as this blessing that this one acquired was either due to his merit or the merit of his forebears. Or perhaps his closest relatives taught him some skill that caused him to amass his possessions; therefore, when he and his seed are removed from them, it is fitting for his relatives who assisted him in this merit to precede all other people.

From the laws of the commandment is that which they, may their memory be Blessed, said in our Mishnah from [the chapter entitled] Yesh Nochalin (Bava Batra 115a), "The order of inheritance is thus: 'If a man dies, etc.' - a son precedes a daughter, and all offspring of a son precede a daughter; a daughter precedes brothers, and all offspring of a daughter precede brothers; the brothers, or the sisters where there are no brothers, precede brothers of the father (uncles); and brothers of the father, or sisters of the father (aunts) if there are no brothers of the father, precede other relatives. This is the general rule: the offspring of any heir precedes the next relation, and the father always precedes his offspring." And in this way that we said, we go and climb up to the beginning of [the lineage]. Therefore, there is not anyone in Israel who was no heir.

And [also] that which they said there (Bava Batra 108a) that a mother does not bequeath [her property] to her children - and this thing is a tradition. And brothers from the mother (but from different fathers) do not inherit each other, as maternal family is not called family. And so, a mamzer (a son from Jewish parents forbidden to marry) - or a mamzer brother - behold, he inherits like other sons (Mishneh Torah, Laws of Inheritances 1:6-7); and even a mamzer son that become an apostate inherits. But a child of a maid-servant or non-Jewess does not inherit, and he is not the father's son for any [purpose]. But the Sages established that a man bequeaths to his wife, if they are fully married; and they gave the matter support from Scripture.

And Rambam (Sefer HaMitzvot LaRambam, Mitzvot Ase 248), may his memory be Blessed, wrote that included in these laws of inheritance without a doubt, is that the first-born receives double - as this is included in the commandment of inheritance. And the explanation of double is two portions, meaning that if there are two brothers, we [divide] the money into three parts and the first-born takes two. And if there are three, we [divide] it into four parts and he takes two, and so forth forever. But the first-born only takes double in properties that are held by the father (Mishneh Torah, Laws of

Sefer HaChinukh

Inheritances 3:1), meaning to say that came into the domain of his father in his lifetime, but not that which is fitting to come to his father, as it is stated (Deuteronomy 21:17), "of all that is found to him." How is this? [If] one of the individuals from whom the father could inherit dies after the father, the first-born does not take double from that inheritance. And so [too,] if the father had a debt that was owed to him (Bava Batra 125b) - even [if it was recorded] in a contract - or if he has a merchant ship [raising revenue] in the sea, the first-born does not have double of this; as this is not 'found to the father.' And so [too,] for this reason, the first-born does not take double of the appreciation of the properties after the death of his father, such as a field yielding grain, or trees bearing their fruit, as these were not extant to his father in his days. If, however, a small tree grew larger not due to an expense - but rather grew on its own - after his father's death before the division [of the property], the first-born does take double of this; as this is considered extant to his father, as it is unchanged in its form.

And the father is believed [when] he says, "This is my son, my first-born" (Kiddushin 74a), or to say, "This is my son" or "This is not my son." As it is written (Deuteronomy 21:17), "But the first-born etc. shall he recognize" - and they, may their memory be Blessed, expounded (Bava Batra 127b), "shall make him recognized by others." And even if someone was presumed to be Reuven's son, if Reuven says that he is not his son, he is believed, and he does not bequeath to him. And Rambam (Mishneh Torah, Laws of Inheritances 4:2), may his memory be Blessed, wrote, "It seems to me that even if the son had sons, [such that] even though [the father] is not believed about him to say he is not his son, for the purposes of family relationships, and he is not presumed to be a mamzer on his word, he is believed for the purposes of inheritance and he will not inherit him.

And also, that which they said (Bava Batra 129b) about this matter, that [if] one says to [someone else], "My properties are yours; and after you, for **x**" - if the first is eligible to inherit, the latter has nothing in place of the first. As since [the first] acquired the properties and he is eligible to inherit them, their is no further interruption of the inheritance because of the stipulation of the bequeather. And with the best commentaries, and proper logic, we learned in the chapter [entitled] Yesh Nochalin (Bava Batra 125b) that even if he says it with an expression of "from now," as for example [if] he said to him, "My properties are yours; and from now, after you for **x**" - nonetheless, the latter has nothing in place of the first, as the first is eligible to inherit (and there is nothing left after the inheritance). But if the first is not eligible to inherit and he said to him, "from now, after you, will be for x," the latter acquires the properties themselves, and the first one [only] receives the income all of his lifetime. And if he did not say, "from now," but rather [just], "My properties are yours; and after you, for x," the latter only receives what is left from the first (Bava Batra 137a, Mishneh Torah, Laws of Ownerless Property and Gifts 12:9). And if the first sells them, the latter never has the power to extract them from the purchaser, as they stay in the possession of the first all the days of his entire for all of his desires - whether to sell them or give them as a gift to anyone he wants. They are so fully in the possession of the first that if the giver said, "My properties are yours; and after you, for x; and after him, for y," if the second one dies in the lifetime of the first, they, may their memory be Blessed, said in the Gemara (Bava Batra 129b), that the properties go back to the heirs of the first. As the [original ceder of the properties] did not leave anything over in his gift to the first, except for [the stipulation] that they would be given after [the life of the first] to the second, and from the second - and through his agency - to the third. And since the second died, and it is impossible for the third to acquire them through the agency of the second - as the giver had said - the properties remain in the hand of whom they are possessed and his heirs forever. And the same is true that we should rule in the way that we said, where he used the expression, "if" - for example [if] he said, "My properties are for x; and if he dies, they should be given to y" (see Tur, Choshen Mishpat 248:4 in the name of Rabbenu Yonah). As we are not coming to rule like this based on the expression, "after you." Rather, the reason of the thing is because we say that the first acquired the properties themselves and its income; and they are possessed in his hand, [unless] we can extract them from him with a strong proof [otherwise]. But where the giver wrote, "My properties are yours; and after you, mine or my heirs"; even though he did not mention the expression, "from now," in this retention, we should rule that if the recipient of the gift dies, the properties return to the giver or his heirs. And even if the recipient of the gift sells [them], the giver may extract them from the hand of the buyer when the recipient of the gift dies. As so did the sages say about this (Bava Batra 137b) - that anyone who retains [the rights to his properties] for himself or his heirs is always as if he stipulates, "This present will be for you to enjoy the profits [only] during all the days of your life."

The general rule of the things that has come up in our hands in this matter after much toil is that so long as the first is eligible to inherit, once the bequeather said, "My properties are yours," it is no longer in is hand to give them to another, even to his heir; since the properties immediately enter the possession of the [first] heir. And afterwards, he is only like one who makes stipulations about the properties of another person. And it is like the matter that is said about this topic in the Gemara (Bava Batra 133a), "He held it has interruption" - it, meaning inheritance - "and the [Torah] stated that it does not have interruption."

And our teachers, may God protect them, taught us what is even greater than this with strong and clear proofs: That even one who says to someone who is eligible to inherit him, "My properties are yours; and after you, to be consecrated property (hekdesh)," or even if he said, "and from now, after you, to be consecrated," the heir acquires the properties and he may sell them or do with them as he desires; and [the one in charge of] consecrated property does not have the power to extract them from the hand of the purchaser or the recipient of the gift for the reason that we wrote. And once the bequeather said to his heir, "My properties are yours," [the heir] acquires the properties, and it is no longer in his hand to consecrate them. Rather, it is like he consecrates the property of others. And regarding what there is to analyze in this matter that at the beginning of the analysis seems difficult - such as that which they, may their memory be Blessed, said (Kiddushin 28b), "his statement for consecrated property is like delivery for regular property," and other things - we have already discussed them back and forth, and have come to precise understandings about all of them, such that the matter has come up clarified as we have written. The matter would be too long if I came to write it all and it is not the work of my book. But if you will merit, my son, and cast your net upon the sea of the Gemara, all of it will come up to you. [These] and the rest of the details of the commandment are elucidated in Bava Batra in the chapter [entitled] Yesh Nochalin (see Tur, Choshen Mishpat 276). And it is practiced in every place and at all times by males and females. And one who transgresses it and commanded - whether he was healthy or on his deathbed - that the one eligible to inherit him, not inherit him, has nullified this positive commandment, provided that he commanded so, with an expression of 'inheritance,' as we have said. And [this is true] even though his words have no substance, as we have written above at the beginning of the topic. And Ramban, may his memory be Blessed, wrote that Rambam, may his memory be Blessed, skipped two commandments, one positive commandment and one negative - and both of them are about the firstborn. As a man is commanded to recognize the firstborn by giving him double, and that is a positive commandment on the father that Rambam skipped. And so too, It warns him about transferring the rights of the firstborn from him. And about this it states (Deuteronomy 21:16), "he may not make into a firstborn the son of the beloved, etc." And the teacher mentioned also did not itemize this warning [as a negative commandment], but rather grouped it all into the commandment of the law of inheritances.

Mitzvah 401

The commandment of the regular [sacrifices] daily: That Israel was commanded that they should sacrifice - through the servants of God, may He be Blessed, who are the priests - two unblemished one-year old lambs as a burnt-offering daily, one in the morning and the second in the afternoon, as it is stated (Numbers 28:2), "Command the Children of Israel and say to them, 'My sacrifice, my bread, etc. two per day, a regular burnt-offering.'" And nonetheless, the main warning is to the court - meaning to say the sages, the decisors of the Torah in Israel, as the work of the community is incumbent upon them. And it is like they, may their memory be Blessed said (Sifrei Bamidbar 142:3), "'And say to them' is a warning to the court."

I have written what went up in my spirit about the simple understanding of the matter from the roots of the commandment of the sacrifices on the commandment of the Temple in the Order of Vayikchu Li Trumah (Sefer HaChinuch 95). And I will also continue according to those reasons in the explanation of the regular sacrifices, to say that we were commanded in this regular service, which is twice a day - with the rising of the sun and with its inclining towards the evening - in order that we be aroused from this action and that we place all of our hearts and all of our thoughts to cling to God, Blessed be He. And we have said several times that a person is acted upon - and his nature is aroused - according to the involvement of his actions. And hence in that a man's nature is designed that he needs to prepare nourishment for himself twice [a day], morning and evening, he is commanded that he place his industry and his occupation in the occupation of the service of his Creator two times [a day] as well, that the service of the servant to himself not be more than his service to his Master. And why all of this (what is its reason)? In order to regularly arouse his spirit and his desire to remember his Creator, and through this to make his actions proper and be Blessed from [God]; as He is One who desires kindness. [It is] as they, may their memory be Blessed, expounded (Sifrei Bamidbar 143:3), "'A fire, of pleasing smell to the Lord' - since I said, and My will was done" - meaning to say, that the entire portion of the Higher from any sacrifice is only His desire, Blessed be He, that the servant do what his Master has commanded him, in order that he be fit to merit His goodness, Blessed be He. From the laws of the commandment - that which they, may their memory be Blessed, said (Yoma 28a) that the time of their slaughter is, of the one lamb of the morning before the rising of the sun, from when the entire face of the East is light, and once in the Second Temple, the time pushed the community and they sacrificed the regular sacrifice of the morning at four hours in the day (Mishnah Eduyot 6:1); and the time of the second lamb of the afternoon is from six and a half hours and onward until the end of the day (Pesachim 58a), but [in fact,] they would always sacrifice it at eight and a half hours and offer it at nine and a half [hours], and these two hours that they would delay it were in order that that they could sacrifice individual and community sacrifices in between, as it is forbidden to sacrifice another sacrifice after the afternoon sacrifice; [that] the process of the regular afternoon sacrifice was like the process of the regular morning sacrifice, except that the one of the morning was sacrificed in the northeastern corner of the room of the slaughterers on the second ring, and [the one] of the afternoon was in the northwestern corner on the second ring, so that it be in front of the sun; and the rest of its details - are elucidated in Tractate Tamid and in the second chapter of Yoma (see Mishneh Torah, Laws of Daily Offerings and Additional Offerings 1).

And this commandment is practiced at the time of the [Temple]; and it is from the commandments that are incumbent upon the community, and especially on the priests. And if maybe, God forbid, they were negligent about it, not to sacrifice it every day, they will have violated this positive commandment. And the mistake is placed upon all of the community of Israel that know about the thing if they have the power in their hands to fix [it] from any angle. And Ramban, may his memory be Blessed, itemized the two regulars [sacrifices] as two [distinct] positive commandments in the tally of the commandments (Sefer HaMitzvot, at the end of s.v. veatah, eem taveen), since the commandments do not impede one another, and the time of this [one] is not the time of that [one].

Mitzvah 402

The commandment of the additional sacrifice of Shabbat: That Israel was commanded to sacrifice two lambs [as a] sacrifice on every Shabbat day, in addition to the regular sacrifice of every day. And it is called the addition of Shabbat, as it is stated (Numbers 28:9), "And on the Shabbat day, two lambs, etc."

I have already written from the roots of the commandment of the additional sacrifices of the holidays in the Order of Emor el HaKohanim regarding the addition of Pesach (Sefer HaChinukh 299) from the angle of the simple understanding. And the addition of Shabbat is also appurtenant to the cluster of additional sacrifices. And the matter is that with the act of the sacrifice, we fix in our thoughts the greatness of the day and its broad holiness, and that 'in six days, the Lord made the heavens and the earth, etc.' - as it is written there. And there I also wrote a little of the laws of the additional sacrifices and the main principle of the matter, as is my custom.

Mitzvah 403

The commandment of the additional sacrifice on each and every month: That we should sacrifice an additional sacrifice on each Rosh Chodesh (first day of the month) on top of the regular sacrifice of every day, as it is stated (Numbers 28:11-15), "And on your new months, you shall sacrifice a burnt-offering to the Lord, two young bulls, one ram, and seven one-year old unblemished lambs [and their grain offerings.] And their libations, etc. And a male goat as a sin-offering to the Lord."

From the roots of the commandment, [there is a need to] preface that it is known to all wise-hearted men that the sphere of the sun and the sphere of the moon act with their power - that is given over to them from the Master of all the powers in this lowly world - great effects upon the bodies of people and and upon all types of other animals. [And] even upon everything that grows in the earth, from the great cedars to the thin grasses - and more generally upon all that is from the four elements, which are below them and under their governance. And so is it written in the Order of VeZot HaBerakha (Deuteronomy 33:14), "With the bounteous produce of the sun, and the bounteous crop of the moons." And it is famous among the masses - young and old - that the power of the moon is noticeable in everything that is done on earth; as is known to those that cut whitish trees, as they do not cut them when the moon is new until five or more days, and those that ply the waters also do not cast off until after five days of a new moon, and so [too,] all people are careful not to draw blood close to its renewal. And several other activities, - big and small - require guarding not to do them when the moon is renewing; to the point that they say that flax found in soaking or in the kettle to cook during the renewal of the moon becomes defective and will not be effective for anything afterwards. And the principal of these things is revealed and known to all, and discussing them at length would be childish. And so since the renewal of the moon brings novelty to the activity of man - and it is all according to the word of the Omnipresent, Blessed be He, and according to His decree - it is fitting for us also to bring novelty, and sacrifice an additional sacrifice over the other days to His name, may He be Blessed; to arouse our souls and to fix in our hearts that all novelties that exist in the world are from Him, Blessed be He, and all of the power of the spheres are only found with God alone. And with this pure and true thought, our souls will rise, and the blessing of God, may He be Blessed, will rest upon our heads.

I have written the laws of the commandment about the matter of the additional sacrifices and and the whole topic - as is my custom - regarding the addition of Pesach in the Order of Emor el HaKohanim (Sefer HaChinukh 299). And I will further inform you here that [when] Rosh Chodesh falls on Shabbat, the song of the addition of Rosh Chodesh pushes off the song of the addition of Shabbat, in order to publicize that today is Rosh Chodesh (Sukkah 54b). And it is well-known that the song of the additions of Shabbat in the Temple was the song of Haazinu. And they would divide it into six parts on six Shabbats. And the sign [to remember this] is hay, zayin, yod, vav, lamed, reish (the first letters of each of the parts), in the way that we read it in the synagogue.

Mitzvah 404

The commandment of the additional sacrifice on the day of the festival of Shavouot: That Israel was commanded to sacrifice an additional sacrifice on the day of the festival of Shavouot, as it is stated (Numbers 28:26), "And on the day of the first-fruits when you bring a new meal-offering to the Lord on your festival of Weeks (Shavouot), etc." And I have already written twice that I have spoken about the matter of the additional sacrifices in the Order of Emor el HaKohanim regarding the addition of Pesach (Sefer HaChinukh 299).

Mitzvah 405

The commandment of shofar (horn) on Rosh Hashanah: That we were commanded to hear the sound of the shofar on the first day of Tishrei, which is Rosh Hashanah - and as we learn in Tractate Rosh Hashanah 2a, "On the first of Tishrei is the beginning of the year (rosh hashanah) for [calculating] years" - as it is stated (Numbers 29:1), "a day of blowing shall it be for you." And even though there is no mention of [how] this blast [should be done], if with a shofar, or with cymbals, or with any other musical instrument; they, may their memory be Blessed, learned from [the oral tradition] (Rosh Hashanah 33b) that it is with a shofar, as we found with regard to the jubilee year, about which it states (Leviticus 25:9), "shofar."

Sefer HaChinukh

It is from the roots of the commandment [that] since a person is physical, he is only aroused by something that arouses, like the way of people during wartime [to] blow and even scream in order that they should be properly aroused for war. So too [is it] on the day of Rosh Hashanah, which is the day determined from antiquity to judge on it all who come to the world, and as they, may their memory be Blessed, said (Rosh Hashanah 18a), "On Rosh Hashanah all creatures pass before Him like benei maron " - meaning to say that His providence is over the action of each and every one individually. And if his merits are greater, he goes out innocent, but if his iniquities are greater such that it is fit to render him guilty, he is rendered guilty for the death penalty, or for one of the decrees, according to that [for] which he is guilty. Hence, everyone must arouse his nature to request mercy over his sins from the Master of mercy, as 'He is a graceful and merciful God, He bears iniquity, rebellion and sin, and removes' [the sin] of those that repent to Him with all of their hearts. And the sound of the shofar greatly arouses the heart of all its listeners, and all the more so, the teruah sound, meaning to say the broken sound (Mishneh Torah, Laws of Repentance 3:4). And besides the arousal from it, there is a memory device in the matter; that when he hears the broken sounds, he break the evil inclination of his heart for the desires of the world and his cravings. As every man prepares his heart and understands things according to what his eyes see and what his ears hear. And this is [the meaning of] what Rabbi Yehudah said (Rosh Hashanah 26b), "We blow from the males (rams) on Rosh Hashanah" - meaning to say, the bent horn of [rams], so that when he sees it, man remembers to 'bend' his heart towards the Heavens. And Rabbi Levi decided the law to be like [Rabbi Yehudah], and the custom of all of Israel is like this.

From the laws of the commandment is that which they, may their memory be Blessed, said (Rosh Hashanah 27b), that the [minimum] size of the shofar is such that a person can hold it in his hand and see it [sticking out] on [both sides] of his hand. And all shofars are fit except for that of the cow (see Ramban in his Sermon for Rosh Hashanah). The explanation is that anything that is a shofar - meaning to say that it is hollow, as the expression, shofar, always implies something that has a cavity - such as the shofar of a [ram] that has a cavity inside of its protrusion, and any shofar in the world that has a cavity as we explained, is fit to blow with it on Rosh Hashanah. [This comes] to exclude the horns of an oryx and other animals, the horns of which are not at all included in the expression, shofar, as they do not have something with a cavity in them, but rather just the protrusion. But the horn of a cow is not fit, even though it is in the category of shofar - as behold, it has a cavity and a protrusion - since Scripture included it with those disqualified, as it called it a horn, as it is written (Deuteronomy 33:17), "His firstborn ox, etc. and his horns are the horns of an oryx." It comes out according to this explanation of ours that all the horns of the world are disqualified to blow with on Rosh Hashanah, except for the horns of [rams] and ewes and also male goats and female goats; as we have not found hollow horns in the world except for these and that of the cow. As all of the horns of all of the [other] animals are not empty, so it comes out that they are not in the category of the expression, shofar. And Scripture has also already taken out that of the cow from the category of the fit and placed it with the category of the disqualified, since it called it with their name. And let it not be difficult in your eyes about these words of ours, that behold Scripture [also] calls the shofar of male goats with the expression of the disqualified, as it is written (Daniel 8:5), "and the goat had a conspicuous horn between its eyes." As this matter was in a prophetic vision, and Scripture informs us that it appeared to the prophet as if it had a horn due to the great strength of the goat - meaning to say [the horn] was strong [in that it was] without a cavity. And the matter is not at all that Scripture is placing it with the disqualified, but rather the opposite, [as is understood] by all who understand. And I have written a little at length here, my son, because this explanation of the Mishnah was newly presented recently, and those who were before, explained it in a different way.

And also, from the content of the commandment is that which they, may their memory be Blessed, said (Rosh Hashanah 27b) that all sounds of the shofar are fit. And they also said that if one scrapes the shofar down until he transforms it into a shell, it is [still] fit. And [so too,] that which they, may their memory be Blessed, said (Rosh Hashanah 29b), that we do not blow the shofar on Rosh Hashanah that falls out on Shabbat, [due to the] decree lest another Israelite take it and move it four ells in the public domain and come to a prohibition [the punishment for which is] stoning. And the

Sages did not decree this in a place where there is a court this is great in wisdom; but it is only [permitted] when they blow there in the presence of the court. And Rambam, may his memory be Blessed (Mishneh Torah, Laws of Shofar, Sukkah and Lulav 2:9) wrote that it needs to be a court ordained in the Land of Israel and that the court have the status of those that sanctified the new moon. But I have heard that the Teacher, Rabbi Yitschak Alfasi, may his memory be Blessed, would blow the shofar in his academy on Shabbat. And you, my son - if you merit [it] - will choose for yourself the [approach that is] better in your eyes.

And also from the content of the commandment is that which they, may their memory be Blessed, said (Rosh Hashanah 33b) that a man is obligated to blow three [sets] of three on Rosh Hashanah, meaning to say three times, tekiah, teruah, tekiah - which comes out that they are six times tekiah (the long uninterrupted blow) and three times teruah. And the understanding of teruah is like its [official Aramaic] translation, yabava. And the [meaning] of yabava is a broken sound, meaning to say, the sound of wailing. It comes out that the Torah commanded us to make a sound similar to wailing from the shofar. But since [different] places in the world differ regarding the matter of wailing - as in one place they wail with heavy sobs, and in another place, with light [yelps] and in [yet] another place, they do [both], heavy and light - it became customary in each and every place to blow the teruah on Rosh Hashanah according to the way each person would wail in his place. And with this, they would [all] fulfill their obligation for the commandment, since the Torah commanded about a voice of wailing. And with whichever one it would be in any place, he would fulfill his obligation with this from the Torah regardless - and even though in his place, they did not wail like this - as he fulfilled the intention of Scripture and made a wail from the shofar on Rosh Hashanah. [This was the case] until Rabbi Abahu rose (Rosh Hashanah 34a) and it was not right in his eyes that Israel should differ regarding the practice of teruah - this one with this and that one with that - as the Torah would become like two Torahs in Israel. [So] he gathered all of the customs and established that they would blow the same [way] in all places and to fulfill the obligation with all of the wailings that are done in the world. He ordained to make the teruah in [all] three ways: like the heavy sobs, which is shevarim ; and like the light [yelps], which is what we call teruah ; and also the way of heavy sobs and light [yelps together], like the custom of one the places where they do it all, according to their [particular] wails. And it comes out according to this that we need to blow three [sets] of three, three times. And the law of the shofar that cracked along its length or width, or was punctured and he plugged it with its type or not its type (Rosh Hashanah 27b); the law of one who puts a shofar inside a shofar; the law of one who blows in a pit or a cellar; the law of a shofar of idolatry or a condemned city or one who vows not to benefit from his fellow (Rosh Hashanah 28a); the law when the listener had intention [to fulfill the commandment] but the [blower] did not; and the rest of its details are [all] elucidated in Tractate Rosh Hashanah (see Tur, Orach Chaim 585)

And it is practiced in every place and at all times by males, but not be females; because it is in the category of commandments determined by time, [from which] women are exempt. And one who transgresses it and did not listen to the sound of the shofar on the day of Rosh Hashanah, according to the order of blows that we said - three [sets] of three, at least - has violated this positive commandment. But if he heard them with an interruption - and even [over the course of] the whole day - he has fulfilled [it]; as they, may their memory be Blessed, said (Rosh Hashanah 34b) that if a person hears nine blows that stretch over nine hours of the day - and even from nine [different] people - he has fulfilled [it]. And I have learned from the sages - may God protect them - that he nonetheless needs to not hear a disqualified sound in between [the fit sounds].

Mitzvah 406
The commandment of the law of the abrogation of vows: That we were commanded in the abrogation of vows, meaning to say that we deliberate about someone who has made a vow, according to what the Torah commanded - as it is stated (Numbers 30:3), "If a man makes a vow, etc.," as it comes explained in [this] section of the Torah. And Rambam, may his memory be Blessed, wrote (Sefer HaMitzvot LaRambam, Mitzvot Ase 95) and this is his language: "And the matter is not that we are obligated to annul regardless. And this matter itself understand from me - when you hear me

counting a law from the laws, it is not [always] that it is a commandment to perform a certain action perforce, but rather the commandment is in our being commanded that we deliberate on the law about this thing. While Scripture has already elucidated and been exacting that a husband and a father can annul [a vow of their wife or daughter], it is the transmission that brought to us that a sage can annul [it] for all, and so too, an oath. And the indication of this is its statement (Numbers 30:3), 'he shall not profane his word' - and they, may their memory be Blessed, expounded (Chagigah 10a), 'He does not pardon [it], but others may pardon it.' And the general principle is that there is no proof to this from Scripture. And they, may their memory be Blessed, already said (Chagigah 10a), 'Annulment of vows flies in the air and has nothing to support it,' except for the truthful transmission only. To here [are his words].

And what apparently comes out of all of this according to his opinion is that in the annulment by an expert sage or three ordinary men of a vow by the commandment of the Torah, and their doing the matter like all that the Torah commands about it - like is proper and like is straight - they will have then fulfilled a positive commandment. But if they annulled the vow not like the commandment of the Torah - for example, [by] two ordinary men or an individual who is not an expert - the punishment for the violation of this positive commandment will be upon them; even though their annulment is not an [effective] annulment. And [it is] like I wrote above regarding the matter of the commandment of inheritances (Sefer HaChinukh 400), that one who says and commands, "My son shall not inherit me" will have the punishment of the violation of the positive commandment upon him, even though his words are void; as he has transgressed the decree of the King that commanded us about the laws of inheritance. However, Ramban, may his memory be Blessed, wrote (in his glosses on the Sefer HaMitzvot LaRambam, Mitzvot Ase 95) that the law should not be counted at all in the tally of the commandments, since it is [just the] negation [of a commandment]. As we were commanded to do everything that comes out of our mouth and that we not profane our words, only according to the father or the husband. To here [are his words]. And 'the words of the wise are grace.'

I have already expanded my words about some of the roots of the matter of the vow and the oath and their annulment in the Order of Vayishma Yitro in the [negative commandment] of "Do not take" (Sefer HaChinukh 30).

From the laws of the commandment are that which they, may their memory be Blessed, said (Nedarim 2a), "All substitutes for [the expression for] vows are like vows, [substitutes for] dedications are like dedications, [substitutes for] oaths are like oaths, and [substitutes for] nazirite vows are like nazirite vows." [This is such that] (Nedarim 10a), "one who says [that a certain object is] konam, konach or konas, behold, these are substitutes for sacrifice (korban); cherek, cherekh or cheref, behold, these are substitutes for dedication (cherem) [to the Temple treasury]; nazik, naziach or paziach, behold, these are substitutes for naziriteness (nazir); shevutah, shekukah or [if] he vows with [the term,] mohi, behold, these are substitutes for oath (shevuah)." And the reason for the matter of these expressions that the Sages said are judged as if a man brought them out of his lips with the proper expression and [that] we do not concern ourselves to require that his mouth and heart be the same - as behold, he did not bring the proper expression from his mouth - is because these expressions imply the matter. Since anyone who hears would decide about it that this is the intention of the one making an oath or vowing. And since it is like this, behold, it is as if he said the thing clearly and properly. As if you don't say like this, it comes out that there would never be vows or oaths from those with speech impediments (see Mishneh Torah, Laws of Vows 1:16). And in truth, this is not [the case].

And so [too,] that which they, may their memory be Blessed, said (Nedarim 2b), that there are four vows which are annulled - meaning to say they are completely annulled, such that we do not require a question to a sage [in order to annul it], and like the opinion of Shmuel in the chapter [entitled] Arbaah Nedarim (Nedarim 21b), as the law is according to him. And these are them: vows of exhortation; vows of exaggeration (nonsense); vows of mistake; and vows of duress. And there in the same chapter, [the makeup of] each and every one is clarified. And we have the textual variant in the Talmud Yerushalmi Nedarim 3:1 concerning vows of exhortation, "Rabbi Zeira said, 'That which you say, is when they were not holding up their words, but if they were holding up their words, they would require dispensation'"; meaning to say, if they were holding up their words - meaning that they did not vow as a vow to exhort, but rather they vowed it with precision - they would require a question to a sage. And the same is certainly true of the other three [vows] that are learned in the Mishnah, that if they were holding up their words, they would require a question of a sage. And nonetheless a sage can annul in any situation, so long as he finds an opening to annul [it], meaning to say that he finds some matter that the vower would say, "If I had known this thing at the time of the vow, I would not have vowed."

And we can open to annul even with something that newly develops (nolad), so long as it is something that commonly develops. But with something new that does not commonly develop, [we do not]. So is it explained in the Gemara (Nedarim 64a). And so [too,] we can open with regret, and as Rava determines in the name of Rav Nachman in Tractate Nedarim 22b - "We open for regret, and make ourselves available to annul, even to the one who has sworn by the God of Israel," which is a severe oath. And [this is] uniquely with regret from the beginning, such as "Is this heart [still] upon you?" [This is] meaning to say that this vower vowed out of anger, and after his mind settled down, he is completely bewildered by his oath and does not want it at all. But if he regrets [it] now because of something new that developed after he vowed, and he wanted his vow until now; this is not effective regret, and we do not open for him at all - as behold, everyone who comes to ask about his vow certainly regrets it now. And if [this type of regret were effective], the Gemara would not have required us to search to find openings for vows. But we find in the Gemara that they did search for openings for vows. But rather the truth is certainly like we wrote, that we need regret from the beginning. And [this is the case] also, since the entire foundation of annulling vows is the claim of error or duress (Shevuot 26a), since the Torah stated (Leviticus 5:4), "a man with an oath" - to exclude duress; and so too, that his mouth and heart are the same. And if so, it is impossible to have mistake or duress during the time of all the oaths depend upon regret from now. But there is a claim of mistake or duress with regret from the beginning; as behold, he now admits that if he knew this, he would not have made the vow from the beginning.

And there are some of the great commentators that wrote that even though we determine that the law is like Rava said [in the name of] Rav Nachman that "We open for regret, and make ourselves available to annul[...] by the God of Israel", now we are accustomed to be strict and [not follow it] as the law. And [so] we do not make ourselves available to the one that swore in the name of the God of Israel, but rather only to that which is similar to the four vows that are learned in the Mishnah. And also, that we do not make ourselves available except for a matter that includes a commandment, such as the making of peace between a man and his wife, or between a man and his fellow, and similar to these matters. And so [too,] did they, may their memory be Blessed, say about this matter, that annulment of vows is with three commoners, and even if they have not learned and reasoned - and that is [only] if when it is explained to them, they can reason, and that one of them have studied nonetheless (Bekhorot 32b). And so too, they said that annulment of vows can be with one if he is an expert. And the same is true in any case that he has permission to annul vows from someone who is ordained, as he [is then considered] like an expert. And there is one that explained it, that so long as he is a great sage among Israel - even today, when we do not have ordination - he is called an expert; but his colleagues disagree with him. And the law of one who recants during the time of speech (immediately after the first speech), that his recanting is an [effective] recanting; that which they said that a father abrogates any vow, but a husband, [only] vows of affliction and things between him and her; the law of one who says, "Any vow that I vow this year," or "from now until ten years" - behold, they are null; the law [that] undifferentiated vows are [understood] stringently, and specified vows are [understood] leniently; the law that a man may not prohibit a thing that is not his; the law of one who says to his fellow, "My loaf is forbidden to you," or "this loaf"; the law of one who vows [not to] benefit his fellow, that he [may] pay his debt [back to him]; the law of the one who vows [not to have] meat, that he is permitted gravy, but if he said, "This meat," he is forbidden even the gravy; the law of one whose benefit is forbidden, that it is permitted to teach him oral law, but not written [law], because we can take a wage for it; the law of that which they said, "With vows, it follows the language of people" - in that place and that language that he vowed or swore; the law of annulment of vows that it is the whole day, meaning night and day, but not [twenty-four] hours, as it is stated, (Numbers

30:6) "on the day of his hearing it"; and the rest of its many details are elucidated at length in the tractate that is composed abut it, and that is Tractate Nedarim (see Tur, Yoreh Deah 233).

And this commandment is practiced in every place and at all times by males, but not by females - as they are not appurtenant to the annulment of vows. And one who transgresses this and annuls a vow, not according to the commandment of the Torah, in the ways that we have written - even though it is not annulled - has violated this positive commandment, as we have written at the beginning of this commandment.

Mitzvah 407
That we not profane our words from vows: That we have been prevented that we not change that which we obligate ourselves in speech (see Sefer HaMitzvot LaRambam, Mitzvot Lo Taase 157) - and even though it is without an oath. And these are vows - for example, a person will say [that] fruits of the world, or fruits of country x or y type of fruits are forbidden to him; and so too, [that] he will say his wife is forbidden to him; and similar to these things - that he is obligated to fulfill them. And about this is it stated (Numbers 30:3), "he shall not profane (yachel) his word." And they, may their memory be Blessed, explained (Sifrei Bamidbar 153:4), that he should not make his word non-sacred (chullin), meaning to say, that he obligates something on himself and not fulfill it. And the language of the Gemara [in] Shevuot 20b [is that] they, may their memory be Blessed, said [times that a person say] konam (a pledge to bring a sacrifice), he [is liable to] transgress because of "he shall not profane his word." And so [too,] with anything that a man vow for a sacrifice or upkeep of the [Temple] or charity or for the synagogue or similar to them, he [is liable to] transgress because of "he shall not profane his word." But with other matters - such as one who vows something to his fellow or who says, "I will" or "I will not do thing x" - even though it is ugly, and it is only small-souled people who do it, he does not transgress because of "he shall not profane his word"; only in the way that we have written. However, about it all is it stated in the Torah (Exodus 23:7), "Keep far from a false thing." And Ramban, may his memory be Blessed, wrote that they are two separate commandments, vows to the Elevated realm and vows of utterance, and as we will write below in the Order of Ki Tetseh in the commandment of fulfilling what comes out of the lips (Sefer HaChinukh 575).

I have already written the root of the commandment regarding the matter of vows and oaths in the Order of Vayishma Yitro in the negative commandment of "You shall not take" (Sefer HaChinukh 30).

From the laws of the commandment is that which they, may their memory be Blessed (Chagigah 10a) said, "He cannot pardon [it], but others can pardon it," such as three commoners or one expert, as we have written in the previous commandment; [that] the same is also true when we ask about sanctifications and about donations to charity, so long as they have not come to the hand of the collector; and [that which] they, may their memory be Blessed, said (Nedarim 59a), even about the priestly tithe or about the challah tithe, we may ask about them, so long as they have not come to the hand of the priest. And the rest of the details of the commandment are elucidated in Tractate Nedarim (see Tur, Yoreh Deah 203).

And this commandment is practiced in every place and at all times by males and females. And one who transgresses it and made a vow or a prohibition upon himself - without an oath - and did not fulfill it has violated this negative commandment. But he is not lashed for it, as there is no act [connected] with it. And that which they, may their memory be Blessed, said (Temurah 3a) that one who swears, or transfers [holiness] or curses his fellow with the name [of God] is lashed, even though there is no act there, is only [when he] swears. But on account of his not profaning his vow or for a prohibition [on himself] without an oath, there are no lashes for it.

Mitzvah 408
The commandment on Israel to give cities within which the Levites may dwell, and they shelter: That Israel was commanded to give cities to the Tribe of Levi to dwell therein, since they do not have a portion in the Land, as it is stated (Numbers 35:2), "Command the Children of Israel, and they shall give to the Levites from the inheritance of their holding, cities to dwell." And it is stated at the end of

the section (Numbers 35:7). "All of the cities that you shall give to the Levites are forty-eight cities." And from these forty-eight cities of the Levites, there were cities that were specified to be a refuge for the killer. However, all of them would shelter him. And with God's help, we will write in the Order of Shoftim in the commandment of the cities of refuge (Sefer HaChinukh 520), what is [the difference] between those specified for this and the others. And they would shelter him in well-known ways, as is explained in Scripture. And it is elucidated in Tractate Makkot 10a.

The root of this commandment is well-known, as the tribe of Levi was from the select of the tribes and prepared for the service of the House of God, and [so] they did not have a portion with Israel in the inheritance of fields and vineyards. But they nonetheless needed cities for them to dwell in - they, and their children and their infants and all of their animals. And because of the greatness of their stature and the fitness of their deeds and the 'grace of their worth,' their land was chosen over the lands of the other tribes to shelter any one that kills by mistake - maybe their land that is sanctified with their holiness would atone for him. And there is another reason in the thing: Since they are people of known [character] in virtues of disposition and respected wisdoms known to all, they would not loath the killer being saved with them and they would not touch him; and even if he would kill one of their friends or redeemers (relatives) - since he killed him 'suddenly and without enmity.' And about this select tribe is it stated (Deuteronomy 33:9), "Who says about his father and his mother, 'I have not seen him'" - meaning to say, that they will never do anything besides [that which is from] the proper path and in line with the truth; and even [in spite of] the love of father and mother and brothers and sons, which is obligated and compelled by nature, and all the more so [regarding] the love of other people. And I have further written another argument about the matter in the Order of Behar Sinai (Sefer HaChinukh 342).

The laws of this commandment are short. And I have written some of the laws in the commandments that are reliant upon it, such as the warning not to sell the field of open space of their cities. And so too, will I write about them, with God's help, in the commandment to separate the cities of refuge in the Order of Shoftim (Sefer HaChinukh 520) - as the three of them are the same topic. And if you desire to know, 'turn and turn in them' (see Mishneh Torah, Laws of Sabbatical Year and the Jubilee 13).

And this commandment is practiced at the time that Israel is dwelling on its land. And it is among the commandments that is incumbent upon the whole community, but especially on the heads of the people. And in the future to come - after inheritance and settlement - we will immediately fulfill this commandment, speedily in our days, amen.

Mitzvah 409
To not kill someone liable before he is brought to justice: That we were prevented not to kill the sinner when we see him doing a sinful act for which he is liable the death penalty, before we bring him to court. Rather, we are obligated to bring him before the court and we bring witnesses in front of [the judges] and they sentence him to what he is liable, as it is stated (Numbers 35:12), "and the killer shall not die before his standing, etc." And the language of the Mekhilta (Sifrei Zuta on Numbers 35:12) is \'Perhaps they should kill him from when he killed or was adulterous? [Hence] we learn to say, 'and the killer shall not die before his standing, etc.'" And even if the Great Court saw him kill, they would all be witnesses and take their testimony to another court to judge him. And they also said in Mekhilta (Sifrei Zuta on Numbers 35:12), "Behold, a community that saw one kill a soul, perhaps they should kill him before he stands in court? [Hence] we learn to say, 'and the killer shall not die before his standing.'"

It is from the roots of the commandment [that] since the matter of capital punishment is a very weighty thing (Rosh Hashanah 26a) which requires the greatest of precision, and the community has been commanded to save the accused with everything that is fit to save him for his sake - not that they pervert the judgement in order to save him, God forbid, and like they, may their memory be Blessed, expounded (Rosh Hashanah 26a, connecting the two phrases in Numbers 35:24-25), "And the community shall judge, And the community shall save," meaning to say that they need to search for his merit and if he has a merit, they should save him, and if not, he should be killed - therefore, we were warned that the judgement should at the very least be brought before the court. And the witnesses that saw the thing with their eyes should never judge him, as maybe from their seeing the matter, they will not be able to search for his merit, as their hearts will arouse them to render him guilty no matter what.

From the laws of the commandment is, for example, that which they, may their memory be Blessed, said (Sanhedrin 73b) that what are these things speaking about that we do not kill the sinner until we bring him to court; when he went and did the sin, but [with] one who is pursuing his fellow to kill him or after a betrothed maiden and they warned him but he did not stop pursuing, even though he did not [formally] accept the warning, we are obligated to kill him and we are warned about it, and as we will write with God's help at the end of the Order of Ki Tetseh in the warning of "You shall cut off her hand; show no pity" (Sefer HaChinukh 600). And the rest of its details are in Tractate Makkot. And this commandment is practiced by males and females at all times, as we are commanded not to kill any sinner - and even though we saw him doing an act that would make him liable for the death penalty in court. And at the time of the [Temple], we are obligated to bring him to court and they judge him. And one who transgresses this and kills the sinner before he comes to the court - even if his judgement was that he would be deemed guilty in court - the ruling for the one who killed him would be like the ruling of a murderer, and he would be killed for it at the time of the [Temple] if there were witnesses.

Mitzvah 410

The commandment on the court to send one who smites a soul inadvertently from his city to the cities of refuge and upon the killer himself to go there: That the courts of Israel were commanded to send one who smites a soul inadvertently from his city and restore him in the cities of refuge, as it is stated (Numbers 35:25), "and the community shall restore him to his city of refuge, etc. and there he shall remain until the death of the high priest." And also, the smiter, he too, is included in this positive commandment, as it is stated about him (Numbers 35:28), "For he shall dwell in his city of refuge until the death of the high priest."

It is from the roots of the commandment [that] since the iniquity of killing is very weighty, as the destruction of the world [comes] through it, to the point that they, may their memory be Blessed, said (Mishneh Torah, Laws of Murderer and the Preservation of Life 4:9) that one who kills a soul volitionally - even if the did all of the [other] commandments - is not saved from judgement, as it is stated (Proverbs 28:17), "A man oppressed by bloodguilt will flee to a pit; let none give him support"; therefore it is fitting for one who killed, that since such a great mishap as this came through his hand, that he should endure the pain of exile for it, which is almost equal to the pain of death - as a person is separated from his friends, and from his birthplace and [instead] dwells with strangers all of his days. And there is also benefit to the world with the commandment - as Scripture elucidates - since he will be saved from his blood avenger through this, such that he not kill him when he has no guilt on his hands; as behold, it was inadvertent. And there is another benefit in the thing, such that the relatives of the slain not see the slayer, the killer, regularly with their eyes in the place that the evil was done. And all 'the ways of the Torah are pleasantness.'

And from the laws of the commandment is that which they, may their memory be Blessed, said (Gittin 70b) that an inadvertent killer is only exiled if the one killed died at the time that he killed him. But if [the killer] injured him - even though they evaluated him to die and he got sick and died - such a one is not exiled, lest [the victim] brought his own death closer, or the wind entered into his wound and killed him. And even if [the killer cut] his two benchmarks (the esophagus and the trachea) but [the victim] remained alive a little, he is not exiled for this.

And [also] that which they said (Makkot 8b) that an Israelite is exiled if he killed a slave or a resident alien; and, all the more so, a slave who killed an Israelite or a resident alien, or a slave who killed a slave, or a resident alien [who killed a slave or a resident alien], as it is stated, "and it shall be for the Children of Israel a statute of judgment, and for the stranger that lives among you." But a resident alien that kills an Israelite - whether volitionally or inadvertently - is killed for it; and a gentile that kills a gentile is not sheltered by the cities of refuge. And [also] that which they said (Makkot 8a), that a son is exiled for the killing of his father and a father is exiled for the killing of his son, and about what are these words speaking - not at the time of learning, but at the time of learning, [if it was] inadvertent as his intention was to teach him and to benefit him with wisdom or with a trade, he is exempt from exile. And so [too,] a teacher with his student likewise. And [also] that which they said (Makkot 10a) that a student that is exiled, his teacher is exiled with him, as it is stated (Deuteronomy 4:42), "he shall flee to one of these cities and live" - and they, may their memory be Blessed, expounded (Makkot 10a), [that] they should do for him [what is needed] that he should live, and "wisdom gives life to he who possesses it" (Ecclesiastes 7:14). And the law of whether a husband or master must pay for the sustenance of a wife, a male slave or a maid-servant who has been exiled there; the law of a killer who died before he was exiled, that we bring his bones there; the law of a killer who killed in his city of refuge, and so [too,] a Levite who killed in his city; the law of who is a hater, about whom it is stated that he killed him with enmity, the law of what they said (Makkot 7b) that anyone who kills a soul with a downward motion is exiled, and even an upward motion for the sake of a downward motion, and anyone with an upward motion is not exiled, and even a downward motion for the sake of an upward motion; the law of a killer that the people of the city of refuge want to honor, that he is obligated to say, "I am a killer," and if they say (to him), "Nonetheless," it is permissible for him to accept [it]; the law of the altar that it shelter an inadvertent killer like a city of refuge, but only its top and with the altar of the Eternal House, and only a priest with the service in his hand, but not someone else, and they would only allow him there for a short time and afterwards they would give him bodyguards and take him to his city of refuge, and about what are these words speaking, about one of those legally liable for exile, but one who was afraid from the king that he not kill him through a provisional ruling and [so] escaped to the altar and placed [himself on it] is saved, and even if he is [not a priest], and we do not ever take him off of the altar, so did I see that Rambam, may his memory be Blessed, wrote. And the rest of its details are elucidated in Tractate Makkot (see Mishneh Torah, Laws of Murderer and the Preservation of Life 5).

And this commandment is observed at the time that Israel is on their land and with the Sanhedrin of seventy-one [judges] sitting in their place that is prepared for them in Jerusalem to judge capital punishments. And if the courts of each and every place transgressed this and did not exile the inadvertent killer, they have violated this positive commandment, and their punishment is very great, because it is a cause for the [possible] spilling of blood.

Mitzvah 411
That the witness not issue a ruling in the case that he is testifying about in capital punishments:
That the witness not speak about the case that he is testifying about in capital punishments, except for his saying his testimony alone - and even though he is educated and wise; as the witness is not made into a judge in capital punishments, as it is stated (Numbers 35:30), "and a single witness should not respond about a soul for death." And Rambam, may his memory be Blessed, wrote (Sefer HaMitzvot LaRambam, Mitzvot Lo Taase 291), "And the negative commandment about this matter is repeated, as it is stated (Deuteronomy 17:6), 'he shall not be killed by the mouth of one witness' - meaning to say, he shall not be killed by the ruling of the witness. And they said in Sanhedrin 33b-34a, '"And a [...] witness should not respond about a soul," whether for innocence or whether for guilt.' And they explained that the reason for this is that it appears as if he is biased in his testimony. And this matter that he cannot respond - whether for innocence or whether for guilt - is only with capital punishments."

Like that which is written in the commandment previous to this (Sefer HaChinukh 409) is from the roots of the commandment.

From the laws of the commandment is, for example, that which they, may their memory be Blessed, said (Sanhedrin 34a) that a witness that testifies about capital punishments and afterwards says, "I have merit to teach about [the suspect]," is silenced; as we do not accept anything from him to rule upon [the suspect], since he is a witness. And to what do these words apply? To capital punishments; but with monetary law, the witness can teach for innocence or guilt, but he may not be counted among the judges (Sanhedrin 34b) and is not made a judge, since a witness is not made into a judge, even in monetary law. And to what do these words apply? To something that needs witnesses from Torah writ; but with something [rabbinic], a witness can become a judge. And because of this, he is made a judge in the validation of contracts; since it is established for us that the validation of contracts is rabbinic (Sanhedrin 18b). As from Torah writ, the signatories of the contract become as if their testimony was investigated in court. And the rest of its details are in Sanhedrin and in Makkot (see Mishneh Torah, Laws of Testimony 5).

And this commandment is practiced by males alone and at the time of the Temple with the Sanhedrin in their place, as then do we judge capital punishments, but not at another time. And it is then that we need the testimony of men. And a witness that testified and transgressed this and spoke, whether for innocence or whether for guilt, has violated this negative commandment. But he is not lashed for it, as there is no act [connected with it]. And Ramban, may his memory be Blessed, explained this verse of "he shall not be killed by the mouth of one witness" (in the negative commandments that he added, commandment 9) [to be] about another negative commandment, and that is not to accept singular testimony in capital punishments. And that is, for example, that the witnesses saw [the suspect], one from this window, and [the other] from another window far from the first, to the point that those [two] standing at the window could not see one another, but they all saw the sinner. And this is elucidated in Tractate Makkot 6b.

Mitzvah 412

Not to take ransom to save the murderer from the death penalty: Not to take ransom, meaning to say, redemption [money] - and even all the money in the world - to save the soul of a murderer, such as not to kill him, as it is stated (Numbers 35:31), "You shall not take ransom for the soul of a murderer who is guilty for death."

And the root of this commandment is well-known - as if the rulers of the land allowed to take ransom from the hand of the murderer, it would come out that anyone greater and wealthier than his fellow would kill him if he got angry at him and give his ransom. And it would come out that the sword of a man would be upon his brother and civilization would be [destroyed].

From the laws of the commandment is that which they, may their memory be Blessed, said (Ketuvot 37b) that even if the blood redeemer wants to exempt him [from the death penalty] and says to the judge that he forgives his blood and that they will take ransom from him - [even] if they want, they are not allowed to take ransom and to exempt him for all of the money in the world; but rather he is killed, like the command of God upon us. And the rest of its details are in Tractate Makkot (see Mishneh Torah, Laws of Murderer and the Preservation of Life 1)

And [it] is practiced at the time of the [Temple] by males and females, as at this time we have no involvement with capital punishments. And they say about [this] that this prohibition is also practiced by females, and even though they do not judge. And the matter is that if maybe at the time of [now] [the Temple] (in the Vilna edition, that time) because of some reason, it will come to the hand of a woman that they will ask from her to save the soul of a murderer on account of money, that she is warned not to take the money and to save him, due to this negative commandment. And one who transgresses this - whether a man or whether a woman - and takes money to save the murderer violates this negative commandment; and his punishment is very great, as it is a cause for the loss of many souls of Israel.

Mitzvah 413

Not to take ransom from one liable for exile to exempt him from exile: Not to take ransom from one liable for exile because he killed inadvertently, to exempt him form exile, as it is stated (Numbers 35:32), "And you shall not take ransom from the one who fled to his city of refuge to return to dwell in the land." And according to this literal meaning, it appears that 'the one who fled' is [in the past], meaning to say, do not take ransom, from one who has fled to his city of refuge, to return to dwell in the land of his ancestors' dwelling.

The root of the prohibition to take ransom from one who kills inadvertently and all of its content is like the content of one who kills volitionally. [So] there is no need to speak about it at length.

Sefer HaChinukh

Mitzvah 414

Not to appoint a judge that that does not know the laws of the Torah: That the Great Court or the exilarch was prevented not to appoint a judge-to-judge people, [who] did not study the wisdom of the Torah and the explanation of its straight and righteous statutes. And even if there are several good characteristics to him, since he is not knowledgeable and an expert in the wisdom of the Torah, it is not fit to appoint him judge. And about this is it stated (Deuteronomy 1:17), "You shall not recognize faces in justice." And so [too,] did they, may their memory be Blessed, explain, (Sifrei Devarim 17:1), "'You shall not recognize faces in justice' - this is [addressed to] one who is appointed to seat judges"; meaning to say that this warning comes to him. And they, may their memory be Blessed, said (Sifrei Devarim 17:1), "'You shall not recognize faces in justice' - lest you say, 'That man is comely' [or] 'strong' [or wealthy or] 'knows all the languages; I will make him a judge.' Hence it is stated, 'You shall not recognize faces' - as it would come out [that] he exonerates the guilty and incriminates the innocent; not because he is wicked, but because he does not know."

The root of this commandment is revealed to all.

Its laws - such as that which they, may their memory be Blessed, said (Midrash Tanchuma 5:3) that just as the one who is fit to be a judge must know the laws of the Torah, so too must he be someone of [good] character traits and a proper man, so that the judged not say to him, "Take out the beam from between your eyes," meaning to say, "adorn yourself [first] and afterwards adorn others" (Sanhedrin 18a); that, behold, it states in the Torah concerning judges (Deuteronomy 1:15), "wise men," meaning to say, those that know the wisdom to judge truthfully, "and known to your tribes," [meaning] that the spirit of men derive pleasure from them, "men of strength," that they are valiant about the commandments, exacting upon themselves and suppress their [evil] inclinations to the point that they do not have any disgrace and any ugliness, and their teaching is beautiful, and [also] included in being men of strength is that they have a brave heart to save the oppressed from the oppressor, like the matter that is stated (Exodus 2:17), "and Moshe rose to save them," and just like our teacher Moshe, peace be upon him, was humble, so too must every judge be humble; and the rest of its details - are elucidated in Sanhedrin in [various] scattered places (see Tur, Choshen Mishpat 18).

And this commandment is practiced in every place and at all times. And one who transgresses it and appoints a judge who is not wise, on account of his wealth or good character traits or from his love for him or on account of the honor of his relatives has violated this [negative commandment]. And his sin is very great, as all of the punishment of the false rulings that this judge ruled from his lack of knowledge are [made] dependent upon him, as he is the cause.

And it appears that [also] included in this commandment is that anyone who the members of the community have chosen to appoint appointees over them for any matter, that they should put all of their attention and intellect [to it], to appoint those appropriate and good for that appointment that the community requires. And he should not be frightened from any man, to appoint someone that is not appropriate. And the Sages said (Avodah Zarah 52b, Sanhedrin 7b) about someone who sets up a judge that is not proper, [that it is] as if he puts up a stone pillar, as it is stated (Deuteronomy 16:22) [soon after the commandment to set up judges], "and you shall not set up a pillar for yourself." And if it is a place where there are Torah scholars in it, they said that it is like planting a tree-god, as it is stated (Deuteronomy 16:21), "You shall not plant a tree-god, any tree, beside the altar of the Lord, your God." And they also said (Sanhedrin 7b) that anyone who appoints a judge because of his wealth, about this is it stated (Shemot 20:20), "You shall not make with Me gods of silver and gods of gold." And they spoke at length about this matter and said (Talmud Yerushalmi Bikkurim 3:3) that it is forbidden to stand [for judgement] in front of a judge who gave money in order that he be appointed a judge. And they treated his honor very lightly, and said about him that the cloak with which he wraps himself should be like a donkey saddle in your eyes. And it was the way of the early Sages to flee from being appointed judges (Sanhedrin 14a), except in a place where there was no one greater than them.

Mitzvah 415

That a judge not fear in judgement: That the judge is prevented from being afraid of a man, to judge a truthful judgement - even if he is a man [that is] destructive, brazen-faced and thick-headed - but rather, he should make the verdict and not put his heart at all to that which may befall him of the [possible] damage [to himself] as a result of the judgment. And about this is it stated (Deuteronomy 1:17), "Do not fear any man." And the language of Sifrei Devarim 17:2 [is] "Lest you say, 'I am afraid of man x lest he kill me or "kill one of the people of my home or lest he burn my stacks or lest he cut down my plantings.' [Hence] we learn to say, 'Do not fear any man.'"

The intellect testifies to root of the commandment.

The laws of the commandment are that which they said (Sanhedrin 6b), "Two [litigants] that come before you in judgment - one is gentle and one is difficult - before you hear their statements, or even after you hear their statements but you do not yet know where the judgment is leaning, it is permitted for you to say to them, 'I am not available to you,' lest he will be found liable, and it will turn out that he will pursue after the judge to kill him. But once you hear their statements and you know where the judgment is leaning, you may not say to them, 'I am not available to you,' as it is stated, 'Do not fear any man.'" And so [too] (Sanhedrin 6b), "A student who is sitting before his teacher and he sees innocence for a poor person and guilt for a wealthy person is not allowed to be silent, as it is stated, 'Do not fear any man.'"

And this commandment is practiced in every place and at all times by males, as judgment is theirs. And one who transgresses this and did not want to judge [a case] from when he knows where the judgment is leaning - as we have said - out of fear of the judged, has violated this negative commandment. And if he also perverts the judgement out of his fear from him, he has violated this negative commandment, besides having violated the negative commandment of "Do not pervert justice."

Mitzvah 416

Not to desire the money of your friend: That we were prevented from fixing in our thoughts to desire what is in the hand of one of our brothers, the Children of Israel; since the fixing of the desire for that thing in our heart will become a cause to create machinations to get it from him - even though it is not his will to sell them - by purchase or exchange or, if we cannot [acquire it] in any other way, by force. And about this is it stated (Deuteronomy 5:18), "you shall not desire the house of your neighbor, etc." And Rambam, may his memory be Blessed, wrote (Sefer HaMitzvot LaRambam, Mitzvot Lo Taase 266), that the two negative commandments - which are "you shall not covet," which is in the Order of Vayishma Yitro, and "you shall not desire" in this Order - are not repeated negative commandments about one matter. Rather, they are two matters. As the negative commandment of "you shall not covet" will prevent him from taking that which someone besides him acquired, in any way - whether with money or without money - if [the owner] does not want to sell that thing. But this negative commandment of "you shall not desire" will prevent him from even the desire for it in his heart. As with the desire, he will come to supplicate him and to pressure him to sell it or trade it for another vessel, no matter what. And even though one of these negative commandments brings its fellow, they are considered two nonetheless. And behold, you [can] see the difference between them. And do not wonder to say, "And how is it in the hand of a man to prevent his heart from desiring the storehouse of every delightful vessel that he sees in the hand of his fellow, whereas he is totally empty of them; and how does the Torah bring a prevention about that which is impossible for a man to uphold?" As the thing is not like this, and only silly evildoers and those that sin with their souls say it. As truly, it is in the hand of a man to prevent himself and his thoughts and his desires from anything that he wants. And [it is] within his control and his cognizance to distance and to bring close his want for all things according to his will. And his heart is given into his hand; to anything that he wants can he incline it. And God - in front of Whom are all hidden things - 'searches all the rooms of the belly, sees the kidney and the heart.' There is not one from all of the thoughts of man - little or big, good or bad - that is hidden from Him; and it is not covered from His eyes. [Hence] He will bring vengeance upon those that transgress His will in their hearts, and 'safeguards kindness for the thousands [of generations] for those that love Him,' who dedicate their thoughts to His service. As there is nothing as good for a man as good and pure thought, as it is the beginning of all actions, and their end. And this is apparently the matter of the 'good heart,' that the Sages praised in Tractate Avot 2:9. And the proof that these two negative commandments are different in their content and considered two [distinct commandments] is that which they said in Mekhilta DeRabbi Shimon bar Yochai 20:14, "'You shall not covet your neighbor's house' (Exodus 20:14), and later it states, 'and you shall not desire,' to make liable for the desire on its own and for the coveting on its own." And there, it [also] says, "From where [do I know] that if he desires, his end will be to covet? [Hence,] we learn to say 'you shall not desire' 'and you shall not covet.' From where [do I know] that if a man coveted, his end will be to steal? [Hence,] we learn to say 'They covet fields, and steal' (Michah 2:2)."

The root of this commandment is known, since distancing theft from among men is useful for all, and the intellect is a trustworthy witness to the thing. And there is no lengthy discussion of [its] laws, as all of its content is elucidated in Scripture (see Tur, Choshen Mishpat 359).

And it is practiced in every place and at all times by males and females. All people of the world are also obligated about it, since it is a branch of the commandment [against] theft, which is one of the seven commandments that all people of the world were commanded. And do not err, my son, with this well-known tally of the seven commandments of the Noachides mentioned in the Talmud (Sanhedrin 56b); as truthfully these seven are [only] like general principles, but they have many details. So you will find that the prohibition of sexual immorality is considered for them to be one commandment as a general principle, but there are details in it; such as the prohibition of the mother, and the prohibition of the sister from the mother's side, and the prohibition of a married woman, and the wife of the father, and the male, and the animal (Sanhedrin 58a). And so [too,] the matter of idolatry is all considered one commandment for them, but there are many, many details; as behold, they are the same regarding it as Israel, since they are liable for everything that an Israelite court would kill about (Sanhedrin 56b). And so too can we say that since they are warned about the matter of theft, that they were also warned about all of its distancings. And my intention is not to say that they are warned about this with a negative commandment like Israel. Rather, they were warned about it more generally in these seven. It is as if you would say, for example, that Scripture warned them, "Each man, shall not come close to the flesh of his relatives; to the mother, to the sister and to all of the family." And so too also with idolatry [that the command be] in general. And so with theft, [it is] as if it was stated to them, "You shall not steal, but distance yourselves from it completely" - and within the distancing is not to covet. But the matter is not like this with Israel, as the Omnipresent wanted to bring them merit, and [so] he multiplied the commandments for them, more than for [the gentiles]; and also in those that we were commanded, He commanded upon them with separate positive commandments and negative commandments - as every one that does one commandment acquires one defender for himself. And the one who transgresses this and fixes his thought to desire that which is of someone else transgresses this negative commandment. But there are no lashes for it, as there is no act [connected with it], yet his punishment is very great; as it is a cause for several mishaps, as is well-known [from] the story of Achav and Navot.

Mitzvah 417

The commandment of the unification of God: That we were commanded to believe that God, may He be Blessed - who is the Mover of all existence, the Master of everything - is one without any combination, as it is stated (Deuteronomy 6:4), "Hear, Israel, the Lord is our God, the Lord is one." And this is a positive commandment, not [just] a statement. But the understanding of "Hear" is, "Accept from me this thing, and know it and believe in it - that the Lord, who is our God, is one. And the proof that this is a positive commandment is their, may their memory be Blessed, constantly saying in Midrash, "On the condition of unifying His name"; "in order to accept the yoke of the kingdom of Heaven upon himself" - meaning to say, the acknowledgement of unity and faith.

The root of this commandment is well-known, as it is the foundation of the faith of all people in the world and it is the strong pillar that every intelligent person relies upon.

From the laws of the commandment is that which they, may their memory be Blessed, said (Berakhot 61b) that every Israelite is obligated about the commandment of unification; since anyone who does not acknowledge His unity, Blessed be He, is as if he denies a fundamental principle [of faith] - as there is no complete [Divine] rulership and majesty without total unity, and the heart of every wise men will distinguish this. And if so, behold, this commandment is included in the prohibition of idolatry, about which we are commanded to be killed in every place and at any time. [This] and the rest of its details are scattered in the Midrash and in [various] places in the Gemara. And there, [there are also] many stories of several Israelites - big and small - may all their memory be Blessed, who were killed for the sanctification of His unity, Blessed be He.

And this commandment is practiced in every place and at all times by males and females. And one who transgresses it and does not believe in His unity, Blessed be He, has violated this positive commandment [as well as] all of the other commandments of the Torah, since they are all dependent upon the belief in His divinity and unity. And he is called a denier of a fundamental principle [of faith], and he is not in the category of the Children of Israel, but rather in the category of sectarians. And God has separated him out for evil, but the one who believes in God and trusts in Him will be raised up. And this is one of the commandments that we said at the beginning of the book that a person is constantly obligated about, meaning to say that the obligation upon him never ceases, not even [for] a small instant.

Mitzvah 418

The commandment of loving God: That we were commanded to love the Omnipresent, Blessed be He (Mishneh Torah, Laws of Foundations of the Torah 2:1), as it is stated (Deuteronomy 6:5), "And you shall love the Lord, your God." And the content of this commandment is that we should think about and contemplate His commands and His actions to the point that we comprehend Him according to our ability and that we delight in His providence with complete delight. And this is [this] special love. And the language of the Sifrei is "Since it is stated, 'And you shall love,'' I would not know how a man is to love the Omnipresent. [Hence,] we learn to say, 'And these things that I command you today shall be upon your heart' (Deuteronomy 6:6) - that through this, you will recognize the One that spoke and the world [came into being]." [This] means to say that with contemplation in Torah, the love will perforce [find its place] in the heart. And they [also] said that this love obligates a man to arouse [other] people, from his love, to serve Him, as we found with Avraham.

The root of this commandment is well-known, as a man can only fulfill the commandments of God, Blessed be He, properly with his love of Him.

The laws of the commandment: That it is fitting for a person to put all of his thought and all of his effort towards the love of God; and he should always evaluate in his heart that all that there is in the world - of wealth, children, power and honor - it is all like nothing and zero and void compared to love for Him, Blessed be He. And he should always strive the whole day at seeking wisdom, so that he will fathom knowledge of Him. [In the final] word, he should use all of his effort to accustom the thoughts of his heart to faith in Him and His unity, to the point that there not be an instant in the day or the night, when he is awake, that he not remembers the love of his Master with all of his heart. And the matter of constantly remembering the love of God is metaphorically like the remembering of the lover who is completely desirous, with his desire to accomplish the bringing of [his beloved] to his home. [These] and the rest of its details are elucidated in scattered places in the Gemara and in the Midrash.

And this commandment is practiced in every place and at all times by males and females. And one who transgresses it and fixes his thought on physical matters and on the vanities of the world - not for the sake of Heaven, but only to delight in them, or to acquire honor in this illusory world to aggrandize his name, not with the intention of doing good to the good and to strengthen the hands of the just - has violated this positive commandment, and his punishment is great. And this is from the commandments constantly upon a person and always incumbent upon him.

Mitzvah 419

The commandment of Torah study: The positive commandment to study the wisdom of the Torah and to teach it; meaning to say how we should perform the commandments, guard ourselves from that which God prevented us and to also know the laws of the Torah according to their true intention.

Sefer HaChinukh

And about all of this is it stated (Deuteronomy 6:7), "You shall teach them to you sons." And our Rabbis, may their memory be Blessed, said (Sifrei Devarim 34:4), "'Your sons' - these are your students. And thus, do you find that students are called sons, as it is stated (II Kings 2:3), 'And the sons of the prophets went out.'" And it is [also] said there (Sifrei Devarim 34:1), "'And you shall teach them (shinantam, which sounds like the word for tooth, hence, make them sharp like a tooth)' - they shall be ordered in your mouth, so that if a person questions you [concerning them], you will not stammer to him, but answer him forthwith." And this commandment is repeated in many places, as it is stated (Deuteronomy 5:1), "and study them and do them," "and in order that you will study them" (Deuteronomy 31:12), "and you shall teach them to your children" (Deuteronomy 11:19).

The root of this commandment is well-known; as with study, a man will know the ways of God, may He be Blessed. But without it, he will not know and not understand, and be considered like an animal. From the laws of the commandment: That which they, may their memory be Blessed, said (Sukkah 42a) [that] from when does a father begin to teach his son Torah? From when he begins to speak, he should teach him, "Moshe commanded us the Torah" (Deuteronomy 33:4), and the first verse from the recitation of Shema, which is "Hear Israel" (Deuteronomy 6:4). And afterwards he teaches him a little [at a time] of the verses of the Torah, until he is six or seven, when he takes him to a teacher of infants. And it is fitting for every intelligent person to put his heart to not overburden the child with study when he is still weak-limbed and weak-hearted, until he he grows and his strength firms, his limbs become vigorous, his bones fill with marrow and he can endure the exertion of study, and that the illness of fainting [spells] not happen to him on account of much exertion upon it. However after his strength firms and his eyes enlighten to understand the voice of his teachers, then is the thing proper and fit; and he is [then] obligated to put his neck to the yoke of Torah [study], and not to loosen it from him, even a hair's breadth. And he should [then] always give him to drink from its spiced wine, and feed him from its honey.

And also, from the content of the commandment is that which they, may their memory be Blessed, said (Kiddushin 30a), "To what extent is a man obligated to teach his son Torah? Rav Yehuda says that Shmuel said, '[Like], for example, Zevulun ben Dan.'" The understanding of [this is that there was] a man in their generation whose name was Zevulun ben Dan, whose father's father taught him Scripture, Mishnah, Talmud, laws, and homiles (aggadot). And they challenged what they challenged about this in the Gemara, and the resolution was that the obligation is to teach him Scripture - which is Torah - like the father's father of Zevulun did, and even though the father's father of Zevulun ben Dan taught him more. And one who adds upon the obligation of the commandment, like the father's father of Zevulun ben Dan, brings a blessing upon himself. And one who was not taught by his fathers who are obligated in this - such as his father and his father's father - is obligated to teach himself when he is an adult and recognizes the thing, as it is stated (Deuteronomy 5:1), "and study them and do them." And if [both] the father and the son needed to study, and the father does not have [enough] in his hand that they can both study, he always [comes] before his son. But if his son is more understanding than he and his [son's] studies are more [effective], his son precedes him. And until when is every man obligated to study Torah? Until the day of his death, as it is stated (Deuteronomy 4:9), "and lest they be diverted from your heart, all of the days of your life" (Mishneh Torah, Laws of Torah Study 1:10). And the Sages emphasized the matter more by way of ethics and to teach people desire [for it] and said (Shabbat 83b) that even at the time of death, a man is obligated to study Torah, as it is stated (Numbers 19:14), "This is the law of the Torah, when a man dies in a tent." And everyone in Israel is obligated about the study of Torah (Yoma 35b) - whether poor or rich, whether healthy or one with afflictions. And they, may their memory be Blessed, already said (Eruvin 54a) that all of the limbs are healed by involvement in Torah. And even a poor person that goes around to [other people's] doors, and even a married man with children - everyone - is obligated to set time for Torah [study] during the day and during the night, as it is stated (Joshua 1:8), "and you shall meditate about it day and night."

And the beginning of a person's judgment after death is because he refrained from study; and as they, may their memory be Blessed, expounded (Kiddushin 40b) from that which is written (Proverbs 17:14), "The beginning of judgment is as one who lets out (poter) water" - meaning to say, [for] one who exempts (poter) himself from 'water,' that is the beginning of the quarrel on his soul after he dies - and 'water' is only Torah, as it is stated (Isaiah 55:1), "Ho; all who are thirsty, go to water." And words of Torah are compared to water because the Torah only endures in a man who is crushed and lowly, but not in a man who is proud; [just] like water also does not stand on mountains, but rather in valleys (Taanit 7a). And so [too,] that which they, may their memory be Blessed, said (Kiddushin 30a) that a man is obligated to divide his time into three parts: a third for involvement with the written Torah; a third for involvement in the oral Torah, meaning to say to accustom himself to be an expert in the text of the Mishnah and the Bereita, that they should be fluent in his mouth; and a third in understanding matters from the root. And he should not place all of his heart to [only] one of them, lest he forget the rest. And [all] three of them are the essence of the Torah, as it is impossible to know it without [all of] them.

And so [too,] that which they said (Bava Batra 21b) that the community in each and every place is obligated to set up teachers of infants, that a city that does not have infants of the house of their teacher will be destroyed and that [up to] twenty-five infants are set up with one teacher. And [also] that which they said (Avot 2:4) that a person not say, "When I will be available, I will study [Torah]," lest he never become available - as a person does not know what a day will bring. As one's involvement in the world renews itself each day and pushes a man from one thing to another and from one bother to another; and [so] it will come out that all of his days will pass in bewilderment if he does not make himself available regardless and push himself to involvement [with] Torah [study]. But anyone who does this and desires blessing will be helped from the Heavens and the bewildering bothers of the world will be lightened from upon him, and the yoke of [other] creatures will be removed from upon him. And [so] he will dwell happily in this world all of his days, and it will be good for him in the world to come. And happy is the one who speaks to a listening year. [These] and the rest of its details are elucidated in Kiddushin in the first chapter and in dispersed places in the Talmud (see Tur, Yoreh Deah 246).

And this commandment is practiced in every place and at all times by males, but not by females, since it is stated (Deutoronomy 1:19), "your sons" - and they, may their memory be Blessed, expounded (Kiddushin 29b), "But not your daughters." And so [too,] a woman is not obligated to teach her son, as anyone who [does not have] the obligation to study, [does not have] the obligation to teach. But even though she is not commanded by Torah writ, nonetheless it is fitting for every woman to make efforts that her sons should not be ignoramuses, and she has good reward [for this] in general (based on Sotah 21a). And there is also reward for a woman who studies Torah. But nonetheless, the Sages commanded (Sotah 20a) that a man not teach his daughter Torah, because the mind of women is weak, and they turn words of Torah into words of nonsense through the poverty of their minds. And one who transgresses it and does not teach his son Torah - until he knows how to read in the Scroll of the Torah and understand the simple understanding of the verses - has violated this positive commandment. And anyone who has the wherewithal in his hand to study in any way is included in this positive commandment. And if he does not fulfill it, his punishment is very great, as this commandment is the mother of them all.

Mitzvah 420
The law of the recitation of Shema morning and evening: That we were commanded every day, morning and evening, to read one verse from the Torah in this Order, and that is "Hear Israel, the Lord is our God, the Lord is one" (Deuteronomy 6:4). And about this verse is it stated (Deuteronomy 6:7), "and you will speak in them in your sitting in your home, in your laying down and in your rising up." And the explanation about this comes (Berakhot 10b) [that it is] at the time that people lay down and at the time that people get up. And it is established to us for the Rabbis (Berakhot 10b) that all of the night until the dawn rises is called the time that people lay down - and like the matter that is written (Leviticus 26:6), "and you will lay down and there is no one that makes to tremble"; and so [too], "it does not lay down until it eats prey" (Numbers 23:24) - since all the time of its laying down is implied. And also, that people are divided in their attributes regarding laying down. There are those that do not lay down until half of the night, and some [not] until its end, and there are some that lay

down immediately at the beginning of the night. And because of this, they said (Berakhot 10b) that the time of the recitation of Shema at night is from the time that the priests retire to eat their priestly tithe - which is the coming out of the stars - until the dawn rises. And the time that people rise up was understood [by] them [to be] from the beginning of the day - meaning to say when the morning is light [enough] that a man can recognize his fellow from the distance of four ells - until three full hours (Mishneh Torah, Laws of Reading the Shema 1:11). And rising up was not understood by them to be all of the day, like laying down; as it is not the way of any person that is healthy to rise up from his bed at the end of the day, or even its middle. And they, may their memory be Blessed, said (Berakhot 9b) about the recitation of Shema of the morning that, in any case, from here onward - meaning from the end of three hours until the end of the day - he who did not read [it] did not lose [out] that he not be able to read it with its blessings.

It is from the roots of the commandment that God wanted to give merit to His people that they should accept upon them His Kingdom and His unity every day and night, all the days that they are alive. As since man is a physical being [that] is seduced by the vanities of the world and drawn by his desires, he certainly requires a constant reminder of the Kingdom of the Heavens to guard him from sin. Hence it was from His kindness to have us merit and He commanded us to remember [this at] these two times, regularly and with great intention. [The] one at the day is to help for all of our actions during the day; as when a man remembers in the morning the unity of God and His Kingdom, and that His Providence and Omnipotence is over everything, and he places to his heart that His eyes are open upon all of his ways and that all of his steps are marked - that he cannot obscure anything from Him and he cannot hide any of his thoughts - will this thought and the acknowledgement of his mouth in the thing not be a protection for him that whole day? And the acknowledgement of the night will also be a protection the whole night. And because the foundation of the commandment is what we mentioned, they, may their memory be Blessed, obligated us about intention of the heart and said that if he did not have intention in his heart, he did not fulfill his obligation. As a man does not remember anything unless he places his intention to it. And this is what they, may their memory be Blessed said in Berakhot 13b in the chapter [entitled] Haya Koreh, "The Rabbis learned, '"Listen Israel, the Lord is our God, the Lord is one" - to here, intention of the heart is required.'" And they required us to lengthen [the word,] one. And [it is] like it was learned over there, "Somchos ben Yosef says, 'Anyone who lengthens [the word,] one, his days and years are lengthened.' And Rav Acha bar Yakkov said, 'But in the [letter,] dalet.' Rav Ashi said, 'And so long as he does not cut short the [letter,] chet.'" And they said there, "How much is this lengthening?" And the answer was until you crown Him in the heavens and in the earth and in the four directions of the world; meaning to say that you have intention that His governance is over all, and that there is nothing obscured from Him and that the existence of all things is through His will.

From the laws of the commandment is that which they, may their memory be Blessed, said (Berakhot 13b) that the obligation of the first verse of the section is from Torah writ - as we have said - but [it is] the Sages that obligated us to read the three sections, which are Shema, 'And it shall be if you listen' [and] 'And He said.' And we begin with reading the section of Shema which has the command about unification of God, may He be Blessed, His love and the study of His Torah, which is the great foundation that everything is dependent upon. And after it is the section of "And it shall be if you listen," which has the command about all the other commandments. And after it is the section of fringes (tsitsit) that also has the command about the remembrance of all the commandments (Mishneh Torah, Laws of Reading the Shema 1:2). And if so, with a person remembering these [things] with intention once every day and another time every night, he will be saved from sin - in any case, if he is intelligent.

And also, from the content of the commandment is that which they, may their memory be Blessed, obligated us (Berakhot 11a) to bless before the recitation and after it: In the morning, he blesses two before it, 'Who creates light' and 'Everlasting love'; and one after it, 'True and solid.' And at night, [he blesses] two before it, 'Who brings the evening' and 'Everlasting love'; and two after it, 'True and faithful,' and 'Lay us down.' And there is no need to speak about them at length, as they are known in all of Israel regarding their introductions, their endings and their wording. And Ezra and his court ordained them, with all of the blessings that are set in the mouths of all of Israel.

And also, from the content of the commandment is that which they said (Berakhot 15a) that one who reads the Shema needs to make it audible to his ear, but that if he did not make it audible to his ear, yet nonetheless read the words with his lips, he has fulfilled [his obligation], ex post facto. And so [too,] that which they said (Berakhot 15a) that one needs to be exacting about the words, yet if he was not exacting about them, he has [still] fulfilled [it]. And some of the commentators said (Meiri on Berakhot 15a) that the matter is not that he did not pronounce the words and the letters. As with this, certainly is it not said that if he was not exacting, he has fulfilled [it]; as anyone who did not read the whole recitation of the Shema has not fulfilled his obligation. Rather, the matter of his fulfilling it if he was not being exacting in them is that he did not put a space between [words that] run into [each other] such as bekhol-levavecha, esev-besadecha, ve'avadetem-meheirah, bechol-levavechem [and] hakanaf-petil ; and so [too,] if the did not sibilate [the letter,] zayin of tizkheru, that needs sibilation; or that he did not lengthen the [letter,] dalet, as it is fitting to do, a priori.

And also from the content of the commandment is that which they said (Berakhot 13a) that between the paragraphs a man asks about the well-being of someone he is obligated to honor and responds to greet any person; and in their middle, he asks due to fear - meaning to the kings of the [other] nations or to [their] great ministers and responds due to honor (Mishneh Torah, Laws of Reading the Shema 2:16). And it has been [much time] that we have not seen someone who is particular towards his fellow at all if he not interrupts [to greet him], even between the paragraphs. [These] and the rest of the many details of the commandment, and all of the matters for which we refrain from the recitation of the Shema are [all] elucidated in Berakhot in the first chapters (see Tur, Orach Chaim 61).

And it is practiced in every place and at all times by males, but not by females; because it is in the category of positive commandments determined by time, [from which] women are exempt. And one who transgresses it and does not read the recitation of the Shema every day and every night at its time - which the Sages fixed for it - has voilated this positive commandment. And Ramban, may his memory be Blessed (at the end of Sefer HaMitzot, s.v. ve'atah, eem tavin), counted the recitation of the Shema in the day as one commandment and in the night as another commandment in his tally of the commandments; since the time of this is not the time of that, and this does not impede on that.

Mitzvah 421
The commandment of the tefillin of the arm: to bind the tefillin of the arm upon the arm, as it is stated (Deuteronomy 6:8), "And you shall bind them as a sign upon your arm." And the explanation comes about this verse, that we bind four sections from the words of the Torah upon our arms. And they are called tefillin when they are bound with straps, as the tradition comes [to explain] about them. And these are these four sections: Two of them are at the end of the Order of Bo el Pharaoh and they are the sections of 'Sanctify your firstborn to me,' until 'you shall keep this statute at its set time from year to year' - which is one section in every exact book [of the Torah]. And the second section is from 'And it shall be when He will bring you,' until the end of the order which finishes [with] 'for with strong-handedness did He take us out of Egypt.' And the third section is at the end of the Order of Ve'etchanan in the Book of Elu HaDevarim (Deuteronomy) - the section of 'Hear Israel,' until 'and in your gates.' And the fourth section is at the end of the Order of Vehaya Ekev - the section of 'And it shall be if you listen,' until 'like the days of the heavens upon the earth.' These four sections are written on one parchment and we roll it like a type of Torah scroll from its end to its beginning. And we place it into a chamber of leather and we pass a strap through one end of the leather. And we bind that leather with the [Torah] sections inside it upon the left upper arm. And since they are bound upon the upper arm, they are resting across from the heart. And they are called tefillin of the arm in every place.

It is from the root of the commandment [that] since people are physical, they are necessarily drawn after their desires; for the nature of all physical things is to seek all which is comfortable for it and is pleasurable - just as a horse or like a mule who understand nothing - were it not that the soul with which God has graced us prevents us, to its ability, from sin. But as it resides in [the body's territory,]

Sefer HaChinukh

which is the earth, and is far removed from its [territory], which is the heavens, it cannot [vanquish] it and [the body] always exerts its strength over it. It therefore nonetheless requires many guards to protect it from its malevolent neighbor, lest it rise up upon it and kill it; as it is in its [territory] and under its hand. And the Omnipresent, Blessed be He, wanted to give us - the holy nation - merit, and [so] He commanded us to set up mighty guards around [the soul]. And they are that we were commanded not to interrupt from [speaking] words of Torah from our mouth's day and night; that we place four fringes on the four corners of our garments; a mezuzah on our doorpost; and the tefillin on our arm and on our head. And all of this is to remind us to avoid the crimes of our hands and that we not stray after our eyes or after the impulse of the thoughts of our hearts. Therefore, they, may their memory be Blessed, said (Zevachim 19a) that the priests and the Levites are exempt from them when they performed the [Temple] service. And as the foundation of the tefillin is as we have mentioned, we are commanded about them (Menachot 36b) that we not remove our thoughts from them. Now, my son, also see how much more power our bodies have than our souls; for despite all this, it sometimes comes up and 'breaks our fence.' May God in His mercy aids us and protect us, amen.

From the laws of the commandment is that with they, may their memory be Blessed, said (Mishneh Torah, Laws of Tefillin, Mezuzah and the Torah Scroll 1:3) that there are ten things about tefillin - whether [it be] in the tefillin of the head or whether of the arm - that are 'laws of Moshe from Sinai.' And one who changes [even] one out of all of them, behold, [his] tefillin are disqualified. Two of them are in the writing and eight are in the cover and the binding of the straps. And these are the two with their writing: That they must be written with ink; and that they must be written on parchment. And these are the eight in their cover (Mishneh Torah, Laws of Tefillin, Mezuzah and the Torah Scroll 3:1): 1) That they be square and their sewing be square, and their diagonals be square to the point that the four corners are all even; 2) that there be the form of a [letter,] shin from the right and the left [sides] on the leather of the head; 3) that he wraps the [Torah] sections in cloth; 4) that he wrap them with the hair of a pure beast or [wild] animal over the cloth, and afterwards, place them inside their leather boxes; 5) that he sew them with tendons; 6) that we make for them an aperture from the leather cover, that the strap may be inserted until it passes and goes though its box; 7) that the straps be black; 8) that their knots be the famous ones like the form of a [letter,] dalet.

And [also] that which they said (Gittin 45b) that only an Israelite can make tefillin and their straps. And the length of the strap of the arm is enough to surround the forearm in the place that they are placed and he ties it from there with the famous knot that needs to be in the shape of a [letter,] yod, and he stretches [it] until the middle finger and he wraps three rings around it on his finger and he ties it. And if it is longer than this, is is [still] fit (Mishneh Torah, Laws of Tefillin, Mezuzah and the Torah Scroll 3:12). And upon which place in the upper arm do we tie it? Upon the biceps - and that is the protruding flesh in the [upper arm] between the shoulder joint and the elbow joint - such that it comes out that when he puts his [upper arm] next to his ribs, the tefillin will be laying across from his heart, and it comes out that he will fulfill, "And these words shall be [...] upon your heart" (Deuteronomy 6:6). And [also] that which they said (Menachot 38a) that the tefillin of the arm does not impinge upon the tefillin of the head, and [that] of the head does not impinge upon that of the arm, because they are two [separate] commandments. And he recites the blessing on that of the head, 'about the commandment of tefillin'; and on that of the arm, 'to place the tefillin.' And about what are these words speaking? When he puts on one of them. But if he put both of them on together, he only recites one blessing; and that is 'to place the tefillin.'

And he first places that of the arm and afterwards that of the head; and when he removes them, he removes that of the head first. And [also] that which they said (Berakhot 9b, (Mishneh Torah, Laws of Tefillin, Mezuzah and the Torah Scroll 4:10) that the time of tefillin during the day is from when one can see his friend until the sun sets, as it is stated (Exodus 13:10), "You shall observe this statute in its proper time from day to day" - and "this statute" is the commandment of tefillin. And Shabbat and holidays - and the same is true of the intermediate festival days - are not a time for the placing of tefillin, as it is stated about them (Exodus 13:16), "And it shall be a sign." And Shabbat days and holidays are a sign themselves, and we do not need another sign.

And [also] that which they said (Shabbat 49a) that tefillin requires a clean body, and they said in the

Sefer HaChinukh

Gemara, "What is a clean body? That he be careful not to pass gas with them [on]." But the matter is not to say that it requires a body clean of sins or of impurity. As every man, even one impure or a sinner is obligated about the commandment of tefillin, so long as he knows to be careful not to pass gas with them [on]. And maybe from being constant with the commandment of tefillin - as they are a great memory device for a person about his service to the Heavens - he will repent from his evil way and purify himself from all of his filth. And the Sages, may their memory be Blessed, obligated us about the commandment of tefillin to educate even the small youths about it, so long as they have arrived to the category [of those] that know to guard them. And from here it can be understood that the opinion of our Rabbis, may their memory be Blessed, was that every man should grab onto this commandment and be accustomed to it, since it is a great fundamental, a protection from sin and a strong ladder to climb with to enter into the service of the Creator, Blessed be He. And maybe the intention of those that are stringent about the holiness of the commandment, and discourage the hearts of the masses with their words from being involved with it, is good. But in truth, through this, there is the prevention of people from several commandments, and [so] it is a great evil. And [this is] even though I know that those that preach these lessons base themselves on the Talmud Yerushalmi Berakhot 2:3, "About a certain man who deposited a glass with his fellow, and afterwards demanded it [back] from him and [the other] denied [having it]." And the owner of the glass said to him, "'It is not you that I trusted, but that which is on your head that I trusted'" - and their intention is to say that there is a desecration of God's name, to be pious about some commandments and to be evil about others. But this is not my home with God (not how I understand the ways of God); as I know that 'there is no righteous man in the world who does good and never sins,' and nonetheless he is not prevented from being involved with commandments when the good spirit of God clothes him to do the good. As who knows whether maybe he will continue in his good path until the time of his death - and death will come suddenly. And they, may their memory be Blessed, have already taught us (Avot 4:2) that "a commandment leads to another commandment" and "the reward for a commandment is another commandment." About all of these things and the good ethics, they, may their memory be Blessed, have preceded us and taught us. And those that want to be wise and add upon their words or take away [from them] are not [involved in] wisdom.

And [also] that which they said (Menachot 34b) that the order of the [Torah] sections on the parchment is thus - that we first write the section of 'Sanctify your firstborn to me,' and afterwards the section of 'And it shall be when He will bring you,' and afterwards the section of 'Hear Israel,' and afterwards the section of 'And it shall be if you listen.' And those that said that we write the 'beings' in the middle - meaning to say the section of 'And it shall be when He will bring you' and the section of 'And it shall be if you listen' in the middle, the section of 'Sanctify your firstborn to me' at the beginning and the section of 'Hear Israel' at the end - did not properly discern the matter. As behold, it is the common opinion of Rashi and Rambam, may their memory be Blessed and Rabbenu Hai that we do not write the 'beings' in the middle, but rather like the order that they are written in the Torah. And the proof is from that which is found in the chapter [entitled] Hakomets in Menachot 34b concerning the order of the tefillin; as they said there that one who reads [them], reads like the order in the Torah. And this text was certainly not found in the [copies of] the books of those people whose opinion was to say that we write the 'beings' in the middle. And regardless, our teachers, may God protect them, agreed now [that it is] like we wrote, that we write them like the order of the sections that are written in the Torah.

And the law of their writing; the law of the crowns in them; the law of one who writes the name [of God] between the lines, or what is the law if [only] one letter from it [is written there]; the law of processing the leather; from which side of the leather are they written; the law if thy were written by a heretic or a gentile; the law that they do not need to be checked - even for a hundred years - like a mezuzah [does]; the law of one who buys tefillin from someone who is not an expert; the law of their sewing with the sinews of a pure beast or [wild] animal; the law of tefillin, the sewing or the straps of which have broken; the law of someone whose tefillin are upon him but needs to eat or to enter the toilet with them, or one who forgot and entered with them; the law of one who enters the bathhouse with them and the rest of the details of the commandment are [all] elucidated in the fourth chapter of

Menachot (see Tur, Orach Chaim 25).

And it is practiced in every place and at all times by males, but not by females; because it is a positive commandment determined by time. And nonetheless, if they want to lay tefillin, we do not protest [against them] and there is reward for them; but not like the reward of a man - as the reward of someone who is commanded [something] and does [it] is not similar to the reward of someone who is not commanded [it] and does [it] (Kiddushin 31a). And in Tractate Eruvin 31a in the chapter [entitled] Hamotseh Tefillin, they, may their memory be Blessed, said that Michal the daughter of Shaul would lay tefillin and the Sages did not protest [against her]. And there they [also] said the wife of Yonah would go up in pilgrimage and the Sages did not protest [against her]. And one who transgresses this and does not lay tefillin of the arm and of the head has violated eight positive commandments (Menachot 44a); as behold, Scripture commanded about the tefillin of the arm and of the head in four sections.

Mitzvah 422

The commandment of the tefillin of the head: To place tefillin on the head, as it is stated (Deuteronomy 6:8), "and they shall be as totafot between your eyes." Behold, I wrote in the previous commandment what is the content of the tefillin, that it is four sections that are written in the Torah, in the Order of Bo el Pharaoh, in the Order of Ve'etchanan and in the Order of Vehaya Ekev. And we were commanded to write these four sections on parchment and to place them on our heads between our eyes and on our upper arm across from the heart. And the matter of these four sections more than other sections of the Torah is because there is in these the acceptance of the yoke of Heaven, the unification of God, and the matter of the exodus from Egypt which forces belief in the creation of the world and the supervision of God over the lower beings - and these are the fundamentals of the Jewish religion. And therefore, we were commanded to place these fundamentals between our eyes and upon the board of our hearts all day; as the wise men of science have said that these two limbs are the residence of the intellect. And when we place these things upon them as a memory device, we are strengthened about them, and we add to the cognizance of the ways of God, may He be Blessed; and [so] we merit life in the world to come. And some of the laws of the tefillin are written above in that of the arm.

And behold I will inform you of the distinction between them in their leather and in their sewing: Know that we make the leather, in which we store [the parchments of] the tefillin of the arm, one chamber; and we place there the four sections that we mentioned, written upon one parchment. But the leather of that of the head we divide into four chambers; and in each one, we put one section from these four sections. And while it is still moist, we make from the leather the resemblance of a [letter,] shin with three heads on the right [side] of the one that is laying the tefillin; and the resemblance of a [letter,] shin with four heads on the left [side] of the one that is laying [the tefillin]. And we insert straps for the head into the extra leather at the end of the chamber, and that is what the Sages called, maaboret, meaning to say that we pass (maavirin) the straps through it. And afterwards we encircle the measurement of the head of the one that lays [them] with the straps, and we make in that place [at the bottom of the back of the head] one knot in the shape of a [letter,] dalet. And it is impossible to describe this in writing, but everyone teaches his students and it is well-known among us, the holy people. And this is the knot of the tefillin that they, may their memory be Blessed, said (Chullin 9a) that every Torah scholar needs to know. And they enumerated it with other things that they said about them that it is fitting to know [how to do] them no matter what. And they are the writing [of the letters], slaughter, circumcision, the blessing of bridegrooms and tsitsit. And the length of the strap of the head is enough to encircle the head with it and tie the knot behind him and that there be enough of it to stretch the two ends of the strap until [they are] across from his navel - or at the very least, that one end is until it is across from his heart and one is until it is across from his navel. And the place of the placement of the tefillin of the head - meaning to say the box of leather that the sections [of the Torah] are placed in - is across from the brain, the place where the brain of a baby is frail (Menachot 37a). And this is the explanation that has been received by us about "and they shall be as totafot between your eyes" - that this is what is called 'between the eyes.' And behold, the one who places it actually between his eyes contradicts the words of the received tradition. And the rest of the details of the commandment and all of its content is like its fellow that preceded [it].

Mitzvah 423
To affix a mezuzah on entrances: To affix a mezuzah on the doorposts of our homes, as it is stated (Deuteronomy 6:9), "And you shall write them on the doorposts of your house and on your gates." And the content of the mezuzah is that we write two sections of the Torah on one parchment - and they are 'Hear Israel,' until 'and in your gates'; [and] 'And it shall be if you listen,' until 'upon the earth.' And we affix them to the doorposts of the opening of the house.

It is from the roots of the commandment that it be a memory device for a person about faith in God every time that he comes into his home and [when] he leaves [it], and like I wrote about the matter of tefillin. And [it is] like the matter that they, may their memory be Blessed, wrote about this commandment (Menachot 33a), "Rabbi Zira said that Rav Matnah said that Shmuel said, 'It is a commandment to place it in the top third.' Rabbah [Rava] said, 'It is a commandment to place it in the handbreadth adjacent to the public domain.' What is the reason? The Rabbis said, 'So that one will be met by the commandment immediately'" (Menachot 33b).

From the laws of the commandment is that which they, may their memory be Blessed, said (Menachot 28a) that these two sections impede each other; and even one writing impedes upon them. [This is] meaning even one letter that is not done properly - such as if the [blank] parchment does not encircle it from its four sides - impedes the [validity] of the mezuzah. And [also] that which they said (Menachot 34a) that the obligation of the mezuzah is to place it on the doorpost of his entrance from the right, as it is stated, "your house (beitecha)" - and our Rabbis explain it [as] your coming (beeatecha), and that when a person picks up [his feet], he picks us his right foot first. And [also] that which they, may their memory be Blessed, said (Yoma 11), "Our rabbis taught, '"And on your gates" - it is one [whether they are] the gates of houses, courtyards, cities, towns, a barn, chicken coops, a hay storehouse, wine storehouses, or oil storehouses, all of them are obligated in [having] a mezuzah. It is possible that I would include a gatehouse, a portico, an open porch, and a balcony [serving as a corridor to several residences. Hence,] we learn to say, "house"; just as a house is designated for residence, so too [only] all that are designated for residence; to the exclusion of these that are not designated for residence. It is possible that I would include even a bathroom, a bathhouse, and a bath for immersion. [Hence,] we learn to say, "house"; just as a house is designed for dignity, so too [only] all that are designed for dignity; to the exclusion of these. It is possible that I would include even the Temple Mount, its chambers and the courtyards. [Hence,] we learn to say, "house"; just as a house is non-sacred, so too [only] all that are non-sacred; to the exclusion of these that are holy.'" And a synagogue is in the category of holy houses (Mishneh Torah, Laws of Tefillin, Mezuzah and the Torah Scroll 6:6), so long as there is no house of residence there. But if there is a house of residence - such as the synagogues of villages within which guests reside - it is obligated.

And [also] that which they said (Yoma 11b) that the mezuzah of an individual is to be checked twice in a seven-year period, and that of a group twice in a jubilee period. And [also] that which they said (Menachot 29b) concerning the crowns, "Rava [Rabbah] said, 'Seven letters in the mezuzah need three [letters,] zayin each, and these are them, shin, ayin, tet, nun, zayin, gimmel, tsaddi (shatnez gets)'" - meaning to say that each letter in the mezuzah from these requires three crowns. And [also] that which they said (Menachot 44a) that one who rents a house outside of the Land [of Israel] and one lives in an inn in the Land of Israel are exempt from a mezuzah for thirty days, but that one who rents a house in the Land of Israel is obligated immediately [to affix] a mezuzah. And [when a landlord] rents out a house to his fellow, it is upon the renter to bring a mezuzah and to affix it, as it is an obligation on the resident. And when he leaves, he can not take it [away] in his hand, unless the house belonged to a gentile (Mishneh Torah, Laws of Tefillin, Mezuzah and the Torah Scroll 5:11). And there are ten conditions that are required of a house before it is obligated in [having] a mezuzah, and these are them:

1) That there be enough [space] to make a square of four ells by four ells;
2) that it have two doorposts;

3) and a lintel;
4) and a roof;
5) and doors;
6) and that the gate be ten or more handbreadths tall;
7) that the house be non-sacred;
8) that it be designed for the residence of a man;
9) that it be designed for residing in dignity;
10) and that it be designed for permanent residence;

And a house that has many openings is obligated in the affixing of a mezuzah in each of them, even though he is only accustomed to entering regularly through one of them (Menachot 44a; Mishneh Torah, Laws of Tefillin, Mezuzah and the Torah Scroll 6:10). And a small opening that is between a house and an attic that people sometimes make at the feet of a ladder, upon which people climb to the attic, is obligated in [having] a mezuzah. And rooms in a house - even a room within a room - are all obligated in [having] a mezuzah, since all of them are made for residing. [These] and the rest of the details of the commandment are [all] elucidated in the third chapter of Tractate Menachot (See Tur, Yoreh Deah 285).

And it is practiced in every place and at all times by males and females. And one who transgresses this and builds a house and puts a roof on it and did not place a mezuzah in it immediately - or rents a house outside of the Land [of Israel] or an inn in the Land and more than thirty days pass him up and he did not place a mezuzah in it immediately - has violated this positive commandment. And even though the time that he was obligated to place it has passed, he is always warned to affix it, anytime he lives in the house.

Mitzvah 424

To not test a true prophet more than is necessary: That we have been prevented to not test a prophet that rebukes the nation and teaches the ways of repentance more than is necessary, once the truth of his prophecy be known. And about this is it stated (Deuteronomy 6:16), "Do not test the Lord, your God, as you tested Him at Massah," meaning to say, "Do not test the rewards of God and his punishments about which He has informed you through His prophets in a way that shall be sufficient for you."

It is from the roots of the commandment [that it is] since harm will be [caused] with superfluous testing of true prophets, as sometimes people that are jealous of him and hurt from his status will disagree with him from this. And the matter of prophecy is not a constant matter to every prophet, as sometimes he will only prophecy a little. And if we burden him each and every time to give a trustworthy sign or a wonder [to show that] he is a prophet, it will be a cause for the people to rebel against him and to frequently take his words lightly. Hence, we have been warned to believe him and not to test him more than is necessary, once he is established with us as good and trustworthy as a prophet. And this matter happened to the true prophets with the false prophets, as [the latter] would contradict their prophecy and quibble about them and contradict their words to the point that one sign after another and one wonder after another was not enough for them.

And likewise included in this commandment is not to do the commandments of God, Blessed be He, by way of testing, such that a person do a commandment to test whether God, may He be Blessed, will reward him in His righteousness; and not from his love of God and his fear of Him. And let it not be difficult to you that which they, may their memory be Blessed, said in the first chapter of Tractate Taanit 9a, "'A tithe shall you tithe (te'aser)' (Deuteronomy 14:22)? Take a tithe (asser) so that you will become wealthy (titasher)." As they have already answered it there and said that in all the commandments is it stated, "Do not test," except in this [one] of tithes, as it is stated (Malachi 3:10), "Bring the whole tithe into the storeroom, [...] and test Me now by this, etc." And the reason for this is like the matter that is written (Proverbs 19:17), "He is lending to God, he who is gracious to the poor" - meaning to say that God, may He be Blessed, has informed us that it is through our financing the servants of His house with tithes that purpose and blessing is found in our money, no matter what, and [that] no matter of sin or iniquity will impinge on it. And the reason for the prohibition of testing about the commandments is because the reward for the commandments is not in this world; and as they expounded in Tractate Avodah Zarah 3a, "Today is the day to do them, but tomorrow" - meaning the world to come - "is [the day] to take their reward." And [about] that which they, may their memory be Blessed said (Bava Batra 10b), "One who says, 'This coin is for charity in order that my son should live,' behold, he is completely righteous" - the wise commentators have answered [that it is when he decides in his heart to give it whether [his son] lives or does not live, as this is not testing God.

From the laws of the commandment is that which they, may their memory be Blessed, informed us about what confirms to us the prophecy of a prophet to the point that we not doubt his words afterwards. It is that he says things that will happen in the world in the future two or three times, and his words [come true] exactly. And we should not obligate him to do a sign or a miracle [that involves] a change in nature, as was done by Moshe, Eliyahu and Elisha. And also, the man that we assume to be a prophet and that we believe needs to be a just man that walks innocently; as it is known that prophecy only rests upon the pious and among men of good deeds (Shabbat 92a). But [regarding] a prophet that promises about an evil that will come, even if it does not come, there is no contradiction to his being a prophet with this. [That is] because God is long of patience and of great kindness and He reconsiders [doing] evil when people repent, like with the people of Nineveh, and like with Hizkiyahu, whose days were added to from the Heavens after the decree that he die. Yet if a prophecy of a prophet that promises about the good does not come true, it is a contradiction to his being a prophet; since any good that God decrees through a sent prophet - even if it is conditional - never returns empty (is always fulfilled). And this is from His abundant goodness and His great kindness. [This] and the rest of its details are in [various] places in the Talmud (see Mishneh Torah, Laws of Foundations of the Torah 10).

And this commandment is practiced by males and females in every place and at all times when a prophet arises for Israel. And one who transgresses it and tests a prophet more than is necessary has violated this negative commandment. But we do not administer lashes for it, since there is no act [involved] with it.

Mitzvah 425

The commandment of killing the seven nations: To kill the seven nations that held our land before we conquered it from them - and they are the Canaanites, the Amorites, etc. - and to destroy them in any place we find them, as it is stated (Deuteronomy 7:2), "you shall totally destroy them." And this commandment is repeated in the Order of Shoftim, as it is stated (Deuteronomy 20:17), "But you shall totally destroy them, the Hittite, the Amorite, etc."

It is from the roots of the commandment [that it is] since these seven nations are the ones that began to do all types of idolatry and every abomination of God that He hated. And hence, in their being the main [source] of idolatry and its first foundation, we were commanded about them, to erase them and to destroy them from under the heavens, [that] they not be remembered and not be counted 'in the land of the living.' And in this commandment of ours about them to destroy them is [also] found a benefit for us, in that their memory will be lost from the world and [so] we will not learn from their deeds. And we also can take a teaching from this that we not turn to idolatry; as in our chasing after each man of this evil family to kill him for their involvement in idolatry, it will not come into the heart of a person to do like his acts, in any manner.

And it should not at all be asked - since their end was to be completely destroyed from the world, why these evil nations were created (see Rambam's Introduction to the Commentary on the Mishnah); as we already know that 'permission is given' to the hand of man to be good or evil, and that God does not force a person to one of them. And since this is so, we can say that these seven nations corrupted their [own] actions and acted evilly to the point that they were all liable for destruction and death. But at the beginning of their creation, they were [also] fit for the good. And we will rely on this reason [for] the commandment of the destruction of Amalek in the Order of Ki Tetse, at the end of the positive commandments in the Order (Sefer HaChinukh 604). And if we want, we can also say that it is possible that they had at one particular time, a time of being proper; and because of that time, they merited to be created. Or maybe we can say that from all of them, one proper man came out; and they merited to be created for his sake; and like the matter that we found one sage about which they, may their memory be Blessed, said (Avodah Zarah 10b) that we was from the [descendants] of Amalek - and that was Antoninos. And it is not impossible with the Creator to create many people for the sake of one, as He, Blessed be He, does not see toil [in this], 'He does everything that He desires.' And He, Blessed be He - who is the One that understands all of our deeds - knows the need of the others for the specific one, that He should create them all for his sake.

From the laws of the commandment is that which they, may their memory be Blessed, said (Sanhedrin 20b; Mishneh Torah, Laws of Kings and Wars 5:1-2) that a king of Israel can not wage [another] war before the commanded war - which is the war of the seven nations that are mentioned, the war of Amalek, and the war of helping Israel from an attacker that comes against them. And with those wars, he does not need to get permission from the court. And the rest of its details are elucidated.

And this commandment is practiced by males and females in every place, and at all times that we have the power to kill them. And Rambam, may his memory be Blessed, wrote (Sefer HaMitzvot LaRambam, Mitzvot Ase 187), "And maybe someone will think that this is a commandment that is not practiced throughout the generations, since the seven nations have already been destroyed. However, this will [only] be thought by someone who does not understand the matter of what is [considered] practiced throughout the generations and not practiced throughout the generations." And the major principle from his words, may his memory be Blessed, is that you need to know that any commandment the performance of which has disappeared because its time has passed - such as the commandments that they had in the wilderness, but not afterwards in the Land; and so [too,] the commandment of apportioning the inheritance which was only for the generation that was [present] for the division of the land upon their entrance into the Land - those like these are the ones that are called, 'not practiced throughout the generations.' But all of the commandments that have disappeared from us because it is not found among us that we can do it - but not because the verse makes its dependent on a specific time, such as the this one of the destruction of the seven nations and Amalek in each and every generation that we find them, and even though we have already done to them that which we are obligated through our King David, who destroyed them to the point that there only remain a small number of them that have scattered and been diluted among the nations until their memory is not known, and it is not even in our [power] now to pursue them and to kill them - nonetheless, this commandment is not called because of this a 'commandment that is not practiced [throughout the generations].' And understand this principle and hold on to it. And one who transgresses this, and one of them comes to his hand - and he is able to kill him without endangering himself through the matter - and he does not kill him, has violated this positive commandment, besides that he violated a negative commandment which is stated about them (Deuteronomy 20:16), "You shall not keep any soul alive," as we will write at the end of the Order of Shoftim with God's help about the commandment not to keep alive one from all of the seven nations (Sefer HaChinukh 528).

Mitzvah 426

To not grace and to have mercy on an idolater: That we should not forgive towards idolaters and that nothing of theirs should be straight in our eyes. [That is] to say that we should distance from our thoughts and not bring up to our mouths that there should be anything of benefit from one who worships idolatry, and that he not brings up grace in our eyes in any matter; to the point that our Rabbis, may their memory be Blessed, said (Avodah Zarah 7a) that it is forbidden to say, "How beautiful is that gentile," or "How fine and pleasant is he." And about this is it stated (Deuteronomy 7:2), "and you shall not grace them." And the explanation of this comes about this, [that it is to say,] do not give them grace, like the matter that we have said. And there are some of our Rabbis that learned from, "you shall not grace them," you shall not give them free presents - and it is all one root. And in Talmud Yerushalmi Avodah Zarah 1:9, they said, "'You shall not grace them' - you shall not give them grace [is] a negative commandment."

It is from the roots of the commandment [that it is] since the beginning of any action of people is the fixing of the thought about the actions and the bringing up of the words upon the language of the tongue [about them]; and [only] after the thought and the speech about them, will he do any action. And therefore, in our being prevented to find benefit and grace in idolaters in our thought and speech; behold, we are prevented through this from bonding with them and from pursuing their love and from learning anything from their evil deeds.

From the laws of the commandment is that which they, may their memory be Blessed, said (Avodah Zarah 65a) about that we do not give free presents to them, that [it is] specifically to one who worships idolatry, but not to one who does not worship idolatry - even though he remains a gentile to eat disgusting animals and creeping animals and all of the other sins like a resident alien. As since he has accepted the seven [Noachide] commandments, we support him and we give him free presents; and they may their memory be Blessed, said (Arakhin 29a) that we only accept a resident alien at a time when the jubilee is practiced. And also that which they, may their memory be Blessed, said (Gittin 61a) that it is permissible to support the poor of the gentiles with the poor of Israel because of the ways of peace. And the rest of its details - are elucidated in Tractate Avodah Zarah (see Tur, Yoreh Deah, 151).

And this commandment is practiced in every place and at all times by males and females. And one who transgresses this and praises worshipers of idolatry, except in a way that brings much greater praise to our nation from praising them, has violated this negative commandment. But there are no lashes for it, since there is no act [involved] with it. Yet his punishment is very great, since it is a cause for a great mishap which has no repayment - as the thing sometimes goes down to the chambers of the belly of the listeners, and all who know knowledge understand this.

Mitzvah 427

To not marry with idolaters: That we should not marry with the nations - and Rambam, may his memory be Blessed, wrote (Mishneh Torah, Laws of Forbidden Intercourse 12:1), "Not with the seven nations and with the other nations" - as it is stated (Deuteronomy 7:3), "You shall not marry with them." And the matter of marriages is that he gives his daughter to [the idolater's] son or his son to his daughter, and as the verse elucidates, "you shall not give your daughter to his son, and his daughter you shall not take for your son." And all the more so one who mates with them [himself], as he himself is included in this prohibition. And we say in Tractate Avodah Zarah 36b [that it is] by way of marriages that the Torah forbade. But even though this verse of "You shall not marry them" is written specifically about the seven nations and in their being converts - and so is it understood by our Rabbis, who said in the Gemara (Yevamot 76a), "In their being converts, they have marriages, in their being gentiles, they do not have marriages" - in that which the Scripture restates [that which is already understood], "you shall not give your daughter to his son, and his daughter you shall not take for your son," it [comes to] include the seven nations and all of the other nations even in their being gentiles. But the seven nations are forbidden even in their being converts because they were the main [source] of idolatry and its first foundation, whereas the other nations are permitted by conversion. But one who has sexual relations on occasion, such as a man who has sexual relations privately with his harlot - this is only a rabbinic prohibition, and it is the prohibition of nashgaz (the Hebrew initials of the four types of women included: menstruant, maidservant, gentile, harlot) mentioned in Avodah Zarah 76a.

It is from the roots of the commandment [that it is that] since most of the masses - in their stupidity - are drawn after the counsel of their wives, if one marries the 'daughter of a foreign god,' she will draw him to worship idolatry. And also, because her children that are born from her will be raised towards idolatry. And woe to the one who disqualifies his seed.

From the laws of the commandment is that which they, may their memory be Blessed, said (Sanhedrin 81a) that zealots would attack one who has sexual intercourse with an Aramean (gentile) publicly in the eyes of ten or more Israelites. And the proof of the thing is the story of Pinchas and Zimri. But the zealot is nonetheless only permitted to attack him at the time of the promiscuous act, and like in the story that happened; as it is stated (Numbers 25:8), "and the woman through her belly." But if he separated [from her], we do not kill him, but [rather] bring him to the court and they administer lashes [upon] him, since he did the act publicly. [If] the zealots did not attack him and the court did not administer lashes [upon] him, we know from the words of tradition that he is [punished] by excision, as it is written (Malachi 2:11-12), "and he who husbands (read here as, who has sexual intercourse with) the daughter of a foreign god. The Lord will excise the man that does it." And a gentile who has sexual relations with an Israelite - if she is a married woman, he is killed over her; but, if not, he is not killed. But a Jew who wantonly has sexual relations with a gentile woman - even [if it is] by way of harlotry - she is nonetheless killed, since a mishap happened to an Israelite through her, like the law of an animal. And this thing is explicit in the Torah, as it is stated (Numbers 31:16-17), "They were the ones that were with the word of Bilaam against the Children of Israel, etc. and any woman that could know a man sexually they killed." [This] and the rest of its details are elucidated in Avodah Zarah and Yevamot and Kiddushin (see Mishneh Torah, Laws of Forbidden Intercourse 2).

And it is practiced in every place and at all times by males and females. And one who transgresses it and marries with the seven nations in their being converts - meaning to say, that he specifies a woman from them for a wife for his son, or he gave his daughter to one of them - the father has violated a negative commandment. But he is not lashed, as there is no act [involved] with it, whereas the son who did the act of sexual relations is lashed. And with the other nations, and so [too,] with the seven nations, in their being gentiles - one who specifies a woman from them to regularly have sexual relations with her, is lashed by Torah writ - from the first relations after he specified her - and she is killed. And if he did not specify her, but only has sexual relations with her once in the way of harlotry, he is struck with lashes of rebellion, by rabbinic writ.

Mitzvah 428
To not derive benefit from the coverings of idolatry and from its auxiliaries: That we were prevented not to benefit from the coverings of idolatry. And even when it is not forbidden to benefit from the idolatry itself - such as if one bowed to something that is not in the holding of a man's grasp (not created by him), like a mountain, an animal or a tree, as it is not prohibited to benefit from them - nonetheless, the covering that is upon them is forbidden to benefit from nonetheless; since they are included in the auxiliaries of idolatry that are forbidden. And about this is it stated (Deuteronomy 7:25), "you shall not covet silver and gold that is upon it and take it for yourself." And even though it is stated in another place more generally (Deuteronomy 13:18), "And nothing shall cling to your hand, etc.," a negative commandment was specified about the covering - as the fools will place their eyes upon them.

It is from the roots of the commandment that [it is] in order to distance any matter of idolatry and anything associated with it.

The laws of the commandment are elucidated in the third chapter of Avodah Zarah.

And [it] is practiced in every place and at all times by males and females. And one who transgresses it and benefits from its coverings - and even the smallest amount - is liable [to receive] lashes.

Mitzvah 429
To not benefit from an offering to idolatry: That we not have anything of idolatry cling with our money, to benefit from it. And about this is it stated (Deuteronomy 7:26), "And you shall not bring an abhorrent thing into your house, etc."

It is from the roots of the commandment [that it is] in order to distance all matter of disgusting idolatry.

The laws of this commandment are also in the third chapter of Avodah Zarah.

And they elucidated for us (Makkot 22a) that one who cooks with the wood of a tree-God is lashed two [sets of lashes] - because of "You shall not bring an abhorrent thing," and because of "And no thing shall cling to your hand from the anathema"; since they are two matters, one is to bring something of idolatry into his domain to benefit from and [the other] is that he benefits from it. As a person shows a desire for it about himself with both of them; and he is lashed for both of them, as we have written. And even though there is one main principle for both of them - and that is benefit, as behold, he is only lashed because of the benefit - nonetheless, once he benefits, he is lashed twice. And [it is] like the matter that we said above in the Order of Emor (Sefer HaChinukh 273) about a high priest that has sexual intercourse with a widow - that he is lashed twice, even though the two negative commandments have one main principle to them, as we have written there.

And it is in the category of this prohibition whether it is the idolatry itself or whether it is its auxiliaries or whether it is its offering, and whether it is the idolatry of an Israelite or of a gentile. And what is [the difference] between this and that? That of a gentile is forbidden immediately from when it is made, as it is stated (Deuteronomy 7:25), "The sculptures of their gods" - from the time that they are sculpted. And that of an Israelite is not forbidden until it is worshiped, as it is stated (Deuteronomy 27:15), "and places it in hiding" - until he does to it things that are in hiding (Mishneh Torah, Laws of Foreign Worship and Customs of the Nations 7:4).

And [also] included in this commandment is that a person should not have cling to his money that God has graced him with justly, other money that is from theft, extortion, interest or from any ugly thing; since all of this is included in the auxiliaries of idolatry. As the evil impulse of a man's heart desires it and brings it to his house - and the evil impulse is called by the name, idolatry; and like they, may their memory be Blessed, said (Bava Batra 10a) that about it is it stated (Deuteronomy 15:9), "lest there be a wanton thing with your heart," and it is written about the matter of idolatry (Deuteronomy 13:14), "Wanton men have gone out from you and have induced, etc." And about monies like this that we mentioned and about the auxiliaries of idolatry - about all of them - is it stated (Deuteronomy 7:26), "and you will be an anathema like it"; meaning to say that all that clings to it is anathema. As the blessing of God is not found in it, and [so] it disappears and is lost; like the matter that they, may their memory be Blessed, said (Bava Metzia 71a) that a small coin of interest makes several treasuries of money disappear. As this comes and destroys that.

And this prohibition is practiced in every place and at all times by males and females. And one who transgresses it and takes anything from idolatry and brings it into his domain and benefits from it is lashed two [sets of lashes], because of "You shall not bring, etc." and because of "And no [thing] shall cling, etc." So wrote Rambam, may his memory be Blessed (Mishneh Torah, Laws of Foreign Worship and Customs of the Nations 7:2).

Mitzvah 430
To bless God after eating food: To bless God, may He be Blessed, after a man eats and is satiated from bread or from the seven types [of food] that are mentioned in the verse (Deuteronomy 8:8) when he is nourished by them. And a loaf made from wheat or barley is called undifferentiated bread; and included in wheat is spelt, and included in barley is oats and rye. And about the seven types that nourish is it stated (Deuteronomy 8:10), "And you shall eat and be satiated, and you shall bless the Lord, your God, for the good land, etc." And this satiation is not the same with very person, but rather every person knows his [own] satiation. And we know the measurement of the satiation of a righteous person is to satiate himself, [by which] I mean to say, only for his sustenance. And the proof that the obligation of the blessing from Torah writ is only after satiation is that which they, may their memory be Blessed, said in the chapter [entitled] Mi SheMeto in Berakhot 20b: Rav Avira expounded, etc. until, He said to them, "And shall I not show favor to Israel, as I wrote for them in My Torah. 'And you shall eat and be satiated, and you shall bless' (Deuteronomy 8:10); yet they are exacting with themselves even if they have eaten as much as a kazayit (the size of a large olive) or a kabeitsah (the size of a large egg)." And I will still expand [upon] this statement in explaining this verse and the laws that come out of the laws of this commandment, with God's help. And I will make known the disagreement that exists among our rabbis in its understanding.

From the roots of the commandment, [there is a need to] preface that, have I not told you, my son in what has preceded, that all glory, all majesty, all the good, all wisdom, all power and blessing are of God, Blessed be He. And the words of people and all of their deeds - whether good or bad - will not add or subtract [from Him]. Hence you must distinguish that in our always saying in the blessings, "Blessed are You, God," or [in our saying,] "May He be Blessed," the understanding is not as it seems, to add blessing to the One who does need any addition, God forbid. As He is the Master over everything and over all the blessing; He renews them and creates them and emanates great abundance from them when his good will is [present] there. Therefore, we must search what is the intention of

Sefer HaChinukh

the matter and not expend our time in that with which we are always involved without any understanding at all. And it is not my thought - I, the one that raises [it] - that my intellect will grasp even like a drop in the ocean of the truth of the matter. As it has already been told to me and I heard from the mouth of sages that there is in these things' strong foundations and wonderful secrets - the Torah sages inform their students [of them] when they are understanding and proper and all of their actions are pleasant. But my will to grasp a little of the reason in these lifts me to speak about it. And maybe silence would have been better, but 'love spoils [sense of what is proper].'

The matter is known and famous that God, may He be Blessed, moves all that exists and created man and put him in control over the earth and over every thing that is in it. And it is from His traits, Blessed be He, that He is of much kindness and that He desires the good of His creatures, and [so] He wants them to be fitting and meriting to receive goodness from Him. And this is really from His perfection, may He be Blessed. As only one who gives to others besides himself can be called perfect in the good - there is no doubt about this to any intelligent person. And since [we are in] agreement [about] this, that we know that it is obligatory from the perfection of His goodness, that His desire is to pour down His blessing upon us, we shall say that the matter of the blessing that we say in front of Him is only a mention to arouse ourselves through the words of our mouths that He is the Blessed One, and the Blessed One that contains all of the goodnesses. And through this good arousal of ourselves and the designation of our thoughts to admit to Him that all of the goodnesses are included in Him and He is the King over them, to send them to all that He desires, we merit through this good action to bring from His blessings upon us. And after this mention and this admission in front of Him, we request from Him that which we need [of] knowledge, or the pardon of our iniquities, or healing, or wealth or anything. And so [too,] after the request from Him, we repeat and admit to Him about this, to say that it comes to us from Him. And this is the opening and the conclusion of the blessings. [The reason for the latter is that we not] be considered like a slave who took a reward from his master and goes away without permission, like a thief. And it comes out according to the premise [created by] this reason that "Blessed" is an adjective, meaning to say it is an admission to Him that He contains all of the blessings. And [about] the expression, "may He be Blessed," that we always mention - which is [in] the reflexive case - we can say that the intention of it is that we are supplicating to Him that it be His will in front of Him to cause the hearts of His creatures to be prepared in front of Him that all should admit to Him and praise Him. And this is the explanation of "may He be Blessed," meaning to say, "It should be Your will in front of You, that all people of the world will relate all blessing to You and admit that everything in the world emanates from You," and that His will be completed - as He wants to do good, as we have said. And the fulfillment of the Will is the purpose of all that ask. And behold, we have found an explanation even for the puzzling expression of "may He be Blessed." And from this understanding (other versions: root), that which they, may their memory be Blessed, said (Chullin 60b) that the Holy One, Blessed be He, craves the prayers of the righteous [is] to say that His desire is that they do an act through which they will merit in front of Him and bring down from His goodness upon them; as He is One who desires to do kindness and to give from His blessing upon them, from the good of His perfection, as is written. And this is the great root to all the good that a man does in this world - that his reward from God [is because] he fulfills His desire, in that He wants the good of the creatures.

And from this root that I have said that the mention of Blessed be He is an admission in front of Him about all of the blessings, that they are His, and that there is a need to make an admission to Him about this at the beginning of the request and at the end so that one not be like a slave that took his reward from his master and then left without permission; the differences that our Rabbis, may their memory be Blessed, fixed for us (Berakhot 11a) in the matter of the blessings - that there are some that open with "Blessed" and also conclude with "Blessed," there are those that conclude [with it] but do not open [with it] and there are those that open [with it] but do not conclude with it - are established, according to my opinion. How is it? Any blessing in the world - that has a request of something from God, may He be Blessed, or the mentioning of a miracle - that is not adjacent to another blessing opens with "Blessed" and conclude with "Blessed"; for example, 'who creates the light' of the morning prayers and 'who brings the evenings' of the evening prayers; and many like them is from the reason mentioned. But any blessing that is not adjacent to its fellow concludes with "Blessed," but does not open with "Blessed," from this reason. As behold, since he admitted and gave governance to God at the end of the blessing that is adjacent to it, and he did not interrupt after this admission with neither a small or big thing, it is not fit to repeat the admission of the acceptance of His mastery twice at once because of the distinction between the requests of that we ask in front of Him. But it is fitting to conclude with "Blessed," since He interrupted with the request of his needs, as it is fit to go back and mention and to give to his heart the acceptance of His Kingship and his Mastery over him. And in this way, you will find the explanation for all of them according to my opinion, if you work them out. And those that have one adjacent that leave this framework - such as the blessing of grooms and Kiddush and Havdalah and others - have already been answered for us by our teachers, may God protect them. And the reason they taught us about some of them is that sometimes these blessings are said not with adjacent ones; and our Rabbis did not want to distinguish and say when it comes with adjacent ones, say it this way, and when without adjacent ones, this. As they always fled from these distinctions in everything that is given over to the hands of the masses, and such is rational.

And any blessing in the world that does not have a request for something from God nor the mention of a miracle for Israel - such as the blessing before food and drink and all pleasures of the body, and so [too,] the blessing of a miracle for an individual - blessings that never have a long text, the matter is known to all who are literate in texts that they all open with "Blessed," and do not conclude [with it]; it is from the reason mentioned: As since he mentioned the Kingship of God and His Mastery and immediately finished his words, it is not obligatory to repeat the mention of "Blessed" a second time; as it would [otherwise] appear as the repetition of something that is not necessary, which is something that is obvious.

And all blessings that are fixed only for the praise of God, such as one who sees the Great Sea or good trees, and so [too,] one who hears the sound of thunder claps, and the rest of the matters mentioned in the chapter [entitled] Haroeh - some of them open with "Blessed" and do not conclude [with it] and some of them conclude [with it] but do not open [with it]. And it is all from the reason mentioned: as the mention of the Mastery at the beginning or even at the end is apparently sufficient for one who mentions praises; since he does not request something for himself and is not reciting a blessing for a pleasure that he wants to receive. As in truth, it is fitting for one who requests something or wants to benefit, to enlighten the opening of his words and to begin with the mention of His mastery, Blessed be He. And this is what they said, that blessings over pleasures open with "Blessed." And so [too,] blessings over commandments open with "Blessed," due to the great benefit that God, Blessed be He, made us profit [through them].

From the laws of the commandment is that which they, may their memory be Blessed, said (Berakhot 35a) that even though the Torah only obligated us to recite a blessing after we are satiated from food, the Sages, may their memory be Blessed, obligated us to recite a blessing also after any thing from which a person derives pleasure - whether it is from the fruits of the seven species for which the Land is praised or whether it is from any other thing. And they learned the thing from their seeing that the Torah obligates a person to bless God after he is satiated from food that sustains his body with strong sustenance. And they went according to this reason and obligated us to recite a blessing even for anything from which a body eats - whether it is something [that nourishes] or is not something that nourishes - so long as a man derives pleasure from it. And so too, they, may their memory be Blessed, obligated us to recite a blessing before eating. And they learned to say this from logic; as it is fitting that a man not benefit from this world without a blessing. [So] metaphorically, they made the blessing like a request for permission from a homeowner to eat from that which is found in his home.

And there are those among our rabbis whose opinion it is that the Torah obligated us to recite a blessing after all of the seven species, such as dates, wine and fig-cakes (see Berakhot 12a) - as it obligated us in truth to recite a blessing after those of them that are nourishing - and said that it was said about all of them, "And you shall eat and be satiated, and you shall bless" (Deuteronomy 8:10). And they also said that satiation from Torah writ it only with [as much as] a kabeitsah; as with this [quantity] the mind of a [hungry] person is put at ease. And I see a bit of proof for their words from that which they said at the beginning of the chapter [entitled] Keitsad (Berakhot 35a), in the give and

Sefer HaChinukh

take which is in the Gemara to find the obligation of blessing from the Torah: It is said over there, "Just as the seven species is something that has benefit and requires a blessing; so too, any item that has benefit, requires a blessing." It appears from this that there is no distinction in the seven species between those that give nourishment and those that do not, such that there is an obligation for blessing from the Torah for all of them. But in any event, I saw in Rambam, may his memory be Blessed, (Mishneh Torah, Laws of Blessings 1:1 and see 3:12 and Kessef Misneh there) and others are with him, such that it appears to me from their words to say that the central obligation of blessing by Torah writ is only on being satiated in the eating of nourishing food, and not on other species, even if they are from the seven species; such as pomegranates, grapes, fresh figs and dates - since they are not nourishing. As the Torah only obligates on nourishing foods; and because of this, [it] put bread adjacent to the blessing - as it is written (Deuteronomy 8:9), "you shall eat bread in it," and then it reverts, "And you shall eat and be satiated." But we shall listen to the great ones in our generation concerning the laws of the Torah.

And after this decision (to follow the great ones of the generation), one who is in doubt if he Blessed the blessing abridged from three (meein shalosh) after any of the seven species is obligated to recite the blessing because of [the] doubt. And so [too,] if he was in doubt [if he recited] the Grace after Meals; and even if he ate less than enough to satiate, he is obligated to recite the blessing - so long as he ate a kabeitsah. But one who eats a kazayit or more until a kabeitsah and is in doubt if he Blessed or not apparently does not have to recite the blessing, as according to everyone, he is not obligated to recite the blessing; as this amount is rabbinic (and a doubt about having fulfilled rabbinic law does not warrant the reciting of a blessing). But according to that which appears to me from the words of the earlier scholars, whenever he has not been satiated from nourishing food, he does not become obligated to recite the blessing because of [the] doubt. And I say that maybe that which we see many from the masses being lenient about the blessing abridged from three, and [yet] no one - even a total ignoramus - being lenient about the grace after meals is from the fundamental principle of the earlier scholars. As their opinion was to say that the central command of the Torah only arises upon satiation from nourishing food. And it appears that way from the simple understanding of Scripture [as well]. It comes out with regards to blessings as follows: The commandment of the Torah is only to recite the blessing after nourishing food - and not before it - and, according to the later scholars, also on the seven species mentioned in the Torah.

And all other blessings - all of them - are rabbinic, except for one of them which is from Torah writ; and this is explicit in the Gemara in Berakhot 21a, and that is the blessing over the Torah before it. And Ramban, may his memory be Blessed, also counted it as a separate positive commandment (on Sefer HaMitzvot LaRambam, Mitzvot Ase 15, where he adds to the count of Rambam). And it appears that the reason for the matter that God, Blessed be He, commanded us in the blessing for the reading of the Torah before it and for food after it is because He, Blessed be He, would only request for the physical to serve Him and to admit His goodness after it received a reward from Him, since the animal portion will only recognize His good after the feeling [evoked by the reward]. But the reading of the Torah is from the intellectual portion, and the intellect knows and recognizes, and understands the benefit before [it] receives it. Therefore, God obligates us to admit [His goodness] in front of Him, before the reading of the Torah. And one who concedes the truth will find reason in my words.

And after this we will speak more generally about the rabbinic obligation of blessings. And that is: To recite a blessing before eating and drinking of anything that has any [good] taste to the palate - and so too, afterwards. And so [too,] they obligated us to recite a blessing over every good smell that we smell before smelling, but not after it. And the general principle of the thing is that they fixed a blessing on everything from which the body derives pleasure. And so [too,] did they obligate us (Pesachim 7b) to bless God and to admit [His goodness] over all the good that He has granted us in our doing His precious commandments. And they said that we recite a blessing over them before their doing. And the matter, according to my opinion, is like the reason mentioned adjacently about the reading of the Torah. And so [too,] they obligated us to recite blessings in praise of the Creator over His very mighty deeds, as is mentioned in the chapter [entitled] Haroeh (Berakhot 54a).

And Ezra and his court fixed the wording of all of the blessings (Mishneh Torah, Laws of Blessings

1:5). And even though they, may their memory be Blessed, said (Berakhot 48b), "Moshe established the blessing of nourishment, Yehosua the blessing over the land," they [only] said this about the essence of the matter. But Ezra and his court fixed the wording of all the blessings. And it is not fitting to add or subtract from their wording; and anyone who makes a change in them is simply mistaken. And nonetheless, ex post facto, we do not make someone who made a change or forgot a little of the wording of the blessing go back [and repeat it], so long as he mentioned its essential meaning and said the conclusion as established. And they, may their memory be Blessed, said (Sotah 32a) that the blessings - besides the mention of [God's] name and the Kingdom of the Heavens - can be said in any language.

And they, may their memory be Blessed, obligated us (Shabbat 24a) to mention the holiness of the day in the Grace after Meals, meaning to say the matter of Shabbat or holidays, as is known. And on the days that a person is obligated to eat [a meal] regardless, we make one that forgot and did not mention it in the blessing go back; and these are the two obligatory meals, which are the first night of Pesach and the first night of the holiday of Sukkot. And the opinion of some commentators is that we also make him go back on every Shabbat and every holiday.

And I will write to you, my son, still a bit more about the laws of the blessings of the meal. And [I shall do so] even though we have spoken at great length about this commandment from my fervor for blessing, though my way is not like this in this work in other places. Every Israelite must wash his hands with proper water before eating bread - meaning to say [this water] was not disqualified from the drinking of a dog and no work was done by it, and for one washing, its quantity is a quarter of a log, which is one and a half eggs. And at the very least, one needs to wash to the joint at the end of the fingers for the eating of bread. And he should recite the blessing, "Blessed are You, Lord, King of the Universe, who has sanctified us with His commandments, and commanded us about the washing of the hands." And he recites the blessing over the eating of bread at the beginning, "Blessed are You, Lord, King of the Universe, who brings out bread from the earth." And if he ate a kazayit of it, he recites the four well-known blessings at the end - 'Who nourishes,' the blessing over the land, 'Who builds Jerusalem' and 'The One who is good and does good,' which they established in Yavneh. And from when he began to recite the blessing over the bread, the blessing over bread exempts anything that comes during the meal, [from blessing] before and after it - whether they are things that nourish, such as the many cooked foods that people make from the five grains, or whether they are all other types of fruits in the world - anything that a person eats to satiate his hunger, to fill his stomach. [And this is the case] whether he eats these things in the middle of his meal or whether after he finishes eating his bread. And so [too] is the law if these things do not come to satiate him but to accompany the bread - the blessing over the bread exempts them before and after [their eating]. And if they come in the middle of the meal neither to satiate nor to accompany the bread, but just as a delight: If it is something that nourishes, such as a cooked food of the five grains, it is exempted [from a blessing] before and after it by the blessing over the bread. But if it is something that does not nourish and it comes as a delight in the middle of the food, such as fruits that people eat as a delight in the middle of the food, he recites a blessing [upon them] before them, but not after them; and included in this delighting is one who eats salted olives and similar things in the middle of the meal as an appetizer for the food, and hence he recites a blessing before it, but not after it. Even though dates are fruits, their law is that of nourishing food and [so] they are exempt before it and after it by the blessing over bread.

[If] many types of fruit were brought in front of him: If their blessings are the same - for example, if all of them are of 'the tree' - he recites the blessing over the one that is [most] beloved to him, and afterwards he eats all of the rest without a blessing. And if none of them are more beloved to him than the rest - if there are from the seven fruits listed in the Torah to praise the Land of Israel among them, he blesses over the one that is earliest in the verse first, and all of [the rest] are exempt from a blessing. But if their blessings are not the same - for example, [some are in the category of] 'fruit of the tree,' and [some are in the category of] 'fruit of the ground' - he recites a blessing for each and every one; and he has that which is [more] beloved to him precede, meaning to say the one that he wants to eat first. And if there is none there that is more beloved to him than its fellow, he has the one that is more important in its blessing precede. And that would be 'fruit of the tree,' since the blessing is more specific to it than 'fruit of the earth,' which includes everything in the earth (including trees). Wine is not included in bread at all and the blessing over bread does not exempt it [from a blessing] (Berakhot 41b). [Rather] it is in the way of a beverage, and [so] we recite a blessing upon it even if it comes in the middle of food. And the Sages, may their memory be Blessed, further established another blessing over wine (Berakhot 59b), when [people] bring a second wine in the middle of the meal or after the meal, besides the one they brought at the beginning - and that is 'the One who is good and does good' - and that is if there are two or more eating. And [the blessing over] wine that is before food exempts all wine that comes after it - whether in the middle of the meal or whether after it (Berakhot 42a). But wine that is in the middle of the food does not exempt wine that is after the food from a blessing [before it]. But from the blessing [after it], Grace after Meals exempts everything; as wine is included in [nourishing] food, since it also nourishes and brings joy.

Final waters (to wash hands at the end of the meal) are an obligation. And it needs to be cold water and that if fall into a vessel or into anything that separates between it and the ground, such as shavings and that which is similar to them. And one who did not eat anything [messy] and did not touch salt during the meal does not require it.

A person must mention the holiness of the day on Shabbat and holidays in the third blessing, like we said. And if he did not mention it and he began 'The One who is good and does good,' he goes back to the beginning (Mishneh Torah, Laws of Blessings 2:12). If he did not begin it but he did finish the third blessing, he says this formula on Shabbat: "Blessed are You, Lord, our God, King of the Universe, who has given Shabbat rest to His people, Israel, as a sign and a covenant. Blessed are You, Lord, who sanctifies the Shabbat." And if it is a holiday, we say, "Blessed are You, Lord, our God, King of the Universe, who has given holidays to His people, Israel, for happiness and joy. Blessed are You, Lord, who sanctifies Israel and the times." And so [too,] Rosh Chodesh (the first day of the month), the intermediate festival days, Channukah and Purim have a mention in the Grace after Meals in the third blessing. But if he forgot [in these cases] and concluded the blessing, we do not make him go back, and we do not mention [the holiday] at all. I have received as a tradition from my teachers, may God protect them, that any one who is careful about Grace after Meals will have his food available with dignity all of his days. [These] and the rest of its details are elucidated in Tractate Berakhot (see Tur, Orach Chaim 188).

And this commandment is practiced by Torah writ in every place and at all times by males. And by females, it is a doubt among our Rabbis whether they are obligated by Torah writ or not. And a man that transgresses this and eats [nourishing] food but does not recite a blessing after it has nullified this positive commandment. And a woman who transgressed and did not recite a blessing has violated a rabbinic commandment, and maybe a Torah commandment. And so [too,] anyone who read Torah in the morning before he recited the blessings that were fixed over the Torah or the blessing 'Everlasting love' (which serves a substitute) has violated a Torah commandment. And therefore, one who forgot if he recited the blessing over the Torah in the morning or not goes back and recites the blessing. And one who transgressed and did not recite any of the other blessings in the world besides the ones we mentioned has only violated a commandment of the Sages, but "one who breaches a fence will be bitten by a snake" (Ecclesiastes 10:8). And He, may He be Blessed, warned about it, 'measure for measure.' And one must be very careful from mentioning a blessing in vain; since there is a severe punishment in the matter, as he mentions the name of [God] for no reason. And the Sages associated (Berakhot 33a) the thing with the negative commandment of "You shall not take the name of the Lord, your God, in vain.' And come and see how careful the early generations were with this, as behold, Shimshon the Nazirite of God married a Philistine woman that he loved in the stream of Sorek. And [yet] he was so careful in mentioning the name of God, not to mention it at all - whether it was necessary or not necessary - that Delilah recognized that he told her everything [in] his heart, by his mentioning God in his words, when he said to her (Judges 16:17), "because I am a nazarite of God" - and as it is written after it (Judges 16:18), "And she saw that he had told her everything that was [in] his heart." And they, may their memory be Blessed, said (Sotah 9b), "And from where did she know?" And there were those of them that [answered that] words of truth are recognizable, and some of them that said [it was] because Shimshon mentioned God among his words - and even though he did not say it by way of an oath, but by way of a narrative.

Mitzvah 431
The commandment of loving the strangers (converts): That we were commanded to love the converts, meaning to say that we be careful not to cause them pain in any thing, but [rather to] do them good and grant them kindness according to what is proper and is possible. And converts are anyone who connects with us from the other nations, that leaves his religion and enters into our religion. And about them is it stated (Deuteronomy 10:19), "And you shall love the stranger, etc." And even though the commandment (Sefer HaChinukh 243) about the Israelite includes him, as it is stated about him (Leviticus 19:18), "and you shall love your neighbor as yourself" - since behold, a righteous convert is included in "your neighbor" - God added for us a specific commandment about his love. And so too is the thing in the prevention against cheating him. As even though he was included in "A man shall not wrong his countryman" (Leviticus 25:17, Sefer HaChinukh 338), Scripture added a specific prevention about him in its stating, "You shall not wrong a stranger" (Exodus 22:20, Sefer HaChinukh 23). And they said in the Gemara (Bava Metzia 59b) that one who wrongs the convert transgresses because of "[A man] shall not wrong" and because of "You shall not wrong a stranger." And so too [with this], he nullifies the commandment of "and you shall love your neighbor" and the commandment of "And you shall love the stranger."

It is from the roots of the commandment that God chose Israel to be a holy nation and wanted to give them merit. And therefore He guided them and commanded them about the ways of grace and compassion and warned them to crown themselves with every beautiful and precious trait to find grace in the eyes of all who see them, [such] that they will say, "These are the people of the Lord" (Ezekiel 36:20). And it is so much the way of pleasantnesses and beauty to show kindness and to grant good to one who leaves his people and all the family of the house of his father and mother and comes to take shelter under the wings of a different nation in his love for it, and in his choosing of truth and his hatred for falsehood. And in our meriting these good traits, the goodness of God will rest upon us and cling to us, and nothing will prevent us from it; as the good will extend to the good ones and the opposite to the bad ones.

From the laws of the commandment - that which they, may their memory be Blessed, said (Bava Metzia 58b) that a person not say to a convert, "Remember your early deeds"; that which they said (Sanhedrin 94a), that a person not disgrace an 'Aramean' in the presence of a convert until the tenth generation, and all of this is not to cause him pain in any regard; the intensification of love that they focused upon them to the point that they said that Scripture equated their love with the love of the Omnipresent, as with them it states, "And you shall love," and with the love of the Omnipresent, "And you shall love, etc.," and that is as I have written in the Order of Mishpatim about the commandment to not oppress the convert, even with words (Sefer HaChinukh 63); and the rest of its details - are in the Midrash and in [various] places in the Gemara (see Mishneh Torah, Laws of Human Dispositions 6).

And this commandment is practiced in every place and at all times by males and females. And one who transgresses it and causes them pain or is negligent in saving them or saving their money, or treats their honor lightly due to their being converts and not having a helper in the nation, has violated this positive commandment; and his punishment is very great, as behold, the Torah has warned about them in several places. And we should learn from this precious commandment to have mercy on a man who is in a city that is not the land of his birth and the place of the family of his fathers. And we should not pass him by on the road when we find him alone and that his helpers are far from him, since we find that the Torah warns us to have mercy on anyone who needs help. And with these traits, we will merit to receive mercy from God, may He be Blessed, and the blessings of Heaven will rest upon our heads. And Scripture hints to the reason of the command when it states, "since you were strangers in the Land of Egypt": It mentions to us that we were previously burnt by this great pain that there is to every man who sees himself among foreign people and in a foreign land. And upon our remembering the great worry of the heart that there is in the matter, and that it already passed over us and that God, in His kindnesses, took us out of there, our mercies for any person like this will overwhelm [us].

Mitzvah 432
The commandment of fearing God: That the fear of God, may He be Blessed, should always be on our faces, that we not sin; meaning to say that we fear with a fear of His punishment and that our hearts not be without fear of Him, the whole day. And about this is it stated (Deuteronomy 10:13), "The Lord, your God, you shall fear." And the proof that this is a positive commandment from the tally of the six hundred and thirteen commandments that we were commanded is that which they said in Sanhedrin 56a by way of the debate about the understanding of "And he who blasphemes the name of the Lord, etc." (Leviticus 24:16): "I will say [that it is] to express, [like that] which is written (Numbers 1:17), 'And Moshe and Aharon took these men that are expressed by name'; and its prohibition is from 'The Lord, your God shall you fear.'" It means to say by way of the debate that maybe we should explain "blaspheme" (nokev), as the expression of [God's] name, alone, without him 'blessing' [it]; and the sin that there would be in this is because he loses the fear - as it is from the fear of God not to mention His name in vain. And they answered there, that one should not say like this, as there are two answers to the thing, "One is that it is necessary that [it involve] the name of God with the name of God, and there is not [this in such a case]" - meaning to say that he must 'bless' the Name with the Name, as in, "Yose should strike Yose!" "And also, it is a [prohibition] of a positive commandment, and a [prohibition] of a positive commandment [is not called] a prohibition" - meaning to say that the verse of "The Lord, your God shall you fear" is a positive commandment.

The root of the commandment of fearing God, may He be Blessed, is revealed to all who see the Sun, as the greatest protection from sin is the fear of His punishment.

And the laws of the commandment are included [in the simple understanding of the Scripture] (in our searching the Scripture) (see Mishneh Torah, Laws of Foundations of the Torah 2).

And this commandment is practiced in every place and at all times and by the entire human species. And this is one of the constant commandments upon a person, that the obligation not ever be interrupted from upon a person, even one instant. And one upon whom the matter of a sin comes to his hand is obligated to arouse his spirit and to place into his heart at that juncture that God, Blessed be He, oversees all of the actions of people and [takes] vengeance according to the evil of the deed. And one who transgresses this and does not [appraise] his heart of this at those times has violated this positive commandment; as this is the specific time [for the] fulfillment of this positive commandment. However, for a person to stand with alacrity and to remember it during all of his times is included in the commandment [as well].

Mitzvah 433
The commandment of prayer: To serve God, may He be Blessed, as it is stated (Deuteronomy 10:20), "and you shall serve Him." And this commandment was repeated several times, as it is stated (Exodus 23:25), "And you shall serve the Lord, your God"; and in another place, it states (Exodus 11:13), "and to serve him with all of your hearts." And Rambam, may his memory be Blessed, wrote (Sefer HaMitzvot LaRambam, Mitzot Ase 5), "Even though this commandment is from the general commandments" - meaning to say that it includes all of the Torah, since the service of God includes all of the commandments - "there is also a specific [commandment] within it, and that is that God commanded us to pray to Him. And it is as they said in Sifrei Devarim 41:25, '"To serve Him with all of your hearts" What is the service that is in the heart? That is prayer.' And in the teaching of Rabbi Eliezer the son of Rabbi Yose HaGalili they said, 'From where [do we know] that the essence of prayer is among the commandments? From here, "The Lord, your God, shall you fear, and you shall serve Him."'"

That which I have written earlier several times is from the roots of the commandment - that all of the good and the blessing land upon people according to their actions and the good of their hearts and the propriety of their thoughts. And the Master of all who created them desired their good and He directed them and facilitated their success through His precious commandments, such that they merit through them. And He also made them know and opened an opening for them such that they attain all of their requests for the good - and that is that they request them from Him, Blessed be He - since the wherewithal and ability for all of their lackings is in His hand; as He will have the heavens answer 'to all that call Him in truth.' And besides informing them of this attribute, He commanded that they use it and and always request from Him all of their needs, and all the desires of their hearts. And besides the attainment of the desires of our hearts, there is a merit for us in the thing, in our arousing our spirit and fixing within all of our thoughts that He is the Master that is good and does good for us and that His eyes are open upon all of our ways, and that He hears our cries to Him at all times and at every instant - 'He does not slumber and He does not sleep, the Guardian of Israel.' And [in this way] He makes us believe in His Kingship and in His ability - without any angle of hesitation - and that there is no prevention and impediment in front of Him for anything He desires.

However, there is no set time for this commandment for us in the Torah. Hence our rabbis are in doubt about the matter: Rambam, may his memory be Blessed, wrote in his great composition (Mishneh Torah, Laws of Prayer and the Priestly Blessing 1:2) that it is a commandment to pray each day. But Ramban, may his memory be Blessed, (on Sefer HaMitzvot, Mitzvot Ase 5) wrangled with him and said that the Torah did not command us to pray every day, and also not (not even) every week, and it does not specify a time about the thing at all. And [that is why] they, may their memory be Blessed always say that prayer is rabbinic (Berakhot 21a). And he says doubtfully that the commandment [from the Torah] is to pray and to cry out in front of God, Blessed be He at a time of distress. Rambam, himself, may his memory be Blessed, also wrote that the number of prayers and the format of the prayers is not from Torah writ and that the Torah does not have a set time for prayer. Nonetheless the obligation of the Torah is to supplicate to God every day and to thank Him, since all of the governance is His, [as] is the ability to fulfill every request. To here [are his words]. And it appears that in that the central commandment of the Torah is this and no more, they, may their memory be Blessed, established for the one who is in a dangerous place and is not able to stand and concentrate in prayer to say, "The needs of Your people, Israel, are great, etc." - as it appears in Berakhot 29a - so as to fulfill his obligation from the Torah.

From the laws of the commandment is that which they, may their memory be Blessed, said (Berakhot 31a) that a man is obligated to pray three times: during the day in the morning and in the afternoon; and one time at night. And these three prayer services were fixed corresponding to the sacrifices, as they would sacrifice the daily sacrifice of the morning and the daily sacrifice of the afternoon in the Temple every day. And they also fixed [prayer] at the beginning of the evening, corresponding to the limbs of the burnt-offering of the afternoon that would be consumed and continue through the whole night. And since this prayer of night corresponds to a matter from the sacrifices that is not an obligation - as, if the burnt-offering of the afternoon was consumed while it was still day, it would not be consumed at night - they, may their memory be Blessed, also said (Berakhot 27b) that the night prayer service is optional - if a man has free time and finds the presence in himself to pray, he prays; and if not, he does not pray, and there is no guilt in that. And nonetheless, in every place today, Israel is accustomed to pray the evening prayer service consistently every night. And once they took it upon themselves in the way of an obligation, every one of Israel is obligated to pray it regardless. And likewise, they, may their memory be Blessed, fixed a fourth payer on Shabbat days and holidays - and that is the one called the additional prayer service (mussaf). And it corresponds to the sacrifice that was added [on these occasions] in the Temple at the time that it was in existence. And they also fixed a fifth payer on Yom Kippur alone - due to the great holiness of the day and because of its being a day of forgiveness and atonement for all - and that is called the sealing (neilah). And the wording of all of the prayers was fixed by Ezra and his court. And on weekdays, they fixed that [we should] pray the eighteen blessings that are well-known in every corner of Israel, besides the blessing about the heretics that was composed by Shmuel the Little with the approval of Rabban Shimon ben Gamliel and his court, as it is found in Megillah 17b (and Berakhot 28b). And what are they? Three of them recount the praise of God, and three are thanks after it and twelve included the requests for the needs of all of Israel. And they, may their memory be Blessed, arranged them according to the order that they are ordered today in the mouths of all of Israel: the first three are in praise of God, may He be

Sefer HaChinukh

Blessed; the middle ones in request of their needs, and the last ones in thanks to God for all of the good that He does with us, Blessed be He. And afterwards their exact order was forgotten. But Shimon HaPakuli knew them and he arranged them according to the intended order, as Ezra and his court had ordered them: to first request intelligence, as if there is no intelligence, there is nothing; and afterwards, repentance, etc., as they are ordered. And on Shabbats and holidays, they only fixed that [we should] pray seven blessings alone, so as not to burden the community on the day of their joy: the first three, the last three and one blessing in the middle which mentions the matter of the day in it - each and every festival and Shabbat according to its content (Berakhot 21a). [This is the case] except for the holiday of Rosh Hashanah, which has nine blessings in its additional service: the three first blessings, the last three blessings and three others, which are malkhiot, zikhronot and shofarot. Everything is as the received tradition in the mouths of all of Israel, even in the mouths of the infants - there is no need to write at length about these matters. However you should know that in the additional prayer service of Rosh Hashanah there is a law that is a novelty from the other prayer services - that the prayer leader (cantor) can fulfill [the obligation of] the one with expertise [in the prayer, as well as] the one without expertise; whereas on other days, he cannot fulfill [the obligation] of the one with expertise. So, will you find the matter if you merit to study in the true path.

And also, from the content of the commandment is that which they warned us much about intent of the heart in prayer. And more [so] in the first blessing, about which they, may their memory be Blessed, said (Berakhot 30b) that we make one who did not have intent in it go back [and repeat it]. And the matter of intent that they obligated going back because of its [absence] appears to be that the person puts into his heart that he is praying in front of God and he is calling to Him, and [that] he empties his mind from all other thoughts of the world and focus it on this. And [also] that which they said (Mishneh Torah, Laws of Prayer and the Priestly Blessing 4:5) that there are things that impede a person from praying, even though the time for prayer has arrived. And among them are purity of the hands; covering the nakedness; purity of the place of prayer; and things that rush a person, such as if one needs [to use the restroom]. And [also] that which they said (Mishneh Torah, Laws of Prayer and the Priestly Blessing 5:5) that there are things about which the one praying must be careful, but we do not impede prayer on their account. And these are them: standing; to direct [himself] that he prays facing the Temple; that he fix his body, meaning to say that he stands with awe and fear - with his eyes down and his heart towards the Heavens and he place his hands on his heart, like a slave standing in front of his master; that he fix his clothing and not stand dressed in the way of commoners; that he make his voice even, not too loud and not too soft; and that he bow during the well-known blessings and these are them - during the fathers (the first blessing) at the beginning and at the end, and during thanksgiving (the penultimate blessing), at the beginning and at the end.

And these are the times of the prayers (Mishneh Torah, Laws of Prayer and the Priestly Blessing 3:1): The morning prayer service is from the sunrise to the end of the fourth hour - and one who transgressed and prayed afterwards before midday has [still] fulfilled his obligation of prayer, but not his obligation of prayer in its time - and one who prays at a pressing time, such as one who wants to get on the road early, can say his morning prayer after the dawn and he will have fulfilled his obligation; the afternoon prayer service is from six and a half hours during the day until the evening; and the evening prayer service is the whole night until the dawn rises. And every person must be careful to pray before he is involved with other tasks, so that he not be negligent.

And the law of one who errs and [misses] a prayer that he must pray the adjacent one twice; the law that one who prays should not interrupt for the sake of any man's honor - even if a king of Israel asks of his welfare, and even if a snake is wrapped on his ankle, he does not interrupt his prayer, [assuming] he knows with certainty that the snake is one that does not kill; [that] also from the content of the commandment is that which they said (Berakhot 8a) that every man is obligated in any case to seek to pray with the community, as the prayer of the community is heard more than the prayer of an individual; and the rest of the details of the commandment are [all] elucidated at length in Tractate Berakhot (see Tur, Orach Chaim 98).

And this commandment is practiced in all places and at all times by males and females. And one who transgresses it and [goes for] a day and a night without prayer at all has violated this commandment according to the opinion of Rambam, may his memory be Blessed. And one who is in difficulty and does not call to God to save him has violated this commandment, according to the opinion of Ramban, may his memory be Blessed. And his punishment is very great as he is like one removes the oversight of God from upon him.

Mitzvah 434
To cling to Torah sages: That we were commanded to associate [with] and cling to Torah sages, so that we learn its glorious commandments from them, and they teach us the true opinions - which are received through them - about it. And about this is it stated (Deuteronomy 10:20), "to Him shall you cling." And the command is repeated in another place, as it is stated (Deuteronomy 11:22), "and to cling to Him." And they, may their memory be Blessed, said (Ketuvot 111b), "And is it possible for a person to cling to the Divine Presence - and behold it is written (Deuteronomy 4:24), 'For the Lord, your God, is a consuming fire'? Rather, one who clings to the Torah scholars and their students is as if he clings to Him, Blessed be He." And from this, our Rabbis, may their memory be Blessed, learned that anyone who marries the daughter of a Torah scholar, or marries his daughter to a Torah scholar or who gives benefit from his property to a Torah scholar is as if he clings to the Divine presence. And they also expounded in Sifrei Devarim 49, "'And to cling to Him' - study the words of aggadah (the homiletical teachings, as through this, you will recognize the One who spoke and the world came into being."

The root of the commandment is revealed - so that we learn to know the ways of God, may He be Blessed.

I have already written some of the laws of the commandment (see Mishneh Torah, Laws of Human Dispositions 6).

And this commandment is practiced in every place and at all times by males. And it is also a commandment upon females to listen to the words of [Torah] sages, so that they will learn to know God. And one who transgresses it and does not associate with them and fix their love in his heart and strive for their good and their benefit at times when he has the ability in his hand to do so, has violated this positive commandment. And his punishment is very great, as they are [essential for] the existence of the Torah and a strong foundation for spiritual salvation; as anyone who is with them often will not sin quickly. And King Shlomo stated (Proverbs 13:20), "He who walks with the wise becomes wise." And our Rabbis, may their memory be Blessed, said (Avot 1:4), "Become dirty in the dust of their feet." And Ramban, may his memory be Blessed, wrote (in his glosses to the Sefer HaMitzvot, Mitzvot Ase 7) that the essence of this commandment is to swear in His name, Blessed be He, to fulfill a commandment. And the proof is from that which they said in Temurah 3b, "From where [do we know] that we swear to fulfill a commandment? As it is stated (Psalms 119:106), 'I have sworn to keep Your just statutes.'" And they answered there that it is derived from "to Him shall you cling," as it appears there.

Mitzvah 435
To swear in His name, may He be Blessed, truthfully: To swear in His name, Blessed be He, at the time that we need to strengthen or establish a thing or to distance it; as with this is there aggrandizement of His statute, may He be Blessed, and [of] the Power and the Loftiness. And about this is it stated (Deuteronomy 10:20) "and in His name shall you swear." And in the explanation, they, may their memory be Blessed, said (Shevuot 35b), "The Torah stated, 'Swear in His name,' and the Torah said, 'Do not swear in His name'" - meaning to say, [just] like an oath that is not needed [should] be prevented, and that is a negative commandment; so too is an oath at a time that it is needed an obligation, and that is a positive commandment. And therefore, we do not ever swear in [the name of] any thing of all the creatures. And they, may their memory be Blessed, said (Sanhedrin 63a), "Anyone who combines the name of [God] with something else is uprooted from the world." However, this is said about one who intends to swear in that thing of the creatures by itself; but one who swears in the heavens or in the sun or in the moon, with the intention of the Master above them that created them - that is not included in the prohibition at all. And we always see that we swear like

this in all of the borders of Israel.

It is from the roots of the commandment that in our establishing our words in His great name, the faith in Him and His supervision over us and over all our words are strengthened in our hearts. And that is a clear thing.

And I have written at great length about the laws of the commandment of oaths and vows in the Order of Vayishma Yitro (Sefer HaChinuch 30) (See Tur, Yoreh Deah 237).

And it is practiced in every place and at all times by males and females. And one who transgresses this and does not want to swear in His name at a time it is needed has violated this positive commandment, according to Rambam, may his memory be Blessed. But Ramban, may his memory be Blessed, wrote (on Mitzovt Ase 7; Ramban on Deuteronomy 6:13) that an oath in His name [even] at a time of need is not a positive commandment at all; that if we want, we swear, and if we do not want to ever swear, there is no [problem] with this. And there is also a commandment in the prevention from an oath, like the matter that they said in Midrash Tanchuma, Matot 1, "The Holy One, Blessed be He, said to them, 'Do not reason that it is permitted to you to swear in My name even truthfully unless there is all of these characteristics with you: "The Lord, your God, you shall fear, and to Him shall you cling." And afterwards, "and in His name shall you swear."'" And if we want, we can say that "and in His name shall you swear" comes to give a positive commandment [alongside the] negative commandment on the one who swears in the name of idolatry; meaning to say, in His name should he swear and not in the name of other gods. And the teacher (Ramban), may his memory be Blessed, already wrote about the matter that they, may their memory be Blessed, said (Temurah 3b) that we swear to perform a commandment, that we derive it from "to Him shall you cling."

Mitzvah 436

To destroy idolatry and its auxiliaries: That we were commanded to destroy all houses of idolatry with all types of destruction - with breaking, with burning, with demolition, with cutting - every type with what is fitting for it; meaning to say with what would be most destructive and quick in its destruction. And the intent is that we not leave a trace of idolatry. And about this is it stated (Deuteronomy 12:2), "You shall surely destroy all of the places, etc." And it is also stated (Deuteronomy 12:3), "But rather, etc. their altars shall you tear down." And it states further (Deuteronomy 12:3), "And you shall tear down their altar." And the proof that it is a positive commandment is that which it said in Sanhedrin 90a, "What is the positive commandment about idolatry" - meaning to say, to destroy it? "Rav Chasda [answered], '"And you shall tear down, etc."'" And the language of Sifrei Devarim 60 is "From where [do we know] that if one cuts down a tree-god and it grows back even ten times that a person is obligated to cut it down? [Hence], we learn to say, 'you shall surely destroy, etc.'" And it is also said there, "'And you will destroy their name from that place' - in the Land of Israel, you are commanded to pursue after them, but you are not commanded to pursue after them outside of the Land."

It is from the roots of the commandment to erase the name of idolatry and all of its remembrance from the world.

And its laws are included in the simple understanding of the verse.

And it is practiced by males and females in every place and at all times; as it is a commandment upon us to destroy the name of idolatry if the power is in our hands (see Mishneh Torah, Laws of Foreign Worship and Customs of the Nations 7:1). But we are not obligated to pursue after them, except in the Land of Israel at the time when our hands are domineering over its worshipers. And one who transgresses it and does not destroy it any time he has the ability in his hand, has violated this positive commandment.

Mitzvah 437

Not to destroy things upon which His name, may He be Blessed, are called: That we should not destroy and erase the things upon which the name of the Holy One, Blessed be He, are called, such as the Temple and holy books and His precious names, Blessed be He. And about all this is it stated (Deuteronomy 12:4), "Do not do this to the Lord, your God." After it was preceded by the commandment to destroy idolatry and to erase its name and to demolish all of its houses and altars, it prevented [it here] and stated, "Do not do this to the Lord, your God." And at the end of Tractate Makkot 22a, they, may their memory be Blessed, said "One who burns consecrated wood is lashed, and its warning is from 'and you shall destroy their name from that place[...] Do not do this, etc.'" And so too did they say there that one who erases the name [of God] is lashed, and its warning is from the very same verse.

The root of the commandment is revealed. As when people approach the holy with fear, with trembling and with perspiration - through that, they will bring into their hearts great fear and awe towards God, Blessed be He.

From the laws of the commandment is that which they, may their memory be Blessed, said (Shevuot 35a) that there are seven names in the prohibition of this negative commandment. And these are them: the name of yod, hay - vav, hay which the sages called the explicit name; and so [too] the name that is written alef, dalet, nun, yod and El, Eloha, Elohim, Shaddai and Tsevaot.

And they, may their memory be Blessed, also said (Shevuot 35a) that any letter that serves as a prefix before the name is permitted to erase, for example the lamed (to) from, "to God." But what serves as a suffix after the name - such as the khaf (your) of "your God" or the mem (your - plural) of "your God," and similar to them - are not erased, since the name [of God] consecrates them. And one who writes [only] El from the word Elohim [that he planned to write], or Yah from yod, hay - vav, hay cannot have it erased because these are names [of God] on their own. But one who writes shad from Shaddai or tsav from Tsevaot - behold, it can be erased. And the rest of the appellations that are used to praise God - for example, Merciful, Graceful, Great, Powerful, Awesome and similar to them - behold, they are like the rest of the holy writings (Biblical texts), which are permitted to erase for the sake of any thing. And [also] that which they, may their memory be Blessed, said (Shabbat 115a) that that which all holy writings (Biblical texts) and their commentaries are included in this prohibition, is from the words of the scribes (rabbinic) - that it is forbidden to destroy them or to burn them. And all of this that we have said is when it is written by a [proper] Israelite, but we burn - and it is a commandment to burn - everything that is written by an Israelite heretic, so as not to leave a name for (remembrance of) the heretics and all of their deeds, whereas we put away that which was written by a gentile (Mishneh Torah, Laws of Foundations of the Torah 6:8). And [also] that which they said (Shevuot 35b) that all of the names with Avraham in the matter of the angels that came to him are holy, and those stated with Lot are profane, except for "Behold now Your servant has found favor in Your eyes" (Genesis 19:19); all the names stated with the mountain of Binyamin (Judges 19-21) are holy, but from all those stated with Micah (Judges 17-18), some are profane and some are holy - el is profane, Yah is holy, except for one El which is holy, and that is "all the days that the house of God was in Shiloh" (Judges 18:31); all that are stated with Navot (I Kings 21) are holy; every Shomo that is stated in the Song of Songs is holy - and it is like the rest of the appellations - except for "a thousand to you, Shlomo" (Song of Songs 8:12); and all kings stated in Daniel are profane except for one, "You are the King, the King of the kings" (Daniel 2:37) - and behold it is like the other appellations. [These] and the rest of its details are found in Tractate Shevuot.

And this prohibition is forbidden in every place and at all times by males and females. And one who transgresses it and erases even one letter from the seven names that we mentioned is liable for lashes. But if he removed one letter from the letters that served as suffixes after them, he would [only] be lashed with lashes of rebellion. And so [too,] one who removes even one stone in a destructive way from the altar or from the chamber or from the rest of the [Temple] yard is liable for lashes.

Mitzvah 438

That one brings all of his vows on the first festival: That anyone who vows or promised any sacrifice to the altar or any thing to the [Temple] upkeep within the year, bring it on the festival that he encounters first after his vow, as it is stated (Deuteronomy 12:5-6), "and to there shall you go. And to there you are to bring your burnt-offerings and other sacrifices, etc. and your vows" - that is a vow, meaning to say, that he said, "Behold, a sacrifice is upon me," and he is always liable for its fulfillment until he sacrifices it - "and your promises" - that is a promise, such as that he said, "Behold, this is a burnt-offering," and if it is lost, he is not liable for its fulfillment. And they said in Sifrei Devarim 63, "'And to there shall you go. And to there shall you bring them' - to establish them as an obligation to bring them on the first festival." And such is the understanding of the verse: Immediately when you go there - which is the first festival - you shall bring the sacrifice.

It is from the roots of the commandment [that it is] because it is not fitting for a person to be lazy about that which he has vowed to do a commandment, as is well-known among people. As they are very careful [about this] in that which they have to do for the commandments of the kings of the earth; all the more so [should they be] with the commandment of the King, the King of kings, the Holy One, Blessed be He. And nonetheless, the Torah did not burden us to go up immediately, lest people will be prevented form [making] vows and promises. [Rather] it warned them to pay off their vows on the festival during which they have to go up there [in any case]. And with regards to transgressing, 'do not delay,' with them, it is not until three festivals - and as we will write with God's help in the Order of Ki Tetseh in the commandment of fulfilling what comes out of the lips (Sefer HaChinukh 574).

From the laws of the commandment is, for example, that which they, may their memory be Blessed, said in Sifrei Devarim 63 [that] "and to there shall you go. And to there shall you bring them" is only stated to fix them as an obligation, that they be brought on the first festival he encounters; and [that] there, they said [that] he does not transgress 'do not delay' until three festivals pass him by, but nonetheless once one holiday passes him and he does not bring it, he transgresses a positive commandment, and so did Rava say explicitly in the Gemara of Rosh Hashanah 6a. And the rest of its details - are elucidated there in Rosh Hashanah.

And this commandment is practiced at the time of the [Temple], as we had permission then to do vows and promises and there was a place for us to sacrifice [them]. But they, may their memory be Blessed, said (Avodah Zarah 13a) that at this time we do not consecrate (sacrifices), and like the matter that we wrote in the Order of Eem Bechukotai (Sefer HaChinukh 350). And even one who transgressed and consecrated [a sacrifice] does not have the ability in his hand today to bring it to the Temple, since the [Temple] is destroyed on account of our iniquities.

Mitzvah 439

Not to sacrifice a sacrifice outside of the [Temple] yard: Not to bring up anything of the sacrifices outside of the [Temple] yard, and this is called offering up outside. And about this is it stated (Deuteronomy 12:13), "Guard yourself, lest you offer up your burnt-offerings in every place" - the understanding of "offering up" is burning. And they said in Sifrei Devarim 70, "this tells me only of burnt-offerings. From where [do I derive the same for] other offerings? [Hence] we learn to say 'and there shall you do all that I command you' (Deuteronomy 12:14). But I still would say that burnt-offerings are [subject] to a positive commandment" - as Scripture states, "there shall you offer up [your burnt-offerings]," which implies only a burnt-offering - "and [also to] a negative commandment" - as Scripture states "Guard yourself, lest you offer up your burnt-offerings," which implies only a burnt-offering. "But other offerings are subject only to a positive commandment" - meaning to say, that one who sacrifices consecrated things outside would only transgress a positive commandment, as Scripture stated, "and there shall you do," and not outside; and a negative commandment that comes from the implication of a positive commandment is a positive commandment. "[From where do I know that they are also subject to a negative commandment? Hence] we learn to say 'there shall you offer up your burnt-offerings.' Burnt-offerings were included [in all of the offerings]. Why were they singled out? To [serve as the basis for] a comparison, and to say to you: Just as burnt-offerings [are characterized by being subject to] a positive commandment and a negative commandment - so [too,] all [offerings] that are [subject to] a positive commandment, behold they are [also subject to] a negative commandment." All of its content is like the negative commandment of slaughtering outside that I wrote in Achrei Mot (Sefer HaChinukh 186).

Mitzvah 440

The commandment to sacrifice all the sacrifices in the Choice House: That we were commanded to sacrifice all the sacrifices in the Temple and not outside of the Land. And about this is it stated

(Deuteronomy 12:14), "But only in the place that the Lord will choose, etc. there you shall offer up your burnt offerings and there shall you do all that I command you." And so is it [found] in Sifrei Devarim 70, "this tells me only of burnt-offerings. From where [do I derive the same for] other offerings? [Hence] we learn to say 'and there shall you do all, etc.' But I still would say that burnt-offerings are [subject] to a positive commandment and a negative commandment" - the explanation of the positive commandment is that which we have mentioned and [of] the negative commandment is from that which is stated in this section "Guard yourself, lest you offer up your burnt-offerings in every place that you see," which mentions "your burnt-offerings" explicitly. "But other offerings are subject only to a positive commandment. [From where do I know that they are also subject to a negative commandment? Hence] we learn to say 'there shall you do, etc.,'" as it appears there, and as it is written above in this Order adjacently (Sefer HaChinukh 439). And the general principle of the matter is that even with other consecrated things, one who sacrifices them outside violates a positive commandment and a negative commandment and is liable excision for it.

It is from the roots of the commandment that in there being a specific place in the world for sacrifices and it having constancy of [being the place] from where one seeks God, the place becomes sanctified, the will of God rests upon it and the emanation of His blessing always emanates upon it. And [so] the hearts of people will be afraid and softened to remember Him, and every man will repent from his evil way and from the violence that is in his palms when he sees it. And if all places were fitting for sacrificing, it would not be like this in all of them; and the thing is well-known. And this is said to the children until they grow in wisdom and understand the wondrous secrets in all the words of the Torah.

In the adjacent (negative) commandment 339, it is written that we have written some of the laws of the commandment in the Order of Achrei. [Those] and the rest of its details are in the end of Tractate Zevachim (see Mishneh Torah, Laws of Sacrificial Procedure 17).

And this commandment is practiced by males and females in every place and at all times. I mean to say that one who transgresses this even at this time and sacrifices a sacrifice outside of the Choice House violates this positive commandment and violates the negative commandment that comes on this, as is written earlier in this Order (Sefer HaChinukh 439). But my intent is not to say that there be an obligation to sacrifice a sacrifice in the Temple now, as it is destroyed. And this is something clear.

Mitzvah 441
To redeem consecrated things upon which a blemish developed: That we were commanded to redeem consecrated [animals] upon which a blemish developed and purchase another animal with their money for a sacrifice. And after the redemption, they go out to being non-sacred and the owners slaughter them and eat them like completely non-sacred [animals]. And about this is it stated, "But in all that your soul desires, you may slaughter and eat meat, etc. the impure and the pure may eat of it, like the gazelle and the deer." After the section mentioned the pure sacrifices and obligated us to sacrifice them "only in the place that the Lord will choose," it stated afterwards about the sacrifices themselves that if a blemish developed in them, that we redeem them and eat them 'in all that our souls desire'; meaning to say that we do with them any of our desires - like the gazelle and the deer, whose body is never holy. And so, the traditional explanation came about it that this verse is only speaking about disqualified consecrated [animals] that they be redeemed.

It is from the roots of the commandment that it was from the kindnesses of God to us to permit us to derive benefit from the sacrificial animals after they develop a blemish - and even though they were already separated to be consecrated and the power of the name of the Heavens rested upon them. God is righteous and does righteousness with His creatures and lightens the rod of His kingship and His loftiness from upon them, and [so] He is not exacting with them to say, "Do not touch the consecrated, since it was Mine even for a moment." And He magnified His kindness with us and obligated the thing with a positive commandment. As if He only left the matter as optional for us, it is possible that we would still be wary by way of piety from touching them. But since there is the fulfillment of a commandment in the thing, no concern remains in the matter. And for this reason, the verse elucidated with a lengthy elucidation, saying, "the impure and the pure may eat of it, like the gazelle and the deer" - meaning to say that no sanctity of the body ever rests on [these two animals], as to say, eat it without any concern at all.

From the laws of the commandment is that which they, may their memory be Blessed, said (Temurah 32a) that if the animal dies before it is redeemed, it is buried, like the law of unblemished consecrated [animals] that die; which is that they are buried, such that no man benefit from them. As redemption after death is impossible, since Scripture requires appraisal and evaluation - as I have written in the Order of Eem Bechukotai (Sefer HaChinukh 353). And if it gave birth before the redemption, we sacrifice the offspring which is unblemished. But if it became pregnant before it was redeemed and it gave birth after it was redeemed, the offspring is forbidden and not redeemed. So what does he do? Adjacent to the redemption of its mother, he invests its offspring with the title of the sacrifice with which its mother was consecrated; as it can not be sacrificed [directly] from the [status] of its mother, since that is a sacntity that has been waived because of its blemish.

And when all disqualified sanctified [animals] are redeemed, it is permissible to slaughter them in the marketplace of the butchers and to sell them and to weigh them by the pound like other non-sacred foods - except for a first-born and a tithe, as they are not slaughtered there. And the reason of the thing is because with other consecrated [animals] their value returns to being consecrated, as we go back and purchase with them a different animal for a sacrifice. And therefore, in order not to reduce their value, we sell them in any place. But with the first-born and the tithe that are eaten with their blemish and for which there is no need to buy a different animal with their value for a sacrifice, we do not slaughter and sell them in the market of butchers. And regarding the blemishes that disqualify a sacrifice, I have already spoken about them in the Order of Emor (Sefer HaChinukh 275). And [these] and rest of the details of the commandment are elucidated in Tracate Bekhhorot and in Temurah and in [some] places in Chllin, Arakhin and Meilah (see Mishneh Torah, Laws of Things Forbidden on the Altar 1).

And this commandment is practiced by males and females at the time of the [Temple]. But now at this time, they, may their memory be Blessed, said (Avodah Zarah 13a) that we do not consecrate [animals]. And the same is true that we do not redeem. And the whole matter is like I have written in the Order of Eem Bechukotai (Sefer HaChinukh 320) - take it from there. And even though I have written there that the consecration of one who consecrates [an animal], even at this time, holds and that there is a need for a correction to the matter, as I have written there - nonetheless regarding redemption, we certainly have to write that it is not practiced at this time from any angle, and like the matter that I wrote there about the law of the evaluations of animals (Sefer HaChinukh 353). You can see the matter from there.

Mitzvah 442

To not eat from the second tithe of grain outside of Jerusalem: To not eat the second tithe of grain outside of Jerusalem. And about this is it stated (Deuteronomy 12:17), "You may not eat in your gates the tithes of your grain." And the verse that comes after it instructs about it that it is referring to the second tithe, as it is stated, "But rather you must eat it before the Lord, your God[...] you and your sons and your daughters, and your slave and your maid-servant." And were it the other tithes, they are for the poor or for the Levites. And I have written regarding what the second tithe is above in this Order (Sefer HaChinukh 473). And I have written the reason for its being eaten in Jerusalem in the Order of Eem Bechukotai in the commandment of the animal tithe (Sefer HaChinukh 360).

From the laws of the commandment is that which they, may their memory be Blessed, said (Makkot 19b) that we are not liable lashes for its eating unless we eat it without redemption after it sees the face of the [Temple]. And so [too,] did they say at the end of Makkot 19b, "From when are we liable for it? From when it sees the face of the [Temple]" (see Sefer HaMitzvot LaRambam, Mitzvot Lo Taase 141). And I have already expanded about the laws of the fixing [of the obligation] of the tithe on fruits in the Order of Vayikach Korach (Sefer HaChinukh 395), and you can see it there if you would like. And the rest of the details of the commandment are elucidated in Tractate Maaser Sheni (see Mishneh Torah, Laws of Second Tithes and Fourth Year's Fruit 3:5).

And this prohibition is practiced by males and females at the time that the obligation of the second tithe is practiced. And in the Order of Shoftim, we will elucidate the time and the place that it is practiced (Sefer HaChinukh 507). And one who transgresses it and ate a kazayit of it outside of Jerusalem is liable for lashes.

Mitzvah 443

To not eat the second tithe of wine outside of Jerusalem: To not eat the second tithe of wine outside of Jerusalem, as it is stated (Deuteronomy 12:17), "You may not eat in your gates, etc. your wine." The entire content of the commandment of the prohibition of the wine is like the content of the commandment of the grain. There is no need to be long of speech about it.

Mitzvah 444

To not eat the second tithe of oil outside of Jerusalem: To not eat the second tithe of yitshar (the understanding is oil) outside of Jerusalem, as it stated (Deuteronomy 12:17), "You may not eat in your gates, etc. your oil." And the whole content of oil is like the content of grain and wine. And the measurement of eating oil to make one liable for it is a kazayit, according to what I heard from my teacher, God protect him. And even though it is a drink, it is held to be eaten by all people. And [even] if we know a few Yishmaelites that drink it, their opinion is nullified by all the rest of the people.

And do not think to say that this negative commandment of "You may not" is a general prohibition, as each and every matter is a negative commandment on its own. And so is it explained in Tractate Makkot (it should say Keritot 4b), "If he ate tithe of grain, wine and oil, he is liable for each and every one." And it challenges there, "And do we administer lashes for a general prohibition?" And it answers it, "The verse is superfluous. How is it? It is written (Deuteronomy 12:23), 'And you shall eat in front of the Lord, your God [...] the tithe of your grain, your wine and your oil.'" [This discussion continues in Makkot 18a:] "Let the [Torah] write, 'You may not eat them in your gates.' Why do I need the [Torah] to enumerate all of them here? [Hence] we understand from it [that it is] to designate for them a negative commandment for each and every one." And this verse of "And you shall eat" is at the end of this Order.

And in Sifrei Devarim 106, it is expounded that, that which this verse mentions "and the first-born of your cattle and your flocks," even though it is for the priests, is coming to compare the tithe to the first-born, etc.

Mitzvah 445

To not eat an unblemished first-born [animal] outside of Jerusalem: That a priest not eat an unblemished first-born [animal] outside of Jerusalem; and so too that a foreigner [non-priest] not eat from a first-born in any place, as the commandment with it is that the priests - the servants of God - should eat it, from the reason that I wrote in the Order of Bo el Pharoah (Sefer HaChinukh 18). And about all of this is it written (Deuteronomy 12:17), "You may not eat in your gates, etc. and the first-born of your cattle and your flocks." And the language of Sifrei Devarim 72 (see [also] Makkot 17a) is "'And the first-born' - this is the first-born. And the verse only comes for a foreigner that ate the first-born, whether before the sprinkling of the bloods or whether after the sprinkling, [to teach] that he transgresses a negative commandment." And the intent is not that the verse does not teach anything except this matter (see Sefer HaMitzvot LaRambam, Mitzvot Lo Taase 144), but rather it is saying that this is [also] included in this negative prohibition. And it comes out that included in it are two matters that we mentioned: prevention of the foreigner from eating an unblemished first-born in any place; and so too, prevention of the priest from eating it outside of Jerusalem. And both of the matters are predicated upon [it being] an unblemished first-born. And there in the Order of Bo el Pharoah, I wrote at what time and in what place the commandment of the first-born is practiced and the disagreement among my teachers - God protect them - about the matter of the first-born at this time. And there is no need to write at length about the reason for its being eaten in Jerusalem, as it is part of the consecrated foods - and as it is written in the Mishnah Zevachim 5:8, "The first-born, the tithe and the Pesach sacrifice offering are low-level consecrated foods (kedoshim kalim), etc." - and I have already lavished my words in several places (Sefer HaChinukh 360) about the reason [for] the eating of consecrated foods in the holy place and their being eaten by the servants of God.

From the laws of the commandment - who is the foreigner regarding the eating of the first-born, the blemishes that disqualify it, the time of its eating - it is all elucidated in Tractate Bekhorot. And a few of these laws are in other places in [the Order,] Kodashim (see Mishneh Torah, Laws of Firstlings 1). And a priest who transgresses it and eats a kazayit from an unblemished first-born outside of Jerusalem, and so [too,] an Israelite in any place, is liable for lashes.

Mitzvah 446
To not eat higher-level consecrated foods: (kodshai kodashim) outside of the [Temple] yard: To not eat - and even priests - from the meat of the sin-offering, and the guilt-offering outside of the 'curtains.' And the masters of the tradition explained that this prohibition is included in "You may not eat in your gates, etc. your cattle and your flocks" (Deuteronomy 12:17). As so did they, may their memory be Blessed, say (Makkot 17a), "The verse only comes with regard to one who eats a sin-offering or a guilt-offering [...] outside the curtains, [to teach that he is transgressing a negative commandment]." And so too, one who eats lower-level consecrated foods (kodashim kalim) outside of the wall [of Jerusalem] is included in this prohibition, like the Gemara comes to teach. As they said there that anyone who eats something outside the place of its eating is [considered], "You may not eat in your gates." And their intention, may their memory be Blessed, in saying, "The verse only comes," is to say that this is also included.

It is from the roots of the commandment to eat every sacrifice in its place so that its eaters will focus their hearts on the atonement for which they are eating. And it is like the matter that they, may their memory be Blessed, said (Pesachim 59b), "The priests eat, and the owners are atoned." And if they ate them in other places, their focus would be dissipated from the matter. This thing is well-known and clear.

The laws of the commandment are in Zevachim (see Mishneh Torah, Laws of Sacrificial Procedure 11).

And this prohibition is practiced in every place and at all times. As even one who consecrated a sin-offering or a guilt-offering today and transgressed and ate a kazayit from them - even the priests - is liable for lashes from this negative commandment, besides the prohibition that [exists] in deriving benefit from the consecrated (see Kiddushin 57b).

Mitzvah 447
To not eat meat of a burnt-offering: To not eat anything of the meat of a burnt-offering, as it is stated (Deuteronomy 12:17), "You may not eat in your gates, etc. your vows that you vow." And the understanding of the verse is as if it stated, "You may not eat any vows that you vow." And our Rabbis, the masters of the tradition, said (Makkot 17a), "'Your vows' - this is the burnt-offering [...] the verse only comes [to teach you] with regard to one who eats the meat of a burnt-offering [whether it is before the sprinkling of the bloods or] after the sprinkling [of the bloods, whether it is] inside the [courtyard or outside the courtyard], that he is [transgressing a negative commandment]. And they, may their memory be Blessed, also said (Sefer HaMitzvot LaRambam, Mitzvot Lo Taase 146) that this negative commandment is a warning for all that misappropriate sanctified foods. I have written in the Order of Vayikach Li Trumah (Sefer HaChinukh 95) that which I know from the angle of the simple understanding about the matter of sacrifices and the benefit that comes out for us in our burning animals in the Great House. And the warning about them that we not eat from them, but rather that all of it be burnt follows from the same reason - it is one connection [that connects them both]. And this warning is specified with the burnt-offering because its commandment is that it be [completely] consumed, but included in this warning is all that misappropriate consecrated foods, as I have written.

And the laws of the commandment are in Tractate Meilah and in [various] places in the Order, Kodashim (see Mishneh Torah, Laws of Sacrificial Procedure 11).

And this prohibition is practiced in every place and at all times by males and females; as even one who consecrated his animal as a burnt-offering today is forbidden to eat anything from it. And one who transgresses it and eats from the meat of a burnt-offering - and so [too,] one who eats from the other consecrated foods as well - has misappropriated and is liable for lashes if volitional, when there are witnesses and a warning, as is well-know in every place. But if he was inadvertent, he must bring a misappropriation (meilah) sacrifice and give back what he misappropriated with the addition of a fifth, as is elucidated in Tractate Meilah. And in the ninth chapter of Sanhedrin 83a, they, may their memory be Blessed, said, "One who is volitional about misappropriation: Rebbi says, '[The punishment is] death.' And the sages say, 'With a warning (a negative commandment).'" And there is also what to consider [to say] that this prohibition and all that is similar to it is only practiced at the time of the [Temple].

Mitzvah 448
To not eat lower-level consecrated foods (kodashim kalim) before the sprinkling of the bloods:
To not eat anything from the lower-level consecrated foods before the sprinkling of the bloods. And lower-level consecrated foods are like the thanksgiving offering and the peace-offerings and that which is similar to them, from those that are enumerated in the fifth chapter of Tractate Zevachim 48. And about this is it stated (Deuteronomy 12:17), "You may not eat in your gates, etc. and your promises" - the understanding of which is as if it stated, "You may not eat your promises." And the masters of the tradition, may their memory be Blessed, said (Makkot 17a), "The verse only comes with regard to one who eats a thanksgiving offering or a peace-offering before the sprinkling of the bloods, [to teach] that he is [transgressing a negative commandment]."
It is from the roots of this commandment [that it is] to place into our hearts that it is always fitting for us to to have benefit to our souls precede benefit to our bodies with everything in the world. Therefore, it is not fitting that the body benefit from eating before the sprinkling of the bloods that comes for the atonement of the soul.
The laws of this commandment are also elucidated in Meilah and in [various] places in the Order, Kodashim (see Mishneh Torah, Laws of Sacrificial Procedure 11).
And this prohibition is practiced in every place and at all times by males and females; as even one who consecrated his animal as lower-level consecrated foods today, and transgressed and ate a kazayit from it afterwards, is liable for lashes.

Mitzvah 449
That the priest not eat the first-fruits (bikkurim) before their placement in the [Temple] yard:
That we were prevented (see Sefer HaMitzvot LaRambam, Mitzvot Lo Taase 149) from eating the first fruits. And about this was it stated (Deuteronomy 12:17), "You may not eat, etc. and the contribution of your hand." And the masters of the tradition explained it (Makkot 17a), "'The contribution (terumat) of your hand' - these are the first-fruits." And it is elucidated at the end of Tractate Makkot 17a, that we are only liable before they were placed in the [Temple] yard. But from when they were placed in the yard, a person is exempt [from punishment] for them. And the language of Sifrei Devarim 72:9 is "The verse only comes [...] with regard to one who eats the first-fruit but did not recite [the recital] over them, [to teach] that he is transgressing a negative commandment." And the understanding of, "because he did not recite over them," is because they were not placed in the yard; but if they were placed there, there is no liability for lashes, even if he did not recite over them. And so too (Makkot 17a; Sifrei Devarim 72:9) there is with them the condition that there is for the second tithe with regards to the liability for lashes, that we are not liable until they see the face of the [Temple] first, and afterwards he eats them before their placement in the yard. In this way is there a liability for lashes for the priest that eats from them. And an Israelite is liable for death by the hand of the Heavens any time he eats from them, even after he recited the famous recital over them. And [that recital] is explicit in the Order of Vehaya Ki Tavo. And they, may their memory be Blessed, said (Mishnah Bikkurim 2:1), "The priestly tithe (terumah) and the first-fruits are liable for [the addition of] a fifth when inadvertent, and death when volitional." And this is exactly like the law of the priestly tithe - because the verse called the first-fruits with the [same] name, terumah, they became

obligated with the laws of the priestly tithe.

And understand, my son, the difference that there is between an Israelite and a priest and remember it. As when a priest eats the first-fruits from when [the fruits] see the face of the [Temple] before they are placed in the yard, he is lashed; and its warning is from "You may not, etc." And do not wonder to say, how can the priest be liable for lashes for them, since he, himself, will eat them after they are placed in the yard. As behold, the same thing is done with the law of the second tithe, that an Israelite is liable for lashes when he eats it outside of Jerusalem, even though he, himself, eats it in the place that is fitting for it. And an Israelite that eats first-fruits is liable for death by the hand of the Heavens any time he eats them; and its warning is from "And any foreigner shall not eat the holy" (Leviticus 22:10), and as I wrote in the Order of Emor el Hakohanim in the commandment that no [non-priest] eat priestly tithe (Sefer HaChinukh 280).

I have written what I have known about the thing from the roots of the matter of the bringing of the first-fruits to the Temple that the servants of God should eat them in the section of Kessef Talveh [in] the Order of Mishpatim (Sefer HaChinukh 91). And the reason for this commandment that the priests not eat them before they are placed in the yard and that Israelites should not eat from them in any manner is drawn from the same root that is written there. Anyone who has intelligence to know the difference between good and evil will find it elucidated and revealed; 'and much contemplation' when there is no need 'is a tiring of the flesh.'

And the laws of the commandment are elucidated in Tractate Makkot.

And this prohibition is practiced by males and females, but only at the time of the Temple (Mishneh Torah, Laws of First Fruits and other Gifts to Priests Outside the Sanctuary 2:5) - since the obligation to bring first-fruits is then. And the liability from Torah writ is specifically with the well-known fruits and the well-known places, as I have written in Kessef Talveh. And even though we said there that the obligation of the commandment of the bringing of first-fruits is only upon the males and not upon the females, a man and a woman are the same with the prohibition of eating them in every place. And [it is] like the matter that they, may their memory be Blessed, said in the Gemara (Bava Kamma 15a) more generally on the verse, "A man or woman, when they they do from all the sins of man" (Numbers 5:6), [that] "The verse made equal a woman to a man for all of the punishments of the Torah." And a priest that ate a kazayit from the first-fruits in the way that we said has violated a negative commandment and is liable for lashes. And so [too,] is an Israelite [violating a negative commandment if he] eats a kazayit from them in any way - meaning whether before they are placed in the yard or afterwards.

Mitzvah 450

To not forsake the Levite, from giving him his gifts: That we have been warned from forsaking the Levites and not to be negligent from filling their portion - meaning to say to not delay their tithes - and all the more so on festivals, as we are warned about them even more, in order to gladden them at the appointed time. And about this is it stated (Deuteronomy 12:19), "Be careful for yourself, lest you forsake the Levite, all of your days upon your land."

It is from the roots of the commandment [that it is] because God, Blessed be He, wanted the good of His people, Israel, that He chose as a people and wanted to give them merit and to make them a paragon in His world - a wise and understanding people - in order that all who see them would recognize them as the seed of the Blessed of God, men of truth and men of repute. And in that this was His will, may He be Blessed, Blessed be He, He brought counsels from afar to cause ways for their occupation to be in wisdom and [that] they would be pouring over it always every day. And [so] He steered them and arranged proper and pleasant customs and dear and strong mores, in order that they 'learn to know God - from their small ones to their great ones' - and their seed would stand and their name would be preserved forever. And from the statutes that strengthened and supported the wisdom among them was for there to be one entire tribe among them without a portion and inheritance in the lands, and that it not go out to the field to plow and to seed and to dig wells [from which] to water. And all of this was to be a cause for it to spend its time, no matter what, to study the wisdoms and to understand the straight ways of God, and they would teach its judgments to their brothers in each and every country and in all of the cities. And therefore, in that this tribe is selected - it and its seed - forever for the occupation of wisdom and understanding, and that all of Israel will [therefore] need to seek Torah from their mouths, agree with their opinions and follow their counsel in everything that they teach them; it was from His will that their brothers provide them all of their sustenance, lest their wisdom get swallowed up, due to the lack of their portion. And from this foundation, the double warning came to all of Israel in this verse with "Be careful" and "lest," that they not forsake and not be negligent at all in all of their matters. And it mentioned about them a warning of the land, as it stated, "all of your days upon your land"; to say, be very careful with them, as your inheritance is the land, but God - who is the One that makes its seeds grow - is its inheritance. [This] means to say, do not think to be proud in front of it because of your inheritance of the land, as it is the master. Or we can say that the mention of the land is to say that he needs you regardless, as you are the master of the inheritance and everyone needs it. As anyone who does not have land - even if he has many monies - requires mercy, since everything is from the land, and there is nothing as solid for a man, that his heart can rely upon it, like it. And the landowners are those that raise choice calves and stuffed geese, they have fattened chickens, doves of the cote, goats and sheep. And in the way that the workers of the land bring of all these things on the holidays to kings of the land and its ministers, so were the Children of Israel warned to do for the Levites. And several warnings were repeated about it in Scripture in several places where it states, "Do not forsake the Levite that is in your gates." And the intent of the matter of its stating, "that is in your gates," is not that he should go to the doors [of people to beg], God forbid. Rather, it is to say that he does not have the inheritance of lands like [the rest of] Israel.

The laws of the commandment are elucidated in Scripture.

And this commandment is practiced when Israel is on their land. And one who transgresses this and forsakes gladdening the Levite and delays his tithes on the festivals has violated this negative commandment. But there are no lashes for it, as there is no act [involved] with it. And anyone with understanding will be able to learn from this commandment to aid and do good to all who are constantly striving for the wisdom of the Torah. As they are the ones that support the true religion, strengthen faith, increase peace in the world, love the creatures, and are joyful with the ordering of the state. All who need grace, 'let him see his face with justice' (tsedek, playing on the word tsedekah, charity); as he has no free time to walk in the streets this way and that for his sustenance. Hence one who has mercy on them and seeks their benefit will receive mercy from the Heavens; and he will eat with them, portion for portion, in the world to come.

Mitzvah 451

The commandment of slaughter: That anyone who wants to eat ([domesticated] beast, [wild] animal or bird) meat first slaughter them as is fit, and that there not be [another way to] permit [it] besides slaughter. And about this is it stated (Deuteronomy 12:21), "you may slaughter from your your cattle or your flock [...], as I have commanded you, etc." And the language of Sifrei Devarim 75:7,16 is, "Just like consecrated [animals] are with slaughter, so too are the non-sacred [animals] with slaughter. [...] 'As I have commanded you' teaches us that Moshe, our teacher, was commanded as to the esophagus and the trachea and as to the [cutting of] the majority of one in a bird and the majority of two, in a beast." The understanding is not that it be such from the understanding of the verse, but rather that upon this commandment came the tradition that it was like this that he was commanded about all the matters of slaughter - as is known to us about the knife, the place of the slaughter [on the animal] on the esophagus and the windpipe and the rest of the matters.

And even though the verse only mentions cattle and flocks, we have known that [wild] animals are included in [domesticated] beasts, since Scripture compares them, as it is written about [domesticated] beasts] disqualified from [having been] consecrated (Deuteronomy 12:22), "But as you eat the gazelle and the deer, so shall you eat it" (Chullin 27b). And birds also require slaughter (Chullin 27b), since it is compared to a beast, as it is written (Leviticus 11:46), "This is the law of the beast and the bird." Yet the sages [further] made an exacting inference, and the tradition supports them, that since Scripture places the bird between the beast that requires slaughter and the fish which has no slaughter

Sefer HaChinukh

- as it is written, "This is the law of the beast and the bird and any living soul that moves in the waters" - it is enough for you with one benchmark (siman, either the esophagus or the windpipe). And from where did they learn to say that there is no slaughter with fish? As it is written about them (Numbers 11:22), "if all of the fish of the sea were collected for them" - just with collection, whether they are collected alive or even dead. And so [too,] all species of locusts do not have slaughter (Keritot 21b), as the expression, collection, is written about them as well - as it is written (Isaiah 33:4), "the collection of the locusts." And also, the verse (Leviticus 11:46) mentions them after the fish at the end of the Order of Bayom Hashmini, as it is stated, "This is the law of the beast and the bird and any living soul that moves in the waters" - these are the fish - "and of any soul that swarms upon the earth" - these are the locusts. And also, because they have scales on their bodies like fish.

I have already written at the end of the Order of Tsav about the prohibition of blood (Sefer HaChinukh 148) and at the beginning of Achrei Mot [about] the commandment of covering the blood (Sefer HaChinukh 187) all that I have known about the matter of distancing that the Torah distanced us from the blood of all flesh. And I say from the angle of the simple understanding that the commandment of slaughter is also from the same reason. Since it is well-known that the body's blood comes out of the neck more than from other places of the body, hence we were commanded to slaughter from there before we eat it. As [in this way] all of its blood will come out from there, and we will 'not eat the soul with the flesh.' And we can also say as a reason for slaughter from the neck with a checked knife, [that it is] in order that we not cause too much pain to living beings. As the Torah [only] permitted man - due to his status - to derive nourishment from them for all of his needs, but not to cause them pain for no reason. And the Sages have already spoken much about the prohibition of pain to living beings in Bava Metzia 32a and in Shabbat 128b, [as to] whether it is a Torah prohibition. And it appears to come out that it is a Torah prohibition (See Mishneh Torah, Laws of Murderer and the Preservation of Life 13:13).

From the laws of the commandment are that which they, may their memory be Blessed, said (Chullin 9a) that five things spoil the slaughter, if one of them happened during the slaughter. And these are them: pausing; pressing; submerging; sliding; and tearing. The content of pausing is, for example, that he began to slaughter the esophagus, and before he slaughtered its majority, he interrupted [the] slaughtering. If he paused with this interruption the measure of enough [time] for another slaughter, his slaughter is disqualified. The understanding of another slaughter is the [time needed to] slaughter the skin and the benchmarks of another beast like it, and like that of small beast (lamb) for a chicken. And there are those that are stringent, that the measure is only enough for the slaughter of the majority of the [two] benchmarks with a beast, and the majority of one benchmark with a bird. But if he slaughters with a bad (meaning dull) knife, even if he goes back and forth the whole day, his slaughter is fit - except if he brings it back and forth after he slaughtered the majority of only one benchmark in a beast; as if he brings a bad knife back and forth on the minority that remains of it like the measure of pausing, his slaughter is disqualified.

The matter of pressing is one who presses the knife, like one who cuts a radish, at the time of the slaughter - meaning to say that he does not bring the knife back and forth - in this manner, the slaughter is disqualified (Mishneh Torah, Ritual Slaughter 3:11)

The matter of submerging that we have received in the tradition is that the knife must stay revealed at the time that we slaughter. And because of this, they, may their memory be Blessed, said (Chullin 30b) that if one covers the knife under one benchmark and slaughtered the second, or even if he covered it under the skin and slaughtered the benchmarks, or even [if he did so] under the tangled wool or even under a cloth (Mishneh Torah, Laws of Ritual Slaughter 3:9, 10) that is very stuck to the neck, the slaughter is disqualified. But it if is not very stuck, it is not disqualified by [a cloth].

The matter of sliding is that which we received that even though the slaughter is from the neck, there are well-known boundaries upon the neck within which the slaughter is fit, but not below [the lower] boundary and not above [the higher one]. And the boundary of the place of slaughter on the windpipe is from the slant of the Adam's apple and below (Chullin 19a) to the top of the small protrusions of the lungs - not until the bottom of the protrusions that are connected to the lungs, but rather their tops. And this measurement is the entire part of the neck that the beast stretches out at the time that it grazes naturally without duress. And on the esophagus (Chullin 44a), one leaves the grasp of a hand above. And below, the measurement is until the esophagus gets 'hairy' - meaning to say that many perforations are found there, in the likeness of the stomach. And some (see Rashi and Tosafot on Chullin 44a) say that the understanding of the grasp of a hand is enough for three fingers, and some say [it is] enough that one grabs it with two fingers from the two sides of the neck, and that is the measurement of the width of one finger. And that measurement is with a [domesticated] beast and a [wild] animal, but with a bird, everything is according to its largeness or smallness. And they said in the Gemara (Chullin 19a) that [in the case of] one who began the slaughter of the windpipe and slaughtered a third, and afterwards moved the knife from the place of slaughtering - meaning above the slant of the Adam's apple - and cut a third, and after that brought the knife back to the place of slaughtering and slaughtered a third, the slaughter is disqualified. As we always need in this law of sliding that the majority of the death of the beast be with slaughter and that at the time of the leaving of life from it - meaning the middle third - that then, the majority is with [proper] slaughter. Anything that is like that is fit; [but if was done] in another matter, it is disqualified. And this [particular] matter of sliding is only found with the windpipe and above adjacent to the slant of the Adam's apple. As below, adjacent to the protrusions of the lungs, its [disqualifying] piercing is with the smallest amount, and the law of sliding one third is not relevant to it at all. And so too, with the esophagus - whether above or whether below - its piercing is with the smallest amount, and the law of sliding one third is not relevant to it at all.

Anyone who is not an expert in these four things that disqualify the slaughter is not permitted to slaughter (Mishneh Torah, Laws of Ritual Slaughter 4:1). And if he did slaughter, it is forbidden to eat from his slaughter. And even if after he slaughtered, they asked him if he was careful about them and he said, "Yes, yes," there is no substance to his words - as since he did not know them at first, maybe he was negligent about them and it is not remembered [by him] at all.

And besides these four things that we mentioned that every slaughterer needs to know, the sages obligated us to know a fifth thing - and even though it is not from the laws of slaughtering [per se] - since this matter always comes up at the time of slaughter, and the beast is made into a carcass with the thing. And if the slaughterer does not know it, he will be feeding carcasses to everyone. And therefore they also said about this [that] it is forbidden to eat from the slaughter of any butcher that does not know it. And this is the prohibition that is called tearing. And its matter is that the windpipe and the esophagus - both of them or even one of them - is torn from the place of their connection with the jawbone and the flesh upon it. And [it is] when they are torn from there completely, or even it they are not torn completely, but rather their majority dangles - [then,] behold it is forbidden. And that is when it is fully detached (Chullin 44a) - meaning to say [that] when we forbid it when its majority is dangling, it is to say that all of it is in this manner, that the dangling is from this [side] and that [side]. As [with] anything that is [detached] in this manner, even that [part of it] which is connected is not connected well, and so, they are considered completely torn. But if the benchmarks were dangling from one side - meaning to say it was detached and torn from the jawbone only in one place - even though the majority was torn - since the tear is only in one place, the minority is connected with a lasting connection [and] that minority saves [it] and it is fit; even though [the tear] is in the majority of the benchmark and there is only [a minority] remaining. And all the more so do we render it fit when the whole benchmark is connected to the flesh on the jawbone, even though the jaw is cut and completely taken out from the place of its connection in the head - the connection of the flesh with the benchmark saves [it]. And it comes out that tearing forbids when the benchmarks are torn in many places, this way and that, in the majority. But in any case, [if it is only] in one place, the prohibition of tearing does not [apply]. And this tearing that we said does not make a beast into a 'torn' (terminally ill) animal. Rather, so have we learned from the tradition, that torn benchmarks cannot be slaughtered - meaning to say that the commandment of slaughter would not be [fulfilled] with torn benchmarks. And hence one who slaughters torn benchmarks - behold, it is as if he did not slaughter, and as if the beast died on its own, such that it is a carcass. And even though they made a bird fit with [only] one benchmark - as we said - so long as one is torn before he slaughtered the other, the slaughter does not permit it and it is forbidden. So have we learned from the tradition? Every one

Sefer HaChinukh

of Israel must know the five laws that we mentioned - pausing; pressing; submerging; sliding; and tearing - to be an expert in them, before he slaughters. And it is forbidden to eat from the slaughter of anyone who is not an expert in them and slaughtered [regardless]. And even if we ask him afterwards and he says, "I am sure that I slaughtered properly," we do not listen to him at all.

And one who wants to slaughter also needs to know the matter of checking the knife - that the Sages required him to check with the fingernail and with the flesh in a knife's three [relevant] directions (Mishneh Torah, Laws of Ritual Slaughter 1:23). And if we feel a nick in it - even the smallest amount - the slaughter [done with such a knife] is forbidden. And it is permitted to slaughter with anything that cuts well that does not have a nick in it at all. And if the knife is found to be nicked after the slaughter, we say that it got nicked with the skin and that the benchmarks were slaughtered with a nicked knife. And we say this when bones were not cut with the same knife after the slaughter - meaning to say that the knife did not touch anything from which it is possible for it to be nicked. But if we know with certainty that something from which it is possible for it to be nicked touched the knife after the slaughter, we assume the nick is from that thing. And anytime we are in doubt if it touched something that [could] nick it or not, we assume it is from the skin. This is what appears [to come out] nicely from the disagreement between Rav Huna and Rav Chasda in this matter at the beginning of the first chapter of Chullin 10a. And [also] the law of that which they, may their memory be Blessed, said (Chullin 3b) that we assume anyone who is found proximate to [the involvement with] slaughter to be an expert. And even if he is in front of us, we do not have to test him, as we rely on the assumption. And there are some commentators that said that if they are in front of us, we do test them. And the rest of the details of the commandment are elucidated in Tractate Chullin in the first two chapters (see Tur Yoreh Deah 1-28).

And this commandment is practiced in every place and at all times by males and females, as even females are warned not to eat from a [domesticated] beast, a [wild] animal or a bird without proper slaughter. And [women] have permission to slaughter - and their slaughter is fit for any person - if they know the laws of slaughter and are expert in them. And the Sages said (Chullin 2a) that even the slaughter of minors is fit, so long as an adult who is an expert in the laws of slaughter sees them slaughter properly. Yet the Sages warned us (Chullin 12a) not to give them to slaughter at the outset, since they commonly blunder, due to their limited intellect, and a loss will be found in the matter.

And one who transgresses this and is not careful about eating the meat of a [domesticated] beast, a [wild] animal or a bird that has one of the five disqualifications that we mentioned happen to them or that was slaughtered with a knife that was not checked has violated this positive commandment, besides having violated the negative commandment of "You shall not eat any carcass," [for which] he is lashed for eating a kazayit of them - as we shall write in this Order, with God's help (Sefer HaChinukh 572). And they, may their memory be Blessed, also said in the second chapter of Chullin 32a, "Everything that is disqualified by its slaughter is a carcass"; meaning to say, any time that the beast is disqualified in the place [on its body] of slaughter - which are the benchmarks - such as if one of the five disqualifications that we mentioned happened to it, or if he slaughtered it with a knife that was not checked, behold, that is called a carcass. "And anything, the slaughter of which was proper and something else caused it to be disqualified, is called 'torn'"; meaning to say, if none of the disqualifications occurred regarding the slaughter, the checking of the knife or the benchmarks, but rather something else caused it to become disqualified - such as it becoming 'torn' with one of the eighteen well-known [ways of being] 'torn,' that I mentioned earlier (Sefer HaChinukh 73) - behold, that is called, 'torn,' which is to say that he gets lashes on account of a 'torn' animal. And even though there are lashes for both of them, the difference to us that comes of it is regarding the warning. And the matter of that which we learned, that everything that is disqualified by its slaughter is a carcass, is not that the main carcass that is mentioned in Scripture should be that which is made into a carcass by its slaughter. As it is certainly an animal that died on its own due to a sickness or with some matter [that causes it to die] that is called an undifferentiated carcass. Rather the author of the Mishnah is coming to teach that anything that is not slaughtered properly is considered like it died on its own.

Sefer HaChinukh

Mitzvah 452
To not eat a limb from the living: That we were prevented that we not eat a limb from the living - meaning to say, a limb that we cut from an animal when it is still alive. And about this is it stated (Deuteronomy 12:23), "and you shall not eat the soul with the meat." And so, they did they say, "'And you shall not eat the soul with the meat' - that is a limb from the living." And we say in Tractate Chullin 102b, "One who ate a limb from the living and meat from the living is lashed twice" - since there are two negative commandments about it: the one which we mentioned; and the second [is] "and flesh torn in the field shall you not eat" (Exodus 22:30), which is a negative commandment about the one that eats meat from the living, as I have written in the commandment not to eat a 'torn' animal (Sefer HaChinukh 73). And the warning for the limb from the living was repeated in another place in Parshat Noach, as it is stated (Genesis 9:4), "But meat with the soul, its blood, you shall not eat."

It is from the roots of the commandment [that it is] in order that we not train ourselves in the trait of cruelty, which is a most disgusting trait. And in truth, there is no greater cruelty in the world then the one who cuts a limb or meat from an animal while it is still alive in front of him and eats it. And I have already written many times [about] the great benefit that comes to us in our acquisition of the good traits and [when] we distance ourselves from the bad traits, as the good will cling to the good. And the good God wants to do good, and hence He commanded us to choose the good. And this is my approach to most of the commandments, according to the angle of their simple understanding.

From the laws of the commandment is that which they, may their memory be Blessed, said (Chullin 101b) that the prohibition of the limb from the living is [applicable to] a [domesticated] beast, a [wild] animal and a bird that are pure, but not to impure ones. And [also] that which they said (Mishneh Torah, Laws of Forbidden Foods 5:3, 4) that the prohibition is one; whether it is a limb that has meat, tendons and bones - such as a hand or a foot - or a limb that has no bone - like the tongue, the testicles, the spleen, the kidneys, the heart and similar to them. However, the limb that has no bone is forbidden because of a limb from the living, whether it is all cut off, or whether part of it is cut off. But a limb that has a bone is not liable on account of a limb from a living animal, until it is separated like its formation - meat, tendons and bones. But if he separated meat from the living, he is liable for a 'torn' animal, as we elucidated, and not on account of a limb from the living. One who eats a kazayit from a limb from the living is lashed for it. And even if he ate a complete limb, [only] if there is a kazayit in it is he liable. [But if there is] less than a kazayit, he is exempted. If he cut a kazayit from the limb according to its formation - meat, tendons and bones - and he ate it, he is lashed, even though there is only the smallest amount of meat upon it. However, if he divided the limb after he detached it and separated the meat from the tendons and from the bones, he is only lashed if there is a kazayit from the meat by itself - and the bones and the tendons do not join with it [to make up] a kazayit, since he has changed it from its formation.

If he divided this limb and ate it a little at a time, if there is a kazayit in what he ate, he is liable; and, if not, he is exempted (Mishneh Torah, Laws of Forbidden Foods 5:4). If he took a kazayit from the limb according to its formation - meat, tendons and bones - and he ate it, he is liable, even though it divided in his mouth before he swallowed it, as that is the way of eating. If he detached the limb from the living and [the animal] became 'torn' in his taking it, and he ate it, he is liable on two [counts], because of a limb from the living and because of a 'torn' animal - as behold, both prohibitions come together (at the same time). And so [too,] one who detached forbidden fat (chelev) from the living and ate it, is liable for two. If he detached forbidden fat from a 'torn' animal, he is lashed [for] three [separate sins]. Flesh that is dangling [from] a beast and a limb dangling [from] it is forbidden if it cannot come back to life - even though it did not separate, but rather was [connected to the animal when it was] slaughtered. But we do not administer lashes for it. And if the beast died, we see it as if it fell while [it was] alive. Therefore, we administer lashes on account of a limb from the living. However, if it could come back to life - behold, it is permitted, if the beast is slaughtered. If the limb from the living was dislocated or one crushed it or ground it - such as if one crushed the testicles or severed them - behold, it is not forbidden from Torah writ; as behold, it has a little life. And therefore it does not stench. But nonetheless it is forbidden to eat it due to the custom practiced by Israel from antiquity; as behold, it is similar to life from the living. If the flesh covers most of a broken bone and most of the circumference of the break, behold it is permissible. But if the bone came outside, behold it is forbidden; and when the beast or bird is slaughtered, he should cut off the limb and a bit from the place of the break and throw it out - and the rest is permitted. If the bone was broken, [even when] the flesh covers most of it - if that flesh was pulverized since it decayed, like the flesh that a physician would scrape off; the flesh that was on it was [full of] holes; the flesh was cracked, or it was scraped like a type of ring; the flesh on top was scraped to the point where only like a peel remained on the flesh; or the flesh was decayed below from all of the bone to the point that the flesh that covers the bone is not touching the bone - in all of these [cases], we instruct to forbid until the flesh is healed. And if he ate from any of these, we administer lashes of rebellion upon him. One who extends his hand into the innards of the beast, cuts off from the spleen, from the kidneys and similar to them, and left the pieces in its innards, and [then] slaughtered it afterwards - behold those pieces are forbidden on account of the limb from the living, even though it is within its innards. But if he cut off from the embryo in its innards and did not remove it and slaughtered it afterwards - behold the pieces of the embryo are permitted, since it did not go outside.

And this prohibition is practiced in every place and at all times by males and females. And one who transgresses it and ate a limb from the living or a kazayit of it in the manner that we mentioned is liable for lashes. And this is one of the seven commandments that are upon all people of the world more generally. But there is nonetheless a difference in the details of the commandment between Israel and the rest of the nations. And it is all as I have written in the Order of Vayishma Yitro (Sefer HaChinukh 26). And it appears that the obligation for the rest of the nations with the limb from the living is whether with pure [animals] or whether with impure [animals]. And so, did the elder instruct (see Mishneh Torah, Laws of Kings and Wars 9:13).

Mitzvah 453

To bring consecrated things to the Choice House (Temple): To bring all sin-offerings, guilt-offerings, burnt-offering and peace-offerings that we have an obligation on ourselves to the Choice House and to sacrifice [them] there. And even though these beasts are outside of the Land, it is an obligation upon us to bring them to the selected place. And about this is it stated (Deuteronomy 12:26), "But your consecrated things that shall be for you and your vows shall you carry and come." And even though the commandment to sacrifice in the Choice House came to us, as I have written in this Order (Sefer HaChinukh 440), nonetheless, this specific commandment comes to us about the sacrifices [from] outside of the Land. And so is it in Sifrei Devarim 77:1-2, "'But your consecrated things' [...] - it is only speaking of his consecrated things [from] outside of the land; 'shall you carry and come,' teaches that he is obligated to care for bringing them until he brings them to the Choice House." And they [also] said there that the obligation is with sin-offerings, guilt-offerings, burnt-offerings, and peace-offerings. And it is possible for us to say that [the reason] a commandment was specified for the consecrated [animals from] outside of the Land, is to warn us about them, because the burden with them is greater than the consecrated [animals from within] the Land, since [the latter] are closer to the [Temple].

But Ramban, may his memory be Blessed, wrote (Sefer HaMitzvot, Mitzvot Ase 85) there is only one commandment with all of the consecrated [animals], whether consecrated [animals from] the Land or whether those [from] outside of the Land; and that we should not make them two commandments. And even though it is true that is expounded in Sifrei to be about the consecrated [animals from] outside of the Land, this is not truly a proof to make them two commandments. And in the third chapter of Tractate Temurah 17b they expounded it in a different way. As there they said, "'But your consecrated things' - these are the exchanged animals; 'that shall be for you' - these are the offspring; 'and your vows' - that is a vow; 'shall you carry and come' - it is possible that they bring them to the Choice House and prevent water and food from them such that they die; [hence] we learn to say, 'And you shall effect your burnt-offering, the meat and the blood' (Deuteronomy 12:27) - in the way that you act with the burnt-offering, so should you act with the exchanged animal, and in the way that you act with the peace-offerings, so should you act with the offspring of the peace-offerings and the animals exchanged for them." The whole content of this commandment is like the content of the third commandment in this Order (Sefer HaChinukh 440) and there is one root to both of them. [Hence] there is no need to be lengthy of speech about it.

Mitzvah 454
To not add to the commandments and their understanding: That we were prevented not to add to the written Torah, nor to the oral Torah. And about this is it stated (Deuteronomy 13:1), "do not add to it." And how is the addition? Rambam, may his memory be Blessed, wrote (Mishneh Torah, Laws of Rebels 2:9), "For example, one who instructs that chicken meat with milk is forbidden by Torah writ - that is adding upon the word of the received tradition. As so did we receive about the understanding of 'you shall not boil a goat, etc.' - that the meat of a [domesticated] beast and a [wild] animal are forbidden to cook in milk, but not chicken meat. And so [too,] if he instructed that meat from a [wild] animal is permitted with milk, he has transgressed on account of 'you shall not subtract.' As this is subtracting, since so did we receive [about the verse's understanding], that the meat of a [domesticated] beast and a [wild] animal are [both] included in the prohibition." To here [are his words].

But most of the commentators (Ravad on Mishneh Torah, Rebels 2:9) would say that 'do not add' is only relevant at all with a positive commandment. And the matter according to what I have heard myself from the mouth of my teacher - may God protect him - is, for example, one that lays two fit tefillin on his head or on his arm; and so [too,] one who makes five [sections] in his tefillin; and likewise, one who takes two fit lulavs in his hand and anything similar to it; and so [too,] one who sits in a sukkah (booth) after the holiday with the intention of fulfilling the commandment of sukkah, even though he know that its time has passed - as we only transgress on account of 'do not add' when one has intent to do the commandment - and so [too,] one who takes the lulav after the holiday and has intent to do the commandment while knowing that the holiday has passed. And so is it in the Gemara in Rosh Hashanah 28b in the chapter [entitled] Rauhu Beit Din, as they conclude there, "Rather Rava says, 'To fulfill [a commandment] does not require intent'" - meaning to say that commandments do not require intent - "'to transgress: during its time does not require intent, not in its time requires intent.'" But [in the case of] one who takes the lulav on the holiday, even a hundred times a day, with intention to fulfill [the commandment] each and every time, there is no [issue] of 'do not add'; and so [too,] one who blows the shofar on the day of Rosh Hashanah, and even many times; and so [too,] anything like this. And there is no need to say that there is no [issue of] 'do not add' here, if one takes a disqualified lulav; and so [too] if he grouped a disqualified specie with [a fit lulav], according to the [legal conclusion] - as it is established for us that there is no need for a grouping. This is the general principle of the matter of this prohibition that my teachers, God protect them, distilled from the words of the Gemara after much effort. And now, my son, you too, if you merit and 'eat from the effort of your palms,' 'you will be happy and it will be good for you.'

It is from the roots of the commandment that the Master who commanded us about the Torah, Blessed be He, is completely perfect and all of His acts and commands are perfect and good. [Hence] adding to them is a deficit - and all the more so, subtracting. This is a clear thing.

The laws of the commandment are in Tractate Sanhedrin 88b, and so too in Tractate Rosh Hashanah 28b, in the chapter [entitled] Rauhu Beit Din, and they also spoke about the matter in Eruvin 96a, in the chapter [entitled] Hamotseh Tefillin.

And this prohibition is practiced in every place and at all times by males and females. And one who transgresses it and adds to the commandments - such as if he makes five [sections] in his tefillin, or lays two fit properly made tefillin on his head, and so [too,] one who takes two lulavs in his hand or anything similar to it, and so [too,] one who sits in a sukkah after the holiday or one who takes the lulav with the intention of fulfilling the commandment, even though he knows that its time has passed - has violated this negative commandment. And he is liable for lashes - [if there were] witnesses and a warning, as is known in every place.

Mitzvah 455
To not subtract from the commandments of the Torah: That we were prevented from subtracting

a thing from that which the perfect Torah commanded us. And about this is it stated (Deuteronomy 13:1), "do not subtract from it." And how is this prohibition? For example, that which they, may their memory be Blessed, said in the third chapter of Rosh Hashanah 28b that if blood that requires one sprinkling is mixed up with blood that requires four sprinklings, "Rabbi Eliezer says, 'It is to be sprinkled four times.' And Rabbi Yehoshua says, 'It is to be sprinkled once - since when you sprinkle four times, you transgress, "do not add," and you perform an act; whereas when you sprinkle once, even if you transgress "do not subtract," you do not perform an act.'" To here [is the excerpt from the Talmud]. We know from this that the negative commandment of 'do not subtract' is in this way and all that is similar to it.

From the roots of the commandment is like the matter that we said in the commandment of 'do not add,' that preceded it. And the rest of all of its matters are like it [as well].

Mitzvah 456
To not listen to one who prophecies in the name of idolatry: That we not listen [to] the prophecy of one who prophecies in the name of idolatry - meaning to say that we not ask him for, and investigate him with, a sign or wonder about his prophecy, as we do with one who prophecies in the name of God. Rather we prevent him from the thing, as is fitting with any criminal or guilty one. And if he persists in his evil, we apply the well-known punishment for which the Torah makes him liable, and that is to kill him with strangulation. And about this is it stated (Deuteronomy 13:4), "You shall not listen to the words of that prophet."

It is from the roots of the commandment [that it is] because error is constantly found with people and their intellects are not strong [enough] to come to the complete truth about things. And [so] the Torah is concerned that maybe the one prophesying in the name of idolatry will seduce a man to his words as a result of the false claims, length of words and argument with the foreigner who speaks lies. And even if he is not seduced by him, maybe he will doubt in his heart to be attracted by some pull in his lies, even for an hour. And even though we know that there is no endurance to his words beyond an hour - since the truth instructs its [own] path and will testify about the words of that prophet that [it is] falsehood in his mouth - nonetheless, the Torah was concerned for us, lest we waste even one hour from all of our days with hesitation about this evil thought.

And the laws of the commandment are in the eleventh chapter of Sanhedrin.

And it is practiced in every place and at all times by males and females. And one who transgresses it and listens to the prophet that prophecies in the name of idolatry - for example, he speaks many words with him or asks for a sign or wonder from him - has violated this negative commandment. But there are no lashes for it, as there is no act [involved] with it.

Mitzvah 457
To not love the seducer: That we have likewise been prevented from bending our ear to the words of a seducer and that we not endear him in any manner. And the content of a seducer is one who seduces one Israelite to worship idolatry, such as one who praises the actions of idolatry to him; and he praises it in order that he will follow it and serve it and leave from under the wings of the Divine Providence. And about this is it stated (Deuteronomy 13:9), "You shall not long for him."

From the roots of the commandment is like the matter that is written in the commandment that precedes it. And its colleague shall speak about all of its laws and practice.

Mitzvah 458
To not leave the hatred towards the seducer: That the hatred of the seducer be fixed in our hearts, meaning to say that we not lighten in the grudge of vengeance upon him for all of the evil that he thought to do. And about this is it stated (Deuteronomy 13:9), "and you shall not listen to him" - meaning to say, do not be amenable to him to remove the grudge of vengeance upon him from your heart. And so did they, may their memory be Blessed, say in explanation of this verse (Sifrei Devarim 89:2), "Since it is stated (Exodus 23:5), 'unload shall you unload with him'" - and Onkelos translated, "unload shall you unload what is in your heart against him," - "it is possible that you should unload

for this one, too; [hence] we learn to say, 'and you shall not listen to him.'"

It is from the roots of the commandment like the matter of the two previous commandments - as it is all to distance every matter of idolatry, that we not stumble in it in any way.

And its laws are in Sanhedrin, Chapter 7. And all the rest of its content is like them.

Mitzvah 459

To not save the seducer: That the seduced is prevented from saving the seducer when he sees him in danger of death and perdition. And about this is it stated (Deuteronomy 13:9), "and your eye shall not be concerned for him." And so did they, may their memory be Blessed, say (Sifrei Devarim 89:3), "Since it is stated (Leviticus 19:16), 'and you shall not stand upon the blood of your neighbor,' it is possible that you do not stand upon [the] blood of this one [too]; [hence] we learn to say, 'and your eye shall not be concerned for him.'"

The root of this commandment is written in the previous [commandments] that come about the seducer. And all of its content is like them.

Mitzvah 460

Not to advocate innocence for a seducer: That the seduced is prevented not to claim something of merit for the seducer. And even if he knows a merit for him, he should not advocate it and not mention it about him. And about this is it stated (Deuteronomy 13:9), "you shall not have pity." And so, did they, may their memory be Blessed, say (Sifrei Devarim 89:4), "Do not advocate innocence for him." And its content is like the other [related commandments] that we mentioned adjacently.

Mitzvah 461

Not to refrain from advocating guilt for the seducer: That the seduced not be silent from advocating guilt for the seducer, but rather that he should advocate if for him. And about this is it stated (Deuteronomy 13:9), "and you shall not cover for him." And they, may their memory be Blessed, said (Sifrei Devarim 89:5), "If you know [claims of] guilt, you are not allowed to be quiet." All of its content is like its colleagues adjacent to it.

And from all of these warnings (negative commandments) about the seducer, I can understand that it is permitted - and also a commandment upon us - to likewise hate evildoers in other sins, in our seeing that they have corrupted their deeds and made them hateful to the point that there is no hope for them; and that they will not listen to the voice of teachers but disparage their words, and will not bend their ear to those that teach them, but damage the 'direction of their faces.' Behold, these are the evildoers about which David stated (Psalms 139:21), "Do I not, Lord, hate Your enemies, and argue with those that come against You."

Mitzvah 462

To not seduce one of Israel to worship idolatry: To not seduce one of Israel to worship idolatry. And one who does so is called a seducer. And about this is it stated (Deuteronomy 13:12), "and they shall not continue to do like this evil in your midst."

The root of this commandment is revealed to all.

The laws of the commandment are, for example, that which they, may their memory be Blessed, said (Sanhedrin 67a), [that] how is the matter of the seduction of the seducer? For example, one who says to his fellow, "Let us go and worship idolatry x," or "Let us go and sacrifice," or "Let us go and burn incense," or "Let us go and pour a libation," or "Let us go and bow down"; or if he said to his fellow in the singular form, "I will go and worship, I will go and sacrifice," or "I will burn incense, I will pour a libation, I will bow down" - whether it is in the singular form or whether it is in the plural form - behold, this is called a seducer. And even though no act was one, such that they did not worship idolatry - not the seducer and not the seduced - nonetheless, their sentence is like that of a seducer because of speech alone. And [also] that which they said (Sanhedrin 67a) [about] one who seduces two, they are his witnesses, and they bring him to court and we stone him upon their [testimony]. And [also] that which they said (Sanhedrin 80b) that a seducer does not require a warning because of the severity of the matter, as it is an evil thing - and so did they, may their memory be Blessed, say (Ketuvot 33a) about plotting witnesses, that they not require a warning due to their great evil, and as we will write with God's help in the Order of Shoftim (Sefer HaChinukh 523). And [also] that which they said (Sanhedrin 67a) [about] one who seduces one, that the seduced is obligated to say to him, "I have fellows that want from this, say it to them also"; and that this is done so that two will testify against him and he will be sentenced by a court. And they, may their memory be Blessed, said further that if he does not want to seduce two, it is a commandment to conceal witnesses for him. And the matter is that he hides witnesses in a place that they will see the seducer and he will not see them, and [then] he enters with him into things that he said to him in isolation. And [then] the seduced answers him, "How can we leave our God in the heavens and serve wood and stones?" And if the seducer recants or is quiet, he is exempted. But if he says to him, "So is it fitting to do and so is it proper for us," those witnesses bring him to court. And with no other death penalty besides this do we conceal witnesses for them. And this whole matter is to distance idolatry. And they, may their memory be Blessed, said (Sifrei Devarim 89:8) that it is a commandment in the hand of the seduced himself to kill him after the court has sentenced him; and about this is it stated (Deuteronomy 13:10), "your hand shall be upon him first to put him to death." And this commandment to kill him is part of the commandment, and we should not consider it as a [separate] commandment on its own. [These] and its other details are in Tractate Sanhedrin.

And this prohibition is practiced in every place and at all times by males and females. And one who transgresses it - whether he is a commoner, a sage or a prophet - and seduces any man or woman from Israel in the way that we said is liable for stoning.

Mitzvah 463

The commandment of investigating the witnesses well: To make a formidable investigation of the testimony and to inquire about it well according to all of our ability, so as to known the root of a thing and its completely exact truth. And from the foundation of this matter, they, may their memory be Blessed, said (Avot 1:1), "Be deliberate in judgment." And it is all so that we can reflect on the thing and know the truth about it; and that we not hurry in judgement, lest we kill the innocent and cause a loss of money, because the truth is concealed. And about this is it stated (Deuteronomy 13:15), "And you shall inquire and investigate and ask well, and behold, the thing is correct truth." And anyone who has eyes in his head will observe and see that the multitude of warnings and repetition of the matter in different words that the Torah repeated about this thing is is to properly warn us about the matter; as it is a great thing and a strong pillar upon which the blood of the souls of the creatures depends.

And there is no [need] to write at length about the root of the commandment, as it is revealed to all.

From the laws of the commandment is that which they, may their memory be Blessed, said (Sanhedrin 40a) that each witness would be investigated with seven investigations, and these are them: In which sabbatical cycle from the seven sabbatical cycles within the jubilee did the event occur that he is testifying about; in which year of the seven years of the sabbatical cycle; in which month of the year; on [which day] of the month; on which day of the six days of the week; at [which hour] of the day; and in what place. And even if he said, "He killed him today," or "yesterday," we ask him all of this. And besides these seven investigations that are the same for all testimony, included in the commandment of investigation is if he testified that [the accused] worshiped idolatry to ask him, "Which idolatry did he worship and with which [type] of worship?" And if he testified that he profaned the Shabbat, we say to him, "With which [type of] work did he profane it and how did he do the work?" And if he testified that he ate on Yom Kippur, we say to him, "What food did he eat, and how much did he eat?" And so [too, for] all that is similar to this.

And besides all of this that we mentioned that are called investigations and inquiries - which are the essence of the testimony and with them the accused is made guilty or exempted - the court would engage in much checking of the witnesses in other matters that are not very essential to the testimony. And since they are not essential, they, may their memory be Blessed, called them, checks. And they said about them (Mishnah Sanhedrin 5:2), "All who increase the checking are praiseworthy." And what is that which is called checks? For example, "What was the killed or the killer wearing?" And likewise, we ask him, "Was the earth on the land that he was killed white or red," and similar to these matters. And they, may their memory be Blessed, said (Mishnah Sanhedrin 5:2) that with the investigations, if one witness was precise in his testimony and the second one said, "I do not know," their testimony is nullified; but with the checks, even if both of them said, "We do not know," their testimony [still] stands - and all the more so, if only one says, "I do not know." And about what are these words speaking? When they did not contradict one another. But if they contradicted one another even in the checks, their testimony is nullified.

And both capital cases and financial cases are included in this commandment, as it is stated (Leviticus 24:22), "One judgement shall there be for you." But the Sages said that in order not to close the door in front of borrowers, that we not require inquiry and investigation of the witnesses of money [cases]. How is this? [If] the witnesses said, "This one lent that one a hundred in front of us in year x" - even though they were not precise about the month and the place in which he borrowed, and not which coin the hundred was [composed of, if] their testimony was the same about the value of the hundred, their testimony stands with that. And about what are these words speaking? About admission, loans, gifts, sales and that which is similar to them. But with cases of penalties, we require inquiry and investigation, and there is no need to say with lashes and exile [that they are required]. And likewise, they, may their memory be Blessed, said (Sanhedrin 32b) that if the judge sees that the case is forged, even with the cases of admissions and loans, he needs to do inquiry and investigation upon them. And if they contradicted one another in the investigations and inquiries, their testimony is nullified; but if they contradicted each other in the checks, their testimony stands. How is this? If the one said, "He borrowed in Nissan," and the other said, "No, rather [it was] in Iyar"; or the one said, "In Jerusalem," and the other said, "No, rather [it was] in Lod." And so [too,] the one said, "He borrowed a barrel of wine," and the other said, "No, rather [it was] a barrel of oil" - this is investigation and inquiry, and [so] their testimony is nullified. But if the one said, "He borrowed a black hundred," and the second said a white hundred - and the value of both of them is the same - or the one said, "They were in the upper floor when he lent to him" and the second said on the bottom floor - this is checks and their testimony stands. [These] and the rest of its details are in Tractate Sanhedrin (Chapters 4 and 5).

And this commandment is practiced regarding money [cases] in every place and at all times by males, as it up to them to administer justice, and not to women. And regarding capital cases, lashes and penalties, it is practiced at the time that the Sanhedrin sits in its place, as I have written in the Order of Mishpatim (Sefer HaChinukh 47, 49). And one who transgresses this and does not investigate the witnesses as is fit has violated this positive commandment; and his punishment is very great, since it is a cause for the [punishing of] people and loss of money that is not according to the law. And [one who does this] is an evildoer and causes the many to sin, giving them the money of others to consume. But [about] one who judges a completely true judgement, they, may their memory be Blessed, said (Shabbat 10a) that his merit is great; and they compared him metaphorically, as if he becomes a partner of the Holy One, Blessed be He, in the act of creation - meaning to say, the preservation of the world and its administration.

Mitzvah 464

The burning of an enticed city and to kill its people: To burn an enticed city and everything that is in it. And a city of Israel [whose inhabitants] have been enticed by wanton men to leave from under the wings of the Divine Presence, and go after the whims of their hearts to worship idolatry, is called an enticed city. And about this is it stated (Deuteronomy 13:17), "and you shall burn the city with fire, and all of its booty."

The root of this commandment is well-known - that evil and sinful men like this that agreed [upon] a bad and disgusting agreement like this together are fit to have their name erased and their memory destroyed from the world, and that there should not be a place of their remembrance in the world at all. And there is no destruction more complete than burning.

From the laws of the commandment is that which they, may their memory be Blessed, said (Sanhedrin 111b) that the city does not become an enticed city - meaning, to judge them with the law of an enticed city, the people of which are killed with the sword and their property is burned with the city - until its enticers are two, or more than two, as it is stated (Deuteronomy 13:14), "Wanton men came out, etc."; and that its enticers are from that tribe and from that city, as it is stated, "from among you, and entice you"; and until they entice its majority, and that the enticed be from one hundred up to the majority of the tribe. But if the majority of a tribe is enticed, they are not judged by the law of the enticed city, but rather as individuals who are stoned and their property is for their heirs, as it is stated, "the residents of the city" - and not a small village and not a large [metropolis], and less than a hundred is a small village, and the majority of a tribe is a large [metropolis]. And the law that a city of refuge and so [too,] Jerusalem cannot be made an enticed city, and so [too,] a city that is on the border cannot be made an enticed city; the law of how we make it into an enticed city, and the warning that we send to it through two Torah scholars; that which they said concerning its plaza; that which they said about the properties of the righteous within it who were not enticed with it; the law of consecrated things within it; the law of the fruit of palm trees within it; the law of the properties of the people of another city that are within it or the properties of the people of the enticed city in another place; and the rest of its details are [all] in Tractate Sanhedrin (Chapter 11).

And this commandment is practiced by males - as justice is theirs - and at the time that Israel is on its land and that the Great Court of seventy-one [judges] is in its place, since we only judge an enticed city through the Great Court. And it is from the commandments that are incumbent upon the community, and [especially] on the Sanhedrin. And if they transgressed this - for example, they knew about one of the cities of Israel that was fitting to be made into an enticed city, and they did not effect the law of the enticed city upon it - they have violated this positive commandment, and their punishment is very great, lest its evil spread to other cities.

Mitzvah 465
To not rebuild an enticed city: To not ever rebuild an enticed city. And about this is it stated (Deuteronomy 13:17), "and it shall be an everlasting mound; you shall not build it again."

The root of this commandment is like the matter that I wrote about in this Order about the burning of an enticed city (Sefer HaChinukh 464).

From the laws of the commandment - that which they, may their memory be Blessed, said (Sanhedrin 111b) about the understanding of "you shall not build," that we do not build it to make it a city, meaning houses like it was, but it is permitted to make it into gardens and orchards; and the rest of its details - are elucidated in the tenth chapter of Sanhedrin. And this prohibition is practiced by males and females at the time that the law of an enticed city is practiced - and that is at the time that Israel is on their land and the Sanhedrin is sitting in its place, as I have written above (Sefer HaChinukh 464).

Mitzvah 466
To not benefit from the property of an enticed city: That we have been prevented from benefiting and taking from the property of an enticed city. And about this is it stated (Deuteronomy 13:18), "And no thing from the anathema shall stick to your hand." And also included in this negative commandment is anything from idolatry, as I have written above in the Order of Vehaya Ekev in the last warning (negative commandment) in the Order (Sefer HaChinukh 429). And in it, I wrote about the roots of this commandment, and all of its content is the same.

Mitzvah 467
To not gash ourselves, like the worshipers of idolatry: To not gash our bodies, like the worshipers of idolatry. And about this is it stated (Deuteronomy 14:1), "you shall not gash yourselves." And this negative commandment is repeated with another word, as it is stated (Leviticus 19:28), "And a marking for a soul, you shall not put onto your flesh, etc." And in Tractate Yevamot 13b, they, may their memory be Blessed said, "'You shall not gash yourselves' is required for itself, as [the Torah] said that that you shall not make a wound." And it is also said there that "You shall not gash yourselves" is for the dead. And in Tractate Makkot 21a, they, may their memory be Blessed, said

that marking and gashing are one thing. And there it is said that one who makes a mark for the dead is liable whether it is with the hand or with a tool; but for idolatry, with a tool, [one is] liable, with the hand, [one is] exempt. As such was their custom to gash themselves in front of the idolatry with a tool, and like the matter that is written (I Kings 18:28), "and they gashed themselves like their statute with swords and spears." And regardless, according to that which appears [to come out] from the words of our Rabbis, may their memory be Blessed, (Makkot 22) the liability of the negative commandment is only about one who gashes himself for the dead or for idolatry. But for one who gashes himself without a reason or from anger about his house that has fallen or his ship that has sunk - even though it is something extremely disgusting and ugly and forbidden - there is no liability of the negative commandment for it.

It is from the roots of the commandment [that it is] in order that we not do amongst ourselves any matter at all that is similar to the worshipers of idolatry, and like the matter that I wrote in the negative commandment of encircling the head in the Order of Kedoshim Tehiyu (Sefer HaChinukh 251). And we have been prevented from gashing over the dead, as it is not proper for the chosen people - those of the wisdom of the precious Torah - to pain themselves about something from the creation of God, except for the matter through which He, Blessed be He, commanded us to pain ourselves, and for the reason that I wrote in the Order of Emor el HaKohanim in the first commandment (Sefer HaChinukh 264). But that we should destroy our bodies and disfigure ourselves like fools is not good for us. And it is not the way of sages and men of understanding, but rather an act of the masses of lowly women that lack intellect, that have not understood anything from the creation of God and His wonders. And Ramban, may his memory be Blessed, wrote (Ramban on Deuteronomy 14:1) [that] from here, there is a support for our Rabbis, may their memory be Blessed, in their forbidding mourning for the dead more than is enough (Moed Katan 27b).

From the laws of the commandment - like that which they, may their memory, said (Makkot 20b) that one who makes a marking is liable one [distinct set of] lashes for each and every marking, and that is when they warned him on it about each and every one, and [that] one who makes one marking for five dead is liable for five [sets of] lashes; and the rest of its details - are at the end of Tractate Makkot. And Rambam, may his memory be Blessed, wrote (Mishneh Torah, Laws of Foreign Worship and Customs of the Nations 12:14) that they, may their memory be Blessed, also expounded that included in this warning (negative commandment) is that there not be two courts in one city [whereby] one follows one custom and the other follows another custom, as this causes disagreement; and the expression, "do not gash yourselves" (titgodedu) is meaning to say, do not create many groupings (agudot, agudot), which means to say that they be differing with one another. [But] from my teacher, God protect him, I have learned that this prohibition is only with one group, some of which differs with [the rest] - and they are equal in wisdom. [In such a case,] it is forbidden for each of their factions to follow its [own] words, as this creates disagreement among them. Rather, they should give and take much among themselves about the thing until they all agree to one opinion. And if it is impossible like this, they should all follow the words of those that are stringent, if the disagreement is about something from Torah writ. But [this prohibition] was not said about two courts that disagree - and they are equal in wisdom. And they brought a proof from the story in Tractate Chullin (it should read Avodah Zarah 40a) - as they said there, "[They] took out the shofar of [Rav to make a proclamation] and forbade it, and [in the same town, they] took out the shofar of [Shmuel to make a proclamation] and permitted it."

And this prohibition is practiced in every place and at all times by males and females. And one who transgresses this and makes a marking any place on his body for the dead or for the sake of idolatry is liable for lashes.

Mitzvah 468

To not make a bald spot for the dead: To not make bald the hair of the head [in mourning] for the dead, like those lacking intellect do. And about this is it stated (Deuteronomy 14:1), "and do not place a bald spot between your eyes for the dead." And this prohibition is repeated about the priests, as it is stated about them (Leviticus 21:5), "They shall not shave a bald spot upon their heads." And we learned from there to make liable [for] upon the head like between the eyes, as it comes in Tractate Makkot 20a. And from this verse [in Deuteronomy], they also learned that there is only liability for a bald spot when it is a bald spot specifically for the dead. And it comes out that with the two verses, there is completion of the commandment and its elucidation: That all - whether Israelite or whether priest - are liable for the whole head, like between the eyes. And you should not ask in this place and in any thing similar to it, why all of the elucidation of the verse is not in one place. For is your mind not put to rest about these matters in many places with my introduction that I wrote to you at the beginning of this book of Deuteronomy?

It is written from the roots of the commandment in the previous commandment.

From the laws of the commandment - that which they, may their memory be Blessed, said that one who made one bald spot for five dead is lashed five [sets of lashes], and that one who makes five bald spots for one dead is [also] lashed five [sets] (Mishneh Torah, Laws of Foreign Worship and Customs of the Nations 12:15) when they warned him on it about each and every one; [that] one who makes a bald spot by hand or with a medication is liable, and even if he submerged his fingers in the medication and placed them in five places on his head at one time, since he made five bald spaces, he is lashed [five sets], even though he only got one warning, since [the bald spots] came at the same time; and the rest of the details of the commandment - are at the end of Tractate Makkot. And all of its content is exactly like the law of its fellow that precedes it.

Mitzvah 469

To not eat from consecrated [animals] that have been disqualified: That we not eat from consecrated [animals] that have been disqualified. And [about] this negative commandment with the consecrated [animals] that have been disqualified, they, may their memory be Blessed, explained in Tractate Bekhorot 34a that it is specifically when we make the blemish in the consecrated [animals], and that they are disqualified by our hand, and afterwards we ate from them - [that] then is there a negative commandment in their eating; and so too, if the sacrifice gets disqualified in any way after its being sacrificed - in this too is there a negative commandment. And about all of this is it stated (Deuteronomy 14:3), "You shall not eat any abomination." And so does it say in Sifrei Devarim 99, "'You shall not eat any abomination' - the verse is speaking about consecrated [animals] that have been disqualified." And there it says further, "Rabbi Eliezer ben Yaakov says, 'From where [do I know] for one who slits the ear of a first-born animal and eats from it, that he is transgressing a negative commandment? As it is stated, "You shall not eat any abomination."'" And they, may their memory be Blessed said further that included in the category of this negative commandment is the warning not to eat notar (remainder) and pigul (that disqualified by thought) - and I have written their content in the Order of Tsav (Sefer HaChinukh 144) - and so [too,] all forbidden foods. And [it is] like the matter that they, may their memory be Blessed, expounded (Chullin 114b), "'You shall not eat any abomination' - anything that I have made abominable to you, behold it is [included] in 'do not eat.'" And nonetheless, it is not called a general negative commandment, since its essence is only coming about the consecrated [animals] that have been disqualified, and the rest of the prohibitions are derived by its implications. [This is] meaning to say that from that which Scripture brought out this warning in a general expression - since it stated, "any abomination," and it did not explicitly state, "You shall not eat the consecrated [animals] that have been disqualified" - because of that, we consider it a specific negative commandment in its essence, that we can learn from its warning to other matters. And accept the truth form the one that says it.

I have already written many times that it is from the roots of the commandments that the Torah [instructs] to prevent us from approaching the holy from touching its edge, [that] it is in order to give awe of these matters to our hearts and to make them precious in our eyes, in order that our spirit be aroused, our thoughts yearn, our hearts be afraid and that a proper spirit be renewed in us, when we come to request forgiveness for our iniquities. And from this, God, Blessed be He, will listen to our prayers and save us from all our troubles and we will be good. And we will also explain the root of this one about this good.

And the laws of the commandment are in Tractate Bekhorot.

And this prohibition is practiced by males and females in every place and at all times. As even though they, may their memory be Blessed, said (Avodah Zarah 13a) that at this time, we many not consecrate - as I have written at the beginning of the Order of Bechukotai (Sefer HaChinukh 350) - nonetheless, one who does consecrate his animal as a sacrifice, [has] holiness rest upon it; and [so] it has the law of consecrated things. And one who places a blemish on it and eats it transgresses this negative commandment and is liable for lashes because of this - when he eats a kazayit from it and there are witnesses and a warning.

Mitzvah 470
To check the signs of a bird: To check the signs of a bird [that distinguish them as being permissible to eat]. And about this is it stated (Deuteronomy 14:11), "You may eat from any pure bird." And so did they say in Sifrei Devarim 103 (see Maggid Mishneh on Mishneh Torah, Laws of Forbidden Foods 2:4), "'You may eat from any pure bird' - that is a positive commandment." I have written all of the content of this commandment, its root, its laws and in which place it is practiced and at what time in the Order of Vayehi Bayom Hashimini (Sefer HaChinukh 153) concerning the examination of the signs of a [domesticated] beast, a [wild] animal, fish, and locusts - as the law of all of them is the same. And over there, I also wrote that Ramban, may his memory be Blessed, differs with Rambam, may his memory be Blessed, in [the latter's] counting of the checking with beasts and other species to be a positive commandment. And he holds that the [verse] only comes to give a positive commandment and a negative commandment to the one that eats from the impure [species]. And there in that same Order, I wrote (Sefer HaChinukh 157) a little of what I heard from my teachers, God protect them, about the signs of birds - and take it from there.

Mitzvah 471
To not eat from the flying swarming creatures: To not eat from the flying swarming creatures, such as flies, bees, mosquitoes and others from these types. And about this is it stated (Deuteronomy 14:19), "And any flying swarming creature is impure for you; they shall not be eaten." And the language of Sifrei Devarim 103 is "'And any flying swarming creature, etc.' is a negative commandment."

And you should know that because the Torah forbade the impure birds and mentioned them by name - since they are few, as I wrote at length in the Order of Bayom Hashmini in the commandment to not eat an impure bird (Sefer HaChinukh 157) - the rest of the birds (winged creatures) remained under the assumption of being permitted. [Hence] it was necessary for Scripture to forbid the flying swarming creatures, in order to inform us that it not included among the permissible - and even though the signs for the pure ones are in the tradition and well-known to us. Or we can say that being that the swarming flying creatures are a type unto its own, it was necessary to forbid them explicitly. And behold, in the Order of Bayom Hashmini, it states (Leviticus 11:13), "And these shall be disgusting for you from the birds," and here it states, "And any flying swarming creature" - a specific negative commandment is put upon them, as birds and flying swarming creatures are two completely different things.

I have written what came up to my thought from the roots of the commandments that come from forbidden foods in the Order of Mishpatim about the prohibition of the 'torn' animal (Sefer HaMitzvot 73). And take it from there. The laws of the commandment are in Tractate Chullin (Chapter 3).

And this prohibition is practiced in every place and at all times by males and females. And one who transgresses it and ate a kazayit from the flying swarming creatures or ate one whole swarming flying creature - even though there is no kazayit in it - since he ate all of it; or he ate a kazayit from it - even though [the creature] is big - is liable for lashes. And I have already written at length in elucidation of the prohibition of swarming creatures and the stringency of the prohibition of a complete creature (beriah) in the Order of Bayom Hashmini, as it its place is there.

Mitzvah 472
To not eat from the meat of a [domesticated] beast, a [wild] animal or a bird that has died by

itself: To not eat from the meat of a [domesticated] beast, a [wild] animal or a bird that has died by itself. And about this is it stated (Deuteronomy 14:21), "You shall not eat any carcass; to the stranger that is in your gates may you give it and he shall eat it, or you may sell it to the foreigner." And I have already written above in this Order in the commandment of slaughter (Sefer HaChinukh 451) the principle that they, may their memory be Blessed, said that anything that is disqualified in its slaughter is also called a carcass. And I also have written about the matter of its impurity in the Order of Bayom Hashmini on the commandment to not eat an impure fish (Sefer HaChinukh 161), and it is a [separate] commandment on its own.

From the roots of the commandment is that which I wrote concerning the prohibition of the 'torn' animal (Sefer HaChinukh 73).

From the laws of the commandment is that which they, may their memory be Blessed, said (Avodah Zarah 67b) that [only] a carcass that is fit for a (gentile) stranger [to eat] is called a carcass and carries liability for its eating; but a carcass that is not fit for a stranger - meaning to say, a putrid carcass - does not carry liability for its eating. And because of this, the verse was lengthy to say, "you may give it to the stranger" - to teach you this. As if it were not so, there is no need to teach us to who to give that which we have. And it should not be said that it is coming to permit its benefit, as it is already written in another place (Leviticus 7:24), "Fat of the carcass and fat of the 'torn' [animal] may be used for any work." And from here they, may their memory be Blessed, learned (Avodah Zarah 65b) the law that exuding taste that spoils is permissible. As we know through this that the Torah only forbids and makes liable for the eating of things that are fitting for people to eat; not for something that disgust a person's soul, as that is considered just like any dirt. And this is the dispensation that is mentioned in the Gemara about forbidden vinegar that fell into split beans, since it spoils them. And from this principle, we have become accustomed to purge vessels in boiling water that have not been used for a day, even though there is not sixty parts in the water corresponding to [the mass] of the vessel - as the absorbed [prohibited matter] that comes out from [it] when it is has not been used in a day is spoiled. And since the absorbed [matter] went out from the vessel due to the power of the water the nature of which is to purge and take out all of what is absorbed in the vessel - even though the vessel sits afterward with the absorbed waters that the vessel expunged into the boiling waters that are less than sixty [parts to it] and goes back and absorbs from it - it is not prohibited through this, as the [absorbed matter] is like a putrid carcass, which the Torah permitted, as we have said.

And maybe you will say, and how is it that we permit to eat even a putrid carcass from the outset. Is there [not a prohibition here of] "Do not be disgusting?" (See Mishneh Torah, Laws of Forbidden Foods 17:29) The answer to this is that whenever it is something small like this and also that it is absorbed in the vessel and spoiled within it and its strength is weakened - in such a manner as this - there is certainly not [a violation of] "Do not be disgusting," and [so] it is permissible from the outset. And you should not at all ask and say [that] if so, how is it that the Torah permitted the vessels of Midian by purging - was not the absorbed [matter] not [yet] spoiled, according to that which was said in the Gemara (Avodah Zarah 67b), that the Torah had only forbidden [and required purging of] a vessel that had been used in the day; as I can say to you that they purged these vessels in much water, which had sixty [parts] corresponding to the [mass] of the vessels (see Tosafot on Chullin 108b, s.v. shenafal).

And from this we can also learn that if one of any of the disgusting swarming creatures in the world fell into the pot - even though there is not sixty [parts] food in the pot corresponding to that swarming creature - that everything is permitted after we remove the body of the swarming creature from the pot. And we do not concern ourselves with that which it exuded at all, since it is from the disgusting things and spoils the taste of the [food]. As behold, this is similar to [the law of] a putrid carcass which is not forbidden, as we have said. And nonetheless, it is necessary that there be two parts of what is in the pot corresponding to the body of the swarming creature, so that it will be nullified by the majority. As if not, the food will be considered like the body of the swarming creature itself, and the Torah forbids its body, even though it is disgusting. [These] and the rest of these many matters are elucidated in Tractate Chullin with the books of the good commentators. And this little that I wrote to you, my son, is not like a small dot on the face of the earth, in comparison with the many laws that are said about this matter. And I have already informed you in several places that my intention is only to arouse your spirit about the matters and I am [just] showing you [items]. But if you merit and Torah become your craft, you will understand all of the things and you will rejoice in them.

And this prohibition is practiced in every place and at all times by males and females. And one who transgresses it and eats a kazayit from a carcass is liable for lashes.

Mitzvah 473

The commandment of the second tithe: To remove the second tithe from the produce in four years of the sabbatical cycle, meaning to say, after we separate the first tithe that is given to the Levites, that we separate yet another tithe. And hence it is called the second tithe. And the law of this tithe is that it be eaten in Jerusalem. And about it is it stated (Deuteronomy 14:22), "You shall surely tithe the produce of your seed." And Scripture elucidates that if the place is far from us and we cannot carry it there except with great burden and much expense, that we can redeem it and bring up its value [to] Jerusalem and spend it there only for the needs of eating and drinking. And Scripture likewise elucidates that the one who redeems his tithe needs to add a fifth to the value - which is to say that if it was worth four dinar, that he eat instead of it [that which costs him] five dinar in Jerusalem. And about this is it stated (Leviticus 27:31), "And if a man surely redeems from his tithe, he shall add its fifth to it." And they, may their memory be Blessed, made a precise inference (Kiddushin 24a): "'From his tithe - but not from the tithe of his fellow; 'a man from his tithe' - but not a woman."

I have written from the roots of this commandment in the commandment of the animal tithe in the Order of Bechukotai (Sefer HaChinukh 360). And even though the matter is clear, its reason is in Scripture, which is "so that you may learn to revere the Lord, your God, all of the days" (Deuteronomy 13:24).

From the laws of the commandment is that which they, may their memory be Blessed, said that we do not tithe the second tithe from one year for [another]. And so is it in Sifrei Devarim 105, "'Each year' - it teaches that we do not tithe from one year for its fellow. I only have [it] for the second tithe, about which the verse is speaking. From where [do I know] to include the rest of the tithes? [Hence] we learn to say, 'You shall surely tithe.'" And they, may their memory be Blessed, said (Rosh Hashanah 2a) that the fifteenth day of Shevat is the new year for the tithe of trees; meaning to say that any tree that has reached the tithing season before the fifteenth of Shevat is tithed with the tithe of that year - that if it is a year of the second tithe, we separate the second tithe from it; and if it is a year of the poor tithe, we separate the poor tithe from it. And I have already written the tithing season for some of the trees, above in the Order of Vayikach Korach in the first commandment (Sefer HaChinukh 395). And it is written there that the central obligation from Torah writ is only upon grain, wine and olive oil, and everything else is rabbinic. And the rest of the many laws of the second tithe are all elucidated in the tractate that is built on this, and that is Tractate Maaser Sheni.

And this commandment is only practiced anywhere at the time that Israel is dwelling on their land and Jerusalem is inhabited - may we merit that our eyes see its goodness. And with the help of God, I will write the places that the first tithe, the second tithe and the priestly tithe are practiced, in the Order of Shoftim in the commandment of the priestly tithe (Sefer HaChinukh 507).

Mitzvah 474

To separate the poor tithe: To remove the poor tithe in the third and sixth year of the sabbatical cycle. And about this is it stated (Deuteronomy 14:28), "At the end of three years, you shall remove all of the tithe of your produce, etc. and you shall leave it in your gates." And in that year, they would separate the poor tithe instead of the second tithe of other years, and not separate the second tithe at all.

From the roots of the commandment of this matter is that which I wrote on the commandment of loaning to a poor person in the Order of Mishpatim (Sefer HaChinukh 66).

From the laws of the commandment are that which they, may their memory be Blessed, said (Mishneh Torah, Laws of Gifts to the Poor 6:7, 10) that the owner of a field through which poor people passed

Sefer HaChinukh

must give everyone of them tithe enough to satiate him, as it is stated (Deuteronomy 26:12), "and they shall eat in your gates and be satiated." And how much is enough to satiate him? From wheat, he should [give] no less than half a kav; from barley, no less than a kav ; spelt, no less than a kav and a half; fig-cakes no less than the weight of twenty-five sela ; wine, no less than half a log ; oil, [no less] than a quarter log ; a quarter of a kav of rice; a litra weight of vegetables; three kav of carobs; ten nuts; five peaches; two pomegranates; and one etrog (citron). If he had a little [produce] and the poor are many, he places it in front of them and they divide it among themselves. And there is no right for the owners to benefit [by choosing who receives] the favor [for] the second tithe that is divided on the threshing floor. [If] a man and a woman come to take, we give to the woman first and afterwards to the man. [These] and the rest of its details are elucidated in Tractates Peah, Maaserot, Demai and in [various] places in [the Order,] Zeraim, and in Makhshirim and Yadayim. And with God's help, I will write in which place it is practiced and at what time, in the Order of Shoftim (Sefer HaChinukh 507).

Mitzvah 475

To not claim a debt that the seventh year passed: To not claim a debt during the sabbatical year, but rather it should be released, and he should not claim it [any] more. And about this is it stated (Deuteronomy 15:2), "he shall not press his neighbor and his brother, etc."

As is my custom, I have have written from the roots of the commandment and all of its content above and adjacently in the positive commandment (Sefer HaChinukh 507) of this negative commandment in this Order. And one who transgresses it and claims his loan after the sabbatical year at the time of the [Temple] has violated this negative commandment. But there are no lashes for it, as there is no act [involved] with it.

Mitzvah 476

The commandment to press the foreigner: To press the foreigner that worships idolatry, to pay what he is obligated to us. And we should not have pity and not have mercy upon him, to prolong the loan. And about this is it stated (Deuteronomy 15:3), "You shall press the foreigner." And so, did they say in Sifrei Devarim 113, "'You shall press the foreigner' - this is positive commandment."

It is from the roots of the commandment [that it is] so that we not teach our souls to have pity and to have mercy upon them, so that we are not pulled after their deeds and their counsel in anything. And Ramban, may his memory be Blessed, wrote (in Sefer HaMitzvot, Shorashim 6) that this is not a positive commandment at all; but rather the matter of the verse is to warn us [to have] pity towards the Israelite with a positive commandment and a negative commandment: And it stated, "Press the foreigner," but not "your brother." And [so] it is a negative commandment that comes from the implication of a positive - about which it is established for us that it is like a positive commandment. And the negative commandment is also elucidated by it, "and you shall not press your brother." And so is the matter exactly with the prohibition of interest, like we will write in the Order of Ki Tetseh (Sefer HaChinukh 573).

The laws of the commandment are included in the elucidation of the Scripture, according to my opinion.

And this commandment is practiced in every place and at all times by males and females. And one who transgresses it and prolongs the time for repayment from a foreigner from the angle of pity upon him alone - and not from the angle of fear of the borrower, or [fear to] lose the debt, or for any other benefit - has violated a positive commandment, according to the opinion of Rambam, may his memory be Blessed. But according to the opinion of Ramban, may his memory be Blessed, one who presses an Israelite for his debt has violated this positive commandment, besides that he violated a negative commandment. But prolonging the debt of a foreigner 'does not raise or lower [a thing]'.

Mitzvah 477

That he releases all of his loans in the seventh [year]: To abandon all of his debts on the sabbatical year. And about this is it stated (Deuteronomy 15:3), "and that which you have with your brother,

Sefer HaChinukh

release your hand." And the warning is repeated about this commandment, as it is stated (Deuteronomy 15:2), "And this is the matter of the sabbatical year, every owner of a debt shall release his hand." And they said in the Tosefta (brought in Gittin 36a), "The verse is speaking about two releases: one is the release of land and [the other] is release of monies."

I have already written in Mishpatim on the commandment of the release of lands (Sefer HaChinukh 84) that which I have known about the root of the commandment; and the release of monies also draws from the same reason - to train our souls in the virtuous traits, the trait of generosity and a kind eye, and to fix great faith in our hearts towards God, Blessed be He. And then our soul will be prepared to receive the good from the Master of all, which is included in blessing and mercy. And also coming from this is a strong fence and partition to distance oneself greatly from theft and from envy for everything that there is to our neighbor. As we will draw an a fortiori argument (kal vechomer) for ourselves by saying, "Even with my money that I lent out, the Torah said to release it in the hand of the borrower when the sabbatical year arrives; is it not all the more so that with not stealing and not having envy for that which is his, that it is fitting for me to distance myself to the [other] extreme?"

From the laws of the commandment is that which they, may their memory be Blessed, said (Arakhin 28b) that the sabbatical year only releases at its end, when the sun sets on the eve of Rosh Hashanah (the new year) of the conclusion of the seventh [year], as it is stated (Deuteronomy 15:1), "At the end of seven years." And it releases even a loan in a deed that [is backed with a lien] on properties. But if he decided a [specific] field for him for the loan, it does not release it. So, wrote Rambam, may his memory be Blessed (Mishneh Torah, Laws of Sabbatical Year and the Jubilee 9:6), but it is a wonder, since Rabbi Yochanan pushed off [this opinion] in the chapter [entitled] Hasholeach (Gittin 37a).

A [revolving] account of a store and the wage of a wage worker is not released. But if they stood them as a loan, it is released. And the same is the law with penalties. The marriage contract (ketuvah) of one who divorces his wife before the sabbatical year is not released unless she damages [its full value] or stood it up against him as a loan. And one who makes a loan upon a pledge, it is not released - and that is when the debt corresponds to the pledge. So wrote Rambam, may his memory be Blessed, (Mishneh Torah, Laws of Sabbatical Year and the Jubilee 9:14). But in the chapter [entitled] Hazahav (Bava Metzia 48a), we say that [it is not released] even though it is only worth half of the debt. And these words are speaking about movable items, but a pledge of land [depends]: in a place that they remove one [from the land], the seventh [year] releases - and a first-born does not take a double-portion, since it is like a total debt; but in a place that they do not remove one [from it], the seventh [year] does not release it. And now that it is established for us that an undifferentiated pledge is for a year - as so was it concluded in the Gemara (Bava Metzia 68a) according to the opinion of some of the commentators - we judge all pledges like a place that they do no remove one, and [so] the seventh [year] does not release a pledge. And a first-born takes a double-portion of it; and the creditor of orphans may collect from it, as it is like their land.

And one who gives over his deeds to the court and said to them, "You collect this debt for me" - [such debts] are not released. As it is stated, "and that which you have with your brother"; and this he already gave into the hand of the court. And from this reason, they, may their memory be Blessed, said (Gittin 37a) that the seventh [year] does not release a debt that orphans have from others - as the [legal status] of Rabban Gamliel and his court is like the [legal status] of the father of the orphans. And after them [the same was true] of all courts in each and every generation. And [so] it is as if they gave over their deeds into the hand of the court. And also, from the content of the commandment is that which they said (Makkot 3b) about one who lends to his friend for ten years, [such a loan] is not released. As when [the Torah] stated, "do not press," [it was] about a debt that is fitting to press - and this one has not yet reached its time to press. And [also] that which they said that one who stipulates about his debt from this fellow, [that it is] on condition that the seventh [year] not release it, behold it releases [nonetheless] - as he is like someone who makes a condition against what is written in the Torah. But if he said to him, "On condition that this obligation not be released, and even in the seventh year" - in this manner, the seventh [year] does not release it; since any condition upon money is upheld, as I have written in the Order of Behar Sinai on the commandment to not lend with interest to an Israelite (Sefer HaChinukh 339). And the rest of its details are in Tractate Sheviit (Chapter 10).

Sefer HaChinukh

And this commandment is practiced from Torah writ in the Land of Israel and in every place by males and females at the time that the Jubilee year is practiced. And I have already written at which time the Jubilee is practiced, above in the Order of Behar Sinai (Sefer HaChinukh 330). But at the time the Jubilee is not practiced, the release of lands and of monies is not practiced by Torah writ (Mishneh Torah, Laws of Sabbatical Year and the Jubilee 9:2, 3). But rabbinically, the release of monies is practiced even at this time and even in everyplace, so that the law of the release of monies not be forgotten from Israel. And I have already written which is the sabbatical year according to the great commentators that know the ways of the Talmud, above at the end of the Order of Behar Sinai at the end of the first commandment (Sefer HaChinukh 330).

And one who transgresses this and claimed a debt from his fellow that the seventh year passed at the time of the [Temple] has violated this positive commandment, besides having violated a negative commandment, as we will write in this Order, with God's help (Sefer HaChinukh 475). And at this time [such a one] has done a rabbinic prohibition. And if the court knows that the seventh [year] has passed it, they are not obligated to press [the debtor] at all, and even at this time. And even though the release of monies is only rabbinic today and it is established for us that a lien is from Torah writ (Kiddushin 13b); nonetheless the law is decided that the sages have the power to push off the word of the Torah in any matter of money, due to the [power] of the court to effectively make property ownerless (Gittin 36b).

Mitzvah 478
To not steel his heart against the poor: Not to withhold kindness and charity from our brother Israelites - and all the more so, from our relatives - in our knowing the weakness of their situation and that we have the ability to assist them. And about this is it stated (Deuteronomy 15:7), "you shall not steel your heart, and you shall not close your hand from your brother, the destitute one" - meaning to say, do not have the traits of stinginess and villainy rule over you, but rather prepare your heart in every way towards the trait of generosity and pity. And do not think that there will be a lack in your money because of the thing; "as because of [this] thing, God will bless you" (Deuteronomy 15:10). And His blessing for one small instant is better for you than several storehouses of gold and silver.

I have written in Parshat Mishpatim from its roots and some of its laws and content, as per my custom.

Mitzvah 479
The commandment of charity (tsedekah): To do charity with the one who needs it, with happiness and out of the goodness of one's heart; meaning to say, that we give from our money to one who is lacking, and to strengthen the poor in all areas that he needs for his sustenance, with all of our ability. And about this is it stated (Deuteronomy 15:8), "you shall surely open your hand to him." And they, may their memory be Blessed, expounded (Bava Metzia 31a), "Even several times." And it is it also stated (Leviticus 25:35), "and you shall strengthen the stranger and the citizen to live with you." And it stated further (Leviticus 25:36), "and your brother should live with you."

I have written what I have known from the roots of the commandment in Mishpatim on the commandment to lend to the poor at the time of his duress.

From the laws of the commandment is that which they, may their memory be Blessed, said (Bava Batra 10b) that the essence of the commandment is to give charity to the hand of a treasurer who should distribute it to the one who needs it; so that the recipient from the hand of the giver not be embarrassed each time he sees him; and also, that the giver not embarrass him about it ever. [Rather] this one does not know to whom he gave it, and that one does not know from whom he received it.

And you, my son, do not think that the commandment of charity applies only for the poor who does not have bread and clothing, since also for the very wealthy can this commandment of charity apply. For example, a wealthy person who is in a place where they do not recognize him and he needs a loan. Or even a wealthy person in his own city and in the place where he is recognized sometimes needs - because of sickness or because of another circumstance - that which you have in your hand and he cannot find it elsewhere. This is also included in the laws of charity without a doubt. Since the Torah always chooses acts of kindness and commands us to fulfill the will of the creatures, the children of the Covenant, in the manner that we can. And the principle of the matter is that anyone that benefits his fellow, whether with money, or food or any other needs - even with good words, words of consolation (Bava Batra 9a) - is included in the commandment of charity and his reward is very much. And may my words enter your ears, as they are good, in the 'ear that examines words.'

And they, may their memory be Blessed, said (Ketuvot 67b) that we trick a poor person who does not want to take [charity] and we give it to him [as] a loan, and afterwards we do not ask it back from him. But we do not pay attention to a wealthy person who torments himself and who has a bad eye with his [own] money. And they, may their memory be Blessed, said (Ketuvot 67b), "'Enough for his lack' (Deuteronomy 15:8) - you are commanded to fill his lack, but you are not commanded to make him wealthy." And Rambam, may his memory be Blessed, wrote (Mishneh Torah, Laws of Gifts to the Poor 9:3) that he never saw and never heard of a city that has ten [or more] from Israel that did not have a charity fund. And they, may their memory be Blessed, said that even a poor person that sustains himself from charity is obligated to [give] charity if he finds someone [more needy] than he, who needs it. And they, may their memory be Blessed, said (Mishneh Torah, Laws of Gifts to the Poor 10:2) that no man ever came to poverty because of doing too much charity (tsedekah), as it is stated (Isaiah 32:17), "And the work of righteousness (tsedekah) shall be peace." And Israel is only redeemed in the merit of charity, as it is stated (Isaiah 1:27), "Zion will be redeemed with justice (tsedekah)." [These] and the rest of its details are in [several] scattered places in the Talmud, but most of them are in Tractate Ketuvot (Chapter 6) and in Bava Batra (Chapter 1).

And it is practiced in every place and at all times by males and females. And one who transgresses it and does not do charity at a time that he is asked for it - or he sees that the thing is needed - and he has the ability in his hand to do it, has violated this positive commandment.

Mitzvah 480

To not refrain from lending before the sabbatical year: To not refrain from lending to those that need, due to fear of the sabbatical year, that it not remove the debt. And about this is it stated (Deuteronomy 15:9), "Guard yourself, lest there be a wanton thing in your heart saying, 'The sabbatical year is approaching.'" And the language of Sifrei Devarim 117 is "'Guard yourself' as a negative commandment; 'lest there be' as a negative commandment" - meaning to say that these two negative commandments come about this matter, one after the other to strengthen [it].

It is from the roots of the commandment [that it is] to strengthen and to fix the trait of generosity in our hearts and to completely distance the trait of stinginess. And there is no more generous person in the world than one who lends out his money while knowing that the time is approaching to release his loan and to lose it for him - if maybe some accident will occur or some circumstance that he will not be able to claim his loan before the sabbatical year. And anyone who understands the ways of the Torah and grasps to understand even a little of the grace of its value knows with certainty that 'one who distributes his money to the ones that need it, will have more added; but the one who refrains from the straight [deeds], it will be for lacking.' As God, may He be Blessed, judges a man according to his deeds, and endows him from His blessing according to his coming close to it. And the trait of stinginess is an iron partition between him and the blessing, whereas generosity is a part of the blessing. And [so] it comes out that the one that practices it is [already] in it. 'The wise man listens and adds insight.'

The laws of the commandment are short [and] included in the simple understanding of the verse, according to my opinion.

And the prohibition is practiced by males and females in any place and at all times. As even at this time, when the release of monies is not practiced from Torah writ, but only from rabbinic writ; nonetheless we are [still] warned to not refrain from lending to the one that needs it out of fear that the sabbatical year - that releases rabbinically at this time and from Torah writ at the time of the [Temple]. And one who transgresses it and refrains from lending to the one who needs it has violated a negative commandment. But there are no lashes for it, as there is no act [involved] with it.

And maybe it will come to your thought, my son, to say, "And why should a person ever refrain from lending because of this; and why was a negative commandment written about this - is it not in our hand to make a condition with him, on condition that it not be released in the seventh [year] and in the way that we always do in our contracts?" Let this thing not confuse you, as the Torah warns us about things, even though it is possible [to circumvent them] with ordinances and conditions.

Mitzvah 481
To not send a Hebrew slave empty: That we not release a Hebrew slave with empty hands from our servitude when he goes out to freedom at the end of six years, but rather that we endow him from our wealth regardless. And about this is it stated (Deuteronomy 15:13), "When you send him free, do not send him empty."

From the roots of this commandment, all of its content and the place of its elucidation are [all] written in the positive commandment of endowment in this Order (Sefer HaChinukh 482).

Mitzvah 482
To endow him upon his leaving to freedom: To give from what we have to the Hebrew slave at the time that he leaves from under our hand to freedom, and we should not send him empty-handed. And about this is it stated (Deuteronomy 15:14), "You shall surely endow him; from your flock and from your threshing floor and from your vat that the Lord, your God, has Blessed you, shall you give to him."

It is from the roots of the commandment [that it is] in order that we acquire for our souls virtuous, dear and beautiful traits; [such that] with a dear and virtuous soul, we will merit the good - and the good God wants to do good for His people. And it is our glory and our splendor that we should have mercy upon the one who served us, and that we give from what is ours as a rite of kindness - besides that which we have stipulated with him to give him his wage. And it is a rational thing - there is no need to be lengthy about it.

From the laws of the commandment - that which they, may their memory be Blessed, said (Kiddushin 16b) that it is one whether the male slave leaves at the end of six years or at the Jubilee year or with the death of the master, and so [too] a female slave that leaves from one of all these or from signs [of physical maturity], behold we endow these, but with the subtracting of money [that allows him to leave mid-term], we do not endow them, as it is stated (Deuteronomy 15:13), "When you send him free," and this one he did not send, but rather the slave caused it with the giving of money that he should leave from under his hand; so [too,] that which they, may their memory be Blessed, expounded (Kiddushin 17a) about that which the verse mentioned flock, threshing floor and vat, that it is with things that have blessing on their own that a man is obligated to endow them, but not [with] monies and clothing; that which they, may their memory be Blessed, said (Kiddushin 17a) that we do not reduce [the endowment] below thirty sela ; that he is obligated to endow him whether the homeowner was Blessed on his account or not Blessed; [that] the endowment of the slave is for himself, and that [the slave's] creditor does not collect from it; and the rest of its details - are [all] elucidated in the first chapter of Kiddushin.

And this commandment is practiced by males and females at the time of the [Temple], as the law of a Hebrew slave is only practiced at the time that the Jubilee is practiced, as I have written in what preceded (Sefer HaChinukh 42). And nonetheless, even at this time, 'the wise man listens and adds insight' - such that if he employed someone from the children of Israel and he served him for a long time or even a short time, he should endow him with that which God Blessed him when he leaves him.

Mitzvah 483
To not work with consecrated things: To not do work with consecrated beasts. And about this is it stated (Deuteronomy 15:19), "you shall not work with your first-born ox." And the rest of the holy things are learned from the first-born, as it appears in Bekhorot 25a.

I have written in this Order on the prohibition of the disqualified consecrated things (Sefer HaChinukh 469) and in several places that from the roots of the commandment is to distance ourselves from getting close to the consecrated things and from touching them.

Sefer HaChinukh

From the laws of the commandment is that which they, may their memory be Blessed, said (Bekhorot 25a) that all consecrated things for the altar - whether higher-level consecrated things or lower-level consecrated things - are forbidden in shearing and work (see Mishneh Torah, Laws of Trespass 1:1, 7); and it is forbidden for commoners (non-priests) to benefit from the consecrated things of God - whether from consecrated things offered on the altar, or whether of the [Temple] upkeep - and anyone who benefits from the value of a small coin has misappropriated. There is no misappropriation of those sacrifices that have become permissible to eat, such as meat of the sin-offering and guilt-offering after the sprinkling of their blood, or the two breads after the sprinkling of the blood of the two lambs. Even if a commoner ate from one of these and similar to them - since they are permissible for some people to benefit from, anyone who benefits from them has not misappropriated. And even if they became disqualified and forbidden to eat - since there was a time that they were permitted, one is not [any longer] liable for misappropriation for them.

Anyone who misappropriates volitionally is lashed and pays the principal of what he damaged of the sacred. And its warning is from that which is stated (Deuteronomy 12:17), "You may not eat in your gates, etc. your vows" - we learned from the tradition that this is a warning to the one that eats meat of the fire-offering - as we said above (Sefer HaChinukh 447), since all of it is for God, may He be Blessed. And the law is the same for the rest of all the consecrated which is only for God - whether it is from the consecrated for the altar or the consecrated of the [Temple] upkeep: If he benefited of the value of a small coin, he is lashed. If he misappropriated inadvertently, he pays what he benefited and an addition of a fifth, and he brings a ram [purchased] with two sela and sacrifices it as a guilt-offering and it atones for him - and this is what is called the guilt-offering of misappropriations, as it is stated (Leviticus 5:15-16), "inadvertently from the consecrated things of the Lord, etc. he shall bring his guilt-offering to the Lord, etc. And that which he sinned from the holy, he shall pay and add its fifth upon it." The payment of the principal with the addition of the fifth and the bringing of the sacrifice is a positive commandment (Sefer HaChinukh 127). The payment of the principal and the bringing of the guilt-offering impede the atonement, but not the fifth; as it is stated about the ram of the guilt offering (Leviticus 5:16), "and he shall be forgiven" - the ram and the guilt-offering impede, but the fifth does not impede [it]. If he brought his misappropriation [offering] before he brought his guilt [payment], he has not fulfilled [his obligation]. If he is in doubt if he misappropriated or did not misappropriate, he is exempted from the payments and from the sacrifice. And the fifth is like the beginning of the consecrated things; and [so] if he benefited from it, he adds a fifth to [the] fifth. And we have already elucidated several times (see Sefer HaChinukh 355) that the fifth is one of four [parts] of the principal, [such that] it and its fifth are five. And there are things that one is not liable for misappropriation from Torah writ, but it is forbidden to benefit from them rabbinically; and one who benefits from them only pays the principle, but does not add a fifth and does not bring a guilt-offering, as is elucidated in Tractate Meilah (Chapter 3).

And all consecrated things for the altar - whether higher-level consecrated things or lower-level consecrated things - are forbidden in shearing and work, as it is stated (Deuteronomy 15:19), "you shall not work with your first-born ox and you shall not shear the first-born of your flock." And the law is the same for the rest of the consecrated things. And one who shears his ox or works with it is lashed from Torah writ. But plucking is not like shearing. And Rambam, may his memory be Blessed, wrote (Mishneh Torah, Laws of Trespass 1:7), "It appears to me that he is not lashed until he shears enough for the double width of a sit, - [so that] it not be more stringent than Shabbat." [If] it is a doubt whether it is consecrated things, such as a beast that was [only a possible] first-born, and similar to it - behold, they are forbidden in shearing and work, but one who shears or works with them is not lashed (Mishneh Torah, Laws of Trespass 1:8). A consecrated beast that contracted a blemish upon it and was redeemed is not permitted for shearing and work and [remains] with its prohibition until it is slaughtered, as we elucidated (Sefer HaChinukh 441). If it is slaughtered after its redemption, its eating is permitted. About what are these words speaking? When their consecration came before their blemish, or [only] a temporary blemish preceded their consecration. But if one consecrates one with a permanent blemish to the Temple, it is only rabbinically forbidden in shearing and work. And [so] if it is redeemed, it is like non-sacred in all matters; and it goes out to be non-sacred, to be shorn and worked - except for the first-born and the tithe. [In those latter cases,] the sanctity rests upon their bodies, and they do not ever go out to be non-sacred to shear and to work, even though they were ones with blemishes from the beginning. It is forbidden to have a first-born or a disqualified consecrated [animal] breed. And it is permissible a priori to pluck the hair from consecrated [animals] in order to show the blemish to an expert. But that hair that he plucked - or that shed from the beast, or from a first-born or from the tithe - behold, it is forbidden to benefit [from] it, even after they were slaughtered because of their blemish. [This is a] decree lest he will delay them, since they are not bringing atonement. But wool that shed from a sin-offering or a guilt-offering is permitted for benefit after being slaughtered because of their blemish; as since they are coming for atonement, he will not delay them. And if it was plucked from a fire-offering - behold, this is a doubt. And behold, all that detached from the consecrated [animals] after they contracted the blemish is permissible for benefit, since he did not pluck it with his hand; except for the first-born, as even that which detached from it after it contracted the blemish is forbidden in benefit. One who slaughters a first-born or the rest of the consecrated [animals] plucks from this [side] and that [side] to make a place for the knife, but he does not move [the hair] from its place. Those consecrated for the [Temple] upkeep are rabbinically forbidden even in shearing and work, but they are not forbidden from Torah writ. Hence one who shears them or works with them is not lashed [from Torah writ], but we lash him with lashes of rebellion. One who consecrates an embryo for the altar, its mother [becomes] rabbinically forbidden in work. They decreed about it, as its work enfeebles the embryo. But behold, it is permitted in shearing, as there is no loss with this to the offspring. If one consecrated one limb of a beast - whether for the [Temple] upkeep or whether for the altar - behold, this is a doubt if it is all forbidden in shearing and work or not. Hence, we did not administer lashes for it. [These] and the rest of its details are in Tractate Bekhorot.

And this prohibition is practiced in every place and at all times by males and females. As even though they, may their memory be Blessed, said (Avodah Zarah 13a) that we do not consecrate a beast for a sacrifice or for the [Temple] upkeep at this time - as we have written many times - nonetheless, the consecration of one who does consecrate [it], is effective. And one who transgresses this and works with a beast [that is] consecrated, in the way that we said, is liable for lashes.

Mitzvah 484

To not shear the wool of consecrated [animals]: That we not shear the wool form a beast of the consecrated. And about this is it stated (Deuteronomy 15:19), "and you shall not shear the first-born of your flock." And all of the other consecrated [animals] are learned from the first-born concerning this prohibition. And all of the content of the prohibition of shearing is like the prohibition of working - it is not fitting to write at any more length about it. Behold, I have written some of the laws of shearing above with the laws of work.

Mitzvah 485

To not eat chamets after midday: To not eat chamets after midday on the fourteenth day of Nissan. And about this is it stated (Deuteronomy 16:3), "You shall not eat chamets upon it." Rambam, may his memory be Blessed, wrote (Sefer HaMitzvot LaRambam, Mitzvot Lo Taase 199), "The word 'upon it,' refers back to the Pesach lamb, the obligation of which to slaughter was in the afternoon of the fourteenth day. And they said from the moment that the time of its sacrifice arrives, 'You shall not eat chamets upon it.' And in Pesachim 28b, they, may their memory be Blessed, said, 'From where [do I know] that one who eats chamets from six hours and onward is [transgressing] a negative commandment? As it is stated "You shall not eat chamets upon it."' And there (Pesachim 4b) it is said, 'According to everyone, however, chamets is prohibited by Torah writ from six hours and onward.' So, have we found the language of all the precise textual variants that were read by the elders of the Talmud? And there is it said about the reason for the prohibition of chamets within the sixth hour, 'The rabbis made an extra distancing, so as not to reach a Torah prohibition.' And one who transgresses and eats chamets after midday is lashed." To here [are his words].

It is from the roots of the commandment [that it is] because the matter of the prohibition of chamets

Sefer HaChinukh

on Pesach is an extremely weighty prohibition, from the angle that it is a great foundation in our religion; since the exodus from Egypt is a sign and wonder that necessitates [there having been] a creation of the world, which is a great pillar upon which the chambers of the Torah rest - as we have written several times. And therefore, any commandment that is in commemoration of the exodus from Egypt is weighty for us and very beloved. Hence from the angle of the great weightiness that there is to it, the Torah warned us to begin it six hours before the set time for that miracle, which is the beginning of the (holiday) fifteenth day. And all of this is in order that we put the weightiness of the commandment and the greatness of its content into our hearts, in our seeing that the Torah makes a fence for us around it.

From the laws of the commandment is that which they, may their memory be Blessed, said (Pesachim 11b) that we eat chamets all [the first] four hours of this day, and we suspend [it] all of the fifth - meaning to say that we do not eat [it], due to the decree because of a cloudy day, and we do not burn [it], but rather we [can] benefit from it, to feed it to any creature or to sell it to a person - and we burn it at the beginning of the sixth hour. And this is an ordinance of the Sages regarding the commandment, in order to distance a person from sin, so that he will not stumble to eat it at the beginning of the seventh hour - which is a Torah prohibition, as we have said. And [it is] also like they, may their memory be Blessed expounded from another verse; as they said there in Pesachim 4b, "It is is written (Exodus 12:19), 'Seven days leaven, etc.,' yet it is [also] written (Exodus 12:15), 'but on the first day, etc.' Behold, how is this? [It is] to include the fourteenth day for destruction [of chamets]." And [so] the understanding of "first" (rishon) would be like [its usage], "Were you born rishon Adam" (Job 15:7), the understanding of which is before. And from that which the verse obligated to dispose of it on that day, we knew that part of that day would necessarily be permitted, as it is impossible to determine the exact first instant of a day and dispose of it then. And since it is like this: That part of the day is permitted, and Scripture did not elucidate which part of it is permissible, we divided it equally from true logic - as if you divide in [any] other way, there will be no foundation to the thing at all. And that is what they said over there, "[The word,] 'but (akh),' divides." And those that explained that akh is chats (divide) in [the letter susbtitution pattern called], "achs, betaa" did not understand the words of the Sages. [This] and the rest of the details of the commandment are in Tractate Pesachim in the first chapter.

And it is practiced by males and females in all places and at all times, even at this time when we do not have the Pesach sacrifice. And one who transgresses it and eats a kazayit of chamets after midday is liable for lashes, according to the opinion of Rambam, may his memory be Blessed. [This is] because he holds (Sefer HaMitzvot LaRambam, Mitzvot Lo Taase 199) that the law is like Rabbi Yehudah, who said that one who eats chamets before Pesach - [by which] I mean on the fourteenth day of Nissan from midday and onward - violates the negative commandment that we mentioned. But Ramban, may his memory be Blessed, disagrees with him (in his glosses to the Sefer HaMitzvot, Mitzot Lo Taase 199). And according to his opinion, there is no negative commandment in this, since the law is like Rabbi Shimon, who disagrees with Rabbi Yehudah. [Rabbi Shimon] says, "Whether it is before its time or whether after its time, he does not violate anything." And he expounds the matter from that which it is written (Deuteronomy 16:3), "'You shall not eat chamets upon it, seven days shall you eat matsot upon it'; at the time that a man is in the positive commandment of 'eat matsot,' there is the prohibition of 'do not eat chamets,' and at the time that he is not in the commandment of eat matsa - which is whether before the time of Pesach or whether afterwards - he is not in the prohibition of 'do not eat chamets.'" And according to the opinion of Rabbi Shimon, the word, "upon it," refers back to the eating of the Pesach sacrifice, which is eaten in the evening. And so is it explicit in the Talmud Yerushalmi Pesachim 1:4 that according to the words of Rabbi Yehudah, the word, "upon it," refers back to its slaughter; and according to the words of Rabbi Shimon to its eating, as it was eaten in the evening. And that which appears in the Gemara, "According to everyone, however, chamets is prohibited," and so [too,] what they said, "The rabbis made an extra distancing, so as not to reach a Torah prohibition" - all of this is true, that there is a Torah prohibition to benefit from chamets after six hours. However, the prohibition that comes upon it is from the commandment to dispose [of chamets] from Torah writ from six hours onward, but certainly there is no negative commandment in it at all - like Rabbi Shimon, like whom we hold. And so, is it explicit there in the Gemara, "[That] according to everyone, however, chamets is by Torah writ from six hours and onward, from where do we [know it]? Abbaye said, 'Two verses are written, etc.'" And the end of his words there are, "Behold, how is this? [It is] to include the fourteenth day for destruction [of chamets]." Behold, it is clear that there is no prohibition about it after midday - according to the [legal conclusion] - except for the Torah commandment of disposing [of it]. Behold, according to the opinion of [Ramban], may his memory be Blessed, this negative commandment of "You shall not eat," is not included in the tally of the commandments. Extend your ear, my son, and listen to the words of the sages - 'these and those are the words of the living God.' And know that that there are seventy faces to Torah, and [that] they are all correct.

Mitzvah 486
To not leave over from the festive (chagigah) sacrifice to the third day: To not leave over anything from the festive sacrifice of the fourteenth day until the third day - and that is the sacrifice that comes with the Pesach [sacrifice] to increase the joy - but rather to eat it all within two days, which are are the fourteenth and fifteenth. And about this is it stated (Deuteronomy 16:4), "and none of the meat of what you slaughter on the evening of the first day shall be left to the morning." And the received (traditional) understanding came upon this (Pesachim 71a) that the verse is speaking about the festive [sacrifice] that comes with the Pesach, [to say] that the time of its eating is up to two days. And about this festive [sacrifice], Scripture stated (Deuteronomy 16:2), "And you shall slaughter the Pesach to the Lord, your God, flock and cattle" - meaning to say, that with the Pesach, he bring another sacrifice; meaning to increase the joy.

From the roots of the commandment is the fixed foundation that we have about the commandment of the matter of the Pesach [sacrifice], which is a strong commandment and foundation in our Torah. And hence we were commanded to make the day of its slaughtering a day of joy; and there is no complete joy for people without the proliferation of meat. And this is [the reason for] that which we have been commanded not to leave over at all to the third day from all of the meat that is slaughtered in honor of the joy of the Pesach. But rather, all of it must be eaten on its day, to increase upon it the gladness and the satiation of joyous occasions. And that which is said here is besides the reason that is written about leaving over [sacrifices in general] in the Order of Tsav (Sefer HaChinukh 143), which 'gives a reason (or, taste) for the better,' in all of the prohibitions of that which is left over.

From the laws of the commandment is that which they, may their memory be Blessed, said (Pesachim 70a) that a man has not fulfilled his obligation of the festive [sacrifice] of the festival - which is also a positive commandment - with the festive [sacrifice] of the fourteenth, as is written in Mishpatim on the commandment to celebrate the festivals (Sefer HaChinukh 88). But he does fulfill his obligation with it for the obligation of the joy of the festival - which is also a positive commandment [as well] - as we have written in this Order (Sefer HaChinukh 488); as the content of the obligation of joy is only to increase meat in order to rejoice, and behold, there is meat [in this]. And from this reason, they, may their memory be Blessed, said (Chagigah 7b) that we have fulfilled the [commandment of the] peace-offerings of joy even with a [a sacrifice that is the fulfillment of a] vow or oath of peace-offerings, and even if we slaughtered them before the festival - so long as he eats from them during the festival. As one does not have to slaughter the peace-offering of joy at the time of the joy. And one also need not slaughter them for the sake of the peace-offerings of joy - as the essence of the commandment is only to increase the joy with meat, as we have said. And [this] and the rest of its details are elucidated in Tractate Chagigah and in [various] places of Tractate Pesachim.

And this commandment is practiced at the time of the [Temple] by males and females; as even women are obligated in peace-offerings of joy - even though [they are] caused by time - just as they are obligated in resting on [the festival of which it is a part]. And one who transgresses it and leaves over anything from this festive sacrifice to the third day is obligated to burn it with fire, as is the law with that which is left over. And hence there is no liability for lashes for this positive commandment, since it is rectified by a positive commandment - from the principle known to us about this.

Sefer HaChinukh

Mitzvah 487

To not sacrifice the Pesach sacrifice on the bamah (altar) of an individual: That we were prevented from sacrificing the Pesach lamb on the bamah of an individual, and even during the time that [a bamah was] permissible. And the matter of the bamah is that before the building of the Choice House, each and every individual from Israel who wanted to offer a sacrifice would build an edifice in any place he wanted and offer his sacrifices there to God, may He be Blessed. And even at that time when it was permitted for them to do so, [that was] specifically with the other sacrifices. But we always only offer the Pesach sacrifice on the community altar, and that is the place where there was the tabernacle there. And about this is it stated (Deuteronomy 16:5), "You may not slaughter the Pesach in one of your gates." And likewise, they, may their memory be Blessed, said at the end of the first chapter of Megillah 9b, "There is no difference between a large (communal) bamah and a small (private) bamah besides Pesach sacrifices."

It is from the roots of the commandment [that it is] to fix the greatness of the matter of the Pesach [sacrifice] and the preciousness of the commandment in our souls, from the reason that I wrote many times about it. And in truth, there is more glory for the commandment when they would do it all together in a specific place, and not each and every individual in the area he desires.

The laws of the commandment are in the first chapter of Megillah.

And this prohibition is practiced at the time of the [Temple] - as then do we offer the Pesach sacrifice - by males and females, as [females] are also obligated in the Pesach sacrifice, and as I wrote on the commandment of the Pesach in the Order of Bo, on [Commandment] 5. And it is possible to say that even at this time, one who transgress and consecrates a lamb as a Pesach and offers it on a private bamah has violated this negative commandment and is liable for lashes.

Mitzvah 488

The commandment to rejoice on the festivals: To rejoice on the festivals, as it is stated (Deuteronomy 16:14), "And you shall rejoice on your holiday." And the first matter that is hinted in joy is that we offer peace-offerings regardless at the Choice House. And [this] is like the matter that is written (Deuteronomy 27:7), "And you shall offer peace-offerings" and it continues, "and you shall rejoice on your holiday." And [concerning] the offering of peace-offerings, they, may their memory be Blessed, said (Chagigah 6b), "Women are obligated in joy" - meaning that even they are obligated to bring peace-offerings of joy. And they, may their memory be Blessed, also said (Chagigah 8a), "Rejoice in all types of rejoicing." And included in this is the eating of meat and the drinking of wine, to wear new clothes, the distribution of fruit and types of sweets to the youths and the women and to play musical instruments in the Temple alone - and that is the joy of the drawing house (simchat beit hashoeva) that is mentioned in the Gemara (Sukkah 50a). All that we mentioned is included in "And you shall rejoice on your holiday." And they, may their memory be Blessed, said in Tractate Pesachim 109a, "A man is obligated to gladden his children and the members of his household on a festival." And it is said there, "It was taught, Rabbi Yehuda ben Beteira says, 'At the time when the Temple is standing, joy is only with meat, as it is stated (Deuteronomy 27:7), "And you shall offer peace-offerings, etc." Now [...] joy is only with wine, as it is stated (Psalms 104:15), "And wine gladdens the heart of man."'" And they said further, "With what should one make them rejoice? Men with what is fit for them, with wine. And women with what is fit for them, with nice clothes." And the Torah also warned us to include the poor and the strangers (converts) and the weak in the joy, as it is stated (Deuteronomy 16:14), "you, the Levite, the stranger, the orphan and the widow."

It is from the roots of the commandment [that it is] because man is designed in [such] a way that his nature requires rejoicing occasionally, [just] like it requires nourishment regardless, and rest and sleep. And God wanted to give us - 'His people and the flock of His grazing' - merit and [so] commanded us to make the rejoicing for His sake, so that we could merit in all of our deeds in front of Him. And behold, He fixed for us times during the year for holidays, to remember upon them the miracles and the goodnesses that He granted us. And He commanded us then at those times to support the physical with something of joy that it needs. And it comes out as a big remedy for us that the satiation of joyous occasions be for His sake and to remember Him; as this thought will be a fence, that we do not go further out than is enough from the straight path. And the one who has reflection without a desire to argue will find reason in my words.

And I have written a few of the laws of the commandment above. And the rest of its details are in Tractate Chagigah and in [various] places scattered in the Gemara.

And this commandment is practiced regarding the joy - but not regarding the sacrifice - in every place and at all times by males and females. And one who transgresses it and does not rejoice himself, the members of his household and the poor according to his ability, for the sake of the commandment of the festival, has nullified this positive commandment. And in the way that we mentioned did they, may their memory be Blessed, say (Avot 2:17), "All of your actions should be for the sake of Heaven."

Mitzvah 489

To appear on the festivals in the Choice House: That we were commanded to have all males appear in Jerusalem at the Choice House three set times a year - and they are Pesach, Shavout and Sukkot. And about this is it stated (Deuteronomy 16:16), "Three times a year all your males shall appear before the Lord, your God." And the content of the commandment is that every man go up to the Temple and appear there with any male child that he has who is able to walk by himself on his [own] feet. And from this obligation of appearing is also that he sacrifice a fire-offering there. And this sacrifice is called the fire-offering of being seen (olat reiah). And there is no measure for this sacrifice - even a dove or a fledgling exempt [one]. And I have already written in Mishpatim on the commandment to celebrate on the festivals (Sefer HaChinukh 88), that which they, may their memory be Blessed, said (Chagigah 10b) [that] three commandments was Israel commanded on the holiday: celebration, being seen and joy. And they would bring a sacrifice for each one of these three commandments and they are called the festive sacrifice, the peace-offerings of joy and the fire-offering of being seen.

It is from the roots of the commandment [that it is] in order that all of Israel see and place upon their hearts, through the act of the sacrifice which awakens the hearts, that all of them - from the small to the great - are God's portion and His inheritance, a holy and chosen people, those that guard His testimonies, the treasure from all the peoples under all of the skies [that] keep His statutes and observe His religion. Hence, they come three times a year to the House of God. And it is like their saying metaphorically, "Behold, we are like slaves to God, entering and coming under the shade of His roof, relying upon His strength forever and ever in the love for Him and in the fear of Him; and no foreigner shall come among us, as we alone are the children of His house." And with this act, our minds are aroused and we place His fear into our hearts and we fix His love into our thoughts, and we merit to receive His kindness and His blessing. And the obligation comes to us only upon the males, since they are the essence of the household, and the infants and wives are attached to them; and when there is control over [the males] as slaves, the control is [also] established over all that is under their hand. And from this foundation was the commandment at the appointed time of the sabbatical year during the holiday of Sukkot made unique, to gather there the men, women, infants and strangers. As that year liberates all and removes the subjugation from all the living - from all flesh - to return everything back under the hand of the Master, the Lord of Hosts. And then during that year the control over those under them is not effective, as there is no domination in the Land at that time. And there is another reason with us for the commandment of gathering (hakhel) - we shall write it in its place in the Order of Atem Netsavim (Sefer HaChinukh 612) with God's help. **From** the laws of the commandment is that which they, may their memory be Blessed, said (Mishneh Torah, Laws of Festival Offering 1:8), that the fire-offering of being seen and the peace-offerings of joy do not push off [the restrictions of] Shabbat or impurity, but they do push off the holiday, even though we do not [otherwise] sacrifice vows and oaths on the holiday. And I have also written some of its laws in the Order of Mishpatim on the commandment of celebration (Sefer HaChinukh 88). And there I wrote by whom it is practiced and by whom it is not practiced and all of its content, as is the custom of the book.

Mitzvah 490

To not go up for the festival without a sacrifice: To not go up to the Choice House on the festival without a sacrifice that we will offer there - and that is the sacrifice that we explained above in this Order (Sefer HaChinukh 489), that is called the fire-offering of being seen. And about this is it stated (Deuteronomy 16:16), "and they shall not appear empty with the face of the Lord." The understanding of "face (pnei)" is like "in front of (lifnei)." And there I wrote from the roots of the commandment and all of its content. And this warning (negative commandment) is not practiced by females, [just] like the positive commandment that comes upon this is not practiced by females.

Mitzvah 491
To appoint judges and officers: To appoint (see Sefer HaMitzvot LaRambam, Mitzvot Ase 176) judges and officers that coerce [others] to do the commandments of the Torah, bring those that are veering from the path of the truth back to it against their will, order that which is fitting to do, prevent disgusting things and enforce the fences against the transgressor - so that the commandments and the preventions of the Torah not require the belief (acceptance) of each and every person. And it is from the conditions of this commandment that these judges should be one level above the other. That is that we set up twenty-three judges in each and every city that is fit for this number, all gathered together in one place from the gates of the city - and that is called a small sanhedrin. And in Jerusalem, we set up a large court of seventy judges, and we stand up one [judge] over these seventy and he is called the head of the academy - and he is the one that the Sages also called, nassi - and they would all be gathered in their place that is designated for them. And in a place that is small of number, such that it is not fit for a small sanhedrin, they should stand up three [that] should judge the small thing and they bring the difficult thing to the [court] that is above them. And likewise, do they appoint supervisors among the people that circulate in the city, the markets and the streets [and] observe the matters of people in commercial buying and selling - so that there not be wrongdoing, even with a small thing. And the commandment that comes about this is that which He, may He Blessed, stated (Deuteronomy 16:18), "Judges and officers shall you place for yourself in all of your gates." And the language of Sifrei Devarim 144 (and see Sanhedrin 16b), "From where [do we know] that we appoint a court for all of Israel? [Hence] we learn to say, 'Judges and officers.' And from where [do we know] that we appoint one [judge] on top of them all? [Hence] we learn to say, 'shall you place for yourself.' And from where [do we know] that we appoint a court for each and every tribe? [Hence] we learn to say, 'in all of your gates.' Rabban Shimon ben Gamliel said, '"For your tribes and they shall judge" - [that] is a commandment on each and every tribe to judge its tribe; "and they shall judge the people" - against their will.'" And this commandment to appoint seventy elders has already been repeated, and that is His, may He be Blessed, stating to Moshe, peace be upon him, "Gather for Me seventy men" (Numbers 11:16). And they, may their memory be Blessed, said (Sifrei Bamidbar 92), "Every place that it is stated, 'for Me,' behold it is an observance forever; and so [is it], 'And they shall be priests for Me, etc.' (Exodus 28:41)" - meaning to say, that it is a permanent commandment and not just temporary, but rather all of the days of the earth.

The root of the commandment is revealed - that with this thing, we will support our religion, in that the fear of our officials and our judges will be on the face of the masses. And from their being accustomed to the good and the straight because of fear, the people will teach their natures to do justice and righteousness out of love, in their recognizing the true path. And [it is] like the Sages say, that much habit is what is behind nature - meaning to say that [just] like nature constrains a man to what it wants, so [too] does a strong habit repeat itself, like a persistent nature that constrains him to always go in the way of the habit. And in the people going in the straight paths and in faith and choosing the good, the good will cling to them and God will rejoice in His creatures.

From the laws of the commandment is that which they, may their memory be Blessed, said (Sanhedrin 36b, and see Mishneh Torah, Laws of The Sanhedrin and the Penalties within their Jurisdiction 1:3) that the greatest of the seventy sits below the nassi, and he is the one called the av beit din. And the rest of the seventy sit according to their years, and according to their wisdom in proximity to the nassi ; meaning to say that each one who is greater than his fellow in wisdom is closer to him, and the ones that are equal in wisdom go according to the most [number of] years. And they all sit in a semi-circle made like half of a round threshing floor, so that they would all see each other. And they would also

Sefer HaChinukh

set up two courts of twenty-three in front of them - one group at the entrance to the [Temple] yard, and one group at the entrance to the Temple Mount. And the greatest in each group is the leader of his group.

We only place (Sanhedrin 17a, and Mishneh Torah, Laws of The Sanhedrin and the Penalties within their Jurisdiction 2:1-2) on the sanhedrin - whether big or small - men that are wise and understanding about the wisdom of the Torah, and also know some of the other wisdoms, such as healing, mathematics, seasons, calculations, astronomy and the ways of the soothsayers, the clairvoyants and the sorcerers, so that they can judge the people in all of these ways if there is a need for it. And we only place on the Sanhedrin priests, Levites and pedigreed Israelites that are fit to marry off their daughters to the priesthood, as it is stated about Moshe (Numbers 11:16), "and they shall stand there with you" - and they, may their memory Blessed, expounded (Sanhedrin 37b), "With those similar to you."

And we never set up a sanhedrin - whether big or small - except [with] ordained judges. And Moshe, our teacher, ordained Yehoshua, his student, with his hands (by pressing his hands upon him), as it is written (Numbers 27:23), "He pressed his hands upon him." And likewise, he ordained the seventy elders that he gathered to himself; and those elders ordained others, and others, others, until the end of all those ordained. However, the ordination of all the generations was not with the hand, like the ordination of Moshe; but rather they would check if the one they wanted to ordain was an expert in the wisdom of the Torah and if he was healthy and complete in his intellect and if was a man that loves truth and hates wrongdoing and all of its content. And after great investigation into his makeup and his wisdom, three ordained sages - or even if only one of them was ordained - would say to him, "Behold, you are ordained." And from that time, they call him, "rabbi," and he has permission afterwards to even adjudicate cases of penalties. And the law that a judge [who is] very old, a eunuch, blind even in one of his eyes or does not have children is not fit to be on a sanhedrin; the law that the kings of the House of David judge and we judge them, but not the [other] kings of Israel, since they are not assumed to be fit like [the House of David]; the law [about] until when the Great Sanhedrin or a small one or a court of three sit [in judgement]; and the rest of its details are [all] elucidated in Tractate Sanhedrin.

And this commandment - meaning the great and small sanhedrins and the court of three - is practiced in the Land of Israel, as ordination is there, but not outside of the Land, since we do not ordain outside of the Land. Yet regardless, anyone ordained in the Land is fit to judge even outside of the Land. And this is what they, may their memory be Blessed, said (Makkot 7a), "Sanhedin is practiced in the Land and outside of the Land." However, they do not have permission to judge capital cases - not in the Land and not outside the Land - except at the time of the [Temple], and at the time when the Sanhedrin is fixed in Jerusalem.

And this is one of the commandments that is incumbent on the community, every [community] in each and every place. And a community that is fit to establish a court among them - as is elucidated in Tractate Sanhedrin 2b - and does not establish it for themselves, has violated this positive commandment and their punishment is very great, as this commandment is a strong pillar in preservation of the religion. And we should learn from this that even though - on account of our iniquities - we do not have ordained [judges] in our days, each and every congregation in every place should appoint among themselves some of the best of themselves to be a power above all of them; to coerce with all types of coercion [as they see fit] - monetary or corporal - for the commandments of the Torah or to prevent anything that is disgusting and anything similar to it from among them. And it is also fitting for those appointed to straighten their [own] ways and to refine their deeds and remove the disparagement of the people from among them; lest the [people] answer their rebuke, that they should [first] remove the beam (their own iniquity) between their eyes. And they should always seek the benefit of their fellows that are dependent upon them, to teach them the true path and to bring peace among them with all their strength. And they should abandon and leave and forget all pleasures from their hearts. And they should put their hearts to this and most of their thoughts and occupation should be about this. And [then] the verse will be established through them (Daniel 12:3), "And the enlightened ones will be radiant like the brightness of the firmament, and those who lead the many to righteousness will be like the stars forever and ever."

Mitzvah 492
To not plant any tree-idols: To not plant any trees in the Temple or next to the altar. And about this is it stated (Deuteronomy 17:21), "You shall not plant for yourself a tree-god, any tree next to the altar of the Lord, your God, etc." Rambam, may his memory be Blessed, wrote about the reason for this prohibition (Sefer HaMitzvot LaRambam, Mitzvot Lo Taase 13) [that it is] since the worshippers of idolatry would do like this in their houses of idolatry to plant beautiful trees there. And [so] to distance anything that is similar to them from the thoughts of people that come to the worship of God, Blessed be He, in the chosen place, we were prevented from planting any tree there. And from the angle of the simple understanding, [this explanation] is likely.

From the laws of the commandment - that which they, may their memory be Blessed, said (Tamid 28b) that the prohibition is not [only] to plant the tree exactly next to the altar like the simple understand of the verse, but rather even one who plants it anywhere in the [Temple] yard is lashed, as the whole yard is called "next to the altar"; [that] whether it is a [fruit] tree or a fruitless tree, it is all included in this and he is lashed for it; [that] to make a fence for this prohibition, the Sages also said that it is forbidden to make a veranda of wood in the Temple in the way that people do in their [own] courtyards, and even though it is by building and not by planting, as it is stated, "any tree (which is also the word for wood)," but rather all fine structures and verandas that extended from the walls that were in the Temple were of stone; and all the rest of its details - are elucidated in Tractate Tamid.

And this prohibition is practiced whether by males or whether by females. And even at this time, one who plants a tree anywhere in the [Temple] yard is liable for lashes.

Mitzvah 493
To not erect a matsevah: To not erect a matsevah in any place. And about this is it stated (Deuteronomy 16:22), "And you shall not erect for yourself a matsevah that the Lord, your God, hates." And Rambam, may his memory be Blessed, wrote (Mishneh Torah, Laws of Foreign Worship and Customs of the Nations 6:6) that the content of the matsevah that the Torah forbade is a tall structure of stones or of dirt; as it was the custom of the worshippers of idolatry to build [it] and to gather around it for their evil service. And therefore, Scripture distanced us that we should not do like it - and even to worship God, Blessed be He, upon it - in order to distance and bring to forget all of the matter of idolatry from between our eyes and from our thoughts. [It is] like the reason that we wrote adjacently about the planting of a tree in the Temple, according to Rambam, may his memory be Blessed. And the building of the [central] altar is not included in this prohibition; as it is stated explicitly about it (Deuteronomy 27:6), "Whole stones shall you build the altar, etc." Rather, [it is] that we not do so in other places.

The laws of the commandment are short.

And this prohibition is practiced in every place and at all times by males and females. And one who transgresses it and erects a matsevah with the intention to worship on it - even to God, may He be Blessed - is liable for lashes.

Mitzvah 494
To not offer a sacrifice of [an animal] with a temporary blemish: That we have been prevented from offering a beast that has a blemish in it, and even if it is a temporary blemish. And about this is it stated (Deuteronomy 17:1), "You shall not slaughter to the Lord, your God, an ox or a sheep that has a blemish on it, etc." And it is elucidated in Sifrei Devarim 147 that the verse is speaking about a temporary blemish.

I have written from the roots of the commandment in Emor el HaKohanim in commandments 277 and 287 (286). And there is also a hint to this in the negative commandment (Sefer HaChinukh 275). The laws of the commandment are, for example, the differences that they, may their memory be

Blessed, said (Bekhorot 37b) that are in a beast between a temporary blemish and a permanent blemish: As any beast that has a permanent blemish in it is redeemed - and it is a commandment to redeem it - as we have elucidated in the Order of Reeh Anochi on the commandment of redeeming consecrated [animals] that had a blemish develop on them (Sefer HaChinukh 441); but if it is a temporary blemish it is not offered and not redeemed, but rather we wait on it until it heals or until it becomes defiled. And about the matter of permanent blemishes and their number, I have already written some of this, as is my custom, in the Order of Emor el HaKohanim in Commandment 287 (Sefer HaChinukh 286). And behold, I will remind you what a temporary blemish is - for example, a wet boil or a growth that is not Egyptian, and so [too,] water dripping from the eye that is not a permanent sickness, and similar to these. [These] and the rest of the laws of the commandment are elucidated in Tractate Bekhorot (Chapter 6).

And this prohibition is practiced at the time of the [Temple], as it was then in our hands to offer sacrifices. And priests and also Israelites, males and females, are included in this prohibition of slaughtering. As since the slaughter of the sacrifices is fit with foreigners (non-priests), so too can we say that they transgress it, if they do it not like the law.

Mitzvah 495
To listen to the voice of the court at all times: To listen to the voice of the Great Court and to do all that they command us in the paths of the Torah - regarding the forbidden and the permitted, the impure and the pure, the liable and the exempt and in everything that appears to them to be a reinforcement and enhancement to our religion. And about this is it stated (Deuteronomy 17:10), "And you shall act according to the word that they tell you." And it is repeated adjacently (Deuteronomy 17:12) to strengthen the thing, "According to the instruction that they instruct you and to the judgement that they say to you shall you act." And there is no difference in this, whether the thing that they see is from their own intellects or is something that they extracted by one of the comparisons through which the Torah is expounded, or something that they agreed is from the secrets of the Torah or they see that the thing is like this in any other way - in everything, we are obligated to listen to them. And the proof that this is from the tally of positive commandments is their, may their memory be Blessed, saying in Sifrei Devarim 154, "'And according to the judgement that they say to you shall you act' - this is a positive commandment."

From the roots of the commandments is that which we wrote in the Order of Mishpatim on the commandment to incline according to the many (Sefer HaChinukh 78).

From the laws of the commandment is, for example, that which they, may their memory be Blessed, expounded (Mishneh Torah, Laws of Rebels 1:2), "'According to the instruction that they instruct you' - these are the decrees and the practices; 'and to the judgement' - these are the things they shall teach from the [Torah] law, through one of the methods that the Torah is expounded; 'from the thing they tell you' - this is the tradition that they received, one man from the mouth of another man." And [also] that which they, may their memory be Blessed, said (Sanhedrin 88b) that at the time that the Great Court is in Jerusalem, any disagreement that existed in any court in its place is asked of the Great Court, and we act according to their word. But now that, on account of our iniquities, there is no court there, any disagreement that there be between the sages in our generations - and the ones that disagree be equal in wisdom - if we are not fit to decide among them and we do not know to where the judgement inclines, we should follow the stringent [opinion] concerning a Torah [law], and follow the lenient [opinion] in scribal (rabbinic) law. And that which they said (Mishnah Eduyot 1:5) that a court is not permitted to revoke that which was forbidden by a court that preceded it, even if it appears to its opinion that the thing is not forbidden according to the letter of the law - so long as it appears that the prohibition has spread in Israel - unless it is greater in wisdom and also in numbers (is composed of more judges) than the court that forbade the thing. And about what are these words speaking, that [the later court] can revoke [it] when [the later court] is greater than [the first court] in wisdom and numbers? When the earlier court did not forbid that thing in order to make a fence for the people for [other] prohibitions. And since this is the law, it is incumbent upon each and every court in its generation to examine the matter and investigate much and to pay attention to each [rabbinic] prohibition that it appears the generation is practicing, not to breach and instruct to be lenient about it (to permit it), lest the [court] that was before it forbade it to make a fence for the people, [and] knew that the thing is permissible by the letter of the law. And 'one who breaches a fence, etc.' And the rest of the details of the commandment are at the end of Sanhedrin (the chapter [entitled] HaNehenakin.)

And this commandment is practiced by males and females at the time that the Great Court is in Jerusalem, as all are commanded to do that which they instruct. And also included in this commandment is to listen and do like the commandment of the judge in each and every generation - meaning to say, the great sage that is with us in our times. And [it is] like they, may their memory be Blessed, expounded (Rosh Hashanah 25b), "'To the judge that will be in those days' - Yiftach in his generation is like Shmuel in his generation"; meaning, that there is a commandment upon us to listen to the voice of Yiftach in his generation, [just] like to Shmuel in his generation. And one who transgresses this and does not listen to the counsel of the great in the wisdom of the Torah in the generation, 'according to everything that they instruct,' has violated a positive commandment; and his punishment is very great, as this is a strong pillar upon which the Torah rests. The matter is well-known to anyone who has intelligence.

Mitzvah 496

To not stray from their words: That we were prevented from disagreeing with the masters of the tradition, peace be upon them, and from changing their words and to not remove ourselves from the commandments in all matters of the Torah. And about this is it stated (Deuteronomy 17:11), "you shall not stray from the matter that they tell you right or left." And they, may their memory be Blessed, said in Sifrei Devarim 154, "'You shall not stray' - this is a negative commandment."

It is from the root of the commandments [that it is] because (see Ramban on Deuteronomy 17:11) the opinions of people are different from one another - never will many intellects agree on things. And the Master of all, Blessed be He, knew that if the intention of the verses of the Torah would be given over to the hand of each and every human being - each man, according to his intelligence - every one of them will explain the words of the Torah according to his [own] rationale; and disagreement about the meaning of the commandments would increase in Israel, and the Torah will become like several Torahs - like the matter that I wrote on the commandment of "to incline towards the many" in the Order of Mishpatim (Sefer HaChinukh 78). Hence our God, who is the Master of all the wisdoms, made our Torah - the Torah of truth - perfect with this commandment; that we were commanded to act within [the Torah] according to the true understanding that was received by our early Sages, peace be upon them; and that we should listen to the sages present [now] that received their words, drank the words of their books, and exerted themselves with many exertions - day and night - to understand the depth of their words and the wonders of their opinions. And with this agreement, we will arrive at the true path in the knowledge of the Torah; and without it - if we are seduced after our thoughts and the poverty of our minds - we will not be successful at anything. And by way of the great truth and praise of this commandment, they, may their memory be Blessed, said (Sifrei Devarim 154), "'You shall not stray from [it] right or left' - even if they tell say to you about right that it is left, do not stray from their commandments" - meaning to say that even if they err in one of the things, it is not fitting for us to differ with them. Rather, we should do like their mistake. And it is better to suffer one mistake, and everything be given over under their constant good opinion; and not that each and every one go according to his [own] opinion. As with [the latter], there would be destruction of the religion, dissent in the heart of the people and total loss of the nation. And because of these things, the intention of the Torah was given over to the sages of Israel. And from this root, they were also commanded that the small group of the sages is subordinate to the group of the numerous, and as I wrote there about the commandment of "to incline towards the many."

By way of this idea that I have raised for you, my son - through it, will I explain to you a certain homelitical teaching, which is in the end of the chapter [entitled] HaZahav in Bava Metzia 59b, regarding the story of Rabbi Eliezer the Great and the "oven of Achnai," which bewilders all who hear it. They said there, "Rabbi Natan met Eliyahu, etc. He said to him, 'What did the Holy One,

Sefer HaChinukh

Blessed be He, do in that hour?' He said to him, 'He smiled and said, "My sons have vanquished Me..."'" - meaning that the Holy One, Blessed be He, was happy that His sons were walking in the way of the Torah and its commandment, to incline after the many. And that which He said, "My sons have vanquished Me," God forbid that there is any victory before Him, Blessed be He. Rather, the explanation about this idea is that in the debate of Rabbi Eliezer with his colleagues, the truth was with Rabbi Eliezer; and like the words of the heavenly voice (bat kol) that decided like him. But even though the truth was with him about this - because of his greater analysis over his colleagues - they could not completely fathom his opinion. And [so] they did not want to concede to him even after the heavenly voice; and they brought a proof from the law set in the Torah that commanded us to always go after the many - whether they say the truth or whether they are mistaken. And about this was the response of the Creator, Blessed be He, "My sons have vanquished Me." Meaning, since they turned away from the true path - for Rabbi Eliezer had surmised the truth about this - and they came upon him from the power of the Torah commandment that I commanded them to always listen to the majority; if so, one must nonetheless concede to them this time - like their words - that the truth be absent. And behold, it is as if the Master of truth was defeated.

From the laws of the commandment is that which they, may their memory be Blessed, said (Sanhedrin 87a), that even though one who transgresses that which the Sages explained about the words of the Torah, transgresses this negative commandment of "you shall not stray"; nonetheless a man does not have the designation of a rebellious judge - known in the Gemara at the end of Sanhedrin 89a, who is liable for the death penalty - until he disagrees with the Great Court (see Mishneh Torah, Laws of Rebels 3:5, 7), and that he is a sage that has reached [the level] of pronouncing decisions [and] is ordained like the [members of the] Sanhedrin, and that he disagrees with them on a matter the volitional transgression of which [brings] excision and the inadvertent violation of which [brings] a sin-offering, and he instructs to do according to his decision or [himself] does the act according to his decision, as it is stated (Deuteronomy 17:12), "who wantonly does" - and not that he only instructs. But if he is a student that has not reached [the level] of pronouncing decisions, and makes a decision; he is exempt, as it is stated (Deuteronomy 17:8), "If a matter is baffling to you" - one who only a baffling thing is beyond him. And so [too,] if he found them outside of the Compartment of Paved Stone (in the Temple) and he rebelled against them, he is exempt, as it is stated, "and you will arise and go up to the place" - teaching that the place causes (is a requirement for) the death penalty.

And the [law is like this], whether he disagrees about something that actually has excision for its volitional transgression (see Mishneh Torah, Laws of Rebels 4:2) or something that brings to something that has excision for its volitional transgression. How is something that has excision for its volitional transgression? For example, that they disagreed about whether a certain woman is [sexually forbidden to a man] or not; if a certain blood renders impure or does not render impure; if a certain woman is [in the category of impurity called] zavah or is not a zavah; if a certain fat is forbidden or not and all that is similar to this. And how is something that brings to something that has excision for its volitional transgression? For example, that they disagreed about the intercalation of the year which [can] bring to the eating of chamets on Pesach; and so [too,] if they disagreed about a law in the monetary laws, such that according to one, the one took money from his fellow legally, and if he married a woman with it, she is married, and one [besides her husband] who has sexual relations with her volitionally is punished with excision, and when inadvertent, liable for a sin-offering, but according to the words of the other, he is exempt, and so [too,] in every matter in which money is to be extracted, such as those obligated by expropriations or evaluations, [the disagreement being about] whether they are liable to give [money] or not liable - that which they took from them [not according to the correct law] is theft, and if he marries a woman with it, she is not married; and so [too,] anything like this. And even if they disagreed about the laws of lashes, he is liable [to be a rebellious elder] as a result of them - as behold, according to the words of the one that [holds] he is not liable for lashes in court, they are obligated to pay the value of his injury, and he would legally take his payments from them.

And Rambam, may his memory be Blessed, wrote about the matter of this negative commandment of "you shall not stray" (Mishneh Torah, Laws of Rebels 1:2) that it is one whether they are things

Sefer HaChinukh

that the Sages learned from the received tradition, or things they learned from their intellects through one of the methods through which the Torah is expounded or things done to make a fence for the Torah - and they are the decrees, the ordinances and the practices (see Rashi on Yoma 74a, s.v. ve'aliba) - in each one of these there things, it is a positive commandment to listen to them; and the one who transgresses any one of them transgresses a positive commandment and a negative commandment. And Ramban, may his memory be Blessed, greatly took a hold upon him [about this] and said (in the Sefer HaMitzvot in his gloss on Shoresh 1): Behold, the rabbi holds that included in the negative commandment of "you shall not stray" is everything that is from the words of the Rabbis - whether it is a rabbinic commandment such as the reading of the Scroll [of Esther] or the Channukah light, or whether it is from the ordinances such as poultry meat with milk and the secondary sexual prohibitions; whether they are active positive, such as three prayers every day or a hundred blessings and lulav on [all] seven [days] in the borders (outside of the Temple), or they are negative, such as anything that is because of a rabbinic Shabbat prohibition on Shabbat and holidays, and so [too,] the second day of a holiday in the Diaspora and the [fast of the] Ninth of Av; and more generally, anything that the Talmud forbids or commands about. And behold, the rabbi builds a fortified wall around the words of the Sages, but it is 'like a spreading breach that occurs in a lofty wall, whose breaking comes sudden and swift'; as it is a rationale [that is found] wanting in many places in the Talmud. As behold, according to his opinion, one who uses what is connected to the ground on Shabbat, such as one who leans on a tree, or one who moves something from the sun to the shade or says to a gentile [to do work] and he does it or even if he takes a large step on Shabbat, he transgresses [both] a positive commandment and a negative commandment from the Torah, and he is fit to be lashed forty [lashes]. But the rabbi exempts him in the Book of Judges (Mishneh Torah, Laws of The Sanhedrin and the Penalties within their Jurisdiction 18:2), because it is given to the warning of a death penalty by the court - as the death penalty of anyone who rebels against their words is with strangulation. And behold, according to his words, he should be lashed according to the opinion in the Talmud that says that we administer lashes for a negative commandment, given to the warning of a death penalty by the court - as is mentioned in the chapter [entitled], Mi Shehichshikh (Shabbat 154b). And according to that opinion, it is fitting to be very stringent in rabbinic laws, as they are all [from the] Torah. There is no difference at all between them and between the commandments explicit in the Scripture; and there [would] be nothing in the Torah more weighty than a rabbinic Shabbat prohibition which is of their words, except that which has a liability of excision or the death penalty by the court - but not anything that has the obligation of a positive commandment or a negative commandment. As behold, according to his opinion, there is the obligation of a positive commandment and a negative commandment in all of their words - the positive commandment of "And you shall act according to the thing that they tell you" And the negative commandment of "you shall not stray."

And behold it is seen that our Rabbis in all of the Gemara say the opposite of this. As behold, they determine all rabbinic cases leniently, as they always say (Beitzah 3b), "A doubt of Torah [law] is to be [ruled] stringent and a doubt of rabbinic [law] is to be [ruled] lenient. And they were lenient regarding a concern of rabbinically forbidden [products being present in a certain food], to say, "As I say" (that we can assume that it is not present). And they said in the first chapter of Pesachim 9b, "I will say that we say, 'As I say,' in a rabbinic [law]; in a Torah [law], can we say, 'As I say?'" And they relied upon minors who are not fit to testify, to testify on that which is rabbinic, as they said (Pesachim 4b), "The checking for chamets is rabbinic, and the Rabbis relied upon them in rabbinic [laws]." And so [too,] regarding perimeters, a minor is believed to say, "The perimeter of Shabbat is to here," [as they] "held that perimeters are rabbinic, and the Rabbis were lenient in the rabbinic," as it is found in Eruvin 58b and in Ketuvot 28b. And they were also likewise lenient in the rabbinic with doubts, as they, may their memory be Blessed, said (Berakhot 21a), "[If] there is a doubt if he prayed or if he did not pray, he does not go back and pray; [if] there is a doubt if he said, 'True and solid' or he did not say it, he goes back" - and they said, "What is the reason? Prayer is rabbinic; 'True and solid' is from the Torah." And not only that, but they were even lenient about things that contradict each other in rabbinic [law] - as they said in the chapter [entitled] Bemeh Madlikin (Shabbat 34a), "[If] two [people] said to him, 'Go out and make an eruv for us'; he made an eruv for one while it was still day, etc.," as it appears there. And it is also seen in the Gemara that we constantly uproot their words on account of a Torah prohibition; as they said in Tractate Shabbat 4a, "If he stuck bread onto an oven [wall], they permitted him to scrape it off before he comes to a prohibition [that is punished with] stoning." And there in Shabbat 128b they said, "Negating a vessel from its preparedness is rabbinic, but the pain of animals is [from] the Torah, and a positive commandment [from] the Torah comes and negates a positive commandment [from] the Rabbis," as it appears there. And this is [something seen] very much in the Talmud - a positive commandment [from] the Torah comes and pushes off a positive commandment [from] the Rabbis. And so [too] with a disagreement among the Sages, they said (Avodah Zarah 7a), "If one [group] was greater in wisdom, follow it; and if not, follow the stringent [one] in that of the Torah, and the lenient in that of the [Rabbis]." And even greater than this, they said (Eruvin 67b), "In that of the [Rabbis,] we first do the act, and then we deliberate." And in the chapter [entitled], Mi Shehichshikh (Shabbat 154b), they said, "What is it that you would say? They were also concerned with a small loss. Hence, it makes us hear" - as it is a novelty with them when they do not push off the words of the [Rabbis], even for a small loss. And they said (Berakhot 19b) that priests can render themselves impure with rabbinic impurity to see kings of the nations of the world; so that if they merit [it], they will differentiate that [which separates] the kings of Israel, etc. And also regarding the punishments of the words of the [Rabbis], they only have excommunication, as they said (Pesachim 52), "We excommunicate for the two days of holiday in the Diaspora." And they said about one who does work on Purim, "Let the master excommunicate him." And in [some] places, they have lashes of rebellion, and that is for one that transgress their words that are similar to [commandments] of the Torah - and those are all the decrees that they decreed from their [own] words - that they lash him until he accepts it upon him or until his soul departs, as is explained in the Tosefta of Sanhedrin. The general rule of the matter is that the words of the [Rabbis] are different in all of their laws from the words of the Torah, that [the one tends] towards leniency, and [the other] towards stringency. But the thing that is clear and clean of any confusion is that this negative commandment of "you shall not stray" is only in that which they, may their memory be Blessed, said in explanation of the Torah - such as things that are expounded through a gezerah shavah or a binyan av or the rest of the thirteen methods through which the Torah is expounded; or about the meaning of the language of the verse itself - and so [too] regarding that which they received as a law of Moshe from Sinai. And it is about this that they, may their memory be Blessed, said that there is a positive commandment and a negative commandment in the thing. And if in this matter, one fitting to pronounce decisions disagrees with the Great Court about that which the volitional transgression [brings] excision and the inadvertent violation [brings] a sin-offering, he becomes a rebellious elder through them - at a time when we judge capital cases. And this is [the meaning of] that which they, may their memory be Blessed, said (Sifrei Devarim 154), "Even if they tell you about the left that it is right"; meaning to say that this is the commandment upon us from the Master of the Torah, may He be Blessed - that we believe the greats regarding what they say, and that the one who disagrees not say, "How can I permit it for myself, since I know with certainty that they are mistaken?" As even if it will be such, it is a commandment to listen to them - as I wrote above at the beginning of the commandment - and like the matter that Rabban Gamliel conducted with Rabbi Yehoshua on Yom Kippur that fell out according to [the latter's] calculation, as is mentioned in Rosh Hashanah 25a.

And there is one condition about this law according to that which they, may their memory be Blessed, said in Tractate Horayot 2b, that if at the time of the Sanhedrin, there was a wise man who was fitting to pronounce decisions or was part of the Sanhedrin, and the Great Court decided not like his opinion, he is not allowed to permit himself the matter that is forbidden according to his opinion, until he gives and takes (discusses) with them about the thing, and after they all - or their majority - agree to the negation of that opinion, confound his rationale against him and come to the conclusion that he is mistaken; [only] then is he allowed to act for himself according to the permissibility about that which it was his opinion to forbid - and it is also a commandment upon this one to accept their opinion regardless. But with the ordinances and the decrees that the Sages made as a protection of the Torah and as its fence, this negative commandment is only a [recommendation], and there is no law of rebellion about them at all. And the rest of the details of the commandment are elucidated at the end of Sanhedrin ([in the] chapter [entitled] HaNehenakin).

And this commandment is practiced concerning the matter of the rebellious elder at the time of the [Temple]. And concerning the matter to listen to the words of our ancient Sages and to our greats in the wisdom of the Torah and to our judges in our generation, it is practiced in all places and at all times by males and females. And one who transgress this and 'breaches a fence' in one of all of that which our Rabbis taught us in explanation of the Torah - such as through one of the thirteen methods or something forbidden from a law of Moshe from Sinai, and like the matter that we wrote adjacently - has violated this negative commandment, besides violating the positive commandment in it. But we do not administer lashes for it, since it is given to the warning of a death penalty by the court with the law of the rebellious elder, and as we wrote.

Mitzvah 497
To appoint a king from Israel: That we were commanded to appoint upon ourselves a king from Israel, so that he can gather us all together and administer us according to his desire. And about this is it stated (Deuteronomy 17:15), "Surely place upon yourself a king, etc." And in Sifrei Devarim 157, "'Surely place upon yourself a king' is a positive commandment."

I have written from the roots of the commandment in the Order of Mishpatim on the negative commandment of the chieftain (Sefer HaChinukh 71). And there I wrote at length about the benefit that is found for a people in there being one person upon them as the head and as the officer; as the order of the people will not be preserved without this. And behold, you see in the books of the Prophets that it comes as a curse when many people are the head in one place - and as it is written (see the book of Judges 9).

From the laws of the commandment is that which they, may their memory be Blessed, said (Mishneh Torah, Laws of Kings and Wars 1:3) that we do not a priori set up a king in Israel except by the word of a court of seventy elders and by the word of a prophet - like Yehoshua, as Moshe, our teacher, and his court appointed him; and like Shaul and David, as Shmuel HaRamati and his court appointed them. And [also] that which they said (in Sifrei Devarim 157), that we do not set up a woman to the monarchy, as it is stated, "a king" - and not a queen. And when they would set up a king, they would anoint him with anointing oil (Mishneh Torah, Laws of Kings and Wars 1:7). And once he has been appointed, he acquires the monarchy for himself and for his sons, as it is written (Deuteronomy 17:20), "in order that he will have length of days upon his monarchy; he and his sons, among Israel." If he [only] left over a minor son, we preserve the monarchy for him until he grows up, as Yehoyada did for Yoash. And anyone who is precedent for the inheritance is precedent for the inheritance of the monarchy. And the big son precedes the small son. And it is not just the monarchy, but all positions of authority - in actuality or as an honorary title from the honorary titles - and all appointments in Israel are an inheritance for a man, such that his son acquires it after him, and his son's son, and his son's son's son forever. And this is when he fills the place of his fathers with the fear of Heaven. But if there is no fear of Heaven in him - even though he has great wisdom - there is no need to say that we do not appoint him to an appointment of the appointments in Israel, but it is [even] fitting to hate him and distance him. And about them, David stated (Psalms 5:6), "[You] have hated all doers of iniquity."

And [also] that which they, may their memory be Blessed, said (Sanhedrin 19b), "'Surely place upon yourself a king' - that his fear should be upon you"; meaning to say that we fear him, trust his words in every matter that he does not command against the commandments of the Torah and that we honor him with the full honor that can be fitting for flesh and blood. And in the hand of the king is the right to kill anyone who transgresses the commandment of the king who is established according to the Torah, or rebels against any matter [pertaining to him]. And there is no angle of iniquity in this, to the point where they, may their memory be Blessed, said (Shabbat 56a) that Uriah became liable for his soul (life), when he said in front of David, "my master, Yoav" (II Samuel 11:11) - as he should not have mentioned mastery about any other man in front of the king. And [also] that which they, may their memory be Blessed, said (Sanhedrin 20b) that in the hand of the king is the power to make a road in the middle of fields and vineyards, and that he may judge people according to what appears to him to be the truth - and even without clear witnesses. And [also] that which they said (Sanhedrin 22a) that we do not ride on his horse; we do not sit on his throne; we do not marry his widow; we do not use his scepter, his crown nor any vessels he uses. And all of this is for his stature and his honor. And when he dies, his vessels are burned in front of his bier. And [also] that which they said (Sanhedrin 19b) that [if] a king forgoes his honor; his honor is not foregone. And all of these things, they are all for the good of the people and for their benefit. And the laws of the king are all like they are explained in the book of I Samuel 8:11-17. [These] and the rest of the details of the commandment are elucidated in the second chapter of Sanhedrin, in the first chapter of Keritot and in the seventh chapter of Sotah. And this is from the commandments that are incumbent upon all of the community; [that is] upon the males, as it is proper for them to do these matters.

And this commandment is practiced when Israel is on their land - and like they, may their memory be Blessed, said (Sanhedrin 20b), "Israel was commanded three commandments in their entering into the land: to appoint a king over themselves, to build the Choice House and to cut off the seed of Amalek." And do not ruminate about my words, my son, to say, "And how can my father count this as one of the commandments practiced by [all] the generations? And is it not that since King David was anointed, that this commandment was withdrawn from Israel; since it is not upon them to appoint another king, as David and his seed are the elevated ones over them 'until Shilo comes,' that the king be from his seed forever - may it be speedily and in our days?" As the content of this commandment is not only to appoint a new king; but rather from its content is all that we have have mentioned - to anoint a new king if there is a cause that necessitates it - but also to set up the monarchy in the hand of the inheritor, to put his fear upon us, to behave [towards] him in everything according to the Torah and according to the well-known commandment. And this is truthfully practiced forever.

Mitzvah 498

To not establish a foreign king over us: That we were prevented from establishing a man that is not from the seed of Israel - and even if he is a righteous convert - [as] king upon us. And about this is it stated (Deuteronomy 17:15), "You may not place upon yourself a foreign man that is not your brother." And they, may their memory be Blessed, said in Sifrei Devarim 157, "'You may not place upon yourself a foreign man' - this is a negative commandment." And likewise, it is not fitting to appoint upon us for anything - not a Torah appointment and not a state appointment - a man that is from the 'congregation of converts,' until his mother be from Israel, from that which is written, "You shall surely place, etc."; and they, may their memory be Blessed, made a precise inference (Kiddushin 76b), "Any placing that you do shall only be from among your brothers."

The roots of the commandment are well-known: Since it is for the appointed head to humble all in everything that he says, it is necessary that he nonetheless be from the seed of Israel - as they are merciful, the children of merciful ones - so that he will have mercy on the people not to make their yoke heavy in any matter from all of the things. And he should love truth, justice and righteousness - as it is known to all that anyone who is from the family of Avraham has all of these good [qualities]; and similar to what the wise men of science said, that the nature of the father is planted in his children. From the laws of the commandment is that which they, may their memory be Blessed, said (Kiddushin 76b) that we only set up a head of authority from the seed of Israel - and even if he is appointed over a watercourse to distribute from it to the fields. And they also said (Kiddushin 82a) that we do not set up one who is a barber, a bathhouse attendant or a tanner [as] king, nor [as] high priest. It is not because they are [intrinsically] disqualified from the monarchy; but rather since their trade is lowly, the people will always disparage them. And one who has done these crafts even one day is disqualified from these positions of authority.

And David and his seed have already acquired the monarchy of Israel. And it is not still in our hands to change it - [just] like it is no longer in our hands to change the priesthood from the seed of Aharon - as it is stated about it (II Samuel 7:16), "your throne shall be established forever." And in the elucidation [of this], they, may their memory be Blessed, said (Kohelet Rabbah 7; Yoma 72b), [that] the crown of monarchy was acquired by David. And all who believe in the Torah of Moshe concede to this. And the rest of the details of the commandment are in [various] places in Yevamot, Sanhedrin, Sotah and Niddah. And I have already written some of the laws of the monarchy, as is my custom, above in this Order on the commandment of appointing a king.

And this prohibition regarding the monarchy is practiced at the time that Israel is on its land in its settlement, and it is from the warnings (negative commandments) that are upon the whole community. And regarding other positions of authority in Israel, this prohibition is practiced in every place that they are. As it is forbidden for them from Torah writ to appoint a man that is not from the Children of Israel over the community.

You can infer from the root of the commandment that it is also forbidden to appoint evil and cruel men over the community. And evil will not depart from the house of the one who appoints them because of relation or from their fear or to flatter them, and 'the violence of that evildoer will fall upon his skull.' And the reward of the one who does not fear from any man - [so as] to benefit the masses with all of his strength - will be from God forever in this world; 'and his soul will recline in the good of the world to come, and his seed will inherit the land.'

Mitzvah 499

That the king not amass many horses: That the king that is ruling over us not amass many horses for himself, besides those needed for his chariot and the chariots of his horsemen; and as it is written (Deuteronomy 17:16), "he shall not amass many horses for himself." And the content of the commandment is that he should not have horses that run-in front of him simply for his glory. And even over one idle horse does he transgress this. However, if he has horses in his stables prepared for war and sometimes his horseman ride upon them, this is not at all included in this negative commandment; as the central matter is only from the angle that we said - that he should not have idle horses always go before him for stature and glory, but rather he should have only one animal upon which to ride.

And the verse already stated the reason of this commandment, which is that he not "bring back the people to Egypt in order to amass many horses, etc." - meaning to say, that he not send from his people that they should establish their residence in Egypt to raise horses there. As the prohibition is only to establish residency there, as they, may their memory be Blessed, expounded (Talmud Yerushalmi Sanhedrin 10:8), "To dwell you shall not return, but you can return for business." And [it is] also so that his heart not become proud by amassing many horses, silver and gold; since the horses' masters become proud due to their beauty and speed.

The laws of the commandment are in the second chapter of Sanhedrin.

And this prohibition is practiced at the time that Israel is in its inhabitation and that we have a king. And this is from the commandments that is only upon the king. And a king that transgresses it and adds even one free horse to be running in front of him - in the way that the other kings of the nations of the world do - is liable for lashes.

Mitzvah 500

To not ever dwell in the Land of Egypt: That we not further go back on the way to Egypt ever; meaning to say that we do not establish our residence in Egypt. And about this is it stated (Deuteronomy 17:16), "and the Lord said to you, 'You shall not further go back on this way again.'" And the prevention of this is repeated three times: They, may their memory be Blessed, said (Mekhilta d'Rabbi Yishmael 14:13:2), "In three places did the Torah warn not to return to the Land of Egypt [...] In the three they returned, and in the three they were punished." And these three places [are] the one we mentioned; the second is "by the way that I said to you, 'You shall not further again, etc.'" (Deuteronomy 28:68); and the third is "as that which you see Egypt today, you shall not further, etc." (Exodus 14:13) - and even though it appears to be [only] a story from its revealed meaning, the tradition comes about it that it is a prevention (a negative commandment).

It is from the roots of the commandment that [it is] because the people of Egypt are bad and sinners. And God, Blessed be He, took us out from there and redeemed us, in His kindnesses, from their hand to give us merit, to walk in the ways of truth. And in His great goodness upon us, He wanted that we not return again to become defiled among them, so that we not learn from their agendum and that we not walk in their disgusting ways, in view of our perfect Torah.

From the laws of the commandment is that which they, may their memory be Blessed, said (Sukkah 51b), that it is not just the city of Egypt which is included in the prohibition, but rather it is forbidden to dwell in all of Alexendria. And from the Sea of Alexendria for the length of four hundred parasangs and for the width of four hundred parasangs is [all included] in this prohibition. And the rest of its details are clear.

And this prohibition is practiced in every place and at all times by males and females. And one who transgresses it and establishes his residence there violates this negative commandment. But we do not administer lashes for this negative commandment, since no act is [involved] with it. As at the time of the entry, it is permitted, and there is no act in his lingering there. And Rambam, may his memory be Blessed, said (Mishneh Torah, Laws of Kings and Wars 5:8) that if a king of Israel conquers the Land of Egypt according to the word of the court, it would be permissible for us to dwell in it. And 'the words of the wise are grace.'

Mitzvah 501

That the king not amass many wives: That the king not amass many wives for himself. And about this is it stated (Deuteronomy 17:17), "And he shall not amass many wives for himself." And the reason for the commandment is elucidated in the verse, as women sway the hearts of their husbands - meaning to say that they seduce them to do what is not fitting to do through the constancy of their competition, their many words and their slipperiness.

From the laws of the commandments is that which they, may their memory be Blessed, said (Sanhedrin 21a) that it is permitted to marry up until eighteen wives, but not more - and even if they are like Avigail, who was righteous, alacritous and good. [This] and the rest of its details are in the second chapter of Sanhedrin. And this is from the commandments which are only upon the king.

And it is practiced at the time that we have a king. And if he transgressed this and took (married) one beyond the eighteen, he is liable for lashes and he must divorce her.

Mitzvah 502

That the king not amass much silver and gold for himself: That the king not amass much plenitude of money - meaning to say that he only have under his hand the amount of what he needs for his chariot and his designated servants. And about this is it stated (Deuteronomy 17:17), "And much silver and gold, shall he not amass for himself."

From the roots of the commandment is that which is elucidated in Scripture, "That his heart not get haughty, etc." (Deuteronomy 17:20).

From the laws of the commandments - that which they, may their memory be Blessed, said (Sanhedrin 21a) that it is for himself that he cannot amass much, but he can amass much for the sake of Israel and for their benefit, meaning to say to protect them and their cities and their places from the enemies; and the rest of its details - are in Sanhedrin (Chapter 2). And a king that transgresses this and sets up his plan to fill his storehouses with money only to fulfill his desire - without his intention being to benefit the people and their defense - has transgressed this negative commandment. And his punishment is very great, as the entire people depends upon the king. Hence he needs to place all of his attention to the good of his people, and not to his own glory and the fulfillment of his desires.

Mitzvah 503

That the king write a second Torah scroll for himself: That it is a commandment on the king that will be over Israel to write for himself a specific scroll of the Torah, from the angle of [his being king], that it be with him always and [from] which he read - besides the other Torah scroll which is a commandment for him, like every one of Israel, to write, as we will write in the last commandment of the book, with God's help (Sefer HaChinukh 613). And about this is it stated (Deuteronomy 17:18), "and he shall write for himself a copy of this Torah, etc."

It is from the roots of the commandment [that it is] because the king is under his own power - no man will pain him over his actions nor rebuke him, and with the staff of his mouth he can plague his land and with the breath of his lips he can kill anyone he wants from his entire people. Therefore he truly needs great guarding, and a proper reminder standing in front of him [so that] he will always look upon it in order to conquer his impulse and turn his heart towards his Creator. And this is [the meaning of] that which they, may their memory be Blessed, said (Sanhedrin 21b), "When he goes out to war, the Torah scroll is with him; sitting in judgement, it is with him; adjourns to eat, it is in front of him." The general rule of the matter is that it not move from in front of his eyes except when he needs to [relieve himself] or enters the bathhouse.

From the laws of the commandment is that which they, may their memory be Blessed, said (Talmud Yerushalmi Sanhedrin 2:6) that it is a commandment to check the Torah scroll of the king from the scroll in the [Temple] yard by word of the court, so that he arrange all of his deeds with righteousness. And I will write the rest of the details of the laws of a Torah scroll, with God's help, in the last commandment of the book. And this is one of the commandments we said at the beginning of the book is only incumbent upon the king. And there is no need to write at which time it is practiced, as the thing is well-known that there is no monarchy in Israel except at the time that their land is in its inhabitation - may our eyes see it soon with the coming of the redeemer, and he shall rule over us in it.

Mitzvah 504

That the tribe of Levi not inherit in the Land of Israel: That the whole tribe of Levi not take a portion in the Land, except for the well-known cities and their open areas, as is elucidated in Scripture. And about this is it stated (Deuteronomy 18:1), "There shall not be a portion and inheritance for the priests, the Levites - the entire tribe of Levi."

It is from the roots of the commandment [that it is] so that all of the involvement of this tribe be in the service of God, Blessed be He, and that they need not work the land. And the rest of the tribes give them a portion from all that they have without [the Levites] toiling for it at all - like the matter that I wrote above on the commandment of tithes in the Order of Vayikach Korach (Sefer HaChinukh 395).

From the laws of the commandment are those apparently included in the simple meaning of Scripture. And this commandment is practiced by the Levites at the time when the Land of Israel is in its inhabitation.

Mitzvah 505

That the tribe of Levi not take a portion in the spoils: That the whole tribe of Levi not take a portion in that which Israel despoiled upon their entering into the land (see Sefer Hamitzvot LaRambam, Mitzvot Lo Taase 170), and in that which they would despoil from their enemies afterwards. And about this is it stated (Deuteronomy 18:1), "There shall not be a portion and inheritance for the priests." And so [too,] does it appear in Sifrei Devarim 163, "'Portion' in the spoils, 'inheritance' in the land." And let not the matter of a general prohibition be difficult for you about this negative commandment (as there appear to be two prohibitions from the same phrase); since two prohibitions come in Scripture about these two negative commandments - and they are, "There shall not be a portion and inheritance for the priests, the Levites," and also afterwards, "And no inheritance shall be for him, etc." (Deuteronomy 18:2). And these two negative commandments themselves are repeated for the priests, as it is stated with Aharon (Numbers 18:20), "In their land you shall not inherit, and there will not be a portion for you among them." And they, may their memory be Blessed, said (Sifrei Bamidbar 119), "'In their land you shall not inherit' - at the time of the division of the land; 'and there will not be a portion for you among them' in the spoils." And even thought the priests were in the tribe of Levi, the prevention is repeated about them for strengthening. And so [too,] all that is similar to this in the Torah, such that it repeats negative commandments in many places - it is all to strengthen the matter or to complete the law when it is not complete from the one negative commandment. And you will understand why God made it lack in one place and completed in another from that which I wrote at the beginning of the book of Eleh HaDevarim (Deuteronomy). And

Sefer HaChinukh

Rambam, may his memory be Blessed, wrote (Sefer Hamitzvot LaRambam, Mitzvot Lo Taase 170), "If we had counted these negative commandments, which are 'In their land, you shall not inherit, etc.' about the priests, additionally to the negative commandments stated about the Levites, etc., it would, according to this comparison, be fitting likewise for us to count the prohibition of the divorcee, the challalah and the zonah for the high priest as three additional negative commandments in addition to the three that came on every priest - whether common or high. And if the speaker say that this is so, we shall answer him with what they, may their memory be Blessed, said in Kiddushin 77b that a high priest is only liable one [punishment] for a divorcee. And were the law to be [that a high priest is transgressing two commandments], he would be liable two for it - one because of [being] a priest, since a divorcee is forbidden to him, and a second from the angle of his being high priest, since she is forbidden to him in a different negative commandment. And from this type itself are the preventions that came to the priests for 'They shall not make a bald spot on their heads, and they shall not shave their beards and their flesh they shall not gash with a gash' (Leviticus 21:5); as they were already preceded for all of Israel more generally, in its stating, 'You shall not round off the corner, etc.' (Leviticus 19:27), 'and you shall not place a bald spot' (Deuteronomy 14:10), 'And a marking for a soul, you shall not put onto your flesh, etc.' (Leviticus 19:28). However these were repeated with the priests to complete the law, as is elucidated at the end of Tractate Makkot 20a. And therefore a priest that transgresses one of these is only liable for one [set] of lashes. And understand this principle and guard it."

It is from the roots of the commandment [that] since they are the servants of God, it is not fit for them to use vessels snatched from the hand of people in war with the sword, the spear and the javelin. As only a thing that has come by way of peace, righteousness and faith should come to the House of God, and not [something] about which the heart of a man or a woman be troubled.

And this commandment is practiced at the time of the [Temple] with the tribe of the Levites. And one who transgresses it and takes a portion of the spoils violates this negative commandment. But there are no lashes for it, since it is possible to transgress it without an act, and it is given to repayment.

Mitzvah 506
To give the foreleg, the jaw and the maw to the priest: That Israel was commanded to give the foreleg, the jaw, and the maw from all pure, slaughtered animals to the priest. And about this was it stated (Deuteronomy 18:3), "This shall be the statute of the priests, etc." The Sages, of Blessed memory, already said (Chullin 134b) about the reason for this commandment that it was in the merit of Pinchas, their father - who was zealous on behalf of his God with regard to the matter of Kozbi, and [was prepared to] surrender his life for the sanctification of [God's] name, to kill a prince from a tribe of Israel - that his children, the priests, merited this present from God forever: The foreleg - corresponding to, "and he took a spear" (Numbers 25:7); the jaw - in the merit that he prayed for the anguish of Israel, as it is written, "And Pinchas stood up and prayed" (Psalms 106:30); and the maw - corresponding to, "and the woman into her stomach" (Numbers 25:8). And we learn from this that one who openly sanctifies the name of Heaven - he and his descendants attain merit in this world, aside from his merit which is kept eternally for his soul in the World to Come.

From the laws of the commandment is that which they, may their memory be Blessed, said (Chullin 134b), "What is the foreleg? That is the right foreleg from the knee until the arm's socket" - which are two limbs, one connected to the other. "And the jaw? From the joint of the jaw until the joint of the trachea" - which is the large ring; with the tongue between them. And we give to the priest the stomach with the fat on it. And the priests have already been accustomed to leave the fat of the stomach for the owners. And also, that which they said (Chullin 132a) that the obligation of the gifts is only with a pure [domesticated] beast and not with a [wild] animal, as it is stated, "whether an ox or a sheep" - and included in the sheep and its species is the billy goat. And they, may their memory be Blessed, also expounded (Chullin 79b), "'Whether an ox' [is] to include a koi" - and even according to the one that says [it is] a creature on its own (a completely separate category); "'whether a sheep' [is] to include a forbidden mixture," such as the offspring that comes of a goat and a sheep. And if it comes from a gazelle and a female goat, he is only obligated for half of the gifts, since it is written, "whether a sheep" - and they, may their memory be Blessed, expounded (Chullin 79b), "Even if it is partially a sheep." But the offspring of a billy goat that copulates with a gazelle is not obligated in gifts at all, since it was a doubt for the Rabbis if we are concerned about the seed of the father or not. And since it is such, the Israelite is able to say to the priest, "Bring a proof that we are concerned about the seed of the father, and I will give you half of the gifts" - and he will not be able [to do so]. And hence I can write that there is no gifts at all with [the offspring of] a billy goat that copulates with a gazelle.

I have already written the opinion of Rabbenu Alfasi, may his memory be Blessed, and other commentators regarding the concern for the seed of the father in the Order of Kedoshim Tehiyu on the commandment of the beast of a forbidden mixture (Sefer HaChinukh 244). And so [too,] from the content of the commandment is that which they, may their memory be Blessed, said (Chullin 132b) that it is permissible to eat from the beast before the gifts were separated. As the law is not like Rabbi Yochanan - who said that the one who eats from it before its gifts are separated is as if he eats unseparated produce - since they are [already] distinguished and distinct in one place; and as a result, they do not make [the rest of it] unseparated. And [this] and the rest of its details are elucidated in Tractate Chullin in the Chapter [entitled] HaZroa, which is distinguished by the laws of this commandment.

And this commandment is practiced with non-sacred animals, but not with those consecrated; by Israelite males and females, but not by priests - since it is written about them, "the statute of the priests from the people," which implies that it is not from the priests. And [this is the case] also because the priests are not called, "people"; and as it is written (Leviticus 16:33), "he shall atone for the priests, and for all the people of the congregation." And the Levites have a special law in this matter; as the priests do not take the gifts from them - since the Rabbis were in doubt if they are called "people," or not. And hence they can not take from them by force of a doubt; but if they took [the gifts], they do not return [them].

And regarding if they are practiced at this time or not, many of the great commentators have already disagreed about this. And what comes out of the discussion in the Chapter [entitled] Hazroa with the good commentary is that they are practiced today. And that is likewise the opinion of Rabbenu Alfasi, may his memory be Blessed, and Ramban, may this memory be Blessed. But we do not have the power over the butchers now to force them to give them to them. 'And those who trust in the Lord shall renew their strength.'

And there in the Chapter [entitled] HaZroa (Chullin 131b), they, may their memory be Blessed, said that we give the gifts to the priestesses [just] like the priests, and even if they are married to an Israelite. And so, it said there, "When Ulla came, he said, 'Give the gift to a priestess.' Hence, Ulla reasoned, 'A priest' - and even a priestess." And there (Chullin 132a), it is also said, "Rav Cahana ate on behalf of his wife" - and so [too,] Rav Pappa and Rav Yeimar and Rav Eidi.

And an Israelite who transgresses this and slaughters a beast and does not give the gifts to a priest or a priestess has violates this positive commandment. And they, may their memory be Blessed, said (Chullin 134b) that if there is no priest or priestess with him; on account of the loss to the priest, he estimates the value and eats it - as they do not have sanctity - and afterwards, he gives the money to any priest that he wants.

Mitzvah 507

To separate the great tithe for the priest: That we were commanded to separate the priestly tithe from the grain and the wine and the oil and we give it to the priest. And this is what is called the great tithe. And about this is it stated (Deuteronomy 18:4), "The first of your grain, your wine and your oil, etc. shall you give him." And they, may their memory be Blessed, said (Chullin 137b), that there is no measure for it from Torah writ. Rather, even one [grain of] wheat exempts a large pile. But the Sages said (Mishnah Terumot 4:3) to separate more. And they said that one who has a moderate eye separated one part in fifty; and they based the thing upon the language, terumah (tithe) - meaning to say, trei memeah (two of a hundred), which is one from fifty.

It is from the roots of the commandment [that] since grain, wine and oil are the essence of people's

Sefer HaChinukh

nourishment and the whole world is the Holy One's, Blessed be He, therefore it is fit for a man to remember his Creator for the blessing with which He Blessed him, and to separate some of it for His sake, Blessed be He, and give it to His servants - which are the priests that are constantly engaged in Heavenly service - before the hand of a man touch it and benefit from it at all. And from this foundation, they, may their memory be Blessed, said that even one [grain] of wheat exempts the pile; as there is no difference between large and small in the remembrance of mastery. However, our Rabbis, may their memory be Blessed, added onto the thing to give a fit measure for it, in order to arouse the heart of a man more. As in man's being physical, he does not put into his heart something small like [he does something] large, that fills his eyes and to which his actions testify more; like it is the way and nature of man to rejoice over much food. And I have already written more of what I have known about the reason for the portions of the priests in the Order of Vayikach Korach on the commandments of the tithe and the tithe from the tithe (Sefer HaChinukh 395-396).

From the laws of the commandment is, for example, that which appears in the Gemara (Rosh Hashanah 12a, and see Tosafot, s.v. tanna derabbanan) that the central obligation from Torah writ - and so [too,] of tithes - is from grain, wine and oil alone, since they are the main nourishment of man. But rabbinically, one is obligated also [on] anything that is human food, that is guarded and the growth of which is from the ground. And even though we found that in the Sifrei, they based the thing on a verse, it was only a memory device (asmakhta) - as I have written in the Order of Vayikach Korach (Sefer HaChinukh 295) with the commandment of the tithe. As there they said, "'The first of your grain': just like grain, wine and oil are human food, its growth is from the earth and it has owners - as it is stated, 'your grain' - so too, all that is similar to them is obligated in priestly tithes and tithes." And they, may their memory be Blessed, said (Talmud Yerushalmi Challah 4:4 and see Mishneh Torah, Laws of Heave Offerings 2:2, 5) that even though vetch is not human food, it is obligated in the priestly tithe and the tithe, since we eat them in years of famine. And rubia (some have the text, tiah), hyssop and thyme that are planted from the outset for man are obligated in the tithe; and so [too,] all that are similar to them. [If] he planted them for animals - even though he reconsidered and designated them for people while they were attached [to the ground] - they are exempt, since the designation of a man while they are attached is nothing. [If] they grew on their own in a courtyard: if it is a courtyard that protects its fruit, behold, they are obligated - as [when] undifferentiated, they are for people; but if it does not protect, they are exempt. Garden seeds - such as turnip seeds, radish seeds, onion seeds and all that are similar to them - are exempt from the priestly tithe and the tithes, since they are not human food. But nigella is obligated in the priestly tithe and tithes. The seed (berries of) clover, of mustard, of white beans, of capers and of caper buds are exempt, because they are not fruits. About what are these words speaking? When he planted them for the seed. But when he planted them for the vegetable, behold, they are obligated, since they are fruits. And so [too,] the berries of capers are obligated, since they are [its] fruit. Coriander that was planted for the seed is exempt from the priestly tithe and the tithes. If they were planted for the vegetable, one must separate the priestly tithe and the tithe from the vegetable and the seed. And so, [too,] shevet: if he planted it for the seed, it is exempt; if he planted it for the vegetable, it is tithed - [both] the seed and the vegetable. As if he took the vegetable to eat, he separates the priestly tithe and the tithes from it, and then he eats; and when it dries and he gathers its seed, he separates its seed.

And also, from the content of the commandment is that which they, may their memory be Blessed, said (Rosh Hashanah 12b) that there is no obligation of priestly tithes and tithes until they come to a third [of their growth]. And so [too,] that which they said that the gleaning, the forgotten, the corner and the small grape strands of an Israelite (which are all reserved for the poor) are exempt from the priestly tithe and the tithes, even though he made a pile of them at home. And so [too,] that which they said (Mishneh Torah, Laws of Heave Offerings 3:4) that we do not take the tithe by weight or by number, but rather by estimation, since a measure is not stated about it in the Torah. And I have already written at the beginning of the commandment that a moderate eye separates one part in fifty by estimation. And he should not put the fruit into a pail or a basket the size of which is known, but he can take the priestly tithe in them [by filling] their half or their third. And it is permitted to separate the priestly tithe from that which is not adjacent; but nevertheless, Torah scholars do not do so. And so, wrote Rambam, may his memory be Blessed (Mishneh Torah, Laws of Heave Offerings 3:20). And that which they said (Kiddushin 41a) that a man can make an agent to separate the priestly tithe and the tithe, as it is stated (Numbers 18:28), "So shall you also separate the priestly tithe" - to include the agent who is likewise a member of the covenant (a Jew) - and many other laws in the Gemara about agency; that which they said (Mishneh Torah, Laws of Heave Offerings 6:1) that the priestly tithe is eaten by priests - whether adults or minors - themselves, their wives, their Canaanite slaves, and even their beasts; and many other laws in the Gemara about this, such as the wife that rebelled, the slave that escaped, the laws of divorce and engagement, and several similar to them; the laws of the priestly tithe concerning its nullification, about which the Sages, may their memory be Blessed, gave a measure of [one part to] a hundred and one; and the rest of its many details are in Tractate Terumot, and some of its laws are scattered in many places of the Talmud.

And the commandment of the priestly tithe - also the commandment of the tithes - is practiced from Torah writ in the Land of Israel and at the time that Israel is there. And so wrote Rambam, may his memory be Blessed, at the end of the first chapter of the Laws of Heave Offerings (Mishneh Torah, Laws of Heave Offerings 1:26), and this is his language, "The priestly tithe at this time is not from Torah writ, but [rabbinic] - even in a place that those that came up from Babylonia held, and even at the time of Ezra - as you do not have the priestly tithe from the Torah except in the Land of Israel at the time that all of Israel is there, as it is stated, 'When you come' (seemingly a reference to Numbers 15:18, which has, 'In your coming') - the coming of all of you, like they were at the first possession, and like they are to return in the future for the third possession, and not like they were at the possession in the days of Ezra, which was a coming of some of them - and hence it was not from the Torah [then]. And so, does it appear to me is the law of tithes [as well], that we are only [rabbinically] obligated at this time - like the priestly tithe." To here [are his words]. And Raavad, may his memory be Blessed, wrangled him about this matter and this is his language: Avraham said, "He did not conceive the law properly - as behold, we establish it [to be] like Rabbi Yochanan - as we say in Yevamot 81a, 'The priestly tithe at this time is from Torah writ' - meaning in the Land of Israel. And it appears that he, himself, wrote this at the beginning of the book. And if there is [truth] to this matter, it is in [the laws of] challah." To here [are his words]. And now if the truth is like the words of Raavad, may his memory be Blessed, we would have had to count this commandment among the commandments that are practiced now in the Land from Torah writ, as well as six other commandments concerning the priestly tithe in the Order of Emor (Sefer HaChinukh 279-284) and one in the Order of Mishpatim (Sefer HaChinukh 72); and two in the Order of Vayikach Korach - the tithe and the tithe from the tithe (Sefer HaChinukh 395-6). But [as for] me, I will set the words of Rambam, may his memory be Blessed, between my eyes and from his well shall I draw - as he is the reason for all of this involvement in the counting of the commandments, for me and for all who came after him. And nonetheless there is none in the world that disagrees that it is also practiced rabbinically in the Land of Shinaar, since it it close to the Land of Israel, and many of Israel go to and come back from there. And they also ordained that we should practice the priestly tithes and the tithes even in the Land of Egypt and even in Land of the Children of Ammon and Moav, since they surround the Land of Israel. And the Land of Israel that is stated in every place is [referring to] the lands that a king of Israel, a Judge or a prophet conquered with the agreement of the majority of Israel. And this is what the Sages, may their memory be Blessed, called the conquest of the many. But a place that an individual from Israel or a family or a tribe gave glory to themselves and conquered is not called the Land of Israel - even if it is within the borders of the land that were given to our father, Avraham. And the law of the places that Yehoshua divided to the tribes - even though they were not all conquered - is like the law of the Land of Israel; so that the majority [of the Land of Israel] not be like the conquest of an individual, when each and every tribe enters its portion. [Regarding] the land that David conquered - such as Aram-Naharayim, Aram-Tsovah, the whole bank of the Euphrates up to Babylonia, Damascus, Achlav, Charan and similar to them - even though he conquered them with permission of the Great Court, they are not like the Land of Israel in every matter. Rather they left the category of outside of the Land and did not enter the category of the Land of Israel. And in every place, they are called Syria. And there are things [for which] their law is like the Land of Israel and there are some [for which] their law is like outside the Land, as you will find in the Gemara in scattered places. And the reason is because he conquered them before he conquered all of the Land of Israel. As had he seized all of the Land of Israel to its borders first and conquered [the other lands] afterwards, they would have been like the Land of Israel for everything. And regarding the priestly tithes, the tithes and the seventh [year], the Sages said that they be like the Land of Israel. But regardless, in the Land the obligation is from Torah writ at the time when Israel is there, like we said according to the opinion of Rambam, may his memory be Blessed; but in those places it is rabbinic at all times. And they, may their memory be Blessed, said (Chagigah 3b) that every place that Israel held when they come up from the exile of Egypt and became sanctified through them - that sanctity was nullified when they were exiled in the first [subsequent] exile, since they only sanctified it by way of conquest alone for the time. But when they came up a second time from the exile of Babylonia with Ezra the Scribe, they sanctified it a second time for the time and for the future to come - meaning to say, a sanctity that stands forever. But nonetheless, the obligation of the priestly tithes and the tithes are only from the Torah there - according to the opinion of Rambam, may his memory be Blessed - when Israel is settled there, and as I wrote adjacently. And some places that they were in - where those that came from Egypt held - those that came from Babylonia the second time did not hold, [but rather] left them and did not sanctify them. And nonetheless, they did not exempt [those places] from priestly tithes and tithes, so that the poor that go up on the seventh [year] would [be able] to rely on them.

It comes out that regarding the commandments dependent upon the Land, the whole entire world is divided into three divisions: the Land of Israel; Syria; and outside the Land. And the Land of Israel is divided into two parts: every place that those that came up from Babylonia held is one part; and the rest that only those that came up from Egypt held is a second part. And outside the Land is also divided into two parts: the Lands of Egypt, Shinaar, Ammon and Moav, where priestly tithes and tithes are practiced rabbinically; and all of the other lands, where priestly tithes are not practiced at all. And what is the land that those who came up from Egypt held? From Rekem, which is at the East of the Land of Israel, to the Great Sea; and from Ashkelon which is to the South of the Land of Israel to Akko, which is at the North. And one who was walking from Akko to Keziv - all the land to his right which is to the East of the path, behold, it is assumed to be outside of the Land, impure from the impurity of the land of the peoples and exempt from the tithe and from the [seventh] year, until it is known to you that this place is from the Land of Israel. And all of the land that is to his left which is to the West of the path, behold, it is assumed to be the Land of Israel, pure from [the impurity of] the land of the peoples and obligated in the tithe and the seventh [year], until it is known to you that this place is outside of the Land. And anything that inclines and descends from the Amanum Mountains and inwards is the Land of Israel; from the Amanum Mountains and outwards is outside the Land. And [regarding] the islands in the sea, we see them as if a string were stretched from the Amanum Mountains to the River of Egypt: from the string and inwards is the Land of Israel; from the string and outwards is outside the Land. And that is its outline.

And one who transgresses this and does not remove the priestly tithe from the grain, the wine and the oil in the Land, at the time that Israel is there, has nullified this positive commandment; and his punishment is very great, as he ate unseparated foods. And I have already written the punishment of one who eats unseparated food in the Order of Emor el HaKohanim (Sefer HaChinukh 284). And with other fruits, he has nullified a positive rabbinic commandment; and according to the opinion of a few commentators, there is an obligation from Torah writ also with other fruits - and like we wrote. And at this time also, one who does not separate the priestly tithe from the fruits of the Land - and likewise, from the fruits of Syria; and likewise, from the fruits of those places that we wrote are obligated in priestly tithes rabbinically, such as Egypt, Shinaar, Ammon and Moav - has nullified a positive rabbinic commandment. But there is no obligation of priestly tithes ever with the fruits of other lands - not from the Torah, and not from the Rabbis.

Mitzvah 508
To give the first shearing to the priest: That we were commanded to give the first shearing of the flock to the priests. And about this is it stated (Deuteronomy 18:4), "and the first shearing of your

flock shall you give him." And the matter of the commandment is that anyone who has a flock of five - whether they are males or females, whether they are lambs or grown sheep, and even if he has sheared them several times - is obligated to give a present from the wool to the priest each time. And there is no measure of this gift from the Torah, but Rav, Shmuel and Rabbi Yochanan said in Tractate Chullin 137b, "The first shearing is in sixty" - meaning to say that he gives him one portion out of sixty. And since Scripture mentioned the expression of giving about this - as stated, "shall you give him" - the Sages said (Chullin 135a) that one who has many shearings and wants to distribute them to many priests, give no less than the weight of five sela when it is cleaned, so that it be fit to make a small garment with it. [It is] not that the Israelite would clean it and afterwards give it to him, but rather that it be fit to make so much [finished] wool after the priest has cleaned it, so that it be a useful gift. And so too did they, may their memory be Blessed, say (Chullin 137b) that the obligation of this commandment is only when there be a flock of [at least] five, such that the shearing amount to sixty sela, and that each one be no less than twelve sela.

And from the roots of the commandment is like the matter that I wrote about the tithe given to the Levites in the Order of Vayikach Korach (Sefer HaChinukh 395); and the priests are the same. Since they constantly serve in front of God and have no inheritance in the lands nor in the shearings, God, may He be Blessed, acquired for them all the needs of their livelihood through their brothers. And behold, He gave them the priestly tithe and the tithe of the tithe, which are their bread and their wine; the gifts of the beast, which is the foreleg, the jaw and the maw and their portion in the consecrated [animals] of the Temple, such that there will be enough meat for their satisfaction. And [since what is] still lacking is shearing for their clothing, he also acquired the first of the shearing for their clothing. And for the rest of their expenses and needs, he also acquired for them the field of possession, the [recovered] theft from a convert [that has died], expropriations and the redemption [money] of first-born [sons].

From the laws of the commandment is that which they, may their memory be Blessed, said (Chullin 137a) that the obligation of this commandment is only with the shearing of sheep, the wool of which is soft and fit to wear. But if the wool was hard and not fit to wear, he is exempt from the first shearing, from the reason that I said - as the priests acquired this for the [purpose] of clothing. But if the wool was red, black or brown, he is [still] obligated in the first shearing, since it is fit for wearing. And the rest of its details are elucidated in the eleventh chapter of Chullin.

And this commandment is practiced by males and females, Israelites and Levites, whether in front of the [Temple] or not in front of the [Temple]. But [it is practiced] only in the Land of Israel, and not outside of the Land; and like Rav Nachman bar Yitschak said in Chullin 136b in the chapter [entitled] Reishit HaGez, "The world acts like the three elders: Like Rabbi Eelayai in the first shearing, etc." - meaning to say that he exempted outside the Land, as it is found there. And one who transgresses it and did not give his first shearing to the priest - when he has shearing that is fit, according to the matter that we wrote - has nullified this positive commandment.

Mitzvah 509

That the priests and the Levites work in the Temple in shifts: That the priests and the Levites work in the Temple in shifts (Sefer HaMitzvot LaRambam, Mitzvot Ase 36) - meaning to say, in [assigned] groupings - and not that the hand of all be involved together in the work; except for the holidays alone, when all would work together - all who would come would [take part] for the joy of the festival. And elucidated in the book of I Chronicles 24-26, is how David and Shmuel divided them, that they made twenty-four shifts of priests and twenty-four shifts of Levites, in order that each of their shifts could work two weeks a year. And in Tractate Sukkah 55b, they may their memory be Blessed, said that on the festivals, the hand of everyone was equal. And about this is it stated (Deuteronomy 18:6-8), "If a Levite would go, etc." - and included in the Levite is a priest, since Levi was the father to all of the tribe - "and he will come in all the yearning of his soul. And he will serve in the name of the Lord, his God, like all his brothers, the Levites, who are standing there [...]. A portion like a portion shall they eat." And the language of Sifrei Devarim 168 is "'And he will come in all the yearning of his soul' - perhaps always" - meaning to say, even not on holidays. "[Hence] we learn to say, 'besides the sales to the fathers' (Deuteronomy 18:8): that which the fathers sold, this one to that one, 'you take on your week and I on my week'" - meaning to say, their agreement in the order of the workshifts, each week its shift. And so did the Translation [of Onkelos Deuteronomy 18:8] explain it, "except for the shift that comes on the Shabbat [of a regular week], as so did our fathers ordain."

It is from the roots of the commandment of known and set shifts [that it is] because all work that is incumbent upon a number of [assigned] men will be done properly, and no laziness or despondency or impatience is found in it. But [regarding] that which is incumbent on the many without there being men [assigned] to do it, sometimes some of them will assign it to others [without their agreement] and sometimes these will be impatient with those about a matter. There is no need to write at length about these things that are well-known about all people in groups. But with a festival, because of the joy [of the festival], they were commanded that the hand of all be equal in them.

From the laws of the commandment is that which they, may their memory be Blessed, said (Mishneh Torah, Laws of Vessels of the Sanctuary and Those who Serve Therein 4:11) that each and every shift would have an appointed man - and he was the head of all of the men of the shift. And he would divide them into households. And on each and every day of the days of the week, the heads of the households would distribute [the jobs, assigning] men to the work, each man his work. And they would change the shifts from one Shabbat day to the next Shabbat day, and rotate accordingly.

And the early prophets established (Mishneh Torah, Laws of Vessels of the Sanctuary and Those who Serve Therein 6:1-3) that twenty-four shifts of proper and sin-fearing men from the Israelites likewise be appointed. And in every place in the Talmud, they are called the men of [the] watch (anshei maamad); meaning to say they are the agents of Israel, to stand over the communal sacrifices, and like the matter that they, may their memory be Blessed, said (Taanit 27a), "Is it possible for the sacrifice of a man to be offered and he not stand over it?" And for every [such] watch, one great [man] would be over them all, and he is called the head of the watch. And this was the custom of the men of the watch: On each and every week, they would gather [and] whoever of them was in Jerusalem or around it, would enter the Temple. But whether in Jerusalem or in the other places, they would gather in the synagogue, pray much, and fast on Monday, Tuesday, Wednesday and Thursday of that week. And the rest of their matters in prayer and in the reading of the Torah is like it is explained in Tractate Taanit and Megillah 22b. And they, may their memory be Blessed, said (Sukkah 55a) that the hand of the shifts of priests and Levites was not equal in everything on the festivals, but rather only in the festival sacrifices, the distribution of the showbread, and the distribution of the two breads of [Shavuot]. But only the shift the time of which is fixed [for then] offers the vows, the oaths and the daily sacrifices, even on the festivals. [That] is to say, "A portion like a portion shall they eat" in the communal sacrifices; but they are not "A portion like a portion" in other things that the fathers already divided and fixed them [for] each and every shift on its week. And a priest (Mishneh Torah, Laws of Vessels of the Sanctuary and Those who Serve Therein 4:7) that had a sacrifice - behold, he could come to the Temple and offer it at any time he wanted, as it is stated, "and he will come in all the yearning of his soul"; meaning to say he can come to offer a sacrifice that is his at any time that he wants. And the skin is his. [These] and the rest of the details of the commandment are in Tractate Taanit and Megillah and at the end of Sukkah.

And this commandment is practiced by the males of the priesthood and the Levites at the time of the [Temple]. And one who transgresses it and protests against the hand of his fellow, that he not works 'in all the yearning of his soul' on the festival, has nullified this positive commandment. And Ramban, may his memory be Blessed, differed about this commandment (in Sefer HaMitzvot, Mitzvot Ase 36) with Rambam, may his memory be Blessed, and said that the working of priests in shifts is not understood from the verse at all - like the opinion of the Teacher, may his memory be Blessed - but rather it is a law of Moshe from Sinai that they divide the service among themselves into groupings. And Moshe, our teacher, was the one that began to divide them first and he made eight shifts - four from Itamar and his party and four from Elazar and his party. So is the received tradition. And that which the verse stated, "besides the sales, etc." is a negation, and not a commandment at all; meaning to say that the priests work 'in all the yearning of their souls' - whether on weekdays, whether on a festival - except if they want and agree to divide the work among themselves into shifts. And we received as a law to Moshe from Sinai that it is proper to do this, so that the work be done orderly and with alacrity. This is the essence of the words of the Teacher (Ramban), may his memory be Blessed.

Mitzvah 510
To not engage in clairvoyance: That we were prevented to not engage in clairvoyance. And Rambam, may his memory be Blessed, wrote (Sefer HaMitzvot LaRambam, Mitzvot Lo Taase 31) that the matter of clairvoyance is the restraint of his ability and thought to [concentrate] on one of the types of movement - like all of the men of [these] abilities all do - that they should tell them what will happen before it does. And truly it becomes realized for them, in that the power of their [concentration] and their quantity from it is very strong. (The explanation of his explanation is) meaning to say that they isolate themselves in their thoughts and fix all of their concentration and all of their feeling to that matter that they want to know. And from the isolation and the strong fixing and the elimination from their thought of all matters of the physical world, their souls mix with the spiritual [forces] that [become aware] of near futures, as is known among the wise men. But nonetheless, they never have the power - and not even in demons - to know the distant futures. And no one can arrive at this great level, except for a true prophet. And even in near futures, the clairvoyants do not fathom the whole truth, but rather [only] most of their words come true. And in this matter itself, not all of the people are the same in it. Rather there are some who have much superiority in these matters, like the superiority of people in strength and [in] other things that some have over others. And the actions of the people with [these] abilities are not [all] the same. As among them are some that isolate themselves in the deserts to focus on this, and from them one that hits the ground with a stick in his hand - blows that come quickly one after the other - and yells out strange yells and leaves his thought and looks to the ground a long time until he understands what will happen. And Rambam, may his memory be Blessed, testified that he saw this once in the West. And among them, there is one who flattens the sand and makes images in it - and this is done by many people in the West. And among them [also] is one who throws small stones in a piece of leather and he stares at them for a long time. And among them [also] is one who does this craft with handfuls of barley and a grain of salt and a charcoal mixed in - and this is famous among us, [as] the Yishmaelite men and women always do it in front of our eyes. And among them [also] is one who throws down a leather belt to the ground and stares at it and speaks. And the intention of all of this is to arouse the ability of the soul that can see. And our perfect Torah distanced us from all of these matters. And about all of this was it stated (Deuteronomy 18:10), "There shall not be found in you a clairvoyant, a soothsayer, a diviner, etc."

And I have already written in the warning (negative commandment) about "do not divine" in the Order of Kedoshim (Sefer HaChinukh 249) what I have known about the reason for these matters. And I saw in the books of the early scholars about the reason for this prohibition, [that it is] because all of these matters mislead the masses. And because some of what the clairvoyants tell them come out to be true, they think that the constellations and powers are the cause of all actions that are in the world. And they can almost be called part of the evil group that say, "The Lord has abandoned the land" (Ezekiel 8:12). And because of this matter which was very famous at the time of the prophets, the prophet said, "My people asks its wood, and its stick will speak to it" (Hoshea 4:12).

The laws of the commandment are elucidated in [various] places in Sanhedrin, in the Tosefta of Shabbat and in the Sifrei (See Tur, Yoreh Deah 189).

And this prohibition is practiced in every place and at all times by males and females. And one who transgresses it and makes himself a clairvoyant in one of the ways from all the matters we have mentioned or in another matter, and tells people things that he sees through his clairvoyance, is liable for lashes - and that is when he does some act in the thing, as we do not administer lashes without an act. But one who asks [something] from a clairvoyant is not under the liability of lashes. Nonetheless, very disgusting is anyone who fixes his thoughts or expends his time on these vanities. As it is not appropriate for one whom God has graced with knowledge and given the true religion as an inheritance to think about these vanities. Rather, he should fix his thoughts on the service of the Creator, may He be elevated, and not fear the words of the clairvoyant; since God, in His kindnesses will change the system of the stars, and nullify the power of the constellations, [so] as to do good to His pious ones. And it is known that we are the holy people, such that we are not under [the power of] a star or constellation - 'the Lord is our inheritance, as He spoke to us.' And [it is] like the matter that we found with the forefathers, that God placed their stature above the ministers above: Like that which is written about Yaakov, "but rather Yisrael will be your name" (Genesis 35:10), "for you have dominated (sarita) with powers, etc." (Genesis 32:29); meaning that God made him a minister (sar) over the [celestial] ministers. And so [too,] is Yitschak called Yisrael, as it is stated (Genesis 46:8), "these are the Children of Israel that were coming to Egypt, Yaakov and his children." And so [too,] Avraham is called Yisrael, as we wrote in the Introduction of the book. And this is [the meaning of] what is written about the matter of the disagreement of the prophet, Eliyahu, with the prophets of Baal, as it stated (I Kings 18:31), "like the number of tribes of the children of Yaakov," whose name was called Yisrael: As he was rebuking them [about] why they were leaving the service of the Master, the Lord of Hosts, who has in His hand to nullify all the actions of the powers and the constellations; and like the matter that He did with the forefathers, such that He put the constellations under their hand. And that is [the meaning] of its stating in that place (I Kings 18:31), "like the number of tribes of the children of Yaakov, to whom was the word of the Lord, saying, 'Yisrael will be your name,'" - meaning to say, that He made him a minister over the [celestial] ministers, to change their system and their power with his merit. [This is] meaning to say, Israel, who are the children of Yaakov, are also ministers over the celestial ministers; and hence it would be fitting for them to not worship anything besides God alone. And so did we find with Yehoshua, who decreed to the sun and the moon to stand - as it is written in Joshua 10:12, "Sun, be still in Giveon, moon in the Ayalon Valley" - and they stood. And so [too,] several pious ones of Israel who changed the system of the constellations [and their power] with their merit. The matter would [take too] long, to bring [the] several stories that happened in Israel about this matter.

Mitzvah 511

To not do magic: That we not make efforts with any act of magic at all. And about this is it stated (Deuteronomy 18:10), "There shall not be found in you, etc. or a sorcerer." And the content of magic is generally well-known to all - that people do machinations without end with types of grasses and stones, or [by] adhering things that people use, one to another. And some of them arrange these evil actions at certain known times or specific months that are fit for those crafts. And the Torah distances us with total distancing from all of these disgusting and ugly things, because they are vanities. And it is not fit for a holy people that holds the true religion to put their thought to these ugly things, but rather only to His service, may He be elevated. As He will fulfill every want of His people for the good, in their being sheltered by His great name, and their placing all of their trust and their reliance upon His kindnesses alone. And since these matters are very remote and ugly in front of Him, Blessed be He, and there is a spark of matters of idolatry in them, He warned us about it with a negative commandment, and made liable for stoning anyone who makes efforts with this if it is volitional, and a fixed sin-offering if it is inadvertent. And it is also from the weightiness of the matter that Scripture warns the court not to forgive one who transgresses this, [more] than with other sins; and as it is stated (Exodus 22:17), "Do not keep alive a witch." And I have already spoken about the roots of this commandment on the negative commandment of "Do not keep alive a witch," in the Order of Veeleh HaMishpatim (Sefer HaChinukh 62).

The laws of the commandment are in scattered places in the Talmud, but mainly in the seventh chapter of Sanhedrin. And anyone who is a judge about it needs to know the wisdom of magic so that he will be able to distinguish about an act that is done, whether it is one of the types of magic or perhaps from the things done through the power of nature and in permissible ways. And [it is] like the matter that they, may their memory be Blessed, said (Shabbat 67a), "Anything that contains [an element] of healing does not contain [the prohibition] on account of the ways of the Amorite." And I have already spoken according to my ability about this, there on the negative commandment of "Do not keep alive a witch." And these matters require great analysis - as behold, acts are found in the Gemara that if we did not know them from their mouth, may their memory be Blessed, we would have forbidden them from a concern about this prohibition. But behold nonetheless, one who raises his soul to enter into these machinations - and compares one thing to another from those things that they, may their memory be Blessed, mentioned [as being permissible] - is like one who opens an opening to go to Gehinnom. And this prohibition is practiced in every place and at all times by males and females.

Mitzvah 512
To not invoke a charm: That we have been prevented from making invocations over anything. And this matter is that a man say things, and say to people that those things [he said] benefit or damage anything. And about this is is it stated (Deuteronomy 18:10-11), "There shall not be found in you, etc. And one who invokes charms." And the language of Sifrei Devarim 172 [is] "It is one if he charms a snake or if he charms a scorpion" - meaning to say, that he says to them things, so that they will not bite him, according to his opinion (see Sefer HaMitzvot LaRambam, Mitzvot Lo Taase 35). And so [too, included] is one who says things over his wound, in order that the pain will leave him. And there are some that explained "one who invokes charms," [to mean] that he gathers snakes or scorpions or other animals to one place with his machinations and his invocations. And it is all included in the prohibition.

And maybe, my son, you will challenge me with that which we have the textual version in Shevuot 15b in the chapter [entitled] Yediot HaTumah, "The song of disturbances (pegaim) with harps and lyres. [...] And he says, 'He that dwells in the secret place of the Highest,' until 'Because You, O Lord, are my refuge' (Psalms 91:1-9). And he says, 'Lord, how many are my enemies become,' until 'Salvation belongs to the Lord' (Psalms 3:2-9)." And the understanding of "disturbances" is meaning to say that the saying of these psalms is beneficial in protection from damages (evil spirits). And they [further] said in Berakhot (see Rif 3a on Berakhot), "Rabbi Yehoshua ben Levi would order these verses and fall asleep." However, the matter is not, God forbid, similar to the matter of invoking a charm that we mentioned. And they, may their memory be Blessed, have already mentioned (Shevuot 15b), "One is prohibited from healing himself with words of Torah." Rather they mentioned to say these psalms that have things that arouse the soul of the one that knows them, to take refuge in God, may He be Blessed, to put all of his trust in Him, to fix His awe in his heart and to rely upon His kindness and His goodness. And from the arousal to this, he will be protected, without a doubt, from all damage. And this is what they answered in the Gemara about this matter, as it challenged there, "And how could Rabbi Yehoshua do that? But doesn't Rabbi Yehoshua say, 'One is prohibited from healing himself with words of Torah?'" and they said, "To protect is different" - meaning to say, the Torah did not forbid that a person say words of Torah to arouse his soul to the good, so that this merit protect him to guard him.

What I have written on the commandment that preceded it is from the roots of this commandment.

The laws of the commandment are in the seventh chapter of Shabbat.

And this prohibition is practiced in every place and at all times by males and females. And one who transgresses it and makes an invocation volitionally is liable for lashes.

Mitzvah 513
To not ask a master of ov: That we not ask a master of ov to inform us of anything. And about this is it stated (Deuteronomy 18:10-11), "There shall not be found in you, etc. and a master of ov." And the matter of this magic is that there are people that do sorcery, the name of which is pitos, which brings up the dead from within his underarm and the questioner listens to the dead answer his questions.

What I wrote adjacently about the matters of magic (Sefer HaChinukh 511) is from the roots of the commandment.

The laws of the commandment are in Sifrei Devarim 172 and in Sanhedrin. And there in Sanhedrin 65a they said that one who does this magic is [liable for] lashes and the one who asks from them is [violating] a warning - meaning to say the obligation of a negative commandment. But there are no

lashes for it, since there is no act [involved] with it.
And this prohibition is practiced in every place and at all times by males and females.

Mitzvah 514

To not ask a yidaaoni: That we not ask a yidaaoni. And this matter is that the sorcerer puts a bone from an animal, the name of which is yidoaa, into his mouth, and that bone speaks through magic. And [regarding] this animal, the name of which is yidoaa, I have seen in a book from the Geonim (early post-Talmudic authorities) that (see Rash on Mishnah Kilayim 8:5) it grows with a large cord that comes out of the ground, similar to the cord of squash and pumpkins, its form is like the form of a man in everything - in the face, the body, the hands and the feet - and it is connected to the cord from its navel. And no creature can approach for the cord's length, since it grazes around it like the length of the cord, and it devours all that it can reach. And when they come to hunt it, they shoot arrows into its cord, until it is separated, and [then] it dies immediately. And in Talmud Yerushalmi Kilayim 8:4, they, may their memory be Blessed, said in explanation of "For your covenant will be with the rocks of the field" (Job 5:23), "It is a man of the mountain, and it lives from its navel. If its navel is separated, it does not live."
The root of this commandment and all of its content - regarding its laws and its obligation - is like the content of the commandment of ov that we wrote adjacently (Sefer HaChinukh 513).

Mitzvah 515

To not inquire of the dead: To not inquire of the dead. And the content of this inquiring (see Sefer HaMitzvot LaRambam, Mitzvot Lo Taase 38) is that there are people that starve themselves and lay down in the cemetery, so that the dead will come to them in a dream and inform that which they asked him about; and there are others who wear well-known clothes and say things and offer well-known incense and sleep alone so that the dead who they want will come and speak to them in a dream. And about all of these types of crafts and similar to them is it stated (Deuteronomy 18:10-11), "There shall not be found in you, etc. or one who inquires of the dead."
What I wrote on the prohibition of magic in this Order (Sefer HaChinukh 411) and in the Order of Mishpatim (Sefer HaChinukh 62) is from the roots of the commandment.
And the laws of the commandment are in Sanhedrin (Chapter 7).
And this prohibition is practiced in every place and at all times by males and females. And one who transgresses it and does any act so that the dead will come and inform him anything is liable for lashes.

Mitzvah 516

The commandment to heed a true prophet: That we were commanded to heed the voice of every prophet of the prophets in everything that they will command. And with the exception of idolatry, even if he commands us to do the opposite of one of the commandments - or even many of them - temporarily, we heed him. As truthfully, since he is a true prophet, all of his intentions are for the good; and everything he does, he does to strengthen the religion and to bring faith in God, Blessed be He. And about this is it stated (Deuteronomy 18:15), "A prophet from among you, from your brothers, like myself, will the Lord, your God, raise up for you; to him shall you heed." And so did they say in Sifrei Devarim 175, "'To him shall you heed' - even if he says to you to transgress one of the commandments temporarily, heed him."
It is from the roots of the commandment [that it is] since the highest level for a man is attaining prophecy, and there is nothing for a man in this world that is true knowledge of things like the true knowledge [he acquires] through prophecy; as it is knowledge that has no hesitation about it, since it comes from the Spring of truth. And there are few people of the world that merit it and rise to it, since the ladder is very [tall] - its foot is on the 'ground and its head reaches the heavens.' And who is the man that fears God and merits and 'goes up to the mountain of the Lord, may He be Blessed, and rises in His holy place?' [It is] one of thousands of myriads of people that reaches this level - and [only] in a generation that is fit for it. Hence the Torah commanded us, that in [it being only] one man in a

generation reaching this level - and he be known among us regarding his manner and the propriety of his actions that he is trusted as a prophet - that we listen to him in all that he commands. As he is the one who knows the true path, and he will guide us in it. And we should not raise our souls to rebel [against his words]; as disagreement with him about anything is a big mistake and a lack of knowing the truth.

The laws of the commandment are elucidated at the end of Sanhedrin (the chapter [entitled] HaNehenakin).

And this commandment is practiced by males and females at any time that a prophet is found among us. And one who transgresses it and does not heed him is liable for death by the hand of the Heavens, and as it is written (Deuteronomy 18:19), "And it shall be that the man who does not heed the words, etc. I will require it of him." And our Sages, may their memory be Blessed, said in Sanhedrin 89a, "The death of three is by the hand of the Heavens: one who transgressed the words of the prophet; the prophet who transgresses his own words; and one who suppresses his prophecy (does not say it)." And all of this is in the understanding of the verse, as it stated "who does not heed (yishma), etc." - and they, may their memory be Blessed, said, "Read in it, 'not heed (yishma),' and read in it, 'not make heard (yashmia).'"

Mitzvah 517

To not prophecy falsely: That we were prevented from not prophesying falsely, meaning to say that no person should say that words were said to him in prophecy from God, may He be Blessed, when God, may He be Blessed, did not say them. And likewise included in this negative commandment is even if he says things that were said in prophecy to someone else, and he falsely says that he was commanded to say them. And about this is it stated (Deuteronomy 18:20), "But the prophet that wantonly speaks something in My name; that which I did not command him to speak, etc." And so [too,] did they, may their memory be Blessed, say in Sanhedrin 89a, "'That wantonly speaks something in My name' - that is the one who prophesies what he did not hear; 'that which I did not command him' - him did I not command it, but to his fellow, I did command it - that is the one that prophesies what was not said to him, but it was said to his fellow."

It is from the roots of the commandment [that it is] since there would be great destruction and much evil to our sacred and perfect religion through this. As the primary truth without limits among people is through the prophets, and [hence] the Torah commanded us to believe them and to follow their correct counsel and their complete intellects. And so when wanton men rise up to say things that God did not command them, they put out slander against prophecy - which is a great principle [of faith] among us, the holy people. And because of them, the heart of all the people will hesitate about true prophets. And there is a great destruction also if a person says what another person was commanded about. As in that this person says that he is prophet and he was commanded about this, and we see that his words are validated like the words of true prophets; we will assume him to be a holy man of God and a messenger of God, and we will believe him. And [so] we will take from his actions as a proof (lesson) for all of our practices. But since his merit and substance are not great [enough] to be the messenger for that prophecy that he said, perhaps he is not fitting to rely upon in everything he says and does. And [so] he will mislead the masses in their following his counsel.

The laws of the commandment are short, and they are in Sanhedrin (the chapter [entitled] HaNehenakin).

And this prohibition is practiced in every place and at all times by males and females. And one who transgresses it and prophesies falsely - meaning to say that he said things in the name of God that God did not say; and likewise, one who prophesies that which God said to his fellow and not to him - is liable for the death penalty. And his death is by strangulation, as it is stated about this (Deuteronomy 18:20), "and that prophet shall die" - and they, may their memory be Blessed, said that any death penalty stated undifferentiated in the Torah is only strangulation.

Mitzvah 518

To not prophesy in the name of idolatry: To not prophesy in the name of idolatry - for example, he says that idolatry x commanded to worship it, and promises a reward for its worshipers and affrights the one who does not serve it with a punishment; as the prophets of Baal and Asherah would say, and like is mentioned in the books of the Prophets. And likewise included in this is if he says that God commanded to worship idolatry x. And the Scripture does not come about this with a specific clear warning, however the punishment of the one who prophesies in the name of idolatry is clear in the Scriptures - that he is liable for death, as it is stated about this (Deuteronomy 18:20), "and the one who speaks in the name of other gods, that prophet shall die." And this death is strangulation, as we wrote adjacently. And we have already known the principle that they, may their memory be Blessed, taught us, "He does not punish unless He warned." And hence we shall say that the warning of this matter was included in "and the name of other gods shall you not mention" (Exodus 23:13), that we wrote in Parshat Mishpatim as a negative commandment of it own about another matter (Sefer HaChinukh 86). And it is not impossible for one negative commandment to prevent several things - and its law is not like the law of a general negative commandment, since the punishment of each and every matter is elucidated. This is the opinion of Rambam, may his memory be Blessed (in the Sefer HaMitzvot LaRambam, Shoresh 14 at the end).

The root of the commandment about all idolatry is well-known.

From the laws of the commandment is that which they, may their memory be Blessed, said (Sanhedrin 89a), "One who says, 'Idolatry x said [or star y], "it is commandment to do this" or "not to do [it],"' even if he approximated the [correct] law, to render impure that which is impure and to render pure that which is pure, his verdict is death" - if volitional when there are witnesses and a warning, as is well-known in every place. [This] and the rest of its details are in Sanhedrin in the eleventh chapter.

And it is practiced in every place and at all times by males and females.

Mitzvah 519

That we not fear from the killing of a false prophet: That we not fear from killing a false prophet (see Mishneh Torah, Laws of The Sanhedrin and the Penalties within their Jurisdiction 14:3) and that we not fear that there be any punishment to us from this. And even if he prophesied about the fulfillment of the commandments - since there is falsehood in his mouth, we do not [receive] a punishment for his death; but rather it is a commandment upon us [to kill him]. And about this is it stated (Deuteronomy 18:22), "do not be afraid from him." And the language of Sifrei Devarim 178 is "'Do not be afraid from him' - do not prevent yourself from advocating guilt for him."

From the roots of the commandment are that which I have written adjacently about one who prophesies falsely.

The laws of the commandment are short, and they are in Sanhedrin (the chapter [entitled] HaNehenakin).

This commandment is practiced at the time of the [Temple] when Israel are in their inhabitation; since [only] then is it in our hand to judge capital cases. And they, may their memory be Blessed, said (Sanhedrin 2a) that we only judge a false prophet with a court of seventy-one [judges].

Mitzvah 520

The commandment to prepare six cities of refuge: To separate six cities of refuge from the cities of the Levites, that they should be designated for the one that slays a soul inadvertently to flee there; to fix and straighten the roads that correspond to the cities - and like the matter that they, may their memory be Blessed, said (Makkot 10b) that they would write [signs] at the crossroads [saying], "refuge, refuge"; and clear the paths, so that there not be anything on them to delay the fugitive from his run. And about this is it stated (Deuteronomy 19:3), "You shall prepare the path for yourself and divide the border of your land into three, etc."

The root of this commandment is well-known and clear - that it be so that the inadvertent killer not be killed by the blood avengers.

From the laws of the commandment is that which they, may their memory be Blessed, said (see Mishneh Torah, Laws of Murderer and the Preservation of Life 8:2, 4) [regarding] these six cities that Moshe separated three of them in Transjordan and Yehoshua separated three of them in the Land of

Canaan, but the ones of Moshe did not shelter until the three of Yehoshua were separated. And if so, why did Moshe separate them? He said, "[If] a commandment comes to my hand, I will fulfill it." And at the time of the King Messiah, we will add another three, as it is stated (Deuteronomy 19:9), "and you shall further add for yourself three cities upon these three, etc." And they, may their memory be Blessed, said (Mishneh Torah, Laws of Murderer and the Preservation of Life 8:10) that all of the cities of the Levites would shelter, as it is stated (Numbers 35:6-7), "and upon them you shall give forty-two cities. All of the cities that you shall give to the Levites, etc." - Scripture compared all of them (the six cities of refuge and the forty-two additional ones). But there is this difference between them - that the cities of refuge shelter, whether knowingly (when the inadvertent killer is seeking refuge there) or not knowingly; whereas the cities of the Levites only shelter knowingly. [Also] a murderer that lives in a city of refuge does not [pay] rent; whereas in the other cities, he [pays] rent. And [also that which] they, may their memory be Blessed, said (Bava Batra 100b) that the width of the path [to the] city of refuge is thirty-two ells; and that on the fifteenth of Adar, the court would send agents to fix the paths - and if they were negligent in the matter, it is as if they spilled blood. And [also that which] they, may their memory be Blessed, said (Makkot 11b) that the perimeter of any city that shelters, [also] shelters. And the rest of the details of the commandment are in Sanhedrin, in Makkot, in Shekalim and in Sotah.

And this commandment is practiced at the time that Israel is dwelling on their land. And it is from the commandment's incumbent upon the king and upon the whole community.

Mitzvah 521

To not show pity upon the killer or injurer: That we were prevented from having mercy upon the one that killed his fellow or removed one of his limbs; that the judge not say, "This poor man that cut off the hand of his fellow or blinded his eye, he did not do it intentionally," and he have mercy upon him from having him repay [the injured] according to his evil. And about this is it stated (Deuteronomy 19:21), "And your eye shall not show mercy, a soul for a soul, etc." And the prevention of this is repeated in a different place, as it is stated (Deuteronomy 19:13), "Your eye shall not show mercy upon him, and you shall purge the innocent blood."

The root of this commandment is well-known - that if we do not punish the injurers and purge the evil from among us, 'a man will swallow his neighbor alive'; and states will not be [properly] civilized. There is no need to speak at length about it.

The laws of the commandment are short [and] elucidated in the language of Scripture.

And this prohibition is practiced at the time of the [Temple] by males, as it is upon to them to administer justice. And the judge that transgresses this and removes his eye from punishing the guilty one according to his evil has transgressed this negative commandment - but there are no lashes for it, since no act is [involved] with it - and his punishment is very great for the reason that we mentioned: That there is destruction to the civilization of the world with this thing. And even outside of the Land, even though we do not have the ability to judge capital cases, every court is obligated to punish their guilt according to that which they [are able] - whether monetarily or, if they can, corporeally - according to what they see that the time requires. For if there is no 'rod always outstretched over the back of the fools,' the preservation of the people is impossible.

Mitzvah 522

To not remove a landmark: That we not remove a landmark. And the content is that we not change a landmark that is between us and someone else to the point that it is possible for the liar to say that the land of another's is his; and likewise, if he changes the indicators of the landmark (border) and sets them firm into the land of his fellow, and say that he did not change it and that the land is his until the landmark. About all of this is it stated (Deuteronomy 19:14), "You shall not remove the landmark of your neighbor, etc." And they said in Sifrei Devarim 188, "'You shall not remove the landmark' - has it not already been said, 'you shall not rob?' [Hence it] teaches that anyone who removes the perimeter of his fellow transgresses two negative commandments. It is possible also outside of the Land. [Hence] we learn to say, 'in the inheritance that you inherit' - in the Land of Israel, he transgresses two negative commandments; outside the Land of Israel, he transgresses one negative commandment." The matter comes out like this: One who removes the landmark of his fellow, even a finger breadth - if it is by force, he has transgressed, "you shall not rob"; if secretly, he has transgressed, "you shall not steal." And this is outside of the Land, but in the Land of Israel, he transgresses two negative commandments.

The root of the commandment about every matter of theft is well-known - as it is something about which the intellect testifies, and it is beneficial for all.

The laws of the commandment are short (see Tur, Choshen Mishpat 376).

And it is practiced in every place and at all times by males and females. And one who transgresses this has violated a negative commandment. But we do not administer lashes for it, because of the well-known principle that we do not administer lashes for a negative commandment that is given to repayment.

Mitzvah 523
To not establish a matter of testimony with one witness: That we have been prevented from establishing the parameters of a punishment upon the body of the convicted - and likewise that we not extract money - according to the testimony of one witness; and even if he is the most fit and wise, or even if he is a prophet. And about this is it stated (Deuteronomy 19:15), "One witness shall not rise against a man for any iniquity or for any sin."

It is from the roots of the commandment [that it is] since the impulse of a man's heart is evil, and sometimes a passion comes to his heart against his fellow; and even if he is an extremely proper man, he is not saved from sometimes sinning. And even if a man stands for [a very long time] upon the ways of righteousness, it is not impossible for him to overturn his thoughts and to become bad. As behold, they, may their memory be Blessed, said (Berakhot 29a) that Yochanan served in the high priesthood and at the end [of his long tenure], he turned into a Saducee; [they also said about him that he was at first a true prophet, and at the end, he became a false prophet]. Hence the thing is fit to not rely upon the heart of a man to punish his fellow according to his testimony; and even if the convicted is a total evildoer and the most common of commoners and the one testifying is the greatest sage in Israel. But when those testifying are two fit men, there is an assumption about all of the seed of Israel that they will not agree to testify falsely. And [this type of] an assumption is [powerful] about all things.

From the laws of the commandment is that which they, may their memory be Blessed, said (Shevuot 40a) about one witness, "'For any iniquity or for any sin' is it that he does not rise" - meaning to say that we do not punish any person according to one witness, monetarily or corporeally; that is the understanding of 'iniquity or sin.' "But he does rise for an oath" - meaning to say that he obligates an oath for the one that he testifies about. For example, if a man said to his fellow, "Give me the hundred that I lent you," [and the other answers,] "I don't have anything [of yours] in my hand," and one witness testifies like the words of the claimant, the defendant is obligated to take an oath. And also, that which they said that even though the Torah did not give believability to one witness to punish his fellow monetarily or corporeally according to him; nonetheless he is believed for prohibitions - and like they said in many places (Gittin 2b), "One witness is believed with prohibitions." [This is] meaning to say, [if] he testifies, "This meat" or "this wine, is forbidden" or "is fit (kosher)," he is believed. And so too [is it regarding] all that is similar to this, with all of the prohibitions of the Torah. And [also that] which they, may their memory be Blessed, said (Makkot 6b) that with monetary cases, we accept individual testimony. How is that? One says, "He borrowed in front of me," and one said, "He admitted it in front of me" - they are combined. And [also] that which they, may their memory be Blessed, said that if one testified in this court and one testified in a different court, one court comes to the other court and they combine their testimonies. And [it is] like we say at the beginning of the chapter [entitled] Get Pashut (Bava Batra 165b), "His colleagues sent to Rabbi Yirmeyah, 'One witness in writing, and one witness orally, what is the law whether they can combine? Two who testified, one in this court and one in another court, what is the law whether one court could come to the other court and combine? Two witnesses who testified in this court and went back and testified in that court, what is the law whether one [of the judges] of each court could combine [with each other to testify as two witnesses]?' He sent [back] to them, 'I am not worthy that you [should have] sent to me. But the opinion of your student leans to them combining.'" And [also] that which they said in Ketuvot 21a in the chapter [entitled] Eeshah Shenitalmanah, that a witness and a judge do not combine in that which is from Torah writ.

And that which they, may their memory be Blessed, said (Mishneh Torah, Laws of Testimony 5:2) that the Torah believed one witness in two places: with a suspected adulteress (sotah), that she not drink the bitter waters; and with a beheaded calf, that it should not be beheaded - meaning to say, if one testifies that he knows about the killing of the one murdered, we do not behead the calf; as the Torah stated (Deuteronomy 21:1), "not known," but behold, it is known to one man. And the Sages believed one witness that testifies for a woman that her husband has died, so that she not be anchored (become an agunah that is not allowed to remarry). And they, may their memory be Blessed, said as the reason of this that she is very exacting after the truth in this. As if she might perhaps marry [as a result] and her [first] husband come afterwards, she must exit from [both marriages], and the offspring [from the second] is a mamzer. And [also that which] they, may their memory be Blessed, said (Mishneh Torah, Laws of Testimony 5:3) that in every place that the testimony of one witness is effective, the testimony of a woman or someone disqualified is also effective; except for the one witness of an oath, as we only obligate an oath with the testimony of one fit witness.

And so [too,] that which they said that sometimes the defendant pays money according to one witness. How is that? (Mishneh Torah, Laws of Plaintiff and Defendant 4:8) One who says to his friend, "It is my hundred in your hand" - and a witness testifies about it; and the defendant says, "That is correct, but you owe me a hundred corresponding to that hundred." Behold, he is obligated an oath because of the testimony of the witness, but he cannot make an oath to contradict the witness, as he concedes to that which the witness testified. And the law is such that anyone who is obligated an oath to his fellow and is not able to make the oath must pay; and we do not ever administer oaths from the testimony of one witness unless the one taking the oath is contradicting the witness, denies his testimony and makes an oath about it. And on account of that reason, Rambam, may his memory be Blessed, wrote (Mishneh Torah, Laws of Plaintiff and Defendant 4:8) that [in the case of] a promissory note that has one witness upon it and the defendant claims that he paid it, [since] he is not now contradicting the testimony of the witness that is testifying about the loan, he must pay. And others (see Raavad there) disagree with him. And so [too,] one who denies [having taken the loan] that has one witness come against him and [then] claimed that he payed or returned the deposit - in all of these [cases], we say that [since] he is obligated an oath and he can not make the oath, he must pay. And in the Gemara in Bava Batra 33b-34a, in the chapter [entitled] Chezkat HaBatim, "There is a story about one who seized a bar of silver from his fellow in front of one witness, and he said, 'That is correct that I seized it from him, but I seized what was mine.' And [the case] came in front of Rav Dimi and he said, 'How should the judges judge this case? To pay [is not possible, as] there are not two witnesses; to exempt [is not possible, as] there is one witness; to have him take an oath that he did not seize it [is not possible, as] behold, he concedes and says, "Yes, I seized it."' And Rabbi Abba was sitting in front of him and said, 'He is liable for an oath'" - meaning to say, because of the words of the witness - "'but he is not able to make the oath, as behold he is not contradicting the words of the witness. And anyone who is obligated an oath and cannot make the oath must pay.'" And this is the law in all that is similar to this.

And one who claimed against his fellow, "I lent you a hundred," and he denied it and said to him, "You never lent me anything ever," and [the claimant] brought a witness in front of him that he had borrowed from him: Since if there had been two [witnesses], he would have been considered a denier and his verdict would have been to pay, behold this one must swear on account of the one witness - since in every place that two obligate him for money, one obligates him in an oath. [If] he came back and said, "I paid it," he must pay without an oath - as he is obligated in a oath on account of the testimony of the one witness, but he is not able to make the oath; as behold he is not contradicting him in the testimony of the loan, but rather he is saying, "I paid." And we have already said that anyone who is obligated an oath that he cannot make must pay. [These] and the rest of the many details of the commandment are elucidated in scattered places in Yevamot, in Ketuvot, in Sotah, in Gittin, in Kiddushin and in all of the Order of Nezikin.

And this commandment is practiced regarding the matter of monetary cases that are practiced today in every place and at all times by males, since it is for them to administer justice. And one who transgresses this and establishes the parameters of the punishment, except for in the ways that we explained - whether corporeal or monetary - with one witness has violated this negative commandment.

Mitzvah 524

To do to the collusive witness like he colluded: That we were commanded to do to the witnesses that testified false testimony according to what they sought to damage the one they testified against with their testimony - whether with money, with lashes or with death. And even though it is possible [for the witnesses to do this damage] without an act, they are lashed; due to the inclusion from the verse (Deuteronomy 25:1), "and they shall justify the righteous one, etc.," as it is found in the chapter [entitled] Arba Mitot (Sanhedrin 25a). And about this is it stated (Deuteronomy 19:19), "And they shall do to him like he colluded to do to his brother." And this is the law of the colluding witnesses mentioned in the Gemara in many places. And the content of collusion is that two witnesses come and contradict the first ones about their testimony - for example, that they say to them, "But how can you testify about thing x? And is it not that on that day that you are saying that story [happened], you were not in the place that you say it happened there, but rather you were with us in a different place?" This is the crux of refutation [of collusive] testimony. And the Torah commanded us to believe the latter witnesses over the first - whether the first were two, or even a hundred or more, as regarding testimony, two is like a hundred, and a hundred is like two.

It is from the roots of the commandment [that it is] to punish any man whose heart became full to testify about a matter that he does not know truthfully and clearly - in that the matter is something that everything that belongs to the creatures, whether monetary or physical, depends upon. And about that which the Torah believed the latter over the first, we do not know a clear reason for it. However one of the sages gave me somewhat of an argument about the thing: As the Torah believes witnesses and there is no doubt that if two fit witnesses testify against three or more people that they killed a soul, we believe them - and even if they contradict the more numerous, since they are witnesses and the others are the parties to the thing. And with colluding witnesses, likewise, since the latter are testifying against the witnesses themselves, to say to them, "You were with us" - which is the central refutation - the first ones [become] parties to the thing and [only] the latter ones are witnesses.

From the laws of the commandment is that which they said (Makkot 5a) that the matter of refutation is upon the witnesses themselves, as we have said - for example that they say to them, "You were with us in place x." But with the matter of contradiction, we do not believe these over those; and the testimony of all of them is nullified. And what is the content of contradiction? For example, that they testify about the testimony itself: that the first group says, "Thing x happened," and the latter says, "It did not happen," or it comes by implication of their words that it did not. And [also] that which they, may their memory be Blessed, said (Makkot 3b) that colluding witnesses are not killed, nor do they pay money nor are they lashed until they are both refuted. And [also] that which they, may their memory be Blessed, said (Makkot 3b) that colluding witnesses do not need warning, but rather once they are refuted, they are judged; and that witnesses that were first contradicted and, afterwards, refuted - behold these are also judged; as they, may their memory be Blessed, said (Bava Kamma 3b), "Contradiction is the beginning of refutation." And [also] that which they, may their memory be Blessed, said (Ketuvot 20a), that we only refute witnesses in front of them, but we contradict witnesses [also] not in front of them. And if they extracted money with their testimony, the court returns the money to its owner, and the witnesses pay according to the amount of money that they thought to make him lose. But with capital cases, it is not like this: As if one is killed according to them and they are refuted afterwards, they are not killed - as so does it come in the received tradition (Makkot 5a), "[If] they did not kill, they are killed, if they killed, they are not killed." And there is somewhat of a reason to give about the matter: [It is] because 'God is present in the congregation of judges.' And were it not that the convicted was guilty because of his [other] evil deeds, the judicial procedure would not have been concluded against him. But rather he was fit for this [punishment], and the judgement against this evildoer was orchestrated from the Heavens. And about similar to this is it stated (Proverbs 15:4), "even an evildoer for an evil day." And since the matter is clarified to our eyes that this man was to die, the Torah did not want that we should kill the witnesses over him. And the analogy about this is one that kills a treifah (someone who is deathly ill) is not killed over him. [And] this one is like that - since we knew in the way that we said that he is guilty in the Heavenly court, [it is considered as if] he had no blood. And the rest of the details of the commandment are elucidated in Tractate Makkot (Chapter 1).

And this commandment is practiced in the Land of Israel at the time that we have an ordained court, since the payments of collusive witnesses are a penalty - and it is well-known that we only judge cases of penalties with an ordained court. And a court fitting to judge cases of penalties that does not 'due to the collusive witnesses like what they colluded to do to their brothers' has violated this positive commandment.

Mitzvah 525

To not be terrified or to be afraid in war: That we have been prevented to not be terrified and be afraid from the enemies at the time of war and not to run away from them. Rather the obligation upon us is to strengthen ourselves against them and to stand in front of them. And about this is it stated (Deuteronomy 7:21), "You shall not be terrified in front of them." And the prevention was repeated in another place, in its stating (Deuteronomy 3:22), "You shall not dread them."

It is from the roots of the commandment that everyone in Israel should place his trust in God, may He be Blessed, and not be afraid for his body in a situation that he can give glory to God, Blessed be He, and to His people.

The laws of the commandment - for example, that which they, may their memory be Blessed, said (Mishneh Torah, Laws of Kings and Wars 7:15) that a man not think at the time of war about his wife, nor his children nor his money, but rather he clear his [mind] from everything, to [focus on] the war. And he should further think that all the blood of Israel is dependent upon him, and [so] if he is afraid and 'he pulls back his right [hand],' it is as if he spilled the blood of all of them - and like the matter that is written (Deuteronomy 20:8), "and that the heart of his brothers not melt like his heart." And it is explicit in the words of the tradition, "Cursed be he who makes the Lord's work a fraud, cursed be he who withholds his sword from blood" (Jeremiah 48:10). And [also] that which they, may their memory be Blessed, said (Mishneh Torah, Laws of Kings and Wars 7:15) that anyone who fights with all of his heart and intention to sanctify God is assured that he will not find injury; and it will be a merit for him and his children, that his house will be established in Israel, and he will merit life in the world to come. And [it is] like the matter that is written (I Samuel 25:28), "for the Lord will surely make a faithful house for my master, since my master fights the wars of the Lord, etc." And the rest of the details of the commandment are in the eighth chapter of Sotah (see Mishneh Torah, Laws of Kings and Wars 6).

And this commandment is practiced by males - as it is upon them to fight - at the time that Israel are upon their land. And one who transgresses this and begins to think and to ruminate and to bewilder himself in war has violated this negative commandment (see Ramban's gloss on the Sefer HaMitzvot, Mitzvot Lo Taase 38) and his punishment is very great, as we have written.

Mitzvah 526

The commandment to anoint a priest for war: That we were commanded to anoint one priest with anointing oil and to appoint him to speak with the people at the time of war, and this priest is called, "the anointed for war." And from this commandment is that the anointed priest should say three verses that are mentioned in the Torah to the people at the time of the war: "Whoever is a man that planted a vineyard, etc. And whoever is a man that built a house, etc., And whoever is a man that has taken (married) a woman, etc." (Deuteronomy 20:5-7). And he adds further words of his own [that] arouse people to war and uplifts them to endanger themselves to assist the religion of God and protect it, and to take vengeance upon the fools that destroy the arrangements of the states. And so, did they, may their memory be Blessed, say in Tractate Sotah 43a, "'And the officers shall speak' - the priest speaks and the officer makes it heard."

The root of this commandment is well-known - since the men of the war need strengthening at the time of war and since a man is heeded more when he is honored, the Torah commanded that the one appointed to strengthen [the troops] be from the priests, who are the select of the people. And the matter that we send back from the war whoever planted a vineyard and did not eat from it, or betrothed a woman but did not [marry] her or built a house but did not dwell in it - and so [too,] the one who is afraid from the sins in his hand - this thing too is appropriate and fit, since all of these people are very weak from [what is needed] to go into war; as their thoughts are very occupied with the things mentioned in Scripture, and they would disincline the hearts of their fellows - and like the matter that is written explicitly (Deuteronomy 20:8), "and that the heart of his brothers not melt like his heart." And so [too,] is it fit to send back the one who is afraid from the sins in his hand, lest others be killed from his iniquity. And all of the paths of the Torah are uprightness and faithfulness.

From the laws of the commandment - that which they, may their memory Blessed, said (Sotah 44b) that we only send back from the battle lines those mentioned in Scripture in an optional war, but in a commanded war, everyone goes out [to war], even a groom from his room and a bride from her canopy; and that which they said (Mishneh Torah, Laws of Kings and Wars 7:4) that after all those sent back from an optional war are sent back, those left arrange the battle lines and appoint army leaders at the front of the people and position strong sentries at the back of all the battle lines [with] iron axes in their hands, and they have the authority in their hands to cut off the shins of anyone who seeks to leave from the war, since the beginning of [an army] falling is fleeing; and the rest of its details - are elucidated in Tractate Sotah (see Mishneh Torah, Laws of Kings and Wars 6,7).

And this commandment is practiced by males at the time that the Land of Israel is in its inhabitation. And this is one of the commandments that is incumbent upon all of the community. And if the people transgressed this, such that they did not appoint an anointed priest among them - as per what we mentioned - and he did not speak the things mentioned in Scripture to the people, they have violated this positive commandment.

Mitzvah 527

To send peace to the cities that we besiege: That we were commanded in our fighting against a city by way of what is optional - that we want to fight against it, and that is what is called an optional war - that we assure them that we will not kill them if they make peace with us and become our servants; meaning to say that they raise a tax for our king and they be subdued under us. But if they do not make peace with us in the manner mentioned, we are commanded to kill all of their males in that city that have reached [maturity], and we take for ourselves the infants and the women and all of its booty. And about all of this, they, may their memory be Blessed, said that it was an optional war. And they said in Sifrei Devarim 200, "If they said, 'We accept the taxes upon ourselves, but not the subjugation,' or 'subjugation, but not taxes' - we do not listen to them, until they accept this and that upon themselves."

It is from the roots of the commandment [that it is] because the trait of mercy is a good trait and it is fitting for us - the holy seed - to practice in all of our matters. Even if the enemies are idolaters, it is for our stature - not from the angle of their being fit for mercy and kindness. And also, because this thing has a benefit to us, that our king have servants that serve him and always raise him a tax, and do his work - if he needs - without his expending any expenses on them at all. And there is no benefit to us in our killing them, since they want to stay subdued under us; but rather there will be destruction in the thing and [in its] teaching us the trait of cruelty; and 'the one who hears [it] will revile us.' And we are commanded about this, to benefit us in all that we have mentioned.

From the laws of the commandment are what they, may their memory be Blessed, said (Mishneh Torah, Laws of Kings and Wars 6:1) that the law of the call for peace is with every place - meaning to say whether in a commanded war or in an optional war. And a commanded war is, for example, [against] the seven [Canaanite] nations and Amalek. And [with] all, if they make peace with us -

meaning to say, they took upon themselves the tax and servitude, and likewise that they took upon themselves the seven commandments - we do not kill a soul from them, and they will be for tribute and serve us. But when they do not make peace, there is a distinction between a commanded war and an optional: That in a commanded war, we do not keep a soul alive; whereas in an optional war we keep their infants and women alive, as we wrote adjacently. And likewise, in an optional war, we leave one side of a besieged city open, that they can run away from there, and as it is found in Sifrei Bamidbar 157. And we learn this from that which is written (Numbers 31:7), "And they gathered upon Midian as the Lord commanded." But in a war against the seven nations, we encircle them from all sides. However, we nonetheless inform them first that if their will is to leave the city and go away, the option is in their hand.

And also from this matter is that which they also said, that whether it is an optional war or a commanded, it is permitted for the front line of the army when they enter into the borders of the gentiles, and they are hungry and and they do not have provisions, to eat [their] foods - and even forbidden foods, such as carcasses, and 'torn' [animals] and pigs - and to drink idolatrous wine. And so did they, may their memory be Blessed, expound (Chullin 17a), "'And houses filed with everything good' (Deuteronomy 6:11) - even [fatty] pigs' necks were permitted to us." And about this is it stated (Deuteronomy 20:10), "When you approach a city, etc." until the end of the section. [These] and the rest of the details of the commandment are in the second chapter of Sanhedrin and the eighth of Sotah. And this commandment is practiced - at the time that Israel is on their land - by males, as they are fit for war. And it is from the commandments that are incumbent upon the community and especially upon the king and the leaders of the people. And if they transgressed this and did not send to the city to call to it for peace and to comport themselves in the way that we mentioned, they have violated this positive commandment.

Mitzvah 528

To not keep alive a soul of the seven nations: That we were warned with a negative commandment not to keep anyone of the seven nations alive in every place that we find them and are able to kill them without danger to our souls. And the seven nations are the Canaanite, the Perizite, the Hivite, the Jebusite, the Hittite, the Girgashite and the Amorite. An about them is it stated (Deuteronomy 20:16), "you shall not keep a soul alive." And even though the truth is that King David killed many of them to the point that he almost finished them [off] and destroyed their memory, nonetheless a few of them remained that assimilated among the [other] nations. And anyone who finds some of them is obligated to destroy them in every place that they are. And I have written all of the content of this commandment at length above in the Order of Ve'etchanan on the commandment of killing the seven nations (Sefer HaChinukh 525). And [so] take it from there.

Mitzvah 529

To not destroy fruit trees: That we have been prevented from chopping down trees when we besiege a city to distress the people of the city and to sadden their hearts. And about this is it stated (Deuteronomy 20:19), "you may not destroy its tree, etc. and you shall not chop it down." And likewise, not to do any damage - such as burning or ripping a garment or breaking a vessel for no reason - entered under this negative commandment and in all of these matters and in all that is similar to them, they, may their memory be Blessed, would always say in the Gemara (Kiddushin 32a), "But behold, he is transgressing on account of 'do not destroy.'" And nonetheless we only administer lashes for one that cuts down a fruit tree, since it is explicit in Scripture. But with other destructions, we [only] give him lashes of rebellion (See Mishneh Torah, Laws of Kings and Wars 6:10).

The root of this commandment is well-known - it is in order to teach our souls to love good and benefit and to cling to it. And through this, good clings to us and we will distance [ourselves] from all bad and destructive things. And this is the way of the pious and people of [proper] action - they love peace and are happy for the good of the creatures and bring them close to Torah, and they do not destroy even a grain of mustard in the world. And they are distressed by all loss and destruction that they see; and if they can prevent it, they will prevent any destruction with all of their strength. But not so are the wicked - the brothers of the destructive spirits. They rejoice in the destruction of the world, and they destroy themselves - [since] in the way that a person measures, so is he measured; which is to say that he clings to it forever, as the matter that is written (Proverbs 17:5), "the one who rejoices in calamity, will not be cleared (of evil)." And the one who desires the good and rejoices in it, 'his soul will dwell in the good' forever. This is known and famous.

From the laws of the commandment is that which they, may their memory be Blessed, said (Bava Kamma 91b) that the Torah only forbade cutting fruit trees when he cuts it down destructively. But it is certainly permitted to cut [them] if he finds a beneficial matter in it, such as the value of the wood become valuable and he wants to sell it; or to remove injury by cutting them, such as [if] it was damaging other trees better than it, or because it was damaging other fields. In all of these angles and in all that is similar to it, it is permissible. And they, may their memory be Blessed, said (Bava Kamma 91b) that it is permitted to cut any non-fruit bearing tree - even when he does not need [its wood] - and [likewise] any fruit tree that is very old, to the point that it only gives a few fruit, for the sake of which it is not worthwhile to toil [on it]. And they, may their memory be Blessed, said with an olive tree, it is permitted to cut anything that makes less than a fourth [of a kav]; and with a palm tree, less than a kav of dates.

And in general, they, may their memory be Blessed, forbade to do anything destructive. And they said about anyone who destroys anything out of rage (Shabbat 105a) that he is like one who worships idolatry, as so is the way of the evil impulse: Today it says to him, "Do this"; and if he trusts it, tomorrow, it will say to him, "Go and worship idolatry" - meaning to say that every person is obligated to rebuke his impulse and to conquer his desire to the point that he makes the intellectual soul dominate the desiring soul, until it becomes its maidservant and [the intellect] dominate it forever and ever. However, they brought in the Gemara (Shabbat 105a) stories of a few sages that showed themselves to be angry and they would throw down some food or some thing from their hand, in order to discipline the members of their household and to give them alacrity. Nonetheless their supervision would always be over them, that they not throw down something that would be destroyed by this. And the rest of the details of the commandment are in the second chapter of Bava Batra (see Mishneh Torah, Laws of Kings and Wars 7).

And this prohibition is practiced in every place and at all times by males and females. And one who transgresses it and destroys fruit trees has violated this negative commandment and is liable for lashes. And for other destruction on other things that are not explicit, we lash him [with] lashes of rebellion.

Mitzvah 530

To behead the calf in the riverbed: That we were commanded to behead the calf in a mighty (the understanding of mighty is that its waters rage - Mishneh Torah, Laws of Murderer and the Preservation of Life 9:2) riverbed. And the matter of the commandment [applies] if we find a dead person in the field or on a path and we do not know who slew him, as it comes explicitly in Scripture. And about this is it stated (Deuteronomy 21:1), "If a slain person, etc." until the end of the section. And this is the matter of the beheaded calf that is mentioned in the Gemara (Sotah, Chapter 9).

It is from the roots of the commandment [that it is] in order that the heart of the people be aroused in their seeing this great procedure - the gathering of the elders of the city and its great men: And they take a cow, which is a large animal, and they go to outside of the city in assembly, and with the masses - since everyone wants to see these things. And all of the listeners will tremble at the sound of its beheading, and their thoughts about the thing will be stimulated. And immediately the heart of anyone who knows about the [murder] will be astounded and his thinking will be aroused to say that which he knows in front of the elders. And through this, the evil ones and the murderers will be destroyed from among them. And besides [this] knowledge, there is much benefit in this great procedure - to show and to publicize among the masses with great publicity that the desire of the elders and intelligent people is is to find the murderer, to exact vengeance from him for the vengeance of the murdered. And so did I find in Rambam (Guide for the Perplexed 3:40).

From the laws of the commandment is that which they, may their memory be Blessed, said (Sotah 45b) that Jerusalem does not bring a beheaded calf; as it is stated about this, "on the land that the

Sefer HaChinukh

Lord, you God, gives to you" - and Jerusalem was not divided [by] the tribes. And likewise, we do not bring a calf if it is found near the border or [near] a town the majority of which are gentiles, as the assumption is that the gentiles killed him. [If] there were two towns there, one of which was closer and one of which was not closer but there is a greater multitude of people there than in the closer one, we go after the further one that has many [people] - as so did they, may their memory be Blessed, say in the Gemara (Bava Batra 23b), "[In a case where one can decide based on] majority or proximity, one goes after majority." And even though majority and proximity are both from Torah writ - meaning that the Torah commanded us to consider proximity and majority - majority is preferred. And from where we measure, from the nostrils of the killed; the law of its beheading, which is with a kofits (a large knife) from behind it; the law of the washing of the hands; the law of [when] the body is found in one place and the head is found in another place; the law of that which they said (Sotah 44b-45a), "'Slain person' and not strangled person, 'on the land' and not covered by a pile of stones, 'fallen' and not hanging on a tree, 'in the field' and not floating on top of the water"; and the rest of its details are [all] elucidated in the last chapter of Tractate Sotah (see Mishneh Torah, Laws of Murderer and the Preservation of Life 6).

And this commandment is practiced in the Land of Israel at the time when it is in its inhabitation, and also in Transjordan. And its obligation is upon the males and especially upon the great men of the city; and like the matter that is written (Deuteronomy 21:3), "and the elders of that city." And that which Scripture states first (Deuteronomy 21:2), "And your elders and your judges will go out," is speaking about the elders of Jerusalem. As so did they, may their memory be Blessed, say (Sotah 44b) that five elders of the Great Court in Jerusalem would go out and measure. And upon them is the commandment of measurement; but upon the elders of the city is the commandment of the calf, of the washing of the hands and of the reciting of those verses, as it is stated (Deuteronomy 21:2), "Our hands did not spill this blood, and our eyes did not see" - meaning to say, the one killed did not come to 'our hands' and we dispatched him without provisions; and 'our eyes did not see him' leave our city and we dispatched him without escort (Sotah 45b).

Mitzvah 531
To not work or sow in that land: That we have been prevented from working or sowing in the mighty riverbed, which is the riverbed where the calf was beheaded. And about this is it stated (Deuteronomy 21:4), "which is not worked and not sown."

What I have written in this Order on the commandment of beheading the calf (Sefer HaChinukh 530) is from the roots of the commandment - that the matter of the beheading is to publicize the matter of the murder, so as to arouse the masses about the thing and that fear enter into their hearts about this evil thing. And from the simple understanding, the prevention of work and sowing there forever, also appears to be from this very reason; in order to forever remind the hearts of all wayfarers that the calf was killed in that place because of the fact that a man was killed on the path - and it stayed barren forever - and their hearts will be moved by this to greatly distance the matter of murder [from themselves]. And if you challenge me about this reason, as the riverbed is not a place for seed; we can answer that it is fit for it, since the Torah prevented us from sowing in it.

The laws of the commandment - that which they, may their memory be Blessed, said (Sotah 46b), "Just as sowing is performed on the land itself, so too, all labor that the Torah prohibited is performed on the land itself," such as plowing and digging and that which is similar to it, but it is permissible to comb flax there and to do any work that is not done on the land itself; and the rest of its details - are at the end of Tractate Sotah. And even though I have written above that the commandment of the law of the beheaded calf is only practiced at the time of the [Temple] when we are judging capital cases, the prohibition of work in the mighty riverbed is apparently forever, if we would know through a bona fide tradition that there was in our land a riverbed where they beheaded a calf at the time that our land was in its inhabitation - as Scripture did not mention a time about the prohibition of work in that place. And if so, we should write it with the commandments that are practiced today in our land. And this prohibition is practiced by males and females. And one who transgresses this and sows in the mighty riverbed is liable for lashes. And thus did they, may their memory be Blessed, say there in the Gemara Makkot 22a: When they mentioned there those liable for lashes, they said, "And behold, there is also sowing in a mighty stream, and its prohibition is from here - 'which is not worked and not sown.'" Behold, it is clarified to us from this that, that which the verse states, "is not worked and not sown" - it is all one warning. [This is] meaning to say that one who works and sows there only transgressed one negative commandment, and we do not make him liable for two negative commandments - for work and for sowing. And we also learned there that there is liability for lashes in the thing.

Mitzvah 532
To execute the law of the one of beautiful form (yefat toar) as is written in the Torah: That we were commanded about the woman of beautiful form to do to her like the statute that is written in this section, as it is stated (Deuteronomy 21:11), "And you shall see among the captives a woman of beautiful form" - meaning to say that she be beautiful in his eyes (see Mishneh Torah, Laws of Kings and Wars 8:3). And the content of the command about her is that the Israelite bring her to his home and command her to shave her head, to grow her nails, to remove from upon her the fine garment that she brought from her home - as such was the custom of the nations, that their daughters would adorn themselves in war for harlotry - and to allow her to cry for her father and mother a month of days, as per her desire. These are the things that are explicit in Scripture about the law of a woman of beautiful form. And it would seem that the obligation of a positive commandment comes on all of these [things].

From the roots of the commandment [is that which] they, may their memory be Blessed, said (Kiddushin 21b), [it is] because the Torah only permitted the one of beautiful form of the captives in view of the evil impulse. As if Scripture had not permitted her, he would marry her [even though it is] forbidden, due to the power of the evil impulse of the heart of man regarding desire. And so, Scripture shut the door in front of him to make her repulsive in his eyes: It commanded to shave her head so as to destroy the form of her fine hair; and to grow her nails so as to distort the form of her hands; and it permitted her to cry for the first month so as to distort her face and to consume her eyes with her tears. Scripture also commanded that she should sit with him in his house while she is doing all of this in the first month. And it is all to make her disgusting in his eyes, that he come in and go out [from his house] and see her in her distortion. And among the commentators, [some] said (Rabbenu Tam in Tosafot on Kiddushin 22a s.v. shelo) that the permissibility of the first intercourse of the woman of beautiful form is in her being a gentile (immediately). And their words are likely, since her permissibility is because of the power of the evil impulse. But [there are others] among them that said that she is not permissible at all until after all of these acts that we mentioned. And from the simple understanding of the verses, it appears like this. And also, in Talmud Yerushalmi Makkot 2:6, they disagreed about this.

The laws of the commandment: That which they, may their memory be Blessed, said (Kiddushin 21b) that [the law of] a woman of beautiful form [applies] whether she is a virgin or [is not] or [even if she is] the wife of a man. But it is not permitted to take two, as it is stated, "her" - not "her and her friend." And [also] that which they said (Kiddushin 22a) to not pressure her in the war, but rather he must isolate himself with her in a house - that he not thinks that the Torah permitted her in any fashion, and even publicly. And she must convert before he marries her as a wife. And after the conversion, he marries her with a marriage contract and betrothal, and the law that pertains to her is like the law of [all] the daughters of Israel. But if she does not want to convert, he puts up with her twelve months and sends her away. And after the month of crying, he waits for her two more months. And (Sanhedrin 21a) if she becomes pregnant from the first intercourse, the offspring is a gentile and not his son for any matter of all the matters - and like the Sages, may their memory be Blessed, said (Kiddushin 68b), "Your son that comes from a gentile woman is not your son, but rather her son." And Tamar, the sister of Avshalom, was from the first intercourse of a woman of beautiful form, whereas Avsahlaom was born after the marriage. And it comes out that Tamar was the sister of Avshalom from [the side of] his mother, and [so] permissible to be married to Amnon. And so, did it state (II Samuel 13:13), "Please speak to the king, as he will not prevent me from you." [These] and the rest of the details of the commandment are in the first chapter of Kiddushin and in Sanhedrin.

And this commandment is practiced at the time that Israel is on its land, as then did they have the power and the ability in their hand to fight wars. And one who transgresses it and does not do the actions that we mentioned has violated this positive commandment.

Mitzvah 533
To not sell one of beautiful of form: To not sell one of beautiful form after the one who desired her had intercourse once with her. And about this is it stated (Deuteronomy 21:14), "And it shall be if he does not want her, he shall send her away for herself, and he shall certainly not sell her for money."

It is from the roots of the commandment to teach ourselves good and precious traits. And I have already written in many places that a precious soul is fit to receive goods and upon it will blessing always descend, and that the good God desired to crown His people with every lovely and refined trait. And there is no doubt that to sell the woman after they lay with her in their laps is from the traits of the wanton and most lowly. The matter is well-known and it is not to be elaborated. And the content of the one of beautiful form, some of its laws and the place of their elucidation in the Gemara and the time that the law of the one of beautiful form was practiced - all of it is written in its positive commandment in this Order (Sefer HaChinukh 532).

Mitzvah 534
Not to make her serve after he has intercourse with her: That we should not make a [captured] 'woman of beautiful form' serve, after intercourse with her. And about this it is stated (Deuteronomy 21:14), "you shall not abuse (titaamer) her, since you afflicted her." The explanation of "abuse" is that is an expression of service. And so, did they say in Sifrei, "'You shall not abuse her' - you shall not take service from her." And the matter is that we should not set her up as a concubine or as maid-servant in bondage. And the matter of the verse is not that we should not have her serve any service that women do for their husbands. [Rather] Scripture prohibits making her into a maid-servant, [just] like it is also forbidden to sell her as a maid-servant, and the intention is one. And so too with the stealing of a soul from his brothers (kidnapping), about which it is written (Deuteronomy 24:7), "and he abused (hitaamer) him" - they, may their memory be Blessed, explained (Sanhedrin 85b), that [it means that] he brought him into his domain and made him serve.

Its neighbor that is adjacent (Sefer HaChinukh 533) speaks about the root of this commandment. And the rest of the matter is written in its [corresponding] positive commandment (Sefer HaChinukh 532).

Mitzvah 535
To hang one who is liable for hanging: That we were commanded to hang one who is liable for hanging by the court. And it is known that all those who are hung are first stoned. And about this it is stated (Deuteronomy 21:22), "and you shall hang him on a pole." And the law of hanging is with a blasphemer and one who worships idolatry only - like the words of the sages in the chapter [entitled] Nigmar HaDin (Sanhedrin 45b), who argue against that [position] of Rabbi Eliezer, who says [that] all those who are stoned are hung.

I have written a little about the roots of the commandments of the four death penalties of the court in the Order of Mishpatim (Sefer HaChinukh 47); that we are commanded to kill those that transgress a few of the commandments in the Torah. And there I wrote the disagreement of Ramban, may his memory be Blessed, with Rambam, may his memory be Blessed, about this matter. And we shall also say that the law of hanging is in order to raise the convict and to publicize him to the eyes of all. Also, when they see the matter of the raising of the pole and the tying of the convict upon it, fear and trepidation will enter their hearts.

From the laws of this commandment are what the Sages, may their memory be Blessed, said (Sanhedrin 46a), that the commandment of those who are hung is [that] after we stone him, we plant a beam into the ground and the pole sticks out from it and [that] we [place] his hands one on top of the other and [that] we hang him close to sunset and untie him immediately and [that] we bury him with the pole that he was hung upon and with the stone that he was stoned with, so that the creatures will not say, "This is the pole that x was hung upon." And if they left him overnight there, they violate a negative commandment, as we will write in this Order (Sefer HaChinukh 536), with God's help. And the rest of its details are in the sixth chapter of Sanhedrin (see Mishneh Torah, The Sanhedrin and the Penalties within their Jurisdiction 4:15).

This commandment is practiced during the time of the Temple, when we had the power in our hands to judge capital punishments; and specifically, by males, as it is up to them to establish justice.

Mitzvah 536

To not leave one that is hung overnight: To not leave the one who is hung overnight on the pole, as it is stated (Deuteronomy 21:23), "You shall not leave his carcass on the pole overnight." This is a negative commandment. The entire matter of the commandment is written in its [corresponding] positive commandment in this Order (Sefer HaChinukh 537), and we shall not be lengthy about what there is no need. And there it is written that even someone who leaves his [relative's] dead body overnight not for his (the dead person's) honor transgresses a negative commandment.

Mitzvah 537

To bury him on the same day, and so [too] all the dead: To bury the one that was hung on that [same] day, as it is stated (Deuteronomy 21:23), "rather you shall surely bury him on that day, etc." And the language of Sifrei here is "'Rather you shall surely bury him on that day' is a positive commandment."

From the roots of the commandment is that which they, may their memory be Blessed, mentioned in the Mishna in the chapter [entitled] Nigmar Hadin (Sanhedrin 46b). As there they said that one who is hung is a curse to God, meaning to say that the creatures should not say, "Why was he hung? Because he cursed the Name [of God]." And it will come out in their mentioning of this and their bringing the thing up in their mouths, that they will be profaning the Name of the Heavens and causing evil to themselves. And the God who desires the good of His creatures prevented them from this because of that.

From the laws of this commandment is that which they, may their memory be Blessed, said (Sanhedrin 46a) that this commandment is not only with one who is hung, but rather even with all those killed by the court - it is a commandment to bury them on the day of their killing. Also included in this commandment is to bury all Jewish dead on the day of their death. And because of this, they, may their memory be Blessed, called a dead body that has no one to be involved in his burial, 'a dead body of the commandment (met mitsvah),' which is to say that it is a commandment upon all to bury him due to this command. And they, may their memory be Blessed, said in the Mishnah mentioned (Sanhedrin 46a) that two grave-sites were set up for the courts, one for those hung and burnt - whose punishment is more severe - and one for those who are killed (decapitated) and asphyxiated - whose punishment is more lenient. And after the flesh has decomposed, we collect the bones of the one convicted to be there and bury them in their fathers' grave-sites. And more details are in the mentioned chapter (See Tur, Yoreh Deah 382).

This commandment is practiced, concerning those killed by the court during the time when capital punishment is practiced; and concerning other Jewish dead in every place and at all times by males and by females, such that it is a commandment to bury them on the day of death. And one who transgresses this, and leaves a dead body overnight not for his (the dead person's) honor, violates this positive commandment, besides violating a negative commandment, as we will write in this Order (Sefer HaChinukh 536) with God's help.

Mitzvah 538

To return a lost item to an Israelite: To return a lost item to its owners, as it is stated (Deuteronomy 22:1), "you shall surely return them to your brother." And in the explanation, they, may their memory be Blessed, said (Bava Metzia 30a) [that] returning a lost item is a positive commandment. And this commandment is repeated in another place in the Torah, as it is stated (Exodus 23:4), "When you encounter your [enemy's] ox, etc., you shall surely return it to (your brother)."

Sefer HaChinukh

The root of this commandment is known - as there is in it a benefit to all, and to the ordering of the state; as forgetfulness exists with all [people, and] also their beasts and all of their animals flee here and there. And with this commandment that is among our people, beasts and vessels will be safe in every place that they may be in our holy land as if they were under the hand of their owners. 'And all of the directives of the Lord are straight, they rejoice the heart.'

From the laws of this commandment are what they, may their memory be Blessed, said (Bava Metzia 21a) [that] there are found items that a person finds in [such] a way or place that he is not obligated to return to their owners, but rather becomes entitled to them himself, as the Torah did not obligate him in these. And [it is] like they said in the Mishnah (Bava Metzia 21a), "These are the found items which belong to him [the finder]: If one found scattered fruit, scattered money, sheaves in the public domain, fig-cakes, baker's bread, strings of fish, cuts of meat, wool as it is from the country, bundles of flax and purple wool." And they said in the Gemara (Bava Metzia 23a), "Rav Zvid said, 'The law is that sheaves in the public domain, behold they are his; in a private domain, if they are in the way of falling, they are his, but if they are in the way of [deliberate] placing, he is obligated to announce [them.]'" And there, they explained how is the way of placing and [how is] the way of falling. And this is with something that has no [identifying] mark, but with something that has a mark - whether it is in the public domain or in the private domain, whether it is in the way of falling or in the way of placing - he is obligated to announce [it. This is the case] except for things that are found in the tide-places of the sea or in the flooding areas of the river. As in those places, even though it has a mark, the Merciful One (in the Torah) permitted it. And they extrapolated this (Bava Metzia 22a) from that which Scripture said, "that is lost from your fellow and you find" - that which is lost from him but found by everyone, which is to say [that] you are obligated to return [it, if it is found] in marketplaces and paths; [and this] excludes that of the river, where it is lost from him and from everyone, [such] that you are not obligated to return it, but rather the finder is entitled to it. And they, may their memory be Blessed, said (Bava Metzia 23a) [that] the reason a person is entitled to a found item that has no mark is because its owner has given up hope on it, which is to say that he has removed his mind and his entitlement from it, since it has no mark or - (Bava Metzia 24a) even when it has a mark - if it fell in the places where owners give up hope from it regardless, for example marketplaces where its majority 'is not from the Children of Israel.' And [so] behold, the one that finds it is like one who becomes entitled to [something] ownerless.

And the laws of the things that a person is obligated to announce and what thing is a mark [on account of which] we return the lost item to its owner; and that which they said about this (Bava Metzia 28a), that size, number, weight and place are marks; and the law of one who says the measure of its length and one who says the measure of its width, or one who says its length and width and one who says its weights; and the law of one who saw a sela (a coin) fall from his fellow and he picked it up before [the owner's] giving up hope or after [his] giving up hope, which is to say after he heard his fellow say, "Woe is to me, for that which I have lost," or similar to it; and the law that they said (Bava Metzia 27a) that a lost item that does not have a worth of the value of a perutah (a very small coin), that he is not obligated to take care of it and not to return it; and that which they said (Bava Metzia 28b) that from when the cheaters proliferated, we say to [the owner], "Bring witnesses that you are not a cheater and take [it]"; and the law of all things that produce [value] and consume or consume and do not produce, [as to] what are their laws, and how much time one has to take care of a cow and a donkey and calves and foals and geese and chickens; and the law of how he should deal with books or tefillin or vessels of wool or flax or other vessels; and that which they said (Bava Metzia 30a) that there are factors [through which] the finder does not become obligated to return the lost item - for example, an elder and it is not according to his honor or a priest in a graveyard; and the rest of the details of the commandment are [all found] in the second chapter of Bava Metzia.

And it is practiced in every place and at all time, by males and females. And one who transgresses this, and finds a found item that he is obligated to return - according to the matter that we have mentioned - and does not return it, has violated this positive commandment, besides having violated a negative commandment, as we shall write in this Order (Sefer HaChinukh 539) about the negative commandments that are adjacent, with God's help.

Sefer HaChinukh

Mitzvah 539
To not avoid his eyes from it: That we should not avoid our eye from the lost item of our brother (Bava Metzia 26b), but we [rather] take it and return it to him. And about this is it stated (Deuteronomy 22:3), "you may not ignore [it]."

The whole matter of this commandment is written in its [corresponding] positive commandment (Sefer HaChinukh 538) in this Order.

Mitzvah 540
To not leave the beast of his fellow falling under its load: That we have been warned that if we see a Jew whose donkey or other beast fell from the weight of its load or from another reason, or if he, himself, is crouching under his load (See Sefer HaMitzvot LaRambam, Mitzvot Lo Taase 270). that we should not leave him on the way and walk [away]; but [rather], we help him and lift up his beast with him, and we stay there until he has set up his load - either on his back or on his beast. And about this is it stated (Deuteronomy 22:4), "You shall not see the donkey of your brother, etc." - and they said in the Sifrei here [that], "'You shall not see the donkey, etc.' is a negative commandment."

And behold, one who transgresses this, and does not aid his fellow on the way, violates this negative commandment and the positive commandment mentioned in Parashat Mishpatim (Sefer HaChinukh 90), about the commandment of removing the load from upon the beast. And there, we elucidated the root of this commandment and all of its matter, as is our custom in this book - see it there (see Tur, Yoreh Deah 272).

Mitzvah 541
To load the load that has fallen [together] with his fellow: That we were commanded to help our brothers when they need to place the load on the beast or on the person, and there is not someone to help them with the thing. And about this it states (Deuteronomy 22:4), "you shall surely pick it up with him." And this, they, may their memory be Blessed, called (Bava Metzia 32a) 'loading (teinah).' And [there] they, may their memory be Blessed, said that we [can] take payment for loading, but for the unloading - meaning to say, to help his brother to unload the load from upon him or from upon his beast - this obligation is upon us to do for free.

And I have written about the roots of this commandment and a few of its laws, with regards to the commandment of unloading in the Order of Mishpatim, about the commandment to remove the load from upon the beast (Sefer HaChinukh 80). And its fellow (that commandment) speaks about all of [the current commandment's] matter.

Mitzvah 542
That a woman should not wear the adornments of a man: That women should not wear the clothing of men and not arm themselves with their weapons. And about this it states (Deuteronomy 22:5), "There shall not be the vessel of a man upon a woman." And Onkelos translated [it], "There shall not be a weapon of a man upon a woman" (see Nazir 59a). And that which is similar [is also prohibited]; since this is the reason that [Onkelos] explained Scripture as regarding weapons - because they are vessels that are completely unique to men, as it is not the way of a woman in the world to go out with weapons. But the same is true, that it is forbidden from the Torah, for them to go out with clothes that it is the custom of the men of that place to use - for example, that she should place a turban on her head or other vessels that are unique to a man (see Targum Jonathan on Deuteronomy 22:5).

It is from the roots of the commandment [that it is] to distance our holy nation from matters of sexual immorality and any matter and any angle whatsoever that contains a stumbling block towards it - as the matter that they, may their memory be Blessed, said metaphorically (Sanhedrin 106a) that our God hates promiscuity. [This] means to say, that in His love for us, He distanced us from promiscuity, which is an exceedingly ugly thing, [and which] takes the heart of a man and pushes it off from the good path and from desirable thoughts, to a bad path and thoughts of stupidity. And there is no doubt that if the clothes of men and women were the same, they would constantly mix - these with those -

'and the world would be filled with promiscuity.' And they also said in explaining this commandment that it is to distance all matters of idolatry, as the way of the worshipers of idolatry was with this. And I found these two reasons in the books of Rambam (Sefer HaMitzvot LaRambam, Mitzvot Lo Taase 40; Guide for the Perplexed 3:37) after I wrote them.

The laws of this commandment are brief. They are included in the simple meaning of Scripture (see Tur, Yoreh Deah 272).

And it is practiced in every place and at all times, by females. And a woman that transgresses this, and wears clothes that are unique only to men in that place that she is in, is liable for lashes.

Mitzvah 543

That a man should not wear the clothes of a woman: That men should not wear the clothes of women, and about this it states (Deuteronomy 22:5), "and a man should not wear the garment of a woman."

What is written concerning the previous commandment is from the roots of the commandment.

The laws of the commandment: That which they, may their memory be Blessed, said (Makkot 20b) that the prohibition and lashes are not only for clothing, but the same is true about their grooming; as anyone who grooms himself with the adornments that are unique to women is obligated in [getting] lashes - for example, one who plucks out white hairs from among the black ones from his head or from his beard; and so [too] one who dyes his hair in the way that women dye theirs. And so did Onkelos translate, "and a man should not groom with the adornments of a woman." And that which they, may their memory be Blessed, said (see Mishneh Torah, Foreign Worship and Customs of the Nations 12:10) that a toomtoom and an androginus (two categories of people the sex of which is in doubt) should, like a woman, not wrap their head; and should, like a man, not shave their head; and [that] if they do so they are not lashed. And so [too,] in every place, we give them the stringencies of men and of women; but if they transgressed, they are not lashed, because they [represent] a doubt. But if they transgressed a prohibition that a man and a woman are equal in, it is not necessary to say about this that they are lashed for it. And its other details are elucidated in Tractate Nazir [in the] chapter [entitled] Shnei Nizirim (Nazir 59a).

And this prohibition is practiced in every place and at all times by males. And one who transgresses this, and wears the clothes of women or grooms himself with the adornments of women - for example, he plucks out white hairs from among black ones or he dyes even one hair - is liable for lashes, from when he plucks it or dyes it.

Mitzvah 544

To not take the mother upon the young: That we should not take a bird's nest - the mother and the chicks or the eggs together - but rather that we should send away the mother. And about this is it stated (Deuteronomy 22:6), "do not take the mother upon the young."

I have written about the roots of the commandment and a few of its laws and all of its matter in its positive commandment in this Order (Sefer HaChinukh 545) - see there. And there we also spoke about this negative commandment; that it is rectified by the positive commandment of "you shall surely send away the mother." And they, may their memory be Blessed, have already taught us in Tractate Makkot 15a in the chapter [entitled] Elu Hen HaLokin [about] all negative commandments that have a positive commandment (that reverses the result of transgressing the negative commandment) - that if he fulfilled its positive commandment, he is exempt [from punishment]; [but] if he did not fulfill the positive commandment and it is [now] impossible to fulfill it, he is liable for lashes. And as it is stated over there, "As Rabbi Yochanan said to the teacher, 'It is taught, "He fulfilled it and he did not fulfill it."'" And that is the correct textual variant (like the variant of Rif and Ramban). And from this opinion we learned that any time the mother dies or another man has sent it away - and even though he has now not negated the positive commandment with his [own] hands, as behold, he did not kill it, but rather it died on its own; and there is no need to say if he killed the mother with his [own] hands - that he is liable for lashes according to everyone. But any time that he sent it before it died - even though he did not send it when he took it [with] the nest - he has not violated the negative commandment nor the positive commandment, since the Torah rectified it with the positive commandment; and behold, he [now] fulfilled it. And [this is so] even though it is not fitting to do so - as maybe the mother will die or the sender [will die] before the sending and he will not be able to fix [it]; and also, since 'enthusiasts are prompt with commandments,' and 'how good is a thing in its time.'

Mitzvah 545
To send away the mother [bird] if he takes it upon the young: To send away the mother from the nest before he takes the young, as it is stated (Deuteronomy 22:7), "you shall surely send away the mother and the young you shall take for you."

It is from the roots of this commandment [that it is] to put into our hearts that the providence of God, may He be Blessed, is upon all of His creatures - with the human species individually, as it is written (Job 34:21), "For His eyes are upon a man's ways, etc."; and upon the other species of animals generally, meaning to say that His desire, may He be Blessed, is towards the existence of the [particular] species. And therefore, no species will ever become extinct from all of the species of creatures, as it is due to the providence of the Living and Existing forever, may He be Blessed, that their existence is found. And when a man places his mind to this, he understands the ways of God and he will see that the continuous preservation of the species in the world - that not one of all of them became extinct and lost from the day they were created, 'from the lice's eggs to the antelope's horns' - is all from His statement and His will about this. And so too, will a man know that when he observes the commandments of his Creator and straightens all of his ways and be of clean hands and a pure heart, that the providence of God will be upon him and preserve his body for much time in this world, and his soul forever in the world to come. And like this did they, may their memory be Blessed, say (Sotah 8a) [that] it is [payment] measure for measure; since when this person places his mind to that which existence and good are with God's providence over things - and not from another cause - he too merits that God should turn to him for the good and make him exist. And about the reward for the existence and the ability [given] since he believed in the Creator about this matter, they, may their memory be Blessed, said in the Midrash (Devarim Rabbah 80:5 on Ki Tetzeh) that a person merits children as a reward for this commandment, which is to say that his existence will continue - as children are the existence of a person and his memory. And they extrapolated this apparently from its stating, "you shall surely send away the mother and the young (banim) you shall take for you," meaning to say, children (banim) take for yourself. As it could have stated, "you shall surely send away the mother" [only] and not [also] "and the young you shall take for you." And about this root, they, may their memory be Blessed, said (Berakhot 33b) that we silence one who says in his prayer, "Have mercy upon us, as You are the Merciful One, since Your mercies extend to the bird's nest." As the matter is not [one of] mercy, but rather it is in order to bring us merit in the way I have mentioned. And they said about this reason in the Gemara there, "It is because he makes the attributes of God into mercy, and they are [actually] only decrees." And the matter is not to say that the Holy One, Blessed be He, does not have mercy, God forbid - as behold, He is called the Merciful One; and they, may their memory be Blessed, said (Shabbat 133b) [that] just like the Holy One, Blessed be He, is merciful, you too have mercy." Rather, their intention is to say that there is no trait of mercy in Him, God forbid - like with people, [such] that the mercy in them is forced by their nature that the Creator, Blessed be He, placed in them. But mercy for Him is from His simple desire - that His wisdom loves to have mercy, because it is a good trait, and all good traits are found with Him. And they said [that] in His commanding us about this, it was not by force of the trait of mercy that He commanded us in the thing; as behold, He permitted their slaughter, since all the species are created for the needs of man. But [rather] the command about this and about 'it and its son,' which is like it, and many other commandments are only like a decree in front of Him, since He decreed about it with His simple desire. And if He had wanted the opposite of this, nothing would force Him [to do otherwise] and no cause would prevent Him, God forbid. [This is,] as opposed to us, who are built with the power of [our] natures, [such] that the trait of mercy impedes us from destroying, or sometimes forces us to do good. This is the matter of their saying [that] they are only decrees, and it is from the root of the thing

Sefer HaChinukh

of that which we mentioned.

And Rambam, may his memory be Blessed, wrote in explanation of this commandment (Guide for the Perplexed 3:48, and some have the textual variant, Ramban in his commentary to the Torah here) and of 'him and his child,' [that] it is because animals have great distress in seeing the pain of their children, like people. As the love of the mother for the child is not a matter that follows the intellect, but rather it is from the effects of the power of thinking that is found in animals, [just] as it is found in people. And Rambam, may his memory be Blessed, wrote about this matter, "Do not answer me with words from the statement of the sages [in] which they say, 'To the bird's nest, etc.' since this is the reasoning of the one to whom it appears that there is no explanation for the commandments, except for them being the will of the Creator. But we maintain the second reasoning, which is that there is an explanation for all of the commandments." And [Ramban] challenged him from that which is found in Bereishit Rabbah 44a, "And for what would the Holy One, Blessed be He, care if an animal is slaughtered from the [front of the] neck or from the back? Behold, the commandments were only given to refine the creatures with them, as it states (Proverbs 30:5), 'Every word of God is refined.'"

And Ramban, may his memory be Blessed, answered the challenges and clarified the matter clearly, completely and nicely. And this is his language that he wrote in his commentary of the Torah: That matter which Rambam, may his memory be Blessed, wrote that the commandments have explanations is something very elucidated, as in each one there is an explanation and a benefit and a refinement for a person, besides the reward for them from the Commander, may He be Blessed. And they, may their memory be Blessed, have already said (Sanhedrin 21b), "For why did He not reveal the explanation of the commandments, etc.?" And they, may their memory be Blessed, expounded (Pesachim 119a), "'And to the clothed elegantly' (which can also be read as, 'and to the one that covers the ancient' Isaiah 23:18) - this is [referring] to the one who covers that which the Ancient of Days (God) covered. And what are they? The explanations of the Torah." And they have already expounded about the red heifer (Bemidbar Rabbah 19:6) that Shlomo said, "I have discerned everything, but the section of the red heifer, I have investigated and asked and searched - 'I said that I could fathom it, but is far from me' (Ecclesiastes 7:23)." And Rabbi Yossi Bar Chinanah said, "The Holy One, Blessed be He, said to Moshe, 'Go and I will reveal to you the explanation of the heifer, but to another, it will be a statute (that is not understood),' as it is written (Zechariah 14:6), 'In that day, there shall be neither sunlight nor cold moonlight' - things that are covered from you in this world, in the future you will gaze upon them in the world to come; like that blind man that becomes able to gaze, as it is written (Isaiah 42:16), 'I will lead the blind by a road they did not know.' And it is written (later in the same verse), 'I have done these words and I have not left them' - as I have already done them for Rabbi Akiva," meaning to say that Rabbi Akiva already knew them in this world.

Behold, they explained that the deterrent to our [understanding of] the explanations of the commandments is only from the blindness of our intellects; and that the explanation of the most difficult one of them was already revealed to the sages of Israel. And there are many such statements in their words - and in the Torah and in Scripture, very many. And Rambam, may his memory be Blessed, mentioned some of them. But [as far] those homiletic teachings (aggadot) with which the Teacher was challenged, according to [Ramban's] opinion, they are about a different matter: that they wanted to say that there is no benefit in the commandments to the Holy One, Blessed be He, Himself, may He be Blessed. Rather, the benefit is for the person, himself, to deter him from harm or a bad belief or an ugly trait or to remember wonders of the Creator, may He be Blessed, [so as] to remember God. And this is [what was meant by] "to refine them with them" - that they should be like refined silver. As the action of the one who refines silver is not without explanation, but [rather] to remove all the dross. So too are the commandments to remove from him any bad belief and to inform him of the truth and to always remind him. And the language of the aggadah itself in Yilamdenu in the section, 'This is the animal' (Midrash Tanchuma, Shmini 8) is "And for what would the Holy One, Blessed be He, care if one slaughters a beast and eats or stabs [it] and eats? Does it help Him or hurt Him at all? Or what would He care whether one would eat pure foods or eat carcasses? 'And if you have been wise, you have been wise for yourself.' Behold, the commandments were only given to refine the creatures with them, as it states (Psalms 12:7), 'The words of the Lord are pure words'; 'The

Sefer HaChinukh

word of the Lord is refined' (Psalms 18:31). Why? So that it will a shield for you."

Behold, it is shown by this that they are coming to say that there is no benefit to Him, may He be Blessed, in the commandments - by way of illustration, that He would need the light that He commanded to light the candelabra (the menorah in the Temple) or that He would need the food of the sacrifices and the smell of the incense, as it would appear from their simple understandings. And even [regarding] the memory of His wonders that He commanded that we do [various acts] in commemoration of the exodus from Egypt and the creation story, the benefit is only that we know the truth and merit from it, such that we be fitting that they be a shield for us. As our honoring [Him] and saying over His praises are considered as nothing and void for Him. And he brought a proof from "the one who slaughters from the [front of the] neck and from the back," to say that all of them are for us and not for the Holy One, Blessed be He. As it is not likely to say about slaughter that there be a benefit and honor to the Creator, may He be Blessed, from the neck more than from the back or from stabbing. But rather they are for us; to guide us in the paths of mercy even at the time of slaughter. And he brought another proof - "or what would He care whether one would eat pure foods" - and these are permitted foods - "or eat impure foods" - and these are forbidden foods, about which the Torah stated (Leviticus 11:26), "they are impure to you": They are only for you to be of clean souls, wise and understanding of the truth. And they said, "And if you have been wise, you have been wise for yourself." They mentioned [the two examples], since the active commandments such as the slaughter [from] the neck are to teach us good traits; and the commandments and decrees regarding the species [that are permitted] are to purify our souls, as the Torah stated (Leviticus 20:25), "and do not make your souls disgusting with the beast and the fowl and with all that crawls on the earth, which I have separated for you to be impure." If so, they are all for our benefit only. And it is as Elihou said (Job 35:6), "If you sin, what do you do to Him? If your transgressions are many, how do you affect Him?"; and (Job 35:7), "What does He receive from your hand?" And this matter is agreed to in all the words of our Rabbis.

And they asked in Yerushalmi Nedarim 9:1 if we can open [an avenue of regret for a vow] with the honor of the Omnipresent in matters that are between him and the Omnipresent. And they answered this question [as follows], "What is the honor of the Omnipresent [that is offended]? For example, a sukkah that [a man] does not make, a lulav that he does not hold, tefillin that he does not don? And that is [what is] understood by the honor of the Omnipresent? It is for [the person] himself that it helps, like that (Job 35:7), 'If you are righteous, what do you give Him; what does He receive from your hand?' [and] (Job 35:6) 'If you sin, what do you do to Him? If your transgressions are many, how do you affect Him?'"

Behold, they elucidated that even the lulav and the sukkah and tefillin - that He commanded that they be "a sign upon your arm and a commemoration between your eyes [...] that the Lord took you out of Egypt with a strong hand" (Exodus 13:9) - are not for the honor of God, may He be Blessed, but [rather] to have mercy on our souls. And they already set this into the prayer of Yom Kippur, "You have separated man from the start and recognized him to stand in front of You, as who will say to You what to do, and if he is righteous, what will he give to You?" And so [too], it stated in the Torah (Deuteronomy 10:13), "for your good"; and so [too] (Deuteronomy 6:24), "And He commanded us to do all of these statutes [...], for our good all of the days." And the intention in all of them is that it be good for us and not for Him, may He Blessed and elevated. But all that we are commanded is [so that] our souls be refined and purified without the dross of evil thoughts and disgusting character traits. And so that which they said (Berakhot 33a), "[It is because] he makes the traits of the Holy One, Blessed be He into mercy and they are only decrees," is to say that God did not worry about the nest of the bird and His 'mercy did not reach' it and its child; as His mercy does not extend to creatures with an animal soul, to prevent us from doing what we need to them. As were it so, slaughtering would be forbidden. But [rather], the reason for the proscription is to teach us the trait of mercy and that we not become cruel. Since cruelty spreads in the soul of a man, as it is known with butchers that slaughter large oxen and donkeys, that they are 'people of blood,' 'slaughterers of men' [and] very cruel. And because of this they said (Kiddushin 82a), "The best of butchers are the partners of Amalek." And behold, these commandments with animals and birds are not mercy upon them, but [rather] decrees upon us, to guide us and to teach us the good character traits. To here are the interpretations of Ramban, may his memory be Blessed.

Behold, my son, I have written to you at length about this to have testify about all of the roots in my book, two trustworthy witnesses - two pillars of the world, great sages and wise men, of refined intellect, and recipients of the secrets of the Torah. As behold you see with your eyes that the opinion of both of them is that there is a reason for the commandments of the Torah [that] benefit people's traits to make them more proper and to accustom them to better all of their actions through them; and that there is no benefit in their performance - God forbid - to the Creator, Blessed be He. And if, however, there are from the commandments that we did not [fully] grasp their explanation due to the smallness of our intellect - because of their great depth and ultimate greatness - we should not prevent ourselves from saying about them all that we have grasped to find the benefit that there is for man in his doing them. And this is my path in all of my speech in this book - that there is a benefit for us found in the commandments; but there is not [benefit] for the One who commands them. And if you put your heart to these words, you will find this intention in all of them. And I have toiled greatly in some of them to succeed with the poverty of my mind to see a small little [part] of the great benefit that is in them. And I have written it on each and every one, 'and this is my portion from all of my toil.'

From the laws of the commandment is that which they, may their memory be Blessed, said (Chullin 139b), "'If you chance upon a bird's nest in front of you on the path' - just like the path which is not acquired by you; so too all, etc. From here they said, 'Doves from the coop and doves from the attic that nested in cubicles and in edifices, and geese and chickens that nested in an orchard, [one is] obligated in sending away; but [if] they nested within the house, and also Herodian doves, [one is] exempt from sending away. [... And] Rav Yehudah... said, '[If] he found a nest in the sea, [he is] obligated in sending away,'" as it is included in the expression, 'on the path,' "as it states (Isaiah 43:16), 'So said the Lord, who makes a path in the sea.'" And (Chullin 12:3) "[If] it was flying - [... if] its wings do not touch the nest, one is exempt from sending. [... If] there were [...] damaged eggs, one is exempt from sending, as it states (Deuteronomy 22:6), '[...] young birds or the eggs' - just as young birds are viable, so too [the] eggs [must be] viable [to fall under the law...]. If one sent her away and she returned, [...] - even [several] times - one is obligated [to send her away again], as it states (Deuteronomy 22:7),' You shall surely send.'" And the rest of the details of the commandment are elucidated in the last chapter of Chullin.

And this commandment is practiced in every place and at all times. And one who transgresses it and takes the mother when she is still on the young, violates this positive commandment, besides violating the negative commandment of 'do not take the mother.' And if the mother died before he sends her away or another person sent her away, he has no remedy to fulfill the positive commandment and to remedy the negative commandment. But if he sent her away before she dies, [the violation of] its negative commandment is rectified; as this negative commandment is rectified by the positive [one], and [it is] as we have written (Sefer HaChinukh 544) about the negative commandment that comes on this, with God's help.

Mitzvah 546

The commandment of a parapet: To remove stumbling blocks and obstacles from our dwelling places, and about this is it stated (Deuteronomy 22:8), "and you shall make a parapet for your roof." And the matter is that we should build a wall around the roofs and around the pits and the ditches and that which is similar to them, so that no creature should stumble to fall in them or from them. And included in this commandment is to build and fix every wall and fence from which it is likely that there come a mishap from it. And that which verse mentioned "for your roof," is [because] the verse spoke in the present (using the most common example). And the language of Sifrei is "'And you shall make a parapet' is a positive commandment" (see Sefer HaMitzvot LaRambam, Mitzvot Ase 184).

It is from the roots of the commandment [that is is] since even though God, may He be Blessed, supervises the details of people's [lives] and knows all of their deeds, and [that] everything that happens to them - good or bad - is through His decree and His commandment according to their merit

Sefer HaChinukh

or their guilt, and like the matter that they, may their memory be Blessed, said (Chullin 7b), "A man does not [so much as] bruise his finger below (i.e. on earth), unless it is announced about him from above (in Heaven)"; nonetheless a person must guard himself from the accidents that are customary in the world. As God created His world and built it upon the foundations of the principles of nature and decreed that fire should burn and that water puts out the flame. And so too, nature requires that that if a large stone falls on the head of a man, that it will smash his brain; or that if a person falls from the top of a high roof to the ground, that he will die. And He, may He be Blessed, graced the bodies of people and blew into them a living soul with a mind, to protect the body from all incidents, and [then] placed the two of them - the soul and the body - within the sphere of the [natural] elements, and [these elements] will move them and act upon them. And since God subjugated the human body to nature - as so did His wisdom require - from the angle of its being physical, He commanded him to guard [himself] from an accident. As nature, to which he is subjugated, will act upon him if he does not guard himself from it.

However, there will a few people that 'the King will desire their glory,' due to their great piety and the clinging of their souls to His ways, may He be Blessed - these are the great pious ones 'who were of old, the men of fame,' like the great and holy forefathers and many of the sons that were after them, such as Daniel, Channiah, Mishael, Azariah and those similar to them, to whom God delivered nature into their hands. And at their start, nature was master over them and at their end - due to the greatness of the elevation of their souls - 'it was reversed,' as they were the masters over nature. As we know with Avraham, our father, that they dropped him into the fiery furnace and he was not injured; and [with] the four (and [with] the three) pious ones mentioned that they placed 'into the burning fiery furnace [...] and [not] a hair on their head was singed.' But most people have not merited this great level due to their sins, and therefore the Torah commands us to guard our dwelling places and our locales, lest death encounter us in our negligence. And we should not endanger our souls by reliance upon miracles; and they, may their memory be Blessed, said (Sifra, Emor 8) that a miracle is not performed for anyone who relies on a miracle. And according to this approach will you see most matters written in every place. Since even in Israel's fighting of a war commanded by the word of God, they would [still] organize their war and equip themselves and do all of the [required] matters, as if they were completely relying on natural processes [to win the war]. And so is it fitting to do according to the matter that we mentioned. And the one who does not argue with the truth from a perverse heart will concede this.

From the laws of the commandment is that which they, may their memory be Blessed, said (Sukkah 3b) that the obligation of a parapet is only in a house that is being used as a residence, but a storehouse or a barn and similar to them [as well as] any house that does not have four square ells is exempt from [requiring] a parapet. And so [too] synagogues and study halls, because they are not made for residence. And [also among its laws is] that which they, may their memory be Blessed, said that if the public domain is higher than his roof, it is not in need of a parapet, as it is stated, "if the faller should fall from it" - and not into it. And the measurement of the height of the parapet is ten handbreadths.

And they, may their memory be Blessed, forbade many things (see Mishneh Torah, Murderer and the Preservation of Life 11:5 and 7) in order to guard ourselves from injuries and bad accidents, as it is not fitting for a person who has intelligence to endanger himself. And therefore, it is fitting that he should put into his mind all of the things that can possibly result in injury. And the one who transgresses [these prohibitions] is rabbinically obligated in [getting] lashes of rebellion. From these [prohibitions] is what they said that a person should not place his mouth under the drainpipe and drink, lest he drink a leech. And they [also] forbade (Chullin 10a) uncovered waters because of the concern, that a poisonous [snake] not have drunk from it. And the measurement of it is [the amount of time] required for the [snake] to come out from the edge of the vessel and drink. And they said about this matter that there are liquids that are susceptible to [the concern] of being an 'uncovered' [liquid] and there are those that are not susceptible to being an 'uncovered' [liquid]. And from this concern itself, they forbade gnawed figs, grapes, pomegranates, squash, pumpkins and cucumbers - even if they are [many] (see Mishneh Torah, Murderer and the Preservation of Life 12:2 and 4). And they said that all fruits that have moistness and are found to be bitten are forbidden. And so too did they forbid that a person not put coins into his mouth, lest there is dry spit of one infected with [skin diseases] upon them - or that there be sweat [upon them], since the sweat of a person is a death potion, except for that from the face. And the rest of its details are elucidated in Bava Kamma and in sections of Sanhedrin and in Yerushalmi Shekalim 1 (see Mishneh Torah, Murderer and the Preservation of Life 11).

And this commandment is practiced in every place and at all times by males and females. And one who transgresses it and leaves his roof or his pit without a parapet has violated this positive commandment and also violated the negative commandment of "you shall not place blood in your house" - as we will write in this Order (Sefer HaChinukh 447), with God's help.

Mitzvah 547

To not leave a stumbling block: To not leave stumbling blocks and snares in our land and in our homes, so that people not die or get injured from them (see Mishneh Torah, Murderer and the Preservation of Life 11). And about this is it stated (Deuteronomy 22:8), "and you shall not place blood in your house." And they said in Sifrei, "'And you shall make a parapet for your roof' is a positive commandment and [that] and 'you shall not place blood in your house' is a negative commandment."

I have written about the roots of this commandment and all of its matter in its [corresponding] positive commandment in this Order (Sefer HaChinukh 546) - and take it from there if you want to know.

Mitzvah 548

To not plant forbidden mixtures in a vineyard: To not plant types of grain in a vineyard, and [also] not hemp or arum (loof). And this type of forbidden mixtures is called forbidden mixtures of the vineyard (kilayei hakerem). And about this is it stated (Deuteronomy 22:9), "Do not plant your vineyard a forbidden mixture." And they, may their memory be Blessed, said (Sifrei on this verse), "[Why] do I need this, is it not stated (Leviticus 19:19), 'your field you shall not plant a forbidden mixture?' It teaches that anyone who keeps a forbidden mixture in his vineyard transgresses two negative commandments." And they, may their memory be Blessed, explained (Kiddushin 39a) that forbidden mixtures of the vineyard are two types of grain seeds with grape seeds. And this is what Rabbi Yishaya said, "He [has not transgressed] until he plants wheat and barley and grape-seed in one fall of the hand," as this is what is implied to them by "forbidden mixtures in a vineyard," meaning to say that you need a forbidden mixture besides "your vineyard."

I have written regarding the commandment of cross-breeding in the Order of Kedoshim Tihiyu (Sefer HaChinukh 244) from the roots of the commandment of forbidden mixtures from the angle of its simple meaning (peshat) as is my custom, and take if from there. And we still need to speak here [about] what the reason is for the new [aspect] of the prohibition, that we need for it a forbidden mixture besides the vineyard. And maybe we shall say that it is from the vineyard being a very important thing and having a very strong nature, that one other type together with it would always be negated and [so] it would not be considered as a forbidden mixture or as anything. And therefore, the verse required two types besides the vineyard. And maybe from the strength of this explanation, we shall also say that the two types that the verse required must be types of grain, which are important for their functions, [just] like hemp and arum, which are important for their functions. But all other types would be negated with the grapevines and are not forbidden by the Torah but only rabbinically. From the laws of the commandment is that which they, may their memory be Blessed, said (Menachot 15a) that the Torah's prohibition of a forbidden mixture of the vineyard is only in the case of types of grain and hemp and arum, but to plant vegetables and other types and grape-seed is [only] forbidden rabbinically. And so [too] did the Rabbis forbid to plant types of grain and also vegetables alongside the grapevines, or to plant a grapevine alongside the vegetable or the grain, because of the concern of interbreeding. Since the grapevine is softer than all other trees, they were more concerned about it. And if he did this - even though he is not lashed - behold, he set [it] apart and it is forbidden to benefit from both of them, and we burn the whole thing. And [we burn] even the chaff of the grain and the wood of the grapevines, as it is stated, "lest it be set aside (tikdash), the crop, the seed, etc." - and they, may their memory be Blessed, expounded (Kiddushin 56b), "Lest it be incinerated by fire (tukad esh)," meaning to say that all of it is fitting to be burnt, as we will write adjacently (Sefer HaChinukh 449). And the rest of its details are elucidated in Tractate Kilayim (See Tur, Yoreh Deah 246).

And the prohibition of forbidden mixtures of the vineyard from Torah writ is practiced by males and females in the Land of Israel alone, and rabbinically even outside of the Land. And even though forbidden mixtures of seeds are not practiced outside of the Land even rabbinically, we have already elucidated in the Order of Kedoshim (Sefer HaChinukh 245) that they, may their memory be Blessed, were stringent with forbidden mixtures of the vineyard to forbid them outside of the Land, since they are so weighty that [even] their benefit is forbidden in the Land, as this reason is explained in the end of the first chapter of Kiddushin 39a.

One who transgresses this, and planted wheat and barley and grape-seed in one fall of the hand in the Land [of Israel], is lashed immediately when he plants them from Torah writ; and outside of the Land, he is rabbinically struck with lashes of rebellion. But concerning the matter of their benefit becoming forbidden, they are not forbidden immediately when he plants them, until after it has taken root, and as they, may their memory be Blessed, said (Pesachim 25a), "[If] it is planted from its start, with the taking root; [if] it has already been planted and increases, with the [further] increase."

Mitzvah 549

To not eat forbidden mixtures of the vineyard: That we are forbidden from eating forbidden mixtures of the vineyard only. And we have already explained in the previous commandment what forbidden mixtures of the vineyard are. And about this is it stated (Deuteronomy 22:9), "lest it be set aside (tikdash), the crop, the seed that you planted and the produce of the vineyard." - and they, may their memory be Blessed, explained (Kiddushin 56b), "Lest it be incinerated by fire (tukad esh)," which is to say that it is not fitting that there be a purpose [from it], as it should all be forbidden in benefit. And the proof that there is a negative commandment in it, is that it is written in its prevention, "lest (pen)." And they, may their memory be Blessed, said (Eruvin 96a) that in every place that it states, "guard yourself," "lest," and "do not" (heeshamer, pen ve-al), it is certainly a negative commandment.

From the roots of the commandment, [there is a need to] preface: The matter is known that in all of the commandments of the Torah, God distances us form a thing according to [the degree] of the stumbling found in it. And there is no doubt that the planting of a vineyard is the cause of wine, which [brings] several stumbling blocks to people. From its desire have many casualties fallen, since [wine] stimulates the 'impulse of the heart of man which is evil,' and it pushes off the good impulse. And all of its counsel is, "Eat, drink and lay down to fall asleep." And [it is] like the matter that is written (Habakuk 2:8), "And surely the one that wine betrays," and the one who separates from it is called holy. And nonetheless God, may He be Blessed, allowed it to us because of its slight purpose for bodies that its found in its slight [consumption]. And since it is only permitted for a great need, the verse obligated us that if also the start of its planting or its seeding will be in such a way that there is an angle of iniquity and sin in it, that we not keep it and that we should not benefit from it at all, but [rather] that it should all be burnt and destroyed from the world. Are all of the stumbling blocks that come out from at it after the end of its ripening not enough for us? [Hence,] it is not good for also its beginning to be in sin, but [rather] all of it should be incinerated - the fruit and the chaff and the wood and everything that is in it.

From the laws of the commandment is that which they, may their memory be Blessed, said (Mishnah Kilayim 5:5), "Whether one plants, or whether one keeps a forbidden mixture in his vineyard" - meaning to say that he saw that a forbidden mixture grew in his vineyard and he left it there - "it has become set aside," meaning it became obligated to be burnt. And that is when they were standing in the vineyard by his will, once he knew about them, in the measure that they increased one two-hundredth from what they were at the time that he knew about them. As they, may their memory be Blessed, said (Pesachim 25a), "[If] it is planted from its start, with the taking root; [if] it has already been planted and increased, with the [further] increase." And, they, may their memory be Blessed, explained from the tradition that this increase is one two-hundredth. And that which we say that they have not become set aside unless he wants their existence is because it is written about them, "which you have planted" - meaning to say, according to his will. And the explanation for this thing is elucidated in the root of forbidden mixtures on inter-breeding and of witchcraft that I have written in their place in the Order of Kedoshim (Sefer HaChinukh 244) and Mishpatim (Sefer HaChinukh 62). And this is what they, may their memory be Blessed, said (Bava Kamma 100a), "[If the] partition of the vineyard is breached (such that a forbidden mixture is created), we say to him, 'Fix [it].'" [This] means to say that even though it increased one two-hundredth while he was still attempting to make the fence, it did not become set aside; since it did not become breached, and it did not stay breached, according to his will. And so [too] they, may their memory be Blessed, said that one who suspends his grapevine over the produce of his fellow, behold, this one set aside his grapevine, but the produce did not become set aside (see Mishneh Torah, Diverse Species 5:8). And for this reason, they also said that - since a person cannot set aside something that is not his - this prohibition is only [operative] by the will of the owners. And because of this, they also said that one who suspends the grapevine of his fellow over the produce of his fellow, did not set aside any one of them. And for this reason, one who plants his vineyard on the seventh year did not set it aside, since in the seventh year the land is ownerless to everyone (see Mishneh Torah, Diverse Species 5:8). And they, may their memory be Blessed, said (Mishnah Kilayim 5:5) that one who plants vegetables or produce in a vineyard or leaves it until it increased one two-hundredth, behold, he has set aside (forbidden) from the grapevines surrounding it sixteen ells in every direction. And one who comes to plant vegetables or produce next to a vineyard must distance it four ells from it. And five vines is called a vineyard; and this is when they are planted in this order: Two across from two and one sticking out as a tail. And they said that we distance produce and vegetables three hand-breadths from a single grapevine in every direction, because the grapevine is soft and the roots of the produce go into it and there is in this a prohibition of [forbidden] grafting. But with other trees which are hard, this concern is not there and one does not need to distance [other plantings] from them at all. And the rest of the details of this commandment are explained in Tractate Kilayim.

And this prohibition not to derive benefit from forbidden mixtures from the vineyard is practiced in the Land of Israel from Torah writ, and outside of the Land rabbinically. And there are those that say that outside the Land - even though the prohibition of planting is practiced there - the prohibition of benefit is only specifically with the forbidden mixtures of the vineyard of the Land of Israel, but their words need support. And the one that transgresses this, and eats or derives benefit from a forbidden mixture of the vineyard of the Land of Israel, is liable for lashes. And even one who eats it not in the way of its enjoyment - meaning to say, he did not derive enjoyment from eating it - is obligated by it and is lashed; which is not the case with all other prohibitions in the Torah, in which we only give lashes for them [if they are consumed] according to the way of their enjoyment - meaning to say that the person derives enjoyment from them. [This is] as Abbaye says in the second chapter of Pesachim 24b, "Everyone concedes about forbidden mixtures of the vineyard that we lash for them even not in the ways of their enjoyment. What is the explanation? Since it is not written about them, 'eating.'" As it is written, "lest it be set aside (tikdash)" - and they, may their memory be Blessed, expounded (Kiddushin 56b), "Lest it be incinerated by fire (tukad esh)." And outside of the Land, one who eats or derives benefit from them transgresses a rabbinic prohibition, according to some of the commentators, as we said.

Mitzvah 550

To not do work with two species of animals: To not plow with an ox and a donkey together. And the same is the case with any two species of animals, when one is pure and the other one is impure. And it is not specifically plowing that is forbidden, but rather the same is true for all types of work - for example, threshing or pulling a wagon [or] any of the types of work. And about this is it stated (Deuteronomy 22:10), "You shall not plow with an ox and a donkey together."

[Concerning] the root of the commandment, Rambam, may this memory be Blessed wrote (Guide for the Perplexed 3:49, see also Ramban on Deuteronomy 22:10) that is it from the root of the prohibition of inter-breeding animals as a forbidden mixture. As the way of workers of the land is to to bring a pair (of animals) from one barn and lest [and there] he would graft them. And the root of the prohibition of inter-breeding I wrote in its place in the Order of Kedoshim Tihiyu (Sefer HaChinukh 244). And after permission of the Master - the teacher mentioned - and concession to his good word, I will also answer my portion. And I say that from the explanations of this commandment is the matter of [causing] pain to animals, which is a prohibition of the Torah. And it is known that for species of animals and fowl, there is great anguish in dwelling with those that are not its species and - all the more so - to do work with them. And [it is] as we see with our eyes with the ones that are not under our hands (undomesticated species) that every bird dwells with its species; and all animals and other species also always cling to their [own] species. And any wise-hearted person will [learn] proper conduct from this, to never put together two people whose natures are different from one another and different in their behavior in any matter - like a righteous person and an evildoer [or] a slight person and an honorable one. Since if the Torah was exacting about the pain that there is to animals - that are not intelligent creatures - from this, all the more so [is this the case] with people that have an intelligent soul, in order to know their Maker.

From the laws of the commandment is that which they, may their memory be Blessed, said (see Sefer HaMitzvot LaRambam, Mitzvot Lo Taase 218 and Mishneh Torah, Diverse Species 9:7) that the obligation of this commandment from Torah writ is only with two species like the ox and the donkey - that one of them is pure and the second one impure, [such] that their natures are very distant from one another. But with two species that are [both] pure or impure - like an ox and a goat, or a donkey and horse - it is not forbidden from the Torah. Rather it is [only] rabbinically that any two species that would [constitute a case of] forbidden inter-breeding are forbidden - and both [domesticated] beasts and [undomesticated] animals are included in the prohibition. And it is the same whether one plows with them or seeds or pulls a wagon with them. And so [too,] if one [person] was sitting in the wagon and one was leading [them] - both of them are lashed, because his sitting in the wagon [also] causes the animal to pull (see Mishneh Torah, Diverse Species 9:9). And even if a hundred [people] led together, all of them are lashed. And [about] that which they said that it is permissible to do all work with a person and an animal, as it states, "with an ox and a donkey" - and not with a person and a donkey or a person and an ox (see Mishneh Torah, Diverse Species 9:10) - the explanation of the matter is according to the root that we mentioned. As the joining of an animal is not distressing for a person, since there is no connection with it at all. And behold, it is like he is doing work with a tree or a stone; and [so] it does not at all come into the designation that we spoke about. And also from the matter of the commandment is that which Rabbi Yitschak said at the end of Makkot 22a, that one who leads an ox of those disqualified from the consecrated is lashed - even though it is one body, the verse made it like two bodies to be lashed for. And the rest of its details are explained in the eighth chapter of Kilayim (see Tur, Yoreh Deah 297).

And this prohibition is practiced in every place and at all times by males and females. And one who transgresses this and seeds or plows or pulls or leads with a forbidden mixture - which are two species, one impure and one pure - is liable for lashes from Torah writ. And he is liable for lashes even if he led them together with his voice alone - like the way of animals that sometimes walk with the coaxing of people, as it is stated, "together" - in any case. They, may their memory be Blessed, made a precise inference from the words of the verse to obligate lashes [even] with speech without a deed. And in [the case of] two species that were [both] impure or pure, that are forbidden to inter-breeding with each other, he is rabbinically liable for lashes of rebellion.

Mitzvah 551

To not wear shaatnez: To not wear clothing that is composed of wool and flax (linen), and that is what is called, shaatnez. And about this is it stated (Deuteronomy 22:11), "You shall not wear shaatnez, wool and flax together."

I wrote a hint about the roots of the commandment in the Order of Mishpatim about the matter of "do not keep a witch alive" (Sefer HaChinukh 62). And Rambam, may his memory be Blessed, wrote about the explanation of the prohibition (in Sefer HaMitzvot LaRambam, Mitzvot Lo Taase 42 and

Sefer HaChinukh

in Guide for the Perplexed 3:37), [that] it is because the priests of idolatry would dress like this at that time. And he wrote further that this matter is still known with the priests that are in Egypt.

From the laws of this commandment is that which they, may their memory be Blessed, said (Yevamot 5b, and see Mishneh Torah, Diverse Species 10:2) that there is only a prohibition from Torah writ of a combination of wool and flax if they are shua, tavui and noz. [This] is to say that the wool is shua by itself, meaning to say, beaten, and tavui (spun) by itself and noz by itself - and the explanation of noz is woven (see Rashi on Niddah 61b and Rabbenu Tam in Tosafot on Niddah 61b) - and so [too] is the flax shua, tavui and noz, by itself; and afterwards he combined them together - for example, he wove them, or even if he tied them one to another, once he tied two knots, this is shaatnez from Torah writ, for which there is lashing. But the whole time that these three [processes] that we have written are not done to them, it is not shaatnez from Torah writ, but [only] rabbinically, according to the opinion of some commentators, and we do not administer lashes for it. But it is forbidden rabbinically if one of the [processes] that we have mentioned - either shua or tavui or noz - is done to them. And this is what they, may their memory be Blessed, said (Mishnah Kilayim 9:9), "the ones alone are forbidden" - meaning to say, rabbinically. And there are some commentators that said that [even] with one of these [processes], it is forbidden from Torah writ - and when they said about this, "forbidden," it is meaning to say from Torah writ.

And they, may their memory be Blessed, said about this matter (Yoma 49a), "Even [if there are] ten beddings, one on top of the other, it if forbidden to [sit] upon them," as we are concerned lest a fiber wrap itself upon his flesh. And they, may their memory be Blessed, said this matter when the forbidden mixture underneath is soft, as then is there this concern of wrapping (see Mishneh Torah, Diverse Species 5:12-13). And this prohibition is rabbinic, as from Torah writ it is permissible, even when they are soft. And [it is] as they, may their memory be Blessed, said, "'It shall not come upon you' (Leviticus 19:19) - but you can set it under you" (see Mishneh Torah, Diverse Species 10:12-13). And in Yerushalmi Kilayim 9:1, they said [that] pillows and comforters - even though they are hard - with full ones, it is forbidden to sit upon them rabbinically, since they double over on the one that is sitting upon them; but with empty ones ([this is what is written] in the Yerushalmi, [though there appears to be an error here in the Sefer HaChinukh, wherein it is written], the soft ones), since there is no concern that they will go on top, it is permissible to sit upon them, since (if) they are hard. And the explanation of the matter is [that it is] because the verse forbids shaatnez with an expression of wearing, meaning to say in the way of wearing is it forbidden and not in another way. And for this reason our teacher, God protect him, permitted us to put hats that are made from felt on our head to guard against the sun, since they are also very hard. And therefore, even though they have a forbidden mixture in them, they permitted them - as it is not the way of wearing something so hard. And there is one who wants to be stringent upon himself with this, and they did not protest against him. And for this reason - that it is the way of wearing that the Torah forbade - they also permitted the sellers of cloth to sell according to their way (to put the cloth on top of themselves) but only when they do not have any intention at all to warm up from it. And nonetheless, the modest and good wholesalers extend clothes from forbidden mixtures on a stick behind them so that they not touch them. And they, may their memory be Blessed, said that there is no measurement to forbidden mixtures - that even one string in a large garment forbids all of it until he removes it (see Mishneh Torah, Diverse Species 10:5). Kelech - which is a type of wool and it grows on stones in the Dead Sea - is forbidden with flax rabbinically, because of the appearance [of sin] (marait ayin). And the rest of the details of the commandment are elucidated in Mishnah Kilayim 9 and in Tractate Shabbat and in the end of Makkot. And this prohibition is practiced in every place and at all times by males and females. And one who transgresses it, and wears a Torah-level forbidden mixture - or covers himself with it - is liable for lashes. And if it is a rabbinic-level forbidden mixture, he is liable for lashes of rebellion. And one who wears a forbidden mixture - and even if he wears it the entire day - is only lashed one [set of lashes]. But one who takes his head out from the garment and puts it back in - even though he does not remove the entire garment - is obligated [lashes] for each and every [time that he does this]. And in what case does it apply that he is only obligated once for [wearing it] the whole day? When they gave him one warning. But if they warned him [several times] and they said to him, "Take it off," and he [continues to] wear it for the time period [needed] in order to put it on and take it off - since they warned him, behold, he is obligated for each and every [such] time period that they warned him about it, and even though he did not take [it] off [and put it on anew].

Mitzvah 552
To marry a woman with a marriage contract and betrothal: That we were commanded to acquire a woman in one of three ways before the marriage. And the sages elucidated these ways (Kiddushin 2a) - that they are money (monetary value), a contract and sexual relations with her. And about this is it stated (Deuteronomy 22:13), "If a man takes a woman and has sexual relations with her," which is to say [that] if a man wants to take (marry) a woman for himself, he should acquire her first with sexual relations. And about that which the verse stated (Deuteronomy 24:2), "And she shall go out [...] and she shall be," the traditional understanding came [to explain] that [just] like the departure (divorce) of a woman is with a contract - as we will write in this Order (Sefer HaChinukh 579), with the help of God - so too is [her] being with him; meaning to say, the acquisition of a woman is with a contract. And they, may their memory be Blessed, also learned (Kiddushin 4b) that she is acquired with monetary value, since it is written about an Israelite maidservant (Exodus 21:11), "and she shall go out, there is no silver (monetary value)" - and the understanding about it came [to explain] (Kiddushin 3b), "'There is no monetary value' for this master, but there is monetary value (when she goes) from another master. And who is he? Her father."

It is from the roots of the commandment that we are commanded to perform an act with a woman [that] indicates the matter of their being a couple before he lays with her, and that he should not have sexual relations with her like he would have sexual relations with a prostitute - without another act between them first. And it is also said, that it is so that she will always put it into her mind that that she is acquired by that man and that she not be unfaithful to him and not rebel against him, and [that] she give him honor and glory like a servant to his master. And with this, their sitting down and their rising up will always be in peace, and civilization will be established according to the will of God, who desired it.

And given that which what I mentioned is from the foundation of the commandment, Israel is accustomed to preform the betrothal with a ring, so that it be a constant reminder on her hand - and even though it is possible to betroth her with the value of a small coin (perutah) alone. However we do not betroth with less than the value of a small coin - as so did they, may their memory be Blessed, say (Kiddushin 3a), "Since she does not transfer herself for less than this," which means to say that she does not consider such a small act to be anything. And [this is the case] even though she is acquired by a contract - [as] even though it does not have the value of a small coin, it is an important act in her eyes; as so [too] are most acquisitions in the world preformed with a contract. And for this reason, an act of exchange (chalifin) does not acquire her; as an exchange is with a vessel, even though it does not have the value of a small coin.

From the laws of the commandment is that which they, may their memory be Blessed, said (Kiddushin 2a) that the one who betroths with money or with monetary value, is required that there be the value of a small coin in it - since, anything that is less than the value of a small coin is not money and a woman is not acquired by it. And he says to her, "Behold, you are betrothed to me with this money or with this monetary value," or "Behold, you are engaged to me," or "Behold, you are a wife to me." And all of Israel is already accustomed to saying, "Behold, you are betrothed to me with this thing like the law of Moshe and Israel." And he gives it to her in front of witnesses. And if there are no witnesses there - and even if they both, the man and the woman, say that he betrothed her - it is not a betrothal (Kiddushin 65a). And it is the man that must say these words - the understanding of which is that he acquired her - and give her the money (see Mishneh Torah, Marriage 3:1,7). But if she gives anything to him and said, "Behold, I am betrothed to you" or any other expression of transferal, she is not betrothed. And so [too], if she gave [it] to him and he said [the betrothal declaration]. But if he gave [it] and she said [the declaration], behold, she is betrothed [from] a doubt [about the actual law] (Kiddushin 6b).

And how is it [when] one betroths with a contract? For example, he writes upon paper or on clay or on a leaf or on all other things, "Behold, you are betrothed to me," or "Behold, you are engaged to me" or [something] similar to these expressions, and he gives this writing to her in front of witnesses - behold, she is betrothed. And he has to write it for this woman and with her consent. But if he wrote it without her consent and not for her - even if he gave it to her with her consent - she is not betrothed. And one who betroths with sexual relations also says to her, "Behold, you are betrothed to me with these sexual relations," and he isolates himself with her in front of witnesses and has sexual relations with her. And it is when he finishes having sexual relations that she is betrothed - as it is most likely that one who betroths with sexual relations has the culmination of sexual relations in mind. And whether he has sexual relations according to her [customary] way or not according to her way, she is betrothed.

And [about] that which they, may their memory be Blessed, said (Kiddushin 5b) that one who says to a woman when he betroths her, "Behold I am your husband," or "your man" or "your fiance," there is no betrothal - it is because the content of these expressions is that he transferred himself to her, and the content of the expression must be that he acquired a wife. For example, [if] he would say, "Behold, you are my wife," or "my fiancee," or "acquired by me" or "Behold, you are mine," or "Behold, you are in my domain," or "obligated to me," "taken by me," "pledged to me," or all that is similar to this - the understanding of which is that he is acquiring a wife - behold, she is betrothed with all of these expressions. And it is all from the root that we wrote. If he said to her, "Behold, you are dedicated for me," or "designated for me," or "Behold, you are my help," "corresponding to me," "my rib (or side)," "my closed one," "my replacement," "my grabbed one," she is betrothed with all of these expressions [from] a doubt [about the actual law]. And that is when he was speaking with her about matters of betrothal, but if they were not speaking about this, she is not betrothed at all with these expressions. And the law of one who betroths a woman by halves; and the law of one who betroths with a debt [owed him] (Kiddushin 6b), and one betroths with a debt and a small coin, and one who betroths with a pledge (Kiddushin 8a); and that which they said that a man can appoint an agent to betroth a wife - whether a specific woman or a woman in general - and so [too], the agent appoint an agent, and the second one a third, and so [forth], and until how many, if the one betrothing had commanded it; and [that] an adult woman can appoint an agent to accept the items of betrothal; and [that] the father acquires the items of betrothal of his minor daughter and that he can betroth her to whomever he wants, even against her will - whether by himself or through an agent - and that a man can say to his minor daughter, "Go and take your items of betrothal"; and [that] a woman can only become betrothed according to her will, but against her will, she is not betrothed - but a man who was forced to betroth, behold, she is betrothed; and [that in a case of] a man who betroths a woman that is a sexual prohibition for him, she is not betrothed (see Mishneh Torah, Marriage 4:12-13), as betrothal is not effective in [the violation] of sexual prohibitions, except for the menstruant woman, whereby betrothal is effective, but it is not fitting to do so - but betrothal is effective in [the violation] of [other] negative and positive commandments, and all the more so in the case of secondary prohibitions; and [that] even though they, may their memory be Blessed, said that a married woman that accepts an object of betrothal from another is betrothed and [yet] that there is no greater sexual prohibition than this - they only said it if it was specifically in front of her husband and from the reason that we posit that her husband divorced her, since she was so brazen-faced to say this [in front of him]; and that which they said (Kiddushin 56b) that one who betroths a woman with that from which it is prohibited to derive benefit - for example, leavened grain products (chamets) on Passover and meat with milk and similar to them and so [too] with all other things the benefit from which is forbidden - she is not betrothed, and even with something the benefit from which is [only] prohibited rabbinically - for example, chamets during the sixth hour of the fourteenth of Nissan - she is not betrothed; and (by association,) our sages in our generation have taught that one who wants to guard his adult daughter from not becoming betrothed to any man, without his consent, should say to her that she should forbid herself any money or monetary value at all that any man should give to her for betrothal without the consent of her father - and the language of sages heals; [as well] as all the rest of the details of this commandment, [which] are many, are [all] elucidated in the tractate that is associated with this and it is Tractate Kiddushin.

And this commandment is practiced in every place and at all times. And one who transgresses this and marries a woman without betrothing her first has violated this positive commandment (see Mishneh Torah, Marriage 1:1-2 and Kessef Mishneh on Mishneh Torah, Marriage 1:1-2 and Lechem Mishnah there).

And the Sages obligated us to recite a blessing upon this commandment - the man betrothing (see Mishneh Torah, Marriage 3:3, and Sefer Mitzvot HaGadol, Assain 41) or someone else on his behalf and he answers, amen - in the way that we recite a blessing on all commandments. As we hold that with blessings over commandments, 'even though he has [already] fulfilled [it], he may fulfill [it] for another.' And the text of the blessing is this: Blessed are You, Lord, our God, King of the Universe, who has sanctified us with His commandments and has separated us from the sexual prohibitions and forbade us the engagements and permitted us marriage through canopy and betrothal. Blessed are You, Lord, who sanctified His nation, Israel, through canopy and betrothal (see Mishneh Torah, Marriage 3:23). This is the text of the blessing over engagement that we are accustomed to say in our land. And our custom is to arrange it over a goblet full of wine, and to recite it after the act of betrothal. And they said that the explanation of this is that since the act of betrothal is dependent upon the consent of another - and that is the woman - it is not fitting to recite the blessing over the commandment before the commandment, as with other commandments. However, Rambam, may his memory be Blessed, wrote (Mishneh Torah, Marriage 3:24), that if he betrothed her, and did not recite the blessing first as with the other commandments, he should not recite the blessing afterwards, as it will be a blessing in vain.

Mitzvah 553

The commandment that the wife of one who 'puts out a bad name' [about her] dwell with him forever: That we are commanded [about] one who puts out a bad name about his wife that she shall dwell with him forever - and even if she is blind or has a skin disease - as it is stated (Deuteronomy 22:19), "and to him shall she be a wife." And included in this law is that the court is commanded also to lash him about that which he put out a bad name falsely and to [fine] him one hundred coins (sela) of refined silver, as it is stated in the section [of the Torah that deals with this]. And they, may their memory be Blessed, explained (Ketuvot 46a) that the warning against putting out a bad name is included in "do not go tale-bearing among your people" (Sefer HaChinukh 236).

From the roots of the commandment [is that it is] to deter villains from engaging in such evil villainy, and like the matter that we will write adjacently below, with God's help, about the law of rape (Sefer HaChinukh 557).

From the laws of the commandment, Rambam, may his memory be Blessed, wrote (Mishneh Torah, Virgin Maiden 3:6-7), "How is the putting out of a bad name? It is that he come to the court and say, 'I had sexual relations with this maiden and I did not find her hymen [intact], and when I inquired about the thing, it became known to me that she was unfaithful to me after I engaged her, and these are my witnesses - since she was unfaithful in front of them.' And the court listens to the words of the witnesses and investigates their testimony. If the thing is found to be true, she is stoned. But if the father brings witnesses and they impugn the witnesses that the husband brought, and it is found that the [first set of] witnesses testified falsely, they are stoned and [the husband] is lashed. And even though there is no action in this but only speech, the Torah obligated him in [getting] lashes, as it is written, 'and they shall discipline him,' and he gives a hundred sela ; and about this it is stated, 'and these are the signs of my daughter's virginity' - these are the witnesses that impugned the witnesses of the husband. If the husband comes back and brings other witnesses and impugns the witnesses of the father, behold, the maiden and the witnesses of the father are stoned, and about this is it stated, 'and if true was this matter.' From the tradition we learned that this section has in it impugning witnesses and impugners of the impugners. If he puts out a bad name about her and she is [now] an adult, even though he brings witnesses that she was unfaithful to him, [if they testified about the time] when she was a maiden (before full legal adulthood), behold, he is exempt from lashes and from the fine. But if it is found that the matter is true, behold, she is stoned, even though she is an adult, since she was a maiden at the time that she was unfaithful." And the rest of its details are in the third chapter of Makkot and in third and fourth chapters of Ketuvot (see Tur, Orach Chaim 177).

And with regards to the lashes and the fine, it is practiced during the time of the Temple, when we were adjudicating the laws of fines. But with regards to her dwelling with her husband forever, [it is practiced] also at the present time - since there is a commandment upon him about this, as this is truly a commandment and not a fine.

Mitzvah 554

That he should not divorce her all of his days: That one who puts out a bad name about his wife and is found to be a liar with his words is prevented from divorcing her forever. And about this is it stated (Deuteronomy 22:19), "he may not send her away all of his days."

I have written about the roots of this commandment and how is the putting out of a bad name and a few of its laws in its positive commandment in this Order (Sefer HaChinukh 553), as is my custom - and take it from there.

Mitzvah 555

The commandment upon the court to stone the one liable: That the court is obligated to pelt with stones one who has transgressed some sins. And one of them is one who has sexual relations with an engaged maiden, as it states (Deuteronomy 22:24), "and you shall stone them with stones." And this is one of the four well-known death penalties of the court - and they are stoning, burning, killing (beheading) and strangulation. And in Sanhedrin 49b in the chapter [entitled] Arba Mitot, Rabbi Shimon and 'our rabbis' disagreed [regarding] which is more severe, stoning or burning. And it is 'our rabbis' that said that stoning is more severe. And the matter of stoning is thus (see Mishneh Torah, The Sanhedrin and the Penalties within their Jurisdiction 15:1): Four ells distant from the house of stoning, we remove the clothes of the man who is obligated in stoning, until he remains naked, and [then] we cover his nakedness in front of him. And a woman is not stoned naked but rather with one garment. And the house of stoning was two stories tall. And he goes up there - [as do] his witnesses - and his hands are tied. And one of the witnesses pushes him on his midriff and he falls to the ground on his heart. And if he does not die from the pushing, the witnesses pick up a stone that was laying there - [weighing] a load for two people - and they release their hands and hurl the stone on his heart. And if he [still] doesn't die, his stoning is by all of Israel, as it states (Deuteronomy 17:7), "The hand of the witnesses shall be upon him first, etc."

I have written a little about the roots of the commandment of the four death penalties in the Order of Mishpatim (Sefer HaChinukh 48).

The laws of the commandment - that which they, may their memory be Blessed, said (see Mishneh Torah, The Sanhedrin and the Penalties within their Jurisdiction 14:4) [that] stoning is more severe than burning, and burning than killing, and killing than strangulation; and [that] anyone who is obligated in two death penalties of the court, whether it is from two sins or from one sin, is sentenced to the more severe; and [that] all those who are liable for death penalties that get mixed up, one with the other and we do not recognize them, are all sentenced to the lighter [penalty] among them (see Mishneh Torah, The Sanhedrin and the Penalties within their Jurisdiction 14:6); [along with] all of the rest of its details - are [all] elucidated in the sixth chapter of Sanhedrin.

And it is practiced at the time of the Temple. And a court that transgressed this, and did not stone one who became obligated in stoning - even if they killed him with a different form of death - has violated this positive commandment.

Mitzvah 556

Not to punish one coerced into a sin: That we have been prevented from judging one who is coerced into doing a sin, which is to say that we should not punish any person for a thing that he does against his will. And about this is it stated (Deuteronomy 22:26), "But to the maiden you shall not do a thing, etc." And this is a negative commandment that includes anyone that is coerced into doing a bad deed; that we should not punish him for it. And explicitly did they, of Blessed memory, say (Sanhedrin

Sefer HaChinukh

27a), "The Merciful One exempts the one coerced, as it states, 'But to the maiden you shall not do a thing.'"

The root of this commandment is known to every person with intelligence - that it is not fitting to punish any creature for that which he does against his will [and] not for his own benefit.

From the laws of this commandment are what they, may their memory be Blessed, said (see Mishneh Torah, The Sanhedrin and the Penalties within their Jurisdiction 20:2) that a court does not kill a person who transgresses out of coercion even one of the three sins that a person is to die for and not transgress - except for if he transgressed and had sexual relations with a forbidden partner; as this is not complete coercion, since there cannot be an erection without volition. But if a woman is coerced to have sexual relations, she is exempt. Even if after the rapist begins to rape her, she says, "Leave him alone," she is [still] exempt, since it is her [evil] impulse that is overpowering her. And the rest of its details are there in Sanhedrin.

And this commandment is practiced in every place and at all times, that we are obligated not to give any punishment to one coerced. And one who transgresses this, and punishes one coerced, has violated this negative commandment and will 'bear his iniquity.' But he does not receive lashes, as it is possible to transgress it without an act - for example, a judge who commanded to lash him or punish him in another manner, since the judge does not perform an act in the thing. And Ramban, may his memory be Blessed, wrote (Shoresh 8 on Sefer HaMitzvot LaRambam, Lo Taase 294) that this negative precept is not a prevention (that we are commanded not to do something), but [rather] it is a negation, that exempts the raped maiden. And [about] that which they said in Sanhedrin, "The Merciful One exempts the one coerced" - this [choice of] expression is truly a proof that it is an exemption and not a [negative commandment].

Mitzvah 557

The commandment on the rapist to marry the one he has raped: That we have been commanded that one who rapes a virgin maiden must marry her as a wife and that he must give to her father fifty silver [shekel-coins], as it states (Deuteronomy 22:29), "And the man who lays with her shall pay the maiden's father fifty [coins of] silver."

It is from the roots of this commandment [that it is] in order to restrain the villains from this evil deed, and that the daughters of Israel should not be as if abandoned. Since if the rapist thinks he can fill his desire with her and [just] walk away, it will be light in his eyes to do so many times. But if he has in mind that she will be tied to him and he will be [held] responsible for the obligation of [her] sustenance, clothing and appointed times, all of his days; and that even if he gets sick of her, he will never have the option of divorcing her; and that he he will have to give to her father fifty silver [shekel-coins] immediately - he will truly suppress his [evil] impulse and prevent himself from doing this villainy that comes with such a penalty. And there is also in this a little comfort for this poor embarrassed woman in that she will stay with him forever, lest another man would embarrass her with this evil thing that happened to her. 'And the ordinances of the Lord are straight, they rejoice the heart.'

From the laws of the commandment, Rambam, may his memory be Blessed, wrote (Mishneh Torah, Virgin Maiden 1:3, 5) [that] any woman that had sexual relations in the field is assumed to have been raped; and any woman that had sexual relations in the city is assumed to have been seduced, until witnesses testify that she was raped. And the Sages said (Ketuvot 39b) that if a raped woman does not want - or her father does not want [for her] - to marry him, we do not force her [to do so]. But if [the rapist] does not want, we force him [to marry her] - even if she is lame or blind or has tsaraat (a skin disease) - and he may not put her out (divorce her) ever. And this [woman] does not have a wedding contract (ketuvah). As what is the reason that the sages established the marriage contract? It was in order that it not be light in the eyes of the husband to divorce her - and he cannot divorce this one. If the woman raped was forbidden to him [to marry] - even if it is from a positive obligation, and even if it is a secondary prohibition, behold this one does not marry her. And so [too,] if he finds something lewd about her after he brings her in, he should [divorce] her, as it is stated, "and she shall be a wife to him" - a wife that is fitting for him.

Sefer HaChinukh

And Rambam, may his memory be Blessed, wrote (Mishneh Torah, Virgin Maiden 1:8) that a rapist or seducer is only obligated in [paying] the fine if he has sexual relations with her according to her [customary] way and with witnesses, but [that] he does not need a warning. And in the fourth chapter of Ketuvot 46b it appears to be the opposite, that in the entire Torah (including rape) there is no difference whether it is according to her [customary] way or not according to her way regarding lashes and [other] punishments, except for only the one who puts out a bad name. And there is no obligation for the fine until she is a full three years old; but from three full years to when she matures, there is a fine for her. And she is called an adult (mature woman) after six months from [when] the lower sign appears, which is two [pubic] hairs, and during those six months, she is called a maiden (see Mishneh Torah, Marriage 2:2). And this is what they, of Blessed memory, said (Ketuvot 39a), "The difference between maidenhood and maturity is only six months." And after she matures (see Mishneh Torah, Virgin Maiden 1:8), there is no fine for her, as it states, "a virgin maiden" - and the explanation that came for it is (Ketuvot 38a), "a virgin" and not one who has had sexual relations; "maiden," and not an adult, or a child bride (memaenet) or a barren woman (aylonit). And the matter of the signs of an aylonit are known. And anyone who has not seen the lower sign and is thirty-five years old and a day - even though she does not have the signs of an aylonit - is assumed to be an aylonit. And whether she has a father or she does not have a father, there is a fine for her. And the Sages enumerated ten women that do not have a fine (see Mishneh Torah, Virgin Maiden 3:9-10), and these are them: an adult; a child bride; a divorcee; an aylonit; an unfaithful woman (sotah); a deaf woman; a convert; a prisoner; a freed slave; and one about whom a bad name has been put out. And all other girls have a fine for them. And anyone that has a fine, has [payment for] embarrassment and damage [in the case when] she is seduced. But if she is raped - even if she doesn't have a fine - she has [payment for] embarrassment, as it is not [any] less than one who injures his fellow [and] who is obligated [to pay] for five things (one of them being embarrassment). And Rambam, may his memory be Blessed, wrote (Mishneh Torah, Virgin Maiden 2:10) that even [in the case of] someone raped, anyone who does not have a fine does not have [payment for] embarrassment, and I wonder [how he could write that]. And the money for these things is the father's - as the Torah appropriated the profit of youth to the father; and if she has no father, it is for herself. And the rest of the details are in Ketuvot in the third and fourth chapter.

And this commandment is practiced with regard to forcing payment of the fine by males during the time of the Temple, when there is the power in our hands to adjudicate the laws of fines; but with regard to the rapist marrying her, even in our times is it a commandment upon him - as the marriage is a commandment and not a fine.

Mitzvah 558
That he not divorce her all of his days: That the rapist is forever prevented from divorcing the one he raped. And about this is it stated (Deuteronomy 22:29), "because he has violated her, he cannot send her away all of his days."

From the roots of this commandments and a few of its laws are written in its positive commandment in this Order (Sefer HaChinukh 557) - and take if from there.

And [about] this negative commandment, they, may their memory be Blessed, said in Tractate Makkot 15a that a positive commandment has already preceded it - and that positive commandment is that which the verse stated, "and to him shall she be for a wife." And there it is said [that] a rapist who divorces his wife - if he is an Israelite, he takes her back [in marriage again] and he is not lashed, since the negative commandment is already rectified by the positive commandment that preceded it, as behold, 'she is to him for a wife'; but if the rapist is a Kohen (a priest) and he divorced her, he is lashed and he does not take her back, as a priest is forbidden [to marry] a divorcee. And since he divorced her, she is not fitting to bring her back any more - therefore he is lashed. And know that if he was an Israelite and he divorced the one he raped and she died before he could take her back or she married another [man] - that behold, since he can no longer fulfill the positive commandment, he is lashed in any event. And even though he did not truly negate the negative commandment with his [own] hands, but rather it was negated by [another] cause - he is liable for lashes, since he is no longer able to fulfill the positive commandment. [This is] like that which is a major principle with us concerning, 'he fulfilled it and he did not fulfill it,' as I wrote in this Order, concerning the commandment of 'sending away the nest' in its negative commandment (Sefer HaChinukh 544).

Mitzvah 559

That a eunuch not marry a daughter of Israel: That one whose sexual organs were damaged by the blow of a person or an animal or a tree - meaning to say, not at the hands of the Heavens - to the point that he cannot reproduce is prevented from marrying a daughter of Israel. And about this is it stated (Deuteronomy 23:1), "No one whose testes are crushed or whose member is cut off shall come into the congregation of the Lord."

About the roots of this commandment are that [one] distance himself [from this] so that he will not damage [his] reproductive organs in any way (see Guide for the Perplexed 3:49). As is known, there are kings that castrate males to appoint them as keepers of women and there are lowly males who want this thing in order to earn the king's table and to benefit monetarily. And we, the holy people - in our knowledge that any eunuch caused by human means will be disqualified from joining any more with a daughter of Israel or to establish a home or the way of marriage - will distance this matter and it will repulse us. And with this argument, we find an explanation for the distinction in the prohibition between that which is damaged by human means and that which is damaged by the hand of the Heavens.

From the laws of the commandment is that which they, may their memory be Blessed, explained (Yevamot 70a, and see Mishneh Torah, Forbidden Intercourse 16:3), "Who is [considered] 'one whose testes are crushed?' Anyone whose testicles were wounded [...]. And [who is considered] 'one whose member is cut off?' One whose penis was cut off." And there are three organs that the male reproduces with: with the penis, and with the testicles and with the paths in which the seed matures - and they are called the testicular ducts. And therefore, from when one of these three organs is wounded or cut or crushed, behold, he is disqualified. And the rest of its details are elucidated in the eighth chapter of Yevamot.

And this prohibition is practiced in every place and at all times, by males. And one who transgresses it - and he is one whose testes are crushed or whose member is cut off - and marries a daughter of Israel and has sexual relations with her, is liable for lashes. But he is permitted to marry a convert or a freed slave. And there are some commentators that have said that he transgresses with sexual relations alone, [even] without marriage, and so is it in the Talmud Yerushalmi.

Mitzvah 560

That a mamzer (a child born from a forbidden marriage) should not marry a daughter of Israel: That a mamzer is prevented from marrying a daughter of Israel. And about this is it stated (Deuteronomy 23:3), "No mamzer shall come into the congregation of the Lord," meaning to say that he should not come to marry a woman from the daughters of the congregation of the Lord. But it is truly permissible for him to enter with them into all of their places of residence and to give and take with them in all things [just] like [any other] one of the children of Israel. And they, may their memory be Blessed, have already said (Horayot 13a) that a mamzer Torah scholar precedes a ignoramus Kohen (priest) in the reading of the Torah (see Rambam on Mishnah Gittin 5:7).

About the roots of this commandment are that since the conception of the mamzer is very bad (see Tractate Kallah 1) - as it is done in impurity and with invalid thoughts and the counsel of sin - and there is no doubt that the nature of the father is hidden in the child, therefore God, in His kindness, distanced the holy seed (of the Jewish people) from him; [just] like He separated us and distanced us from all bad things (see Guide for the Perplexed 3:49).

From the laws of the commandment is that which they, may their memory be Blessed, said (Yevamot 49a and see Mishneh Torah, Forbidden Intercourse 15:1) that the mamzer that the Torah forbade is one that is born from the sexual prohibitions mentioned in the Torah, except from a menstruant women - as a son from her is defective, but he is not called a mamzer. And whether it was under coercion or volitional, in any case, he is called a mamzer. And [if] a gentile or a slave has sexual relations with a daughter of Israel, the offspring is fitting (as opposed to being a mamzer) - whether she is single or whether she is the wife of a man, whether it is under coercion or whether it is volitional. But [if] a gentile or a slave has sexual relations with a mamzeret, the offspring is a mamzer, but if a mamzer has sexual relations with a gentile woman, the offspring is a gentile - and if he converts, he is fitting immediately, like all of the converts of the nations (Yevamot 45b and see Mishneh Torah, Forbidden Intercourse 15:3-4). And if he has sexual relations with a slave woman, the offspring is a slave. And if [his master] freed him, the offspring is fitting, like other freed slaves - and they are permitted to come (marry) into the congregation of Israel. This is the general principle: A son that comes from a slave woman or a gentile woman or from a slave or from a gentile or from a mamzer, the offspring is like [the woman] and we do not pay attention to the [identity of the] father at all. And because of this thing, the Sages permitted (Kiddushin 69a) a mamzer to marry a slave woman, in order to 'purify' his children - as behold, he frees them and they are found to be free men. And a mamzer is permitted to marry a woman convert and a woman mamzer is permitted to marry a convert, as it states, "into the congregation of the Lord" - and the congregation of converts is not called a congregation - and [in these cases,] the offspring follows the defective one (see Mishneh Torah, Forbidden Intercourse 15:7,9). And even [if] a convert marries [another] convert, [their] son is permitted to [marry] a mamzeret, from the reason that we mentioned - even though his conception and his birth were in purity (after they converted). And [this is the case] even [for] his children and grandchildren until the name of gentileness is removed from them, meaning to say that it is not known that he is [descended from converts]. But [if] a convert marries a daughter of Israel or a son of Israel marries a convert, the offspring is an Israelite in all matters and forbidden to marry a mamzer woman. And the rest of the details of the commandment are elucidated in the eighth chapter of Yevamot and at the end of Kiddushin (see Tur, Even HaEzer 4).

And this prohibition is practiced in every place and at all times, by males and females. And one who transgresses it, and is a mamzer and marries a daughter of Israel - or [if] an Israelite marries a mamzeret - once he has sexual relations after the betrothal, they are lashed, both he and her. But [if] he had sexual relations and did not betroth her, they are not lashed - as you do not have anyone who is lashed for sexual relations without betrothal in all of the negative commandments of the Torah, except for a High Priest with a widow, as I have written in its place in the Order of Emor el HaKohanim (Sefer HaChinukh 273). This is the opinion of Rambam (Mishneh Torah, Laws of Forbidden Intercourse 15:7,9), but there are commentators that have written that they are lashed for sexual relations only, [even] without betrothal (Raavad on Mishneh Torah, Forbidden Intercourse 15:2).

Mitzvah 561

That an Ammonite or a Moabite not enter the Congregation of the Lord: That we should not marry with the males of the Children of Ammon and Moav forever, and even after they convert, as it is stated (Deuteronomy 23:4), "An Ammonite or a Moabite may not come into the Congregation of the Lord forever."

What is explained in the section (of the Torah where it is mentioned) "because of the matter that they did not greet you with bread and water [...] and that he hired against you, etc." is from the roots of the commandment a. And the verse [thus] informed us of the greatness of the virtue of acts of loving-kindness, and the [need to] distance oneself from villainy and stinginess. And therefore He commanded us to fix a hatred for them; as they were wicked and abominable to show the fullness of their evil and villainy - not to greet a large congregation of those tired from the road, passing their border, with [even] bread and water; and that Moav hired Bilaam against them to curse them. And even though the Egyptians subjugated us and caused us pain for a long time, we only distanced ourselves from them to the third generation. And through this we knew that it is better for a person to do several sins rather than one great villainy - since in his willingness to do the ugly villainy and not to be concerned about revealing his opinion and his [lack of] embarrassment in front of the many peoples, he shows through it the evil of his constitution and the fullness of his lowliness. And [he also shows] that there is no way to fix and adjust himself to fix his deeds, and [that] his perversion is strengthened until 'it cannot be fixed.' And it is not fitting to mix such a person into the holy and Blessed nation.

From the laws of the commandment is that which they, may their memory be Blessed, said (Yevamot 76b) that specifically the males of the Children of Ammon and Moav - them and their sons forever - are the ones forbidden to come into the congregation, but the females are permitted immediately when they convert. And they said in explanation of this that it is since it is the way of the man to greet, but not the females; which is to say that their hand was not in this villainy when [the men] did not greet Israel with bread and water - since it is not the way of a woman to go out. And God would not twist justice to punish the woman for the villainy of the man - God forbid, that God would [allow such] evil. And the rest of its details are elucidated in the eighth chapter of Yevamot and at the end of Kiddushin (see Tur, Even HaEzer 4).

And this prohibition was practiced before King Sancheriv of Assyria came up against Jerusalem and exiled Israel, and also jumbled all of the nations and mixed them with each other - as he ruled over the whole [known] world. But after Sancheriv jumbled the nations and the Children of Ammon and Moav were mixed with the other nations of the world, all are permissible immediately after they convert; as there is an assumption that anyone who separates and comes to convert is separating from the other nations who are a majority (more numerous) with relation to the Children of Ammon and Moav and with relation to the Egyptians and the Edomites, as we will write about them adjacently (Sefer HaChinukh 563,564), with God's help. And therefore we do not investigate anyone who converts in our time at all - as to which nation he is; but rather he is immediately permitted [regardless of the] nation he is from.

Mitzvah 562
Not to seek their peace in a war: That we have been prevented from making peace with Ammon and Moav forever. And this matter is that God commanded us that when we besiege countries that we should request [terms of] peace with them before the war, and as I have written in the Order of Shoftim about the commandment to call out for [terms of] peace in an optional war (Sefer HaChinukh 527). And with Ammon and Moav, we have been prevented from this practice. And about this is it stated (Deuteronomy 23:7), "You shall not seek their peace or their welfare, etc." And so did they did they say in Sifrei, "It is implied from that which is stated (Deuteronomy 20:10), 'When you approach a city to fight against it, etc.' Is it possible also here? Therefore [the verse] teaches us to say, 'do not seek their peace.'"

That which I have written in the previous commandment; is from the roots of the commandment - that they were villainous to the point that they are not fitting for peace and welfare. But [rather] cruelty against them is worthy and virtuous, as we said (see Mishneh Torah, Kings and Wars 6:6).

The laws of the commandment are included in the simple meaning of the verse and in that which we brought from the language of Sifrei. And this prohibition is practiced by the males, who are the fighters of war. At the time that Israel was on its land [and] that they were fighting with Ammon and Moav, they were [bound] by this prohibition, from making peace with them. But today, in our times, we do not have the power to fight. And also, these nations have already lost their names in the jumbling of Sancheriv, as we mentioned in the previous commandment.

Mitzvah 563
Not to distance an Edomite of the third generation from coming into the congregation: Not to distance the seed of Esav after they convert - which is to say that we should not prevent ourselves from marrying with them, as there is no prohibition, like there is with Ammon and Moav; but rather, they are permissible after two generations. And about this is it stated (Deuteronomy 23:8-9), "You shall not despise an Edomite, since he is your brother, etc. Children that will be born to them in the third generation shall come into the Congregation of the Lord." And the third generations is the grandson of the convert. And they, may their memory be Blessed, said (Yevamot 78a) about a pregnant Egyptian woman that converted while she is still pregnant, that her son is called the second [generation], even though his conception was while the mother was still an Egyptian.

Sefer HaChinukh

The root of this commandment is revealed - that it is to inform us that we should not treat the seed of Esav [as] prohibited and that we should not distance them via an a fortiori argument (kal ve'chomer) from the Children of Ammon and Moav: to say that [since] God distanced us from Ammon and Moav because of one time that they did not greet us with bread and water, is it not all the more so with the Edomites and the Egyptians who caused so much pain to Israel? Hence, this warning about them came to us that we should not prevent ourselves from marrying them. Since the subjugation that they subjugated us was a decree upon us from God, it is not fitting that we fix a hatred in our hearts about it. And they are called our brothers in their converting and coming to be shielded under the wings of the Divine Presence. But with Ammon and Moav, there is another reason for hating them, and that is the matter of the great villainy that they found in their hearts to do - everything is as I wrote above adjacently (Sefer HaChinukh 561).

From the laws of the commandment is that which they, may their memory be Blessed, said (Yevamot 78a) [that if] an Egyptian marries [another] Egyptian and she converts while she is still pregnant, the offspring is called the second [generation], as it states, "Children that will be born to them, etc." - and the verse makes it dependent on the birth; and [that if] an Ammonite convert marries an Egyptian woman, the offspring is an Ammonite, [but in the case of] an Egyptian convert that married an Ammonite woman, the offspring is an Egyptian. This is the general principle: With the [gentile] peoples alone, it goes after the males, and like we find that Scripture relates them to the males, as it is stated (II Kings 20:12), Baladan the son of Baladan. [But if] they [both] convert, it goes according to he less [advantageous]. And the rest of the details of the commandment are elucidated in the eighth chapter of Yevamot and at the end of Kiddushin (see Tur, Even HaEzer 4).

This prohibition that we are prevented from distancing them after they have converted is practiced in every place and at all times by males and females. And one who transgresses it, and decides in his mind not to marry into them - even after two generations - from the angle that they troubled Israel or from the angle that he has fixed a hatred in his heart for them because they came from another people, has violated this negative commandment. And we do not give lashes for it, since there is no act [involved] with it.

Mitzvah 564

To not distance an Egyptian of the third generation: That we were prevented from distancing and despising an Egyptian [such that we not] marry with him in the third generation after he converts (see Sefer HaMitzvot LaRambam, Mitzvot Lo Taase 55). And about this is it stated (Deuteronomy 23:8), "you shall not despise an Egyptian, for you were a stranger in his land." All the content of this commandment is like the previous content of the Edomite. [Hence] there is no reason to write at length about it.

And do not understand from our words that we are commanded to get married with an Egyptian or with an Edomite after the third generation. As this is not the intention of the verse - to command us to marry with them, God forbid. And the pedigreed families in Israel [need] not come down from their virtue to marry with them. But [rather,] the verse prevents us from distancing marriage with them with the claim that it is forbidden; and it informs us that there is no prohibition at all with them, and as we wrote adjacently above.

Mitzvah 565

That one impure should not enter the Temple mount: That anyone who is impure is prevented from entering the camp of the Levites (see Sefer HaMitzvot LaRambam, Mitzvot Lo Taase 78), the embodiment of which for the generations is the Temple mount. And about this is it stated (Deuteronomy 23:11), "If anyone among you has been rendered unclean by a nocturnal emission, he must leave the camp, and he must not enter the camp." And so did they, may their memory be Blessed, say (Pesachim 68a), "'He must leave the camp' - that is the camp of the Divine Presence; 'and he must not enter the camp' - that is the camp of the Levites. Ravina challenged it strongly, 'And I could say, this and that are the camp of the Divine Presence, and [the latter part of the verse] is to [make one] transgress [both] a positive and a negative commandment.' If so, the verse should have written, 'he should not come into'" - which is to say that, if so that it was only speaking about one camp, it should have stated, "he should not come into it," as it already mentioned 'camp' at the beginning of the verse. "[So] why do I need, [the word,] camp? To give him a different camp" - which is to say that since it mentioned 'camp' another time, the verse was hinting to a different camp - and that is the camp of the Levites, that any one who is impure should not enter it.

I have written about the roots of distancing impurity from the holy place a few times in my book (Sefer HaChinukh 362).

The laws of the commandment are elucidated in the first chapter of Tractate Kelim (see Mishneh Torah, Admission into the Sanctuary 3).

And this commandment that one impure should not enter is practiced both by males and by females at the Temple Mount even in our days, and like the matter stated by the verse (Leviticus 26:31), "and make your holy places desolate" - and they, may their memory be Blessed, expounded (Megillah 28a), "Their holiness is upon them even when they are desolate." And [it is] as I wrote above (Sefer HaChinukh 184, 363).

Mitzvah 566

The commandment to set up a place in which to defecate: That we were commanded that when our soldiers go out to war that we set up and designate a set place (see Tosefta Megillah 3:15) for the soldier, in which every man can go out to take care of his needs; so that their 'needs' not be [found] in very place and between the lodgings, like the [other] peoples do (Sanhedrin 104b). And about this it is stated (Deuteronomy 23:13), "And there shall be a yad for you outside the camp, etc." And the language of Sifrei is "A yad is always a place, as it states (I Samuel 15:12), 'and behold, he established a yad.'"

It is from the roots of the commandment [that it is] like the matter that is written in the section of the Torah [wherein this is mentioned), "Since the Lord, your God, moves about in your camp [...], let your camp be holy" which is to say that the souls of Israel always cling to the Divine presence. And all the more so are all of them of clean souls in the camp; since anyone who was fearful from the sins in his hand already left and went back to his home, and there [only] remained the good ones - in which the spirit of God dwells among them. And it is fitting for them to stand in cleanliness, as is known and famous - since cleanliness is from the good traits that bring the holy spirit, and like the homily of Rabbi Pinchas ben Yair in the first chapter of Avodah Zarah 20b. And there is also praise to the people in this, when gentile messengers come and see that their camp is holy and clean from all filth (see Guide for the Perplexed 3:48).

The laws of the commandment are included in the simple meaning of the verse.

And it is observed at the time of the Temple by males, since they are the fighters, not the females. And one who transgresses it, and does not set up a place for himself outside of the camp and dirties the place of the camps, violates this positive commandment. And his punishment is very great, since he caused the Divine Presence to withdraw from the camp of Israel. And [it is] like it is written, " let Him not find anything unseemly among you and turn away from you" - which is to say that, in your being among dirt, you will distance yourself from the good.

Mitzvah 567

The commandment to set up a spike to dig with: That there be to each one of the soldiers a spike - or another tool with which it is fitting to dig - suspended with his war gear, in order that he dig with it a place in the ground to take care of his needs in a way that is prepared for this (see Sefer HaMitzvot LaRambam, Mitzvot Ase 193 and Mishneh Torah, Kings and Wars 10). And about this is it stated (Deuteronomy 23:14), "With your aazen you shall have a spike" - the explanation of (the word,) your aazen is your weapons.

And the root of this commandment and all of its content is in the commandment that is before it. And since this verse has come to our hand, we will write the midrash about it; that they, of Blessed memory, affixed to it in the gemara, when they said (Ketuvot 5b), "Why are the fingers of a person made like spikes" - which is to say, tapered? "So that if a person hears a thing that is not proper, he should put his finger into his ear (ozen), as it is stated, 'With your aazen you shall have a spike' - do not read, 'your aazen,' but rather your ozen.'"

Mitzvah 568
Not to turn over a slave that fled from his master: That we have been prevented from returning a slave that fled form his master outside of the land, [who came] to the Land of Israel (see Sefer HaMitzvot LaRambam, Mitzvot Lo Taase 254). And even if his master is an Israelite, we do not return [the slave] to him. But [rather], we free him and write down his value as a debt on himself. And about this is it stated, (Deuteronomy 23:16), "You shall not turn over a slave to his master." And so is it elucidated in Tractate Gittin 45a, that the verse is speaking about a slave that fled from outside of the Land to the Land of Israel. And they said there that the law about him is that we write a contract with his value [as a debt] for him and we [also] write a contract of [his] freedom; and that we not return him to slavery in any way - since he entered the chosen valley of purity to serve God, may He be Blessed, there.

That which we mentioned is from the roots of this commandment - that God wanted for the honor of the land, that one who flees to there be saved from slavery; in order that we place the honor of the place into our hearts and fix the awe of God, may He be elevated, into our hearts, when we are there. And all of this is to help His people and to give them merit, as He is one Who desires kindness.

The laws of the commandment are elucidated there in Tractate Gittin.

And this commandment is practiced even in our day by males and females, as all are warned not to return him to his master, since he has fled to the Chosen Land. And one who transgresses this and seizes him and returns him to his master, has violated this negative commandment. But according to what appears, there is no obligation for [getting] lashes, since the obligations is only when he returns him to slavery; and maybe his master will no longer enslave him - and we do not give lashes, [in the case] of a doubt.

Mitzvah 569
To not oppress a slave who has fled to us, from outside the Land, to the Land [of Israel]: That we have been prevented, that we not oppress the slave that flees to us from outside of the Land. And about this does it state (Deuteronomy 23:17), "He shall live with you in any place he may choose among the settlements in your midst, wherever he pleases; you must not oppress him." And the language of Sifrei is "'You must not oppress him' - that is verbal oppression" - meaning to say, that we not curse him or disgrace him with words; and all the more so with actions.

And that which I wrote about with the negative commandment of oppressing the convert in the Order of Mishpatim (Sefer HaChinukh 63) is from the roots of the commandment are, since both of them are the same. And therefore, just like God, may He be Blessed, added a negative commandment with the oppression of a convert because of the weakness of his soul, from his being a foreigner among the [Jewish] nation; so too did He add the negative commandment of oppressing the slave, as he is [even] more weak-souled and disgraced than the convert. [It is] such that you not say, "This is a slave and there is no concern about him, and we would not have a sin upon us in oppressing him verbally." And we know with certainty that this convert and this slave - whom we have been warned about oppressing them even with words - both, accepted the Torah upon themselves. [This is] meaning to say that this convert is a righteous convert (a ger tsedek, as opposed to a ger toshav, who is not a convert, but rather a resident alien) and that this slave is a slave that was circumcised and immersed in order to become a slave. And I wrote a few of the laws about verbal oppression and monetary oppression there - concerning oppression of the convert and, so too, concerning the negative commandment of oppression of the fellow Israelite - in the Order of Behar Sinai (Sefer HaChinukh 338).

And this prohibition not to oppress the slave that fled from his master to the Holy Land is practiced by males and females at all times. And one who transgresses this, and oppresses him - whether verbally or whether monetarily - has violated this negative commandment. But there are no lashes [for it], since it is possible to transgress it without doing an act.

Sefer HaChinukh

Mitzvah 570

Not to have sexual relations with a woman without a marriage contract and betrothal: That we have been prevented from having sexual relations with a woman without a marriage contract and betrothal. And about this is it stated (Deuteronomy 23:18), "No daughter of Israel shall be a prostitute." And Rambam, may his memory be Blessed, wrote (Sefer HaMitzvot LaRambam, Mitzvot Lo Taase 355) and this is his language: "The negative commandment about this matter has already been duplicated with a different language in the verse (Leviticus 19:29), 'Do not desecrate your daughter to make her a harlot' - and the [following is the] language of Sifrei Kedoshim 7:3, '"Do not desecrate your daughter" - this is one who gives over his single daughter not for the sake of marriage and also [a woman] who gives herself over not for the sake of marriage.' And hear from me for what [reason] this negative commandment of strong language was duplicated, and for what was it added to (see Mishneh Torah, Virgin Maiden 2:17): That which He already made precede from His laws that one who has sexual relations with a virgin - whether it be a seduction or a rape - is not obligated any one of the punishments, except only to [give] money and to marry the woman with which he had sexual relations, as it is explained in the verse, would let it come into our thoughts that since this thing only requires the payment of money, that this law goes according to the procedure of financial law. And [if so, just] like a person has the right to give whatever of his money to his fellow and he leaves it to him to do his will with that which is [now] his; so too has [the father] the right to take the maiden with him and to give her to a man to have sexual relations with her, since that is his law that is fitting to him - meaning to say the fifty shekel-coins of silver that go the father of the maiden. And this [father] will also give her on condition that he takes from him such and such dinar-coins. And he is prevented from this [thought] and it is told to him, 'Do not desecrate your daughter to make her a harlot.' Since that which is My law with her to only take money, however, is only when there is an incident when a man seduces or rapes [her]; but when the matter is with the consent of both of them together and it is public, there is no permissibility to this at all from any angle. And He showed the explanation for this and stated (Leviticus 19:29), 'lest the land fall into harlotry and the land be filled with depravity.' [This is] since the existence of seduction and rape is limited, but when the matter would be by choice and consent, it would spread and fill the land. And this reason is very nice and it enhances the verse. And similar to this is all that which the Sages have mentioned and all that they agreed upon regarding the Torah laws." To here is his language, may he be Blessed. And Ramban, may his memory be Blessed, wrangled with him about this (in his critique of Sefer HaMitzvot LaRambam, Mitzvot Lo Taase 355) and said that this negative commandment of the prostitute is not coming to warn one having sexual relations without a wedding contract and betrothal, as the wedding contract is neither a commandment nor a form of acquiring a woman, at all, according to the Torah. But [rather] the main negative commandment [here] is coming to warn not to have sexual relations with a woman that is forbidden [in marriage] to the man having sexual relations in such a way that betrothal would not be effective for him with her. As they, may their memory be Blessed, elucidated in the Gemara (Yevamot 61a), that the harlot (zonah) that is mentioned in every place in the Torah is none other than a woman who an Israelite has sexual relations with, when betrothal would not be effective for him with her. And this is the harlotry that the Torah distanced and loathed forever and [here] it warned the [man] and the [woman] about it. And so too from the foundation of this matter is that the verse warns the court that they should not let a woman be abandoned among them, since her end will be to have sexual relations with men that she is forbidden to [in marriage], to the point that betrothal is not effective for them with her. As there is no doubt that a woman abandoned to the many will not be exacting afterwards 'between a piece of permissible fat and a piece of forbidden fat.' And so too does it warn the father of the girl about this explicitly in another verse; that he should not abandon her to harlotry and not to give her over to one who cannot have betrothal with her. And about this is it stated, "Do not desecrate your daughter to make her a harlot." And it is all from the reason mentioned - since she will have sexual relations with one who she is forbidden to [in marriage]; not from the reason of marriage contract and betrothal, as is the opinion of Rambam, may his memory be Blessed.

And Ramban, may his memory be Blessed, also said that when the master of the Targum (Onkelos), translated [the verse as], "Never shall a woman of Israel be [married] to a man slave, and a man shall not marry, etc.," he combined with this that we should not be mixed up with the slaves, as it is also sexual relations [of a couple for which] betrothal is not effective. And because of this, is it stated in this language: "No [daughter of Israel] shall be, etc." Since had the verse stated, "There shall not be among you a male prostitute or a female prostitute," slaves would have been included in the category of the prohibition; since they are also obligated in the commandments, except for those places where they are excluded - when Israel is explicitly specified, as with stealing a soul, wherein it is written there, "from his brother, from the Children of Israel." And so too, here, where it states, "from the daughters of Israel" and "from the sons of Israel" - it is implied that the warning is to Israel alone; not to the slaves. And about the matter of this prohibition about "There shall not be a male prostitute," I have already written the disagreement that [exists] between the two sages mentioned there in the Order of Achrei Mot concerning the negative commandment of male cohabitation (Sefer HaChinukh 209), see there.

I have written what I know about the roots of the matter of distancing depravity in the Order of Achrei Mot (Sefer HaChinukh 188) and in the Order of Vayishma Yitro about the negative commandment of "do not commit adultery" (Sefer HaChinukh 35).

And the laws of this commandment are elucidated in Tractate Kiddushin (see Tur, Even HaEzer 6). And this prohibition is practiced in every place and at all times by males and females. And one who transgresses it, and lays with a single woman, is liable for lashes - [both] he and her - even if the man having sexual relations with her can have betrothal with her, according to the opinion of Rambam, may his memory be Blessed. But according to Ramban, may his memory be Blessed, a single man and a single woman who have sexual relations are not liable, except if she is sexually forbidden to him, to the extent that betrothal is not effective for him with her, as we have explained. And included in this prohibition is also that it is upon a court, that knows that there is among them a woman who has abandoned herself, to eliminate this evil from among them. But they do not have a liability for lashes, as they are not doing an act; but their punishment is very great - since the entire degradation of the generation is attributed to one who has the ability in his hand to protest and does not protest.

Mitzvah 571

Not to bring the fee of a prostitute or the price of a dog: That we have been prevented from bringing the fee of a prostitute or the price of a dog towards the altar. And about this is it stated (Deuteronomy 23:19), "You shall not bring the fee of a prostitute or the price of a dog into the house of the Lord, your God."

About the roots of this commandment are that since a sacrifice comes to purify the thoughts of a person and to make his deeds proper with this act - and as I wrote in the Order of Vayikach Li Terumah (Sefer HaChinukh 95) - and since his sacrifice is coming from the fee of a prostitute, which is a filthy sin; maybe he will think about this evil matter at the time of his sacrifice and his thought will be disqualified by his thinking this evil and disgraceful thought. And so also with the price of a dog, for this reason: As a sacrifice brings a man to the atonement of his soul, and like the matter that when his sacrifice is slaughtered and cut into pieces, it is fitting for the owner of the sacrifice to think that it was fitting to do to him such, to his [own] body, for the matter of the sin; were it not for the kindness of God, may He be Blessed, that was upon him, to take from him a little of his money as atonement. And with this action, it is fitting for him to soften his heart and soften his soul about its sins, to the point that it repents and has regret about what it has done, and agrees to not continue to sin any more - and like I wrote in its place about the matter of sacrifices and in the Order mentioned. And it is known that dogs are brazen-souled, and maybe from his thinking about them and their strong nature, his soul will strengthen itself, and he will become stiff-necked [against] regretting his sins, as is fit for him. And if I recount, my son, that these are words for children, you should be aroused by them, and 'take the explanation of the elders.'

The laws of the commandment: That which they, may their memory be Blessed, said (Temurah 29a, see Mishneh Torah, Things Forbidden on the Altar 3:8) that the fee is that which he says to the woman, "Behold, this thing is to you for your wage." And it is one whether the prostitute is a gentile or a slave or an Israelite that is sexually forbidden to him, or from those that are prohibited by negative commandments. And so [too], the fee of a male is included in the fee of prostitute, but the fee of his wife when she is menstruant is not within the prohibition of the fee. And one who resolves with the prostitute to give her one lamb - if he gives her another, even if he does this with a thousand lambs, they are all forbidden as the fee (see Mishneh Torah, Things Forbidden on the Altar 3:11). And there is no prohibition of the fee and the price except with their bodies - therefore, the prohibition only applies to something that is fitting to offer on top of the altar (see Mishneh Torah, Things Forbidden on the Altar 3:14-15). And if one gives her a sanctified animal as a gift, it does not become forbidden, as the consecration already preceded and took possession of it. And what is the price of a dog? This is the one that says, "Behold, this lamb for that dog." And even if he gave him several lambs for one dog, they are all forbidden. And the remainder of its details are elucidated in the sixth chapter of Terumah (see Mishneh Torah, Things Forbidden on the Altar 1).

And this prohibition is practiced by males and females during the time of the [Temple]. And one who transgresses it, and sacrifices the fee of a prostitute or the price of a dog - even with the sacrifice being invalid - the one who brings it is liable for lashes; like one who sacrifices a blemished animal, as we explained in the Order of Emor el HaKohanim. And Ramban, may his memory be Blessed, calculates the fee of a prostitute and the price of a dog as two [separate] commandments in his tally of the commandments.

Mitzvah 572

That the borrower not give interest to an Israelite: That we have been prevented from giving interest to an Israelite (see Sefer HaMitzvot LaRambam, Mitzvot Lo Taase 236), and, so too, from taking it. And about this is it stated (Deuteronomy 23:20), "You shall not take interest from your brother, interest of money, interest of food, interest of any thing, etc". And the [traditional] explanation comes about this: "Do not take interest" means, do not have interest taken from you, which is to say, do not give interest - as the one who gives it is the one who has it taken from him. And in the elucidation, they said in the chapter [entitled] Eizehhu Neshekh (Bava Metzia 75b) [that] the borrower transgresses on "Do not take interest" and on "you shall not place a stumbling block before the blind" (Leviticus 19:14). And had this preventing of this not come explicitly, I would have reasoned that it is the lender that is forbidden from taking it, but [that] if the borrower wants to forgive and is willing to be oppressed, that it would be permitted - in the manner of [other] oppression, where it is the oppressor that is transgressing, not the oppressed.

I have written what I known from the roots of the prohibition of interest and its distancing from the Children of Israel in the Order of Mishpatim (Sefer HaChinukh 68). And in the Order of Behar Sinai (Sefer HaChinukh 343), [I have written] a little of the laws of interest - as is my custom - and all that is needed for this commandment, as is the custom of the book. And take it from there.

Mitzvah 573

To lend to the gentile with interest: That we were commanded to request interest from the [other] peoples when we lend to them and that we not lend to them without interest. And about this is it stated (Deuteronomy 23:21), "Take interest from the foreigner." And likewise, is it permitted to borrow from them with interest? And they said in Sifrei, "'Take interest from the foreigner' - that is a positive commandment; 'and from your brother, do not take interest' - that is a negative commandment."

It is from the roots of the commandment that it is fitting for us to do acts of loving-kindness only to the nation that knows God and serves in front of Him. And by refraining from kindness with other people and doing it with these, it becomes clear that the main love and pity on them is [coming] from the angle of their following the Torah of God, may He be Blessed. And behold, with this intention, there will be reward for us in our refraining from kindness to them, [just] like [there will be] in our doing it to the children of our nation.

From the laws of the commandment is that which they, may their memory be Blessed, said (Bava Metzia 71a) that it is a commandment to prioritize a free loan to an Israelite over lending to a gentile with interest; and that which they said (Bava Metzia 72a and see Mishneh Torah, Creditor and Debtor

5:1) that [if] a gentile borrowed money from an Israelite with interest - even though he converted - [the Israelite] should collect from him all the interest that accrued until he converted; so that they will not say, "He converted to not pay the interest." And in the same manner that we were commanded to request interest from them, so too is it permissible to give them interest; since the verse only prohibited [taking] interest of an Israelite - the matter is known. And they, may their memory be Blessed, said (Bava Metzia 71b and see Mishneh Torah, Creditor and Debtor 5:4) that [if] a gentile borrowed money from an Israelite and wanted to pay back [the loan] and found another Israelite and [that Israelite] said, "Give it to me and I will give you the interest from it, in the [same] way that you give it to the Israelite," it is permissible. But if [the gentile] stood [this Israelite] in front of the Israelite [lender] - even though the gentile gives the money to the hand of [the Israelite borrower] - since [the gentile] gave the money with the knowledge of the Israelite [lender], behold it is fixed interest (and forbidden). And they, may their memory be Blessed, said (Bava Metzia 70b and see Mishneh Torah, Creditor and Debtor 5:2) that even though their interest is permissible according to the [letter of the] law, it is [still] forbidden for an Israelite to lend to them with fixed interest, more than what he needs for his livelihood; so that he not be accustomed to always be with him and learn from his deeds. But it is permissible to take 'the dust of interest (avak ribit),' even if it is more than what he needs for his livelihood - since he will not be so accustomed to be with him for the sake of the 'dust of interest.' And a Torah scholar may lend whatever he wants, as there is no concern about him that he will learn from [the gentile's] deeds; since 'wisdom emboldens the sage and guards him forever.' And the rest of its details are elucidated in the chapter [entitled] Eizehhu Neshekh in Bava Metzia (see Tur, Yoreh Deah 159, 160).

And [it] is practiced in every place and at all times by males and females. And one who transgresses it and lends without interest from the perspective of kindness alone - not from the hope about him that he will profit from him from another angle, or because of the ways of peace - has violated this positive commandment. And Ramban, may his memory be Blessed (in his critiques of the sixth root and at the end of his critiques of the Sefer HaMitzvot LaRambam) does not count this positive commandment in the calculation of the [613] commandments. And he says that this verse only came to give a positive [as well as] a negative commandment for one who lends to an Israelite with interest. And this is the intention of the midrash in Sifrei, in its saying that this is a positive commandment. And so does it appear from the words of the Gemara at the end of the chapter [entitled] Eizehhu Neshekh. But with all of this, 'we walk in the way of the king' - 'we will not veer to the right or left' from [Rambam's] calculation. And great is the one whose mistakes are numbered (few in number).

Mitzvah 574
Not to delay his vows for more than three festivals: That we not delay the vows and pledges and other sacrifices that are an obligation upon us. And about this is it stated (Deuteronomy 23:22), "When you make a vow to the Lord, your God, do not delay fulfilling it." And the tradition came (Rosh Hashanah 4b) [to explain] that we only transgress this negative commandment when three pilgrim holidays have passed after he made the vow. I have written clearly about the whole matter of this commandment in its positive commandment in this Order (Sefer HaChinukh 575) - and take it from there.

Mitzvah 575
To fulfill what has come out of his lips, as he vowed: That we have been commanded to fulfill all that we have obligated ourselves in speech, from oaths and vows and [similar] to it. And about this is it stated (Deuteronomy 23:24), "You shall keep what has come out of your lips, etc."

And Rambam, may his memory be Blessed, wrote (Sefer HaMitzvot LaRambam, Mitzvot Ase 94), "And they already separated the words of this verse and placed a [different] matter on every word of it. And nonetheless what comes out from all that I have mentioned to you is that it is a positive commandment for a person to fulfill that which he speaks about to obligate himself in any thing. And the language has already been duplicated in this commandment, and that is its stating (Bemidbar 30:3), 'like all that comes out of his mouth, he shall do.'" To here are his words.

Sefer HaChinukh

And Ramban, may his memory be Blessed (in his critique of Sefer HaMitzvot LaRambam, Mitzvot Ase 94) wrangled with him about it and said that he grouped two commandments here - which are different in their laws and their contents - into one. As this verse of "what comes out of your mouth, etc." is stated about the matter of what a person obligates himself to God, may He be Blessed, whether they be in matters of sacrifices or charity moneys, and that is what is stated, "as He will surely demand it from you" - which is to say, that He will seek from you the money that you vowed to Him - and your delaying it will be a sin. And so, they, may their memory be Blessed, said (Rosh Hashanah 4a), "Those who are obligated for dedications [to the Temple]; appraisals; consecrations; sin-offerings; guilt-offerings, burnt-offerings; peace-offerings; charity [monies]; tithes; first-borns; [animal] tithes; a Pesach sacrifice; gleanings; forgotten sheaves; and corner fields - once three festivals passed him, he violates 'do not delay.'" But regarding everything that a person obligates himself to in optional matters - which the sages called, 'utterance (bitui),' and that is if he vows or swears, "I will eat," or "I will not eat," "I will go to place x," or "I will not go," and all that is similar to this - this does not come into the category of this commandment. And this is why the verse needed to promise, "If you refrain from vowing, you will incur no guilt." And nonetheless, with vows of utterance, there is another commandment specified for it, and that is the section of [the Torah about] vows in the Order of Roshei HaMatot, where it is written (Numbers 30:3), "taking an oath imposing an obligation on himself, he shall do all that has come out of his lips" - and they, may their memory be Blessed, explained (Sifrei on Numbers 30:3) [that this is speaking about a vow] to forbid the permitted.

And another difference between vows of utterance and vows to the Elevated realm is that with vows to the Elevated realm there is no need to mention [the word,] 'vow' with them, but rather he says, "This animal is a sacrifice," or "This vessel is for the upkeep of the [Temple]," or "for the poor." And with this alone, he is obligated to fulfill the words of his mouth, by the positive and the negative commandment mentioned in this verse; such that if three pilgrim holidays passed and he did not fulfill his vows, he transgresses, 'do not delay.' But regarding, 'do not profane his words,' he only transgresses when he transgresses the vow in a way that it impossible for him to fulfill it ever. But concerning optional matters, he needs to mention 'vow' with them - or something that indicates it, for example, what they called 'hands of the vows (yadot hanedarim) or utterances.' But if he only said words, [such as] "I will eat this loaf," or "I will walk to place x," or "I will give this portion to the rich Mr. x," he has not obligated himself in a positive commandment at all. [Still,] it is fitting for anyone who God has graced with intelligence to fulfill all of his words [evne in such a case]. And we say so [too] that he does not transgress, 'do not delay,' with vows of utterances - and even after several pilgrim holidays.

And what comes out of all this according to the opinion of Ramban, may his memory be Blessed, is that we count [it as] one positive commandment that a man fulfill what comes out of his mouth with the vows to the Elevated realm; and we count [it as] another commandment to fulfill the vows and oaths of utterances.

I have written about the roots of the commandment in the Order of Reeh Anochi Metsaveh about the commandment of the sacrifices on the first pilgrim holiday (Sefer HaChinukh 438).

From the laws of this commandment are that which they, may their memory be Blessed, said (Rosh Hashanah 6a), that [vows of] charity obligates a person to do it immediately; and they said in explanation of this, [that it is] because, "Since behold, the poor are standing" - which is to say that since it is in his hand to fulfill the commandment immediately, the obligation of the positive commandment is also upon him immediately. And nonetheless regarding the matter of not transgressing, 'do not delay,' we do not transgress until three pilgrim festivals have passed one by - as the Torah made liable more generally regarding all vows of the Heavens about 'do not delay' after three pilgrim holidays, and not before; and like the words of the bereita that I wrote about this commandment adjacently. This is the opinion of some of the commentators. But there are some of them that said that we are liable with charity immediately when he does not pay, even about 'do not delay.' And they said that there is a difference between what a person obligates himself in - for example, charity - and what a person does not obligate himself - like gleanings, forgotten sheaves, and corner fields. As with what he obligated himself to, and it is in his hand to fulfill - [something]

Sefer HaChinukh

that has these two [elements]; for example, charity - he is immediately liable for 'do not delay.' But with gleanings, forgotten sheaves, and corner fields, he did not obligate himself to [do] them. And [with] sacrifices, in which he did obligate himself to [do] them, it is not in his hand to sacrifice them immediately - and therefore, he does not transgress for them until after three pilgrim holidays. Merit, my son, and you will examine their words. And the rest of the details of the commandment - meaning to say the exact clarification, meaning to say to warn a person to do what he is obligated to do, and how he can save himself from this when a doubt comes into what he said - it is all elucidated in places in Shevuot, in Nedarim, and at the end of Menachot and so too, in Kinnim.

And this commandment is practiced in every place and at all times, by males and females. And one who transgresses it and does not fulfill his word, with vows to the Elevated realm - for example, sacrifices and vows for the upkeep of the [Temple] during the time of the Temple - immediately when it is possible for him to fulfill it, and as we wrote in the Order of Reeh Anochi (Sefer HaChinukh 438), negated this positive commandment. And when three pilgrim holidays have passed by him and he has [still] not fulfilled his word, he has transgressed the negative commandment of 'do not delay,' and [it is] as we will write in this Order with God's help (Sefer HaChinukh 574). And in our day, one who vows charity and does not pay it to the beadles or the poor - if there are some there - on the day that he vows it, he has negated this positive commandment and also transgressed 'do not delay,' immediately - according to the opinion of a few commentators. And if he delays doing the thing for three pilgrim holidays, he has transgressed, 'do not delay,' according to the words of everyone.

And regarding the obligation of vows of utterance, we have already designated a commandment for them - that one is obligated to fulfill them - in the Order of Roshei HaMatot, as we have said. And if he delayed fulfilling them to the point that they have been negated - such that it is no longer in his hand to fulfill them - then we say about them, that he has negated the positive commandment of "he must carry out all that has come out of his lips," and [violated] the positive commandment of "he shall not profane his word" (Sefer HaChinukh 406) - but not before then, and even if several pilgrim holidays have passed by him.

Mitzvah 576
The commandment to allow the wage-worker to eat from the attached [produce] upon which he is working: That we have been commanded that the wage-worker eats at the time of his work from that which he is working upon - when that thing is something that grows from the earth and its production has not been completed. And about this does it state (Deuteronomy 23:25), "When you enter your neighbor's vineyard, etc." And the [traditional] explanation [that] came about it (Bava Metzia 87b) is that the verse is speaking about a wage-worker. And so [too] did Onkelos translate, "When a wage-worker." And so is it likewise written, "When you enter your neighbor's field of standing grain, etc." And they, may their memory be Blessed, explained in the chapter [entitled] Hasokher et Hapoel (Bava Metzia 88b), that we learned from these two verses that a person eats that which is connected at the time of the production's completion. And they elucidated there that it would be insufficient to learn that which we need [to learn] from one of the verses without the other.

It is from the roots of the commandment [that it is] to teach the Children of Israel to have a nice soul and goodwill; and through this the blessing of God will descend upon them. And it is true that fastidiousness towards the worker, that he should not eat that upon which he is toiling, while he is still toiling - and all the more so, if they are involved with that which grows from the ground, about which a person is joyful with the blessing of God that He has given him - is an indication of villainy and a very bad temperament. And I have already written several times that the curse and evils will cling to the evil and that good thing will cling to the good - 'a specie with its specie.'

From the laws of the commandment is what they, may their memory be Blessed, said (Bava Metzia 87a), what is the difference between someone involved in what is detached and someone who is involved with what is attached: That the one involved with what is detached eats until he finishes his work, and once he finishes his work, it is forbidden for him to eat. But the one who is involved with what is attached - for example harvesting and reaping - only eats when he has finished his work. For example, the harvester and the reaper, would eat after they have filled the basket (see Mishneh Torah,

Hiring 12:2). This is the law of the Torah, but the Sages said [that] because of returning a lost object to the owner - meaning to say, that they not idle form work - that they should eat while walking form one row to another and in their returning [from the vat]. And one who idles during the time of work, and eats, transgresses a negative commandment. And about this is it stated, "you must not put a sickle to your neighbor's grain," as we will write in this Order adjacently in its negative commandments with God's help (Sefer HaChinukh 577). And also that which they said about this matter (Bava Metzia 89a), that one who milks and one who churns and one makes cheese, and all that is similar to it does not eat, because [milk products] are not things that grow from the ground; [and] one who thins out onions or garlic - even though he detaches small ones from among the big ones - does not eat, because this is not the end of production; and it is not necessary to say that guardians of gardens and orchards and all that is attached to the ground do not eat at all. And [also] that which they said (Bava Metzia 89a) that the worker does not eat from something, the production of which is completed concerning tithing and challah-tithing. One who harvests and one who threshes and one who winnows and one who separates and one who reaps olives or grapes and one who crushes and all that is similar to these [types of] work eat from Torah writ. And the guardians of threshing floors and mounds and anything that is detached from the ground, the production of which has not been completed regarding tithes, eat from the laws of [what is practiced] in the state, but not from Torah writ, since a guardian does not do an act (see Mishneh Torah, Hiring 12:8-9). And with someone who does an act, there is no difference between when he does it with his hand or his foot or even with his shoulder - all of them eat from Torah writ. If he was involved with figs, he cannot eat grapes, as it states, "in your neighbors' vineyard, and you may eat grapes" - meaning to say, and not something else. And one involved in this grapevine should not eat grapes of a different vine. And it is forbidden for the worker to suck the grapes, as it states, "and you may eat [grapes]" - and not sucking. And he should not eat a gluttonous eating, as it states, "and you shall be satisfied" - but not more. And the rest of the details of the commandment are elucidated in the chapter [entitled] Hasokher Hapoalim in Bava Metzia.

And [it] is practiced in every place and at all time by males and females. And one who transgresses it and does not allow his wage-worker to eat in the mentioned manner, has violated this positive commandment.

Mitzvah 577

That the worker not take into his hand more than his eating: That the wage-worker is prevented from taking more than his eating, from that [upon] which he is working (see Sefer HaMitzvot LaRambam, Mitzvot Lo Taase 268). And about this is it stated (Deuteronomy 23:25), "you may eat as many grapes as you want, until you are full, but you must not put any in your vessel." The whole matter of this commandment is also elucidated in its positive commandment in this Order (Sefer HaChinukh 576). And one who transgresses it - whether a man or a woman, in all places, at any time - and takes more than his eating, from that which he is working [upon], has violated this negative commandment. But we do not give lashes for it, since it it is a financial matter, which is given to repayment. And the general rule which they, may their memory be Blessed, said (Makkot 16a) already preceded us - that we do not give lashes for any negative commandment that is given to repayment. And if you will ask, "And why was there a need for this negative commandment on this, is it not within the category of theft?" The answer is that it is since it appears to the worker that there would not be a sin in his taking that which grows from the ground at the time of the harvest or the reaping - as it is the way of people not to be concerned with the thing so much, [as opposed to how] they are concerned with that which they have inside the house. Therefore, it was from the kindnesses of God, may He be Blessed, to increase the warnings about it, in that which stumbling is common. And it is like the matter that they, may their memory be Blessed, said (Makkot 23b), "The Holy One, Blessed be He, wanted to give merit to Israel; therefore, He increased for them Torah and commandments."

Mitzvah 578

That the worker not eat during work time: That the wage-worker not eat during his work from the thing with which he is involved. Even though it is permitted to eat from it not during work - and that is when he is going from row to row - when he is working with that which is connected to the ground, it is not permitted to eat during work time (see Sefer HaMitzvot LaRambam, Mitzvot Lo Taase 267). And about this is it stated (Deuteronomy 23:26), "but you must not put a sickle to your neighbor's grain." As they, may their memory be Blessed, said (Bava Metzia 87b) [that the word,] "sickle" is to include all that requires the sickle, and at the time of the sickle - meaning to say at harvest time, do not harvest for yourself. And it is already known that this verse is coming [to refer] to a wage-worker. And the explanation of "When you come" is meaning to say, when you come to your wage-work to be involved with the owner of the field; as Onkelos translates it, "When you are employed" (Onkelos Deuteronomy 23:26).

The matter of this commandment is also elucidated in its positive commandment in this Order (Sefer HaChinukh 576). And one who transgresses this - whether it be a man or a woman, in every place and at any time - and puts a sickle to the grain of his neighbor in the way that we have explained, has violated this negative commandment. And we do not give lashes for it for the reason mentioned in the previous commandment.

Mitzvah 579

That one who wants to divorce his wife divorce her with a bill (get): That we were commanded that if we want to divorce our wives, [it is required] to divorce them in writing. And about this writing the verse states, "a book of cutting" - and it is what our rabbis, may their memory be Blessed, called a bill (get); and so too the Translator, translated it as a book of get (Onkelos Deuteronomy 24:1). And about this does it state (Deuteronomy 24:1), "and he writes her a book of cutting, gives it to her, and sends her away from his house."

It is from the roots of the commandment [that] since woman was created to help man and she is like a beloved vessel for him - and like the matter that they, may their memory be Blessed, said (Sanhedrin 22b), "A woman only makes a covenant with the one who makes her into a vessel" - since that is the case, it was from His will, Blessed be He, that anytime his soul be sick of this vessel, that he should put her out of his house. And for this reason, there are some of our Rabbis that say in the gemara (Gittin 90a) that he can divorce her even if she burnt his cooked food - meaning to say, even for a small thing - since she is only like a valuable vessel in the home. And there are some of them that say that since this vessel is in His image and His likeness, and God granted to her - for his need and his honor - eyes to see, ears to hear and an intelligent soul, it is only fit for him to put her out and send her away from him for a large claim, and as the matter that is stated in the verse, "because he finds something lewd about her." However, according to everyone, if he finds a big thing, it is fit for him to divorce her for the reason that I mentioned - since she was only created for his sake. And since she is a bitter spirit for him and his soul despises her, he is under no compulsion to be with her in any case (as do some of the nations, who make a covenant with a woman [that is] a strong covenant until [one of them reaches] the grave below; and [so] she does not fear separation if she is licentious in his eyes and destroys everything in the house and burns everything that he has with fire - from the heaps to the standing grain to the olive grove). Nonetheless, the Torah commanded us that when we send her away, that he not send her away with speech alone, lest this be a stumbling block for us and it become a snare - that there be licentiousness among our nation, such that the adulterer claim that her husband divorced her; and also that divorce be very prevalent. Accordingly, now that we have been obligated to write the words in a book and to have witnesses testify, any [woman] that claims to be divorced, must show a deed [to that effect]. And there is also [another] benefit in the matter - as through this, sometimes the man will calm down and regret from [wanting to] divorce her. And 'great is peace.'

From the laws of the commandment is that which they, may their memory be Blessed, said (Kiddushin 41a) [about] this get that we mentioned, [that] the man must give it into the hand of the woman or into the hand of her messenger (agent); since the messenger of a person is [considered to be] like him. And [also] that he can give it into her courtyard, and she is divorced with that. And that is if she is standing in the midst of her domain, as the get is disadvantageous to her; and we have someone incur a disadvantage only in their presence. And that which they also said (see Mishneh Torah, Divorce

Sefer HaChinukh

2:1-2) that that which it states in the Torah, "and he writes her a book of cutting" - the intention is not that he writes it with his hand. Rather it is one, whether he writes with his hand or he tells another to write and give it to her. And it is one whether he gives it into her hand or he says to another to give it to her. It is only written, "he writes," to let us know that she is only divorced by writing. And it is only written, "he gives," to say that she not take it on her own. And one who says to two [others], "Write a get and sign it and give it to my wife," behold these can write and sign and give [it] to her - and behold, they are his messengers and they themselves are the witnesses. And it is impossible for there to be a giving of a get without witnesses; as it states, 'according to the mouth of two witnesses shall the matter stand.' And it is impossible for her to be a sexual prohibition today - [such] that one who has sexual relations with her is [subject to] death by the court - and tomorrow be permissible, without witnesses. And therefore they, may their memory be Blessed, said that if he gave her a get between himself and herself - and even with one witness - it is not a get at all. And to what do these words apply? To the script of a scribe. But if the husband wrote it in his own script and one witness signed it, behold, this is an invalid get. And further ahead, we will elucidate what the difference is between an invalid get and one which is not a get at all.

And there are ten things (see Mishneh Torah, Divorce 1:1) that are called the fundamentals of divorce from the Torah, and these are they: 1) that a man can only divorce from his [own] will - and among them is the one who is coerced by Israelites until he says, "I want"; 2) that the divorce should be in writing and in nothing else; 3) that the matter of that which is written be that he is divorcing her and removing her from his acquisition; 4) that its matter should be something that cuts (separates) between him and her; 5) that it be written for that purpose; 6) that the get not lack another action after its writing, besides its giving; 7) that he gives it to her; 8) that he gives it to her in front of witnesses; 9) that he give it to her for the institution of divorce; 10) that the husband or his messenger be the one giving it to her. And all of these are elucidated in the meaning of the verses. And the rest of the things with a get - for example, the signing of the witnesses, and similar to it - are all from the words of the scribes. And the essence of a get is that (Gittin 85a) the man says to his wife, "I, x, divorce you, y, and behold, you are permitted to any man. And nonetheless, all of Israel have become accustomed to writing it in Aramaic, even though it is permissible to write it, a priori, in any language. And this is the text of the get that everyone is accustomed to in our land.

On x day of the week, that is the so and so [date] in the month x (and if Rosh Chodesh is two days, we say, in such and such day of the first month or the second month, since a postdated get is invalid, which is not the case with other contracts), which is in such and such a year from the creation of the world, according to the counting that is accustomed to count with in the place x, how I, x the son of y, from place x - and any other name and the like that I or my fathers or my place or the places of my fathers have - determined from my own will [such] that I was not under duress, that I released and left and divorced you: you, x the daughter of y from place x - and any other name and the like that you or your fathers or your place or the places of your fathers have - that you were my wife from before now. And now, I released and left and divorced you, [such] that you be endowed and in charge of yourself to go and marry any man you determine. And no one should protest against you from my name [for that] from this day and forever. And behold, you are permitted to any man; and this is from me for you a book of divorce and a get of release and a letter of dissolution, like the law of Moshe and Israel.

And the witnesses sign below. And the people have become accustomed to writing it with twelve rows, like the number [of the numerical equivalent of the letters in the word,] get (Tosafot on Gittin 2a:1, s.v. hamevi). And we only write, 'like the law of Moshe and Israel' on the last line.

And so too do we write a get of emancipation (from slavery) with twelve lines. And the text of the get of emancipation is like the text mentioned [above], except for the language of emancipation that we change in it. And this is it:

On such day of the week, that is the so and so [date] in the month **x**, which is in year **x** from the creation of the world, according to the counting that we count in the place x, which is situated on river **x** or on the shore of the sea, how it is that I, **x** the son of **y**, from place **x** - and any other name and the like that I or my fathers or my place or the places of my fathers have - determined from my own will

Sefer HaChinukh

[such] that I was not under duress, that I released and emancipated and left you, you, x who now lives in place x - and any other name and the like that you or your place have - that you were my slave from before now. And now, I released and left and emancipated you, [such] that you be endowed and in charge of yourself. And no one should protest against you from my name [for that] from this day and forever. And behold, you are to yourself, and behold, you are a free man, and you and your seed are permitted to enter the congregation of Israel. And no man has authority over you or your seed; and this is from me for you a book of emancipation and a letter of dissolution and a get of release, like the law of Moshe and Israel.

And we write, 'like the law of Moshe and Israel' on the last line, and the witness's sign.

And the universal custom is to warn the man divorcing to nullify any [future] objection or objection of an objection (see Mishneh Torah, Divorce 6:20). And we say to him that he should say, "Write this get for the sake of my wife x." And we place him there next to the scribe. And nonetheless, if he has gone after he ordered to write the get and to sign and to give it, we give it and we do not concern ourselves with [his possible death], as we place him under the assumption of [someone still] alive. And they, may their memory be Blessed, warned us, that we should not write in the get, veden, with [a] letter, yod, lest the reader read [it as] vedin (and the law), and its understanding would be to say, the statute will be between you and me; and a get requires clear language [that is] void of doubt. And so too, they said not write eegeret with [a] letter, yod, lest the reader read [it as] ee gart (if you became a stranger), which would be to say, if you were unfaithful; and he should not write lemechach with [a] letter, yod, lest the reader read [it as] lee michach (it is laughable to me), which would be to say, it is laughter to me; and he should not write tehavian and tetsavian ('shall be' and 'determine' in the singular) with two letters, yod, lest the reader read [it as] tehavyena and tetsavyena (in the plural), which would be to say, that he is speaking to two women, and it comes out that that he is not divorcing this one, but rather two others. And so too, he should lengthen the [shape of the letter] vav in tarukhin and shevukin ('divorce' and 'left' in masculine), lest it resemble a yod and its understanding would be tarikhin and shevikin (in the feminine), meaning to say, that she left him. And in this manner, we must be careful with every expression and every [word] that is written in the get, such that it not be ambiguous (see Mishneh Torah, Divorce 4:13). And so too, the writer must be careful in the writing that the script be a lucid one, such that children who are not foolish but not wise can read it (see Mishneh Torah, Divorce 4:10). And he can write in any language and in any script, so long as the language and script are clear in the manner that we have mentioned. And Israel has already become accustomed to writing in the Aramaic language and the Ashuri (standard Hebrew) script (see Shulchan Arukh, Even HaEzer 126:2).

And behold, my son, I will write a little of the text of general contracts. And even though this is not included in this commandment and its subject, the word, get that we have spoken about is a general word for all contracts, and [so] this is included in the word. Before anything, I will say that it is fitting for all proper witnesses to investigate and to understand the essence of the things to which they will testify, whatever the matter may be; and that they inform the involved parties to inform them of all the stipulations between them in a clear language, and to review all of the things in front of them until they comprehend them well. And [they should not act] like the foolish witnesses, who strip people of their cloaks and their possessions and their properties 'by the tail of their cloaks.' [The parties] whisper a little into the ears of the silly masses and, before they inform them [properly - such] that they understand the essence of the stipulations - they go and write and sign according to what is good in their eyes about them, until they [strip] them clean of their possessions. And the Lord, our God, did not give us, the holy people, this [way] to do anything that is not the way of truth. And therefore, the prohibition against deceptions is repeated in the Torah three times, as it is written in three places (Leviticus 19:33, 25:14, 17), "a man shall not wrong his people."

And our Rabbis, may their memory be Blessed, also informed us in several places in the Gemara to establish every thing according to the truth of the matter, and according to the thought of the sellers and the buyers; and that we not fashion the judgement entirely according to their words, but rather according to the intention of the people, when their intention is clear to us. And [it is] like the matter that they, may their memory be Blessed, said in Ketuvot 97a in the chapter [entitled] Almanah

Sefer HaChinukh

Nizunet, [that] if one sold and [subsequently] did not need the [liquid cash], the sale goes back; and that is [in the case] when he revealed his thought, that it was because he needed the money to do such and such with it that he made the sale. And we also say in Kiddushin 50a in the chapter [entitled] Haeesh HaMekadesh Bo Ubeshlucho, "A certain man sold his possessions with the intention of going up to the Land of Israel; he went up but he did not settle [there]. Rava said [about this], 'Anyone who goes up has the intention of settling, and he did not settle'" - which is to say [that] the sale goes back. Behold, their opinion was to say that all actions should be concluded according to the truth and the intentions of the doers. And this is a straight path that a person should choose for himself and [so] be successful in all of his deeds.

The customary text among us for contracts of sales, of gifts, of behests and of giving over rights is this: We, the undersigned witnesses, know clear testimony that x the son of y told us, "Be witnesses for me and acquire [this testimony] from me and give it to Rabbi b the son of c, that it be a proof and a benefit for him, because I have taken and received from his hand such and such money and sold him for it, x vineyard (or field or house), as is indicated and marked off by its indications and its borders, and these are the borders of that place: on side **x**, such, and on side y, etc." - until he marks it off from its four sides. "Everything that is within these borders have I, **x**, sold with a complete sale and acquisition, from now, for the money mentioned, etc." And afterwards, he specifically mentions [the various] aspects of that place - for example, trees, stones, beams, walls, roofs. And all of this is for the embellishment of the contract. And he needs to mention its height and depth (Bava Batra 63a). And so [too] have they become accustomed now to write on loan contracts, "On condition that the seventh year not remove it." As, if not, the seventh year would remove it; since we hold that the removal of money [debts on the seventh year] is practiced outside the land rabbinically, as I have written above (Sefer HaChinukh 477).

And they, may their memory be Blessed, also said (Bava Batra 167a) about this matter of contracts that a person should not write the sum of three to ten at the end of a line, lest [the one holding it] forge it and write thirty instead of three or forty instead of four or fifty instead of five (which in Hebrew only requires the addition of more letters at the end of the word), etc. And if it came out at the end of a line, we go back [and write it again] two or three times, and [then] it is possible that it will come out in the middle of the line. And they likewise said (Bava Batra 165b) that if 'one hundred' is written at the top, and 'two hundred' at the bottom - or the opposite - that it always goes according to [what is written at] the bottom. And they likewise said (Bava Batra 167b) that we write a contract for the seller or the borrower, even if the purchaser or the creditor is not with him. But we only write contracts for sharecropping or contractual work or arbitration - or any act of court - with the knowledge of them, both. And Rabbi Yitschak bar Yosef said in the chapter [entitled] Get Pashut (Bava Batra 161b) that a person must write down the existence of all erasures, entirely. And he also needs to review the subject of the contract on the last line, since we do not learn from the last line (and the review is not essential). And because of that, if the witnesses spaced their signatures one [extra blank] line below the writing, [the contract is still] fit. And that which they have become accustomed to writing 'everything is firm and valid' (Tosafot on Bava Batra 162a:1, s.v. lefi) is because the expression does not invalidate a contract and - even if we did learn from it - there is nothing [harmful] in this. And Rava said there (Bava Batra 163a) that a contract wherein he and his witnesses [write] on top of the erasure is fit. And Rav Shisha, the son of Rav Eedee said in the chapter [entitled] HaZahav (Bava Metzia 47a) that we write in the contracts, "And I acquired from him, with a vessel with which it is fitting to acquire." "With a vessel" is to exclude that of Rav Sheshet, who said that we can acquire with cows; "which it is fitting" is to exclude that of Shmuel, who said that we can acquire with a dung vessel (maroka); "to acquire" is to exclude that of Levi, who said with the vessels of the one who is making the acquisition - and Rav, and [perhaps] Rav Ashi said that that "which it is fitting" is to exclude that from which it is forbidden to derive benefit.

And the text of a contract of occupancy is like this: In front of us, the undersigned witnesses, x gave to y the keys of place **x** that he sold to him, as is written and signed in the sale contract that he made for him, and whose witnesses were b and c. And in front of us witnesses, **x** said to **y**, "Go and possess and acquire [it]." And the [afore]mentioned Rabbi y opened and locked [it] in front of us and occupied it with complete occupancy, and that which happened at [that] time.

The text of a contract of selling an obligation: I, **x**, sell you, **y**, the contract of the debt of **z**, in as **z** is in debt to me, as he is holding such and such; and you will acquire [the obligation] and all that is liened to it, by the force of this contract and the delivery of the contract. And if the contract is not in their hands, he gives over his possession of it, by way of its attachment to four ells of land. And [about] any oral contract, they, may their memory be Blessed, said (Kiddushin 48a and see Tosafot on Bava Batra 77b:1, s.v. Rav Pappa) that it can only be acquired in the presence of the three of them (the creditor, the borrower and the purchaser of the obligation). And this is from the three things that they, may their memory be Blessed, said (Gittin 14a) that they are traditional laws without an explanation.

The text of a will: We, the undersigned witnesses, went into Rabbi x, to visit him and found him ill and stuck in bed; and his words were lucid in his mouth, and his mind was clear to answer yes to [what was] yes, and no to [what was] no. And he said to us, "Behold, I am ill and I am worried lest I will die from this illness. I request from you to be the witnesses for my will, and behold, I command in front of you because of death to give to my son, y, such and such and to my other son, such and such, and to z such and such." And after all of his words, they write, "The [afore]mentioned Rabbi **x** commanded all of this in front of us because of death, and we know clearly that he departed (died) from this illness to the House of his World and left us and all of Israel alive."

The text of a contract of court validation (notarization): In the sitting of three as one, have we now made valid this contract that is before us, we the undersigned [members of the] court. And it has become clear to us that the signatures of these witnesses signed above in this contract are the signature of their hands, and we have permitted and validated them as is fit. And behold, it is approved and established. And they sign their names.

And the rest of the details that come out of the matters of a get and other contracts are elucidated in the tractate that is built on it, and that is Tractate Gittin and in Bava Batra in the chapter [entitled] Get Pashut and in a few scattered places in the Talmud.

And this commandment of divorce bills is practiced in every place and at all times. And one who transgresses it and divorces (sends away) his wife and does not write her a get - like the commandment of the Torah, and in the manner that our Sages, may their memory be Blessed, explained - has violated this positive commandment. And his punishment is very great, since her legal status is that of a married woman, and [yet] he treats her as if she is divorced [which will lead her to act accordingly]. And the punishment of [having sexual relations with] a married woman is well-known, as it is from the most severe sins in the Torah.

Mitzvah 580

That he not bring back his ex-wife from when she has married: That we have been prevented from bringing back a woman after we have divorced her and she has married another. And [that is] specifically when she married or became engaged (with formal erusin); but if she was promiscuous after he divorced her, it is permissible to bring her back. And about this is it stated (Deuteronomy 24:4), "The first husband who divorced her may not take her to wife again." And this is speaking about after she married another - as it stated first, "and becomes the wife of another man." As if it is before she married [another], it is permissible to bring her back; and it is also appropriate to do so, if she is not an evildoer.

It is from the roots of this commandment [that it is] in order to distance all matters of licentiousness and anything similar to it. And I have already written in the Order of Achrei Mot (Sefer HaChinukh 188) and concerning the negative commandment of "Do not commit adultery" in the Order of Vayishma Yitro (Sefer HaChinukh 35) [about] the multitude of harm that is [involved] in licentiousness, and the matter is known. And like the matter of licentiousness is it for a woman to go out from one [man], and have relations with others, and afterwards to come back to the first.

The laws of this commandment are in [various] places [in] Yevamot (see Tur, Even HaEzer 10).

And this prohibition is practiced in every place and at all times by males - as the warning to not bring them back comes to them. And nonetheless, women are also included in the prohibition, even though the main negative commandment is upon men. And Ramban, may his memory be Blessed, (15 in the negative commandments according to the opinion of Ramban, in Sefer HaMitzvot LaRambam) enumerates two negative commandments in this: One is not to bring back an ex-wife after she has married; and the [other] is that the husband should not have sexual relations with his wife after she has been promiscuous while she is still [married] to him.

Mitzvah 581

That a groom should not go out from his home the whole year, even for the needs of the community: That the groom is prevented from going out from his house the entire [first] year, meaning to say to go on distant trips. And also, the army officer is prevented from taking him out by force, meaning to say, from taking him out to war or to do work needed for the war - for example, to supply water and food to his brothers or to fix matters in the city, to guard it from the enemy. And about this is it stated (Deuteronomy 24:5), "nor have any purpose assigned to him." And they said in Tractate Sotah 44a, "'He shall not go out with the army' - it is possible that with the army he shall not go out, but he should fix weapons or supply water and food; [hence] it is taught to say, 'nor have any purpose assigned to him.'" And they inferred further,"[it is] 'to him' that you do not assign, but you do assign to others," meaning to say to those that return from the war because of weak-heartedness, or because of the dedication of a house or vineyard. And there they also said, "And since it comes out from 'nor have assigned to him,' why do I have 'he shall not go out with the army?' To have him transgress on two negative commandments."

And I have already written that which is needed about this commandment, according to the fashion of the book, in its positive commandment in this Order (Sefer HaChinukh 582) - take it from there.

Mitzvah 582

The commandment that a groom rejoice with his wife for one year: That we have been commanded that a groom rejoice with his his wife for one year - meaning to say that he not travel outside of the city to go out to war, nor for other matters, [such that] he would dwell without her for many days; but rather he should dwell with her for a whole year from the day of the marriage. And about this is it stated (Deuteronomy 24:5), "he shall be exempt one year for the sake of his household, to give happiness to the woman he has married."

It is from the roots of the commandment that God, may He be Blessed, had it come up in thought in front of Him to create the world; and His desire was that it be inhabited with good creatures born from male and female that mate properly - as licentiousness is an abomination in front of Him. Therefore, He decreed upon us - the nation that He chose to be called for His name - that we should dwell with the woman that is designated for us to raise seed, for a whole year from the time that he marries her. [This is] so that [his] nature becomes used to her and to have [his] desire cling to her and to bring her form and all of her acts into the [heart] - to the point that all the acts of another woman be foreign to his nature; as every nature generally seeks and loves that to which it is accustomed. And from this, a man will distance his path from an [other] woman, and he will turn his thought to the woman that is fitting for him; and the offspring that she will bare him will be proper, and the world will bring up grace in front of its Creator. And that is [the understanding of] what they, may their memory be Blessed, said (Sotah 44a) that it is the same whether one marries a virgin, or a widow or a levirate (yivamah) - he is obligated in this; as all of them are fitting for this according to the explanation mentioned [above], but not one who brings back the woman he has divorced.

From the laws of the commandment is that which they, may their memory be Blessed, said (Sotah 44a, see Mishneh Torah, Kings and Wars 7:11), that the whole year, he does not go out to war and he also does not supply water and food to his brothers who are at war, and he does not place barriers for the city and he shall have no purpose assigned to him; as it states, "he shall not go out with the army nor have any purpose assigned to him" - meaning to say, not the needs of the war and not the needs of the city. And the rest of its details are elucidated in the eighth chapter of Sotah.

And this commandment, regarding that the people of the city not force him to go to war, is practiced at the time of the [Temple], as then we would sometimes go out to war. And regarding that which it is fitting for every man to gladden her and to dwell with her for a year, it is practiced in every place and at all times. And one who transgresses it and separates from her within the year to stay without her for many days - even with her dispensation - has violated this positive commandment. And nonetheless, it appears that [in the case of] one who wants to go away for the matter of a commandment or to gladden his friends - with the intention of returning joyfully after a few days - there is no violation of the commandment. And there are some that say it is permissible [to go away] with her dispensation (See Shulchan Arukh, Even HaEzer 64:1 and Beit Shmuel and Chelkat Mechokek there).

Mitzvah 583
That we not take as surety vessels in which life-sustaining food (ochel nefesh) is made: That we have been prevented from taking as surety vessels that are the means for the preparation of food for people - for example (see Sefer HaMitzvot LaRambam, Mitzvot Lo Taase 242), a vessel for grinding and a vessel for kneading and a vessel for cooking and a vessel for slaughtering animals and the others of what are grouped as that with which we make life-sustaining food. And about this is stated (Deuteronomy 24:6), "A handmill or an upper millstone shall not be taken in pawn, for that would be taking someone's life in pawn." And the language of the Mishnah (Mishna Bava Metzia 9:13) is "And they did not refer only to a mill and an upper millstone, but anything that is used to make life-sustaining food, as it states, 'For that would be taking someone's life as a pledge.'"

And Rambam, may his memory be Blessed, wrote (Sefer HaMitzvot LaRambam, Mitzvot Lo Taase 242), "And it remains for us that we explain to you their saying (Mishnah Bava Metzia 9:13), 'and he is liable for two vessels, as it states, "A handmill or an upper millstone shall not be taken in pawn, for that would be taking someone's life in pawn"' - as this brings us to thinking that they are two commandments; and all the more so in their saying (Bava Metzia 115a) that we make liable for the handmill on its own and for the upper millstone on it own. And this matter is that anyone who takes a vessel in which we make life-sustaining food as surety transgresses a negative commandment, as we shall explain; and one who takes many vessels - all of with which we make life-sustaining food - as surety is liable for each and every vessel; for example, if he takes as surety a vessel for grinding and a vessel for bread and a vessel for kneading. And this is like one who takes in pawn the garment of Reuven's widow and the garment of Shimon's widow and the garment of Levi's widow - that he transgresses for each and every garment. However, the law in question is about one who takes in pawn two vessels - and he makes life-sustaining food with all of them - but the cannot suffice with (use) one without the other, and [so maybe] he should [only] be liable for one vessel; or perhaps we should say that since they are two vessels, he should be liable for each and every one by itself. And they elucidated for us that he is liable for two vessels, and even though the work is done through the gathering of both of them - for example, a handmill and an upper millstone, with which one cannot grind without the other. Such that if he takes in pawn a handmill and an upper millstone, it will be like he takes in pawn a vessel for the dough and a slaughtering knife - and they are two vessels, each of which has its [own] work. And this is the matter of that which they said, 'and he is liable for two vessels' - not that they are two commandments. And this is the language of Sifrei about this matter that I have elucidated to you - they said, 'Just like a handmill and an upper millstone are two distinct vessels but serve for one work and we make liable for this on its own and for this on it own; so too all two vessels that serve for one work, one is liable for this on its own and for this on it own.' The elucidation of the thing and its matter is [that] even though we use it for one work, he is liable for this on its own and for this on it own. And if he takes it in pawn, we take it from him and return it to the craftsman."

The root of this commandment is known, that is for the betterment of the world and the needs of its civilization.

From the laws of the commandment is that which they, may their memory be Blessed, said (see Mishneh Torah, Creditor and Debtor 3:2) that with regard to this prohibition, there is no difference if he took it in pawn with his hand or through the court - from any angle, he is liable for them. And if he took it in pawn, the court returns it - [even] against his will. And our teachers, may God watch over them, explained that this prohibition is only to take the vessels mentioned in pawn when it is not at the time of a loan. But [in exchange for] a loan, it is certainly permissible to take in pawn all the vessels in the world. As it is no worse than selling - as we do not prevent a person from selling all of his vessels, or to put them in pawn. And since some of the great sages of the world erred about this, I have written at length about it. And one who takes in pawn many vessels with which we make life-sustaining food and did not return them before they were burnt or they got lost is liable for lashes for each and every one - and even from two vessels that do one work, like a handmill and an upper millstone or that which is similar to it, he is liable for two lashings. And that is when they were burnt before he returned them. And the rest of its details are elucidated in the ninth chapter of Bava Metzia. And this prohibition is practiced in every place and at all times.

Mitzvah 584

To not detach signs of tzaraat (a Biblical skin disease): That we have been prevented from cutting off signs of tzaraat or to burn it to the point that its appearance changes. And about this is it stated (Deuteronomy 24:8), "Be careful with the blemish of tzaraat, etc. And the language of Sifrei is "'Be careful with the blemish of tzaraat' is a negative commandment." And the language of the Mishnah Negaim 7:4 is "One who removes the signs of impurity or burns the healthy patch of skin transgresses a negative commandment."

I have written about the roots of this commandment in the Order of Eeshah Ki Tazria [regarding] 'and do not shave the scab' (Sefer HaChinukh 170).

Among the laws of the commandment is what they, of Blessed memory, said (see Mishneh Torah, Defilement by Leprosy 10:1) that one who detaches signs of impurity - whether all of them or part of them; or even if he burns a healthy patch of skin, completely or even partially; whether from [his] flesh or from a garment or from the house; whether before the priest sees the blemish or during the days of tentative quarantine or during the days of definite quarantine or even after he is [deemed] exempt - in all of these, he transgresses a negative commandment and is liable for lashes. About this it states, "Be careful with the blemish of tzaraat to guard exceedingly and to do like all that the priests, the Levites, instruct you to do; as I commanded them, be careful to do" - meaning to say, "as I commanded them, be careful to do" and do not remove or cut off the blemish. And the well-know principle already preceded us (Makkot 13b) that in every place where it states, "be careful," or "lest" or "do not," it is nothing but a negative commandment. And they, may their memory be Blessed, said (see Mishneh Torah, Defilement by Leprosy 10:1) that a person is only lashed for this when his actions are effective for him - meaning to say that in the removal of that which he removed of the blemish, there remained less than the required amount [for impurity] in the remnant. But if there remained the amount [needed] for impurity in the remnant - for example, if there was a bright spot and there were three white hairs in it and he detached one, or if he burned part of the healthy skin and there remained part of it the size of a lentil - he is not lashed; as behold, he is [still] impure as at first. And so [too], all that is similar to this. But we [rather] strike him with lashes of rebellion. And the matter is not like this with a scab, as he is not lashed for a scab in his shaving part of the scab - until he shaves all of it, as I wrote in its place in the Order of Eeshah Ki Tazria (Sefer HaChinukh 170).

And they, may their memory be Blessed, said (Shabbat 132b) about the matter of this prohibition that one who has tzaraat on his foreskin should not have a concern about circumcising, as the positive commandment of circumcision pushes off this negative commandment; [just] like we hold in every place, that a positive commandment comes and pushes off a negative commandment. And that is when it is impossible to fulfill the positive commandment without the negation of the negative commandment - for example, this [case of] circumcision with tzaraat. And the sages, may their memory be Blessed, learned (Yevamot 3b) that this law was not said generally with all negative commandments, but rather only with a light negative commandment, meaning to say one that doesn't come with excision (karet). [This is] as in the case of the negative commandment of "You shall not wear shatnez " (Deuteronomy 22:11), which we push off with the positive commandment of "You shall make for yourselves tassels." And so too, this negative commandment of not cutting off his bright spot, where there is also no excision - with these and and with similar to them, behold, the thing is as if the Torah said explicitly, "I have not prevented you in the case of this positive commandment." But with any negative commandment that comes with excision, we do not push [them] off because of a positive commandment. Since the verse was so stringent about it to obligate him excision, behold it is as if it stated explicitly, "Do thing x, so long as you will not need to transgress negative commandment y in doing it." And the rest of the details of this commandment are elucidated in Tractate Negaim (Chapter 7).

And this prohibition is practiced in every place and at all times by males and females, such that one who contracts tzaraat and recognizes the signs of his tzaraat is not permitted to cut them off. And one who transgresses this and detaches them in the way that we mentioned, is liable for lashes.

Mitzvah 585

To not take surety from a debtor by force: That we have been prevented from taking surety from a debtor - meaning to say a borrower - with our hands by force, bur rather through the command of a judge and through his agent; that we should not jump and come to the house of a debtor and take surety from him or grab a surety from him when we find him in the marketplace. And about this is it stated (Deuteronomy 24:10), "you must not enter his house to seize his pledge" - and it is not specifically the house [that was intended], but the same is true of one who grabs it from his hand in the marketplace. And the language of the Mishnah Bava Metzia 9:13 is "[If] one lends to his fellow, he may not extract surety except through the court, and he may not enter his house to take the pledge, as is written (Deuteronomy 24:11), 'You must remain outside.'"

It is from the roots of the commandments [that it is] so that people not be as if abandoned and violence increase in the land; that the big one swallow up the small one and take surety from him by force without fear from him, and that the small one not be able to get his case against the big one from fear of his stature. And so, the verse equalized them, such that one not take surety for his debt from his fellow, but rather that it all be done according to the law. And with this will there be a betterment in the civilization of the world - as is the desire of its Creator, that it be [properly] inhabited.

From the laws of this commandment is that which they, may their memory be Blessed, said (see Mishneh Torah, Creditor and Debtor 3:4) that it is one whether it is the creditor or the agent of the court, he is not allowed to go into the house of the debtor and take surety from him; but rather the debtor must bring the pledge outside to them. [If so,] what is the difference between an agent of the court and the [creditor] himself? That the agent of the court is permitted to strip the surety from the hand of the creditor by force when he finds him outside; whereas the creditor is not permitted to strip it from him, until the debtor hands it over with his consent. And the rest of the details of this commandment are elucidated in the ninth chapter of [Bava] Metzia.

And this prohibition is practiced in every place and at all times by males and females. And one who transgresses it, and takes surety from his debtor - whether at home or outside - by force, has violated this negative commandment. But there are no lashes for it, since it is rectified by a positive commandment, as it states, "You must return the pledge to him." But if he did not fulfill the positive commandment in it and the pledge get lost or burnt - such that it is impossible to fulfill it any longer - he is liable for lashes. And [it is] like the matter that we wrote regarding the sending of the nest (Sefer HaChinukh 544) - as we hold like Rabbi Yochanan who said to the teacher, "It is taught, 'He fulfilled it and he did not fulfill it'" (Makkot 16b). And the creditor takes the surety for the payment of his debt according to its worth, and claims the rest from the debtor according to law. This is the opinion of Rambam, may his memory be Blessed (Mishneh Torah, Creditor and Debtor 3:4). And he also wrote that the creditor is liable for lashes the entire time that the surety is lost, since it is no longer in his hand to fix the negative commandment [that he transgressed]. And I wonder [about this] - since this is [an issue of] money, why can he not become exempt [from lashes] by repayment?

Mitzvah 586

To not prevent surety from its needy owner: That we have been warned not to prevent the surety from its owner at the time that he needs it, but rather to return it to him - a vessel for the day during the day, and a vessel for the night during the night. And about this is it stated (Deuteronomy 24:12), "you shall not go to sleep in his pledge." And the language of Sifrei is "Do not go to sleep when the pledge is with you, but rather return it when he will not have with what to replace it, from the weakness of his poverty" - as the verse (Exodus 22:26) explains, "It is his only clothing, the sole covering for his skin."

I have written the whole content of this commandment in its positive commandment (Sefer HaChinukh 587) of "You must return the pledge to him" in this Order. And one who transgresses this and does not return the surety to the needy man when he needs it has violated this negative commandment. But we do not give lashes for it, as it is a negative commandment that does not an act [involved] with it.

Mitzvah 587

To return the surety to the owners at the time that he needs it: That we were commanded to return the surety to its Israelite owners at the time that it will be needed by him; meaning to say that if the surety is something that a person needs during the day - for example, the tool for his work - he should return it to him during the day, and the borrower brings it back to him during the night, and if it is a vessel that he needs during the night - for example, bedding or a blanket - he should return it to him during the night, and the borrower brings it back to the creditor during the day. And the language of Mekhilta, Mishpatim 186 is "'You must return it to him before the sun sets' (Exodus 22:25) - this is the clothing of the day, that you must return it to him [the whole day. That you must return the clothing of the night] for the whole night, from where [do I know it]? [Hence] we learn to say, 'You must surely return the pledge to him at sundown' (Deuteronomy 24:13). From here they said, we take the clothing of the day for surety during the night and the clothing of the night during the day." And the proof that this is from the count of positive commandments is that which they, may their memory be Blessed, said in the Gemara in Makkot 16a that the negative commandment of "you must not enter his house to seize his pledge," is a negative commandment that is rectified by a positive commandment - and [that] positive commandment is "You must surely return."

It is from the roots of this commandment that God, may He be Blessed, desired, in His goodness, the good of His creatures and their merit and wanted that they should teach themselves the traits of kindness and mercy in order that they merit the good. And [it is] like the matter that I wrote in Parshat Mishpatim in Sefer HaChinukh 66 and in many commandments.

From the laws of the commandment is that which they, may their memory be Blessed, said in the chapter [entitled] HaMekabel (Bava Metzia 113a) [that] one who gives a loan to his fellow is not permitted to take surety from him - meaning to say [if it is] not in court. And if he takes surety from him, he is obligated to return the surety - the bedding during the night, and the plow during the day. To what do these words apply? When he takes surety when it is not at the time of his loan. But if he takes surety at the time of his loan - for example, he lends to his fellow based on the surety - he does not need to return it at all. And until when does he have to [keep] return[ing] the surety? Forever.

And if you shall ask, "If so, what does the surety help;" it helps that the debt not be withdrawn on the seventh year - as we hold [that] a loan with surety is not withdrawn by the seventh year, and as I have written concerning the commandment of the sabbatical year below (Sefer HaChinukh 577). And, so too, it helps with the matter that this surety does not become [classified as] movable goods with regards to the son of the borrower - as we hold that the [inherited] movable goods of orphans are not liened to the creditor, unless the borrower acquired it for the creditor explicitly - as is the way that we do it today in our contracts. And since this surety is in the possession of the creditor - even if the borrower dies when it is in his home - it does not become movable goods with regards to his sons. Rather, the creditor extracts it and he is paid [for the debt] from it. It also helps him that if he wants to be paid for his debt, he sells it and is paid from it - if the borrower does not want to redeem it. As they only said that he has to return it forever, if the creditor does not want to be paid from it for his debt. And if the surety is from vessels that are not required for work during the day and for cover at night, they, may their memory be Blessed, said (Bava Metzia 113a and see Mishneh Torah, Creditor and Debtor 3:6) that we leave it with him for thirty days; so that the borrower can look for money to repay him. And if he has not paid for it after thirty days, [the creditor] sells it in court. And the rest of its details are elucidated in the chapter [entitled] HaMekabel in Bava Metzia.

And this commandment is practiced by males and females in every place and at all times. And one who transgresses it and does not return the pledge in the way that we wrote above has violated this positive commandment - besides having violated a negative commandment, as we shall write [about] it, with God's help (Sefer HaChinukh 586).

Mitzvah 588

To give the wage of a wage-worker on its day: To give the wage of a wage-worker on its day; and we do not delay his wage to a different day, as it is stated (Deuteronomy 24:15), "You must pay him his wages on the same day." And they, may their memory be Blessed, elucidated in the ninth chapter of Bava Metzia 111a, that whether it is an Israelite wage-worker or even a resident alien, there is an obligation to pay him on its day; but the negative commandment that comes upon this is not [applicable] with a resident alien.

What is elucidated in the verse is from the roots of the commandment - as, in general, every wage-worker needs his wage for his sustenance. Therefore, it is not fitting to delay his sustenance; and like the matter that is written, "for he is needy and urgently depends on it." And they, may their memory be Blessed, explained (Bava Metzia 112a) [that] for this wage did he go up the ramp and suspend himself in the tree. And God, in His kindnesses, commanded us to train ourselves in the traits of mercy and kindness, and that we should bring the required portion to every creature in his time of need, in order that we merit and receive His goodness - as He is One who desires to do good, as I have written many times.

From the laws of the commandment is that which they, may their memory be Blessed, said (see Mishneh Torah, Hiring 11:1-2) [that] it is one whether it is the wage for a person or the wage for an animal or the wage for vessels - [for them all,] he is obligated to give [the wage] to its owners at its time. And what is its time? A day wage-worker collects the whole night; and about this is it stated, (Leviticus 19:13), "the wages of a laborer shall not remain with you until morning." And a night wage-worker collects the whole day; and about this is it stated, "You must pay him his wages on the same day." And a day hourly wage-worker collects the whole day and a night hourly wage-worker collects the whole night. A monthly wage-worker, a weekly wage-worker, a yearly wage-worker, a seven-year wage worker - [if] he leaves during the day, he is paid [that] whole day, [and if] he leaves during the night, he is paid [that] whole night. And [also among its laws] is that which they said (see Mishneh Torah, Hiring 11:3) that contractual work is like wage-work concerning this commandment - that once he has finished the work and returned it to its owners, [the employer] is obligated to give [the worker] his wage on that day. But if he did not return the work to its owners, [the employer] does not transgress [by delaying payment]. And it is like the matter that they, may their memory be Blessed, said (Bava Metzia 112a), "One who gives his cloak to a craftsman - when he has finished it and informed him, even after ten days - the whole time that it is in the hand of the craftsman, he does not transgress." And also what they said (see Mishneh Torah, Hiring 11:4) that the employer does not transgress unless the wage-worker makes a claim against him; but if he does not make a claim or if [the employer] does not have anything with which to pay him, [the employer] does not transgress; as the verse only obligated him when he has it in his house or he can pay him [otherwise] - but if he is not able to pay him on the same day unless he loses much of his [property], the verse did not apparently obligate him to do so. And nonetheless, it is fitting that the money be in the hand of any intelligent person before he hires the workers. And [regarding] one who hires someone on the eve of the Shabbat and is pushed off from paying because of Shabbat, the law would be that he does not transgress the law of the Torah in this, as once it is pushed off, it is pushed off; but he is obligated rabbinically because of 'do not say to your neighbor, "Go and come back."' And the rest of its details are elucidated there in Bava Metzia [in the] ninth chapter.

And this is practiced in every place and at all times by males and females. And one who transgresses this and does not pay his wage-worker according to the matter that we have written, has violated this positive commandment - besides having violated its negative commandment, as we will write in this

Sefer HaChinukh

Order, with God's help (there is nothing about this in this Order, but it is likely that the reference is to what he writes in Parshat Kedoshim).

Mitzvah 589
That a relative not testify, one about the other: That we have been commanded not to accept the testimony of some relatives about some relatives. And about this is it stated (Deuteronomy 24:16), "Parents shall not be put to death for children, nor children be put to death for parents" - and concerning this came the traditional understanding (Sanhedrin 27b) [that it means that] fathers should not be put to death from the testimony of the sons, and sons should not be put to death from the testimony of the fathers. And the same is true of financial cases - that we do not believe some relatives about some relatives. However it is mentioned regarding laws [involving] death sentences by way of hyperbole - that we should not say, since this is [causing] the loss of life, we should not suspect the relative about him, but rather do like his testimony; since his testimony is to lose the life of his relative. And even though the verse only mentioned the fathers and the sons, the same is true of several of the other relatives. But it mentioned sons and fathers by way of an example; saying that [even though] one loves the other very much, and [yet the Torah] stated that also these are not believed that one should condemn the other and - there is no need to say - exonerate [him]. And the same is true of some of the [other] relatives, as the tradition about them has come to us - and we shall mention them in the laws of the commandment, with God's help.

It is from the roots of this commandment [that] since the essence of all human matters is dependent upon testimony of people - like the matter that I wrote at the beginning of my book - therefore, the Omnipresent wanted to distance [us from] making [improper] judgment among people; [and] only [to make it] with strong and true testimony that is clean from any suspicion. And to strengthen the matter, He distanced us from all the testimony of relatives - even to condemn; lest the habit spread with this to accept him also to exonerate. And this matter is from the ways of the perfect Torah to always distance us from snares and things that are close [to them]; that damage be found from them to people. And there is another benefit found from the matter [and that is that] since relatives always dwell one near the other, their dwelling and being together [makes it] impossible for them to be saved from sometimes quarreling, one with the other. And if we would believe their testimony - one against the other - perhaps in their constant anger [of] one against the other, their anger would momentarily rise and they would come in front of the court and condemn their heads to the king. And once his anger abates, the relative will almost strangle himself from worry about his relative and about his [own] deeds. And all the ways of God are straight.

And from the laws of this commandment is that which they, may their memory be Blessed, said (see Mishneh Torah, Testimony 13:1) that the disqualification of being related from Torah writ is only with the family of the father - and they are the father with the son and with the son of the son; and the brothers from the father with each other, and their sons with one another; and there is no need to say, the uncle with the son of his brother. But with the other relatives from the mother, and so [too] the relatives from the side of marriage, their disqualification is [only] rabbinic. And this reasoning is taught in the last mishnah in the chapter [entitled] Zeh Borer (Mishnah Sanhedrin 3:4), which is all the extant law, according to the opinion of a few commentators. But from [the commentators], there are [other] great ones - sages and wise ones - that decided [that] even all of the sibling relatives from the mother, and so [too] his brother-in-law and step-son and all that are not fit to inherit, are [all] disqualified from Torah writ, [just] like the [corresponding] relative on the father's side - as they learned [to include] them in the Gemara, from the inclusion of the verse, [based on its mentioning the word,] fathers, fathers twice. And their proofs are in their books - merit, my son and you will distinguish the truth.

And (see Mishneh Torah, Testimony 13:3-5) the brothers with each other were called by the Sages, the first (level of separation) with the first; and so, the father with his son is also called like this, the first with the first. And the children of the brothers with each other are called the second with the second; and the sons of the sons of the brothers are called the third with the third. And it is established for us that a third with a first is [a] proper [witness], and, all the more so, a third with a second - and it is not necessary to say that a third with a third is proper. But a second with a second is disqualified - and it is not necessary to say that a second with a first is disqualified. And according to this, the father is disqualified with his son and with his son's son; but he is proper with the son of his son's son - as he is a third with a first. But there are a few commentators (Rashbam on Bava Batra 128a:18), the opinion of which is to say that that all those that come from the 'thigh' of a person are disqualified for him. And the brother with his sister are likewise called a first with a first, like with brothers. And in the same way that we count with males, the first generation and the second and the third, so [too] is it counted with the females (see Mishneh Torah, Testimony 13:6).

And so [too] is this matter with what they, may their memory be Blessed said (see Mishneh Torah, Testimony 13:6) that anyone who is disqualified with [a specific related] woman, is [also] disqualified with her husband, since the husband is like one body with his wife in this matter. And so too, we say that anyone who is disqualified to testify about the husband is likewise disqualified from testifying about his wife; as the husband is like his wife, and the wife is like her husband. And we say 'a husband is like his wife' once, but we do not say 'a husband is like his wife' twice [over]. For example (as a result), the son-in-law of his brother-in-law (the brother of his wife's sister) is proper to testify for him, as it is his brother-in-law who is disqualified to him because of his wife's sister - who is a sexual prohibition for him. But the son-in-law of his brother-in-law is not disqualified to him, because he is married to the daughter of the sister of his wife, who is disqualified to him - since 'a husband is like his wife' about this matter is not said twice [over]. But any time that both of the women are sexual prohibitions to him, we do say 'a husband is like his wife' twice [over]. For example, two men that are married to two sisters are disqualified from each other, as both of them [together] are sexual prohibitions for both of them; and so [too], the husband of his step-daughter, as both are sexually forbidden to him; as behold, they are 'a woman and her daughter,' and so [too] anything similar to this. This is what comes out of the gemara, according to what my teachers have taught me - God should guard them with the good explanations.

And they said about this matter in Ketuvot 28a that relatives are [accepted] to testify when he is an adult, about the writing of his father or his teacher or his brother that he saw when he was a minor. And the disqualification of being a relative is with the laws [involving] death penalties and with financial cases - whether the witnesses are relatives of the litigant or the guarantor or to each other or to the [judges of the] court or the court [is related] to the litigant or the court is related to each other. Regarding the matter of one who was a relative and became distant (no longer a relative), we hold that he is proper (Sanhedrin 28b); and even if there are sons there - as the law is not like Rabbi Yehudah, who holds that if there are sons there, he is disqualified.

Brothers on the mother's side [only,] can testify for one another (see Mishneh Torah, Testimony 13:12-14). As behold, there is no relation between them at all - except that the brother of this one is [also] the brother of that one, and that is not considered a relation. And a man and his wife are a first with a first. Therefore, a husband cannot testify for her son and not for the wife of her son, and not for her daughter and not for the husband of her daughter and not for the wife of her brother. And regarding this matter, when he is engaged to his wife, she herself is disqualified, but her relatives are not, until he marries her. And, as a general rule, our teachers, may God protect them, taught us concerning the matter of testimony that anyone who knows testimony for his fellow and was originally proper - meaning to say he was not disqualified to him - and became disqualified to him in between, and then returned to being proper - for example, that he became distant - is proper to testify for him. [This is the case] even though he became disqualified in between. But if he was disqualified originally - even though he became proper in the end - he is disqualified. And it is not necessary to say that one who was originally proper and became disqualified in the end is disqualified; as he is disqualified at the time of the testimony. And the rest of the details of this commandment are elucidated in the third chapter of Tractate Sanhedrin.

And this commandment is practiced, with regards to financial cases that are observed today, in every place and at all times by males, as it is upon them to receive testimony - since they are the ones that judge, and not females. And one who transgresses this, and accepts the testimony of a relative that is not fitting to testify and judges according to his testimony, has violated this negative commandment.

But we do not give lashes for it, since there is no act [involved] with it.

Mitzvah 590
To not sway the judgement of a stranger or an orphan: That the judge is prevented from hiding his eyes, to sway the judgement of a stranger or an orphan. And about this it states (Deuteronomy 24:17), "Do not sway the judgement of a stranger or an orphan, etc." I have written what is needed about the matter of swaying judgement above in the Order of Kedoshim (Sefer HaChinukh 233) and Mishpatim (Sefer HaChinukh 81), according to the way of this book - and take it from there.

And one who transgresses this, and sways the judgement of a stranger, violates two negative commandments - the one is that mentioned here and the second is "Do not do injustice in judgement" in the Order of Mishpatim (Leviticus 19:15). And if [the judged] was a stranger and an orphan, [the judge] violates three [commandments]; one because of [being a] stranger, one because of [being an] orphan - that are [both] mentioned here - and one because of "Do not do injustice in judgement." And there is no doubt that the main warning here is to the men, as they are the charge of justice. But, nonetheless, women are [also] included in this negative commandment (see Mishneh Torah, The Sanhedrin and the Penalties within their Jurisdiction 2).

Mitzvah 591
To not take the garment of a widow as surety: That we have been prevented from taking surety from a widow, as it states (Deuteronomy 24:17), "you shall not take a widow's garment in pawn." And the language of the mishnah is (Mishnah Bava Metzia 9:13) "From a widow, whether she be poor or she be rich, we do not extract surety."

It is from the roots of the commandment that God was concerned about his creatures and wanted to give us merit to acquire the trait of mercy for ourselves; and [so,] He commanded us that we should pity the widow - as her heart is broken and worried - and not take surety form her. And all the ways of the Torah 'are pleasantness, and all of its paths are peace.'

From the laws of this commandment is that which they, may their memory be Blessed, said (Bava Metzia 113a) that we not take surety form a widow - not by oneself, and not through the court (see Mishneh Torah, Creditor and Debtor 3:1). [This] is to say, in no way at all do we cause her pain to take surety from her, as it is stated, "you shall not take a widow's garment in pawn." And the rest of its details are elucidated in the ninth chapter of Bava Metzia.

And this prohibition is practiced in every place and at all times by males and females. And regarding one who transgresses it and takes in pawn her garments or her vessels or anything from all that she has - not during the time of the loan - we return it to her against his will (see Mishneh Torah, Creditor and Debtor 3:1). And if she admits the debt to him, the court forces her to pay him that which she owes him. And if she denies [it], she takes an oath and is exempted. And if the surety gets lost or burnt before he returns it, he is liable for lashes. So wrote Rambam, may his memory be Blessed; but certainly, the debtor accepts to pay the payment of his debt. And, if so, I wonder how it is [that he should] be lashed and [also] pay.

Mitzvah 592
To leave what is forgotten to the poor: That we were commanded when we forget a sheaf in the field to leave it there, and that we not return to take it when the thing becomes known to us. And about this is it stated (Deuteronomy 24:19), "and you forget a sheaf in the field [...]; it shall go to the stranger, the orphan, and the widow" - meaning to say, leave it there for them.

It is from the roots of the commandment [that it is] since the poor and destitute - in their sin and in their poverty - suspend their eyes upon the produce, in their seeing the owners of the field sheaving their sheaves 'according to the blessing of the Lord that He gave to them'; and they think in their heart, saying, "Who will give that it will be like this for me, to gather sheaves into my house - and if only I could bring one, I would rejoice in it"; and hence it was from His kindnesses towards His creatures, may He be Blessed, to fulfill this desire of theirs when it occurs that the owner of the field forgets it. There is also a benefit for the owner of the field, that he acquires through this a goodly soul; for truly through the trait of generosity and a Blessed soul that does not place its heart upon the forgotten sheaf and leaves it to the destitute - on those with such a soul - does the blessing of God descend forever.

And from the laws of the commandment is that, which they, may their memory be Blessed, said (Mishnah Peah 6:6 and see Mishneh Torah, Gifts to the Poor 5:18), "If a sheaf has [a volume of] two seah and he forgets it, it is not [considered] forgotten" - as it states, "and your forget a sheaf" - not a stack. And [also] that which they said (Mishnah Peah 5:7 and see Mishneh Torah, Gifts to the Poor 5:18), "A sheaf that is forgotten by workers and not forgotten by the property owner, or that is forgotten by the property owner and not forgotten by the workers," or that it is forgotten by both of them, but there were others there that did not forget it - it is not [considered] forgotten until it is forgotten by every person. And the rest of its details are elucidated in Tractate Peah (see Tur, Yoreh Deah 332).

And this commandment is practiced by males and females in the places that priestly tithes and tithes are practiced. And I have already written at length [about] the whole matter of priestly tithes and tithes and the places where they are practiced in the Order of Shoftim, concerning the commandment of separating the great tithe (Sefer HaChinukh 507). And one who transgresses this and returns to go back to take it has violated this positive commandment and shows about himself [that he has] an evil soul.

Mitzvah 593

To not go back to take what is forgotten: That we have been prevented from taking the sheave of what is forgotten, as it states (Deuteronomy 24:19), "and forget a sheaf in the field, do not turn back to get it" (See Sefer HaMitzvot LaRambam, Mitzvot Lo Taase 214). And the commandment of what is forgotten is also [applicable] with trees.

And this negative commandment is from the negative commandments that are rectified by a positive commandment - as anyone that transgresses and takes from what is forgotten is obligated to return it to the poor, as it states, "it shall go to the stranger, the orphan, and the widow." And I have written in this Order regarding the sending away of the nest (Sefer HaChinukh 544) [about] any negative commandment that is rectified by a positive commandment, [that if] he performs the positive commandment, he is not lashed. But if he does not perform the positive commandment and it is also impossible to perform it any longer - and for example, [if] the thing were lost or burnt - he is lashed. And the example of this is with the corner of the field, the reaping of which is a negative commandment (Sefer HaChinukh 217): And if he reaps it, he is not liable for lashes for the reaping; as behold, he is able to 'fix what he distorted' [by] giving it to the poor in its sheaves. And even if he threshed the wheat and ground and baked it, he can give the required amount of 'the corner' to the poor from the bread; and behold, it is still in his hand to fix [the sin] and [so,] he is not lashed. But if an accident happens that all of that wheat gets lost or it gets burnt, he is lashed; as behold, it is impossible for him to still perform the positive commandment in it. And [so,] he has already transgressed the negative commandment and he can not fix [it]. And this is called in the Gemara, 'he did not fulfill it.' And if he lost the wheat in his [own] hands or ate all of it, all the more so is he liable for lashes for it. And this is called, 'he negated it,' in the Talmud, as he was the cause for the negating of the negative commandment in his hands - a negation that no can longer be fixed. And [about] that which they said in Makkot 16a at the end of the chapter [entitled] Elu Hen HaLokin concerning the commandment of sending away the nest regarding 'he fulfilled it and he did not fulfill it,' "We only have this and one other [case]" - and it is known that the other is 'the corner' - as it is concluded there, "But rather 'this and one other' is about that," meaning to say, [about] 'the corner,' and the matter stays like that - their intention is not that it wants to say that only sending away the nest and 'the corner' have this law of 'he fulfilled it and he did not fulfill it.' But rather their intention was to say 'the corner' and all that have a similar law - such as fallen grapes, that which is forgotten, the fallen sheaves, and the bunchless grapes - as each one of these is a negative commandment that [involves] an act, and it is [just] as likely with them to have all that is likely with 'the corner,' regarding 'he fulfilled it and he did not fulfill it' or 'he negated it and he did not negate it.' As the verse from which we learned that in 'the corner' there is a positive commandment, is that which is written about it (Leviticus 19:10), "you shall leave them for the poor and the stranger." And with the sheaf of what is forgotten and the others mentioned, there is likewise about them, "you shall leave them for the stranger and the orphan and the widow," or "it shall go to the stranger, the orphan, and the widow." And take this matter and understand it, as it is a little hidden, in that the language in the Gemara is somewhat unclear - in that which they said, "We only have this and one other [case]."

I have written about the roots of the commandment and its content in the positive commandment of that which is forgotten in this Order (Sefer HaChinukh 592).

Mitzvah 594

The commandment to lash the evildoer: That the court was commanded to lash those transgressing some of the commandments of the Torah, and this is the matter of lashes mentioned in the Gemara - and like the matter that I have written in each and every commandment that has the liability for lashes with it, and as I will [likewise] write in that which I will write in the future, with God's help. And about this is it stated (Deuteronomy 25:2), "and the judge shall have him lie down and be given lashes in his presence, as his guilt warrants, etc."

It is from the roots of the commandment [that] since Israel are called the children of the Omnipresent, He, may He be Blessed, wanted to discipline them for their sins, so that they return to Him and, in the end, merit the world that is completely good - and like the matter that is written (Proverbs 19:18), "Discipline your son while there is still hope, and do not set your heart on his destruction." And based on this principle, they, may their memory be Blessed, said (Makkot 22b) that we estimate [the strength of] the one liable for lashes, such that he not die from the wound of the lashes. And they would lash him according to that which they appraised him that he can withstand from the flogging and not die. And even after they estimated him and started flogging him - if they saw they he is not able to withstand the estimate that they estimated about him, they leave him; as we say in the chapter [entitled] Elu Hen HaLokin in Tractate Makkot 22b, "[If] he is partially flogged and they saw that he is not fit to take that which they estimated about him, he is exempt."

From the laws of the commandment is that which they, may their memory be Blessed, said in the chapter mentioned (Mishnah Makkot 3:12-14), "How do they lash him? His two hands are bound on each side of the column and the administrator grabs his clothes. If they are torn, they are torn (so be it), and if they become unstitched, they become unstitched, until his heart (chest) is uncovered. And a stone is placed behind him and the administrator stands on it. And a strap of calfskin is in his hand, doubled over once into two [straps] and a second time into four [straps] and there are two [other] straps going up and down with it. The [strap's] handle is a hand-breadth [long] and [the strap] is a hand-breadth wide and its tip reaches to the mouth (beginning) of his stomach. And he lashes him one third [of the lashes] on his front and two thirds on his back [...] The reader would read, 'If you do not guard to do [...] And the Lord will increase your beatings, etc.' (Deuteronomy 28:58-59)." And the rest of its details are elucidated in the mentioned chapter of Tractate Makkot (see Mishneh Torah, The Sanhedrin and the Penalties within their Jurisdiction 6)

And this commandment is practiced in the Land of Israel, which has an ordained court. And they, may their memory be Blessed, said, in Tractate Sanhedrin 2a, "Flogging is with three," which is to say that a court [of] three ordained [judges] gives lashes. And it is not necessary for the matter of lashes to have a court of twenty-three. And a court that transgresses this and does not give lashes to one liable for lashes, violates this positive commandment. And [such a court's] punishment is very great, since it is through fear of judgement that religion is kept by the masses.

Mitzvah 595

To not increase in flogging him: That the judge has been prevented from flogging the sinner extensive floggings. And the elucidation of this matter is like this: That the limit of lashes for anyone who is liable for lashes is forty strikes minus one, as has come through the tradition (see Sefer HaMitzvot LaRambam, Mitzvot Lo Taase 300). And he should not flog anyone until he has appraised the flogging, that it should be according to the ability of the one struck, and his years and his constitution and the form of his body. And if he can withstand the flogging of the complete maximum punishment, he flogs [him accordingly]. And if he cannot withstand it, [the judge] flogs [him] according to his ability [to withstand it]. And there is never less than three strikes, and the fullness of the count of the number of strikes is always forty minus one, as we have said. And this prevention comes [that he not] increase striking him even one strike upon this number or upon that which the judge appraised that he can withstand. And about all of this is it stated (Deuteronomy 25:3), "you shall not increase." And so did they say in Sifrei, "If he increases, he transgresses a negative commandment. [From here] I only have if he increases on the forty. From where [do I know that it also applies] to each and every estimation that the court estimated about him? [Hence] we learn to say, 'You shall not increase, lest you increase.'"

And the Sages reduced one of the forty in the understanding of the negative commandment of 'do not increase.' So wrote Rambam, may his memory be Blessed, (Mishneh Torah, The Sanhedrin and the Penalties within their Jurisdiction 17:1), and it is a wonder [to say such a thing], according to [that which is written in] the Gemara. And this prohibition is a warning to hit anyone of Israel. And if we are warned about not striking the sinner, is it not all the more so with all other people? And the sages, may their memory be Blessed, prevented us from even hinting to strike. They said (Sanhedrin 58b), "Anyone who raises his hand against his fellow to hit him is called an evildoer, as it states (Exodus 2:13), 'and he said to the evildoer, "Why do you strike your fellow?"'"

The root of this commandment is revealed to all - as it is not right and it is not fitting to hit a creature, except according to his evil [in order] to discipline him at the behest of the court.

From the laws of the commandment is that which they, may their memory be Blessed, said (see Mishneh Torah, The Sanhedrin and the Penalties within their Jurisdiction 16:2) [that] when we estimate how many strikes the sinner can withstand, we only estimate with [a number] of strikes that is divisible by three. If they estimated about him that he could take twenty, we do not say to lash him twenty-one - since they are divisible by three - but rather we lash him eighteen. And [regarding] one who was estimated for lashes, and when they began to lash him, he broke down and defecated or urinated, we do not lash him any more, as it states (Deuteronomy 25:3), "and your brother be degraded before your eyes" - from when he is degraded, he is exempted. If the strap split before they finished lashing him - even after the first strike - he is exempted. [If] they tied him to the column and he took off the strings with his strength and ran away, he is exempt. Anyone who has sinned and is lashed goes back to being [considered] proper, as it states, "and your brother be degraded" - once he is degraded, he is your brother. And even [about] all those obligated in excision that received lashes, they, may their memory be Blessed, said (Makkot 23a) that [they are] exempted from their excisions. And the rest of the details of the commandment are explained in Tractate Makkot [in the third chapter].

And this prohibition is practiced concerning not hitting any Israelite in every place and at all times by males and females. But concerning the prohibition of not increasing the lashes, that matter is only practiced at the time of the settlement of the land [of Israel], when we had a court that was fit to give lashes. And one who transgresses this (see Mishneh Torah, The Sanhedrin and the Penalties within their Jurisdiction 16:12), and flogged an Israelite a great flogging, such that he is obligated for it the payment of a small coin (perutah) or more - is not liable for lashes, since it is a negative commandment that is given to repayment. And it is established for us [that] a person does not get lashed and [also] pay. But if he flogged an Israelite a small flogging, such that he is not obligated for it the value of a small coin (perutah) or more - he is liable for lashes. And I say that it is fitting to say that this law is a novelty that the Torah [presented].

Mitzvah 596

To not muzzle an animal at the time of its work: To not prevent an animal from eating that which it is working on, at the time of its work - for example, when it threshes grain or carries straw from place to place on its back - as we do not have permission to prevent it from eating from it. And about this is it stated (Deuteronomy 25:4), "You shall not muzzle an ox in its threshing."

It is from the roots of the commandment [that it is] to teach ourselves that our souls be a good soul that chooses what is right and clings to it and pursues kindness and mercy. And in our accustoming, it to this - even with animals that were only created to serve us, to be concerned for them to distribute to them a portion of the toil of their flesh - the soul will take for itself the way of this habit; to do good to people and to guard from taking access away from them for anything that is appropriate for them, and to repay their reward according to all the good that they do and to satiate them with that upon which they toiled. And it is fitting for the holy chosen nation to follow this way.

From the laws of the commandment is that which they, may their memory be Blessed, said (Bava Metzia 89a, see Mishneh Torah, Hiring 13:1-2) that the prohibition of muzzling is when the animal is involved with that which grows from the ground, whether it is attached or removed. And it is one whether it is an ox or it is any type of beast or animal, whether they are impure or pure - they are all included in this prohibition. And it is one whether it is threshing or it is [involved] in any type of work with that which grows from the ground. And "ox in its threshing" is only stated because it is common. And one who muzzles a worker is exempt. And it is one whether one muzzles [an animal] during the time of the work or before the work and it does the work afterwards - he is guilty for muzzling. And the law of threshing with the cow of a gentile (Bava Metzia 90a), and one who says to a gentile, "Muzzle my cow and thresh with it"; the law if what it is working with is bad for its intestines; the law of a cow that is walking on grain (Bava Metzia 89b); and the rest of its details are elucidated in the seventh chapter of Bava Metzia (see Tur, Choshen Mishpat 338).

And this prohibition is practiced in every place and at all times by males and females. And one who transgresses it and muzzles his cow and threshes with it is liable for lashes (Bava Metzia 90b). And even if he muzzled it with [his] voice, he is lashed - for example, [if] he prevents the cow from eating with the call of his rebukes. As the twisting of the lips in this is considered a major act, to give him lashes for it, as is apparent from Sanhedrin 65b. (And it is a wonder: what is different here from other places where we do not lash for a negative commandment that has no [true] act.) And one who rents an animal and muzzles it is lashed and repays the owners - four kav for a cow and three kav for a donkey.

Mitzvah 597

That a levirate wife not marry another until she is released: That every man of Israel is prevented from having intercourse with the levirate wife while she is still bound with the levirate husband. And about this was it stated (Deuteronomy 25:5), "the wife of the deceased shall not be married to a stranger, outside the family; the levirate husband shall have intercourse with her."

I will write what I have known about the roots of the commandment of levirate marriage in its positive commandment in this Order (Sefer HaChinukh 598). And there I will also write some of the laws of the commandment and its content, as is the custom of this book. And one who transgresses it and has intercourse with a levirate wife while she is bound to the levirate husband is liable for lashes. And the essence of this warning is upon men, but she is also included in the prohibition [such] that she should not go and get married to any man until she is released from the levirate husband. And it is possible that if she transgresses and has sexual relations while she is still bound to the levirate husband, that she is also [included] in the liability for lashes (see Tur, Even HaEzer 173).

Mitzvah 598

The commandment of levirate marriage: That one whose brother died and did not leave children was commanded to take the wife of his dead brother as a wife. And this is what is called yibum in the Torah and [in] the words of our rabbis, may their memory be Blessed. And about this was it stated (Deuteronomy 25:5), "the levirate husband shall have intercourse with her, etc."

It is from the roots of the commandment [that it is] since the woman that a man marries, behold, she is like one of his limbs - as so does nature necessitate because of the story of the first father, as one of his ribs was taken and from it did God build woman - and since this man died with no sons, that there should be a portion from him for his memory and to fill his place in the world in the service of his Creator. And also there is no memory of him in the physical world besides this woman, who is the bone of his bones and the flesh of his flesh. And [so] it was from the kindnesses of God to him to establish seed from her for him, through his brother - who is also like half of his flesh - in order that this seed take his place and serve his Creator in his stead, and so that he merit through him in the world of souls, where he is. As it is known that a son gives merit to the father; as so did they, may their memory be Blessed, say (Sanhedrin 104a), "A child gives merit to a father, a father does not give merit to a child." And truthfully likewise does the living brother that fathered the children from the levirate wife also get a share in them for himself, and he also gets merit in their merit. Nonetheless, not all of the merit will go to him; but rather his brother will take his portion because of the big portion that he has in them - and that is the wife that fell to his portion first, as we have said.

And according to that which we mentioned, when the verse states (Genesis 38:9), "But Onan, knowing that the seed would not be his," its sense [in terms] of the simple meaning is to say that not all of the merit of the seed would be his, as his brother would take a part in it; and he was not [interested] in partial merit. And also because maybe the main merit is to the dead brother, since he is like the owner of the field and the living brother is like a sharecropper - and like the well-known matter about sharecroppers, that there are some that provide their own seed. And this is what they, may their memory be Blessed, said (Yevamot 22b) that any time that his brother has any memory in the world - a son or a daughter or grandchildren from another woman, and even an illegitimate son (mamzer) or daughter - that they exempt his wife from levirate marriage; [such] that it appears from this that the matter is only to memorialize his name and to give him a portion and merit in this physical world (see Guide for the Perplexed 3:49). And behold, with my knowing that there is a major principle and a correct explanation about this commandment with the Kabbalists, I will rely upon what I wrote at the beginning of my book. And there I penned my apology, that I do not silence myself from writing my thoughts about the simple understanding of the explanations of the commandments, in order to stimulate the spirit of the children to ask questions about them to their elders and their teachers. By [their] dealing with them, perhaps, a merit will come through me in the revelation of the truth of their matters, and I will merit with them in my place.

From the laws of this commandment is that which they, may their memory be Blessed, said (Yevamot 13b and see Mishneh Torah, Levirate Marriage and Release 1:1) that the commandment of levirate marriage [applies] whether she was the wife of his brother from marriage or even from engagement (erusin). And [also] that which they said (Yevamot 17b and see Mishneh Torah, Levirate Marriage and Release 1:7) that regarding the matter of levirate marriage and release and inheritance, only brothers [born of] the father are considered brothers; even though regarding the issue of mourning and the issue of testimony, even brothers [born of] the mother are called brothers. And [also] that which they said (Yevamot 43b and see Mishneh Torah, Levirate Marriage and Release 9:12) that [if] one has many wives and dies but does not leave a child from any of them, one of the brothers has levirate marriage with, or releases, one of [the wives] and they all become permissible [to marry]. And he is not able to have levirate marriage with two - not he and not one of his brothers; as it states, "who will not build up his brother's house" - and the [traditional] explanation that comes about this is (Yevamot 44a) "One house shall he build" - meaning to say, [it is only for] one brother, and he does not build two houses. And also, if he does this, he transgresses the positive commandment, as it states, "he shall have intercourse with her" - and the Sages, may their memory be Blessed, expounded, "And not with her and with her rival wife."

And from the outset, the commandment to perform the levirate marriage is upon the eldest (Yevamot 24a and see Mishneh Torah, Levirate Marriage and Release 2:6). And, so too, they can only release one [wife]; and once she is released, she and all of her rival wives become forbidden to the releaser and to all of the other brothers, by the words of the scribes (rabbinically) - like secondary relations. But there are certainly no Torah prohibitions on them - once his brother died without children, the prohibition on his wives departed. Hence, betrothal is effective, as it is with secondary relations. And [in the case of] one who releases his levirate wife, just like she is forbidden to him, so too are her relatives forbidden to him - and we have mentioned the relatives [concerned] in the Order of Achrei Mot. And, likewise, she is forbidden to his son and to his brother. The general principle of the matter is that, behold, she is like his wife that he divorced. And, so, if the levirate wife died before the levirate marriage [or] release; behold, her law regarding her relatives is that she is like his wife that died [in his lifetime]. And all of these prohibitions are rabbinic.

Sefer HaChinukh

And that which they, may their memory be Blessed, said (Yevamot 41a) that the levirate wife should not perform levirate marriage and not be released until she waits ninety days - excluding the day of death and the day of the levirate marriage, or the day of the release - was in order to distinguish between the seed of the two brothers. And [about] that which they said that she should not be released during this time, they learned that thing from an inference in the Gemara (Yevamot 41b). And they, may their memory be Blessed, said about this matter (Yevamot 35b) that if the first brother leaves his wife pregnant and she has a miscarriage after he dies, behold, she must perform levirate marriage or be released. But if she gave birth and the newborn came out alive, she is exempt from the levirate marriage and from the release. And even if the newborn died immediately [is she exempted] by the law of the Torah. But the Sages said not to exempt her until it becomes definitively known that the newborn completed its months [of gestation]; but if it is not known, she should be released and not perform levirate marriage.

And so did they, may their memory be Blessed, say about this matter (Yevamot 53b and see Mishneh Torah, Levirate Marriage and Release 2:3-4) that one who has intercourse with his levirate wife - whether it is accidental or premeditated, whether it is under duress or volitional, whether he was premeditated and she was accidental or under duress or she was premeditated and he was accidental or under duress, whether she was awake or asleep, whether he had sexual relations with her according to her [customary] way or even not according to her way, and it is the same whether he [only began] or finished intercourse - behold, he had levirate marriage and acquired her [in marriage]. And to what do these words apply? When he had the intention of having intercourse. But if he did not have the intention of having intercourse, he did not acquire [her in marriage]. And from the words of the scribes (Yevamot 52a) is it that the levirate husband should not have intercourse with his levirate wife until he has betrothed her in front of witnesses - and this is what is called, 'maamar' in the Gemara. And this 'maamar' does not [constitute] a complete acquisition regarding a levirate wife; as the Torah stated, "the levirate husband shall have intercourse with her" - behold, that the matter of levirate marriage depends on intercourse.

And they, may their memory be Blessed, also said (Yevamot 79b and see Mishneh Torah, Levirate Marriage and Release 6:8) about this matter that there are women that are exempt from levirate marriage and also from release. And these are them: the wife of a eunuch of the sun (caused by nature) or of an andrigonos; the wife of someone mentally incapacitated; the wife of a minor; a sterile woman; and one who is sexually forbidden to the levirate husband. As it is stated, "that his name may not be blotted out in Israel" - to exclude a eunuch of the sun and an andrigonos, the names of which are [already] blotted out; since they are not capable of having children from the beginning of their creation, they are like their own species. And it states, "The first son that she bears shall be" - to exclude a sterile woman, who is not capable of having children from the beginning of her creation. "The wife of the deceased shall not be married to a stranger, outside the family" - to exclude the wife of someone mentally incapacitated or a minor, that do not have marriage at all. "He shall take her as his wife" - to exclude one who is sexually forbidden to the levirate husband, that do not have taking (marriage) for him to them. And the sages counted (Mishnah Yevamot 1:1) fifteen women that do not have taking, that exempt their rival wives from release and from levirate marriage. And they said also (see Mishneh Torah, Levirate Marriage and Release 6:6-7) that there are some women that perform levirate marriage but do not get released, and there are some that get released but do not perform levirate marriage. And there are some that do not perform levirate marriage and do not get released. And there are from the brothers also those that are fit for levirate marriage and release, and some who are not fit for levirate marriage nor for release - and they have no connection [to the woman] at all - and there are some that are fit for release but they are not fit for levirate marriage, and there are some that are fit for levirate marriage but not for release. And the rest of the many details about these matters are all complete in the tractate connected to it and that is Tractate Yevamot.

And this commandment is practiced in every place at all times by males. And one who transgresses it and does not do levirate marriage with his levirate wife - meaning to say that he does not have intercourse with her one time, which is the essence of this positive commandment - or does not exempt her with release, has violated this positive commandment.

Sefer HaChinukh

Mitzvah 599

The commandment of release (chalitsah): That we have been commanded (see Sefer HaMitzvot LaRambam, Mitzvot Ase 217) that the levirate wife removes the shoe of the levirate husband from upon his foot when he does not want to marry her as a wife. And about this is it stated (Deuteronomy 25:9), "and she removes the shoe from upon his foot."

It is from the roots of the commandment [that it is] since this woman is fitting to serve this man instead of his brother from the reason that we gave above regrading the commandment of levirate marriage and [yet] he does not want her. [Hence] the Torah commanded that she perform this act of service of removing the shoe for him - which is the service of a slave acquired publicly in front of the court - to show to all that she was completely acquired to him, and that it would have been fitting for him to perform levirate marriage with her for the reason mentioned in the previous commandment. And because he does not want to do what is incumbent upon him - to establish a name for his brother - she goes out from under his hand and spits in front of him; to make known that she is completely separated from him and not subjugated to him any longer, [such] that she should give him honor in any matter. Rather, he is considered like a stranger that is not concerned about spitting in front of him. And from now on, she goes and can marry anyone she wants.

From the laws of the commandment is that which they, may their memory Blessed, said (Yevamot 17b), "'When brothers dwell together' - to exclude the wife of a brother who was not in his world"; meaning that [then] she does not have an obligation of levirate marriage and not of release - for example, [if] this brother was born after his brother [that was married and had no children] died. And that which they also inferred (Yevamot 17b), "'Brothers together' - that are together in inheritance, to exclude brothers [born only] from the mother," who are not obligated in levirate marriage and release. "'And has no (ein) son' - look into (ayen) him" (Yevamot 22b). [This is] meaning to say that if the brother did have a son or daughter from any place, or the son of a son or the son of a daughter or the daughter of a daughter or any one that came out from his 'thigh' - there is no commandment of levirate marriage or release there, for the reason that we mentioned concerning the commandment of levirate marriage.

And this is the order of the release (chalitsah) as we have learned it from our Rabbis, may their memory be Blessed, in the Gemara (Chapter 12 of Yevamot - Mitzvat Chalitsah) - and so is it practiced today: Three men are chosen that know how to read what they are obligated to read to the levirate husband and the levirate wife - and they are called judges. And they add to them [two] others with them, so that there be five to publicize the matter - or [even] up to ten (Yevamot 101b); and such is the practice of the people. And the five judges are careful (Yevamot 104a) that they not be related to each other or to the levirate husband or the levirate wife. And [then] they say to each other, "Let us go to place x, and set a place for the release of y" - since so did Rava say (Yevamot 101b), "The judges have to set a place." And they [all] go there and the judges sit and the levirate husband and the levirate wife stand - as if in judgement, wherein the judges are sitting and the litigants are standing. And there is no impediment in this - such that if they did it [with the levirate husband and the levirate wife] sitting, the release is not disqualified by this. And afterwards, the judges ask the levirate husband if he is thirteen years and a day old and has produced two [pubic] hairs, and they also find out clearly that the woman being released is the wife of the dead brother of this releaser - as Rava said (Yevamot 106a), "We do not release if we do not recognize." And when they know all of this with certainty and the matter is clear to them, they also ask the woman if she ate that day. And if she ate, we do not release on that day, [as] we are concerned lest she ate things that bring her to spitting; and we need the spitting to be from her - as Rava said (Yevamot 106b), "[If] she ate garlic and spit, [or] if she ate a clod of dirt and spit, it is nothing; 'and she spits' - we need it to be from her and [this] is not." Nonetheless, this thing does not impede [it], and if they released her in this way, their release is fit, ex post facto - as behold, the spitting being from her does not impede [it].

And afterwards, if the court sees that the levirate husband and the levirate wife are [legally] fit for one another, they start with the levirate husband (Yevamot 106b) and say to him, "If it is pleasing to you to perform levirate marriage, perform [it] - and, if not, release [her]." And if he wants to release her, he takes a hard sandal that is all leather, or a soft sandal, since all of the people have already become accustomed to it (Yevamot 102a). And he should be careful that it all be stitched with leather (Yevamot 102b), and that it not be exceedingly large, but rather medium - so that he can walk with it - and also not too small, but rather it should at least cover the majority of his foot. And, from the outset, he should release [her] with his shoe and it [should be] the right shoe; however, ex post facto, this does not impede [it]. And there should be two straps of leather or of hair sewn into the shoe (Yevamot 107b), and they should be big enough to wrap it around his foot. And he should put the shoe on his right foot; and he [should be otherwise] barefoot and not with stockings, so that it not 'upon that which is "upon."' And if he released [her] with the left foot, his release is disqualified (Yevamot 104a). And he should be careful that the shoe not be so tall that it goes over his knee - as this is also 'upon that which is "upon."' But [if it is] below the knee, it is certainly not 'upon that which is "upon."' And afterwards, he ties the straps around his foot, and he ties two knots. And the levirate husband stands next to the wall or next to a post and presses his foot onto the ground - as Amimar says, "That one that releases needs to press his foot" (Yevamot 103a).

And afterwards (Yevamot 106b), the court has the levirate wife recite in the holy tongue [the relevant passage] from, "My levirate husband refuses" until "he does not want to perform levirate marriage with me." And she should be careful not to pause between "does not" [and] "want," but rather read these two words at one time without a pause, so that it does not sound like "want[s] to perform levirate marriage with me." And they have the levirate husband recite, "I do not want to marry her."

And afterwards, the levirate wife comes next to the levirate husband and she approaches him and unties the straps without any assistance from the levirate husband at all. And [then] she removes the shoe from his foot - and also in this, the levirate husband does not assist at all. Rather, he stands next to the wall and presses his foot properly onto the ground. And it is all [done] standing, as we have said. And according to our Gemara (Bavli Yevamot 102a), she removes [the shoe] with either her left hand or her right hand - as we do not find an exactitude about this in the Gemara. But in Yerushalmi Yevamot 12:1, they said that she needs to remove [it] with the right hand. Hence, the [woman] should concern herself [about this] and, from the outset, remove [it] with the right. And if she has no hands, she should remove it with her teeth, [even] from the outset, and as it is explained in the Gemara (Yevamot 105a).

And afterwards "and she spits in his face" - spit that the judges can see - as Rava says (Yevamot 106b), "The judges need to see the spit that came out of the mouth of the levirate wife." And "we need [...] that the spit reaches in front of the face of the levirate husband," as we say in the Gemara. [It is] such that if he is tall and she is a midget and the wind caught it [upwards], we call this "in his face"; but if she is tall and he is a midget and the wind caught it [upwards], it does not help at all - as we need that it 'reaches in front of the face.' However, after it 'reaches in front of his face,' if the wind caught it, we have no [concern about] it.

And afterwards, the court has her recite in the holy tongue from, "Thus shall be done to the man" until "the unshoed one." And afterwards, all who are standing there answer, "The unshoed one, the unshoed one," three times. As it is taught (Yevamot 106b), "Rabbi Yehudah said, 'One time we were sitting in front of Rabbi Tarfon, and a levirate wife came to remove [the shoe]. He said to us, "All of you answer, 'The unshoed one,' three times in the holy tongue."'" And they said in the Gemara (Yevamot 106b), "Rav Yehudah said that Rav said, 'The commandment of release is [that] she reads and he reads, she removes and spits and reads.' What [novelty] do we infer - it is [already in] our mishnah? We infer that [this is only] a mitzvah (an ideal fulfillment of the commandment), and if [the order] is reversed, we have no [concern about] it." And so is the law.

And after she removes [the shoe] in court as is fitting, the court writes her a contract of release, so that she can get married to [anyone in] the marketplace with it. And Rabbi Alfasi, may his memory be Blessed, wrote in his Laws (Rif Yevamot 35b in his pagination) and this is his language: "And so the writing of the release contract has to be lined with lines and not [written] with [inferior] ink, and he needs to write, 'In the place of the sitting of three as one,' and the three sign it, and [that is] only if they know how to read it to others."

And this is the contract of release: On **x** day that is this number in the month **x**, which is this number

[year] from the creation of the world, according to the number that is accustomed in the place x, we the judges, some of which are signed below, are in the sitting of three as one in the court. And x the daughter of y came down in front of us, the widow of z, and she brought close in front of us a man, whose name was **b** the son of **c**. And so did she say to us, 'This **b**, the son of **c**, the brother - [born] from the father - of z the son of c, who married me and died and left our rabbis and all of Israel alive, but he did not leave a son or daughter that would inherit and would be related and bring out his name in Israel. And this b, his brother, is fitting to perform levirate marriage with me. And now, our rabbis, my judges, say to him, "If you want to perform levirate marriage with me, perform [it]." And, if not, let him extend his right foot in front of you, and I will untie the shoe from upon his foot and spit in his face.' And we have ascertained it, that this b is the brother of z, [born] from the father, and we said to him, 'If you want to perform levirate marriage with her, perform [it] - and, if not, extend your right foot to her in front of me, and she will untie your shoe from upon your foot and spit in your face.' And he answered and said, 'I do not want to perform levirate marriage with her.' Immediately, I had this x recite, 'My levirate husband refuses to establish a name in Israel for his brother; he does not want to perform levirate marriage with me.' And also [with] this b, I had him recite, 'I do not want to marry her.' And he extended his right foot and she untied his shoe from upon his foot and spat in his face - spit that was visible to us from her mouth to the ground. And again, I made this x recite, 'Thus shall be done to the man who will not build up his brother's house!' And again, I had her recite, 'And he shall go in Israel by the name of the family of the unshoed one.' And we, the judges, and all who were sitting there, answered after her, 'the unshoed one,' three times. And once this event happened in front of us, we have permitted this x to go and marry any man she wants, and no one should protest against her [for that], from this day and forever. And this x requested this contract of release, and I have written it and signed it and given it to her to own, like the law of Moshe and Israel. And three [judges] sign on it."

And the rest of the details of this commandment are elucidated in the tractate connected to the laws of levirate marriage and release, and that is Tractate Yevamot. And for this, is it called Yevamot (levirate marriages) and not Chalitsot (releases) - because they, may their memory be Blessed, said (Yevamot 39b), "The commandment of levirate marriage precedes the commandment of release."

And it is practiced in every place and at all times by males. And one who transgresses this and does not want to perform levirate marriage with his levirate wife nor to release her, because of the evil of his heart, has violated this positive commandment.

Mitzvah 600

The commandment to save the pursued with the life of the pursuer: That we were commanded to save the pursued from one who is pursuing him to kill him, and even [at the expense of] the life of the pursuer - meaning to say, that we are commanded to kill the pursuer if we are not able to save the pursued unless we kill the pursuer. And about this is it stated (Deuteronomy 25:12), "You shall cut off her hand; show no pity." And they said in Sifrei (see Sefer HaMitzvot LaRambam, Mitzvot Ase 247), "'And she seizes him by his genitals' - and just like that place is distinguished by a danger to life (sakanat nefashot) and it says about it, 'You shall cut off her hand'; so too anything that has a danger to life, behold it is [included] in 'You shall cut off her hand.' And from where [do I know] that if he cannot save him with only her hand, that he is obligated to save him with her life? [Hence,] it teaches us to say, 'show no pity.'" And that which the verse stated "the wife of one," [is because] the verse was speaking according to what is common; as the wife of a person is always with him and tries to save him from his attacker with all of her strength; but it is the same with any person.

It is from the roots of the commandment [that it is] since God, may He be Blessed, created His world and wants its settlement; and the settlement of the world is established by the delivery of the weak from the hand of the one stronger than he. And also, because the eyes and heart of the pursued are always to God to deliver him from the hand of his pursuer. And [it is] like the matter that is written (Ecclesiastes 3:15), "and God seeks the pursued" - meaning to say that the pursued seeks God and pleads with Him. Therefore, Blessed be He, commanded us to help him.

From the laws of the commandment is that which they, may their memory be Blessed, said (Sanhedrin

Sefer HaChinukh

72b and see Mishneh Torah, Murderer and the Preservation of Life 1:6-7) that even if the pursuer is small and the pursued is bigger than him in every regard, everyone is obligated to save [the pursued], and even [at the expense of] the life of the pursuer. And to what do these words apply - that we save with the life of the pursuer? When it is impossible for us to save [the pursued] with one of the limbs of [the pursuer]; but if it is possible to save him with one of the limbs and he saved him with his life - this is spilling of blood (murder). And so did our Rabbis, may their memory be Blessed, say (Sanhedrin 49a) about the death of Avner when Yoav killed him: As it is written there (II Samuel 3:27), "and he died for shedding the blood of Asahel, his brother." And the tradition came about this that Yoav had a claim against Avner for the blood of Asahel, and judged him in a case of the Sanhedrin (High Court) - which means to say that he killed him for a claim for which it would have been fitting to [receive] death according to the Sanhedrin: He said to him, "Why did you kill Asahel?" Avner said [back] to him, "He was a pursuer." Yoav said to him, "You should have saved yourself with one of his limbs." Avner said to him, "I did not know how to aim at him [in that way]." Yoav said to him, "You aimed onto his fifth rib! And you did not know how to aim at him?" And about this is it stated, "he died for shedding the blood of Asahel, his brother."

And they, may their memory be Blessed, said (Sanhedrin 72b and see Mishneh Torah, Murderer and the Preservation of Life 1:7) regarding the matter of a pursuer, that - even if he did not [formally acknowledge] the warning - since they warned him and he continues to pursue, [it is as if] he has no blood, and it is permissible to kill him.

And based on the reason of a pursuer, they, may their memory be Blessed, instructed (see Mishneh Torah, Murderer and the Preservation of Life 1:9) in [the case of] a woman who is having difficulty giving birth, to cut up the fetus in her innards - whether with a drug or whether by hand - because it is like a pursuer behind her to kill her. And if it stuck out its head, we can not touch him; as we do no push off one life for [another] life, and this is the way of the world.

And it is one, whether it is one who pursues behind his fellow to kill him, or after one of all of the sexual prohibitions which [involve] excision to those that have sexual relations - we save them with the lives of their pursuers. And the same is true of one pursuing behind [another] male to have sexual relations with him. But [in the case of] one pursuing behind an animal - and so [too, with] one running to do one of all of the other sins in the Torah, even to worship idolatry - we do not kill him until he does the sin, as we judge him in a court. [That is] since the tradition only came about these two sins alone that we save with the life of the pursuer. But with all the other sins in the Torah, we bring him to court and they judge him. And the rest of the details of the commandment are elucidated in the eighth chapter of Tractate Sanhedrin.

And [it] is practiced in every place and at all times by males and females. And one who transgresses it and is able to save the pursued and does not save him with one of the limbs of the pursuer - or even with his life - has violated this positive commandment, besides having violated two negative commandments, which are "show no pity" and "do not stand by the blood of your neighbor" (Leviticus 19, 16); as we will write in the negative commandments (Sefer HaChinukh 601). And his punishment is very great - as if he destroyed a life from Israel.

Mitzvah 601

To not have concern about the pursuer: That we have been prevented from having compassion for the life of the pursuer. And the elucidation of this commandment is like I have written in its positive commandment in this Order (Sefer HaChinukh 600): That the tradition came to us about two sins - which are murder and sexual prohibitions - that if we see him pursuing to do one of them, we must always prevent him with all of our strength. And if he does not want to desist with words from doing the sin, and we are able to save from his hand the man or woman pursued, with one of his limbs, we must chop it off. And if it is impossible for us to save the pursued if we do not kill the pursuer, we must kill him. And about this comes the prevention to us, that we should not have compassion upon him; but rather we should kill him nonetheless - if it is impossible for us to save the pursued in any other way than by [taking] his life. And about this is it stated (Deuteronomy 25:12), "You shall cut off her hand; show no pity." And the language of Sifrei is "'You shall cut off her hand' teaches that you are obligated to save him with her hand. And from where [do I know even] with his life? [Hence,] it teaches us to say, 'show no pity.'"

And the roots of the commandment and its content is elucidated - as is the custom of the book - in its positive commandment (Sefer HaChinukh 600) in this Order.

Mitzvah 602
To not hold over deficient weights and measures: That we have been prevented, that we not hold over the deficient weights and scales in our homes - and even if we don't take and give (measure) with them in our purchases and in our sales, lest it be a snare. And about this is it stated (Deuteronomy 25:13), "You shall not have in your pouch alternate weights, larger and smaller." And so [too] (Deuteronomy 25:14), "You shall not have in your house alternate measures." And so did they, may their memory be Blessed, say in Bava Batra 89b, "It is forbidden for a person to hold over a deficient or oversized weight in the midst of his home, and even if it is [used as a] bedpan for urine."

And Rambam wrote (Sefer Hamitzvot LaRambam, Mitzvot Lo Taase 272), "And do not think that they are two [distinct] commandments since they are two negative statements [in the Torah]. Indeed, [the two statements] have come to complete the laws of the commandment, such that two types of size are included - and they are the weight and the measure. [It is] as if it stated, 'You should not have two sizes, not in measurement and not in weight.' [It is] like 'You shall not take interest from loans to your brother, whether in money or food or anything else that can be taken as interest' (Deuteronomy 23:20) - which is all one negative commandment. As it is not by the duplication of expressions that [the number of] commandments increase, when it is all one matter. And so [too with] 'no leavened bread shall be found with you, and no leaven shall be found' (Exodus 13:7), which is [all] one negative commandment, since it is [all] one matter. Rather, [the two expressions] are stated to complete the elucidation of the matter." I have written about the roots of this commandment - as is my custom in this book - in the Order of Kedoshim Tehiyu (Sefer HaChinukh 259) regarding the commandment of just scales and the warning (Sefer HaChinukh 258) not to lie with [the scales]. And from there you can see what you need about this [commandment].

And it is practiced in every place and at all times by males and females. And one who transgresses it and holds over a deficient weight or a deficient scale in the midst of his home - and even if he does not ever weigh with them - has violated this negative commandment. And there are no lashes for it, as there is no act [involved] with it; and also, even if he transgressed it and weighed with them, it is given to repayment. And it is already known that we only give lashes for a negative commandment that is not given to repayment.

Mitzvah 603
To remember what Amalek did to us: That we were commanded to remember what Amalek did to Israel - that he began to harass them when they left Egypt, before any other nation or kingdom raised their hand against them; and as the matter is stated, (Numbers 24:2) "Amalek is the first of nations." Its [Aramaic] translation (Onkelos Numbers 24:2) is "The first battle of Israel was Amalek" - because everyone was afraid of them when they heard of God's great hand that He used for them in Egypt. But the Amalekites, due to their evil hearts and evil disposition, did not turn their hearts to all of this, and harassed them [by waging war]. And as a result of this, Amalek was able to remove the great fear from the hearts of the other nations. And it is like the matter that our Rabbis, may their memory be Blessed, analogized it (Pesikta Rabbati 12, Midrash Tanchuma on Devarim 25:17) to the analogy to a large boiling pot that no person could enter and [then] one [individual] comes and jumps and enters it. Even though he is burnt, he cools it for others. And about the memory of their matter is it stated (Deuteronomy 25:17), "Remember what Amalek did to you on your journey, after you left Egypt."

It is from the roots of this commandment [that it is] to put into our hearts that anyone who distresses Israel is despised in front of God, Blessed be He; and that according to his evil and his great deceptive damage, will be his downfall and bad [occurrences], as you find with Amalek: That due to [the fact that] he committed a great evil to Israel - that he began to harm them - Blessed be He, commanded us to 'destroy his memory from the earth' and root it out after him, until its end (see Sefer HaMitzvot

Sefer HaChinukh

LaRambam, Mitzvot Ase 189).

From the laws of the commandment is that which our Rabbis, may their memory be Blessed, said (Megillah 18a) that the obligation of this remembrance is with the heart and with the mouth (see Sefer HaChinukh 330). As so is it in Sifrei, Parshat Bechukotai (at the beginning), "'Remember what Amalek did' - could it be with the heart? When it says 'do not forget' - behold, [this refers to] the forgetting of the heart. Behold, what is [the purpose of] 'Remember?' That it should be recited in your mouth." To here is [what is written] in Sifrei. [It is] in order to not forget the thing, lest the enmity be weakened and be removed from the hearts over the length of time.

We do not know an established time in the year or the day for this remembrance with the heart and the mouth, such as we are commanded to remember the exodus from Egypt every day and every night. And the reason [for the latter] is that that remembrance is a fundamental principle of religion, and as we have spoken about this in detail in many other places in this book. But the reason for remembering what Amalek did, is only that the hatred in our hearts not be forgotten. And for this, it is enough to remember the matter once a year, or in two years, or in three years. And behold, in all the places of Israel, they read the Book of the Torah over a year, or two or three - at the very least. And behold, they fulfill this commandment with that. And perhaps we should say that the custom of Israel to read Parashat Zachor on a specific Shabbat each and every year is [as a law from the] Torah. And it is due to this commandment that they fixed it like that. And it is always the Shabbat before Purim. And the law should be to read it on Purim day, because it is from the matter of the day, since Haman the wicked was from the seed [of Amalek]; but in order to make known that before the miracle [of Purim], we were commanded in this remembrance, they fixed the [reading] before Purim. However they made it adjacent to Purim, in the way that they, may their memory be Blessed, say (Berakhot 21b) in [certain] places, "they placed the matter adjacent to it."

This commandment is practiced in every place and at all times by males, because it is upon them to wage war to avenge the enemies - and not upon women. And one who transgresses this and did not remember and recite with his mouth what Amalek did to Israel ever has violated this positive commandment, and also violated the negative commandment that comes upon this - which is "do not forget," as we will write in the negative commandments (Sefer HaChinukh 604) with God's help.

Mitzvah 604

To blot out his seed from the world: That we were commanded to blot out the seed of Amalek and to destroy his memory from the world - male and female, old and young. And about this is it stated (Deuteronomy 25:19), "you shall blot out the memory (zekher) of Amalek" - as all are included in "the memory." And a great man of the generation (gadol hador) already erred in the vocalization of this word - and that was Yoav ben Tzeruiah - and he left over the females from them. As many were those that did not pay careful attention when they learned this verse and Yoav jumbled [it] and read "male" (zakhar) instead of "memory" (zekher), as it comes [down] in Bava Batra 21b in the chapter [entitled] Lo Yachpor.

The matter that we wrote in the commandment that precedes it is from the roots of the commandment. The laws of the commandment are short and they are elucidated in the eighth chapter of Sotah.

And this is from the commandments that are incumbent upon the entire community; and like the matter that they, may their memory be Blessed, said (Sanhedrin 20b), "Three commandments were commanded to Israel at the time of their entrance to the land: to appoint themselves a king; to build themselves the Choice House (the Temple); and to cut off the seed of Amalek." And in truth is it that the obligation to kill them and destroy them from the world is also incumbent upon every male individual from Israel - if they have the power in their hands - in every place and at all times, if he finds one from all of their seed. And one who transgresses this and one from the seed of Amalek [chances upon] him - and he has the wherewithal in his hand to kill him - and he does not kill him, he has violated this positive commandment.

Mitzvah 605

To not forget what he did to us: That we have been prevented from forgetting that which Amalek did with us - meaning to say, his starting to harm us [before anyone else]. And about this is it stated (Deuteronomy 25:19), "do not forget." And is written in Sifrei [that] "Remember" is with the mouth [and] "do not forget" is with the heart - meaning to say do not cast down hatred of him and do not remove it from you soul, in the manner that you will forget it.

From the roots of this commandment and all of its content is written in its positive commandment in this Order (Sefer HaChinukh 603) - and take if from there and quench your thirst.

Mitzvah 606

The commandment of recital over the first-fruits: That we were commanded when bringing the first-fruits to the Temple to recite these verses in this section over them; and they are from, "My father was a wandering Aramean" (Deuteronomy 26:5), until "behold I have brought the first of the fruit of the land that the Lord gave me" (Deuteronomy 26:10). And about this is it stated (Deuteronomy 26:5), "And you will answer and you will say in front of the Lord, your God, etc." And they, may their memory be Blessed, called this commandment, (Sotah 32a), "the recital of the first-fruits." I have written about the commandment of bringing them in the Order of Mishpatim (Sefer HaChinukh 91); and the commandment to bring them is likewise repeated in this section. And we already known that many of the commandments are repeated in the Torah; and all of them are for a great matter or necessity.

It is from the root of the commandment [that it is] since a man arouses his thoughts and draws the truth in his heart with the power of the words of his mouth. Therefore, in that God did good to him, and in that He Blessed him and his land to bear fruits, and he merited to bring the fruits to the House of our God; it is appropriate for him to arouse his heart with the words of his mouth and ponder that everything arrived to him from the Master of the universe, and he recount His kindnesses, may He be Blessed, upon us and upon the people of Israel, more generally. Therefore, he begins with the subject of Yaakov, our father, whom God rescued from the hand of Lavan, and the subject of the slavery of the Egyptians over us and His, Blessed be He, rescuing us from their hand. And following the praise, he requests from Him to eternally bestow the blessing on him. And from the arousal of his soul with the praise of God and His goodness, he will merit that his land be Blessed. Therefore, God commanded us about this, since He desires kindness.

From the laws of the commandment is that which they, may their memory be Blessed, said (Mishnah Bikkurim 1:5) that the obligation of the commandment of the recital of the first-fruits is not upon all that bring first-fruits to the Temple, as there are those that bring [them] but do not recite. And these are them: a woman; a tumtum; and an androginos (the latter two being those the sex of which is in doubt) - since these are not able to say, from "the land that the Lord gave me," as the land was only distributed to definite males. And so [too,] trustees do not recite, as they bring first-fruits for the sake of others. And so [too,] the slave and the agent do not recite, as they also cannot say, You "gave me" - as the land is not theirs.

And from this matter we should learn to be very exacting, and to be careful about the language in our prayers and supplications in front of God, Blessed be He - not to say anything in front of God without great precision. And remember this, my son, and keep it.

And they, may their memory be Blessed, also said (Mishnah Bikkurim 1:4) about this matter that converts bring them and recite, even though the land was not distributed to them. As it was given to Avraham first, and he was called "the father of many nations" (Genesis 17:4) - meaning to say that anyone who converts is considered like his son.

And they, may their memory be Blessed, said (Mishnah Bikkurim 1:6) that one who acquires two trees within his fellow's field brings [them] but does not recite, as they were in doubt in the Gemara (Bava Kamma 81b) whether one who acquires two trees [receives] the land or not. But one who acquires three [trees] brings and recites. [These] and the rest of the details of the commandment are elucidated in Tractate Bikkurim and in the seventh chapter of Sotah.

And this commandment is practiced at the time that the Temple is in existence, but only in the Land of Israel - as it is stated (Exodus 23:19), "The first fruits of your land you shall bring to the House of the Lord, your God" - by males, but not by females, as we have said. And rabbinically, they would bring first-fruits at the time of the [Temple] from the cities of Sichon and Og and from Syria. And one who transgresses this and brings first-fruits, but does not recite over them at that time, has violated this positive commandment.

Mitzvah 607
The commandment of declaration of tithes: That we have been commanded to declare before God, Blessed be He, and to state with our mouths in His Temple, that we took out the legally-required tithes and priestly tithes from our grain and from our fruits, and that none of them is remaining in our possession that we have not given. And this is called the commandment of the declaration of tithes. And about this is it stated (Deuteronomy 26:13), "And you shall say before the Lord, your God, 'I have disposed of the holy from the house, etc.'"

It is from the root of the commandment [that it is] since the uniqueness of man and his great praise is his speech, such that with it, he exceeds all the types of creatures. As were it from the angle of the other movements, other animals also move like him. And hence there are many people that are more afraid to disqualify their speech - in that it is their great splendor - than sinning in deed. And in that the matter of tithes and priestly tithes is a big thing - and also because the sustenance of the servants of God is dependent upon them - it was from His kindnesses upon us so that we do not sin with them, to warn us about them to separate them and that we not touch and benefit from them in deed; and also that we testify about ourselves with our mouths in the Holy house that we did not lie about them and we did not withhold anything of them. And so much [is required], so that we be very careful about the matter.

From the laws of the commandment is, for example, that which they, may their memory be Blessed, said (Megillah 20b) [that] we only make this declaration during the day, and that the whole day is fit for the declaration of the tithe, and that it can be said in any language (Sotah 32b). And [the proper execution of] its commandment is in the Temple, as it is stated, "in front of the Lord, your God." But if he makes the declaration in any place, he has fulfilled [it]. And there cannot be anything left of any of the gifts with the one making the declaration, as he says, "I have disposed of the holy from the house." And when does he make the declaration? After the third year in which we separate the poor-tithe, in the fourth year which is after it on the last day of Pesach; and so [too,] in the seventh [year]. And the rest of its laws are elucidated in the last chapter of Tractate Maaser Sheni.

And this commandment is practiced at the time of the [Temple] by males. And one who transgresses it and did not make this declaration about the tithes at the time of the [Temple] has violated this positive commandment.

Mitzvah 608
To not eat the second tithe in bereavement: To not eat the second tithe in bereavement. And I have written the content of the second tithe in the Order of Reeh Anochi (Sefer HaChinukh 473). And the content of bereavement from Torah writ is that one who has one of his relatives die on him is obligated to mourn for them - that day that [the relative] dies and he buries him, he is called a bereaved (onen). And they, may their memory be Blessed, said explicitly that only the day of death and burial is the main bereavement from Torah writ. And [that is] specifically the day, but not the night, as it is stated (Leviticus 10:19), "And I ate the sin-offering of the day" - and they, may their memory be Blessed, expounded (Zevachim 100b), "'The day' is forbidden, but it is permitted at night." And about this is it stated (Deuteronomy 26:14), "I have not eaten from it in bereavement" - meaning to say that if he ate from it in bereavement, he would have transgressed. And it is not only second tithes that it is forbidden to eat in bereavement, but rather one who eats any consecrated foods in bereavement is lashed for them (Mishneh Torah, Laws of Second Tithes and Fourth Year's Fruit 3:7).

It is from the roots of the commandment [that it is] because the consecrated foods are the table of the Higher realm, and it is not fitting for someone who is worried and very hurt in his heart to approach the table of the King. And by way of an analogy, it is like the matter that is written, "for one should not enter the gate of the king with sackcloth" (Esther 4:2). And another reason is because atonement of the owner is found in the eating of the consecrated foods - and like the matter that they, may their memory be Blessed, said (Pesachim 59b), "The priests eat, and the owners are atoned." And there is no doubt that when they would eat their consecrated foods, they would eat them with great concentration and with complete minds and [that] all of their thoughts and movements would be proper in front of God. And in a person being distressed, worried and trembling on the day of his relatives's death, his mind and concentration will not be settled at all. And therefore, it is not fit to eat the consecrated foods of the Heavens [at that time]. And the matter is fit in the eyes of the one who says it (the author).

From the laws of the commandment - that which they said (Mishneh Torah, Laws of Second Tithes and Fourth Year's Fruit 3:7) that the liability for lashes upon the one that eats the second tithe in bereavement is only upon the one that eats it in Jerusalem; that which they said that we administer lashes of rebellion upon the one that eats in bereavement from rabbinic writ, and that bereavement from rabbbinic writ is the night after the burial day, and so [too,] all the days that the dead body stays over between the day of death and the burial (Mishneh Torah, Laws of Second Tithes and Fourth Year's Fruit 3:6); and the rest of the details of the commandment and the statutes of bereavement - are elucidated in the eighth chapter of Pesachim and the second of Zevachim.

And this prohibition is practiced by males and females at the time of the [Temple], as there were tithes from Torah writ then. And one who transgresses this at that time and ate a kazayit of consecrated foods or second tithe in bereavement from Torah writ is lashed.

Mitzvah 609

To not eat the second tithe in impurity: To not eat the second tithe in impurity - and even in Jerusalem - until it is redeemed (Sefer HaMitzvot LaRambam, Mitzvot Lo Taase 150); as the essential rule for us is that we can redeem second tithe that has become impure, even in Jerusalem, as it is elucidated in Tractate Makkot 19b. And about this is it stated (Deuteronomy 26:14), "I have not disposed of it while impure" - and it is as if it said, "You shall not dispose of it while impure," meaning to say, "You shall not eat from it while impure." As since God commanded us that we should say, "I did not do this and that," behold it is as if He commanded us, "Do not do this." And for that reason, these expressions in this verse are considered negative commandments. And behold, the end of the verse states, "I have heeded to the voice of the Lord, my God" - meaning to say that He warned us about all this.

I have written in many places in this book what I have known from the roots of distancing impurity from consecrated foods (see Sefer HaChinukh 362).

From the laws of the commandment is that which they, may their memory be Blessed, said (Makkot 19b), "'I have not disposed of it while impure' - whether I am impure and it is pure or whether I am pure and it is impure" - meaning to say, that from each one of these two angles, we administer lashes for them. And this is when he eats it in Jerusalem, which is the place of its eating. As so did they, may their memory be Blessed, explain, that we only administer lashes for it there. But one who eats it in impurity outside of Jerusalem is not lashed for it, but we do administer rabbinic lashes of rebellion upon him. [These] and the rest of its details are elucidated at the end of Makkot.

And this prohibition is practiced by males and females at the time of the [Temple], as we had tithes from Torah writ [then].

Mitzvah 610

To only expend monies of the second tithe for eating and drinking: To only expend monies of the second tithe for the needs of eating and drinking. And about this is it stated (Deuteronomy 26:14), "and I did not give from it to the dead; I have heeded to the voice of the Lord, my God" - meaning to say, "I have not expended from it for a thing that does not sustain the body."

You will understand the reason of the matter, of why we were commanded to only expend it for the needs of eating and drinking and we cannot expend it even to acquire silver and gold vessels or slaves or other things, from what I wrote in the Order of Reeh about the root of the commandment of the second tithe (Sefer HaChinukh 473) - take it from there.

From the laws of the commandment is that which they, may their memory be Blessed, said (Mishnah

Maaser Sheni 2:1) that it is permitted to expend on things with which he can anoint his body - as anointing is included in eating and drinking, since it is similar to nourishment, to strengthen and benefit the body. And [also] that which they said (Mishneh Torah, Laws of Second Tithes and Fourth Year's Fruit 3:10) that it is forbidden to expend its monies upon anything besides eating, drinking and anointing, and even if it is for the matter of a commandment - and the language of Sifrei Devarim 303 is "That I did not buy from it a coffin and a shroud." And they, may their memory be Blessed, [also] said (Mishnah Maaser Sheni 1:7) that any time that he expended anything except for eating, drinking and anointing, the repayment for it is that he should spend money corresponding to it and eat the needs of a meal with it in Jerusalem. And it appears that since there is repayment for it, there is no liability for lashes. [These] and the rest of its details are elucidated in Tractate Maaser Sheni.

And this prohibition is practiced by males and females at the time of the [Temple], since we then had tithes from Torah writ. And one who transgresses this and expended monies of the second tithe on anything except for eating, drinking and anointing at that time has violated a negative commandment and pays money [of the same amount] from his wallet, and buys the needs of eating from it and eats them in Jerusalem, as we said.

Mitzvah 611
The commandment to walk in - and make oneself similar through - the ways of God, may He be Blessed: That we were commanded to perform all our actions in the way of straightness and goodness with all our strength and to incline all our affairs that are between ourselves and others towards the way of kindness and mercy; as we have known from our holy Torah that this is the way of God, and this is God's desire for His creatures so that they merit God's goodness - as He desires kindness. And about this is it stated (Deuteronomy 28:9), "and you shall walk in His ways." And this commandment was further repeated in another place, as it is stated (Deuteronomy 10:12, 11:22), "to walk in all His ways."

And they, may their memory be Blessed, said (Sifrei Devarim 49), in explanation of this commandment, "Just like the Holy One, Blessed be He, is called merciful, so too you be merciful; just like the Holy One, Blessed be He, is called compassionate, so too you be compassionate; just like the Holy One, Blessed be He, is called righteous, so too you be righteous; just like the Holy One, Blessed be He, is called holy, so too you be holy." And the whole matter is to say that we should teach ourselves to follow good actions like these and glorious traits through which He, may He be Blessed, is described by way of analogy - to say that He acts with these good traits towards His creatures. But He, Blessed be He, is more elevated than any great elevation; as we do not have the power or the knowledge to grasp the greatness of His elevation and the largeness of His kindness - nor do any of the creatures (Mishneh Torah, Laws of Human Dispositions 1:6). And in this way that we have [explained], the prophets called God all [these] appellations: righteous; straight; strong; of great kindness; of long patience. When they said, "of long patience," the matter is not, God forbid, that there ever be anger in front of Him ever. As why should He get angry - it is in His hand to kill and to make live, to destroy the world and to create; and there is none who says to Him, "What are you doing." Also because anger is a lack of perfection in the one getting angry, whereas all perfection is His, may He be Blessed. Rather the matter is in truth like the way that we described - meaning to say that they are the elevated traits with which He acts towards His creatures; and that we should study and follow His ways, in imitation of Him.

And maybe, my son, you will think to come to me with that which is written (Psalms 7:12), "and God gets furious every day" - and they, may their memory be Blessed, said (Berakhot 7a), "And how much is His fury? An instant." And you, my son, should not err in this, God forbid, that there be evil to God, and that your heart believe about Him, Blessed be He, anything but all perfection. And the matter of anger only happens in us from the angle of our being inferior physical beings. And in truth the fury that they mentioned about Him is only by way of analogy to a matter of the world. Their intention [with it] was to say that in that the majority of people in the world are pulled after their desires and there are many among them that worship the sun, the moon and the constellations - and even trees and stones - the world constantly becomes liable for extinction. And maybe the reason for their saying that His fury is for an instant every day is that since the world is judged according to its majority and that the world becomes liable because of their bad deeds on each and every day; they, may their memory be Blessed, compared that small moment when a sinner completes the majority [of the world's actions] with his sin, to the fury of God. As everything is fit at the instant for extinction from the power of [God's] trait of justice, except that [His] trait of kindness immediately determines [otherwise] and preserves it. And accept this, my son, from me until you hear [something] better than it.

The root of this commandment is well-known to all, as it and its root are one thing.

Its laws are also short. Its content is generally that a man choose for himself in all of his matters and in all of his actions - whether in eating, drinking, [commerce], words of Torah, prayer, conversation or in any other thing - the good and moderate path; and never to remove himself to the extremes. And about this general principal, they, may their memory be Blessed, said (Sotah 5b) that a man always examine his dispositions - meaning to say that he think about his affairs, to do them in the moderate and good path. And they based this upon a verse, as it is written (Psalms 50:23), "and to him who orders his way, I will show him the salvation of God" - they expounded (Moed Katan 5a), 'Do not read it [as] "and orders (vesam)," but rather "and evaluates (vesham)."'

And this commandment is practiced in every place and at all times by males and females. And one who transgresses it and does not make efforts to straighten his ways, to conquer his impulse, to improve his thoughts and deeds for the Love of God and to fulfill this commandment, has violated this positive commandment.

Mitzvah 612

To gather all of Israel on the festival of Sukkot: That we were commanded that the people of Israel gather in its entirety - men, women, and infants - at the closing of the sabbatical year on the festival of Sukkot on the second day of the festival, and read a little from the book of Mishneh Torah in their ears, which is the book of Deuteronomy. And about this is it stated (Deuteronomy 31:12), "Gather all the nation - the men, the women, and the infants, etc." And this is the commandment of gathering (hakhel) that is mentioned in the Gemara; like the matter that they said in the first [chapter] of Kiddushin 34a, "But behold, gathering which is a positive commandment that is caused by time, and women are obligated!" And they explained at the end of the topic, "We do not learn from general rules," which means to say that truthfully women are obligated in this commandment.

It is from the roots of the commandment [that it is] because the entire essence of the people of Israel is the Torah; and through it are they separated from every nation and language, to be meritorious for life of the forever - eternal pleasure that is not surpassed by anything among the creatures. Therefore since their entire essence is in it, it is fitting that everyone should gather together at one point in time to hear its words, and for the voice to go out amongst the whole nation - men, women, and infants - to say, "What is the great gathering, that we have all been gathered together?" And the answer would be, "To hear the words of the Torah, which is our entire essence and glory and splendor." And they will come from this to tell of the great praise and the splendor of its value; and its yearning will enter all of their hearts. And with this yearning for it, they will learn to know God and merit good, and 'God will be happy with His creations' - like the matter that is written in explanation of this commandment "and in order that they will learn and fear the Lord."

From the laws of the commandment is that which they, may their memories be Blessed, said (Sotah 41a, Mishneh Torah, Laws of Festival Offering 3:3) that the king was the one that was obligated to read it in their ears. And he would read it in the women's yard [of the Temple]. And he reads while sitting, but if he read while standing, behold that is praiseworthy. And from where does he read? From the beginning of the book of Eleh HaDevarim (Deuteronomy) until the end of the section of Shema Yisrael (Deuteronomy 6:9), and he skips to Vehaya im shamo'ah and finishes that section (Deuteronomy 11:13-21), and [then] skips to Aser te'aser (Deuteronomy 14:22) and reads from Aser te'aser, according to [its proper] order, until the end of the blessings and curses, up until "besides for the covenant which He made with them in Chorev" (Deuteronomy 28:69), and stops. And how does he read (Mishneh Torah, Laws of Festival Offering 3:4)? They blow trumpets throughout Jerusalem, and bring a big stage - and it was made of wood - and stand it up in the middle of the Women's Courtyard, and the king walks over and sits on it, so that they will hear his reading, and all of Israel that came for the Festival gather around him. And the sexton of the [Temple] synagogue takes a Torah Scroll and gives it to the head of the synagogue, and the head of the synagogue gives it to the assistant [high priest], and the assistant gives it to the high priest, and the high priest gives it to the king, in order to glorify him through the many people. And the king receives it while he is standing, and if he wants, he sits. And he opens it and recites a blessing, in the way that everyone who reads from the Torah in the synagogue recites a blessing; and he reads the sections which we said, and recites a blessing after it, in the way that they recite the blessing in synagogues. And he adds seven [blessings], and these are them: "Be pleased, Lord our God, with Your people Yisrael and their prayer" (Retseh); "We are thankful to You" (Modim); "You chose us from [among] all the peoples" (Atah bachartanu), until "who sanctifies Israel and the times" - behold, three blessings like their [usual] imprint; [in] the fourth he prays for the Temple and finishes it, "the One who dwells in Zion"; [in] the fifth he prays for Israel, that their kingdom should stand, and concludes it, "the One who chooses Israel"; [in] the sixth he prays for the priests and concludes it, "sanctifies the priests"; in the seventh he supplicates and prays, according to that which he is able, and concludes it, "save, Lord, Your nation Israel, for Your nation Israel needs to be saved. Blessed are you, Lord, who listens to prayer."

This commandment is practiced at the time when Israel is on their land. And one who transgresses this, whether man or woman, and did not come on this appointed time to hear the words of the Torah - and so [too,] the king, if he does not want to read - has violated this positive commandment. And their punishment is very great, because this commandment is a strong pillar and great honor for the religion.

Mitzvah 613
For everyone to write a Torah scroll for himself: That we were commanded that each man in Israel must have a Torah scroll (Sefer HaMitzvot LaRambam, Mitzvot Ase 18). If he wrote it with his [own] hand, this is praiseworthy and very dear; and as they, may their memory be Blessed, said (Menachot 30a), "If he wrote it" - meaning to say, with his hand - "Scripture attributes [it] to him as if he received it from Mount Sinai." But one who is unable to write with his hand must pay someone to write it for him. And about this it is stated (Deuteronomy 31:19), "And now, write for yourselves this poem and teach it to the Children of Israel" - meaning to say, write for yourselves Torah, which contains this poem.

It is from the roots of the commandment [that it is that] since it is well-known about people that they do all of their things according to what is prepared for them, therefore He, Blessed be He, commanded that there be a Torah scroll prepared with him, that he can always read from it and that he not need to walk for it to the house of his fellow; 'so that he will learn to fear the Lord,' and know and understand His commandments that are more precious and desirable than much gold and fine gold. And we were commanded - each and every one of Israel - to make efforts about this, even if his fathers left him one. [This is] so that scrolls proliferate among us and we can lend them out to the one whose hand not be able to purchase it; and also in order that each and every one of Israel read from new scrolls, lest their souls be sick of reading in the old scrolls that their fathers left them.

And know, my son, that even though the main obligation from Torah writ is only about a Torah scroll, there is no doubt that each one should also make [copies] of the other books that were composed about the understanding of the Torah - according to [his] ability - from the reasons that we said; and even if his fathers left him many of them. And this is the way of all God-fearing men of stature who were before us, to establish a study hall in their house, for scribes to write many books, according to the blessing of God that He gave to them.

From the laws of the commandment is that which they [explained] (Menachot 30a and see Mishneh Torah, Laws of Tefillin, Mezuzah and the Torah Scroll 7:4-9) how do we write a Torah scroll: Its writing [should be] refined, good and pleasant; and he should leave the space of a letter between each and every word, and the space of a line between each and every line. And the length of each line should be thirty letters, enough so as to write, "to their families (lemishpechoteichem)" three times.

Sefer HaChinukh

And that is the width of each and every column, and not that the line be shorter than this, so that the page not be like a letter; and not longer than this, so that his eyes not stray in the writing. If a word of five letters chanced upon him, he should not write two [letters] within the column and three [past] the column, but rather he should write three within the column and two [past] it. If there is not enough [room] in the column in order to write three letters, he leaves the place empty and begins from the beginning of the [next] line. If a word of two letters chanced upon him, he should not throw it between the columns, but rather return to the beginning of the [next] line. If at the end of a line, a word of ten letters - or less or more - chanced upon him, and there is not enough [space] in the line to write all of it within the column: if he can write half of it within the column and half of it [past] the column, he writes [it that way]; but if not, he leaves the place empty and begins [it] from the beginning of the [next] line.

And he leaves four rows empty without writing between each and every book (Chumash) - not less and not more - and begins the [next] book from the beginning of the fifth line. And when he finishes the Torah, he needs to finish it in the middle of the row at the end of the column. If there are many rows left in the column, he should continue to shorten [the content of the script in each line] and begin from the beginning of the line - but not to end the line - and plan [it] until "in the eyes of Israel" (the Torah's last words) is in the middle of the line at the end of the column.

And he should be careful (Mishneh Torah, Laws of Tefillin, Mezuzah and the Torah Scroll 7:8-9) about the big letters and the small letters, the dotted letters and the letters the form of which is unusual, such as the bent [letter] peh, and the twisted letters - like the scribes copied, one man from another. And he should be careful with the crowns and in their numbers - there is a letter that has one crown upon it and there is [another] letter that has seven upon it. And all of the crowns are like the form of a [letter,] zayin, [that] are as thin as a strand of hair. And all of these things are only said for an ideal [fulfillment of the] commandment. And [so] if he diverged [erred] in this refinement or was not exacting with the crowns, but he wrote all the letters as fits them; or if he made the lines closer or further or lengthened them or shortened them - since he did not have one letter cling to [another] letter and he did not miss or add or destroy the from of [a single] letter, and he did not make a change in the open paragraphs (petuchot) or in the closed paragraphs (setumot), behold this is a fit Torah scroll. [These] and the rest of the details of the commandment are elucidated in Tractate Menachot [in] the third chapter, and in the first chapter of Bava Batra and in Tractate Shabbat.

And it is practiced at all times and in every place by males, as they obligated in Torah study - and so too, to write it - but not females. And one who transgresses this and does not write a Torah scroll, if it is possible for him in any way, has violated this positive commandment. And his punishment is very great, as it is the cause of the study of the commandments of the Torah, as we have said. And anyone who fulfills it will be Blessed and wise - he and his sons - as it is is written, "And now, write for yourselves this poem and teach it to the Children of Israel."

www.ingramcontent.com/pod-product-compliance
Lightning Source LLC
Chambersburg PA
CBHW081426070526
44586CB00020B/2505